THE WRITER'S HANDBOOK

The Writer's Handbook

Edited by
SYLVIA K. BURACK
Editor, The Writer

Publishers   THE WRITER, INC.   Boston

CONTENTS

BACKGROUND FOR WRITERS

HOW TO WRITE—TECHNIQUES

GENERAL FICTION

ix

BACKGROUND FOR WRITERS

1

CULTIVATING THE LIBRARY HABIT

BY JOHN JAKES

LIBRARIES ARE MAGICAL PLACES. There's nothing quite like strolling the hushed aisles, letting your eye rove along dimly lit shelves. Each spine, each title, seems to beckon with a promise of incredible wonders, surprises and adventures.

Libraries not only take us into new and exciting realms, but also help us grow. They answer questions, solve problems, enable us to better ourselves. If I did not have the library habit—which is passed on by families—I certainly couldn't research and write the first chapter of a historical novel.

Whatever the need—from simple escape reading to learning gourmet cookery, or evaluating mutual funds, or confronting dire illness—as my son, Mike, said in his 20s, when he set out to master the handling of small boats: "There's always a book."

I've never forgotten those words. A majority of Americans know how true they are. According to the American Library Association, 66 percent of us use one of the nation's 15,000-plus public libraries annually. And the usage numbers go up each year.

But finding the books we need or want, when we want them, is getting harder. Our libraries are in trouble. And we'd better take notice and remedy the situation before one of our nation's most precious assets becomes a skinny, starving shell of its old self.

With today's tax dollars stretched to the limit, states and towns facing a budget crisis find the library a tempting target. But when they do, bad things happen. Services are curtailed, hours shrink. Worst of all, libraries are closing all over the country. Even in the Great Depression, I don't know of *one* library going out of business.

It's a terrible situation—and here's the paradox: Americans as a whole don't want it to happen! Individually, we want our libraries to succeed. We want *more* for them, not less.

3

So what's wrong? I'm afraid we must round up the usual suspects—politicians and their Frill Mentality. This is a mindset that perceives public libraries as less important than unfilled potholes.

The Frill Mentality is sometimes bolstered by the assertion that libraries are dinosaurs, doomed to extinction by the computer age. I doubt it. I suspect it will be many years before every home has a computer and the money and expertise to use it.

And will we then give up the children's story hours? Book discussion groups? The librarian who helps us find exactly what we're searching for?

But the Frill Mentality is widespread and insidious. It attacks the very life blood of our nation—information, knowledge. Because a library isn't just some pleasant, dusty building under the trees that's nice to have but not really essential. I believe passionately that the library is one of the cornerstones of a healthy community. It gives us the opportunity to encounter great ideas, great minds, great art.

And spare me the argument that reading is declining because of TV. It may be true in some quarters, but I've seen TV adaptations of my novels drive hordes of new readers straight *to* the libraries, hunting for Jakes books. Some of those readers send me letters saying mine is the first novel they've ever read.

What, then, can you or I do as individuals do to protect and promote our public libraries?

• First, get the facts and figures. Is your library adequately funded? If not, what's a reasonable higher goal to work toward? If you have a good local or county library board, its members can be helpful here.

• Second, watch for elected or appointed officials who exhibit symptoms of the Frill Mentality. If one of them starts blathering about "unnecessary" library hours and "expendable" services, jump on that person with calls or letters. If he or she is unreasonable, elect someone else next time.

• Third, for muscle in your own locality, it helps to have an organized Friends group. If there's one where you are, join it. If there isn't, start one. Friends of Libraries U.S.A. (1326 Spruce St., Suite 1105, Philadelphia, PA 19107) will be glad to help.

4

Finally, as a strategic objective, work to have the library operating tax removed from the general tax fund, and always put it to a public vote separately.

"There's always a book," our son said. That's a promise we absolutely have to keep.

2

IS THERE A SECRET TO GETTING PUBLISHED?

BY KATHERINE PATERSON

ONCE UPON A TIME THERE WAS A WOMAN who wanted to write. No, delete that first sentence. Once upon a time there was a Maryland housewife with first two, then three, then four children under the age of six who was constantly composing in her head and furiously writing down the bits whenever she had a moment, who wanted desperately to publish. She became a celebrated, award-winning commercially successful writer of books for children and lived happily ever after. The end.

What a minute! That's no story.

What do you mean "that's no story"? You have "once upon a time" and "happily ever after." What more could anyone want?

A middle! A story must have a beginning, a middle, and an end.

But that's the boring bit. Delete "boring," insert "depressing." Besides, it's a story the audience will know all too well. The slogging away at manuscripts she has no hope will ever see the light of day— the wistful attendance at writers' conferences—the seven dismal years of self-addressed envelopes jammed into the mailbox—the coffee-stained manuscripts that have to be painfully retyped before they can be submitted to yet another seemingly heartless editor—the drawers of printed rejection slips—the wondering if it is worth the headache, not to mention the postage. She doesn't think about the time—her time evidently has no value.

Through the years, she tries everything—stories, poems, articles, fillers—but nothing sells except one story and one poem. The tiny magazines that buy them immediately fold.

She is, obviously, not meant to be a published writer. She doubts that she has any talent at all. In all other ways, she is a fortunate

6

woman—she has a good husband and four happy, healthy children. Isn't that enough? Why can't she be content?

But if she'd been content in the middle, the happily ever after wouldn't have happened.

What you've just read is an internal debate between my creative side and my business side. The business side is, frankly, a bit surprised that anyone would ask me to speak about "writing for the market." Years ago she made noble efforts to steer me toward writing something that might be marketable, but it became sadly evident that I was simply incapable of that kind of writing. The creative side wants me to tell the middle of the story, hoping it might help other weary writers, though she's not quite sure how. . . .

So, I pulled myself together and called my editor to tell her that I'd been asked to speak on writing for the market. "What are you planning to say?" she asked nervously. "Well, that's what I'm trying to figure out," I said. "What do *you* think I should say?"

"Well," she said, "I'm right now reading through the slush pile, and I wish everything weren't so market driven. I think people should write what they need to write."

"Can I quote you on that?" I asked.

"No, wait a minute. I have to phrase this very carefully. Writers have to know what's being published today and what's selling. It's not enough to go to libraries. Writers have to go to bookstores to find out what's being published and what's selling. But, having said that, I believe they should write what they need to write."

"Do you think new writers have a chance today?"

"It's harder," she admitted, "though it's always been hard. But today there are fewer editors willing to read slush-pile submissions. Though I can't understand it. How are they going to find good first novels if they don't read slush-pile submissions?"

No wonder my story turns out well. Does anyone in the world have such a terrific editor?

But back to the middle of the story. The question I suppose I need to address is how I got from there to here—how the frustrated, practically unpublished housewife became, if not exactly a household name, at least a respected and well-paid writer.

Let me say first of all that no one has been more surprised by my success than I have. But everyone seems a bit surprised. When people first meet me, I watch the way they think I ought to. Here's this woman, not nearly so clever as I, they're thinking, and she's supposed to be this well-known writer. Then often, surprise moves to questioning— or to be more specific, to what is sometimes known as the "trick" question. Which is, what is your trick? There must be some trick, some secret that you know that I don't. So, be generous, tell me your secret, so I can be rich and famous like you.

It doesn't do to say that there is no trick. The person will just think you're being selfish. And advice, even good advice, comes without a guarantee. It reminds me of the Mother's Day card I got from one of my sons this year: "Mom," it says, "all the advice you gave me growing up is still as clear in my mind as the day you gave it—And to this day, I always look both ways before accepting candy from strangers. . . ." Hm-m.

But, anyhow, for what it's worth, here it is: The middle of the story— the trick—the secret—the advice. It boils down to what my editor suggested: I did read what was being written in the field of children's books, but when I sat down to write, I wrote what I *needed* to write, I wrote what I *wanted* to write, what, as it turned out, I *could* write.

There is a wonderful story about the writer Conrad Aiken who during his lifetime received awards and critical respect, but very little in the way of actual money. During the 1920s and 1930s, he was a struggling writer with a house full of children to support. He was publishing, but only in toney little literary magazines too high class to insult contributors by paying them for their work. But what Aiken needed most of the time was cold, hard cash.

He decided to change his ways. Forget literature. Write something that would put groceries on the table. He went about his assignment scientifically. Taking most of the almost non-existent family budget, he bought copies of all the magazines that paid real money to writers for their stories. There were a lot more of them in those days than there are, alas, now: *The Saturday Evening Post, Liberty, Collier's.* He studied and analyzed all the stories in these publications until he figured out the key. Then he deliberately wrote a *Saturday Evening Post* story, one he was sure the editors would not be able to resist.

Well, of course, the *Post* rejected his "perfect" story, as did all the other high-paying magazines. (His "Silent Snow, Secret Snow" was eventually published in some obscure place, but it has been repeatedly anthologized in the years since Aiken's death as an example of a great literary short story.)

The moral of this cautionary tale is, you can study the market to a fare-thee-well, but in the end, you write what you can.

When children ask me where I get my ideas, I turn the question back on them. Ideas are everywhere—a dime a dozen. But before I write a book, I look at the idea, or rather, the complex of ideas I am proposing to turn into a story, and I ask two questions: Is it worth all the trees? And, the second question, which gets more relevant for me with every passing year—is it exciting enough, important enough for me to live with it for the year, two years, maybe three years of my ever-shortening life that it will take me to write it?

You may wonder why I ever write a book—so do I. And yet I do, because, like you, somehow I must. It's what I do. But I only write books that I truly need to write—that matter deeply to me.

I began to write my first novel back in those grim days when nothing I wrote was getting published. A lady in the church where my husband was pastor felt sorry for me, home with all those little children. She took me on as a kind of good work. "How about attending a writing class through the county adult education program?" she asked. She knew I was trying to write, but without success. It sounded great—Mom's night out. I started in a general writing course. Then the next year I took a course on Writing for Children. I was writing something—a story or a poem—every week, and publishing nothing, when it occurred to me that if I could write a story a week, I might be able to write a chapter a week. And at the end of the year I would have a book.

I wanted to write a story set in Japan, because I had lived there for four years, back when I was a competent single woman, and I was a little bit homesick for Japan. If I wrote a story set in Japan in the past, I would have an excuse to read Japanese history, something I loved doing. I don't think I ever knew that if I did that I would be committing historical fiction. I wasn't thinking about genre, I was thinking about story. I'm sure I didn't know that a book for children set in 12th-century Japan would be for all practical purposes totally unmarketable.

But a novel has to have more than fascinating setting and well-paced plot. It has to have an emotional core. It has to be written out of passion. And the heart of this novel set in 12th-century Japan came

9

from an unexpected source. It came to me from my then five-year-old daughter.

Lin was born in Hong Kong in the fall of 1962. When she was about three weeks old, she was found on a city sidewalk by a policeman and taken to an orphanage out in the New Territories, where she lived for more than two years before she came to be our daughter. Her initial adjustment was horrendous, and again when we moved from New Jersey to Maryland in 1966, a lot of it came unglued and had to be redone. But by 1968 when she was five, life had settled down pretty well for her. Still, there were times when for no reason we could discern, the bright, happy little daughter she had become would disappear. And in her place would be a silent waif. It was as though the child we knew had simply pulled down a curtain that we could not reach through, often for several days at a time. And it scared me to death. Where had she gone? What was going on behind that blank stare? And how on earth could I reach her? I had tried everything—cajoling, begging, holding her. Nothing worked. One evening I was in the kitchen making supper and she came in. Without a word she climbed up on a high kitchen stool and sat there, her tiny body present, but the rest of her completely closed away. I tried to chat with her in a normal tone of voice. There was no answer, no indication that she even heard. The harder I tried, the more tense I became.

Finally, I did what any good mother would do under the circumstances, I lost my temper and screamed. "Lin," I yelled, "how can I help you if you won't tell me what's the matter?"

She jerked to life, her eyes wide open. "Why did that woman give me away?" she demanded.

And then it all began to pour out. Why had she been given away? We'd never told her that she was a foundling. It seemed too harsh— just that her mother had not been able to keep her and wanted her to have a home. I repeated this, adding that I was sure her mother hadn't wanted to give her away, and wouldn't have if there had been any possibility that she could take care of her. Was her mother alive? Was she all right? I couldn't answer her questions, but she let me try to comfort and assure her. She never again, even in adolescence, pulled down the curtain in just that way.

She is a mother herself now—a wonderful, loving, funny mother, giving our baby grandchild all the care that she herself never had but that somehow she knows how to give. She is a wonder, and I cannot tell you how I admire her.

But what she gave me that day was not only herself, but the emotional heart of the story I wanted to write. What must it be like, I wondered, to have a parent somewhere that you do not know?

I look at this book—*The Sign of the Chrysanthemum* is its title— and it's no marvel to me now that I had difficulty finding a publisher. It is set in the midst of the civil wars of 12th-century Japan. The central character is a thieving bastard who is searching for the father he never knew. The girl he cares about ends up in a brothel; I didn't put her there because I wanted to scandalize my readers, but because a beautiful thirteen-year-old girl in 12th-century Japan who had no one to protect her would, most likely, end up in a brothel, and the penniless teenage boy who loved her would be powerless to save her.

Now at some point I must have realized that I hadn't seen a lot of books for young readers along this line, but when I wrote *The Sign of the Chrysanthemum* I wasn't, to be honest, worrying about readers. I was writing a story I needed and wanted to write, as honestly and as well as I knew how.

For those of you who have been wondering about the difference between novels for young readers and adult novels, the adult bestseller at about the same time my book was published—a bestseller that was breaking every sales record since *Gone With The Wind*—was the sentimental tale of an overachieving seagull *Jonathan Livingston Seagull,* by Richard Bach. Then how on earth did my book ever see the light of day?

It almost didn't. It made the rounds of various publishers for more than two years. And then a miracle happened. It was taken out of the seventh or eighth publisher's slush pile by a young woman just out of college who read it and loved it. She took it to the senior editor, who had just come back from a visit to Japan and who was and is a woman of vision in the field of children's books. She has always dared to publish books that she feels will open up unknown worlds for children. She had no illusions that the book would sell well, but she wanted young readers to have a chance to read the book, and she wanted the writer to have the chance to write more books.

Though *The Sign of the Chrysanthemum* has never sold well in hardback, it sells remarkably well in paperback. This is particularly satisfying to me, because children and young people buy paperbacks, and it means that the book is reaching the people I am writing for.

Well, that's pretty much the middle of the story. It is harder to place a first novel now. The corporate giants who control most of the New York publishing houses do not have the vision of my first editors. Fewer chances are being taken.

There was a depressing article a few years ago in *Harper's Magazine* entitled, "Reading May Be Harmful to Your Kids." It included the twenty best-selling paperback children's books of that year. Nine of the top ten had the words "Teenage Mutant Ninja Turtles" in the title. There were only two genuine books on the whole list. One of these, number fifteen, was E. B. White's *Charlotte's Web,* published in 1952, and the other, number twenty, was Maurice Sendak's *Where the Wild Things Are,* published in 1963.

So those of us who haven't the patent on Ninja Turtles might just as well devote our energies to writing something we really care about. And which, not incidentally, may be the only thing we really can write.

It is well to remember that by the time you write a book for the market and that manuscript has gone through the long process of selling itself to an editor and being published, the market may have long before gone somewhere else and left your book far behind. But a beautifully written book, a well-crafted story, a work of honest human feeling and deep passion, like the stories of Conrad Aiken, E. B. White, and Maurice Sendak, will never go out of style. And I still believe there will be a few horribly underpaid, sensitive, unjaded young people ploughing through the slush pile who will find your manuscript and take it to one of the rare remarkable editors left in the business, who will dare against all trends to put it between covers.

It will take a miracle, of course. But who am I to deny the existence of miracles?

12

3

YOUR DREAMS ARE MODELS

BY T. ALAN BROUGHTON

EVERY NIGHT, NO MATTER WHAT our vocations, each of us spends some time in a process that is very like the making of a poem or story. We dream. In fact, scientists have demonstrated that if we don't dream, we become disoriented, distracted, even at times nearly schizophrenic in our waking hours. Similarly, to be without great poems or stories would be to enter the state of a deprived sleeper, and without the finest art, our lives would be the worst kind of madness in which we would be insane but would not know it.

Perhaps we have misinterpreted the nature of our lives anyway. When we look at trees we think those unseen, toiling roots and tendrils are there merely to support the flourishing leaves and branches and blossoms. But perhaps the true life of the tree is underground. Is it possible that in our lives we arc awake merely to provide material for the essential business of living—sleep and dreams and those long hours when we sink back into the deepest centers of existence?

Spend the week dreaming. You will anyway, but for a few weeks keep a notebook by your bedside. When you wake, or more likely, half-wake, from a dream, turn on a light or flashlight, grab a pencil, write down what you can—never in generalizations ("crazy dream at two," "scary nightmare at 3:30"), but in all the details you can recover ("Mother was wearing Aunt Ida's nose, but even that could not disguise her because she kept telling me to take off my boots in the house"). Don't wait until morning, because the dream will not be there then, only its aura, or perhaps a snippet or two before even that goes. Like the lame boy who cannot keep up with the other children, you will be left outside the hill with only a vague sense of the music the Pied Piper was playing.

Because dreams are elusive. They are as elusive as the glints of poems and stories we sometimes have but will lose if we do not write

13

them down. That is why writers often keep notebooks—not as a daily record of what they did or did not do, but as a storehouse for those hints and suggestions offered by all the quickly passing flotsam of the world outside us that we notice only because of the tendencies of our individual minds. What catches me in the words of an overheard conversation in the doctor's waiting room will not lure another writer. Each of us leaps instinctively at what is needed for understanding and completion.

Getting the dream down on paper takes the quick, deft motions of the hunter of nightcrawlers. In the circle of your flashlight, lying long and flat in the damp, night grass is the fat, moist worm that dares to be less cautious in a world without sunlight and gulls. You must jab quickly to keep it from slithering away, down its hole. But the problem is: Which end is loose, which is still in the hole? A wrong guess means losing it, maybe even not catching a fish you might have caught with this, and only this, special worm. Get it before it retreats, put it in your pail, and save it for a good day. Then, when you have that dream, and others, you may use them for poems or stories, but first look hard at where your dreams came from, think hard about how they came to you. The *process* of dreaming itself should give you assurance that the task of writing can be done and also how you can do it.

We are talking here about imagination and how it accepts and transforms the experiences of our lives. All of them, especially the ones we don't want or didn't even know we had. Dreams show us something about how poems and stories are made and how they are made convincing.

1. Dreams are not abstractions. They are concrete, specific enactments. Weird sometimes, but always emotionally convincing because they are so totally specific that our emotions cannot help but give in to them. Above all, notice how we *experience* dreams. They are not explained to us. The essential act of making poems, like that of reading, is immersion in the detailed world of things we know through our senses.

2. Note how easily the dreaming mind moves from association to association. We are making metaphors in our dreams, yoking together illusions of all the physical senses we have. Situations we would not logically connect are rearranged and brought into a seamless unity.

14

Images we did not know we had in us emerge—vivid, surprising, highly sensuous. Some people dream predominantly in visual images, some in colors, and others mix sound and smell. Studies of various poets have shown how one uses a certain sense more than another, subliminally influencing the reader's perceptions of their poems. The marvel of a Keats is how richly he uses all the senses and even brings them together in complex mergings, called synaesthesia. The "logic" of dreams is the logic of poems and stories. What makes sense to the *emotions* is what makes meaning.

3. Dreams leave out as much as they include, but what they leave out may be the essence of what is being shown to us. How often we wander through a dream, knowing that what is happening is merely the dramatization of what cannot be fully shown because it is ultimately so powerful, so mysterious that even these extraordinarily affecting moments are only hints. "Tell all the truth, but tell it slant," Emily Dickinson says. And Willa Cather, in speaking of short stories, reminds us that "whatever is felt on the page without being specifically named there—that, one might say, is created." The art of saying is the art of silence, or as Tolstoy indicates, art has focus, "and this focus must not be able to be completely explained in words."

4. A corollary to this suggestiveness is the assurance that you have a very good editor already in you. Notice how much is edited from your dreams. Only what is essential to the complex effect is present. Emphasis should be on the complex. Emotions are not pure and simple; they come mixed—love and aversion, fear and attraction. Remember that you experience confusion at times in a dream, but the dream in itself is never confused. It has confused you by its own eloquent and significant means. Through condensation a poet can achieve intensity, memorability, and evocation.

5. Dreams should give you faith in your ability to use your own experience to create a poem, yet not be limited by its literal or historical circumstances. Some of the images in your dreams, you may believe, are totally unrelated to anything you have seen or known; they are so divergent from any reality you thought you had experienced. There is no need to trace them all down. This is not therapy. But believe now in how remarkable your innate faculty is for invention.

15

You are free to imagine whatever you need to imagine in order to make the world of story or novel, or to create the images of poems. Remember how in your dreams you turned to all those stores of memory you did not even know you had. At the moment of writing, you let go of all you have learned from reading and studying, and sink into those layers that are partly you and partly the memory of the species. As Rilke said in *Letters to a Young Poet,* "...and even if you were in some prison, the walls of which let none of the sounds of the world come to your senses—would you not then still have your childhood, that precious, kindly possession, that treasure-house of memories? Turn your attention thither."

6. Partly yours, partly the species. Here is the most miraculous aspect of the imagining that merges dream and writing. Melded in the dream are all the experiences of your own life from which you make selections and all the dream life of the human species you are part of. When you wake in the morning to tell your dream at the breakfast table, you may find little more response than the crackling of someone else's Rice Krispies. Dreams are private, we each have our own, and we are not always very much interested in listening to someone else's rather than reading the newspaper. But when you do find a sympathetic listener, and if you are fairly adept at turning the night's events into words, you will find that your listener is amused, sometimes shocked, even thoughtful about what you have to say, and she may even respond with a dream of her own that is similar.

In art we use the term "universality" for such common understanding, and without it the work would remain only the private muddle of an inarticulate, single person. But the essential thing to remember is that the universal is reached only through the particular. Repeating the words "I love" over and over and over in pentameter for fourteen lines gives the reader a steady diet of iambs but does not make a great love sonnet.

7. But imaginative dreamers are not necessarily fine pocts. Confidence can be fostered by seeing how all the machinery for making poems and stories is in each of us, that every night of our lives we are practicing. But there is an important difference between dreaming and writing. Words. What we dream is in the involuntary release of our brain cells pretending to do what they perform during our waking

16

hours—bringing us news from the world outside us. But poems and stories are words—*only* words.

So the essential element in all this is talent. If it is any consolation to beginning writers, they should know that the disappointment they experience shortly after they have attempted to write something is lifelong; that almost all writers, no matter how long they write, admit again and again that words are not sufficient for everything the mind shows them; that hope resides mainly in the belief that the next poem or story will work better. But why shouldn't that be so? Would we want any substitute for our brain, want anything we could make to be greater than it? We seem doomed never to understand our most vital organ...if that is doom. Such ignorance may be simply what enables us to remain imaginative, creative, hopeful. You can find out whether you have a sufficient talent only by spending a lifetime looking for it. You will know soon enough if you have none at all, because you will lose any interest in the search.

In dreams and in the imaginative use of words, the experience of the individual and of the species comes together in a creative act. In making poems and stories, we wander into new landscapes holding firmly to that talisman of the tribe—language—hoping to come back and share a dream formed well enough to join the waking dreams of our species.

4

WHAT IS SUCCESS?

BY JOANNA HIGGINS

UNTIL RECENTLY, I'VE FELT LITTLE NEED to think about success in any systematic way, or to question conventional definitions. It was something to dream about, but in my case it was also something that seems to happen only to others. Since the publication of my first book, though, after twelve years of writing, I *have* been thinking about it, especially when friends say, "You must be *so* excited!"

I agree, of course, not wanting to deflate their enthusiasm. But I don't add that it's not as exciting as the book's acceptance, months ago. And nowhere near the stratospheric excitement I felt while *writing* the stories.

Here's the thing. If I'm not writing, if I haven't written that day when I wanted to, needed to, and could have, had I managed my time better, then in my own eyes I'm not much of a success at that moment. Nor do I feel "victorious" or "prosperous" or "famous," all synonyms of the word. Just a little disconcerted, in the presence of that awesome gap between illusion and reality.

All this has led me to come up with my own definition for success, a personal, existential one: success as *process* as well as result. Journey as well as arrival. For without the journey, there can be no arrival. No success story.

Here, then, are the tenets of my definition:
• Success, above all, is writing—daily, if possible. A little bit or a lot. Writing: making words appear where there were none before—on page or computer monitor. Writing when I feel like it—and when I don't, when I'm high on some idea or in a slump or anywhere in between, when I've been "accepted" or "rejected." Writing. Journal entries, essays, lines of poetry, character sketches, plot ideas, fragments of description, bits of dialogue, three pages, one page; even letters,

but really get into them, take time, craft them and enjoy the crafting; don't skimp.

• Success is having a system to help you work through your frustration over rejections. I give myself a day or two, sometimes, to mope, then go out and buy a new ream of paper and say to myself, "Well you have to keep going now until you use this batch up, *then* you can quit, if you want to." The date for this decision, like the millennium, is always pushed ahead, and in the meantime, I get more words down.

• Success is schooling myself to acknowledge and praise previous accomplishments, including—and most important—the writing done that day, not devaluing these victories in light of what I hope to achieve but haven't—yet. So, once in a while I take time to look over a list of my published work and say to myself, "Now, *there*. See?" This exercise also helps the rejection blues. Which leads to the next tenet:

• Success is thinking positively. This really works. The unconscious needs to hear good things. Say, "I can *do* this. It's going to take lots of time and effort and patience, but I can do it, and it'll be terrific. So let's get moving!" And off we go. But if I allow myself to whine—"Oh, I don't think I can do this novel, this poem, this story, I'm not good enough, I'm no writer, look at all these rejections! I'm too old (or too young), too inexperienced, too tired, too fragmented, I have no time, no talent, no one believes in my work, how am I supposed to *write*!"— guess what? Words wither. Pages stay blank or hopelessly botched. What follows is more internal whining—about writer's block. A vicious circle. The real pity is that so much valuable time and energy are spent in the creation of—nothing. Fight these "negs" with positive imagery. Last thing every night, first thing every morning, say a kind of writer's prayer: *I can do this, I will do it.* Repeat ten times. Then see yourself doing it, and sit down and write. That is success.

But exerting one's will and inculcating discipline shouldn't obscure the fact that a sense of *play* is at the heart of all creativity. *Play,* and the freedom—and joy—that true creativity embodies. I once took a beginner's class in acrylic painting and was struck by how much fun it was, learning to mix colors and create the illusion of shapes and perspective on canvas. Another woman in the class, far more accomplished than the rest of us, seemed awfully anxious and tense. Why?

19

I asked her, when she was obviously so good. She said she'd really enjoyed painting when she first began, but as she started entering competitions, winning prizes, getting commissions, the less she enjoyed painting, and the more stressful it all became.

I immediately thought of parallels to writing. Entering contests, getting rejected, sending a manuscript out again and again over the years, having one's work continually judged in competition with others'— especially in a glutted market—how truly hard it is to retain that sense of play, to be joyful in the doing. *To have fun.* There's bound to be some emotional erosion over time. Success provides the nutrients necessary to rejuvenate the soil: Design a *writer's* sabbatical. Take a course in a field other than writing. Or read works that speak deeply to the writer's soul. My favorites include Dorothea Brande's *Becoming a Writer* and John Gardner's *On Becoming a Novelist.*

• Success is also finding time to read for pure pleasure, so we don't ever forget what we're about, as writers: To give pleasure—through the stories, poems, or creative essays we write. It's important to read the best writers in order to develop an instinct for "the best" and to cultivate it in our own work.

• Above all, success is forgetting about success and just doing the work at hand: finishing a first draft, setting it aside before rewriting, then digging deeper, maybe after weeks of doubt, misgivings, premature judgments, and all the other "negs" we need to fight. It is sending out that story again and again, while continuing to work on other things. *No matter what.*

Prizes, accolades are fine—wonderful, in fact—as testimonials to where we've been. Where I *am,* though, at the moment is what counts. Right now I'm at my desk writing, and it feels just great. Congratulations are definitely in order.

5

WHAT MAKES A WRITER TICK?

BY WARREN KIEFER

EVERY WRITER DREADS THE BORE who says, "You're just the person I always wanted to meet, because I've got this incredible, surefire idea for a runaway bestseller and a fantastic film. You write it and we split the money."

My most common defense is to pretend I'm deaf and immediately focus my attention elsewhere. Writers are still vulnerable, however, to the other kind of literary groupie whose question is, "Where do you get your ideas?" He or she may be less obsessed than the one who thinks he has a story to tell, but just as ignorant of what makes a writer tick.

And what *does* make a writer tick? Lots of answers have been suggested by writers themselves, and all of them are probably true. Ego is a powerful goad. Writers tend to be uncommon egotists even when they hide behind pseudonyms or ghostwrite other people's books. But there's nothing wrong with ego if it keeps them working. A lack of confidence, in fact, is tough on talent.

The desire to see one's name in print has usually been enough to drive more than one recalcitrant talent to work hard enough and long enough to overcome early rejection and finally to succeed.

But incentives provide only a partial answer to the key question. If there were a recipe for creating an original, pleasurable, readable, salable manuscript and getting the finished product sold and published, it might read something like this: one part *idea,* two parts *talent,* and three parts *motivation* seasoned with *patience.* Trim excess fat from idea, simmer in talent, mix in motivation, and bring to a boil. If patience runs thin, add fresh discipline until it stands by itself.

A reading public is essential, of course, and luckily it is still out there. It may be fickle, biased, or poorly prepared, but then again, it probably always was. Dickens complained when his editors asked him to write down to his readers, while Proust held the public in such

21

contempt he wrote only for himself. Most working writers cannot afford such luxury, but must reach out to their markets, regularly. Today's reading public may be more inclined to rent a video or spend eight dollars going to a ninety-minute film than twenty dollars on a book that lasts a lifetime, but that is of no concern to the writer. Without him video and film wouldn't be there either.

So one starts with the idea. I can't speak for an entire profession, but if I hadn't been brimful of story ideas clamoring to get out, I never would have become a writer. I've never had a problem coming up with themes, characters, and/or plots. The real problem is selection.

Assuming you have a good idea, you can first ask yourself a few simple questions to make sure it is good enough.

Is it truly original, or has it been used before? If it has been used before (and most good ideas have), will your treatment of it be sufficiently fresh or outstanding to give it a chance anyway in a highly competitive market?

Is it of compelling interest to others outside your immediate family and circle of admirers?

Are the characters you envision strong enough to sustain the idea (as well as the writer and the reader) throughout the hundreds of pages necessary to express it?

If the answer is "no" or even a reluctant "maybe" to any of the above, the idea should be shelved without a second thought.

Over the years I've stocked files with notes on storylines that include enough dramatic incidents, dynamic relationships, and intriguing situations to fill a hundred books. I've overpopulated these files with real or imaginary characters whose idiosyncrasies include inventories of everything from the color of their socks to the quality of their minds.

Most of this material I'll never look at again, but the process of writing it down and filing it feeds that data bank of the mind I call the creative subconscious. What I retrieve later may be insignificant, or it may become the driving idea behind a new book. The filing itself is a refining process, and even if the material never sees print, it filters into my daily work, coloring and affecting what I write and perhaps defining my literary style.

Talent is obviously vital and not something one acquires like a suntan but has from birth, like 20/20 vision, hand-eye coordination, or good muscle tone. Yet talent can't succeed without motivation. A writer must want to write more than anything else. Mark Twain described this compulsion as a curse worse than madness, as debilitating as a disease, while Balzac said it was an itch he had to scratch with his pen every day.

Motivation is no substitute for talent, however, any more than money can take the place of motivation. A person anxious to get rich can choose from a hundred professions more remunerative than writing. There are always a few writers—like Stephen King or Danielle Steel—who reach the top income bracket, but according to the Authors Guild, $7,000.00 is the average annual income for professional writers, placing them well below the poverty level.

Assuming one has the talent, the motivation, and the stamina to write, one still needs the time. But that, too, is relative. Full-time employment usually takes only forty hours of a 168-hour week. Allowing for a job, sleep, food, and exercise, anyone with a little self-discipline can always wring another forty writing hours from an ordinary week.

But even with the time to write, when does one decide the idea is important enough to form the basis of a novel, and how does one extrude a publishable work from the bare bones of the idea? In my case, this happens only when I feel the need to explore something in greater depth than I can through my normal habits of thought or random conversation with friends. The make-believe space afforded by the novel allows me to ask questions, probe character, plumb emotions, and circle closer to a clearer understanding of the human condition.

For example, I have always found the question of identity absorbing. Who are we, each of us, really? How many roles do we play in life and how do we perceive others in the roles they play? Race, gender, age, profession, height, weight, education, and cultural background all figure in the identity equation. Alter any one to the least degree and you have a different person. This has been a recurring theme in my work.

I dealt with it first in *The Lingala Code,* a suspense novel about war and violence in Africa. The man telling the story is a U.S. ambassador, married and with children, who had once been an Air Force fighter pilot and CIA agent. Flashing back to his days in the Congo with the CIA, he tells how he investigated the murder of his best friend, nearly got himself killed, and wound up with a red-headed French girl he eventually married. The reader assumes he is white until the very end of the book when I reveal that he is black. This changes nothing basic

23

about the character, but it sharply alters the reader's perception about race and identity, which was my precise intention. The book won the Edgar Allan Poe Award as the year's best mystery novel and brought in hundreds of letters from readers both black and white, who said they'd had to rethink the story in view of their own unconscious prejudices and assumptions.

In *The Stanton Succession,* I returned to the question of identity and people's perception of others, but in an entirely different way. One of the main characters, a corporation vice-president of immense charm and demonstrated ability, is exposed on page 12 as an ex-convict who had once served time in prison for fraud, forgery, and embezzlement. The shock of learning this gives the company president a fatal heart attack, and infighting begins for the successor of his job.

The Stanton Succession is told from the point of view of the company's Wall Street attorney, a man of some rectitude and conscience who nevertheless lets himself be drawn deeper and deeper into a web of corporate criminal intrigue as he balances questions of law and morality against the rampant greed, fear, and ambition around him. His deep misgivings about abandoning old shibboleths in favor of a new morality of convenience reflect my own concern for a society that sometimes seems to be telling us that anything goes as long as you can get away with it.

Unlike my lawyer character, I tend to have ambiguous feelings about the law. And I had some hard questions I hoped to explore in depth while writing the book. I was taught to respect and fear the law, but I also mistrust it, particularly when I see educated, respectable people who know better ignore its moral intent and violate its social constraints in order to further their personal ambition or fill their pockets. In writing *The Stanton Succession,* I found myself asking whether the fault was in the law or in us.

Perhaps there are no clear answers to such questions, but writing a novel does offer a unique way to examine them. Besides entertaining readers, good fiction should also bring both author and reader a little closer to otherwise elusive truths about ourselves and how we relate to the world around us.

For the novelist who likes to enjoy himself at other people's expense, writing a book is a wonderful way to get even. But getting even can also involve a serious shift in one's perception of others, as I once found out to my dismay. I made the main villain in one of my early books a sinister, nasty charmer of the kind who'd sell crack to his kids if there was a buck in it. I modeled him on a former boss in such a way that anyone who knew the real-life man could not fail to see him in my fictional portrait. It was revenge on my part, pure and simple, from the gray in his hair to the flaws in his character. I made the hero of the story his opposite—a younger, handsome, decent sort of fellow with all the right instincts.

A few days after the book was favorably reviewed by *The New York Times,* I received a call from my old boss.

"Congratulations, big shot."

"Ah . . . well . . . thanks."

"When can we do lunch?"

"Well, I dunno . . . let me look at my agenda and . . ."

"Quit stalling. I read your book." He was never one to suffer indecision if he could steamroll his way over you.

I showed up at the restaurant ten minutes early. I told myself I should have talked to a libel lawyer beforehand, and when I saw his grim expression as he walked in, I was sure of it. He sat down heavily and laid an enormous package on the nearby chair. "You did one hell of a job on me," he said flatly. "I give you that."

"Well, look, you know, don't take it . . . I mean . . ."

"Don't take it personally? How am I supposed to take it? The minute I got past the first page I saw what you'd done."

"No harm was meant. . . ." I lied.

"I loved it."

"You. . . ?"

". . . loved it! I recognized myself as the main character immediately. You made me younger and better looking than I really am, but that's O.K.—poetic license, right? Otherwise you got me down to a T. I didn't realize you knew me that well. I liked the heavy, too. He was a well-drawn character." He winked. "I can guess who you had in mind there, but I'll never tell."

I was stunned that he could ever have imagined himself as the hero, and I had no idea whom he thought I'd used as the model for my villain. I simply stared in disbelief as he wrestled his package closer and opened it. Inside were twenty copies of my book with a list of all the people he wanted them inscribed to.

25

6

BOOKS ON TOP

BY E. ANNIE PROULX

EVERY OTHER WEEK SOMEONE SAYS THAT books are dead or dying, that just around the corner is the black hour when they will be curiosities like stereopticon slides or milk stools—probably the same thing they said when radio was invented, when television flickered its way into our living rooms.

To some the phrase means sluggish book sales in the recent and lingering recession; to others it means that the old gray novel ain't what it used to be. Not a few associate the obliteration of distinguished literary houses and imprints in the age of the corporate takeover as synonymous with the inevitable disappearance of books. The hearse followers mournfully announce that no one reads these days, can't read, won't read. It doesn't strike them as peculiar that there is a fierce scramble among corporate interests to buy the publishing houses that put out these dying books.

It's possible that the premature obituaries merely cover our confusion about the clouded direction of change in the culture. As the big publishers try for bestsellers at the expense of serious books, it is increasingly the small publishers and university presses that are finding and publishing the books of interesting new writers.

Books once rather scornfully considered grist for the small publisher's mill are catching the reading public's interest. Among the new books published last year were important works of fiction from Arab-Americans, African-Americans, Chinese-Americans, Mexican-Americans, Caribbean-Americans, Native Americans, and others. The so-called gay and lesbian novel is beginning to escape the genre closet and stand on bookstore shelves alongside traditional works.

Book groups, an old idea, are everywhere. Books are moving into motel and hotel rooms, where a year ago one could find only a single title in a black binding. Now thousands of copies of Joel Conarroe's *Six*

American Poets engage travelers in lonely rooms across the continent. There are guidebooks to used bookshops, and a few imaginative independent booksellers thrive in the shadow of ever-increasing numbers of superstores.

Those who say the book is moribund often cite the computer as the asp on the mat. But the electronic highway is for bulletin boards on esoteric subjects, reference works, lists and news—timely utilitarian information, efficiently pulled through the wires. Nobody is going to sit down and read a novel on a twitchy little screen. Ever.

In a curious way, the computer emphasizes the unique virtues of the book:

The book is small, lightweight and durable, and can be stuffed in a coat pocket, read in the waiting room, on the plane. What are planes but flying reading rooms?

Books give esthetic and tactile pleasure, from the dust jacket art to the binding, paper, typography and text design, from the moment of purchase until the last page is turned.

Books speak even when they stand unopened on the shelf. If you would know a man or woman, look at their books, not their software.

§ 7

LONESOME HILLS, PURPLE SKY

BY NANCY SPRINGER

ON THE MORNING I WAS TO LEAVE for a few days' visit to my mother, just before I awoke, I had a vivid dream:

I was at Mom's house. Well, sort of. It seemed to be the house I grew up in, but isolated in a strange landscape of uninhabited chartreuse hills under a bruise-purple sky. For some reason a book manuscript of mine was lying out under that dark sky. I had taken it along to work on, apparently, but it had never made it through Mom's door. It lay stranded, a stolid chunk of paper, on the front lawn, where a passing motorist flicked a cigarette on it and set it afire. I tried again and again with my bare foot to stamp out the fire, but it kept coming back like the flame on one of those trick birthday candles. I called for help, but no one came. Finally, a drizzly rain started falling, and I put the fire out.

Only the first few pages of the manuscript were charred. I left it in the rain and was packing my suitcase to go home when I realized I had forgotten my manuscript and ran outside to get it. It was gone. I felt frantic, bereft. I ran and ran, then I spotted the end of it, a long computer-paper ribbon, and gather it into my arms. Was that all of it? No. One the other side of the road I saw more. I scrambled down the steep embankment and started to cross, but a car was speeding at me, it was going to hit me, then . . . .

I woke up, of course.

Usually, I do not pay much attention to my dreams. On those rare occasions when I can remember them, I find them regrettably lacking in plot. I wasn't going to be writing for a few days anyway. There would be no use in taking a manuscript to my mother's place. So I left my office behind and drove three hours down the road. During the next few days, Mom and I shopped, and watched game shows, and ate too much fried chicken.

28

Driving back home at the end of my visit, I found myself thinking again about that damn dream, which was for some reason still vivid in my memory.

The main thing I remembered about it was the feeling of being pulled in two directions, trying to be in two places at once. The manuscript was outside, with the sky and the rain and the lonesome hills; my family was inside, around the table in the warm kitchen. I was constantly feeling as if I ought to be out when I was in, and in when I was out; running back and forth between my family and my writing, in danger of being torn in half.

Over the years, I have talked with many beginning writers who have expressed a feeling that their writing is not understood or taken seriously by family and friends. Most of them also hoped that, once they were published, this would change, that once they were earning money by their writing, relatives would be more willing to let them write, be more approving, more interested and supportive.

Yes and no. Yes, now that I am many times published, my family is very good about allowing me uninterrupted writing time. But no, as one who is eighteen books down the road, I have my dream as evidence: In a way things haven't changed all that much.

Nor should they. I am convinced now that some loneliness, some sense of separation, is at the heart of the writing process. People who are happy and well-adjusted and leading full lives don't write—they don't feel the need. Show me a writer, and I will show you somebody standing with nose pressed to the windows. If you feel distanced, it is not necessarily something your family has done to you; it may just be part of who and what you are. As a writer, you will always be to some extent an observer, an outsider looking in.

As a writer, you are a somewhat discomfiting person to know, let alone to be related to. A writer is one of those people who will forget everything else to go chasing after a book, as I did in my dream. If family members are reluctant to acknowledge the writer in us, it is not necessarily because they don't understand us; it may be because they understand us all too well.

"Everything goes by the board: honor, pride, decency . . . to get the book written," William Faulkner once said. "If a writer has to rob his mother, he will not hesitate; the *Ode on a Grecian Urn* is worth any number of old ladies."

29

Faulkner was more honest than most of us. Sexist, possibly, but honest.

Most family members instinctively know about writers. They know about the fire that burns inside us. They know our priorities are different from theirs. They know that even when we are with them, part of us is always somewhere else. But it's rough on them, too, the aura of separation and distance that we have. They sense it, and therefore, the less they think of us as writers, the less they have to face the danger of losing us.

What was my vivid, crazy dream trying to tell me? I guess the writer part of me did not like the idea of losing three days of work. Viewing it entirely from a writer's point of view, my dreaming self sees the world as hostile to writers and writing. Motorists seem intent on killing me. Family is obtuse, oblivious to fire, and nobody is looking out at the wild, beautiful hills across which the most important thing in my life is blowing away.

Driving home to where my office and my works-in-progress blessedly awaited me, I thought a lot about all this. My mother had not asked how my writing was going. I had not even told her about the exciting phone call from my agent, telling me about my latest book sale. Strange.

No, not so strange, because I knew she would just say, "That's nice. Congratulations, dear. Would you like some crossword puzzle books to take home?" Much as my husband had said, "Great, honey! What's for dinner?"

So what did I ever do about it all, when I got home? What does a writer ever do about anything? I wrote this article. And as I wrote, I realized a few things:

—I am a mature, productive writer who does not need coddling.
—Rather than feeling torn in half, I could consider myself as having the best of two worlds.
—Crossword-puzzle books and what's for dinner are not bad things.
—Being inside the house is cozy and warm.
—I have a family, not a following of groupies.

Would I really want it any other way?

Still . . . above the yellow hills of my dream hangs a purple sky. The wind blows lonesome, bringing the rain.

30

8

FROM TYPEWRITER TO COMPUTER SCREEN

BY RICHARD EDER

"ONCE YOU GET USED TO YOUR COMPUTER, you'll never want to use your typewriter again." So everyone assured me after the newspaper I write for cut back the staff that transcribes typed manuscripts into the word-processing system.

Right. After the factory power-loom, you'll never want to hand-weave again. After you spray the crops with weed-killer, you'll never need to hold a hoe. After you try aluminum siding on your house, you'll never nail another clapboard. And after you eat frozen peas, you'll never shell fresh ones.

"Wait a month," they said, as I fretted about the disembodied quality of the green glowworms on the computer screen, compared with the sharp definition of typed strokes on paper; and worried about growing wordy out of sheer ease, or becoming turgid out of the screen's tendency to make a blur between the look of a tight springy sentence and a soft, pillowy one.

Right. And: "Wait an hour or two," Circe told her mariner guests when they complained of bristly noses and a difficulty in standing upright. Sure enough, it was no time at all before they were finding a mud wallow more satisfactory than sheets, and no need to iron; acorns better than moussaka and easier to prepare; and their companions' squeals as eloquent as Demosthenes' oratory, which by then would have been all Greek to them.

It's an old scruple, by now; surely just about everyone who writes has made similar grumbling noises on the way from typewriter to computer screen. Why come in at this late date with my own? It is like reviving, after all this time, the silly concern of some farmers that electricity would "leak" from high-tension wires and do harm, or the fears of gently-nurtured women 100 years ago about exposing their

31

complexions to the sun, or the notion that computerized record keeping could somehow threaten privacy. Yes.

"You'll end up loving it." I do, in a way, and that's the trouble. Just as predicted, the initial fumblings and rebellions subside; the technological barrier is not really all that formidable. Great fun, not to mention convenience, in using three keystrokes to hurl around whole paragraphs as if they were thunderbolts; in avoiding the laborious tedium of retyping; in not merely correcting a page of false starts, but totally annihilating it. No longer is it lying balled up by the wastebasket—it's gone.

The allure goes deeper than that. Writing is a lonely affair. How companionable the hum when you switch on, a minute or two before you can start writing. By the time you do start, it is no longer a matter of setting off on a solitary expedition from the everyday populated known, to the everlastingly unpopulated unknown. It is like entering a conversation that is already going on, joining a two-person committee where the other member has already arrived and is making coffee.

The computer's hum is a hum of approval. Every word you quietly stroke in is greeted with the same purr, the same pulsing green recognition. It is a writer's play school: That was interesting, Johnny, after Johnny has given a disjointed report about his collection of toilet paper rolls. How different from the tortured glower a bad sentence gives us back from the typed page. "Go on, go on, good," says the sentence on the screen. "Make me better, you hopeless idiot," says the sentence on the page.

Writing began as inscribing, on stone and clay, and later on papyrus parchment and paper. There was the stroke and the resistance and what happened when they met. Writing was never pure idea any more than friendship is pure conquest.

The quality of the encounter varied, of course; the gravity of chiseling rock is not the same as that of typing on paper. There were those who lamented the loss of stylistic élan as the quill-pen's difficulties eased into the successive convenience of the steel-nib dipping-pen and the fountain pen.

Today, there are writers who feel unable to express themselves even on a typewriter, and stick to pen or pencil. Despite the differences, the stylus, pen and typewriter were all inscribing on something. The word-processing computer breaks the encounter entirely. There is no resist-

32

ant material. There is only the glowing light of what is intended, without the marks of what is achieved. "It is not writing, it is skywriting," a friend said years ago, when the computer was just coming in. He was a writer then; he is an editor now, and every day he scrolls the sky down to see what has floated in.

It could be argued, and is, that this is an ascent into sublimity, into unimpeded self-expression. We write on the sky, we are archangels. We are free of the hostile look of our bad prose squatting across our path like a toad. We are alone with the approving hum. We are part of the great communication machinery; the machinery that polishes resumés until they shine, that bestows precocious authority on student papers while fixing their spelling, and that makes manuscripts longer and longer. While hospitably recording our intentions, it is programmed with the intentions of its designers. Who are they, and who hires them? Probably this sounds paranoid; no doubt their purpose is benevolent. But at best, they are slipping their layer of benevolence in between the dust of creation and the breath that brings it to life.

The first pieces I wrote on the computer were marked by sentences swollen with jargon and useless connective phrases. Things are better, and I suppose I am about as intelligent as I ever was. I try to clean up lines as I apply a pen to the paper printout. But I have the suspicion that I have retreated into my intentions, that I am operating with fewer windows, and achieving greater fluency and less reality. Writing threatens to become more of a chess problem and less of a chess game.

Since writing began, its implement or implements were a kind of working companion, a small mutt that helped round up the sheep of our imaginations. The dog has grown until it is beginning to dwarf the sheep. Is it eating them?

9

FIVE WAYS TO HANDLE REJECTIONS

BY MARY WARREN

REJECTIONS SLIPS PLUNGE MOST WRITERS into the doldrums. Here are several ways to help you avoid the "poor me" syndrome.

1. *Persistence pays off.* At the age of 11, I mailed out my first manuscript. I had read about Frances Hodgson Burnett, author of *The Secret Garden.* As a young girl, she sent a story to a magazine, stating "My object is remuneration."

I hurried to the dictionary, looked up *remuneration,* discovered it meant "being paid for the work you do," and sat down to copy three of my poems in careful penmanship. I added Frances Burnett's terse statement to the letter I included and sent the poems off to *The Saturday Evening Post.*

"My object is remuneration." How those editors must have chuckled! I did receive a rejection slip, the first of many. But there was a kind note, too, commending me for my creative effort and encouraging me to keep on writing.

Successful authors often reveal how many rejections they received. For instance, Catherine Cookson was told at the beginning of her fruitful career that her writing was so poor she should abandon any idea of writing for publication. Alex Haley claimed he wrote steadily for five years before receiving a letter from an editor instead of a printed slip. Dr. Seuss received *twenty-seven* rejections before his first book *To Think That I Saw It On Mulberry Street,* was accepted. Jane Yolen, Colleen McCullough, and Madeleine L'Engle all have similar stories about rejections.

Persistence means sending your work out not once or twice, but *many* times. I submitted my first juvenile novel, *Walk in My Moccasins,* four times before Westminster Press wrote the most exciting letter of acceptance I've ever received.

Do your homework, and consult current market lists. When you select the first target for your manuscript, choose five additional possibilities. If your manuscript is returned, reread it and if you spot flaws, correct them. Then send it off to the next market on your list without delay.

2. *Polish and revise.* Ask yourself the following questions: Does my manuscript look professional? Are the grammar, punctuation, and spelling correct? Is the type clean and easy to read? Is the piece well organized? Examine every page, and cut any expression that seems trite or overused. Don't send out a manuscript that lacks originality. You can use an old theme or plot, as long as you give it a new twist.

Was the market you selected appropriate? Did you send a short story to a magazine that uses only articles? Did you send the complete manuscript to an editor who stated unequivocally in the listing, "Always query first"?

Be ruthless with your revisions, with one exception: If, after reading a returned manuscript several times (with a lull of several days or weeks between readings), you judge it to be high quality . . . trust your intuition. Don't tinker with it. Instead, make a new list of possible markets and, one by one, try them all.

3. *Pay attention to valid criticism.* If you receive an editorial comment along with your returned manuscript, weight it carefully, remembering that different editors have different tastes. If you get a similar comment from other editors, try making the suggested changes. For instance, if two or three editors note that your mystery plot is intriguing but your heroine seems stereotyped, take this into consideration as you revise. Develop an original heroine who will remain in the mind of a reader long after the book has been read.

Forget accolades you receive from relatives and friends. The only friends who ever see my unpublished manuscripts are professional colleagues who read my work with a trained eye. They can be objective. A good critique group, especially one with members who have some degree of publishing success, will prove invaluable.

4. *Develop a positive attitude.* As a writer you probably will hit long dry periods. I do. After selling 23 books and numerous articles, I still receive rejection slips, but I have found a way to sweeten my sour

mood whenever that happens. I view each rejection as a *practice piece* instead of a failure! It makes a enormous difference in my attitude.

Your rejections or practice pieces are not useless. If you fail to sell a manuscript after numerous rejections, try incorporating one of the characters or one of the article ideas into a different piece of writing. A plot germ too thin for a novel, for instance, may be exactly right for a short story.

5. *Put perennially unsold manuscripts away for a while.* Don't fly into a tizzy after the twentieth rejection and discard a manuscript; however, don't leave those rejected manuscripts hidden forever. Sort through them from time to time, study current markets, send them out again. Markets change. Editors change. So does the taste of the reading public. Publishing houses may have been flooded with cat stories or historical romances ten years ago, but perhaps a new company is ready for something in one of those fields now.

On the other hand, as you look over your rejections and come upon a manuscript you *know* will never see publication because hours of revision cannot make it hit the mark—what then? You can do one of three things:

Leave it in your file—which will add to unnecessary clutter.

Throw it away—in many cases, a sensible action to take.

Collect your unwanted manuscripts in a scrapbook titled *The Unpublished Works of Frank Carpenter* or whoever *you* are. This, come to think of it, is an elegant idea! "Unpublished" sounds more appealing than "rejected," doesn't it? Why stash unpublished stories and articles and novels in boxes when you *could* punch holes in the pages and bind them in looseleaf notebooks? Keep these notebooks on a bookshelf where you can look at them for fresh insights, or share them with interested writing colleagues, family, and friends.

So . . . don't shed crocodile tears over rejection slips or paper your walls with them, as some writers claim they do. As a starter, try these five feasible ideas.

36

10

Writer's Block—and What to Do About It

By Jeffrey Skinner and Stephen Phillip Policoff

Now here's a subject and a cry near and dear to every writer's heart: I can't think of a single thing to say!

You wake bright and early. You note the weather and the stirring of the few birds earlier than yourself carrying on their bird business in the yard. You brew the coffee, eat your bran muffin, settle in to that magical corner of your room. In the past, this spot has reliably carried you to the height of the American Parnassus. You touch extra-fine-point felt-tip pen to paper. Two hours pass and, upon lifting pen from paper you discover . . . a dot! It's round! The same color as the ink in your pen! Never mind that every pencil within reach may now be sharpened to acuity, and your desk beautifully organized and dusted for the first time in six months, and a second pot of coffee consumed, and all neighborhood bird life and car movements scrupulously observed and mentally noted. You have not written a word.

This is an old story. Every writer has a tale of woe to tell about going blank, dry, empty, blocked. Even when I first began writing and would turn out poems at an alarming rate, day after day, I eventually got wind of this thing called writer's block and, of course, immediately came down with an acutely painful case of it. "I'm afraid," I said archly to a friend, "that each poet has a finite stock of images given to him in a lifetime, and that I may be approaching the end of my store."

The problem is that we have amnesia. Sometimes we forget that we have written before, that we are essentially the same person, and that we will touch that true place of poetry within us and write again. We mistake a momentary pause for a permanent condition. I don't know why writers are so susceptible to this fear; perhaps because, by temperament, we have such a strong interest and investment in the very notion of permanence.

In any case, it is common among writers to experience periods of block, or dryness, or times when the muse does not return our calls—however we choose to characterize those stretches when nothing comes, and we simply do not write. And the fact that virtually every one among us, in this loose tribe called writers, at one time or another, or repeatedly, shares this problem, should and can be the beginning of our calm as we face writer's block individually. We are not alone; others have worked through blocks to write more and better than ever before, and so can we. So the first thing to do when facing the scary void of writer's block is to relax, to rest easy in the knowledge that you *will* write again.

The fact is that there are probably times in any writer's life when it is a good idea not to be writing. "To every thing," Ecclesiastes said, "there is a season." The marathoner must rest at the end of a race, and poet who has written hard under the white heat of inspired composition has also expended great energy and needs time to regroup and recover mentally, physically, and spiritually. This is natural, and it may well be that an inability to write the next poem, at the time you want to write it, is a deep expression of the body/mind/spirit's need for solitude, silence, new reading, or simply just loafing around. Loafing is good: "I loaf and invite my soul, I lean and loaf at my ease observing a spear of summer grass," said Walt Whitman. All of us, in this time and this country, are more driven than is good for our souls. Walt had the right idea. There is a time for writing, and there is a time for contemplation, for just being.

After we have taken a few deep breaths, gained some healthy perspective on the problem, and had our proper fill of loafing, there are some concrete steps we can take to "prime the pump"—to slip back into the writing head. I'll list a few that have worked for me and for other poets I've known. As with all my suggestions, not every one will work for you, but if you keep trying I'm pretty sure that something will, by and by, shake loose inside, letting the words through again.

Vary writing locations

Generally, it's a good idea to establish a writing routine, if at all possible: writing in the same place, at the same time, for the same

38

period, every day. This is the ideal, but any schedule approaching this regularity can work.

Writing under these circumstances becomes a sort of conditioned response; somehow the body/mind/psyche learns through repetition that there is a time and place to write and slips faster and deeper into the writing mode with familiarity and practice. The unconscious (whatever that may mean) gets into the act.

An hour a day on a regular basis is better than ten hours all at once at unpredictable intervals. We understand only too well how hard this is to put into practice in our harried world, but we also have experienced (at those blissful times when we were able to write on a regular, daily basis) the benefits of such perseverance.

This is one of those general principles that was made to be broken. And if you are blocked, vary your writing routine. Maybe just the thing you need to stir up fresh stuff is to write in the park instead of at your desk; to write first thing in the morning, if you are a usually a night writer; to use a pen instead of a typewriter or a typewriter instead of a pen. Writers tend to be ritualistic, at least about writing process and paraphernalia, and sometimes turning our usual ritual on its head can result in a poem (or a story or a play) we never dreamed could come from us—one that can "stand on its hands." Experiment!

Give up the fixed ideas you've had about your own writing ("I can write only when it's absolutely quiet") and try the opposite. You can change the rules of the game. Why not? It's your game.

Vary your reading

Writers tend to be readers ("A writer is a reader who is moved to emulation," said Saul Bellow), so we probably don't have to tell you how important it is to the enrichment of your own work to read the work of others. But it is. Read the work of those who are doing, this moment, what you want to do—living, publishing poets and fiction writers. Read lots of it. You're not going to like all of what you read, but that's natural; nobody likes all of anything. But we hope you find enough to fall in love with: those chosen writers that seem to speak to you personally, whom you read with absolute wonder that they know so much about your inner life, who change you in ways sometimes more profound than the three-dimensional, living-color people you speak to and dance with and love and can't stand, every day. The passion of our reading feeds the passion of our writing, in some way both mysterious and absolutely real.

So if we find ourselves in a slump, we can easily change one of the things that most directly and deeply affects our writing: our reading. As in location, sometimes it's very fruitful to make a radical change— to pick up the kind of book we never thought we'd be interested in, something ordinarily far from our tastes. If we have a passion for Kurt Vonnegut, we might try the more mainstream (but also highly readable and accomplished) novels of Anne Tyler. If our tastes in poetry ordinarily run to the high-speed surrealism of, for example, James Tate, we might try the firmly grounded, statuesque poems of Louise Gluck. If you don't know enough about the scene to find such new resources, ask your friends for recommendations.

But this suggestion about varying your reading does not only apply to "fine literary writing." Most writers are voracious readers of anything printed. There is nothing wrong with "escapist" literature! Or instruction manuals, biographies, fairy tales, geology textbooks, rock star interviews, science journals, *People* magazine, or, anything in words—it can all be grist for the writer's mill. Pick up the *National Enquirer* at the supermarket checkout. Maybe the two-headed baby story will spark your next story or poem. We don't suggest that you make this kind of thing your only pleasure reading; it's essential that you read the best published examples of contemporary fiction and poetry and lots of it. But ideas come from the oddest places, and for a writer to divide all printed matter into the two categories of *literature* and *trash,* boasting of the former and sneering at the latter, is simply self-imposed limitation. It's more liberating to think of ourselves as scientists of the sentence, the line, the word; on some level every specimen is worth examining. Read with an alert sensitivity to language, and everything you read will give you something—perhaps the beginnings of your next poem or story.

Jump-starts

Freewrite in your journal to help you rev up your creative engine and jump-start your failed battery. Write down everything that comes into your head. Describe the smirk on a colleague's face; scold your friend on the page; write the stupidest, foulest things you can think of. Any writing helps the act of writing seem less daunting.

Write a letter, not a real letter but one that you have no intention of mailing. Write a letter to someone you admire but could never bring yourself to talk to. Write a letter to the friend you wish you had. Write a letter to someone in which you say everything you've ever wanted to say—then throw it away. Or, better still, read it over; maybe you'll find a poem lurking in there; maybe there's a character you've invented without even knowing it.

Exercise. Creative people often use physical exercise as a way of forcing their minds to work in a different way. Sitting and brooding over the blank page in front of you is probably the worst thing you can do. Jog around your neighborhood; take your dog for the longest walk he's ever been on; go for a swim; ride your bike to that secret place where you can scream, and no one will hear you—or care, anyway. But while you're doing these things, be sure you keep your eyes open, and observe everything around you. Be a sponge; soak up the atmosphere, even if it's the same atmosphere you see every day.

People-watch—intensively. If you can, go somewhere, sit down, and watch the world go by. Go to the mall, the local diner, the donut shop, the bus station, the train station, a busy downtown street—somewhere, anywhere, as long as there are lots of people going by. Bring your journal, and just sit and watch. Sooner or later someone will do something or say something or walk by wearing a weird hat, and maybe you'll get an idea. Maybe you won't, but you will have removed yourself from the place where ideas are not flowing, and put yourself in a position to make them flow. There is probably no better way to invite ideas than simply to allow yourself to observe and think and laugh.

Sit in the dark and listen to music. The idea is to jolt your mind out of its usual mode of thinking, and try to get into a sort of trance state. That's what freewriting does, to an extent, and what physical exercise does. Some music nudges us into that state. You must experiment with the sort of music that will work for you. It probably won't be the kind of music you listen to for fun, to dance to, or when you're bored. Instead, try some instrumental music—classical or jazz—or what is often called "New Age" music, music that washes over you, like waves of the ocean. You may hate it, but the point is that this sort of music (and weirder music, like that of Philip Glass and Laurie Anderson) often acts in an almost hypnotic way and may coax your imagination out of hiding.

41

Go to a museum. Looking at pictures, especially unusual ones, or pictures you are unfamiliar with, can be a valuable goad to the creative process. If there's no museum accessible, go to the library or to a bookstore and look at art or photography books. Try to find an image or two that intrigues you or gives you the creeps, then without trying to figure out why you like or hate it, write down everything you can remember about it: what it made you think of, what you think the artist was up to, what you saw in that picture.

There are lots of other gambits that writers have dreamed up to coax them out of writer's block. Ernest Hemingway always stopped for the day in mid-sentence so that when he returned the next day, he would have a way of beginning again without thinking about what he was doing.

Remember, too, that all writers write badly most of the time. All writers—young ones, old ones, famous ones, desperate ones. Feeling compelled to write brilliantly, or even passably well, all the time is a sure-fire way to thwart your ability to write at all.

Ultimately, the most important lesson to be learned from writer's block is this: You just have to write. You can put it off, you can worry about it, you can tear up each page because you hate it so much, you can swear you'll never write again, but still you know that you will. Writing is the best cure for not writing. Writing nonsense, writing stuff you know stinks to high heaven, writing because you want to, have to write—that's all that counts.

🙞 11

How to Deal with Non-Writer's Block

By Phillip M. Margolin

Until I was thirty, I had a severe case of non-writer's block, a mental disease that keeps many potential writers from taking the step from having an idea to writing it. I had never met a published writer, so I assumed (1) that they all had the writing ability of Shakespeare and the I.Q. of Einstein, and (2) that I would never be one of them because I did not. Now, twenty years after the publication of my first short story, with a novel that made *The New York Times* bestseller list, an Edgar nomination, and a movie under my belt, I still find it hard to believe that I am a published writer. The insecurity bred by non-writer's block is hard to shake. I hope this piece will cure some of the people with this disease and help them become published writers.

What is the most important part of a writer's anatomy?

The most important part of the writer's anatomy is not the brain, where ideas are born, or the hands that transfer those ideas into concrete form, but the backside. I'd never met a published fiction writer until I published my first short story. I was in awe of published writers. Since my work has been published, I have had the pleasure of meeting many writers. They are very bright and very nice, but they are no more creative or intelligent than my non-writing friends. In my experience, the big difference between published and unpublished writers is that published writers sit down and write. If what you write is good, it will probably be published some day; if it is never published, you've had the fun of writing.

"I don't have time to write."

This type of thinking is a clear symptom of non-writer's block. I wrote my three novels while practicing law full-time and raising two children. How did I find the time? If you play golf or bridge or have a hobby, how much time do you spend on those activities? I write my novels on the weekend. I'm at my word processor by eight in the morning and write until eleven when the family is ready to do things. Every once in a while, I will write for an hour or two before going to work or take a day off. When I have a week's vacation, I write. While other people are out on the golf course, I'm pounding away on my word processor. If you think of writing as a hobby, then the mystery is solved.

Here are two other ways to think about time:

A. If you write one page a day for a year, you will have a 365-page manuscript. If you write two pages a day, you'll have *War and Peace*.

B. If you have no contract for the book you are writing, check your actuarial table. It will tell you how much time you have to complete your novel. No contract + no deadline = plenty of time to finish your book.

If you have a full-time job as I do, I suggest you write a detailed outline before you start writing your novel. This outline will help you get back into your book if you have to leave it for days at a time because of your daytime job.

Write your first draft without worrying about the quality of the writing or how much sense the book makes. Get all your ideas out of your head and on to paper. Once you have finished this bad first draft, you will really have written a very detailed outline. Now you can spend time rewriting and editing to make the bad outline into a good book.

Never write to publish; always write for fun.

People with non-writer's block do not write because they are afraid they cannot write anything worth being published. You should write because you have an idea and want to turn it into a novel. You should never write just to be published. Writing should be a happy experience without any pressure. Defending murder cases is exciting, but stressful. I write to escape from the real world. I want to have only fun when I write, and no responsibility to anyone but myself.

I have written three novels that have been published. I have also written novels that have not been published. I can honestly say that I had as much fun writing the unpublished novels as I did writing my best-selling *Gone, But Not Forgotten*. Of course, I did not know that

Gone, But Not Forgotten would be published when I wrote it. Its success has been a great thrill for me, but I had the most fun the year I spent writing and editing the book. If you write for fun, you will always enjoy writing. If your book is published, that's gravy.

Is there a difference between publishable and unpublishable?

In 1974, at the age of thirty, I sold "The Girl in the Yellow Bikini," a short story, to a mystery magazine. This gave me the confidence to try to write a publishable novel. I had submitted short stories before, but they had all been rejected, so I reread "The Girl in the Yellow Bikini" and the stories that had been rejected to find out what was so different about my successful venture.

"The Girl in the Yellow Bikini" is about a man who loses his job just before his wife leaves him. It is summer, and he is alone and depressed. A beautiful woman moves into the house across the street and sunbathes in a yellow bikini. At first, our hero watches her as a voyeur. Then, because he is bored, he decides to try to find out as much as he can about his sexy-looking neighbor without meeting her or her finding out. Eventually, there is a double murder and blackmail.

There were two significant differences between my unpublished stories and my successful story. "The Girl in the Yellow Bikini" had (1) a believable and unpredictable plot and (2) believable characters with whom the reader could identify.

I have read a number of manuscripts over the years from people who wanted to publish. Many of them suffered from either having no plot or having a plot that made no sense. Here are some tips on developing a plot:

A. Don't start writing until you have your ending. There is nothing worse than spending twenty years writing the great American novel only to find you cannot end it. You can always change your ending, but you must have something toward which to write.

B. A plot must have twists and turns. If readers can figure out your ending in chapter one why should they read to the end? Set up your readers. Convince them they know what is going on, then pull the rug out from under them. If you fool a reader once, he will never trust his judgment again. This advice does not just apply to mystery novels.

You must also create believable characters with whom your reader

45

can identify. My hero in "The Girl in the Yellow Bikini" was lonely, unemployed, and unloved. Many readers have lost a job at some time in their lives or had an unhappy romantic experience. They could identify with my hero, and that made them care about what happened to him. This meant they would want to read to the end of the story to see if my hero came out O.K.

Your characters should have limps, pimples, and histories, and they must be psychologically consistent throughout the book. Insecure characters should not become steely, self-assured individuals without something in the plot to help them change.

Rewrite, rewrite, rewrite.

As a general rule, nothing you write the first time is any good. You will think your first draft is good or else you would not have written it, but if you put it away and reread it a day or so later, you will see it really needs work.

To evaluate your writing properly, you must have no ego involvement in it. That means you must be willing to cut anything that does not work well in the story, no matter how beautifully it is written. You must also be open to criticism.

I love to have an editor tear my book apart. I do not always agree with what an editor says, but I listen because I know he wants my book to be excellent and is trying to help me make my book better.

I hope these writing tips have been useful. I also hope you are writing, because the tips only help if there are words on paper. Now sit down, boot up your word processor, or sharpen your pencil. If you care about writing enough to read this article, you are probably excited enough about writing to start doing it.

12

TALKING ABOUT WRITING

BY URSULA K. LE GUIN

PEOPLE COME UP TO YOU if you're a writer, and they say, I want to be a writer. How do I become a writer?

I have a two-stage answer to that. The first-stage answer is this: You learn to type (or to word-process). The only alternative is to have an inherited income and hire a full-time stenographer. If this seems unlikely, don't worry. Keyboards are easy to learn.

Well, the person who asked, How do I become a writer, is a bit cross now, and mumbles, but that isn't what I meant. (And I say, I know it wasn't.) I want to write short stories, what are the rules for writing short stories? I want to write a novel, what are the rules for writing novels?

Now I say Ah! and get really enthusiastic. You can find all the rules of writing in the book called *Elements of Style,* by Strunk and White, and a good dictionary—I recommend the *Shorter Oxford*; Webster's is too wishy-washy. There are only a very few rules of writing not covered in those two volumes, and I can summarize them thus: Your story may begin in longhand on the backs of old shopping lists, but when it goes to an editor, it should be typed, double-spaced, on one side of the paper only, with generous margins—especially the left-hand one—and not too many really grotty corrections per page.

Your name and its name and the page number should be on the top of every single page; and when you mail it to the editor it should have enclosed with it a stamped, self-addressed envelope. And those are the Basic Rules of Writing.

I'm not being funny. Those are the basic requirements for a readable, therefore publishable, manuscript. And, beyond grammar and spelling, they are the only rules of writing I know.

All right, that is stage one of my answer. If the person listens to all that without hitting me, and still says All right all right, but how *do* you become a writer, then I can deliver stage two. How do you become a writer? Answer: You write.

It's amazing how much resentment and evasion this answer can arouse. Even among writers, believe me.

The most frequent evasive tactic is for the would-be writer to say, But before I have anything to say, I must get *experience*.

Well, yes; if you want to be a journalist. But I don't know anything about journalism, I'm talking about fiction. And of course fiction is made out of experience, your whole life from infancy on, everything you've thought and done and seen and read and dreamed. But experience isn't something you go and *get*—it's a gift, and the only prerequisite for receiving it is that you be open to it. A closed soul can have the most immense adventures, go through a civil war or a trip to the moon, and have nothing to show for all that "experience"; whereas the open soul can do wonders with nothing. I invite you to meditate on a pair of sisters. Emily and Charlotte. Their life experience was an isolated vicarage in a small, dreary English village, a couple of bad years at a girls' school, another year or two in Brussels, and a lot of housework. Out of that seething mass of raw, vital, brutal, gutsy Experience they made two of the greatest novels ever written: *Jane Eyre* and *Wuthering Heights*.

Now of course they were writing from experience; writing about what they knew, which is what people always tell you to do; but what was their experience? What was it they knew? Very little about "life." They knew their own souls, they knew their own minds and hearts; and it was not a knowledge lightly or easily gained. From the time they were seven or eight years old, they wrote, and thought, and learned the landscape of their own being, and how to describe it. They wrote with the imagination, which is the tool of the farmer, the plow you plow your own soul with. They wrote from inside, from as deep inside as they could get by using all their strength and courage and intelligence. And that is where books come from. The novelist writes from inside.

I'm rather sensitive on this point, because I often write science fiction, or fantasy, or about imaginary countries—stuff that, by definition, involves times, places, events that I could not possibly experience in my own life. So when I was young and would submit one of these things about space voyages to Orion or dragons or something, I was

48

told, at extremely regular intervals, "You should try to write about things you know." And I would say, But I do; I know about Orion, and dragons, and imaginary countries. Who do you think knows about my own imaginary countries, if I don't?

But they didn't listen, because they don't understand. They think an artist is like a roll of photographic film: You expose it and develop it and there is a reproduction of Reality in two dimensions. But that's all wrong, and if any artist tells you "I am a camera," or "I am a mirror," distrust them instantly; they're fooling you. Artists are people who are not at all interested in the facts—only in the truth. You get the facts from outside. The truth you get from inside.

O.K., how do you go about getting at that truth? You want to tell the truth. You want to be a writer. So what do you do?

You write.

Why do people ask that question? Does anybody ever come up to a musician and say, Tell me, tell me—how should I become a tuba player? No! it's too obvious. If you want to be a tuba player you get a tuba, and some tuba music. And you ask the neighbors to move away or put cotton in their ears. And probably you get a tuba teacher, because there are quite a lot of objective rules and techniques both to written music and to tuba performance. And then you sit down and you play the tuba, every day, every week, every month, year after year, until you are good at playing the tuba; until you can—if you desire—play the truth on the tuba.

It is exactly the same with writing. You sit down, and you do it, and you do it, and you do it, until you have learned how to do it.

Of course, there are differences. Writing makes no noise, except groans, and it can be done anywhere, and it is done alone.

It is the experience or premonition of that loneliness, perhaps, that drives a lot of young writers into this search for rules.

Writing cannot be shared, nor can it be taught as a technique, except on the most superficial level. All a writer's real learning is done alone, thinking, reading other people's books, or writing—practicing. A really good writing class or workshop can give us some shadow of what musicians have all the time—the excitement of a group working together, so that each member outdoes himself—but what comes out of that is not a collaboration, like a symphony performance, but a lot of

49

totally separate, isolated works, expressions of individual souls. And therefore there are no rules, except those each individual makes up.

I know. There are lots of rules. You find them in the books about The Craft of Fiction and The Art of the Short Story and so on. I know some of them. One of them says: Never begin a story with dialogue! People won't read it; here is somebody talking and readers don't know who, and so they don't care, so—Never begin a story with dialogue.

Well, there is a story I know, it begins like this:

"*Eh bien, mon prince!* so Genoa and Lucca are now no more than private estates of the Bonaparte family!"

It's not only a dialogue opening, the first four words are in *French*, and it's not even a French novel. What a horrible way to begin a book! The title of the book is *War and Peace*.

There's another Rule I know: Introduce all the main characters early in the book. That sounds perfectly sensible, mostly I suppose it is sensible, but it's not a rule, or if it is somebody forgot to tell it to Charles Dickens. He didn't get Sam Weller into the *Pickwick Papers* for ten chapters—that's five months, since the book was coming out as a serial in installments.

Now you can say, all right, so Tolstoy can break the rules, so Dickens can break the rules, but they're geniuses; rules are made for geniuses to break, but for ordinary, talented, not-yet-professional writers to follow, as guidelines.

And I would accept this, but very grudgingly. Put it this way: If you feel you need rules and want rules, and you find a rule that appeals to you, or that works for you, then follow it. Use it. But if it doesn't appeal to you or work for you, then ignore it; in fact, if you want to and are able to, kick it in the teeth, break it, fold staple mutilate and destroy it.

See, the thing is, as a writer you are free. You are about the freest person that ever was. Your freedom is what you have bought with your solitude, your loneliness. You are in the country where *you* make up the rules, the laws. It is a country nobody has ever explored before. It is up to you to make the maps, to build the cities. Nobody else in the world can do it, or ever could do it, or ever will be able to do it again.

Absolute freedom is absolute responsibility. The writer's job, as I see it, is to tell the truth. The writer's truth—nobody else's. It is not an easy job. You know how hard it is to say to somebody, just somebody you know, how you *really* feel, what you *really* think—with complete honesty? You have to trust them, and you have to *know yourself,* before you can say anything anywhere near the truth. And it's hard. It takes a lot out of you.

You multiply that by thousands; you replace the listener, the live flesh-and-blood friend you trust, with a faceless unknown audience of people who may possibly not even exist; and you try to write the truth to them, you try to draw them a map of your inmost mind and feelings, hiding nothing and trying to keep all the distances straight and the altitudes right and the emotions honest. . . . And you never succeed. The map is never complete, or even accurate. You read it over and it may be beautiful, but you realize that you have fudged here, and smeared there, and left this out, and put in some stuff that isn't really there at all, and so on—and there is nothing to do then but say O.K.; that's done; now I come back and start a new map, and try to do it better, more truthfully. And all of this, every time, you do alone—absolutely alone. The only questions that really matter are the ones you ask yourself.

13

DON'T YOU KNOW YOU'RE BEAUTIFUL?

BY ARN SHEIN

ONE OF MY ALL-TIME FAVORITE movies is *The Inn of the Sixth Happiness,* a 1958 film starring Ingrid Bergman and Curt Jurgens. In one memorable scene, Jurgens asks why she never married and Bergman tells him she's not pretty.

"Don't you know you're beautiful?" he asks.

Long pause . . . reflective look . . . tilted head . . . shy smile.

"Once in her life," says Miss Bergman, "every woman should have that said to her. I thank you for being the one who said it to me."

Nearly 16 years later, poor health forced me to end a long and happy career as sports editor and columnist of a New York daily newspaper. Recognizing my need for a psychological lift, my wife talked me into joining a creative writing class. Smart woman! The old juices flowed once again and, with the help of an understanding teacher, I soon began pounding out one personal experience article after another.

It has long been my contention that if *you* don't think every word you put to paper is a gem, neither will the reader. And since I have never in my life written anything that I didn't think deserved a Pulitzer, I began sending my articles to upper-echelon magazines.

Over the next four years, I discovered that the editors of those publications didn't necessarily agree with my assessment. During that period, I amassed an impressive array of rejection letters—94 in all. My confidence was shaken, but each time an article came back in my self-addressed, stamped envelope (SASE), I stubbornly pulled out the red pencil, worked diligently to improve the copy, and sent it back out to another top-rated magazine.

The SASEs continued to find their way back to my mailbox. Most of the rejections were cold, impersonal form letters, without even a salutation. I was a no-name. Occasionally, a few editors would include a personal note with their rejections. And sometimes those notes included the suggestion that I must learn the difference between writing for a newspaper and a national magazine.

As you might imagine, with 94 submissions and 94 rejections, it's easy to have periods of self-doubt and depression. Mine became so bad at that stage that I went for many months without sending a single line of copy out into the world.

Then I began writing my autobiography. Perhaps that was my escape hatch, a way of continuing to write without having to face constant rejection. After completing the first 150 pages, I sat down to read what I had written. True to form, I came to the immodest conclusion that this was Pulitzer Prize stuff.

Then I had an inspiration. Putting my autobiography aside, I pulled out my old rejected articles to see if I could smooth out the rough edges. One of those, "Ida's Friend, God," was an inspirational piece about my late mother. It had already been turned down by at least a dozen of the finest magazines on the market. But that, I told myself, was when it had all those rough edges.

In my 60th year, I decided to give one of the country's leading women's magazines first crack at this resurrected piece. About a month later, I opened my mailbox, only to be greeted by the sight of that large, ugly manila envelope. This time, however, the rejection letter was a bit different. It was a far cry from a form letter.

"Dear Mr. Shein," it began.

Hey! It's got my name on it!

"Dear Mr. Shein: Thank you for sending us your very moving essay. Ida sounds like a truly unusual and terrific lady. That's why I'm especially sorry to have to say that we don't see a spot for the story in our magazine. Thanks, though, for giving me the chance to read and enjoy your piece."

Encouraged by those words, I smoothed out still another rough edge or two and shipped my article to *Reader's Digest*. It wasn't long before, on opening my mailbox, I was confronted by that big envelope—and a rejection letter.

Once again, however, the letter was different:

"Dear Arn:"

Dear Arn?

"Dear Arn: This won't quite work for *The Digest,* but it seems like a natural for *Guideposts.* I'd send it right off if I were you."

It was signed by a senior editor.

It was my 96th consecutive rejection letter. But there was something startlingly different about numbers 95 and 96. I raced out, made a copy of the *Reader's Digest* letter and sent if off to *Guideposts* with my own cover letter, the customary SASE, and my article, "Ida's Friend, God." On the 28th day after mailing the article, I opened my mailbox. There *was* a letter, a *thick* letter . . . from *Guideposts.* I pulled the contents out of the envelope and began reading the letter from the senior staff editor.

"Dear Mr. Shein: *The Digest* editor gave you good advice. Your story is beautiful, and we'd like to buy 'Ida's Friend, God.' Here's our offer in the usual legal language. *Guideposts* will pay you . . ."

But I kept looking at those first few incredible words: ". . . beautiful . . . we'd like to buy . . . will pay . . ."

I opened a file drawer, pulled out a copy of my article and stared at it. I didn't read it; I just stared at it. There was a long pause, a reflective look, a tilted head and a shy smile.

"Don't you know you're beautiful?"

Once in his life, every free-lance writer should have that said to him. I thank you, *Guideposts,* for being the one who said it to me.

14

ONE FICTION WRITER'S BEGINNINGS

BY EDITH PEARLMAN

AS A SCHOOLGIRL ESSAYIST, I wallowed in facts. I liked any subject I could do research on, and I could produce respectable pages on Altruism through the Centuries as well as on Flatworms or the Development of the Tram Railway.

But I had no powers of invention. Asked to imagine myself on a desert island, I consulted a botanical encyclopedia and described the likely flora. As for my prose style, it was, to be charitable, consistent. In every sentence the predicate lumbered after the subject, each wearing some squashed old adjective.

I was a flop at letter-writing, too. I could throw off a thank-you note or a postcard; but anything longer, anything that required a reach of heart toward heart, rendered me wordless. For the whole of my thirteenth year I had a pen pal in Wales, shackled to me by an eager English teacher; but my Cardiganshire friend stopped answering my weather reports.

Then, at fifteen I fell into a one-way correspondence. My father, in a hospital in another state, was very sick . . . recuperating, the family liked to say; dying, as it turned out. My mother was with him. I missed her, and I missed him very much, and I wrote to him frequently—page-long efforts like those the Welsh school girl had tired of. Date. Salutation. How are you I am fine. Today in Latin we learned the Ablative Absolute. We lost the hockey game, but who cares. Tonight for dinner we ate burnt fish. See you soon I hope.

I hadn't minded subjecting the Welsh girl to this dispirited stuff once a month; but my letters to my father were going out twice a week, and even I was bored with them. One evening, after the salutation, I paused. The bedroom was warm. The nosegays on the wallpaper repeated themselves *ad infinitum* or perhaps *ad nauseam* . . . I could learnedly allude to that, I supposed; but showing off wouldn't aid my father's Recuperation.

I lifted my pen between two fingers, just the way he lifted his cigarette. That day after school I had attended confirmation class with the Rabbi. The class had talked about a chapter in Exodus which deals with the nature of charity. I had added nothing to the discussion, being occupied with my algebra homework. Now I sensed that the afternoon's reality might be made entertaining. I looked over my shoulder to make sure I was alone. Then I took a drag on the pen and bent to my work.

With only the mildest of misgivings, I deformed our decent Rabbi. I made him sly and insinuative. He hinted at a salary raise while he babbled about self-lessness, lecturing skinflint fathers through their captive children. "The Cantor appeared just as I was making my getaway," I fabricated. "A deck of cards stuck out of his back pocket. 'Come, All Ye Faithful' he bellowed to his cronies—apostatically, out of season, and out of tune."

I put down the pen. I was drenched; but as I have said the room was warm.

"Dad loved your letter," said my mother in the next telephone call. "He showed it to all the nurses." I didn't say anything. "I hope you don't mind," she hastily added, interpreting my silence as indignation when it was in fact bliss. I was imagining my father sitting up in his hospital bed, handing my final draft to four young women in starched dresses. One after another they peruse it; all together they burst into applause. He beams. The surgery he has undergone has left some lines of pain on his handsome face, but my letter is smoothing them. He is wearing the silk dressing gown we gave him on his most recent birthday.

The next week, I advanced from caricature to improvisation. I created Cora and Dora, look-alike pals whose scrubbed faces did not conceal their unwholesome attachment to small animals. When the biology class was forced to dissect a frog, Cora, overidentifying with the creature, fainted. Dora had to drag her out. I coolly slit the frog ventrally, and described the glistening interior, the egg sac, the unsophisticated heart, and the sweet troubling aroma of formaldehyde.

In my mind's eye, my father had improved enough to wear pin stripes and a Countess Mara tie.

"Keep them coming," said my mother.

I kept them coming. Under my hand, by my hand, the day's happenings became anecdotes . . . sketches . . . stories.

Some weeks later my father was returned home from the far-away hospital—pale, wall-eyed, with a voice like a sob. He was wearing striped pajamas, wrinkled and stained. My heart stopped, or seemed to. A few days later he was gone forever.

"A wonderful man. You have an enviable heritage," my principal wrote; and of course that was true. I had enjoyed a happy childhood. And though I had failed to cure him, I had tried. My attempt turned out to be strenuous on-the-job training. Through draft after draft I'd learned that prose could be spiced by simile and metaphor and the metaphoric verb—and I had learned that in this effort to reduce language to its flavorful essence, the hapless apprentice would sometimes boil a whole paragraph off the page. That the predicate can sometimes precede the subject I had also discovered. And more: The reader can be trusted to figure out the moral for himself.

Writing letters to my father taught me to cut ties to the literal. I was unmoored—or, more hopefully, I was launched. These days I continue to write letters, though my editors call them stories. The work remains a labor of love for an Ideal Reader who requires distraction, not instruction; who enjoys a version of truth but is indifferent to facts; who wears an opera cape and a top hat, though he lies in a hospital bed.

§ 15

IMAGINING WHAT YOU DON'T KNOW

BY PAULA FOX

I HAVE BEEN UNABLE TO PUT out of my mind, though I have tried, a sentence I glimpsed in the last paragraph of an interview with a novelist that appeared in a national magazine a few years ago. The novelist, when asked about her plans, replied, "Now that I have succeeded as a writer, I'm looking for new forms of stimulation."

Such fatuousness is not exceptional, perhaps not even surprising during these days when one of the more intrusive catchwords has become *lifestyle,* with its implication that how one lives is entirely by choice, by will, and when the director of a national self-help organization announces from his platform that "We must applaud everything equally and give up the useless habit of evaluation."

Life is not a style, any more than death is a style, although if we give up the "useless habit of evaluation," we may not be able to tell the difference. And as for succeeding as a writer, a claim that in the days of my own youth no writer would have been caught dead making, and wouldn't, I venture to say, have secretly thought, here is what Cesare Pavese says about such self-congratulation in his diary, *This Business of Living:*

> Complacency is a deficiency whose penalty is a special perennial adolescence of the spirit. It is doubt which alone can make us probe and glimpse the depth of consciousness.

I have written and published six adult novels and twenty books for young people. Save for an occasional sentence, a paragraph here and there, I haven't been content with my work. "Eased" is closer to describing the sense of deliverance I feel when the last galley is corrected, when I am, for a time, free of the enveloping tension of work.

During those quiet days, a kind of truce prevails in me. I am relatively untroubled, either by doubt or certainty, volatile states in any

58

case. In fact, for a little while, I rest almost in a torpor, its surface only faintly ruffled by mild, vague thoughts. I can hardly recall, in this state, the days of the years when work was like digging a trench in hard ground. I forget the times of confusion, of tedium, of a failure of nerve, of pulling myself together once more to go to my workroom, wishing the telephone would ring, resenting it when it does, wishing for any distraction, yet dreading all distraction. I forget, too, the moments when writing seems nearly effortless (there are few of those!), and a voice seems to speak through me. And I forget the deep pleasure of an absorption so complete that time itself weighs nothing.

Before the book is actually published, any judgment of mine on the possible failure or success of the book I have written bears on how effectively reviewers will encourage or discourage readers from buying it and reading it; the significance of that kind of success or failure is that it will—or will not—result in buying me time so I can begin once again.

The calm is soon over. A few reviews trickle in. A painful prospect opens up. My book will not be understood by anyone. It will not be read by anyone. Or if it is read and written about somewhere, it will be by that same happy and successful novelist whose words I quoted at the start of this article. And she will say about my book: It has not succeeded! Let the writer seek a new form of stimulation!

Hard and unremitting labor is what writing is. It is in that labor that I feel the weight and force of my own life. That is its great and nettlesome reward.

It is not easy to convince people who take writing courses just how much labor is required of a writer.

After all, their mouths are full of words. They need only transfer those words to paper. Writing can't be really difficult, like learning to play the oboe, for example, or studying astrophysics.

Pavese, in his diary, also writes:

They say that to create while actually writing is to reach out beyond what-ever plan we have made, searching, listening to the deep truth within. But often the profoundest truth we have is the plan we have created by slow, ruthless, weary effort and surrender.

Most students of writing need little convincing about the deep truth they have within them, but they are not always partial to "slow, ruthless, weary effort." Few of us are. Yet there comes a time when you know that ruthless effort is what you must exert. There is no other way. And on that way you will discover such limitations in yourself as to make you gasp. But you work on. If you have done that for a long time, something will happen. You will succeed in becoming dogged. You will become resolute about one thing: to go to your desk day after day and try. You will give up the hope that you can come to a conclusion about yourself as a writer. You will give up conclusions.

The English critic, John Middleton Murry, wrote:

A writer does not really come to conclusions about life, he discovers a quality in it. His emotions, reinforcing one another, gradually form in him a habit of emotion; certain kinds of objects and incidents impress him with a peculiar weight and significance. This emotional bias or predilection is what I have ventured to call the writer's mode of experience; it is by virtue of this mysterious accumulation of past emotions that the writer, in his maturity, is able to accomplish the miracle of giving to the particular the weight and force of the universal.

People who see themselves as having succeeded so thoroughly at writing there is nothing left for them except to search out fresh fields of endeavor are not, in my view, in the right profession. Conclusions about life are just what such authors like best. They wish to believe there are answers to everything, and everything is defined by them as that for which they have answers.

I think that the character, the temperament, of their products, exhibit a kind of perverted social-workerism. And their fiction trivializes even as it sentimentalizes our lives no less than did the older, didactic literature of the past, toward which these new didactic writers often express such lofty contempt.

These are not tellers of tales, imaginers. They are answerers, like those voices on the telephone, which, for a fee, can provide a caller with a prayer, a joke, sexual stimulation, weather reports, or a list of antidotes in case one has swallowed poison.

In *The Tragic Sense of Life,* Miguel de Unamuno tells of Solon weeping over the death of his son. When asked why he is weeping, since it will avail him nothing, "That," replied Solon, "is why I was weeping."

Complacency is a deadweight on the spirit. It smothers imagination. But one rarely hears talk about imagination, especially in the classroom. This is partly due, I think, to an insidious kind of censorship. Censors have always been around, wanting to ban books because they contain some sexual or social or political content that frightens or repels them.

But the new censors tell us that, as writers, our only valid subject is ourselves, or those identical to ourselves, as though we were clumps of clones distributed about the earth. Men are to write only about men, women about women, black people about black people, and so on.

What a foretaste of the intolerable boredom that lies ahead! What is to be done with Tolstoy's reflective hunting dog, with Gogol's Nose, with Turgenev's singers of the Brezhin meadow, with Sancho Panza's imaginary kingdom, with all the men and women and children and ghosts and gods and animals that have been imagined and made living for us in all the stories that witness and record our pleasures and our sufferings, the mystery of our lives?

Narrowing, ever narrowing, the new censors, their tiny banners inscribed with ominous declarations: *I can't identify with that! I can't relate to this!* seem to want to ban humanity itself, in all its disarray and difference!

"Maybe we're here," the poet, Rainer Maria Rilke, said, "only to say: house, bridge, well, gate, jug, olive-tree, window—at most, pillar, tower—but to say them, remember, oh! to say them in a way that the things themselves never dreamed of so intensely."

As I write Rilke's words, I think of the great silence into which we hold up our small bundle of words; it is like the blue light of our small planet glimmering in the darkness that is all around.

16

DIGGING UP THE FACTS

BY RICHARD S. SMITH

THE STORY HAD BEEN PROGRESSING SMOOTHLY, almost effortlessly, until I got to the part where my protagonist, Matthew McClure, was forced to open the lid of a coffin. This stopped me dead, if you'll pardon the expression.

I did not have the foggiest idea how a coffin lid works.

Does anybody? Maybe undertakers and grave robbers, I thought, but I have never had the misfortune to exchange pleasantries with either of them.

What I wanted to say in the story was something like this: "Matt reached under the coffin, unfastened the latch, and raised the lid quickly so that . . ."

But is it a latch? Maybe coffins have more of a catch. Or a hasp, bolt, fastener, clinch, clip or clasp. And it might be located on the top, rather than on the bottom.

It's not that I'm too lazy to do a little research now and then, but this was ridiculous. Would any of my readers really care? Yes, they would. A casket manufacturer, for instance. I could already see the sales manager's irate letter:

Dear Mr. Smith:
After reading your story, "Six Feet Under," I realize how true it is that writers should write about what they know. You obviously wouldn't know a casket if it fell on you. The lid will open only if you release the fradestan buckle which is located, not under the coffin, but just to the left of the catary elbow coupler near the head handle. So now you know. And when your time is nigh, and you feel death's soft breath on your cheeks, remember our name. Our coffins are known as the Cadillacs of the industry. Incidentally, why wait? If you order now, we can offer you a ten percent discount.

Heaven help me I should get such a letter.

But to get back to my story, the situation was as follows: Matthew, a North Carolina mountain man, is attending the funeral of his eccentric brother, Arvel. Just as the coffin is being lowered into the ground, Matt remembers a pledge he made to Arvel on his deathbed. He promised to bury with him two of his most prized possessions: his harmonica, on which he could play only one tune, "Home on the Range," and his box of dead bugs.

Are you still with me?

Anyway, Matthew forgets all about it until it's almost too late. The two items are still not in the casket as it begins to disappear into the hold, so he has to have it brought back up to the surface. To make matters even worse, Arvel's body has not been embalmed (to save the family, which is very po', money) and by now the flesh is ripe enough to fall off the bones. So what Matt has to do is get the lid up as fast as possible and slide the bugs and harmonica in before something foul slides out.

I called the library and asked if they had any books on the construction of caskets. They wanted to know if I was serious. I said, "Hell, yes, I'm *dead* serious. This knowledge is absolutely essential to the authenticity of a story I'm writing."

They suggested I call a funeral home.

O.K. There were fifteen of them listed in the phone book, confirming my suspicions that death, while not very advantageous to the deceased, must be highly profitable for those who care for the remains.

My first call was to the Swan Song Mortuary, where I got a busy signal. The phone was also busy at the Eternal Rest Funeral Parlor, the Last Sleep Embalmment Center, and a joint called Terminally Yours. Business must be booming, I thought. Had a horrible plague struck the area? I finally got an answer at a place called The Debt Which Cancels All Others.

"I'm a free-lance writer," I said. "In the story I'm writing one of the characters has to open a coffin. How does the lid work?"

There was a long pause, followed by a chuckle, and then, "Is that you, Marty?"

"Marty?" I said.

"Come on," said the voice. "I know it's you. Ha-ha. That's really a good one. How does the lid work."

I hung up and dialed the Swan Song again. This time I got an answer and briefly explained my problem.

"Is the coffin a single or double-lidder?" the man asked.

63

"What's the difference?"

"Well, with a single-lidder, the whole lid comes up. On the double model, only the top half raises, the half where the deceased's head is located. The lower half of the body remains covered with the bottom half of the lid."

Isn't research wonderful? I had already learned something new and useful, but it didn't alter the fact that I had no particular coffin preferences.

"Make it a double," I said absently.

"It's really very simple," the man said. "by the way, my name's Fogg, as in London."

"Mine's Smith," I said. "As in under the spreading chestnut tree."

"I could probably explain it over the phone," said Fogg, "but I think it would behoove you to come in and let me demonstrate."

Sure. Why not? I needed a break, anyway. I said goodbye to the wife and told her I was going into town to look at some coffins. She immediately turned deathly pale, if you'll pardon the expression.

"My God!" she cried, clawing at her hair curlers. "I didn't even know you were ill!'

It took the better part of an hour to pacify her.

Fogg was a tiny gnome of a man who looked a little like Yoda in *Star Wars*. Long, pointy ears, scraggly hair, and a wrinkled face. After introductions, he led me through a dark chamber, with a single candle burning, to a well-lighted room in which there was a coffin surrounded by racks of flowers. The top half of the double lid was open, and I noticed there was a gray-haired old man in it, taking the long sleep. Was Fogg going to demonstrate the lid functions on a coffin that was occupied? Yes, he was. He started to lower the lid over this poor old guy's face, and I began to feel the way I did when the horse kicked me in the stomach.

"Couldn't you demonstrate on an empty one?" I asked.

"I'm afraid we don't have any empty ones at the moment," he said. "The minute they come in, we fill them."

"Oh," I said.

He was pointing to some kind of doohickey on the side of the lid, but I was staring at the old guy. I couldn't take my eyes off him. He was the first dead person I had ever seen. Yes, I thought, research is truly wonderful. Now I know what a corpse looks like. Actually, he didn't look too bad. A splash of rouge on his cheeks for color, gray hair carefully combed, nice suit, shirt and tie. He probably looked better here in the other world than he had in the real one.

"If you press this and turn it counter-clockwise," Fogg was saying— but I had turned my head at the sound of voices behind me. Six other people, three men and three women, had entered the room, and I suddenly found myself in the middle of a group of bereaved friends or relatives. Slowly, they all began to file past the open coffin, the women wailing, knuckling their eyes, sniffling, blowing their noses and muttering, "poor Emil," the men merely looking down silently at the body. Fogg had retreated to the rear of the bier.

This was enough for me. Maybe some other time; right now I need some fresh air. A casket, after all, is not a computer. It's only a box. Since I'm in charge of the story I can do anything I want to. I'll have Matthew build a homemade one out of pine, to my specifications, of course. Six feet long, two feet wide, and two feet deep. The latch will be one of those simple little hooks they put on screen doors. Nothing complicated. Arvel will never know the difference, and think of the money Matthew can save.

And that's exactly what I plan on doing, one of these days. Maybe tomorrow. Next week would be even better. I'd get at it right away, but after all that running around, doing important and valuable casket research, I'm dead tired.

If you'll pardon the expression.

17

ARE YOU A WRITER?

BY CHUCK MEYER

ARE YOU A WRITER? TRY THIS QUIZ:

* Write three verbs that describe yourself.
* Write three adjectives that describe yourself.
* Write three nouns that describe yourself.

If at least one of those descriptive words was "writing" or "writer," then you have passed the first test. If *none* of the words was related to writing (poet, screenwriter, artist, playwright, etc.), then you may *enjoy* writing, you may even be good at it, but it is likely to take a lower priority for your than for someone who *must* write.

Writers *have to* write. It is not a choice; it is what many writers call a pleasurable compulsion. If, between writing pieces—books, poems, articles or musings—you get anxious, agitated, nervous, depressed, or downright ornery, this is a *good* sign. If you find that you can't *not* write, then you are truly influenced by one of the Muses, for better or for worse.

Many people want to write but claim they cannot find the time. Writers don't *find* time; they *make* time. Even with the busiest schedules, a real writer will make room for thirty minutes or an hour of writing a day. Whether you keep a journal, jot random notes for the next article or mystery, edit a manuscript, or (luxury of luxuries) whip out your notebook computer to pick up where you left off the previous night, these very *acts* of writing are requirements (not options) in a writer's life.

Writing is not a matter of waiting until you *feel* like it, feel "inspired" or "in the mood." In fact, writing has nothing to do with feelings or motivation: It has to do with *discipline*. If you are a writer, or want to become one, you will make the time, daily, to sit and stare at the paper or the computer screen and record what emerges. What you write needn't be perfect; you can always fix it later. If you wait until you *feel* like it, you'll never *do* it.

Waiting for the "right" place makes as much sense as waiting for the "right" time or feeling to start. The only requirement for a "place" of writing is that it be relatively quiet, though some people do their best in crowded noisy environments. Writers write anywhere: in airports, restaurants, parks, on beaches, planes, in their backyards, kitchens, and even in the bathroom.

If you *are* a writer or aspire to be one, here are nine suggestions for success:

1. Write. Don't wait for the "right" time or place. As the Nike slogan says, "Just do it."

2. Persist. Persistence pays off. Keep at it. Never give up. Remember that *Gone with the Wind* was rejected 32 times. *The Wizard of Oz* had to be self-published, because no publisher wanted it.

3. Network for everything—ideas, publishers, markets. Join a local writers' group and ask for comments on your work (even though you know it's perfect just as it is).

4. Balance assertiveness and self-belief with openness and willingness to change. You have to be audaciously egocentric to think that anything you produce is worth reading by anyone else. But you needn't let that trait get in the way of criticism that may ultimately make your work even better.

5. Take risks. You have nothing to lose but fame and money. Write the outrageous piece. Say what you think. Tell the story the way it wants to be told. Send it to major publishers. The worst they can do is say "No." No successful writers became best sellers without taking risks. Neither will you.

6. Lighten up. You have to maintain a healthy sense of humor about this enterprise to survive the compulsion to write. Laughter, including sarcastic and ironic humor, provides the distancing necessary to accept useful criticism, to see your work as others see it (without the defensiveness of authorship).

7. Timing is everything. A lot of things simply depend on *luck*. You

may not have a lot of control over this, but given the odds, if you are persistent enough, you might in the right place at the right time with the right reader or editor. Remember that the reason your manuscript was accepted may be that you were lucky they didn't look at the one under it in the stack.

8. Be generous. Writers succeed by honestly critiquing each other's work, and by supporting and praising each other's accomplishments. When publishing contracts are offered, negotiate fairly, not out of greed.

9. Keep in mind your mission as a writer. To be inspired or commanded by the Muses is to carry on their mythic tradition and mission.

The nine Muses remained young and beautiful forever, so they continue to evoke within us new images for us to convey through our writing. They could see into the future, and they encourage us to do the same with our words. They could banish all grief and sorrow, and inspire mortals to reach deep inside and beyond themselves, something each writer must do each time he or she picks up the pen.

Their mother was Mnemosyne, the goddess of Memory. She is particularly important, for memory is the basis of hope. And writers inspire our individual and collective memories to recall, to relate, to see in our words and images who we are and who we have been. The task of writing calls us—and our readers—to remember, and therefore, to have hope.

Are you a writer? You are if you have to be.

18

BRAINSTORMING

BY MARY E. MAURER

SOMETIMES I FIND IT DIFFICULT TO JUGGLE my roles as wife, mother, chauffeur, gardener, cook, dishwasher, *and* writer. I wish I had more time just to think and read and come up with brilliant ideas. But, since my time is limited, I've developed a plan that keeps twenty-five ideas on my desk ready to be researched, outlined, and turned into publishable prose.

You and I probably have a lot in common. You're a pretty good writer. You can take ideas and shape them into articles that educate and entertain. Sometimes after about a dozen rewrites, you even like what you've written. You sell enough articles to be reasonably pleased. You could probably write 365 days a year if you had something to write about. Well, if ideas are your problem, try brainstorming.

Here's how it works: Take a piece of typing paper and fold it into quarters. Get out your favorite pen. No pencils, no erasers, and no typing! Clear off your desk or sit at the kitchen table. Now relax. Take a deep breath and close your eyes for ten seconds. Stretch your arms above your head and then shake them at your sides. Feel better? Great. The calisthenics aren't actually necessary to brainstorming, but most writers need more exercise.

Now, in the middle of each quarter section, write the name of a favorite subject. Think about each subject one at a time, for at least ten minutes. As you think, jot down *anything* that comes to mind. Doodle. Underline the subject. Draw arrows. Don't stop. Don't edit. Don't be critical. Just move that pen. When you get tired of one subject, go to the next one.

At first you may find this difficult. Ask yourself a few questions. Why do you like to write about this subject? Have you sold any articles about it? Have you read anything about it lately? Have you done anything related to the subject? Do you have friends who are concerned

69

with some aspect of the subject? Does your local college teach a related course?

At the end of an hour you should have at least a dozen ideas for new articles. You may have to do some more thinking to develop some of the ideas, but you should have plenty of material to work with. My last brainstorming session yielded twenty ideas. I've already written eight of them and sold four. There are at least four others that are worth pursuing. What about the others? Who cares! Every idea won't be a winner. You don't have to write an article about every idea on the sheet; you don't even have to write about every *good* idea. And you can write about other ideas that aren't on the sheet at all. Brainstorming just keeps the ideas flowing.

The following illustrates my brainstorming method:

I **Preschool**	**II** **Travel**
III **Gardening**	**IV** **How-To**

Square 1: **Preschool**

1. Who Makes the Rules? How to decide on good classroom rules your kids will really follow.

2. Clean Up the Mess. How to get kids to clean.

70

3. Egg Carton Crafts. Five of my favorite ideas.

4. Art Center. How to set up a successful art area.

Square 2: **Travel**

1. Dude ranch. Interview owner of local dude ranch.

2. Barking dogs. Why do people always take their dogs camping with them and then let them bark half the night?

3. Driving drowsy. How do you stay awake during long trips? What can you avoid taking, eating, doing, to make you more alert?

4. How to take better travel pictures.

Square 3: **Gardening**

1. Favorite plants. Pick one or two for "profiles."

2. Butterflies. How to attract them to the garden. What do you plant, when?

3. What are the best seed catalogues?

4. How do you figure out seed catalogues? What do all those symbols mean? How do you know if a plant will grow in your area?

Square 4: **How-To**

1. Write about the history of gardens and tell people how to re-create cottage gardens with "heirloom" plants.

2. How do you encourage your child to do well in school without being a nag?

3. Tell people how to complain.

4. Tell people how you get your ideas for articles.

I sit down and do this about once a month. I usually try to pick a time when I've gotten a rejection that's actually typed, not printed, on real letterhead with a personal note. I'm talking about ecstatic, confident, powerful, justified, enthusiastic, and eager to face the typewriter once again! That's when you want to do your brainstorming!

You can use the same method for writing fiction. Write down four character names, or four countries, or four occupations, or four colors, and see how many story ideas develop. Use brainstorming when you're

71

stuck in the middle of chapter six and can't figure out how to get your hero across the moat. Write down four reasons why, and then doodle around them for an hour. Draw pictures of the moat. Scribble. Write "swim," "jump," "fly," "walk on water." You'll surprise yourself, and maybe you'll surprise your readers.

19

CHOOSING A WRITERS CONFERENCE

BY SHIRL THOMAS

FROM MY OBSERVATIONS AS A CONFEREE, as well as a speaker and workshop leader at writers conferences, I have found that those who attend often feel shortchanged, for a variety of reasons: They may find speakers uninterested, hard to approach, or disappointing; are unclear about a conference's procedures and available services; or feel that they don't get the most out of workshop sessions, particularly when writers at varying levels of competence are in the same group.

There are countless writers conferences—local, regional, and national; they can be as short as one day or as long as one week. The conference locale, cost, and theme or focus can vary greatly; subject matter may be geared to beginners or cover advanced writing or marketing techniques. So, how do you decide if a particular conference is worth the time and money? One important factor to consider is your motivation. Are you writing for love of the written word, or striving for a professional career? Prospective goals can make a difference in your determination.

If you write primarily for self-expression, speakers who deal extensively with the literary marketplace or small presses would be of interest. These "little" magazines often publish only experimental works and poetry, and usually offer modest compensation—sometimes, "payment in copies only." However, they are receptive to beginning writers who can gain valuable experience from contributing to these markets and have a better chance of getting published.

If you have professional goals, attending workshops on business and marketing would be beneficial, along with hearing speakers from the more prestigious magazines and publishing houses, as well as literary agents who could be helpful in placing your work later on.

In any case, some research is necessary before making an informed decision about attending one conference over another. Here are some guidelines:

1. Does it fit your needs?

You should have a direct interest in the market categories represented. Most conferences will offer a range of several different fields, while others are organized around a specific theme or topic, such as "Writing for Children" or "Articles in the Making." Find out in advance what market categories will be covered. Do they match your writing interests?

For example, if workshops and seminars emphasize "whodunits" and you're concentrating more on "how-tos," you may want to choose a different conference. (There is much to be said, however, for mixing fiction techniques with nonfiction styles.)

2. What type of help will be offered?

There are four popular conference formats: lectures; workshops; writer discussion groups; and speaker roundtables, or a combination of two or three. Choose the one most appropriate to your taste and needs, taking into account whether a conference is geared to your level of writing. Ask yourself these questions: Will discussions include beginning fundamentals or be restricted to more advanced techniques and the business side of writing? Will detailed instruction be offered? Will there be an opportunity to have your manuscript critiqued at the conference? By whom? Other conferees, or workshop leaders—editors, publishers or agents? May manuscripts be sent in advance and appointments set up so that you can be sure of being able to discuss your work with a professional? Should you bring a writing sample— or a portfolio?

Determine the level of your participation well in advance, and be prepared to take advantage of these opportunities.

NOTE: Make sure any material you do bring with you is professionally typed and ready for the market. No first drafts!

3. Who are the speakers?

Research the qualifications of speakers and the genres and specific areas they will cover, and decide whether they warrant your time and effort. Will appointments for private consultation be available? If not, ask whether speakers will have question-and-answer sessions or will mind being approached by participants at the conference. And when the time comes, remember: Don't be too timid or too pushy.

4. How much will it cost?

In addition to the registration fee, will the costs for food, lodging, and travel fit your budget? Conferences at luxury hotels may be prohibitive, so you may want to consider going to a conference held on a college campus. (Don't expect to recoup expenses with the money you'll make from your writing!)

5. What are the proposed schedules?

Will there be a conflict in the schedules for the lectures or workshops in which you have a special interest? If so, will you be able to buy tapes of the overlapping seminars? Do you object to early-morning or late-evening sessions?

NOTE: If you are restricted by time or finances, you may want to check to see if you can be a part-time participant.

Attending the right conference at the right time can open doors of opportunity for a writer, provide an often needed change of scenery, a fresh point of view, and insight into how others are pursuing the craft. Although some writers may find the prospect of being around professional authors intimidating, keep in mind that successful published writers were once beginners, too, and are usually sensitive to newcomers' trepidations. Though some speakers' egos may interfere with the goal of addressing writers' concerns, most are dedicated to assisting writers and are prepared to help—otherwise, they would not agree to participate.

If you leave a conference feeling only that it provided entertainment or perhaps a diversion, then there may have been little merit in having attended. But if the time spent at a writers conference helps you improve, or has given you a push in the right direction, then it was a worthwhile endeavor—whether you write for the love of the craft or with the goal of becoming a professional. In any case, it's a personal choice. Decide what you want to derive from the experience, and then go for it.

How To Write—Techniques
GENERAL FICTION

20

BEGINNINGS

BY BARNABY CONRAD

SINCLAIR LEWIS ONCE TOLD ME of his pride in seeing a woman on board the *Queen Elizabeth* settle into a deck chair and open a copy of his new book. His joy was short-lived when he watched her read the first page, then walk to the rail and drop the book over the side of the ship.

The first page—even the first sentence—of your article, short story, novel, or nonfiction book is of paramount importance.

When an editor takes your piece out of its manila envelope you will not be there at his elbow to say: "Keep reading! It really gets good later on!"

There'll be no "later on" if the editor is not intrigued right off the bat. He or she does not necessarily have to be shocked, startled, or amazed, but the editor, putting himself in the place of a reader, must be tantalized enough to read further. A well-drafted opening immediately tells the editor that he is dealing with a good writer; professional writers seldom write a dull first page. We can break down the various ways of starting an article or a story into twelve general categories. In the old days these categories might be applied only to fiction, but nowadays the boundaries between fiction and nonfiction have become blurred.

Let's look at those categories one by one:

1. *Setting*

In the past, books almost invariably started with a purely physical description: a New England drawing room, an Alpine meadow, a western landscape, or a dark and stormy night in London. Some writers who wish to give the reader an immediate sense of place and mood still prefer the description opening. By and large, static description is more appropriate for book-length fiction.

But if you choose to begin by describing scenery, weather, or by, say, taking inventory of a parlor, you must write it very well if you are to engage the attention of the reader. Here is the second paragraph of F. Scott Fitzgerald's novel, *Tender Is the Night*:

The hotel and its bright tan prayer rug of a beach were one. In the early morning the distant image of Cannes, the pink and cream of old fortifications, the purple Alp that bounded Italy, were cast across the water and lay quavering in the ripples and rings set up by sea-plants through the clear shadows.

2. *Setting plus characters*

A more common, economical, and exciting way to begin is by combining *characters with setting*.

Using this combination, the writer reveals something about a character as well as describing the place that the plot is to be played out, and may even suggest a hint of the conflict to come.

I'll make up an example: Instead of simply describing a setting sun in detail, let's open with the protagonist watching and reacting to that sunset:

Clem watched as the dying sun turned his beloved log house and the barn and his horse to a golden hue, and his gut twisted at the thought he might lose it all. And up there in those beautiful blue hills were two men and a bitter woman who wanted to see him dead.

Here a wary protagonist is shown in a specific setting, plus having something happening, the reader does not yet know what.

3. *Thematic*

A method of beginning a story opposite to starting with a happening is to start off with a philosophical idea or truism, or generality. Here is an example from Jane Austen's *Pride and Prejudice*:

It is a truth universally acknowledged that a single man in possession of a good fortune must be in want of a wife.

Then there is Tolstoy's famous opening line from *Anna Karenina*:

Happy families are all alike; every unhappy family is unhappy in its own way.

But after starting with a leisurely generality, these authors immediately shifted gears and went to a specific happening to get their story in motion!

4. *Factual*

A factual type of beginning should be an attention-grabber whether for a fiction or a nonfiction work, as in this realistic, no-nonsense opening I've made up for an article on the Chernobyl disaster:

On April 26, 1986, an explosion in Unit No. 4 at the Chernobyl nuclear power station set the reactor's graphite core ablaze, jeopardizing the entire reactor complex and spewing into the winds radioactive debris that threatened human health and the food chain even beyond the vast area of Ukraine. More than thirty of the reeactor operators, guards, and local firemen who fought to contain the damage and extinguish the fire died from radiation poisoning.

An equally effective beginning about the disaster could borrow from fictional techniques using dialogue:

"God, it was so terrible and I was so scared," said Natasha Trompesky, an elderly survivor of Chernobyl. "I felt the ground tremble and heard the noise and I thought of my husband still inside."

Hemingway, a former journalist, liked the factual sounding beginning for his fiction; witness *The Old Man and the Sea*'s first sentence:

He was an old man who fished alone in a skiff in the Gulf Stream and he had gone eighty-four days now without taking a fish.

Who, where, what, when in one sentence!

Then there is the purely factual beginning for the purely factual article or book. A couple of years ago *The New York Times* asked a dozen famous writers what their favorite beginning to a book was. Elmore Leonard, the great suspense writer, had picked the beginning of my book *La Fiesta Brava*:

On August 28, 1947, a multi-millionaire and a bull killed each other in Linares, Spain, and plunged an entire nation into deep mourning. The bull's name was Islero, and he was of the Miura strain. The man's name was Manolete, and he was the essence of everything Spanish.

5. *Emotional: Aim for the heart!*

Beginnings that appeal immediately and directly to a reader's emotions are among the most successful. Take staff writer Alan Abrahamson's lead in a *Los Angeles Times* account of a murder:

On a pleasant autumn afternoon in Northridge, Froggy, Chunky, and Nini killed the neighborhood lady.

Chunky and Nini, who were 15 and 12, stabbed her 11 times. Their sister Froggy, 16, stayed at home and turned up the volume on the family's two stereos to drown out the screams from next door.

The neighbor, 62-year-old librarian Meta Frances Murphy, had befriended the girls, often treating them to snacks or driving them to and from school. It was a crime that made no sense—and still doesn't.

How could one not read on?

An emotion-evoking beginning in fiction is a sure-fire way of luring the reader into your story.

How about this one, from Ambrose Bierce's short story "An Imperfect Conflagration":

Early one morning in 1872 I murdered my father—an act which made a deep impression on me at the time.

Almost 100 years after that was written, Allan Folsom's hugely successful 1994 thriller *The Day After Tomorrow* starts out:

Paul Osborn sat alone among the smoky bustle of the after-work crowd, staring into a glass of red wine. He was tired and hurt and confused. For no particular reason he looked up. When he did, his breath left him with a jolt. Across the room sat the man who murdered his father....

The reason this strikes an immediate chord in the reader, of course, is that subconsciously we wonder how *we* would react and what would *we* do if we encountered a person who had murdered one of our parents.

Writers can also arouse emotions in the reader subtly and quietly, as in the opening sentence of Mary McCarthy's *The Company She Keeps*:

She would leave him, she thought, as soon as the petunias bloomed.

Or for a more brazen attention getter here's Mary Breasted's lead into her novel *Why Should You Doubt Me Now?*:

If there is a fate that can befall a man worse than having the Virgin Mary appear in his bedroom just as he is about to seduce the most beautiful apprentice horoscope writer in Dublin, Rupert Penrole did not know of one.

82

6. Action

Action beginnings are effective because of the all-important fact: Action is character!

By action we mean any significant movement, endeavor, activity, or event engaged in by people (or, in some cases, animals).

The action may be violent, as in the opening of Ambrose Bierce's "An Occurrence at Owl Creek Bridge," where a young man is about to be hanged:

> A man stood upon a railroad bridge in northern Alabama, looking down into the swift water twenty feet below. The man's hands were behind his back, the wrists bound with a cord. A rope closely encircled his neck.

But the story or article can also start with action as simple as a Little League game or a church wedding, or a birth, or a graduation, or a knock at the door, or a funeral, or an arduous trek, as in Jack London's short-story masterpiece, "To Build a Fire":

> Day had broken cold and grey, exceedingly cold and grey, when the man turned aside from the main Yukon trail and climbed the high earth-bank, where a dim and little-traveled trail led eastward through the fat spruce timberland.

7. In medias res

Rather than setting the scene or describing the situation in detail beforehand, the writer plunges the reader directly "into the middle of things." Here is Frederick Forsyth's beginning of *The Day of the Jackal*.

> It is cold at 6:40 in the morning of a March day in Paris, and seems even colder when a man is about to be executed by firing squad. At that hour on March 11, 1963, in the main courtyard of the Ford d'Jury a French Air Force colonel stood before a stake driven into the chilly gravel as his hands were bound behind the post, and stared with slowly diminishing disbelief at the squad of soldiers facing him twenty metres away.

We don't know who the man is or what he has done to deserve execution or whether the sentence will be carried out.

But! We want to find out. And that, after all, is the name of the game.

Robert Ludlum, Elmore Leonard, Robert Parker, Ed McBain, and Judith Krantz, to name a few among many other best-selling novelists, also favor the *in medias res* beginning.

8. *Dialogue*

Everyone practices—and enjoys—eavesdropping, especially if the subject and person speaking are interesting and exciting. Readers, therefore, respond immediately to a story (or article) that starts with people talking, particularly if there is tension or conflict in their dialogue. For example:

"I didn't realize the gun was loaded," mumbled a distraught Mark Smith yesterday outside his Brentwood home.
His neighbor, Juan Gomez, restrained by friends, shouted: "You'll pay for this, you weasel! Ask your wife!"

Having caught our attention, the writer gives the facts of the situation.

Here are some diverse examples of stories that begin with dialogue; they have nothing in common except that they provoke our interest or tell us something about the protagonist or simply get the story going:

Aldous Huxley's "The Giaconda Smile":

"Miss Spence will be down directly, sir."
"Thank you," said Mr. Hutton, without turning around. Janet Spence's parlourmaid was so ugly—ugly on purpose, it always seemed to him, malignantly, criminally ugly—that he could not bear to look at her more than was necessary.

Eudora Welty's "Petrified Man":

"Reach in my purse and git me a cigarette without no powder in it if you kin, Mrs. Fletcher, honey," said Leota to her ten o'clock shampoo-and-set customer. "I don't like no perfumed cigarettes."

9. *Characterization*

Starting with a description of a protagonist or antagonist is valid. Observe this familiar opening:

Scarlett O'Hara was not beautiful, but men seldom realized it when caught by her charm as the Tarleton twins were.

This not only introduces our heroine but takes us firmly into the first scene of Margaret Mitchell's epic novel.

To begin *Lord Jim*, Joseph Conrad gives the reader an immediate and graphic physical description of his character and, at the same time, works in some of the man's character and profession:

84

He was an inch, perhaps two, under six feet, powerfully built, and he advanced straight at you with a slight stoop of the shoulders, head forward, and a fixed-from-under stare which made you think of a charging bull. His voice was deep, loud, and his manner displayed a kind of dogged self-assertion which had nothing aggressive in it. It seemed a necessity, and it was directed apparently as much at himself as at anybody else. He was spotlessly neat, apparelled in immaculate white from shoes to hat, and in the various Eastern ports where he got his living as ship-chandler's water-clerk he was very popular.

10. *Author-to-Reader*

"Call me Ishmael," Herman Melville's narrator warmly invites the reader in *Moby Dick.*

This is a disarming, confidential, effective and somewhat old-fashioned way to begin a story. The writer addresses the reader directly. Here is Edgar Allan Poe seemingly confiding in the reader as he begins his chilling tale "The Tell-Tale Heart":

True!—nervous—very, very dreadfully nervous I had been and am! But why will you say that I am mad?

Study Mark Twain's chatty—and artful—opening to *The Adventures of Huckleberry Finn*:

You don't know about me without you have read a book by the name of *The Adventures of Tom Sawyer*, but that ain't no matter. That book was made by Mr. Mark Twain and he told the truth, mainly.

Note how much Twain accomplishes in these few sentences, gaining the reader's confidence on behalf of his protagonist and establishing the narrator's voice.

Isak Dinesen begins *Out of Africa* with this simple paragraph which sounds as though she were conversing with a friend:

I had a farm in Africa, at the foot of the Ngong Hills. The Equator runs across these highlands, a hundred miles to the North and the farm lay at an altitude of over six thousand feet. In the day-time you felt that you had got high up, near to the sun, but the early mornings and evenings were limpid and restful, and the nights were cold.

11. *Diary, Epistolary or Reflective*

Such contemporary works as the long-running play "Love Letters" by A.R. Gurney, *Fair and Tender Ladies* by Lee Smith, *A Woman of*

Independent Means by Elizabeth Forsythe Hailey, and the *Griffin and Sabine* trilogy by Nick Bantok are told entirely in letters.

Many stories and novels begin with the device of a character finding a note or receiving a letter that starts with some form of "When you read this I'll be dead (married, gone, living in Tahiti, etc.)."

Josephine Humphreys, in the beginning of her sensitive novel *Rich in Love*, has her young heroine come across a curt note from her mother telling her father that she is leaving him; in a poignant scene the girl rewrites the letter in gentler language so as to soften the blow for her beloved father.

Alice Walker's *The Color Purple* is told in letters and journal style and starts out with the intriguing sentence:

"You better never tell nobody but God. It'd kill your mammy."

12. *Interrogatory*

Starting with a question is a fairly common way of starting a story.

"Jee-zus," he thought as he heard the first strains of Lohengrin. "What have I got myself into?"

A question opening is frequently used to begin suspense stories to involve the reader as soon as possible in the action and situation:

What time was it? Adam looked at his watch for the tenth time. Where were those guys? The dynamite was set to blow in ten minutes and they weren't here! What was keeping them and where was Kate now that he needed her so desperately?

Larry McMurtry starts his novel, *Some Can Whistle*, about a writer's long lost daughter suddenly entering his life, with this question:

"Mister Deck, are you my stinkin' Daddy?" a youthful, female, furious voice said into the phone.

The first words of your novel, story, or article may be the most important in terms of salability. Therefore as you sit down to start to write, consider these suggestions and options:

1. Try to pick the most intriguing place in your piece to begin.

2. Try to create an attention-grabbing image of a place if that's where you must begin.

3. Raise the reader's curiosity about what is happening or is going to happen in an action scene.

4. Describe a character so compellingly that we want to learn more about what happens to him or her.

5. Present a situation so vital to our protagonist that we must read on.

6. And most important, no matter what method you choose, *start with something happening*!

Hone your opening words, for just as stories aren't written but rewritten, so should beginnings be written and rewritten. Look at your opening and ask yourself, "If I were reading this, would I be intrigued enough to go on?"

And remember: Always aim for the heart!

21

WHAT WE WRITE ABOUT WHEN WE WRITE ABOUT LOVE

BY NANCY WILLARD

THE FIRST BOOK I EVER WANTED to steal was a slim blue paperback called *Tales of French Love and Passion*. It showed a woman in a low-cut gown and elbow-length gloves eyeing a man with a goatee and moustache: the devil, I supposed, or one of his minions. Because the devil wore a striped polo shirt and a beret, I assumed he was on vacation—a cruise, perhaps. The woman was giving him a sly smile; she had one arm raised, as if she were waving at someone just out of the picture.

I was twelve, going on sixteen. Every summer my mother and sister and I moved from Ann Arbor, Michigan, to a ramshackle cottage sixty miles away, in the sleepy settlement of Stoney Lake. My father, who was teaching summer school, drove to Stoney Lake every Friday after his last class, and on Sunday he drove the family car back to Ann Arbor.

All week long the old men of Stoney Lake went fishing and the young men went to work in town or at the gravel pit across the lake, and the mothers and grandmothers sat on their front porches and watched the dust rise and fall in the dirt road, and gossiped in Italian, and so the air hung heavy with their secrets. Only our house felt as dull as a convent.

Thank God for my mother's younger sister, Nell, whose chose to spend the first month of her summer vacation with us and whose *Tales of French Love and Passion* showed me what I was missing. She kept the book on the nightstand, next to her Madame DuBarry Beauty Box, and her favorite story, "Room Eleven," was no secret; when I picked up that slim blue volume, it obligingly opened to p. 33:

She picked all her lovers from the army and kept them three years, the time of their sojourn in the garrison. In short, she not only had love, she had sense. . . . She gave the preference to men of calm allurement, like herself, but they must be handsome. She also wished them to have had no previous entanglements, any passion having the power to leave traces, or that had made any trouble. Because the man whose loves are mentioned is never a very discreet man.

After having decided upon the one she would love for the three years of his regulation sojourn, it only remained to throw down the gauntlet.

> —From *Stories of Love and Passion: A Collection of Complete Short Stories Chosen from the Works of Guy de Maupassant*

Not for her second-graders at Northville Elementary did Nell pluck her eyebrows, oil her eyelashes, and rouge her cheeks. She was young, pretty, and thrice divorced. When she scanned the *Oxford Weekly,* she was appalled to find that God hosted all the regular social events announced in its pages; even square dancing was held in the basement of the Methodist church. The only gatherings that escaped His watchful eye were auctions.

The auctions always took place on somebody's front lawn. On one hot Sunday in July, we stood in the crowd that milled around the front yard opposite the high school, listening to the to the auctioneer's patter and laughing at his jokes.

Nell bid on whatever looked like a bargain. Who knows why we suddenly want what we don't need? When an upright piano was pushed into view and the auctioneer shouted, "What am I bid for this piano?" my mother bid ten dollars.

"Ten dollars!" sneered the auctioneer. "Madam, I'd buy it myself for ten dollars if I had a place to put it. Look at the work on this thing."

"Do it play?" called a voice from the back of the crowd.

"Play? Play?" The auctioneer touched middle C. "Can anyone here give us a demonstration?"

Nell was on the platform in an instant. She pulled up a kitchen chair, and she played "You Are My Sunshine" and "Four Leaf Clover," then eased into the rippling improvisation she used to quiet her second-graders.

"Twenty!" shouted the voice in the back.

"Twenty-five!" shouted my mother.

"Twenty-five going once, twenty-five going twice—"

The auctioneer paused. The silence was deafening.

"All done at twenty-five!"

"My God," whispered Mother, "where will we put a piano?"

While the auctioneer's assistant was smoothing Mother's five-dollar bills and tucking them into the cashbox, Nell was talking to one of the movers, a man whose sweat-soaked shirt stuck to his back in ragged patches. He was the only mover with black hair, and it fell around his eyes in tight curls. Nell signaled to my mother.

"His name is Lou Lubbock," she said. "For two dollars, he'll move the piano on his pick-up truck."

By the time Mother had counted her change, Lou had rolled the piano up a ramp into the back of the red pick-up and was sitting in the cab beside a man whose face we couldn't see.

"Did you tell him where we live?" asked my mother.

"I told him to follow us," said Nell.

"You did?" exclaimed Mother. "Who's that old gentleman with him?"

"His father."

The piano, which had looked almost diminutive among wardrobes and breakfronts at the auction, appeared monstrous when Lou tried to bring it through the front door of the cottage. Mother cast anxious glances at Lou Lubbock's father. He did not look as though he'd ever moved anything heavier than a telephone book.

"Won't go through the front door," he remarked, as the two men set the piano on the grass.

"I guess we'll have to take it back to the auction," said Mother. She sounded relieved.

"What doesn't go through the door goes through the window," said Lou. "Trust me."

With the practiced hand of a burglar, he pried out the top half of the big window in the living room and pushed his father through. Then he lifted the front end of the piano, letting it straddle the sill.

There was a sudden thud, and all at once the piano was standing in the living room as if had always been there. As Lou Lubbock took his leave, somewhere between our front door and his truck, he invited Nell to go roller skating.

That summer Nell kept company with the piano mover and I read *Tales of French Love and Passion* and mooned around the visible borders of their passion like a twelve-year-old voyeur. But when school started in September and our teacher asked us to write about what we did on our vacation, did I write about Aunt Nell and the piano mover? No. I wrote about the lake, the fish, and the turtles. What I learned about love that summer sank out of sight but not out of mind. Like so many visitors from the invisible world, those memories come unannounced and never when I call them.

Writers believe they choose the stories they want to write, but this is an illusion. Our stories choose us, and they are as patient and sure as the heroine in that tale I found on my aunt's nightstand. Not until ninth grade did I meet it again when I happened to check out of the school library a modest gray hardcover called *The Complete Stories of Guy de Maupassant*. As I reread it with astonishment and awe, the longing that had infused the summer of the piano mover washed over me. I wanted to write a love story. And de Maupassant made it look so easy.

There are two ways of beginning such a story. The first lets you know right away that you're reading a love story. The second does not; indeed, it takes pains to hide its true intent. A beginning of the first kind can make you feel you're eavesdropping on a telephone with a party line. Here is the opening of John Updike's "Love Song for a Moog Synthesizer":

> She was good in bed. She went to church. Her I.Q. was 145. She repeated herself. Nothing fit; it frightened him. Yet Tod wanted to hang on, to hang on to the bits and pieces, which perhaps were not truly pieces but islands, which a little lowering sea level would reveal to be rises on a sunken continent, peaks of a subaqueous range, secretly one, a world.
> —From *Problems and Other Stories*, by John Updike (Alfred A. Knopf)

What Updike gives us is a close-up: the raw surface of the lover's confusion as he picks over the bits and pieces of a relationship, puzzling over them, gathering them into the lap of a long sentence, trying to understand love through the sum of its parts.

Now turn the telescope of the lover's vision around. The moment you step back and put a little distance between you and the characters, you have space to examine their motives, as Alice Walker does here in the opening sentence of her story, "The Lover": "Her husband had wanted a child and so she gave him one as a gift, because she liked her husband and admired him greatly."

No writer can surpass Isaac Babel for opening sentences that perfectly balance distance with immediacy. Take the beginning of a story called "First Love," which, by its very title, announces its subject—a dangerous practice for the novice writer:

> When I was ten years old, I fell in love with a woman called Galina. Her surname was Rubtsov. Her husband, an officer, went off to the Russo-Japanese War and returned in October, 1905. He brought a great many trunks back with him. These trunks, which weighed nearly half a ton, contained Chinese souvenirs such as screens and costly weapons. Kurma the yardman used to tell us that Rubtsov had bought all these things with money he had embezzled while serving in the engineer corps of the Manchurian Army.
> —From *The Collected Stories*, edited and translated by Walter Morison (Criterion Books)

Though Babel's impassioned opening sentence seems to give the whole story away, he follows it, not with a description of Galina, but with three purely factual statements: her name, her husband's occupation, and what he brought home from the war. The last sentence in the paragraph turns from fact to rumor and gives us a little of the husband's character through the eyes of the yardman. The husband is a crook. Babel knows that part of telling a story well is holding back and that Chekhov's advice on writing about grief also applies to writing about love:

> When you . . . wish to move your reader to pity, try to be colder. It will give a kind of backdrop to . . . grief, make it stand out more. . . . Yes, be cold. . . .
> —From *Chekhov,* by Henri Troyat (Ballantine Books)

Why am I seeking advice from Chekhov? Because Nell's story is knocking at a locked door in the back of my mind, and I can't find the key to let it out. The key is the right voice to tell it. Should the teller be a twelve-year-old child, narrating the events with an innocent eye? Or the child, grown up now, looking back? Should I tell it in the voice of my mother, looking askance? Or should I hand the story over to Aunt Nell, who is not looking at all but stepping headlong into love?

Here's one possible way into the story:

> The piano went for twenty-five dollars, plus three dollars extra if you wanted the auctioneer's assistant to move it. Nell asked him if he would move it for two as she and her sister were short of cash. Watching him push it up the ramp into his pick-up truck she thought, I could run away with that man.

The instant I've written these lines, I know I'm lying. It was not love at first sight. Every evening Lou Lubbock called for Nell in his pick-up truck, and every night I dozed but did not fall asleep until two in the morning, when his truck clattered down the dirt road to our house, and Nell let herself in through the kitchen door, and my mother tiptoed downstairs in her nightgown. Together my mother and Nell sat in front of the empty fireplace and went over the day, piece by piece. A hole in the floor under my bed gave me a clear view of the living room. If I pressed my ear to the hole, I could catch most of their conversation. It might go something like this:

> Mother: So where did he take you?
> Nell: We went roller skating.
> Mother: Oh, you love roller skating.
> Nell: Not with him. He's a terrible skater. All he wants to do is eat.
> Mother: Where'd you eat?
> Nell: He took me to the Harvest Table.
> Mother: That's a nice restaurant.
> Nell: But he chews with his mouth full. And he always has dirt under his nails. I said to him, "Lou, just because you work on cars all day doesn't mean you can't wash up afterwards."
> Mother: Why do you go out with him?
> Nell: Because he's there.

Oh, he was certainly there. Though he was always on her mind, she made it clear to us that she would leave him at the end of the summer. Even she would never have called what passed between them love.

Who knows better than Chekhov the power of love that begins with mild curiosity and ends with obsession? In "The Lady With The Pet Dog," a man has an affair with a woman he meets at a resort hotel, expecting to forget her when the affair ends, as he has forgotten other women. In a single paragraph, Chekhov shows us the lover's inability to forget:

> A month or so would pass and the image of Anna Sergeyevna, it seemed to him, would become misty in his memory, and only from time to time he would dream of her with her touching smile as he dreamed of others. But more than a month went by, winter came into its own, and everything was still clear in his memory as though he had departed from Anna Sergeyevna only yesterday. And his memories glowed more and more vividly. In the street he followed the women with his eyes, looking for someone who resembled her.
> —From *The Portable Chekhov,* edited by Avrahm Yarmolinsky (Viking)

To tell Nell's story the way it happened, I need the kind of beginning that doesn't appear to be part of a love story at all. Take, for example, the opening of Rachel Ingalls' "Faces of Madness."

Four other boys in William's class shared his name. At home he was Will. At school someone else was called Will; two were Bill, and one went under a middle name. Only William was given the full, formal version.
—From *The Literary Lover,* edited by Larry Dark (Viking Penguin)

Nothing in the opening hints at how the main character, William, will spend his life and fortune looking for the woman his parents prevented him from marrying.

After the summer ended, Nell rarely mentioned Lou Lubbock. A week before Christmas, one of the women who lived in the cottage next door called to say Lou's truck had skidded on a patch of ice and flipped over on him. "He was trapped for six hours before he died," she added. "Thank God he was alone when it happened."

That winter when Nell came to visit on weekends, I could feel the ghost of Lou Lubbock listening, invisible and helpless, as she told the story of how she'd met her first husband in the laundromat. She'd just put two quarters into the dryer.

"I went to get a Coke from the machine, and he snuck over and opened the door of the dryer and threw all his stuff in with mine. When we tried to sort it out, my bra was hooked around his undershirt. One thing sort of led to another."

Now let me interrupt myself with a story which I hope will illuminate the problem facing any writer who has ever set out to write a love story. Three years after the summer of Nell and the piano mover, my sister, who was living in a sorority house in Ann Arbor, accepted the fraternity pin of the boy she was dating, and called home, four blocks away, to announce the good news.

"I've been 'pinned'!"

I was fifteen and thought the choice of words was unfortunate; it made me think of wrestlers on a mat, of butterflies skewered under labels. But to those wiser than I, it meant she was one step away from being engaged. It also meant that on a Monday night in the middle of May the whole fraternity would assemble under her window and serenade her. Of course my mother and father and I were not invited. But she explained that if we brought binoculars and hid behind the trees or in the bushes that flourished in the front yard of the First Presbyterian Church across the street, we could get a view of the whole ceremony.

On the appointed evening, my mother and father concealed themselves behind two large oaks, and I tucked myself into a honeysuckle bush between the church and the parking lot, with its single car, and waited for the show to begin. The fragrance of honeysuckle filled me with a nameless sorrow. Because I had the worst view, my mother had entrusted me with the binoculars. The sorority house was dark save for a single upstairs window, at which my sister stood, holding a candle so that love could find her. Presently I heard the clatter of footsteps in the distance. What appeared to be a well-trained army of salesmen was marching toward my sister's light, two by two, on the opposite side of the street. They assembled under her window, and after a small silence—during which I could almost hear the squeak of a pitchpipe—they burst into song.

A love song, no doubt. I've forgotten the words. In the middle of it, the young man paying court to my sister held up something large and lobed—his heart, I thought, till it lit up and through the binoculars I saw it was a model of his fraternity pin. Was it my fear of the dark that made me turn the binoculars away from my sister to the parking lot? What did it matter that I had the worst view of the pinning ceremony? I had an extraordinary view of the couple necking in the car in the parking lot.

Writing a love story is a little like finding yourself with a pair of binoculars in your hand, caught between passion and scruples, ceremony and sex. If you err too far in either direction, you can end up on the side of pornography or romance. The difference between a love story and a romance is one of intent. When you write a romance, you carefully follow where many have trod, so that your readers can recognize the genre through its conventions. But in a love story, you try to show love as if your characters had just invented it. Follow your characters, and they will give you the story, but you can't tell ahead of time exactly where they'll lead you. Rousseau's advice for writing a love letter is also useful for writing a story: ". . . you ought to begin without knowing what you mean to say, and to finish without knowing what you have written."

Love has its roots in the particular and the ordinary. Surely one of the writer's greatest challenges is to show how imagination can transform an ordinary human being into one whose absence turns day into night, heaven into hell, happiness into an abyss. Weather, light, fragrance, memory and loneliness have more to do with the alchemy of love than beauty or grace; Maurice Chevalier once remarked that "many a man has fallen in love with a girl in a light so dim he would not have chosen a suit by it." For showing that alchemy, I know of few writers who can surpass Thomas Mann in this passage from "Tonio Kroger":

> Strange how things come about! He had seen her a thousand times; then one evening he saw her again; saw her in a certain light, talking with a friend in a certain saucy way, laughing and tossing her head; saw her lift her arm and smooth her back hair with her schoolgirl hand, that was by no means particularly fine or slender, in such a way that the thin white sleeve slipped down from her elbow; heard her speak a word or two, a quite indifferent phrase, but with a certain intonation, with a warm ring in her voice; and his heart throbbed with ecstasy . . .
> —From *Death in Venice and Seven Other Stories.*
> Translated by H. T. Lowe-Porter (Vintage Books)

We are in love, and love what vanishes; isn't that why the sight of a thin white sleeve slipping down a girl's arm can break someone's heart? While lovers lie in each other's arms, the world is singing an older tune: "Golden lads and girls all must/ As chimney-sweepers, come to dust."

But though the teller vanishes, the tale does not. Several years ago when I started to work on a novel called *Sister Water,* the voices of women—in the living room at two in the morning—these voices I thought I'd forgotten did not forget me. As I wrote the chapter in which the main character receives word that her husband has been killed in a car accident, I knew what Aunt Nell would say.

"Death is so ordinary," she whispers. "Write about love."

22

CREATING A CHARACTER THE READER HAS NEVER MET

BY SHELBY HEARON

LAST SPRING, I GOT A LETTER from a talented former student, a fine writer who said she was stuck working on her novel. She didn't know where to go with it. What did I suggest? I knew she had sold her first story to *Mademoiselle,* and had an agent, so I didn't take her predicament lightly. Her impasse is one all writers share. And I sent her back a postcard that summed up the basic rule for writing fiction:

> Dear Elizabeth,
> Forget everything else and create a character the reader has never met before.
> Love,
> Shelby

I think we all know this is the secret heart of fiction. When we recall those books we most loved growing up, or discovered last year and passed around to our friends, we loved them because they introduced us to someone we had never met before and couldn't get out of our minds.

I saw in the bookstore that my writer friend Max Apple had a nonfiction book about his grandfather, who, at 93, had gone off to college with him. The book is called *Roommates.* And I thought, for Max, his granddaddy (who later, at 103, moved into the house with him and helped him out when his first wife was very ill) is the unforgettable character. But for a fiction writer, the young man who went off to college with his 93-year-old granddaddy in tow would be the person readers couldn't forget. What became of him? How did it work out? What did he do on dates, when he was studying, after he (they) graduated? I wouldn't use the real-life events: Max Apple remarries, this time a vital rabbi, and writes a bestseller about his grandfather. If it were fiction, I'd start with the idea of someone doing something we'd never encountered before, would never have imagined, and can't forget once we've read it.

I was thinking along the lines that we have to make sure the character we are creating is not just one of a class of people (boy coming of age, unhappy wife, victim and killer, star-crossed lovers, old man has a change of heart), but someone who, although in that class, is at the same time distinct from it. A misfit or a standout, a winner among losers, a loser among winners, a participant among observers, an observer among participants. A lemon in a bowl of cherries. That is the attraction of books in which someone with limited mental capacities is born to a family of Ph.Ds, or someone who breaks the tape for the 100-meter dash has parents who are home eating chips and watching the game on TV.

So I made that my first rule for writers: Write about someone who is not like everyone else in the group. I recalled the stories I'd judged or taught in the past year, trying to figure out what had made a select few out of hundreds stick in my mind. The plots themselves did not sound that different. There was a boy meeting a man in a mall; a minority student from the Texas Valley accepted to Yale; a Cuban woman tearing her legs fleeing her country; a security guard duped into crime; a probation officer deciding to help one more kid before throwing in the towel; an unmarried woman in the sixties deciding to keep her baby; a divorcée who recited in her mind like a litany all the men she'd ever been with when she met someone new. But what made these memorable, made them recalled not as stories similar to other stories I'd read, was that the people in the stories were unforgettable.

The writer of each had chosen some specific detail that still stood out in my mind. And had taken this one characteristic or habit or way of behaving and exaggerated it. Emphasized it. Enlarged it. Made that particular quirk or dream the starting place and built on that. So that the one alive, interesting, revealing part of the character became the kickoff, the yeast, from which the whole person could grow into someone I, the reader, had never encountered before. And about whom I wanted to know much more.

But this turned out to be only half the story. I realized it wasn't enough to create bizarre people with odd handicaps in weird predicaments having peculiar epiphanies. And I realized that "memorable" doesn't just mean strange; that freaky situations don't necessarily create depth of character.

In a recent *New York Times Book Review,* I read about a book by the real woman who became known as Jane Roe in *Roe* v. *Wade,* and I was intrigued at once. Here was not the person I'd expected to encounter, but rather someone in jeans, who worked in a bar, and wore a bandanna around her left leg in what was supposed to be a signal that she didn't have a girlfriend. What a wonderful fictional character that would make, I thought. Someone so unlikely, becoming a symbol for all of us. Then when I read the review of a novel about a teenager who loses his hearing after swimming in a forbidden pool, I realized that here was the missing key to how we create someone the reader has never met before. It is not enough to make your character unusual; your character must also teach us something new.

I went back to the Max Apple book and thought, if I were writing a fictional account of a boy going off to college, rooming with his granddad, I would need to be saying to the reader: We are all roommates on this planet, as reluctant and mismatched as we sometimes are. We are all going through the school of life together. And I understood that what had caught my interest about the woman who became Jane Roe was not only that she was unlikely candidate, but that her life made the point that those we least expect to can become symbols of something larger and finer and more important than our individual lives. I read again the review of the illicit swimmer and realized that what had made me want to buy the book was the suggestion that the tale was going to say that we are all deaf to our parents, that our children are all deaf to us. That in each case the character would be someone we had never met before because the character would be telling us a truth we had not thought about before.

I remembered those *Reader's Digest* features on "My Most Unforgettable Character" that I'd read as a girl: where the person, usually a parent or a teacher, but perhaps a bum or a stranger on a train, teaches us a lesson. That the person remains unforgettable not only because of special quirks, language, attitudes, but also for the way they make the writer, and us, the readers, see something we had not seen before about our lives.

I thought back to my gifted student, Elizabeth, and her own life. A lovely WASP woman who fell in love with a Jewish man, already a father, married him, had two more babies. And I asked myself: What would I do with that in a fictional way to make a fictional Elizabeth you had never met before? Certainly I would detail special things about her likes and dislikes, oddities about her upbringing, some funny, perhaps sad, thing she always did when she met someone she liked, something she kept hidden in a drawer, maybe, that no one ever saw, a talisman—all those details we use to build character. But then, to make her someone you had never met before, I would also have to let her tell you something true that you had never thought about that way before. Perhaps that all of us marry strangers, that all of us couple with people whose lives we don't share and can never wholly know, that every marriage is mixed, a mixed-bag, a mixed-metaphor, a mixture of intimacy and distance.

That got me thinking about my own recent novel, *Life Estates,* and the two women in it and readers' responses to them. And I saw that in my own case there was more to creating someone readers had never met before than just unusual loves and hates, attitudes and possessions, being different from others in the group. The novel is the story of two women who have been friends for forty years, since boarding school, and takes place the spring and summer before one of them dies. Harriet, the one who lives in east Texas, at fifty-five is very vain about her Betty Grable legs. She has an emerald green bedroom and wears emerald green satin mules and robe. She has a deer rifle in the corner by her bed and carries a .38 caliber handgun in her beaded evening bag. When she has to start chemotherapy, she arranges to get an eye-tuck at the same time. She has a crush on a man fifteen years younger.

Readers either loved her ("how spunky," "how brave") or hated her ("what a narcissistic twit," "what a self-centered snob"). But it was Sarah that they remembered, the woman in western South Carolina with the braid down her back, the wallpaper shop, the black lab named Gentle Ben, the peach orchards, the seventy-year-old lover, the daughter pregnant with her fifth son. They remembered her not because of these details, but because she refused to accept the money provided for her by her banker husband's will. The idea of men supporting their wives from the grave seemed to Sarah a denial of death, and sexist besides. And it was this declaration, this decision, and what it said about her view of life and loss and men and women that caused readers to remember her. It wasn't only because she possessed a juxtaposition of contradictions they hadn't encountered before, as was the case with Harriet, but because her actions caused them to think about something in a way they hadn't thought about before.

And so I dropped another postcard to my former student, now working away on her novel about a younger sister, and said:

Dear Elizabeth,
Don't forget that the character we have never met before must also teach us something we have never learned before.
                         Love,
                         Shelby

23

THE TRUTH ABOUT FICTION

BY NANCY SWEETLAND

WHEN I WAS YOUNG, each night after we were tucked into our beds, my mother would pull a straight-backed chair into the hall between our doors and open a book. As we drifted off to sleep, we also drifted off to Wonderland with Alice, to England with Mary Poppins, or down the river with Tom Sawyer and Huck Finn. Oz. Avonlea. Sunnybrook Farm. I thrived on those stories. Those people, those places, were a real part of my world. I had been, you might say, baptized into the religion of reading.

Then agnosticism hit me. At the age when most youngsters begin to doubt the Word, the word *I* began to doubt was fiction. Those stories— well, they were just made up, not real at all. Only a dummy would waste time on *that*!

I devoured all the biographies I could carry home, including Wanda Gag's fat journal that took me almost a month to read—and I was a fast reader. If I started a book, I finished it, like it or not. I learned— and likely, forgot—the stories of a lot of important people.

Next phase, places. Curious about the world, about personal experiences, I rafted on the *Kon-tiki,* sifted through digs in Egypt, crossed mountains with Halliburton.

Married by this time, I read voraciously, while my husband studied for his degree . . . sociology books, psychology. . . . When I became a mother, my children wanted books, and they wanted *stories,* stories they could understand, stories that could take them to faraway places, stories to drift to sleep on. Remembering my childhood pleasures, I began with Mary Poppins. They loved her, as I had expected. But I thought *I'd* be bored in the reading. No so.

There were lessons in *Mary Poppins.* I didn't remember *that*. Children could be naughty, and it wasn't always bad. Or that everyone

102

doesn't need to know everything; sometimes mystery is nicer . . . and certainly more fun.

Huck Finn—lots of lessons in living from old Huck . . . and the Wizard of Oz . . . and Alice. I fell down the rabbit hole again, and I began to wonder: Was it possible that I had learned a lot about life from my "serious" reading, but not much about the *living* of it? Had I learned *what* people had done, but not why, or how they felt about it?

I had read English history, but until I read Dickens, I never knew the desolation of huddling around a small coal grate to dispel the bone-chilling damp of London's winter air. I *knew* those people . . . felt their frustrations, their suffering. In their lives—as in mine—there were no absolutes. People dealt with situations, and I asked myself, would I have acted differently? (A question I never considered while reading nonfiction.) And, without realizing it, I learned about the period as well—the dress, the customs, even the furniture. From the fiction writer, the social historian.

In my pursuit of reality, I had missed many of the truths of living. And I realized that, throughout the ages from the time of cave children, storytelling was the thread from which our heritage is woven. It's how we learn to cope, because history *does* repeat itself. Times, customs, and specific situations change, but people still react with fear, hope, envy, love, or joy.

Roberta Simpson Brown, teacher, storyteller and author of *The Walking Tree and Other Scary Stories,* believes that children learn to handle fear vicariously by experiencing it—and they *do* experience it when they read or listen to her ghostly stories that maybe—just *maybe*—could really happen. But that's not all they experience. I think storytelling does something else, perhaps even more important: It allows children's imaginations to soar. Could *they* think up a story like *that*? Maybe that isn't just a closet door in their room; maybe it's an opening to a whole world, like *Narnia*.

I have a small collection of fairy tale books from various countries, mostly old, with favorite stories from when I was a child. Names are different, and there are variations, but by and large they convey the same message: Never give up. If you can't climb the mountain the first time, try again. If the king demands a stupendous feat for the poor young lad to win the princess, well, he's up to it. Good will triumph, and the wicked will be punished. Wonderful! They sky isn't really falling. Not today, anyway.

"All the truths we live by are unprovable," said Madeleine L'Engle. "It is the believable character, acting in believable situations that makes those truths real."

Love. Can you define it? Yet if you remember Rhett Butler and Scarlett O'Hara, can you doubt it?

Envy. Joy. Hate. People living their emotions make realities of "undefinables."

I'm a born-again reader. That's *true*.

Searching for *truth*. That's fiction.

24

SPEAKING OF FICTION . . .

BY SIDNEY SHELDON

Q. *How long, on the average, does it take you to write a novel—from idea to finished manuscript? Do you ever work on two books simultaneously?*

A. I take anywhere from a year to two years to write a novel. I may finish a first draft in 3–4 months. I then spend the rest of the time rewriting until the manuscript is as good as I know how to make it, before the publisher ever sees a word. When I was writing TV and motion picture scripts, I used to work on 3 or 4 projects simultaneously. When I write a novel, I work only on the novel.

Q. *How have your experiences and relationships with people been reflected in your novels?*

A. Some wise person once said that writers paper their walls with themselves. Everything that a writer sees or hears usually winds up in some form in his or her work. Many novels are autobiographical to a large extent. I've used incidents in my life in many of my books.

Q. *Do you create a "profile" for your characters prior to starting a novel?*

A. I think doing a profile for a character prior to starting a novel is a good idea. I work a little differently. My characters come to life in my novels as I dictate the story.

Q. *Many writers, especially inexperienced writers, have difficulty establishing a voice in their fiction. How can they go about finding their voices?*

A. The way to find a voice is to make your characters real. I once planned to write a novel using only dialogue and no description. The readers would know who was speaking purely from the character's way of talking. The only reason I didn't go ahead with it was that I found out that a French writer had gotten there first.

Q. *Why do so many successful first novelists have problems writing their second novels? How should they go about addressing these problems?*

A. One of the reasons that some successful first novelists have problems writing their second novel is that they are intimidated, afraid that they can't live up to their first success. Some writers seem to have only one novel in them, especially if that novel is autobiographical. Carl Reiner wrote a wonderful play called "Exit Laughing," about a playwright who wrote a smash hit and had trouble writing a second play until he moved back into the poverty-stricken life he was living when he wrote his hit play.

Q. *How do you account for novels that get generally enthusiastic reviews but do not sell?*

A. If a novel gets enthusiastic reviews and doesn't sell well, it's usually because either the publisher is doing a bad job of selling it, or because the critics are expressing personal opinions that are not shared by the reading public.

Q. *How, if at all, have movies and your screenwriting experiences affected your novel writing?*

A. The motion pictures, TV shows and Broadway plays I've written have made a great difference in my life as a novelist. They have taught me to keep the action moving and to write dialogue that's realistic.

Q. *Knowing how difficult it is to break into screenwriting, what realistic advice can you give to the aspiring screenwriter?*

A. It's almost essential to have an agent submit your screenplay to a studio because of the fear of plagiarism suits. The best way to get an agent is to have a finished screenplay to show. A list of agents can be found in the Yellow Pages of most metropolitan area telephone books, or in directories at the public library. The Writer's Guild of America (in New York City and Los Angeles) may also be helpful.

Q. *How important is it for writers to travel the world, broaden the range of their experiences, and get a first-hand feel for a place and its people?*

A. It's important for writers to broaden their experiences as much as possible. This doesn't necessarily mean traveling around the world—most writers can't afford to do that—but you can have emotional and physical experiences wherever you may live.

Q. *How do you research your novels? Of the various research techniques—libraries, interviews, visits to settings—which do you find most useful?*

A. I do extensive research in my novels. I won't write about a city that I haven't visited or about a meal that I haven't eaten. If finances make this difficult to do, I would suggest using the voluminous research capabilities of any good public library.

Q. *Why are so many of your main characters female? What are the options with and limitations of female and male protagonists?*

A. Most of the protagonists in my novels are females. I enjoy writing about women. I think they're more interesting than men, more complex and more vulnerable. Since my novels have an element of suspense and danger in them, vulnerability is important.

Q. *Do you write scenes in the order they will appear in the novel? Or do you write key scenes first and arrange them later?*

A. Many writers will plot out their books in advance. I read that Jerzy Kosinski used to get up in the morning and a look at the huge board he had, where each scene in the book was numbered. He would then pick out the number (a love scene, a murder scene, etc.) and write the scene he was in the mood to do that day. I write my books in sequence from beginning to end.

Q. *What are some of the devices you have found most successful in keeping your readers turning the pages?*

A. The most successful device in keeping readers turning pages is to end each chapter on a note of suspense. Mickey Spillane wisely said that the first page of a novel will determine whether someone buys the book, and the last page determines whether that person will buy your next book.

Q. *How do you determine whether your manuscript is ready to be sent off to the publisher?*

A. I write as many as a dozen drafts. A writer knows when his book is finished, in the same way that an artist knows when his painting is finished.

Q. *Which parts of the writing process—if any—do you find easier now than when you were starting out?*

A. Every novel becomes more difficult than the last because of a fear of disappointing the reader.

Q. *Given that writers are always studying people they meet or observe for character ideas, would you consider a fiction writer to be a better judge of character than a non-writer?*

A. Fiction writers are better judges of character than anyone else. They are also more intelligent and purer in heart.

25

REVISING YOUR FICTION MANUSCRIPT

BY JOHN DUFRESNE

REVISION IS NOT A MATTER OF CHOICE, yet many beginning fiction writers either resist, resent, or misunderstand its importance. When we read an impressive ten-page story, we may not be aware of the numerous discarded pages that preceded the finished product. If you were taught that writing is product and not process, that it's the articulation of thought and not thought itself, then revision may seem like punishment for not getting it right the first time. But writing is not supposed to be easy or extemporaneous. The writer has the duty and the opportunity to rework a story to try to find the best word, phrase, or scene, or do it over again until it is right.

If you are like Dorothy Parker, your revision begins with the first sentence of the first draft. She claimed that in writing seven words she revised five. The writing process itself is repetitive, erratic, messy. Planning, drafting, and revising seldom proceed in a linear fashion and, perhaps, should not be thought of as distinct tasks. All three go on in the first draft, as well as in the second and the tenth. But if we think of revision as a "seeing again," then we might say it starts when you have a beginning, middle, and end to your story. Now you can read it. Now you can see what you've said and sense what still needs to be said.

Revising means casting a critical eye on your work, and doing so makes the revision different from your first draft. You reorganize material; examine words, phrases, and paragraphs; consider character and plot; look at beginnings, endings, transitions, and composition. You add, delete, reshape. You examine your choices. There are a thousand steps in the process. It is in the revision stage that your imagination becomes deeply engaged with your material, when you come to know your characters and begin to perceive their motivations and values. Revision is not the end of the creative process, but a new beginning; it's a chance not simply to clean up and edit, but to open up and discover.

When you've completed a draft of your story, it's a good idea to set the manuscript aside and return to it later. Each time you read it over, you'll see something new. Read it aloud and note the places where the rhythms are smooth or hard, the prose graceful or awkward, a character's diction consistent and revealing, or jarring and unconvincing. Note the connections and tangents. Listen to your story. What is it trying to tell you? Try to visualize your characters, and before you go on to the next draft, imagine what they're doing or what they think they're doing and how they feel about it.

As the creator of a piece of fiction, you see what no one else sees. That's your job. Just as you notice every significant detail about your character's appearance—the thin scar on his left index finger, say—so you notice the confusing shift in tense, the awkward transition, the intrusive or extraneous adverb. You see what you wrote, not what you thought you wrote.

You look at your current draft and you ask yourself the right questions: Have I shown and not told? Is every scene necessary? Have I chosen the point of view that is likely to add interest and afford the reader clear access to the central conflict? Is the plot a causal sequence of events or a simple chronology? Has my central character changed? If so, how? Is the purpose of the change clear? Does each character have a distinctive voice? Have I made it difficult enough for my central character to get what she wants? Is the setting evocative? the theme fresh? Are the details vivid, precise, and revealing?

Answer the questions honestly. Make all necessary changes, and see if they necessitate additional ones. The substitution of a single word may sharpen the vision of an entire story. A character's precisely described gesture may be as effective as a page of exposition. Ask yourself more questions: What is my story about? Was that my intention? What emotional experience do I want the reader to have? Have I made that happen? Is the story as clear as it can be? If a scene drags, cut it; if dialogue rambles, tighten it. Make every word count.

All these rewrites and changes can't be done at once. Some writers may revise as they go along. Each of us has a different approach and process and needs to learn what works best. But for every writer, the first draft is an act of discovery; then the real labor begins. Be ruthless. The story should improve with each revision. Make a list of your "obsessions." Challenge your characters to take responsibility for their actions. Read each draft closely, because you must find the solution to the problems in the story itself. You begin to write better than you thought you could. You fix the problem, a new one appears, you persevere, and write on. If you never revise, you never learn to write. You see that the made-up characters you have created have become vivid and intriguing people who live interesting, but often heart-breaking, lives. You begin to resent the time spent away from them.

I write many drafts longhand, because it slows me down, gives me time to think. I change sentences, words, phrases as I write, often recopying the entire annotated draft from the first line to the point at which the corrections get so messy and confusing that I have to stop and make a fresh copy. In this way, I get to feel the rhythm of the prose, hear the tone of the narrative voice.

When I'm finally satisfied that the elements of plot are in place and I think I know what my characters want, I type this draft into the computer. I print it out, then put the copy away for a few days. When I read it again, I immediately begin to tear it apart. What I couldn't see in the heat of writing usually becomes clear now. I see that a story that I thought was good can be made even stronger. I make the changes, wait, reread, and start over.

There are some common stylistic problems that you will want to address in each stage of revision or at some point before the manuscript is finished. The following checklist may help you do that. By "challenge," I mean take out the offending word or phrase, read the piece again and only if the word or words in question are essential should you put them back in.

1. *Challenge every adverb.* Mark Twain said, "The adverb is the enemy of the verb." Often, what we need are not two words, one qualifying, thus weakening, the other, but one stronger word. Not "He walked unsteadily" but "He staggered." Adverbs modifying verbs of attribution are particularly intrusive and offensive. "'I see the problem,' she said confidently." *Show* us her confidence; don't tell us.

2. *Challenge every adjective.* Like adverbs, most adjectives are un-necessary. Often the adjectival concept is in the noun. A night *is* dark, an ache painful, a needle sharp. Color is often redundant, as in *blue* sky, *green* grass, and so on. Other adjectives are too conventional to

be either vivid or significant, like a *tender* heart or a *sly* fox. An adjective should never be simply a decoration; it must always be essential.

3. *Challenge every verb with an auxiliary.* Replace passive voice verbs with active ones that are immediate, clear, and vigorous. "I kissed her" is better than "She was kissed by me"—and shorter. Also, replace progressive forms of verbs with the simple tenses: "I brewed coffee" indicates a more definite time than "I was brewing coffee." (On the other hand, be sure to use the past perfect tense if denoting an action completed before a time in the past: "My mother had already called the plumber by the time I arrived.")

4. *Challenge the first paragraph.* Sometimes the first paragraph helps get the story going, but often it merely introduces the reader to the story we are about to tell. Action may actually begin in the second paragraph.

5. *Challenge the last paragraph.* If the last paragraph unnecessarily summarizes or explains the meaning of the story, cut it out.

6. *Challenge every line that you love.* Delete every word that is there only for effect, every phrase you think is clever, every sentence for which there is no purpose or point. Your concern must be with the characters and not with your own wit or style. Check your list of "obsessions" and correct them. Watch for your "pet" words—"just," "very," and "that" are common offenders—and delete them if they're not essential. Or perhaps your first-person narrators do too much telling and not enough showing, or you tend to shift tenses needlessly.

7. *Challenge every exclamation point.* Like adverbs, they are intrusive.

8. *Be alert for every cliché* or hackneyed word or phrase, every overused or unnecessary modifier. If you've heard it often, don't use it.

9. *Cut every nonessential dialogue tag.* In a conversation between two people you may need only a single tag:

"Doris, I'm home," Lefty said.
"In the kitchen, dear. Did you remember the milk?"
"Got it right here."

The new paragraphs clearly indicate who is speaking. When you're attributing dialogue, use "said" or "asked." Anything else focuses attention away from the dialogue.

10. *Eliminate those colloquial introductory words* in dialogue, like "yes," "no," "well," "oh," etc. What follows usually tells enough.

11. *Eliminate everything you're not sure of.* If you doubt whether a sentence, word, or behavior belongs, it doesn't.

12. *Read the draft aloud and listen* for awkward and repetitious words, inadvertent rhyme, faulty rhythm.

13. *Proofread* for clarity, consistency, grammar, punctuation, economy. And then proofread again.

Revision is not just a time to edit. It's a time to invent and surprise, to add texture and nuance. In writing fiction, you must be honest and rigorous. You cannot judge your characters or want to say something so much that you manipulate them, twist the plot, or ignore what *their* reactions and responses would be. You owe it to your characters to do justice to *their* lives. Revision continues until you feel that you have done all you can to make the story as compelling and honest as possible. Ask yourself if you care enough about these characters to put in the time, energy, and thought it takes to work a story into its best possible shape. If you quit, if you don't revise, then you don't care enough.

26

BACK IN A FLASH

By GAIL RADLEY

FLASHBACKS OCCUR SO NATURALLY in everyday life that you may scarcely notice them. In fiction a flashback is a valuable device for conveying information and revealing character and motivation. Whether you are writing juvenile or adult works, short stories or novels, a few simple techniques will enable you to ease in and out of the past gracefully.

There are times when the current events of a story just don't carry the full impact without background information. These are good times to consider flashbacks. In my juvenile novel, *The Golden Days,* it is important that the reader know eleven-year-old Cory's background of disappointment and abandonment to appreciate why he is having trouble trusting his new foster parents. I conveyed this information in a quick montage of memories:

. . . he could remember [his mother] much better than he could remember his father. She had been with him longer—until he was nine. He remembered her staring out the window for what seemed like hours, while he tugged at her hand and begged her to play. He remembered burying his face in her long blond hair while she rocked him, and how her face twisted up when she screamed at him. He remembered chasing her down the stairs and running after that beat-up old Volkswagen van until he could run no more. He remembered the hollow feeling when he realized she wasn't going to stop and he couldn't catch up to her—and how he wished for tears that did not come until nightfall. She had put a loaf of bread, a jar of peanut butter, and a jar of Marshmallow Fluff on the kitchen table and walked out of his life.

Without this passage, and the passages that describe Cory's previous foster fathers, it would be difficult to sympathize with Cory when he rebuffs his foster parents' overtures.

When the information is dramatic and central to the story, you may want to expand the flashback into a scene that allows the reader to experience its impact fully. In *Cracker Jackson,* by Betsy Byars, a boy

114

learns that his former baby sitter is being abused by her husband. Two
things are critical to Jackson's response—his fear and his love for the
sitter. Byars established both with a flashback:

> Jackson's earliest memory was of fear.
> Alma, his new baby sitter, had taken him down to the creek behind the
> apartment house to wade. He was five years old, but he had never been allowed
> to wade before, and stomping around in the muddy water made him happier
> than he had known it was possible to be.
> When he and Alma got out of the creek, they noticed there were some brown
> things on their ankles. Jackson was pleased, and Alma was, too.
> "What are they, Cracker? Mine don't want to come off, do yours?"

In the next two pages we learn that the "brown things" were leeches.
We see Mrs. Hunter's horror when she discovers them and hear her
restrained anger toward Alma. We experience Mrs. Hunter's caution
and fear as contributing to Jackson's fears. But his fear does not surpass his devotion to Alma:

> "Is Alma coming back?" Jackson asked as he and his mother went up the
> stairs.
> The leech danger had passed. He now had on his hightop, orthopedic, Stride-
> Rite shoes, laced tight. He was safe.
> "Is she?" Alma was his newest, youngest, and already his favorite baby sitter.
> The only answer his mother would give was the one he hated most: "We'll
> see."
> His mother did let Alma come back, but Alma was never at ease with his
> mother after that.

Flashing in

Notice that Byars introduced the flashback by having Jackson evoke
a memory, which is a commonly used and effective technique for sig-
naling a shift into the past. Sometimes the character is actually reliving
the memory at the point in the story where it occurs. But too much
stopping to remember makes the reader uneasy. Byars has avoided this
problem by making the transition into flashback through narration,
rather than by having Jackson lapse into reminiscence.

There are many ways of introducing a flashback other than evoking
memory. Katherine Paterson moves into a flashback boldly in *Jacob
Have I Loved* with the phrase "This is the story that the old people
told." The story concerns the past of a former resident of a tiny island
community who has recently returned. Since his identity and purpose

115

in returning are mysterious to Louise, the main character, and since he figures importantly in the story, the episode deserved to be set off in such a prominent way. A shift to the past perfect tense—which you may have noticed in the preceding examples—eases the transition. Note that the past perfect need only be used for a sentence or two. Simple past tense can be used for the main part of the flashback:

> This is the story that the old people told: Captain Wallace and his son, Hiram, had let down their sails and were waiting out the storm. The lightning was so bright and near that it seemed to flash through the heavy canvas of the sail. . . . [Hiram] had rushed out from under his sail cover, taken an ax, and chopped the mast to the level of the deck. After the storm passed, they were sighted drifting mastless on the Bay and were towed home by an obliging neighbor. . . . Not long after, he left the island for good. . . .
>
> Unless, of course, the strong old man rebuilding the Wallace house was the handsome young coward who had left nearly fifty years before.

Usually, you will want to slide into a flashback less conspicuously. There is a whole range of subtle transitional words and phrases that can announce your flashing into a different time zone, such as "once," "yesterday," and "when she was in fifth grade." Watch for such phrases in your reading.

Flashing out

When returning to the time of the story, continue in the past tense for a sentence or two. Use of a common link makes transitions smoother—and flashbacks are no exception. In the preceding Paterson example, Hiram Wallace, past and present, provides the necessary link. An object, an idea, or a feeling are other possible links you can use. Put in another transitional word or phrase, such as "now" or "today," to further clarify the return to the present.

Of course, any time you ask readers to step out of the chronological time flow, you run the risk of losing or confusing them. This is especially true for young readers who live in the here and now, and for whom it is easy to become confused by a disjointed chronology. So use flashbacks judiciously. Allow your reader the opportunity to care about what is happening in the story's present. Don't break into a tense or emotional scene with a flashback: You have worked too hard to build that emotion to step away before it is completed.

The alternatives

You don't need to rely on flashbacks whenever you want to say something about the past. Consider alternatives. If the scene is important enough to dramatize, you might begin your story at that point in time. Jerry Spinelli summarizes the first ten years in the life of *Maniac Magee* in under three pages. *Jacob Have I Loved* actually begins at the end of the story, with the main character returning to the island where she grew up. The remainder of the book recalls her growing-up experiences there, and her early history is briefly summarized.

Another alternative is to work the information in through dialogue or narration. If your story is told from the main character's viewpoint, you will *have* to present background information about other characters through dialogue and narration. *The Golden Days* is told through Cory's viewpoint. But background information about his elderly friend Carlotta is important. Cory learns her story along with the reader—through dialogue:

"Tell me about when you were with the circus, Carlotta."
A little puff of sound escaped her, and Cory waited. "When I was sixteen, I saw Philo's circus. It was the first circus I had ever seen." There was a silence in which Cory settled himself cross-legged on the rollaway bed. . . . Then Carlotta spoke again, her voice low and soothing. "I thought this was the most beautiful thing in the world. The costumes flashing like colored stars, the animals so strong and wild. Only later did I understand how trapped they were, and how faded the stars. . . ."

Realism is the watchword for presenting the past through dialogue and narration. Your characters must not sound as if they have stepped out of the story to give the reader a necessary bit of information. Listen to the words. Does the dialogue sound natural? Does the narration seem too weighed down with information? Does the story seem to stop when the information begins?

Information can also be conveyed through official reports. My novel-in-progress, *Dear Gabby,* uses a newspaper article to tell some of the story. Since reading the newspaper figures naturally into the story, it does not seem contrived. A detective story might lend itself to using police reports, a school story could naturally use school records.

Although the flashback is not the only way to present past information, it is an important device. Using a flashback, you can highlight past events quickly, or invite the reader to step back and experience the past with your character. And with careful use of verb tenses and transitions, you can slip into the past and be back in a flash.

27

POINT OF VIEW IN THE SHORT-SHORT STORY

BY MARIAN BATES

FOR BOTH CREATIVE AND COMMERCIAL REASONS, my favorite fiction form is the short-short, a preference that resulted from a process of trial and error. Some years ago, in less complicated times, I wrote a short story about the problems of a young girl emerging from childhood. Her shyness and resulting inability to make friends easily is compounded by an over-protective mother as well as by the unattractive braces on her teeth. (I used the braces as a symbol of childhood as well as the device by which the story is resolved.) When the braces are removed, the girl sees a new image of herself in the mirror and acquires self-confidence and a sense of self-esteem for the first time. This makes it possible for her to convince her mother that her childhood is over, and the time has come to let go.

When I finished the story and read it through, I was unhappy with it. While the beginning and end worked well, the middle seemed over-long and dragged out. There was a solution, I thought: I had never tried the short-short form before, but how hard could it be to pick up a pencil and cut my story to size, from 3,500 words to a thousand? Impossible, was the answer. That was how I discovered how unique the short-short story form is.

First and foremost, every word must count. In structure, a short-short must have a beginning, middle, and end, as in other fiction, but there the similarity stops. There is no room for intricate plot complications, lengthy descriptions, or numerous scene changes. For the same reason, it is crucial that the short-short author select the right viewpoint character—the one through whom the story can be told with the greatest economy. In my original story, I had chosen the girl as the pivotal character, but in rethinking it as a short-short, I decided that the mother should play that role, and provide the most significant emotional turning point in the story: the mother's bittersweet acceptance of the fact that her only daughter's childhood is over.

I was still not ready to begin writing. Now that I had my viewpoint character, I had to decide on the point of view, that is, the method of narration I would use. Most fiction writers prefer to write in the third person, which allows the most flexibility. With third person you can (if you wish) know everything about everybody, because you have personally created all the characters. That makes it easy—sometimes fatally, flatfootedly so—to lay out the lines of the plot and reveal each character's innermost thoughts and emotions. Using this omniscient point of view, it is even possible to switch viewpoint to a second character—or a third, a fourth—bearing in mind that you must do it deftly to avoid reader confusion. Or you can settle for less than omniscience, but still use the third-person point of view within whatever limits, wide or narrow, you want to set for yourself.

Writing in the first person (my preference) allows no such leeway. You must stay within the persona of the "I" of the story, which can be limiting. It can also be hard, because in using all those "I said"s and "I thought"s, you can be seduced into substituting your own persona for the character's, jarring to readers—unless the character really *is* you in disguise.

However, there is one outstanding advantage in the first-person approach: There is no faster, surer way to draw the reader directly into the heart and mind of the pivotal character. And in the case of my mother/daughter story, first person was a perfect fit, since I identified with the mother, being one myself (no daughters, though!).

I began the story in its new short-short form this way:

When Jennifer came beaming out of the orthodontist's office into the waiting room, I looked up from the magazine I was reading.

"Well, Mother, what do you think? Don't I look fabulous?"

It was Jennifer, and it wasn't Jennifer at all. The braces were gone. She was smiling, lips wide apart framing straight, perfect teeth. That much was brand-new, heart-stopping, beautiful. What I couldn't comprehend was the familiar, unfamiliar rest of her. Her shoulders, normally hunched forward so that the long butterscotch hair fell across her face, were flung back assuredly, accentuating small, lovely breasts, a slim waist, and narrow but discernible hips.

I knew I should have been as ecstatic as my daughter obviously was, sharing this longed-for moment with her, but all I felt was dismay. More than her braces had been left behind in the examining room, I thought, with a physical stab. It was as though her childhood had been left in the dentist's office too.

In the body of the story, the daughter is asked out on her first date. The boy's car develops clutch trouble; he calls from a gas station to say the car is being fixed and that he and the daughter will be late getting back. The mother's first impulse (which she struggles to resist) is to jump into her car and bring her daughter home.

At this point in the story, the problem was to show the mother working her way through the painful process of "letting go," taking care to make her change of heart believable to the reader. What I needed was additional insight into her character, insight she herself, as the viewpoint character, has to achieve. The question was how to accomplish it in very little space. After several false starts, I decided to use a memory from her childhood to confirm and strengthen the story's resolution:

. . . but my own mother had managed what I was struggling to achieve. . . . The years rolled back. I had been younger than Jennifer was now—a new town, a new school, and on the day I had to report for the first time, I begged my mother to come with me.

She had looked at me thoughtfully. "I will, Laura, if you insist, but I don't really want to. I think you can do this by yourself. Will you please try?"

Years later I had asked my mother about that day. She had smiled.

"The minute the door closed behind you, I wanted to run after you, take your hand, walk with you. . . . It seems now I held my breath for the entire day until I looked out and saw you skipping home, a new friend on either side. I was so proud—of you, of course—but more of myself."

From this point on, the story wrote itself. When the daughter returns at last, "glowing like a roomful of Christmas trees," she tells the mother that there has never been a day as special as this in anybody's life anywhere in the entire world, and that the mother, by not interfering, is the one who made it perfect.

I used the braces again as a metaphor to bring the story full circle. When the mother is in bed at last, after what has seemed the longest evening of her life, it ends this way:

Drifting into sleep, I said a final, wistful good-bye to Jennifer's beautiful braces.

In another short-short story of mine, "Where Tomorrow Waits," the "I" of the story is Susan, a young woman too proud to admit she misses her small-town boyfriend when he, in a similarly mulish mood, visits her in the big city. Again, a symbolic object—Susan's grand-mother's candy dish and the associations it brings with it—provides a compressed but effective way of breaking the emotional logjam needed for the story's resolution.

A few words about another technique—writing from the male char-acter's point of view, if you're a woman. (Male writers don't seem to need any encouragement to do the reverse; from the beginnings of the English novel—witness Samuel Richardson's *Pamela* and *Clarissa*—men have used a female persona whenever it seemed right to do so.) Indeed, there is no reason not to adopt whatever voice, male or female, young or old, is best suited to tell your story. If as the writer you—and by extension the reader—can identify with a male hero, step into his shoes, think and feel as he does in that dimension of his life you have chosen to explore, you'll have no problem.

Remember, too, that we are not talking about *War and Peace* here (though even if we were, the principle would be the same), but about light romantic fiction. And in that form, a male protagonist works par-ticularly well; traditionally, the heroine has filled the central role, so a certain spice is added when the tables are turned.

My first story using the male character's point of view, "The Wonder of Jenny," was about a man who falls in love with a warm, generous caring girl, only to discover later that the very traits that drew him to her are a source of trouble in their relationship. Jenny's instinct for helping people thwarts Ben's efforts to be the focus of her attention, the center of her world. As he puts it:

There was a Good Samaritan streak in Jenny's nature a mile wide, and if I didn't learn to live with it we were both going to be miserable. Maybe she wasn't the girl for me after all. . . .

In creating Ben I had to walk a careful line. I wanted to portray him as a likable, sympathetic character, because I *knew* him and cared about what happened to him; at the same time, I had to show his unappealing self-centered side, or there would have been no conflict and therefore no story. The turning point comes when he finally real-izes that unless he can learn to share at least some of Jenny's thoughtfulness for others, he will lose her. But he has to come to that realization *his* (masculine) way to make his conversion believable.

Endings

Does your short-short have a happy ending? Of course! Hadn't I known from the beginning that Ben and Jenny belonged together?

But before character, before point of view, before anything, comes plot. True, an imagined character sometimes becomes so real to a writer that he or she creates his or her own story. But most of the time, it's a situation that brings the characters to life. The idea for "Wedding Bell Blues" (another of my stories with a male protagonist) came from a snatch of conversation I overheard in a checkout line after a week of sitting at my typewriter fruitlessly searching for a short-short theme. The women behind me were discussing a wedding they'd been to. The gist of it went something like this:

> **First woman:** "I couldn't believe it when Doug showed up at Kate's wedding, could you?"
> **Second woman:** "I couldn't believe she invited him! Did you know he had bought her a ring just before she told him she was going to marry Brian?"

That was all, but it was enough to get me thinking. Looked at one way, it was a sad little snippet, but most young men, as we all know, are resilient creatures when it comes to romance. Just suppose, I thought to myself, "Doug" were to meet an ex-girlfriend of the groom at "Kate's" wedding—where else more likely?—and. . . . My imagination was off and running. Two days and three drafts later I had my story. Here the problem was to avoid a possible sad-sack connotation of two losers in love getting together on the rebound; using the first person for the engaging hero seemed the quickest way to head it off.

Today, few magazines actually have a special "short-short" fiction category. But as the demands on pages once allocated for fiction grow, a writer's ability to use this demanding but space-saving story form can be a marketing advantage.

One final word of advice: Often, other things being equal, a story with a seasonal or holiday theme may be just what an editor is looking for, if you can write it in time for the appropriate issue. But keep in mind the monthly magazines' long production lead time, at least three to six months.

§ 28

PLOTTING

BY ROBERT BARNARD

ONE THING THAT IS ALWAYS TRUE about my plots is that they come like Yeats' peace on the Lake Isle of Innisfree, "dropping slow." I have never been able to sit down and work a plot out in detail, have never begun a book knowing exactly what is going to happen. Agatha Christie, I believe, could do that, and it made the actual writing of her books a fast and comparatively straightforward process. My plots come to me, little by little, over a long period, and that period includes the time when I am writing the early chapters. This makes the plot-ideas notebook that I presume every writer has particularly important in my case.

It sits on the mantlepiece, and it mostly gets written in when I am listening to music in the evening. Many of the things that get noted down are simply phrases—funny twistings of clichés, for example, or odd things I have heard people say. But the first ideas for books will almost always be there, as well as subsequent changes, accretions, minor characters, twists that may mislead readers, and so on. Often I go back and read through the book, say if I am looking for an idea for a short story, and I don't remember the ideas that got there years ago, sometimes don't even understand what the scrawl was actually getting at, the idea that was behind my shorthand noting down of it.

I've gotten into a routine of writing a book between October and spring, with the interruption of Christmas to catch my breath in mid-book. This leaves late spring and summer for rewriting, revising, and writing the odd short story or magazine piece. At some stage during this "fallow" period, I will also decide which book for which I have some ideas will actually get written next. This doesn't always work out quite as I expected, and sometimes an idea will "take hold" of me and demand to be written *now,* as I remember my book called *The Skeleton in the Grass* did. I then take a new notebook and collect all the ideas I have had relevant to the new novel. That inevitably means that more ideas start coming, centering on the new project. All these I put at the beginning of the notebook.

Of course, the new ideas do not all concern the new plot: Some are, again, what we might call "little funnies," others are details of character, descriptions of houses, towns, and so on. But all have a tangential relationship to plot—plot is character in action; locales mirror the atmosphere that the plot needs, and sometimes prove an essential component in the actual murder (like the ruined castle on a steep declivity in my mystery novel, *Fête Fatale*). I am always very conscious that I have to write a book of two hundred pages or so, and have to have enough material, enough *story,* to fill those pages interestingly. My historical crime novel, *To Die Like a Gentleman,* written under the pseudonym Bernard Bastable, took me twelve years to write; it didn't take that long because it was long, but because it was short. The material didn't quite warrant two hundred pages, and, since I thought that what I had written was very good, I didn't want to spoil it with padding or by introducing subplots that detracted from the main interest. In the end, I had to take a deep breath and make a conscious decision to write a book rather shorter than usual.

I hope this suggests that to me, unlike E. M. Forster, the novel does and should tell a story, and I in no way regret this. How could I, whose main love is the Victorian novel, which so gloriously does tell a story? I laugh about a review that said that one of my books "has about as much tension as a wet noodle" (and, in passing, the convolutions of a wet noodle is not a bad image of a whodunit, which should be nicely tangled), but if I thought it was true, I would regard it as a serious charge: There must be tension, and there must be enough interest in what is happening to keep the reader reading. Otherwise, any piece of fiction that aspires to be popular literature has failed.

Often during the summer months I write the first chapter of what is to be the next book. First chapters to me are vital. If you don't believe me, read the first chapter of *Dombey and Son,* which simply compels one to read on, and compare it with the first chapter of *Martin Chuzzlewit,* which is a heavily laboured bore, and must have put countless people off a brilliant novel. The main thing is to seize the readers' interest, but also to give them the *feel* of the book, right from the start. One of the reasons I have mostly resisted having a series detective is that he dictates the feel, the tone, the atmosphere—call it what you will—of any book he or she is in. Agatha Christie regretted using Poirot in a book called *The Hollow,* and I think this was because it was a more serious book than usual, with greater depth of characterization, and Poirot simply did not fit in.

As well as setting the feel of the book, that first chapter in my case usually includes one or more of the central characters, and usually centers on the victim. I like to know the corpse before he becomes a corpse—having the character of the corpse gradually revealed after his death does not, for me, have the same immediacy. My bodies usually come around page sixty, or even later, and tend to be pretty unpleasant characters. This is for my own sake: When I have killed off characters I liked (as in *Fête Fatale,* and *A Corpse in A Gilded Cage*), it upsets me, and I feel rotten about it. And of course the nature of the victim's unpleasantness will be a major factor in setting the tone of the book: Is his or her unpleasantness dangerous, vicious, rather comic, or what?

Just before getting down to write, I start dividing the second half of the notebook into chapters and noting what each chapter will include. This I do about two or three chapters ahead: When I start the book I have, say, the first three chapters mapped out, and chapters get planned bit by bit as I write. All I've said has implied the cardinal element in my plotting: I get ideas as I write. Holding a pen is the most powerful stimulant to ideas (I'm sure tapping away at a word processor wouldn't have at all the same effect). So though I start the book with ideas, and have the main characters pretty firmly in mind—probably the victim, probably the murderer, too—I still have lots of room to maneuver, lots of minor characters to invent, lot of minor clues to think up. Charlotte Brontë started one of her juvenile pieces of fiction with the chilling words: "There is, reader, a sort of pleasure in sitting down to write, wholly unprovided with a subject." Oh no, there isn't, Charlotte, not for the reader, one is tempted to retort. On the other hand, a novel begun with a broad idea, a general notion of the most important characters, a sense of its tone, does have a sort of vitality and energy that a novel begun with everything already mentally in place will often lack.

Let me end by offering hostages to fortune in the shape of the two books I am planning. At this writing, I am not quite sure which of the two will be written first. One is a Robert Barnard novel called (very provisionally) *The Masters of the House*. The first chapter, already written, has a woman dying in childbirth and her husband going quietly mad with grief, or guilt, or something. The children of the house start a process of concealing their father's condition and taking over their own fates. I know who is going to get killed, I think I know who did it, and what is going to happen at the end of the book. More than that I don't know.

The other book is a Bernard Bastable called, definitely, *Dead, Mr. Mozart*. It is set, musicians may be puzzled to hear, in England in 1820. I have some main characters: Mozart, the manager of an opera company, a wealthy patron and his singer-mistress, King George IV, his mistress, and so on. I know roughly what is going to happen in the early chapters, but I am not at all sure who is going to get killed and know nothing about who killed him/her or why: This probably means this will not be the one that gets started first.

Let me say in conclusion that the above is not meant as any sort of prescription, merely as a description: This is what I do. I have no idea whether my practice sets a good example or a bad one for others. But I do in general believe that you have to allow yourself a bit of leeway, room to invent and expand while the book is being written. Whatever scheme for plotting a work of fiction is adopted, it has to be one that enables the work to stay fresh during the months or years that the actual writing takes. One must start a book with the ability to free-wheel, even though every chapter one writes necessarily limits that freedom.

29

WHEN IS A STORY A SHORT STORY?

BY SUSAN R. HARPER

"THIS IS ON ITS WAY TO BEING a powerful short story," I once wrote on a manuscript—in fact, I've written something like that on any number of them, over the years. "But it isn't a short story yet," is how the second sentence goes, followed by sentences that offer thoughts on how it might become one.

The author of the piece I'm recalling right now asked to have his story read in class; he wanted it judged by a jury of his peers. I had to think about that for a minute; I never deliberately leave students open to embarrassment. But there's nothing inherently embarrassing about an early draft that falls short or isn't working—at least, there shouldn't be. Not in a workshop, anyway. That's what workshops are for. Besides, perhaps I'd been wrong: judged the story too harshly, missed its point. I've been crashingly wrong about stories at times.

I read the story out loud to the class, as I almost always do. That way the authors remain anonymous, and the criticism is directed toward the work, not the writers. I was careful to present the story as well as I could, as if I myself had written it. Then I asked for comments, first on what was working well (we usually begin with that), and then on what seemed not to work.

There was a lot to like in the story, everyone agreed: The characterizations were strong, the point of view consistent and convincing, the setting well evoked. . . . But? The comments suddenly became vague: "I didn't care for the ending."—a useless observation except that it did point to a problem area and got the group talking about it. "I wasn't ready for it to end."—a *bit* more helpful. "I don't know," said one young man. "Are we sure it *had* an ending? I felt more as if it had just quit. Like a plane that's supposed to come in for a landing, but instead just drops out of the sky."

128

"But did you have any idea *where* it would land?" asked another student.

"No," the first admitted.

"I didn't either. There wasn't any sense of a destination, or any suspense about whether or not the character would get there—wherever 'there' is."

"Right," someone else said. "It isn't that you don't care. The main character's too real for that; you can't be indifferent to him. But you don't know where he's headed, or what really matters to him. So when things happen to him, you don't know how you're supposed to feel about them."

Tell me a story

What's interesting to me about those comments is the way they spontaneously and almost innocently reveal what readers expect from a short story. There wasn't anything hifalutin' about the remarks—nothing technical or showoffy. People were just groping around for how they felt about that story.

Their feelings, I think, go all the way back to childhood, and beyond, to the beginnings of the human race. As we learned in high school biology, each of us repeats, in our individual lives, the whole history of our species. A lovely and intriguing thought! It assigns each generation more to absorb; it makes the "front ends" of our lives seem (in the abstract, at least) like speeded-up movies; and it offers one explanation, at least, for why things seem more frantic and more complicated with each succeeding generation.

When we sit around a long table in a seminar in San Francisco and listen to a story, we are doing something almost as old as humankind: gathering around a fire. And we are doing something we probably did when we were children. As soon as we became truly verbal, one of our requests was "Tell me a story."

What did we mean by that? I think that in a funny way I had a chance to find out as a kid. My parents came from a long line of raconteurs, and my father in particular was and is a very good storyteller. He has led an adventurous life, so he's continually adding to his repertoire, but the old stories are the ones we've heard the most and know the best. Even now, when we get together for a holiday or a reunion, we ask for these old stories by name. "Tell us 'Punk's Hack,'"

129

we say. "No, how about 'Ham and Eggs and Gravy Legs'?" They are stories we've heard from childhood.

But I was a child of the forties and fifties, the era of the "shaggy-dog story"—a long, rambling narrative, the point of which was that it had no point. This type of story was, for some perverse reason, hilarious to my dad. So once in a while, if we asked for a story, we got a shaggy-dog story, told by him with great amusement and greeted by us with something close to mutiny. "That wasn't a *story*," we'd protest. I'm sure my father thought we were a pretty humorless bunch. But I can still remember my real disappointment, the sense of having been cheated. I wanted something with a *point,* something that started at A and went to B (or G, or Z). It was this desire, in fact, that the shaggy things exploited and mocked. So we weren't wrong in feeling that we were somehow being laughed at.

Were our desires different from most people's? Look at what the class members were implicitly looking for in the story I read aloud. They wanted an ending, certainly: an ending they were prepared for. "A destination," one of them called it—implying a journey: a shape of the whole story, as if it were a trajectory. "Suspense," one of them mentioned. Another talked about getting a sense of "what really matters," so that "when things happen to [the character], you . . . know how to feel about them."

The slice-of-life question

The key question in a short story workshop is: "What was the author's intention?" That is what we as readers must divine, if we are to do justice to the writer's work. In the last analysis, the writer may not do what we want, but has he achieved what *he* wanted?

That was the question at which our discussion arrived, and we were up in the air about answering it. "Since I couldn't tell where the author was going with this story," said the woman, "I never knew whether he or she got there."

Then a new voice joined the discussion. "I had the feeling that we were being shown something—like, say, a snapshot," he said, "and being asked to draw our own conclusions." And how had he felt about that? Was that a valid thing for a story to do?

"I guess anything is valid," he said (a true child of the seventies). "But how I felt was, well—it was as if I'd been given a test and had never found out if I'd passed. I always want to know the *author's* conclusions. Otherwise, why read an author's stuff, right?"

At that point, we turned to the author, who could hardly wait to speak. "That was the whole *idea*," he said. "The story did just what I wanted it to do. It presented a slice of life. Period. The rest is up to the reader. It's *supposed* to make you feel frustrated; it's *supposed* to bring you face to face with life, and with the inevitability of making decisions and drawing conclusions and being alone in your judgments."

"O.K.," I said. "The author has done what he set out to do. His story affected us as he hoped it would. In that sense, he's entirely satisfied.

"The basic question now is: Has he written a short story? Does this piece have the hallmarks of what we call by that name? Or is it something else?"

"What else could it be?" someone asked.

If it's Tuesday, this must be fiction

One of the assumptions people fall into sometimes is that if a piece of writing is "creative" (as opposed to purely factual and expository) and if it's prose, it must be a short story. "What else could it be?"

The answer is that it could be a prose poem, or a novella, or a "short short story," or a vignette, or a character sketch. Each of these has particular attributes that distinguish it from the others. So-called slice-of-life stories usually turn out to be vignettes—brief incidents or scenes, or short descriptive sketches; moments, places in time, rather than trajectories—and I felt that the piece we were considering was probably a vignette. Because they're static, vignettes can't stand alone. And in that sense, they don't fulfill our expectations of the short story.

The short story, in fact, like the sonnet, can inspire (and fulfill) the most extravagant expectations. And even in its simplest, purest form, it is as rigorous, as rigidly circumscribed by "rules," and as demanding as the sonnet, though it doesn't have a prescribed number of lines or words or syllables, or a rhyme scheme with a name. But it has been interpreted—by writers, readers, and critics alike—with wide latitude. It flows between broad banks, retaining its fluidity and grace. Yet, like any chemical compound, including water, it has a specific structure that can be diagrammed, and a specific set of elements that go to make it up. These aren't arbitrary, and they aren't optional; they are what make a short story a short story rather than a vignette or a prose poem or a shaggy-dog story.

Like the child in the old television advertisement who is playing in the snow while waiting for his mother to make soup for lunch, we have certain definite expectations. "Is it soup yet?" the child calls in to his mother as she stands at the stove, stirring something in a pot. The child is expecting a hot liquid to be set before him in a cup or bowl. But if, when he sits down, his mother serves him tea—a hot liquid in a cup or bowl—he will protest, "This isn't soup!" We will expect the same response if she offers him oatmeal or chili. Soup is soup.

Call me a short story

We don't just decide that a piece of prose is a short story because we want it to be or wish it could be or don't know what else it is. We *know* whether a piece of prose is a short story by what is in it.

I'm thinking now of the injured man lying in the street, who cried out to a nearby hippie, "Call me an ambulance." Nodding, the hippie responded, "Like, man, you're an ambulance." I realize that the fact that this is one of my favorite awful old jokes shows the extent to which I am my father's daughter. But it's still true that if we dub something a short story without even thinking about it, we're as bad as the hippie. We're discouraging the author from understanding his or her work, and from confronting the standards by which it is measured. The short story is called a demanding form for good reason. And we don't write one by accident. Look at what Edgar Allan Poe wrote when he offered—more than 150 years ago—the critical definition of the short story that still stands today:

In the whole composition there should be no word written, of which the tendency, direct or indirect, is not to the one pre-established design. And by such means, with such care and skill, a picture is at length painted which leaves in the mind of him who contemplates it with a kindred art, a sense of the fullest satisfaction.

Pre-established design? At length? This is not the description of a casual process, but of a painstaking and specific (and perhaps lengthy) one. A rewarding one, too, for at its best it leads to that "sense of the fullest satisfaction" for reader and writer alike.

30

SPIRIT OF PLACE

BY EVA IBBOTSON

SOME YEARS AGO I was staying in a hill village in the south of France with a friend who has made her home there. Wandering along by the old ramparts on the way to the *épicerie* to buy our bread, we came on a lovely, near-derelict house with a fig tree growing through the kitchen roof, valerian sprouting from the gutters, and a heavenly view over vineyards and olive trees toward the mountains.

"Is it for sale?" I asked, caught by the dream of house-hunting, of escaping into a different life, that everyone has when they are holidaying in the sun. And my friend said, "No. It belongs to an old lady but she won't sell the house because it's in her soul."

So there it was, untenanted, falling down, but not for sale because of its occupancy in the old lady's soul—and it is still there, I understand, because souls don't age like bodies, and however old the old lady is by now there will still be room in her soul for much-loved houses.

I suppose if I have to describe a place that will matter to us as fiction writers—places that will give our stories uniqueness and resonance— then I would say they are places that for one reason or another are in our souls. But how do places get there? Why are some places beautiful or interesting or threatening, but somehow outside what we write— not really greatly our concern—whereas others, no more beautiful or unusual, never leave us alone till we have given them life again on the page?

There's no simple answer, I suppose. A child brought up within the sound of the sea, if taken inland or to the city very early on, will always hold up a conch, so to speak, to hear the sound of the waves. Children reared in the mountains can adapt perfectly well to flat places, to cities, but in times of trouble turn their faces to the hills, real or imagined. For me, the open sea won't do: It's too sad, too limitless. . . . I love water, but I need it contained in arms of land, I need trees to

133

be reflected in it. . . . I need, in short, an echo of the Austrian lakes where I spent my childhood summers. So, yes, places can get into the soul in those early years, and what lodges inside the soul remains.

Childhood and familiarity, then, will make a place special, as will love, which seems to be an inescapable requisite of the creative process. For you can catch places from people that you love, or catch places because there you have loved and been in love. I caught the opera house in Manaus from a man I was very much attached to long ago. He came back from a business trip and told me that many years ago the rubber barons had built a fabled opera house a thousand miles up the Amazon, where music was played while howler monkeys climbed on the roof. He told me that Caruso had performed there, and Sara Bernhardt, and I listened as I would not have listened to someone I had not loved, and lo, in my soul there grew this many-splendored thing, the opera house. Ten years later, when I had parted from this man, and life had taken me elsewhere, I wrote a book about it, in which a "Company of Swans" in a ballet travel there, and one of them finds fulfillment. . . .

I caught places from someone else I loved very dearly—my mother. She was Austrian, and the city I caught from her was the city of her birth, Vienna, which has been the setting of so many of my books. It was not the solemn city with its heavy Ringstrasse that I caught from her, not the stuffy Vienna of the Emperor Franz Joseph, but the city of her stories, the city where her uncle kept a carp in a bath for Christmas and tried to shoot it with his shotgun on Christmas Eve and missed. I have written again and again of this city which my mother herself did not love but knew, and which I loved because I loved her, and reinvented.

For make no mistake about it, some serious reinvention has to take place before a locale moves out of the soul to do useful work on the page. Whatever the love, or perhaps hatred—for hatred may also attach us passionately to a place; it is only indifference that does not work for us as writers—that pervades us, we must approach atmosphere and locale with an eagle eye and a large pair of mental shears.

Some time ago I was asked to help a new writer with a historical novel that she was finding troublesome. This writer was an avid researcher, and since the book was set in the ancient world, she read that great historian Herodotus from cover to cover. She scarcely stopped for weeks, and soon partially digested chunks of this splendid man appeared in the novel, effectively blocking the action. I coined a phrase for what had happened: *Herodotisation*—and teased her out of it; after a lot of pruning, the novel eventually saw the light of day.

Herodotisation is easy to fall into; the purple passages gleaned from learned tomes, triumphantly inserted into the text, are as dangerous as being dull and featureless. Look how restrained the great masters are: Dickens's *Our Mutual Friend* contains famous descriptions of the Thames, for the heroine is the daughter of a waterman who makes his living robbing corpses that float by on London's river. In my memory, the book opens with rich, dense, intensely atmospheric evocations of the Thames at night, yet look at the first sentence:

> In these times of ours, though concerning the exact year there is no need to be precise, a boat of dirty and disreputable appearance with two figures in it, floated on the Thames between Southwark Bridge which is of iron and London Bridge which is of stone. . . .

What could be simpler, yet what could be more effective, than the juxtaposition of the ancient stone bridge with the newer, brasher one of the Victorian's favorite ironwork, thus setting both place and time? And a paragraph later he writes:

> Allied to the bottom of the river rather than the surface by reason of the slime and ooze with which it was covered and its sodden state, the boat and the two figures in it were obviously doing something they often did and were seeking what they often sought.

And now we are already there with Gaffer Hexham and his lovely daughter who must be rescued from her awful life.

Or take Charlotte Brontë, the mistress of atmosphere, whose "Thornfield" stands for all the inimical wuthering, the windswept loneliness that accompanies a doomed romance? Mr. Rochester's decision to wed Jane Eyre even though he has a wife still living is accompanied by the fiercest storm in living memory—but how is it described?

> But what had befallen the night? The moon was not yet set and we were all in shadow—I could scarcely see my master's face, near as I was. And what about the chestnut tree? It writhed and groaned while the wind roared in the laurel walk and came sweeping over us.

135

And there is scarcely more except the news, the following morning, that the chestnut tree has been struck by lightning—yet I remember this as a great paean, as pages of description in which the fury of the elements is called up.

Lawrence Durrell said that a man is born twice—once in the place of his actual birth and once in the place where he learned to write. It is this second place that I am trying to describe in my new book: a school housed in a dilapidated castle beside an Austrian lake—a place where I went myself as a child and scribbled my first stories. I wanted to describe the beauty of the castle as it was when it was built and so I wrote:

> In the count's pleasure gardens, morning glory wreathed itself round olean-der bushes, jasmine tumbled from pillars, stone urns frothed with geraniums and heliotrope. . . .

So far so good. But I go on to describe an orchard in which peaches and apricots ripen and a flight of stone steps leading down to the water where black swans come to be fed.

No, that's overkill. I rein back, eliminate the black swans. But I miss them; I love black swans. Shall I trade them for the apricots and peaches?

And so I go on, sometimes for hours, taking out swans, putting in oleanders, backward and forward, forward and back. But in the end, with luck, I'll get there—because that place, if anywhere on earth, is in my soul.

31

CIRCUMSTANTIAL EVIDENCE: SOURCE OF FICTION PLOTS

BY LEILA DAVIS

CREATING A CHARACTER BASED ON circumstantial evidence presents a writer with a different approach—and challenge. Law enforcement officers are often faced with that situation, a classic example being the "contents of a dead man's pockets." Identification may be missing, leaving as clues only what "John Doe" carried and wore. For example:

1) In John Doe's pockets they may find: a key chain with gold-tone golf cart medallion and seven assorted keys, nail clippers, black comb, two large rubber bands, partial book of matches from Tony's, one white shirt button, golf tee, receipt for three rolls of film, partial pack of mint Tic Tacs, two ticket stubs from a hockey game, a ⅜-inch brass nut, three nickels, six pennies, one quarter. A crumpled grocery list with these items: grapefruit, bread, coffee, chicken, light bulbs, Coors, cheese, carrots, tuna, hamburger, meat sauce, VCR tapes. No wallet was found.

The police have already taken the body to forensics; fingerprints and dental charts may eventually identify the man. Let's assume his body was found on the shores of Lake Michigan. Given the size of the Great Lakes, a boat could capsize and/or sink without ever being noticed or reported.

One writer might invent the following story: The victim, Mark, a cautious man, always stashed his wallet in the cabin so he wouldn't lose it if he fell overboard. He needed the ⅜-inch brass nut to repair the boat railing. Brass fittings are expensive, used mainly where equipment is subjected to a high degree of corrosion, such as a cabin cruiser. Mark also enjoys golf, but neither golf nor his boat gives him enough exercise to control the weight he's gained from frequent meals at Tony's Ristorante. The shirt button, strained to the limit, popped into his lasagna, and ended up in his pocket.

He'd left the three rolls of film on July 7 to be developed, pictures taken during a holiday get-together with other boating/golfing enthusiasts. Mark bought the groceries for the weekend he had custody of his son, who tapes movies off Dad's cable TV. The pair spent one evening at an exhibition hockey game.

Quite another story could be developed by a novelist: Randy, with the same items in his pocket, is found in an alley, victim of a mugger. Randy plays golf with the same foursome every week during the golfing season. The author imagines the button came off when Randy forgot to undo the left sleeve before pulling off his shirt in his rush to make starting time. He and one of his golf buddies are also rabid hockey fans, vocal in expressing their opinions. After a game, they often stop at Tony's to hash over the highlights of the day's game.

Smoking is not allowed in Randy's office, so he sucks a Tic Tac when he can't have a cigarette. The brass nut is to repair his leaking kitchen sink, too long neglected by the apartment manager. Randy pulled the large rubber bands off the bundle of magazines and letters delivered that day.

In addition to the key to his apartment and two car keys, he has a key to his basement storage locker, another to the apartment of one of his golf partners, as well as one to his parents' home, and one to his office. But, inexplicably, his key to the executive washroom is missing. Against company policy, Randy was having duplicates made. When his boss hears that Randy was killed, he's more upset about the missing executive washroom key than about Randy's death.

And here's a third possibility for developing a story from the same "evidence": Joe has never really liked golf, but his wife, Vanessa, loves it; he's more her caddy than her partner. The key chain was a stocking stuffer at Christmas, and now he carries on it a key to the apartment of his mistress, Melanie, who shares his love of hockey, a game Vanessa considers "common" and "vulgar." Melanie also shares Joe's interest in restoring antique cars. She picked up the brass nut for him at the hardware store where she works, and where they met. She and Joe occasionally meet at Tony's Lounge, a bar with a dim interior and high-backed booths.

The film is still at the drugstore where he'd left it because Joe's handwriting is so illegible that the envelope with the developed pictures is filed under Joshua, not J. Fisher. Vanessa has been nagging him for losing the pictures of their Miami vacation, but it was the crumpled grocery list she found in Joe's pocket that signed his death warrant. On it are chicken, hamburger, meat sauce. An ardent animal rights' activist and a vegetarian, Vanessa would never have asked Joe to buy these items. Enraged by his infidelity, she hired a hit-man to shoot Joe and make it look like a robbery.

2) Women usually carry handbags, and a woman carrying a Gucci handbag with gold-plated fittings is very different from one who carries a denim patchwork bag. Alison carried a red leather shoulder bag, gold-tone trim, one outside pocket, with one inside zipper pocket. Suppose a purse-snatcher removes Alison's wallet before disposing of the handbag in a trash can?

The person who discovers it opens the purse and finds these items in the zipper pocket: a twice-folded $20 dollar bill inside an address book, two community theater season tickets, a Hilton sewing kit, three Band-Aids, four safety pins, a pair of silver hoop pierced earrings. Loose in the purse are a black ball-point pen, a short Garfield pencil with worn-down eraser, three keys on a key ring, a small memo pad, a checkbook with scenic mountain "designer" checks, a receipt for dry cleaning—one suit, two sweaters—a packet of Kleenex tissues. Also in the purse is a floral cosmetic kit containing Clinique cosmetics—pink lipstick, mauve eyeshadow, brown/black mascara—a medium beige compact, comb, mirror, emery board, and an open pack of Tums. In the outside pocket are sunglasses and a Hallmark pocket calendar noting birthdays, anniversaries, teacher conference dates and orthodontist appointments for her daughter.

A writer may conclude that Alison is an upper-middle income mother. Her cosmetics are in a separate bag, not rattling around the bottom of her purse, demonstrating organization and the importance she places on her makeup. She can afford to keep $20 stashed away for emergencies, and supports the local theater. She has her sweaters dry cleaned, not hand-washed at home. At least one child has braces, seldom covered in full by dental insurance. The fact that she's willing to pay for her daughter's orthodontia and to arrange conferences with her teacher indicates a caring mother, but the Tums show she sometimes suffers from indigestion. Her scenic checks are another little

139

luxury. Imprinted with her name and address, they may get her handbag back.

The Band-Aids, safety pins, sewing kit, tissues, and extra earrings indicate she's prepared for emergencies. With an address book in her purse, she has instant access to necessary information when she's away from home.

An alternative view casts Alison as a second-grade teacher keeping track of parent conferences and *her* orthodontist appointments. As an adult, she's opted to have the dental work her parents couldn't afford when she was a child. Her allergies led her to choose Clinique cosmetics, and the earrings were left at her home by an absent-minded guest. Alison plans to return them when she sees the woman at the next meeting of the community theater play selection committee. On the way to school, she dropped her husband's clothes at the cleaners; Alison is allergic to wool.

The red leather handbag was a birthday present from her mother, who lectures Alison about becoming dowdy. Mom also ordered the checks, a reminder of the annual family ski vacations in Vermont. Her mother's final gift was the address book listing all their relatives, including some Alison would like to forget.

A pupil gave Alison his Garfield pencil for her birthday. The memo pad is a necessity for a woman who writes notes to herself about everything. With her sensitive eyes, Alison wears sunglasses outdoors year-round.

3) Lacking a John Doe with pockets for you to explore, or a lost handbag, try to analyze character traits of fellow diners. Imagine a thirty-something couple seated across from you at a moderately priced restaurant at six on a weekday evening. The man is wearing a conservative suit but a flashy tie. His companion's raspberry suit is accented with a large pearl and rhinestone brooch. Both wear wedding rings.

He starts with a cocktail, but she shakes her head and drinks ice water. They share an appetizer of crab-stuffed mushrooms, then go on to soup, caesar salad, hers with peppercorn dressing, his with Roquefort. When the entrees arrive, he has a thick filet mignon that covers a platter, with large baked potato and sour cream on the side. She ordered chicken Kiev on a bed of rice. Later, the waitress brings two glasses of champagne, and offers congratulations. After clinking their glasses in a toast, the woman takes a few sips, then sets it aside. His dessert is "Chocolate Sin Pie," hers fresh strawberries and yogurt. Before leaving, she places three $20 bills on the table, under the check. What could the occasion be?

They could be celebrating an anniversary, or the birth of their first child. The early hour suggests they plan to go elsewhere after dinner, or perhaps their babysitter has an early curfew on a school night. The woman may have chosen not to drink much because she's on a medication that precludes alcohol, or she's more conscious of her health. In their haste to leave home, she forgot to give her husband the cash she'd picked up at the bank that day. Budget-conscious, they keep their credit cards locked in a desk at home unless they're traveling, also forgotten on this occasion.

But the writer reveals this couple is not married to each other. They're business rivals in the firm both work for. She lost her bet that she could outdo his sales figures for the month. Fearful that her husband—a tight man with a dollar—may find out how much the dinner cost, she paid cash, inwardly seething because her co-worker chose the most expensive items on the menu. The waitress offered congratulations after the man boasted they were celebrating a major triumph at work.

Whatever your basic information, try viewing it from at least three angles. "Circumstantial evidence" too often depends on personal interpretation. That's why it's seldom accepted in a courtroom. You see the teenager next door, with his deafening boombox and reckless driving, as a menace to society. To his girlfriend, he's a second Tom Cruise. His father glows with pride when he thinks of his son as a future partner in the family tire dealership. And you're *all* right.

32

WHAT DIALOGUE CAN DO FOR YOUR STORY

BY WINIFRED MADISON

ONE OF THE BEST WAYS to bring a story to life is to let your characters talk. In fact, if they are truly alive, you can hardly keep them from doing so. But they must talk in their own way, not the writer's. One of the first steps in developing believable dialogue involves becoming a good listener, even if it means "professional eavesdropping" from time to time. Listen carefully to people talking, not only your family and friends, but also strangers in restaurants, buses, supermarket lines and just about everywhere else. You might want to jot down overheard conversations, and later read them as if you were an actor learning lines, so that you get used to the sound of voices other than your own.

Here are seven good reasons for using dialogue:

(1) Speech is one of the most valuable keys to a person's character. It is amazing that so many writers who take great pains to describe a person's physical features, hair, eyes, height, et cetera, leave out one of the most telling attributes of all. What a character says and how he says it reveal his temperament, education, social background, intellect, emotion, and attitudes, and how he interacts verbally with other characters tells us even more.

(2) It gets rid of the problem most writers face—the familiar SHOW, DON'T TELL. When characters are having a conversation, they are alive. This is "showing" exactly what they said, not "telling" about it.

(3) Dialogue breaks up the formidable blocks of paragraphs which, if not relieved, may drive readers away. Since reading is a visual experience, your story is more intriguing when bulky paragraphs are set off by the short staccato sentences of dialogue.

(4) Dialogue can provide an effective way of beginning a story. It may throw the reader directly into the plot, pique interest immediately, and create the mood of the story, as in the following examples:

SEATTLE, TUESDAY, 10:15 A.M.

"Ms. Moira Connolly?"

"That's right. Who's speaking, please?"

"Detective John Kearns, Homicide Division, New York Police Department. Sorry to bother you, ma'am, but I'm afraid I have some bad news. . . ."

—Laura Hastings, *The Peacock's Secret, Good Housekeeping,* February 1994

"It must look like an accident. Can you arrange that?"

—Sidney Sheldon, *Memories of Midnight*

"Gracie darling, will you marry me?"

"Yes."

"What?"

"Yes."

—Iris Murdoch, *An Accidental Man*

One day, I was already old, in the entrance of a public place a man came up to me. He introduced himself and said, "I've known you for years. Everyone says you were beautiful when you were young, but I want to tell you I think you're more beautiful now than then. Rather than your face as a young woman, I prefer your face as it is now. Ravaged."

—Marguerite Duras, *The Lover*

Of course not all stories have to begin with dialogue, but if yours doesn't get off the ground right away, you might consider trying dialogue.

(5) The spoken word is capable of enormous power. Words can be dangerous as bombs, insidious as snakes or mellowing as tranquilizers.

Example: The husband of a feminist refers to all women as "gals" to annoy his wife, and when she flares up, he repeats it. Here, hypothetical dialogue showing how this argument might heat up is more effective than a narrative description would be.

"Aunt Sal may be pushing seventy, but she's a great gal," Richard says.

"She's not a *gal.* I wish you'd stop using that expression. She's a *woman,*" Myrna says.

"But, darling, you're such a great *gal* yourself, and your aunt's a great *gal,* too. And you sister. All great *gals!*"

"Richard, stop that this minute."

"You're such a cute *gal* when you're angry."

(6) Dialogue may be used to advance plot. Here's a possible beginning for a short story I may write some day: Two women are talking about their previous weekend:

"Janie, I couldn't wait to tell you. On Friday I met this guy in Denny's of all places. What a dream! I can hardly believe it."

"Guess what! I met a fabulous guy too. At the party on Saturday. What's yours like?"

"Romantic. Sensitive. Sweet. We talked for hours over coffee. He said he'd been looking for me all his life but never realized it until he saw me."

At this, Janie's eyes narrow. Her voice is no longer dreamy.

"Hold on! He said that to you, too? Cynthia, what does he look like?"

"Medium height. Gorgeous dark eyes. Long black lashes. Why?"

"And a gold earring? And his name is Doug?"

"Yeah. How did you know?"

"Oh my God, Cynthia, it's the same guy I met Saturday!"

(7) Fiction writers often face the problem of introducing action that has taken place before the story begins. Dialogue may be one way of doing this. Here is part of a story that may serve as an example:

My grandmother is telling me to hurry up and get to the airport.

"He'll be expecting you, honey. He's come all this way just to see you. You better get moving, Jeannie."

"I'm not going."

"Jeannie, he's your father."

The word 'father' sticks in my throat, halts my breathing. Once more I am ten years old, hiding up in a tree, clinging to a limb. He orders me from below, looking up.

"Jeannie, you get the hell down from there."

"No."

"You do like I say. I'm your father. C'mon down now. I mean NOW . . . or else."

Don't move. Don't say anything. Don't go down.

"You gonna stay up there all night, Jeannie? Okay, I kin wait as long as you. Every minute means another strap across your butt when you do come down."

It's years later but I still feel the lash of the belt again and again and again.

At last I answer my grandmother. "Let him wait."

Dialogue also has its pitfalls. Here are some to watch out for:

(1) If you record the ordinary conversations of most individuals verbatim, you will find them filled with interruptions and exclamations of all sorts. Sentences may be peppered with "you know," or "right?" as if the person addressed wasn't bright enough to understand what was said. A literal transcript of a conversation may describe a person convincingly, but most of the time it is boring when heard, boring when written, and even more boring when read.

(2) Slang. You want to show you are with it, so you use the latest vocabulary. Be careful, since slang gets dated quickly, and by the time

your story appears, idioms that were colorful when you wrote it will
have long been out of fashion. Keep alert for changes in language, and
use slang with discretion.

(3) The verbal menace. For the most part, people do not talk in long
unrelieved paragraphs, except one or two individuals we are all apt to
know. When we see one of them coming, even if it's a friend, we might
"remember suddenly" we have an appointment elsewhere and regret
that we must leave. And so, if your characters go on and on and on,
your reader may find he or she has an appointment somewhere else,
possibly with another book.

If you cannot circumvent a long speech, it may help to interrupt it
now and then, perhaps with comments from the listener, a change in
the weather, or the ring of a telephone, whatever seems appropriate
to keep the story in the present time.

(4) Stereotypes. Your characters may be three dimensional, but if
you do not consider their speech carefully, they may become cardboard
cutouts. For example, not all cab drivers grunt in barely understandable English, nor do all executives bark out orders. Not every criminal
sounds like a member of the Mafia or a gang. Some do, of course, but
many speak without any particular distinction and certain con men
show such an excellent command of English they could be taken for
college professors, some of whom, in fact, fail to talk in the polished,
academic manner we would expect.

(5) Accents can be subtle and tricky. They exist everywhere. Even
in our country, although we all think we are speaking English, there is
a multiplicity of dialects. Writing phonetically is a nightmare, and reading it is even worse. The solution is simple. Don't do it at all. Dropped
letters and misspellings are usually unacceptable.

Still, since an accent is so characteristic of an individual, you don't
want to lose it entirely. If you can catch the lilt or rhythm of foreign
speech, this may work well to suggest an Irish brogue or a southern
drawl. Occasionally a well-known idiom, *au revoir, hasta la vista* or
ciao, may be acceptable. Many writers let a character speak English
but indicate that he may have a Scottish burr as thick as tweed, or a
suggestion of a Boston background, or whatever is appropriate.

What was once thought a distinct accent that defined certain ethnic
groups has changed, thanks to television, mobility and shifts in population, making speech more uniform. Many people are sensitive about

their accents and resent it when they think you have misrepresented them. Move carefully in this dangerous area.

(6) The "he said, she said" problem is hardly a problem at all. It is all right to use "he said" or "she said" without tag lines. If you have a long dialogue between two people and the "he said, she said" would be too repetitive, skip it but let one speaker occasionally address the other by name so that your reader can keep track of who is speaking.

(7) The tone of a speaker's voice can say more about your character than blocks of description. An angry voice, a muffled voice, a sweet flute-like voice, a throaty voice—the variety is endless. When one character opens his mouth, it sounds like a sonic boom, whereas another may speak so softly nobody can hear what she's saying. Individuals may bellow or purr, growl or whimper. Occasionally it's all right to say that "he roared" or "she whispered," but don't overdo it. The same need for restraint applies to adverbs. Rather than use the adverb "angrily," for example, show how angry the character is by what he says.

Developing your skill in dialogue is an ongoing and worthwhile exercise. This important tool will enable you to reveal a deeper understanding of your characters to your readers.

33

HOLD THAT EDGE OF EXCITEMENT

BY PHYLLIS A. WHITNEY

THERE ARE A GOOD MANY EXCITING MOMENTS IN a writer's life. These happenings are all the more gratifying because of the rejections and discouragement that have gone before. I will never forget my first encouragement from an editor, or the first acceptance and appearance of my words in print. Of course I felt ecstatic when I held my first book in my hands.

However, I'm sure that the true "high" for any writer of fiction lies elsewhere. Fortunately, it is something that can come again and again, and we learn to treasure and encourage it. I mean that magical moment when the first glimmer of an idea for a story stirs in our minds. There can be a sense of marvelous "shimmer" around the flashing of those early indications of a story (or novel) to come. We always feel that *this* will be the best thing we've ever written.

While this miracle can occur for me in an instant—perhaps when I'm not even searching—it is something I may carry about with me for days or weeks, while the shining nucleus in my mind gathers more of its special sparkle, developing as if by magic. Perhaps creativity in any field is one of life's most satisfying experiences. That it doesn't last must be accepted and dealt with, so that it can be transferred to something that exists in the real world.

At first, the experience can be so invigorating that I need to hold back and not run around telling everyone what a remarkable book I am going to write. After seventy-three books, I can still be eager and even naive, though I know by this time that too much talking is a sure way to dampen the glow—and possibly even kill my own interest in what is happening.

Getting the idea down on paper in some form is much safer than bragging about it. Even a few words can capture it sufficiently so it won't get away for good. I do know, by now, that this glimmer is only that, and it won't be ready to become a full story or novel for quite a while. So, impatient though I may be, I have learned to wait.

When I was twelve years old, I discovered that I enjoyed making up stories. I could tell exciting stories to neighborhood children, making them up as I went along and delivering them with a dramatic flair that made up for their shortcomings. But I wanted something more permanent that could be read over again—by others, and by me.

My young brain teemed with stories, and I began to set them down on paper. I started out gloriously with story after story, but only now and then did I finish one. Whatever I wrote was never as wonderful as the dream. I was in too much of a hurry, and when I found I had created only the beginning of a story and must then find out where I was going, I lost interest. The magic disappeared and I gave up repeatedly.

There are two kinds of writers. I envy the writer who *can* run with the initial idea and develop it into a story or novel. (I have a private theory that these writers may need even more revision than I want or expect to do.) But my mind doesn't work that way; I can't find my story by writing it immediately, so I will deal here with my sort of writer. *We* need to find out where we're going before we attempt to write. I have developed a few methods that I use to hold onto that early shimmer and help it to grow. Or to be reborn. Somehow, in the course of three hundred pages or more, I must keep the initial excitement going so my interest will stay high until I finish the project.

How long that first edge of excitement will last differs with each book. I spend time with my notebook, developing my characters, collecting odds and ends of plot, discovering my direction, simply jotting down whatever comes to me—until the moment I *must* write. This always arrives before my planning is complete, and I know better than to deny the urge. At least I may get the opening for my story down. So I reward myself by writing several pages. My actors come onstage and begin to live. This is good for future planning, and I don't mind when the desire to write dies and I must go back to work on my characters and plotting.

When I read over what I've written, exhilaration runs high again, and I want to share this remarkable piece of writing with a reader. I never seem to learn, but perhaps it doesn't matter, since one part of my brain is being realistic and doesn't expect too much too soon. Of

148

course, what I want is warm applause, approval—the same response to the "shimmer" that *I* have been feeling, even though I know that I am the worst possible judge of my own work when I am too close to the creative phase to see its faults.

Usually, my chosen reader, knowing the game, provides encouragement, with a hint of gentle suggestion that brings me down to earth. Sooner or later, I take another look at the first chapter and see if I can do a better version with a little more thought. For the beginner, there may be a danger in asking for criticism too soon. Our excitement over that first shining vision can be damaged all too easily. It's a lot safer to get the work done before we call on that necessary reader/critic.

Though I no longer expect that high point of excitement to last, I know it will return to engage and delight me—and keep me going. The writing of several hundred pages cannot be achieved on a single wave of exhilaration. Still, I can manage to lose myself in individual scenes that I feel are good. Along the way, wonderful new ideas attach themselves, and I take unexpected turns that lift me to the heights again. Fiction writers are allowed to be emotional people. If we write coldly and automatically, it will show.

It isn't wise to wait for these spurts of inspiration to come from out of the blue. I ask myself deliberate questions: What unexpected action can a character take at this point? What surprise event can I supply that will be logical and lift the story? I dream, see pictures in my mind, invent—and encourage lightning to strike repeatedly.

Let's consider three types of excitement that are involved in fiction writing. First and most important is the author's feeling about the story he or she is going to write. That's what I've been talking about. The second is the excitement the characters themselves feel as they play their roles in the story. If you examine what will excite each character and move him or her to action, you'll raise the excitement level.

The third type concerns the reader. If your interest and the interest of the characters remain high, the reader will live your story and take satisfaction from the experience. As writers, our purpose is to make the reader feel emotion along with the characters. But how does a writer retain that high interest level, often so difficult to achieve, when it's necessary to work on the same novel for months, or even years? Boredom for what we're writing and loss of perspective remain a real threat.

To avoid this and keep a certain freshness about the work, I make it a rule not to go back very far over what I've written. When I start work each day, I read only the last finished pages before moving ahead. This gives me a needed impetus to continue. Though I am dying to know what I've done and whether it's any good, I never allow myself to look back for more than a few pages—not for a while, anyway.

Eventually the time comes when I begin to feel sure that what I've written is a mess. I lose interest and courage. Since I expect this to happen, I now go back and read all those earlier pages that I'd stayed away from—read them up to the point where my writing stalled. They always seem much better than I expected, and I'm caught up again in the excitement of the story and can move ahead. I find that I even know my characters better after that rereading. This can be repeated a number of times in the course of writing a novel.

Often I receive letters from young writers—or even older ones who are still beginners—who are experiencing "writer's block." "Writer's block" is not a label I believe in. These pauses and stoppages are never incurable. We learn to set aside the "real" world with its worries and sorrows that can pull us away from our fictional scenes. The healing that results from our writing can be remarkable. We learn to turn the blows life gives us into stories, thus helping not only ourselves, but perhaps our readers as well. Nothing that happens to a writer ever needs to be wasted. We adapt and change and *use,* whether a happening is good or bad. For me the only writer's block occurs when excitement over my creation dies and my interest is suddenly gone. That could be fatal if I accepted the condition!

The problem came home to me repeatedly in the writing of my Charleston, South Carolina, novel, *Woman Without A Past.* I found myself breaking one of my own major rules: *to give my main character a strong, life-or-death drive*—a struggle she must engage in and deal with in order to save herself. In the course of writing this novel, I often failed to achieve this and my excitement for the story died along the way.

In the early stages of the novel, my heroine took action only when she was forced to by the characters around her. *They* all had plenty of drive and purpose, much of it tremendously important to them. My heroine's one goal was to solve the mystery of her birth. But that wasn't strong enough in itself and she drifted along without much drive behind her actions. I worried about her, but couldn't seem to correct the flaw. When I asked myself what she was striving for, fighting for, I came up with nothing strong enough. I ploughed through dull (to me) transition scenes, hoping I could fix them later. (Transition scenes are always hard for me to make interesting, so that was nothing new.)

During this struggle (on my part, if not on my heroine's) I called in every device I knew to keep myself interested in a character who wasn't fighting for her life, or for much of anything else. I examined my other characters—interesting enough—to discover how they would challenge my heroine and force her to act. This worked pretty well. My own interest quickened, and my excitement level rose—at times.

When the action sagged, I worked on emotion. It is all too easy in the middle deserts of a novel to lose contact with the main character's feeling. Each writer must find a way to recover lost emotion. Some play music that moves or stirs them; others take long walks that seem to free the creative mind. Or you may have a trusted friend—not necessarily another writer—with whom to discuss the problem. There are times when talking helps.

My own method is to read. Certain fiction speaks to me. I read, not to imitate or to get ideas, but to find a mood. My attention will wander from the page as something touches some emotion in me. Then I can write, because I have transferred that feeling to my main character. I rewrite the wooden love scene, and this time it works. Once you evoke your memories, they are endlessly useful and can be adapted to the needs of the scene you are working on. My heroine, I find, has a good deal to worry about.

I have also discovered that a good way to cure my loss of interest is to feed something new into my mind. Long ago, when I was teaching writing at New York University, I adopted a slogan: *Interest follows action.* When students would look at me blankly, with not a story idea stirring, I'd tell them to go out and *do* something new. Study something they knew nothing about—have fresh experiences. These need not be earthshaking, but just something to open the possibility of exploring a new field. They were always surprised that their own interest came to life when they took this sort of action, and very quickly they found themselves filled with fresh story ideas. First, you *do* something, and then you get interested. It never fails. While writing *The Singing Stones,* I went up in a hot air balloon. I had no idea how I could get that into a story—but it churned away at the back of my mind and gave me a lovely climax scene.

So when I was baffled by my problems with *Woman Without A Past,* I investigated a new subject, for me: what is known in the psychic field as "channeling," when a voice (from another dimension?) speaks through a living person. Or through a story character! My interest came to life, and I was able to develop several scenes that tied in with the plot. I even investigated cats for this novel, reading several books about them so I could understand and write about the cat in my story. Research about practically anything that will fit in can give you more material than you can handle. You, your characters, and your readers will profit from what you learn.

Nevertheless, when I finished the book, I had no great confidence in what I'd written. I knew there were some good dramatic scenes, and my Charleston setting offered wonderful material. Yet, my heroine's drifting continued to worry me, and I waited anxiously for editorial response. To my surprise, my agent and my daughter thought the story strong, exciting, satisfying. No one seemed to notice that my main character was more done-to than doing. By all the rules I know, it wasn't supposed to work—but it did. Why?

It took me some time to find the answer, and it's a useful one. I discovered the explanation in a book by Dwight Swain: *Creating Characters.* One of the goals he lists for a character is "relief from. . . ." Now I knew why my heroine had succeeded in spite of the author! I had written about a sympathetic young woman who is much put-upon (that's important) and who deserves to win out in the end. The goal of *relief-from-adversity* is legitimate and can be very satisfying to the reader.

A great deal of anxiety can be involved, in spite of having the main character take only minor action on her own. Often she is afraid, and this helped with my own interest as I became aware of her desperate, threatened state. She certainly needed relief from a number of unpleasant actions by other characters.

Anxiety can be a good tool to think about and use. However, I don't recommend that this rather negative goal be the sole direction of your main character. In my next novel, I shall make sure that my main character has a strong drive against tough opposition, though I'll certainly use the element of "relief-from" as well.

All such methods and devices are part of a writer's tool kit. We use them to keep our characters in a state of excitement that will convey itself to the reader and will grow from our own effort to hold that first shimmer of an idea alive—that edge of magical excitement that is the best reward of all to the fiction writer.

34

WHERE DO YOUR STORIES COME FROM?

BY RICK HILLIS

WHEN YOU TAKE YOUR FIRST EXPLORATORY STEPS onto a blank page, you're probably farther ahead if you're treading on something a tad more concrete than an idea. I'm talking about nuts and bolts: scene, character, tone of voice. As many short stories sprout from an interesting character you want to follow around for a bit, a curious image, a musical line of description, or even a mysterious title you keep scribbling onto cocktail napkins, as from any idea you might have.

Pre-formulated thoughts and politically correct opinions are not good short story fodder. Issues such as homelessness, child abuse, racial or sexual discrimination seem at first to be exactly the sort of topic a short story writer should take on. These ideas matter. You think they will make the kind of art that moves people to action!

But trying to cram big issues into seventeen pages is a lot like trying to shoehorn a whale into a wetsuit. In order to get your point across you have to manipulate the story's components so they add up right. Characters spout dialogue that sounds suspiciously like ventriloquism. They creak robotically, predictably, through moments more didactic than delicate and poetic. No mystery. No surprise. No discovery. The "epiphany" at the end clanks down like a hobnail boot.

Why? How come the story failed? Can't be the idea. There's nothing wrong with a noble idea.

In the real world, maybe not. But in the world of fiction, trying to dramatize conventional wisdom makes for a story that's too broad, too easy, too uncomplicated. None of the messy gray area that is the heart of most stories.

But now that a writer has this ball and chain of an idea and has invested time in a story, has something, no matter how lifeless, on the page, he or she will revise and rework and polish in a vain attempt to breathe life onto the page, changing everything *except* the idea. During the course of writing a story, things change. You make discoveries. Patterns emerge that weren't in your original game plan. In the end, the story may be about something totally different from what you intended, maybe something wholly different from what you believe at the moment.

In order for the story to become itself, characters, images, whole passages of prose you have sweated over often have to be sacrificed for the good of the story. Don't worry—these are spare parts to be used in another story. But knowing this doesn't help. Parting is always tough, especially parting with an idea. The idea *is* the story, right? That, in a nutshell, is the trap. An idea makes you want to create literature *before* you've built a story.

The best "idea" you can have for a story is to think in scenes. Stories are composed largely of scenes. The camera in close-up, paying close attention to detail, and the action unfolding dramatically at about the same pace as the time it is taking you to read it. Many stories are one long scene.

"Limbo River," the title story in my collection, is a good example of how a writer may build a story from image to image, discovering through these images and the scenes they spark, the story's central theme.

"Limbo River" came out of an image I had of a boy swirling around in a ride at a cheap fair. It was a cage. He was upside down, could see the stars between his running shoes. I'd just been at such a fair, and the experience triggered a memory of riding upside down on a similar ride when I was a kid.

On a napkin, I jotted down the image of the boy's "screaming at the stars between his shoes." I didn't know what the image suggested or why the boy was screaming, but it felt right to me, enough so that I not only thought about it, I wrote a mini scene to go with it, getting down as much detail as I could remember from the fair (broken bolts and nuts, cigarette butts, popcorn, change flying out of pockets on a ride, the sense of night). Here's the tail end of it:

It was a mesh cage that spun and orbited around a greasy hub like a planet around a star. There were broken bolts and nuts in the popcorn and cigarette butts scattered around the base, but we didn't care. "We're here for a good time, not a long time," Marcel laughed. And as he said this our cage jerked,

155

lifted us into the night sky, and we spun upside down, and Marcel's change flew out of his pockets, whizzed past our ears like shrapnel. My heart tore free of my chest and I felt it in my mouth. We dove toward the ground, but at the last minute were scooped up, swirling through the blackness, me and Marcel, screaming at the stars between our shoes.

This could be the ending to any number of stories dealing with any number of ideas. But the important thing to me was that it seemed to *be* an ending, part of a climactic scene. Everything suggested a past history: It was night; there seemed to be a complicated bond built over time between the characters; the broken-down ride through the darkness seemed like the end of a journey; and the "stars between our shoes" suggested the arrival of some sort of personal philosophy. Something had changed in the boy to get to the point where he felt whatever he felt on that ride. Now all I had to do was find the rest of the pieces to fit the puzzle.

About the same time as I wrote the fair ride scene, another image came to mind, something I'd seen. Because of drought, a stream was drying up, and down river from a dam, huge fish were captive in isolated pools. You couldn't catch them because it was illegal to fish within a hundred yards of the dam.

Somehow I thought this image fit with the fair ride image. There seemed to be a connection between the freedom of the ride and the flowing river, and the same way that the ride's cage was a prison image, so were the shrinking, isolated pools in the river.

I could say it was intuition that made me link these images, and that intuition is a large part of writing fiction. And it is. But the truth is the images were linked because I wanted them to be. They were good material, and I wanted to use them in a story, so I made them fit.

Images that reinforce and build upon what's come before, like everything in short fiction, can accomplish several things at once. They can serve as events, flashbacks, humor, description. They are often the phrases that close out or open scenes, loaded with implication and beauty and tension. They are the joints of the skeleton of a story. And often, both for the writer and the reader, they hold the seed of what will become the story's idea. Throughout "Limbo River," I consciously remained on track, by reinforcing the basic ideas of the first images with more images that worked similarly:

156

"The Trip took so long, we felt like bugs trapped in a jar"; "Ralph was swimming back and forth across the dark blue cage, slamming the windows, the wire mesh"; "The pen was located out where the blue vein of river wound through scrub prairie land"; " I went and nosed my car into a creek"; "By then the (drowning) victims were misshapen balloons hung up in the debris after spending all winter locked in their frozen bodies under the ice. . . ."

All but one of the stories in my collection *Limbo River* came about in this way. The one exception is "Blue," which, ironically, is one of my better stories. From the beginning, "Blue" was an idea. And I thought the idea was a winner. It had to be; it was all I had. Here it is: A woman gets hired on a pipeline construction crew. It's her one chance to have a solid, good-paying job. Her redneck coworkers are threatened. Sparks fly. O. K. It doesn't sound that great, but reduce any idea to a phrase or two, and it's going to sound idiotic. I think I liked this idea because it was the only one I'd ever had for a story— that, and I'd done pipeline work, so I had imagery stockpiled, ready to use when the story took shape.

But, it wouldn't take shape. In the first version of the story I tried to save my idea (the woman encountering the rednecks) so I could spring it on the reader in a climactic shootout. No matter how hard I revised, scenes seemed toenailed together, characters moved as if I were jiggling marionette strings. I was killing time until about page fourteen—*voila!* I could finally make this cardboard woman appear in the welding shop. And then, boy-oh-boy, the welders are not thrilled. Change had visited the men's traditional workplace, but dammit, it was time things changed!

Horrible, and I knew it was horrible, but I didn't know why.

One of the terrible things about an idea-driven story is that once the idea has hold of you, it won't let go. The more trouble you have doing the idea justice, the more precious and important it seems. It takes over. It haunts you.

About three or four years after I first started taking runs at "Blue" (I was calling it "The Wobble" then), it finally dawned on me that everybody knows that if a woman joins a pipeline, sparks will fly and things will be tough. That's no climax scene, no epiphany . . . it's a *beginning*.

So I wrote:

Lubnickie slams the truck door and leaps up the ramp to the shop. Nothing new about that, but this morning Murdoch grabs his arm as soon as he steps inside, gives him a shake, gets his goddamn attention.

"You seen them yet?"

"Don't even think like that," says Lubnickie.

But when his eyes get used to the dark and he sees them, it's true. Three of them, two in their early twenties with faces like they got off at the wrong bus stop, the other one older, maybe thirty or so, and hard looking. She's got on men's jeans and dirty running shoes with the toes worn through on top. Her hair is reddish, tied from her face with a green scarf. One of the younger ones has on dress shoes with pointed heels and keeps lifting her feet one at a time like a flamingo . . .

By beginning with what I thought would be the climactic scene, exposing the idea on the first page, I stumbled on the prime short story axiom:

Start as close to the main action as you can. If your story is about a guy being stood up at the prom, don't begin in kindergarten.

Great. On the other hand, what happens next? Now that I'd opened with Norma encountering Ed in the welding shop, I'd written the sum of what I knew about the story by the end of the first page. I had no idea what was going to come next until out of nowhere:

Norma, the older of the women, fixes her eyes on a spot on the wall where no one is leaning. She is nervous, more frightened than she would ever admit, especially to herself. But seeing these cocky men with their pressed jeans and polished boots makes her think, *screw everybody.* Screw the younger ones with the muscle cars and designer jeans that cost more than the parka she's worn through at the elbows. Screw the older guys with their grade-eight educations, color TVs, second cars, houses with nice lawns, big weddings for their daughters, holidays in the summer. She knows who they are, because she's seen their wives in the mall, spending money their husbands made. . . .

So Norma had some real anger in her. Maybe even a chip on her shoulder. I hadn't realized that about her until I wrote it. Not only that, *I was in her mind, telling the story through her experience* as well as Ed's!

Which leads to a couple more axioms—or close to it: *Stories are not about issues or events* (sexism on the job, for example); they are about how these events affect *people.* Also when writing about a gathering of people, an outsider forced to be on the inside will provide an interesting point of view. For example, Norma can observe details Lubnickie would overlook. Everything is old hat to him.

By dispatching the rigid idea on the first page, I let myself be surprised and discover the natural structure of the story. Juxtaposing parallel moments between characters, each from their own points of view, came out of the blue. But once I had it, I knew the characters would drive the narrative. A day later the story was finished.

By setting out to dramatize an idea, it's unlikely you'll get beyond it. Three of a writer's chief tools—intuition, risk, and playfulness— will be left in the toolbox, and you won't enjoy one of a writer's great highs: discovery. Unless, in the end, you manage to say more than you intended (or even knew you knew), writing is just painting by numbers. It's not the idea you begin with that matters. It's the one you come away with.

35

REWRITING—WITH A FOCUS

BY REX BURNS

IF THERE IS A SINGLE CAVEAT THAT will help a writer strengthen the structure of a detective story or any piece of fiction, it would be, Know What You Want to Say. That is, if you know precisely the conclusion of your work before you start, you will discover the way to get there, and usually discover it with the least effort. But if, like me, you are not so lucky, if you're not quite sure what you're groping toward in a story, if the process of creating is a process of discovery for you, then there's no easy way, but only the hard one: Rewrite. And rewrite. And . . .

To say rewrite may be good advice, but it's a pretty vague directive. I rewrite for various purposes: In addition to going through a manuscript to correct basic spelling, language, and punctuation errors, I find other problems that may require me to do more rewrites. For example, one pass through a manuscript might be to look at diction, to be certain that the words I used achieved not only clarity, but euphony and effectiveness. Are there too many -ing endings too close together ("Seeing and hearing the running dog, Fred . . ." *vs.* "Fred jumped up")? Another kind of rewrite might look closely at sentences to see if the length suits the action. Did I vary my sentence patterns effectively? Did I use unnecessarily convoluted sentences? What excess words can I cut?

Less cosmetic but more fundamental is the rewrite that focuses on such elements of narrative structure as plot, multiple story lines, and in mysteries, puzzle.

The conventional distinction between story and plot—"story" is what happens, "plot" is why it happens—is a convenient and generally accurate one. Plot does answer the whys of an action: Why does Fred visit his father? Why does his father feel as he does toward Fred?

160

When we start to understand the whys of actions, we say, "Aha—the plot thickens!"

But plot has at least two main aspects, and examining them separately can often contribute to your perception of the manuscript and, thus, to how well the rewrite works. Let's call these the *psychological* and the *mechanical* aspects. Henry James argued that plot and character were synonymous, and there's truth in that: Psychological motivation, derived from character, often explains a lot of the whys of an event. Fred, a selfish young man, is greedy for his inheritance and, to sate that greed, he tries to convince his rich father that he is a dutiful son. That's the *psychological* reason behind Fred's decision to visit the old man.

The *mechanical* aspect of plot is the result of forces external to a character. For example, for years, Fred has ignored his father, except to ask for money, but now the old man has a terminal illness. This external circumstance prompts Fred to visit his father before it's too late. Moreover, the combination of Fred's past behavior and the discovery of his father's illness, both external to the father's character, generate in the father resentment and suspicion of his son's sudden solicitude.

Recognizing this distinction between the psychological and the mechanical aspects of plot by careful rewriting can help you focus the story more sharply. Depending upon the length of the story, Fred's greed, for example, can be explored for development and consistency. What made him so selfish? Was it a trait inherited from an over-acquisitive grandmother? Was it the result of his being the smallest at the dinner table? Was he imitating a similar fault in his father? Or has he a sense of alienation from other people? In other words, by singling out the psychological aspect of plot for rewriting, you can more readily trace the protagonist's character through the story and assess it for probability and consistency. On the other hand, by focusing on the mechanical aspect, you can rewrite in anticipation of an event: Is it likely that Fred could avoid his father for years and yet ask him for money? Is it possible that the old man has terminal cancer? Could Fred easily arrange a visit home?

Broken down into a series of questions like this about the sequence of events and their psychological or mechanical causes, the job of rewriting becomes not just one of determining the believability of an

161

action, but also of seeing the proper proportion of narrative space required to describe that action. So the writer can see more clearly which events are the most vital and consequently most likely to demand "scenic" treatment. Conversely, actions identified as less vital can be treated by mere reference or inference. For example, Fred may have a memory of fighting for that last slice of bread on the dinner table, but perhaps the event with the greater psychological impact, and therefore necessitating greater detail, was seeing his father, as master of the house, help himself first to the best. Or, the father's cancer could be mentioned briefly in a letter or telephone call, while Fred's decision to go back home might call for somewhat more expanded treatment.

The relationship between Fred and his father might be sufficient for a short story or a one-act play, but a novel would require more strands. Fred's mother or sister or brother may come on stage. There may be longtime servants present or a family lawyer to draw up a new will. In other words, given that Fred's is the central story, other story lines might also exist. Often when I'm partway through writing a novel, I've discovered that my protagonist or chief villain needs an accomplice, or that the suspense element calls for a red herring, or the pacing of the action requires the tension provided by adding another suspect. Thus, even before a book is completed, I usually face a rewrite to look closely at multiple story lines.

Again, an analysis of the psychological and mechanical aspects of plot often applies to the secondary story lines as well. Fred's mother, for instance, may have suffered silently in the conflict between her son and her husband. What events have caused her to be silent? Does she eventually speak out? Why? But in addition to examining these issues, you must also ask how (and whether) the secondary line clarifies or adds tension to or resolves issues in the main narrative. If Fred's mother does finally speak out, what effect does that have on the main narrative? Or do the actions of an old and privileged servant contribute to the father-son conflict? If so, how? What about Fred's sister Mary? What has she been doing all these years, and how does she feel about her brother's sudden reappearance? Note further that in making revisions in these other story lines, the extent of their effect on the central narrative will determine their importance and consequent space appropriate in the overall structure.

Sometimes, a subsidiary story line will gain in importance either in the first draft or in the rewrite. If it's in the first draft, my practice is to let it grow, because at that point I don't usually know where the story's going. But in the rewrite stage, painful though it may be, my method is usually to share and pare. Does the subsidiary story line compete with the main story and blur the focus, thus requiring you to cut? Where and how can it be expanded to add enrichment—thematic or psychological—to the principal narrative? Obviously, there's no clear-cut answer to these questions, but the relationship between the subsidiary story line and the central narrative helps clarify the development and presentation needed. Is it important that Fred's sister has an illegitimate child? It is if her father sees that child as a better son than Fred has been, or if Fred believes that's the case; it is if the child is old enough and willing to act in some way that affects the main story. If, however, that child serves no purpose in the central narrative, then it may be best to delete it or not even put Fred's sister, poor thing, through the trauma of an unwanted pregnancy.

A third element that the writer of mystery and detection fiction must emphasize is puzzle, which is often confused with plot. *Who*dunit is often related to *why* it was done, and thus the confusions. But whereas the writer must deal with both plot and puzzle, readers are often interested primarily in puzzle, while plot is only on the fringe of their attention. You must keep this difference in emphasis in mind as you write. Who was it that knocked on the door two hours after Fred returned home, and why? What was it that Fred's sister didn't want overheard when she was on the phone? Why was the lawyer standing outside the door when Fred and his father had their first meeting in years? And where did the old and trusted servant disappear to on the night Fred's father was murdered?

Such puzzling elements may or may not be integral to the structure of the story. If that is the case, however, chances are that they have already figured as mechanical aspects of the plot. But if they are solely elements of the puzzle, they can be considered or possibly added in a rewrite as useful red herrings, or used to heighten tension, or even be used as genuine clues in either the primary or the secondary story line. Again, in dealing with puzzle elements, the principle of effective rewriting is the same: analysis of the element, focus of attention on that element, and assessment of its relationship to the narrative's climactic ending.

36

READING AS A WRITER, WRITING AS A READER

BY SHARON OARD WARNER

LAST WEEK I RECEIVED A LETTER from a novelist friend. She began by telling me about her hectic summer schedule. Her new novel has just been published, and she's about to leave for her first big tour of bookstores. She included a scrawled list of cities and dates, so many that I felt a little daunted, sitting comfortably on my front porch. So far, twenty newspapers are committed to reviewing her book, and of course she's worried about what the reviewers will say. Will they be generous, and if they are, will their good words translate into sales? But that's not all she had to say. She also reported that her adult daughter has come down with chicken pox in Europe and is now confined to an American hospital. Do I know how awful chicken pox is in adults? (As a matter of fact, I do.) And how do you suppose my friend ends the letter? This way: "I'm reading Jane Hamilton's *Map of the World*. It's a knockout."

Writers are first of all readers—avid, life-long readers who consume books the way other people do hamburgers or beer. As children, we crave the cool silence of libraries and summer afternoons draped over an armchair, the hours we spend suspended between the real world and the one we hold between our two sweaty hands. We covet the feel of books, their rigid covers and the pages that blow in the breeze. When our eyes scan a book we've just borrowed or bought, we writers feel buoyed with anticipation, hopeful and content.

Most often, though, we are taught to consider writing and reading as separate activities. We do one or the other, and most of us would agree that reading is the easier of the two. Sometimes, if we sit down dutifully in front of the computer or typewriter, we reward ourselves with an hour of reading. Other times, we put off writing by reading. I've certainly indulged in this sort of guilty reading over the years, although I no longer call it procrastination. Now, I dip briefly into books before I write in order to remind myself that I am first of all a reader, that I write because I read. For me at least, the two activities have been mingled; it's difficult to say where one leaves off and the other begins.

What do I mean? Well, lately, I've been writing my first novel after many years of devoting myself to short stories. When I began this novel two years ago, short stories were what I knew how to write—familiar territory, so to speak—and I was inclined to approach the first chapter of my novel as I would have a short story: with a vague sense of theme, or a strong image, or maybe even a bit of dialogue.

I'm not suggesting that I launched into the novel itself without a plan; I had a plan and one hundred note cards to prove it. I also had legal pads full of notes on my main characters, but none of those things told me how to begin the first chapter of my book. What does a novelist want to accomplish in the first chapter of a novel? A chapter shares some common features with a short story, but when push comes to shove, the two are also different. Just how different, I wasn't sure.

In some ways, I have found short-story writing a useful apprenticeship for that longer endeavor, the novel. To begin with, short-story writers get ample experience developing characters. In fact, one of the disappointing parts about writing stories is that you just get good and comfortable with a character when the story is finished. It's a little like going to a two-week camp, where you begin by bunking with strangers and end by parting with friends. The goodbyes are wrenching, but they're also clean because you haven't spent enough time with these people to get good and sick of them.

Short-story writers also learn the A to Z of settings. We eventually realize that characters are like the rest of us: They live in particular rooms in specific cities; they despair of cigarette wrappers in the gutters or atrazine in the farm fields; they suffer through cold snaps and sweat when the weather is humid. They even have their own ideas about interior decorating. Some characters line their mantels with Coke bottles from all fifty states, while others prefer Precious Moments figurines or half-burned candles.

All this experience holds the writer in good stead when it comes to writing the first chapter of a novel. But where plotting is concerned, short-story writers draw up short. We're like day hikers who suddenly find ourselves at the foot of Mt. Everest. It's a hell of a climb, and we have no idea where to start or how long it will take to get there. This is especially true for those writers in the habit of writing "sudden fiction," although even longer stories are a little thin where plot is concerned.

Take "Cathedral," by Raymond Carver, for instance. I admire this story and wouldn't change a word of it, but in some sense, not much really happens. A blind man has dinner with a couple; they drink a lot and smoke a lot; and then the husband and the blind man draw a cathedral together. That's the gist of the story—that's what happens on the outside, anyway. But if you've read the story, you realize I've left out the important part: After spending an evening with a blind man, the narrow-minded main character of Carver's magnificent story has been given sight, or rather, insight. He has experienced what we short story writers call an epiphany. Unfortunately, epiphanies do not a novel make.

If experience is not the best teacher when it comes to writing chapter one, what's a short-story writer turned novelist to do? The answer is simple: Read a good book. To get a sense of what's crucial to include in the first chapter of your novel, try taking a look at the initial chapters of novels you admire. Reread the first chapter of three novels you have read recently, and then ask yourself this question: What did the writer do in the first chapter to get my attention and keep it? Make a very specific list. These will be your objectives in writing a first chapter.

Once you begin your first chapter, you'll find it's necessary to change gears. Reading as a writer will only take you so far. Eventually, you'll have to write as a reader, too. Otherwise, the book won't get done. Now, I'm not suggesting you become a critic. That comes later, after you've written chapter one and all those subsequent chapters. For the time being, while you're getting something down on paper, you should read as a fan. We all need fans, don't we? According to my novelist friend, we need as many fans as we can get. So be a fan of your own work. Write the sort of novel you love to read. Chances are that if you truly enjoy reading as you write, others will enjoy reading *what* you write.

While this may seem an obvious bit of advice, some of us have to learn our lessons the hard way. For instance, a few years ago, I had a bit of success with selling stories to a particular women's magazine.

When summer came around and I had a little more time, I decided to write a story specifically for the editor of this one women's magazine. Likely, you can guess the result. Here's part of the letter I received from the fiction editor: "I have found that whenever a writer tells me she or he wrote a story especially for us, it lacks a certain special quality that we are looking for—a quality that comes, I think, only when the writer is writing a story she or he wants or has to write for personal reasons." She was right. My reasons weren't personal at all. I was in it for the buck, not for the joy of the process. Since I seldom read women's magazine fiction, I didn't really care about what I was writing.

Fortunately, when I began my novel, I knew better than to write for an editor or the market or a favorite teacher. Instead, I wrote the kind of novel I like to read. Where a first chapter is concerned, here are a few suggestions for writing as a reader:

1. In Chapter One, introduce at least one character who is both familiar and yet somewhat puzzling. As the writer, you should know and understand this character to the degree that you've done your homework—written character inventories and profiles. But as a reader, you must feel some mysterious pull to this person, some curiosity or intrigue. In his essay "The Magic Show," Tim O'Brien writes that "the object is not to 'solve' a character—to expose some hidden secret—but instead to deepen and enlarge the riddle itself." Part of the pleasure of intimacy is the element of surprise. This should also be true of writers and their characters.

2. Don't allow your first chapter to get bogged down in exposition. Because we're beginning something big, as novelists we often feel the first chapter should indicate seriousness of purpose. And nothing is more serious than page after page of summary and description. Nothing's more deadening to write or read, either. If you must begin with exposition, dispense with it quickly, and be on your way to writing a scene. Readers yearn for scenes, for life taking place. That's where the unexpected is likely to happen, and the unexpected is what keeps readers and writers (one and the same for our purposes) turning the pages. Here's the opening sentence to Rosellen Brown's *Before and After:* "She wasn't on ER, never was during the day when she had

167

patients, but they called her in on it." Immediately, we are immersed in a scene. What's going to happen? What's she been called in on?

3. Get your plot underway immediately. After reading the first chapter of my novel, an editor remarked that she was happy to see something significant happening in the first twenty pages. (The character I introduce in Chapter One attends a pro-life rally, where she witnesses a car accident.) Short-story writers turned novelists often proceed slowly because they're used to the exposition/complication/crisis/climax mode of story development. In something as big as a novel, they may reason, surely the first chapter should be devoted to exposition alone. Here's where thinking as a reader comes in handy. Readers crave action, and they're most likely to stay interested in characters who are *doing* things, preferably interesting, inexplicable things.

4. As you climb slowly toward the summit—the end of your novel—return to the first chapter for inspiration and guidance. Be your own best reader. Often, part of the larger design of the book is imbedded in your initial chapter. This design can manifest itself in different ways. For instance, the first chapter of my novel ends with the accident. As I progressed through the novel, I began to see that accidents of various sorts were the novel's means for exploring the notion of fate. Not surprisingly, then, the culminating incident in the book is also an accident, one which is, in many respects, the logical outcome of the accident in Chapter One.

5. Lastly, enjoy yourself. Have fun with the first chapter and with the rest of the book, too. I can honestly say that writing my first novel has been a pleasure, and I'm convinced that my enjoyment of the process has as much to do with my love of reading as it does my love of writing. For me, writing is a way of responding to what I read; it's a way of conversing with myself and others, a way of paying homage to all those writers who have written so beautifully and so well.

37

DIALOGUE: THE MEANING BEYOND THE WORDS

BY TIM SANDLIN

THE FIRST NIGHT OF MY FICTIONAL FICTION CLASS, I walk to the front of the room, open the roll form conveniently provided by Central Wyoming College, and begin.

"George Singleton."

"Yo."

"Irene Bukowski."

"Present."

One by one, I call their names and they respond.

"Here."

"You got me."

"Yes."

"It is I."

One girl doesn't say anything, just raises her hand a half-inch off the desk.

"Accounted for."

"Sorry, I'm late."

And with each response, I learn something about the characters. The "Yo" guy will write comic pieces that start with the hero waking up hung over. The girl who won't speak will write a poem featuring death. The "It is I" girl won't take criticism, "You got me" is sneaky, and "Sorry, I'm late" will drop out after we read his first story.

Your snap judgments based on one or two words of dialogue may not match mine, but the point is that each member of the class gave a different response. And they stayed in character.

In real life, half the class would say "Here" and the other half raise their right hand about chin high, but this is fiction, and fiction is not real life. Don't forget that. If you write so realistically you can't stand the thought of that much diversification in a group, skip calling the roll and go right to the scene where each student says a few words on "Why I'm taking this creative writing class."

Won't be any repeat answers there.

In fiction with energy, no two characters put any one thought the same. There are four primary ways to build a character—description, dialogue, and action, plus thought in your viewpoint people. To pass up the smallest opportunity to differentiate and build on your fictional people is a waste. Worse, it's stagnant. Even a story about stagnation can't be stagnant.

Several years ago in a show called "Charlie's Angels," three women with teeth and hair brought bad guys to bay with perkiness and spunk. But without dialogue. As far as the lines went, the women were interchangeable. Mostly, they took turns saying, "Come on, Charlie."

In putting words on paper, no one has enough teeth or hair to get away with this sloppiness. P. G. Wodehouse believed every sentence in a book must have entertainment value. That may or may not be true with every style of book, but it sure is true of dialogue. If the reader doesn't learn something new every time he ventures between the quotation marks, the writer has botched his or her job.

So what are these gems the reader is supposed to learn between the squiggly floating marks? Oversimplified, dialogue must do four things—show character, advance plot, give information, and set the voice, tone, and scene.

Show character. There are people in the English-speaking world of a certain cultural and educational background who actually say, "It is I." Imagine that. The secret is to nail down a character as quickly as possible. If you have her say "It is I," then follow up with a tight bun on her head and dark purple nail polish, you've pretty much done the job. Give her some matching action and send her down the road.

The idea is to supply one or two details that are so distinct, the reader can fill in all the others. A character who says, "I'm going to snatch you kids baldheaded," won't wear the same clothes or drive the same car as a character who says, "I have difficulty interfacing with children."

Even non-dialogue is dialogue. The girl who wouldn't answer but held up her hand a half-inch revealed character by not speaking. From there, you can have her go with the grain by keeping her in sweaters four sizes too large and afraid to ride on an elevator unless it's empty, or you can blast against the grain—and be almost as trite—by turning her into a sex-crazed tigress when she lets down her hair.

Not speaking often says more than speaking, especially in tense climactic showdowns. It's a lot easier to write a scene where a man punches out his boss than a scene in which his anger is beyond words, and he walks away. That makes sense. By definition, "beyond words" is harder to put into words than a punch in the nose.

Here's a trick for keeping your characters in character. When I wrote a book about two 13-year-olds and their awkward struggles to overcome strange upbringings, I found my old junior high yearbook from 1963. Whenever one of my kids said something precocious, wise, or cornball, I looked at a photo of my 13-year-old classmates, and said, "Could this have come from Ronnie Craig's mouth, or Ann Humphrey's, or Annette Gilliam's?" The answer was usually "No," and the line got thrown out.

Advance action. This one should be self-explanatory. Story is how characters react to conflict, and much of the conflict between people in our modern world is caused by words. Communication—the thing that is supposed to resolve problems—actually causes more than it resolves.

We advance action by arguing, seducing, planning, slighting, gossiping, giving ultimatums—I could go find a thesaurus and stretch this into twelve column inches, but you get the idea.

Here's another place where fiction differs from real life. Most of those heart-to-hearts you have with your mother/husband/wife go in circles and dead-end. The same thoughts are constantly reported in slightly different ways, and when all this communicating is done, nothing has changed.

You don't have time for this jive in fiction. Each conversation must end with some condition different from what it was at the beginning. The relationship between the speakers has been slightly altered, or someone has grown wiser, or the speakers—at the very least, the readers—have information they didn't know before. Your viewpoint character is in more trouble or thinks he is moving closer to the solution to the conflict. Or maybe all she's done is order lunch. Ordering lunch reveals more about a character than his or her resumé.

171

A sidetrack on dialect. Anyone who tries it is braver than I am. Mark Twain pulled it off. John Kennedy Toole pulled it off. People think Eudora Welty pulls it off, but if you read her work carefully, you'll see she does it more with sentence rhythm and word choice than by dropping g's off walkin' and talkin'.

Check this out from her "My Life at the P.O.":

I says, "Papa-Daddy, you know I wouldn't any more want you to cut off your beard than the man in the moon. It was the farthest thing from my mind. Stella-Rondo sat there and made that up while she was eating breast of chicken."

Not a misspelled word in the quote, yet after I read this story to my class, they all swore it was written in Deep Mississippi dialect.

Give information. This is the easiest one to mess up. The worst example I can think of in conveying information through dialogue happens on the soap operas.

MAMA: "I saw Mildred Kinnicknick at the grocery store yesterday."
DAUGHTER: "Is that the same Mildred Kinnicknick whose father was tried for murder, then he got off by claiming insanity because he'd eaten too many Twinkies and whose mother used to be married to Doc Watson, then she divorced him and married his brother Spud, only now she's back with Doc but carrying the baby of his older brother Bubba?"
MAMA: "Yes."

Uh-uh. Dialogue doesn't work that way. To get information across, you have to be sneaky. This is part of the Show-Don't-Tell lesson you've heard 200 times. Don't say, "I see you wear glasses." Do say, "Your glasses are always dirty." This gets across that the character does wear glasses, and it also says something about his personality that they're always dirty and it says something about the speaker's personality that she notices the dirt and is brazen enough to comment on it.

This is especially true when you use dialogue to foreshadow. In mysteries by unskilled writers, there's always a line where someone says, "I notice you have a gun in your closet," or "We're spraying the rose bushes with Fetadetamiacin today, so don't stick any petals in your mouth or you'll die." Right then, I know that 200 pages from now, the gun or the Fetadetamiacin will pop up and kill somebody.

172

Foreshadowing, especially in mysteries, has to be done so when readers come to the place where the gun is used, they're totally surprised, but then they think about it and say, "Gee, that makes sense."

Anticipated surprises—they're what make endings fun. And the sneakiest way to foreshadow without getting caught is in dialogue.

Set the voice, tone and scene. Choosing the tone may be the most important decision you make when starting a story. I was once assistant editor at a literary magazine, and I read something like 200 stories in a weekend. Every one of those stories was competent—not a total loser in the batch—but what made an exceptional story rise above the others were the voice and tone.

The Holy Trinity of fiction is plot, character, and voice—Father, Son, and Holy Ghost. And, like the Holy Ghost, voice is the hardest to understand. Voice is that attitude of the writer to the story. It's the attitude of the writer toward his or her readers.

Sometimes I have my students write a two-page story, then rewrite it Erma Bombeck-style, then Edgar Allan Poe-style, then Louis L'Amour. The growth of these stories is amazing. And the easiest place to establish these styles is in the dialogue. People in Valley Girl High School speak differently from people in 1880s Bitter Creek or Transylvania. People about to be murdered on the moors speak differently from people chasing down the blue light special at K Mart. Doesn't take a Guggenheim grant to figure out that one.

Not everything to do with dialogue happens between the quote marks. The reader has to know who is talking and in what tone of voice. For this we use dialogue tags.

Dialogue tags seem to come in styles, like hats. What worked in 1932 looks slightly ridiculous now. There are no absolute rules in writing dialogue tags or anything else. If it works, you got away with it. But there are certain ways to playing it that work more often than not.

The easiest tag is none. Compare—Laurie crossed her arms on her chest. "Why do you say that?" to— "Why do you say that?" Laurie asked defensively.

If you can set the tone of the speech with a bit of action, you're better off than "Blah-blah," he said, adverb. If it isn't crystal clear who is speaking, use *he said* or *she said*. Once every couple of pages, sneak in a *he asked*. Don't, under penalty of personal castigation, use *he stated, she observed, the boy piped, George groaned,* or any other word for *said.* If you want George to groan, have him do it first.

> George groaned. "I can't get up this morning."
> Not—"I can't get up this morning," George groaned.

Trust me on this. You can't groan and talk at the same time.

And, if at all possible, avoid adverbs in dialogue tags. In the 1950s, riding the wave of the Hemingway revolution, adverbs were words to be avoided like the plague. I look at them as tools, and no tool should be banned forever.

However, use them with care. Hand grenades don't kill—people who throw hand grenades do kill. Pretend the adverb, when used in a dialogue tag, is a hand grenade. Don't play with it.

A word about typographical tricks. Say your character is really hacked off.

"GET OUT OF MY HOUSE." "Get out of my house!"
"Get out of my house."

Every editor in America is going to hate two of those three sentences, but I can't tell you which two, because it depends on the editor. Personally, I'd rather snort barbwire than use an exclamation point, and I can't even think of a metaphor disgusting enough to compare to dialogue in ALL CAPS, so I'm stuck with italics. Some editors can't stand italics. It's a pet peeve deal. If possible, work it into the action.

> George smashed a glass on the linoleum floor.
> "Get out of my house."

If that isn't strong enough for you, try one of the other three. I highly recommend against any combinations. *"GET OUT OF MY HOUSE!"*

And the worst, absolutely bottom-of-the-barrel method of expressing quoted frenzy is multiple punctuation.

"Get out of my house!!?!"

This was once Batman-style, but no more. I just looked in one of my son's *Ghost Rider* comic books, and do you think Mephisto himself screams questions!? Heck, no @#%&!

Of course, as soon as I say that, someone will mail in an example of James Joyce and the double exclamation point. Which brings us back to rule number one: There are no rules.

SPECIALIZED FICTION

38

A NOVEL BY ANY OTHER NAME . . .

BY ELIZABETH GEORGE

I'VE FOUND THAT ONE OF THE BENEFITS of achieving the status of published writer is that I've been able to meet and talk with hundreds upon hundreds of readers and unpublished writers since my first novel hit the bookstores in 1988. My role when asked to speak to neophyte writers is to give a shot-in-the-arm discourse about persevering through doubts and dead ends that go hand in hand with completing a project, as well as weathering the maddening frustrations of trying to get someone to read, to represent, to believe in, and—*mirabile dictu*—to purchase their work.

But every so often, a conversation develops that carries me in another direction, prompting me to evaluate what I do when I sit down in front of my word processor every day and, more important, why I do it.

I had such a conversation not long ago with a psychologist-cum-novelist who told me that he intended to write mystery novels only until such a time as he became good enough to write "a real novel." The fact that a mystery (or thriller or crime or suspense or psychological) novel is indeed "a real novel" possessing all the requirements of "a real novel" appeared to escape him. As far as he was concerned, writing a mystery was going to be a way to practice his craft, rather like baking cookies in the hope that one day he could work himself up to the challenge of a layer cake.

Let's ignore the questionable sense our psychologist displayed in sharing this peculiar literary plan of action with a mystery-suspense writer. Instead, let's examine what he failed to realize about the well-crafted mystery. First, it *is* a novel of character, of plot, of setting, of dialogue, of metaphor, of allusion, of landscape, of drama, of conflict, of love, of death, and most important, of imagination. And second, to deny the mystery-suspense its place among the world's "real novels"

177

is to deny a place among "real novelists" to such writers as Thomas Hardy *(Desperate Remedies),* William Faulkner *(Intruder in the Dust),* Charles Dickens *(Bleak House),* Wilkie Collins *(The Woman in White),* Edgar Allan Poe *(Murders in the Rue Morgue),* Dorothy L. Sayers *(Gaudy Night),* George Eliot *(Silas Marner),* Nathaniel Hawthorne *(The House of the Seven Gables),* and more recent writers like Alice Hoffman *(Turtle Moon),* Scott Turow *(Presumed Innocent),* Kem Nunn *(Pomona Queen),* and a host of others whose mysteries and suspenses have stood and will stand the test of time.

This is not to argue that there are no deplorable mystery-suspense novels being written. On the contrary, dozens of writers seem to turn them out on an annual basis. But the novelist who commits herself to the process, the product, and the passion of writing is, believe me, writing "a real novel" from start to finish.

The mystery-suspense novel provides the writer with a natural structure, and it is perhaps because this structure exists in the first place that the uninformed neophyte writer might evaluate the mystery-suspense as a lesser creature in the world of literature. The natural structure is generally the same: A situation of grave import (like a murder) has occurred or is threatening to occur or a dramatic question is presented to the reader; this situation or this dramatic question must be resolved in some way by the final pages of the book. But it is what the individual writer does with this natural structure that can, and often does, alter the tiresome label "piece of genre fiction" to "literary classic."

Because a given structure exists, the writer of the mystery-suspense can choose to provide her readers with little more than a skeleton of a novel and still get away with constructing a whodunit that not only entertains, but also stimulates the reader's perspicacity. In this sort of novel, the hero or heroine—be the character a spymaster, a police detective, a private investigator, an FBI agent, or an amateur sleuth caught up in unexpected circumstances that try the intellect if not the soul—marches fairly directly to the conclusion of the story, encountering the expected road blocks, clues, red herrings, and conflicts along the way. Or the writer can take that same skeleton and hang upon it the organs, muscles, and flesh of subplot, theme, character development, exploration of social issues, and the complex psychology of human relationships. It's my belief that the novels that stand the

178

test of time, that move out of genre because of their refusal to be bound by the mundane rules of genre, follow this latter course of action.

To write a mystery-suspense that is "a real novel" is to write largely about character. In these novels, the characters and the circumstances engendered by those characters drive the story forward, and not vice versa. Characters do not exist to be set pieces in a contrived drama whose value is ultimately revealed in a single indecipherable clue or a "gotcha" ending whose sole purpose is surprise rather than provocation of thought. Mystery-suspense novels that are "real novels" end where they begin: with an examination of the human heart—in conflict, in despair, in peace, in anguish, in love, in happiness, in fear.

When a writer decides to create a novel of character within this genre of mystery-suspense, she challenges herself to move beyond the simple mechanics of plotting, to drive from her mind the temptation to adhere to a formula, and to take a risk. She decides to begin with character and to use character as the foundation for the hundreds of pages and thousands of words that will follow that character's creation.

This is what I have attempted to do with my novels, which are sometimes called literary mysteries, sometimes novels of psychological suspense, sometimes detective stories, sometimes police procedurals, sometimes British novels, but are always—at least to my way of thinking—"real novels" from start to finish. I begin with a kernel of killer, victim, and motive. I plant that kernel into the soil of imagination, and I begin to people a world in which killer and victim move.

In peopling the world of the novel, I create individuals. I begin with their names, knowing that the name I give to a character will have a large influence upon the way a reader feels about him. So when I wanted the victim in *Missing Joseph* to be seen as a gentle and thoughtful country vicar, I named him Robin Sage, just as when I wanted the schoolboy bully in *Well-Schooled in Murder* to be believable as a mutilator of self and others, I gave him the name Clive Pritchard with the hard sound of that initial *C* and the surname reminiscent of a farming tool.

Once I have named my cast of characters, I begin the process of making them real. Each is given a personality that has—as we all do— a core need in life. Perhaps the core need is to be seen as competent, perhaps it is to be in control of self and others, perhaps it is to belong, to be of service, to be perceived as authentic. The character's personal-

179

ity arises out of his backstory, which may or may not become part of the novel but is indeed part of the groundwork that leads up to the writing of the novel. The character's backstory includes his family relationships, his growing up, any pivotal events that shaped him, his friendships or the lack thereof. Within this backstory is woven the character's interior landscape: what his agenda is with other characters, what his throughline is for the entire novel, how he reacts to stress, what he experiences as joy or pleasure. To this are added the telling details that will appear in the novel and act as a means by which the reader can view the character in a more direct light: that peculiar article of clothing worn by a teen-aged boy but once belonging to his absent father; that bullet-like line of ear studs and the silver nose ring donned by the girl who always wears black; the hairlip covered inadequately by a mustache; the perfect sitting room with no mote of dust floating in the air; the bitten fingernails; the choice of artwork; the music listened to; the car driven; the condition of the curtains hanging at the windows; the collection of tea cups lovingly displayed. The character is given a place of birth, a place in society, and a place within his individual family. He is described physically, mentally, psychologically, and emotionally. And when that is done, he stands on the brink, ready to come to life in the manuscript itself.

But my preliminary work does not end here. Because the novel will not exist in outer space, I must create an inner space for it. This is its setting. The setting may be a place as simple to construct as was the Yorkshire village of Keldale in *A Great Deliverance* where a farmer met a hideous end in an old stone barn. What was required of that little village: two pubs, an inn, a churchyard containing the grave of an abandoned newborn, a huge ruined abbey with a legend descending from the time of Cromwell. Having seen many such villages and abbeys during my time in Yorkshire, I needed only to assembly my photographs and map out my locations.

Or setting may be as challenging as the creation of Bredgar Chambers, the public school founded by Henry VII that sat in West Sussex and served as the setting of *Well-Schooled in Murder*. Here I needed all the accouterments of the English public school—the great chapel, the dining hall, the houses of residence, the quadrangle, etc.—and the only way to make them authentic was to blend myself into the world of the English public school for a period of time until I knew it well enough to create my own, from its prospectus to its architecture.

Or setting may require that I bring a real place to life, jockeying its streets and buildings a little in order that it might accommodate just one more college. This was the case in *For the Sake of Elena,* where St. Stephen's College was slid into the new space I created between Trinity College and Trinity Hall. But to make it real—and thus to integrate it into an atmosphere that felt authentic to the reader—St. Stephen's had to be a place of architectural significance, for such is the case of every college in the city of Cambridge.

With setting and characters well in hand, I begin to outline the plot. Sometimes I use a step outline only, creating a preliminary list of scenes with fragments of information to guide me in the construction of those scenes. Sometimes I use a running plot outline, in which entire sections of the novel are outlined in depth, including description, narration, and dialogue. And sometimes I have to feel my way slowly into the novel, allowing an initial scene or the glimpse of a character to dictate what will follow.

The story I ultimately tell grows out of all of this: these characters who have been created in my imagination from that initial kernel of killer, victim, and motive; this setting that I have labored over like a loving god; this plot that I am always unsure of, partly in terror of, but determined to carry onward. And when that story has reached its conclusion, if it's successful and not a tosser, it comprises plot and subplot, internal and external conflict, theme, drama, moments of re-flection and evaluation, landscape, setting, metaphor, and allusion.

It is, because of how it has been written, in every way a real novel.

39

WRITING GHOST STORIES

BY JOAN AIKEN

Like one that, on a lonely road
Doth walk in fear and dread
And, having once turn'd round, walks on
And turns no more his head:
Because he knows a frightful fiend
Doth close behind him tread.
—Coleridge *(The Rime of the Ancient Mariner)*

WHY DO WE READ GHOST STORIES? Partly out of curiosity. No one—
except Lazarus—ever *has* come back from the dead; most people, at
one time or another, wonder if there is another life, if souls linger after
death, if the effect of some violent happening can remain, like an imprint or an echo, affecting the locality where it took place. And the
discoveries of modern science do nothing to diminish such specula-
tions; the knowledge that matter is not at all what it appears to be,
that space is full of gravitational waves, and time wholly different from
our conception of it, makes the idea of ghosts—*revenants,* "the ones
who come back," as the French call them—more credible, not less.

Ghosts themselves have changed, though. In contemporary stories,
they no longer clank chains and trail white sheets; they do not inhabit
ruined abbeys and crumbling castles. They are to be found in subway
trains and elevators, peering out of TV screens and car windows, sending postcards through the mail, or uttering threats over the telephone.
Ghosts are more sophisticated than they were in the days of our grandparents, but they are just as potent.

In the course of my writing career I have put together five or six
collections of ghost/horror stories, and among my novels, three short
ones had definitely supernatural themes (*The Shadow Guests, Voices*—
in the United States retitled *Return to Harken House*—and *The
Haunting of Lamb House*); significantly, all of those have sold rather
better, and continued to stay in print longer, than my non-supernatural

works. And a tiny ghost tale, *The Erl-King's Daughter,* actually found its way onto a best-seller list. All of which proves, to me at least, that readers like ghosts and need them. Perhaps ghost stories are a kind of homeopathic remedy against real terrors: Take one a day to guard against anything of this kind happening to you. Most modern readers lead lives which are, to a great extent, insulated from primitive fears. But this, I believe, leads to a build-up of unacknowledged anxiety that may be liberated and drawn to the surface by the artificial alarms of ghost stories.

Henry James said that ghost stories were on a par with fairy tales, and there is a generally accepted theory that the human race needs fairy tales and myths; that children who grow up without this kind of mental nourishment are permanently impoverished. Perhaps it is such people, deprived of fantasy in their early years, who turn so eagerly to ghost stories in adult life.

Be that as it may, ghost stories do seem to be in perennial demand; any writer who gets into the ghostly habit may be sure of regular requests from editors for "a Christmas ghost story," "a summer holiday ghost story," or one related to some theme for a specialized anthology. I once even—believe it or not—received a request for a "Regency ghost story." And even more incredibly, I happened to have, in my unsold story drawer, a manuscript that, with a little editorial work, would suit the purpose: a story I had written in my twenties about a girl bedeviled by the ghost of a swashbuckling Restoration ancestor. A few changes of costume and dialogue shifted Lord Harlowe from the reign of Charles II to that of George III. And this reinforced the lesson drummed into me by my first literary agent: Never throw any work away; something that is not wanted now may be just what editors are asking for in five, ten, fifteen years.

That story (it was called "Peer Behind the Scenes") was a lightweight, not meant to be taken seriously; but if you can write a *real* ghost story, the sort that keeps the reader breathlessly attentive through half a dozen pages of mounting tension, torn between an inclination to shut the book and think of something else, and an inability to do so—and if you can then finish the story with a genuine freezing *frisson*—then you may be sure of a permanent market for anything you are able to produce. And, of course, if you can do this, you hardly need me to be making suggestions about the technique of writing ghost stories. But one may always pick up a clue or two from the ideas of other practitioners.

It is never too late to study the advice of the masters. M. R. James, who might be called the Grand Old Man of ghost-story writing, said that *reticence* was just as necessary in a ghost story as horror and malevolence; and with this I most emphatically agree. It is always a mistake to ladle on the grue too fast and too lavishly; just a delicate touch at a time achieves a much stronger effect.

Henry James, the other old master of the supernatural, likewise advised that the writer should make use of what he called his "process of adumbration," that is, making the reader use his own imagination to envisage the horror that threatens the hero. "Only make the reader's general vision intense enough . . . and that already is a charming job . . . his own experience . . . will supply him quite sufficiently with all the particulars.

This is brilliant advice. It was brilliant when Henry James wrote it, and it has lost none of its force now.

The worst, the most frightening stories, are those in which the reader is not told precisely what happens, but is left to guess. Another thing that James said, in discussing *The Turn of the Screw,* is still sadly true: If the threat in the story is to children, it makes it much worse. This has been a period of dreadful happenings: Wars, floods, earthquakes, bombs, every kind of horror has been presented on TV news. But to me the worst, most unforgettable image was during the hunt in Liverpool for the killers of a three-year-old boy whose body had been found: His abduction by two older boys had actually been recorded on a shopping-mall TV. I cannot think of anything more dreadful than the hazy picture of those two young, thin figures receding into the crowd with the little, trustful one going off between them.

Of the stories by M. R. James that after nearly a hundred years still hold great potency, the most terrifying is "Oh Whistle and I'll Come to You." Yet, what happens? The hero picks up a whistle, and has a dream of a half-glimpsed creature chasing a terrified man through the dusk along a wintry beach. At the climax of the story, the bedclothes from the unoccupied bed in his hotel room assemble themselves into a shape and come at him. He sees a face *of crumpled linen* (James's italics). But what could a creature made out of bedclothes really do to an active, golf-playing university professor? The secret of the story is

184

that the reader is not given time to ask such a question; he is completely caught up in the carefully assembled and graded action: first, the character of Parkins, a fussy, fidgety, old-maidish academic; then the detailed description of the English east-coast area, the hotel, the "pale ribbon of sand intersected by black wooden groynings" [breakwaters], and the monastic ruins where Parkins picks up the whistle.

The story seems to proceed at a leisurely pace, but all along the way, small hints are dropped. Parkins, having picked up the whistle, glances back and sees "a rather indistinct personage who seemed to be making great efforts to catch up with him but made little, if any, progress." He makes little of this glimpse—though the reader makes more—but it serves to remind him of the moment in *The Pilgrim's Progress* where Christian sees a foul fiend coming over the field to meet him. And from then on, tension builds steadily. When Parkins tries to blow the whistle, there is a sudden gust of wind, and an image comes into his mind of a desolate, windswept landscape, with a solitary figure. He then has the frightening dream, and the reader is conned into thinking that perhaps all the fear, all the threat, is in Parkins's own mind. But no; the bedding on the second bed is disturbed at night and a local boy, outside, is terrified by the sight of a white figure—"not a *right* person"—in the hotel bedroom window. Notice that all through the story the impressions given the reader are always as observed by one of the characters in the story. And even in the final climax, it is through Parkins's eyes that we see: "The spectator realized, with some horror and some relief, that it must be blind, for it seemed to feel about it. . . ." (The fact that the creature is blind makes it *more* frightening, not *less*.)

Does a writer have to believe in ghosts himself in order to be able to portray them?

My answer to that is no, or, at least, it depends on what you mean by ghosts. I do not believe in sheeted spectres clanking chains, and I have not seen anything of the kind. But I know several people who have experienced supernatural manifestations. (One was my stepfather, an entirely rational, level-headed, skeptical person.) I have had experience with telepathy and nonnatural happenings, and I am perfectly ready to believe that paraphysical phenomena take place all around us all the time, but we have hardly begun to be aware of, or to understand them. I have lived in various old houses in which odd things happen, some of which I used in a story called "The Legacy." "Would you shut the window, Basil?" said my aunt Helen. "The curtain keeps billowing in." But, behind the curtain, the window was already tight and locked. Also in that house, a pair of shoes were found in the cellar, inexplicably packed with foil milk-bottle caps. Nobody could have done this, and there was no reason for it. That is generally the case with supernatural, or paranormal occurrences: They are odd, trivial, meaningless. The art of the ghost story writer is to turn these inexplicable little oddities into something meaningful and threatening.

The way I build a ghost story is to start with what I call *the moment*—the climax, though it may not be the end. The classic example of this is the person waking in a fright, putting out a hand in the dark, and the hand goes into a *mouth,* hot and wet, with sharp teeth. . . . Other examples: You ring the bell of a familiar house, but when the door is opening, the interior is completely unfamiliar, and the person who opens the door is a stranger. You answer the phone, and the voice of a long-dead person says, "See you later." You confidently put your hand in your pocket for keys and encounter—what? Something hideously out of place.

E. F. Benson was a great exponent of The Moment; several of his stories, such as "Naboth's Vineyard," rise to an almost unbearably frightening climax. But I think the best of all is in another M. R. James story, "The Treasure of Abbot Thomas," in which, following clues, a treasure hunter climbs down a spiral stair into a well, and opens a door in the masonry, only have Something slither out and *put its arms round his neck.*

In my case, The Moment comes first. Then follows the slow, structural part of working back to causes and building up to the scene. To whom has this happened? Why? And, tremendously important, where? To be frightening, a story does not have to be set in some wild, desolate Edgar Allan Poe-type region. Elizabeth Bowen, who wrote some very haunting supernatural stories, used modern housing estates and prosperous stockbrokers' residences. One of her most sinister ghosts is a taxi driver.

E. F. Benson tended to build his stories on a traditional pattern: Some evil, violent episode has occurred in the past—murder, hostility, cruelty, oppression. Into the place where this happened comes a present-day character who somehow contrives to disturb old vibrations and set off a replay of what took place before. The present-day protagonists may come to a sticky end. Or there may be some kind of exorcism. This is a reliable framework; the skill lies in making the setting as real, and the characters as sympathetic as possible, so that the reader may become involved and empathize more and more, up to the moment of climax.

I find it enriching to the story if the protagonists have aims and intentions and plans of their own, so that there are two themes intertwined, as happens so often in life. The story, therefore, is not simply A goes to Place X and sees Ghost B, but A, having decided to leave his wife and children and go off with C, arrives at Place X and meets Ghost B; whereupon the writer is at once given various interesting choices: Does C also see the ghost? If not, why not? Is A seeing the ghost because he is in a vulnerable psychological state? Does this affect his relationship with C? And so on.

A couple of years ago, I was approached by the National Trust, the body that cares for ancient houses in England, and asked if I would like to write a story about one of their properties. Enchanted, I at once said, Yes, I would like to write a story about Lamb House. This ancient house stands at the top of the hill where I was born, in Rye, Sussex, England. Up to 1918, it belonged to Henry James, who wrote many novels there, including *The Turn of the Screw;* after his death, it passed into the hands of E. F. Benson, who wrote his Lucia books and many ghost stories there. Then later, it was occupied by Rumer Godden, who had several strange psychic experiences (described in her autobiography *A House with Four Rooms*). Both James and Benson had fallen in love with the house, and both said they had practically been *summoned* to live in it by what seemed a meaningful chain of events. Comparing their lives, I found many interesting parallels: They both came from large, talented families; their sisters had breakdowns; they had supernatural experiences. . . . I began planning a series of three tales, one to be wholly invented, preceding the lives of James and Benson, but linking them. I thought I would write the stories about James and Benson each in a pastiche of their own style, and the climax of each would be the type they themselves used in ghost stories: In the case of James, a kind of nebulous, sinister fade-out; in Benson's case, a more robust and dramatic confrontation with the Powers of Evil, ending in an exorcism.

At this point the National Trust got in touch with me and said they were afraid that Lamb House was not at all suitable for such a project, as there was no shop on the premises in which the book could be sold.

But by that time (several months had elapsed) I was fired with enthusiasm and wrote the book anyway and had a lot of fun inventing appropriate happenings. (Both men had written ghost stories—which I took pains to read—using Lamb House as a setting. Although mine was not a book that would ever reach a best-seller list, I was lucky enough to find publishers on both sides of the Atlantic, and even in Spain and Germany, and it did rather better than expected for such an oddity. Which shows that there is always a market for a ghost!

Like all writers, I keep a notebook—a whole series of notebooks—in which I jot down ideas for future stories. Many of these might develop into ghost stories: "Hotel wallpaper with spooky little catlike creatures." "Somebody whose memory skips a day. Why?" "Churchyard full of grave slabs that look like a chessboard." "Floor covered with fingernails." "Sign: DANGER. Keep clear of unpropped body." "Taking ghost on travels."

These are all waiting for The Moment.

Being a writer is not at all unlike being a medium. Sometimes the message comes through loud and clear. Sometimes you simply have to wait for it.

40

WHY HORROR?

BY GRAHAM MASTERTON

FEW PEOPLE UNDERSTAND that writers are writing all the time.

To think that a writer is writing only when he or she is actually hammering a keyboard is like believing that a police officer's job is "arresting people."

Even while they're not sitting down at the word processor, writers are writing in their heads. Inventing stories. Playing with words. Thinking up jokes and riddles and metaphors and similes. These days, I write both historical sagas and horror novels. Most people relish historical sagas, but I'm often asked, "Why do people like horror?"

I think they like horror novels because they depict ordinary people dealing with extraordinary threats. They like to imagine, what would *I* do if a dark shadow with glowing red eyes appeared in my bedroom at night? What would *I* do if I heard a sinister scratching inside the walls of my house? What would *I* do if my husband's head turned around 360 degrees?

I've found my inspiration for horror stories in legends from ancient cultures, and my research into how these demons came to be created by ordinary men and women is fascinating. Each of them represents a very real fear that people once felt, and often still do.

There are beguiling men who turn into evil demons. There are monsters that suck your breath when you're asleep. There are gremlins that steal children. There are horrible gorgons that make you go blind just to look at them, and vampires that drain all of the energy out of you. There are zombies who come back from the dead and torment you.

My favorite Scottish demons were the glaistigs, hideous hags who were supposed to be the ghosts of women haunting their former homes. They were frequently accompanied by a child who was called "the little plug" or "the whimperer." If you didn't leave out a bowl of milk for the glaistigs, they would suck your cows dry or drain their blood. Sometimes a glaistig would carry her little whimperer into the house, and bathe it in the blood of the youngest infant in the house, and the victim would be found dead and white in the morning.

Now, this is a legend, but you can understand what genuine fears it expresses. A woman's fear of other women intruding into her home, as in the film, *Fatal Attraction*; a man's fear of losing his livelihood; parents' fear of losing their children to malevolent and inexplicable illnesses, such as crib death. What I do is take these ancient demons, which are vivid and expressive manifestations of basic and genuine fears, and write about them in an up-to-date setting, with modern characters.

The very first horror novel I wrote was called *The Manitou*. A manitou is a Native American demon, and in this novel a 300-year-old medicine man was reborn in the present day to take his revenge on the white man. I was inspired to write that by *The Buffalo Bill Annual, 1956*.

Since then I have written books based on Mexican demons, Balinese demons, French demons and Biblical demons, two dozen in all, and I'm working on another one about the Glasgow woman who makes a pact with Satan so that her house disappears every time the rent collector calls.

I started writing horror novels at school, when I was 11. I used to read them to my friends during recess. Reading your work out loud is always invaluable training. When I met one of my old school friends only recently, he said, "I'll never forget the story you wrote about the woman with no head who kept singing 'Tiptoe Through the Tulips.' It gave me nine years of sleepless nights, and I still can't have tulips in the house."

Horror books seem to sell well all over the world, with some notable exceptions, like Germany. The French love horror, and the Poles adore it. In France, *Le Figaro* called me "Le Roi du Mal," the King of Evil. I was the first Western horror novelist to be published in Romania, home of Dracula. I received a letter from a reader this week saying, "I have to write to congratulate you on a wonderful book, rich with ideas and shining with great metaphors. Also very good printing, and excellent paper, which is appreciated here because of bathroom tissue shortage."

How extreme can you be when you write horror? As extreme, I think, as your talent and your taste permit, although gruesomeness is no substitute for skillful writing. I had several complaints about a scene in my book *Picture of Evil,* in which the hero kills two young girls with a poker. People protested my graphic description of blood spattering everywhere. In fact, I never once mentioned blood. All I said was, "He clubbed them to death like two baby seals." The reader's imagination was left to do the rest.

It is catching the mood and feel of a moment that makes your writing come to life. Most of the time you can dispense with whole realms of description if you catch one vivid image; catching those images requires thought and research. When I write historical novels, I frequently rent period costumes which my wife and I try on so I can better understand how my characters would have moved and behaved when wearing them. How do you rush to meet your lover when wearing a hobble skirt? How do you sit down with a bustle?

We also prepare food and drink from old recipes, using cookbooks by Fannie Farmer, Mrs. Beeton, and Escoffier. One of the least successful period drinks we prepared was the King's Death, drunk by King Alfonso of Spain in the Men's Bar of the Paris Ritz. The King's Death is made with wild strawberries marinated in Napoleon brandy, then topped up with half a bottle of champagne—each! We served it to some dinner party guests, and they became incoherent and had to go home.

Whether you're writing history or horror, thrillers or love stories, the most important technique is to live inside the book instead of viewing it from the outside. Your word processor or typewriter is nothing more than a key that opens the door to another world. When I'm writing, I step into that world, so that it surrounds me. So many writers as they write look only forward at the page, or screen, forgetting what's all around them.

Think of the rain on the side of your face and the wind against your back. Think of what you can hear in the distance. Think of the fragrances you can smell. Most of all, *be* all your characters: Act out their lives, act out their movements and their facial expressions, and speak their dialogue out loud. Get up from your keyboard sometimes, and do what you've imagined; then sit down and write it. The Disney artist Ward Kimball used to draw Donald Duck by making faces in the

191

mirror. You can do the same when you're writing about the way your characters act and react.

Your best research is watching real live people living out their real lives. Watch every gesture, every nuance, listen to people's conversations and accents. Try to propel your story along at the pace that *you* would like to read it. Avoid showing off in your writing; all that does is slow down your story and break the spell you have been working so hard to conjure up. How many times has your suspension of disbelief been broken by ridiculous similes, like "her bosoms swelled like two panfuls of overboiling milk."

Two similes that really caught my attention and which I later used in novels were an old Afrikaner's description of lions roaring "like coal being delivered," and the hideous description by an Australian prisoner of war of two of his fellow prisoners being beheaded: "the blood spurted out of their necks like red walking-sticks."

To my mind, the greatest achievement in writing is to create a vivid, spectacular novel without readers being aware that they are reading at all. My ideal novel would be one that readers put down, and discover that they're still in it, that it's actually come to life.

The other day I was reading *Secrets of the Great Chefs of China,* and apart from the eel recipe, where you throw live eels into boiling water and have to clamp the lid down quickly to stop them from jumping out of the pot, the most memorable advice the book gave was, "A great chef prepares his food so that it is ready for the mouths of his guests; it is both a courtesy and a measure of his professionalism." That goes for writing, too.

§ 41

IT'S NO MYSTERY

BY CAROLYN G. HART

WHAT CAN MAKE *YOUR* MYSTERY an editor's choice? The answer is no mystery—or it shouldn't be.

Superb books grab the editor in the very first paragraphs, the very first lines.

Superb books are as individual and as idiosyncratic as crusty Aunt Edith or affable Cousin Charles.

So these, in my view, are the two essential elements for a successful mystery novel:

Action.

Voice.

Action is creating the story as the reader watches.

Voice is the unmistakable reflection of the author's personality.

If your novel successfully combines action and voice, editors will vie to publish you.

I've always loved beginning novels with action, and in my Death on Demand mystery series, I use a technique I adore: the vignette.

A vignette is a small, swift cameo of a scene, featuring a character who is important to the novel in an act that relates to the theme of the novel.

Here are the opening sentences of the vignettes in the fourth book in the series, *Honeymoon with Murder:*

Vignette One: Jesse Penrick didn't miss much on his solitary nocturnal rambles. Lights at an odd hour. A visitor never before seen. An unfamiliar car.

Vignette Two: Lucinda Burrows darted through the crowd, her brown alligator heels clicking excitedly against the concrete. She'd done just as instructed, and the whole operation had gone without a hitch.

Vignette Three: The perfect crime. Who said it couldn't be done?

Vignette Four: Ingrid Jones had no idea she was being observed, she and the whole expanse of Nightingale Court.

What is accomplished? The reader is immediately plunged into the action. The reader knows things are happening, and the reader is made a part of the action.

Perhaps the single most enervating and deadly mistake a beginning writer makes is in trying to tell the reader what is happening.

Never *tell* a reader anything.

Let the reader become a part of the scene.

Look at it this way: People who read are smart or they wouldn't read. They've been going to films all their lives. When the movie opens with a chase scene, big guys with guns chasing Michael Douglas down an alley, the viewers don't know what's going on, but they are quite willing to find out *as the story unfolds.*

Let your story unfold.

For example, in *The Christie Caper,* my protagonist Annie Laurance, owner of the Death on Demand mystery bookstore, is planning a celebration of the centennial of the birth of Agatha Christie. What could be more boring than beginning a book with that information? For example, Annie might be talking on the telephone with her mother-in-law, Laurel, and she could tell Laurel, "I'm going to have a convention here on the island to celebrate the centennial, etc., etc."

That is telling the reader. Instead here is the beginning of the opening chapter:

Annie counted the magnums of champagne. Four. Five. Six. Surely that would be enough. She whirled on her heel and dashed out of the storeroom.

I don't *tell* the reader anything. The reader is there as Annie frantically readies the bookstore for an evening cocktail party for the convention attendees.

Action. Use it. Enjoy it. Live that scene, and your reader will live it, too.

There is always a way to provide information through action. When I received the editorial letter on *Deadly Valentine,* my editor suggested that readers needed to know more about the people who would be the focus at the Valentine Ball *before* the Ball began.

I created a scene before the party, when Annie and her mother-in-law, Laurel, walk down to the pier and look at the houses around Scarlet King lagoon, where Annie and Max live in their new house. If they'd walked down to the pier and Annie had simply described the houses and their occupants, it would have been what writing teachers call "tea party conversation," that is, the contrived exchange of information in a scene that doesn't move the story. Instead, there is action because of a subtle struggling between Laurel and Annie, Laurel intent upon gaining information, Annie reluctant to part with it. What makes it credible is that Annie is certain Laurel has some ulterior motive in asking for this information, and, as the reader discovers later, indeed Laurel did. This moves the story along and, at the same time, it satisfies the author's objective of introducing to the reader some of the people who will be at the Valentine Ball. Often, the author has several objectives in a scene in addition to the objectives of the characters. The characters' objectives in this scene are twofold: Annie wants to find out what her madcap mother-in-law is up to, and Laurel is quite determined to learn all about the neighbors.

Action can be mental. In *Design for Murder,* I used a vignette to give readers a clear picture of Corinne Prichard Webster's character:

. . . Her eyes narrowed, and she no longer looked at her reflection so she didn't see the transformation. At one instant, the mirrored face was soft and beguiling, almost as beautiful with its classic bones, silver-blonde hair, and Mediterranean blue eyes as on her wedding day at nineteen almost forty years before. Then, as Corinne Prichard Webster thought about her niece, Gail, throwing herself at a totally unsuitable man, the face hardened and looked all of its fifty-nine years, the eyes cold and hard, the mouth, thin, determined, and cruel.

In *A Little Class on Murder,* Annie is teaching a course at a college in Chastain on the Three Great Ladies of the Mystery: Agatha Christie, Dorothy L. Sayers, and Mary Roberts Rinehart. This is Annie's first teaching venture, and she's very self-conscious and certainly doesn't want anyone in the class whom she knows. I decided (unknown to Annie, of course) to enroll in the class Annie's ditzy mother-in-law, Laurel, her most opinionated customer, Henny, and the curmudgeon of Chastain, Miss Dora.

The day arrives for Annie's first class:

She was skimming her lecture notes when she stiffened, her senses assaulted.
Scent.
Sound.

195

Sight.

The scent came first. The unmistakable fragrance of lilac, clear and sharp and sweet.

Annie's hands tightened in a death grip on the sides of the lectern. Surely it couldn't—

It could.

Laurel swept through the doorway, beaming, of course. . . .

In short order, Miss Dora and Henny also arrive.

. . . The back of her (Annie's) neck prickled. That thump behind her!

It took every vestige of her will to turn her head to face the door to the hallway.

Thump. Thump. Thump.

Quick, purposeful, decisive thumps.

The ebony cane with its black rubber tip poked around the corner, followed by its mistress.

The tiny old lady (Miss Dora) stood motionless in the doorway. . . .

And then . . .

Oh God.

The sight framed in the doorway was almost too much for her to accept. Laurel was bad enough. Miss Dora would cast a pall on the Addams family tea party.

But this—

It wasn't as though she didn't recognize the costume: a large gray flannel skirt with a droopy hem, a full blouse with a lacy panel down the front, a shapeless rust-colored cardigan, lisle stockings, extremely sensible brown shoes, and hair bobbing in springy sausage-curl rolls.

"Henny," she moaned.

And poor Annie is facing her first class.

The reader saw it happen.

Action is yours for the asking. Pretend you're training a camera on your characters. Watch the scene unfold *with* your readers.

And with action, you will discover voice.

How you see the world, how you create scenes, will be a product of your personality, your experiences, and your willingness to dare.

Voice is perhaps the easiest element to recognize in successful fiction and, for uncertain writers, the most difficult to attain.

What is voice? It is the quality of writing that makes a passage instantly identifiable. If you handed me five unidentified pages written by Nancy Pickard, Sara Paretsky, Dorothy Cannell, and Joan Hess, I would have no difficulty at all in knowing who wrote what. Because each author's voice is so distinctive, so unmistakable.

This is perhaps the most elusive concept in writing. Maybe a few don'ts will make it clearer.

If you look at the bestseller lists, then write a book and send it to an agent or editor, saying this is just like Robert B. Parker or Mary Higgins Clark, that book won't sell.

Don't try to be another Parker or Clark. Don't imitate. Study, observe, absorb, but when you write, write it your way. You must write a book that absolutely no one in the world could have written except you. Each human being is unique. The passions and prejudices, the obsessions and revulsions that drive each person are different. Take advantage of this. Listen to your heart. Then you will have a voice.

You must write a book that matters enormously to you, not a Native American mystery because Tony Hillerman is hot, or a cat mystery because Lillian Jackson Braun is hot, or a serial killer because Thomas Harris is hot.

This isn't to say you can't set a book in New Mexico. Walter Satterthwaite and Judith Van Gieson are using that locale, but their books are succeeding because they are unmistakably their own, not Hillerman spinoffs.

If I look deeply into the books I have written, I realize that paramount to me is the exercise of power in relationships. This is my obsession, the element that fuels my books. I want everyone to be accountable for the way they treat others, so that is my focus.

And the way I write?

I love language. The sound of words matters to me. Is my fiction distinctive enough for readers to mark the words as mine? I can't answer that. That is for readers to say. But I know there are passages in what I have written that reflect the essence of my soul.

That is the price a writer pays to achieve voice. The writer must be willing to reveal what matters most of all to him.

If I were to select a passage that perhaps says the most about me, it would be from my novel, *Dead Man's Island*. This is the first novel in a new series featuring a retired newspaperwoman, Henrietta O'Dwyer Collins, as the protagonist. She's known as Henri O, a nickname given to her by her late husband, Richard, because he said she provided more surprises in a single day than O. Henry ever put in a short story.

Dead Man's Island is the story of a woman who responds to a call for help from a voice out of her past. She travels to a private island where murder and a hurricane threaten the survival of the stranded guests.

Toward the close of *Dead Man's Island,* Henri O awaits the return of the storm:

As I stood, fatigue washed over me. It would be so easy to drop down beside Valerie and close my eyes, let the warmth of the sunlight touch me with fingers of life and let my mind drift, taking memories and thoughts as they came.

But anger flickered beneath the exhaustion.

I suppose I've always been angry. That's what drives most writers, the hot steady consuming flame of anger against injustice and dishonesty and exploitation, against sham and artifice and greed, against arrogance and brutality and deceitfulness, against betrayal and indifference and cruelty.

I would not give up.

This passage is what Henri O is all about.

Should you as a reader care, this passage also tells you everything you'd ever need to know about me, the author. So when you write a book that offers your heart and mind and soul to readers, it will have voice.

Your voice.

42

How the Westerns Are Won

By Jacqueline Johnson

FOR MANY YEARS, the Western novel genre has been subject to speculation about its impending demise. The present is no exception, despite the resurgent interest in Western movies. The inevitable questions are: Is the Western novel a dying breed? Or is the Western making a comeback? Who really is the next Louis L'Amour?

Fans of the genre are ardent and loyal, though not as numerous as we would like. The future of Westerns depends on whether the industry can attract stronger and more steady sales. Publishers are shrinking their lists—and while that may be good news for those titles remaining, as this should boost sales, it is bad news for writers trying to place their work. If a publisher does buy your manuscript, you cannot expect to sit back and wait for your royalty checks. Given the relatively small market for Westerns, it is crucial that the author take the initiative on local promotion. Publishers routinely send press releases and review copies to some outlets, but you should become the expert on how to publicize your work in your own hometown, your state, your regional media. There are countless book titles out in the world, with hundreds more being released all the time. Why should a newspaper or magazine review your book? What is there about this particular vengeance tale (or train robbery story, etc.) that should send readers to the nearest library or bookstore with your name on their lips?

Good enough isn't good enough

Most people who take the time to write a novel, and who go to the trouble to learn how and where to submit their work, are able to write reasonably well. There is much competition for a few slots. For every manuscript that is accepted, many are turned away. One of the hardest things about a rejection is not knowing why your proposal or manuscript was not accepted.

Editors do send writers encouraging notes, occasionally letters. But we often limit our response to terse comments because we handle too many submissions to give each a detailed individual reply. Writers who have felt the frustration of rejection forms often hunger for a clue about why their work was not accepted. Those who do get a note or a brief comment may find themselves asking, "What does *that* mean?"

Here are some tips on how to decode editorial criticism of your work. You might not agree with everything an editor tells you, but you may be able to use the feedback to your own advantage, either by refining your work to fit your chosen market, or by reassessing which market is more suitable for what you want to write.

Avoiding plot pitfalls

Consider these options if an editor says your story . . .

"—is not substantial enough." Either not enough happens to move the story along or there is a lot going on, but the story lacks impact. One solution may be to delve more deeply into the story, looking at the characters or the setting from an angle that lets the reader know what is special about this particular story.

"—is all atmosphere and characterization." A plot is too inconsequential if nothing significant is at stake for the protagonist. By the novel's end, something should be resolved, though that doesn't mean tying all the loose ends into a neat (or happy) ending.

"—does not hold our interest." The novel may have started off well, then became too predictable or too like many other stories of its kind. This type of comment may signal that you should submit your manuscript elsewhere, since editorial taste and needs do vary from one publishing house to another. If you get a similar response from several sources, you may need to look into some lesser-known (but historically accurate) locations or events as inspiration on your next project.

"—is not credible." This comment infuriates some writers, many of whom have done meticulous research. However, if the story does not ring true for the reader, the fact that it really happened is a moot defense. You may need to explore the motivations of your characters more deeply, or use more detail to set up a crucial scene so the reader doesn't feel manipulated, misled, or duped.

"—is too long/too short for our format." Find out the length (or other) requirements of prospective markets. Although a publisher might be willing to make an exception in your case, it is unlikely that a major deviation from the guidelines will be made to accommodate your work. Cut down on the number of rejections and the time your work is tied up in transit by first familiarizing yourself with the publisher's books to see whether your work fits in with current offerings.

Correcting characterization flaws

If your characters are perceived as being "too stiff or one-dimensional," try to flesh them out more. Let the reader see the character outside the context of the main storyline; show another side of him or her. (Romance is often used for this purpose, but there are many kinds of relationships and situations that can give a character more personality and depth.)

"Clichéd characters" are an occupational hazard for genre writers because of the prevalence of stock types, like the strong, silent hero whose vocabulary is limited to "Yup" and "Nope," and who lets his guns (or his fists) do his talking. Don't rely on stereotypes as a shortcut or a substitute for credible characterization.

Controlling the flow of storytelling

If the pace of a story is "too slow," prudent trimming can bring it into sharper focus and speed it along.

When the pace is "too feverish," the writer may be overloading the story with one calamity after another. Even in an action-packed genre, the reader may need time to catch his breath and mull over what has happened after an especially intense scene. A good Western's impact is not measured by how high the body count is, but by how much the reader is affected by what is transpiring in the novel.

Fine-tuning the tone

Every genre has its own parameters that identify it. Even within this category, there are differences between traditional Westerns and historical Westerns, series Westerns and Novels of the West, and so on. At Walker and Company, where I've been editing Westerns for nine years, traditional Westerns run 65,000 words, are set exclusively in the Old West, and tend not to be:

"—too dreary." Life in the Old West was undeniably tough, and the traditional Western usually does have the presence of danger, a threat of some kind of violence. But exaggerated, relentless villainy and violence can make a story oppressive.

"—too like a romance novel." A cowboy's affections aren't limited to his horse. There are courtships, marriages, and affairs in Westerns, but intimate relationships are unlikely to be the sole focus of the book.

"—too like a young adult novel." Although our Westerns are read by people of all ages, they are edited for adults. Oversimplification and excessive exposition are not suitable for us.

Regardless of whether writing genre or mainstream fiction, novelists face many of the same obstacles, from overcoming writer's block to coping with the frustrations of rejection. People who are unfamiliar with the range of work within category fiction are often surprised by the literary quality of some of the top-of-line books. Fans of this genre know that the best Westerns have never been merely shoot-'em-ups, but some of the most memorable and beloved novels in the spectrum of American fiction.

$\wr$43

THE USES OF SUSPENSE

BY ANDREW KLAVAN

WANT TO LEARN about writing suspense fiction? Try this simple experiment at home. Invite a friend over to your house, preferably someone better-looking than you are and with more money. Let's call him Nigel. Let's say he's been trying to make time with your wife. (Women can try this experiment, too! It's easy! Just change Nigel's sex!) Seat Nigel in a chair close to yours, one of those wooden Windsors with the fanning spoked backs. Now, for approximately fifteen minutes, engage Nigel in conversation about something excruciatingly dull: the latest deficit debates, say, or Madonna's inner life.

A yawn-fest, am I wrong? O.K. Now, tie Nigel to the chair with a strong rope (this is where that spoked back comes in handy). Produce a .38 caliber revolver with only one bullet in it (prepare this earlier). Spin the revolver's wheel so you don't know where the bullet is, and then level the barrel at Nigel's head. Continue the conversation on exactly the same subject in exactly the same way as before—except, every minute on the minute, pull the trigger of the gun.

I think you'll find that those next five minutes of conversation—if there are five more minutes of conversation—are a lot more interesting and suspenseful than the first fifteen, especially to Nigel. Thus, you have just demonstrated several important aspects of the nature of suspense. And, as I hope and pray you'll be spending the rest of your life in some sort of high-security institution, you should have a lot of time to think about them, too.

But what exactly have we learned? To begin with, suspense is not about the things that are happening; it's about the things that might happen, that threaten to happen. Obviously, if you'd merely continued chatting away about the deconstructionist profundities of "Like A Virgin," there would have been no suspense at all, though you might eventually have been given tenure. But it's also true that if you had simply whipped a fully loaded gun out and blown Nigel away, it might have been surprising, it would certainly have been messy, but the suspense factor would still have stood at zero. Suspense is in the pauses between the pulls of the trigger; between the time the reader knows what might happen and the time it actually happens or doesn't.

It follows from this that the more readers know about the threat to your characters, and the earlier they know, the more suspense there is. All sorts of interesting stories can be told in which the audience, mystified, waits to be enlightened. But in suspense fiction, whatever else you hold back, your readers should be in on the threat of danger as soon as possible and as much as possible.

For example, in a novel I wrote called *Don't Say A Word,* the story revolves around a psychiatrist, his wife and child, and a beautiful but disturbed young woman who becomes his patient. For the first hundred pages or so, the psychiatrist tends to his practice, plays with his child, makes love to his wife, and treats the young woman. Then, the psychiatrist's little girl is kidnapped, and he spends the rest of the book in a desperate attempt to get her back. I like to think that those first hundred pages are interesting and mysterious and compelling and all that, but if they're suspenseful, it's because of the ten-page prologue during which the bad guys worm their way into an apartment that has a view through the psychiatrist's window. They brutally murder the old lady who lives there and set up camp, watching every move the psychiatrist makes. When the psychiatrist plays with his child, the reader knows they're watching. When he makes love to his wife, the reader knows they're watching. And because of what they did to the old lady, the reader knows that whatever the bad guys eventually do to the psychiatrist, it's going to be very bad. Right up front, I tell the reader who the bad guys are, what they're like, and whom they're after. The only mystery about them is their motive, which has nothing to do with the present danger and so can be saved for a revelation at the end. The less I can hold back, in other words, the more the reader comes with me for the ride.

Of course, any editor or agent will tell you to begin a suspense novel with a scene of danger or violence like that. But it's amazing how often they want you to cut out precisely the piece of information that switches on the suspense. In this particular case, they liked the old lady getting killed, but they didn't want me to mention that it was the psychiatrist the bad guys were watching. Editors and agents know that a little violence at the beginning sells books, but somewhere along the line someone told them that you're not supposed to give too much away. I think, to create suspense, you should give as much away as you can. So in the event you should meet with this problem, try saying something like this: "Sweetheart—baby—you're the best editor or agent I've ever met, and I love you like my own brother, and I'm going to give that a lot of thought, let me tell you." Then leave it in.

This brings us to the next lesson we learned from killing Nigel (and what an oleaginous little son-of-a-gun he was, wasn't he?). Once you have established suspense, once readers know exactly where the danger lies, you really have a lot of room to work in. Even if you and Nige are discussing the latest trade agreement and its effect on deficit spending, no one's attention is going to wander once you've pulled out that gun. Likewise, in a work of fiction, the firm pressure of suspense gives you the time you need to establish your characters, work out your plot elements, expound your ridiculous metaphysical theories, or hawk your half-baked political notions—whatever meat your story feeds on. In *Don't Say A Word,* I wanted to draw a fairly full picture of this psychiatrist's life; I wanted readers to see his fault-lines, where he might crack once the going got tough. The killing of the old woman and the men watching through the window, gave me time to do a fairly in-depth study of the man, all the while keeping the pressure on.

This use of suspense is particularly important to me because of the kinds of books I write. I don't generally deal with stories about world leaders or terrorists or guys in ties who grab the phone and shout, "Get me Quantico! Now!" I like stories like that quite a lot actually, but as a writer, I'm more interested in the inner worlds of regular people, and I generally make up stories in which the glitches and nightmares of those inner worlds are played out in reality. Now, if you introduce the President of the United States as a character, readers all know he's important, and if you bring in the best FBI agent west of the Tappan Zee, readers know he or she is likely to be where the action is. But establishing the inner worlds of clerks and housewives, small-time shrinks and would-be poets—and drawing readers into their ordinary lives—takes more time and involves a lot of mundane action. Suspense—the danger that the audience can see coming—gives you that time and brings those actions to life.

205

But the effect of suspense on commonplace events can be brought into play in all sorts of ways, scene by scene. I love to create episodes in which something perfectly ordinary happens while the reader (one hopes) tears his hair out wishing it would stop. In my novel *The Animal Hour,* one of my heroes, Oliver, gets trapped into what is to him the horrible situation of *having tea with his grandmother*! The way it works out is this: Oliver is trying to prevent the murder of his grandmother, which he knows will take place at a certain time. He trails the villain, who knows the plan of his grandmother's house. Both she and Oliver also know that Granny has a very bad heart; any sort of fuss will likely cause the old woman to die. So, when Oliver tries to force the villain out of the room, she, in turn, offers to make everyone a lovely cup of tea. As a result, Oliver, a hulking bear of a man, is forced to sit through a dainty tea party with Granny and the villain, while the minutes tick away toward the time of the killing.

What I like about this situation is that the trivial is heightened with the threat of death, and since both the trivial and the threat of death are always with us, it provides the story with a sort of metarealism. If you do it well enough, you can make the reader feel that even the dullest tea party takes place under an inexorably ticking clock. Which, of course, it does.

Finally, the now-famous Nigel Experiment demonstrates a more sub-tle aspect of suspense and one that is, in my opinion, too rarely put to good use; that is, suspense is amoral. It slams the reader into the endangered character's point of view, no matter who that character is or what he's done. Let's say we tell the story of our experiment from Nigel's viewpoint. We know he's a no-good sort of guy; just look at him: Anyone who's richer and better-looking than you are probably deserves whatever he gets. But when you pull that gun out, when your finger begins to tighten on the trigger, readers can't help putting themselves in his place. Every time the hammer goes back, they'll worry about him and fear for him, whether they like him or not. You can take it to the limit—a thief, a rapist, a killer. Write the scene from his point of view, put him under threat of danger, and part of the reader's mind will automatically root for him to escape.

This gives the suspense writer a wonderful opportunity to drag read-ers kicking and screaming into the lives of the very people they most condemn. What's more, you can do it without romanticizing the villain, without pardoning his behavior, and without even explaining that his mother never loved him and that's why he's such a bad hat. I suppose you could say that danger—suspense—forces the reader to recognize the villain's humanity without losing sight of his own moral verities.

Nowhere have I seen this done better than in Simon Brett's novel *A Shock to the System*. I adapted this book for the movie that starred Michael Caine, and what I most wanted to recreate in the film was the way Brett used suspense to make the reader an accomplice to murder. The story involves a man who begins to realize that he can kill his way to the top of his profession. At first, he escapes through pure good luck. But with each successive killing, he becomes more and more adept at covering his tracts. Brett didn't stint in his depiction of the homicidal personality. His protagonist is bitter, vengeful, impotent, sweaty-palmed, and full of petty deceit (I stinted a little in my screenplay: Movie stars don't play impotent). All the same, whenever something threatens to go wrong with one of the killer's plans, whenever the police seem to be closing in, the audience holds its collective breath. They don't want the bad guy to get away exactly; they just don't want him to be caught right now. As a result, bit by bit, they are drawn into the killer's activities nearly as completely as he is himself. I love that. It's wicked and it's funny, but it also reminds us that even the things of darkness must ultimately be acknowledged as our own.

So, though Nigel is no longer with us, we can take comfort in the fact that he gave his sleazy little life to show some of the methods through which suspense can be well used. Indeed, I think if he were here today, what he would tell us, in his smarmy way, is that all fiction is merely a series of thrills, some deeper and more subtle than others, but thrills all the same. In suspense, the basic thrills are pretty obvious and immediate, and they naturally lend themselves to being used mechanically and on the cheap. Used skillfully, though, they give the writer the time and the narrative drive he needs to pull his readers into heightened worlds of thought and sensation that are, at the same time, not much different from everyday life. Well, that's what Nigel would've said. He was a verbose, pompous guy, what can I tell you? I never liked him.

§ 44

SERIES CHARACTERS: LOVE 'EM OR LEAVE 'EM

BY ELIZABETH PETERS

CONAN DOYLE LEARNED TO LOATHE Holmes so intensely, he tried to murder him. At the opposite end of the spectrum are such writers as Dorothy Sayers, whose affection for Lord Peter Wimsey has prompted a certain amount of rude speculation. What is it about series characters? Is there a happy medium between loving and loathing them? Do the advantage of series characters outweigh the disadvantages? Should you, if you haven't done so already, consider starting a series?

In addition to the non-series Barbara Michaels novels, I write three different series, featuring Jacqueline Kirby, librarian; Vicky Bliss, art historian; and the notorious Amelia Peabody, Victorian gentlewoman Egyptologist.

None of the novels in which these three characters first appeared was intended to be the beginning of a series. The reason the series developed is simple and crass: There was a demand. I don't know why publishers suddenly decided that series characters were "in." They had always been popular, as witness Holmes, Poirot, Wimsey, et al., but it was not until ten or fifteen years ago that interest resurfaced. Now, many mystery writers have a series character, and those who do not are being pressured to create one.

The demand of the market is important. If publishers aren't buying a particular type of book, there is not much point in writing it, except for your own satisfaction. However, it is a big mistake to write only for the market, and a bigger mistake to do something you detest simply for the sake of sales.

There are certain disadvantages to a series. It does limit the author to some extent; a given plot may not be suitable for your character. Another disadvantage is that you have to reintroduce the character in every book, and it requires some skill to tell a new reader what he needs to know without boring those who have read earlier books and without slowing the action. Publishers want series, but they also insist that each book stand on its own. This may not be literally oxymoronic, but it's darned hard to do.

However, this last problem is simply one of craftsmanship, and I find that the advantages of a series character far outweigh the disadvantages. Over the space of several books, you can develop the character far more richly and convincingly than is possible in one book, and I believe character has become increasingly important in the mystery novel. Readers are no longer satisfied with stereotypical robots—the Young Lovers, the Detective, the Sinister Lawyer, and so on. The most successful writers of the New Golden Age have succeeded in large part, not so much because of the ingenuity of their plots, but because readers like their characters and want to know more about them.

And, in my opinion, the author should feel the same way about the characters. If, as you hope, the series is a success, you are going to live with these characters for a long time. If you don't like them, they will get on your nerves, and you will either loathe them or become horribly bored by them. (Readers are less likely to become bored than you are. If they do lose interest in your characters, you will know about it; they will stop buying the books.) But there's no reason for you to take on a task you despise when, with a few relatively simple tricks, you can learn to enjoy your characters and look forward to the next visit with them. After writing seven books in the Amelia Peabody series, I am finding her and her family more fascinating every time around.

The most important thing is to begin by creating realistic characters. This may sound paradoxical when applied to Amelia, but in fact she is far less of a caricature than some readers believe. I had read an enormous number of contemporary novels, biographies, social histories, and travel books before I began writing the series, and there are many real-life parallels to Amelia's career, opinions, and behavior, as well as those of her eccentric husband, Emerson. Even Ramses, their catastrophically precocious son, is based to some extent on actual Victorian children, and, to an even greater extent, on normal boys of all eras who exhibit similar tendencies.

If the protagonists of the novel are properly conceived, they will behave consistently and comprehensibly. Of course this requirement

209

is true of character development in general, but it is particularly important with series characters, whom the reader comes to know well. One useful result of consistently drawn characters is that you will find their personalities often determine the way the plot is going to develop. By now I am so familiar with the behavioral patterns of the Emersons that I have only to set up a situation and describe how they will inevitably react.

Just because a character is consistent, however, doesn't mean his behavior should always be predictable. In fact, seemingly irrational behavior makes a character more realistic; real people don't always behave sensibly either. Yet, if we examine the true motives that govern their behavior, we find it is not inconsistent, that we ought to have anticipated it. It is the author's task to establish this. The reaction you want from a reader is a shock of surprise, followed immediately by a shock of recognition: "Oh, yes, of course. I ought to have realized . . ." that despite her constant criticism of her son, Amelia would kill to protect him; that though Emerson complains about his wife's recklessness, he is secretly amused by and appreciative of her courage; that while Ramses sounds like a pompous little snob, he is as insecure as are most young children.

The best way of establishing character is through actions rather than words. This is particularly true if you are writing in the first person. Amelia describes herself as hard-headed and unsentimental, but it should be apparent by page ten of the first book in the series that she is a soft touch who acts on impulse, and then has to scramble desperately to find logical reasons for her actions.

But the smartest thing I did with the Amelia series wasn't done deliberately; it was pure serendipity, or luck, or as I would like to believe, "a writer's instinct."

Crocodile on the Sandbank, the first book in the series, ended like any conventional romantic mystery novel, with Amelia happily married to the hero. This should have been the end of the story; conventional literary wisdom maintains that the protagonist of a series should remain single and therefore open to further adventures, amatory and otherwise. But when I decided to resurrect Amelia, I had to resurrect Emerson as well. I mean, there he was. Worse—he and I had got Amelia pregnant. Emerson may have done it on purpose, but I certainly didn't. The demands of a husband interfere considerably with a heroine's activities as a detective; the demands of a baby are almost impossible to dismiss.

If I had intended *Crocodile* to be the first in a series, I wouldn't have been as specific about dates. Not only did Amelia inform the reader of her age (curse her!), but historical events mentioned in the book tied it to a particular year. As the series continued, there was no way I could get around this, or fudge the date of Ramses' birth, or keep him and his parents from aging a year every twelve months.

I decided to regard these developments not as limitations but as challenges. Could a spouse and a baby be advantages to a heroine, instead of the reverse?

There are two ways of dealing with a detective's spouse. The first and perhaps most common method is to make the spouse a minor character (babies are particularly useful in keeping wives in the background). I chose the second alternative: husband and wife operating as equal, active partners in a genuine team. Note that word *equal*. I wanted my readers to feel that it would be inconceivable for either Amelia or Emerson to function independently of the other.

Insofar as the romantic element was concerned. . . . Well, that was another challenge. I couldn't see any reason husband and wife shouldn't be enthusiastic lovers as well as affectionate, supportive mates, but in order to maintain the "sexual tension" editors are always demanding, the marriage had to be questioned, even threatened, periodically. Rivals who crop up from time to time keep both Amelia and Emerson on their toes (so to speak). In the Amelia novel *The Snake, the Crocodile and the Dog,* I resorted to an even more drastic expedient, which resulted in a severe, potentially destructive strain on their relationship. However, the real conflict stems from the personalities of the major characters themselves. Amelia's air of smug self-confidence conceals a painful inferiority complex, particularly with regard to her personal appearance. She'll always be jealous of more beautiful women, and Emerson will never stop wondering what *really* happened when his wife was in the clutches of her devoted admirer the Master Criminal. Their marriage will never be boring and neither of them will ever take the other for granted.

The birth of Ramses presented even greater difficulties, and more provocative possibilities. In the second book of the series, I hadn't quite come to grips with the difficulties, so I did what most writers do with inconvenient babies: I left Ramses at home and allowed his parents to continue their activities without him. By the third book, *The Mummy Case*, I was ready to cope not only with Ramses, but with the tripartite relationship.

During this novel, Ramses developed into one of the most perniciously obnoxious children in all of mystery fiction—or so I have been told. I'm rather fond of the poor little devil myself, and I do not respond politely to readers who want me to drown him. However, by the fifth book I decided he was getting a little out of hand, so I copied a device by another writer, and introduced two children who were so awful they made Ramses look sympathetic by comparison. They also forced Amelia to reevaluate her feelings for her son. He becomes a full and active participant in his parents' adventures, supplying both comic relief and much-needed assistance in critical situations. His participation stems naturally and inevitably from his own character traits, which are the result not only of heredity but of upbringing; as he matures he will undoubtedly play a larger and quite different part. His relationship with his parents will change as well; a young adult can't (or shouldn't!) be treated like a child.

So the baby, who might have been a liability, is developing into an individual with considerable future potential. Ramses is about to enter adolescence, and I await this development with much interest.

The minor characters who populate a series are almost as important as the protagonists, and this, I think, is another way in which the New Golden Age mysteries differ from those of the first Golden Age. Instead of a single sidekick or bumbling foil from Scotland Yard, the Emersons have acquired a group of friends, enemies, and hangers-on who form a pool from which I can draw: Gargery, the cudgel-wielding butler; Kevin O'Connor, the brash young reporter; Abdullah, the loyal foreman; Evelyn, Amelia's sister-in-law; Nefret, the golden-haired beauty who has won Ramses' adolescent heart; and above all, Emerson's hated rival, the Master Criminal. The utility of a cast of supporting characters should be obvious. Like the major characters, they have changed and developed during the course of the books, and their occasional reappearances add to the reader's feeling that these are real people with decided personalities and distinctive foibles.

This is why I do not anticipate ever becoming bored with my series characters. Like real people, they change. Like real people, they are not always predictable. I have a rough idea of what is going to happen to them, but I could not emulate Agatha Christie and write the last book in the series now. I don't know what the Emersons are going to do until they do it—but when they do it, I am not really surprised. "Of course. I should have known. . . ."

From a purely practical viewpoint, there is one simple way to avoid being bored by your series characters: Don't confine yourself to a single series. Some writers can do this; I don't believe I could. The Barbara Michaels novels give me the opportunity to use plot ideas that don't fit any of the series characters, and the two other series I write as Elizabeth Peters allow me to employ themes and interests unsuited to Amelia and company.

To a lesser extent—probably because I have written less about them—Vicky and Jacqueline are also maturing and changing. Jacqueline has become a best-selling writer of romances, a development she regards with a distinctly jaundiced eye, and somewhere in her background there is a Mr. Kirby. Who is he and what happened to him? Some day I may find out.

As for Vicky, she's not getting any younger, and when I began *Night Train to Memphis,* I decided it was time for Vicky to sort out her feelings, not only for the dashing Sir John Smythe, but for her exasperating but engaging boss, Herr Direktor Schmidt. By the time I finished the book, I was a trifle surprised, and decidedly intrigued, to discover how Vicky, as well as John and Schmidt, have changed since they first appeared on the literary scene.

And that, dear Reader (to quote Amelia), is the real trick. Let your characters grow; allow them to mature and develop; put them into situations that will force them to exhibit hitherto unsuspected aspects of their personalities. The other day I was talking with a friend who inquired interestedly, "Is Vicky going to get pregnant in this book?" My reaction was instantaneous, spontaneous, and, I am afraid, typical of the generation in which I was raised. "Pregnant?" I squawked indignantly. "She isn't even married!"

I am fairly sure Vicky's reaction would be, if not identical, equally indignant. But one never knows. At least *I* never know, and that's why I like writing about my series characters.

If you don't like yours and can't make them into people whose company you enjoy, be brutal. No, not that brutal; I do not recommend killing off major characters, no matter how much you detest them. You can be sure some of your readers have become attached to them and will resent you for bumping them off. Just ignore them for a while. Shrug and smile politely when readers ask when you are going to return to Harry or Jennifer or whoever. Start another series, with characters who do appeal to you. You may find, after enough time has elapsed, that Harry and Jennifer aren't as repellent as you thought. If they still don't appeal to you, let them languish in the limbo of forgotten literary figures. The bottom line is simple: Enjoy your characters or leave them alone.

45

BEYOND GOOD AND EVIL

BY JOHN LUTZ

IT'S THE LAST CHAPTER of a mystery novel. The characters are assembled, the detective is present, the solution of the crime and identification of the criminal are at hand. The miscreant has made a fatal mistake and is about to pay for it, another example of virtue triumphing over villainy.

Though this is a hackneyed situation in mystery fiction, it still occurs, but often with a new twist that adds interest. And even if it doesn't occur as described above, in the manner of an Agatha Christie or Nero Wolfe novel, it happens in some form or another in most contemporary mysteries because it must. There should be a summing up, a catharsis and a tying of loose ends that reward the reader with a sense of closure. The reader has to know if he or she has guessed correctly. The reader longs for the mental "Aha!" as the pieces click into place, and all is known. In the better mysteries, those that are fairly clued, with endings cleverly foreshadowed, the "Aha!" is accompanied by an "Of course!"

Mysteries are popular. This is the true golden era for the reader as well as the writer. Because of the popularity and salability of mysteries, there are more good ones being published today than ever before. Also because of this immense popularity, added demands are made on the mystery author.

Mystery readers and mystery editors are always looking for books that push the envelope of formula. Sure, the basic components might be the same: scarred and tough private eye or cop such as Philip Marlowe, or superior intellectual type such as Sherlock Holmes, or genteel but steel-trap-minded elderly woman in the manner of Miss Marple. Mystery readers are familiar with the rest of the galaxy of pivotal characters that solve their fictional crimes. Along with these protagonists are the traditional cast of victims and villains, red herrings, love interests, police contacts, etc. Writers are always trying to do something original with the standard model that readers love, to twist it, remold it, get around, under, through or over it. To transcend it.

Something like this occurred when female private eyes began appearing in greater numbers in the seventies and early eighties, a development that helped to cast the mystery in the light of modern literature and in large measure explains its widespread popularity today.

The track is faster. Now more than ever originality and quality are necessary. Wooden characters, stilted dialogue and contrived situations won't do. A mystery must first be a good novel, then a good mystery.

But one aspect of the mystery novel has lagged behind the others. Much is made of character, situation, and setting, but theme is sometimes given short shrift. Theme, which in simple terms is *What a Book Means,* is not dealt with as often or as effectively as the other elements of fiction, even though it has become increasingly important. Good will triumph over evil—that seems to be the extent of the theme in some novels. (Not to suggest that it wouldn't be good enough in the real world.) That the bad guy (or gal) is brought to justice—and the case is closed—seems to be all that's required.

But it isn't enough. Not for most readers. Today's mystery readers demand and deserve something more.

Some of the best of the female mystery writers explore and provide interesting insights about the changing role of women in society, and they incorporate it in their work without seeming to preach. The best of the private eye novels provide character studies and social commentary. The detective (amateur or professional, private or law officer) is like a novelist within the novel, assessing people, evaluating their relationships with each other and with the world around them, turning over rocks to discover what's beneath them and to examine the strata of society, all to make connections, to draw conclusions, to illuminate. The mystery—especially the detective novel—is a wonderful and enduring literary device that should be used to full potential.

The modern mystery should be much more than a simple deductive puzzle; it should mean something. Today's mystery writer should be concerned, and concern the reader, with more than the basic question of whether the villain will get away with the crime. In my recent novel *Torch,* set in Florida, private investigator Fred Carver is forced to

216

contemplate (along with the reader) the institution of marriage and the nature of the elusive human quality we call character. My intent was to provide the reader with something richer and more revealing than a deductive puzzle to be solved in the last chapter. The characters in the novel are changed by the mystery; they are affected as they reach conclusions about questions posed along the way. The novel goes beyond the identification and arrest of the guilty party. It has, I hope, a larger meaning.

Of course, as with most writing techniques, this isn't as simple as it first seems. Theme can be tricky. The idea here isn't to tell the reader *about* the theme, but to present the characters and story and let them speak for themselves, so that the novel resonates as something more than a simple account of how a criminal is tripped up. The intent of most writers—and mystery writers are no exception—is to give a novel depth and meaning. The important thing to remember is that the old rule of showing rather than telling is especially important when it comes to theme.

In the mystery, as in most good fiction, the most effective tales usually stem from character. If you are writing about criminals double-crossing each other, try to make them act out of more than simple greed. Maybe the characters don't merely want more than their share of the money; maybe they *need* it for some private and crucial reason. Or perhaps it is competition for a love interest that also motivates them, or a yearning for political power, or an inherent distrust in them that is the result of something in their backgrounds. And they should have backgrounds, not presented in a page-and-a-half of personal history that reads like a resumé, but subtly woven into the fabric of the novel. They shouldn't do things merely because the author has designated them as the bad guys.

The basic elements of fiction are character, situation, setting, and theme. Character is the most important element, and the most useful in establishing theme. There are exceptions to this, as in stories in which people are battling hostile environments, but even in this sort of fiction, it's wise to emphasize character rather than the other elements. Character—people—is what most good fiction is about. So if your criminals double-cross each other for political power, this affords you the opportunity to highlight as your theme the corruption of such power and how it has affected your characters. If romance is the motivation, we all know the multitude of possible themes available. Even if simple material greed is the motivation, there is much to be said about its ramifications. Possibly this greed illustrates something about the corrosive lure of gold or diamonds, or the pull and destructive force of dealing in illegal drugs for profit.

Even the master of the deductive puzzle, Sir Arthur Conan Doyle, employed theme to engage the reader. Often it was Holmes's patriotism that prompted him to take a case and see it through to completion.

In "The Naval Treaty," Holmes works on a case that has international ramifications. And even when his cases are more limited in scope, they are lifted out of the ordinary and lent a grander meaning by the unnatural and encompassing evil of his arch enemy Professor Moriarty. As Holmes declares of Moriarty in "The Final Problem":

He is the Napoleon of crime, Watson. He is the organizer of half that is evil and of nearly all that is undetected in this great city.

The theme here is not merely good versus evil, but good versus evil on an almost mythic scale. This is a difficult plateau to reach, made easier for Doyle by the fact that his detective Holmes was of mythical proportions when the story was written.

If setting is important in your story, as in a tale of shipwreck survivors together in a lifeboat, or a camper trapped by the elements, or plane wreck survivors making their way through jungle or desert back to civilization, how your characters respond to the test of their courage and endurance, as well as to each other and whatever potential for gain is involved, offers plenty of opportunity for good mysteries and meaningful themes. The saga of people rising to physical challenge has always made for good fiction and always will.

Situation can also lead to the expression of theme. Love triangles, moral dilemmas, traumatic emotional events, torturous mental states, all potentially lead to theme and can be occurring as the main character and the reader puzzle out the mystery.

Dashiell Hammett's Sam Spade and Raymond Chandler's Philip Marlowe are quintessential American loners, solitary operators guided by their own moral codes that often get them into conflict even as they solve their cases. And their apartness lends them a certain objectivity useful in presenting theme. The novels in which they appear are as much social observation and moral commentary as they are about criminals brought to justice. In *The Maltese Falcon,* Spade tries to get Brigid O'Shaughnessy to understand his actions:

Listen. When a man's partner is killed he's supposed to do something about it. It doesn't make any difference what you thought of him. He was your partner, and you're supposed to do something about it.

In the same novel, Spade comments:

"The cheaper the crook, the gaudier the patter."

In the first of these two brief passages, Spade's personal code and motivation are clearly spelled out, which makes the novel something more than a simple account of an investigator's case and provides it with a moral base and a theme. In the second, the reader gets a succinct commentary on the people in Spade's world, and learns of his distance and objectivity even though he moves in that world.

Character. That's what theme preferably should be about, even when utilizing the other elements of situation and setting. And if you think about theme as you compose, usually there will be an opportune and appropriate time to illustrate it.

In the aforementioned *Torch,* the investigator Carver expresses the rewards and desirability of doggedness and fidelity quite directly, as he muses over the actions of his lover Beth Jackson while they sit and watch the ocean:

Carver glanced over at her impassive dark features. She amazed him sometimes by being even more uncompromising than he was. But then she'd survived by not compromising about certain things, by keeping a part of herself whole at the center of the damage.

It was surprising how often uncompromising people, if they were discriminative in their choice of battle, were ultimately proved right.

It was called character.

We were here and then gone in this world, and character was the thing that made a difference, that made it all mean something.

There is the theme. The introspection occurs near the end of the novel and, I hope, sums up what the novel is about. And what it is about is something more than a determined investigator who overcomes odds to solve a case and bring a criminal to justice.

219

There will always be room for the basic deductive puzzle mystery if it is clever and intriguing enough. But with so many mysteries to choose from, readers are becoming increasingly sophisticated and demanding.

As mystery writers, we'd be wise to remember we are constantly challenged to stay a step ahead of them.

The game's afoot.

46

Writing Literary Science Fiction

By Elizabeth Hand

Mention the notion of "literary" science fiction to most people, and they'll think you're crazy. At the least, they'll think the term's an oxymoron. After all, science fiction is for kids and Trekkies, simplistic laser-gun rocket-ship stuff, with a few contemporary trappings—cyberspace, genetic engineering—thrown into the primordial soup. Right?

Wrong. Sure, a glance at the bestseller list on any given week will turn up the usual glob of TV and movie novelizations, but a closer look at the pages of *Locus* and *Science Fiction Chronicle*—two trade magazines for writers of science fiction and fantasy—shows that there are a number of writers with more on their minds than getting the crew of the *Enterprise* from Planet A to Galaxy Z.

Since the heyday of the space opera as practiced by the likes of Robert Heinlein and Isaac Asimov, a whole new generation of writers has come of age, people who grew up reading not just *Starship Troopers,* but novels like Thomas Pynchon's *Gravity's Rainbow,* and their literary style is as likely to have been influenced by the Lost Generation as by the TV show, "Lost in Space."

What exactly *is* literary science fiction? Well, it's hard to categorize, for one. Robert Silverberg coined the term "neuromantics" to describe those writers who bore the influence of William Gibson's hard-edged novel *Neuromancer* behind their mirror shades, and Robert Irwin came up with "cyberbyzantinism" to describe my own work. But books of this ilk—and there are many, ranging from the superbly baroque, multi-volume epics of science fiction writers Gene Wolfe and Paul Park, to the late Angela Carter's sublime forays into the genre—can be distinguished by a few common features.

First, these literary science fiction authors share a love of—almost an obsession with—*language*. Not the ersatz "futuristic" language of so many bad sci-fi movies, but *real* language, the language of Shake-

221

speare and Conrad and Blake. Here is a descriptive passage from Gene Wolfe's *The Shadow of the Torturer,* the first volume of *The Book of the New Sun.*

> The space about it had been a garden in summer, but not such a one as our necropolis, with half-wild trees and rolling, meadowed lawns. Roses had blossomed here in kraters set upon a tessellated pavement. Statues of beasts stood with their backs to the four walls of the court: hulking barylambdas; arctothers, the monarchs of bears; glyptodons; smilodons with fangs like glaives. All were dusted now with snow. I looked for Triskele's tracks, but he had not come here.

In fewer than a half-dozen sentences, Wolfe has cast a spell. He has drawn an entire world for us—an archaic, dreamy and somewhat ominous place, removed from yet somehow akin to our own world. And he has done this in a very clever way, buy substituting archaic or uncommon terms for their more mundane counterparts—*krater, necropolis, monarch* instead of vase, graveyard, king. For his stone menagerie, he has resurrected extinct mammals such as the *glyptodon* and *smilodon,* and created a portmanteau word in *barylambda,* which derives from the Greek *barus,* for heavy, and *lambda,* a letter of the Greek alphabet but also a type of moth. In his book, horses are called *destriers,* and members of the guild of torturers are *lictors.* The beauty of such words lies not only in their strangeness, and thus their ability to summon up a strange world, but in their *rhythm*—another indispensable part of stylish writing. Witness one of Wolfe's ethereal sentences, brought down to earth by the substitution of everyday language—

> Flowers bloomed in vases on the checkered sidewalk.

Not quite the same, is it? But this sort of magic is available to anyone; I have used it in my own books, and so have many other writers. A few tools are necessary, chief among them a fascination with words and a sense of play. You'll also need a good dictionary—and by this I don't mean a pocket-sized American dictionary, but a *real* dictionary, *the* real dictionary, the one no writer should be without: the *Oxford English Dictionary,* called *OED.* The *OED* is expensive, but is available in a good public or college library. In addition to being an absolutely wonderful source of unusual words and phrases—words like *famulus, roborant, cordelier*—it comes in very handy for Scrabble.

That's one easy-to-find tool; what about another? Well, this is an obvious one, but a good thesaurus should be on every writer's desk. Roget's is the standard, and *Roget's 21st Century Thesaurus* is now available, but I prefer an old 1930s vintage Roget's I found at a tag sale years ago. It has marvelous listings of bizarre phrases and words not found in more up-to-date volumes, including a fascinating rundown of various methods of divination, including *Crithomancy* (by the dough of cakes) and *Geloscopy* (by the mode of laughing).

Now, lest you think some of these things seem too archaic for science fiction, I read just this week of a contemporary society where funeral effigies of the dead are made of sugar and devoured by the bereaved. And that brings us to another aspect of style, one that has particular bearing upon sf writing—namely, the creation of a new yet somehow believable world or culture that differs in some significant manner from our own. This can be done by fairly straightforward means, as in *1984,* which posits a totalitarian future England; or it can be done more subtly, as in Philip K. Dick's novel, *The Man in the High Castle,* which takes place in an invented world in which the Japanese won WWII. Until fairly recently, most science fiction didn't venture too far from this sort of thing—invented worlds that would not stretch the imagination of someone still living in the 1950s, when rocket ships were still *ne plus ultra,* and people had not yet grown disenchanted with the promises of Big Science.

But in the last ten or fifteen years, science fiction has moved beyond the fifties, with its emphasis on war games and stories for boys. As the global village has expanded the parameters of music, film, and the fine arts, so it has stretched the imaginations of science fiction writers.

Just as a few artful sentences told us quite a bit about Gene Wolfe's Urth, so the following selection from Paul Park's novel, *Soldiers of Paradise,* gives us a number of clues about *this* world—without bludgeoning us with hard facts:

"Watch that," cried the landlady, a middle-aged slattern with painted lips and cheeks, and teeth stained blue from kaya gum. "That's all I need. That's murder on the premises, even if it's only tenth degree." She leaned over the stove to peer doubtfully at the furry, purselike body.

"Nothing to be afraid of," said Mock. "What's one more dead rat?"

"You can't be too careful," muttered the landlady . . . "All those rats are numbered."

223

Here the slum-ridden city of Charn created by Park owes much to the cities of present-day India, where Park has traveled extensively. The landlady with her blue-stained teeth is the sf counterpart of any number of Hindi women, spitting red juice from chewing betel leaves; the crime of murdering a rat mirrors the Hindu proscription against taking a life—even an animal's life. In his three-volume *Starbridge Chronicles,* Park deftly weaves Indian folklore, religion, and culture into a startlingly beautiful, and compellingly strange, evocation of interstellar life. For most of us, the streets of Calcutta would be as bizarre as those of Aldebaran. Yet the subtle connections between Charn and a world recognizably our own give the Starbridge books an exotically contemporary flavor not found in more mainstream science fiction works. Learning about an environmental or cultural milieu other than one's own—be it the barrio, the Amazon, the world of teenage hackers or Carmelite nuns—can infuse an otherwise drab world with the aura of the marvelous. It's also a good way to avoid the sort of literary xenophobia that has afflicted too many genre writers afraid to peer beyond television's "Deep Space Nine," or Dungeons & Dragons-style *faux*-medievalism.

Point of view is another means by which you can jolt your fiction out of the every day. Here's an example from Pat Murphy's Nebula Award-winning story, "Rachel in Love":

> She thinks that perhaps she made a mistake. Perhaps her father is just sleeping. She returns to the bedroom, but nothing has changed. Her father lies open-eyed on the bed. For a long time, she huddles beside his body, clinging to his hand.
>
> He is the only person she has ever known. He is her father, her teacher, her friend. She cannot leave him alone . . .
>
> Outside, somewhere in the barren land surrounding the ranch house, a coyote lifts its head to the rising moon and wails, a thin sound that is as lonely as a train whistling through an abandoned station. Rachel joins in with a desolate howl of loneliness and grief. Aaron lies still and Rachel knows that he is dead.

This is a heartbreaking depiction of the pangs of loss and desire that come with first love, but the protagonist, Rachel, is not a human girl but a sentient chimpanzee. Murphy's prose style is simple and elegant, its realistic atmosphere a far cry from the sinister decadence of Urth or Charn. Yet, Murphy's use of an unexpected point of view gives her tale depth and poignancy. John Crowley's classic novel, *Engine Sum-*

224

mer, does the same thing in a very different manner, using as narrator a young man known as Rush That Speaks. I won't spoil the novel by revealing the ending; suffice it to say that the narrator is not quite who—or what—he appears to be.

So we see that the tools used to create a more "literary," stylish, science fiction, are not all that different from those used in writing any kind of prose. But as in fashion, so in fiction—it's not *what* you wear or write, but the flair and panache with which you do it. Next time you set words to paper in your science fiction, turn up your nose at the literary equivalent of fast food—the standard sf burger-and-fries, the tired old clichés about aliens and space travel and traditional gender roles. Instead, opt for something new and strange, be it a world drawn from Balinesian dance instead of the ballet, or a baby-toting cybernetic heroine whose role model is *Dr.* Spock, instead of Mr. Spock. Your readers will thank you; and *you'll* enjoy this sort of gourmet writing more than that other greasy kid stuff.

47

Off to See the Wizards

By Fraser Sherman

Fantasy fiction deals with the impossible. In most fantasy fiction, the impossible takes the form of magic—ghosts, wizards, genies. In other fantasy stories, there are no magicians or spells; things simply happen that defy reality (a lot of *Twilight Zone* stories fit this category).

Fantasy can be cheap and crude or literary and pensive: Subgenres include urban fantasy (magic in modern cities); imaginary world fantasy (the author makes up his own setting); epic fantasy (on the sweeping scale of a Cecil B. DeMille film); and fantasy romance (romances in which one lover is a witch, elf, etc.). These aren't firm boundaries: Some stories fit more than one genre, and many don't fit any.

How do you get started?

If you think fantasy sounds interesting, start by reading fantasy fiction written in different styles, by different writers, old classics, and current bestsellers. If epic fantasy intrigues you, start with *the* classic, J. R. R. Tolkien's *The Lord of the Rings* trilogy, in which Frodo Baggins and his friends save the world of Middle-Earth from the dark lord, Sauron. Then go on to other epic writers—Stephen Donaldson, Raymond Feist, Melanie Rawn—and study their variations on the subgenre.

If epics don't appeal to you, try another subgenre; when you find one you like, start thinking of ideas. Coming up with a novel twist on the books you enjoy is one way to jump-start your imagination. Fifteen years ago, I noticed that none of the novels about King Arthur dealt with the legend he would someday return to Britain, so I wrote a book in which the legend comes true. It never sold, but it got me started writing.

Keeping magic under control

Many short stories fit into the "impossible" style of fantasy, like Walter Tevis's "Rent Control," in which a couple discovers their love can stop time. No one calls it magic, no one explains it; it simply happens. Most fantasy novels focus on more overt, "real" magic, which presents problems writers won't find in any other genre, because when you break the laws of nature—as magic does—where do you draw the line? A story in which magic can do literally anything would be unworkable—but how do you set limits on the impossible?

To start with, decide what the magic in your story can do: control the weather? control peoples' minds? summon demons? turn water to wine? And what does it take to make it work: a snap of the fingers? spoken spells? human sacrifice? Does it draw on a power source that can run dry? Can anyone work magic, or only wizards who've studied it for years?

Finally, what is it magic can't do? Is the only limit the witch's power ("Teleporting us such a distance is beyond even my sorcery!"), or are there more specific restraints? In Jack Vance's *Dying Earth* stories, wizards wield spells so powerful, even the mightiest magicians can't retain more than two or three in their minds at a time. When they use those up, they're powerless until they memorize more.

If you can't answer these questions yet, get started on your story anyway, and see what sort of magic the plot requires. Once you know that, rewrite until it looks as if you had the magic thought out from the very beginning. Whether you derive your rules before you start writing or not, you have to honor them; to make readers believe the impossible, the impossible has to be consistent.

So do people. Given a goal, characters should use all their abilities to strive for it; having them act stupidly simply because your plot calls for it is cheating. Once you establish that your magician can fly, you can't have her trapped on the edge of a cliff without explaining why she can't fly off. Was she exhausted from her previous spell-casting? Were there gale-force winds overhead? Did a stronger wizard cancel her spell?

The more powerful the wizard, the tougher this gets; if a wizard has power enough to destroy his enemies before Chapter One is over, how do you stop him? Particularly if he's one of the good guys—powerful evil wizards can unbalance a plot, too, but at least having the heroes outmatched looks interesting; having the villains overwhelmed never does.

Here are some ways to rein in magic:

227

• There are no strong wizards. If all magic can do is light a candle or clean the laundry, it won't upset your story much.

• Magic works only under specific circumstances. If wizards can cast spells only through their Wands of Power, smashing the wand makes them powerless.

• A magic talisman—a ring, a sacred necklace, an ancient sword—neutralizes magic; as long as a character possesses it, he's safe from enemy magic.

• The magician has a weakness. *The Lord of the Rings* hinges on Sauron's having placed most of his power in the Magic One Ring; when Frodo destroys the ring, Sauron can't survive.

• The magician has personal reasons for holding off: He wants to destroy his hated enemy face-to-face, or to wait until they've unearthed the lost treasure he seeks. (In Disney's *Aladdin,* the hero is used for just such a purpose.)

Robert E. Howard does a fine job limiting magic in his Conan the Barbarian story, "The People of the Black Circle." The story opens with the evil Black Seers casting a death-spell on an enemy king: When they face Conan, readers might expect them to kill him as easily, but the Seers make it clear death-spells are anything but easy:

> Even the arts you call sorcery are governed by cosmic laws; not until the heavens were in the proper order could they perform the necromancy. [By a stolen lock of hair] a soul is drawn from its body and across gulfs of echoing space.

Reading this, we see that the Seers can't just strike Conan dead; when they use poisoned mists, spiders, and landslides against him instead, we know it's not solely because the author's going easy on his hero.

Don't be too obvious about using limits to make the plot work; it's one thing to be manipulative, another to be obviously manipulative. And again, be consistent: You can't have a wizard exceed the limits you've set, simply because the plot needs him to. (For more on making magic work, I highly recommend Orson Scott Card's *How to Write Science Fiction and Fantasy.*)

Background: make it real

To make the impossible parts of a fantasy credible, the rest of the story has to drip with realism. If you set a story in medieval France, you'll need to know how people back then lived, ate, traveled, fought. If your story involves witches manipulating the stock market, learn how the stock market normally works and what real stockbrokers are like.

Even in imaginary worlds, realism matters. Jungles don't spring up next to deserts. Cities develop because they're in strategic sites or on trade routes, not because you threw a dart at a map. The people in those cities will have religions, governments, jobs, and sports to keep them busy. Detail will make your invented world more believable. If it seems like a lot of work, "steal" a culture from our world as a starting point. Many good fantasies have used medieval Europe, ancient China, or Arabia, changed the names and some details, and created fine imaginary worlds.

Such worlds should have a consistent tone: Avoid modern elements that strike a false note, like football games, power lunches, or match boxes. If you must use them, at least change the names ("We call this game ram, since the two teams are always ramming each other."). Lin Carter's out-of-print *Imaginary Worlds* covers tone, creating credible cultures, and fleshing out fantasy with realistic details; it's worth scrounging around to find a copy.

Filling the reader in

Now you've worked out the rules of magic and the ways of your imaginary world. You've decided demons fear moonlight, and that the emperor is an ineffective, ceremonial monarch. How do you explain all that to the reader?

Keep in mind you don't have to explain everything. A reader picking up a fantasy knows it's about magic. Stories of knights, witches, dragons, and unicorns are familiar enough not to need explanation, at least in a medieval setting. (If the unicorn's running loose in Times Square, readers will have questions.)

If you write something stronger and more exotic, use more exposition; as in other genres, it can be done in dialogue, if you make it believable. A master wizard might explain the rules of magic to his apprentice, but not to another master wizard who already knows them. Nor would two courtiers lecture each other on court politics they're both familiar with. In fact, avoid lectures altogether; both the information and the dialogue need to be interesting.

229

Alternatively, forget dialogue and tell readers the rules straight out. Don't do this in the first paragraph; first get the readers hooked, then introduce information when appropriate. You can do this in various viewpoints: first-person ("I haven't trusted witches since they overthrew our king."); omniscient ("Five years ago, the Coven of Silence overthrew King Agarri."); or limited omniscient ("Raven tensed; it was said witches could smell people still loyal to the king.").

Characterization: the hero problem

Fantasy fiction has its own version of cardboard characters: heroes whose exploits emphasize their magic swords, their powerful spells, and their brawny muscles, not their inner selves. That's a mistake; if a hero's worth reading about only because of his muscles and magic, he's not worth reading about at all.

Conan, often derided as a stick figure, triumphs not merely because of his strength, but because of his courage and grit; it's not his muscles that save the day, but his stubborn refusal to surrender. In *The Lord of the Rings,* Frodo Baggins is an ordinary soul, far outclassed by the power of his companions; this makes him all the more heroic when he struggles on against all odds to destroy the One Ring. If your heroes had no special powers, would they be as interesting?

Fantasy heroes can be afraid or flawed; they might prefer staying home with a good book to saving the world. But when the moment comes, if they're worth being heroes, they'll face overwhelming odds, conquer their fears, and shout "No!"

And if they can do that, and if the rest of your world looks real— you've written a heck of a fantasy.

230

$\underset{\text{\tiny §}}{}48$

FROM GUMSHOE TO GAMMA RAYS: HIGH-TECH ADVANCES IN CRIMINAL INVESTIGATION

BY ROBERT L. SNOW

NOT LONG AGO in Indianapolis, we solved a four-year-old murder that we had previously believed would go unsolved. The victim had been bound and then strangled with an electric cord ripped from a lamp. Although at first we thought we might get lucky when an evidence technician lifted a partial fingerprint from the lamp, the fingerprint, it turned out, didn't match anyone connected with the case or acquainted with the victim, so the case stalled for four years.

The incident that broke the case came about because Indianapolis, like most major cities, has recently installed an Automated Fingerprint Identification System (AFIS). This very expensive computer compares fingerprints fed into it with the millions that can be stored in its memory. In setting up the system, the technicians needed to do a number of test runs, and they decided to use the fingerprint from this murder during one of the tests. Within a half hour, the computer gave us a suspect, a young street hustler who, when confronted by detectives, confessed to the murder and named his accomplice.

This incident started me thinking about all of the technological advances that have been introduced into law enforcement during just the last five or six years, and how important they can be to writers. Although police work in the 1990s still involves bringing the bad guys to justice, how the police do this has changed, and writers of mysteries, police procedurals, or those who simply include the police in a novel or short story must know about these changes because if they don't, somewhere a reader will spot the mistakes and omissions and point them out!

With the introduction of AFIS, fingerprints have increased dramatically in importance in solving crimes, particularly in cases where there are no suspects. Before AFIS, if there were no specific suspects, there was really no practical way to search through the fingerprint file of a large city like Indianapolis, which has 4,000,000 individual fingerprints on file; any fingerprints recovered in a major case that didn't match the suspect's were kept in an open file, and only as time was available were they *manually* compared against the fingerprints taken from newly arrested people. Occasionally, we would be lucky and hit a match. Now, however, a fingerprint recovered at the scene of a crime can be inserted into the AFIS computer, and its recognition points compared at enormous speed with the millions of prints already in the computer's memory.

The actual collection of fingerprints has also gone high-tech in the last five or six years, and writers need to be aware of these changes. The traditional method for collecting fingerprints involves brushing fingerprint powder onto smooth surfaces. But on many surfaces fingerprints are not visible, and in many cases—particularly when large areas are involved—the traditional method is not only messy but often impractical.

Thanks to recent developments in light technology, however, the detection of these fingerprints is now much easier. Scientists have found that the amino acids and other compounds in fingerprint residue will fluoresce under certain lighting conditions. Because of this discovery, police officers are now able to detect previously invisible fingerprints by using such devices as a Laser Print Finder, a pulsating laser beam, and Luma-Lite, a high-intensity light source. The beam of these light sources causes the amino acids and other compounds to produce glowing fingerprints that can be seen by wearing special goggles.

Finding the fingerprint is only half of the job. It must then be recovered, and rather than going high-tech, police use a simple substance to do this: the chemical cyanoacrylate, which is the main ingredient in Super Glue. Objects with fingerprints are placed in a closed container with cyanoacrylate that is either heated or simply allowed to vaporize naturally. The chemical vapors stick to the fingerprint residue and then harden.

Several years ago in California, the police recovered a vehicle believed driven by the infamous "Nightstalker." A structure was built around the car and filled with cyanoacrylate vapor. A print recovered from the car was sent to the AFIS computer in Sacramento, where a match was made, and the "Nightstalker" arrested.

In addition to fingerprints, there is another personal identifier that suspects often leave behind at the scene of a crime: samples of their DNA in the form of blood, saliva, semen, or other bodily fluids. Contained in most human cells, DNA is the blueprint for a person's body, and it is now accepted as an identifier by a number of courts. While still in its infancy, DNA testing will become extremely important to the police departments of the future. Unfortunately, however, there is currently no AFIS computer for DNA, as there is for fingerprints, and so a suspect must be available in order for a match to be made. In a number of celebrated cases, however, DNA analysis has been used to free suspects rather than convict them, since it can prove that the semen, blood, or other substance left at a crime scene was not theirs.

Many times, there are no fingerprints, DNA, or live witnesses at a crime scene, but again, science has filled the gap. The police are now able to do "criminal profiling" from the evidence left at a crime scene, from the type of crime it was, and from how the crime was committed. This profiling will often suggest the perpetrator's age, sex, race, educational level, and other attributes, even though there were no witnesses.

Several years ago in Indianapolis, a woman was kidnapped from a shopping center, raped and murdered, and then left in the trunk of her car. Even though there were no witnesses to the crime, through criminal profiling we were able to develop a clear enough picture of the perpetrator to identify a likely suspect, who was arrested and later convicted of the crime.

Since the apprehension of criminals can quite often be dangerous, as in the murder case above, safety devices for officers have also gone high-tech. For example, while body armor has been around for many years, until recently it was so bulky and hot—and so obvious—that many officers decided just to take their chances. Within the last few years, however, body armor for police has become thinner, lighter, cooler, and much less obvious, and now in many high-crime areas almost all officers wear it.

Science has also improved on the old standard nightstick or billy club. Police officers today are much more likely to be carrying a PR-24, or side-handled baton, which can be used, in martial arts fashion, much more effectively than the old nightstick. And liquid tear gas has

233

been replaced by a new chemical that is much more potent and effective, disorienting a person as well as irritating the eyes and nasal passages. One form of spray now offered even uses the chemical found in red peppers.

Along with saving lives, however, saving time has also become high-tech, and computers are now firmly established in law enforcement. They are everywhere, from Computer-Aided Dispatching to in-car terminals, from in-car navigational systems to computer mug shot terminals that can age, remove hair, grow beards, add moustaches, etc. And of course, many police departments now routinely computerize their records.

Writers also need to know that in the last five or six years video cameras have become standard law enforcement equipment. Crime scenes are now routinely videotaped, as are suspect line-ups and confessions. A number of police departments are also installing video cameras in police cars to record everything the officer sees and hears through the windshield. These are, of course, of immeasurable help in convicting anyone committing a crime that's visible through the windshield, and they have actually recorded the murder of police officers by the occupants of stopped vehicles.

The above examples are only a few of the dozens of recent innovations in law enforcement technology that writers need to be aware of if they want their work to be authentic. There are many more, including laser-sighted weapons, night-vision goggles, Tasers (electric stun guns), multi-channel walkie-talkies with scrambling capability, signalling devices that allow the police to track stolen cars, robots for high-risk entry, quick and accurate kits for field testing drugs (police officers NEVER, NEVER test drugs by tasting them!), and many more high-tech advances.

There are several ways for a writer to learn about these high-tech advances: reading police journals such as *Law and Order* (1000 Skokie Boulevard, Wilmette, IL 60091); *Police* (6300 Yarrow Drive, Carlsbad, CA 92009); or *Law Enforcement Technology* (445 Broad Hollow Road, Melville, NY 11747). If these are not available in your local or community library, try the library at a university that has a Criminal Justice program. You might also try inviting a police officer to your writers club meeting; most police departments will send an officer to groups that request them, and they are usually glad to discuss the details of their work and investigation procedures.

Still another way for writers to get a firsthand view of police work in action: Most large police departments have ride-along programs for citizens who want to see police work up close. Be prepared, however, for salty talk, filthy homes, and bloody situations, which are all part of police work. And if, as occasionally happens, you ride on a slow night when nothing is happening, don't be discouraged; this will give you eight uninterrupted hours to pick the officer's brain.

I suspect that some writers, particularly those without a firm grounding in the sciences, will be discouraged by all of this new police technology because they don't believe they'll be able to understand it. Don't be. Your viewpoint character doesn't have to have the in-depth knowledge of a scientist, but if you want your work to ring of authenticity *you* must know at least as much as the police do.

49

"Rules" for the Classic Whodunit

By Herbert Resnicow

Mystery novelist P. D. James once said that when she decided to become a writer, she chose mysteries as her field because mystery fiction is the most difficult to write, and if she could write mysteries well, she could write anything.

The classic, fair-play whodunit, the puzzle mystery, is the most demanding sub-genre of this most formidable genre, and is the hardest to write. The essence of the whodunit is that a puzzle is central to the plot. Puzzles are made to be solved; a puzzle has a unique solution available to anyone who can arrange its elements in the right pattern so that the solution is inevitable. Problems, on the other hand, are not easily or satisfactorily solved, and are often not solvable. All people have problems involving work, money, health, family, religion, personal relationships, etc. In life as well as in fiction, some problems are solved by murder; problems provide the motive for the murder in whodunits.

The classic whodunit is a complex and fascinating word game and, like all games, it is defined by its rules. There is a competition implicit in all whodunits. Ostensibly a duel to the death between the murderer and the detective, the whodunit is truly a contest between the reader and the author. In any game played between a professional (the author) and an amateur (the reader), the rules should favor the amateur.

The reader has only two rules to obey: Don't look at the end first—this is giving up without a fight—and don't tell anyone else whodunit. The rules for you, as the author, are far more stringent, and there are many more of them.

1) You are writing a story, so your first consideration is to write a good story, one that is interesting, believable, and entertaining. The writing should exhibit charm, wit, and humor, and there should be no *gratuitous* sex, violence, horror, or nausea. Like any good workman, you must be skilled in the use of the tools of the trade. The story

should be tight, no longer than it has to be, with neither puffing nor filler visible. Your characters should be well-rounded, with the personality and temperament of the characters revealed in their words and actions and not defined solely by what they own. Foreign accents should not be transliterated, but indicated by rhythm, vocabulary, and word order. Provide names for characters that are easily distinguishable, no two beginning with the same combination of letters nor rhyming with other names in the story. In short, write well.

2) The crime must be murder, the worst crime of all, and the killer's motive must be strong enough to induce an amateur to commit murder. The victim, the killer, and all the suspects should be people who are important to the plot as individuals. All the suspects must be real suspects, and the killer must be one of the suspects; don't bring in a new face just before the final chapters. The murder should be premeditated or, if it's a crime of passion or an unintended killing, it should be ingeniously covered up. The killer should be an intelligent, competent amateur; the crime elegantly planned and executed, a "perfect crime," which, but for the brilliant detective, would go unsolved. A solution is possible not because the killer made a mistake, but because a perfect crime by an interested party—random killings are excluded—is necessarily of such complexity that, when the clues are fitted together in the proper pattern, the solution becomes clear and the murderer known.

3) Clues should be clearly presented, preferably more than once. All information given to the detective must be given to the reader. The detective should not be superhuman; his actions must be reasonable and possible. The clues should permit two lines of reasoning: inductive, applying a general rule to a specific situation, and deductive, putting together bits of data to make a coherent pattern. Never use rare drugs, animals, bacteria, weapons, or complex technology. Roles must be clearly defined and consistent; the detective is not the murderer. Information given to readers must be accurate; do your research. Red herrings are out, as are gratuitous suspicious actions by suspects who know they are being watched. There must be no clumsy withholding of information by witnesses, though lying is permissible if there is a good reason for it. Above all, the story must be internally consistent and, where it meets the real world, externally accurate.

4) There cannot be any subhuman foolishness, such as not phoning

the police when suspicious characters lurk about, or having the heroine meet the killer at midnight on a deserted pier. Don't use old-fashioned techniques, such as addressing the reader, or step out of the story frame with pre-knowledge such as "had I but known" or "that was the last time I was to see him alive." The detective may be bigger, stronger, and smarter than most people, and it's fun if he's unusual, even picaresque, but he must not be superhuman. Let him be capable of making mistakes and wrong decisions, of being outwitted and outmuscled, of having human feelings and problems. Don't depend on luck or coincidence to help the detective, nor let him overhear a whispered conversation by the killer or find a letter of confession in the next-to-the-last chapter. Guesswork is *out*.

5) The lead characters should grow and change as a result of the murder. You're writing a story, not just presenting a puzzle, so provide at least one *intrinsic* subplot involving the major characters and the innocent suspects. If you begin with an exciting action scene, you will need at least one flashback, but keep the number and length of flashbacks to a minimum to avoid slowing down the story. A linear story, preferably occurring over a short period, helps the reader keep the story line straight.

6) Don't overdescribe. If the color of the heroine's hair is not a factor in the story, don't mention it; let the reader's imagination take over. Where possible, use the kind of locale that a reader is probably familiar with, so you don't have to spend time describing the Devonshire meadows in detail. If your story requires an esoteric setting, show the differences between that setting and Main Street succinctly, by action within story, rather than by pages of description. Choose a profession for the detective that allows him to spend his time, money, and energy on the case; if he's a cop or a D.A., he's restricted by law in many ways. Don't spend time describing the detective's drinking, smoking, drug use, etc., except as it reveals character or mood, and do it only as needed. Avoid "lower depths" locales and characters and such clichés as the hoodlum-philosopher or the prostitute with a heart of gold.

7) Don't treat the police and D.A.'s as idiots; they are not. If they had the freedom the fictional detective has, there'd be a lot less ramp-

ant crime. Have the authorities give the detective reasonable cooperation, but not to the extent of risking their jobs. If they have information
the detective needs, find a practical way for him to get it.

8) Don't make the victim an angel or the killer demented or thoroughly evil. The killer should be an amateur who has not killed before
and doesn't plan to kill again. No serial killers, psychopaths, or random
killings are allowed in the classic whodunit, nor are professional killers,
gangsters, terrorists, or government organizations. The method of
murder and cover-up should be practical and workable and not dependent on plans working out perfectly. The killer's gain should be propor-
tionate to the money, time, effort, and risk he spent committing the
murder and commensurate with what he could lose by using any other
method of solving the problem.

9) Be realistic. A killer won't collapse or confess when faced with a
minor discrepancy in his statements. The murderer should, as most
people would, deny everything and fight against the accusation until
he is faced with an even less palatable alternative and/or is offered an
amelioration of his punishment coupled with a case good enough to
warrant an indictment. All his actions should be compatible with those
of someone capable of plotting a perfect murder.

10) The *whydunit* is an intrinsic part of the whodunit, but a *howdunit*—an impossible crime or a locked room puzzle—adds another
dimension to the story; the pleasure of greater complexity and a puzzle
within a puzzle. However, the howdunit should not be added gratui-
tously; it must be the natural outcome of the situation and the characters, and the most efficient way to accomplish the killer's ends. Above
all, don't show the gears.

11) There is an ethic implicit in a whodunit. Just as the author must
be honest and play fair with his readers, so must the story uphold the
generally agreed-on moral system (the Ten Commandments). The story
must be moral in that BAD is punished, GOOD is rewarded, and the
universe is restored to harmony and balance. The murderer must be
caught and made to pay the appropriate penalty under the law.

12) The solution must be satisfyingly complete, leaving no unan-
swered questions or loose ends. There must never be any use of supernatural, or even highly improbable, influences.

13) In first-person narration, *all* the thoughts and actions of the narrator that reflect on the puzzle in any way must be presented to the reader clearly and unequivocally. This makes it almost essential to use a Watson, preferably one who is intelligent and whose skills and talents complement the brilliant detective's. It also adds to the fun if the Watson has reason to be in some ways critical of the detective.

14) If long-distance murder is used—such as planting a bomb on an airplane, or shooting from a mile away—it brings in so many possibilities that the puzzle is greatly diluted and the number of suspects greatly increased. The method of murder in a classic whodunit should require the killer to be near the victim, and to use ordinary, easily available methods of murder—stabbing, strangling, clubbing, injecting poison, etc.

15) It is highly desirable to have the murder committed or discovered early in the story, so the puzzle is whodunit, not when-will-the-author-get-down-to-business. It also adds to the suspense if there is a deadline for the detective to struggle against; something undesirable that will happen to him or his associates if the killer is not found by a certain time. It also helps if every chapter ends with a cliffhanger, a page-turner, a bit of bad news, or the anticipation of certain disaster.

If it takes only ten rules to get into heaven, why should it require more than that to write a classic whodunit? Elementary: It's harder to write a good whodunit than to get into heaven. Actually, there can be no *rules,* as such, for writing a whodunit (or any other kind of story) well; these are rules for writing badly, reversed. As an experiment, try writing a tightly plotted, fair-play whodunit breaking several of the rules. It will be easy, and it will be bad. A further tip: Don't start to write a whodunit with the rules posted on the wall in front of you; mechanical writing does not charm. Before you write, read the rules over a few times, internalize them, and put them away. Write as well as you can. When you're finished, put the manuscript away for a week. Reread it with the rules in front of you. Blue-pencil every instance in which you broke a rule, then rewrite. And reread. And rewrite. And rewrite. And rewrite. No one promised you it would be easy. But the game is worth the candle.

§ 50

RESILIENT WESTERN WRITING

BY JACK CURTIS

IN A WORLD OF PUSH-BUTTON electronic entertainment, the traditional genre publishers face a rapidly shrinking market that will send them like Conestoga wagons into the museums unless they can find new, resilient vitality.

Clearly, the Western must keep changing to hold its readership, and because my publishers, Pocket Books, encourage original Western writing, I can concentrate on creating three-dimensional novels of the West. I am able to examine contemporary problems such as political show biz, corruption in high places, law officers overriding constitutional rights, science-business versus humanism—all vital issues for this generation of readers—within the context of the Old West.

In my Sam Benbow mystery-western series and other western novels, I start by looking for an especially villainous character in an especially villainous situation. In *Wild River Massacre,* he is a politically motivated general preparing to make capital from the slaughter of Cheyennes (based upon Custer's massacring men, women, children, and a thousand horses at Washita). Another villainous character, in *The Fight for San Bernardo,* is a corrupted Captain of the Texas Rangers attempting to steal the communal lands of a Mexican-American village. Another is a doctor in Dodge City using cast-off Indian derelicts for his fertility experiments.

None of these characters would ever fit into a conventional Western, yet they produce amazingly strong, suspenseful plots. It is in the plot that I find the opportunity to make the book multidimensional, abandoning formula and searching out a theme and situation that will have appeal to modern readers.

Once I've found my villain, I write a short biography of him so that I will know him well. I want to know his age, appearance, attitude, and enough of his background so that his motivation is understandable and credible. I do the same for the six or eight auxiliary characters, but with less detail. In doing this, unexpected resources can appear out of nowhere, as in *The Mark of Cain,* where I discovered one of my characters, a demented bounty hunter, had once been a member of the Southern aristocracy; he could slip back into those times by decorously waltzing around the saloon with a sporting gal. He's a back-shooting skunk all right, but he has his reasons and his own tormented morality.

Of course, Sam Benbow speaks in the first person, which makes the writing more difficult, since he is limited to what he can see, hear, feel, and deduce, but brings him as close as possible to the reader. Using the third person distances the reader from the characters but is easier to write because the third person knows so much about what is going on.

I try to make a fairly comprehensive outline, but almost always find that the story veers off into unknown regions that are usually of greater value in terms of originality and spontaneity. I also make it a point never to talk about an unwritten project because for me it's a sure way of losing interest. Writers have a special psychology which involves baring their souls in a thoughtful and entertaining way, and they are willing to wait for whatever accolades may come along. The dilettante talks of his work for immediate gratification, and once the applause has died down, he has no reason to work further on that story.

A free-hand map of the area involved and, if necessary, the floor plans of relevant structures are excellent aids. In the case of *Target: Grant,* I mapped a hotel and named each room's occupants so that I knew where they all were and why. I often try to listen to a bawdy Western folk song to give me a basic rhythm and a little sauce for the reader, even though my background music is usually Bach.

I begin each of my Western novels with a dramatic scene that will disturb Sam Benbow emotionally and set his mood for what follows. In *Wild River Massacre,* a boy playing at being an Indian is killed by an unknown sniper, provoking Benbow's sense of justice and forcing him to solve not only that crime, but other murders that follow. Other first scenes might show his revulsion for the killing he encounters in his work, or a sense of loneliness as the years slip by. Sometimes it's simply the desire to do the job well and then get out of the business. Whatever it is, it is shown in a strong, eye-opening scene, much like the short teaser in teleplays.

From that scene evolves the three-act structure. The first act will drag the hero into increasing problems only gradually revealed to him. In *Wild River,* Benbow learns that the General killed the boy, but before he can take action on that knowledge, the General is murdered. The second act defines the problem more clearly and puts the hero in more jeopardy. Here Benbow considers seven very different characters as suspects in the General's murder. In the third act, he works these problems out, understands them, and solves them the best way he can. It turns out that the General's murderer is his terminally ill flack, who is trying to regain his integrity and atone for the cowardly massacre.

Another device, which I learned from writing teleplays, is to use a "front story" and a "back story." The front story in *The Fight for San Bernardo* is Sam's mission to seek out the truth about the Texas Rangers and to solve the problem. The back story is his bitter awareness that he has killed too many young men (set up in the first scene), albeit in self-defense, to continue. In his resistance to violence, he is nearly beaten to death by the Rangers and must return to violence in order to survive. For the first time in history the Mexicans are victors in the battle to keep their land. In the end, both these stories or problems converge and force the denouement.

While some writers proclaim authenticity is the First Commandment, I don't mind fudging with dates and geography if it helps the story along. I have a unique library of old Western memorabilia, including the handwritten inventory of a large general store in San Francisco circa 1880, with each item from cocaine to bloomers to black powder priced out. *Campaigning with Crook,* by Captain Charles King, printed in 1890, is one of the books in my personal collection that served me well in writing *Wild River Massacre.* I own an old set of spurs upon which are crudely welded triangles cut from a solid gold brooch. One of these triangles is engraved with the cowboy's name, Joe. I also have what is believed to be the only Cavalry saber that was used in the battle of Little Big Horn. Because of my collection and because of a plentitude of experiences, I don't feel that it's necessary to use a card file to write a book of fiction, believing that the honesty and urgency of the story are more important than the type of bit in the horse's mouth.

My discipline for working is simple. Being a fan of the late Georges Simenon, I became curious about his method of locking himself in a room and writing a book in twelve days. The first time I tried it, I was sweating brain matter every day, groaning and screaming to get the necessary number of pages, no matter their value. Writing a 180-page manuscript in twelve days requires a minimum of fifteen pages a day. After a day or two of this self-imposed pain, I discovered that my enthusiasm became so heightened in the mad rush to gain the page quota that often I'd run over several extra pages.

This is a difficult discipline but I find that after a month of carefully rewriting and revising the hurried-up first draft, I'm eager to start another. So it goes. A week of planning, researching, mapping, getting my nerve up, then the twelve-day plunge and sprint, followed by a month of shaping and detailing to finish and polish. In this way I can easily write six first-class Western novels a year.

Without strong promotion, the new wave of Westerns remains one of the best kept secrets of the book trade. It may be that some day a Western novel will be as rare and precious as a good poem, but I hope that younger readers are passing on their discovery of our changes by word of mouth, and with resilient writers, the Western will prevail.

❦ 51

SCIENCE IN SCIENCE FICTION: MAKING IT WORK

BY JOAN SLONCZEWSKI

"WHERE DO YOU GET THOSE *IDEAS*?" That is the number one question I get as a writer of science fiction. The next question is, how do you make science ideas into a story? Most important, how do you extrapolate from known science to make it convincing and intriguing?

First it's important to realize that there are various kinds of science fiction today, in which science functions differently. Michael Crichton builds a thriller around technical details, even tables of data; character and "art" are less emphasized. Ursula Le Guin writes anthropological science fiction, emphasizing the social sciences and subtleties of character. A recent trend is the "future historical" novel such as Maureen McHugh's *China Mountain Zhang,* in which scientific extrapolation provides details of a vivid future setting for everyday people. My own work explores the interactions between science and society, and the human beings caught between them—even when, as in *A Door into Ocean,* we are not sure at first who is "human."

As a writer, you need to decide what role (if any) science extrapolation can play in your work. In fact, much of what is labeled "science fiction" today could as easily be labeled fantasy; and if your own style is distinctive enough, that may be the route for you. On the other hand, to take science seriously requires special attention. I can suggest some approaches that work for me.

Where to find ideas

The freshest ideas come straight from experience in an actual scientific laboratory. In my own lab and those of my colleagues, I regularly experience natural phenomena stranger than the strangest of science fiction: a superconducting magnet that suspends paper clips in the room next door; a dish of bacteria that generate thousands of muta-

245

tions overnight; a flask of chemicals that "magically" turns color every few seconds. As a research scientist, and a teacher needing to range widely, I have an advantage. But any writer can telephone a research lab and even request a visit; most scientists love to talk about their work. INTERNET bulletin boards are another good source of expertise.

Next to the lab itself, the best source of ideas is research journals such as *Science* and *Nature*. These sources provide primary research reports of the latest discoveries, those of interest to a wide range of scientists. While the reading is a challenge even for a veteran scientist, most of the exciting finds reported here will never reach the popular science magazines. For example, I came across a report in *Science* of a bacterium that actually eats uranium. This fit right into the plot of my science fiction novel *Daughter of Elysium,* which required an organism to eat something no other creature would touch!

For readable reviews of emerging fields, use periodicals aimed at the scientifically literate readership such as *Scientific American* and Sigma Xi's *American Scientist.* Be wary of newspapers and the less sophisticated popular science magazines, whose accounts are likely to be superficial and contain errors.

Once you have a good idea, it's worth checking it out with experts, just as you might check out any other aspect of setting. Thus you can avoid obvious bloopers, as well as ideas considered total clichés by experts who would otherwise be sympathetic to your work. For example, physicists told me that an anti-gravity device would be written off as a cliché, but the use of a white hole as an energy source might be taken seriously.

In the end, you can take heart from the fact that "mistakes" may not be fatal, as far as popular success is concerned. Frank Herbert's bestseller *Dune* showed settlers on a desert planet distilling water from the air. This would work in an Earth desert only because Earth's atmosphere carries water from the oceans. Even if your science is "right" when the book is written, some aspects are bound to get outdated soon. *A Door into Ocean* depicted women who generate children by fusion of ova. Even before the proofs reached me, research had shown this to be impossible because paternal chromosomes carry essential modifications.

246

Credibility and consistency

What makes an idea "credible," then, is hard to define. Getting the facts exactly "right" and up-to-date is helpful; yet if none of your assumptions or extrapolations could be challenged, your work would not be science fiction.

Interestingly, the more common complaint I hear from inexperienced writers is that the "real science" they have carefully researched is declared false or unbelievable by readers or editors. What do we do when truth is stranger than fiction?

One way to make your ideas credible is to tie each invention to some easily verifiable event or fact on Earth. This can be done more or less subtly as a sort of in-text footnote. When Crichton shows his dinosaurs chomping through steel bars, "like hyenas," he offers a fact that I could verify. We can be sure that some hyena enthusiast out there will complain loudly if he gets it wrong! Similarly, when I created an alien organism with infrared vision in *The Wall around Eden,* I noted that known animals such as rattlesnakes possess infrared sensor organs. The focusing lens of the alien "eyes" was of sodium chloride, an infrared-focusing substance that living creatures commonly contain in their bodies.

Another source of credibility is consistency: Make sure that your facts and extrapolations, however reasonable on their own, make sense together in the story. If your imagined planet has twice the mass of earth, what is its gravity? The composition of its atmosphere? How close is it to its sun, and how long does it take to complete a year? Do the native animals on such a planet have thick, ponderous limbs, or delicate long ones? If voracious monsters descend upon your space visitors, what fauna do they normally prey upon?

The biological questions are frequently overlooked. In *Door into Ocean,* I created an entire ecosystem complete with microbial plants to photosynthesize, small phosphorescent grazers, both aerial and marine predators of a range of sizes, and scavengers, "legfish" that crawl up upon floating vegetation.

It may seem exhausting and frustrating to get all the parts to work together, but this extra craft is what distinguishes stories like *Dune* from more forgettable attempts. In my own work, I have come to rely upon a layered approach, in which I start at the beginning, write in a chapter or two until inconsistencies build up, then start all over from

247

the beginning and try to get a couple of chapters farther. Inevitably the first chapter gets rewritten twenty times; but the reward is that my last one virtually writes itself.

A writer who develops a particularly complex worldview, or "universe," may choose to write several books within the same universe, exploring different aspects of its setting or theme. Just as Doris Lessing wrote a series of novels about Martha Quest in Africa, Ursula Le Guin wrote several books, including *Left Hand of Darkness,* within one imagined universe, where humanity's far-flung colonial worlds are linked by the "ansible" communication device. One must however take care to come up with enough fresh material to justify each new story in its own right.

Explaining your ideas

The biggest mistake is to lecture your readers, however intriguing an idea may be. The writer must blend science ideas seamlessly with all other aspects of experience that form the story. As always, "show, not tell" is the rule.

Try to let science ideas lead into character development, and vice versa. An example of this process occurred as I wrote *A Door into Ocean,* in which a population of women called Sharers inhabit a planet covered entirely by ocean. One day a researcher in my laboratory excitedly showed me a flask of purple protein he had just isolated from photosynthetic bacteria. When light shined upon the protein, it bleached clear, as it absorbed the light energy. This demonstration gave me the idea that my aquatic women characters would carry purple bacteria as symbionts in their skin, providing extra oxygen underwater. When their oxygen ran low, the Sharers' skin would bleach white dramatically. This ability to "bleach white" later developed a spiritual significance as well; the Sharers can enter a special kind of trance, called "whitetrance," which enables them to endure extreme physical stress while upholding their religious beliefs.

Another example from *A Door into Ocean* works in the opposite direction, of character development leading to science: The Sharers use Gandhian pacifist resistance to repel an armed invasion of their planet. I sought a metaphor from science to help describe the unexpected success of their resistance, which from the invaders' limited perspective seemed doomed to fail. The metaphor had to fit into the perspective of the Sharers, who have advanced biological technology. I hit upon the idea of "electron tunneling," a phenomenon in which electrons can penetrate a seemingly impenetrable energy barrier. Electron tunneling occurs in the hemoglobin molecule as it collects oxygen in the blood, so the Sharers would know about it.

Some explanation is always necessary; the trick is, how much. It helps to weave necessary explication into dialogue, a sentence at a time, at a point where events demand it. For example, in *Daughter of Elysium,* a visiting scientist (new to the planet) discovers that his discarded culture dishes have come alive and are trying to gobble up his two-year-old son. A student comes to the rescue and explains that the "intelligent" culture-dish material (composed of billions of microscopic robots) has malfunctioned; it is designed to enclose tissue cultures, not children.

This example, by the way, also illustrates the time-honored gimmick for explaining any new setting: the naive "visitor," who needs everything explained. It works, if you don't make the lecture too obvious and do keep the plot moving. Michael Crichton's *Jurassic Park* essentially consists of a long lecture on cloning dinosaurs, kept moving by a fast-paced, and blood-thirsty, series of events.

One approach to the problem of explanation is to include all that the story seems to need in the first draft, even though you know it's too much for the reader to take. In later drafts, cut it drastically. Omit terms known only to experts, or redefine in simple language. (*Oogenesis* is "making eggs.") A typical science course introduces more new words than a first year of language. So try to use scientific terminology as you would use words from a foreign language—sparingly, for effect.

An occasional phrase of jargon may be worth keeping if it takes on a life of its own in the story. In *Daughter of Elysium,* I did keep one phrase of fetal development about the "primordial germ cells" which undergo a lengthy migration to reach the developing gonads before the fetus is born. The phrase set up a distinctive metaphor for the life journey of my central characters. But countless similar phrases were cut or redefined before my final draft.

How science and technology can advance plot

Complex technical information is best fed to the reader a little at a time and in such a way that it feels "inevitable" where it comes up.

This task is a challenge, but if done skillfully the development of ideas can advance your plot, heightening dramatic tension, much more so than if you had revealed all the implications at the start.

Daughter of Elysium depicts research connecting fetal development and aging, a field of daunting complexity. My opening chapter shows how the fetal heart tube forms and begins to pulse; later chapters depict more subtle processes of cells and tissues, and much later, the critical molecular events that determine whether the embryo will live or die—or live without aging. In between, various subplots incidental to research take up the scientist's time, much as they would in real life. Often the subplots make an ironic contrast to his work; for instance, when he faces his dying relatives back home, who will never benefit from his research on aging.

Another role for science in your plot can be to show how various characters react to change, and are themselves changed (or not). In *A Door into Ocean,* the invaders of the ocean world respond to the Sharers' life science in diverse ways. Some simply try to destroy it, and none of the bizarre setbacks they face changes their outlook. Others become intrigued by the new science, with its implications for their own medicine and agriculture. A few even take up the symbiotic purple microbes into their own skin.

The points I've made about finding ideas and using them have served me well in my own novels, and have worked for other writers too. At the same time, it is important not to get lost in the science. Remember that what makes a science fiction novel "work" in the long run is what makes any good novel work: connection, consistency, and characters that make us care.

§ 52

TIME, TRUTH, AND THE READER

BY JANE AIKEN HODGE

TRUTH AND TIME are twin problems for the historical novelist. Are you going to stick religiously to the historical facts of your background, and how are you going to make sure that your characters' fictional time, the events of their lives, mesh with the historical frame in which you have set them? I think there is some room for compromise in both cases, less over truth than over time. And you can save yourself a great deal of trouble by thinking hard about both problems in the early stages of planning your historical novel.

Of course, the basic facts of history are sacred. If you make the Confederate instead of the Union Army win the Battle of Gettysburg, you will lose your reader's confidence, and that is fatal. Nor can you alter dates. I think it is useful, in this context, to imagine yourself always being read by an expert in the field. Please them, and you will convince everyone, including yourself. There is no mistaking the absolute ring of truth in a solidly researched novel.

When it comes to using real people, probably as background to your story, there has to be a bit more latitude, but again you want to avoid making them do or say anything totally out of character. The best thing is to get to know them well before you start. And the more famous they are, the more careful you will need to be. If you introduce, say, the Duke of Wellington, or Abraham Lincoln, you will need to mind how you go. If Abraham Lincoln were to light a cigarette and say, "That's OK," then, I, the reader, would lose confidence in you as author and stop reading your book. Georgette Heyer, a past mistress of historical accuracy, used to weave quotations from, for instance, the Duke of Wellington's letters into her text, and they give a splendid ring of truth. Or you can use bits of actual recorded conversation, which will both give conviction and help you to tune your ear to the way your character talked, so as to get it right yourself.

I had a little trouble with someone called Lord William Bentinck in my novel *Escapade*. I decided to take a pair of heroines to Sicily in 1811, because they needed to get out of England, and with Napoleon in control of the rest of Europe, that was the only place they could go. So I looked into Sicily and found a most interesting situation. The Queen, Maria Carolina, was at daggersdrawn with this Lord William, who was sent out to take over as British Minister that summer. So I sent my heroines out on the same boat on which he sailed, and began by cheerfully providing him with a wife and children through whom they could all make friends.

Luckily for me, I went back to the library at this point and discovered a whole lot more information about Lord William. He was a most interesting, difficult character, with an evangelical wife and no children. I had outrun my research and had to go back, unravel the whole chapter, and knit it up again. It came out much better, as difficult bits often do, because I now knew enough about Lord William to make sense of him. I had met the queen before in a previous book, *Shadow of a Lady,* so I knew something about her; she was a passionately indiscreet letter writer, which helped. In fact, I got very fond of her, and there was a dangerous moment when she showed signs of taking over the book. I longed to drag it out to tell the sad end of her story, when Lord William won and drove her into exile, but this would have meant trouble with time. I would have had to keep my heroines in suspended animation for a couple of years, and it was not that kind of story. I sadly consigned the Queen's later adventures to a postscript, for anyone who had gotten fond of her, too.

The problems of truth and time are often linked like that. It is hard to tell, when planning the book originally, just how long things are going to take to happen. I often find that events move faster than I expect, so that the fictional climax turns up before I have come to the historical moment for which it was planned. That is trouble. In my book, *Windover,* I had meant to end with the infamous treason trials of May, 1794, but things speeded up, and the book was ready to end in the autumn of 1793. I went back to my source books and was luckier than I deserved. I found that a similar set of panic arrests and trials happened in Scotland in autumn, 1793. Word of them, reaching London, served to precipitate my crisis. Happy discoveries of that kind are some of the extra pleasures of the historical novel, but should not be counted on. The more you know in advance about the period on which you are working, the happier you will be, and the better your results.

There is a truth of language and detail, the small print of history, as well as of fact, and, in my view, it is equally important. It is the small details that give the feel of the period. The main reason I write historical novels, aside from the pure pleasure of it, is that I pine for a world with a moral structure, as against the moral and aesthetic chaos we suffer today. I write (and read) historical novels to recreate a world of rules and standards of behavior. My heroines conduct their lives by rules quite different from those (if any) that obtain today, and it is vital to keep the reader conscious of this. You need at the same time to keep readers aware that this is a different world, with different rules, and keep them gripped by the story.

Here, too, it seems to me to be a question of intelligent compromise. I have never set a book earlier than the time of the American Revolution because I feel that the language from then on is near enough to modern English so that such compromise is possible. There is no need for *pish* or *tush,* for *zounds* or *gadzooks.* One can remind the reader, perhaps with an Austen usage here and there, or a glancing reference to a *pelisse,* a *fichu* or a *fan,* that these are people who do not speak or think quite as we do today. Too much of it, and you risk losing the reader. I am very cautious with dialect and cockney, since I find, for instance, Walter Scott's Scotch novels unreadable, and have the same blank about anything heavily Irish. No use writing what one would not read oneself.

It is a kind of balancing act. You must keep your reader aware that your heroine is living by different standards, but be careful not to make her seem alien, or, worse still, priggish. You could call this the Fanny Price problem. Many modern readers of *Mansfield Park* identify with the naughty Crawfords instead of with good little Fanny. Jane Austen was writing with a different set of rules, and it is amusing to remember that contemporary critics tended to fault her books for not having a high enough moral tone. But then, she was daughter and sister of clergymen; religion was part of the air she breathed. It is part of the miracle she was that *Mansfield Park* is the only one of her books in which this does prove a possible barrier between her work and our more free-thinking age. I am surprised that no modern publisher has reissued her rogue book, *Lady Susan,* the story of a splendidly spirited and amoral adventuress, told largely in her own letters.

In my last two books, my heroines have been in revolt against the excesses of strait-laced puritanism, but I look on this as dangerous ground, to be gone over as lightly as possible. Religion is an explosive subject, to be handled with care. I have rather the same reservations about costume. It always comes as a shock to me when I get the jacket design for a new book, and there is my beloved heroine in poke bonnet and clinging muslin. This is not the way I think of her. Of course, that's what was worn then, but it was contemporary dress to them; they were not aware of it (unless they were fashion mad) and nor do I want my reader to be. We should think of them just as young women. It is one of the few points on which I differ from Georgette Heyer. I am bored by those long, detailed descriptions of every color and every frill, laboriously gleaned from *La Belle Assemblée* or *The Mirror of Fashion.* This seems to me an ostentation of research that risks alienating the reader.

Which is the one thing one must never do. In these days of fast everything, it is amazing to turn to a novel by Walter Scott and see the leisurely winding chapters with which he sets his scene. No time for that today. They had time in the nineteenth century. We do not. Or think we do not. You have to catch your readers quickly and never let them go. It is amusing to see how many novels open with a dramatic scene, culled from almost anywhere in the story, then fill in the background at leisure, bouncing around in time, maybe using several narrators to do so. I prefer to begin at the beginning, and keep the story simple, but then, what is the beginning? This is never so obvious as it might seem and it is vitally important. Get it right, and you are well away. A beloved Doubleday editor made me cut several first chapters of *Here Comes a Candle,* in which I had carefully built up to what is now the dramatic opening scene. It was painful at the time, but looking at it now, I see how right she was. And the work on the early chapters was not wasted. I had found my way into my characters and their situation. One should never underestimate the value of a good editor. More precious than rubies, they are.

Here Comes a Candle illustrated another interesting problem of the historical novel. My hero had an autistic daughter, but of course the word had not been invented, nor the condition recognized. This is true

of all kinds of medical terms and conditions; the whole of post-Freud-
ian psychological jargon is out of the question, and what a blessing
that is. The subconscious did not exist, nor the Oedipus complex, nor
a lot of other things one can manage very nicely without. I have an
anorexic heroine in my new book. I hope readers will recognize the
condition, but they will most certainly not find the word.

Plants are something else that must be handled with care. Your hero
or heroine looks out at the garden, and what does he/she see? I thought
of decorating my Sicilian gardens with bougainvillaea and cautiously
looked it up in my favorite book of reference, the 1911 edition of the
Encyclopaedia Britannica. And what a fascinating story I found. It
was introduced from South America by Captain de Bougainville, who
tried to colonize the Falklands for France, survived the French Revolution, was decorated by Napoleon, and died at 82 in the year of my
book, 1811. Fascinating story; maybe I'll use it some day, but no bougainvillaea in the Sicilian gardens. It seems unlikely that it would have
been anything like established by 1811.

I have not dealt at all with the kind of historical novel that uses real
people for its central figures, because this is a game with totally different rules, and a very dangerous one at that, particularly when the
characters are from the recent past. Splendid to recreate Alexander
the Great for us, but to write books, for instance, vilifying Charles de
Gaulle, and altering history to do so seems to me to be breaking a
basic rule of the game.

Another of the games one plays with one's readers is trying to get
enough basic information about time and place across without boring
them into stopping reading. Dialogue is a great help here, as Alice so
famously pointed out. Characters can discuss the events of the day, at
the same time establishing themselves in the reader's mind and filling
in their historical context. Much better that they should tell each other
things than that you should prose on about them direct. After all, the
writing of fiction is a kind of conversation, only the other party keeps
silent. It is not much use going on with your story if your audience
has crept away, one by one, from around the campfire. First you must
catch them, then you must hold them. I think there is a great need,
these days, for good old-fashioned storytelling. The straight novel has
gone so far upmarket as to be almost invisible; the thriller has gone

savage, and the mystery has gone glum. If you want to tell a plain romantic tale you must put it in disguise. Fantasy builds worlds of its own with its own rules; the historical novel recreates the rules of the past. It means that for both of them that delightful old-fashioned thing, the happy ending, is still a practical possibility.

53

WHEN YOUR SLEUTH WEARS A BADGE

BY MARGARET MARON

WHEN I BEGAN MY FIRST MYSTERY novel about Sigrid Harald, a self-conscious, awkward young woman who would be competent in her professional life but inept in dealing with her emotions, I simply intended to create a continuing character who could sustain my interest over a series of books and who had plenty of room for personal growth. My main worry was that I might not find enough plausible ways to involve her in one murder after another if she were a complete amateur; so, à la Willie Sutton when asked why he robbed banks ("Because that's where the money is!"), I naïvely made her a homicide detective because that's where the bodies were!

In short, Lieutenant Sigrid Harald of the New York Police Department was to be a traditional sleuth who just happened to wear a badge. New York's routine violence could provide more than enough background cases; I planned to concoct classic puzzles to occupy the foreground.

In the U.S., where each aspect of the mystery genre must fit into a neatly labeled category, using a police character automatically—and often mistakenly—tags that book a "police procedural." For me, the term "procedural" conjures up a novel fascinated with hardware, official hierarchies, and all the mechanical details of a technical investigation. More hardboiled in tone than traditional murder mysteries, the police procedural tends to emphasize the gritty *noir* side of city life. The victim is usually a random choice, devoid of personality, and merely serves as an excuse for readers to watch members of a homicide squad interact with each other as they investigate the crime. Of relatively little importance in these American procedurals are the killer's character and motivation.

Although true procedurals can be interesting to read, I didn't want to write them. Much closer to my own taste was what the British call "the police whodunit"—classically plotted puzzle mysteries with strong emphasis on character development, mood and setting. Ngaio Marsh, P.D. James, and Colin Dexter in England, Tony Hillerman and Susan Dunlap in America are good examples of this aspect of the genre.

In a *procedural,* the main emphasis is on *how* and *who,* not *why,* and we know that the killer will be unmasked as soon as enough witnesses have been interviewed and enough man-hours have been logged. The reader is merely a spectator.

In the police *whodunit,* the best writers "play fair," thus letting the reader become a participant who, if all the red herrings are eliminated, may actually solve the crime one step ahead of the police sleuth. Investigative processes are kept subordinate to the lives of the main characters.

When I began, I probably knew more about New Scotland Yard than about the New York City Police Department; and *One Coffee With,* my first Sigrid Harald novel, reflects my disinterest in technicalities: Details are focused and specific in the college scenes (a place familiar to me), vague and generalized in the scenes set in her office. *Death of a Butterfly* was much the same, but I had begun doing some research, and by the third book, the results were increasingly creeping onto my pages even though I still regarded actual police work as the least interesting part of Sigrid's life.

When I described the boredom of a routine stakeout or let an officer gripe about how long it takes the FBI to run a fingerprint, it was merely to add verisimilitude to the background. For me, the important thing was to show how Sigrid Harald was changing and growing as a person. Everything else was window dressing. Yet, as a professional, I tried to make my window dressing as accurate as possible.

I visited the bookstore at John Jay College of Criminal Justice and came home with used textbooks on gunshot wounds, arson investigations, and methods of police patrol. (My current forensics bible is *Practical Homicide Investigation: Tactics, Procedures, and Forensic Techniques.**) I borrowed books from the public library and browsed in the true crime section of used bookstores. Eventually, I even en-

---

**Practical Homicide Investigation* is part of a series edited by Vernon J. Geberth and published by CRC Press, 2000 Corporate Blvd. N.W., Boca Raton, FL 33431.

rolled in various criminalistics courses at my local community college. These teach the practical nuts and bolts of technical investigation and are usually geared toward police officers who want to move up in the ranks. Just listening to their slang, their turns of phrases, and their "war stories" provided reams of colorful details.

Through the years, I've found it relatively easy to get my facts straight when dealing with the investigation of the murder itself. Most medico/legal professionals will talk to you about postmortem cooling, lethal doses, blood-splatter patterns, etc., once you've explained clearly and concisely why you want to know. To find local experts, I usually start with the secretary of a specific department in a nearby college or teaching hospital. I describe the information I need and ask to be connected with a user-friendly professor or doctor. If the first one I get sounds harried, I apologize and ask if I can call later or if he could recommend someone else. Then when I call that "someone else," I can say, "Dr. X suggested that you might explain to me. . ."

If no one local can answer my questions, I've discovered that almost anyone in the country will answer a courteous letter, especially if I make it seem irresistibly easy. I decide beforehand what facts I absolutely must have and keep my questions as specific as possible. Triple-spacing between questions encourages the expert to answer directly on my letter so that all she has to do is jot down the facts and slip the sheet of paper into the self-addressed, stamped envelope which, of course, I have enclosed.

By contrast, getting the housekeeping details of precinct stations has been my biggest headache. Who reports to whom, what forms are used in which situations, who hands out the paychecks, to whom do the officers or detectives call in sick? These are the day-to-day background details that make a novel ring true and are much too easy to get wrong.

Networking outward from those early criminalistics classes, I met and talked with real-life police detectives and civil service clerks from many different commands. Over the years, they've given me updated organizational flow charts and guided me through their bureaucracy's constantly changing red tape.

Whenever I visit a detective's office, I take note of the sights and smells along a corridor, the stacks of papers piled on overflowing file cabinets, the mix of plainclothes and uniforms. "Who makes the coffee?" I ask. "How often do you use the pistol range in the basement? How do you requisition ballpoint pens and legal pads?"

In *Past Imperfect,* my seventh book about Sigrid Harald and the people in her life, Sigrid's personal complications were still very much in the foreground, yet the mystery itself—the murder of a colleague— required so many scenes that could take place only inside her station house that I kept getting hung up on minutiae I really didn't want to know—or use.

Less procedure and more whodunit, I reminded myself grimly. As I slogged through the final pages of in-house politics and bureaucratic trivia, I promised Sigrid, "Just get us to the end of this book, and you'll never have to see the inside of a police station again except to pick up your paycheck."

"I've already requested automatic deposit," she told me.

54

SETTING IS MORE THAN PLACE

BY WILLIAM G. TAPPLY

AN INTERVIEWER RECENTLY ASKED ME WHY I choose to set my mystery novels in New England instead of, say, Nebraska. I was tempted to answer with the old vaudeville punchline: "Everybody's got to be somewhere." Every story has to have a setting.

Instead I told the interviewer the simple truth: My choice of New England was easy—New England is where I've lived my entire life. It's what I know best. I couldn't write about Nebraska.

I define setting broadly. It's more than place. Setting comprises all the conditions under which things happen—region, geography, neighborhood, buildings, interiors, climate, weather, time of day, season of year.

I feel fortunate. My New England provides me with a rich variety of settings from which to select. I can send my narrator/lawyer/sleuth Brady Coyne from the inner city of Boston to the wilderness of the Maine woods, from the sand dunes of Cape Cod to the farmland of the Connecticut Valley, from exclusive addresses on Beacon Hill to working class neighborhoods in Medford. New England has whatever my stories might call for.

New England also gives me the full cycle of the seasons and all the weather and climate that accompany them. It gives me Locke-Ober and pizza joints, museums and theaters, factories and office buildings, mansions and apartments, skyscrapers and fishing lodges, condominiums and farmhouses.

I don't know about Nebraska. I suspect that if I lived there and knew it as intimately as I know New England I'd find a similar wealth of possibilities. I have, in fact, sent Brady to parts of North Carolina and Montana that I'm familiar with. What's important is knowing my settings well enough to invoke the details that will bring them to life and be useful in my stories.

261

Settings must strike our readers as realistic. A realistic setting persuades readers to suspend their disbelief and accept the premise that our stories really happened. The easiest and best way to do this is to write knowledgeably about real places, places where our readers live or have visited, or, at least, places they have read about or seen pictures of. Readers, I have learned, love to find in a novel a place they know. They enjoy comparing their impressions of Durgin Park or the New England Aquarium with Brady Coyne's. They like to hear what strikes Brady as noteworthy about Newbury Street, the Combat Zone, the Deerfield River, or the Boston Harbor.

You must get actual places precisely right or you risk losing your readers' trust. No matter how much you might dislike it, you cannot avoid research. You *must* hang out in the places you intend to write about. Observe the people, listen to the sounds, sniff the smells, note the colors and textures of the place. I have spent hours loitering in Boston's Chinatown and prowling the corridors in the East Cambridge courthouse. I've wandered around the Mt. Auburn Hospital and the Peabody Museum, looking for the telling detail that makes the place unique and that will allow me to make it ring true for every reader who has been there.

Research need not be unpleasant, in fact. I make it a point to eat in every restaurant I write about, no matter how familiar it already is to me, at least twice—once just before writing the scene to fix it in my mind, and once again afterward to make sure I've rendered it accurately.

A realistic setting doesn't really have to exist, however, and the fiction writer shouldn't feel limited to using actual places if doing so will alter the story he wants to tell. A fictional setting can still be true. My rule of thumb is this: If the setting you need exists, use it; if it doesn't exist, make it up but make it true. I built Gert's on the North Shore and Marie's in Kenmore Square—where no such restaurants stand— because my stories demand there be restaurants like them there. Readers are continually asking me how to find Gert's and Marie's, which I take to mean that I have rendered them realistically.

I made up a hardscrabble farm in Lanesboro and a horse farm in Harvard—fictitious but realistic places in actual Massachusetts communities. In my first Brady Coyne novel, I moved a rocky hunk of Rhode Island coastline to Massachusetts, committed a murder there, and named it Charity's Point because that storyline required it. I've had readers tell me they believe they have been there. In *The Vulgar Boatman,* I invented the town of Windsor Harbor. Had I tried to set that tale in a real community north of Boston, too many readers would have known that no events such as the ones I invented actually happened there. They would have been unable to suspend their disbelief.

Gert's and Marie's, the farms in Lanesboro and Harvard, Charity's Point, and Windsor Harbor were like the characters that populated the books. Although they were not *real,* they were all *true*—places like them exist, and they *could* be where I put them.

Setting can—and should—serve as more than a backdrop for the action of the story. The conditions under which the action occurs should do double or triple duty for you. Setting can create mood and tone for your fiction. The places where they live and work can reveal the personalities and motivations of your fictional characters. Places, weather, climate, season of year, and time of day can cause things to happen in a story as surely as characters can.

Shakespeare and Conan Doyle understood how setting can establish mood and foreshadow events. The "dark and stormy night" had its purpose, as did the spooky mansion on the remote moor or the thick fog of a London evening. Contemporary writers can use thunderstorms and abandoned warehouses and the barrooms and alleys of city slums in the same way. Robert Louis Stevenson once said, "Some places speak distinctly. Certain dank gardens cry aloud for murder; certain old houses demand to be haunted; certain coasts are set apart for shipwrecks." Find such places. Use them.

But be wary. Such obvious settings can too easily become literary clichés. Misuse them, or overuse them, and they lose their punch. Clever writers understand the power of going against stereotypes. Seek subtlety and irony. Murder can be committed on a sunny May morning in a suburban backyard, too, and when it does, the horror of it is intensified by the contrast.

Carefully selected details of setting can delineate the characters who populate the place. Match the pictures or calendars that hang on every office wall with some trait of the man who works there. Is the policeman's desk littered with half-empty styrofoam coffee cups? What kind of tablecloths does your restaurant use? What music is piped into the elevator of the office building? Does a week's worth of newspapers litter the front porch of that Brookline mansion? Does a specimen jar containing a smoker's lung sit on the desk of the forensic pathologist? Does the lawyer keep a bag of golf clubs in the corner of his office? Does a stack of old *Field & Stream* magazines sit on the table in the dentist's waiting room? Such well-chosen particulars can reveal as much about a character as his dress, manner of speech, or physical appearance.

Think of your settings as characters in your stories. Settings need not be passive. They can act and interact with your characters. Rainstorms cause automobile accidents. Snowstorms cover footprints and stall traffic. Laboratories contain chemicals that spill and release toxic fumes. The bitter cold of a Boston winter kills homeless people. Water released from a dam raises the water level in a river and drowns wading fishermen.

Your choice of setting may, at first, be arbitrary and general—the city where you work, the village where you live. But as you begin writing, you will need to search out particular places where the events of your story will unfold. Visit them often enough to absorb them. If you're lucky, you'll find that your real settings will begin to work for you. You'll see a person whose face you'll want to use. You'll overhear a snatch of conversation that fits a storytelling need. You'll note a detail you didn't expect that suggests a new direction for your plot. On one backgrounding mission to a rural farmyard, I came upon a "honey wagon" pumping out a large septic tank. This suggested to me an unusually grisly way for a villain to dispose of a dead body; this murder method found its way into my story.

The secret of a successfully rendered setting lies *not* in piling exhaustive detail upon repetitive particulars. There's no need to lug your typewriter around a room describing the designs of the furniture, the colors of the rugs and drapes, the brands of the whiskey on the sidebar. Extended descriptive passages, no matter how poetic and clever, only serve to stall the momentum of your story and bore your reader.

Setting is important. It serves many purposes. But don't get carried away. It *is* only a setting, the conditions in which your characters can play out their conflicts. The key to creating effective settings lies in finding the *exactly right* detail that will suggest all of the others. Be spare and suggestive. Look for a water stain on the ceiling or a cigarette burn on the sofa. You may need nothing else to create the picture you want in your reader's imagination. As Elmore Leonard says, "I try to leave out the parts that people skip."

❦ 55

WRITING "TRUE" CRIME: GETTING FORENSIC FACTS RIGHT

BY STEVEN SCARBOROUGH

THE STORY READS LIKE THIS: Mitch Sharp, the skillful detective, solves the "Casino Slasher Case" by tracing cloth fibers and a drop of saliva found at the murder scene to the stealthy criminal.

What's wrong with the facts in this scenario? This simply can't be done. The evidence is scientifically dubious. When is a case plausible, and when does it stretch reality? A writer can know only by examining the type of forensic evidence necessary for the events of the story and then by doing the appropriate research.

Fingerprints

Fingerprints are the most conclusive form of forensic evidence; they are the only type of evidence that does not require corroborative proof. Though the probability of finding that elusive fingerprint or that single strand of hair is low, it can be woven into your story if you include the proper background. Fingerprint processing of a toenail and an eyeball of a murder victim in the *Red Dragon* is not only technically correct, but it also lends a gritty credence to Thomas Harris's novel.

Fingerprints command the most attention in court, and they should get equal billing in your crime story. In a city of about 300,000, fingerprints lead to the identification, arrest, or conviction of nearly one person every day.

While fingerprints are readily retrieved from glass, shiny metal, and paper, they are difficult to recover from fabric, textured objects, or finished furniture. Surface to surface, the methods of recovery differ, so the writer should know the proper processes for recovering incriminating fingerprints. It will make a story both interesting and accurate.

In *Presumed Innocent,* Scott Turow gives us an impressive account of the questioning of a fingerprint witness in court. His only lapse is in describing blue fingerprints developed on glass with ninhydrin powder. Ninhydrin, a liquid chemical brushed on paper, produces a purplish fingerprint. The common graphite powder method is used on slick surfaces such as glass.

A dramatic punch to your story might be to recover prints from one of your victims, and it can be done. Iodine fumes are blown over the body with a small glass tube and a silver plate is pressed against the skin to lift the print. However, at this time prints can be recovered only within two hours from a live person and within about twelve hours from a deceased one.

Is your antagonist trying to incriminate someone else? Maybe he has considered forging a fingerprint? Forget it; his attempts are sure to be futile. It is nearly impossible to recreate an accurate die of someone's fingerprint. A cast can be made, provided he has a willing or dead hand to cast. Yet, even then the resulting print will be reversed or backward if transferred to an object.

A fingerprint expert cannot testify to how long a fingerprint will last on an object. General rules suggest that a fingerprint will last days, not weeks, outside in the weather; weeks but not months in a residence; and a month would not be long for a fingerprint left on a mirror, especially if encased in a drawer or a safe. Fingerprints have been chemically recovered years later on the pages of a book.

When tracing someone from latent fingerprints, the investigator must have the suspect's name and fingerprint record on file to make a positive match. Lawrence Block captures the essence of fingerprints in *The Burglar Who Painted Like Mondrian*:

> . . . you can't really run a check on a single print unless you've already got a suspect. You need a whole set of prints, which we wouldn't have, even if whoever it was left prints, which they probably didn't. And they'd have to have been fingerprinted anyway for a check to reveal them.

Historically, fingerprints have been filed using a ten-print classification system; without recovering latent fingerprints of all ten fingers, a person could not be identified. In the 1980s, the AFIS (Automated Fingerprint Identification System) computer was introduced, enabling jurisdictions with access to the computer to link a single latent fingerprint to a suspect previously fingerprinted. Writers should remember that AFIS computers cost over a million dollars, and your quaint Vermont village will not have one. The well-connected fictional investigator should know someone at a large agency or the FBI for a record check.

Body Fluids

Fingerprints may be the most positive form of identification, but what if your perpetrator does not leave any? In the absence of fingerprints, body fluids are a common type of evidence found at a crime scene. If an intact sample of adequate size is recovered, body fluids can be analyzed to obtain a DNA genetic profile that can be compared with the suspect's or examined for blood type.

Blood, semen, and saliva are all excellent media for determining a DNA match. DNA (deoxyribonucleic acid) is the blueprint of a person's genetic makeup and is absolutely unique for each individual.

Contrary to common belief, hair will not reveal a person's DNA pattern. Have your victim yank out a clump of hair with the skin cells to make a DNA match.

The equipment necessary to analyze DNA is highly specialized and costly. Again, if your story is set in a quaint village, it may not be feasible to run a DNA check. It also may take months to get results from one of the few laboratories that do DNA analysis. This need not be a negative; think of the desperation, the agony, of waiting for results while your killer still stalks.

Body fluids can be analyzed by the local crime lab to help your detective. An important factor associated with body fluids, including blood types, is secretor status. A secretor puts out, i.e., secretes, his ABO blood type into peripheral body fluids such as semen, perspiration, etc. It is possible for your fictional serial rapist to avoid any link to his body fluids by being one of the 15 per cent that are non-secretors.

What does blood type tell the investigator? Normally a blood type places a person in a broad portion of the general population. A community might have 45 per cent of its members with O blood, 40 per cent with A blood, and so on. Therefore, if standard ABO typing is done, the results are of little value because of the large population with that blood type.

Additional blood grouping techniques, specifically enzyme and protein analyses, enable the forensic chemist to assign a suspect to a narrower population. Your fictional crime lab should not give your detective a match on blood from the crime scene. They can limit only the number of people in your town that have that type of enzyme blood group.

The special equipment needed for thorough blood analysis is costly, and it is probable that numerous crimes go unsolved because sufficient testing is either too expensive or neglected.

Other evidence

Hair can be of forensic value. Strands found at the scene of the crime can be compared to a suspect's for similarities in color, shape, and texture, but it is difficult to determine race or even sex. An author can write that some of the suspects were eliminated because analysis concluded that their hair was not similar or consistent with the hair found at the crime scene.

Footwear prints, recovered by photography, fall into the class category. Except for the exceptional case, shoeprints can only be said to be made by the same type of shoe. Footwear, or any class type evidence (hair, fiber, ABO blood type) by itself would normally not be enough to convict your suspect in a court of law.

Handwriting cases rarely get into court. A handwriting expert renders an opinion after examining several varying factors such as letter height ratio and slant. If the writing is similar, then degrees of match probability are reported.

Criminals usually disguise their writing. It is unlikely that a kidnapper's ransom note, written in block letters will lead to the identity of your brutish villain. Words in blood dribbled on a wall may provide a strong clue and add color to your story, but they will not enable a handwriting examiner to point to your murderer.

Striations on a bullet are unique, much like the ridges of a fingerprint. Therefore, a bullet can be traced to a gun using the scratches or lands and grooves imprinted on it by the barrel of a gun. Unfortunately, if the barrel is damaged or changed, or if the bullet is mangled, the examination will be inconclusive. Careful scrutiny is necessary before including a firearms match in your murder mystery.

Thomas Harris was very skillful in weaving his forensic research throughout his novel. FBI Agent Will Graham explores the gamut of forensic evidence from fingerprints to blood typing to bite marks. *The Red Dragon* could be used as a forensic model for crime writers.

The increasing sophistication of today's readers is a two-edged sword: Readers are no longer satisfied with, "He was the only one tall enough who had a motive." A writer trying to add more realism to a story need not shy away from scientific evidence, but he must check his forensic facts for accuracy. Credibility is the key to a successful crime novel. Just as a character's action may lead the reader to say, "He wouldn't do that," an erroneous forensic fact can turn off the reader. Do your research well, and you will be rewarded by readers clamoring to pick up your latest authentic crime story.

56

CHARACTER: THE KEY ELEMENT IN MYSTERY NOVELS

BY JAMES COLBERT

BY DEFINITION, TO BE A MYSTERY a novel must have a murder at the beginning that is solved by the end. And by convention there must be a solution, whether or not there is an apprehension. This is the contract assumed by the reader when he or she picks up a book classified as a mystery. Yet despite this murder-solution requisite, mysteries offer the writer greater freedom, a basic structure around which to work plot, setting, and most important, character.

Without doubt, character is the most important element of a mystery. A clever plot helps, certainly, as does a strong sense of place, but those elements are secondary, best used to show how the central character thinks and responds to events and environment. One writer may have a native Floridian solving murders while another may send a New York City detective to Florida. While Florida, of course, remains the same, the interesting thing for the reader is to see how the character responds, how he or she integrates the sense of the place into an overall experience. The same is true of the plot. No matter how interesting, unless uncovered by a central character readers find engaging, events take on a flat, two-dimensional quality. "Just the facts, ma'am. Just the facts" has its place, all right, but that place is in a newspaper, not a mystery.

So how does a writer go about portraying an engaging character? The answer to that is as multi-faceted and as complex as the character must be, and it is accomplished one small step at a time. Think of a police artist putting together a composite sketch of a suspect. Thin sheets of transparent plastic, each with slightly different lines are laid one over another, composing different parts of the face until a whole picture emerges. While the medium is different, the technique is not dissimilar to the one a writer uses. First sheet: How tall is the character, and how much does he weigh? How is he built? Second sheet: What color hair does he have? What are his distinguishing characteristics? Third sheet: What is the setting, and what is the character thinking? Small elements are put together, one over another, until a whole picture emerges.

Where the police artist leaves off with the physical portrait, however, the writer is just beginning because the reader wants to know, well, what's this guy really *like?* Is he threatening or non-threatening? Well-read or illiterate? Optimistic or pessimistic? What kind of car does he drive? What does he eat? The nuances, eccentricities, habits, way of thinking and quirks are what separate a description of a character from one who starts to *live*; and all those things are revealed as the character responds to his surroundings and reacts to events—in a very good mystery, dynamic events make the character *grow.*

Growth and change are intrinsic, inevitable elements of the human condition. The growing and the changing, however, usually occur very slowly, day by day, not very noticeably. Within the usually limited time frame of a novel, this change is often very difficult to portray, but the mystery has the advantage of a dynamic structure. A murder occurs at the beginning and is solved by the end. Events, feelings, new understandings are speeded up, compressed into a very short time. As a result, it is credible that the characters change fairly quickly in response. Really successful mysteries allow the reader not just to know a character but to grow with him, to learn his lessons as he did, without actually having to endure the violent crime. Observe Burke in Andrew Vachss's novel, *Blossom,* or listen to the first-person narrator in Scott Turow's *Presumed Innocent.* Notice how they change during the course of the book. Observe what they learn and how the new understandings affect them. And watch how, with the characters firmly in hand, the authors thrust them into the events that form the respective plots.

Plots are usually very simple ideas extended. Even the most complex plot can be described briefly. (Excellent examples of this can be found in your Sunday paper, in the film listings, where even very involved movies are summarized in a line or two.) But unlike the step-by-step development of characters, plots appear complex at the outset and become more and more simple. Elements are stripped away rather than added. What appears confusing, even chaotic, at the start makes sense later on when other motives and actions are revealed: In retrospect, all the twists and turns make sense. The reader is left with a clear sense of order, a good sense of character, and, one hopes, a strong sense of place.

Evoking a place is stage setting in its most basic form. Remember, it is crucial to have the stage set for the central character—and not the other way round. Overlong descriptions of a place and a recitation of facts about it are best left to travel guides, which is not to say that setting is *un*important. But it *is* secondary. When successfully used, setting becomes the character and helps to reveal his or her foibles and way of life. In John D. MacDonald's Travis Magee novels, Travis Magee's houseboat, for example, is very much a part of Travis Magee, accommodating, even making possible, a way of life that is so much a part of him that when he travels, he seems to embody one *place* confronting another. Readers envy Travis the beachbum freedom of his life, and we understand how it feels to leave the beach and go, say, to New York City or to Mexico—or, for that matter, just to go to work. The setting is integral to Travis Magee and enriches the whole series; but while it may be difficult to imagine him anywhere else, the fact is, readers can. (MacDonald even tells us how to go about it whenever Travis considers his options.) For the writer, however, the single most important facet of technique, as important in its own way as making character primary, is to make use of what you know.

If presented well, there is no human experience that is uninteresting. Very good books have been written about what might, from all appearances, be very mundane lives. Yet mystery writers too often feel the need to write not what they know but what they perceive they *should* be writing about. As a result, the characters they create do not ring true, or in particular, they are tough when they should not be, or have no real sense of what violence is really like. But despite the hard-boiled school of detective fiction, it is *not* necessary for a central character in a mystery to be either tough or violent—the book can, in fact, be just as interesting when a character conveys some squeamishness or distaste for violence. Not all detectives have to be built like linebackers and display a penchant for brutal confrontation.

The simple fact is, what you know is what will ring true. Andrew Vachss writes about violence and violent people because he knows his subject; but Tony Hillerman eschews that and writes about Navajo

Indians, which is what *he* knows. Scott Turow, the lawyer, writes about legal proceedings. All three have written very good books. But since Dashiell Hammett's *Continental Op,* far too many mystery writers have felt it mandatory to make their investigators tough, even when the writer has no notion of what real toughness is all about. The result is facade rather than substance—and the reader will sense it. In fiction, certainly, there is a need for imagination, but the imagination must spring from knowledge, not speculation. The most credible, most substantive books are those in which the author's grasp of his or her subject shows through. Allow your character to know what you know and do not attempt to impose on him what you feel he *should* know. Your character will appear shallow if you do, shallow, and most damning of all, contrived. With respect to that, it is important, too, that you consider your story first, *then* the genre it happens to fall into.

With my first novel, *Profit and Sheen,* I wasn't even aware that I had written a mystery until the first review came out. What makes me appear rather dense in one way worked to my advantage in another: I told my story as well as I knew how and was completely unencumbered by any feeling of restriction. The point is, tell your story as well as you know how and see how it comes out. *Then* worry about genre. If you start out with the expressed intent of writing a mystery, well and good; if you follow the rules. But if what you have in mind is a story with only some elements of a mystery, tell your story first and do not try to change it to conform to some vague idea of what a mystery should be. Your publisher will classify your book for you; genre classification is a subjective thing, nothing more than a handle, really, an easy and convenient way of breaking down different works into groups more for marketing purposes than for readers.

There are, of course, other aspects of writing a mystery to consider, but these are more difficult to pin down. Most notable among them, however, are point of view and voice. Selecting the right point of view is extremely important, because it determines what the reader will and will not learn. Voice is, really, the application of point of view to a consistent rhythm, a *voice* the reader hears. More often than not, point of view is intrinsic to the writing itself (the writer will begin "I . . ." or "He . . ."), but voice requires a certain conscious effort on the writer's part, an attempt to convey the story consistently through or around the central character—even when that central character's vision is rather limited or, to the writer, unattractive. The success of the voice is directly related to how true the writer remains to his character and how willing the writer is to remain "transparent."

If you work within the given structure, writing a mystery is not so different from writing any other kind of novel. Good mysteries do, in fact, have all the elements common to all good fiction: engaging characters, strong sense of place, compelling plot, believable voice. Allow the structure to work for you, write as honestly as you know how, and everything else will fall into place.

NONFICTION: ARTICLES AND BOOKS

♦ 57

The Way of a Biographer

An Interview with Ron Chernow

Q. What elements go into selecting the subject of a biography? Does he or she have to be an important figure who would be familiar to a large audience, or simply one who fascinates and intrigues the biographer?

A. Let me reply in terms of crude commerce, then somewhat more elegantly in terms of art. An obscure writer chooses an esoteric biographical subject at his or her peril. The novice biographer should find a book that will sell on the strength of the subject—the author, after all, being unknown. As a writer's career progresses and his name looms larger on the dust jacket, he will have correspondingly more freedom in choosing topics, for he will (presumably) have faithful readers. To assume that a book will sell solely on the strength of strong reviews, without any preexisting interest in the subject, is a risky strategy for the tyro and a prescription for heartbreak. It always helps if you can picture a particular group of people who will be passionate about reading your book.

Turning to art, I have several criteria. I prefer epic tales, teeming with characters and covering a rich slice of history. I like a story so vast that I have freedom to roam, to shape and arrange, to impose a pattern on the flux. As any novelist will testify, a multitude of contrasting personalities heighten each other's reality. A powerful saga should also have a mighty theme buried in it or it will be just a diverting chronicle instead of a serious, absorbing history. The theme, ideally, should be one of topical significance. For instance, in writing *The House of Morgan,* I used the story of the J. P. Morgan empire as a prism through which to view the evolving world of high finance over a 150-year period. *The Warburgs* was my lens for examining the development of the remarkable Jews of Germany.

In writing history, I think it essential to present a fresh view of the

277

subject, to subvert stereotypes, to uncover major revelations. To this end, I will undertake a book only if I know of large caches of unpublished, largely untouched papers, scattered about in various archives, which promise dramatic new disclosures. To my mind, those documents are far more important than the prospect of cooperative family members—unless, of course, those family members happen to control the literary rights to the documents. In which case, they should be treated with the greatest delicacy.

Q. Many contemporary biographies are simply titled *X: A Life*. But how much of the "life" has to go into biography, and how does the biographer decide what to include and what to omit? What criteria are used in making such a selection?

A. At the outset, a biographer feels swamped by the material and wonders how the wilderness of random facts can be tamed into the formal garden of a book. Early in my research, I tend to jot down information with a nervous, indiscriminate pen. What finally simplifies matters is the emergence of the central theme, which becomes the glue, the binding agent, for the book. Once you find that principal focus, the material quickly divides itself into the essential and the superfluous. The panic subsides. Then you can climb back in from the window ledge.

Q. When, as in your case, you choose a whole family to write about—the Morgans and currently the Warburgs—do you attempt to embody their "personae" and the events and times in which they lived, as well as their influence on those events, and how they were influenced by them?

A. What I have learned in the course of doing two sagas is that you can spoon-feed people enormous amounts of information if you sugarcoat it with narrative. To that end, I keep people fixed in the foreground. Once you engage readers in the emotions of your characters, their minds expand, become more receptive, and absorb more information than they ever thought possible. In the end, readers are immensely grateful if you can give them a history lesson in a palatable, entertaining form.

Of course, you have to keep sketching in historical background, if the reader is to fathom what these people represent. The clumsy writer will pause, clear his throat, offer a history lesson, then resume the narrative. The artistic biographer will try to sketch in background without breaking the story's flow, inserting the material so deftly that characters and events appear completely intertwined.

Q. How much of their relationship with their family, friends, associates, and characters from the world in which they lived and worked do you draw on?

A. I intermingle the public and private lives as much as possible. From an ethical standpoint, the fact that he is a devoted husband or father may not redeem the ruthless tycoon, but it certainly makes him real. Character is most clearly revealed in relationships, particularly those fraught with conflict. To the extent possible, I take a kaleidoscopic approach and try to capture my people from different angles. It might seem that this would produce a blurry, diffuse portrait of the person. In fact, since we are all implausible compounds of good and evil, it makes the people seem more vivid and credible. I always look for paradox, irony, and complexity and like to go against the grain of received wisdom. For me the research gets interesting when I discover information that completely refutes my cherished little theories about the subject.

Q. What is the danger of a biographer's falling in love with his research and how do you decide when enough research is enough—or too much?

A. It is, of course, also dangerous for a writer to detest his subject and dwell morbidly on his deficiencies. But in general the besetting sin of much contemporary biography is the writer entranced by his subject and "making a case" for his importance. Writers tend to believe that if they elevate their subject's importance, this will enhance their own status. Yet I think that readers prefer subtle discriminations to crass boosterism. I don't like books in which the subject seems implicitly on trial and the author feels obligated to act as counsel for the defense or as prosecuting attorney.

Perhaps the surest signal that it is time to write is when your bank account slips into overdraft. Aside from that, I know that I am ready

279

to write when the people cease to surprise me and I'm hearing everything for the second or third time. This means that I have reached the point of diminishing returns and will only be adding shading or detail to the portrait, not broad new strokes.

Q. It has been said that biography uses elements of fiction and nonfiction to create the world and the people portrayed. Do you subscribe to that point of view, and if so, which techniques from fiction—dialogue, for example—have you used in writing your biographies?

A. Here I must confess that I am a novelist *manqué,* an old English major, and that at age twenty (to paraphrase George Bernard Shaw) I knew Shakespeare's characters better than my own contemporaries. So I give stories a novelistic shape by habit and training as well as by choice. If I have done anything unique in economic history, it's because I bring an alien, literary sensibility to bear. (As they say, in the realm of the blind, the one-eyed man is king.) I use many novelistic techniques: viewing events through the eyes of characters, changing the points of view, revealing personalities through incidental details, and saturating my books with anecdotes. At the same time, I try to adhere scrupulously to the facts. For instance, I don't claim to know what people were thinking, unless I have documentary evidence to prove it. And I don't reconstruct dialogue. That sort of thing only cheapens the writing and belittles the people, turning them into stale, storybook characters.

Q. Do you believe that a biographer should follow the chronological approach, or the dramatic conflicts of the span of history that you cover—in the case of the Warburgs, many, many decades?

A. I believe in the importance of chronology, but not in some plodding, inflexible manner. I want the reader to watch the characters grow and to view them, not as fixed and immutable, but in a state of development. I find it jarring when a biographer shuttles back and forth too freely over time, for it roughly shakes me awake from the pleasant spell cast by the narrative. On the other hand, I object to the tedious technique of narrating unrelated developments at once, just because they happened to occur the same year. This approach flattens and trivializes events by giving things of different value equivalent weight. So I would opt for chronology, but within certain limits.

Q. What, beyond the lifeline of birth, education, career, death, do you feel a biographer must include to portray the life or lives of the subject(s)?

A. I don't have a simple rule on this one. I always recommend to young writers that they follow the gravitational pull, the subterranean tug, of the subject. If they're mysteriously drawn to some aspect of a person's life—however trifling it might first appear—it probably contains some deeper truth. I monitor my own responses to my research. For instance, if I find myself regaling dinner parties with certain anecdotes about my subject, I know that I have stumbled upon stories that probably possess the person's essence. If I keep turning over certain details about my subject while out for a stroll, I know they must be pregnant with meaning. In the end, I assume that I am an Everyman, a proxy for my readers, and that what fascinates me will do the same for them.

Q. Should a biographer express his point of view and attitude (pro or con) about his subjects, or is the objective approach desirable, or, indeed possible?

A. Whether we like it or not, we are constantly betraying our feelings about our subjects. But while I don't think that pure objectivity is possible, it serves as a useful, constraining ideal that saves us from self-indulgent subjectivity. I prefer to let the point of view emerge from the narrative rather than have a nosy narrator butting in with his opinions. This doesn't mean that my approach is less opinionated, but it does mean that the narrative has enough independent life that the reader can form a contrary opinion. A writer should always include information that undercuts his "thesis" about the subject; only the hack will suppress it. This not only adds to the book's fairness, but makes the subject more lifelike.

Q. What are the special problems of writing the "multiple" biography (*The Warburgs, The House of Morgan*)? What role does the historical setting play?

A. The multiple biography taxes the author's craftsmanship more than any other nonfiction genre. You have so many strands to weave

281

together. In both of my plump books, I wanted to present the whole menagerie of characters as actors in a unified story. An earlier book on the Warburgs had put each famous family member in a separate, watertight chapter. That's boring and artificial, because the characters come alive only in dealing with each other. So I stressed those things— the evolution of the Jews in Germany, the fate of the Warburg bank and library, the rise of the state of Israel—in which family members, who might have led otherwise separate lives, suddenly joined in common cause.

This is also where the historical setting becomes extremely important. It is the atmosphere that bathes the characters, lending unity to their disparate lives. I don't know that you need to have affection for your characters, but you do need to love the period in which they lived.

Q. Do you favor the "great man" or the "great events" approach?

A. I don't think that one can have great men without great events. Many observers thought Franklin Roosevelt a lightweight, a mediocrity, until the Depression brought out his flair for innovation and his capacity to inspire a disconsolate citizenry. Without the Second World War, Winston Churchill would never have emerged from his political wilderness. The biographer wants to see how people behave under the pressure of events, those agonizing moments so intense as to force hidden character traits to the surface. What makes historical writing so much fun is that history flows through your characters. As T. S. Eliot once said, we cannot help but be modern. You don't have to choose between people and events because in good historical writing, they aren't really separable.

$58

FACTS AND THE NONFICTION WRITER

BY TRACY KIDDER

WHEN I STARTED WRITING NONFICTION a couple of decades ago there was an idea in the air, which for me had the force of a revelation: that all journalism was inevitably subjective. I was in my twenties then, and although my behavior was somewhat worse than it has been recently, I was quite a moralist. I decided that writers of nonfiction had a moral obligation to write in the first person—really write in the first person, making themselves characters on the page. In this way, I would disclose my biases. I would not hide the truth from the reader. I would proclaim that what I wrote was just my own impression of events. In retrospect it seems clear that this prescription for honesty often served as a license for self-absorption on the page. I was too young and self-absorbed to realize what should have been obvious: that I was less likely to write honestly about myself than about anyone else on earth.

I wrote a book about a murder case in a swashbuckling first person. After it was published and disappeared without a trace, I went back to writing articles for the *Atlantic Monthly*. For about five years, during which I didn't dare attempt another book, I worked on creating what many writer friends of mine call "voice." I didn't do this consciously. If I had, I probably wouldn't have gotten anywhere. But gradually, I think, I found a writing voice, the voice of a person who was informed, fair-minded, and always temperate—the voice, not of the person I was, but of the person I wanted to be. Then I went back to writing books, and discovered other points of view besides the first person.

Choosing a point of view is a matter of finding the best place from which to tell a story. The process shouldn't be determined by theory, but driven by immersion in the material itself. The choice of point of view, I've come to think, has nothing to do with morality. It's a choice among tools. On the other hand, the wrong choice can lead to dishonesty. Point of view is primary; it affects everything else, including voice. I've made my choices by instinct sometimes and sometimes by experiment. Most of my memories of time spent writing have merged together in a blur, but I remember vividly my first attempts to find a way to write *Among Schoolchildren,* a book about an inner-city teacher. I had spent a year inside her classroom. I intended, vaguely, to fold into my account of events I'd witnessed there a great deal about the lives of particular children and about the problems of education in America. I tried every point of view that I'd used in previous books, and every page I wrote felt lifeless and remote. Finally, I hit on a restricted third-person narration.

That approach seemed to work. The world of that classroom seemed to come alive when the view of it was restricted mainly to observations of the teacher and to accounts of what the teacher saw and heard and smelled and felt. This choice narrowed my options. I ended up writing something less comprehensive than I'd planned. The book became essentially an account of a year in the emotional life of a schoolteacher.

My choice of the restricted third person also obliged me to write parts of the book as if from within the teacher's mind. I wrote many sentences that contained the phrase "she thought." I felt I could do so because the teacher had told me how she felt and what she thought about almost everything that happened in her classroom. And her descriptions of her thoughts and feelings never seemed self-serving. Believing in them myself, I thought that I could make them believable on the page.

For me, part of the pleasure of reading comes from the awareness that an author stands behind the scenes adroitly pulling the strings. But the pleasure quickly palls at painful reminders of that presence— the times when, for instance, I sense that the author strains to produce yet another clever metaphor. Then I stop believing in what I read, and usually stop reading. Belief is what a reader offers an author, what Coleridge famously called "That willing suspension of disbelief for the moment, which constitutes poetic faith." All writers have to find ways to do their work without disappointing readers into withdrawing belief.

In fiction, believability may have nothing to do with reality or even plausibility. It has everything to do with those things in nonfiction.

I think that the nonfiction writer's fundamental job is to make what is true believable. But for some writers lately the job has clearly become more varied: to make believable what the writer thinks is true (if the writer wants to be scrupulous); to make believable what the writer wishes were true (if the writer isn't interested in scrupulosity); or to make believable what the writer thinks might be true (if the writer couldn't get the story and had to make it up).

I figure that if I call a piece of my own writing nonfiction it ought to be about real people, with their real names attached whenever possible, who say and do in print nothing that they didn't actually say and do. On the cover page of my new book I put a note that reads, "This is a work of nonfiction," and I listed the several names that I was obliged to change in the text. I feared that a longer note would stand between the reader and the spell that I wanted to create, inviting the reader into the world of a nursing home. But the definition of "nonfiction" has become so slippery that I wonder if I shouldn't have written more. So now I'll take this opportunity to explain that I spent a year doing research, that the name of the place I wrote about is its real name, that I didn't change the names of any major characters, and that I didn't invent dialogue or put any thoughts in characters' minds that the characters themselves didn't confess to.

I no longer care what rules other writers set for themselves. If I don't like what someone has written, I can stop reading, which is, after all, the worst punishment a writer can suffer. But the expanded definitions of "nonfiction" have created problems for those writers who define the term narrowly. Many readers now view with suspicion every narrative that claims to be nonfiction. But not all writers make up their stories or the details in them. In fact, scores of very good writers do not—writers such as John McPhee (*Coming into the Country*), Jane Kramer (*The Last Cowboy*), J. Anthony Lucas (*Common Ground*). There are also special cases, which confound categories and all attempts to lay down rules for narrative. I have in mind especially Norman Mailer's *Executioner's Song,* a hybrid of fact and fiction, labeled as such, which I loved reading.

Most writers lack Mailer's powers of invention. Some nonfiction writers do not lack his willingness to invent, but the candor to admit it. Some writers proceed by trying to discover the truth about a situation, and then invent the facts as necessary. Even in these suspicious times, a writer can get away with this. Often no one will know, and the subjects of the story may not care. They may approve. They may not notice. But the writer always knows. I believe in immersion in the events of a story. I take it on faith that the truth lies in the events somewhere, and that immersion in those real events will yield glimpses of that truth. I try to hew to a narrow definition of nonfiction partly in that faith and partly out of fear. I'm afraid that if I started making things up in a story that purported to be about real events and people, I'd stop believing it myself. And I imagine that such a loss of conviction would infect every sentence and make each one unbelievable.

I don't mean to imply that all a person has to do to write good nonfiction is to take accurate notes and reproduce them. The kind of nonfiction I like to read is at bottom storytelling, as gracefully accomplished as good fiction. I don't think any technique should be ruled out to achieve it well. For myself, I rule out only invention. But I don't think that honesty and artifice are contradictory. They work together in good writing of every sort. Artfulness and an author's justified belief in a story often combine to produce the most believable nonfiction.

§ 59

PROFILE WRITING

BY SYLVIA WHITMAN

NEXT TIME YOU UNLOAD YOUR CART at the supermarket, check out what enquiring minds are reading. Headlines tease with the triumphs of Madonna and the travails of Princess Di. In a word: gossip. Even magazines that carry more cachet—that would never think of putting on the cover some mother who just gave birth to a space alien (unless he were the spitting image of Michael Jackson)—feature similar faces: Maria Shriver, Bill Clinton, Barbara Walters. As editors will testify, people fascinate people.

Fortunately for writers, that attraction has created a tremendous demand for profiles, from cameos of hot business owners, to biographies of offbeat scientists. If you socialize with the glitterati, you may need only to string together sentences to entrance a publisher. But connections won't make or break you in this field. Free lancers will find markets for the lowdown on any interesting person, celebrated or not.

Choosing the person

Fame sells. What superstars think isn't even feature fluff nowadays; it's news. The lucky few who make a living writing celebrity profiles earn their fat paychecks, however: Cozying up to stars requires patience and chutzpah.

Many of the rich and famous hire publicists to fend off writers. Busy actors usually don't chat on spec. While an assignment from a national magazine may open the door for you, "names" often demand quid pro quo—their photo on the cover, a plug for their latest project. Some celebrities require questions to be submitted in advance. If the latest heartthrob does grant you an interview, you may find your conversation has all the intimacy of a royal audience.

Dead celebrities offer a good alternative for writers outside of the

New York-L.A.-D.C. loop of cultural elitism. First of all, they're never too busy or too prickly. Secondly, they can't recant their quotes during the limbo between an article's acceptance and publication. On the other hand, the grave does lessen a star's newsworthiness, so a writer must try to give the profile a timely peg. That means working long enough ahead to allow for a magazine's lead time. A year before the 75th anniversary of the Girl Scouts, I started circulating a query about Girl Scouts founder Juliette Gordon Low. Think birthdays and decade milestones. I once sold to an airline magazine a retrospective that claimed, "Forty years after his death, W. C. Fields still reigns as the Dark Prince of American humor."

Beginners do well to follow the environmentalist motto: Think globally, act locally. Find someone close to home whose story deserves an audience. Local and regional publications love to introduce readers to their neighbors. Start with a topic. Who spearheads historic preservation in your town? Who shelters AIDS babies? Who runs an eco-store? When a city magazine asked me to write about child abuse, I contacted a Parents' Anonymous group and profiled an incest victim who had started to bully her own kids but was seeking help to break the cycle.

Hunt for people with extraordinary talents. By browsing widely, you may discover that the guy next door is better known outside the community than locally. After *The Wall Street Journal* described investment banker Anthony Gray as the Orlando money manager with a "Midas touch," a weekly in town enlisted me to interview him for a cover story. Few residents of Central Florida had ever heard of him.

Far more often, I pitch articles about local folks to national magazines. I mine my daily newspaper for likely candidates—someone with an unusual hobby, a recent award, or a bright idea—then pan through their backgrounds for an angle. While living in New Orleans, for example, I read a feature about a judge who assigns book reports to young offenders. Surely children's book writers would appreciate that. Indeed, the kids' lit trade magazine *Horn Book* bought my profile. Talking to the judge in chambers, I learned not only about her taste in literature, but also about the frustrations of administering juvenile justice. The wheels started clicking: law. I sold a revised version of the article to *Student Lawyer*.

The beauty of profiles lies in the many different ways you can slant them. Is your subject female? Try women's magazines. Does she work?

Hit professional journals. Where did he grow up? Query his hometown paper. Where did she go to college? Pitch an alumni magazine. Did he serve in the armed forces? Interest a military publication.

Recently, I learned about hotelier and philanthropist Henri Landwirth, who has opened an all-expense-paid resort near Disney World exclusively for terminally ill children and their families. First, I queried general-interest magazines with this story, but *Parade* had already run a profile on him, and others turned me down. Since Landwirth was nearing retirement age, I tried senior-citizen publications but again met rejection. Landwirth, a Holocaust survivor, said something that stuck in my mind: "I can relate to children who have no control over their lives. As a child, I had no control over mine." Wouldn't Jewish readers empathize with his motivation? Sure enough, a Jewish quarterly bought the manuscript.

Setting up the interview

It's not whom you know but how well you get to know them that counts. Usually, you get only one shot—one interview. You need to milk that conversation for all it's worth.

I try to schedule the meeting well in advance, at the subject's convenience. I also press for an open-ended time slot so I can have as much time as necessary. It takes a while for people to let down their defenses.

I prefer to tag along with someone on the job—or at least to meet on the interviewee's personal turf, whether home or office. "Midas" investor Tony Gray let me spend a morning in his office—a wonderful boon, since he had a speaker telephone, so I eavesdropped on traders angling for a piece of the stock action in the $1.5 billion pension fund Gray manages.

Look around. Knickknacks and photos often prompt questions. And observing someone in action supplies details that round out a profile. By taking our county appraiser to lunch, I could tell the readers of *Orlando* magazine that at age 79, he still climbs the stairs to his second-floor office and still considers a ham sandwich a grand meal.

Take photographs whenever possible—with the subject's permission, of course. Not only will the offer of a "package" tempt editors, but I find that pictures free me from objective physical descriptions—brown eyes, short hair, etc. When writing the piece, I can then focus on subjective details. I wanted to convey my impression of Kids Village founder Henri Landwirth as a businessman whose heart led him out of the executive suite: "A slim man at ease in a tie, he speaks softly with a European accent. Yet the children understand him . . ."

Lacking visual cues, I ask more probing questions during phone interviews, which sometimes stretch for hours. To protect her privacy, the incest victim I reached by phone didn't reveal her name. But I pried for enough information about her daily routine for readers to believe she was a normal, stressed-out parent:

> Like most working mothers, Chris lives by the clock. Every weekday she wakes up at 5:30 a.m., dresses, mobilizes her three daughters, makes breakfast, drops the kids at school, works a full day as an interior designer, and picks up the kids at day care. Barring kickball games and teacher conferences, she usually arrives home around 5:30 p.m.—except on Tuesdays, when her 6-year-old takes ballet, and Wednesdays, when her 5-year-old dances, and Thursdays, when she buys groceries. . . .
>
> On Mondays, Chris and her girls grab supper, maybe a bowl of cereal if they're rushed, and head to a church in Leon County. There . . . Chris and eight to 10 other [parents] discuss how and why they're not going to hurt their kids.

To prepare for interviews, I review all the information I have about my subject, but I make sure to verify what others have written. I jot notes and questions—but never in stone: Since I'm hoping for heartfelt comments, I aim to keep the conversation spontaneous.

For accuracy and later verification, most writers tape their interviews, provided the speaker agrees. Unless I'm worried about getting sued or planning to use extended or technical quotes, I don't use a tape recorder. Machines unnerve some subjects. Taking notes forces me to listen closely, and sometimes while I'm scribbling away, trying to catch up, my interviewee fills the pause with a golden afterthought.

Lastly, I solicit comments from friends, colleagues, a spouse. How to track them down? Ask the subject. Pals talk more freely when you have a referral, and unless you're writing about a controversial figure, fans serve just as well as critics. They often confirm your judgments but spare you from going out on a limb. When I wrote an article about Manlin Chee, winner of an American Bar Association award for public service, I let a legal-aid coordinator in Greensboro, North Carolina, describe her: "If you see Manlin, you would say she's a hippie. . . .

But what you see is not what you get. . . . She's just the person you want behind you, whatever your case."

Putting it on paper

I enjoy writing profiles because of their cohesiveness. I never have to drop bread crumbs to find my way back to the focus: Who is this person?

Chronology forms the outline for chunks of the article—where he came from, what she's doing now, what he hopes to accomplish in the future (or, in the case of a dead person, what she left as a legacy). Of course, I scramble the order of these blocks to pique a reader's curiosity. In the profile about the founder of the Girl Scouts, I started not with her privileged childhood in Savannah, but with her doldrums in the wake of a miserable marriage:

Although Juliette Gordon Low had just succeeded in recovering a fair share of her late husband's estate from his mistress, middle age looked as bleak as tundra. "I am just an idle woman of the world, with no real work or duties," she wrote from England to her mother around 1906.

From there, I fast-forwarded six years, to the mustering of the Girl Scouts who gave her life purpose. Then I rewound to her family history—dwelling on the resourceful women who influenced "Daisy" Low and the evolution of her daffy charm.

I always plant a statement or two in the lead about my subject's claim to attention, if not fame. At the same time, I try to establish a theme. In a profile of textile artist Lisa Williamson, I opened with her talking about a pair of sculptures in her yard, since yin and yang inform so much of her work. Writing the rags-to-riches story of Hector Hernandez for a teen magazine, I emphasized that as the son of migrant farm workers, he grew up a workhorse, not a clotheshorse:

. . . "My family shopped at the Salvation Army—long before that was trendy." Now as a designer for the prestigious Robert Comstock label, Hernandez helps to dress the most fashionable men in America.

Think of how you introduce a new acquaintance to an old friend: This is X—who works at X. She's the X who started X. Yeah, yeah, the one who X'd. Cool, huh?

No article ever writes itself, but you and your subject share the work in a profile. You take turns at the mike. The writer arranges, condenses, describes, explains; the subject speaks in a loud, clear voice. Since tone reveals character, I insert a lot of direct quotes. Readers discovered Manlin Chee's modesty the way I did, by her humorous account of law school: "I went through my first year in a fog. . . . All I knew was Perry Mason." Yet I avoid transcribing monologues. Most people ramble. If the subject supplies the gems, then the writer must play jeweler, crafting a proper setting for every quote.

There's more to people than what they say, so a profile should include some of the writer's impressions. Does the subject flit from topic to topic like a hummingbird or lumber like a bear? You are the reader's intermediary: What strikes you? I noticed that high-rolling investor Tony Gray "does not dress the part of a tycoon—no silk, no monograms, just a watch and a wedding ring." Even if I'm casting someone as a hero or a villain, I often add asides that illustrate human contradictions. "Hippie" Manlin Chee told me that she sat through *Easy Rider* covering her eyes and ears because of the film's violence and profanity. Real people have many dimensions.

I usually save one of the better quotes for the last paragraph. When designer Hector Hernandez summed up his fashion philosophy, I tagged it for a conclusion: "Style is something personal; it's what you wear at home when no one's looking; it's who you are without airs." Then my editor tacked on another sentence about his rise up the ladder of success. Which brings me to a general lesson: Never make promises about the published form of a profile. No matter what a subject or a writer says, editors always get the last word.

60

BECOME A TRAVEL WRITER

BY MARGERY MILNE

BECOME A TRAVEL WRITER, beckoned an advertisement in a recent popular magazine. It encouraged readers to travel to the Arctic. "Take our Alaskan Voyage," it said. "Watch whales, dolphins, arctic foxes and more; then write about what you've observed. You will have a travel article about Alaskan wildlife that could be a winner." That sounds easy enough, especially if you are willing to travel to Alaska.

But is it that easy to be a travel writer? Do you have to travel far from home? You could be that lucky but it takes much, much more. One of my students told me he was interested in being a travel writer, but first he had to take time out to go to Boston from New Hampshire to be interviewed for a job. I suggested that he record his travel experiences and observations along the way and that by doing so he would accomplish much more than just a job interview. He returned with an incredible account of the changes that had occurred along the route since the time he was a teenager. With the thought of writing a travel piece in mind, he tuned into his senses and was amazed at what he observed, proving that to be a travel writer, you must be alert and aware and prepared for every sight and experience. If you stop, look, and listen in your travels near or far from home, you can find adventure that could be worth sharing and a discovery worth writing about.

Record your personal experiences when you travel. This could be in any one of several forms. The best way to remember events is to write them down daily in a journal. When friends departed recently to drive across the United States to spend several months in California, I gave them a tape recorder so they could comment on their experiences and observations as they drove along. Usually I record my travel activities with dated slides that help me remember when I visited an area as well as the sights I saw. This avoids mixing up locations later when I put slides on a videotape and add narration or music.

293

Small, everyday encounters can sometimes provide the most interesting experiences. When traveling, take note of whatever excites you; it will no doubt excite your reader as well. Write articles similar to ones you like to read. Look in the newspaper travel section for various excursions; and view trips through the eyes of a child because what seems to captivate children could be of interest to others. Jot down key words you hear from fellow travelers or your tour guide. Descriptive phrases enhance your writing, so rather than write about going to Spain, compel your reader by writing about travel to "tantalizing" Spain. Keep alert for that discovery you will make on your trip as it becomes a special experience to remember. When you are writing, simple style is better than such murky phrases as: "Individuals who make their abode in vitreous edifices are well advised not to launch petrous projectiles." How much simpler to say, "People in glass houses shouldn't throw stones."

Seeking sources for your travel stories requires reading and analyzing travel magazines and just about everything else. So many articles on travel show that the market is rich in opportunities. The main task is to mold your article to fit the trend. The current focus seems to be ecotourism—travel and the environment—family travel experiences, and ethnic values and diversity.

More people than ever are traveling at home and abroad with all sorts of intriguing interests, so that no matter where you travel, anywhere and everywhere, there is something to explore and write about. Articles on travel in special groups such as elderhostelers, families with children, or people with particular hobbies appear frequently. Recently, I returned from lecturing on travel writing on a huge cruise ship, on which a group of physicians was holding meetings on medicine. There you have an idea for a travel piece: doctors talking about medicine getting together on a ship and at the same time seeing the sights as they travel the world. That would make a much more intriguing travel article than a meeting at a large hotel on some tropical island.

Do you feel upbeat about your travel article idea? Then you should query or write the appropriate editor. When I traveled to Wyoming and camped at Jackson Hole, I was so enthralled watching and photographing, close-up, moose and their young, that I wrote a query letter detailing my travel observations to *The New York Times Magazine* editor. He responded with a telegram: "Send the article and include photos." Having only one roll of exposed film, I sent it to him, along with the article, and the piece was published a week later.

Later, while traveling in the jungles of Panama, I was so impressed with my findings that I wrote the same *Times* editor. Again he responded favorably, and my article appeared with full-page photos. Did the photos help this travel piece? From further experiences, I know a good story doesn't always need photos. After sending a query letter and getting a supportive response, I submitted a different piece on the rain forests of Panama (without photos) to the *Illustrated London News*.

Conferring in advance with an editor of a magazine or newspaper may excite you to get going and write. The editor of the *Portsmouth (NH) Herald* met with one of my students who had shown her ability in writing a travel piece after visiting Ireland. The editor liked it so much that he encouraged her to write similar articles about travel in New England. A series by her was subsequently published in the Sunday section of the newspaper. Having one piece accepted often leads to further assignments.

If you have an opportunity to confer with an editor before you write your piece, you should explain why your topic is suitable for that publication. For example, in advance of a trip to Disneyland, I asked the editor of my hometown paper whether he'd be interested in a travel piece on this tourist attraction. He encouraged me to go ahead, but advised me that there would be no payment. I decided that having my name on the piece would still make it worth writing. Getting bylines helps make your name known, and editors will later recognize you as a writer. I'd carried a letter from the newspaper editor saying that a travel piece on Disneyland was of interest to his publication. When I arrived, I was given a special badge to admit me and my companion everywhere, and also a folder of photographs for use with the article. With such kind help and recognition, I felt rewarded.

Many aspiring travel writers want to begin by writing for *National Geographic*. My advice to them is to try for publication in smaller magazines: First get published, then get recognized.

I am often asked how to write travel articles. There is no secret to doing it; just write as you would any other article—naturally. Tell stories of your experiences as if you were relating them to a friend; be humorous, suggest ways you could improve the trip to make it more

295

enjoyable, or less costly. Write about something you find unusual. If it is new to you or attractive to you, it could be appealing as well to others.

When I traveled to the Soviet Union, I wondered what subject I could find to write a travel piece about. I wanted something unusual; the environment and nature particularly appeal to me. Yet I wondered, is it possible to find anything in that devastated land? It came to me in a flash at the end of my two-week visit: I had noticed the quantities of amber displayed by street vendors and in shows and saw people searching for amber along the beaches. These treasured souvenirs, I decided, were just right for an unusual travel piece.

When I returned home, I read books on amber, and became so excited with my findings that I sent off a query letter to the Sunday travel editor of *The Boston Globe*. Back came the letter asking for my article, which I called "The Baltic Sea of Amber." A request for photos followed. I had lost my camera in Moscow, but my companion had some remarkable pictures, which I sent, and they were published along with my piece several months later, when the *Globe* featured travel to the Soviet Union.

Newspapers have a schedule for publishing travel pieces on particular places, usually related to the seasons: Florida and the Caribbean in winter, New England in the fall. Ask for the paper's schedule so that you can submit your travel manuscript well in advance of the scheduled issue. (The same applies to magazines.)

An inspiration for a travel article is all you need to get started. Follow it with a strong query letter to the travel editor of the right publication. If there is editorial interest in your proposal, check your facts and start your lead-in as intriguingly as you can. For example, my "amber" story began:

While visiting the Soviet Union, I discovered something special. It was amber, a honey-colored resin that was part of a living thing 50 million years ago. Like the yellow glare of sunlight, the amber glittered in shops as I moved from Leningrad to Moscow, increasing in quantity and quality as I came close to the Baltic Sea.

You may wish to include some history, as I did:

Amber was revered by the ancient sun worshippers. In fact, the Egyptians worshipped it more than gold. Rooms that had walls of amber and furnishings

296

of amber were given to Peter the Great. During war time, it was dismantled and hidden. The hiding place is no longer known; a similar room is being constructed.

If your travel writing appeals to your editor, it will appeal to your readers, and you are on your way to becoming a travel writer!

61

WRITING THE FEATURE ARTICLE

BY RITA BERMAN

THERE IS A GOOD STEADY MARKET for feature articles. Readers are always looking for ways to improve themselves. Pick up any magazine at the newsstands. What do you see? Articles on how to cope with a teenager or a baby, make tasty meals in 30 minutes, take off ten pounds. How to live longer, happier, wealthier, understand and buy art, learn word processing, or—how to write. All of these feature articles are aimed directly at the reader.

The content of a feature article is more important than the author's name, so the unknown writer has as good an opportunity as the well-known one to have an article accepted, provided that the manuscript is well done and meets the editor's needs.

"Find facts that are new and known by few," an editor told me when I began my writing career. Sounds gimmicky, but it's good advice. Remember that a feature article focuses on the human-interest angle of facts, but this is not a hard and fast rule. Many feature articles are instructive or informational: how-to, how-I, or how-you. The principles of these how-tos (also known as service articles) are that you state the problem, offer a solution, and end with a result. Your advice must guide the readers through the steps taken so that they, too, can recreate your success. Other features are based on interviewing an expert or recognized authority in the field you wish to write about, then in your article, sharing their experiences and knowledge with the reader.

You must do a lot of thinking and planning, as well as gathering and organizing facts. You need to consider the subject of the article; how much readers will be interested in that subject; possible markets; sources that could provide ideas and facts; who might be interviewed for the article; and whether illustrations or photographs may be needed.

By the time you have collected notes, material, photographs, or illustrations, the article may be taking shape in your mind. Before writing your feature, organize your thoughts and material. Know what you want to put into your article, but don't try to keep it all in your head. *Use an outline to get started and stay on track.*

1. On your worksheet, write the working title, which could change after you've written the piece, or as you go along.

Titles are the bait you use to attract editors and readers. Most magazine titles rarely exceed six to eight words. A good title should suggest the contents and tone of the story. Titles cannot be copyrighted, but avoid using one that might be confused with a previously published piece.

2. Jot down a list of words, phrases, or sentences to remind you of all the items and points you wish to cover in your feature.

3. Decide what kind of lead to use to attract the reader:

The question lead: What can you do to get a million dollars?
The controversial statement: It's easy to get a million dollars.
The case history or anecdotal lead: I made my first million—the easy way.
A statement of fact: There are more millionaires than ever.
A descriptive lead: A million dollars in gold lay gleaming in the vault.

A strong lead is crucial in feature writing because this is what draws the reader into the article, and immediately after the lead, you proceed in a way that will sustain that reader's interest and provide the reason or justification for your lead.

This transition from the lead to the text is sometimes referred to as the bridge, hook, angle, or peg of the story.

Example: For one feature, "How We Sold Our Home" (published in *Army, Navy, Air Force Times*), I used a grabber lead about military families being familiar with change-of-station orders, and how we had led a nomadic existence for 12 years.

4. After your lead, what kind of bridge will you use to hold readers' interest?

In my feature, a paragraph stating that about 7 million homes change hands each year provided the bridge; the rest of the piece was my personal story. I involved the readers by informing them that selling our house without using a real estate broker saved us thousands of dollars. That was my response to the reader's natural "what's in it for me?" question. No matter what the subject—going on a cruise, or trying to avoid paying more taxes—readers always ask, "What's in it for me?"

5. The body of your piece. What anecdotes, examples, or facts will you use to prove the point you want to make? For a how-to piece this is where you will describe the pitfalls, things that didn't work, as well as tips that will lead to a satisfactory conclusion.

I continued my home sale feature by describing a few simple steps that should be followed when selling without an agent. Then I was off into the body of the story, repeating and expanding the reasons for selling the house ourselves, and describing how we did it: preparing the house and grounds; pricing the house realistically; and how we saved time and money when we conducted the sale.

6. The conclusion. A final strong paragraph should wrap it all up effectively for the reader.

My last paragraph for "How We Sold Our Home" echoed my lead by referring to military families and their nomadic way of life. This helped reinforce the message to the military readers of *Army, Navy, Air Force Times* that they too might be moving and selling a house sometime in the future.

Do not try to write any of the sections in final form at this stage. The outline should be used as a guide to prompt the flow of thoughts and to keep you moving in the right direction. It will be particularly helpful if for any reason you have to put the article aside.

Writing the rough draft

With the outline to guide you, you will be ready to begin writing your feature. Write directly and simply, as if talking to your readers. Short paragraphs. Write to be understood, not to impress. As your piece begins to take shape, you will have to consider what transitions are needed to take the reader from example to example, and how you will tie the whole thing together. Keep the feature story flowing toward a strong closing paragraph to balance the hard-hitting lead.

Use subheads and a blurb so that readers can grasp the main idea quickly. A blurb is a summary of what the article is about. You need to know this yourself in order to write the feature. If you are unable to compress the scope of the feature into a sentence or two, perhaps you need to think about it some more.

For informational articles, sidebars and boxes keep the article tight and give it impact. In "How We Sold Our Home" I included a box headed "What do real estate terms mean?" listing key words and definitions such as *appraisal, closing costs, earnest money.*

Tell the reader how and where to get more information on the topic, including addresses and phone numbers, if available. If the how-to was based on interviews, give your sources credit for their remarks.

Accuracy is essential in how-to articles, so recheck your facts before you send out the manuscript.

Revision

You should spend almost as much time on revising and rewriting as you spent on thinking, planning, and writing your rough draft. Are the points in good logical order? The best possible words? It's fun to cross out words you have written and substitute new ones that are clearer and give sharper meaning to your story.

If a sentence sounds awkward on rereading, rephrase it. Chop a long sentence into two. Write in simple sentences rather than long, compound or complex ones.

Allow some time to elapse between the first and second draft. If I wait for a day or two, sentences or sections that need reworking seem to leap off the page. Try to read the article aloud, or better still, tape it. Listening to your words will uncover writing weaknesses.

Write to space

The only way you can cut a feature, if it ends up being too long, is to prune throughout. An alternative is to write to space from the outset. Do this by assigning a specific number of words to each section of your outline. As a guide, for a 1,500-word piece you might allot 50 words for the introduction, 150 words for the bridge, 1,200 words for the body of the piece, and 100 words for the conclusion. An average page of typing contains 250 words (25 lines of 10 words), so 1,500 words should run approximately six pages.

Getting the feature published

The usual publication outlet for features is in the monthly or quarterly magazines, thousands of which are published in all regions of the country. New magazines hit the newsstands every month, and the old ones change their formats. In addition, magazines sold by subscription only also have a constant need for steady, reliable writers who can write interesting features. Names and addresses of consumer, special interest, trade, and a host of other magazines can be found in the back of this book; select the best possible markets for your feature.

Many listings request that writers query instead of submitting a completed manuscript. By querying, you find out if—and where—there is interest in your piece. Make a list of markets to query, and send for writers guidelines before you write your query letter. Guidelines provide information on topics that are wanted, word length, preferred submission format, whether photographs are needed, the rights bought, pay scale, and other useful information about editorial needs.

Select one publication and submit a query letter. If you draw a negative response, revise the letter and work your way through the market list. After you get a go-ahead from an editor, you can prepare the article to meet the magazine's editorial needs, and thus increase your chances of being published.

62

LETTER TO A YOUNG ARTICLE WRITER

BY DONALD M. MURRAY

YOUR PIECES ARE FILLED with interesting, specific information; they have a clear focus; they are well written; but they are not likely to be published without revision.

What they lack is what professionals call an edge. The idea does not contain the tension that attracts and holds a reader. Note the first paragraph of my letter. It contains a surprise, an apparent contradiction, a conflict, something unexpected that engages the reader in a conversation. "What does he mean? The articles are written well, with focused information, and they are *not* publishable?" the reader asks, and the writer responds.

Your articles are pleasant and predictable. They do not have an urgency, a significance, an unexpectedness, a tension that will draw in a reader who is not already fascinated by your subject.

Editors find it difficult to describe what is missing in such good writing—and so do I. The problem is not with what is on the paper but what is not. Editors are looking for what they have not seen and cannot command. If editors know what they want, they can order it from professionals on their staff or from familiar free lancers like me. Doris Lessing said, "You have to remember that nobody ever wants a new writer. You have to create your own demand."

The demand is created when a writer expresses an individual, authoritative point of view toward our familiar world in a voice that is appropriate to the topic and the writer's attitude toward it. The voice communicates authority and concern.

Your ideas do not have an essential tension. Some of my daybook lines that have led to writing include:

"I cheered when we dropped the atomic bomb." [I was in the paratroops and scheduled to jump into Tokyo.]

"I'm lucky I had a sickly childhood." [It forced me to exercise my imagination.]

"I'm glad I have an old wife." [We have a shared history.]

"It was good there was no Little League when I was a kid." [We played sandlot ball and were not over-organized by competitive parents.]

My habit is to seek the tensions within my life and the lives of those around me. I inventory what sparks a strong emotional reaction: irony, anger, despair, humor, pain, pleasure, contentment, fear.

I read the mental and daybook or journal notes I make as I lead my life, asking such questions as:

- What surprises me?
- Where's the tension?
- What should be and what is?
- Where's the conflict?
- Where will these ideas, issues, people collide?
- What's the problem?
- What's different from what I expected?
- What are the implications—for me, for my readers?
- What are the connections?
- What contradicts?

Margaret Atwood says, "Good writing takes place at intersections, at what you might call knots, at places where the society is snarled or knotted up." Mary Lee Settle says, "I start my work by asking a question and then try . . . to answer it."

As I question myself, I hear fragments of language. These are rarely sentences, although they may be. Usually they are just phrases, words in collision, or words that connect in unexpected ways. Recently I wrote a column about my grandson learning to walk. The line came from his father, who said Joshua had "to learn to fall to learn to walk." That was an idea; it contained a truth expressed in a line that had a surprising tension.

I record such lines and scratch when they itch. A lead—the opening sentences or paragraphs—can hold an article in place so I can explore it in a draft written days or weeks later. For example, the other day I was doing errands with my wife when I had the following experience, and I immediately wrote (in my head), "have to get glasses tightened." When I got home, I turned the line into a lead:

We are driving to Dover, New Hampshire, to shop when Minnie Mae says, "I have to get my sunglasses tightened."

I pull up to Whitehouse Opticians and Minnie Mae asks, "Why are we stopping here?"

"To get your sunglasses tightened."

"They are home on my desk."

[She's just talking. I hear a problem to be solved.]

I have an idea, but that's not enough. In John Jerome's wonderful book on nonfiction writing, *The Writing Trade: A Year in the Life* (Viking, 1992), which should be on your desk, he quotes a colleague as saying that a 600-word essay needs about an idea and a half. That articulated an important truth about all articles for me.

My grandson's learning to fall so he could learn to walk was a good idea, but it was not enough. In writing the article I connected his need to learn to fall with writers, artists, scientists, and entrepreneurs, who need to experience instructive failure to succeed. Then I had an essay.

The anecdote demonstrating the difficulty I (who always want to solve a problem) have communicating with my female companion who is just commenting on life, is an interesting and amusing idea. It articulates a tension most male and female readers have experienced. But it is not yet publishable. I will write it when I come up with the essential extra half of an idea or, more likely, when I start drafting the piece and discover the extra half during the writing.

Your articles stop short of that significant half of an idea, that moment of discovery of a significant extra meaning that you and your reader share in the writing and reading of the essay.

To find that extra meaning I have to write with velocity so that I am thinking on paper, saying what I do not expect to say. Of course you will consider and reconsider, write and rewrite this discovery draft, but for me, it is essential to discover what I have to say by saying it. If I know just what I am going to say when I first start to write an article, the draft is flat, uninteresting. When I discover meaning during the writing, as I have in writing this letter to you, I may have something to share with readers that editors will want to publish.

Good luck. Draw strength from the fact that you can gather specific, revealing information; that you can focus it; that you can write a clear running sentence and a paragraph that develops and communicates a thought or feeling, and then go on to find the edge, the tension, that will make editors accept your articles and invite you to write more.

305

63

WRITING A LIFE

BY LINDA SIMON

"BIOGRAPHY WORKS IN MYSTERIES," wrote Leon Edel, the masterful biographer of Henry James. "That is its fascination." Many biographers have likened themselves to detectives trying to find a missing person—their subject—by searching for clues in letters, diaries, photographs, and whatever other artifacts survive as evidence of their subject's life. Working in public archives and private collections, biographers read intimate revelations, discover secrets, and ultimately come to know their subjects better, perhaps, than they know their own friends and family. The work of a biographer can be difficult, frustrating, and time-consuming; but, as Edel tells us, biography has many rewards. Biographers learn not only about the particular details of their subject's life, but also the historical, cultural, and social context in which they lived; not only about the particular problems and decisions that their subject faced, but something about human nature, about the dreams and desires that we all share. As a result of their search into someone else's life, biographers often learn something about themselves.

Choosing a subject

Who makes a good biographical subject? If we look at library shelves, we find that in the past biographies were written about famous men—and a few women. The biographical subject usually was a hero: someone who had accomplished some great feat, held an important political position, or made a lasting contribution to the arts. The biographer paid homage to this person's greatness by portraying his life as exemplary. Catherine Drinker Bowen, who wrote biographies of such great men as Justice Oliver Wendell Holmes and John Adams, tells us that writing about heroic figures was, for her, an uplifting experience:

To spend three years or five with a truly great man, reading what he said and wrote, observing him as he errs, stumbles, falls, and rises again; to watch his talent grow . . . this cannot but seize upon a writer, one might almost say transform him. . . . The ferment of genius, Holmes said, is quickly imparted, and when a man is great he makes others believe in greatness. By that token one's life is altered. One has climbed a hill, looked out and over, and the valley of one's own condition will be forever greener.

Biographers today, however, are not likely to share Bowen's belief in heroes. Experience, observation, and a dollop of Freudian psychology has disillusioned many of us. We tend to believe that all people have their weaknesses, flaws, and dark sides. We look for complexities and contradictions—and we find them, even in men and women who have enacted great deeds.

Although many biographies are written about famous men and women, increasingly we find biographies about those who lived relatively ordinary lives. Jean Strouse, for example, decided to write about Alice James, a minor historical figure compared with her brothers, the novelist Henry James and the philosopher William. Alice James, Strouse wrote, "made no claim to have carried on an exemplary struggle or to have achieved anything beyond the private measure of her own experience. To make her into a heroine (or victim-as-heroine) now would be seriously to misconstrue her sufferings and her aims." Still, Strouse believed that Alice James's experiences could illuminate for readers the context of women's lives in the nineteenth century. She believed that writing about "semi-private lives" helps us to enter the world of ordinary men and women—the world, after all, in which most of us live.

If biographers today have a wide range of subjects to choose from, how does one decide? Who is a good subject? Simply put, a good subject, like an interesting friend, is someone whose stories we like to hear, someone we would like to introduce to other people. A good subject is not always likable, but never dull. It is someone whose story has not yet been told, perhaps, or in any case, has not yet been told the way we understand it. We may feel a connection with this subject because we share similar experiences or sensibilities; or we may feel admiration, even envy, for the subject's life. We may be attracted to someone who lived in an exciting time and place, even if that person did not contribute greatly to the excitement. Always, we feel that there is a mystery to be solved: Something about this person is not yet known, and we want to discover it.

I had been reading books by and about American expatriates in Paris, simply for the pleasure of it, when I noticed that Gertrude Stein emerged again and again in memoirs of the period. Surely Stein is an interesting historical figure: an experimenter in poetry and prose whose unconventional appearance and personality made her the center of attention wherever she went. I liked Stein's raunchiness, self-confidence, and literary daring. As I read biographies of Stein—again, simply for the pleasure of immersing myself in the period—I noticed that her companion, Alice B. Toklas, seemed to be a mysterious figure. Was she a kind, protective supporter of Stein? Was she a cold-hearted manipulator? Most biographers portrayed Stein as a dominant force in the household, but was Toklas really in charge? These questions motivated me to see Toklas as a potential biographical subject: She presented a problem for me; she was a mystery.

Although Alice Toklas lived a "semi-private" life in comparison with Gertrude Stein's, still she lived an extraordinary life in comparison with, say, my grandmother or uncle, who did not cavort with the likes of Ernest Hemingway, Pablo Picasso, and F. Scott Fitzgerald. But anyone's grandmother or uncle might be a suitable biographical subject. If your grandmother was an immigrant who kept diaries and sent letters to relatives in her native land, if your uncle was a health food guru who traveled the world teaching new ideas about nutrition, they may be interesting subjects for a full-length biography or a shorter study: an article in a historical journal, for example, or a chapter in a collection of biographical sketches. As a potential biographer, however, you need to ask the same questions about these subjects that you would ask about anyone else: Would my grandmother or uncle interest other people? Is there sufficient source material to give me enough biographical information for my study? Is there a mystery about this person that I want to solve?

Finding clues

Once biographers find a subject, they need to assess whether sufficient biographical material will be available to them. Biographers can write only about someone who has left a paper trail, including letters, journals, creative writing, works of art such as films or paintings, interviews. The biographer must have access to material that can document the subject's life.

If you have chosen a subject who has been written about before, existing biographies can help you to locate archives where there is material about your subject. I knew from biographies of Gertrude Stein that the Stein archives were housed in the American Literature collection at Yale University's Beinecke Library. Many of Toklas's letters were housed there as well. But to find other material, I began a search in the reference room of my local library. There, I examined such sources as the *National Union Catalogue of Manuscript Collections* and the *Directory of Special Libraries and Information Centers* to locate other archives where I guessed that I might find Toklas correspondence or other material. I wrote to these libraries, visited some, ordered photocopies, and began to assemble my own files of source material.

The reference room of a good library contains many directories that lead researchers to archival material. Some of these directories are specialized—focusing on women's history, science, or art, for example. Reference librarians are helpful and knowledgeable about these sources. I have discovered these professionals to be a biographer's best friend.

If you find few sources in library archives, the search becomes a bit more complicated. If your subject has survivors, you need to find out whether material that you need may be in private collections: the attic of your subject's grand-niece or the basement of your subject's ex-wife. Sometimes, survivors are cooperative; sometimes, however, they feel threatened by an interloper who may discover information about the family's life that they wish to be kept private. Although many biographies have been written in the face of survivors' hostility, some biographers find such a situation uncomfortable and stressful. If you are among them, you may want to choose another subject.

Doing it

Researching and writing a biography is not a quick project. It takes time to locate material, time to assemble sources, time to track down clues. You may find yourself spending years formulating a chronology of your subject's life. Anyone beginning a biography needs to have developed strong research skills. Historical writing is good practice, and so is newspaper reporting. Gradually, biographers develop a sense of intuition about their subject, discovering that they can anticipate their subject's reaction to a new acquaintance or a new experience.

Suddenly, they feel it is time to write. When I was working on a biography of Thornton Wilder, I went to visit a charming man who had been a close friend of Wilder's. He began to tell me some stories about Wilder's life—his experiences in the theater, his days as a soldier, his literary friendships—and I found that I could finish sentences: These were stories that I knew in even more detail than Wilder's friend. When I returned home, I began to write the book.

Some biographers write as they research, sketching in the parameters of a life, filling in details as they find them. Some biographers spend twenty years involved in their subject's life, although not all of those years are spent researching and writing. Few writers are able to work on a biography full time, so other tasks—teaching, translating, even doing the laundry—intervene in the research and writing process. Yet biographers admit that even when they are not actually conducting research or writing, their subject becomes a companion, someone they think about often. They begin to see events in their own lives through their subject's eyes; they reflect on their own experiences in light of what they learn about their subject. Biography invites introspection. Personal introspection—thinking about why people behave as they do, about the forces that shape us and the way we affect other people—is good training for the biographer's work.

Biographical problems

In the past few years, biographers have come under attack as being nothing more than burglars, rifling through lingerie drawers and laundry bins, looking for the worst about their subject. Joyce Carol Oates coined the term "pathography" to apply to biographies that present subjects as neurotic, psychotic, depressed, incestuous, alcoholic, or suffering from other antisocial maladies. But these biographies reflect our current intellectual climate more than they reflect the craft of biography.

Certainly the kinds of questions that biographers ask about their subjects have changed over time. Biographers have been influenced by the work of psychologists and social scientists; they examine their subjects from different perspectives, depending on their own ideas

310

about personality development and the cause and effect of behavior. A biography of John Kennedy, written in the 1960s, would have ignored questions about family rivalry and sexual infidelity that biographers feel free to ask twenty years later. A burgeoning interest in biographies of women, beginning in the 1970s, changed both the kinds of questions that biographers asked and the subjects that they chose to write about. In creating a sense of the reality of someone's life, biographers have come to see that the superficial interactions and daily routine may not define an individual. This delving deeply into another personality may seem to some an invasion of privacy. But responsible biographers take their task seriously: They want to find a missing person. Without their efforts, their subject would simply disappear, fade from memory, be lost to history. Biographers keep spirits alive.

64

WRITING ABOUT BUSINESS

BY LYN FRASER

RECENTLY PERUSING MAGAZINES at my local library, I found that almost two-thirds covered business or business-related topics in some way. Given the reading public's tremendous interest in business, writing on this topic offers an exciting challenge to the free-lance writer. The abundant market potential encompasses books, local and regional newspapers, newspaper syndicates, and all kinds of magazines—general interest, women's, men's, travel, sports, and many with specialized topics.

Finding ideas can be as easy as figuring out how to deal with some of the everyday problems or situations you encounter and how they could be presented in article form. For instance, you could write about how to select from the staggering number of options available when you open a checking account, or how to decipher confusing financial statements, or even how to manage the finances of a local club or organization to which you belong. Interview a successful small business executive you know of, or profile an innovative company in your area.

Whatever the topic, I have found three elements that are essential to being consistently successful in business writing: a) knowing the subject thoroughly; b) finding a market that matches the topic; and c) communicating the technical content of your subject in a readable, understandable style.

Know your subject

Business writing is not an area for bluff. Whether you are writing a book, an article, or a short column, research your topic and know it thoroughly before you attempt any writing for publication. To acquire the necessary background, you may have to read articles and books, talk to experts, or take a course. Complete whatever study and discussion you need to raise your own level of understanding to the point that you can explain the information to others. Even if you are writing a profile of a successful businessperson, you will need enough background to understand what she or he is saying in order to write about it effectively.

Like other writing specialties, business writing is one in which becoming an expert in some area helps establish a writing base. By developing an expertise in business financial statements, I turned a part-time teaching, part-time writing job into a career as a full-time freelance writer. When I taught students how to interpret financial statements, I found that all the available books on the subject were either too long or too technical. In 1984 I proposed a book to Reston Publishing Company (subsequently acquired by Prentice Hall) that would explain financial statements to an audience with little or no background in accounting. That book is now in its third edition and generates a stable, predictable income, which I supplement with income from magazine articles and other writing.

Another advantage of knowing a subject well is that editors will sometimes get in touch with you when they want an article written about that topic.

Find the right market

Markets for business writing abound, with choices ranging from local newspapers to major book publishers. For beginning free-lancers, the best markets are probably regional and special-interest magazines. Begin by considering the publications you read on a regular basis, then head for the nearest library or newsstand and read what interests you there. Another helpful resource is the market list of trade journals and business magazines provided in the back of this book.

Never rule out a magazine just because it does not have a business section. Many general magazines publish articles on financial and business subjects. You might discover that a seemingly unlikely publication will be interested in a business piece. I have just completed an article for a national environmental magazine about a nature group that financed the acquisition of a bird sanctuary using an innovative fund-raising approach: selling bonds to its members. If the magazine's editorial focus interests you and your topic is related, try your idea on the editor. Unless your topic is extremely "hot," most magazines prefer that you query first, which means sending a letter outlining your proposal and describing your qualifications.

Always read several copies of any magazine you plan to query. If you cannot find a copy at a library or newsstand, write for a sample copy. Send for writers guidelines—which many publications have—and *follow them*.

Another possibility for getting started is in your local newspaper's business section or op-ed page. Even though the initial pay for such writing may be low, these publications generate clips that you can use to help sell your writing on a regional or national level. Also, a local newspaper article can sometimes be sold to a newspaper syndicate for wider distribution.

Although the competition at the national magazine level is intense, there are many national magazines open to free-lance business writers. You might also consider attending a writers conference that has a business magazine editor as a speaker or workshop leader. An in-person contact can be an enormous help. Always take a portfolio of your published work and a short bio that includes a list of your credits and your areas of expertise. By building a publications base at the local and regional level, you will establish your credibility as a business writer and increase your chances of selling material to national publications.

Translation and interpretation

The language of business is unfamiliar to many readers. Even those with business backgrounds may find reading about business subjects tough going. Writing effectively about business involves several forms of translation:

1) *Turning technical data into clear, understandable language.* Making the numbers of business accessible involves careful selection of what to include as well as adequate explanation of the statistics in the text of an article. Use examples, as well as tables and sidebars, to support key points. In some cases, it is most effective to rely on quotes from interviews with experts to "tell" the factual data. Blending well-designed tables, graphs, and charts with clearly explained text and quotations from persons knowledgeable about the topic will help create a reader-friendly article.

314

2) *Including analysis and interpretation as well as description.* Providing and explaining the data are only two steps in business writing. In addition to the basic facts, the effective business article must interpret the information, and focus on underlying causes and future implications.

Whenever possible, let experts provide the analysis. In a recent article on the rental housing shortage in our area, I wanted to explain why little new building had occurred. Rather than providing the explanation myself, however, I cited an area lender: "Current regulations make it burdensome and frustrating to lend for new construction. And even if someone can find property at the right price to build or owns the dirt already, substantial equity in the 40% to 50% range would be required to support the project." This quotation added authenticity and liveliness.

By adding analysis the business writer takes the reader beyond information that she or he could gather and explains *what it means.*

3) *Connecting the facts to the reader.* Even if the figures are well presented and the analysis is excellent, you still have to lure readers so they will want to read your piece. Start with a question or series of questions that will be answered in the article; or describe a real situation that is related to the topic as a "hook" for the reader. Summarize one or more tantalizing points that will be covered in the article and explain the key implications.

For the rental housing shortage article, I began with the plight of a student-friend who was unable to find an apartment to lease; an accompanying photograph showed her reading the classified ads in the newspaper. This lead gave the story an immediate appeal to renters, rental property owners, prospective developers, lenders, and to the university community.

To summarize: Knowing your subject, finding the right markets, and effectively interpreting the material will bring you success as a business writer.

315

65

BREAKING INTO MAGAZINE ARTICLE WRITING

BY CHARLOTTE ANNE SMITH

WHEN MEETING A WRITER, many people comment that they've always wanted to write. The question is, do they really want to write or do they want to have written? There is a vast difference, and the response to this question, in my opinion, is one of the primary ways to weed out the people who truly want to be writers from those who think being a writer would be glamorous.

There are some other questions that can help clarify these two desires, and you need to ask them of yourself before you embark on this often frustrating, extremely rewarding profession. And, yes, it is a profession, but resign yourself to being asked what you *really* do for a living.

Do you have a passion for the written word? Are you the despair of your family because wherever you are, there is always a pile of books, magazines, and paper? Do you think being a writer would be just the best life ever? Are you one of those people that just *have* to write? If you are, don't give up. That is a pretty good test to determine if you should be a writer.

Now that you have passed that test, let's talk about magazine writing. Nonfiction is easier to break into than fiction—not easy, just *easier*—because there are so many more markets for articles than for short stories. But there is still a lot of competition. In order to sell, you have to be aware of certain basic facts of magazine publishing.

First, be professional. How can you be professional if you've never sold anything? If you've written the right article for a particular magazine and present it in a professional manner, the editor doesn't usually need to know and may not even care if it is your first effort.

Whether you approach an editor by query or in a cover letter accompanying your article, state what is unique about it, compared to others on the same subject. It can be firsthand knowledge, access to documentation or interviews others have not had, specialized training in that field, or just a different viewpoint—i.e., a woman writing about football, a farmer about Wall Street.

For example, I have farmed, raised cattle, operated a bird-dog training kennel, performed in rodeos, trained horses, raised four children, taught Sunday school, played a musical instrument, sung in public, done standup comedy, refinished and reupholstered furniture, built two houses, fished, camped and hiked, and been a professional writer for 24 years. There are publications related to all of these things, and I have sold articles dealing with all of them. My experiences made my articles believable.

You can also use the experiences and expertise of others. My brother was a police officer for years; I have a friend who is a world-renowned livestock auctioneer specializing in thoroughbred horses; others are famous musicians, writers, artists, or just interesting people doing interesting or unusual things. I live in an area whose industries include oil and gas production, coal mining, and agriculture, and I have sold articles on all of these subjects. Some were technical, and I relied on my sources to fill in what I didn't know. The editor didn't care who the expert was, just as long as my article was accurate and the whole thing was readable.

How you present your manuscript is important. Don't submit one full of misspellings and typos. In this day and age, you are going to need equipment that will enable you to turn out a professional-looking manuscript. If you use a typewriter and your finished manuscript is covered with correction fluid, make a clean copy before you submit it.

Just because a market listing says, "replies in two weeks," don't get all upset if you don't hear from the editor by then. (If, on the other hand, the response time goes on much longer than originally indicated, you should contact the editor; things do get lost or forgotten.) If the listing says "don't call," then don't call, and if it says, "query; don't submit the complete manuscript," then follow those instructions. And *don't* send your manuscript by fax unless you know the editor wants to receive submissions that way.

One of the most common complaints editors have about free lancers—and it is a justifiable one—is that they're unfamiliar with the market. Don't send a poem to a publication that never publishes poetry, or an article on cooking wild game to a vegetarian magazine. Write for a sample copy of your target market, buy one on the newsstand, if available, or read several back issues in the library. Carefully reading the magazine you're aiming for will give you a feel for its subject matter, tone, and style. You can get specific information on word length, photo requirements, and method of submission by assiduously studying the market lists in this book.

Don't think that your words are so precious they can't be deleted or changed. Often a rewrite to change length or focus or to include additional information will make the difference between a rejection and a sale. The editor is the buyer; work with him or her. However, it is permissible to object to a suggested change that will destroy the meaning of the article, or will affect your credibility, since credibility is the one commodity a nonfiction writer must maintain to survive.

Ideas for articles are everywhere. If you can't recognize a potential article idea, you're in the wrong business. Everything you see, hear, feel, smell, taste, and touch is a possible article with a potential market. It is your job to make the match. Whatever your interest—a sport, craft, food, profession, hobby, lifestyle, religion—there is a publication (sometimes several) out there devoted to it. Find those magazines, study them, and then develop your article ideas. Markets are everywhere; look for them. Never pass a newsstand without checking it for publications with which you aren't familiar. While waiting for a train in Victoria Station in London, I picked up several magazines on horses and agriculture in England. Soon after I got home I sold an article to a British publication, *Sporting Horse*.

Almost every field has a publication that wants profiles. Consider your family and friends. What professions are they involved in? What are their recreational interests? Have they had a traumatic experience? Won an award or contest? Lived to be 100? The answers to these questions should generate many article ideas.

Train yourself to remember. You never know when what you see, hear, or read will be just right for an article. A fact learned long ago may give you the authenticity needed to make a sale today; an anecdote stored in your memory may be just the thing to put your personal stamp on an article.

Be realistic about what you expect to accomplish. Realize there will be months when you may not make any sales, and many publications still send checks with only two figures on the left of the decimal point. There is also a limit to how much work you can turn out in a given time, and this has to be taken into consideration when you are estimating your potential income. Don't quit your day job the day you decide to become a writer, or even on the day you make your first sale.

Often you won't be paid until weeks or months after you submit your work. Even publications that pay on acceptance may not actually accept the article until several weeks after it is received.

Aim as high as you can. If there are two publications into which your article would fit, always query or submit first to the one that pays more. If one pays on acceptance and the other on publication, but the amount is about the same, go with the pay-on-acceptance publication.

Don't work free. A publication doesn't expect its printer, advertising staff, typesetters or anyone else to work free, so why should the writer? Without the writer they don't have a publication.

I will make two exceptions to that rule. If you find a new publication that may be a steady market and can work out an agreement for payment in the future, go ahead, but have a firm understanding. This will give you credits to show editors, and they don't have to know you weren't paid.

The other exception is a publication dealing with something you are trying to promote—a religion, political viewpoint, or social issue, for instance.

Decide if you want to specialize. If you have expertise in a given field, you may want to write exclusively for that area. However, you may qualify in more than one area and that can make your work more interesting for you and your readers.

Don't expect to get rich, but keep in mind that there are good things in life besides money. I don't know of any other profession as enjoyable, that gives you the freedom to do what you want to do when you want to, that opens up the opportunity to meet so many interesting people— or that would have allowed me to be hugged by Roy Rogers.

66

SCIENCE WRITING TODAY AND TOMORROW

BY PATRICIA BARNES-SVARNEY

I AM TRULY SURROUNDED by my work: My computer runs on megabytes and RAMs; my car moves because of sparks and subsequent combustion, and sports more digital equipment than I care to imagine; and even my gym has the latest techno-gizmo to tell me just how many calories I've used up on a five-mile (albeit stationary) "bike ride." I cannot seem to get away from science and technology—but as a science writer, I do not mind, because it is more fuel for my science articles.

Science and technology encompass all our lives. If you find your hands sweating during the latest Space Shuttle launch, or you enthusiastically tell your friends the reasons why tsunamis crash along a coastline, you may be a potential science writer. And you do not have to be another Albert Einstein, Richard Feynman, or Isaac Asimov to succeed at it.

I became a science writer through the back door. I was a professional scientist who analyzed water samples and plotted flooding along sinuous river systems. A side trip back to college changed my life: The day my professor handed back the first draft of my thesis and said, "This reads like . . . well . . . an article for the general audience," sealed my fate. I have thanked her insight for ten years now.

You do not have to be a scientist or have a science background to write articles and books about science and technology. In fact, it may be helpful for you not to have a science background, because then you won't be caught up in the science jargon. If you are interviewing an astronomer on interstellar objects who says that MACHOs are found at the periphery of our galaxy, you would not just nod your head. You would ask him or her to explain—not only the acronym (Massive

320

Compact Halo Objects)—but why MACHOs are important to your article.

The best part about science and technology writing is the range of topics from which you can choose—and each of those subjects can be further broken down into narrower topics for other articles. Topics include the physical sciences, (geology, chemistry, etc.); biology (plant, human, viral, bacterial); space science; or medical science. Many science writers also delve into technology: computers, robotics, and electronics. Under technology, a science writer may describe remote sensing techniques used to detect and track volcanic eruption plumes across the planet; or under medical science, show how using supercomputer modeling can help us understand how drugs react within the body.

Science writing does not have to be about current scientific developments; it can also be about science in the past or future. Science past had its wonderful moments of serendipity; science future has its promise of a better life. And do not overlook science fiction for article ideas. After all, most people know about "warp drive," an idea often referred to on "Star Trek." A science writer might ask, "Can we go faster than the speed of light? If we could, what type of propulsion would be needed to catapult a spaceship to such speeds?"

Although there is a myriad of topics to choose from, all science and technology writing must apply to and excite the readers. Will they be able to use the discovery in the present or future? Will it help their children to live happier lives? Does the topic stimulate their imagination, and is it enjoyable to read? Or will the story tell them about a person, place, or thing that they never knew about before?

Now that you have decided to try your hand at writing science, you will need the following:

• *Intense curiosity.* When you are curious about a subject in science, you are more apt to dig deeper, ask for more explanation—and your enthusiasm will show in your writing. An editor once told me, "The attention span of the reader is directly proportional to the writer's interest in the story."

• *An interest in the research.* You may have all the curiosity about a subject, but you also need the tenacity to do the research. Science writers today have it easier than they did in the past: We have access to tremendous amounts of information, not only in libraries, but through

321

computer communication services, where you can find articles on your subject and leads to help you find other sources.

• *Ability to recognize a good idea for a science article.* A good idea for a science article is not "DNA"; a good science article idea is how DNA is being used as genetic "fingerprints" in crime investigations— and how it is also under fire because the technique is so new. Article ideas are everywhere, but the science writer has to know how to focus on that one kernel of interest.

• *Contacts and sources to interview.* A science writer's most valued possession is his or her contact/source list: past interviewees (experts in the fields you are writing about), reference librarians, earlier contacts from science conferences, public information offices of science-oriented institutions, organizations, and universities—and, of course, other science writers.

• *Insistence on accuracy.* The science writer's creed, to borrow from Thoreau, should read, "Simplicity, simplicity—not to mention accuracy, accuracy."

• *Good interpretative skills.* Science writers have a serious responsibility to their readers: They must interpret and present what they uncover in their research and interviews in a clear and interesting way. This interpretation is not always straightforward. I have heard it compared to translating Japanese into English: There are nuances of the Japanese culture integrated into their language that cannot be translated into English. It is often the same with explaining science to the general audience, and as Nobel physicist Richard Feynman once said, not all science can be explained in a basic way. But do not use this as an excuse; a science writer must do the best he or she can to get the subject across to the reader.

Coming up with a good science article idea is not as difficult as it seems. There are many sources that spark ideas: newspapers, science journals, news releases, computer communication services (the ubiquitous "information highway"), and numerous publications from universities and science-oriented organizations—also other people's conversations: I began to research my article on microrobots (for *Sky Magazine*) when I overheard two people joking about "minimachines" taking over the planet Mars. The real microrobots may never take over the red planet, but the suggestion triggered the idea. It also started me

322

on the trail of just how far we have come in space-oriented microrobotic research.

After you come up with a specialized science topic, your first stop should be the library to check on magazines. Read through current magazines and explore magazine topics in the *Readers' Guide to Periodical Literature* (and similar indexes) from the past year or so. This will help you avoid writing about an idea whose time has come and gone; also you will not send a query to a magazine that has just published an article on the same subject with the same angle. If your idea seems to be on track, then gather basic information on the subject from science magazines, brochures, encyclopedias, or books.

Next comes the query, usually a less-than-one-page "outline" (in text form) of your proposed article. The query presents your idea, sources, and credentials to the editor. A word of caution: Know your magazine. Do not send a query on industrial robotics to *Woman's World,* or an idea on the future of the American/Russian cooperation on the Space Station to *Sailing*; but also remember that certain non-science magazines will take science or technology topics, including some inflight and general-interest magazines. Know your science magazines, too: Articles for *Omni* have a different slant from those for *Popular Science.*

The day the editor says, "Go for it," is the day you take all your basic information and outline-query letter, and get to work. Now is also the time to call on your sources for interviews. Some science writers write a sketchy first draft to their article before the interviews—a way to organize their thoughts and frame the questions to ask the interviewee in some semblance of order; other writers do a first draft after the interview. In either case, you will need a list of questions to ask your experts. Always remember that the only dumb question is the one you did not ask.

Writing a publishable science article takes the ability to explain complex concepts without baffling or confusing the readers. One of the best approaches is to discuss the subject or idea in terms the reader can relate to. For example, in my article on agriculture in space (for *Ad Astra*) I wove familiar gardening terms (and references to many gardening problems) into the piece so the readers could relate to growing plants in the Space Station and beyond.

Another strategy to give your science article life is to use anecdotes.

Usually, your interviewees have interesting stories to tell, such as how their discovery was made, or about the first patient to use their new drug. Since the general public often thinks of science as another world, descriptions of the scientists and their surroundings will "humanize" your article, showing that the expert has the same idiosyncrasies that we all have—right down to worries about money or celebrations of victories.

Of course, there are two more qualities that keep all science writers going: patience and perseverance. It takes patience to get an interview with a busy scientist (and sometimes you will not get the interview at all); and patience to see your words in print. Plus, it takes perseverance to understand the intricacies of your science article—and to keep up with the new science discoveries that pop up every week.

There is more than enough science to provide you with subjects for science articles. As a science writer just remember that the universe is now your beat.

⸎ 67

GIVE READERS WHAT *THEY* WANT— AND NEED

BY SAMM SINCLAIR BAKER

BEST-SELLING NOVELIST Stephen King was quoted in *Publishers Weekly* as saying, "Don't give them what they want—give them what you want." In my opinion, that statement should be reversed if you want to write nonfiction that will sell. Your basic guideline—which can make the difference between sale and rejection—is: *Give them [readers] what they want, not what you [the writer] want.* You must concentrate on serving the reader. That doesn't mean you're greatly restricted in your subject matter: Your articles can inform, elevate, entertain, and teach.

As with every type of writing, you want to attract and involve readers in your articles quickly and personally. A sure way to accomplish that is to appeal to readers' *self-interest,* and show them how they will benefit from what you are telling them in your piece. Keep in mind always the old saying: "Feed your pets what *they* want, not what *you* prefer to eat."

To make your articles most effective, keep the readers' problems and needs foremost and write the best you can, clearly and simply. Above all, focus on the stated or implied you-you-you. In articles and nonfiction books, too much I-I-I is likely to trigger no-no-no from editors. When you recheck and revise your manuscript, cut out every extraneous "I"; insert "you" wherever it fits. That's what will grab and hold editors and readers.

How the YOU-factor works

The superior value of "you" over "I/me" in most nonfiction was proved to me beyond doubt by an ad I worked on years ago for a then new gardening product, "Miracle-Gro." In a preliminary test, the ad

325

was headlined, "How to Grow a Miracle Garden"—a general appeal. The resulting orders were satisfactory, but not great.

We then reran the ad in the same publication, making the headline just one word longer: "How *you* can grow a Miracle Garden." The seemingly minor change increased by many times the draw of the first ad. That dramatic experience taught me the enormous power of the YOU-factor, which I then applied to writing my thirty nonfiction books (including three blockbuster best sellers) and many articles on a variety of subjects.

Since then, the actual word "you" or the implied you has been the guiding sell-word for all my nonfiction. I urge you to consider that in what you write from now on. Also, check your rejected manuscripts for sufficient stress on the YOU-factor. You'll see how even minor changes can often enliven and increase the power of the piece, grab your reader, and sell. Emphasis on *you* can be a significantly valuable guideline in your nonfiction writing.

Concentrate on the reader

Here are two devices I use that you can try for yourself: First, I print the word YOU on a small card and set it up on my desk where I see it intermittently as I write.

Second, I find a newspaper or magazine photo of a person who represents the reader I'm aiming to reach. For a diet article or book, I focus on a photo of an overweight couple. If you are writing about health topics, choose a photo of individuals of varying ages, depending on the market you are addressing.

Whatever the subject, you must make sure that it has an appeal that will grab the reader in a personal way. An article in *Smithsonian Magazine* started this way:

> You really feel your age when you get a letter from your insurance agent telling you the car you bought slightly used the year you got out of college can now be considered a "classic." "Your premiums will reflect this change in your classification," the letter said. I went out to look at the car and could almost hear my uncle's disapproving voice. "You should never buy a used car . . ."

Check how many times "you" and "your" keep the reader bound closely to the page. Also note that most individuals are involved at some time in buying a car, new or used, so the topic has universal appeal.

An article on golf in *Modern Maturity* states:

Sharpen your game with seven points from senior pros . . . that will give you power and accuracy. . . . Whatever your problem, you can take the solutions we recommend straight to the practice ground or the course.

Again, note the lure of a popular subject—golf—and how the reader is then brought in intimately by the use of "you" and "your." See how this personalizing technique is far more effective than a general approach.

In the first of my three diet book bestsellers, *The Doctor's Quick Weight Loss Diet,* the reader is hooked in the opening paragraph this way:

The prime aim of this book is to help you take that weight off quickly, and then to help you stay slim, healthy, and attractive. Here you'll learn exactly how in clear, simple, proved ways never told before.

Because the subject of diet is of deep concern to tens of millions of people, I was able to sell dozens of dict articles. The field is wide open for you today. Another point: Never bypass the possibility of milking a subject on which you've scored.

In my inspirational book, *Conscious Happiness,* I had to establish a special, close personal connection with the reader quickly. The opening lines were:

Conscious happiness is free. It can enrich your life tremendously—yet it doesn't cost you a cent from now on. But nobody else can pay for it and give it to you as a gift. You must earn it yourself by wanting it enough so that you work at it daily. Once you attain it, you can keep and enjoy its great benefits for the rest of your more rewarding life.

Note again how the variations of "you" linking the reader to the text repeatedly serve to reach and hold the reader's attention. As for the subject, who doesn't want to be happy?

Convinced more than ever by results I gained in my writing from the selling power of "you," I used those writing techniques for *The Complete Scarsdale Medical Diet,* which started selling immediately after publication and zoomed to become the bestselling diet book of all time.

Right near the start, the writing captured readers this way:

Most meaningful for you are reports from overweight people. Their statements, which came unsolicited through the mail, are all-important as proof that the diet that worked wonderfully for them can do the same for you too. . . .

The clear lesson you can derive from this boils down to three words: *Involve the reader.* Heed this advice and you'll have a far better chance of receiving acceptances instead of rejections on your future nonfiction submissions.

Captions on the covers of major magazines are good examples of the emotional connection that the writer must evoke in the reader. For example, from *Ladies' Home Journal:* "When Your Man Doesn't Give You What You Need." The opening of an article in *McCall's* reads:

Quick! Can your toddler swim? Has your five-year-old expressed an interest in a musical instrument? Does your 12-year-old keep up socially? . . . No? Well, what are you doing wrong?

Note carefully for your future guidance that in another issue of *Ladies' Home Journal,* there are several pages with "you" in the overall headings; *YOU—Relationships & More,* with subsections: *High Anxiety, Ways to Make Your Weekends More Fun . . . Five Things Never to Say in the Height of an Argument.* This is followed by *FINANCE: How Safe is Your Money?*

This is succeeded by an article: "Barbra's New Direction" that starts, "When you first walk into Barbra Streisand's large but cozy apartment . . ." See how the sentence leads *you* personally on the guided tour.

Consider how the following *Reader's Digest* article projects the YOU-factor in the opening line: "Your thoughts influence feelings and behavior and therefore the state of your body. Awareness of this can be an important difference in treating problems of overweight. *Study yourself . . .*" Note the repetition: "*your* thoughts . . . *your* body . . . study *yourself.*"

In short, study the market you are trying to sell to, the subjects that are most timely for that readership, and the best ways to attract the interest of those readers intimately.

Seeking to affect the reader deeply, Walt Whitman wrote, "The whole theory of the universe is directed unerringly to a single individual—namely to You." That wise and enduring concept applies just as effectively today.

The all-important pointers offered to you here will help you profit from your writing now, and from now on.

❦ 68

TURNING YOUR SKILLS INTO ARTICLE SALES

BY DENISE VEGA

HOW MANY TIMES HAVE YOU picked up an article and lamented, "If only I had expertise in a particular area, I could make lots of sales"?

I'm willing to bet you *are* an expert. You just don't know it yet. By applying strategies I've used successfully in writing service pieces, you can identify your expertise, develop an article, and get it to market.

Me? An expert?

Being an expert doesn't require a Ph.D. or years of experience in a particular field. It just means knowing a great deal about a specific topic. To discover your expertise, start with these two questions:

What interests me? Review your daily life. When you pick up a magazine or newspaper, what articles do you read first. Are they political? Human interest? Are they about children? Sports? Business? Women's issues? What community, sports, or entertainment events do you attend? What type of movies and books do you like? Most people pursue several interests in their recreational reading and activities.

What am I good at? Examine your activities over the last several months, starting at home. Do you make fabulous meals without recipes? Have you recently repaired your car, sink, or television? Did you find a unique way to remove a stain or deal with a child's discipline problem?

What about outside activities? Is your daughter's soccer team one of the best because of your coaching skills? Have you helped others on a literacy project? Do people come to you when they need to work out a problem, complete their tax returns, or locate a reputable repair person?

What about your job? Are you good at organizing projects, delegating tasks and getting things done on time? Are you the idea-generator?

The cost-cutter? Did you devise the system to improve office efficiency by 20%?

Choose one of these areas and jot down as many facts and pieces of information as you can. Explore such areas as techniques or steps to performing a task (if it's how-to oriented); its unique aspects; the local or famous people involved, and relevant background or history. When did you first become interested in the project, and why?

When you realize that you know a lot about a topic, examine it for its potential as an article. As an example, I chose coaching a girl's soccer team; though I'm not a coach, I discovered I knew something about it from talking with friends and family and observing games.

Brainstorming markets and ideas

Once you've narrowed your topic, you can use a variety of market resources to brainstorm article ideas. With coaching in mind, I flipped open the April issue of *The Writer Magazine* and turned to the special market lists: *Juvenile, Young Adult, College and Career,* and *City and Regional.*

Picture the target audience for each of these markets (their age and interests, for example) and determine the focus for that audience. Write down your ideas, either as a title or one-sentence synopsis. Force yourself to come up with at least one idea for each market, even if you're not thrilled with the results. Not every idea will be marketable, but the exercise should stretch your creativity and broaden your marketing horizons.

Here's my list for coaching:

Juvenile: Kids like to read about themselves; individual success; overcoming odds; learning a skill. Possible article: "Sarah's Success" (about one girl on the team who has made tremendous progress).

Young Adult: Teens also like to read about themselves; individual success; unusual teenagers. Possible article: "Coach Sue: The Joys and Travails of a Volunteer Soccer Coach" (an interview with a high school student who coaches).

College and Career: College students like to know about current trends on campus; how to manage their time and how to help pay for their education. Possible article: "Whistle Blower: How to Referee Your Way Through College" (becoming a certified referee and finding work).

City/Regional: These magazines focus on a particular geographic area, so topics should reflect the area as well as provoke interest. "Recreational Sports in Denver: How Competitive Are They?" (Do kids have as much pressure in community-sponsored leagues as they often do on school-affiliated teams?)

That's brainstorming from just four general markets, without looking at individual magazines. And each article idea could lead to others. For example, "Sarah's Success" might appear in a children's magazine with an "overcoming the odds" slant, then later in a children's health-oriented magazine with an exercise/fitness slant. Once you get started, ideas begin to tumble over one another.

Filtering ideas

The following questions will help determine the worth of each idea:

(1) *Does the idea excite and intrigue me?* If you're not interested, no one else will be, either. After looking over my coaching ideas, I'm most excited about "Whistle Blower: How to Referee Your Way Through College." The title is catchy and I like the idea of providing students with a unique way to finance part of their education. I'm also hoping the topic is unusual enough to grab an editor's attention.

(2) *Is it something I can write with confidence?* Even if the topic is only an offshoot of your actual area of expertise, you should still have some working knowledge of it. If you don't have the information at your fingertips, you should know where to get it.

(3) *Are there similar pieces on the topic?* Consult *The Readers' Guide to Periodical Literature* and back issues of your target magazines to discover if your topic has been covered recently. If you find one or two titles on your subject, read the pieces to determine how to make yours different.

(4) *How much research will I need to do?* If you must do extensive research, factor it into your enjoyment quotient, as well as time and effort versus payment ratio.

Once your idea has passed the salability test, you can begin to structure it to see exactly what you've got.

The expert weigh-in

Here you flesh out the topic to determine if you have enough for a full-fledged article or merely a filler piece. List the main area you will address in the article, leaving ample room to write beneath each main topic afterward. If you can't come up with at least three strong areas, you probably don't have enough for a full-length article.

Beneath each main topic, note the points you'll highlight, including whom you might quote, what anecdotes (actual or possible) you want to use, and any instructions you need to include (if it's a how-to piece).

Here is my outline for "Whistle Blower":

WHISTLE BLOWER
How to Referee Your Way Through College

Introductory Paragraph—Actual referee quote or anecdote
The Demand for Referees
- Statistics on the number of organized sports in the country; growth predictions
- Statistics on the number of referees
- Possible quotes by coaches who have had trouble finding enough referees

How to Become a Certified Referee
- Who requires certification and why
- What's involved in certification (time, cost)

How to Get Referee Jobs in Your Area
- Whom to contact
- How to improve your chances

What to Expect as a Referee
- Payment
- Time commitment
- Dealing with angry parents, coaches, players (quotes from referees)

Closing Paragraph—Circle back to opening anecdote or quote in introduction.

Getting your expertise to market

Once you have a solid outline, choose two to four possible magazines for your piece; to narrow your list, read back issues and request writers guidelines. (You may have done this as part of determining if the topic has been covered recently.) Next, you'll need to query or write the entire article. Though many magazines prefer queries, it may make sense to send the entire piece, especially if you're new to writing or to a particular magazine. Whatever you decide, make sure you know the market and have tailored your query letter or article as closely as possible to the magazine's needs.

In your cover letter or query, include all the experience that makes you an expert on the topic, noting how long you've performed a particular activity, any courses or workshops you've taken (or taught), and any certification or special recognition you've received.

Then, send it out, forget about it, and start working on your next idea. Your expertise will pay off sooner or later, and you'll have a credit to add to the next article you propose or submit.

§ 69

CONDUCTING THE "SENSITIVE" INTERVIEW

BY KATHLEEN WINKLER

A DAUGHTER WHO WAS STALKED and killed by a former lover. Surgery that left impotence in its wake. An abortion kept secret for years. A past that includes painful abuse.

Occasionally in your writing career you may find yourself interviewing people about topics that are very hard to talk about. Sometimes it's because they are physically unpleasant or embarrassing. Sometimes it's because they are emotionally wrenching. In either case, you as the writer have a great challenge: to make your subjects feel comfortable enough to share sensitive, intimate experiences with you so your readers can benefit from them.

An awkward interviewer, trampling on the subject's sensibilities, will not only not get a good story, but can also do great damage to the subject, who may never again trust anyone enough to open up.

A skilled and sympathetic interviewer, on the other hand, will not only elicit a moving story from the subject, but may actually help him or her come to terms with an experience kept hidden or repressed for years.

It all depends on how you go about it.

As a medical writer for fifteen years, I've interviewed people on such intimate topics as sexual function, emotional responses to physical scars from surgery, and life-threatening illness. In the course of writing *When the Crying Stops: Abortion, the Pain and the Healing* (Northwestern Publishing House), I interviewed twenty women about their abortion experiences and subsequent reactions. Some of these women had never told their stories to anyone before the interview.

As a result of these often painful interviews, I've developed an approach to sensitive interviewing and some helpful ways to make such interviews easier for me and for the subject, and more productive.

I believe that the number one rule for interviewing on any topic, especially a sensitive one, is respect for the person sitting across from you. Always keep in mind that he or she doesn't *owe* you anything. In most cases your subject is telling his or her story out of a simple desire to help others cope with the same or a similar problem, with no expectation of any kind of reward. The subject, therefore, has the right to decide how much to share. While as the interviewer you can encourage the sharing and make it as free of stress as possible, you must not try to force the person to reveal more than he or she is willing to. The subject has the right to end the interview at any point, or to say, "I don't want to talk about that"—and you must respect that decision.

There are some things you can do to make a sensitive interview as tension-free as possible for the subject, and, at the same time, get the information you need to write an honest and moving piece.

• Since it's absolutely essential to use a tape recorder during the interview—especially if there are likely to be any legal aspects to the piece—ask the subject for permission to do so, explaining that you want to be sure your quotes are accurate. But get the permission on tape before you begin.

• Preparation is important. Never try to "wing" an interview. Learn as much as you can about the person in advance. If the story is likely to have a psychological or medical slant, do your research: Familiarize yourself with the problem and the various treatments and side effects. In dealing with a social problem—child abuse, spouse battering, etc.—read current background material on all aspects of it.

• Prepare your questions carefully ahead of time. Start with the general, less threatening questions and move on to those dealing with the more difficult, personal aspects of the experience. Begin by asking about the subject's childhood and the events that led up to the traumatic experience. This will help relax your subject and get the dialogue flowing.

• When you arrive at the interview, the subject is likely to be nervous. A warm smile, a handshake, and a friendly comment—"I'm so happy to meet you; I think it's wonderful that you are willing to share your experience with others"—will go a long way toward putting the subject at ease.

• If your subject is especially nervous, confront that fact—don't ignore it—saying, "I know this may be difficult for you. That's understandable. Many people are uneasy at first, but it won't be as hard as you may think."

• Start with a disclaimer, if you think it will help. Say, frankly, "I hope you will want to share your thoughts and feelings, but I won't pressure you to say any more than you want to." If you have agreed to anonymity for the subject, emphasize at the outset that you will not, under any circumstances, break that promise.

• Use broad, general questions at first, asking such non-threatening questions as, "Tell me a little about yourself: Where are you from? What was it like growing up in your family? How did you get along with your siblings? Parents?" If this leads to an appropriate opening, you might follow the answer with, "Can you tell me a little more about that?" Obviously avoid questions that can be answered with "yes" or "no." Have a summary question ready for the end—"What's the most important effect this experience has had on you? What is the most helpful thing you would like to share with the readers?"

• Move gradually, in chronological order, through the part of the person's life that is relevant to the story. If the subject wanders and gets off track, bring the interview back to the main topic by saying something like, "We're going to get to that in a minute, but right now I'd like to hear more about—." A little humor never hurts: "Hold on a bit; we're getting way ahead of ourselves."

• When you are ready to deal with the sensitive topic, warn the person by saying, "We've come to the point where I need to ask you some more specific questions about what happened." If the subject becomes emotional, confront that directly, saying, "Go ahead and cry if you feel like it. I certainly understand. I would have cried, too, in that situation." Don't try to hide your emotional reaction; if you actually do respond with tears, that's O.K. I've never done a sensitive interview in which the subject cried and I didn't shed a few tears, too.

• Give your subject plenty of time to respond to your questions. If she or he stops at a critical point, pause, too, and then make a casual comment to start the conversation flowing again: "That must have been very hard for you. What happened next?" Keep your voice warm and sympathetic.

• Never make a judgmental comment. Obviously, remarks like, "How could you have done that?" are taboo, but so are even subtle gestures or verbal responses, no matter how repellent you may find what the subject says.

• Get on tape the subject's wishes about using real names in your feature.

• When you have finished the interview, thank the person warmly, and leave your card so she or he can reach you if she wishes to give you some additional information. Don't be reluctant to call her back for clarification or more details. Store the tapes in a fireproof safe. It is not advisable to show the subject a transcript of the tape recording or the manuscript prior to its publication.

Though telephone interviews on sensitive subjects can be done, they do present a different challenge. Sometimes the anonymity of the phone allows a nervous subject to talk more freely, it can in some instances be inhibiting.

• Always tell the person that the phone interview is being tape recorded. I usually say, "I'm taping this, so you don't have to worry about talking slowly enough for me to take notes."

• As in a face-to-face interview, you must establish a personal relationship over the telephone, which presents some difficulties. Chat casually at first, in a warm, friendly tone, asking about the weather, how the person likes living in his or her hometown, how he or she spent the weekend. Get to know the subject a bit before jumping into the interview.

• Schedule your phone interview at a time when you are not likely to be interrupted. Disconnect your call-waiting! Late night often works best for me. There's something about quiet houses and low lights that encourages the flow of conversations.

Talking to people about their most intimate, personal problems and experiences can be exhausting and emotionally draining, for you as well as for your subject. Don't schedule too many such interviews back to back or you may find yourself on overload. Allow time for a break between interviews.

Some of your subjects may well be in need of professional counseling and may try to put you into the role of the therapist. Remember that your job is only to ask the questions and listen—which may in itself be therapeutic for the subject. Never offer advice. It may in some

338

instances be appropriate to ask, "Have you ever had professional help in dealing with this problem? You might find it helpful."

Sharing the darker sides of pain often helps the teller and the reader to know that they are not alone, that other human beings have had similar experiences and survived.

As writers, we have a tremendous responsibility in doing sensitive interviews. We have a responsibility to our subjects not to betray their trust. And, in addition, we have a responsibility to our readers to present these stories as honestly and with as much empathy as we can. Conducting ourselves with the utmost professionalism is the only way to live up to it.

§ 70

TRUE CRIME THAT PAYS

BY KRIST BOARDMAN

FOR THE ASPIRING WRITER, CRIME DOES PAY. If you're willing to do some research and master the techniques of detective magazine writing, you can develop a market for yourself that will pay frequently and reasonably. Detective magazines specialize for the most part in true homicide cases. Sold on newsstands, these magazines feature criminal cases in the United States and other countries where police and court records are accessible to the public and journalists.

Usually, these stories are about *closed cases*. This means that a suspect has been arrested, tried, convicted, and sent to prison. There are exceptions to the closed case rule, but beginning true crime writers need not be concerned with them until they have mastered the craft and are contributing to the magazines regularly.

Where do you find a crime story to write about? Any old murder will not do. Though the annual murder rate in the United States now approaches 25,000, you must be selective. To find out what murders have been committed in your area, read the local or metropolitan sections of your newspaper. When you find a case that involves a homicide, clip and date it. Continue to gather clippings. With some practice, you will be able to separate good prospects for true crime features from those that will not work. If the case involves a lot of detective work and has some interesting and unusual twists, it is probably a good possibility for a crime magazine article.

You will notice that crime coverage in metropolitan newspapers usually differs from that in county weeklies. Reading the major dailies— which often publish news of major criminal cases in their home states, not just in their metropolitan areas—is an excellent way to gather leads on cases from all over the state, but those news accounts may be very tersely written, without the details you need for a good true crime article. County weeklies, on the other hand (which cover a smaller area), frequently carry in-depth coverage of particular cases being tried in their communities.

Having identified a good magazine possibility, send a query to a detective magazine editor. Detective magazine editors are usually receptive to new writers who have had some previous writing experience or demonstrate a keen interest in learning how to write these articles. In your query, include the type of crime, names of the victim and suspect, approximate date of the crime, locale, weapon used (if any), a short description of what happened, and the outcome of the case if it has already gone on trial. You can do this prior to the trial, but in that event, don't work on your piece until you get the editor's approval to do it and unless there is a conviction.

The best true crime features are well researched. Go to the courthouse where the criminal case was tried and look up the court file or official record. You can skip over the tedious legal deliberations and go right to what happened, as outlined in the original complaint by the police or prosecutor. Also take careful note of important evidentiary material, such as medical examiner reports, testimony of forensic experts and lab results requested by the police.

In addition, check the files of the county's newspaper of record in the county library. Photocopies of news reports will be helpful when you're describing what happened during the trial.

If the murder case was solved easily, you probably won't have enough material for a 5,000-word story. In that event, remember that there are many other good crimes for you to look into; refocus your efforts on them. More than once, I've found that though my original article never panned out, I nevertheless established new contacts that led me to other publishable ones I was previously not aware of.

Before leaving on a research trip, review your news clips and, if necessary, call ahead to the police department or prosecutor in the jurisdiction concerned to ask if they will talk to you about the case. Your chances of having them cooperate are considerably better if you approach them when their case has already been tried and the criminal has been convicted. An advance call also saves you unnecessary time and expense on trips. Another way to economize is to target several cases in a particular geographical area, so that you can do all your research on them at the same time.

In your research, you want to touch all of the bases, if you can. You

NONFICTION: ARTICLES AND BOOKS

may find that interviews are hard to come by, or that court officials are not cooperating in making key documents available, or that the case was not covered in the local media. By consulting all your sources, you will usually be able to get enough material for your story without compromising accuracy.

There is no hard-and-fast way to gain the cooperation of police and prosecutors, but it's always worth a try. Frequently, they appreciate having their firsthand perspectives recorded in a detective magazine. (Police and prosecutors are among the most avid readers of these publications.) Sometimes, police and prosecutors will roll out the red carpet and give you excellent, detailed, accurate accounts of crimes that even their local newspapers missed.

If they can't or won't help you, don't be discouraged; they often operate in highly political environments and under bureaucratic constraints that prevent them from talking to you. You have to learn to take this kind of rejection in stride.

When you have completed your research, you are ready to write your article.

To create a compelling narrative that will keep readers and editors asking for more, there are important techniques to follow.

Begin your manuscript with the commission of the crime, or the events leading up to its discovery. For example: It is five o'clock on a February morning in a medium-sized city. The air is chilly, and the sun has not yet risen. The trash man who comes into the alley to empty a dumpster is shivering and moving quickly to stay warm, exhaling clouds of dimly seen vapor. He notices a body on the ground in front of his truck, and thinking a homeless person is sleeping there, he nudges the body with his foot, but there is no response. He then rolls the body over, and in the murky rays of dawn, sees a bloody, battered face at the head of a lifeless torso. In the headlights of the trash truck, he sees a bloody hammer on the pavement several feet away.

As an editor of a group of detective magazines used to say, there is no need for a true crime writer to write dramatically. Murder is inherently dramatic, without literary embellishment. Just write the facts; in my opinion, understatement is a most powerful form of writing and is appropriate for this medium.

Your article may then explain something about the town where these events occurred, either before or after discovery of the body, to establish setting and also to indicate the frequency of crime in that locale. Perhaps the police have very few homicides to deal with, or maybe murder is commonplace in the area. Either situation will affect the behavior and attitude of the responding investigator and his coworkers.

A uniformed officer arrives first, followed by a detective and a crew of evidence technicians. Usually, the detective takes charge and becomes the central character in your narrative. You adopt him as the protagonist in your account and follow him through his paces until the defendant is apprehended and goes to court.

What kind of identification was on the body? If there was none, what clues were used to establish identity? What about that bloody hammer nearby? Whose fingerprints—if any—were on it? Whose blood? What type? What does the medical examiner establish as the probable time of death, and is the investigator able to find witnesses who saw or heard anything unusual in the area at that estimated time of death? What else did the detective find? How did he respond? These are questions that your investigator will be asking and to which you will want to provide your readers answers all along the investigative trail.

You should also tell your readers something about the primary investigator and his close associates. If you were able to interview the detective, you will have a feel for him, as well as for some specific details about his life and career. The detective may have a partner or a supervisor, and all three may have played unique roles that you will want to explain.

An important element of the police inquiry is the identity of the victim—not just name, address, and occupation, but what in the life of the victim led to his or her murder. Through interviews with his or her friends, coworkers, employers, acquaintances, boyfriends, girlfriends, spouses, the detective will try to reconstruct what the victim's life was like just prior to his death. These different angles produce a profile of the victim's life and world and help narrow the field of suspects to those who interacted with him.

Always remember that except for the victim, suspect, police, and court officials—judges and attorneys—you should not use actual names in your story. A witness identified by name in court documents should be described in your story only as the trash man, a neighbor, a girlfriend, or a relative. The same rule applies to the names of busi-

343

nesses. *This restriction is a must for detective magazines,* because it protects them from lawsuits from persons claiming invasion of privacy.

Avoid revealing the identity and motive of the suspect until you have exhausted every other aspect. I call this style "writing backwards," or backing into the denouement of your story; it prolongs the suspense and pulls the reader along. You want to focus on the clues, the blind alleys of the investigation, other possible suspects, and even possible red herrings, until it's virtually impossible to avoid giving up the identity of the suspect. This keeps the reader in suspense about the resolution of the case until the very end.

This technique is totally different from straight newspaper reporting, which tends to explain the outcome first and then goes back and fills in the details.

Frequently, the most interesting character is the perpetrator of the crime. Once he's been identified as a suspect, you will want to tell more about him and the motivations that led him to commit his crime. His personality often has a direct bearing on the outcome of the case: Is the suspect an abused, mentally disturbed person simply acting in self defense, or is he a vicious and calculating repeat offender who enjoys making his victims suffer? Is he someone in between these extremes? The judge usually takes all of these factors into account when determining a sentence, and the defendant's character might become a point of contention that should be mentioned in your article.

The court trial can be as dramatic as the steps that led up to it. Significant quotations from court testimony, interviews, and news articles can be used to illustrate how the case was resolved.

Now that you have written your 5,000-word manuscript and checked it for factual and grammatical accuracy, get whatever photos you can. This is not always easy, and you must be resourceful. You should ask official sources for crime scene photos, photographs of key evidence, pictures of defendants and suspects. Take your camera to interviews and ask the prosecutor and detectives for permission to photograph them. If they can't give you pictures, ask if you can make copies of their pictures. This is less than ideal but much better than nothing. If official photos are totally unavailable, take your own photos of the scene of the crime and the courthouse where the case was tried. Try to find some pictures of the defendant and victim from local newspapers. Sometimes local newspaper photographers or their newspapers will be willing to share pictures in exchange for a credit line in a national magazine or for nominal payment. If possible, do all this when you are gathering material; being able to mention to an editor that you have photographs or artwork available will increase your article's salability.

The true crime magazine story offers the serious and committed writer the opportunity to get published regularly, and to hone his craft in a market that constantly looks for new material. I also feel that the true crime writer has a mission: to let the world know that the unfortunate victims of murder have not been forgotten, and that serious efforts were made to bring the criminals to justice.

⧉71

NINE LEADS TO ARTICLE SALES

BY LOTTIE ROBINS

TWENTY YEARS AGO, THE INSTRUCTOR OF A NONFICTION COURSE I was taking walked into the first class, fidgeted with some papers for a few minutes, then suddenly approached a young man in the front row. Pointing a finger at him, the instructor said, "Hey, you!" The young man looked up, startled.

"Did you hear me?" the teacher asked.

"Of course," came the quick reply.

"Good," said the teacher, walking back to his desk. "That's how to begin an article. You grab the reader's attention and say as few words as possible to make him listen, during which time you introduce your theme."

That teacher's dramatic illustration has stayed with me ever since.

Factual approach

Who, what, where, when, and why are usually the rules for the first sentence in a news article. For example, in a feature article entitled, "Home Schooling," published in *The Woman's Newspaper of Princeton,* my opening read:

> Our son Jesse is a bright, normal boy of ten who reads five books a week, loves to browse through the encyclopedia, adores science fiction, and hates to take showers. He likes to swim and go to museums, adores his two-year-old sister, and hates to clean his room.
> Today Jesse is attending a small private school. But from second grade through fourth, he was a home schooler, and although I do not have a degree in education, I was his only teacher.

Instead of straight facts, I bring an active character into the story, give his name, paint a word picture, give an important fact about the narrator (my daughter, in this case), and state where Jesse is today in his education.

The fictional approach

To avoid sounding like a textbook, try the anecdotal lead, which is excellent for a subject without too much fictional or dramatic material. If you are planning to become a serious nonfiction writer, learn some fiction techniques and start collecting anecdotes.

In "I Can Hear the Water Running" *(The Woman's Newspaper),* I used a story that had been told to me. My article began:

A number of years ago, a friend in her early 40's told me she had been deaf since the age of six and had just had surgery that restored her hearing. The biggest thrill, she told me, was when she awoke from the anesthetic and the nurse turned on the tap in the adjoining bathroom and she could hear the water running. It was like a symphony.

If I had begun with the history of hearing aids, or the statistics of how many hard-of-hearing people there are, I would probably have lost my audience immediately.

Begin with a character

To write an article for which you don't have statistics or for which they aren't really essential, plunge right in with a character who has a problem related to your theme. Here's my opening for "Start Your Own Singles Club" (published in *Pennysaver*):

Josephine is 51, recently divorced, and feels out of place with her married friends, even though they include her for a social evening in their home.

As I also wanted to draw in the male reader, two paragraphs later I introduce George, age 60, just widowed.

The Act I setting

After meeting two women who ran a personal service for senior citizens and deciding to write about them, I tried a half dozen openings before I came up with one I felt was just right. The reason I chose the following "stage setting" for "Help for the Elderly Housebound" *(Lady's Circle)* was that it best served my purpose to describe the service:

347

The telephone rings: "My elderly mother needs a series of X-rays that will take several days. I work and cannot take her. Can you escort her?"

I then listed two more telephone calls, using the same style, and continued:

Picking up the telephone and saying yes, they will be glad to help, is Personal Service of the Lehigh Valley, in Guthsville, PA.

The shocker

Sometimes, for a very dramatic emotional article, it is best to begin with a shocking statement, such as the one I used for "A Boutique to Save Babies" *(Life and Health):*

Scott died when he was five and a half. He was born on December 29, 1969, a delightful blonde boy with fuzzy hair and big blue eyes. He came from the hospital healthy, hungry, and spry.
Scott had Tay-Sachs disease.

Sometimes, when you wish to shock your reader into action, using the "you" technique is advisable. This method is excellent when your article is an exposé with a warning. In an editorial in *Seniorgram,* the author does just that: "Senior citizens, beware of the smooth-talking sales persons who tell you they're going to send you medical equipment that Medicare will pay for."

Ask a question

By opening with a question, you are getting your reader to think, and to participate in the answer. The question can come in the first sentence, or follow a few introductory remarks.

In "Seniors Go Back to School" *(Pennysaver),* I plunged in with:

Do you recall dropping your children off at a college dorm and wishing you, too, were going to experience the fun of college life?

Quotations

A popular type of opening is a quote from an authority, giving the person's title, background, and area of expertise. For my article, "Adult Condominiums—Why They Are for You" *(The Woman's Newspaper),* I open with the following quote, with permission of the realtor:

"New Jersey has more adult condominium developments than any other state in the metropolitan area," says Arlene Mulry, sales representative at Weichert Realtors.

Dialogue for human interest

Dialogue is one of the most important attention-grabbers a writer can use. For an article that needs drama, this type of opening will keep your editor reading beyond the first sentence. When I queried *The Saturday Evening Post* about an article on cults, the editor cautioned me that the story had to be dramatic as well as traumatic. In order to introduce both our son and us, I opened with:

"Mom, you've got to accept it. I have to give up everything I love for Reverend Moon and his Divine Principle," said Arthur, our twenty-two-year-old son, over the telephone. "My art, my drums, my apartment, my girl friend."

Make a statement

Lastly, if you cannot come up with any of the above catchy openings, then begin with a statement . . . but make sure it's an eye-opener, and keep your sentences as short as possible, each one having directly to do with your subject. Here's the opening for "Is the Law Abusing Women?," by Michael G. Dowd (*Woman's Day*):

My job is to defend women charged with killing the men who have abused them. I meet my clients in jail.

Here the opening not only gives the author authenticity, but in one short statement invites the reader to come into the jail with him.

With all these openings to choose from, pull out all your rejected manuscripts, and to grab your readers' and editors' attention, do what my instructor did years ago: Say "Hey, you! Are you listening? Because I've got something to say that you won't want to miss."

DO'S AND DON'TS

• When using first person, set the scene, the time, and the subject matter in the first sentence.
• If you are writing on a topic that requires authority, such as medicine, the law, social issues, literature, or even sports, be sure to identify

yourself in the first paragraph, and if possible, in the title, i.e. Tom Jones, M.D.

• If you are writing about a holiday, mention it not only in the title, but in the first paragraph.

• When writing about an ethnic group, be sure your reader knows, in the very first sentence, which group you are writing about.

• Make your lead catchy but not more dramatic than your article.

• Don't use long descriptive passages.

• Do use short sentences and small paragraphs.

72

FROM TRAVEL TO TRAVEL ARTICLES

BY MARY MAYNARD DRAKE

REMEMBER YOUR LAST VACATION? The sunset glow on the sea . . . the witty guide . . . the intricate handcrafts . . . the superb golf course . . . the crusty warm breads . . . the lasting impressions of another culture. . . .

You can share these experiences with others, and earn money, too— as a travel writer.

Travel writers are as varied as the people, places, and adventures they write about, but they all share one essential trait: a love of travel and new experiences, for no matter how exotic the destination, travel writing is work, not a vacation.

Where to start

Start with an idea, a destination with a unique angle or a timely hook.

You don't have to travel to faraway places. You can write about a local museum, historic house, park or event that intrigues you and attracts out-of-town visitors. For example, I've sold newspaper travel articles about tours of Ben & Jerry's ice cream factory, the antique planes at Owls Head Museum, and viewing fall foliage by boat along the Maine coast.

New attractions in your area also make good travel subjects for major newspapers. My accounts of whale watching on the East Coast, mountain biking in Vermont, skiing inn to inn in New Hampshire, and kayaking in the Florida Keys sold readily when the activities first became popular.

However, unless you can provide an unusual angle about famous museums, important bicentennials, or ongoing attractions, newspaper travel editors will opt for the wire service story, rather than pay you for yours.

Turn your vacation into a working trip

Before departing, read whatever you can find about your destination in travel magazines and tourist guides. Then you'll have an idea of what you want to see and photograph. But don't make your plans so rigid that you can't adjust them once you arrive.

Talk to locals who can tell you about unusual sites not recommended by the AAA, chambers of commerce, and tourist bureaus. A Dunedin, Florida, coffee shop waitress suggested an uncrowded hiking trail; a museum docent in Portland, Maine, recommended her favorite "undiscovered" restaurant; a B&B host in Kauai steered us to a remote waterfall for swimming; and a Balinese man took us to a Hindu cremation ceremony. These bits of local lore helped enliven my writing.

When gathering information for an article, collect all the maps, menus (with prices), and brochures you can. (If you don't want to carry all that paper around, ship it home in large manila envelopes that you've brought with you.)

Take notes while sightseeing, or write in a diary every day. To tape or not to tape is a major question. It's often easier just to jot down the important points during a tour guide's spiel. During long talks, some writers quietly dictate important facts and figures into their tape recorders.

Tape formal interviews with officials or experts, always asking their permission first. Take notes, too, and as soon as possible after the interview, listen to the tape with notes in hand. I expand my notes and key specific quotes, so I can find them quickly when I go to write my article.

Good pictures often clinch a sale and may mean placing your travel article in a better market for more money. Use an automatic 35 mm camera and make sure you learn how to use it. You don't need an elaborate state-of-the-art single lens reflex camera with interchangeable lenses at first, though you'll probably want one eventually.

Take a variety of vertical and horizontal pictures—close-ups, medium range, and distance. Editors usually use an expansive horizontal photo as a lead-in for a travel article, plus smaller close-ups and medium views of people, action, and scenery. Magazine cover shots are vertical.

Thirty-five mm color slides (transparencies) are most versatile. Most newspapers, and almost all magazines, require slides for color pictures and can convert them into black-and-white photos, if necessary. (Specialty labs also can make slides from color negatives.)

Take more pictures than you think you'll need. I often shoot two rolls a day for an article, taking normal, slightly underexposed, and slightly overexposed shots of each view when possible. That is the best way of getting a perfectly exposed picture, and it's a lot cheaper than having to return to the location (when the action and/or light conditions will be different).

Don't depend upon photos from tourist bureaus or public relations firms, except in an emergency. The quality of their slides and prints varies greatly, and the shots may not suit your article.

Query before you write

As a beginning travel writer, be realistic when seeking a market. Your daily or weekly newspaper or regional magazine will probably be your best first outlet. Hone your skills and build up a portfolio of published articles before you approach *The New York Times, Travel & Leisure,* or any other major publication. But don't aim *too* low; if you have a unique idea, go for it. And *never* give your travel article away free.

Before querying, study your prospective market by writing for writer's guidelines and reading several issues. Determine the readership (upscale vs. family budget), style (first-person vs. third-person, formal vs. colloquial English), length, and other factors. Note which publications will not accept articles resulting from free or subsidized trips offered to writers by special events or sites, visitors bureaus, or public relations firms. (Those publications are often good markets for beginning travel writers who pay their own expenses.)

Write your query, describing your idea in one or two paragraphs for a newspaper, less than a page for a magazine. Include a photocopy of one or two of your best travel articles, a short biography, and a self-addressed stamped envelope (SASE).

Two or three times a year I send queries with a paragraph each on two to five subjects, giving availability dates and a self-addressed post card, to travel editors of 20 or so newspapers with non-overlapping circulation areas. I then submit the articles for which each editor gives me a go-ahead. When querying a new editor, I also enclose my resumé, an SASE, and a color copy of one of my recently published travel articles that used my color photographs. When a major paper rejects any or all of that series of ideas, I immediately query smaller papers in the same area on the rejected topics.

Editors retire, get promoted and/or have their free-lance budgets cut, so I constantly seek new, more important, better paying markets.

Writing the article

When describing your destination, put yourself in the reader's shoes. Give an honest report, not a public relations puff piece, and include negatives when appropriate. Make your article succinct, but colorful. Most newspaper travel articles run 1,000 to 1,200 words, plus a sidebar of how to get there and specifics on amenities, costs, and phone numbers. Magazines usually run a range of longer feature articles and shorts of varying lengths.

Be professional. Meet your deadline; and double-check your facts, figures, and phone numbers for accuracy. Send a complete package of error-free, double-spaced typed or computer-generated text and slides, unless the editor requests otherwise. Always include an SASE. I send only duplicate slides, unless a magazine editor specifically requests originals (in which case I insure them).

To the growing number of newspaper editors who don't accept queries, I send one article at a time, a brief cover letter, and an SASE. To save postage, I suggest the editor discard an unwanted manuscript and return only my slides.

Keep adequate records of the expenses and income related to your travel writing. I also keep records on the status of each article as it progresses from idea to published-and-paid-for.

Newspapers are buying fewer travel articles from free-lance writers, but new specialty magazines are a growing market, and people are always eager to read about exciting, relaxing, and intriguing places to visit or dream about.

Keep refining and marketing your travel writing. Then you too can share your vacation impressions in print.

73

BIOGRAPHER AT WORK

BY GALE E. CHRISTIANSON

THE BIOGRAPHER BONDS HIMSELF to his subject in a union more symbiotic than matrimony. Almost never are the two separated during the long months and years of their association, for dreams and nightmares are as much the stuff of writing lives as the countless hours passed in airless archives or mornings wrestling with the blank page.

Thus your subject must be a companion whose character faults, which magnify in the glare of intense scrutiny, are offset by accomplishments sufficiently redeeming to override skepticism and assuage doubt. Such was the case for me with the great Isaac Newton, the subject of my first biography. Though mean-spirited and given to withering tirades against those who challenged his scientific ideas, the inventor of calculus, the mortal who flung gravity across the void, is forever woven into my tapestry of the blessed.

My feelings for Loren Eiseley, the anthropologist, literary naturalist, and author of some of this century's most elegant and evocative essays, are rather more ambivalent. While writing Eiseley's life, I was gradually overwhelmed by his tendency to cast events in conspiratorial hues and to blame everyone but himself for his sufferings. To put it simply: Had I known what I was getting into with Eiseley, I think I would have passed.

Yet the biographer should also be cautious when his prospective subject seems too companionable. Identifying too closely with the subject violates the constraints essential to writing biography. Psychoanalysts term this process "co-creation" or the "commingling of consciousness." Setting out to write the life of another, the biographer is actually carrying on an interior dialogue with himself, while plying his own emotional terrain.

After choosing a subject, the real work begins. Almost every serious biographer (we are not here concerned with so-called celebrity biog-

355

raphies or what I call tabloidism) must face the daunting prospect of burrowing deep into one or more archives. But it is well to complete as much background reading as possible before immersing yourself in the primary sources. Since it is not only unwise but impossible to attempt to include everything about a life, however important, the researcher must be selective. The late Barbara Tuchman characterized biography as a prism of history, while others have likened it to fine portraiture. Leon Edel, best known for his multivolume life of Henry James, speaks of "the figure under the carpet," whose true identity can be resolved only by carefully scrutinizing the tea leaves of research. Whatever the method or the metaphor, the biographer must create a unique angle of vision by fitting keys to locks that yield only to the right questions.

Some biographers enter archives armed with little more than a pencil and a generous supply of 3″ by 5″ cards; others carry laptop computers whose clicking keyboards serve as a constant distraction to those with a sensitive ear. My preference is the portable archives made available via photocopying. With photocopies at one's fingertips, dates, quotations, and myriad other details can be rechecked as often as need be, thus minimizing the number of inadvertent errors that steal into a manuscript.

Moreover, the biographer's perspective is subject to change. This is especially true when dealing with letters, diaries, and notebooks, which may require several readings. Notes are inevitably incomplete and have a way of growing cold during the months or possibly years that may pass before the author returns to them.

But most important to me is that an exact copy recharges the atmosphere as the original did when I first viewed it in the archives. Photocopies are the catalysts of inspiration and of musing, and serve as a constant reminder of the responsibility one bears to one's subject.

Finally, the more quickly material is gathered the sooner one can return home. The costs of photocopying are but a fraction of what it takes to hole up in major cities, where archives tend to be found.

To my continual surprise, I am often asked if I research the *whole* life before I begin to write it. The answer is an emphatic "yes," for, to paraphrase Kierkegaard, a life must be lived forward but it can only be understood backward.

No writer can tell another when enough research is enough, when

356

science must yield to art. This is a personal matter based on a hidden clock whose ticking is as individual as the human thumbprint. But one thing is certain: There will never be a book without writing, and without self-imposed deadlines, the writing will never begin.

To biographers of people who have only recently died, primary sources constitute more than words and images captured on paper. These include the house in which one's subject came into the world, and perhaps left it; the church in which he attended Sunday school; the neighborhood streets along which he bashfully walked hand in hand with his first love; and, if one is very lucky, the living memories of those who grew up with him and took his measure "way back when."

Interviewing friends, relatives, and colleagues of your subject is a tricky albeit rewarding business, best left until you are conversant with the archives. It is only at this point that the right questions can be asked. The web of memory is often very delicate, and responds most sympathetically when probed by a gentle and informed petitioner. And the more you address the same questions to various individuals, the sounder the process. Above all, listen. It is often the seemingly little things these people say that turn out to be the most important.

And what about writing the life of a living person? Having never done so, I can only say, *caveat emptor!* Since the life is not a finished thing, its telling will be superceded by future works based on a sounder perspective. Access to information may also be a problem, even if the subject is cooperative in the beginning. What is gladly given with one hand can be angrily snatched away by the other, especially if the subject's views and those of the biographer clash. With so many other wonderful subjects to choose from, why run the risk?

In her often cited account of Shakespeare's imagined sister, Virginia Woolf asserted that the writer must have "a room of one's own." What is true of the novelist and the poet is no less true of the biographer. "You must have a room, or a certain hour or so a day," wrote the mythographer Joseph Campbell, "where you don't know what was in the newspapers that morning, you don't know who your friends are, you don't know what you owe anybody, you don't know what anybody owes you." This is the place of creation where the writer brings forth what he or she is—and is to be.

Saturated with facts and documents, the writer confronts a ream of blank pages. Do not be surprised or dispirited if nothing happens right away, for obviously a book never writes itself. Someone, presumably the author, must shape the narrative while deciding which details to retain or to cut, which gestures to play up or to play down, which lines to quote or to omit.

A biography can begin at any point in a subject's life, from birth to the deathbed, from the moment when lightning struck, to the transforming pain caused by the loss of a loved one. The tale begins by fitting one of those precious keys into a lock, turning it, and bidding the reader to enter. During my research on Loren Eiseley, for example, it became clear that he had idealized his father, an itinerant hardware salesman who reminded me of no one so much as Willy Loman. Thus the book begins with three-year-old Loren in the arms of Clyde Edwin Eiseley, gazing into the midnight sky of a chill and leafless Nebraska spring in 1910, an incident Loren recounted in an essay penned many years later. The two are transfixed by Halley's comet.

"If you live to be an old man," his father whispered, "you will see it again. It will come back in seventy-five years."

"Yes, Papa," the boy replied dutifully. Tightening his hold on his father's neck, he promised that when he grew old, he would gaze on the comet a second time and remember the person he would always care for more than any other.

Once you begin, set yourself a challenging yet reachable goal. Mine is some 1,000 words a day, the equivalent of about three typed pages. When the gods are kind, as happens on occasion, the total may double, but more often than not I fall a few paragraphs short. I also try to finish a day's writing at a point which will stimulate the creative flow the next morning, the psychological equivalent of priming the pump.

There is much to be gained by reading fine literature while trying to approximate it oneself. The genre does not matter: Novels and essays, short stories and narrative histories, poetry and plays all serve to deepen one's sensibilities.

Your actual voice can also help to locate your literary voice. At day's end, or night's if you are an owl, read your edited work back to yourself aloud. You will not find it easy to ignore dissonant sound waves. Take pleasure in selecting chapter titles as well as epigraphs, if you plan to use them. A copy of *Bartlett's Familiar Quotations* interleaved with scores of ragged markers is a positive sign that you are well on your way. As for the biography itself, keep in mind the fact that Hemingway

358

had thirty titles in reserve, should his editor veto *For Whom the Bell Tolls*.

In time—if you have the determination and the talent—something will happen. You will experience one of those very special days when the narrative voice and the mind become one. It will not last; the days of the storm petrel must inevitably follow. Yet you will also find, when rereading your manuscript for the twentieth time, that you were not appreciably better on your best days than on your worst. Your mind has been operating at two levels, the one conscious but illusory, the other subconscious but real. You have subtly programmed yourself to remain within certain boundaries, both scholarly and aesthetic. You have found your own way of identifying with your subject, and mutual suspicion has yielded to trust. The pages, so pitifully few in the beginning, are piling up with satisfying regularity. You are a biographer.

359

74

REVIEWING BOOKS

BY EDWARD HOWER

HAVE YOU EVER THOUGHT IT WOULD BE FUN to get paid for reading the latest books, and then for saying what you think of them? Then maybe you should think about reviewing books.

Getting started

You don't have to be an established book reviewer for your work to be published. A lot of hometown newspapers—including the local shopper's weekly—are glad to have reviews of books by local authors or about the area. Regional and special-interest magazines also run reviews, so if you're an expert on a particular part of the country or on some specialized subject, you should query those publications. If you have a book in mind that you'd like to review, say why you think the publication's readers might like to read about it—and why you are especially qualified to review it. An editor who is interested will respond by phone or letter to discuss it.

Early in your career, you may have to obtain your own copy of the book you select to review; you can do so by writing to the publisher's publicity department, saying that you want to review the book for whatever publication you have in mind. If you can get a note from the publication's editor indicating that he or she is interested in seeing your review, include this with your letter to the publisher. After you've published some reviews and editors get to know your work, they may send you bound galleys of forthcoming books—pre-publication paperback editions—in response to your letters to the publicity director.

Don't be surprised if you're paid nothing or almost nothing for your reviews, at first. Count it as a learning experience. I was paid only $5 apiece for my first several reviews in a local weekly, but later I used clips of these reviews to show to the editors at *The New York Times, The Boston Globe, The Chicago Tribune, Newsday,* and the other newspapers I write for today. Now I do about two reviews a month at $100 to $400 each. I also get free hardcover editions, which I can keep after reviewing them.

Once you've reviewed a few books, include photocopies of your published reviews with your next query letters to editors. Don't be afraid to mail out multiple queries, and to send follow-up letters if you don't hear from the editors after a few weeks.

Your letter should include a description of the kind of books you especially like; my specialty is contemporary fiction and books about the Third World. Other reviewers specialize in women's issues, American history, nature, sports, boats, or science. If your interest is too narrow, you may not get many responses to your queries, so it's a good idea to indicate that you'll be glad to review a wider range of books.

Each August and January, *Publishers Weekly* lists books, by publisher and date, that will be published in the coming season. Look through these issues in the library for titles that match your special interests. With your letters to editors include a short list of the books you'd be interested in reviewing for them.

Learning the trade

How do you learn to write reviews? First, as you read, take notes on the plot and content, and jot down comments you may want to make later. It's amazing how much more closely you read a book when you have pencil in hand. You can also learn a lot about reviewing by reading published reviews in newspapers and magazines. Many national and regional publications have book review sections or columns, often somewhere near the back.

It would be worth your while to spend time in the library looking through recent volumes of *Book Review Digest* and *Contemporary Literary Criticism,* valuable references that publish extracts from reviews of earlier books by most major authors. They're also useful for getting capsule plot summaries of books that you might not have time to read—good background for your own reviews.

You'll soon discover that a good review includes these elements:
• a lively opening: one or two brief paragraphs that mention the name of the author and the title and often some brief information about the author, as well as any past works, prizes, etc.

- a summary of the plot (if it's a novel) or of the main purpose and subject of a work of nonfiction
- the reviewer's opinion of the book's strengths and weaknesses
- a wrap-up sentence or paragraph that gives the reader a final impression of the book

The opening

Composing a good lead paragraph is the most challenging part of review writing. The purpose is to catch your readers' attention, making them eager to read what you have to say.

To get started, take notes. Ask yourself some questions:
- What's the main theme that runs through the book?
- What's special about the book, compared to others like it?
- What impact did the book have on me?

You're likely to find your lead in your answers.

The name of the author and the book title are often included in the first paragraph, but sometimes you can start with the book's most important idea, as if the review were an article on the book's subject.

Here's how I began the review of a satirical novel about college life that was published in *The New York Times:*

College campuses have been in turmoil for some time now. No, the students haven't been acting up. It's the professors who have been leaving trails of blood along the hallways of academe, bludgeoning one another over questions about what's called "political correctness."

Then, a couple of sentences later, I named the author (Ishmael Reed) and title *(Japanese by Spring).*

In the first paragraph, I called it a "funny, explosive new novel." Generally, I think it's a good idea to indicate very briefly at the beginning what you think of a book. An adjective or two will do, and you can expand on it later.

In reviewing nonfiction books, you can open with a short background to the topic the book covers, especially if the subject is likely to be unfamiliar to some readers. For instance, a review of mine in the *San Francisco Chronicle* started like this:

The recent news from South Africa has been both exhilarating and alarming. The nation seems on the verge of freedom, yet its people are rioting among themselves.

362

The next sentence gives the book's title, author, and some relevant information about him:

No recent book can better clarify South Africa's dilemma than *The Mirror at Midnight,* by Adam Hochschild, a former editor and co-founder of *Mother Jones* magazine.

The summary

People read reviews primarily to find out whether they want to read a book. You need to give them a taste of what's between the covers. When reviewing fiction, tell your reader something about the main characters but summarize only *some* of the plot. Nothing's more infuriating for both an author and would-be reader than to have a reviewer give away what happens in the end! I usually summarize the first third to half of the plot of a novel, omitting the subplots, and stop where a conflict is about to be resolved, a character is about to make a decision, or a major action scene is about to begin.

Reviews of nonfiction books, on the other hand, should provide an overview of all the important information. Include significant dates, people, places, and ideas, and a statement of how the author arrived at his or her conclusions.

Choosing good quotations from the book can make it come alive for your readers. Look for especially witty, moving, or powerful quotes, and describe the context in which they were made. But limit the quotations to no more than a sentence or two, unless an editor has given you the go-ahead to write a long review. Don't forget to give page references after each quotation, so that your editor can check them.

The opinion

Some reviewers don't mind trashing a book, and some seem positively to enjoy it. Not I. If I can't find at least something to like in a book's first twenty or thirty pages, I sent it right back, so another reviewer can try it. There are a lot of good books that deserve attention, so why waste my time on those I think unworthy? I do write mixed reviews, though; few books are without flaws, and it's my job to be honest with my readers about what I find in the books I'm reviewing.

When forming your opinion of a book, you might start by asking yourself these questions:

- What did this author set out to do?
- How well did he or she succeed?
- Did the book move me in some way?
- What did I like about the book?
- What did I dislike?

It's also helpful to divide your evaluation into two categories:

- Content: what the author said.
- Style: how he or she said it.

When considering the content of a work of fiction, ask yourself:

- Were the characters interesting and convincing?
- Did the plot hold my attention to the end?

As for style, decide what to say about the author's language.

- Was it simple, stilted, poetic?
- Impersonal, formal, moving?
- Hackneyed or original?

Try to come up with some fresh descriptive words. My rule: Any hackneyed adjectives that appear in a blurb are out of bounds for my review.

In reviewing nonfiction books, content is more important than style, though you do need to say whether or not the writing is clear and readable. Consider:

- How thoroughly and thoughtfully did the author cover the material?
- What is the author's major focus? Why?
- Were the conclusions justified by the material that the author presented?

You may disagree with the book's conclusions, but you must make every effort to be objective, not to argue with the author and say how *you* would have written it.

The wrap-up

Make your ending short, finding some strong words that sum up your opinion of the book. If possible, echo a statement you made in your opening paragraph.

At the end of my review of Ishmael Reed's *Japanese by Spring,* I echoed my opening statement, using different language and adding a twist:

. . .this clever, outrageous novel is just the sort of weapon we need in the war against academic pedantry.

The last paragraph of my review of Adam Hochschild's book echoed its opening, and, taking it one step further, added what I thought was the work's most important accomplishment:

The Mirror at Midnight is an ambitious and thoughtful book. It's strength lies not only in explaining what has been happening in South Africa, but in letting us empathize with its people.

Remember, your goal is not just to finish writing about a book, but to put a memorable ending on the review itself, making it a first-rate piece of journalism that you'll be proud of long after the book has been forgotten.

75

WRITING AND SELLING IN THE NEWSPAPER MARKET

BY JOHANNA S. BILLINGS

ALTHOUGH IT'S NOT EASY TO BREAK INTO the newspaper market as a staff writer, nevertheless, local newspapers are literally begging for free-lance writers, or "stringers," to cover events that the staff writers can't get to.

Both daily and weekly newspapers use stringers. Weeklies generally accept beginning writers because often their staffs are less experienced. Smaller suburban dailies are likely to be receptive to new writers, but the larger dailies usually demand journalism experience.

Breaking in

The best way to sell your work to newspapers is to sell yourself first. Once you have chosen a newspaper, find out who the editor is, and then send a cover letter, including a resumé highlighting your writing credits and "clips" if you have any. A follow-up call should get you an interview, which may be rather informal, especially if you already have some writing experience.

Because most editors are not looking to buy just one article, they seldom want query letters. Instead, they want to cultivate a working relationship with stringers to whom they can give assignments regularly.

As a stringer, you will be doing both "hard news," which refers to government- and other issue-oriented articles, and "features," which include interviews/profiles and community events.

There are no standard rules for article length. Some newspapers have no length guidelines at all; others will tell you before you begin to write exactly how long an article should be.

Article length in newspapers is expressed in inches. The number of words to an inch depends on the size of print and column width of the paper. At the newspaper at which I am currently a stringer, a nine- or ten-inch story is about 800 words, but the same number of words might be eleven or twelve inches at another newspaper.

If you've written for other markets such as magazines, be prepared for a much faster pace. Since newspapers publish roughly thirty times as often as magazines and therefore need thirty times the input, if you want to succeed, you have to write good articles—fast.

Often, particularly at daily newspapers, a stringer will get an assignment without much advance notice. You may get a call Monday afternoon asking if you can cover something that begins at 7:30 that night. And if you're writing for a morning paper, you will be expected to have the story written and in final form by 11 p.m. or midnight.

The "musts"

Both hard news and features are written in much the same way. They must incorporate these elements:

The five W's. *What* is the story about? *Who* is affected by it? *Where* is it happening, and *when*? And most important, *why*? Doing this well means paying attention to details. How much something costs, an address, a person's age, the number of people attending an event are all small details that will make your story complete.

Accuracy. This may seem so basic that it doesn't warrant a mention, but it is crucial. No reader will continue to buy a newspaper if the facts are not reported accurately. And editors will not keep stringers who cannot produce accurate copy.

So, when you conduct an interview or cover a meeting or event, make sure you understand exactly what happened and how, what effects it will have and why it is important. If you have any questions, read previous articles on the subject, or ask sources, editors, and other writers. Then, write your story. When writing about a complicated issue, I try to get phone numbers of key people to call if questions come up while I'm writing.

Balance. Newspapers strive to represent both sides of every story, not the opinion of the writer. If, for example, a zoning board votes to allow an oversized parking lot, explain why the board made that decision. If it wasn't a unanimous vote, be sure to quote people who voted *for* and *against* it. And just as important, be sure to talk to the business people and anyone living nearby who will be affected by the decision.

Let the words of the people you quote speak for themselves, even if you disagree. But remember, the opinions expressed should advance your story, or provide new information, not just repeat information.

The hook. Entice readers at the beginning of your piece with the most interesting item. Newspapers generally present articles in the "inverted pyramid" style, that is, using the most important item first, with the least important at the end. But using the inverted pyramid style is not a hard-and-fast rule. Many of the newspapers I've worked for encourage more flexibility, allowing writers to begin a story with an anecdote or something to catch the reader's attention.

Relevance. Most readers will ask, "What does it mean to me?" before deciding to read on. Put yourself in readers' shoes and ask yourself that question—before you begin writing. For example, what will the zoning hearing mean to the average person reading a story about it— or to the person who is not directly affected but lives or works in the community? Will the new parking lot affect traffic flow? Will a traffic light be necessary? Why did the petitioners need or want a bigger parking lot? Have any residents voiced objections to the new lot? If so, who? Talk to them. Include their opinions in your story.

Generally, the more you include people in a story, the better it will be. If you find that "John Doe" is upset about the new lot, you might lead your story with, "John Doe moved to his present home thirty years ago because he wanted to live in a rural setting. But soon, he will be living next door to So-And-So's new parking lot." Then describe the zoning hearing and decision, moving quickly to represent the views of the zoning board and business owner to make sure your story stays balanced. Personalizing even a hard-news article will make it more interesting to read (and more fun to write).

Do the same with features and stories about community events. Interview people and find out why they came to an event and what they liked or disliked. You might hear about inefficient or rude ticket sales people, something the sponsors would never tell you. Having this information will give your story pizazz.

The fresh approach. This is particularly important when writing about community events. Without new ideas, the preview and after-the-event story can be essentially the same, year after year. It's your job as a stringer to make sure you don't write the same story that appeared in the paper last year. A fresh approach is especially crucial at a weekly because the story might not appear until six days after the area daily already covered it.

While working for a paper in suburban Philadelphia, I did a preview story on the upcoming annual Philadelphia Folk Festival. I had interviewed some volunteers who camped out on the site months before the festival to get the grounds ready, and began my story by focusing on a couple of them. I then gradually worked my way into the nuts and bolts of the festival—how many people were expected to attend, the dates, and the special attractions. The volunteers' experiences served as the thread that tied all the elements of the story together.

Features about individuals who "overcame great obstacles" or "remain positive despite the obstacles" have been done over and over, so taking a fresh perspective is very important. Don't editorialize; just let the person's words speak for themselves, and readers can form their own conclusions.

One last rule: Stringers are often assigned the stories that staff writers can't get to or don't want. But don't look at this as an obstacle. As a stringer, you'll have the luxury of having the time to develop really interesting features.

At first, all your work will be on assignment by the editor. But once you feel comfortable with the business and the writing, you will feel free to suggest ideas for future articles. If it's a viable idea, you'll get the assignment.

§ 76

How to Write and Sell the Regional Historical Article

By Carol Bennett McCuaig

THERE IS A GROWING DEMAND for historical articles in regional publications. The good news for the free lancer in this field: There are more markets available today than ever before.

What are your choices for your article on regional history?

• The regional magazine
• The local weekly newspaper
• The weekend edition of your daily newspaper
• A national magazine

Although a slightly different approach is required for each of these, some common rules of thumb apply, no matter where you plan to submit your work.

Subject matter should not be too general. Zero in on one aspect of your theme. Look for an unusual angle. Forget about such ho-hum topics as bygone school days or the trials of the hardy pioneer. Those have been done to death. Readers—and editors—expect something fresh and entertaining.

The oft-stressed maxim that you should "write what you know" doesn't apply here. Writers of popular history usually begin with an idea that is fleshed out after they've done considerable research. Although you may start out in one direction, after you've done your research, the finished article may have a totally different slant, depending on what your sleuthing turns up.

What *should* be stressed is that complete accuracy is absolutely essential. In years to come, students and historians will rely on your information, and any mistake will be perpetuated.

When writing a regional history, you must gear the piece to the interests of a particular region or community. Query an editor before you do any extensive research or write your article, so you'll be sure to go in the right direction—if you get an assignment. Needless to say, you need to do some preliminary research before sending off a query to prove (to yourself as well as the editor) that you can carry the task through to completion.

The regional magazine

By their very nature, regional magazines are narrow in focus, and many accept only material that has a tie-in with their geographical area. It is, therefore, best that you begin by writing about your own county or neighborhood.

If you live in Arizona, for example, does this mean that you're excluded from contributing to New England publications? Not at all, as long as you give them what they want—which won't be a piece about the Grand Canyon.

Weekly newspapers

A great place for the free lancer to break into the market is the local weekly newspaper. Their editors seldom have time to respond to letters, so phone and make an appointment. Don't choose the day before the paper comes out, when everyone in the office is working at a hectic pace!

If you hope to write a column, take several examples (500 to 1,000 words) of the kind you propose to write (or clips if you've had some published) with you to the interview. If you know that an anniversary is coming up, such as the town centennial, ask the editor if he is planning a special edition to celebrate the event. Appropriate free-lance articles may be welcome.

What sells local newspapers and magazines? Names, names, names! The more local names you can work into historical articles, the better, but not long "laundry lists" that just take up space and bore the reader. Do mention by name the crew of the first train that came into town, or the first people elected to the local council.

While most publications pay their columnists, not all local newspapers can afford to, and remuneration may be in copies only. Consider doing the work on a volunteer basis anyway, so you'll have clips to show other editors, and a proven track record.

Daily newspapers are a little different. Although their main focus is world news, some print a weekend feature section. Write a one-page

371

query and mail it in with your resumé, clips of your published work, and an SASE (self-addressed, stamped envelope). Editors come and go, so call the paper to get the name of the person in charge of the appropriate department.

National magazines

There are a number of big-circulation magazines that print historical material, and yes, you may sell your regional article to them, if it has a universal theme. For example, if you have access to unpublished letters or diaries that shed light on some local aspect of the American Civil War, the editors may well be interested.

Where to find ideas

• Visit your local museum or library, which may keep files of clippings and letters relating to local people and events.

• Talk to retirement home residents, who may have witnessed certain incidents. In 1911, a large section of an Ontario town was destroyed by fire; when writing about the tragedy eighty years later I was able to use the stories of more than a dozen people who had actually witnessed the devastation.

Always try to double-check the facts to avoid using incorrect names and dates.

• Were any famous people born in the community you're writing about? I once wrote a piece on author Leslie McFarlane, who was born in the town where I was working. Under the pseudonym Franklin W. Dixon, he ghosted the first nineteen books in the Hardy Boys series. He also write four Dana Girls books under the name Carolyn Keene.

• Study plaques at historic sites.

• Read local history books, which may give you clues you can follow up on and use in your own way with a new angle and focus.

• Back issues of local newspapers, usually found on microfilm at local archives, are also a rich source of information.

While searching through 1890s issues of a community newspaper, I noticed that a great debate had raged for many weeks over whether cows should wear bells. At that time, many households kept a cow, and these animals wandered at large, causing havoc in neighborhood gardens.

Some people favored bells so they could hear the cows coming. Others found the constant noise disturbing. This prompted me to write a short piece, "The Great Cow Bell Controversy," an interesting period piece, which was published in a newspaper supplement.

If you have old photos to illustrate your article, include one or two photocopies with your query letter: They may help you to net an assignment. When asked to submit the actual prints, submit duplicates, not originals. Photos are easily lost, and you might never see them again.

Never write on the back of a photo. Write caption details on a photocopy. The photo must be clear, but size doesn't matter. The publication can adjust it to fit the space available.

Selling your historical article

As always, it's important to choose the right market for your work. The most common error made by free-lance writers is their failure to identify the requirements of a particular publication.

Check the listings in the back of this book. Read the entries in the history section, and the list of regional magazines, but don't stop there. Your work may find a home in general-interest publications, too.

Read the magazine for which your work is intended. Look for a copy in your local library, or send for a sample copy and writer's guidelines, enclosing an SASE for a reply.

The increasing trend towards recording the past means that editors constantly need new material!

§ 77

THE MARKET FOR OP-ED ARTICLES

BY GENIE DICKERSON

THERE'S A LOT OF CONFUSION ABOUT OP-ED articles, the free-lance essays that newspapers publish opposite their editorial pages. Papers buy two kinds of op-ed pieces: personal experience and opinion or analysis. Most op-ed rejections result from the writer's confusion and blending of the two types.

Let's take the personal experience piece first. This offers writers the best and easiest way to get published by a newspaper. All that's required is 1) simple, clear, tight writing, and 2) an experience in some segment of public affairs.

Included in this type might be first-person narratives by a foreign defector, for example, or by personal victims of some horror. The whistleblower, the disaffected union worker, the member of an ethnic minority who has been discriminated against—all these may have special stories they want to tell. Any topical firsthand experience will work.

I've had op-ed articles published on my problems with neighborhood squirrels and on a conversation I overheard while having breakfast at a restaurant. Virtually everyone has at least one personal story that would interest newspaper readers.

Analysis or opinion op-eds

The analysis type of op-ed article usually sheds light on a public concern, or expresses a new point of view or opinion, but it does not involve personal experience. Here the writer uses the third person and turns out an impersonal commentary. The tone of an analysis should be firm and somewhat formal; its vocabulary is more likely to use polysyllabic words from the Latin, and the style is more sophisticated and knowledgeable. Facts and statistics must be verifiable. For instance, just because a person is sick and tired of the government's

374

budget deficit doesn't necessarily mean he should get paid to have his opinion set into print. The reader deserves more.

In dollars, how big was the deficit last year? Who is to blame? When did the problem begin? Do the United Kingdom, Germany, and Japan also run budget deficits? What evidence is there for these statements? The writer must present the facts in a logical essay and tie them together with an answer to one more question: What's the solution?

Experience is helpful but not necessary. I've sold opinion pieces on income tax, freedom of the press, and public funding for the arts, without having any special knowledge. Research at the library can fill in. Telephone inquiries to such sources as government bureaus and senators' offices are another good option.

With analytical op-eds, it's especially important to stick to one subject. Tossing in gratuitous comments on secondary issues may alienate readers needlessly. Avoid blanket criticisms of large groups like conservatives, liberals, ethnic groups, teenagers, college students, etc. Try to lead readers to look at an issue from a new angle without insulting any person or class. Balance should permeate the piece.

Writers of analytical op-eds should omit unnecessary personal facts: age, religion, race, political party preference, lifestyle choices, etc. If the writer seems to have an ax to grind, he'll lose the reader. The greatest pitfall in op-ed writing is mixing the personal, emotional narrative type with the impersonal, intellectual analytical type.

The first sentence is the most important part of any op-ed. It should be clever and concise, telling just enough about what is to come to hook the reader. The next most important sentence is the last one of the article, which should summarize the main point.

Humor is another valuable element in an op-ed. If the article can raise a smile or a laugh, so much the better. Although op-eds aim basically to provoke thought and discussion, the writer should offer readers some frosting on the cake. Although this sort of writing cannot be used in hard news reporting, it sells op-ed articles. But don't go too far. Fluff, purple prose, and padding will only bring rejections.

Titles and headlines

Newspaper headlines run longer than most magazine titles and often contain a verb. Also, individual newspapers use their own capitalization styles. Follow the style of the paper to which you submit. The paper may change your heading, but at least you have suggested a workable one and have shown your knowledge of the newspaper's style.

Follow normal manuscript form—typed, double-spaced—and include an SASE. Payment rates for op-ed pieces range from nothing to several hundred dollars, with larger-circulation papers paying the higher rates. Op-eds longer than the usual 700 to 800 words also command the higher-range fees, but few papers buy long pieces.

The best op-ed markets are hometown papers. Some newspapers refuse to buy from out-of-area writers, but most op-ed editors of metropolitan papers welcome the freshness brought by writers outside their region. Address the manuscript to "Op-Ed Editor" or to the editor by name. A few op-ed editors prefer queries, but many topics would be cold before the query was answered. Check the query policy of your targeted paper.

Whether or not to send a cover letter with the manuscript depends on what you've got to say in it and who the editor is. If you have relevant expertise, then a cover letter (or a bio line at the end of the manuscript) is in order. Rarely do op-ed editors welcome footnotes or a bibliography. If you have tearsheets on the same subject as the submitted manuscript, include them as support for your knowledge of the subject. Generally, however, the editor would rather just get to your manuscript without spending time reading extras.

If you prefer to test the waters before jumping into op-ed writing, try a short letter to the editor, similar in content to pieces published on the op-ed page. A success or two will build your self-confidence.

376

78

Rx for Health Writing

By R. M. Adams

*A collection of facts is no more science than a heap of
stones is a house.*

—Lewis Thomas

In no area has the information explosion been greater than in
health and medicine. Scientists always have something new to say,
ergo, getting ideas is a cinch. Start by scanning newspapers for 10 days
(include two Sunday editions). Pick three or four topics that interest
you and decide which one would affect reader health most directly.

Consult the *Readers' Guide to Periodical Literature* under two topics: health and medical/medicine. Make a list of the subcategories.
For example, under "medical dynamics" the topics include: education,
electronics, equipment, ethics, examinations, facilities, fakers, fees,
genetics, geography, histories, and hypnosis. Under each category are
titles of published articles. This will give you the "big picture" of health
issues in the popular press.

It can also be helpful to visit the pressroom at a medical convention
to read the press releases.

When a topic has appeared frequently in these sources, it may mean:
1) the issue has been beaten to death, or 2) reader interest is still high.
You must decide, based on the market you wish to target, what is still
a viable topic.

Markets

Check the market sections in the back of this book. Peruse newsstands. New publications appear frequently and getting in on the
ground floor is easier than approaching an established magazine.

As you study the markets, you'll notice that health/medical publications for the general reader tend to fall into one of two categories:

377

1. Prevention/lifestyle
2. Disease/treatment

You must pick which fork in the road you wish to take.

Some publications are devoted exclusively to health matters. Because health and medicine are such popular topics, almost any magazine will consider a timely, well-written piece on a health issue that affects its readers, particularly those for older readers such as *Modern Maturity* and *Mature Years*.

Magazines move and change their names and editors, so confirm the current editor and address.

Background

At this point let's say you have decided to write about early detection of breast cancer and have two or three markets in mind. Of course, you will have read back issues and sent for writers' guidelines.

Next, you'll need to read extensively on diagnostic approaches: mammography, breast self-examination, etc.—deep background research. If you have no experience and little knowledge about health issues, this reading is even more important. Research is essential to any good article, but in medical writing, it may *be* the article.

Background research cannot be rushed. In addition to obtaining the latest facts, the object is to gain perspective: Where does your specific topic fit into the general subject? Are there issues related to sociology, psychology, ethics and the law? With breast cancer, early diagnosis is the key; related fields would be the psychology of dealing with a potentially fatal disease or mastectomy, as well as possible complications of treatment.

If you get confused or encounter too much jargon, go to the children's section of the public library and read books on the same topic. Begin with a large city library, then move to a medical school library (anyone has access, but you may not be able to check out materials; plan to spend some money on photocopying key articles).

Other sources of information and free literature are non-profit health agencies like the American Heart Association, American Cancer Society, etc. The government printing office also has inexpensive publications on health and medicine, as do the National Institutes of Health (NIH) in Bethesda, Maryland.

Interviews

You need to consult "experts," because information in books is 18 to 24 months old by the day of publication. One way to find experts is through the commmunications department of a local medical school.

Once you have chosen a few specialists to interview, the following process is recommended:

1. Make appointments to interview them in person; avoid using the phone.

2. Use a tape recorder. This is more important for interviews for health articles than for any other type of inverview, because of the complexity of the subject matter, and the potential for misquoting.

3. Do your homework, both on the topic and the interviewee.

4. Prepare relevant questions in advance.

5. Ask for explanations when anything isn't clear.

6. Repeat what has been said to check your understanding of it.

As long as you give proper credit in the piece, most people will be willing to talk to you.

Putting it together

Before you start writing, make an outline and write the closing. If you can't write a satisfying ending, you either don't have a meaningful theme, or your thinking is still fuzzy. If the former applies, you may have to abandon the project. Often you won't recognize a dead-end piece until you attempt to write the ending.

Assuming you just needed to sharpen your thinking and are able to write a definitive closing, proceed to write the lead. Make it lively but not dramatic. Hook the readers; make them want to know more.

With the lead and ending in good shape, the middle is easy. Given length constraints, this is where you distill and contract (never expand; you should always have more material than you can use).

A word about how to resolve differences of opinion among your experts: DON'T! Just report what they said. Honest differences of opinion enhance your article. Pieces on controversial subjects or presenting major disputes are best. Some timely topics for medical articles might include the following: aging, AIDS, attention deficit disorder, birth control, cancer, computers in medicine, drug abuse, endocrinology, medicine and ethics, health insurance, home remedies, immunology, implants (breast, penile), leisure sports injuries, medical technology, mental health, new drugs, organ transplants, phobias, prenatal diagnosis, profiles (physician/astronaut, Nobel laureates), self-help strategies, space medicine, stress reduction, teen pregnancy, universal health care, use of animals in research, and women's health issues.

Last words

Medical writing is a fertile field because the flow of new information is endless, and the potential for helping thousands of people is rewarding. If you specialize, you'll have a competitive edge over other free lancers.

To begin, publish wherever you can, then with a few clips, move up to loftier periodicals. Use "medicalese" sparingly.

If you continue to write medical articles, you'll soon find you know more medicine than most writers and certainly more journalism than most health professionals.

❦ 79

How to Write a How-to That Sells

By Gail Luttman

ANY ACTIVITY THAT INTERESTS YOU—from canoeing to cooking to collecting Civil War relics to cutting your own hair—is a potential how-to article. And whether you are an expert or a novice, you are qualified to write about it.

Where to start

The most successful introductions to how-to pieces state a problem and then propose one or more possible solutions, perferably those relating to the seven basic human motivators.

Ego—Does your solution to the problem improve the way you look, the way you feel about yourself, your ability to relate to others?

Economy—Does it save money, protect the environment, improve quality without increasing cost?

Health—Does it give you more energy, promote safety practices, increase your psychological well-being?

Romance—Does it enhance sex appeal, create a cozy atmosphere, improve personal relationships?

Family—Does it entertain children, foster loyalty, help research family history?

Leisure—Does it enliven holiday activities, provide an engrossing hobby, help plan exciting vacations?

Individuality—Does the activity appeal to the universal desire for uniqueness by offering something new, different or better?

These motivators often overlap. A hobby may bring in income. Dieting may improve both health and self-image. An inexpensive bungalow of unusual construction may serve as a romantic retreat. The more motivators you appeal to, the greater interest you will generate in your how-to.

Moving on

After piquing the reader's interest, offer a brief explanation of what the activity involves, couched in enthusiastic words that inspire confidence. Can the skill be learned in five easy steps? Fifteen minutes a day? Does it require a special setting, or will a corner of the garage do? What special tools or materials are needed?

Rather than barrage readers at the beginning with a large number of tools or materials required, you may want to list them in a sidebar, a separate boxed-off article that accompanies the main story. Sidebars are a great way to include data or lengthy explanations without interrupting the narrative flow. Some editors favor articles with one, two, or even three sidebars if the article is very long or complex.

Definitions of unfamiliar terms might go into a vocabulary sidebar, especially when they are numerous; on the other hand, if special words are few or are easy to define, it is better to explain their meanings as you go along.

Whenever possible, describe new concepts by drawing a comparison with something familiar. In a piece about building stone walls, for example, a description of the proper consistency of mortar as "buttery" sparks instant recognition.

Complicated procedures don't seem quite as confusing when written up in short, uncomplicated sentences of the sort found in cookbooks. Explicitness also ensures clarity. Vague directions such as "measure out six to eight cups of water" or "cut two to three yards of string" leave the reader wondering which of the two stated amounts to use.

Clarity is also improved by separating general principles from specific procedures. If you are writing about how to build a chicken coop, for example, after the introductory remarks, explain how the layout and dimensions are established, then include some specific plans. In a how-to about cooking a Christmas goose, first describe how to roast the goose, then offer some favorite recipes. In that way you'll satisfy both the creative reader who likes to improvise and the less adventuresome reader who feels more comfortable with step-by-step instructions.

The final and best way to ensure clarity is with illustrations. The less commonplace the subject, the more important photographs and sketches become, and they are essential when dimensions are involved. In addition, the market is more receptive to illustrated how-tos. But don't despair if you are not an accomplished photographer or artist; many how-to magazines have illustrators who will enhance your article with clear, easy-to-follow illustrations.

Organization

The subject of a how-to usually dictates whether to organize the steps chronologically or to start with simple procedures and work toward difficult ones. If two steps are to be taken at the same time, it is important to make that clear. In bread baking, for instance, point out that yeast should be softening in warm water while the other ingredients are being measured.

Repetition can help or hinder reader understanding. Too much repetition causes readers to lose interest. In a short article, a brief reference to the original explanation is usually all that's needed. But if the article is very long or complex and the explanation is relatively short, repetition is better than asking readers to flip pages back to find the required information.

Include a timetable for each step to help readers gauge their progress. How long does concrete take to set? Eggs to hatch? Wine to ferment? Do varying conditions influence timing? Can or should any deliberate measures be taken to speed things up or slow them down? What specific signs might the reader watch for as the project nears completion?

Finally, what can go wrong? Think twice before including a separate how-not-to section or a trouble-shooting sidebar. Faced with a long list of things that can go wrong, a reader might understandably wonder whether the whole thing is worth the bother. But, in general, as long as a how-to is clearly written and well organized, it doesn't hurt to point out danger spots along the way.

Research, including interviews with appropriate experts, supplies background that adds depth and authority to how-tos, thereby increasing reader interest and credibility. It also helps a writer discover whether his experiences are typical or not. If not, avoid making sweeping or questionable generalizations.

When consulting authoritative sources, watch out for regional variations in the terms and methods you plan to describe, especially when you're writing for a national magazine. Mention chicken wire and a southerner is likely to picture what the westerner calls livestock fencing. Talk about reupholstering a divan or davenport, and there are readers who won't realize you are discussing a couch or a sofa. Before you write your article, look up alternative terminology from other areas.

Voice

Of course, the target audience determines how to approach your subject. If you are describing a new weaving technique to experienced weavers, you may use standard terms freely without defining them. But you should define any words that are specific to the new technique and you should definitely explain why the new technique is worth learning.

It is your job as a how-to writer to make certain that all readers achieve the same level of information by the time they reach the heart of your piece, and to do it without talking down. You can manage this by pretending you are writing a detailed letter to an interested friend.

You will find your most effective how-to voice by writing your article as if you were addressing a particular person who engages you in especially lively conversation. If you can't think of anyone suitable, invent someone. By writing expressly for that single reader, real or fictitious, you will delight all your readers with the personal tone of your how-to.

Playwriting

༄ 80

ADVICE TO PLAYWRIGHTS

BY JANET NEIPRIS

WHEN I BEGIN A PLAYWRITING CLASS, the first lecture is FIFTY RULES TO FOLLOW WHEN WRITING A PLAY. Of the fifty rules, forty-nine are structural; only the fiftieth is practical. That rule is, "Make certain you love this project, that you have passion for this play, because you will be working on it for five to ten years, and it is passion that will sustain you." Talent is only one part of playwriting, craft is another, and the third, and perhaps most important, is perseverance.

Recently, I began to write a play at the suggestion of an artistic director of a theatre. The subject—the life and loves of an eminent American playwright—was fascinating, filled with opportunities for research, and eminently commercial. It would be hard to believe this project would not excite any living playwright.

So, I began. But, the more research I did, and the more I learned, the less I was in love with the subject. It remained a good idea, but not for me. The director, who had suggested the play and had promised a staged reading of it, called to ask, "Do you hear the play singing yet?" "No," I replied, "but that will come."

Well, it never did. So, after six months of work, many scenes outlined and written, but no fire from inside, I abandoned the project. It was the most courageous thing I've ever done as a playwright, and with it came the conviction that I was never going to write about something I didn't love. From that moment on, I was certain my actions matched the practical advice I always give young playwrights: WRITE FROM THE HEART.

WRITING YOUR PLAY

1. First, always write out of *passion*. Passion is what sustains perseverance. You have to believe that the play you are writing *must* be written, and that you are the only one who could tell the story you want to tell in exactly this way.

2. Second, you should be convinced your play is worth developing *artistically,* that its subject matter is of significance and is identifiable to an audience. Always remember you are crafting a piece of dramatic literature. Significant doesn't necessarily mean recreating the Civil War on stage, but rather, that you are writing about a subject that is common to the human heart.

3. Then, you must be convinced your play is worth developing *commercially,* and that an audience will want to pay to come to see it. Your play should either entertain, question, or challenge, and at best, do all three.

4. Always write with the *practical* elements in mind—the set design, costumes, and props. For example, an action that involves fifty elephants or twenty minor characters or a waterfall is certainly impractical, both technically and financially. The writer can, however, be practical without compromising his or her art. For example, if a waterfall is integral to the plot, maybe slides could be suggested, or a backdrop, or sound.

5. Make sure your play is not exactly like this season's hit. The theatre traditionally honors quality, craft, and originality. To create, after all, means to make something where there once was nothing. To create suggests imagining.

6. Write a play that does more than simply mirror reality. Reality is never enough for a complete artistic piece. It is only a beginning. If the audience wanted simple reality, they could just open their windows and look out. Also, be certain never to use a real name for any of your characters. It is the playwright's job to *start* with reality, then *transform* it into a dramatic story.

7. Don't expect to get your script right the first time. You are trying to portray *unique* characters in *conflict,* which leads to *confrontation, resolution,* and *change.* The first draft serves to help you find out what you are writing about. The subsequent drafts, the *rewrites,* are about craft.

8. Before you send the manuscript out, make certain it is the best you can make it. Competition is high, but so is expectation when any publisher or theatre receives a new play. The first chance is the best chance, so you want to give editors, artistic directors, literary managers, possible producers, and readers the best script possible.

How to Break In
Getting an agent

Do you need an agent in order to get a play produced? Not necessarily, as many theatres and contests do accept scripts that are not represented by an agent. However, having an agent will make it easier to ensure that your script gets a reading. In cases where a regional theatre does require representation, an agent is a necessity. In addition, an agent can be helpful in negotiating a contract with a theatre, a contract that represents you, the playwright, professionally and financially.

1. Get a list of drama agents from one of the following sources:

a. *Dramatists Sourcebook,* published by Theatre Communications Group (TCG), 355 Lexington Ave., New York, NY 10017.
b. *The Dramatists Guild Quarterly,* Summer Directory, published annually by the Dramatists Guild, 234 W. 44th St., Sardi Building, New York, NY 10036.

2. Research *which* agents represent *the kind of plays you write* by reading volumes of *The Best Plays* and *Short Plays* published annually and available in most public libraries. Additional sources include the general drama sections of large bookstores and libraries.

3. Write query letters to agents of interest to you, describing your play briefly and any possible readings or productions of the play. Also, if you have a recommendation from another writer, you can mention the name, but get permission from the writer first.

Then, ask the agent if you may send a script. If you've had no answer a month after sending your script, send a short polite letter asking about its status.

Getting a reading or production

1. Go to local productions in order to familiarize yourself with local directors and actors. Start a notebook listing actors and directors you are interested in working with in the future.

2. Subscribe to *The Dramatists Guild Quarterly,* which lists production possibilities and contests, many of which include production opportunities.

389

3. Purchase a copy of the *Theatre Directory* from Theatre Communications Group, 355 Lexington Ave., New York, NY 10017. This lists regional theatres and rules for submission of scripts.

4. Join a local theatre group that does play readings and productions. There are such groups in many communities, either attached to a regional theatre or working independently.

5. Try to set up a reading locally or even in your own home. First, discuss your script with a local professional director. Make a list of questions you want to ask about themes, tone, focus, possible cuts, and casting. If you can't make a connection with a local director, you might try to direct this first read-through yourself.

Then, cast the play with local actors or friends. The main purpose of this first reading is for the playwright to "hear" the play. This reading will serve both as an opportunity to plan your second draft of the play, and also for you to align yourself, if possible, with actors and directors in your community. It never hurts to have an actor or director interested in your script. A passionate actor or director who has a script he or she wants to perform or direct is a gift to any playwright.

Getting the play up and alive in any way you can means the project is *in process,* and the *process* of readings and workshop productions (limited rehearsal, staging, and performances) is what ultimately leads to productions.

Don't expect perfection from a reading or production. You are trying to master your craft and improve your playwriting skills. The purpose of early readings or productions is to do your best work, take notes, then rewrite.

Be patient. Playwriting is about talent, craft, and most of all, perseverance and patience. Remember that Beckett sent out the completed draft of *Waiting For Godot* thirty-two times before it was accepted for production.

Getting published

Publishers of plays are listed in the *Dramatists Sourcebook*. A play can only be published if it has been produced, has received good notices, and is deemed commercial, meaning that it will have a future life in regional, community, high school and college theatres. Plays also get published as part of contests.

390

So, in order to be published, you need either to have a production or win a contest. There are exceptions to these rules, but they are rare. The major publishers of plays are the Dramatists Play Service and the Samuel French Company, as well as Baker's Plays, which publishes children's plays. There are, however, a growing number of smaller and reputable dramatic publishing companies.

Also, there are many young playwrights' competitions throughout the country. If you are a student, consult your English or drama teacher for details. Many of these contests include publication.

Remember, the play belongs to you. Ultimately, if the work is good and you have the endurance of the long distance runner, you will write the play, rewrite, be produced and be published.

81

Before You Try Broadway . . .

By Anna Coates

As a Los Angeles-based writer, script analyst, and devotee of community theater, I see a lot of plays that could have been a lot better, and I read a lot of scripts that probably should have been shredded at birth.

Which is not necessarily a bad thing.

One of the functions of little theater is to give the playwright a chance to see what works and what doesn't—not on the page, but on the stage, with living, fumbling, stumbling actors. The playwright's duty—alas, oft-neglected—is to figure out what doesn't work, and why, and if necessary to cut and chop or even to begin again.

And in a world that seems unjustly biased toward screenwriters—from Joe Eszterhas and his three-million-dollar *Basic Instinct* to Joe Schmoe and his twenty-thousand-dollar B-flick advance—the playwright has one wonderful advantage over the screenwriter. In addition to basic moral superiority, of course.

The playwright can learn as he goes.

The playwright may aspire to Broadway, but he has a crack at many lesser triumphs along the way. He can tinker with his work, tightening here and lengthening there. Even after he surrenders a script to a director's interpretation, he may continue to edit and rewrite, with or without the director's blessing.

Markets for a stage script can be divided into four categories: *community theater, experimental theater, "legitimate theater"* (aka, the Big Time), and *publication/TV.*

Of course, the categories aren't mutually exclusive. Community theater can mean a show performed on a makeshift stage in a church basement, or an elaborate and well-funded production staged as part of the regular "season" of a repertory house. (You understand, of course, that the term "well-funded" is relative!) Student productions are another type of community theater, and in some college towns they are eagerly awaited as the only theater available.

Community theaters like to produce well-known plays by established playwrights. That gets a little tired when you're seeing *Our Town* or *Streetcar* for the fifth time in six years, but if you think about it, it makes sense. Working with tiny budgets, directors tend to pick shows that are proven winners with broad appeal. They keep in mind that audiences—not to mention casts—may be unseasoned, and will react most favorably to mainstream fare.

This doesn't mean your original light comedy or social drama can't find a home with a little theater—of course it can. But you may need extra patience to find the right house to handle its premiere.

And yes, local companies will occasionally get crazy and go for *experimental theater.* But you're more likely to come across it in a city like Los Angeles or New York with a heavy concentration of actors and writers, an abundance of venues, and a weird (whoops, I mean *varied*) range of tastes.

If you're slathering to do your play on the Great White Way, or at least on cable TV, back up and slow down.

The road to Broadway (and Off-, and off-Off) wends its way through many a community theater and college campus. Sure, your play might be one of the fifteen selected by the O'Neill Theatre Center's National Playwrights Conference. On the other hand, it might be one of the fifteen hundred they reject. And it's within the realm of possibility—just faintly, there at the border—that you'll zap out your first rough script to a cable television company and get a fat check and a contract by FedEx a week later. Certainly, if you're confident about the quality of your work you should try.

But for most mere mortals the way to earn a few credits and learn the ropes is to have their work produced by a small local theater or an undergraduate director.

And that should be pretty easy. After all, an undergraduate director is really just a college kid. And local theaters pay nothing—or maybe carfare—and ought to be happy to get what they can get. Right?

Well, no.

The great majority of scripts submitted to student directors, to little theaters, and to contests will never be produced or optioned because they are badly written.

It's not because the writers are without talent. There is almost always—no, *always*—something positive I can say about a piece of writing, and I'll go out of my way to figure out what it is. Still, it's frustrating and annoying to read script after script in which plots are direct rip-offs from current movies or standard stage productions, down to characters' names and dialogue. Sure, we all know there are only three basic storylines. The trick is to make yours seem fresh.

What directors and readers and editors look for in a script is a storyline that flows and that is logical *within context*. Think about the eternal *Ten Little Indians*. Now, the idea of a disgruntled murderer gathering nine victims and bumping them off slowly and cleverly, one by one, is a bit preposterous, especially in this day of Uzi machine guns and other high tech timesavers. But so cleverly is this story crafted that contemporary audiences are able to lose themselves in the drama and the terror, and suspend disbelief—for ninety minutes, at least.

Realistic dialogue

Beyond plot, what you should be most concerned with is that your script be peopled by believable characters who use realistic, interesting dialogue. Trust me, if you write a terrific story and a potential producer thinks it needs a modified end, or an older main character, or a different setting, she will let you know. Those are very fixable flaws and an excellent piece of work won't remain homeless because of them.

What will get "no thanks" is a hackneyed plot, flat, stereotyped characters, and trite, wooden dialogue.

Stilted dialogue is a common problem. If you want to know how real people speak, listen to them.

Don't be afraid of contractions! You'll seldom hear a person say, "I do not know what I am going to do about it." Most people will say "I don't know what I'm going to do about it." (The exceptions might be a person speaking stiffly, for emphasis, or a non-native speaker. For instance, on the television series *Star Trek: the Next Generation*, Mr. Data's "un-contracted" speech helps define his android character. This device is effective because the other cast members speak naturally.)

When in doubt, read your dialogue aloud.

People sometimes—uh, pause, when they speak. And sometimes

they begin sentences with *and* or *but*. But I find writers, are, well . . . reluctant to use hesitation in dialogue.

If you want your hero to say, "Gloria, I—I'm confused. This feeling is so strong. And I don't know what's happening between us," then don't write "Gloria, I am confused. This feeling is so strong. I do not know what is happening between us."

Remember that theoretically the actor should utter only the lines you write. Yes, he may get fed up and throw in an ad-lib and the director may decide to use it. In that case you, the playwright, have not done your job. Dialogue that *works* doesn't tempt actors to rewrite.

(As I'm chasing you with the hickory switch, remember that an early production of your play is your chance to cut and polish for later audiences. Maybe the church-basement director won't allow you to rewrite dialogue mid-production, but you certainly may do so before you resubmit your play to larger regional companies.)

The professional look

Budding playwrights I have found avoid commas although I'm not sure why. Without commas the actors may forget to breathe if you follow me or at least they'll be confused.

An occasional *tpyo* is no big deal, but when every other line of a script contains misspellings like "ocaissional," "privledge," "thier," and "perference," can you blame me for concluding that the writer was just too lazy to consult his dictionary?

Grammar mistakes are irksome, too. No, you don't need perfect diction to write a good script. On the other hand, a writer who aspires to be a professional should certainly know the difference between "lie" and "lay." Your heroine may choose to lay on the bed, but that's a pretty good trick if she's alone in the room. And anyway, isn't this a G-rated production?

The writer should know whether his characters are doing well or doing good (or both). He should know whether that cool rebel flaunts rules or flouts them, and why that kid's new puppy can't be a gift from Daddy and I.

He should know if it's proper to contract *it is* as *its* or if it's not.

Of course, people don't speak perfectly, and judiciously placed solecisms make dialogue ring true. But when *every* character confuses literal and figurative, and says fortuitous when he means fortunate, or infer when he means imply, I begin to suspect the blunders aren't the characters' but the writer's own.

Get the simple stuff straight: Split infinitives will continue to easily slip by me. Likewise sentence fragments.

Dialect trips up a lot of playwrights. No, you don't have to be African-American to create a character who speaks "Black English," and you don't have to be Chinese to write about a fellow from Beijing. But spare me your "G'wan, man, I be jivin' yo' funky sef'" and your "Solly, no speaky Engrish" and most of all, your Southern Belles who say "y'all" when they're speaking to only one person.

If you must indicate a dialect, do it like this:

BELLE

Why, I declare!
(Belle's thick Southern accent makes this sound like, "wha, ah declayuh.")

You need indicate this only once. The director will get the idea, and so will the actress. And both of them will thank you.

Try to keep your set directions to a minimum. Just tell us we're on a pretty beach at sunset, and let the set designer worry about the golden sun and the cry of the gulls and the sails like white wings against the horizon. And keep in mind that the more sets and props your play calls for, the more it will cost to produce.

Keep blocking—the stage directions that show the actors when and how to move—to a minimum. Entrances and exits must be indicated, of course, and long slow clinches are fun to write. But if Tom enters angry, the director will guess that he might slam the door. If Suzy is doing an audience aside, the director will definitely place her downstage. If the phone rings, he can figure out that Jan will need to cross to answer it. O.K.? So indicate movement when necessary to advance the story, and don't leave your actors rooted in place like young saplings. But do have mercy and let the poor director have something to do.

It's scary for a writer to pack up her work and send it out for strangers to peruse. Presumably the fledgling playwright reminds herself that stage companies—local to pro—*want* to like her work. They, like you, are in this biz for the love of the written and spoken word. And besides, who wouldn't like to discover the next Sam Shepard?

What amazes me is that with this in mind, so many scripts are sent out flawed not only in the ways we've discussed above, but badly typed and poorly photocopied.

Neatness counts. Your third-grade teacher told you that and you probably relearned it in college when your psych professor showed you a study indicating that of two term papers *identical* in content the one typed neatly earned higher grades than one full of typos and cross-outs.

So what's the trouble?

I know. It takes a long time to type a hundred pages, doesn't it? It hardly seems worthwhile to retype the whole thing every time you add a couple of paragraphs or take one away.

Stop! You're breaking my heart!

The fact is, if you want to be taken seriously, your script must look professional. That means 8½″ × 11″ white paper, black ink, margins at the top, bottom, and sides, numbered pages, and invisible corrections or none at all. Absolutely no strike-outs.

Submit a photocopy, never the original. If your script is returned to you clean, there's no reason not to send it out again, but spare us the dog-eared, coffee-ringed, penciled fourth-timers! No one likes to feel like last choice.

The standard format for a play script, adjusted according to number of acts and intended medium and audience, is available from many sources, including books from your local library. But you won't be penalized for indenting dialogue seventeen spaces instead of fifteen, or for numbering your pages at the top center instead of at the top right.

Cover letters

Whether you are submitting your work to a little theater, a contest committee, a cable television director, or a magazine editor, address your cover letter to a specific person *with whom you have spoken,* and who has agreed to look at your work. And I don't want to hear any whining about the cost of toll calls. First of all, most of these people aren't going to want to sit and chat (until they've read your script and realize you're brilliant and incredibly talented). And secondly, are you interested in getting produced or in sitting around complaining about an unavoidable business expense?

If you're submitting your script to a contest or television company, write ahead to request specific instructions about format, formal copyright registration, and whether a signed release is required. But when you want a local theater director to look at your work, it's still necessary to call ahead. By calling in advance, you can make sure that you have the correct contact name and address and that the director is willing to consider your work. Why waste time if she's not? Many directors will look at new plays only between seasons, and if you mail your script to a college theater department in June, it's likely to gather dust at least until September. And remember that your work should *always* go out with the copyright symbol (©) that indicates "copyright protected" at the right-hand top of the cover page.

Like your call, your cover letter should be brief. "Here's the script we talked about, and thanks for your time" will do. If you want to, add a few lines to mention your credits, if you have any, or your credentials, if they're germane. If your script is a comedy about a dairy farmer, and you happen to live on a dairy farm, say so.

Don't send a script replete with four-letter words to a children's playhouse, no matter how the kids in your neighborhood talk. And keep in mind that an all-nude sex comedy isn't likely to play in Peoria.

If you've done your homework and kept set and prop requirements to a minimum, you can say so in your cover letter. But don't use your cover letter to sell the script; it must sell itself. Don't write, "This is a wonderful, rip-roaring comedy full of hilarious moments in the wacky life of a dairy farmer."

With all the pitfalls I've described, what's the worst mistake aspiring playwrights make?

It's not confused plotting or flat characterization or trite dialogue. It's not sloppy typing or garbled cover letters. It's not even forgetting to put your name and phone number somewhere it can be found.

The worst mistake budding playwrights make is *not trying*. Not writing that script, or not polishing it, or not sending it out. Or sending it out only once, then giving up.

You may place your first script its first time out. Or you may place your tenth, its tenth time out, then watch it move along through little theaters and repertory ensembles. And as you look back on all the rejections, you'll realize that you learned something from every one.

I'm rooting for you, so get busy. And, hey—see you on Broadway!

82

CONFLICT: THE HEARTBEAT OF A PLAY

BY D. R. ANDERSEN

EVERY PLAYWRIGHT IS A DR. FRANKENSTEIN trying to breathe life into a page for the stage. In a good play, the heartbeat must be thundering. And the heartbeat of a play is conflict.

Simply put, conflict exists when a character wants something and can't get it. Conflict may sometimes be internal—as when a character struggles to choose between or among opposing desires. For example, Alma in Tennessee Williams's *Summer and Smoke* longs to yield to her sexual yearnings but is prevented by the repressed and conventional side of her nature.

Conflict in drama may also be external—as when a character struggles against another *character* (Oscar and Felix in Neil Simon's *The Odd Couple*); against *society* (Nora in Ibsen's *A Doll's House*); against *nature* (the mountain climbers in Patrick Meyers' *K2*); or against *fate* (Sophocles' *Oedipus*).

In most plays, the conflict is a combination of internal and external struggles. In fact, internal conflict is often externalized for dramatic impact. In Philip Barry's *Holiday,* for instance, the hero's inner dilemma is outwardly expressed in his attraction to two sisters—one who represents the safe but boring world of convention, and the other who is a symbol of the uncertain but exciting life of adventure.

Granted that a conflict may be internal or external; that a character may be in conflict with another character, society, nature or fate; and that most plays are a combination of internal and external conflict, many plays that have these basic elements of conflict do not have a thundering heartbeat. Why? These plays lack one, some, or all of the five magic ingredients of rousing, attention-grabbing-and-holding conflict.

The five magic ingredients

I. *Never let your audience forget what your protagonist wants.*

You can achieve this in a number of ways. Often the protagonist or another character states and periodically restates in dialogue what is at stake. Or in some plays, he explains what he wants directly to the audience in the form of a monologue. As you read or watch plays you admire, take note of the obvious and ingenious techniques playwrights use to tell the reader or audience what the characters' goals are.

Sometimes the method used to keep your audience alerted to your protagonist's goal/concern/need is a direct reflection of the protagonist's personality. In the following three short passages from my play *Graduation Day,*[1] a mother and father with very traditional values have a conversation while waiting to meet their rebellious daughter, who has told them she has a big surprise. Notice how the protagonist— Mrs. Whittaker—nervously and comically manipulates the conversation, reminding her husband and the audience of her concern for her daughter Jane:

MRS. WHITTAKER
(Knocking on the door)
Jane. Jane. It's Mom and Dad.
(Pause)
No answer. What should we do, Tom?
MR. WHITTAKER
Let's go in.
MRS. WHITTAKER
Suppose we find Jane in a compromising situation?
MR. WHITTAKER
Nobody at Smith College has ever been found in a compromising situation.

* * *

MRS. WHITTAKER
Tom, you know, this was my freshman room.
MR. WHITTAKER
Of course, I know.
MRS. WHITTAKER
And Jane's. It was Jane's freshman room too, Tom. Remember?

* * *

MR. WHITTAKER
Mary, you get in the craziest moods at these reunions. I may never bring you back again.

---

1. First produced by Playwrights Horizons in New York, starring Polly Holliday.

MRS. WHITTAKER
Do you know why you fell in love with me, Tom?
MR. WHITTAKER
I fell in love with you the minute I saw you eat pancakes.
MRS. WHITTAKER
That's a sound basis for a relationship. Tom, where do you suppose Jane is? And more frightening, what do you suppose she wants to tell us? She said just enough on the phone to suggest that she's going to be bringing a boy here for us to meet.
MR. WHITTAKER
A man, Mary, a man.
MRS. WHITTAKER
Oh, God. I never even considered that possibility. Suppose Jane brings a fiancé—our age—like Pia Zadora did.
MR. WHITTAKER
Don't you want Jane to live her own life?
MRS. WHITTAKER
No. Especially not her own life. Practically anyone else's. But not her own.
MR. WHITTAKER
What *do* you want for Jane?
MRS. WHITTAKER
I don't see why Jane can't fall in love with a plain Harvard Business School student, let's say. Someone who'll be steady and dependable.

And so it goes. The protagonist discusses a number of topics, but she inevitably leads the conversation back to her overriding concern. Mrs. Whittaker's desire to see her daughter do the right thing and marry wisely is always uppermost in the mind and conversation of the character.

In this one act, a comic effect is achieved by having Mrs. Whittaker insistently remind the audience what she wants. Once you have clearly established what a character wants, you can then write powerful and often hilarious scenes in which the audience, already knowing the character's point of view, is able to anticipate his reaction.

II. *Show your protagonist struggling to achieve what he wants.*
This principle is, of course, the basic writing advice to *show,* not tell, and it was a major concern for me when I was writing *The House Where I Was Born.*[2]
The plot: A young man, Leo, has returned from the Vietnam War, a

2. First produced by Playwrights Horizons in New York.

psychosomatic mute because of the atrocities he witnessed. He comes back to a crumbling old house in a decaying suburb, a home populated by a callous stepfather; a mother who survives on aphorisms and by bending reality to diminish her despair; a half-crazy aunt; and a grandfather who refuses to buckle under to the pressures from his family to sell the home.

I set out to dramatize Leo's painful battle to free himself of memories of the war and to begin a new life. However, each time I worked on the scene in the play when Leo first comes home, his dialogue seemed to trivialize his emotions.

Then it occurred to me that Leo should not speak at all during the first act; that his inability to speak would *show* an audience his suffering and pain far better than his words could.

At the end of the third act, when Leo regains some hope, some strength to go on, every speech I wrote for him also rang false. The problem, I eventually realized, was that as playwright, I was *telling* the audience that a change had taken place, instead of *showing* the change as it took place.

In the final draft, I solved this dramatic problem by having Leo, who had loved music all his life, sit down at the piano and begin playing and singing Christmas carols while his surprised and relieved family joined in.

First silence, then singing, served my play better than mere telling.

III. *Create honest, understandable, and striking obstacles against which your protagonist must struggle.*

Many plays fail because their characters' problems seem too easily solved. I wrestled with this issue when I was writing *Oh Promise Me*,[3] a play that takes place in a private boarding house for the elderly. The play's original title was *Mr. Farner Wants a Double Bed*. The plot involved the attempt of an elderly man and woman—an unmarried couple—to share a double bed in a rooming house run by a repressed and oppressive owner. I wanted to explore contemporary attitudes toward the elderly, particularly as they concerned sexuality.

The more I played with the idea, the more I repeatedly heard an inner voice saying, "Chances are the couple could find some place to

3. Winner of the Jane Chambers Memorial Playwriting Award.

live where nobody cared if they were married or not." This voice—
like the audience watching a play without an honest, understandable,
convincing obstacle for the protagonist—kept saying, "So what?"

The writer's response: "Suppose, instead of a man and a woman,
the couple is two men." Here was a real obstacle: Two elderly, gay
men, growing feeble, want to sleep together in a double bed under the
roof of an unsympathetic and unyielding landlord.

Suddenly, the play was off and running.

IV. *In the final scene or scenes, make sure your protagonist achieves
what he wants; comes to understand that there is something else he
wants; or accepts (defiantly, humbly, etc.) that he cannot have what
he wants.*

If we spend time in the theater watching a character battle for something, we want to know the outcome—whatever it may be.

In my psychological thriller *Trick or Treat*,[4] Kate, a writer in her
forties, has been badly burned in a love affair and is unable to decide
whether to accept or reject a new relationship. She is involved at present with Toby, a younger man, but—as the following dialogue reveals—
she insists on keeping him at a cool distance.

KATE
That does it, Toby. We're getting out of this place.
TOBY
Okay. Tomorrow we'll check into the local Howard Johnson's.
KATE
I want to go home—to New York—to my own apartment.
TOBY
Okay. Okay. If you insist. Besides, Howard Johnson's is not to be entered
into lightly.
KATE
Huh?
TOBY
It's an old college rule. You'd never shell out for a room at Howard Johnson's—
unless you were *very* serious about the girl.
KATE
I'll remember that. The day I agree to check into a Howard Johnson's—you'll
know I've made a serious commitment to our relationship.

In the course of the play, Kate faces a number of trials—including
a threat to her life—as she tries to expose the fraudulent leader of a

---

4. First produced by the Main Street Theater, New York.

religious cult. Through these trials—with Toby by her side—Kate comes to realize that she's ready to forget the past and give herself over to a new relationship. This critical decision is humorously expressed in the last seconds of the play:

KATE

Do you love me, Toby?

TOBY

Yes, I do. I found that out tonight . . . when I thought I might be losing you forever. Do you love me?

KATE

Yes. And I can prove it.

TOBY

How?

KATE

Take me to Howard Johnson's—please! Take me to Howard Johnson's!

The curtain falls and the audience knows that the heroine has made an unequivocal decision.

V. *Make sure that the audience ultimately sympathizes with the protagonist's yearning to achieve his goal, however outlandish his behavior.*

This may be the most important of the five magic ingredients of conflict. It may also be the most elusive. To oversimplify, in a good play, the protagonist must be very likable and/or have a goal that is universal.

In the plays I've had produced, one character seems to win the sympathy of the audience hands down. In my romantic comedy *Funny Valentines,*[5] Andy Robbins, a writer of children's books, is that character. Andy is sloppy, disorganized, and easily distracted, and—this is his likable trait—he's painfully aware of his shortcomings and admits them openly. Here's Andy speaking for himself:

ANDY

Judging by my appearance, you might take me to be a complete physical and emotional wreck. Well, I can't deny it. And it's gotten worse—much worse—since Ellen left. You know that's true.

---

5. Published by Samuel French; winner of the Cummings/Taylor Playwriting Award; produced in Canada under the title *Drôles de Valentins.*

Andy is willing to admit his failings to old friends and strangers alike. Here he's talking to an attractive young woman he's just met.

ANDY
You don't have to be consoling just because I haven't finished a book lately. I won't burst into tears or create a scene. No. I lied. I might burst into tears—I'm warning you.
ZAN
I didn't mean to imply . . . *(She laughs.)*
ANDY
Why are you laughing?
ZAN
You stapled your shirt.
ANDY
What's so odd about that? Millions of derelicts do it every day.
ZAN
And your glasses are wired together with a pipe cleaner.
ANDY
I didn't think twine would be as attractive.

In addition to liking Andy, audiences seem to sympathize with his goal of wanting to grow up and get back together with his collaborator and ex-wife, Ellen.

Whether you're wondering where to find an idea for a one-act play or beginning to refine the rough draft of a new full-length work or starting rehearsals of one of your plays, take your cue from the five magic ingredients of conflict. Whatever your experience as a playwright and whatever your current project, understanding the nature of dramatic conflict and how to achieve it will prove invaluable at every point in the writing and staging process.

* * *

Five exercises for creating dramatic conflict
Try these exercises to develop your skill in handling conflict.

1. Choose five plays you like. Summarize each in one sentence, stating what the protagonist wants. For example, Hamlet wants to avenge his father's murder.
2. Write one page of dialogue in which character A asks character B to do something that character B doesn't want to do. Have character A make a request in three different ways, each showing a different emotion—guilt, enthusiasm, humility, anger.

3. Write a speech in which a character talks to another character and conveys what he wants without explicitly stating his goal.

4. Choose a famous play you enjoy. Rewrite the last page or two so that the outcome of the conflict for the protagonist is entirely different from the original.

5. Flip through today's newspaper until you find a story about a person—famous or unknown—who interests you. Then summarize the story in one sentence, stating what the person wants. For example: X wants to save an endangered species of bird. Next list the obstacles the person is facing in trying to get what he wants:

   • A developer wants to build a shopping mall where the remaining members of the endangered species live.

   • Pollution from a nearby factory is threatening the birds' food supply.

Finally, write several short scenes in which X (the protagonist) confronts the people (the antagonists) who represent the cause of each obstacle. (In this example, the antagonist would be the developer or the owner of the factory.) Decide which of the scenes you've written is the most dramatically satisfying. Identify the reasons you think it is the best scene.

83

ACT ONE, SCENE ONE: BEGINNING A PLAY

By JEFFREY SWEET

NOT SO VERY LONG AGO, IT WAS COMMON PRACTICE to start a play with a pair of secondary characters in a scene that ran along these lines:

MARY: Young Gregory was out late last night. He finally came back at three in the morning.
JOHN: Did he say anything about where he was or why there's such a big dent in his car?
MARY: No, but he'd had too much to drink, I can tell you that.
JOHN: I wonder if this has anything to do with the letter he received yesterday. The one that made him turn so pale.
MARY: I couldn't say. But this morning at breakfast you could have cut the tension between him and his parents with a knife.

All right, I'm exaggerating, but not by very much. The introductory conversation between two servants, or two gossips in the neighborhood, or a character newly returned from travels asking about events during his absence often kicked off the action. If you can call this action.

The idea behind such scenes was to pump the audience full of the information necessary to understand the subsequent events. Playgoers used to sit patiently for the first ten minutes or so knowing that enduring this sort of exposition was the price they had to pay in order to get to the good stuff. And I'm not talking only about plays by forgotten hacks. The only reason for the lame passage between Camillo and Archidamus in Act One, Scene One of Shakespeare's *The Winter's Tale* is to help the audience get its bearings. (Just because Shakespeare is the best doesn't mean he didn't make his share of mistakes.)

Generally speaking, plays start faster than they used to.

I think this is partially the result of television. Tune into a prime-time drama series, and you'll see something like this in the pre-credits action:

Stand-up comic onstage, telling jokes. Audience laughing. A woman in black carrying a purse slips in through the stage entrance. She moves to a door marked "Dressing Room," enters the room and closes the door behind her. Inside, she switches on the light, looks around, sees a framed photo of an attractive lady sitting on the make-up table. Suddenly, she smashes the photo onto the floor so that the glass from the frame breaks. Onstage, the comic says goodnight and takes his bows. In a cheerful mood, he goes to his dressing room. He switches on the light, takes a step and hears a crunch. He looks down on the floor and sees he has stepped on the glass from the smashed frame. Then he hears a voice: "You were really cooking tonight, Charley. You were killing them." He turns and sees the woman standing behind the door, pointing a small pistol at him. Sweat builds up on his lip. "And I always thought 'die laughing' was an expression," she says. Now she smiles. The camera pulls in on her finger on the trigger. Fade out. Bouncy music kicks in and the credits begin.

Do you want to know who the woman is, why she smashed the picture and whether she's going to ventilate Charley? You've got to stay tuned past the credits and the opening batch of commercials. If you do, you'll probably be willing to sit through some less immediately compelling stuff setting up other characters till the story returns to Charley and his mysterious visitor. And then, odds are, having invested this much time, you'll stick around for the rest of the show. By beginning with a provocative but unexplained incident, the story has been launched, caught your attention and given you enough reason to take the ride to the last stop.

The craft of writing for television has necessarily been affected by the nature of the audience's relation to the medium. Aware that the audience, holding channel changers in their hands, can switch to a competing program at any time, the writers know they have to serve up immediate and pressing reasons for viewers to stick around. Obviously, few are likely to stick around if the show starts with the equivalent of two servants relating offstage events. So a TV script tends to start with a scene that builds to a pressing dramatic question.

Of course, audiences don't come to the theater with channel changers in hand. But, after years of watching the box in their living rooms and getting used to the pacing of tales told there, they come to the theater in the habit of being plunged into the heart of the story quickly. To grab the playgoer fast, many contemporary playwrights have borrowed a leaf from television's book by beginning their plays with characters in the middle of high-energy sequences equivalent to the one introducing Charley's dilemma.

John Guare's remarkable play, *Six Degrees of Separation,* starts with two of the leading characters, Ouisa and Flan Kittredge, excitedly telling the audience about their narrow escape moments before from some unnamed threat, checking to see that none of their valuables has been stolen, savoring how close they may have come to death. Having established their hysteria, Guare then has them take us back several hours to a lower-key scene anticipating the arrival of a friend who is to join them for dinner. With the benefit of hindsight, we know that they will shortly be hyperventilating, and so we watch carefully to see what part this dinner will play in the chain of events that leads to their alarums.

Guare could very well have *started* with the Kittredges discussing their dinner plans and then proceeding with the rest of the play as written. Doing this would not have meant omitting any of his story. But, by kicking the play off with the two in such an agitated state and then flashing back, Guare makes the audience sit up and take notice from the first moment. No coy wooing of the playgoer here; he snares our interest instantly. Knowing that the flashback holds the answer to the question, "What's making the Kittredges so upset?," the audience pays closer attention to the lower-key scene that follows than they would have if the play had started with that scene.

I'm not suggesting that all plays should begin in the middle of action, but quite a few would be improved if they did. I asked the members of a playwriting workshop I run to bring in scripts they were working on, and, as an experiment, we read excerpts from them, each time starting on page ten. In all but two cases, the writers decided their plays actually began better on their tenth pages than on their firsts.

What information was contained in the missing pages? My students discovered that most of it was implicit in the scenes from page 10 on. By beginning in the *middle* of dramatic action—instead of setting up the circumstances in the first ten pages—the playwrights gave the audience the fun of figuring out the circumstances for themselves. Gone were the dull stretches of characters entering the stage, pouring drinks, and slipping in nuggets of self-introduction. Gone, too, were the one-way phone calls designed to sneak in exposition. Rather than switching on and warming up the scripts' motors and then coaxing them up to speed, the plays now had a sense of urgency from the word go, and that urgency made them compelling.

The opening of a play not only gets the story started, it also makes a contract with the audience. The first few minutes virtually announce, "This is the kind of play we're doing," and the audience sets its expectations accordingly. We watch different genres with different expectations. It is very important, then, for the opening of your script to set the audience's expectations correctly. If you break a promise to a friend in real life, you're likely to lose the trust and confidence of that friend. Break a promise to the people who have paid to see your play, and they will respond with confusion and irritation. If, for instance, you begin your play with a pair of bewigged fops trading quips in blank verse, you'd better not suddenly switch in the middle of the second act to a modern psychological thriller. Raising the curtain on a solo figure in black tights on a bare stage miming the life cycle would be a misleading introduction to a Neil Simon-style domestic comedy.

This may sound like very obvious advice, but some very savvy theatrical talents nearly lost a great musical because of such a miscalculation. *A Funny Thing Happened on the Way to the Forum* was trying out in a pre-Broadway engagement in Washington in 1962. According to all accounts, the show was substantially the one we've come to know, but the audiences weren't taking to it. The laughs were few and far between, and each night a dismaying chunk of the audience disappeared at intermission. The perplexed creative team—which included such celebrated figures as George Abbott, Larry Gelbart, Bert Shevelove and Stephen Sondheim—asked director-choreographer Jerome Robbins to take a look and tell them where they were going wrong.

After the performance, Robbins informed them that the problem was with the opening number, a light-hearted little tune called "Love is in the Air," which promised a romantic frolic. What followed instead, however, was an evening of broad jokes, slapstick, and farcical intrigue. Robbins said what was needed was an opening that *promised* broad jokes, slapstick, and farcical intrigue. An opening, he insisted, should promise the audience what in fact a show is going to deliver.

Composer-lyricist Stephen Sondheim went to his piano and wrote a song entitled, "Comedy Tonight," which did just that. According to legend, as soon as it was put in, the reaction to the show turned around

411

completely. What had previously played to indifference now brought cheers. *A Funny Thing Happened* went on to New York, where it received glowing reviews and was proclaimed a hit, all because the opening was changed. It is now counted a classic musical comedy.

Not only do you establish the genre of a show in the first few minutes, you also establish stylistic rights. At the beginning of *Six Degrees of Separation,* Guare swiftly signals the audience that he reserves the right to 1) have any of his characters, at the drop of a hat and without self-consciousness, address the audience directly, and 2) with the briefest of transitions, leap to any other time or place in the story. And, indeed, throughout the script, both major and minor characters feel no compunction about making eye contact with a theater full of playgoers and speaking their minds. What's more, scenes move abruptly back and forth in time and jump, without second thought, from the Kittredges' fancy apartment to Central Park to Greenwich Village and wherever else it is necessary to go to witness the essential events of the story. And, oh yes, the number of laughs at the show's beginning clearly indicates the audience is in for a comedy.

It is a truism among musical theater writers that the opening number is usually the one you write last, because it is only after you've finished the rest of the show that you know what the opening should prepare the audience for. Straight plays are structurally less complicated than musicals, but upon completing a draft, a smart dramatist looks closely at the opening few pages to see if they correctly establish the world and style of the two hours to follow. The audience isn't likely to go through your door if you don't offer them the key to unlock it.

84

BLUEPRINT FOR WRITING A PLAY

BY PETER SAGAL

IF I WEREN'T A PLAYWRIGHT, I'd be an architect, which on certain days I think is the finest kind of artist there is, because architects create art that is indisputably useful, necessary: Architecture is the art that stitches together the seams of the physical environment. But since I can't draw, I can't do math, and I'm too lazy to undergo all that study, I have to settle for being a playwright. I comfort myself, though, by imagining plays as architecture: art defined by its function, articulated by structure, inspired by the truths about the people who are to use it. Plays, like architecture, are, or should be, useful; they should express their beauty through purpose sheathed with ornament.

So one should go about the business of writing a play with all the dedication, discipline, knowledge, etc. that any fine art requires, but something else, too—something shared again with architecture, and that is a sense of *responsibility*. The architect knows that his or her building may or may not be admired by passers-by, but most definitely it will be used; a mistake on the drawing board may result in discomfort and displeasure for unknown thousands whom the architect failed by making a building that may have been fashionable or pretty but did not *work,* though architects ask people to live and perform their professional and personal functions within such a building. We playwrights ask less but still something substantial: We ask for time. Give us two or three hours of your life, two or three hours that can never be replaced, and we will enclose you in a soundproof room, turn off the lights so you can't read, and forbid you to talk, and we promise that it will be worthwhile.

Your first responsibility as a playwright is to waste no one's time. Consider your audience's attention as a precious gift, a gem, and if you fumble, it's lost forever. Time is a sacred thing, because everyone has only a finite supply of it.

Your job as a playwright, then, is to create a series of events, conversations, and images so important that it's worth asking the audience to give up their lives for a while and listen. I think this is the most difficult task in all writing, with the possible exception of book-length epic poetry. You do not have the expansive freedom of the novelist, or the factual safety net of the journalist. There's no tolerance for sloppiness; writing a play is done with a gun to the head. Here's how to do it:

Love your art

The theater won't pay you, won't comfort you, will provide you with little reward, and for that reward will drain your blood. In the best case your writing will be subject to the whims and caprices of actors, technicians, directors, producers; in the worst case, it will be ignored. If very, very successful, it will reach a tiny fraction of the people who watch "Married With Children" on TV, and your financial remuneration will be an even tinier fraction of the amount received by the writers who produce that work and others like it. Don't write for the theater if you want to write for television or the movies, or even for Broadway, which is a fictional place, like the Big Rock Candy Mountain. Write for yourself; write because if you don't you'll go crazy. Write because nothing else in your life compares to the power of creating your own worlds. Write plays because you believe that the experience of people gathering in a theater to see a play is nothing less than sacred. If you don't have the strength of this quasi-religious conviction, then the trials ahead could well overwhelm you.

Study your art

I am continually amazed by how many aspiring playwrights are ignorant of dramatic writing outside of a narrow canon of recognized giants: Shakespeare, Tennessee Williams, Arthur Miller, David Mamet, Sam Shepard, etc. In many cases, the writer sets out to imitate one or more of them. One problem, of course, is that these writers are geniuses, and you can't just imitate their work.

The other problem is that they *aren't* geniuses at all; they were and are working writers who slogged away for years and years, and most of them did their slogging in the theater. There isn't a single great writer for the theater who did not spend a long apprenticeship: Shake-

414

speare, for example, started with the Lord Chamberlain's Men as an actor, writing plays himself only after he had performed uncounted dozens of other, now unknown works.

Such a lengthy servitude isn't necessary, but it is foolish not to recognize such problems as how to make the stage relevant to your life and the lives around you. If you live in a city with an active theater scene, go all the time, particularly to the new plays; the failures will be as educational as the few successes. If you don't have that luxury, then read as much as you can: Read your peers in American playwriting (Tony Kushner, Marlane Meyer, Neal Bell, Jose Rivera, Migdalia Cruz, Wendy Hammond, etc., etc.) and their counterparts in Great Britain; read plays from non-English speaking and non-Western traditions. You will come across hundreds of good ideas and save yourself from making thousands of mistakes. It is idiotic to try to invent the theater from scratch every time you sit down. Depart and rebel, by all means, but know what you are rebelling against.

I am very skeptical of books and articles that offer "rules" for writing, which is why I refuse to offer any specific suggestions to aspiring playwrights, such as, "start in the middle," "make the exposition active," etc. I have arrived at my own set of principles of dramatic writing, but they describe not so much how to write a play, as the kind of play I like. For every one of those rules, there's an exception, and in many cases, the exceptions are brilliant plays. For example, I don't like to have my characters address the audience, offering information about the other characters. That means I'll never write *The Glass Menagerie* or *The Marriage of Bette and Boo,* or even *Henry V,* among the many other plays I admire. The theater, more than any other form of writing, is a living thing: It grows and changes, departing from what just happened and pointing toward what's next. Rules hinder evolution. Further, when you sit down to write, you should be writing from an interior vision of what *your* play *is,* not some acquired idea of what *a* play is *like.* Television writers follow rules, because people who watch television know what they want and watch TV, expecting to get just that. This is the opposite of theater.

Practice your art

Writers in any form have to confront and control the hunger for acclaim. In the theater, this becomes even more difficult because, first, you are collaborating with actors and other artists who are eager to make their mark, and more important, your work is read out loud to large groups of people who might very well make loud noises that indicate approval (or disapproval). It becomes very tempting to get those words out of the word processor, into the hands of actors, and up in front of the audience, and to let the magic of the moment make up for any shortcomings. However, if you remember what I said about responsibility, you will see that this is a pernicious urge to be avoided. The rules of discipline, writing, and constant revision hold as much in playwriting as in poetry—don't buy into the old adage that a playscript is a "blueprint" and can slide by on heart alone. It *is* a blueprint, and it had better be a perfect blueprint or this house won't stand.

So write, write, write; experiment with sound and language and vision and structure. Do not be indulgent. Do not be lazy. Do not put less than perfect words on a stage and hope that the audience will buy them. Don't try to dazzle. Don't coast. Whatever you put on a page, make it your own. Remember, when you sit down to write a play, you are taking the future of an ancient and fragile art form in your hands: A bad play strikes another blow at it, in these wounded and wounding times; a good play breathes new life into the theater, and sends it striding on into a few more hearts, which may, in turn, nourish it after us.

POETRY

⸙ 85

The Poetry Scene Today

By David Kirby

We all know that technology grows in leaps and bounds. Today's computers, for example, make yesterday's models look like Victorian steam engines in comparison. And poetry changes, too. A hundred years ago, formal poetry dominated the scene. Then free verse came along. And now new free-verse forms appear every day. That doesn't mean that formal poetry has disappeared; to the contrary, formal poets are inventing new poem-types of their own. Exactly what kinds of poems are being written today, and how can you write them?

As I see it, there are not just two choices, free verse and formal poetry, but actually six distinct kinds, each with its own particular characteristics.

(1) **Improvisational free verse.** There are really two very different kinds of free-verse poems being written these days, improvisational free verse and formal free verse. Improvisational free verse is like jazz; you make it up as you go. It represents the most obvious extension of what might be called the Walt Whitman tradition in poetry. A poet is most free when he or she is improvising, and thus improvisational free verse has the widest range of the six kinds we're considering here; it extends all the way from the one-stanza poem based on a single insight or observation to the poem that runs for several pages and encompasses a much wider variety of experience.

As written by writers as different as Gwendolyn Brooks, Frank O'Hara, Imamu Amiri Baraka, and William Stafford, the shorter and relatively simple kind of improvisational poem is the most common; it is the kind of poem that most poets are writing these days, and it is what comes to most readers' minds when they think of poetry.

But if you are a free-verse poet who is looking for a challenge, you might consider the long improvisational poem, which may be composed of several parts and, for variety's sake, use several contrasting styles. Allen Ginsberg's 1956 Beat masterpiece "Howl" is an excellent example of the long improvisational poem, as are the works of such poets as Norman Dubie, Laura Jensen, Caroline Knox, and Gary Snyder.

(2) **Formal free verse.** This may sound like a contradiction to you, but think of it as a kind of writing that combines the best of the formal and free-verse traditions. Formal free verse is a kind of poetry that has the elegant appearance of formal poetry yet takes advantage of the comparatively greater range of expression we associate with free verse. In its simplest terms, a poem of this kind is a free-verse poem with stanzas and lines of equal length.

Try this: Take one of your free-verse poems, count the number of lines in it, and divide them into stanzas of equal length. Say you have a thirty-line poem; you could make two fifteen-line stanzas, fifteen two-liners, five stanzas of six lines each, six stanzas of five lines, and so on. You don't want to break arbitrarily, of course, but you'll find that the different possibilities will change the way in which you read the poem. After a while, one of them will make more sense than the others. If there is a climactic development near the middle of the poem, for example, then the two fifteen-line stanzas would result in two distinct parts, and the poem as a whole would gain a certain dramatic flair.

But if your original is twenty-nine or thirty-two lines long instead of thirty, you'll have to add a line or cut two. Don't be discouraged: That extra line may just make the point you've been trying to make all along. Or the two you remove may be weak lines that you didn't recognize as such until you had to cut. It never hurts to take another look at a poem, and the formal free-verse method will have you doing just that.

Your final version will be just as expressive as your original, even if you have to add or cut a line or two, yet it will have about it the aura of dignity and composure that the great formal poems have. Every reader wants to have confidence in the poets he reads, and that formal look is an excellent way to establish the poet's authority; it says, "Behold my great shape, dear reader; you haven't read a word yet, but already you can see that a lot of work went into the making of me." Your poem looks good, yet it says what you want—what more could you ask? That's why more and more poets are writing formal free verse these days. Look at the work of Robert Bly, Robert Creeley,

James Dickey, and Adrienne Rich. My poem, "Sub Rosa," is an example:

Sub Rosa

Maps would be literal if the normal order
were other than it is: letters would appear across
the faces of cities, and roads would become red lines.
Pages would fly out of books as well and then out
  of windows
to form trees in the yards of the literary.

The trees would shrink to seedlings and then seeds,
which would disappear up the anuses of birds
who would drop them where trees have never grown.
Gasoline would run out of cars and down hoses
into the earth, where it would turn into dinosaurs

who would escape through giant rents in the crust
to lurch down streets crowded with witches,
Manicheans, Confederate soldiers, Hunkpapa Sioux.
Everywhere things would extrude, exfoliate;
poems would be replaced by their meanings.

As for us, nothing would change.
For already when we lie down together or go for
  drives
or simply sit across the table from one another,
each look, each word, each touch bears out
the secret history of the world.

(3) **The New Formalism.** In a sense, there's nothing new about the New Formalism. It's really the Old Formalism being practiced by poets today, so that makes it new. As always, formal poetry requires some very specific skills. If free verse achieves its highest level of success through the appearance of risk and daring (invariably the result of hours of detached, objective revision, of course), formal verse accomplishes what it does through skillful use of rhyme and meter. Occasionally you'll hear someone complain that "poems don't rhyme any more," but that may be because the poems rhyme so subtly that the rhyming isn't apparent. Very few poets use tick-tock AABB rhymes these days. And galloping meters have been replaced by softer rhythms.

Consider these lines that begin Marilyn Hacker's poem "Fourteen" (from her collection *Assumptions*):

421

> We shopped for dresses which were always wrong:
> sweatshop approximations of the lean-
> lined girls' wear I studied in *Seventeen*.
> The arms pinched, the belt didn't belong. . . .

Here, the poet uses a loose iambic pentameter line, but her ABBA rhyme scheme and her enjambment (or run-on lines) keep the poem from having a singsong sound. The result is a highly formal poem whose emotions are nonetheless expressed in a very natural and unaffected-sounding way. Other poets writing formal verse these days include Van K. Brock, John Hollander, X. J. Kennedy, Barbara F. Lefcowitz, Maura Stanton, and Stephen Yenser.

(4) **Prose poetry.** So far, I've discussed the three main kinds of poetry you're most likely to encounter in books and magazines these days. But another kind is often found there also, and, like free verse, it's an old form that simply gives the appearance of being new. You can find prose poems in the Bible, and they also began appearing in the West in the nineteenth and early-twentieth centuries.

A prose poem is actually a free-verse poem written in paragraphs rather than stanzas, which means that it relies on the allusive, surreal effects of poetry while it disdains the conventions of stanzas and line breaks. There's no hard and fast rule about what goes into a prose poem, but many of them tend to read like fables or dreams or fairy tales. For example, an untitled Charles Simic poem, in his book *The World Doesn't End,* begins: "I was stolen by the gypsies. My parents stole me right back. Then the gypsies stole me again. This went on for some time." A poem like this is intended to induce a dream-like state, and its prose form contributes to that effect, since the action is continuous and without break. As opposed to the impressive grandeur of the formal or the formal free-verse poem, there's a casualness to the prose poem that seduces the reader. A prose poem is like a letter that is found on the sidewalk; who can resist picking it up? William Carlos Williams, Gertrude Stein, and John Ashbery have all written very different kinds of prose poetry, and more poets seem to be trying this appealing form every day.

(5) **Language poetry.** Rather than describe language poetry, let me begin with a stanza from a poem in Michael Palmer's book *Sun:*

Ideas aren't worth anything
Today space is splendid
The mountains have come loose
Let's unmake something

If the meaning of these lines isn't terribly clear, that's the point: Language poets are trying to break free from the restrictions of conventional middle-class attitudes toward art and life. As a result, their poems often seem bizarre and disorienting. But what poet hasn't strung words together randomly just to hear how they sound? More than any other kind of poetry, language poetry probably embodies the quality that drew most poets to their craft in the first place: the sheer music of it. Consider the poems of Charles Bernstein, Lyn Hejinian, Susan Howe, David Melnick, and Ron Silliman.

(6) **Performance poetry.** If you've ever read a poem and thought, "This would really sound good read aloud," it may be because that poem was written exactly for that purpose. Poets have often sent me their books, but today more and more are sending me tapes of their work as well. When most people hear the phrase "performance artist," they think of some self-dramatizing, avant-garde type, but the oral tradition is as old as the ancient Greeks, and Caribbean and African poets still chant their poems aloud today. If you live in a big city like New York or Chicago, you may be aware already of the "Poetry Slam" contests that take place in bars and coffee houses. Otherwise, contact your local university's English department to find out whether poetry readings are held on campus, and if so, when and where they take place. Also, look for *Stand-Up Poetry,* a collection of performance pieces edited by Charles H. Webb and Suzanne Lummis.

As a poet, surely you've found in this survey a kind of poetry similar to what you are writing at present. Therefore, you might now consider writing a kind of poem you've never tried before. You could end up taking your poetry in an entirely new direction. At the very least, you'll find you've written a "starter" you can use when you go back to the kind of poem you usually write.

86

POETRY AND MEMORY

BY JAMES APPLEWHITE

MEMORY IN THE WIDEST SENSE governs all I do as a writer, since words, along with the skills acquired for relating them, are stored there. Yet, we aren't aware of the wonder of memory until it falters. Aging makes certain words, especially proper nouns, more difficult to access, in that organic computer-storage we call memory. We're surprised by any difficulty, because the vocabulary, syntax and formal skills we begin learning in childhood have always been spontaneously on hand for our use, as naturally as breathing or walking. Language with its rooting in memory, when we realize its scope and complexity, seems almost miraculous: this vast store to which we're continually adding and, if losing some, not much, in proportion to the total, which seems endlessly elastic.

The operation of memory was central to the argument of E.D. Hirsch's *Cultural Literacy*—a discussion highly relevant to the writer, who always was at first a reader. The words we're reading, apparently, remain only temporarily in a short-term memory, unless they're connected to some pre-existing network of things known. We remember by association, or linkage, and so reading with comprehension requires, in a sense, reading with recognition. We have to recognize the relatedness of what we're newly taking in, to what we already have stored, if there is to be significant understanding and retention. Hirsch argues, therefore, that the new knowledge acquired by the eyes and nerves from words must be connected into the networking of memory, things newly observed attaching themselves to things previously learned.

This means that our understanding of the present, this immediate, passing moment, is conditioned by, and contingent upon, memories from the past. Our eyes interpret not only the letters of words and sentences on the basis of previously acquired knowledge, but also the whole range of experience. We can't conceptualize things, or speak, or write, or take a walk, without using memory.

Writing a poem is therefore an act of memory. The process of arranging old and familiar words into a new order, to embody those conceptions and emotions that always seem different and individual, draws on the long-term storehouse of memory. Writing a poem dramatizes this almost imponderable relation of the present to the past: this moment of consciousness dependent on the deep reservoir of experience. This record of earlier time would lie mute and passive without the moment's articulation. And any current cognitive act would be thin and anonymous without the years' accumulated layers of memory—this basis of who we are. To see a tree as a tree is an act of pattern recognition requiring the past.

Certain poems feature memory explicitly, while all poems implicitly depend on its power. Perhaps such poems are especially moving (I had almost said *memorable*) because they remind us of the relation of the thoughts we think, this minute, to all those preceding thoughts that we cannot now particularly recall, but feel in their cumulative legacy. When the present mind feels the form and texture of a vast, earlier time-scale, one it cannot in detail recall or read, the result may be a profound aesthetic emotion. It is like looking at the ruined masonry of a Gothic abbey: You cannot know the exact history behind these walls and arches, yet you feel the resonance of the past beneath the fissured surface.

I don't think it profitable for a writer to try to *use* memory, directly. Memory is always allowing itself to be used, but won't be coerced; there are better strategies than head-on pressure. Memory has its own processes and its own selectivity. Scenes, faces, bits of story that rise up spontaneously are thus more likely to have an emotive significance than those memories we might deliberately call up.

Really to remember is often to reencounter a part of experience, perhaps distant from present life but still related to it. Profound memory can continue the assimilation of a part of our lives we'd thought we'd finished with, but hadn't. The poetic use of memory is therefore not really separate from that larger meditative attempt to make sense of our lives, of which poetry is part.

As poets, we can intensify this process by focused thinking, not so much on the past itself, as on those issues that *involve* the past: issues

425

of personal identity, confrontations with disappointment or loss, plans for the future that we see as completing long-cherished hopes and ambitions. Just as in keeping a dream-journal one learns to remember dreams better, so consistent meditation and writing can make the past and one's own buried emotions available for poetry. We don't always know how or what we really feel about certain matters—especially those areas of experience involving our childhood. My own experience has shown me that the driving force behind memory is not merely the desire to call up earlier days, but the deeply felt need to reencounter unresolved issues and emotions—the need to understand, to come to terms with, past time.

During the last several years, I've been working on an interrelated set of autobiographical and literary essays. My book of poems, *A History of the River* (Louisiana State University Press), presented a kind of cultural history of my region of the South, ranging from the curing rituals for bright leaf tobacco, through farm artifacts, such as Mason jars, sausage grinders, and mule-drawn plows, through patterns of farmhouse births and deaths and home burials. I was moved to portray the change of the world, as the time-order associated with these earlier objects and practices gave way to the more recent time, surrounding tractors, electrical appliances, mercury vapor farmyard lights, and television sets.

Last spring, I began to write a sequence of more formal poems focused directly on the experience of time. All of them seemed to involve streams, rivers, lakes or the ocean. I thought of them tentatively as *Meditations on Water*. Though my explicit subject was time and its river-like shapes as it flowed by, I was also trying to show how experiences accumulate in the mind, just as a lake holds water which is mostly out of sight. Here is a poem that began as I thought of boat rides on a lake as a child, and the home movies taken there, that extended and represented memory:

Remembering Home Movies on Water

My father cranks the outboard motor. His face
  looks tender
in the camera's fixed light. Beside me sits my
  mother
in her one-piece suit, peering ahead through time,

426

her face a sphinx-prediction of puzzlements to come:
my amazement at the world, uncertain identity,
courage against death and illness but inability
to assert my own need and course. That route
seemed plowed by the boat's expanding wake,
     the pout
of my mother's lips a judgment on his unwisdom:
this fated, accelerated design, the masculine
     momentum
she deplored and embraced. I also apparently wish
     not
to go on, though summers continued with another
     boat
and larger motor and myself at the helm, driver
so harshly one evening across the wave-cut river
that my girl in front carried bruises across her back
for a week. Her father cursed but she raised her neck
to my lips. I piled weight and muscle into this role
my mother derided, working in the concrete hole
beneath the cars, greasing as automatically as my
     parents
had inserted me into life: these disguises it permits,
these inherited expressions raised dumbly toward
     storm,
as we rush into the imitations from which we've
     come.
Now in this present so seemingly distanced, world-
     different,
I paddle across these circling mirrors to contemplate
their curious accumulation and reflection. Afternoon
sky changes blue into green. Clouds puff dryly
     in the sheen
that's liquid yet develops, a film to be viewed.
Gazing into depths I feel the years' dumb plunges
     flood
back and as Freud knew, that drowned world never
     will change.
I sit on its surface and suffer, accept, mourn,
     rearrange
myself in relation to this deadly dynamic I always
     take
to bed and don't escape: this lost ponderous hidden
     lake.

The lake's depth holds a reservoir of past time that is like the contents of the unconscious. The narrator, in sad recognition that this
underwater world "never will change," is somewhat consoled by his

sense that the present offers the possibility of new attitudes and relationships to this fixed past.

Other poems I'm working on grew out of recent experiences canoeing or sailing or running beside the Eno River near my house. It seemed that both through my writing and my involvement with water, I was trying to put the first part of my life and the second part together. In one of the poems that resulted, I used memory very centrally, though that had not been my original intention. The kind of writing and thought I'd recently been involved with apparently prepared the way for a spontaneous memory-event, which provided the narrative of the poem.

I had gotten back home almost too late for my customary run by the river, but went out anyway, along the dimming trails of the Eno State Park off Cole Mill Road. I ran deep into the forest and next to the river for a while, its slick quickness maintaining light on the surface, while the trees beside lost detail, becoming humps of shadow. On my way back to the parking area, I passed down into a vale where night had almost fallen. Lightning bugs winked, yellow-green and moving, and a sense of my childhood home came back, at first as a presence and tone without action or shape. A voice from the distant parking lot became a voice from a neighbor's porch. I felt the community gathered around me again and remembered the preacher's term, "communion of saints." When I'd made my slow way back out to the road, I had the shape of a poem in my head. I wrote it out the next day, in the slant-rhymed couplets I've been using lately for meditations. These rhymes, partial and less fully heard, let me say things more explicitly and deliberately, keeping the arguments and questions I want to voice now within the realm of the poetic. Here is the poem.

A Run with the Double River

I returned from the looping trail to Bobbitt's Hole,
finishing in darkness, walking a last half mile.
The footpath dimming among hardwoods angled
   down,
where air felt heavy as breath and a water shone.
Suddenly it was old summer, as lightning-sparks
of insects glowed near and large. A steepening
   of rocks
lay seamed with times like coal, under layers of

428

noises.
An owl called, a vole rustled, a sighing like voices
came from trees toward the road. Deeply, I
   remembered:
a time without events, the shadow over a town that
   slumbered
into twilight as the lightning bugs like momentary
   sight
rose sparkling, the scene as if seeing itself in a
   night
wherein minds added up to an awareness and were
   calm.
It felt like our Sunday congregation singing a hymn.
Nothing had gone. Faces of friends, parents, old
   men
I hardly knew looked renewed, individual yet not,
   grown
together in this hum, this single continuing
   evening tone
that collected the drone of the electric fan and dove
   alone
on telephone wires into one thing—all made simple
   again,
as when a garden's leaves rise together after a rain.
But in what medium is this cloud of presences
   stored?
My church had told me of saints gathered unto the
   Lord.
It praised occasions when our single, ephemeral
moments melt together and we feel what is like the
   eternal:
the form within the flowing, shape where past years
   are.
I had entered this under-knowledge, like the river
   aware
of itself. We'd sat as static muttered in our porch's
   radio;
the stories of voices from the chairs around sounded
   low
and ceaselessly, like cicadas crowded into a single
   tree.
The stars pierced near and real. There was no TV.
Such memories seem transmitted by genes instead
   of by wires,
though the footage catalogued in archives aspires
to be this library of the blood. Two currents run
   together,
as clouds and stars paint these streams with passing
   glitter.

429

The TV in the house with its insistent, loud alarm
distracts from profounder dreaming, yet shows the
   charm
of the race. Its goddesses arouse us to love, and
   heroes kill.
This presentness seems a surface. The river's motion
   is still
though its depth holds a pressure of all early instants,
which roil and swerve and pulse. We run as water
   glints,
as it flashes into a consciousness, that the sky
   imprints
like a source. Each red leaf splashes upon it, come
into a mighty sequence, unique, subsumed in time.

Part of my life I've felt the past as a burden upon me, even as an oppression. I am a southerner, and share in the South's problem of history: the feeling I grew up with of having been anticipated by those fathers and grandfathers and greatgrandfathers who'd bequeathed me the world in which attitude and actions seemed already determined, or overdetermined. More recently however, I've felt my separation and freedom from a regional history which, not in the national consciousness (and sometimes in my own estimation), seems only a stereotypical relic—a formulaic reiteration—of exhausted prejudice, pride, and grievances.

What felt so fresh about this descent into a small ravine in the edge of night was the immediacy of a past that had neither gone stale nor dwindled into cliché—a past as the presences that inform one's identity, without obtruding their individual outlines. I experienced past time as a reunion of one part of the self with another. My current personality felt itself for a moment within a gathering of presences who had reappeared from deep in my earlier life. They were (and are) a part of who I am, though I'm not usually aware of that fact.

So as the poet sits writing, figures and images out of the past may sometimes crowd about. My schoolteacher uncle used to tell me of Odysseus in the land of the dead, and of how the spirits of the heroes and heroines of his land collected around him. Since he was still alive, they wanted him to hear their story, and perhaps to tell it again among the living. The prophet Tiresias also came forward, and told Odysseus how he was to get home again successfully. Odysseus may stand for the poet in relation to deep memory. He or she gathers stories out of cultural and personal history: old stories that will be seen in the new form of their retelling. Like Odysseus, the poet learns from the past how to get back home to the present, how to live in it more vitally, how to proceed into the future. When we've come to the past as free persons, able to accept and internalize its mighty echo, it can send us along our way, abler and more confident, surer of our mission, and of who we are.

A poem is given shape by the poems remembered, collectively, from all the poet's earlier reading: sonnets, blank verse meditations, various kinds of free verse—by the sounds of emphasis and closure, the chiming of stanzas and of rhyme. Poetry is an old story that comes alive again with the new idea. The names and the events and the rhymes are similar but never quite the same. So I say again, the way to use time and memory as a writer is to let it use you. This involves respect toward the past, but not worship. *We* the living are the custodians of all record; we are the only minds of all history now able to reanimate its stories. Ours are the only voices through which the past can speak, in becoming the present and future. Ours is the equal of any time, because it has all times within it. But the empowerment of the past lies buried, unless we can find ways to experience it as alive. The poet occasionally needs to surrender some of his or her conscious intention, even some of the present sense of self, in order to be visited by the times and presences held in the deeper layers of memory. What we remember without usually being aware of it may help us become more truly ourselves as poets.

87

WRITING THE NARRATIVE POEM

By DEBRA ALLBERY

SOMETIMES AN ORDINARY WORD takes on a mild halo—*patience, provenance, correspondence*—so that the mind in its restless scanning lingers a second to repeat it. Sometimes it's an image that insists—the heavy silhouette of a woman walking toward a row of mailboxes, the last snags of white in a cotton field. The dream-image of a dog, sleek and abject, spotlit, crawling across a gravel road; he glances up at you and the picture fades. Each of these triggers the same recognition of *story*—and each, in time, with careful attention and patience, might become a poem.

I could attempt these "stories" in prose, but I know from experience what would happen. The margins would begin to creep in from either side with each revision; sentences would tighten and straighten themselves into lines. And I'd gradually grow frustrated, ready to cut to the chase, to the reason I was writing in the first place—aiming not so much toward the construction of plots and fleshing-out of characters, but toward the discovery inside a particular moment. For me, a poem is the most natural means toward that discovery.

The narrative poem relates an event in time—a memory, perhaps, a dream: *once, this happened.* Its synopsis might be ordinary, unassuming *(once when I was a child I crossed against the light),* or more startling *(I once lived across the street from a man who killed by dismemberment).* Something in your present has called forth and fixed upon this triggering moment; you write the poem to find out what it has to say about then, about now. In *Memory and Enthusiasm* W.S. DiPiero says that narrative poetry tells "states of becoming," that it "enacts the process of things." In the finished poem the "process of things" is revealed; the significance of that moment, and its relation to the present, becomes clear. The poem may grow out of a fragment, a small story, but the understanding it imparts has a wholeness. The larger story suggests itself around it.

The "narrative" label in contemporary poetry is a loose one. We're not talking here of ballads or epics, but of a general storytelling approach. I wouldn't say that all my poems are narrative, but it's a method I'm drawn to; I like the slight distance it provides, as well as the intimacy of tone it allows. Like a prose story, a narrative poem may concern itself with descriptive passages, characterizations, even dialogue, but it must of course meet any poem's requirements of compression, economy, rhythmic intensity, emotional risk-taking. I try to use as few brushstrokes as possible. Or, to switch the metaphor, the narrative poem should aim to have, as Robert Lowell said of Robert Frost's poetry, "the virtue of a photograph and all the finish of art." It might have a plain and conversational style or a highly rhetorical one, but in no case are its lines merely chopped-up prose. A flexible blank verse has served many narrative poets well, but you might find that shorter or variable line lengths produce musics more suited to your subject.

And your subject? Whatever insists. Whatever, with patience, is revealed. A word repeats itself to you to tell you that there's something important in it you haven't yet heard. An image appears, reappears, and you slowly begin to trace its provenance, detect correspondences. The color of the dog is the color of dust in a cotton field. The woman looks up at you as she lifts her hand to the mailbox. The poem sets its story into motion.

Here are two of my narrative poems* that illustrate the form:

Instinct

Winter was running out before I was ready—
gray clouds scudding flat-bottomed above
the cornfields and small huddles of houses,
the cold low-roofed light breaking open.
There wasn't any work. I took longer walks.
One day I boarded a bus and stepped off here
with two suitcases and my last twenty.

---

*"Next-Door Neighbors" and "Instinct," both of which originally appeared in *The Iowa Review,* are reprinted from Debra Allbery's collection, *Walking Distance* (University of Pittsburgh Press, 1991).

I found a room in this house, three floors
of women keeping out of each other's way.
Lucille, the rickety shadow above me,
has rented her attic room for life.
She scrubs our kitchen sink every morning,
a ritual with rubber gloves and cleanser,
and water boiled in white enamel bowls.

A cellist has moved into the room below me.
She practices at odd hours, scraping
bow against strings, irregular, urgent—
rasping pitches of some mental schism.
It's a quiet house except for her, except
for the undertones of pipes, doors closing,
phones ringing in rooms with no one home.

I hung a bird feeder from the fire escape
outside my window, but they haven't discovered it.
It's not a place birds would think to land.
I watch that little house swinging in gusts
of north wind against a backdrop of brick.
I'm considering South Dakota, Alberta.
Everywhere you move people ask you why.

As far as I know this is part of the story,
these slight intersections of contiguous lives.
The cellist's song rises like the undersides
of memory, the migratory calls of something winged
and flightless. Lucille hangs a sign on the
   basement doorknob
whenever she descends with trash or laundry,
Dont lock this door I am down there.

Next-Door Neighbors

Grant Street was one long Sunday afternoon
in February or March, a few yards of brown grass
thinning and matted, or rubbed away hard.
Our house stayed dark with my mother's pleurisy,
and it made me angry, the way she kept trying
to raise herself up to clean rooms or fix supper.
Then she'd lie down again on the couch, covering
herself tight with two blankets, chilling.
It was Sunday afternoon, foggy, and my father
was playing his Hank Williams record.
He's dozing at the end of the couch, his hand
on my mother's feet, and I go outside to sit
on the porch. Mr. Carter from across the street

pulls up grinning on his Harley and asks me
if I want to take a ride, and I do, but I don't
like his eyes, and besides, I'm not allowed to,
and shake my head no. I'm ten or eleven
with a younger brother and sister somewhere,
but my seeing is short-ranged and telescoped—
cardboard taped to the Carters' front window,
the busted taillight on our old white Comet,
yesterday's *Register,* "The World at Your
    Doorstep."

Mrs. Carter appears in the broken-paned window,
another black eye, and pulls down the blind.
My mother had called Mrs. Carter to ask if
she'd come over and blow cigarette smoke into
    her earache,
she had read somewhere that it helped.
But Mrs. Carter said sorry, she couldn't leave the
    house.
I'd yelled at my mother then why didn't she go
to a doctor, I slammed the door and was sorry.
Now I'm sitting on the step, biting the polish
off my nails. I don't like my coat, it's reversible
and has imitation fur. The snow edging the empty
    street
looks like coal. Next year Mr. Carter will go
to the electric chair for killing an old man
and his wife and hiding their pieces in his car trunk.
One night I'll forget to kiss my father goodnight
before he drives off to the factory with just one
taillight working, and I'll worry to sleep seeing that,
certain he'll die. I pray for goodness
and mercy every night, I want too many things.

🌀 88

THE SHAPE OF POETRY

BY PETER MEINKE

THERE'S BEEN A LOT OF INTEREST LATELY among young writers in the New Formalism, which is basically a good thing—writers should know what form has to offer, which forms their voice might be compatible with—just as painters and musicians benefit from working with a variety of materials and instruments.

But New Formalism is not an interesting subject, because it's irrelevant to the main question: Are the poems good or not? Writing a villanelle or a sonnet is neither a virtue nor a sin. The point is, does it work? Just as "free verse" often disguises laziness of thought and execution, "formal verse" often sugar-coats a bloodless triviality.

My theory is that every poem, formal or free, has an ideal shape, and the job of the poet is to find it. (I suppose this is partly what Gerard Manley Hopkins meant by his term "inscape"—the "pattern" of a poem.) There is no limit on these shapes but I believe some poems truly want to be free and all over the page, and some want to be haiku or sestinas. A poet, as he or she is working on the early drafts of a poem, has to recognize which way the poem is leaning (of course, to do that, you have to acquaint yourself with the possibilities—no one can write poetry who doesn't spend a lot of time reading it).

Here's the title poem of my book, *Liquid Paper:*

Liquid Paper

> Smooth as a snail, this little parson
> pardons our sins. Touch the brush tip
> lightly and—abracadabra!—a clean slate.
>
> We know those who blot their brains
> by sniffing it, which shows
> it erases more than ink
> and with imagination anything
> can be misapplied . . . In the Army,

our topsergeant drank aftershave, squeezing
my Old Spice to the last slow drop.

It worked like Liquid Paper in his head

until he'd glide across the streets of Heidelberg
hunting for the house in Boise, Idaho,
where he was born . . . If I were God
I'd authorize Celestial Liquid Paper
every seven years to whiten our mistakes:
we should be sorry and live with what we've done
but seven years is long enough and all of us

deserve a visit now and then
to the house where we were born
before everything got written so far wrong.

In the first few drafts of this poem, it was all in one stanza, a regular (or irregular) free verse poem, about half again as long as the final version. I think it's best to write uncritically for as long as you can, until you come to a stopping point or run out of steam. When I had done that, I began to think about what was the best structure for the poem; it was clear that although the lines tended to be about the same length, it wasn't going to be regularly rhymed or metered: no clusters of rhymes or near-rhymes looking to get organized, no iambic pentameter motor throbbing below the surface.

The next thing I noticed was that the line, "It worked like Liquid Paper in his head," was more or less in the middle, so I isolated it. I liked the idea of its being by itself (like Liquid Paper clearing a little space). Dropping lines and phrases here and there, I shaped the poem so the same number of lines preceded and followed that line.

Now I had a funny-shaped poem, with two stanzas of about a dozen lines surrounding a skinny one-line stanza. It was a little hard to read, to follow. I looked for the first natural break, which came after "a clean slate" in the third line, so I made that a three-line stanza (that seemed right: it *was* a clean slate). I then tried writing the poems with three three-line stanzas surrounding the middle line. That wasn't bad, but never quite worked just right. The poem didn't want to be in three-line stanzas.

It took me a while to recognize that this was a poem with a religious thrust. I had begun just by staring at this familiar little black and white bottle and seeing what I could think about it, where it would lead me (poems are seldom really about their ostensible subject, which is just

437

an excuse to enter the poet's mind). When I realized I had used the number "seven" twice, that led me to the symmetrical final shape of three/seven/one/seven/three—those numbers all having religious significance. The point about all this shifting around is to find the shape in which your poem most clearly and vividly expresses itself. Few readers will notice what you've done—just as no one can see the backbone that holds up your body—but it's extremely important that you've done it: It supports your poem.

One advantage of working in this way is that it's easier to know when you're finished. Although it may be true that poems are not so much finished as simply abandoned, there's a greater chance that the poem will feel finished when you put the last touches on a satisfactory shape. As I stared at "Liquid Paper" in its final stages, I could see that in the (now) second stanza there was a leap of imagination between "misapplied" and "In the Army"; and this was more or less balanced by a similar leap in the fourth stanza, between "born" and "If I were God." I wouldn't have noticed this if I hadn't already broken the poem down into these particular stanzas, but now that I did, I worked on creating a mirror image, dropping a few words, and adding the ellipses, making a sort of four/three: three/four split within the seven-line stanzas. So who cares? I care, the way a painter may stare with dissatisfaction at his painting, and then add a little touch of red to the bottom left hand corner and say, "That's it!" Though no one else will notice, the painter knows he has finished his painting.

I hope when you read "Liquid Paper" it seemed perfectly natural, as if this is just the way it popped out of my head. As Yeats wrote:

> A line will take us hours maybe;
> Yet if it does not seem a moment's thought,
> Our stitching and unstitching has been naught.

The sound of the poem is shaped, too, from the beginning alliterations to the combination at the end of "done," "long," "all," "then," "born," "wrong." Of course, some of these were present in the very first draft, but many were added, and—more importantly—much was jettisoned to outline the sound that I saw already imbedded there.

I hope also the poem sounds "true"—I think it's a true feeling. But some "facts"—as opposed to "truth"—had to be sacrificed for the shape of the sound. For example, my poor old sergeant really did drink my Old Spice, and that fit perfectly well because "Old Spice" goes nicely with "misapplied." But I was stationed in Schweinfurt, not Heidelberg—and I think the sergeant was from Orlando. Obviously, for all kinds of "sound" reasons, Heidelberg and Boise, Idaho, work a lot better here. "Until he'd glide across the streets of Schweinfurt" might have been "true," but the sound is so awkward it breaks up the thought.

Another, maybe simpler, example is the following poem:

Soldiers With Green Leggings
Villa Schifanoia, 1987

Father and daughter marched between
the erect cypresses, moss turning

the dark trunks green
on the north side

like soldiers with green leggings
and he wanted to say

Let us lay down our swords
(how pompous like a father!)

and she wanted to say
Let's open our doors

(how sentimental like a daughter!)
but the music in their heads

kept playing so they held
their chins high, stepping

together left right left right
smart as any parade and soon

the trees marched with them
ground rumbling like distant cannon

birds whirling like bewildered
messengers until a white flag

rose from the castle
and they fell to their knees

to sign the treaty:
any treaty—my treaty, your treaty.

This poem went through many "shapes" until I came up with those couplets, marching unpunctuated side by side down the page, mirroring the two people in the poem. An early draft began like this:

Father and daughter walked between the erect cypresses, moss turning the trunks green on the north side, like soldiers with green leggings. He wanted to say, Let us lay down our swords and she wanted to say, Let us open our doors . . .

Changing it into couplets focused the poem and led to the parenthetical additions, as well as other changes which were much clearer to see with the new structure (i.e., the military emphasis).

There will always be disagreement between those who favor "spontaneity" and little rewriting (Allen Ginsberg, for example), and those (like Yeats) who "labor to be beautiful." Nothing wrong with this. Every poem is a mixture of lines that have just been "given" to us—the inspiration—and those that we have worked on to fulfill the great promise of the original lines—the perspiration. Of course, we tend to be "given" more lines when we're well prepared. Ginsberg began by writing Blakean rhymed poems. As Alexander Pope wrote:

> True ease in writing comes from art, not chance,
> As those move easiest who have learned to dance.

If you are one of those writers whose lines (mostly) come out best on the first try—God bless. I'm jealous. And of course, this happens to everyone, even me, once in a while, like being dealt four aces. But as advice to writers, I'd be lying if I didn't say that I think ninety-nine percent of first drafts benefit from rewriting. Severe rewriting, serious shaping. An inspiration is not a poem, but if it's a real inspiration, with hard work and an eye to the shape it's struggling to be, it can become one.

§ 89

YESTERDAY'S NOISE: THE POETRY OF CHILDHOOD MEMORY

BY LINDA PASTAN

How sweet the past is, no matter how wrong, or how sad.
How sweet is yesterday's noise.
    —Charles Wright, "The Southern Cross"

I WROTE AN ESSAY TEN YEARS AGO CALLED "Memory as Muse," and looking back at it today I am struck by the fact that in the poems I write about childhood now the mood has changed from one of a rather happy nostalgia ("Memory as Muse") to a more realistic, or at least a gloomier, assessment of my own childhood and how it affects me as a writer ("Yesterday's Noise"). Let me illustrate with a poem called "An Old Song," from my most recent book.

An Old Song*

How loyal our childhood demons are,
growing old with us in the same house
like servants who season the meat
with bitterness, like jailers
who rattle the keys
that lock us in or lock us out.

Though we go on with our lives,
though the years pile up
like snow against the door,
still our demons stare at us
from the depths of mirrors
or from the new faces across a table.

And no matter what voice they choose,
what language they speak,
the message is always the same.
They ask "Why can't you do
anything right?" They say
"We just don't love you anymore."

441

As A. S. Byatt said about herself in an interview: "I was no good at being a child." My mother told me that even as a baby I would lie screaming in the crib, clearly terrified of the dust motes that could be seen circling in the sun, as if they were a cloud of insects that were about to swarm and bite me. By the time I was five or six, I had a series of facial tics so virulent that I still can't do the mouth exercises my dentist recommends for fear I won't be able to stop doing them. I'm afraid they'll take hold like the compulsive habits of childhood that led my second-grade teacher to send me from the room until I could, as she put it, control my own face. There was the isolating year (sixth grade) of being the one child nobody would play with, the appointed victim, and there was the even more isolating year (fourth grade) of being, alas, one of the victimizers. There was my shadowy room at bedtime, at the end of a dark hallway, and, until some worried psychologist intervened, no night light allowed.

I thought about calling my last book *Only Child* because something about that condition seemed to define not only me, but possibly writers in general who sit at their desks, necessarily alone, for much of the time. In some ways, of course, it defines all of us, born alone, dying alone, alone in our skins no matter how close we seem to be to others. I tried to capture my particular loneliness as a child, my difficulty in making friends, my search for approval, in what I thought would be the title poem of that book:

Only Child*

Sister to no one,
I watched
the children next door
quarrel and make up
in a code
I never learned
to break.

Go Play!
my mother told me.
Play! said the aunts,
their heads all nodding
on their stems,
a family of rampant
flowers

442

and I a single shoot.
At night I dreamed
I was a twin
the way my two hands,
my eyes,
my feet were twinned.
I married young.

In the fractured light
of memory—that place
of blinding sun or shade,
I stand waiting
on the concrete stoop
for my own children
to find me.

At a reading I gave before a group of Maryland PEN women, someone who had clearly not read beyond the tables of contents of my
books introduced me as a writer of light verse. I remember thinking
in a panic that I hardly had a single light poem to read to those expectant faces, waiting to be amused. Did I have such an unhappy life,
then—wife, mother, grandmother, with woods to walk in, books to
read, good friends, even a supportive editor?

I am, in fact, a more or less happy adult, suffering, thank God, from
no more than the usual griefs age brings. But I think my poems are
colored not only by a possibly somber genetic temperament, but also
by my failure at childhood, even when I am not writing about childhood
per se. And more and more, as I grow older, those memories themselves insist upon inserting themselves into my work. Perhaps it is the
very way our childhoods change in what I called "the fractured light
of memory" that make them such an inexhaustible source of poetry.
For me, it is like the inexhaustible subject of the seasons that can be
seen in the changeable light of the sun, or the versatile light of the
imagination, as benign or malevolent or indifferent, depending upon a
particular poet's vision at a particular moment.

I want to reflect a little then on those poems we fish up from the
depths of our childhoods. And for any teachers reading this, I want to
suggest that assigning poems to student writers that grow out of their
childhoods can produce unusually good results, opening up those frozen ponds with what Kafka called the axe of poetry.

Baudelaire says that "genius is childhood recalled at will." I had a
19-year-old student once who was not a genius but who complained

443

that he couldn't write about anything except his childhood. Unfortunately, his memory was short, and as a result, all of his poems were set in junior high school. He had taken my course, he told me, in order to find new subjects. I admit that at first glance junior high doesn't seem the most fertile territory for poems to grow in. On the other hand, insecurity, awakening sexuality, fear of failure—many of the great subjects do exist there. It occurred to me that when I was 19, what I usually wrote about were old age and death. Only in my middle years did I start looking back into my own past for the subjects of poems. This started me wondering about the poetry of memory in general. Did other poets, unlike my young students, come to this subject relatively late, as I had? As I looked rather casually and unscientifically through the books on my shelves, it did seem to me that when poets in their twenties and thirties wrote about children, it was usually their own children that concerned them, but when they were in their late forties or fifties or sixties, the children they wrote about tended to be themselves.

Donald Justice, in an interview with *The Missouri Review,* gave as good an explanation of this as anyone. He said, "In the poems I have been thinking of and writing the last few years, I have grown aware that childhood is a subject somehow available to me all over again. The perspective of time and distance alter substance somewhat, and so it is possible to think freshly of things that were once familiar and ordinary, as if they had become strange again. I don't know whether this is true of everybody's experience, but at a certain point childhood seems mythical once more. It did to start with, and it does suddenly again."

There are, first of all, what I call "Poems of the Happy Childhood," Donald Justice's own poem "The Poet At Seven" among them. But for poets less skilled than Justice, there is a danger to such poems, for they can stray across the unmarked but mined border into sentimentality and become dishonest, wishful sort of recollections. When they are working well, however, these "Poems of the Happy Childhood" reflect the Wordsworthian idea that we are born "trailing clouds of glory" and that as we grow older we are progressively despiritualized. Even earlier than Wordsworth, in the mid-17th century, Henry Vaughan anticipated these ideas in his poem, "The Retreat."

I mention Wordsworth and Vaughan because in looking back over the centuries at the work of earlier poets, I find more rarely than I expected poems that deal with childhood at all. Their poems are the exceptions, as are Shakespeare's 30th Sonnet and Tennyson's "Tears, Idle Tears." Perhaps it wasn't until Freud that people started to delve routinely into their own pasts. But nostalgia per se was not so rare, and in a book called *The Uses of Nostalgia: Studies in Pastoral Poetry,* the English critic Laurence Lerner comes up with an interesting theory. After examining pastoral poetry from classical antiquity on, he concludes that pastoral poems express the longing of the poets to return to a childhood arcadia, and that in fact what they longed to return to was childhood itself. He then takes his theory a step further and postulates that the reason poets longed for childhood is simply that they had lost it. He writes, "The list is varied of those who learned to sing of what they loved by losing it. . . . Is that what singing is? Is nostalgia the basis not only of pastoral but of other art too?" Or as Bob Hass puts it in his poem "Meditation at Lagunitas," "All the new thinking is about loss./ In this it resembles all the old thinking."

But though there are some left who think of childhood as a lost arcadia, for the most part Freud changed all of that.

We have in more recent times the idea of poetry as a revelation of the self to the self, or as Marge Perloff put it when describing the poems of Seamus Heaney, "Poetry as a dig."

The sort of poems this kind of digging often provides are almost the opposite of "Poems of the Happy Childhood," and they reflect a viewpoint that is closer to the childhood poems I seem to be writing lately. In fact, a poem like "Autobiographia Literaria" by Frank O'Hara actually consoles the adult by making him remember, albeit with irony in O'Hara's case, how much more unpleasant it was to be a child. If the poetry of memory can console, it can also expiate. In his well-known poem, "Those Winter Sundays," Robert Hayden not only recreates the past but reexamines his behavior there and finds it wanting. The poem itself becomes an apology for his behavior as a boy, and the act of writing becomes an act of repentance.

If you can't expiate the past, however, you can always revise it— and in various and occasionally unorthodox, ways. Donald Justice in the poem "Childhood" runs a list of footnotes opposite his poem, explaining and clarifying. Mark Strand in "The Untelling" reenters the

445

childhood scene as an adult and warns the participants of what is to occur in the future.

Probably the most ambitious thing a poem of childhood memory can accomplish is the Proustian task of somehow freeing us from time itself. Proust is perfectly happy to use random, seemingly unimportant memory sensations as long as they have the power to transport him backwards. When he tastes his madeleine, moments of the past come rushing back, and he is transported to a plane of being on which a kind of immortality is granted. We can grasp for a moment what we can never normally get hold of—a bit of time in its pure state. It is not just that this somehow lasts forever, the way we hope the printed word will last, but that it can free us from the fear of death. To quote Proust: "A minute emancipated from the temporal order had recreated in us for its apprehension the man emancipated from the temporal order." Proust accomplished his journey to the past via the sense or taste, but any sense or combination of senses will do. In my poem "PM/AM," I used the sense of hearing in the first stanza and a combination of sight and touch in the second. Here is the second:

AM**

The child gets up
on the wrong side of the bed.
There are splinters
of cold light on the floor,
and when she frowns
the frown freezes on her face
as her mother has warned her it would.
When she puts her elbows roughly
on the table her father says:
you got up on the wrong side of the bed;
and there is suddenly
a cold river
of spilled milk.
These gestures are merely formal,
small stitches in the tapestry
of a childhood she will remember
as nearly happy. Outside
the snow begins again,
ordinary weather
blurring the landscape
between that time and this,
as she swings her cold legs
over the side of the bed.

But did I really say: "A childhood she will remember as nearly happy"? Whom are you to believe, the poet who wrote that poem years ago or the poet who wrote "An Old Song"? As you see, the past can be reinterpreted, the past can be revised, and the past can also be invented. Sometimes, in fact, one invents memories without even meaning to. In a poem of mine called "The One-Way Mirror Back," I acknowledge this by admitting: "What I remember hardly happened; what they say happened I hardly remember." Or as Bill Matthews put it in his poem "Our Strange and Lovable Weather"—

> . . . any place lies about its weather,
> just as we lie about our childhoods,
> and for the same reason: we can't
> say surely what we've undergone
> and need to know, and need to know.

This "need to know" runs very deep and is one of the things that fuels the poems we write about our childhoods.

But the simplest, the most basic thing such poems provide are the memories themselves, the memories for their own sakes. Here is the third stanza of Charles Simic's poem "Ballad": "Screendoor screeching in the wind/ Mother hobble-gobble baking apples/ Wooden spoons dancing, ah the idyllic life of wooden spoons/ I need a table to spread these memories on." The poem itself, then, can become such a table, a table to simply spread our memories on.

Looking back at some of my own memories, I sometimes think I was never a child at all, but a lonely woman camouflaged in a child's body. I am probably more childlike now. At least I hope so.

---

*"An Old Song" and "Only Child" appear in *Heroes In Disguise,* Norton, 1991.
**"AM" is from *PM/AM:New and Selected Poems,* Norton,1982.

90

WRITING POETRY FOR CHILDREN AND YOUNG ADULTS

BY PAT LOWERY COLLINS

FOR YOUNG CHILDREN, A POEM IS A DEEPLY SATISFYING way of looking at the world. Fascinated at first by rhyme for its own sake, they soon begin to appreciate poetry that deals with simple concepts. They love slapstick, the wildly impossible, the ridiculous, word play, fanciful questions, clever and unexpected conclusions, twists and turns. They dote on repetition, used to great effect in *A Fine Fat Pig,* by Mary Anne Hoberman, in which the word abracadabra, used as an exclamation, precedes each line describing a zebra.

They revel in the action rhymes, finger play, and later, jump rope games, that depend on onomatopoeia, hyperbole and alliteration, as well as in such farcical verse as *Merry Merry FIBruary,* by Doris Orgel. Using these last two devices and the fun of a deliberate fib, the claim is made that "On the first of FIBruary/Setting out from Hackensack/ My Aunt Selma, in a seashell/ Sailed to Samarkand and back."

Poetry books for this age group are heavily illustrated, not only to complement the words, but also sometimes to explain them. And since poets are usually very visual writers, they will often provide the artist with exciting possibilities for illustrations without really trying.

The combined *Hector Protector* and *As I Went Over the Water* by Maurice Sendak is an unusual case in which poems and illustrations are all of one piece. Words emphasizing the text pepper the illustrations, and much of the action is in the pictures instead of the words. But in most cases, poems, even for the very young, rhymed or unrhymed, should be able to stand on their own.

Sometimes a single poem is used as the entire text for a picture book, illustrated so as to enhance or help to develop a concept or story. The text of my nonfiction book, *I Am an Artist,* is actually one long poem conveying the concept, through the finely detailed paintings of Robin Brickman, that art is a process which begins with our experiences in the natural world.

It's been my observation that children in the middle grades (ages 9–12) are no longer as fascinated by rhyme. To some degree they want a poem to be as profound as what they are experiencing in life, something that takes them seriously. Yet, they still look for poetry that is simple and unlabored. *Haiku,* three unrhymed lines (in Japanese they must consist of 17 syllables) offering an unusual perspective on a spark of reality, is a perfect vehicle. Writing in this form is not as easy as it sounds. To provide an example, I struggled to produce: "Evening/is quietly stitching/the seam of night."

Children of this age are intrigued by the subtlety of haiku, and its shortness is irresistible to those just learning to put their own thoughts on paper.

But humorous, silly verse, either in such traditional forms as the limerick or in new and inventive ways, still holds great appeal. Thus the information that "Oysters/are creatures/without/any features," provided by John Ciardi in *Zoo Doings,* may be better remembered than the multiplication tables.

It is also a good time for books such as *Alice Yazzie's Year,* by Ramona Maher, in which unrhymed poems, each one complete in itself, taken together tell a story of a year in the life of a Navajo girl, a year that holds such mysteries as the birth of a lamb. We are told that "The new lamb sucks/The pinyon burns low/The lamb goes to sleep/ His nose is a black star."

Poems about parents quarrelling or grandparents dying are often interspersed with poetry in a lighter vein in collections for this age group. One that does this effectively is *Knock at A Star,* collected by X. J. Kennedy and Dorothy M. Kennedy.

Language for its own sake becomes the focus again for readers about eleven to twelve, when communication with peers, intrigue, and secrets are important. Poetry is then a vehicle to express feelings without exposing them. Tools for this are found in nonsense sounds, obscure meanings, double meanings, rhyme, and, of course, humor. The mystery of nonsense—even an entire made-up language—seems to hold the same allure as it had for the four-year-old. Young readers are all too willing to accept the special logic of Lewis Carroll's "Jabberwocky" and will have no trouble figuring out that when the Jabberwock "came

449

whiffling through the tulgey wood/And burbled as it came," the "beam-ish boy" slays him as his "vorpal blade went snicker-snack!"

But these same children are also looking for poets able to look at life in the ways that they do. The poetry of Walter de la Mare has a timeless appeal because he affirms feelings that are universal. His book *Peacock Pie* was first published in 1913 and has been in print ever since. I'm currently illustrating a collection for Atheneum called *Sports, Power and Dreams of Glory, Poems Starring Girls,* edited by Isabel Joshlin Glaser, that affirms the dreams and aspirations of young women in such poems as "Abigail," by Kaye Starbird*, which ends by saying, "And while her mother said, 'Fix your looks,'/ Her father added, 'Or else write books.'/ And Abigail asked, 'Is that a dare?' And wrote a book that would curl your hair."

Teenagers may establish a passionate identification with one particular poet as they look for role models, a sense of history, a way to understand the world as it changes in and around them. By this time, they have probably been made aware of the mechanics and craft of poetry and are intrigued by experimentation. They can appreciate any poet whose vision is not too obscure. Because of the need of adolescents to deal with strong feelings and disturbing issues such as death and suicide, they are often attracted to poets with dysfunctional lives, for example, Sylvia Plath and Anne Sexton.

Most poetry for this age group appears in anthologies related to a single theme, to a city or to some historical period.

My own feeling is that even though the poetry you are compelled to write may turn out to have a special appeal for this age group, you will be competing with Shakespeare, T. S. Eliot, Walt Whitman, Emily Dickinson, and a cast of thousands. Of course, there is a lot of wonderful poetry out there for young children too, but not enough of it. And here I think the masters of today are a good match for those of yesterday and have an edge because they speak to the familiar.

But knowing your audience is only a beginning. There are a number of other things you should bear in mind in writing poetry for young people.

Don't fall victim to the mistaken notion that writing poetry for children of any age is easier than writing for adults. Your perspectives and topics may be different, but the skills you must bring to task are the same, skills honed through years of reading good poetry and working to develop your craft. Your most important assets will be a good memory and a strong awareness of the child within you.

It is a common misconception that almost anyone can write poetry for children. It's true we can get away with serving them peanut butter sandwiches for dinner, but it better be creamy peanut butter or the kind with just the right amount of nuts. Just so, the quality of poetry we give our children should be the best available, from the very beginning of their awareness of language.

Another misconception is that almost any idea for a children's book should be written in rhymed verse. Quite the opposite is true. Although there are exceptions, even reasonably good verse will not necessarily make for a more compelling text, and bad verse can, in fact, be deadly. So many "first" manuscripts in verse are submitted to editors that there is almost a universal resistance to them. Here I must admit to being an offender myself with my first book for children, *My Friend Andrew.* Looking back, I realize that any advantage I may have had was somehow knowing enough to keep it simple.

Things I personally object to, not under the control of the poet, are anthologies that include bad poems simply because they're by "good" poets, and minor poems by major poets because they're short; uneven collections by one poet or many; and anthologists who completely overlook contemporary poems and poets. The inability of some editors to recognize good poetry or to appreciate a child's ability to understand abstract concepts is a real problem.

Besides being as meticulous when writing poetry for children as you would be in writing for adults, you should, under penalty of a one-way trip down the rabbit hole, avoid all of the following:

• Poetry that talks down to the reader or is used as a vehicle to deliver a moral or message, unless it is written with good humor, as when Shel Silverstein, in his *Where the Sidewalk Ends,* admonishes readers to "Listen to the Mustn'ts."

• Near rhymes. They stop children in their tracks and detract from the flow of the poem. An example would be "lion's" rhymed with

451

"defiance" and "cat" with "hate" in the poem "My Old Cat," by Hal Summers. *(Knock at A Star)*

• Rhymes that are too cute, convenient, or overused. "Rain" rhymed with "Spain" comes to mind.

• Lazy images. Even well-known poets sometimes do this, settling for the most obvious image, metaphor, or simile as in "wide as the sky."

• Rhyme for rhyme's sake, not because it will assist in saying what you want to say in the most interesting way. If, as with the book, *Madeline,* by Ludwig Bemelmans, it would be hard to imagine your own story being told in any other way, then, by all means, go for it. (I felt this way about *Andrew.*)

• Subject matter inappropriate for the intended age group, sometimes directed more to the parent than the child, or dealing with subjects outside the child's experience.

• Distorted rhyme that's hard to read aloud. Always read your own work aloud to avoid this.

• Poetry that is florid and old-fashioned, written in the accepted style of an earlier period.

• Poetry that is too complex or obscure. Young readers won't want to struggle to understand what may be very personal imagery.

• Writing presented in the form of a poem that isn't poetry by any stretch of the imagination and isn't even good prose.

• Writers who believe they must write like another poet in order to be published.

There was only one Dr. Seuss. If he had insisted on being another Edward Lear, we would have missed his unique vision and voice. If you aren't sure enough of your own voice, keep studying the work of poets you admire—their pace, rhyme schemes and structure—and keep writing until you find how to say what you want to in ways uniquely yours.

Like Valerie Worth, in her *All the Small Poems,* you may have wonderful, quiet perceptions to express about everyday objects and happenings. Borrow her microscope if you must, but wear your prescription lenses and present the world through your observations and special talents, having in mind that building a poem is much like building a block tower: You will be balancing one word or line against another; arranging and rearranging; dropping one word, adding another, until the poem begins to say what you had in mind all along or what may never before have occurred to you. When a poem really comes together, really "happens," it is a moment like no other. You will feel like the child whose tower at long last has reached the sky.

Today, the market for children's poetry is quite different from what it was in the inhospitable 1980s. Then, there were a few poets who had cracked the barrier somewhat earlier and continued to be published, but a limited number of new names came on the scene. Thanks to the firmer financial footing of most book departments for young readers, to some editors who realize that poetry rounds out a list, and to the demand by teachers and librarians, there is currently greater opportunity for new poets. A number of publishing houses are actively seeking poetry for children, but they are highly selective and still apt to overlook a talented newcomer in favor of a poet more likely to turn a profit.

But the field of poetry has never been considered a lucrative one. There are exceptions, as with any art form, and for some poets, who continue to put their words down on paper napkins and laundry lists, there is really no escape.

⸙ 91

WRITING THE POETIC SEQUENCE

BY JEFFREY SKINNER

I'D LIKE TO URGE YOU TO A LITTLE GRAND AMBITION. I realize the oxymoronic character of that phrase, but the poetic sequence as practiced today often contains elements of both transcendence and homeliness, like much of our "postmodern" art, and life. So, please, bear with me.

If we grant that the Adam and Eve of American poetry, Walt Whitman and Emily Dickinson, invented the modern poetic sequence—long, lyrical poems in more or less free-standing sections, connected by tone, texture and theme (rather than by the narrative event and heroic characters of epic)—then it seems natural that every American poet since has at least attempted a long poem to contend with and extend the work of their progenitors.

T. S. Eliot's *The Wasteland,* Ezra Pound's *Cantos,* William Carlos Williams' *Paterson,* Hart Crane's *The Bridge* are some examples of modern poets that come most readily to mind. In the next generation, we might think of John Berryman's *Dream Songs,* Robert Lowell's sonnet sequences, Sylvia Plath's "final" poems. And, to name only a few contemporary examples: Louise Gluck's *Ararat,* Charles Wright's *China Trace,* and Sharon Olds' *The Father.*

This is a cursory list, though even within it one can find an astonishing range of concerns, diction, style, and strategy. I know it's intimidating to begin by mentioning such monuments as *The Wasteland,* but I give them as historical precedent only, not as competitive model. Remember—I said a *little* grand ambition. It is ambitious enough to attempt a sequence on one's own, without bringing Eliot, et al, along for the ride.

We are a diverse and fragmented society, and our poetry reflects this fact. Flexibility of mind and spirit are demanded of us. The juggling act our lives can so easily become is sometimes cause for anxiety, but the other side of this coin is great freedom. At no other moment in history have poets had the opportunity to mix so freely high and low culture, formal and free verse, and language that simultaneously encompasses the diction of the street, the home, the office, the academy and—well, any speech at all—even the jargon of meteorologists.

So—we are free to write a book of sestinas based on the characters in the old Perry Mason television show (*The Whole Truth,* by James Cummins), or a sonnet sequence on rock and roll icons (*Mystery Train,* by David Wojahn). Or we can use free verse and lean more on obsessive character or theme for structuring—as in Sharon Olds' searing vignettes of a father's death *(The Father),* or Charles Wright's book-length sequence of meditative lyrics on the meeting of Eastern and Western views of spiritual regeneration *(China Trace).* The possibilities are infinite. We need not begin with a grand, elevated idea.

How *do* we begin a poetic sequence? Often, the beginnings of a sequence have come for me when I have written a poem I felt did not say all I wanted to say on the subject. But at the same time, I knew that the poem as written was finished: It had a completeness that could not be expanded without distortion. The poem suggested an overarching idea or zone of concern that I wanted to explore from different angles. I sensed that if I continued to build on what the initial poem had established, the resulting group or sequence might acquire an added dimensionality, a depth of field, that the first poem alone did not possess. I felt the pull toward sculpture, if you will, as opposed to the flat canvas.

Here is a poem I wrote some years ago:

Prayer to Owl Hiding in Daylight

Zealot in the trees, hot tiny speck
glowing in the dark of God's endless palm,
forgive me my absences! The clinically depressed
tenements of Bridgeport
ejected me into this calm, and now
there is too much rain, the leaves are pleading,
the green runs. All day, invisibly, you take notes,
like a businessman writing a novel
on his time off, a pale blue spark
snapping between your ears.
When will you visit? We desire visitations
but lack discipline to call them

on, and only our best shoes are shining.
I want claw, want your gold
headlights, your roomy coat of feathers.
I want to sleep days and work nights,
praising silence in high branches.
I want the microtonics of steel
drained from my blood. Oh the eclipse
has come and gone: show yourself.
You'll find my true love and me dreaming
on each other's shoulders, as the baby
breathes out tiny flowers in her crib
and the war continues, silently, elsewhere.

I don't know where this poem came from. Or, to be more precise, I don't know where the first line came from—"Zealot in the trees, hot tiny speck." The words drifted into my mind like a song on the radio; I tuned in. I did not discover until later in the writing that the "Zealot" was an owl. When I did, the poem began to move much faster, and I completed the last third rapidly. Only after it was finished did I notice that the poem was a kind of address, or supplication to the owl. That realization gave me the title.

Now I had a poem that was recognizably mine in language and allusion (new baby, Bridgeport tenements, businessman writing a novel), but that also harked back to earlier periods and cultures, when poetry was taken seriously as ritualistic invocation, a concrete way of knitting together the human and natural worlds, often through the mediation of animals. The poem also seemed conscious of the distance between these two worlds; there was a kind of implied acknowledgment of poetry's functional loss, a sad irony that struck me as essentially contemporary in tone.

These contradictions seemed resonant, and I wanted to explore them further. I began writing other "prayers to animals," setting for myself certain "rules": Each poem must address an undomesticated animal (or insect); I must take the animals as they are, without wrenching them from their natural environment or giving them supernatural attributes; each poem must include my world *as it is,* without idealization; and I must ask something of each animal, something I truly desire. I allowed myself to vary the form of the poems: "Prayer to Sparrow in Two Seasons" was written in tercets, with an iambic pentameter base; "Prayer to Cottonmouth Blocking the Road to the Pond" seemed to require couplets; "Prayer to Wasp on the Eve of Its Execution," an extended block of varied two- and three-beat lines; and so forth.

I ended up with about fifteen poems in the sequence. It was exciting to follow the implications of an idea, and writing the poems was, as Frost says, "serious play." I did not think about the "great American poetic sequence." I just looked about me for animal subjects, and wrote the next poem.

And this is the attitude I'd suggest you take when writing a sequence: Let yourself be swept up in the idea, yes, but remember that the section or piece you are currently working on deserves your complete attention, and that, day by day, the whole will take care of itself. *Agi quod agis;* Do what you are doing . . .

I have also written a number of sonnet sequences, a formal challenge that comes down to us trailing a long history and its own set of rules. I don't know exactly why the sonnet remains of perennial interest to poets in succeeding generations, but since its invention and right into the present time, the form has drawn poets to test both its resources and its limits. It may be that the sonnet is, in its compactness, and in the buried logic of its movement, a more accurate analogue of human consciousness than anyone has guessed. The poet David St. John calls poems "maps of consciousness"; perhaps the sonnet is, simply, an ideal grid for the linguistic cartographer. . . .

Theory aside, it's clear to me after years of writing and teaching that the formal strictures of a sonnet or sonnet sequence release a paradoxical freedom in the poet. By concentrating on the "boundaries" of fourteen lines, rough iambic pentameter, and end-rhyme, my students find themselves saying surprising, insightful things they just would not have arrived at by writing "free verse." Such discoveries are compounded in the sonnet sequence, where at a certain point the form itself becomes second nature—no longer an impediment of any kind, but rather a powerful tool for unearthing the new.

I have two daughters, now eight and ten years old, but both toddlers when I wrote this poem:

> I wanted a boy, of course, wanted to create
> in my own image, ambitious little god that I am.
> But the long years spent chasing women immoderate-
> ly stacked karma: now I'm surrounded by them.
> Human flowers, your natural smell intoxicates

457

and the fine blond hair I smooth, reading books,
consoling a fall. My own boyhood aches
in me still, burnished wind of summer dusks
comes back: bike-riding through dinner, stickball,
mumbletypeg in the marvelous junkyard; running,
running the long dark length of Grandma's hall
to leap her scented quilt. . . . Oh I've lost nothing,
and need no small version of myself to keep
boy pleasures. A daughter takes a farther reach.

After reading this over, it occurred to me that it might be the beginning of something larger. It engaged many of the themes important to me at that point in my life: the relation of parenting to one's own childhood; the dangerous tendency to view children as extensions of the self; the eternally fascinating and difficult subject of gender difference; and the anxieties raised by simply bringing children into a complex world.

In addition, the poem gave a hint ("your natural smell intoxicates") of the stance succeeding poems might take: they could be written *to* my daughters. The address to a loved one is a time-honored strategy in sonnet sequences and, as is probably obvious by now, I am in favor of the use of traditional poetic form, as long as that form is refreshed and remade by living, contemporary language.

But at that point in their lives neither of my daughters could read; the younger one was not yet talking. How could I suspend my own disbelief in writing poems to people who could not possibly understand?

The solution came in the form of a title for the sequence: "Sonnets to My Daughters Twenty Years in the Future." The poems, or poem, as I now saw it, would be addressed to the women my daughters would become. I would write a "time capsule" poem. This freed me to speak of adult matters in adult terms, though I would still be writing to my flesh and blood. The prospect was, again, exciting, and I plunged in, writing sonnet after sonnet.

I varied the pattern, using both Shakespearean and Petrarchan models. I relied on an iambic pentameter "back beat," though there is much metrical variation in the finished sequence. I also took considerable liberties with end-rhyme exactness, using off, slant, and approximate rhymes whenever I thought it appropriate. My primary goal, while retaining the strong echo of the sonnet form in the reader's mind,

458

was to stay as close to current American speech (as I hear and use it in conversation) as possible. Whatever interest the resulting sequence has, apart from subject matter, is due in large measure to the tension between traditional form and colloquial usage. Purists may object, but to me there is nothing more boring than the tick-tock of a sonnet written to metronomic perfection. *Make it new!* Pound says, and to do that, whether writing in form or free verse, poets must use the language of the time and place they have been given.

One of the advantages of attempting a sequence is that, whatever the eventual success or shortfall of the piece as a whole, one generally ends up with at least a few sections that are salvageable as poems in their own right. When I was writing the sonnets to my daughters, I made it my goal to write fifty of them. But when I reached somewhere around number forty, I felt the impulse fading; the sonnets were becoming mechanical, repetitive. I wrote to my old mentor and friend Philip Levine for advice. "Stop writing," he replied, "when you get tired of reading them." This seemed like excellent counsel; I closed up shop on the sequence and chose and arranged the twenty best sonnets to include in my second collection of poems.

Writing the poetic sequence allows us a kind of relaxed concentration. We escape the pressure of having to say all we know in a single section or poem. Each section opens the way, associatively, to others. The "grid" of a larger structure frees us from the invention of new form every time we set pen to paper. We have the spur of ambition, tempered by the necessity to attend to whatever specific piece of the whole is before us at the moment.

However you begin your sequence—whether with a line, or a poem in which you sense hidden seams of rich material, or the excitement of a formal pattern, or a subject—at some point you will have to decide whether the *idea* of the sequence is important enough to engage you, deeply, on many levels. The writing of a poetic sequence is the construction of a small world, and the heady intensity of that work can be its own reward. Go ahead—try a little grand ambition. You have nothing to lose, and much of delight and discovery to gain.

92

Poets, Learn Your Trade

By Robert Mezey

I HAVE BEEN ASKED TO OFFER some useful advice to beginning writers and I shall address myself to young poets, since poetry is the art I know best. I confess that I feel a little uncomfortable in this role of wise old counselor, being neither particularly old nor particularly wise and, in fact, in want of advice myself. (What wouldn't I give for a conversation with Robert Frost or John Crowe Ransom or W. H. Auden. There are many things I should like to ask them about this beautiful and difficult art.) Also, I am all too aware that the precepts that immediately spring to mind are the ones that veteran writers always hand out to the young. Nevertheless I will mention a few of them; they are easily summarized, they are no less true for being clichés, and they bear repetition.

First of all, live. Experience, observe, reflect, remember—try to be one of those on whom nothing is lost (in Henry James' great phrase). It is not necessary that your experience be wide, only that it be deep. Think what Emily Dickinson managed to live without—sex, travel, drugs, a career, a lifestyle—and yet few Americans have ever lived as fully, as intensely as she. Live your life. One cannot write out of books.

Read, for after all, one does write out of books also, and poetry is made of poetry. Reading and writing are inseparable; if you are not a reader, you are not a writer. Read history, novels, science, whatever you like, and above all, poetry. As in life, so in reading: Deep is better than wide. And read the best—not your mostly dismal contemporaries, but what has lasted hundreds and thousands of years: Homer, Virgil, Dante, Shakespeare, the King James Bible. Read continually.

Revise what you have written, and then revise it again. You don't want to work all the life out of it, but precision and liveliness and an air of spontaneity are the fruit of long hours of writing and rewriting, of trial and error. First thought is *not* best thought, and poetry, unlike jazz, is not improvisation. In fact, first thoughts tend to be banal, unfocused, conventional, not quite coherent. Most poems require a number of drafts—maybe twenty; maybe fifty. Don't be too easily satisfied.

Those are perhaps the three essential commandments. (If they are not easily obeyed, it may be that you are not destined to be a poet.) But I want to tell you something that nowadays not many others would tell you or even assent to. You must learn to write verse. Not "free" verse, but verse—numbers, measures—call it what you will. It is what poetry has always been written in until the last century or so, and indeed it is only over the last few decades that nonmetrical verse has become the norm (if something which, by definition, violates the norm can *be* a norm). Before you break the rules, you need to know the rules; before you seek novelty, you ought to demonstrate that you know the ancient craft. That is no more than simple honesty and humility. You cannot properly call yourself a poet otherwise. A poet who cannot compose in verse is like a painter who cannot draw or a scientist who does not grasp the scientific method. Besides, as you acquire facility, you will find that verse-making supports your sentences, generates ideas, leads you where you might not otherwise have gone; and you will find what many poets have long known, that free verse is not easier than metrical verse, but much more difficult, and very few can write it well. As André Gide said, art is born of constraint and dies of too much freedom.

How can you go about learning to write in meter? As poets have always learned, by reading good verse and trying to imitate its sounds. You may need to count on your fingers at first, to be sure that you have the permitted number of syllables and the accents in the right positions, but soon you will be able to play by ear. It is useful to have some theoretical understanding, but in the end, an iambic pentameter is a line that sounds like an iambic pentameter, and you must know it the way you know the tune of an old familiar song. Be careful where you look for instruction: Many teachers don't know much about the meters, and these days most poets don't either, and the books can be misleading or flat out wrong. George Stewart's book *The Technique of English Verse* (Holt, Rinehart & Winston) is good; so is James McAuley's *Versification* (Michigan State University Press), the shortest and maybe the best; so is Derek Attridge's *The Rhythms of English*

Poetry (Longman). (Remember that good prosodists, though they hear the verse much the same way, may use different terminology or different symbols of scansion.) Be sure you read good models; many contemporary poets who write in meter, or what they call meter, do it atrociously: It is obvious that they don't know how the game is played. You can't go wrong with Marlowe, Herbert, Jonson, Milton, Pope, Tennyson, or Frost, or a hundred others. If you want to read the best of your own times, look for Philip Larkin, Edgar Bowers, Donald Justice, Richard Wilbur, Anthony Hecht, the late distinguished American poet, Henri Coulette, and there are a few others.

All the good poets make up a great free university, which you can attend at any hour of the day or night, choosing whatever teacher you like. Whatever you do, read aloud, both the verse of your models and your own, and listen to it carefully. (It might help to listen to it on tape. It might help to listen to records or tapes of good poets who also read well: Frost, Justice, Larkin, Wilbur, Ransom.)

Once you get the tune fixed in your head, you will have it forever, and you will recognize it in all its many varied patterns. You should, at the very least, be able to write pentameters, tetrameters, and trimeters (the longer and shorter lines are more difficult), and in both strict iambic and loose; common measure and ballad meter; rhymed couplets, tercets, and quatrains; blank verse and passable sonnets. The better you can write in meter, the better you can hear the old verse, and, to some extent, vice versa. And it is essential that you hear the great English poems as they were meant to be heard and that you have some idea of what those poets were trying to do. Otherwise you will have a very imperfect understanding of the poetry of your own language, and that is a serious deficiency in a poet. (Not to say in any cultivated man or woman—after all, accentual-syllabic verse, its invention and development, is one of the glories of our civilization.)

Once you have achieved some mastery of your craft, you can have a go at free verse if you like. Having learnt something about making verse lines that are really lines, you are likelier to do better than if you had never written anything but free. And you may well discover that for all its charms, free verse cannot do nearly as much as metrical verse can, in expressing feeling, in clarifying thought, in varying tempo, in delineating nuances of tone or subtleties of meaning, in emphasizing, modulating, elevating, clinching both ideas and emotions, and above all, in bringing about that perhaps magical phenomenon that poetry alone is capable of: making us feel that the sounds of the words *are* what is being said, that the sounds somehow deepen, enlarge, enact, embody—in a sense, create—the reality behind them. As Henri Coulette once wrote, "Meter is thinking; it is the basis of intimacy between reader and writer."

These are some of the powers of meter and rhyme, and only the profoundest, sincerest, and most original poet can put them aside, and then only if he knows what he is putting aside. I am no Yeats, God knows, but I urge you, young poets, to do what he urged *his* young fellow poets to do: Learn your trade. Sing whatever is well made.

§ 93

REACHING TOWARD FORM IN YOUR POETRY

BY GREG GLAZNER

ANY ASPIRING POET LOVES to read poems. It's safe to guess that if you are writing poetry, you have been keeping a mental list of other people's poems—your favorites—for a while now. My list began when I was ten years old. I was fascinated by several of Robert Frost's poems, thanks to a first-rate teacher. (Mrs. Grimes wasn't perfect; she also taught us a terribly sentimental poem, written by a WWII fighter pilot, which began "Oh, I have slipped the surly bonds of earth / And danced the skies on laughter-silvered wings." I still remember the whole poem verbatim.)

Having ignored poetry during my junior high and high school years, I encountered Frost again during my first year in college. "The woods are lovely, dark, and deep," Dr. Brunner half-chanted over the lectern, and my list of favorite poems began growing again—and changing. Over the next fifteen years, poems by Rilke, Stevens, Whitman, Yeats, Dickinson, Kinnell, Milton, Roethke, and many others surpassed Frost's on my list of favorites, but poetry remains as alive for me now (in different ways, of course) as it was when I was a fourth grader, discovering "Stopping by Woods on a Snowy Evening" for the first time.

The love of reading poems is the first drive you need to become a serious poet. Chances are, if you have read this far, you already possess it. The second drive, the desire to develop craft, is especially important in the beginning years. And the third, a fascination with the way form and style turn into content, implying a world, is especially important after some technical problems have been handled.

Even some of the greats have struggled with technique—and the struggle isn't limited to poets. Early on, Charlie Parker, arguably the greatest musician in the history of jazz, was known as the worst saxophone player in Kansas City. Apparently, he was bad enough that after the word got out, he couldn't even get an audition. So for a period of two or three years, he practiced relentlessly with his friend Dizzy Gillespie, racing through scales, working up various classical pieces. He claims to have practiced eleven to fifteen hours a day. No wonder his mature solos would later sound so effortless, so full of vigor and surprise. His reservoir of technique freed him to focus almost all of his immense talent into creating an unprecedented kind of music. He didn't have to think about getting the notes right.

Maybe it's true that poets, like jazz musicians, want nothing more than to break into a spontaneous, intelligent music. If so, the most important lesson to learn at the outset, so that later on it can become as natural and as unconscious as breathing, is this: Almost all of a poem's power comes from what is suggested, not from what is stated outright. And of the many ways that poetry can suggest things, three seem to give beginning poets the most difficulty: voice, tone, and image.

When I use the word "voice," I mean the personality implied by the poems' diction and syntax. Maybe such a distinction already sounds arcane, but it isn't; we instinctively delight in voice in our everyday lives. Consider this fictitious personal example: Over the Christmas holidays, when the whole extended family convenes at my parents' house, somebody gives my mother a new puppy, a three-month-old Great Dane which promptly eats part of the couch. My grandfather happens onto the scene of the crime first, smiles, and says, "I reckon we're just about ready to get shed of a dog." My brother David comes in and says, "So, looks like Rover here jumped the gun on lunch." And my mother addresses the dog directly: "Oh, come on. You know better than that!"

The point is that the way people talk tells us much about their personalities. And the speaker of a poem, while not identical to the poet, must sound authentic in his or her speech patterns. So when a beginning poet brings into one of my workshops a poem which opens, "The moss-infested river flowing forth from the verdant mountains. . . . ," the voice problem jumps out immediately. For starters, the diction is generally pitched too high to be believable. But the overly formal speaker who calls the mountains "verdant" wouldn't use the adjective "moss-infested" in the same breath. So there is a problem with consistency as well. By dropping the diction level and getting the focus away from adjectives, the student writes, "Out of the green mountains, the river choked with moss . . ." and gains much credibility. The voice sounds intelligent, but not stilted.

Beginning poets aren't alone when they encounter substantial difficulties in early drafts of a poem. During the year it took me to write "From the Iron Chair," the nine-page title poem of my book, I filled over three hundred notebook pages with drafts, struggling much of the way. As I worked on the fourth section in particular, the problems in the early drafts all seemed to have to do with tone. By "tone," I mean, of course, the overall mood of a piece of writing.

The first few lines went well enough; only relatively minor changes were necessary. Here are those lines as they appear in the book:

> Down the well of old need,
> down the concrete steps,
> splintered rails, and leaf-rot
>
> of the half-demolished hotel,
> my cousin—one of the last illegal tenants—
> opened the door to his basement.
>
> Inside, there was vodka on his breath
> and a blue-gray static on the air.
> He adjusted a TV wired
>
> to the battery of a car
> and offered me a beer. All I did
> was lean back and take it to my bones,
>
> at twenty that first firing and eviction,
> this last inhabited room
> smelling of booze & glimmering
> like the interior of an age. . . .

Up to this point, the tone was nostalgic, tough, and visceral all at once. It seemed honest. But in what was to follow, the poem took a wrong turn. Here are the next few lines as they appeared in the first draft:

> The weight of twisted beams and bricks
> rose in the mind, at once
> imaginary and real, as if the future

> had a demolished superstructure—
> a brute, invisible weight
> and the glut it took to forget it.

What happened to the power of the remembered experience? The tone of "rose in the mind, at once / imaginary and real, as if the future / had a demolished superstructure" is detached, cerebral, so that in context, the lines seem forced and powerless. Here is the same passage rewritten for tone—for the *feel* I had unwittingly abandoned:

> We stared into the tube
> as if it were enough to change us,
>
> even as the invisible brute weight
> of bricks and twisted beams
> crushed itself closer like the future.
>
> Twice the ceiling groaned, and I leaned
> closer to the sentimental violins.
> For an hour my cousin stiffened with me. . . .

While tone and voice work to create the sense that a poem has come from a believable, human origin, images bring the subject matter alive through the senses. Imagery is absolutely central to the work of most poets. Certainly, some great writers have been able to use abstract statement powerfully in poetry; Wallace Stevens comes to mind as a modernist who did so. But in most poems written by beginners, a direct statement of feelings or ideas not embodied in imagery will ring so false and flat that it will ruin the poem. William Carlos Williams' directive, "No ideas but in things," seems tailor-made for aspiring poets learning their craft. Keeping Williams in mind, a young poet whose love poem contains the line "In your absence, I am sleepless with longing," revises it to read, "You are gone, and the streetlight sets off / its blue-white fires across the sheets." The revision gains its power by appealing to the senses of sight and touch. The poem is an aesthetic experience, not amateur philosophy and not diary entry. For most poets, imagery is a crucial way of making a poem live. As the poet Miller Williams once said, "Film it."

Imagery, tone, voice, and many other aspects of craft are addressed in poetry workshops available in almost every corner of the country. A writing workshop can be an excellent way for a poet to improve rapidly, assuming that the teacher is both a good poet and a good teacher—and that the student is motivated. But when, after years of hard work, a poet reaches the level of technical competency, writing as well as thousands of poets whose work fills hundreds of literary magazines in America, what next? What follows the long apprenticeship?

In short, transcending one's own self-imposed strictures. Doesn't the serious poet, having learned to write a modest kind of poem, try to live his way beyond it, reaching toward an understanding of the forms that experiences themselves assume? Think of Galway Kinnell's early poems, heavily influenced by the formalism of the 1950s (some of these are very fine, by the way), and his *The Book of Nightmares,* which moves through the most fundamental, archetypal experiences in jagged, free-verse lines, full of a dark, celebratory, American music. Think of Dickinson cloistered in her father's house, fusing the common measure of the church hymn with her intelligence and solitude, forging her small, powerful hymns to doubt. Think of Charlie Parker breathing out rush after rush of chromatic flourishes, sailing beyond the melody like someone discovering a new kind of grace for an age when all the moorings have come loose.

Young, anyone can set out "like something thrown from the furnace of a star," as Denis Johnson puts it. Poetry touches us easily then, as long as we have the good fortune—as I did in the fourth grade—of being exposed to it in an intelligent way. But for some of us, the experience has such power that we go on to become writers ourselves, governing our lives by the rich, unpredictable cadences of the human voice. In the end, we never know for sure whether we succeed in writing important poetry. But the process—reading, crafting, reaching toward form—is a way of aspiring toward meaning with one's whole being. Anything less is just fooling around with verse.

JUVENILE AND YOUNG ADULT

§ 94

WRITING NONFICTION FOR CHILDREN: QUESTIONS AND ANSWERS

BY JAMES CROSS GIBLIN

AMONG THE FIRST AND MOST FREQUENT QUESTIONS asked of writers of children's nonfiction is *Why did you choose to write nonfiction?* My answer is that I'm not sure I did "choose." Instead, nonfiction probably chose me—and it happened at a very early age, as I have a hunch it happens for many nonfiction writers.

When my mother read me Inez Hogan's *The Navajo Twins,* I was fascinated by the description of an arroyo near the twins' home. I lived in Northeastern Ohio and had never seen anything like the desert landscape in which the story was set. In fact, I became so fascinated by it that I went around the house chanting the word *arroyo* over and over, indicating that even at age five I was intrigued by the unusual word and the odd bit of information. And I've continued to be intrigued by such things in my adult life. That's probably why I've explored offbeat subjects like chimney sweeps, eating utensils, windows, and chairs in many of my nonfiction books.

Take a look back at your own childhood. You may detect an early interest in animals, history, airplanes, gardening, or some other subject area that you could draw on for your nonfiction writing if you haven't already.

The next question is generally *Where do you get the ideas for your books?* The answer is, from all sorts of places. The trick is to recognize a good idea when one comes along.

For example, some years ago I saw an exhibit of antique and modern chairs at the Cleveland Museum of Art. The range and variety of chairs on display amazed me, and I thought, "There might be a children's book in this." I picked up the brochure that accompanied the exhibit and, after reading it, was even more convinced of the idea's possibilities.

At the New York Public Library, I delved into several histories of furniture and then drafted a proposal for a book of my own. My editor responded enthusiastically to the idea, and soon I had a contract for *Be Seated: A Book About Chairs.*

Often an idea is suggested to a nonfiction author. For example, after I spoke at one conference, I was asked by a librarian if I'd ever thought of writing a book about unicorns. A month later, at another conference, I was asked the same question.

The second query coming so soon after the first made me think seriously about the idea. Like many writers, I keep a file of newspaper and magazine articles concerning topics that interest me, and I seemed to remember clipping several pieces about unicorns. I riffled through the file, and found three scientific articles dealing with the mythical creature. I reread them, and that was the beginning of my research for *The Truth About Unicorns.*

Wherever an idea comes from, it must strike a deep chord in you, the author. Otherwise, you won't be able to sustain the drive needed to research and write a nonfiction book—a process that can take years. For example, I've jotted down many ideas for books and countless others have been suggested to me, but only a few have called to me the way those for *Be Seated* and *The Truth About Unicorns* did.

Another frequent question is *How do you decide what age group to write for?* The answer depends on three factors that are closely intertwined: (a) your inclinations as an author; (b) the age group you feel would have the strongest interest in the material; and (c) the requirements of the marketplace.

Many nonfiction topics can be explored for all age groups. For example, biographies of George Washington could be—and have been— written for preschoolers, children in the elementary grades, and young adults. I chose to write my biography of Washington as a picture book for first- and second-graders, because I liked the challenge of the picture book format, and because the publisher wanted a biography for that age level.

Other topics are clearly suited to one age group more than another. My book about the deciphering of the Rosetta Stone would be beyond the comprehension of preschoolers and most children in first and second grade. However, it could have been directed toward either the upper elementary or the young adult level.

I decided on the former because I knew that most youngsters study ancient Egypt in the sixth grade. Consequently, I assumed *The Riddle of the Rosetta Stone* would find its largest audience if it were aimed at that age level, and the book's sales so far prove I was right. This shows how important it is to have a sense of the market when you're deciding on the age group for a nonfiction book.

The next question is one of the most basic: *How do you do research?* There's no simple, clear-cut answer to that since each book requires its own research plan, and some are much more complex than others. I usually start the process by letting my mind wander and asking myself, "What subtopics branch out naturally from the main topic?"

For example, with *Let There Be Light,* a history of windows in various cultures and periods, I began my bibliography with books about the history of architecture. From there I got more specific, adding titles about life and dwellings in Africa, the Middle East, the Far East, and the Arctic. Before I was through, I also read books and articles about the Crystal Palace exhibition in Victorian London, the infamous *Kristallnacht* in Nazi Germany, and in this country, the urban riots in which so many windows were smashed during the 1960s.

All of this research gave me a solid foundation on which to build *Let There Be Light.* Like most nonfiction authors, I used only part of the material I'd gathered in the actual writing. But I believe readers can sense the rest, lending credibility and authenticity to the finished book.

Still another question might seem insulting at first hearing, but it's probably not meant to be taken that way: *Do nonfiction writers have to be concerned with literary style?* Of course we do, if we're serious about our work. And a definition of style offered by the French poet, playwright, and filmmaker Jean Cocteau would seem to have a special application to children's nonfiction: "Style is a simple way of saying complicated things."

That definition of Cocteau's is a goal you should constantly aim for in your writing, especially when you're explaining a scientific concept or sketching in the historical background of an event. How do you achieve it? Here are some steps you may find helpful. First, go over the facts in your research notes for a particular section or chapter until you've virtually memorized them. That way you won't have to refer to the notes too often and will be free to draft the text in your own words. Then, work and rework each paragraph until it says what you

473

want to say in the way you want to say it. Besides simplicity, strive for rhythm in the writing. Listen to each sentence in your head as you compose it, and if the words don't flow smoothly, fiddle with them until they do.

Some reviewers have said my books have a "conversational style." If that's true, I think it's because I try to make each sentence *speakable*. That's a distinct advantage today, when even nonfiction books for older children are often read aloud in the classroom.

In the last fifteen or so years, there has been much more emphasis on the visual aspect of children's nonfiction books. So it's not surprising that authors are almost always asked *Are you involved in the illustration of your books—and if so, how?*

Not only am I involved, but—like many nonfiction authors—I'm responsible for gathering most of the illustrations that appear in my books. For example, with *The Truth About Unicorns* I assembled photographs of paintings and tapestries depicting the mythical animal from art museums around the world. To supplement these, I also found pictures of the real narwhal and the one-horned Indian rhinoceros at natural history museums.

However, I was unable to locate illustrations of ancient Greek, Roman, and Chinese unicorns, so the publisher commissioned an artist to draw pictures of them. To help pay for the drawings, I agreed to take a reduced royalty. I felt this was a small price to pay in return for a more attractive and salable book.

Some nonfiction authors still think their work is done when they turn in a manuscript to an editor, and refuse to concern themselves with the illustrations. They're making a big mistake, in my opinion. For if a book isn't well designed and illustrated, it has little chance of succeeding in today's nonfiction marketplace.

Finally, writers are sometimes asked a question which frankly annoys me: *Now that you've mastered nonfiction, would you like to try your hand at fiction?*

The question is annoying because—like the similar question often asked of children's writers, "Would you like to write adult books some day?"—it implies that nonfiction writing is somehow inferior to fiction.

I refuse to accept that notion, probably because I've written my share of fiction and in many ways find that writing nonfiction is a greater challenge; you have to absorb and present a huge amount of information in a clear, accurate, and entertaining manner. Like a writer of fiction, you must find a way to write freely and spontaneously. But at the same time—unlike a fiction writer—you always have to be on guard to make sure you're not omitting or distorting any necessary facts.

It's not easy to rise to this challenge and achieve a happy balance between spontaneity and control, but when you do, the result can be uniquely satisfying. That's why I, for one, would never want to give up writing nonfiction in favor of fiction.

95

Is It Good Enough for Children?

By Madeleine L'Engle

A while ago when I was teaching a course on techniques of fiction, a young woman came up to me and said, "I do hope you're going to teach us something about writing for children, because that's why I'm taking this course."

"What have I been teaching you?" I asked her.

"Well—writing."

"Don't you write when you write for children?"

"Yes, but—isn't it different?"

No, I assured her, it isn't different. The techniques of fiction are the techniques of fiction, and they hold as true for Beatrix Potter as they do for Dostoevsky.

But the idea that writing for children isn't the same as writing for adults is prevalent indeed, and usually goes along with the conviction that it isn't quite as good. If you're a good enough writer for adults, the implication is, of course, you don't write for children. You write for children only when you can't make it in the real world, because writing for children is easier.

Wrong, wrong, wrong!

I had written several regular trade novels before a publisher asked me to write about my Swiss boarding school experiences. Nobody had told me that you write differently when you write for children, so I didn't. I just wrote the best book I possibly could; it was called *And Both Were Young*. After that I wrote *Camilla*, which has been reissued as a young adult novel, and then *Meet the Austins*. It's hard today for me to understand that this simple little book had a very hard time finding a publisher because it's about a death and how an ordinary family reacts to that death. Death at that time was taboo. Children weren't supposed to know about it. I had a couple of offers of publication if I'd take the death out. But the reaction of the family—children as well as the parents—to the death was the core of the book.

Nowadays what we offer children makes *Meet the Austins* seem pale, and on the whole, I think that's just as well, because children know a lot more than most grown-ups give them credit for. *Meet the Austins* came out of my own family's experience with several deaths. To have tried to hide those deaths from our children would have been blind stupidity. All hiding does is confuse children and add to their fears. It is not subject matter that should be taboo, but the way it is handled.

A number of years ago—the first year I was actually making reasonable money from my writing—my sister-in-law was visiting us, and when my husband told her how much I had earned that year, she was impressed and commented, "And to think most people would have had to work so hard for that!"

Well, it is work, it's most certainly work; wonderful work, but work. Revision, revision, revision. Long hours spent not only in the actual writing, but in research. I think the best thing I learned in college was how to do research, so that I could go right on studying after I had graduated.

Of course, it is not *only* work; it is work that makes the incomprehensible comprehensible. Leonard Bernstein says that for him music is cosmos in chaos. That is true for writing a story, too. Aristotle says that what is plausible and impossible is better than what is possible and implausible.

That means that story must be *true*, not necessarily *factual*, but true. This is not easy for a lot of people to understand. When I was a school child, one of my teachers accused me of telling a story. She was not complimenting me on my fertile imagination; she was accusing me of telling a lie.

Facts are fine; we need facts. But story takes us to a world that is beyond facts, out on the other side of facts. And there is considerable fear of this world.

The writer Keith Miller told me of a young woman who was determined that her three preschool children were going to grow up in the real world. She was not, she vowed, going to sully their minds with myth, fantasy, fairy tales. They were going to know the truth—and for truth, read fact—and the truth would make them free.

One Saturday, after a week of rain and sniffles, the sun came out, so she piled the children into her little red VW bug and took them to the Animal Farm. The parking lot was crowded, but a VW bug is small, and she managed to find a place for it. She and the children had a wonderful day, petting the animals, going on rides, enjoying the sunshine. Suddenly, she looked at her watch and found it was far later than she realized. She and the children ran to where the VW bug was parked, and to their horror, found the whole front end was bashed in.

Outraged, she took herself off to the ranger's office. As he saw her approach, he laughed and said, "I'll bet you're the lady with the red VW bug."

"It isn't funny," she snapped.

"Now, calm down, lady, and let me tell you what happened. You know the elephant your children had such fun riding? She's a circus-trained elephant, and she was trained to sit on a red bucket. When she saw your car, she just did what she was trained to do and sat on it. Your engine's in the back, so you can drive it home without any trouble. And don't worry. Our insurance will take care of it. Just go on home, and we'll get back to you on Monday."

Slightly mollified, she and the kids got into the car and took off. But she was later than ever, so when she saw what looked like a very minor accident on the road, she didn't stop, but drove on.

Shortly, the flashing light and the siren came along, and she was pulled over. "Lady, don't you know that in this state it's a crime to leave the scene of an accident?" the trooper asked.

"But I wasn't in an accident," she protested.

"I suppose your car came that way," she said, pointing to the bashed-in front.

"No. An elephant sat on it."

"Lady, would you mind blowing into this little balloon?"

That taught her that facts alone are not enough; that facts, indeed, do not make up the whole truth. After that she read fairy tales to her children and encouraged them in their games of Make Believe and Let's Pretend.

I learned very early that if I wanted to find out the truth, to find out why people did terrible things to each other, or sometimes wonderful things—why there was war, why children are abused—I was more likely to find the truth in story than in the encyclopedia. Again and again I read *Emily of the New Moon,* by Lucy Maud Montgomery, because Emily's father was dying of diseased lungs, and so was mine. Emily had a difficult time at school, and so did I. Emily wanted to be a writer, and so did I. Emily knew that there was more to the world that provable fact, and so did I. I read fairy tales, the myths of all nations, science fiction, the fantasies and family stories of E. Nesbit. I read Jules Verne and H. G. Wells. And I read my parents' books, particularly those with lots of conversation in them. What was not in my frame of reference went right over my head.

We tend to find what we look for. If we look for dirt, we'll find dirt, whether it's there or not. A very nice letter I received from a reader said that she found *A Ring of Endless Light* very helpful to her in coming to terms with the death of a friend, but that another friend had asked her how it was that I used dirty words. I wrote back saying that I was not going to reread my book looking for dirty words, but that as far as I could remember, the only word in the book that could possibly be construed as dirty was *zuggy,* which I'd made up to avoid using dirty words. And wasn't looking for dirty words an ugly way to read a book?

One of my favorite books is Frances Hodgson Burnett's *The Secret Garden.* I read it one rainy weekend to a group of little girls, and a generation later to my granddaughters up in an old brass bed in the attic. Mary Lennox is a self-centered, spoiled-rotten little heroine, and I think we all recognize at least a little of ourselves in her. The secret garden is as much the garden of Mary's heart as it is the physical walled garden. By the end of the book, warmth and love and concern for others have come to Mary's heart, when Colin, the sick boy, is able to walk and run again. And Dickon, the gardener's boy, looks at the beauty of the restored garden and says, "It's magic!" But "magic" is one of the key words that has become taboo to today's self-appointed censors, so, with complete disregard of content, they would add *The Secret Garden* to the pyre. I shudder. This attitude is extreme. It is also dangerous.

It comes down to the old question of separate standards, separate for adults and children. The only standard to be used in judging a children's book is: *Is it a good book?* Is it good enough for me? Because if a children's book is not good enough for all of us, it is not good enough for children.

479

96

WRITING FOR TODAY'S YOUNG ADULTS

BY MAUREEN CRANE WARTSKI

WHEN I TOLD A STUDENT THAT I had been writing for young adults for over twenty years, she commented, "I'll bet you've seen a lot of change in that time."

Yes, and no. *Plus ça change. . . .* really. Adolescence has always been a tumultuous voyage, full of soaring mountains, valleys of incredible beauty, and seemingly impassable rivers full of crocodiles. To take the metaphor one step farther, though the journey remains the same, the landscape changes as the years go by.

Writing for today's young adults is admittedly a challenge. Issues that would have been unthinkable or at least controversial even in the early 80s—AIDS, condom distribution in school, homosexuality, sexual harassment, and children carrying guns—are openly discussed. Scientific progress has made miracles commonplace: The Hubble telescope illuminates the darkness of space, and the information superhighway is but a phone call away. Television brings an almost surreal immediacy to wars and disasters that happen hundreds or thousands of miles away. DNA, genetic engineering, and incredible medical advances lead us to the brink of the twenty-first century.

Keeping abreast of this brave—and often frightening—new world certainly requires work, but creating plots for today's young adult readers is not as daunting as it appears. For, although this readership demands books that reflect modern problems and some of the dangers and risks have changed, the qualities necessary to deal with them—altruism, moral courage, self-knowledge, and simply love—remain the same. Human nature is a constant. Emotions remain the common denominator of every person. Honesty, joy, loneliness, despair, humor, and pain are the bedrock of all human experience.

This being the case, I find it helpful when plotting fiction for today's teenagers to keep in mind what I call the four Cs—*Character, Conflict,*

Climax, and *Conclusion.* The first C is the most important, for to my mind fiction stands or falls by its protagonists. But, though the young adults we write about in the 90s are bright and well informed, and may appear confident and unfazed by situations that might have stymied their predecessors in the 80s, they are not as secure as they seem as they confront today's awesome problems.

Conflicts are everywhere. Whether an inner-city dweller or a youth living in the suburbs, today's child is sure to be faced by a host of difficulties that all too often begin at home. The traditional family is no longer a given, and divorced parents, single parents, warring parents, and abusive parents proliferate.

And then, there is the outside world to worry about. Consider that a single recent issue of the local newspaper carried news stories about a teenager whose school lockers were sprayed with hate slogans (racism, hatred); about young refugees from Bosnia arriving in New England (war and the terrible echoes of genocide); and an account of a sniper opening fire at an elementary school. Family crises, war, crime, drugs, AIDS, prejudice, and sexual harassment are only a few of the ills that can beset modern youngsters.

For my novels, I have drawn freely from real-life situations. In the first chapter of *My Name Is Nobody,* for example, Rob stands on the edge of a building while a crowd beneath him chants, "Jump, why don't you jump?" This incredibly cruel scene was taken almost verbatim from a newspaper article. In *Dark Silence,* Randy Wilmot realizes that her new neighbor, Delia, is being abused by her father—a frighteningly familiar scenario. In *A Boat to Nowhere* and *A Long Way from Home,* young Vietnamese confront the racism, war, and death that are plaguing us here and abroad. In *Belonging,* Jenny Dowling witnesses a death brought on at least partially by substance abuse, and she must choose whether or not to tell the truth or lie to protect her friends.

There are, of course, less dramatic conflicts, especially in shorter fiction. In my short story, "A Daughter Of the Sea," a Vietnamese girl deals with both subtle and overt prejudice at school. In one of my *Boys' Life* stories, "Where Eagles Fly," a college-bound boy is excited but also frightened at the prospect of leaving home. And in "The Silent Storm," another *Boys' Life* story, a young mountain climber wonders if he wants a hearing-impaired youth as a partner during a difficult climb.

Decisions are what it is all about, and the third "C" in the plotting chain, the climax, is the logical result of the characters' actions, which have also changed.

In many of my mysteries, I have brought the protagonists face to face with considerable difficulty. Jenny, in *Belonging,* keeps her guilty silence until one of her friends attempts suicide. Now, Jenny knows, she *must* act. Horrified at the extent of Delia's injuries, Randy in *Dark Silence* must decide whether or not she can trust her despised stepmother. In *A Boat to Nowhere,* Kien has to choose whether or not to abandon his newfound friends and be saved, or stay with them and perish. Rob, in *My Name Is Nobody,* tries to escape ridicule and his own despair by sailing a boat into a stormy sea. Then his friend and mentor, Kurt Doyle, comes after him, suffers a heart attack and falls into the raging sea. Can you feel the tension in the seemingly insurmountable danger?

In creating our characters we equip them with tools to overcome danger. This is most important since young readers are today as eager for role models as their predecessors. Confronted by situations they cannot avoid, they often turn to fiction for non-judgmental, non-threatening guidance.

Humor is one of those necessary elements: The ability and the courage to laugh at themselves not only stands fictional characters in good stead, but also spices up action, provides relief from tension, and helps the reader lighten up as well. For instance, Jenny uses a slew of funny maxims to keep her emotional balance. She says, "Jenny Dowling's second rule of thumb goes—there's no use crying when the ice cream cone falls in the dirt."

Then there is accountability. Admittedly scarce in today's society, it is a quality I am careful to build into my protagonists. Thus, confronted with a situation in which she must either face ostracism from her peers or lose her own self-respect, Jenny does not whine or blame others, but faces the music. Likewise, Randy enlists her stepmother's aid; Kien, the heretofore selfish street child, decides that he would rather die with the people he has come to love; Rob grows past pain and despair in order to save his mentor. You see, if your fictional characters are surely and strongly crafted, they will confront their problems head on, and possibly battered but unbowed, reach the conclusion.

Two warnings about the last C: conclusion. You should never use a conclusion to preach or editorialize. It should give closure to your novel or story. This does not mean that you should go on and on; in fact, one of my most satisfactory conclusions used only four words at the end of an action-filled, do-or-die escape scene in *The Lake Is on Fire.* Nor should writers "pretty up" endings so that everybody lives happily ever after. Life is not like that, and *deus ex machina* seldom works in fiction. No, a conclusion simply means that a logical point has been reached in the narrative and that the protagonist is signing off. If your story is good enough, your characters' adventures will continue in the readers' minds, and you may even get letters requesting a sequel, sometimes with advice on how to write it. Young adults are very definite about suggestions, which is one reason I value workshops and classroom visits where I can note changes in the dress, attitudes, concerns, and hear the vocabulary of my readers. I also get their reactions, which are helpful to me in writing future books.

"Your book was really good, but it was boring in the beginning," one student stated firmly, making me resolve to pace my opening chapters more carefully. Another assured me that I'd done a good job in *My Brother Is Special.* "It gave me a better understanding and feeling for retarded people."

Young adults are straightforward and often blunt, but I trust their instincts. When I was writing *Belonging,* one of my (adult) friends questioned my decision to have fifteen-year-old Jenny betray her peer group. It was, my friend pointed out, something that teenagers would *never* do, and if Jenny were to rat, she could never, never be forgiven.

Shaken, I put the question to the participants in one of my high school writing workshops. "Sure she should tell. Definitely," one young person exclaimed. "Yes, she should," another added thoughtfully, "but it isn't going to be easy."

A young adult's voyage toward self-discovery is never easy, and a writer who chooses to chronicle this journey will undoubtedly find pitfalls and difficulties. But there will also be vistas of surprising beauty, events along the way that astonish and delight.

It is an experience that I, for one, would not want to miss.

97

NEWS THAT'S FIT FOR FICTION

BY EVE BUNTING

RECENTLY, A PROMOTIONAL POSTER for several of my books, designed to look like the front page of a newspaper, carried this headline:

EXTRA, EXTRA, READ ALL ABOUT IT!
ALL THE FICTION THAT'S FIT TO PRINT

The format was no accident. The editors had already commented on how often the stories I write come straight from newspaper headlines. . . . well, not straight exactly, but by a fairly direct route. My theory, unconsciously known to me but never actually stated, is that if a story is dramatic enough, heartbreaking, poignant, or funny enough to be considered by newspaper editors and published for millions of people to read, it's a good story.

In my case, I read the newspapers that come to our home rather superficially. But when an article or essay catches my attention, it gets my full attention. Never have I said at this point, "I will write a book about this." What I have said is "Wow! What an interesting story." Sometimes I clip the piece, sometimes I don't. When I don't I'm often sorry and find myself, days or weeks later, trying to track it down on microfilm in my library, unsure of the date when I read it, unsure *where* I read it. I'm tracking down the story because I can't forget it. And that is the key. If I can't forget it, that story has touched me in some deep, heartfelt way. At that point I say: "I want to write about it."

Before I begin, though, there are four questions to consider—the first I've already answered:

(1) Does the story deeply affect me?

(2) Will it also affect young readers, or does it simply touch on my personal interests and concerns?

484

(3) Can I write it so I have a young person as the protagonist, or is it altogether too adult?

(4) Can I see in this an underlying truth that will unfold as the story unfolds? If not it has only surface value and I don't want to do it.

If all of these questions can be answered in the affirmative I am ready to go on to the "thinking through" process, which to my mind is the most valuable time I spend on any book. I will not know it all when I start. That "miserable middle" will still be shadowy. But I will have a strong skeleton, and the theme or unstated message will be fixed in my mind along with a forceful and unflinching ending that I can work toward.

I was sitting one morning at my breakfast table reading my paper. There was a brief paragraph about two young boys who had been walking home from a party the night before. They walked single file along a road where there was no sidewalk. A car came behind them, on the wrong side of the highway, driving at high speed. It hit and killed one boy. The other jumped to safety. "That was the all of it," as we say in Ireland.

But not for me.

The story took hold of my mind and my heart. I imagined the scene . . . the dark road, the shriek of brakes, the car driving on, the boy who had jumped walking unsteadily to where his friend lay motionless on the road, calling his name, knowing he was dead.

I asked myself the four salient questions and was able to answer "yes" to all of them. When I'd thought it through, I had the outline of a plot that told of a quest to find the driver of the killing car, a story of guilt, of revenge, and the maturing of a boy who realizes that things and people are not always what they seem and that revenge can never truly erase sorrow.

Here is the opening paragraph of A Sudden Silence, the scene that I visualized so clearly when I first read that sad article in my morning paper.

It was Saturday the 20th of June at 11:30 pm when my brother, Bry, was killed. I'll never forget that date, not if I live to be an old, old man. Coast Highway, shadowed between its tall pole lights, the car suddenly behind Bry and me as we walked single file in the thick grass at the highway's edge. The

485

glare of its white beams; the roar as it passed me where I'd dived sideways, belly down; the thud as it hit him. I'll never forget it.

Naturally, I did not use the boys' real names or the real setting. But the story began with a real happening in the way that so many of my stories do.

One Sunday, I opened the "View" section of my *Los Angeles Times* and saw a group of bizarre pictures. Life-sized wooden dolls, wide-eyed, staring, stood in the front yard of a small, wooden house. There was a photograph of an elderly couple and a close-up of one of the dolls. The accompanying story told of how the couple had always wanted children but had not been able to have them. The husband, a wood carver, made these dolls for his wife, and they became her children. She found or made clothes for them, she gave them names and talked to them. They "talked" back. I stared at the doll. He stared at me. I was mesmerized, hooked. One of the dolls was on view in an art gallery on La Cienega Boulevard in Los Angeles. I visited it. Oh my! The hook was definitely in place.

Could I give these elderly people a real child who would tell my story? Of course. He could be a nephew who is orphaned and comes to live with his mysterious relatives and their even more mysterious children. I called him Matt and gave him a little sister, someone to protect from ghostly or insane happenings. Would young readers be as entranced by the spookiness of this kind of story as I? I'd bet on it. And what would Matt learn? I saw that clearly from the beginning. Aunt Gerda, who is at first to be feared because she is "not like anyone else," is found to be kind, loving and compassionate to the two orphaned children. Is love stronger than fear? In my stories, yes. In life, too.

"Are the ghost children really real?" children ask in their letters.

"If you think they are," I answer.

It's impossible to give a definitive yes or no. Because the author isn't too sure herself, and it's that kind of uncertainty that makes writing fun! And writing *The Ghost Children* was definitely fun.

Sharing Susan was probably taken more directly from a newspaper article than any other book I wrote. Who didn't read about the little girl, accidentally changed with another baby at birth, everyone unsuspecting until one of the girls died. Then the wrenching, heartbreaking complications arose. Should a child be taken from the only parents she has known for thirteen years and sent to strangers who will be her mother and father from now on? The dramatic, misery-making possibilities tore at my imagination.

The writing of *Sharing Susan* presented difficulties. When I write, I usually try to "get rid of the parents" early in the story. That way I am not tempted to have a passive character as my protagonist. I can create one who is independent, who makes decisions on her own, and who can solve her problems without adult help. (Other than her early training, of course, which taught her to be courageous, honest, self-reliant and to ask for help only when it involves her own safety or the safety of others.) I try to send the parents off on a vacation or business trip in Chapter 1 or 2. Or I can have my protagonist go stay with a relative, or go to camp, or keep him or her in school most of the time. Often a mother or father may be out of the picture entirely, and I have a one-parent family that reflects today's society.

In *Sharing Susan,* I had two sets of parents, and many of the decisions being made were *about* Susan, not *by* her. I was forced to have a lot of introspection, slow stuff for young readers. One of my challenges was to keep the plot moving. Strong characterization helped enormously. I had two very different sets of parents with different lifestyles: four complex individuals. My inclination here was to portray one set of parents as mean, demanding, unyielding. That way I could have lots of confrontation and add to Susan's anguish in leaving her familiar home. But I wanted to avoid that trap, which is certainly a cliché and is also scary. A child in such a situation must go where she is sent. What if something like this happened to me, a young reader might ask. Horrifying enough without any additional terror. The book and the idea did spike a lot of imaginations, though, and I must say that most of those who wrote letters to me seemed less than horrified!

Dear Eve:
I've always suspected these weren't my real parents. I am *so different.* Please tell me how I can find out if *I* was changed at birth.
Your friend. . . .
P.S. Up until now I thought I was adopted or left on their doorstep, but they say no. This seems more likely.

Because I know about children's imaginations, I did try to show how extremely rare such an occurrence would be, and I was careful to portray the adults as wise and caring, making the best of a tragic situation and acting in Susan's best interests—at least the way I hope they would be.

In the book, as in real life, I think, Susan is at first prepared to hate her new, upstart mom and dad. She is totally disinterested in the fact that she will have a brother. She enlists her relatives to help her stay where she thinks she belongs, and when that doesn't work she makes her own plans. She'll be so hateful, so ill-mannered, so rotten to that new little brother that these impostor parents will want to send her back. Susan's efforts gave me an opportunity to have Susan "do" instead of being "done to."

In the resolution, Susan understands that she will always be part of both sets of parents, that it is O.K. to love the new ones, too, and that in no way is it disloyal to the mother and father who have cared for her since they brought her home from the hospital, their wonderful, brand-new little girl. She understands that the more love you give, the more you have left to give. And so, happily, Susan is shared.

"But this really happened. Can't you be sued?" I'm asked.

No, it didn't really happen.

I took reality as a jumping-off place, a springboard to my story. My book has different people, acting out in different ways. I am careful never to use the same characteristics, physical, or as far as I know, psychological, of the original players. For instance, in the newspaper article that sparked *Sharing Susan,* the child's biological parents had six or seven other children. In *Sharing Susan,* they had only one. I knew no follow-up to the "real" story until much later, when my book was completed. This was the reality for me. This was what happened. It was Susan's ordeal, and mine. No one else's.

So, read voraciously and clip like a fiend.

Get excited.

Pause.

Question.

Think.

Write.

Take all that fiction that's fit to print—and make it your own.

98

WRITING MULTICULTURAL BOOKS FOR CHILDREN

BY KAREN MCWILLIAMS

LONG BEFORE EUROPEANS, LATIN AMERICANS, and Asians immigrated to this country, the United States was "multicultural." Hundreds of Native-American tribes with unique languages, religions, and customs lived throughout the Americas. Today, with the continuing arrival of immigrants from around the world, most schools have many students from a variety of cultures. Teachers, librarians, and parents, therefore, are demanding more multicultural children's books, so that their pupils can better understand each other as well as learn about and have pride in their own culture. Many publishers are now actively seeking multicultural material in order to meet this growing demand.

All of the mainstream editors I queried stated that 10–20% of their titles are multicultural, and that they would publish more if well-written manuscripts were submitted to them. Furthermore, small presses specializing in multicultural and bilingual books have sprung up within the last decade. Some bilingual publishers publish simultaneously in English and another language, most often Spanish, while others publish bilingually within the book. Some presses specifically look for books about a particular culture that are written by an author belonging to that culture, but most will consider *any* well-written, well-researched manuscript.

Most children's books are classified as preschool and picture books, for kindergarten through third grade; first chapter books for beginning readers; middle-grade novels for more advanced readers; and young-adult novels for preteens through teenagers. But whatever age level you write for, you must make your plot exciting and your characters compelling. And your book should show what the particular culture you are writing about has in common with other cultures, as well as what makes it unique.

Perhaps you wonder how a non-Chinese, for example, can write a convincing middle-grade novel about a Chinese-American family. To do this successfully, you must never write off the top of your head. If you have never lived in China, Taiwan, or Hong Kong, or had Chinese friends, you will have to do extensive research in libraries, archives, and museums. In addition to consulting encyclopedias, books, and watching videos, look in *The Readers' Guide to Periodical Literature* to find the most recent magazine articles about China, especially about Chinese who have relocated to the United States.

Visit the children's section of your library for fiction and nonfiction on China, and other multicultural books written at the grade level in which you are interested. Also, try to locate Chinese or Chinese-Americans living in your region, and talk to people who have lived or traveled in China. You can even visit Chinese restaurants in your area to steep yourself in the culture. Remember, it is better to overdo your research, later omitting most of it from the final version of the manuscript.

The picture book, *I Hate English,* by Ellen Levine, is a perfect example of what it is like to be a foreign child adjusting to life in the United States. Mei Mei had been a good student in her school in Hong Kong, but when her family moved to New York she couldn't understand her teacher or classmates. She hated New York, and she hated English, as revealed in the following excerpt from the book:

> Such a lonely language. Each letter stands alone and makes its own noise. Not like Chinese. Sometimes English letters fight each other. "We will go on a class TRIP," the teacher said in English. T-R-I-P, thought Mei Mei. The letters "T" and "R" bang against each other, and each keeps its own sound. Not like Chinese.

Little by little, Mei Mei understands more English but refuses to speak it. Then her cousin takes her to a Chinatown tutoring center where an American teacher coaxes her—with some difficulty—into speaking English. Once Mei Mei starts to speak English, she becomes a chatterbox in both English and Chinese.

When you have finished your research, how do you make your writing convey the real essence of a Chinese family living in the United

States? Study the many ways in which foreign cultures are presented in multicultural books: Picture books are often written in correct English, and the only way the reader knows the book is multicultural is from the illlustrations. In other cases, writers may occasionally use words and phrases from a particular culture as well as word reversals, such as switching the order of the subject and verb, to give the feeling of a foreigner speaking English.

In the fictional biography, *Ahyoka and the Talking Leaves,* by Peter and Connie Roop, Sequoia, a Cherokee father, and his daughter invent a written language for their tribe. They use words from the Cherokee language as well as description reflecting the Cherokee love of nature:

He must be drawing *agaliha,* sunshine, Ahyoka thought. A difficult word-picture, almost as difficult as anger.

and

Books are as rare around here as wings on bears.

The authors did their research at the Cherokee National Museum, Tsa-La-Gi Ancient Village, the University of Oklahoma, and Sequoia's Home, operated by the Oklahoma Historical Society.

Since middle-grade and young-adult novels are much longer than picture books, they usually include more dialogue and detailed description. In Gary Paulsen's young-adult Newbery Honor Book, *Dogsong,* it is obvious from the following description that the author has either lived on the frozen tundra, where his young Eskimo protagonist lives, or has done extensive research:

On the wall were sealskin mukluks. He took them down and felt inside. The grass bottoms were still good and he pulled them on, tied them up around his calves over the bearskin. Then came the squirrelskin inner parka with the hair out soft and fine, like leather silk . . .

In the young-adult Newbery Honor Book, *The Moves Make the Man,* Bruce Brooks uses dialogue that gives a *sense* of how a poor inner-city African-American boy would speak and think:

I took right to the idea of French class, and I took right to the lingo itself too. The teacher was this white woman named Madame Dupont, but she wasn't French though it was a French name. After three days, which we learned how

491

to pronounce a few basic things and the pronouns and the rules for verbs, after that we were allowed only to speak French in class! Anybody talking in English, they got themselves ignored. Right there in a school and you could not talk English! Man, that room was something special to me, a little world by itself. . . . I never realized before then how much my way of talking was what made me who I thought and other people thought I was.

The mannerisms, vocabulary, and fashions of each new generation differ from earlier ones, so it is important to research and become familiar with the age group for which you're writing. If you don't have contact with middle school or high school students, volunteer at a school or chaperone a youth group to observe them in action. Also, watch television programs popular with teenagers. When writing your book, be careful not to use words unfamiliar or not in common use in other parts of the country or fad words that may soon be out of date. And remember, it is important for you to give your dialogue a *sense of dialect* or the vernacular, but never write exactly the way young people speak or your novel will be unreadable.

Finally, publishers usually require complete manuscripts for picture books and novels, but will accept (and in many cases demand) proposals for nonfiction. If you are not Hispanic but have written a Hispanic novel, include a cover letter stating your qualifications—majoring in Latin American studies in college or experience working with migrant farm workers with Hispanic backgrounds. Include a resumé of your background that is relevant to writing multicultural books for children, and a list of your most recent book or magazine publishing credits, if any, noting the names of the publishers, dates of publication, grade level for which they were intended, number of pages, color photos, number of copies sold, and tearsheets of any reviews. Also, list your multicultural volunteer work or relevant teaching experience.

NOTE: Before submitting your manuscript to a publisher, you may want to consider sending it to The Center for Multicultural Children's Literature, sponsored by HarperCollins and Scott Foresman. First, request an application to submit with your story. A committee of experienced authors and illustrators will then review it, and if the committee feels your story has potential, a mentor will be assigned to you

492

according to the culture, age, level, style, and genre of your manuscript. The CMCL has high standards, too, and cannot accept every submission for review. For an application, write to: The Center for Multicultural Children's Literature, HarperCollins Children's Books, 10 East 53rd Street, New York, NY 10022.

§ 99

WRITING THE JUVENILE SHORT STORY

BY GLORIA D. MIKLOWITZ

"Now stop that, Blackie," Rufus ordered, crouching before the dog. He wished Blackie would stop straining against the leash holding him to the hydrant. He wished he didn't have to leave him like this. Every time he came to visit Steve at the hospital he felt the same way.

"Down, Blackie, down!" Rufus tried to sound mean. Then he rose and turned his back to the dog. If he didn't hurry, he'd miss visiting hours, and he hadn't seen Steve in two days. Each visit was harder than the last. Ever since the motorcycle accident when Steve lost his arm, it had gotten worse. Rufus would come into the ward and see his friend Steve turned to the wall, closed up, wan. He'd tell him about school, about Karen, about his family. But Steve would only say, "Go away. Leave me alone."

"He just doesn't have the will to live," one of the doctors said. A big lump formed in Rufus's throat. What could he say today to make Steve care again? What could he give him or do that would bring the old spark back?

THERE'S THE OPENING FOR A PURPOSE ACHIEVED plotted story. Rufus's purpose is shown quickly. He loves his friend, but Steve has lost interest in life. The story question becomes: How can Rufus help his friend want to live?

By the end of 2,000 carefully chosen words, about eight double-spaced typed pages, Rufus will have achieved his purpose. He will have done so after making several efforts that fail, always through action. Finally, he will succeed through *ingenuity, courage,* or some *special ability.*

Most short stories and all novels have a shape, a skeletal form, a *plot.* One of the most often used is PURPOSE ACHIEVED.

In my book *After the Bomb* (Scholastic), Philip's purpose is to save his mother, who was badly burned after a nuclear bomb destroyed Los Angeles. Throughout the book, Philip tries, fails, tries again, sometimes making progress toward his goal but often losing ground. Through his persistence and courage, he succeeds in getting his mother to a burn center—a classic PURPOSE ACHIEVED plotline.

Another plot type is MISUNDERSTANDING, DISCOVERY, AND REVER-

SAL, in which the hero misunderstands something important—that personal integrity is more important than belonging to a group, for example. Through two-thirds of the story, he acts on this misguided premise, then (through an action scene) discovers he's wrong and reverses his behavior. In a final scene, the hero shows his change of belief, again through action.

No story succeeds, no matter how well worked out the plot, without several other elements, the most important of which are the CHARACTERS. The hero or heroine must be someone the reader likes and cares about. To develop flesh-and-blood people, you need to know a lot about them before you start: age, appearance, attitudes, family, hobbies, likes and dislikes; how they think and feel about themselves and others; what they want from life; what they fear, dislike in themselves and others. In short, you want to create characters like people, like you and your readers. Write a page or two about each character and put it aside. Later, it will help you write more convincingly.

Who is your *antagonist?* In a short story there's room for only one. The antagonist is the person (usually) who tries to prevent the hero from getting what he wants or tries to make the hero do what is wrong. This "villain" supplies much of the opportunity to develop conflict. He needn't be all bad. Even in real life villains often have redeeming features, loving their children, perhaps, or being kind to animals.

An antagonist need not be a person. Imagine a boy who is afraid of heights but must overcome that fear to save a friend. Scaling the height becomes the antagonist. Man against himself or against nature has provided the material for many a story.

When considering the characters in your story, remember: Each must have a reason for being there, or out he goes!

SETTING: Life doesn't happen in a vacuum. A story takes place *somewhere*—in a specific place. Visualize a stage as you begin a scene. What's on it? A couch? Pictures on the wall? An exercise bike? Bring your characters into this setting and *show* through their action, dialogue and inner thoughts what their problems are and how they are dealing with them.

VIEWPOINT: In most short stories, there's a single viewpoint character: your protagonist. He or she will tell the story, but how? In first person ("Now stop that, Blackie," *I* ordered.) or third person personal ("Now stop that, Blackie," *Rufus* ordered.")? In either case, everything

495

must be seen or heard and reacted to by the viewpoint character. No action can take place without the viewpoint person being there to observe it or take part in it. For example, in first- or third-person personal viewpoint, you can't write a scene in which several friends are talking about the hero *unless* the hero is able to hear what's happening.

In juvenile short stories and novels, the main character must solve the problem himself. Wise advice from a parent or friend may be heard but not heeded. The hero must decide on his own what's best for him.

With plot, character, setting, and viewpoint worked out, what next?

Start assembling scenes that will *show* the problem and how the hero is trying to solve it. Each scene must do at least one of three things, preferably two, and even better all three: 1) move the story forward through dialogue, inner thought, and/or action; 2) show us how the character *feels;* 3) give information.

Look at the first paragraphs of the Rufus story. Rufus reprimands his dog, but he does it kindly, so we like him.

The narrative (non-dialogue) gives Rufus's inner thoughts, which provide the reader with information and feelings. (We learn that he visits Steve often and is becoming discouraged.) The narrative moves the story forward to the hospital, where the next scene will take place. By the end of the third paragraph, the story question and plot type are clearly defined. The story question becomes: What can Rufus do to make Steve want to live? The plot type is PURPOSE ACHIEVED. The setting is the hospital, and viewpoint is third person.

By the end of the third paragraph, the reader knows Rufus will attempt all the things he considers. And he does. The rest of the story develops his efforts: He reasons with his friend. It does no good, so he accuses him of cowardice in an effort to shock him out of his lethargy. Failing that, he spends his hard-earned money on a gift, but Steve responds with anger. This is the dark moment. Rufus leaves the hospital certain he can't achieve his purpose. On the way out, he meets Steve's doctor, who remarks that Steve needs a reason to go on, "someone to love, something worth getting on his feet for, something that will make him forget the loss of his hand."

Now Rufus knows what to do. Have you guessed what he'll give Steve? Right. Blackie, the dog he loves almost as much as he loves his friend. In the final scene, he drops Blackie on Steve's bed and tells him the dog is now his. Steve protests, and Rufus turns away. When

Blackie licks Steve's cheek, Steve reaches out with his good arm and pets the dog. The reader knows that everything will be O.K. now.

When the rough draft of your story is done, it's time to look at it with the cold eye of an editor. Maybe you wrote it in one sitting in a white heat. Put it aside for a few days, then read it as if you had never seen it before. Does each scene do what it should? Is each character needed and well defined? Have you gone into too much detail on setting or inner thought? Can you use one word where you've used three?

Is the THEME—the moral statement your story makes, the wisdom you wish to impart—clear? Each story should have a theme buried within it. In *After the Bomb,* the theme is, "never give up"; in the Rufus story, "love is the best gift."

Writing a short story—considering everything that must be part of it—may seem contrived and even confining, but it need not be. Every good story incorporates plot, character, setting, viewpoint, and theme. While some writers instinctively know how to use these elements, most of us need to be reminded.

Master these elements, and you'll write a better short story. Master them and writing the *novel* will even be more manageable.

Short Story Checklist

1. Does your story have a plot type? Is it PURPOSE ACHIEVED (through ingenuity, courage or a special ability?) or MISUNDERSTANDING, DISCOVERY, AND REVERSAL?

2. What is the story question, in one sentence?

3. What is your theme, the moral statement you want to make? Is it developed through the story's action?

4. Have you shown the story problem within the first page? Is there action in those first paragraphs?

5. Do you have conflict through an antagonist, nature, or the main character's personal flaw?

6. Does the hero solve his own problem?

7. Is the story told through one person's viewpoint?

8. Have you avoided solving problems through coincidence?

9. Does the story build through several scenes to a climax in which the hero seems to have lost the battle? Then, does the solution follow quickly?

10. Have you checked every word, sentence, paragraph to see if it belongs or can be improved?

100

RESEARCHING NONFICTION FOR YOUNG READERS

BY NORMAN H. FINKELSTEIN

IF YOUR NONFICTION FOR YOUNG PEOPLE reads like good fiction, you've got a lot going for you. But no matter how well you tell a tale, there is no substitute for factual, accurate and reliable research. Your readers deserve nothing less.

Don't be put off by stories of nonfiction writers who spend years traveling from one research site to the next to rummage through musty archives and records. You do not need to quit your day job to replicate the lifetime work of scholars.

The financial rewards you will reap as a writer of juvenile nonfiction can rarely support intensive academic research.

Remember, you are writing for young adults and not for doctoral candidates. That means you can generally rely on the basic research of others found in secondary sources for much of the information and data you will need. Still, your writing can succeed only if you make the complex scientific or historical research of others readable and understandable to young readers. Condescension is never permissible.

Where to start? You'll often find succinct overviews and up-to-date information in newspapers and general circulation magazines. I usually consult *The New York Times Index* first. Although it may seem cumbersome, it is also the quickest and most reliable way to locate specific information.

Once I make a list of relevant articles, their dates of publication and page numbers, I then turn to the library's *New York Times* microfilm collection (usually going back to the mid-nineteenth century) for the original full-text articles. Most libraries have reader-printers, so, at a small per-page cost, I can make copies of the relevant articles and take them home for more careful reading.

For magazine articles, there are indexes available in most public libraries; some even provide full text for selected articles. The tried-and-true *Readers' Guide to Periodical Literature* is still the classic key to articles in popular magazines. It is also available as *Wilsondisc* on CD-ROM, which provides abstracts for many articles. These summaries are useful tools in themselves to help narrow your search to the most appropriate articles. The newer *Magazine Index,* also on CD-ROM, provides full-text articles.

I also recommend skimming major books and scholarly journal articles on your topic. Become familiar with the scope of existing research. Soon, you will begin thinking of yourself as one of that field's leading experts. (Don't let that go to your head, however. After all, you are only a beginning expert!) Once you have achieved a general familiarity with the personalities, language, and nuances relevant to your topic, you can then get down to the gritty work of tracking down more specific information.

Writing eight nonfiction books for young readers has taught me a simple, common-sense approach to locating information. I follow a research trail that moves from the general to the specific, using one source to lead to another. My most important tool is a well-organized notetaking system. Use whatever method you wish. The important thing is to build a database of information sources. (Although I am a firmly committed computer user for my writing, I use 4×6 index cards for this stage, a separate card for each information source, print, nonprint or human.)

Where appropriate, I jot down the bibliographic data on books or articles I will need later for footnotes and/or bibliography. (Don't forget the call number and name of the library in which you found a specific book, in case you wish to return to it later.) For human resources, I write down addresses, phone numbers, and where I found the names mentioned. Tracking down information and sources is much like a detective game. One clue leads to another.

Here is my unpatented, common-sense, two-step research plan for tracking down sources:

First, visit the public library.

The preceding quick review of selected published material has already given you a general acquaintance with your topic. Now it's time to build on your basic knowledge by consulting other sources. Jot down a list of possible subjects and key words that describe your topic. A useful initial source I frequently use is a good encyclopedia index. To make sure your words coincide with those used by your library's catalogue, you might also consult the *Library of Congress Subject Headings* volumes (available in all public and university libraries). These headings are almost universally used by libraries. You can also get hints on headings you had not previously considered by checking the subject headings in the Cataloging in Publication (CIP) sections of the books you find. Most books published within the past decade display that information on the copyright page.

Today's newer computerized catalogues enable you to do versatile in-depth searches. Once you have compiled a list of possible books, go to the shelves and pull those that interest you. As you leaf through the books, pay particular attention to two important, yet usually overlooked sections where a good researcher can find lots of useful leads: the acknowledgment page and the notes/bibliography section.

Writers are usually a polite and friendly lot, and they like to thank everyone who helped them on their way to publication. On many acknowledgment pages you will find the names of scholars, librarians, or archivists who helped that writer. Also, footnotes may refer to sources you might not otherwise discover on your own. Bibliographies will guide you to yet other books and journal articles.

Pay particular attention to the mention of specific archives or libraries and the people who work there. That's how I found out about archives I previously didn't know existed, such as the MacArthur Archives in Norfolk, Virginia, and the American Library of Radio and Television at the Thousand Oaks, California Public Library. The result: rewarding research trips to invaluable depositories of memorabilia, documents, and photographs I would have otherwise overlooked.

Although, as I have mentioned earlier, my major research utilizes published secondary sources, I try to include some original research to highlight events or scenarios that my young readers may enjoy or find particularly relevant and to make my book unique.

Before you pawn the family silver and phone the airlines to book expensive reservations to exotic research sites, sit down, pour yourself a fresh cup of coffee, and write letters. I have always found the archivists and librarians I contact by mail to be more than willing to help locate data. Many times, basic research questions can be answered by telephone or letter.

If you have a computer and a modem, try to get an inexpensive Internet connection. (Local universities are the best source for an account, but you will probably need an affiliation. Commercial sources, such as Compuserve, are also available.) Then, from home you can search library catalogues and other databases throughout the world for relevant titles and even full text articles. You could use E-Mail to correspond with experts in your field who may also be on-line.

Don't forget your public library's reference room. There, you will find all sorts of directories and indexes to special museums, archives, libraries, and associations. Browse for additional specialized directories, such as the *Encyclopedia of Associations, The Research Center Directory,* or the *Directory of Special Libraries* to locate specific places with information on your topic. *The Official Museum Directory* may also be useful. For writers looking for historical sources, I recommend the *American History Sourcebook,* edited by Joel Makower. You may be surprised at the number of historical societies and special interest membership groups. There seems to be a society or library for nearly any topic you could possibly imagine.

By now you are thinking, "So many sources, so little time!" There is a wonderful one-volume reference book I often use to consolidate my searches. *The New York Public Library Book of How and Where to Look It Up* (Prentice-Hall, 1991) should be on every nonfiction writer's bookshelf. It includes a list of major reference books on many subjects as well as specific government and special collection sources. Addresses and telephone numbers make it easy for you to get in touch with credible sources.

Second, write letters—to everyone!

In spite of the rising cost of postage, the post office is a writer's most useful research tool. Use the names you've put on the index cards, and write letters to the experts who helped other writers, and to directors of the specific special interest libraries you've tracked down in the directories. Directories of addresses are available in the library or on-line through several data retrieval services. Most people you write to will be gracious and helpful. If they themselves cannot help you with your particular needs, they will often direct you to others who can.

Be professional and businesslike in your correspondence. Type or word process your letter. Use imprinted stationery. Identify your research topic, and introduce yourself. Don't ramble. Have you been previously published? What is your particular interest in the topic? When you write libraries or archives, ask about specific research policies. Would you be welcome to visit? Are there any restrictions on the use of materials? What about copying services? Does the library maintain a photo file that you could use? Are there charges for specific services? What permissions will you need to reproduce material in your book, and, if there are rights and permissions charges for quoting excerpts or reprinting photographs, what are they?

Whenever possible, address your query to a specific person. Provide enough information about your research topics and your credentials to establish your credibility. The more information you provide (as briefly as possible) the easier it is for the archivist or librarian to help you.

Creativity is a full-time job. I firmly believe that every writer worth a publishing contract needs to develop a lifelong affinity for the ancient art of browsing. I've never met a bookstore or library that I didn't like. I learn a lot from roaming through bookstacks and skimming a wide variety of newspapers and magazines, and even the Yellow Pages. I often stumble across unexpected facts and research sources.

Finally, when your book is published, don't forget to cite the sources *you* used, and remember to thank all those wonderful individuals who helped you research your subject. Then, someone else down the road will be able to rely on your experiences just as you were helped by writers who preceded you.

101

DISCOVERING STORIES FOR PICTURE BOOKS

BY BARBARA ABERCROMBIE

YOU ASK YOURSELF WHAT COULD BE SO HARD about writing a picture book? It ought to be easy: a short simple story for little kids . . . kind of an apprenticeship for writing adult fiction. So you write a short simple story you think children will like, but when you send it out to publishers it only generates rejection slips. You wonder if there's some sort of trick to discovering stories that will sell. A right way to do it, maybe a formula.

There isn't a trick, of course, or a formula, and if there's a right way to write picture books for children, it's simply being honest about your own feelings. *Your* feelings, not what you think children should or should not feel.

What were *your* secret fantasies when you were little? Did you want to fly? Did you wish you could talk to your cat, or vice versa? Did you want a larger family, or to be an only child? Were you ever confused about who you were and what was expected of you? Did you sometimes have the best intentions in the world but find your actions misinterpreted? Did you want to be bigger? Better? Braver? Did your parents ever embarrass you? Did you feel guilty about being embarrassed? Did you feel too tall, too short, too thin, too fat?

You may notice that things don't change all that much when we grow up. What we dreamed of, found joy in, hid from, or hoped to change as children often still concerns us as adults, and out of these concerns can come the best stories for picture books. It took me a long time to realize this. When I first attempted writing for children, I believed I could think and plan my way into a story. But instead, the idea for my first picture book, *Amanda & Heather & Company,* came to me as an image, a flash of memory: I remembered how it felt to be a little kid on an elevator and able to see only adult knees.

I can't tell you how or why this image popped into my head. But I can tell you that by paying attention to the feeling it gave me, of being very small and not understanding adults and their strange rituals, a story evolved about two little girls puzzled by the strange ways grown-ups enjoy themselves at a party. There's nothing about elevators in the story, but there is an illustration (by Mimi Boswell) showing Heather, very small, looking up at a sea of adult knees.

From writing my first picture book, I learned this lesson: Pay attention to your feelings, respect them, and recognize the paradox of thinking that your emotions are unique, yet at the same time *universal*.

One way to get direction into how you felt in the past is through sense memories—concentrating on whatever you absorbed through your five senses during a specific experience. Try it with the following list (you might want to make up your own list later). After each image, shut your eyes for a few moments, relax, and imagine seeing, smelling, tasting, touching, or hearing whatever the image suggests. Choose a specific period in your childhood and pay attention to the feelings that surface with the memory.
Imagine:

* the smell of your classroom the first day of school
* trying on a brand-new pair of shoes
* listening to the sounds of a summer night after you've gone to bed
* eating hot cereal in your kitchen on a cold winter morning
* holding a kitten and running your fingers through its fur
* walking barefoot through grass
* the sound of your parents' voices when they're angry
* opening a present you've longed for (or not getting a present you've longed for)
* your bedroom: what your bed looks like, the things you collect, your favorite toys, the view from the window
* playing a game with your best friend: the sounds, surroundings, feel of the ball or cards or whatever the game is played with

Notice also from this exercise how few words it takes to evoke feelings and memories.

In a picture book as in a poem, each word counts and echoes. In fact, I think a picture book is closer to a poem than to any other form of writing. The story needs to be compressed, yet at the same time each line requires weight and concentration. Dr. Seuss (Theodor Geisel) spoke of "boiling the thing down to the essentials." Simplicity and specific images (including metaphors) are essential. And your story must entertain as well. The sounds and rhythm of the language are vital. Children like to hear a good picture book read over and over again (something rarely true of novels or other forms of written material), but won't want to listen if the story isn't fun.

To understand the power of a picture book, the range and depth and sheer fun it can offer a child, read Maurice Sendak's *Where the Wild Things Are.* Read it over and over, and you'll understand how and why a picture book can endure and resonate, as a poem can. Read *The Story of Ferdinand* by Munro Leaf, too. Written over fifty years ago, this children's classic about a gentle bull who just wants to sit quietly and smell the flowers is an example of what can be done with plot, character, language, humor, and meaning in less than three pages of text. Read and study picture books that were your favorites when you were a child, then read at least fifty examples of picture books that are being published today—not for formulas or rules, but for information and to see what is possible. The best way to learn how to write is to read what you want to write. (This sounds obvious, but I'm always amazed at how many people try to write for children without ever reading what's being published today.)

How do ideas for picture book stories come to you? All I really know for sure is that out of the writing itself comes the story. You take a flash of memory, a true-life incident, a dream, or an observation, and you start writing. You take a cat from your own life and give it to two children in your imagination. You remember what it feels like when a pet is missing. You try what-ifs. What if the father lives in the city with a new wife? What if the girls visit them every weekend? And then suddenly you realize how that situation would connect to the fact that the cat has two homes.

Sometimes inspiration for picture books can come from experiences we have as adults, and then the story itself grows from a blend of reality and imagination. Charlie, the cat in my picture book *Charlie Anderson,* was actually a cat my parents adopted and that, they later discovered, had a second family. I wrote his story through the eyes of two little girls, but only as I wrote did I discover that Sarah and Elizabeth also have two families—a mother in the country and a father and stepmother in the city. I didn't start out to write about children who have two homes because of a divorce; I followed Charlie's life and discovered a more meaningful story as I wrote.

Another source of inspiration for picture books can be an urge to rewrite history, a need to change a sad, factual ending to a happy or more satisfying one. Newspapers can be gold mines for stories you'd like to rewrite. A few years ago I read a letter to Dear Abby about a pet pig named Hamlet who thought he was a dog. His life came to a sad yet predictable end (his name a self-fulfilling prophecy) when his owner had to give him up because of complaints from her suburban neighbors. The grieving owner wrote to Abby to let the world know how good-hearted pigs are and what wonderful pets they make. I was moved by the letter and couldn't get it out of my mind. Finally, I began a story about a pig that would have a happy ending. I worked on it for a long time before I discovered what the story was really about. My pig, renamed Henry, wants to fit into the family that adopted him. He first tries to be a baby, then one of the cats, and then one of the dogs, but he never really belongs or feels appreciated. He can't find happiness because he's always trying to be something he isn't; he feels he's the wrong color, his fur or tail isn't right, or he's too fat. My happy ending has Henry living out the rest of his natural life in a petting zoo, where he's loved and admired for what he is—a magnificent friendly pink pig.

I wrote this story for myself, to make me feel better about the real-life pig who wanted to be a dog. Picture books aren't written for children *out there* in desperate need of being shown the right way to feel and think and live. The child we're really writing for is right inside us. We're writing for the children we were, and the adults we are now. We still want to hear stories that make us laugh at ourselves and the weirdness of the world; stories that tell us we're not the only ones who get into trouble or danger or feel crazy sometimes; stories that will comfort us in the dark.

507

102

To Be a "Storyteller"

By Zilpha Keatley Snyder

In the years since I began writing books for young people, I have occasionally been referred to by critics and even by friends as a "storyteller." Sometimes as a "natural" or even an "accomplished" storyteller. But even when such an appellation is obviously meant to be complimentary I have found that my reaction is slightly ambiguous.

For me, the sobriquet "storyteller" invokes some particularly poignant and powerful memories, memories of childhood habits and idiosyncrasies that in fact are, I believe, closely related to my present approach to writing fiction for young people. Therefore I thought it might be appropriate to begin a discussion of my writing techniques with a few words about how I happened to have earned, at a rather early age, the not always complimentary title of "storyteller."

As a child, growing up in a rather narrow and limited environment, I learned early on to entertain myself by "making stuff up." I made up games, wildly imaginative scenarios based on everything I had ever heard or read, but winging on past learned facts and data into the realms of sheer illusion. And I also told stories—and soon learned that telling stories can get you in trouble.

I got in trouble when, for instance, in the midst of giving oral book reports, I threw in some really exciting events that the original author might very well have included if he/she had happened to think of them. And I got in even more serious trouble when I succumbed, in the course of describing some interesting occurrence to my parents, to my chronic urge to make any story really worth telling. Even among young friends, who could be quite accepting of my urge to embellish at Halloween when I was esteemed as a concocter of really scary ghost stories, I was at times put down as a "storyteller." And so I was forced long ago to confess to a certain lack of truthfulness as one of my major sins, in spite of the fact that I seldom told lies, which to my way of thinking, is something quite different.

And how does this confession relate to the techniques that I have developed over the years in the course of writing twenty-eight books for children and young adults? It relates, I think, in the following ways.

I still begin a story by indulging in what has always been for me a form of self-entertainment. I look for a character or characters and a beginning situation that cries out to be explored and embellished—or "embroidered," as my mother used to say reprovingly. This beginning situation must be something that connects directly to my long-established urge to find excitement, mystery, and high emotion in the midst of even the most prosaic circumstances. And over the years I have found that if such an element is lacking, I should not look for other reasons to continue work on that particular story idea.

For me at least a theme to develop, a problem to explore, or a message to be delivered, doesn't do it. I know because I've tried. I have started books with a particular message in mind, only to find that my plot mires down and my characters refuse to come to life.

This is not to say that my stories contain no references to problems that have been of concern to me, or causes I would like to promote. I just find it better to start with the joy and excitement of letting my imagination run wild—and let the messages take care of themselves—because they can and will. Messages are, I think, unavoidable. Anything a writer cares or feels deeply about will inevitably find its way into what he or she writes. However, I have found that it is better, when I start out on a new literary journey, to let messages climb into the back seat on their own, rather than to invite them to take the wheel.

So what happens then, after the initial excitement of discovering a sufficiently intriguing combination of characters and setting? Then, of course, comes the hard work—careful methodical plotting, planning and developing. Hard and demanding work, but always buoyed up and carried along by that storytellers' excitement over a situation that simply begs to be "embroidered."

For me, this hard work begins by preparing a looseleaf notebook, taking out the scribbled and doodled-over pages collected during my previous writing endeavor, and adding new, invitingly pristine paper after each of the section dividers. The first section must have blank, unlined paper, because it is there that I will draw maps and/or floor plans.

This urge to draw maps or floor plans may be unique. At least I haven't met any other writers who seem to follow such a strange procedure. I draw town plots when a small town or village is the setting for a new story, clarifying for myself the location of the protagonist's home in relation to other pertinent sites—such as the location of his or her school, best friend's home, sites of important happenings, etc. Then there are the floor plans of a house, if a house is important to the story, particularly a "big old" house, as has been the case in several of my books. Or, as in a recent book, a castle. Drawing that floor plan after studying several castles during the course of a European trip was a particularly intriguing effort.

I don't know what this "map complex" means, except that I know I do have a strong visual sense, and it is important to me to have a vivid mental image of the place I'm writing about. Place or person.

And so—on to persons. The next divider in my notebook is labeled CHARACTER SKETCHES. In this section I start a number of pages with the names of my main characters and begin to jot down what I know about them, not only their general appearance but their strengths and weaknesses, joys and sorrows, loves and hates, family relationships. Everything, down to minor personality quirks. I don't try to finish these descriptions before I begin to write the story. I simply begin with initial impressions, and leave lots of room to add or change information as we get better acquainted.

After the pages for central characters there follow a few pages for minor characters—simply the names I have chosen for them and a sentence or two about their relationship to the story. Such a listing comes in handy when, for instance, you are nearing the end of a book and the occasion requires you to mention a minor character—perhaps a teacher, a mailman, or bus driver—and you find that you have forgotten what you'd named him. Without this list, you'll be endlessly flipping pages, or scrolling through chapters, looking for an elusive name.

Usually after a few days or weeks of daydreaming, map drawing, and character sketching, I begin the actual writing—a preliminary stab at the first chapter or two to get a handle on the tone, style, and feel of the story. But then I pause to work on the all-important next section of my notebook: PLOT.

On the PLOT pages I do what I sometimes describe as "writing the book report before the book is written." I know there are some fine authors who, after getting to know their characters and beginning situation, simply start to write and "just see what happens." I also know it doesn't work for me. It's fun, I'll admit, but it just doesn't work. The usual result is that my characters immediately get themselves into predicaments that I can't get them out of in any logical manner. Also, I really can't understand how one can do the necessary foreshadowing of events, if one is unaware what these events will be.

So as I slowly and carefully (because this is one of the most demanding and crucial steps in the whole process) write the one or two pages of my PLOT section, I clarify in my own mind the barebones storyline that I will be following. Of course I don't, at this point, know everything that is going to happen in the story. Totally unexpected events—surprising and sometimes wonderfully exciting—are certain to occur as the story progresses. But what I must know is the major problem or mystery to be solved—and *in particular,* the final climax of the story and its resolution. Then, the story can zig and zag as new characters come on scene, or minor events occur, without causing the story to wander off into uncharted wastelands—as long as the writer always keeps one eye on the resolution that is the final goal.

Having completed the PLOT section I move on to the CHAPTER OUT-LINES, which will be done one at a time as I begin each new chapter.

Each CHAPTER OUTLINE consists of one page divided into two columns, one of which is titled *Action* and the other *Exposition.* On the left-hand side, as I begin each new chapter, I jot down a few notes about the on-scene events that need to happen in the next few pages. And on the right-hand side, I remind myself of information that needs to be presented to the reader—all the background material, descriptions, character development, etc., that should be included in the chapter. I find this brief outline helps me remember to weave expository material into dialogue and action continually, rather than dropping it in occasionally in huge clumps.

The next section of my notebook is labeled REWRITE, and it consists of brief notes that I make as the writing progresses to remind myself that I should, perhaps, "look for a good place to foreshadow Grub's reaction to Robinson's death," for instance. Or perhaps, "go over Chapter Nine to see if some cutting would pick up the pace."

511

Such notes are usually made when 1) someone in my writer's support group (seven writers who have been meeting twice a month for over twelve years) points out a flaw; 2) after hearing from my editor who has just read the manuscript; 3) I suddenly discover, all by myself, that what I've written is less than perfect.

And that's about it except for one final section labeled RESEARCH, which is self-explanatory. I may refer to this section relatively little when I'm writing a book like *Libby on Wednesday,* a contemporary story set in California, but when I wrote *Song of the Gargoyle,* which has a medieval setting, the research section was almost book length.

So there it is, my own personal "Notebook Method," which has evolved slowly over the years since, at the age of eight, I resolved to be a writer after it dawned on me that there were people in this world who, instead of being scolded for being a "storyteller," actually could make a career of it.

103

CALLING IT QUITS

BY LOIS LOWRY

"You put what in it?" my son asked, his fork halfway to his mouth.
"Ginger snaps," I repeated. "Crushed ginger snaps."
"I thought that's what you said." I watched while he put his fork
back down on his plate and then pushed the plate away from him. It
was clear to me that my son, normally a good sport, was not going to
eat my innovative beef stew.

It was clear to me, after I tasted it myself, that he had made the
right decision.

SOMETIMES IN THE PROCESS OF CREATING, it is very difficult to know
when to quit adding things.

Some years back, I received in the mail the first foreign edition of
my first young adult book, *A Summer to Die*. Fortunately it was
French. Later I would receive, with a gulp of astonishment, the Finn-
ish, the Afrikaans, the Catalan; but this first one was French. French
I can read.

And so I leafed through the pages, savoring the odd, startling sense
of recognition that I had, seeing my own words translated into another language.

On the last page, I read the line of dialogue with which I had concluded the book. "'Meg,' he laughed, putting one arm over my shoulders, 'you were beautiful all along.'" There it was, in French.

But there was something else, as well. I blinked in surprise, seeing
it. In French, the book concluded: "They walked on."

They walked on? Of course they *had* walked on, those two characters, Meg and Will. I knew they had, and I trusted the reader to know
that they had. But I hadn't written that line. The translator had.

I don't know why. I can only guess that the translator simply couldn't
resist that urge that makes all of us throw a crushed ginger snap into
the stew now and then.

Knowing when to stop is one of the toughest tasks a writer faces.

Is there a rule that one can follow? Probably not. But there is, I think, a test against which the writer can measure his ending, his stopping place.

When something more is going to take place, but the characters have been so fully drawn, and the preceding events so carefully shaped that the reader, on reflection, knows what more will happen, and is satisfied by it—then the book ends.

In essence, you, as writer, will have successfully taught the reader to continue writing the book in his mind.

What about the concept of resolution, then? Isn't the writer supposed to tie up the loose ends of the story neatly at the conclusion? And if everything is neatly packaged and tied, then how on earth can something more take place?

Your story—your plot—your theme—is only a portion of the lives of the characters you have created. Their lives, if you have made them real to the reader, are going to continue in the reader's mind.

Your role is only a part of that process. And you need to know when and how to get out when your role is finished. As author, you tie up and resolve the piece of a life you have chosen to examine. Then you leave, gracefully. The life continues, but you are no longer looking at it.

You have engaged and directed the imagination of the reader; and then you have turned the reader loose.

Writing this, I looked at the endings of some of my own books, to see if they followed any kind of pattern.

In one, *Anastasia on Her Own,* a mother and daughter are laughing and tap-dancing together up a flight of stairs.

In *Find a Stranger, Say Goodbye,* a young girl is packing to go away; she is deciding what to take and what to leave behind.

The narrator and her mother in *Rabble Starkey* are together in a car, heading into a somewhat uncertain future. (Not coincidentally, that book is published in Great Britain under the title *The Road Ahead.*)

The forms of these endings are different. Some are descriptive, some consist of dialogue. Some are lighthearted, others more introspective.

But they do seem to have a few elements in common.

514

They all include the main character—sometimes more than one—in the final scene.

Each of them, in various forms, reflects a sense of motion, of flow, of moving forward.

And each in its own way contains a kind of conclusive statement.

Anastasia fell in behind her mother and tried to follow the complicated hops, turns, and shuffles her mother was doing. Together they tap-danced down the hall and up the stairs. It was silly, she thought; but it was fun. And it sure felt good, having her mother back in charge.

—Anastasia on Her Own

It was the throwing away that was the hardest. But she did it, until the trunk was packed, the trash can was filled, and the room was bare of everything except the memories; those would always be there, Natalie knew.

—Find a Stranger, Say Goodbye

She sped up a little, driving real careful, and when we went around the curve I looked, and it was all a blur. But there was nothing there. There was only Sweet Hosanna and me, and outside the whole world, quiet in the early morning, green and strewn with brand new blossoms, like the ones on my very best dress.

—Rabble Starkey

The common elements that you can see and hear in those ending paragraphs are a little like the basics in a good stew; maybe you could equate them to a garlic clove, a bay leaf, and a dollop of wine.

As for the crushed ginger snaps? The ingredient that qualifies as overkill and makes the whole thing just a little nauseating?

Well, I confess that those three passages have one more thing in common. Each one was tough to end. Like the translator who added another sentence to my book, I wanted to go on, too. I wanted to add crushed ginger snaps: more sentences, more images, embellishments, explanations, embroidery.

And if I had? Take a look:

She sped up a little, driving real careful, and when we went around the curve I looked, and it was all a blur. But there was nothing there. There was only Sweet Hosanna and me, and outside the whole world, quiet in the early morning, green and strewn with brand new blossoms, like the ones on my very best dress.

What would the future hold for us? I had no way of knowing. But I remembered how, in the past years, my mother had worked and saved to bring us

515

this far. I looked at her now, her eyes intent on the road, and I could see the determination . . .

Et cetera. You can't read it—I couldn't *write* it—without a feeling of wanting to push your plate away. It's too much. It's unnecessary. It is, in a word, sickening.

The letters I get so often from kids provide me, unintentionally, with a reminder of the impact of a good ending. Boy, if anyone in the world knows how to *end,* it's a kid writing a letter.

"Well," they say, "I have to quit now."

104

Thirty Seconds, Eight Drafts, Three Years—and Then a Book

By Norma Fox Mazer

Some years ago, I was in a school speaking to the youngsters about writing, books, and reading. The librarian had worked hard, the pupils had been reading steadily, and there were countless copies of my books in their hands.

At the end of the day, the librarian drove me back to my motel and on the way told me there'd been an "incident" in the school that day. Two boys had grabbed a girl, pulled her into a corner and molested her. Many people were upset: the girl, the teachers, the principal, the boys, and quite soon it was possible that more people were going to be upset. There were parents to be considered. Newspapers and TV might get wind of this. With her hands off the wheel for a moment, the librarian sketched a "what a mess" statement in the air, and I muttered agreement.

I was tired, and listening to this tale, I became gloomy, angry at those boys and at males in general. When were they going to get it? Not meaning, get the brunt of it, but just *get it*—up there, in the brain. When were they going to wake up, smell the coffee, and start acting like human beings instead of dumb posts with legs?

We were both silent for a few minutes. Then the librarian said, "And you know, the whole thing happened in thirty seconds." All at once, I was alert. All sorts of systems started humming and buzzing in me. My brain woke up with an almost audible click. I flushed and looked at this librarian with intense gratitude and almost as intense suspicion. Did she realize what she had just said? I didn't want her to know that her words had needled their way into my skin.

". . . the whole thing happened in thirty seconds."

Astonishing. My heart beat hard. I was like a dog with a bone, afraid it would be taken from me. I scribbled those words on a piece of paper.

When I looked at it five minutes later, it was indecipherable. No matter. I could no sooner have forgotten what she had said than I could have forgotten the names of my children. But still, taking no chances, I wrote it down, only it came out this way: "Thirty seconds that changed the world."

Then I scribbled a few phrases: "Thirty seconds . . . it all happened in thirty seconds, less than a minute . . . the random and chaotic nature of life . . . the confluence of events and personalities . . . like raging streams that pour together at some point and swell into a flood . . . do one small thing, everything changes. . . ."

From the moment the librarian said those words, I knew I wanted to write a story, and that it would be about those thirty seconds, and I knew, too, that it would be told by one of the boys. Months passed. I wanted to write the book, but I couldn't. I had other commitments, other projects to finish. At last, the time opened up. It was nearly a year later. The only thing I had done in that year to prepare to write this book was to carry around inside me that phrase that was so potent for me. "Thirty seconds that changed the world."

And, then too, I had remembered a retarded woman I'd met in a bookstore in Philadelphia five or six years before. She had come rushing up to tell me with the glowing face of an eight-year-old child that it was her birthday, that she was thirty-three today, that her mommy had given her money to buy a new Nancy Drew book. I smiled at her and wished her happy birthday. She flung her arms around my neck, gave me a smacking kiss, and said, "You are my favorite person! You are a lovely, lovely person!"

Ever since, I'd wanted to write her into a story. I didn't know why she should be in this story, but she had haunted me for so many years, I made up my mind that she would be. I began writing about a boy named Rollo, a nice guy, a big guy, a football player who covers up how much he hates playing. And I wrote about Rollo's two friends and Valerie, a girl he can't stand, who's artistic, short-tempered, outspoken, and tackless. All of these kids come from good homes, are outstanding in school. I didn't know any of this when I started writing. I found out as I wrote. And I found out, too, that Rollo had a retarded sister named Kara.

Now that the book is finished, I see clearly how important Kara is to balancing and building the character of her brother, Rollo, through whom much of the story is told. When we know Kara, and when we know how Rollo acts toward her, we also know that, despite what he will do to Valerie, there's good in him. And Kara is important, also, to the working out of the plot. The gaps that might have been in the story without Kara! No wonder it scares me that her appearance was so seemingly accidental. But then, so much in the writing of a novel is accidental, or at least not deliberate.

Anne Roiphe, the novelist, said of a book she wrote, "The facts were all lies, but the book was all true." That's what I hope for when I write. I don't care about the facts. I don't give a damn about facts. I heard something that day in the car, a tiny piece of truth, a fragment, maybe about thirty seconds worth, and three years and eight drafts later, I had a book called *Out of Control.*

How close is my story to that original incident, to the truth of that school and what those kids did and the details of that day? I have no idea, but I have no reason to think it's close at all. I never saw those kids in the "incident." I never found out what really happened to the girl or what happened to any of them afterwards. I never heard or knew a single other detail than what the librarian had told me on that ten-minute ride. The people in my book are my creations; they are born not to parents but out of my head. The "truth" I hope for concerns the emotions, the feelings, and the thoughts of the characters, and the reverberations of the event. And though it might be discouraging to a young writer for me to say this, I still say that most of these things cannot be planned, but must emerge from the tension between character and story, must emerge as you write.

I was working hard to finish the book when instead of spending every hour in front of the computer, I found myself mesmerized in front of the television, watching the Clarence Thomas confirmation hearings. Listening to Anita Hill tell her story. Watching the wrenching issues of what goes on between men and woman played out on national television.

Since then, the issue of sexual harassment in the schools has gained national attention. *The New York Times* ran a front-page article about sexual harassment; *Seventeen* printed a graphic and deeply disturbing article on the same topic, and *Newsweek* had an article about sexual harassment in the *elementary schools.*

Someone said to me, "Your book is really needed. Great timing!"

but the truth of it is, it was pure dumb luck. I know that if someone had told me to write that book, I wouldn't have done it. I couldn't have. I needed the spur of that phrase about "thirty seconds." I needed the needle in my brain. And should someone come to you today and tell you the market is crying for a book on Subject X and why don't you do it, I would say to you . . . *Don't.*

I believe that the path to publication for the new writer and the secret of survival for the published writer are the same: Follow the yellow brick road. Your heart should go before you. Write what comes to you as passion or curiosity or a nagging of the conscience that you can't put aside. Then you will have something splendid, something that no one else could have written but you.

EDITING AND MARKETING

§ 105

EVERYTHING YOU NEED TO KNOW ABOUT LITERARY AGENTS

BY NANCY LOVE

GETTING STARTED IN THE BOOK writing business isn't getting any easier. To the great frustration and annoyance of both writers and literary agents, many large publishing houses no longer accept unsolicited manuscripts. Gone are the slush piles of yore and the excitement when an assistant editor found a gem buried in all those masses of paper. I hear from writers that some editors still do respond to query letters— as opposed to proposals or manuscripts—and instead of a stock, "We don't read unsolicited submissions; get an agent," may actually invite a submission.

For better or for worse, though, agents have increasingly become the keepers of the gates to book-publishing heaven. It's not good for agents when many of us feel as if we're drowning in unsuitable submissions, and it's worse for writers who, in most cases, have to get an agent's attention before they can even try to get an editor's attention.

Who *doesn't* need an agent?

But not everyone needs an agent. Who doesn't? Writers of poetry, articles, and short fiction for magazines can do best on their own, and in fact, probably won't find an agent who will represent them. Writers of text, academic, and professional books—in other words, non-trade (bookstore) books—traditionally sell their own books.

As for writers of trade books, the most successful on their own are the well-connected and the persistent. The well-connected know who they are. They have friends or family who will open some doors for them, or have been approached by a publisher to write a book; or they are so well-known that they need only put out the word for offers to come pouring in. Those in this category will often work with a lawyer who can negotiate and vet the contract.

As for the persistent, they are those hardy and fearless souls who believe they can unlock the doors themselves, and often do, though they often have to approach smaller publishing houses. Some self-publish and can do well if they have a well-defined market—like the Chinese cookbook writer in San Francisco who sells her books at conventions and to people who take her Chinatown tours. A couple I now represent sold 40,000 copies of their self-published book on the joys of Eastern sex through catalogues and advertising and their workshops. Eventually, the business of selling books was taking too much of their time, and I sold reprint rights for their book to a large publishing house only too happy to take over the decidedly unglamorous nitty gritty of the business of promoting and selling.

When do you start looking for an agent?

If you write fiction, after you have finished writing a novel (and have polished it; don't send a "first draft"), you could start your search. Most editors won't read unfinished first novels, therefore, I won't either. There are exceptions to this general rule, of course. Someone famous or with other writing credits can go to an agent with a partial manuscript. A writer with a success or two to his credit will usually be able to show his editor a synopsis of the next book. The advice I always give for short story collections is to try to get some of the stories published in magazines or quarterlies before going for a book.

As for nonfiction, you are ready to talk to an agent when you have a proposal (there are lots of books that will tell you how to do it). If you have some credentials as a journalist, however, an agent might be willing to talk over some ideas with you. If you are a doctor or a physicist or a police officer with an idea but no time or writing skills, a query letter and/or a telephone call is probably your best avenue to an agent who may be able to find a writer to help with a proposal.

Why do you need an agent?

What can an agent do for a writer that a writer can't do for himself or herself, besides having access to editors and saving the writer time?

Here are some of the services that I perform for writers. You decide whether you can do the same or better yourself.

Pre-selling or Getting the Book Together

• When I am approached by editors or packagers with book ideas, I go to the writers I represent, or to others I think would be suitable. Or *I* might come up with ideas that I pass on to my writers.
• Collaborations also often originate with agents. Or if a writer comes to me with a collaboration offer already in place, I can help to negotiate it and try to keep it on course if there are problems.
• Those of us with editorial skills like to think we can make your good ideas better. Often the writer's original idea for fiction or nonfiction needs shaping, focusing, or a little fine-tuning. Maybe it only needs a better title. There's no point in going out with either a nonfiction book proposal or a novel that isn't the best it can possibly be.

Selling

This is what everyone knows agents do. But what does it mean?

• Matchmaking: Selling a book is not like selling widgets. Putting the right editor in the right publishing house together with the right project is more like putting together the right partners in a marriage. John's wife just had a baby so he's going to love this parenting book. Publishing house A favors conservative books and their editor B likes controversial books, so he'll go for this book about how the radical left is corrupting Congress.

• Deal-making: So what's the trick? you might ask. Just take the most money and run. I wish it were that simple. Often the best way to get the most money is an auction, but you can't have an auction without at least two bidders. Three or more would be better. At this point, I call on any reserves of knowledge about herd mentality that might work to stampede the reluctant-to-bid to the table; or if the auction falls through, I regroup to try to get the offer raised. This is the time to stand firm.

There are often other considerations as important to a client as money. For example, what resources will the publisher commit to promoting the book? Control of foreign rights or entertainment rights might be an issue. All these are part of the basic deal that sometimes requires both delicacy and strength to put together.

• Negotiating the contract: Then there are all those fine points in every boilerplate contract. It's my job to know which ones are soft and will yield if I tough it out and which ones are probably engraved in stone. I can hear myself saying, "Well, if you can't give me better percentages on discounts, then give me a cap on how many books can be sold at that discount." Naturally, the more clout a writer has, the easier it is to get concessions. The agent for a writer of three successful books is obviously in a better position to make demands than when she was negotiating a contract for the writer's first novel.

Pre-publication

• Collecting the money. Actually, this starts with signing the contract and in the best cases continues for years after the book comes out. The agent is the collector of advances, royalties, subsidiary rights money. I spend a lot of time tracking and chasing clients' money, and checking royalty statements. I assume it is my responsibility to keep publishers honest and payments on time.

• Acting as liaison between writer and editor, between collaborators, and if necessary between writer and company lawyer on libel and privacy issues. In the best of all possible worlds, nothing goes wrong; in the real world here are a few scenarios from hell that might drag me in as mediator or go-between:

The book is late. Can we get an extension?

The editor leaves. The book is now an "orphan."

The collaborators have stopped talking to each other, and no one knows how or if the book will be completed.

• Promotion and marketing. As it gets closer to publication, I like to do a reality check on the plans of publisher and writer for promoting the book. Sometimes everything is humming along nicely without me. Sometimes I am the one who sets up a meeting of the writer and public relations team (and special sales force if appropriate). I might suggest outside publicity help or coach a writer in the ways she can do it herself.

After publication, I might find myself drawn into the promotion drama when systems break down—where are the books? why can't the writer get on "Oprah"? and other crises.

526

• Handling subsidiary rights either alone or with subagents. Aggressive pursuit of first serial, entertainment, foreign and other rights is an important link in the money chain and can continue well after the publication of the book.

These are the tangible tasks I find myself occupied with in my role as an agent. The intangible ones might include support, encouragement, and hand-holding, but probably the most important role of an agent is being sensitive to the dreams and goals of each individual, and to help writers reach those, whatever they are, whether money, recognition and/or the pride of having made a contribution to society.

How do you find an agent?

A personal recommendation is the best. Take a lesson from businessman/writer Harvey Mackay and hit your Rolodex. He has thousands of cards on his, but you probably have more possibilities in yours than you realize. Is there a newspaper or magazine editor you've worked with who could suggest an agent, or a writer who has an agent to share? How about your old roommate from college who had a book published? You get the idea. Put the word out and get those phone lines buzzing.

I heard an ingenious idea for identifying a likely agent from a writer who had checked out the acknowledgments in a published book that was similar to his—and found me. It's one way of finding an agent who is successful with your kind of book.

Then, of course, there are listings in reference books for writers. Perhaps the best lists are those that have been pre-screened. For instance, members of the Writers Union rate agents and provide this information to other members. If you belong to the American Society of Journalists and Authors, they will supply you with a list of their members' agents.

Another valuable list is the members of the professional society of agents, the Association of Authors' Representatives, which you can obtain for $5.00 plus a legal-size self-addressed, stamped envelope with 52¢ postage from its office (10 Astor Pl., 3rd Floor, New York, NY 10003). To be eligible for membership, agents have to meet certain book sale requirements and be sponsored by other members. The requirements for listings in *Literary Market Place,* while not as stringent, at least are designed to screen out dabblers and the inexperienced.

527

Once you've put together a target or targets, the next step is a query letter or a telephone call for information about how the agent prefers to receive submissions. For nonfiction, some of us prefer a query letter first, others a proposal and sample chapters. For fiction, some agents want a query letter, others like sample chapters and a synopsis, still others prefer a full novel. (Always include a self-addressed, stamped envelope if you want your proposal or manuscript returned.)

Agents vary not only in how they want to be approached, but also in what the next steps are in consummating a relationship once the agent offers to represent you. If possible, it is a good idea to meet in order to judge whether the chemistry is right. But at the very least, it's important to discuss the agent's client list, method of operation, and terms. I have an Author-Agent Agreement that spells out the terms of my representation. If the agent of your choice doesn't, be sure you ask questions about charges for expenses that will be passed on to you; what the commission is for subagents, who handle foreign and movie or TV rights; and the provisions for dissolving the relationship if either party decides to pull out.

You will probably want to ask other questions about the working arrangement. Will you be informed of submissions and rejections? Will the agent do multiple or single submissions? I just read a letter from an agent who told a writer that she was sending back his novel because she didn't continue to submit after she had four rejections. I send out many books twelve, even twenty-four times, if that's what it takes to sell them, and I don't think I'm that unusual. Agents differ in many ways, large and small.

I know there's a certain euphoria that settles in when an agent wants to sign you up; I've been on that end myself. But you have to remind yourself that this is a serious business arrangement. You are entrusting your career to a person who will have an important role in your life. Do you trust him/her? Is his/her vision for your future the same as yours? In other words, the question you should ask yourself is not just, How do I get an agent? but How do I get an agent who is right for me?

❧ 106

WIELDING YOUR BLUE PENCIL

BY DENNIS L. PETERSON

THE ESSENCE OF SUCCESSFUL WRITING is the ability to edit oneself. Only dreamers would think that their initial, unedited scribblings are ready for publication. They gripe about the unreasonable and undiscerning editors who continually reject their submissions. On the other hand, writers who have learned to edit what they've written are the ones who are likely to get published.

By following seven steps in editing yourself, you're not likely to be heavily edited by editors and *are* likely to get your work published.

1. Swallow your pride. William Zinsser, a famous proponent of self-editing, wrote, "You have to have the toughness to separate your work from yourself, to look at your piece objectively and make it as good as you can."

Few writers can admit that their writings are imperfect at best and can be improved. Writers tend to guard jealously their literary creations; that attitude almost guarantees failure.

Every word is fair game for the editor's blue pencil. The wastebasket is our best friend, and the blue pencil runs a close second. Most successful writers will agree that "half of life is the act of revision."

2. Cut the fat. Cutting the fat means that no word or phrase can remain in your manuscript unless it has a justifiable purpose, carries its own weight, or supports another word or idea. It also means saying the most in the fewest possible words and saying it as simply as possible.

I learned this important lesson early in my free-lance career when an editor returned one of my submissions and stated that he was willing to publish it—if I would cut it in half! My initial reaction was, "But I've already cut it to bare bones. Any further cuts will kill the thing!" But my desperate financial situation and my desire to be published in that particular magazine prompted me to comply. So I cut and pasted the manuscript, occasionally rewriting entire sections and inserting transitions where necessary, until I had it down to the desired length. It was accepted and published and gained a modicum of acclaim for its humbled author.

A weakness of many writers is to attempt to sound more authoritative than they are or to impress readers by using long words. The best writers, however, take complex ideas and state them simply. The wise writer will heed the advice of the sage who said, "Never try to impress people with the profundity of your thought by the obscurity of your language. Whatever has been thoroughly thought through can be stated simply."

3. Choose the best word. Closely associated with cutting the fat is the art of choosing the right words to deliver your thoughts effectively. Choosing the precise word, especially selecting the right verb (which is often the most important word in the sentence), is vital. More confusion and misunderstanding result from improperly used words than for any other reason. And when your words are wrong, your ideas are misunderstood, the intended message is garbled, and communication ceases.

Finding just the right word can at times be difficult and involves more than a cursory glance through *Roget's Thesaurus*. It requires careful thought and often some trial and error until the right word "clicks." As Mark Twain said, "The difference between the right word and the nearly right word is the difference between the lightning and the lightning bug."

In word choice, the following rules of thumb apply:
a) A short word generally is preferable to a long word.
b) A concrete term is clearer than an abstract idea.
c) A specific word is better than a broad generality.
d) Common words are more understandable than jargon.
e) Clichés should almost always be avoided.

4. Check your grammar and usage. Using a word incorrectly or making a mistake in grammatical construction is the mark of a careless writer. Readers are often confused by the lack of agreement between a pronoun and its antecedent or between a subject and its verb. Dangling participles, misplaced modifiers, and dozens of other grammar and usage problems not only can cause reader confusion but also can turn an editor against your manuscript.

One way to avoid such problems is to develop an ear for correct usage, but that takes time and experience. There is no substitute for a sound knowledge of grammar. This does not require a college degree in English. Simply check a good college handbook on English usage (e.g., *Harbrace College Handbook, Chicago Manual of Style,* or *Gregg Reference Manual*), and then try to follow the rules.

5. Vary your sentences. Don't use the same sentence structure and length. If you tend to write short, simple sentences, avoid Dick-and-Jane-reader choppiness by occasionally joining two simple sentences to create a compound sentence; link two related simple sentences with a semicolon; or use a few complex sentences.

6. Use active voice. Good writing requires action. There is nothing wrong with using the passive voice from time to time, but sentences using the active voice are shorter, livelier, more direct, and more effective. For example, although the meaning is clear when one writes "The ball *was hit* by John" (passive voice), action is injected into the piece when one writes "John *hit* the ball" (active voice). Substituting a more descriptive verb, such as *clobbered,* adds even more action.

7. Cool it! Trying to edit a piece while it's still "hot" is never a good idea. After working on a piece for several hours (or perhaps days), during which you have revised and reread it several times, your mind begins to accept what you have written as perfect—even when it isn't. Favorite words and pet phrases become so fixed in your mind that you are less likely to see and correct problems. Set your manuscript aside to cool, and on rereading it, you'll discover that many of the awkward phrases or wrong words will jump right out at you, suggesting fresh alternatives.

The same approach works for catching spelling and usage errors in your writing. Reading the piece after it is "cold" will enable you to see not only misspelled words but also correctly spelled but improperly used words that even computer spell checkers could not identify.

One of the challenges of writing is that writers can learn something new about self-editing every time they sit down with pen and paper or word processor. That's why they must be willing to cut, edit, and revise.

There's always room for improvement. As Art Linkletter wrote, "When you are in the world of communication, you can never be perfect. But you can always be better."

❧ 107

GETTING OUT OF THE SLUSH PILE

BY HAROLD UNDERDOWN

AS PART OF MY JOB AS A CHILDREN'S book editor, I read many unsolicited manuscripts. I'd like to pass on some of my experiences, since it's people at my level whom many of you are reaching with submissions, and we, not more senior editors, need new authors.

I'll start where the process begins—the dreaded "Slush Pile": I could be polite and talk about "unsolicited manuscripts," but that is not how people in publishing refer to them, though we use the term with a mix of frustration, bemusement and hope—frustration with the volume of material we have to deal with, bemusement at some of the more misguided submissions, and hope that there'll be something interesting in it today (and if not today, then tomorrow). In any case, the slush is a potential goldmine for a publisher, so most publishers really do read the slush, though they are not always well organized at it.

In the slush pile, certain kinds of manuscripts predominate, and you should aim to distinguish your work from this kind of material, which readers are tired of seeing. So here's a list of some kinds of manuscripts of which I see too many.

Hot topics: Anything in the news brings a brief flurry of manuscripts, from picture books to novels, that in some way "cover" the topic. Desert Storm was one popular source. "Green books" are more generally hot, and often overwhelmingly pedantic and focused on topics like recycling, which is overpublished; a recent submission—"Tony Two-Liter Gets Recycled." The Clintons' cat and the rain forests are big, too. But how many books can be published on a particular topic? Not many. . . .

Personified objects: This category ranges from the mundane (Clyde the Cloud who teaches you about the weather) to the bizarre (Harry the Horizon Line). We get a lot of these simple picture book stories, all of them meant to teach something, either practical information or

533

values. This used to be a common kind of picture book, but it's not being published much today.

Hot characters: New spins on Santa, the Easter bunny, characters from cartoons. Leaving aside the problem with using copyrighted characters, which some people don't seem to be aware of, it is simply difficult to come up with a *truly* original approach to a well-known character.

Anthropomorphized alliterated animals: This includes Sally Squirrel, Carter Carp and Billy the Bossy Beetle. We get hundreds of stories that fall into this category, many by authors who seem to think a story is only a story for children if it has a talking animal with a cute name. But, all too often, their characters work neither as animals nor as stand-ins for children.

Isn't———(insert name) cute?: Authors writing about their own pets or children, or about grandparents who have wonderful relationships with their grandkids, feel their stories are very meaningful, but all too often children would find them like looking at 200 snapshots of a neighbor's little genius.

Verse: Many people will attempt to write like Dr. Seuss; *they try and they try—it just isn't much use.* I can't do it myself. Verse really has to work perfectly in stories or poetry collections for kids, or it sounds just horrible.

Series: Some people put a lot of time and effort into developing a whole series of picture books or novels, as in a recent proposal I saw for 32 picture books about two brothers' adventures on a farm. Unfortunately, hardcover publishers almost never would sign up more than one book at a time, and the effort that went into the series is wasted.

Genre novels: This category includes formulaic middle-grade mysteries and adventure stories, YA romances and memoirs of teenage years by adults. Though competently written and possibly as good as published work, they don't hold the attention of the eager slush reader, who needs to find something *different*.

"Accepting yourself" stories: This is a classic story line in children's books, of course. But how many variations on the story of the Ugly Duckling do we need? We get lots!

Avoid these types if you want to catch the eye of a reader like me. It *is* possible to get a new spin on an old subject, but will your reader necessarily notice that you have done so? Strike out into new territory!

Be original and you will get the reader's attention (eventually—though there are many stories of famous books that were rejected before being taken on).

I also see a lot of peripheral material submitted with manuscripts, none of which helps to get my attention:

Illustrations—Unless you are certain you are cut out to be an author/illustrator, don't send any. They can just get in the way of the reader's visualizing the story.

Fancy paper, colorful envelope, Express Mail—all suggest you don't know the standard procedure and convey an unfortunate hint of desperation.

Resumé, qualifications—don't bother to include unless your experience is truly relevant. Writing a technical manual for adults, for example, is not something a reader needs to know about.

Agents—we're getting more and more submissions from people who call themselves agents, but as we don't know them manuscripts are treated like other slush. New authors from *known* agents—same thing. You'll find it hard to get a good agent until you're published, and so you would do better to direct your efforts at publishers.

Cassettes, slides, etc.—these are just a distraction. Most readers don't have the necessary equipment in their offices.

Marketing plans and series ideas—most editors feel they know or their marketing department knows how to market a book and whether a book could become a series.

I have developed a cynical rule of thumb. The more work someone does on peripherals, the less work they have put into the manuscript, and this neglect will probably show.

Does it help to address your submission to a particular editor? I think editors' names are useful only if you have actually made a real contact with someone, either through an encouraging letter or meeting her/him at a conference. Otherwise, the manuscript goes into the slush pile. It can also be counterproductive to use names if your information is not absolutely current or if the person you have sent your middle-grade novel to does only nonfiction. And since beginning editors aren't well known, you can miss them—the ones you want to reach—if you target someone more established. Above all, do not phone and ask for names. Assistants resent it—the implication is that you don't trust them or the reader to pick out the promising stuff—and even if you get a name, you'll probably just end up in the slush, after a slight pause on the editor's desk.

How *can* you get someone's attention? There are two ways that can work:

1. Find a niche, and trumpet this fact in your cover letter (which should be no longer than half a page, or it won't be read). Check *Children's Books in Print,* other reference guides and your library. Find ways to differentiate your manuscript from what is already out there. Do you have a new angle on a familiar subject? Say what it is. This works best in nonfiction, of course, but may also apply with picture books and fiction. In any case, you should always know what similar books exist. Reading the major review magazines—*Horn Book, Booklist, School Library Journal, Publishers Weekly*—can also help keep you up-to-date, and *PW* is particularly useful for news of publishers, gossip, trends, etc.

2. Work on the manuscript. Be tough on yourself. Many manuscripts we get seem not to have been revised, critiqued in any way—writers' workshops are thus a very good idea. As a small side note, local writing contests are not a good measure of your story being ready for publishers. We get occasional manuscripts with a proud cover letter saying it won such-and-such a contest—but these invariably read like good short stories for adults with children as characters, and that is why they won. Feedback from professionals, not friends or family, is probably the most valuable.

In the end, the manuscript has to speak for itself. Simply send your polished manuscript with SASE and a letter pointing out its unique angle to the Submissions Editor (or some such title) of a given imprint.

Try not only new companies, but also regional, specialty, or niche publishers. And do not neglect magazines. You gain valuable experience working with an editor and also get yourself a track record. I know I pay more attention to someone if they have been published; it shows the author is committed to his writing.

The best way, in the end, to get out of the slush pile is to write what you are passionate about. Strive to get beyond competence to something only you can write about in a particular way. Find an editor who shares your passion. If you aren't passionate about your writing, after all, there's simply no reason to be in this field. There's no guarantee that you will get out of the slush pile, and even if you do, you aren't likely to get rich from your writing. So it helps if you get something out of the writing itself. Good luck in your efforts! Luck is another thing that helps. . . .

108

COMMON QUESTIONS ABOUT COPYRIGHTS

BY HOWARD ZAHAROFF

TO BE A GOOD WRITER, YOU MUST UNDERSTAND THE BASICS OF WRITING. To be a published writer, you must understand the basics of manuscript submission and the editorial process.

And to be a successful writer, the owner of a portfolio of published manuscripts, you must also understand the basics of copyright law. As a lawyer who practices in the field, I promise that this isn't too hard. Let me prove it by answering a dozen questions that free lancers often ask.

Before doing so, a few comments. First, the answers I give are based on U.S. law. International issues are mostly ignored. Second, my focus is mainly on works first published or created after March 1, 1989, the last major revision of the Copyright Act (which I refer to below as the "Act"). Third, although the Copyright Office cannot provide legal advice, its Circulars and Public Information Office (call 202/479-0700) provide guidance on many of the following issues. (Start with Circular 1, "Copyright Basics.") There are also many excellent books available, such as Ellen Kozak's *Every Writer's Guide to Copyright & Publishing Law* (Owl, 1990).

1. *What can be copyrighted?* Copyright protects nearly every original piece you write (or draw, compose, choreograph, videotape, sculpt, etc.): not just your novel, article, story or poem, but the software program you create, the advertisements and greeting cards you published, and the love letters you wrote in high school. But copyright does not protect your ideas, only the way you *express* them.

2. *What protection does copyright provide?* A "copyright" is really a bundle of rights. The copyright owner (whom we'll call the "proprietor") controls not only the right to copy the work, but also the rights

537

to prepare "derivative works" (i.e., adaptations, translations, and other modifications), to perform or display the work publicly, and to make the "first sale" of each copy of the work.

3. *What is the duration of copyright protection, and is it renewable?* For works created or first published after 1977, copyright generally lasts 50 years after the death of the author. However, for anonymous or pseudonymous works, or works made "for hire" (see below), the term expires 100 years from creation or 75 years from publication. There are no renewals. (For works published before 1978, the term is 28 years, with right to renew for 47 additional years. See Circular 15, "Renewal of Copyright.")

4. *How do you obtain a copyright?* Copyright protection arises *automatically* as soon as you put your ideas into tangible form. Thus, once on paper, canvas, video, or computer disk, your creation is protected by law.

5. *Is a copyright notice required for protection?* No. Until recently a notice was required on all *published* copies of a work. ("Published" simply means distributed to the public; it does not require printing in a periodical or book.) However, on March 1, 1989, the United States joined the international copyright treaty known as the Berne Convention and removed this requirement for works published after that date.

Still, including a copyright notice alerts everyone to your claim and prevents an infringer from pleading "innocence" (that is, that he had no idea your work was copyrighted). Thus, good reasons remain for including notices on all published copies of your work, and for insisting that your publisher do so.

If you are concerned that your *unpublished* work may be used or copied without permission (e.g., you are circulating copies of your most timely and accomplished piece within your newly formed writers group), you can't lose by including a notice.

6. *What should my copyright notice say?* A proper notice has three elements:

- The international copyright symbol © or the word "Copyright." Most publishers use both. (The abbreviation "Copr" is also acceptable.)
- The year in which the work is first published. (For unpublished works, you may omit a date.)

538

- Your name, or a recognizable abbreviation (e.g., International Business Machines Corporation may use "IBM").

In general, notices should be displayed prominently at the beginning of your work, although any reasonable location is acceptable. If your piece will appear in a magazine, anthology, or other collective work, a single notice in the publisher's name will preserve most of your rights. However, including a separate copyright notice in your own name will clarify that only you, *not* the publisher, has the right to authorize further uses of your work.

7. *Must I register my work with the Copyright Office?* Although registration is not required for copyright protection, it is a precondition to suing for infringement of the copyrights in any work first published in the U.S. (and in the unpublished works of U.S. citizens and residents), and enables you to recover both attorneys' fees and "statutory damages" (i.e. damages of up to $100,000, determined by the judge, which the proprietor may elect to recover from the infringer in lieu of proving and recovering actual losses).

You can register your copyrights at any time during the term of copyright. However, registration within three months of publication generally preserves your rights to all infringement remedies, including statutory damages, while registration within five years of publication provides special benefits in legal proceedings.

8. *How do you register a work?* Copyright Office Form TX is the basic form for nondramatic literary works. Form PA is used to register works of the performing arts, including plays and movies. These one-page forms cost $20 to file and are fairly easy to complete (but only if you read the accompanying instructions!). Adjunct Form GR/CP allows writers to reduce costs by making a single registration for all works published in periodicals within a 12-month period. (You can order forms and circulars over the Hotline, 202/707-9100).

When you apply you must submit one copy of the work, if unpublished, and two copies of the "best edition" of the work, if published. (Only one copy of the best edition is required for contributions to collective works.) The "best edition" is the published edition of highest quality, determined by paper quality, binding, and other factors listed by the Copyright Office (see Circular R7b). For example, if the work was published in both hard and soft covers, the hard cover is normally the best edition.

9. *Should I register my work?* In most cases, no. If your work was published, your publisher may have registered it. If not, failure to register costs you mainly the option for *immediate* relief and statutory damages. Moreover, infringement is the exception and, where it occurs, often can be settled without lawsuits or registration. Besides, most writers earn too little to justify the cost of registration (certainly for articles, poems, and other short works).

10. *What is "public domain" and how can you find out what's there?* Works that are not protected by copyright are said to be in the "public domain"—i.e., freely usable by the public, without the need to get permission or pay a fee. This includes works in which copyright has expired or been lost, works for which copyright is not available, and works dedicated to the public. Although there are many exceptions, *in general* the following are in the public domain:

* Works published more than 75 years ago.
* Works published more than 28 years ago, if the copyright was not renewed.
* Works published without a proper copyright notice before 1978.
* Works published without a proper notice between January 1, 1978 and February 28, 1989 (although the Act enables the proprietor to correct this failure).
* Works created by employees of the Federal government as part of their duties.

For a fee the Copyright Office will examine the status of a work. (See Circular 22, "How to Investigate the Copyright Status of a Work.")

11. *What is fair use?* The Act allows the limited use of others' works for research, teaching, news reporting, criticism, and similar purposes. These permitted uses are called "fair use," although the Act never defines that term. Rather, it lists factors to consider, including the purpose and character of the use (e.g., for-profit vs. teaching), the nature of the work (e.g., a science text vs. a poem), the amount and substantiality of the use, and its effect on the market for the work.

Here are some basic rules that should help you stay on the right side of the law (and help you recognize when someone's use of your work doesn't).

- **Copying for noncommercial (e.g., educational) purposes is given wider scope than copying for commercial use.** For example, in general you may quote less of the published writings of a politician in a television docudrama than a history professor may quote in journal articles.

- **Copying factual material gets more latitude than copying fiction.** Fiction contains more of the "originality" protected by the Act: characters and events, sometimes even time and place, derive from the writer's imagination. Facts cannot be copyrighted.

- **Parody is a permissible use, as long as it does not appropriate too much of the original.**

- **Copying from unpublished works without permission is usually considered unfair.** This was illustrated in a 1989 case concerning an unauthorized biography of Scientologist/SF writer L. Ron Hubbard. Referring to an earlier case, in which Random House was enjoined from publishing an unauthorized biography of J. D. Salinger because it infringed copyrights in his unpublished letters, the court wrote that "unpublished works normally enjoy complete protection" from unauthorized publication. (However, legislation is being considered that would expand the application of fair use to unpublished works.)

- **The Act permits certain uses of copyrighted works by libraries, archives, educators, charitable organizations, and others.** See sections 108–110 of the Act and Circular 21.

These rules are complex. Therefore, if you intend to copy more than a negligible amount from another person's work without permission, write to the publisher or copyright owner. Don't take a chance.

12. *What is a "work made for hire," and who owns the rights to these works?* The creator of a work generally owns the copyrights. There is an exception, however, for "works made for hire." Here it is the party who commissions and pays for the work, rather than the actual creator, who owns the copyrights. So when is a work "for hire"?

First, unless expressly excluded by contract, all works created by employees within the scope of their employment are "for hire." (This will normally not include works created on your own time that are unrelated to your employment.) So if you are employed by a newspaper, or hired by a software publisher to write documentation, your employer owns the copyrights in the works you've been paid to create. If you use copies of these works at your next job, you are infringing on your former employer's copyrights.

Second, certain specified categories of works (including translations, compilations, and parts of audiovisual works) are considered "for hire" if they have been specially commissioned and a signed document identifies them as "for hire." Therefore, *if you are not an employee and you haven't agreed in writing that your work is "for hire" (or otherwise assigned your rights), you will generally continue to own the copyrights in your work* even if others paid you to create it (although they will have the right to use your work for the express purposes for which they paid you).

You may wonder about the division of rights when your article, story, or poem is published in a magazine (or other collective work) and there is no written agreement. The Act supplies the answer: The publisher acquires only the right to publish your piece as part of that collective work, of any revision of that work, and of any later collective work in the same series. You retain all other rights, so you are free to revise or remarket your piece.

The above is a *general* discussion of the copyright law as it applies to freelancers. Myriad qualifications and exceptions are not included here. Before making any important copyright decisions consult a knowledgeable copyright lawyer, the Copyright Office, or a trusted publisher or agent with an up-to-date understanding of the law.

542

〜 109

Agents: What Every Writer Should Know

By Todd Wiggins

DESPITE THE PROMINENT ROLES that literary agents play in the publishing industry, many writers remain confused as to an agent's precise function, or at least how to go about getting one.

Does every writer need an agent? Not necessarily. The writer of short stories, magazine articles, and academic texts can often manage perfectly well without one; but for the writer who hopes to place a book-length work with a major publishing house, or who is writing juvenile and young adult fiction, there is a very simple rule: *Find an agent. Period.*

The function of literary agents

Unpublished writers, especially those unfamiliar with the publishing world, often question the need for literary agents, as well they might. After all, an agent will claim between ten and twenty per cent of the income from sales of the book. But unagented writers usually spend months or even years submitting their material to publishers to no avail, for a very simple reason: Most major publishers do not accept unagented submissions, and return them unopened.

Editors at the major publishing houses receive thousands of submissions each year. Each editor manages an annual list of fifteen to twenty books, most of them by veteran authors, and can accept only about five new projects a year. As a result, an editor devotes most of his or her workday to books that have already been contracted. New manuscripts are read at night or on weekends, so it's not surprising that editors prefer submissions from reputable agents who have placed a number of successful books over the years, and whose judgment is therefore trusted.

There are a few publishers who do accept unsolicited manuscripts, but writers must be prepared to wait—often for months—until that rare day when someone, usually the editor's assistant, has the time to glance over submissions. On the other hand, a submission from a well-known agent will always be greeted with enthusiasm and will be read within two or three weeks. In extraordinary cases, a particularly "hot" book will be bought the day after submission. If that book has been sent to a number of publishers, the buyer will obtain the rights after a frenzied auction. This is every writer's dream, and only an agent can make it happen.

Yet there's still far more to agenting than cachet among editors. Very infrequently, a first-time author succeeds, unaided, in placing his or her work with a major publisher. The editor who buys such a book will immediately suggest that the writer find an agent and will provide a few recommendations. Editors *prefer* to deal with agents. An agent acts as a buffer between writer and editor during certain moments— e.g., contract negotiations—when disagreements can be taken personally and poison their relationship. Also, editors would rather negotiate with someone who is familiar with book contracts, and who will know which points are negotiable and which aren't.

The writer who still insists upon going it alone, even after his book is accepted, is heading for big trouble. Publishing contracts are written in language that most people would find unintelligible, stipulating, among other things, who is to be paid, and how much. It is no secret that the boilerplate in any such contract is biased in favor of the publisher; but a seasoned agent will have a good idea of how much a manuscript is worth and how best to obtain that price.

Even after the basic deal is agreed to, there begins the intricate process of how the subsidiary rights of the book (i.e., book club rights, foreign rights, film rights, audio rights, etc.) will be licensed. In a standard publishing contract, the publisher receives 50% of all income from these rights, and will not release the author's share until the book's advance has been earned out. Depending on the quality of the book, an agent can retain some or all of these rights for the author. Then, using his contacts among foreign publishers and film producers, he can sell these rights independently, and retain all proceeds (less his commission) for the author.

Depending upon the marketability of the book, an agent will be able to insert a number of perks into the contract for the writer's benefit

544

and find creative ways to increase the writer's income. Some authors, for example, receive large bonuses for every week their books appear on *The New York Times* bestseller list; the higher the position, the higher the bonus!

An agent, in general, is the writer's best advocate, not to mention (on occasion) moneylender, psychologist, and nanny. If a publisher violates an author's interests, the agent will act immediately—and get results. Of course, the unagented writer is also free to complain to his editor, but his objections understandably will have less impact. A powerful agent does lucrative business with publishers every day, and it does not pay the publisher to make him or her unhappy.

Selecting the right agency

You will have noticed that I often speak of the "good agent" or "powerful agent." The only thing worse than having no agent is having a bad one—and there are many.

There are hundreds of literary agencies in America. To a writer, this might seem a good thing, in that there will be a greater chance of the author's getting an agent to represent his or her work. Unfortunately, this isn't true. For one thing, many writers waste precious money on agents who charge "reading fees"—that is, agents who charge money simply to evaluate a manuscript for representation. Many other agencies will evaluate a manuscript free, and then charge a "signing fee" if the writer's work is accepted. In reality, these agents charge money because they are unable to make enough from the commissions of successfully placed manuscripts—and some writers are naïve enough to pay. Hence, the first rule in selecting an agent is: *Never hire an agent who charges money up front.* All reputable agencies make their money *only* from commissions. And while most agencies will charge a writer for incidental costs in submitting a manuscript—photocopying, express mailing, etc.—they do so *only after the manuscript has been sold to a publisher.*

The second rule in hiring an agent involves reputation. Despite the abundance of agencies, most of today's successful writers—those who make the bestseller lists, or those who publish to critical acclaim—are represented by a small, elite group of agents, most of whom are located in or near New York City. Since trade publishing is centered in New York, such proximity allows agents to meet regularly with editors and to build a wide network of personal contacts. A few prominent agents do live elsewhere, however, and a writer should ultimately choose an agent based upon credentials and past successes.

Here, then, are the steps a writer should take when seeking an agent:

1. Make a list of all the current books that have influenced your writing, or belong in the same genre.

2. Glance through the acknowledgments of each book. Does the author mention the name of his or her agent? If not, write down the name of the publisher.

3. Call the publisher and ask for the Subsidiary Rights Department. You will be transferred to an assistant, who may be willing to provide the name of the author's agent.

4. To broaden your list further, consult one of the many guides to literary agencies available at your local bookstore. *The Literary Market Place,* found in the reference department of most public libraries, includes a list of agents. You may also obtain a list of agents (for $5.00 plus a 52¢ legal-size SASE) from The Association of Authors' Representatives, Inc., 10 Astor Pl., 3rd Fl., New York, NY 10003.

5. Narrow your list to five or ten agencies. If you don't already have the name of individual agents, call each agency to find out who specializes in your type of book.

Some other points are also worth considering. For example, an agent may be good at selling manuscripts, but is he or she a good editor? Some writers, envisioning publishing's gentlemanly past, justifiably assume that editing is done by the publisher. On the contrary, most editors today merely *acquire* manuscripts and do not line-edit them. More and more, a book that is presented to a publisher must be in nearly perfect form, and require only minor alterations. For the talented writer whose work has some rough edges, this can spell trouble. Countless manuscripts exhibit great promise but are declined because they require what the publisher considers too much work. A question presents itself: Can an agent fill the role of editor?

The answer varies. Some agents are accomplished editors, and work closely with their authors from first outline to final draft. Others do little or no editing. The more work an agent does, the more likely his or her name will appear on the acknowledgments page of the relevant book.

Another point. Some agencies have stables of world-renowned authors, but may not provide the sort of personal, friendly attention that many authors would cherish. Thus there is a case to be made for choosing a small or mid-sized agency in lieu of one of the giants. (An agency with fewer than ten employees is considered small; an agency with ten to thirty employees is mid-sized; an agency with more than thirty employees is large.) Some of the biggest publishing contracts have been negotiated through smaller agencies. In any case, the agent's track record should speak for itself.

The best way to get an agent

Now begins the real fun. But first, a note of caution:

Some (to my mind) disturbing trends have occurred in publishing in recent years. Multinational conglomerates have gobbled up family-run publishers. Sales executives, and not editors, are the decision-makers at many houses. Record advances have not been recouped, and profits have shrunk. And while more books are being sold than ever, *they are coming from fewer and fewer authors.*

Today, it seems that book buyers are not spending more money, but rather, are sticking with a small group of veteran authors with solid reputations. Every now and then a new author will join this club, and another will drop out.) All this is discouraging for the first-time author, especially the novelist. Publishers are fixated more than ever on the bottom line, and are taking fewer and fewer chances on unknown authors, especially those whose work is not obviously commercial. Still, some 200 first novels do get published annually. An agent, to stay alive, must place books with publishers, and so today, the foremost question in any agent's mind when evaluating a manuscript is: *Will it sell?*

Agents, like publishers, receive thousands of submissions each year. Bearing this in mind, you should submit your manuscript in the best possible form, then prepare your first mailing. The protocol here is very specific, and your chances of acceptance are greatest if it is followed to the letter.

Most prominent agents require the first submission in the form of a query letter. Prepare one to each agent on your list, and address it to him or her by name. The length of your query letter should ideally be one page, and never more than two. After a paragraph of introduction, briefly synopsize the contents of your book. For novels especially, you should be direct and to the point; and for any type of material, you should name similar books in its field or genre and then state *how yours is different and better.* Your last paragraph should contain a short personal biography, and list any publishing credits you have or any career work or travel experience that relates to your book.

The tone of a query letter should be polite, warm, and unassuming. Agents are human, and will respond to such a letter more favorably than one that is aggressive or boastful. Allow an agent two months for a reply; if he has not responded by then, call to ask the status of your book.

You may send a query letter to many agents at once, but most agents insist upon reviewing the actual manuscript on an exclusive basis. If an agent does ask to see your manuscript, when you send it, state that he may read it exclusively for a period of thirty days, after which you may try another agency.

It is *imperative* that you enclose a self-addressed, stamped envelope for the return of your material, or at least for a letter of reply. Agencies will not spend the money to return rejected material, or even to cover the cost of a simple rejection letter.

Another rule. Since agents, like editors, spend their days managing the affairs of established clients, they are inclined to route to their assistants the telephone calls of anyone they do not know. A good assistant will be able to answer any questions you have about the submissions process, and might even nudge his or her boss on your behalf. For verification of your manuscript's arrival, send it by Certified Mail, Return Receipt Requested.

Acceptance!

When an agent agrees to represent you, a number of things will happen. You will first be given an agency contract. A good first test of an agent is whether he or she will patiently walk you through this agreement and explain any points on which you need clarification. In broad terms, you should agree to a 15% commission on your book's domestic earnings and a 20% commission on foreign sales. It is customary, as mentioned earlier, for the writer to pay for incidental costs involving her work, but only *after* that book is sold to a publisher.

Most agreements last for a year, after which they can be cancelled upon written notice by either party. Keep in mind, however, that an agent who sells your book will be entitled to a commission for the life of its copyright, regardless if you change agents later on.

You might also ask the agent for the phone numbers of one or two clients who can vouch for his or her services. The agent's willingness (or lack thereof) to grant this request might well be an indication of how he or she will treat you in the future.

Should you sign on with the agency, your agent will prepare your manuscript for submission and send it on to various editors who specialize in your sort of book. From that point on, you must sit and wait.

Having an agent does not assure your success. When all is said and done, the quality of your work is the most important factor in your career. A good agent, though he or she cannot promise you a deal, *can* guarantee that your book will go as far as it deserves to, and that you get the best deal in the process.

110

How to Write Queries That Sell

By Nancy Cornell

ARMED WITH AN IDEA FOR A TERRIFIC article, you are ready to join hordes of other free lancers in the magazine writing field, right? Wrong! Before writing the article, you have to sell the idea. An irresistible query letter will put you ahead of the mass of other free lancers.

You must make your query appropriate, professional and intriguing to an editor to get your name out of the slush pile and onto a check. Here are six tips for writing a good query:

1) Target appropriate markets, and study them carefully. Read several current issues of the magazine you want to write for. I asked for a sample copy of *Key Horizons,* a closed-circulation magazine (sent only to certain people), and enclosed a large, self-addressed stamped envelope (SASE).

The closer your query matches the articles in the magazine, the better your chance of getting an assignment. Are the magazine's articles written in first person or third? Do they use lots of anecdotes and quotes or more straight exposition? Does the magazine favor human-interest pieces, technology, travel? How long are the articles? After perusing a few copies, you'll recognize the magazine's editorial format.

2) Know the reader. Look at the ads, because they reflect the readers' demographics. Is the model nibbling caviar in a five-star restaurant? Then a proposal entitled "Cost-Cutting Hostels" is about as appropriate as a fur coat in Tahiti. Publications know whom they want to reach—so do successful writers.

Pictures in *Key Horizons* showed models with gray hair and a few wrinkles, ads for hearing aids and retirement centers. Readers of this magazine lead active lives on retirement dollars. Since *Key Horizons* ran a food story in each issue, my query on the benefits of cooking healthful, low-cost meals with peppers interested them.

Editors want articles like the ones they publish, but not the same one they just published. "Browse a dozen copies of the magazine so you don't unknowingly repeat ideas that have run recently," advises former editor and publisher of *Playboy* Nat Lehrman. "This may seem elementary, but the most common complaint heard about writers in an editorial office is: 'Don't these writers read the magazine?'"

3) Be brief. Keep queries to one page, and make the first paragraph, at least the first sentence, sing. Though swamped with submissions, editors notice good queries. My query consisted of three informative, short paragraphs. The first paragraph hooked the editor, the second briefly outlined the article and named an expert I would interview, and the third told some of my writing experience. A zippy title headed the letter.

Analyze your target magazine's article titles. Are they in the form of questions or statements or labels or rhymes? Perhaps they are statistical, paradoxical, or a play on words. Determine the average word length of the titles. Attention to such details helps set your work apart from the competition. Of course, editors often change your title; my title, "Hot 'n' Healthy," became "Hot Stuff." I wish I'd thought of it!

4) Present your query professionally. If a professional-looking query with a promising idea and title reaches an editor the same day as a similar idea filled with grammatical errors and scrawled on mauve stationery, guess which writer gets the go-ahead.

Think of your query letter as a job application, your stand-in for a personal interview. Like an applicant, the letter must be neat, grammatical, and respectful of the editor's time. It must sell itself.

Fussy English teachers pale in comparison to fastidious editors. Misspelled words, typos, or grammatical errors have no place in a professional writer's business.

Since writers and editors rarely meet face to face, a query is often their first contact. Using good quality white or off-white paper for your letterheads, envelopes, and business cards is a must. Though the initial expense may seem high, it's worth the cost, because editors are more disposed to read attractively presented queries.

Letterheads should include your name, address, telephone number, and FAX number, if you have one. Do not have the word "writer" printed on your letterhead, but do put a descriptive word like "Writer" or "Travel Writer" on your business cards. Don't use vertically printed or odd-sized business cards that won't fit into a business card file.

5) After you've written an irresistible query on your professional-looking stationery, send it to the appropriate person at the magazine, not just The Editor. Look at the masthead and address it to a person by name. Skip the publisher and editor-in-chief; aim instead for an editor about the middle of the masthead. If you can't tell if it's a man or a woman, then address the editor by the full name: Dear Leslie Black. Or better still, call the magazine to check the editor's name and exact spelling (and gender, if there is a question about it). This is especially important if the sample issue you have is more than a couple of months old, as editors often move from one publication to another.

6) Keep careful records of queries and follow up on them. On a simple tracking chart, note the date you mailed the query, subject of your proposed article, name and address of the publication, and the name of the editor. Allow room on the chart to note the response and other pertinent information. A weekly glance at the chart will keep you up to date on your queries.

The following is an example of a query letter that used all six tips and resulted in an article published in *Key Horizons* magazine:

Brenda Pace, Editor
Key Horizons
950 N. Meridian, Suite 1200
Indianapolis, IN 46204

Dear Ms. Pace:

Hot 'n' Healthy

Now there's proof positive. Peppers not only taste good but they also help those who eat them to stay healthy. One jalapeno contains more of vitamins A and C than three oranges. Peppers contain no fat and few calories. In addition, delicious Mexican food is easy and inexpensive to prepare.

How would you like my feature story on the healthy habit of eating tasty hot peppers? Along with verified health facts, pepper history and tips for use, the story will include interviews with pepper authorities including Pace Foods' Dr. Lou "Pepper" Rasplicka. I can provide recipes and illustration.

I am a contributor to *New Choices, American Way, Modern Maturity,* and other national publications. Clips and an SASE are enclosed for your convenience. Thank you for considering this query.

Best regards,
s/Nancy Cornell

Key Horizons responded to my query in an unprecedented 12 days; more often, replies take four to six weeks. If there's been no response within that time I send a postcard that reads: "Dear [editor's name]: I wonder if you received my query entitled [name of query] mailed to you on [date]. If not, please let me know, and I'll be happy to send you a copy. If you are still considering it, fine. Take your time. But if you can't use it, please let me know so I may submit it elsewhere."

Surprisingly effective, this polite request usually gets a quick response and, on more than a few occasions, an assignment. Maybe the editor is considering the query and simply needs encouragement.

Because an editor's inaction effectively removes your proposed article from circulation while it's in his or her hands, writers often submit simultaneous queries, sending the same idea (not the same letter) to more than one appropriate publication at the same time. The practice makes good business sense. What if more than one editor wants you to go ahead with your idea? You should be so lucky!

Be sure to send an SASE with your query to assure a reply. Most editors will not respond if you fail to do so. Successful writers get more assignments than rejections because they treat writing as a business, not a hobby. When you get a "go-ahead" in response to your query, write that article in an entertaining and informative manner. Try to make the written piece even better than the query that got you the assignment.

WHERE TO SELL

Where to Sell

This year's edition of *The Writer's Handbook* includes more markets and listings than ever before, and writers at all levels of experience should be encouraged by the number and variety of opportunities available to them. Editors, publishers, and producers rely on free lancers for a wide range of material—from articles and fiction to play scripts, poetry, opinion essays, and how-to and children's books—and many are very receptive to the work of talented newcomers.

Still one of the best markets for beginning free lancers is the field of specialized publications, including city and regional and travel magazines, and those covering such areas as consumer issues, sports, and hobbies and crafts. Editors of these magazines are in constant need of authoritative articles (for which the payment can be quite high), and writers with experience in and enthusiasm for a particular field, whether it's gardening, woodworking, bicycling, antiques, bird watching, bridge, or car repair, can turn their knowledge into article sales. Such interests and activities can generate more than one article if a different angle is used for each magazine and the writer keeps the audience and editorial content firmly in mind.

Magazines devoted to the special concerns of families and parents represent another market with great potential for free lancers, and the dramatic increase in the number of publications in this area has inspired the creation of a new category in the market section of this edition called Family & Parenting. The market for technical, computer, health, and personal finance writing is also very strong, with articles on these topics appearing in almost every publication on the newsstands today. For these subjects, editors are looking for writers who can translate technical material into lively, readable prose, often the most important factor in determining a sale.

While some of the more established markets may seem difficult to break into, especially for the beginner, there are thousands of lesser-known publications where editors will consider submissions from first-time free lancers. City and regional publications offer some of the best opportunities, since these editors generally like to work with local writers and often use a wide variety of material, from features to fillers. Many newspapers accept op-ed pieces, and are most receptive to pieces on topics not covered by syndicated columnists (politics, economics, and foreign affairs); pieces with a regional slant are particularly welcome here.

It is important for writers to keep in mind the number of opportunities that exist for nonfiction, because the paying markets for fiction are somewhat limited. Some general-interest and women's magazines do publish short stories; however, beginners will find these markets extremely competitive, with their work being judged against that of experienced professionals. We recommend that new writers look into the small, literary, and college publications, which always welcome the work of talented beginners. Payment is usually made only in copies, but publication in literary journals can lead to recognition by editors of larger circulation magazines, who often look to the smaller publications for new talent. In addition, a number of regional, specialized, and Sunday magazines use short stories and are particularly interested in local writers.

The market for poetry in general-interest magazines continues to be tight, and the advice for poets, as for fiction writers, is to try to get established and build up a list of publishing credits by submitting material to literary journals. Poets should look also to local newspapers, which often use verse, especially if it is related to holidays or other special occasions.

New playwrights will find that community, regional, and civic theaters and college dramatic groups offer the best opportunities for staged production in this competitive market. Indeed, many of today's well-known playwrights received their first recognition in regional theaters, and aspiring writers who can get their work produced there have taken a significant step toward breaking into the field. In addition to producing plays and giving dramatic readings, many theaters also sponsor competitions or new play festivals.

The market for television and feature film scripts is limited, and most writers break into it only after a careful study of the medium and a long apprenticeship. Writers should be aware of the fact that this market is inaccessible without an agent, and for this reason, we list several agents who are willing to read queries for TV scripts and for screenplays.

While the book publishing field remains extremely competitive, beginners should be especially encouraged to know that more than 200 first novels were published in the past year. Writers often feel that publishers bring out or promote only the work of already established best-selling authors, but the truth is many publishing houses have committed themselves enthusiastically to launching new novelists. An increasing number of publishers are broadening their nonfiction lines as well, and editors at many hardcover and paperback houses are on the lookout for new authors, especially those with a knowledge of or training in a particular field. Writers of juvenile and young-adult books will be pleased to hear that in response to a growing audience of young readers and increased sales, many publishers are greatly expanding their lists of children's books.

Small presses across the country continue to flourish—in fact, they are currently publishing more books by name authors and more books on mainstream subjects than at any other time in recent years—offering writers an attractive alternative for their manuscripts.

Writers seeking the thrill of competition should review the extensive list of literary prize offers, indexed for the first time in this edition. Many prize sponsors are intent on promoting the as yet unpublished author, and have established writing contests open only to newcomers. Nearly all of the competitions are for unpublished manuscripts, and offer publication in addition to a cash prize. The prestige that comes with winning some of the more established awards can do much to further a writer's career, as editors, publishers, and agents are likely to consider the future work of the prize winner more closely.

Those writers who are interested in retaining the services of an agent will want to consult the list of literary agents, newly expanded in this edition to include the type of material each agent represents, whether the work of unpublished writers will or will not be considered, and the commission and operating fees each agent charges his or her clients. (Only those agents that do not charge reading fees are included.)

All information in these lists concerning the needs and requirements of magazines, book publishing companies, and theaters comes directly from the editors, publishers, and directors, but editors move and addresses change, as do requirements. No published listing can give as clear a picture of editorial needs and tastes as a careful study of several issues of a magazine or a book catalogue, and writers should never submit material without first thoroughly researching the prospective market. If a magazine is not available in the local library or on the newsstand, write directly to the editor for the price of a sample copy. Contact the publicity department of a book publisher for an up-to-date catalogue or a theater for a current schedule. Many companies also offer a formal set of writers guidelines, available for an SASE upon request.

ARTICLE MARKETS

The magazines in the following list are in the market for free-lance articles of many types. Unless otherwise stated in these listings, a writer should submit a query first, including a brief description of the proposed article and any relevant qualifications or credits. A few editors want to see samples of published work, if available. Manuscripts must be typed double-space on good white paper (8 ½ x 11), with name, address, and telephone number at the top left- or right-hand corner of the first page. Do not use erasable or onion skin paper, since it is difficult to work with, and always keep a copy of the manuscript, in case it is lost in the mail. Some publishers will accept and prefer work submitted on computer disk, usually noting the procedure and type of disk in their writers guidelines.

Submit photos or slides *only* if the editor has specifically requested them. A self-addressed envelope with postage sufficient to cover the return of the manuscript or the answer to a query should accompany all submissions. Response time may vary from two to eight weeks, depending on the size of the magazine and the volume of mail it receives. If an editor doesn't respond within what seems to be a reasonable amount of time, it's perfectly acceptable to send a polite inquiry.

Many publications have writers guidelines, outlining their editorial requirements and submission procedures; these can be obtained by sending a self-addressed, stamped envelope (SASE) to the editor. Also, be sure to ask for a sample copy: Editors indicate the most consistent mistake free lancers make is failing to study several issues of the magazine to which they are submitting material.

GENERAL-INTEREST PUBLICATIONS

ACCENT/TRAVELOG—P.O. Box 10010, Ogden, UT 84409. Attn: Ed. Staff. Articles, 1,000 words, about travel, having fun, fitness, sightseeing, the ordinary and the unusual in foreign and domestic destinations. "Avoid budget approaches and emphasize the use of travel professionals." Must include excellent transparencies. Queries with SASE required. Guidelines. Pays 15¢ a word, $35 for photos, $50 for cover photo, on acceptance.

AIR & SPACE—370 L'Enfant Promenade, 10th Fl., Washington, DC 20024–2518. George Larson, Ed. General-interest articles, 1,000 to 3,500 words, on aerospace experience, past, present, and future; travel, space, history, biographies, essays, commentary. Pays varying rates, on acceptance. Query.

AIR FORCE TIMES—See *Times News Service.*

AMERICAN HERITAGE—60 Fifth Ave., New York, NY 10011. Richard F. Snow, Ed. Articles, 750 to 5,000 words, on U.S. history and background of American life and culture from the beginning to recent times. No fiction. Pays $300 to $1,500, on acceptance. Query.

AMERICAN JOURNALISM REVIEW—8701 Adelphi Rd., Adelphi, MD 20783. Rem Rieder, Ed. Articles, 500 to 5,000 words, on print and electronic journalism. Pays 20¢ a word, on publication. Query.

THE AMERICAN LEGION—Box 1055, Indianapolis, IN 46206. John Greenwald, Ed. Articles, 750 to 2,000 words, on current world affairs, public policy, and subjects of contemporary interest. Pays $400 to $2,000, on acceptance. Query.

AMERICAN VISIONS, THE MAGAZINE OF AFRO-AMERICAN CULTURE—2101 S St. N.W., Washington, DC 20008–4011. Joanne Harris, Ed. Articles, 1,500 words, and columns, 750 to 2,000 words, on African-American history and culture with a focus on the arts. Pays from $100 to $1,000, after publication. Query.

ARMY TIMES—See *Times News Service.*

THE ATLANTIC MONTHLY—745 Boylston St., Boston, MA 02116. William Whitworth, Ed. Non-polemical, meticulously researched articles on public issues, politics, social sciences, education, business, literature, and the arts. Ideal length: 3,000 to 6,000 words, though short pieces, 1,000 to 2,000 words, are also welcome and longer text pieces will be considered. Pays excellent rates.

BON APPETIT—6300 Wilshire Blvd., Los Angeles, CA 90048. Barbara Fairchild, Exec. Ed. Articles on fine cooking (menu format or single focus), cooking classes, and gastronomically focused travel. Query with samples of published work. Pays varying rates, on acceptance.

BOSTONIA: THE MAGAZINE OF CULTURE OR IDEAS—10 Lenox St., Brookline, MA 02146. Attn: Ed. Articles, to 3,000 words, on politics, literature, music, art, travel, food, and wine. Pays $150 to $2,500, 30 days after acceptance. Queries required.

CAPPER'S—1503 S.W. 42nd St., Topeka, KS 66609–1265. Nancy Peavler, Ed. Articles, 300 to 500 words: human-interest, personal experience for family section, historical. Payment varies, on publication.

CAR AUDIO AND ELECTRONICS—21700 Oxnard St., Woodland Hills, CA 91367. Bill Neill, Ed. Features, 1,000 to 2,000 words, on electronic products for the car: audio systems, security systems, CBs, radar detectors, cellular telephones, etc. Pays $300 to $1,000, on acceptance.

CHANGE—1319 18th St. N.W., Washington, DC 20036. Attn: Ed. Dept. Well-researched features, 2,500 to 3,500 words, on programs, people, and institutions of higher education; and columns, 700 to 2,000 words. "We can't usually pay for unsolicited articles."

CHATELAINE—MacLean Hunter Bldg., 777 Bay St., Toronto, Ont., Canada M5W 1A7. Attn: Ed. Dept. Articles, 1,500 to 2,500 words, for Canadian women, on current issues, personalities, medicine, psychology, etc., covering all aspects of Canadian life. Send queries to Elizabeth Parr, Sr. Ed. "Upfront" columns, 500 words, on relationships, health, nutrition, fitness, parenting; send queries to Diane Merlevede, Man. Ed. Pays from $350 for columns, from $1,250 for features, on acceptance.

THE CHRISTIAN SCIENCE MONITOR—One Norway St., Boston, MA 02115. Lawrence Goodrich, Features Ed. Articles, 800 words, on arts, education, food, sports, science, and lifestyle; interviews, literary essays for "Home Forum" page; guest columns for "Opinion Page." Pay varies, on acceptance. Original material only.

COLUMBIA—1 Columbus Plaza, New Haven, CT 06510–3326. Richard McMunn, Ed. Journal of the Knights of Columbus. Articles, 500 to 1,500 words, on a wide variety of topics of interest to K. of C. members, their families, and the

Catholic layman: current events, religion, education, art, etc., illustrated with color photos. Pays $250 to $500, including art, on acceptance.

THE COMPASS—365 Washington Ave., Brooklyn, NY 11238. J.A. Randall, Ed. True stories, to 2,500 words, on the sea, sea trades, and aviation. Pays to $1,000, on acceptance. Query with SASE.

CONSUMERS DIGEST—5705 N. Lincoln Ave., Chicago, IL 60659. John Manos, Ed. Articles, 500 to 3,000 words, on subjects of interest to consumers: products and services, automobiles, health, fitness, consumer legal affairs, and personal money management. Photos. Pays from 35¢ to 50¢ a word, extra for photos, on publication. Buys all rights. Query with resumé and published clips.

COSMOPOLITAN—224 W. 57th St., New York, NY 10019. Helen Gurley Brown, Ed. Guy Flatley, Man. Ed. Articles, to 3,000 words, and features, 500 to 2,000 words, on issues affecting young career women. Query.

COUNTRY—5400 S. 60th, Greendale, WI 53129. Dan Matel, Man. Ed. People-centered articles, 500 to 1,000 words, for a rural audience."First-person articles about contemporary country experiences especially encouraged." (No articles on farm production techniques.) Taboos: tobacco, liquor, and sex. Pays $75 to $100, on acceptance. Query.

COUNTRY JOURNAL—P.O. Box 8200, Harrisburg, PA 17105. Peter V. Fossel, Ed. Articles, 500 to 1,500 words, for country and small-town residents. Helpful, authoritative pieces; how-to projects, small-scale farming, and gardening. Pays $100 to $500, on acceptance. Send SASE for guidelines. Query with SASE.

DALLAS LIFE MAGAZINE—*The Dallas Morning News*, Communications Ctr., P.O. Box 655237, Dallas, TX 75265. Mike Maza, Man. Ed. Well-researched articles and profiles, 1,000 to 3,000 words, on contemporary local issues and personalities. "Dallas peg is a must." Pays from 20¢ a word, on acceptance. Query.

DAWN—2519 N. Charles St., Baltimore, MD 21218. Kevin Peck, Adv. Dir. Illustrated feature articles, 750 to 1,000 words, on subjects of interest to black families. Pay varies, on publication. Query.

DESTINATION DISCOVERY—7700 Wisconsin Ave., Bethesda, MD 20814. Rebecca Farwell, Ed. Amplifies and develops (but does not review or retell) the topics and genres covered by the Discovery cable TV channel, including science and technology, nature and ecology, human adventure, history, people and places. "Our objective is to approach nonfiction subjects in a literary style. We are always looking for writing with strong 'you are there' feeling. Articles are commissioned by staff, though queries are sometimes considered." Send letter of introduction, resumé, areas of expertise, and published clips.

DIVERSION MAGAZINE—60 E. 42nd St., Suite 2424, New York, NY 10165. Tom Passavant, Ed.-in-Chief. Articles, 1,200 to 2,500 words, on travel, sports, hobbies, entertainment, food, etc., of interest to physicians at leisure. Photos. Pays from $500, on acceptance. Query. Currently not accepting outside material.

EBONY—820 S. Michigan, Chicago, IL 60603. Lerone Bennett, Jr., Exec. Ed. "We do not solicit for free-lance material."

THE ELKS MAGAZINE—425 W. Diversey Pkwy., Chicago, IL 60614. Fred D. Oakes, Ed. Articles, 1,200 to 3,000 words, on business, sports, and topics of current interest, for non-urban audience with above-average income. Informative or humorous pieces, to 2,500 words. Pays $150 to $400 for articles, on acceptance. Query.

563

ESQUIRE—250 W. 55th St., New York, NY 10019. Edward Kosner, Ed.-in-Chief. David Hirshey, Deputy Ed. Articles, 2,500 to 6,500 words, for intelligent adult audience. Pay varies, on acceptance. Query with published clips; complete manuscripts from unpublished writers. SASE required.

ESSENCE—1500 Broadway, New York, NY 10036. Susan L. Taylor, Ed.-in-Chief. Linda Villarosa, Ed. Provocative articles, 800 to 2,500 words, about black women in America today: self-help, how-to pieces, business and finance, health, celebrity profiles, and political issues. Short items, 500 to 750 words, on work, parenting, and health. Query required. Pays varying rates, on acceptance.

FAMILY CIRCLE—110 Fifth Ave., New York, NY 10011. Susan Kelliher Ungaro, Ed.-in-Chief. Articles, to 2,000 words, on "women who have made a difference," marriage, family, and child-rearing issues; consumer affairs, health and fitness, humor and psychology. Query required. Pays top rates, on acceptance.

GLAMOUR—350 Madison Ave., New York, NY 10017. Ruth Whitney, Ed.-in-Chief. Pamela Erens, Articles Ed. Editorial approach is "how-to" for women, 18 to 35. Articles on careers, health, psychology, interpersonal relationships, etc. Fashion, health, and beauty material staff-written. Pays from $1,000 for 1,500- to 2,000-word articles, from $1,500 for longer pieces, on acceptance.

GLOBE—5401 N.W. Broken Sound Blvd., Boca Raton, FL 33487. Robert Taylor, Man. Ed. Factual articles, 500 to 1,000 words, with photos: exposés, celebrity interviews, consumer and human-interest pieces. Pays $50 to $1,500.

GOOD HOUSEKEEPING—959 Eighth Ave., New York, NY 10019. Joan Thursh, Articles Ed. Articles, 2,500 words, on a unique or trend-setting event; family relationships; personal medical pieces dealing with an unusual illness, treatment, and result; personal problems and how they were solved. Short essays, 750 to 1,000 words, on family life or relationships. Pays first-time writers $500 to $750 for short, essay-type articles, $1,500 to $2,000 for full-length articles, on acceptance. "Payment scale rises for writers with whom we work frequently." Buys all rights, though the writer retains the right to use material from the article as part of a book project. Queries preferred. Guidelines.

GRIT—1503 S.W. 42nd St., Topeka, KS 66609. Roberta J. Peterson, Ed.-in-Chief. Articles, 500 to 1,200 words, on health, consumer topics, people, home, garden, friends and family, Americana, and travel. Short fiction, 2,500 words (must be addressed to Fiction Ed.). SASE required. Pays 15¢ to 25 a word, extra for photos. Query. Send SASE for guidelines and theme calendar.

HARPER'S BAZAAR—1700 Broadway, New York, NY 10019. Elizabeth Tilberis, Ed.-in-Chief. Articles for sophisticated women on current issues, books, art, film, travel, fashion and beauty. Send queries with one- to three-paragraph proposal; include clips and SASE. Rarely accepts fiction. Payment varies.

HARPER'S MAGAZINE—666 Broadway, New York, NY 10012. Attn: Ed. Articles, 2,000 to 5,000 words. Query. SASE required. Very limited market.

HARROWSMITH COUNTRY LIFE—Ferry Rd., Charlotte, VT 05445. Attn: Ed. Dept. Feature articles, 3,000 to 4,000 words, on country living, gardening, community issues, shelter, how-to and do-it-yourself projects. Short profiles of country careers, news briefs, and natural history. Pays $500 to $1,500 for features, from $50 to $600 for department pieces, on acceptance. Query with SASE required. Guidelines.

HISTORIC PRESERVATION—1785 Massachusetts Ave. N.W., Washington, DC 20036. Anne Elizabeth Powell, Ed. Feature articles from published writers,

1,500 to 4,000 words, on residential restoration, preservation issues, and people involved in preserving America's heritage. Mostly staff-written. Query.

HOUSE BEAUTIFUL—1700 Broadway, New York, NY 10019. Elaine Greene, Features Ed. Articles related to the home. Pieces on architecture, design, travel, and gardening. One personal memoir each month, "Thoughts of Home," with high literary standards. Pays varying rates, on acceptance. Query with detailed outline and SASE. Guidelines.

IDEALS—P.O. Box 148000, Nashville, TN 37214–8000. Lisa Thompson, Ed. Articles, 800 to 1,000 words; poetry, 12 to 50 lines. Light, nostalgic pieces. Payment varies. SASE for guidelines.

INQUIRER MAGAZINE—*Philadelphia Inquirer*, P.O. Box 8263, 400 N. Broad St., Philadelphia, PA 19101. Ms. Avery Rome, Ed. Local-interest features, 500 to 7,000 words. Profiles of national figures in politics, entertainment, etc. Pays varying rates, on publication. Query.

INSIDE MAGAZINE—226 S. 16th St., Philadelphia, PA 19102–3392. Jane Biberman, Ed. Articles, 1,500 to 3,000 words, on Jewish issues, health, finance, and the arts. Queries required; send clips if available. Pays $75 to $600, on publication.

KEY HORIZONS—Gateway Plaza, 950 N. Meridian, Suite 1200, Indianapolis, IN 46204. Joan Todd, Man. Ed. General-interest articles and department pieces, 300 to 1,500 words, for readers ages 50 and older. Topics include personal finance, cooking, family trends, domestic travel, and puzzles. No nostalgia, domestic humor, fillers, or poetry. Pays $25 to $500, $25 to $50 for photos, on publication.

KIWANIS—3636 Woodview Trace, Indianapolis, IN 46268. Chuck Jonak, Man. Ed. Articles, 2,500 to 3,000 words, on home; family; international issues; the social, health, and emotional needs of youth (especially under age 6); career and community concerns of business and professional people. No travel pieces, interviews, profiles. Pays $400 to $1,000, on acceptance. Query. Send SASE for guidelines.

LADIES' HOME JOURNAL—100 Park Ave., New York, NY 10017. Jane Farrell, Articles Ed. Articles on contemporary subjects of interest to women. "See masthead for specific-topic editors and address appropriate editor." Query with SASE required.

LIFE IN THE TIMES—See *Times News Service.*

LISTEN MAGAZINE—55 W. Oak Ridge Dr., Hagerstown, MD 21740. Lincoln Steed, Ed. Articles, 1,000 to 1,200 words, on problems of alcohol and drug abuse, for teenagers; personality profiles; self-improvement articles, and drug-free activities. Photos. Pays 5¢ to 7¢ a word, extra for photos, on acceptance. Query. Guidelines.

LOS ANGELES TIMES MAGAZINE—Times Mirror Sq., Los Angeles, CA 90053. Bret Israel, Ed. Articles, to 5,000 words: general-interest news features, photo spreads, profiles, and narratives focusing on current events. Pays to $4,000, on acceptance. Query required.

MCCALL'S—110 Fifth Ave., New York, NY 10011. Attn: Articles Ed. Articles, 1,000 to 3,000 words, on current issues, human interest, family relationships. Payment varies, on acceptance. SASE.

MADEMOISELLE—350 Madison Ave., New York, NY 10017. Dana Cowin, Man. Ed. Articles, 750 to 2,500 words, on subjects of interest to single, working women in their twenties. Reporting pieces, essays, first-person accounts, and humor. No how-to or fiction. Query with clips. Pays excellent rates, on acceptance. SASE required.

MERIDIAN LIFESTYLES—(formerly *People in Action/Sports Parade*) Box 10010, Ogden, UT 84409. Attn: Ed. Dept. Personality profiles, 1,200 words, of celebrities in sports, entertainment, fine arts, science, etc. Celebrities must be nationally or internationally known for their participation in their field, have positive values, and be making a contribution to society. "High-quality color transparencies are a must; query for details." Pays 15¢ a word, $35 for photos, $50 for cover photos, on acceptance.

METROPOLITAN HOME—1633 Broadway, New York, NY 10019. Attn: Articles Dept. Service and informational articles for residents of houses, co-ops, lofts, and condominiums, on real estate, equity, wine and spirits, collecting, trends, travel, etc. Interior design and home furnishing articles with emphasis on lifestyle. Pay varies. Query with clips.

MODERN MATURITY—3200 E. Carson St., Lakewood, CA 90712. J. Henry Fenwick, Ed. Articles, 1,000 to 2,000 words, on careers, workplace, human interest, living, finance, relationships, and consumerism, for readers over 50. Photos. Pays $500 to $2,500, on acceptance. Query.

THE MOTHER EARTH NEWS—24 E. 23rd St., 5th Fl., New York, NY 10010. Christine Cauchon, Asst. Ed. Articles for rural and urban readers: home improvements, how-tos, indoor and outdoor gardening, family pastimes, health, food, ecology, energy, and consumerism. Also "Funny Fotos." Pays varying rates, on acceptance. (No payment for "Funny Fotos.")

MOTHER JONES—731 Market St., Suite 600, San Francisco, CA 94103. Jeffrey Klein, Ed. Investigative articles, political essays, cultural analyses. "OutFront" pieces, 250 to 500 words. Pays on acceptance. Query.

MS.: THE WORLD OF WOMEN—230 Park Ave., 7th Fl., New York, NY 10169. Attn: Manuscript Ed. Articles relating to feminism, women's roles, and social change; reporting, profiles, essays, theory, and analysis. No poetry or fiction. Pays market rates. Query with resumé, clips, and SASE.

NATIONAL ENQUIRER—Lantana, FL 33464. Attn: Ed. Dept. Articles, of any length, for mass audience: topical news, the occult, how-to, scientific discoveries, human drama, adventure, personalities. Photos. Pays from $325. Query or send complete manuscript. SASE.

NAVY TIMES—See *Times News Service.*

NEW WOMAN—215 Lexington Ave., New York, NY 10016. Karen Walden, Ed.-in-Chief. Articles on personal and professional relationships, health, fitness, lifestyle, money, and career issues. Editorial focus is on self-discovery, self-development, and self-esteem. "Read the magazine to become familiar with our needs, and request guidelines with SASE. We look for originality, solid research, and a friendly, accessible style." Pays varying rates, on acceptance.

NEW YORK—755 Second Ave., New York, NY 10017. Edward Kosner, Ed. Peter Herbst, Man. Ed. Feature articles of interest to New Yorkers; focus is on current events in the metropolitan New York area. Pays $850 to $3,500, on acceptance. Query required; not responsible for unsolicited material.

THE NEW YORK TIMES MAGAZINE—229 W. 43rd St., New York, NY 10036. Attn: Articles Ed. Timely articles, approximately 3,000 words, on news items, forthcoming events, trends, culture, entertainment, etc. Pays to $2,500 for major articles, on acceptance. Query with clips.

THE NEW YORKER—20 W. 43rd St., New York, NY 10036. Send submissions to appropriate Editor (Fact, Fiction, or Poetry). Factual and biographical articles for "Profiles," "Reporter at Large," etc. Pays good rates, on acceptance. Query.

NEWSWEEK—251 W. 57th St., New York, NY 10019-1894. Attn: Ed. Dept. Original opinion essays, 1,000 to 1,100 words, for "My Turn" column; must contain verifiable facts. Submit manuscript with SASE. Pays $1,000, on publication.

OMNI—324 W. Wendover Ave., Suite 205, Greensboro, NC 27408. Keith Ferrell, Ed. Articles, 750 to 3,000 words, on scientific aspects of the future: space, machine intelligence, ESP, origin of life, future arts, lifestyles, etc. Fiction, 2,000 to 10,000 words, should be sent to Ellen Datlow, Fiction Ed., *Omni,* 1965 Broadway, New York, NY 10023. Pays $750 to $2,500, on acceptance. Query.

PARADE—711 Third Ave., New York, NY 10017. Sarah R. Cohen, Articles Correspondent. National Sunday newspaper magazine. Factual and authoritative articles, 1,000 to 1,500 words, on subjects of national interest: health, consumer and environmental issues, the family, sports, etc. Profiles of well-known personalities and service pieces. No fiction, poetry, games, or puzzles. Pays from $1,000. Query.

PENTHOUSE—1965 Broadway, New York, NY 10023-5965. Peter Bloch, Ed. Lavada Blanton, Features and Fashion Ed. General-interest or controversial articles, to 5,000 words. Pays to $1 a word, on acceptance.

PEOPLE IN ACTION/SPORTS PARADE—See *Meridian Lifestyles.*

PEOPLE WEEKLY—Time-Life Bldg., Rockefeller Ctr., New York, NY 10020. John Saar, Asst. Man. Ed. "Vast majority of material is staff-written." Will consider article proposals, 3 to 4 paragraphs, on timely, entertaining, and topical personalities. Pays good rates, on acceptance.

PLAYBOY—680 N. Lakeshore Dr., Chicago, IL 60611. Peter Moore, Articles Ed. Sophisticated articles, 4,000 to 6,000 words, of interest to urban men. Humor, satire. Pays to $3,000, on acceptance. Query.

PLAYGIRL—801 Second Ave., New York, NY 10017. Charmian Carl, Ed.-in Chief. Articles, 2,500 to 3,000 words, for women ages 18 to 54. Query with clips. Fiction and nonfiction. Pays negotiable rates.

PSYCHOLOGY TODAY—49 E. First St., 11th Fl., New York, NY 10010. Hara E. Marano, Ed. Bimonthly. Articles, 4,000 words, on timely subjects relating to human behavior or the national psyche. Pays varying rates, on publication.

QUEEN'S QUARTERLY—Queens Univ., Kingston, Ont., Canada K7L 3N6. Boris Castel, Ed. Articles, to 5,000 words, on a wide range of topics, and fiction, to 5,000 words. Poetry; send no more than 6 poems. B&W art. Pays to $400, on publication.

READER'S DIGEST—Pleasantville, NY 10570. Kenneth Tomlinson, Ed.-in-Chief. Unsolicited manuscripts will not be read or returned. General-interest articles already in print and well-developed story proposals will be considered. Send reprint or query to any editor on the masthead.

REAL PEOPLE—950 Third Ave., New York, NY 10022-2705. Alex Polner, Ed. True stories, to 500 words, on interesting people, strange occupations and hobbies, eye opening stories about people, places and odd happenings. Pays $25 to $50, on publication; send submissions to "Real Shorts," Brad Hamilton, Ed. Query for interviews, 1,000 to 1,800 words, with movie or TV actors, musicians, and other entertainment celebrities. Pays $100 to $350, on publication. SASE required.

REDBOOK—224 W. 57th St., New York, NY 10019. Diane Salvatore, Sr. Ed. Toni Gerber Hope, Health Ed. Articles, 1,000 to 2,500 words, on subjects related to relationships, marriage, sex, current social issues, crime, human interest, health, psychology, and parenting. Payment varies, on acceptance. Query with clips.

ROLLING STONE—1290 Ave. of the Americas, 2nd Fl., New York, NY 10104. Attn: Ed. Magazine of American music, culture, and politics. No fiction. Query. "We rarely accept free-lance material."

THE ROTARIAN—1560 Sherman Ave., Evanston, IL 60201–3698. Willmon L. White, Ed. Articles, 1,200 to 2,000 words, on international social and economic issues, business and management, human relationships, travel, sports, environment, science and technology; humor. Pays good rates, on acceptance. Query.

SATELLITE ORBIT—8330 Boone Blvd., Suite 600, Vienna, VA 22182. Phillip Swann, Ed. Television-related articles, 750 to 2,500 words, of interest to the satellite and cable TV viewer: personality profiles, general sports pieces, items on hardware. Query with clips. Pay varies, on acceptance.

THE SATURDAY EVENING POST—1100 Waterway Blvd., Indianapolis, IN 46202. Ted Kreiter, Exec. Ed. Family-oriented articles, 1,500 to 3,000 words: humor, preventive medicine, destination-oriented travel pieces (not personal experience), celebrity profiles, the arts, and sciences. Pieces on sports and home repair (with photos). Pays varying rates, on publication. Queries preferred.

SMITHSONIAN MAGAZINE—900 Jefferson Dr., Washington, DC 20560. Marlane A. Liddell, Articles Ed. Articles on history, art, natural history, physical science, profiles, etc. Query with clips and SASE.

SOAP OPERA DIGEST—45 W. 25th St., New York, NY 10010. Jason Bonderoff, Roberta Caploe, Man. Eds. Investigative reports and profiles, to 1,500 words, about New York- or Los Angeles-based soaps. Pays from $250, on acceptance. Query with clips.

SOAP OPERA UPDATE—270 Sylvan Ave., Englewood Cliffs, NJ 07632. Dawn Mazzurco, Richard Spencer, Exec. Eds. Soap-opera oriented articles, 750 to 1,250 words; fillers to 500 words. Pays $200, on publication. Queries preferred.

SPORTS ILLUSTRATED—1271 Ave. of the Americas, New York, NY 10020. Chris Hunt, Articles Ed. Query. Rarely uses free-lance material.

STAR—660 White Plains Rd., Tarrytown, NY 10591. Attn: Ed. Dept. Topical articles, 50 to 800 words, on human-interest subjects, show business, lifestyles, the sciences, etc., for family audience. Pays varying rates.

SUCCESS—230 Park Ave., #7, New York, NY 10169–0014. Scott DeGarmo, Pub./Ed.-in-Chief. Profiles of successful executives, entrepreneurs; management science, psychology, behavior, and motivation articles, 500 to 3,500 words. Query.

TIMES NEWS SERVICE—Army Times Publishing Co., Springfield, VA 22159. Attn: R&R Ed. Articles that are informative, helpful, entertaining, and stimulating to a military audience for "R&R" newspaper section (formerly "Life in the Times"). Pays $75 to $100, on acceptance. Also, 1,000-word articles on careers after military service, travel, books and home entertainment, finance, and education for *Army Times, Navy Times,* and *Air Force Times.* Address Supplements Ed. Pays $125 to $200, on acceptance. Guidelines.

THE TOASTMASTER—P.O. Box 9052, Mission Viejo, CA 92690. Suzanne Frey, Ed. Articles, 1,500 to 2,500 words, on decision making, leadership, language, interpersonal and professional communication, humor, logical thinking, rhetorical devices, public speaking in general, profiles of great orators, speaking techniques, etc. Pays $100 to $250, on acceptance.

TOWN & COUNTRY—1700 Broadway, New York, NY 10019. Pamela Fiori, Ed.-in-Chief. Considers one-page proposals for articles. Include clips and resumé. Rarely buys unsolicited manuscripts.

TRAVEL & LEISURE—1120 Ave. of the Americas, New York, NY 10036. Nancy Novogrod, Ed.-in-Chief. Articles, 800 to 3,000 words, on destinations and leisure-time activities. Regional pieces for regional editions. Pays varying rates, on acceptance. Query.

TROPIC—*The Miami Herald*, One Herald Plaza, Miami, FL 33132. Tom Shroder, Exec. Ed. Essays and articles, 1,000 to 4,000 words, on current trends and issues, light or heavy, for sophisticated audience. No fiction or poetry. Limited humor. Pays $200 to $1,000, on publication. SASE. Allow 4 to 6 weeks for response.

TV GUIDE—Radnor, PA 19088. Barry Golson, Exec. Ed. Short, light, brightly written pieces about humorous or offbeat angles of television and industry trends. (Majority of personality pieces are staff-written.) Pays on acceptance. Query.

VANITY FAIR—350 Madison Ave., New York, NY 10017. Attn: Submissions (Fact, Fiction, or Poetry). Pays on acceptance. Query.

VILLAGE VOICE—36 Cooper Sq., New York, NY 10003. Sarah Jewler, Man. Ed. Articles, 500 to 2,000 words, on current or controversial topics. Pays $75 to $450, on acceptance. Query or send manuscript with SASE.

VISTA—999 Ponce, Suite 600, Coral Gables, FL 33134. Carmen Teresa Roiz, Ed. Articles, to 1,500 words, for English-speaking Hispanic Americans, on job advancement, bilingualism, immigration, the media, fashion, education, medicine, sports, and food. Profiles, 100 words, of Hispanic Americans in unusual jobs; photos welcome. Pays 20¢ a word, on acceptance. Query required. "Sample copy and guidelines free on request."

VOGUE—350 Madison Ave., New York, NY 10017. Attn: Features Ed. Articles, to 1,500 words, on women, entertainment and the arts, travel, medicine, and health. General features. Query.

WASHINGTON POST MAGAZINE—*The Washington Post*, 1150 15th St. N.W., Washington, DC 20071. Liza Mundy, Man. Ed. Essays, profiles, and Washington-oriented general-interest pieces, to 5,000 words, on business, arts and culture, politics, science, sports, education, children, relationships, behavior, etc. Pays from $1,000, after acceptance.

WISCONSIN—*The Milwaukee Journal Magazine*, P.O. Box 661, Milwaukee, WI 53201. Alan Borsuk, Ed. Trend stories, essays, humor, personal-experience pieces, profiles, 500 to 2,500 words, with strong Wisconsin emphasis. Pays $75 to $750, on publication.

WOMAN'S DAY—1633 Broadway, New York, NY 10019. Rebecca Greer, Articles Ed. Articles, 500 to 2,000 words, on subjects of interest to women: marriage, education, family health, child rearing, money management, interpersonal relationships, changing lifestyles, etc. Dramatic first-person narratives about women who have experienced medical miracles or other triumphs, or have overcome common problems, such as alcoholism. Query; unsolicited manuscripts not accepted. SASE required. Pays top rates, on acceptance.

WOMAN'S WORLD—270 Sylvan Ave., Englewood Cliffs, NJ 07632. Attn: Ed. Articles, 600 to 1,800 words, of interest to middle-income women between the ages of 18 and 60, on love, romance, careers, medicine, health, psychology, family life, travel; dramatic stories of adventure or crisis, investigative reports. Send SASE for guidelines. Pays $300 to $900, on acceptance. Query.

WORKING WOMAN—230 Park Ave., New York, NY 10169. Lynn Povich, Ed. Articles, 1,000 to 2,500 words, on business and personal aspects of working women's lives. Pays from $400, on acceptance.

YANKEE—Yankee Publishing Co., Dublin, NH 03444. Judson D. Hale, Ed. Articles, to 3,000 words, with New England angle. Photos. Pays $150 to $1,000 (average $750), on acceptance.

YOUR HOME/INDOORS & OUT—Box 10010, Ogden, UT 84409. Attn: Ed. Staff. Articles, 1,000 words with good color transparencies, on fresh ideas in home decor, ranging from floor and wall coverings to home furnishings. Latest in home construction (exteriors, interiors, building materials, design, entertaining, and lifestyle), the outdoors at home (landscaping, pools, patios, gardens, etc.), home management, and home buying and selling. Avoid do-it-yourself approaches. Emphasize the use of professionals. Queries required. Guidelines. Pays 15¢ a word and $35 for photos, $50 for cover photo, on acceptance.

CURRENT EVENTS, POLITICS

AFRICA REPORT—833 U.N. Pl., New York, NY 10017. Margaret A. Novicki, Ed. Well-researched articles, 1,000 to 2,500 words, by specialists on current African affairs. Include photos. Pays $150 to $300, on publication.

THE AMERICAN LEGION—Box 1055, Indianapolis, IN 46206. John Greenwald, Ed. Articles, 750 to 2,000 words, on current world affairs, public policy, and subjects of contemporary interest. Pays $500 to $2,000, on acceptance. Query.

THE AMERICAN SCHOLAR—1811 Q St. N.W., Washington, DC 20009–9974. Joseph Epstein, Ed. Non-technical articles and essays, 3,500 to 4,000 words, on current affairs, the American cultural scene, politics, arts, religion, and science. Pays to $500, on acceptance.

THE AMICUS JOURNAL—Natural Resources Defense Council, 40 W. 20th St., New York, NY 10011. Kathrin Day Lassila, Ed. Investigative articles, book reviews, and poetry related to national and international environmental policy. Pays varying rates, on acceptance. Queries required.

THE ATLANTIC MONTHLY—745 Boylston St., Boston, MA 02116. William Whitworth, Ed. In-depth articles on public issues, politics, social sciences, education, business, literature, and the arts, with emphasis on information rather than opinion. Ideal length is 3,000 to 6,000 words, though short pieces, 1,000 to 2,000 words, are also welcome. Pays excellent rates, on acceptance.

CHURCH & STATE—8120 Fenton St., Silver Spring, MD 20910. Joseph L. Conn, Man. Ed. Articles, 600 to 2,600 words, on issues of religious liberty and church-state relations. Pays varying rates, on acceptance. Query.

COMMENTARY—165 E. 56th St., New York, NY 10022. Norman Podhoretz, Ed. Articles, 5,000 to 7,000 words, on contemporary issues, Jewish affairs, social sciences, community life, religious thought, culture. Serious fiction; book reviews. Pays on publication.

COMMONWEAL—15 Dutch St., New York, NY 10038. Margaret O'Brien Steinfels, Ed. Catholic. Articles, to 3,000 words, on political, social, religious, and literary subjects. Pays 3¢ a word, on acceptance.

CURRENT HISTORY—4225 Main St., Philadelphia, PA 19127. William W. Finan, Jr., Ed. Country-specific political science articles, to 20 pages. Hard analysis written in a lively manner. "We devote each issue to a specific region or country. Writers should be experts with up-to-date knowledge of the region." Queries preferred. Pays $300, on publication.

ENVIRONMENT—1319 18th St. N.W., Washington, DC 20036–1802. Barbara T. Richman, Man. Ed. Articles, 2,500 to 5,000 words, on environmental, scientific, and technological policy and decision-making issues. Pays $100 to $300, on publication. Query.

FOREIGN SERVICE JOURNAL—2101 E St. N.W., Washington, DC 20037. Articles of interest to the Foreign Service and the U.S. diplomatic community. Query. Pays to 20¢ a word, on publication.

THE FREEMAN—Foundation for Economic Education, Irvington-on-Hudson, NY 10533. Beth Hoffman, Man. Ed. Articles, to 3,500 words, on economic, political, and moral implications of private property, voluntary exchange, and individual choice. Pays 10¢ a word, on publication.

INQUIRER MAGAZINE—*Philadelphia Inquirer*, P.O. Box 8263, 400 N. Broad St., Philadelphia, PA 19101. Ms. Avery Rome, Ed. Local-interest features, 500 to 7,000 words. Profiles of national figures in politics, entertainment, etc. Pays varying rates, on publication. Query.

LABOR'S HERITAGE—10000 New Hampshire Ave., Silver Spring, MD 20903. Stuart Kaufman, Ed. Quarterly journal of The George Meany Memorial Archives. Publishes 15- to 30-page documented articles of original research for labor scholars, labor union members, and the general public. Pays in copies.

MIDSTREAM—110 E. 59th St., New York, NY 10022. Joel Carmichael, Ed. Articles of international and Jewish concern. Pays 5¢ a word, after publication. Allow 3 months for response.

MOMENT—3000 Connecticut Ave. N.W., Suite 300, Washington, DC 20008. Suzanne Singer, Man. Ed. Sophisticated articles, 2,500 to 5,000 words, on Jewish topics. Columns, to 1,500 words, on American Jewry, pluralism, and current issues in the Mideast and Israel. Pays $50 to $400, on publication.

MOTHER JONES—731 Market St., Suite 600, San Francisco, CA 94103. Jeffrey Klein, Ed. Investigative articles and political essays. Pays $1,000 to $3,000 for feature articles, after acceptance. Query required.

THE NATION—72 Fifth Ave., New York, NY 10011. Victor Navasky, Ed. Articles, 1,500 to 2,500 words, on politics and culture from a liberal/left perspective. Pays $75 per published page, to $300, on publication. Query.

THE NEW YORK TIMES MAGAZINE—229 W. 43rd St., New York, NY 10036. Attn: Articles Ed. Timely articles, approximately 4,000 words, on news items, trends, culture, etc. Pays $1,000 for short pieces, from $2,500 for major articles, on acceptance. Query with clips.

THE NEW YORKER—20 W. 43rd St., New York, NY 10036. Address the Fact Eds. Factual and biographical articles, for "Profiles," "Reporter at Large," "Annals of Crime," "Onward and Upward with the Arts," etc. Pays good rates, on acceptance. Query.

ON THE ISSUES—Choices Women's Medical Ctr., Inc., 97–77 Queens Blvd., Forest Hills, NY 11374–3317. Ronni Sandroff, Ed. "The Progressive Woman's Quarterly." Articles, up to 2,500 words, on political or social issues.

Movie, music, and book reviews, 500 to 750 words. Query. Payment varies, on publication.

THE PROGRESSIVE—409 E. Main St., Madison, WI 53703. Erwin Knoll, Ed. Articles, 1,000 to 3,500 words, on political and social problems. Pays $100 to $300, on publication.

PUBLIC CITIZEN MAGAZINE—2000 P St. N.W., Suite 610, Washington, DC 20036. Peter Nye, Ed. Investigative reports and articles of timely political interest, for members of Public Citizen: consumer rights, health and safety, environmental protection, safe energy, tax reform, trade, and government and corporate accountability. Photos, illustrations. Payment negotiable.

REASON—3415 S. Sepulveda Blvd., Suite 400, Los Angeles, CA 90034. Attn: Eds. "Free Minds and Free Markets." Articles, 850 to 5,000 words, on politics, economics, and culture "from an individualist's perspective." Query. Pays varying rates, on acceptance.

REGARDIE'S—1010 Wisconsin Ave. N.W., Suite 600, Washington, DC 20007. Richard Blow, Ed. Profiles and investigations of the "high and mighty" in the DC area. "We require aggressive reporting and imaginative, entertaining writing." Pays 75¢ a word, on publication. Queries required.

ROLL CALL: THE NEWSPAPER OF CAPITOL HILL—900 2nd St. N.E., Washington, DC 20002. Stacy Mason, Ed. Factual, breezy articles with political or Congressional angle: Congressional history, human-interest subjects, political lore, etc. Political satire and humor. Pays on publication.

SATURDAY NIGHT—184 Front St. E., Suite 400, Toronto, Ont., Canada M5A 4N3. Kenneth Whyte, Ed. Canada's oldest magazine of politics, social issues, culture, and business. Features, 1,000 to 3,000 words, and columns, 800 to 1,000 words; fiction, to 3,000 words. Must have Canadian tie-in. Payment varies, on acceptance.

VFW MAGAZINE—406 W. 34th St., Kansas City, MO 64111. Richard K. Kolb, Ed. Magazine for Veterans of Foreign Wars and their families. Articles, 1,500 words, on current issues and history, with veteran angle. Photos. Pays to $500, extra for photos, on acceptance. Guidelines.

THE WASHINGTON MONTHLY—1611 Connecticut Ave. N.W., Washington, DC 20009. Charles Peters, Ed. Investigative articles, 1,500 to 5,000 words, on politics, government, and the political culture. Pays 10¢ a word, on publication. Query.

WASHINGTON POST MAGAZINE—*The Washington Post,* 1150 15th St. N.W., Washington, DC 20071. Liza Mundy, Man. Ed. Essays, profiles, and general-interest pieces, to 5,000 words, on Washington-oriented politics and related issues. Pays from $1,000, after acceptance. SASE required.

WHO CARES: A JOURNAL OF SERVICE AND ACTION—1511 K St. N.W., Washington, DC 20005. Leslie Crutchfield, Heather McLeod, News and Features Eds. Chloe Breyer, Photo/Creative Ed. Articles, 1,000 words, on service programs throughout the country for "Partners in Change." Features, 1,500 to 2,500 words, on specific issues related to service and action. "Entrepreneur" pieces, 1,500 to 2,500 words, focus on the business of starting a successful nonprofit. "On Campus," 800 words, on unique service programs that involve college students. "Faith in Service," 1,000 to 1,500 words, on connections between service and spirituality. "Who's Who and What's What," 100- to 400-word news blurbs on service and action. Also, humorous essays, 800 words, and first-person narratives, related fiction, and other creative essays, 800 to 2,000 words. No payment for unsolicited articles. Payment for assigned pieces varies, on publication.

REGIONAL AND CITY PUBLICATIONS

ADIRONDACK LIFE—P.O. Box 97, Jay, NY 12941. Tom Hughes, Ed. Features, to 5,000 words, on outdoor and environmental activities and issues, arts, wilderness, profiles, history, and fiction; focus is on the Adirondack region and north country of New York State. Pays to 25¢ a word, 30 days after acceptance. Query.

ALABAMA HERITAGE—The Univ. of Alabama, Box 870342, Tuscaloosa, AL 35487–0342. Suzanne Wolfe, Ed. Quarterly. Articles, to 5,000 words, on local, state, and regional history: art, literature, language, archaeology, music, religion, architecture, and natural history. Query, mentioning availability of photos and illustrations. Pays an honorarium, on publication, plus 10 copies. Guidelines.

ALASKA—808 E St., Suite 200, Anchorage, AK 99501. Tobin Morrison, Ed. Articles, 2,000 words, on life in Alaska. Pays varying rates, on acceptance. Guidelines.

ALOHA, THE MAGAZINE OF HAWAII—720 Kapiolani Blvd., 4th Fl., Honolulu, HI 96813. Cheryl Chee Tsutsumi, Ed. Articles, 1,500 to 2,500 words, on the life, customs, and people of Hawaii and the Pacific. Poetry. Fiction. Pays $150 to $500 for full-length features, on publication. Query.

AMERICAN DESERT MAGAZINE—P.O. Box 1303, Desert Hot Springs, CA 92240. Joan Brooks, Pub./Ed. Quarterly. Articles, 1,000 to 2,500 words, related to the southwest deserts: desert history, natural features, survival, Native American culture, profiles. Pays 3¢ a word, on publication. Guidelines.

APPRISE– P.O. Box 2954, 1982 Locust Ln., Harrisburg, PA 17105. Jim Connor, Ed. Articles, 1,500 to 3,500 words, of regional (central Pennsylvania) interest, including profiles of notable Pennsylvanians, and broadly based articles of social interest that "enlighten and inform." Pays 10¢ a word, on publication.

ARIZONA HIGHWAYS—2039 W. Lewis Ave., Phoenix, AZ 85009. Robert J. Early, Ed. Articles, 1,600 to 2,000 words, on travel in Arizona; pieces on adventure, humor, lifestyles, nostalgia, history, archaeology, nature, etc. Departments using personal experience pieces include "Mileposts," "Focus on Nature," "Along the Way," "Event of the Month," "Back Road Adventures," "Hiking," and "Arizona Humor." Pays 35¢ to 55¢ a word, on acceptance. Guidelines. Query.

ATLANTA—1360 Peachtree St., Suite 1800, Atlanta, GA 30309. Lee Walburn, Ed. Articles, 1,500 to 5,000 words, on Atlanta subjects or personalities. Pays $300 to $2,000, on publication. Query.

ATLANTIC CITY MAGAZINE—P.O. Box 2100, Pleasantville, NJ 08232. Ken Weatherford, Ed. Lively articles, 200 to 2,000 words, on Atlantic City and the southern New Jersey shore, for locals and tourists: entertainment, casinos, business, recreation, personalities, lifestyle, local color. Pays $50 to $600, on publication. Query.

BACK HOME IN KENTUCKY—P.O. Box 681629, Franklin, TN 37068–1629. Nanci P. Gregg, Man. Ed. Articles on Kentucky history, travel, craftsmen and artisans, Kentucky cooks, and "colorful" characters. Limited personal nostalgia

573

specifically related to Kentucky. Pays $25 to $100 for articles with B&W or color photos. Queries preferred.

BALTIMORE MAGAZINE—16 S. Calvert St., Suite 1000, Baltimore, MD 21202. Ramsey Flynn, Ed. Articles, 500 to 3,000 words, on people, places, and things in the Baltimore metropolitan area. Consumer advice, investigative pieces, profiles, humor, and personal experience pieces. Payment varies, on publication. Query required.

THE BIG APPLE PARENTS' PAPER—36 E. 12th St., New York, NY 10003. Susan Hodara, Ed. Articles, 600 to 750 words, for New York City parents. Pays $50, on publication. Buys first NY-area rights.

BIRMINGHAM—2027 First Ave. N., Birmingham, AL 35203. Joe O'Donnell, Ed. Profiles, features, business, and nostalgia pieces, to 2,500 words, with Birmingham tie-in. Pays $50 to $175, on publication.

BLUE RIDGE COUNTRY—P.O. Box 21535, Roanoke, VA 24018. Kurt Rheinheimer, Ed. Bimonthly. Regional articles, 1,200 to 2,000 words, that "explore and extol the beauty, history, and travel opportunities in the mountain regions of Virginia, North Carolina, West Virginia, Tennessee, Kentucky, Maryland, South Carolina, and Georgia." Color slides or B&W prints considered. Pays $200 for photo-features, on publication. Queries preferred.

BOCA RATON—JES Publishing, Amtec Ctr., Suite 100, 6413 Congress Ave., Boca Raton, FL 33487. Marie Speed, Ed. Articles, 800 to 3,000 words, on Florida topics, personalities, and travel. Pays $50 to $500, on publication. Query with clips required.

THE BOSTON GLOBE MAGAZINE—*The Boston Globe*, Boston, MA 02107. Evelynne Kramer, Ed. General-interest articles on local, national, and international topics and profiles, 2,500 to 5,000 words. Query and SASE required.

BOSTON MAGAZINE—300 Massachusetts Ave., Boston, MA 02115. Attn: Man. Ed. Informative, entertaining features, 1,000 to 3,000 words, on Boston-area personalities, institutions, and phenomena. Query. Pays to $2,000, on publication.

BUFFALO SPREE MAGAZINE—Box 38, Buffalo, NY 14226. Johanna Van De Mark, Ed./Pub. Articles, to 1,800 words, for readers in the western New York region. Pays $75 to $125, $25 for poetry, on publication.

BUSINESS IN BROWARD—P.O. Box 7375, Ft. Lauderdale, FL 33338–7375. Sherry Friedlander, Ed. Bimonthly. Articles, 1,000 words, on small business in eastern Florida county. Pay varies, on acceptance. Same address and requirements for *Business in Palm Beach County.*

BUSINESS IN PALM BEACH COUNTY—See *Business in Broward.*

BUZZ: THE TALK OF LOS ANGELES—11835 W. Olympic Blvd., Suite 450, Los Angeles, CA 90064. Allan Mayer, Ed.-in-Chief. Articles, varying lengths, of particular relevance to readers in southern California. Query. Pays $1 a word, within 30 days of acceptance.

CALIFORNIA BUSINESS—1427 Bay St., Suite 2000, San Francisco, CA 94123. Umberto Tosi, Ed. Articles, 500 to 3,500 words, on California-based businesses. Payment varies, on acceptance. Query.

CAPE COD LIFE—P.O. Box 767, Cataumet, MA 02534–0767. Brian F. Shortsleeve, Pub. Articles, to 2,000 words, on current events, business, art, history, gardening, and nautical lifestyle on Cape Cod, Martha's Vineyard, and Nantucket. Pays 10¢ a word, 30 days after publication. Queries preferred.

CARIBBEAN TRAVEL AND LIFE—8403 Colesville Rd., Silver Spring, MD 20910. Veronica Gould Stoddart, Ed. Articles, 500 to 3,000 words, on all aspects of travel, recreation, leisure, and culture in the Caribbean, the Bahamas, and Bermuda. Pays $75 to $550, on publication. Query with published clips.

CAROLOGUE—South Carolina Historical Society, 100 Meeting St., Charleston, SC 29401–2299. Stephen Hoffius, Ed. General-interest articles, to 10 pages, on South Carolina history. Queries preferred. Pays in copies.

CHESAPEAKE BAY MAGAZINE—1819 Bay Ridge Ave., Annapolis, MD 21403. Jean Waller, Ed. Articles, 8 to 10 typed pages, related to the Chesapeake Bay area. Profiles. Photos. Pays on publication. Query.

CHICAGO—414 N. Orleans, Chicago, IL 60610. Shane Tritsch, Man. Ed. Articles, 1,000 to 5,000 words, related to Chicago. Pays varying rates, on acceptance. Query.

CHICAGO HISTORY—Clark St. at North Ave., Chicago, IL 60614. Claudia Lamm Wood, Ed. Articles, to 4,500 words, on Chicago's urban, political, social, and cultural history. Pays to $250, on publication. Query.

CHICAGO TRIBUNE MAGAZINE—*Chicago Tribune*, 435 N. Michigan Ave., Rm. 532, Chicago, IL 60611. Attn: Ed. Profiles and articles, to 6,000 words, on public and social issues on the personal, local, or national level. Prefer regional slant. Query. Pays $250 to $1,500, on publication.

CITY SPORTS MAGAZINE—2201 Third St., San Francisco, CA 94107. Craig Bystrynski, Ed. Articles, 300 to 3,000 words, on participant sports, family recreation, travel, and the active lifestyle. Pays $50 to $500, on publication. Query. Limited market.

COMMON GROUND MAGAZINE—P.O. Box 99, McVeytown, PA 17051–0099. Ruth Dunmire and Pam Brumbaugh, Eds. Quarterly. General-interest articles, 500 to 5,000 words, related to central Pennsylvania's Juniata River Valley and its rural lifestyle. Related fiction, 1,000 to 2,000 words. Poetry, to 12 lines. Fillers, photos, and cartoons. Pays $25 to $200 for articles, $5 to $15 for fillers, and $5 to $25 for photos, on publication. Guidelines.

CONCORD NORTH—See *Network Publications.*

CONNECTICUT—789 Reservoir Ave., Bridgeport, CT 06606. Charles Monagan, Ed. Articles, 1,500 to 3,500 words, on Connecticut topics, issues, people, and lifestyles. Pays $500 to $1,200, within 30 days of acceptance.

CRAIN'S DETROIT BUSINESS—1400 Woodbridge, Detroit, MI 48207. Mary Kramer, Ed. Business articles, 500 to 1,000 words, about Detroit, for Detroit business readers. Pays $100 to $200, on publication. Query required.

DALLAS LIFE MAGAZINE—*The Dallas Morning News*, P.O. Box 655237, Communications Ctr., Dallas, TX 75265. Mike Maza, Man. Ed. Well-researched articles and profiles, 1,000 to 3,000 words, on contemporary local issues and personalities. Pays from 25¢ a word, on acceptance. Query required.

DELAWARE TODAY—P.O. Box 2087, Wilmington, DE 19899. Lise Monty, Ed. Service articles, profiles, news, etc., on topics of local interest. Pays $75 to $125 for department pieces, $50 to $500 for features, on publication. Queries with clips required.

DETROIT FREE PRESS MAGAZINE—*Detroit Free Press*, 321 W. Lafayette Blvd., Detroit, MI 48231. Attn: Ed. Articles, to 5,000 words, on issues, lifestyles. Personality profiles; essays; humor. Pays from $150. Query preferred.

DETROIT MONTHLY—1400 Woodbridge, Detroit, MI 48207. John Barron, Ed. Articles on Detroit-area people, issues, lifestyles, and business. Payment varies. Query required.

DOWN EAST—Camden, ME 04843. Davis Thomas, Ed. Articles, 1,500 to 2,500 words, on all aspects of life in Maine. Photos. Pays to 20¢ a word, extra for photos, on acceptance. Query.

EASTSIDE PARENT—Northwest Parent Publishing, 2107 Elliott Ave., #303, Seattle, WA 98121. Ann Bergman, Ed. Articles, 300 to 2,500 words, for parents of children ages 12 and under. Queries preferred. Pays $25 to $200, on publication. Also publishes *Seattle's Child, Portland Parent*, and *Pierce County Parent.*

ERIE & CHAUTAUQUA MAGAZINE—317 W. Sixth St., Erie, PA 16507. K. L. Kalvelage, Man. Ed. Feature articles, to 2,500 words, on issues of interest to upscale readers in the Erie, Warren, and Crawford counties (PA), and Chautauqua (NY) county. Pieces with regional relevance. Pays after publication. Query preferred, with writing samples. Guidelines available.

FLORIDA KEYS MAGAZINE—P.O. Box 2921, Key Largo, FL 33037. Gibbons Cline, Ed. Articles, 1,000 to 2,000 words, on the Florida Keys: history, environment, natural history, profiles, etc. Fillers, humor. Photos. Pays varying rates, on publication.

FLORIDA WILDLIFE—620 S. Meridian St., Tallahassee, FL 32399–1600. Attn: Ed. Bimonthly of the Florida Game and Fresh Water Fish Commission. Articles, 800 to 1,500 words, that promote native flora and fauna, hunting, fishing in Florida's fresh waters, outdoor ethics, and conservation of Florida's natural resources. Pays $50 to $300, on publication.

THE GAZETTE—The Sunday Magazine of the *Pittsburgh Post-Gazette*, The Pittsburgh Press, 34 Blvd. of the Allies, Pittsburgh, PA 15230. Mark S. Murphy, Ed. Well-written, well-organized, in-depth articles of local, regional, or national interest, 3,000 to 4,500 words, on issues, personalities, human interest, historical moments. No fiction, hobbies, how-tos or "timely events" pieces. Pays from $500, on publication. Query.

GOLDENSEAL—The Cultural Ctr., 1900 Kanawha Blvd. E., Charleston, WV 25305–0300. Ken Sullivan, Ed. Articles, 1,000 and 3,000 words, on West Virginia history, folklife, folk art and crafts, and music of a traditional nature. Pays to $200, on publication. Guidelines.

GRAND RAPIDS—549 Ottawa N.W., Grand Rapids, MI 49503. Carole Valade Smith, Ed. Service articles (dining guide, travel, personal finance, humor) and issue-oriented pieces related to Grand Rapids, Michigan. Pays $35 to $200, on publication. Query.

GULF COAST GOLFER—See *North Texas Golfer.*

HAMPSHIRE EAST—See *Network Publications.*

HAWAII—Box 6050, Mission Viejo, CA 92690–6050. Dennis Shattuck, Ed. Bimonthly. Articles, 1,000 to 5,000 words, related to Hawaii. Pays 10¢ a word, on publication. Query.

HIGH COUNTRY NEWS—Box 1090, Paonia, CO 81428. Betsy Marston, Ed. Biweekly. Articles, 2,000 words, and roundups, 750 words, on environmental issues, public lands management, energy, and natural resource issues; profiles of western innovators; pieces on western politics. "Writers must take regional approach." Poetry. B&W photos. Pays $2 to $4 per column inch, on publication. Query.

HONOLULU—36 Merchant St., Honolulu, HI 96813. Ed Cassidy, Ed./Pub. Features highlighting contemporary life in the Hawaiian islands: politics, sports, history, people, arts, events. Columns and department pieces are mostly staff-written. Queries required. Pays $300 to $700, on acceptance.

ILLINOIS ENTERTAINER—2250 E. Devon, Suite 150, Des Plaines, IL 60018. Michael C. Harris, Ed. Articles, 500 to 1,500 words, on local and national entertainment (emphasis on alternative music) in the greater Chicago area. Personality profiles; interviews; reviews. Photos. Pays varying rates, on publication. Query preferred.

INDIANAPOLIS MONTHLY—950 N. Meridian St., Suite 1200, Indianapolis, IN 46204. Deborah Paul, Ed./Pub. Sam Stall, Man. Ed. Articles, 1,000 words, on health, sports, politics, business, interior design, travel, and Indiana personalities. All material must have a regional focus. Pays varying rates, on publication.

INQUIRER MAGAZINE—*Philadelphia Inquirer*, P.O. 8263, 400 N. Broad St., Philadelphia, PA 19101. Ms. Avery Rome, Ed. Articles, 1,500 to 2,000 words, and 3,000 to 7,000 words, on politics, science, arts and culture, business, lifestyles and entertainment, sports, health, psychology, education, religion, and humor. Short pieces, 850 words, for "Up Front." Pays varying rates. Query.

THE IOWAN MAGAZINE—108 Third St., Suite 350, Des Moines, IA 50309. Karen Massetti-Miller, Ed. Articles, 1,000 to 3,000 words, on business, arts, people, and history of Iowa. Photos a plus. Pays $200 to $600, on publication. Query required.

ISLAND LIFE—P.O. Box 929, Sanibel Island, FL 33957. Joan Hooper, Ed. Articles, 500 to 1,200 words, with photos, on wildlife, flora and fauna, design and decor, the arts, shelling, local sports, historical sites, etc., directly related to the islands of Sanibel, Captiva, Marco, Estero, or Gasparilla. No first-person articles. Pays on publication.

JACKSONVILLE—(formerly *Jacksonville Today*) White Publishing Co., 1650 Prudential Dr., Suite 300, Jacksonville, FL 32207. Larry Marscheck, Ed. Service pieces and articles, 1,500 to 2,500 words, on issues and personalities of interest to readers in the greater Jacksonville area. Department pieces, 1,200 to 1,500 words, on business, health, travel, real estate, arts and entertainment, sports, food. Home and garden articles, 1,000 to 2,000 words. Query required. Pays $200 to $500, on publication. Guidelines.

JOURNAL OF THE WEST—1531 Yuma, Manhattan, KS 66502-4228. Robin Higham, Ed. Articles, to 20 pages, on the history and culture of the West, then and now. Pays in copies.

KANSAS!—Kansas Dept. of Commerce, 700 S.W. Harrison, Suite 1300, Topeka, KS 66603-3957. Andrea Glenn, Ed. Quarterly. Articles, 5 to 7 typed pages, on the people, places, history, and events of Kansas. Color slides. Pays to $250, on acceptance. Query.

KENTUCKY LIVING—P.O. Box 32170, Louisville, KY 40232. Gary Luhr, Ed. Articles, 800 to 2,000 words, with strong Kentucky angle: profiles (of people, places, events), history, biography, recreation, travel, leisure or lifestyle, and book excerpts. Pays $125 to $300, on acceptance. Guidelines.

LAKE SUPERIOR MAGAZINE—P.O. Box 16417, Duluth, MN 55816-0417. Paul Hayden, Ed. Articles with emphasis on Lake Superior regional subjects:

historical and topical pieces that highlight the people, places, and events that affect the Lake Superior region. Pictorial essays; humor and occasional fiction. Quality photos enhance submission. "Writers must have a thorough knowledge of the subject and how it relates to our region." Pays to $400, extra for photos, after publication. Query.

LOS ANGELES MAGAZINE—1888 Century Park E., Suite 920, Los Angeles, CA 90067. Lew Harris, Ed. Articles, to 3,000 words, of interest to sophisticated, affluent southern Californians, preferably with local focus on a lifestyle topic. Pays from 10¢ a word, on acceptance. Query.

LOS ANGELES READER—5550 Wilshire Blvd., Suite 301, Los Angeles, CA 90036. James Vowell, Ed. Articles, 750 to 5,000 words, on subjects related to the Los Angeles area; special emphasis on feature journalism, entertainment, and the arts. Pays $25 to $300, on publication. Query preferred.

LOUISVILLE—One Riverfront Plaza, Louisville, KY 40202. John Filiatreau, Ed. Articles, 1,000 to 2,000 words, on community issues, personalities, and entertainment in the Louisville area. Photos. Pays from $50, on acceptance. Query; articles on assignment only. Limited free-lance market.

MANCHESTER—See *Network Publications.*

MEMPHIS—MM Corp., Box 256, Memphis, TN 38101. Tim Sampson, Ed. Articles, 1,500 to 4,000 words, on a wide variety of topics related to Memphis and the Mid-South region: politics, education, sports, business, history, etc. Profiles; investigative pieces. Pays $75 to $500, on publication. Query. Guidelines.

MICHIGAN LIVING—1 Auto Club Dr., Dearborn, MI 48126–9982. Len Barnes, Ed. Travel articles, 300 to 2,000 words, on tourist attractions and recreational opportunities in the U.S. and Canada, with emphasis on Michigan: places to go, things to do, costs, etc. Color photos. Pays $55 to $500, (rates vary for photos), on acceptance.

MID-WEST OUTDOORS—111 Shore Dr., Hinsdale, IL 60521–5885. Gene Laulunen, Ed. Articles, to 1,500 words, with photos (no slides), on where, when, and how to fish and hunt, within 500 miles of Chicago. Pays $25, on publication.

MILWAUKEE MAGAZINE—312 E. Buffalo, Milwaukee, WI 53202. John Fennell, Ed. Profiles, investigative articles, and service pieces, 2,000 to 6,000 words; local tie-in a must. No fiction. Pays $400 to $900, on publication. Query preferred.

MINNESOTA MONTHLY—15 S. Ninth St., Suite 320, Minneapolis, MN 55402. Debbie Mazzocco, Man. Ed. Articles, to 4,000 words, on the people, places, events, and issues in Minnesota. Pays $50 to $800, on acceptance. Query.

MONTANA MAGAZINE—P.O. Box 5630, Helena, MT 59604. Beverly R. Magley, Ed. Recreation, travel, general interest, regional profiles, photo-essays. Montana-oriented only. B&W prints, color slides. Pays 15¢ a word, on publication.

MPLS. ST. PAUL—220 S. 6th St., Suite 500, Minneapolis, MN 55402–4507. Brian E. Anderson, Ed. In-depth articles, features, profiles, and service pieces, 300 to 7,000 words, with Minneapolis-St. Paul focus. Pays to $1,000.

NASHUA—See *Network Publications.*

NEBRASKA HISTORY—P.O. Box 82554, Lincoln, NE 68501. James E. Potter, Ed. Articles, 3,000 to 7,000 words, on the history of Nebraska and the Great Plains. B&W line drawings. Pays in copies. Cash prize awarded to one article each year.

578

NETWORK PUBLICATIONS—100 Main St., Nashua, NH 03060. Rick Broussard, Ed. Nancy Williamson, Man. Ed. Lifestyle and business articles with a New Hampshire angle, with sources from all regions of the state, for the company's 4 regional monthlies: *Nashua, Manchester, Concord North,* and *Hampshire East*. Query. Payment varies, on acceptance.

NEVADA—1800 Hwy. 50 East, Suite 200, Carson City, NV 89710. David Moore, Ed. Articles, 500 to 700 or 1,500 to 1,800 words, on topics related to Nevada: travel, history, profiles, humor, and place. Special section on Nevada events. Photos. Pay varies, on publication.

NEW FRONTIERS OF NEW MEXICO—P.O. Box 1299, Tijeras, NM 87059. Wally Gordon, Ed./Pub. Fiction and in-depth nonfiction, to 3,000 words, related to New Mexico and the Southwest. Humor, to 1,000 words. Poetry, to 100 lines. Pays $25 to $200, on publication.

NEW JERSEY MONTHLY—P.O. Box 920, Morristown, NJ 07963–0920. Jenny DeMonte, Ed. Articles, profiles, and service pieces, 1,500 to 3,000 words; department pieces on health, business, education, travel, sports, local politics, and arts with New Jersey tie-in, 750 to 1,500 words. Pays $25 to $100 for shorts, $400 to $600 for departments, $600 to $1,750 for features, on acceptance. Query with SASE and magazine clips. Guidelines.

NEW MEXICO MAGAZINE—Lew Wallace Bldg., 495 Old Santa Fe Trail, Santa Fe, NM 87503. Attn: Ed. Articles, 250 to 2,000 words, on New Mexico subjects. No poetry or fiction. Pays about 30¢ a word, on acceptance.

NEW ORLEANS MAGAZINE—111 Veterans Blvd., Metairie, LA 70005. Errol Laborde, Ed. Articles, 3 to 15 triple-spaced pages, on New Orleans area people and issues. Photos. Pays $15 to $500, extra for photos, on publication. Query.

NEW YORK—755 Second Ave., New York, NY 10017. Kurt Andersen, Ed. Sarah Jewler, Man. Ed. Feature articles on subjects of interest to New Yorkers. Pays varying rates, on acceptance. Query required.

NORTH DAKOTA HORIZONS—P.O. Box 2639, Bismarck, ND 58502. Diane Kambeitz, V.P. Communications. Quarterly. Articles, about 3,000 words, on people, places, and events in North Dakota. Photos. Pays $75 to $300, on publication.

NORTH GEORGIA JOURNAL—P.O. Box 127, Roswell, GA 30077. Olin Jackson, Pub./Ed. History, travel, and lifestyle features, 2,000 to 3,000 words, on North Georgia. History features need human-interest approach and must be written in first person; include interviews. Photos a plus. Pays $75 to $250, on acceptance. Query.

NORTH TEXAS GOLFER—9182 Old Katy Rd., Suite 212, Houston, TX 77055. Steve Hunter, Ed. Articles, 800 to 1,500 words, involving local golfers or related directly to north Texas. Pays from $50 to $425, on publication. Query. Same requirements for *Gulf Coast Golfer* (related to south Texas).

NORTHEAST MAGAZINE—*The Hartford Courant,* 285 Broad St., Hartford, CT 06115. Lary Bloom, Ed. Articles and short essays, 750 to 3,000 words, that reflect the concerns of Connecticut residents. Pays $250 to $1,000, on acceptance.

NORTHERN LIGHTS—Box 8084, Missoula, MT 59807–8084. Attn: Ed. Articles, 500 to 3,000 words, about the contemporary West. "We look for beautifully crafted personal essays that illuminate what it means to live in the Rocky Mountain West. We're looking to bust the Hollywood stereotypes." Pays 10¢ a word, on publication.

NORTHWEST PARKS & WILDLIFE—See *Northwest Regional Magazines.*

NORTHWEST PRIME TIMES—10829 N.E. 68th St., Kirkland, WA 98033. Neil Strother, Pub./Ed. News and features of the Northwest for readers 50 and older. Pays $25 to $50, on publication. Limited market.

NORTHWEST REGIONAL MAGAZINES—P.O. Box 18000, Florence, OR 97439–0130. Attn: Dave Peden or Judy Fleagle. All submissions considered for use in *Oregon Coast, Oregon Parks, Northwest Travel*, and *Northwest Parks & Wildlife.* Articles, 800 to 2,000 words, pertaining to the Pacific Northwest, on travel, history, town/city profiles, parks, and nature. News releases, 200 to 500 words. Articles with photos (slides) preferred. Pays $50 to $350, on publication. Guidelines.

NORTHWEST TRAVEL—See *Northwest Regional Magazines.*

OKLAHOMA TODAY—Box 53384, Oklahoma City, OK 73152–9971. Jeanne M. Devlin, Ed. Articles, 1,000 to 4,000 words: travel; profiles; history; nature and outdoor recreation; and arts. All material must have regional tie-in. Queries preferred. Pays $75 to $750, on acceptance. SASE for guidelines.

ORANGE COAST—245-D Fischer Ave., Suite 8, Costa Mesa, CA 92626. Robin Manougian, Ed. Articles of interest to educated Orange County residents. Pieces, 1,000 to 1,500 words, for regular departments: "Escape" (local travel), "Coastwatch" (services and products), "Short Cuts" (local phenomena), "Guide" (local private schools, weight control centers, art galleries, etc.), and "Close-Ups" (local personality profiles). Feature articles, 1,500 to 2,500 words: investigative, social issues, business trends, and other local topics. Query. Pays $250 for features, $150 for columns, on acceptance. Guidelines.

OREGON COAST—See *Northwest Regional Magazines.*

OREGON PARKS—See *Northwest Regional Magazines.*

ORLANDO MAGAZINE—P.O. Box 2207, Orlando, FL 32802. John Kiely, Ed. General-interest articles and department pieces, lengths vary, for residents of central Florida. Query with clips.

OTTAWA MAGAZINE—192 Bank St., Ottawa, Ont., Canada K2P 1W8. Rosa Harris-Adler, Ed. Articles, investigative journalism, and profiles, 1,500 to 2,000 words, relating to the social issues and cultural and consumer interests of Ottawa City. Query with 5 or 6 article ideas, resumé, and published clips. Pays 30¢ to 50¢ a word, on acceptance.

OUTDOOR TRAVELER, MID-ATLANTIC—WMS Publications, Inc., P.O. Box 2748, Charlottesville, VA 22902. Marianne Marks, Ed. Scott Clark, Assoc. Ed. Articles, 2,500 to 3,000 words, about outdoor recreation, travel, place and events in VA, NC, WV, MD, PA, DE, DC, and NJ. Departments include "Destinations," 450 to 600 words, practical and descriptive guides to sports destinations; "Getaways," short pieces about inns and B&Bs, usually seasonal and including outdoor activities; Book Reviews, 200 words. Pays $500 to $650 for features; payment varies for departments, on publication. Guidelines.

PALM SPRINGS LIFE—Desert Publications, 303 N. Indian Canyon Dr., P.O. Box 2724, Palm Springs, CA 92263. Jamie Lee Pricer, Ed. Articles, 1,000 to 2,000 words, of interest to "wealthy, upscale people who live and/or play in the desert": food, interior design, luxury cars, shopping, sports, homes, personalities, desert issues, arts, and culture. Pays $150 to $400 for features, $30 to $60 for short profiles, on publication. Query required.

PENNSYLVANIA MAGAZINE—Box 576, Camp Hill, PA 17001–0576. Albert E. Holliday, Ed. General-interest features with a Pennsylvania flavor. All articles must be accompanied by photocopies of possible illustrations. SASE required. Guidelines.

PERSIMMON HILL—1700 N.E. 63rd St., Oklahoma City, OK 73111. M.J. Van Deventer, Ed. Published by the National Cowboy Hall of Fame. Articles, 1,500 to 2,000 words, on Western history and art, cowboys, ranching, and nature. Top-quality illustrations a must. Pays from $100 to $250, on publication.

PHILADELPHIA—1818 Market St., Philadelphia, PA 19103. Eliot Kaplan, Ed. Articles, 1,000 to 5,000 words, for sophisticated audience, relating to Philadelphia area. No fiction or poetry. Pays on acceptance. Query.

PHOENIX MAGAZINE—5555 N. 7th Ave., Suite B200, Phoenix, AZ 85013. Richard Vonier, Ed. Articles, 1,000 to 3,000 words, on topics of interest to Phoenix-area residents. Pays $300 to $1,000, on publication. Queries preferred.

PIERCE COUNTY PARENT—See *Eastside Parent.*

PITTSBURGH—4802 Fifth Ave., Pittsburgh, PA 15213. Christopher Fletcher, Ed. Articles, 850 to 3,000 words, with western Pennsylvania slant. Pays on publication.

PORTLAND MONTHLY MAGAZINE—578 Congress St., Portland, ME 04101. Colin Sargent, Ed. Articles on local people, legends, culture, and trends. Fiction, to 750 words. Pays on publication. Query preferred.

PORTLAND PARENT—See *Eastside Parent.*

RECREATION NEWS—P.O. Box 32335, Washington, DC 20007–0635. Sam E. Polson, Ed. Articles, 1,500 to 2,000 words, on recreation for government workers in the Washington, DC area. Light, first-person accounts, 800 words, for "Sporting Life" column. "Articles should have a conversational tone that's lean and brisk." Queries preferred. Pays $50 for reprints, to $300 for cover articles, on publication. Send SASE for guidelines.

RHODE ISLAND MONTHLY—18 Imperial Pl., Providence, RI 02903. Vicki Sanders, Man. Ed. Features, 1,000 to 4,000 words, ranging from investigative reporting and in-depth profiles to service pieces and visual stories, on Rhode Island and southeastern Massachusetts. Seasonal material, 1,000 to 2,000 words. Fillers, 150 to 250 words, on Rhode Island places, customs, people, events, products and services, restaurants and food. Pays $250 to $1,000 for features; $25 to $50 for shorts, on publication. Query.

THE RHODE ISLANDER MAGAZINE—*Providence Sunday Journal,* 75 Fountain St., Providence, RI 02902. Elliot Krieger, Ed. Articles, 500 to 3,000 words, with a New England focus. Pays $75 to $500, on publication.

ROCKFORD MAGAZINE—99 E. State St., Rockford, IL 61104. Craig Schmidt, Ed. General-interest magazine covering Rockford and northern Illinois. Feature articles, 2,500 to 3,500 words, and departments, 1,500 to 2,000 words, on city and area personalities, politics, events, business, family, travel destinations, home improvement and decor, dining, etc. "Nothing predictable or routine." Query with samples and clips required; no unsolicited manuscripts. Payment varies, on acceptance.

RUNNER TRIATHLETE NEWS—P.O. Box 19909, Houston, TX 77224. Lance Phegley, Ed. Articles on running for road racing and multi-sport enthusiasts in TX, LA, OK, NM and AR. Payment varies, on publication.

RURAL LIVING—4201 Dominion Blvd., Suite 101, Glen Allen, VA 23060. Richard G. Johnstone, Jr., Ed. Features, 1,000 to 1,500 words, on people, places, historic sites in Virginia and Maryland's Eastern Shore. Queries preferred. Pays $150 to $200 for articles, on publication.

RURALITE—P.O. Box 558, Forest Grove, OR 97116. Attn: Ed. or Feature Ed. Articles, 800 to 2,000 words, of interest to a primarily rural and small-town audience in OR, WA, ID, NV, northern CA, and AK. "Think pieces" affecting rural/urban interests, regional history and celebrations, self-help, profiles, etc. No fiction or poetry. No sentimental nostalgia. Pays $30 to $400, on acceptance. Queries required. Guidelines.

SACRAMENTO MAGAZINE—4471 D St., Sacramento, CA 95819. Krista Hendricks Minard, Ed. Features, 2,500 words, on a broad range of topics related to the region. Department pieces, 1,200 to 1,500 words, and short pieces, 400 words, for "City Lights" column. Pays $75 to $300, on publication. Query.

SAN DIEGO MAGAZINE—4206 W. Point Loma Blvd., P.O. Box 85409, San Diego, CA 92138. Virginia Butterfield, Assoc. Ed. Articles, 1,500 to 3,000 words, on local personalities, politics, lifestyles, business, history, etc., relating to San Diego area. Photos. Pays $250 to $600, on publication. Query with clips.

SAN DIEGO READER—P.O. Box 85803, San Diego, CA 92186. Jim Holman, Ed. Literate articles, 2,500 to 10,000 words, on the San Diego region. Pays $500 to $2,000, on publication.

SAN FRANCISCO EXAMINER MAGAZINE—*San Francisco Examiner*, 110 Fifth St., San Francisco, CA 94103. Attn: Ed. Articles, 1,200 to 3,000 words, on lifestyles, issues, business, history, events, and people in northern California. Query. Pays varying rates.

SAN FRANCISCO FOCUS—2601 Mariposa St., San Francisco, CA 94110–1400. Amy Rennert, Ed. Service features, profiles of local newsmakers, and investigative pieces of local issues, 2,500 to 3,000 words. News items, 250 to 800 words, on subjects ranging from business to arts to politics. Payment varies, on acceptance. Query required.

SEATTLE—701 Dexter Ave. N., Suite 101, Seattle, WA 98109. Giselle Smith, Ed. City, local issues, home, and lifestyle articles, 500 to 2,000 words, relating directly to the greater Seattle area. Personality profiles. Pays $100 to $700, on publication. Guidelines.

SEATTLE WEEKLY—(formerly *The Weekly, Seattle's News Magazine*) 1008 Western, Suite 300, Seattle, WA 98104. David Brewster, Ed. Articles, 700 to 4,000 words, from a Northwest perspective. Pays $75 to $800, on publication. Query. Guidelines.

SEATTLE'S CHILD—Northwest Parent Publishing, 2107 Elliott Ave., #303, Seattle, WA 98121. Ann Bergman, Ed. Articles, 400 to 2,500 words, of interest to parents, educators, and childcare providers of children under 12, and investigative reports and consumer tips on issues affecting families in the Puget Sound region. Pays $75 to $400, on publication. Query required.

SENIOR MAGAZINE—3565 S. Higuera St., San Luis Obispo, CA 93401. Attn: Ed. Articles, 600 to 900 words: profiles, travel pieces, articles about new things, places, business, sports, movies, television, and health; book reviews (of new or outstanding older books) of interest to senior citizens in California. Pays $1.50 per inch; $10 to $25 for B&W photos, on publication.

SILENT SPORTS—717 10th St., P.O. Box 152, Waupaca, WI 54981. Attn: Ed. Articles, 1,000 to 2,000 words, on bicycling, cross-country skiing, running, canoeing, hiking, backpacking, and other "silent" sports in the upper Midwest region. Pays $40 to $100 for features; $20 to $50 for fillers, on publication. Query.

SOUTH CAROLINA HISTORICAL MAGAZINE—South Carolina Historical Society, 100 Meeting St., Charleston, SC 29401–2299. Stephen Hoffius, Ed. Scholarly articles, to 25 pages with footnotes, on all areas of South Carolina history. Pays in copies.

SOUTH CAROLINA WILDLIFE—P.O. Box 167, Columbia, SC 29202–0167. Attn: Man. Ed. Articles, 1,000 to 2,000 words, with regional outdoors focus: conservation, natural history and wildlife, recreation. Profiles. Pays from 10¢ a word. Query.

SOUTHERN CULTURES—Ctr. for the Study of the American South, Manning Hall, UNC-CH, Chapel Hill, NC 27599–3355. Alecia Holland, Man. Ed. Articles, 15 to 25 typed pages, on folk, popular, and high culture of the South. "We're interested in submissions from a wide variety of intellectual traditions that deal with ways of life, thought, belief, and expression in the United States South." Pays in copies.

SOUTHERN OUTDOORS—5845 Carmichael Rd., Montgomery, AL 36117. Larry Teague, Ed. How-to pieces, 800 to 1,200 words, and 2,000-word how and where-to articles on hunting and fishing, for fishermen and hunters in the Southern states. Pays 20¢ a word, on acceptance. Query.

SOUTHWEST ART—5444 Westheimer, Suite 1440, Houston, TX 77056. Susan McGarry, Ed. Articles, 1,200 to 1,800 words, on the artists, art collectors, museum exhibitions, gallery events and dealers, art history, and art trends west of the Mississippi River. Particularly interested in representational or figurative arts. Pays from $400, on acceptance. Query with slides of artwork to be featured.

THE STATE: DOWN HOME IN NORTH CAROLINA—128 S. Tryon St., Suite 2200, Charlotte, NC 28202. Scott Smith, Man. Ed. Articles, 750 to 2,000 words, on people, history, and places in North Carolina. Photos. Pays on publication.

SUNSET MAGAZINE—80 Willow Rd., Menlo Park, CA 94025. William Marken, Ed. Western regional. Limited free-lance market.

SUNSHINE: THE MAGAZINE OF SOUTH FLORIDA—*The Sun-Sentinel,* 200 E. Las Olas Blvd., Ft. Lauderdale, FL 33301–2293. John Parkyn, Ed. Articles, 1,000 to 3,000 words, on topics of interest to south Floridians. Pays $250 to $1,000, on acceptance. Query. Guidelines.

TALLAHASSEE MAGAZINE—P.O. Box 1837, Tallahassee, FL 32302–1837. Dave Fiore, Ed. Articles, 800 to 1,500 words, with a positive outlook on the life, people, and history of the north Florida area. Pays on acceptance. Query.

TEXAS HIGHWAYS MAGAZINE—P.O. Box 141009, Austin, TX 78714–1009. Jack Lowry, Ed. Texas travel, history, and scenic features, 200 to 1,800 words. Pays about 40¢ to 50¢ a word, $80 to $550 per photo. Query. Guidelines.

TEXAS MONTHLY—P.O. Box 1569, Austin, TX 78767–1569. Gregory Curtis, Ed. Features, 2,500 to 5,000 words, and departments, to 2,500 words, on art, architecture, food, education, business, politics, etc. "We like solidly researched pieces that uncover issues of public concern, reveal offbeat and previously unreported topics, or use a novel approach to familiar topics." Pays varying rates, on acceptance. Queries required.

TIMELINE—1982 Velma Ave., Columbus, OH 43211–2497. Christopher S. Duckworth, Ed. Articles, 1,000 to 6,000 words, on history of Ohio (politics, economics, social, and natural history) for lay readers in the Midwest. Pays $100 to $900, on acceptance. Queries preferred.

TOLEDO MAGAZINE—*The Blade*, Toledo, OH 43660. Sue Stankey, Ed. Articles, to 5,000 words, on Toledo-area personalities, events, etc. Pays $50 to $150, on publication. Query with SASE.

TROPIC—*The Miami Herald,* One Herald Plaza, Miami, FL 33132. Tom Shroder, Exec. Ed. General-interest articles, 750 to 3,000 words, for south Florida readers. Pays $200 to $1,000, on acceptance.

TUCSON LIFESTYLE—Old Pueblo Press, 7000 E. Tanque Verde, Tucson, AZ 85715. Sue Giles, Ed.-in-Chief. Features on local businesses, lifestyles, the arts, homes, fashion, and travel in the Southwest. Payment varies, on acceptance. Query preferred.

TWIN CITIES READER—5500 Wayzata Blvd., Minneapolis, MN 55416. David Carr, Ed. Articles, 2 to 4 printed pages, on local public affairs, arts, and general-interest subjects, for readers ages 25 to 44. Pays $5 to $8 per inch, on publication.

VALLEY MAGAZINE—16800 Devonshire, Suite 275, Granada Hills, CA 91344. Bonnie Steele, Ed. Articles, 1,000 to 1,500 words, on celebrities, issues, education, health, business, dining, and entertaining, etc., in the San Fernando Valley. Pays $100 to $350, within 8 weeks of acceptance.

VERMONT LIFE—6 Baldwin St., Montpelier, VT 05602. Tom Slayton, Ed.-in-Chief. Articles, 500 to 3,000 words, on Vermont subjects only. Pays 20¢ a word, extra for photos. Query preferred.

VIRGINIA—The Country Publishers, Inc., P.O. Box 798, Berryville, VA 22611. Lisa Cain Curran, Ed. Quarterly. "Written for and about people, places, events, and activities in, around, and affecting Virginia." Features, 2,000 to 2,500 words; articles, 1,200 to 1,800 words; humor, folklore, and legend, to 2,000 words; fiction, 1,000 to 1,500 words, with regional setting or reference; related poetry, to 32 lines. Department pieces, 500 to 700 words. Photos. Pays $200 to $300, 30 days after publication.

VIRGINIA BUSINESS—411 E. Franklin St., Suite 105, Richmond, VA 23219. James Bacon, Ed. Articles, 1,000 to 2,500 words, related to the business scene in Virginia. Pays varying rates, on acceptance. Query required.

VIRGINIA WILDLIFE—P.O. Box 11104, Richmond, VA 23230–1104. Attn: Ed. Articles, 1,500 to 2,500 words, with Virginia tie-in, on conservation and related topics, including fishing, hunting, wildlife management, outdoor safety and ethics, etc. Articles must be accompanied by color photos. Query with SASE. Pays 10¢ a word, extra for photos, on publication.

WASHINGTON POST MAGAZINE—*The Washington Post*, 1150 15th St. N.W., Washington, DC 20071. Liza Mundy, Man. Ed. Personal-experience essays, profiles, and general-interest pieces, to 6,000 words, on business, arts and culture, politics, science, sports, education, children, relationships, behavior, etc. Articles should be of interest to people living in Washington, DC, area. Pays from $100, on acceptance. Limited market.

THE WASHINGTONIAN—1828 L St. N.W., Suite 200, Washington, DC 20036. John Limpert, Ed. Helpful, informative articles, 1,000 to 4,000 words, on DC-related topics. Pays 50¢ a word, on publication.

WE ALASKANS MAGAZINE—*Anchorage Daily News*, Box 149001, Anchorage, AK 99514–9001. George Bryson, Ed. Articles, 500 to 1,000 words, and features, 3,000 to 4,000 words, on Alaska topics only. Profiles, narratives, fiction, and humor. Pays $50 to $150 for short articles, $300 to $600 for features, on publication.

THE WEEKLY, SEATTLE'S NEWS MAGAZINE—See *Seattle Weekly*.

WESTERN SPORTSMAN—P.O. Box 737, Regina, Sask., Canada S4P 3A8. Brian Bowman, Ed. Informative articles, to 2,500 words, on hunting, fishing, and outdoor experiences in Alberta, Saskatchewan, and Manitoba. How-tos, humor, cartoons. Photos. Pays $75 to $300, on publication.

WINDY CITY SPORTS—1450 W. Randolph, Chicago, IL 60607. Shelley Berryhill, Ed. Articles, to 1,500 words, on amateur sports in the Chicago area. Queries required. Pays $100, on publication.

WISCONSIN—*The Milwaukee Journal Magazine*, Journal/Sentinel, Inc., Box 661, Milwaukee, WI 53201. Alan Borsuk, Ed. Articles, 500 to 2,500 words, on business, politics, arts, environment, and social issues with strong Wisconsin emphasis. Personal-experience essays, profiles and investigative articles. Pays $75 to $700, on publication. Query.

WISCONSIN TRAILS—P.O. Box 5650, Madison, WI 53705. Lucy J. Rhodes, Assoc. Ed. Articles, 1,500 to 3,000 words, on regional topics: outdoors, lifestyle, events, history, arts, adventure, travel; profiles of artists, craftspeople, and regional personalities. Fillers. Pays $150 to $500, on publication. Query with SASE.

WISCONSIN WEST MAGAZINE—2645 Harlem St., Eau Claire, WI 54703. Attn: Ed. Articles on current issues for residents of western Wisconsin: profiles of restaurants, weekend leisure activities and getaways, and famous people of western Wisconsin; and historical pieces. Short humor. Payment varies, on publication.

YANKEE—Yankee Publishing Co., Dublin, NH 03444. Judson D. Hale, Ed. Articles and fiction, 500 to 2,500 words, on New England and New England people. Pays $500 to $2,500 for features, on acceptance.

YANKEE MAGAZINE'S TRAVEL GUIDE TO NEW ENGLAND—33 Union St., Boston, MA 02108. Janice Brand, Ed. Articles, 500 to 2,000 words, on activities, attractions, places to visit in New England. Photos. Pays on acceptance. Query with outline and writing samples required.

TRAVEL ARTICLES

AAA WORLD—1000 AAA Dr., Heathrow, FL 32746–5063. Douglas Damerst, Ed. Articles, 600 to 1,500 words, on consumer automotive and travel concerns. Pays $200 to $800, on acceptance. Query with writing samples required. Articles by assignment only.

ACCENT/TRAVELOG—Box 10010, Ogden, UT 84409. Attn: Eds. Articles, 1,000 words, on travel destinations, ways to travel, and travel tips. Pays 15¢ a word, $35 for color photos, on acceptance. Query with SASE.

ADVENTURE ROAD—The Aegis Group Publishers, 30400 Van Dyke Ave., Warren, MI 48093. Mike Brudenell, Ed. Official publication of the Amoco Motor Club. Articles, 1,500 words, on destinations in North America, Mexico, and the Caribbean. Photos. Pays $500 to $1,000, on acceptance. Query.

AIR FAIR: THE MAGAZINE FOR AIRLINE EMPLOYEES—6401 Congress, #100, Boca Raton, FL 33487. Debra Fredel, Ed. Travel articles, 1,800 words, with photos, on shopping, sightseeing, dining, and nightlife for airline employees. Prices, discount information, and addresses must be included. Pays $250, after publication.

AIR FORCE TIMES—See *Times News Service.*

AMOCO TRAVELER—K.L. Publications, Inc., 2001 Killebrew Dr., Suite 105, Bloomington, MN 55425. Mary Lou Brooks, Ed. Quarterly. Membership magazine for Amoco Traveler Club. Articles, 1,500 to 1,800 words, on North American travel and destinations. "Writing should be tight, reportorial, and colorful." Pays $350 to $450 for first rights; $125 to $150 for reprints, on publication.

ARIZONA HIGHWAYS—2039 W. Lewis Ave., Phoenix, AZ 85009. Richard G. Stahl, Man. Ed. Informal, well-researched personal-experience and travel articles, 1,600 to 2,000 words, focusing on a specific city or region in Arizona. Also articles dealing with nature, environment, flora and fauna, history, anthropology, archaeology, hiking, boating. Departments for personal-experience pieces include "Focus on Nature," "Along the Way," "Back Road Adventures," "Hiking," and "Arizona Humor." Pays 35¢ to 55¢ a word, on acceptance. Query with published clips. Guidelines.

ARMY TIMES—See *Times News Service.*

BLUE RIDGE COUNTRY—P.O. Box 21535, Roanoke, VA 24018. Kurt Rheinheimer, Ed. Regional travel articles, 750 to 1,200 words, on destinations in the mountain regions of VA, NC, WV, TN, KY, MD, SC, and GA. Color slides and B&W prints considered. Pays to $200 for photo-features, on publication. Queries preferred.

CALIFORNIA HIGHWAY PATROLMAN—2030 V St., Sacramento, CA 95818–1730. Carol Perri, Ed. Travel articles, to 2,000 words, focusing on places in California and the West Coast. "We prefer out-of-the-way stops with California Highway Patrol tie-in instead of regular tourist destinations." Query or send complete manuscript with photos. SASE required. Pays 2 ½¢ a word, $5 for B&W photos, on publication.

CANADIAN—199 Avenue Rd., Third Fl., Toronto, Ontario, Canada M5R 2J3. Grant N. R. Geall, Pres./Pub. Inflight magazine of Canadian Airlines International. Travel pieces, 800 to 1,000 words. Payment varies, on acceptance. Query.

CANADIAN DIVER & WATERSPORT—See *Diver Magazine.*

CARIBBEAN TRAVEL AND LIFE—8403 Colesville Rd., Suite 830, Silver Spring, MD 20910. Veronica Gould Stoddart, Ed. Lively, informative articles, 500 to 2,500 words, on all aspects of travel, leisure, recreation, and culture in the Caribbean, Bahamas, and Bermuda, for upscale, sophisticated readers. Photos. Pays $75 to $550, on publication. Query.

CHILE PEPPER—P.O. Box 4278, Albuquerque, NM 87196. Melissa Jackson, Assoc. Ed. First-person food and travel articles, 1,000 to 1,500 words, about spicy world cuisine. Queries required. Payment varies, on publication.

COLORADO HOMES & LIFESTYLES—7009 S. Potomac, Englewood, CO 80112. Laurel Lund, Ed. Travel articles, 1,200 to 1,500 words, on cities, regions, establishments in Colorado and contiguous states. Roundups and travel pieces with unusual angles, sidebar, and photos. Pays $150, on acceptance. Query.

CONDE NAST TRAVELER—360 Madison Ave., New York, NY 10017. Irene Schneider, Sr. Ed. Uses very little free-lance material.

THE COOL TRAVELER—P.O. Box 273, Selinsgrove, PA 17870. Bob Moore, Pub./Ed. Bimonthly. Articles, 800 words, including excerpts from diaries and letters written while traveling. "We emphasize 'what happened' rather than 'what to see.' " Travel-related poetry. Pays to $20, on publication.

CRUISE TRAVEL—990 Grove St., Evanston, IL 60201. Robert Meyers, Ed. Charles Doherty, Man. Ed. Ship-, port-, and cruise-of-the-month features, 800 to 2,000 words; cruise guides; cruise roundups; cruise company profiles; travel suggestions for one-day port stops. "Photo-features strongly recommended." Payment varies, on acceptance. Query with sample color photos.

DIVER MAGAZINE—295–10991 Shellbridge Way, Richmond, B.C., Canada V6X 3C6. Peter Vassilopoulos, Pub./Ed. Illustrated articles, 500 to 1,000 words, on dive destinations. Shorter pieces are also welcome. "Travel features should be brief and accompanied by excellent slides and/or prints and a map. Unsolicited articles will be reviewed only from August to October and will be considered for *Diver Magazine* and *Canadian Diver & Watersport*." Pays $2.50 per column inch, on publication. Guidelines. Limited market.

EARLY AMERICAN LIFE—Box 8200, Harrisburg, PA 17105–8200. Mimi Handler, Ed. Travel features about historic sites and country inns, 1,000 to 3,000 words. Pays $100 to $600, on acceptance. Query.

ENDLESS VACATION—Box 80260, Indianapolis, IN 46280. Helen W. O'Guinn, Ed. Travel features, to 1,500 words; international scope. Pays on acceptance. Query preferred. Send SASE for guidelines. Limited market.

FAMILY CIRCLE—110 Fifth Ave., New York, NY 10011. Sylvia Barsotti, Sr. Ed. Travel articles, to 1,500 words. Concept travel pieces should appeal to a national audience and focus on affordable activities for families; prefer service-filled, theme-oriented travel pieces or first-person family vacation stories. Pay rates vary, on acceptance. Query.

FRIENDLY EXCHANGE—P.O. Box 2120, Warren, MI 48090–2120. Adele Malott, Ed. Articles, 700 to 1,500 words, of interest to active midwestern and western families, on travel and leisure. "Must have 'people' orientation." Photos. Pays $400 to $1,000, extra for photos. Query required. Guidelines.

GREAT EXPEDITIONS—Box 18036, Raleigh, NC 27619. George Kane, Ed. Articles, 700 to 1,800 words, on socially responsible, adventurous, budget-conscious travel and unusual destinations. Pays $30 to $80, on publication. Guidelines.

INDIA CURRENTS—P.O. Box 21285, San Jose, CA 95151. Arvind Kumar, Submissions Ed. First-person accounts, 1,200 words, of trips to India or the subcontinent. Helpful tips for first-time travelers. Prefer descriptions of people-to-people interactions. Pays in subscriptions.

INTERNATIONAL LIVING—824 E. Baltimore St., Baltimore, MD 21202. Kathleen Peddicord, Ed. Dir. Newsletter. Short pieces and features, 200 to 2,000 words, with useful information on investing, shopping, travel, employment, education, real estate, retirement, and lifestyles overseas. Pays $100 to $400, after publication.

ISLANDS—3886 State St., Santa Barbara, CA 93105. Joan Tapper, Ed-in-Chief. Destination features, 2,500 to 4,000 words, on islands around the world as well as department pieces and front-of-the-book items on island-related topics. Pays from 25¢ to 50¢ a word, on acceptance. Query with clips required. Guidelines.

LIFE IN THE TIMES—See *Times News Service*.

587

MICHIGAN LIVING—Automobile Club of Michigan, 1 Auto Club Dr., Dearborn, MI 48126. Len Barnes, Ed. Informative travel articles, 300 to 2,000 words, on U.S. and Canadian tourist attractions and recreational opportunities; special interest in Michigan. Pays $55 to $500 (rates vary for photos), on acceptance.

THE MIDWEST MOTORIST—12901 N. Forty Dr., St. Louis, MO 63141. Michael Right, Ed. Articles, 1,000 to 1,500 words, with color slides, on domestic and foreign travel. Pays from $150, on acceptance.

NATIONAL GEOGRAPHIC—17th and M Sts. N.W., Washington, DC 20036. William P.E. Graves, Ed. First-person articles on geography, exploration, natural history, archaeology, and science. Half staff-written; half written by recognized authorities and published authors. Does not consider unsolicited manuscripts.

NATIONAL MOTORIST—Bayside Plaza, 188 The Embarcadero, San Francisco, CA 94105. Jane Offers, Ed. Quarterly. Illustrated articles, 500 to 1,100 words, for California motorists, on motoring in the West, domestic and international travel, car care, roads, personalities, places, etc. Color slides. Pays from 10¢ a word, on acceptance. Pays for photos on publication. SASE required.

NAVY TIMES—See *Times News Service.*

NEW WOMAN—215 Lexington Ave., New York, NY 10016. Karen Walden, Ed.-in-Chief. Armchair travel pieces; women's personal-experience and "what I learned from this experience" pieces, 800 to 2,500 words. Pays $500 to $2,500, on acceptance. Query required.

NEW YORK DAILY NEWS—220 E. 42nd St., New York, NY 10017. Gunna Bitee Dickson, Travel Ed. Articles, 700 to 900 words, on all manner of travel. Price information must be included. B&W or color photos or slides. Pays $100 to $200 (extra for photos), on publication.

THE NEW YORK TIMES—229 W. 43rd St., New York, NY 10036. Nancy Newhouse, Travel Ed. Query with SASE required; include writer's background, description of proposed article. No unsolicited manuscripts or photos. Pays on acceptance.

NORTHWEST PARKS & WILDLIFE—See *Northwest Regional Magazines.*

NORTHWEST REGIONAL MAGAZINES—P.O. Box 18000, Florence, OR 97439. Attn: Dave Peden or Judy Fleagle. All submissions considered for use in *Oregon Coast, Oregon Parks, Northwest Travel,* and *Northwest Parks & Wildlife*. Articles, 1,200 to 2,000 words, on travel, history, town/city profiles, parks, and nature. News releases, 200 to 500 words. Articles with photos or slides preferred. Pays $50 to $300, on publication. Send SASE for guidelines.

NORTHWEST TRAVEL—See *Northwest Regional Magazines.*

OREGON COAST—See *Northwest Regional Magazines.*

OREGON PARKS—See *Northwest Regional Magazines.*

OUTDOOR TRAVELER, MID-ATLANTIC—WMS Publications, Inc., P.O. Box 2748, Charlottesville, VA 22902. Marianne Marks, Ed. Scott Clark, Assoc. Ed. Articles, 2,500 to 3,000 words, about outdoor recreation, travel, places and events in VA, NC, WV, MD, PA, DE, DC, and NJ. Departments include "Destinations," 450 to 600 words, practical and descriptive guides to sports destinations; "Getaways," short pieces about inns and B&Bs, usually seasonal and including outdoor activities; Book Reviews, 200 words. Pays $500 to $650 for features; payment varies for departments, on publication. Guidelines.

RV TIMES MAGAZINE—Royal Productions, Inc., Box 6294, Richmond, VA 23230. Alice P. Supple, Ed. Articles and fiction, 500 to 2,000 words, related to outdoor or leisure activities, travel attractions in the MD, VA, NJ, NY, DE, and PA areas. Pays 7¢ a word (to $90), on publication.

RV WEST MAGAZINE—Prescomm Media, Inc., 4125 Mohr Ave., Suite E, Pleasanton, CA 94566–4750. Roger K. Burchill, Ed. Travel and destination articles, 1,000 to 1,500 words, on where to go and what to do in the 12 western states with your recreational vehicle. Color or B&W prints must accompany articles. Occasional fiction, 1,000 to 1,500 words, with an RV slant. Pays $1.50 per column inch, on publication. Guidelines.

SACRAMENTO MAGAZINE—4471 D St., Sacramento, CA 95819. Krista Hendricks Minard, Ed. Articles, 1,000 to 1,500 words, on destinations within a 6-hour drive of Sacramento. Pay varies, on publication. Query.

SPECIALTY TRAVEL INDEX—305 San Anselmo Ave., #313, San Anselmo, CA 94960. C. Steen Hansen, Co-Pub./Ed. Semiannual directory of adventure vacation tour companies, destinations, and vacation packages. Articles, 1,000 words, with how-to travel information, humor, and opinion. Pays 20¢ per word, on publication. Slides and photos considered. Queries preferred.

TEXAS HIGHWAYS MAGAZINE—P.O. Box 141009, Austin, TX 78714–1009. Jack Lowry, Ed. Travel, historical, cultural, scenic features on Texas, 200 to 1,800 words. Pays about 40¢ to 50¢ a word; photos, $80 to $500. Guidelines with SASE.

TIMES NEWS SERVICE—Army Times Publishing Co., Springfield, VA 22159. Attn: R&R Ed. Travel articles, 700 words, on places of special interest to military people for use in "R&R" newspaper section (formerly called "Life in the Times"). "We like travel articles to focus on a single destination but with short sidebar covering other things to see in the area." Pays $100, on acceptance. Pays $35 for color slides or prints. Also, travel pieces, 1,000 words, for supplements to *Army Times*, *Navy Times*, and *Air Force Times*. Address Supplements Ed. Pays $125 to $200, on acceptance. Guidelines.

TOURS & RESORTS—See *Travel America.*

TRANSITIONS ABROAD—18 Hulst Rd., Box 1300, Amherst, MA 01004–1300. Clay Hubbs, Ed. Articles for overseas travelers who seek an in-depth experience of the culture: work, study, travel, budget tips. Include practical, firsthand information. Emphasis on travel for personal enrichment and education and on establishing meaningful contact with people of host country. "Eager to work with inexperienced writers who travel to learn and want to share information." B&W photos a plus. Pays $1.50 per column inch, after publication. Query preferred. Guidelines.

TRAVEL AMERICA—(formerly *Tours & Resorts*) World Publishing Co., 990 Grove St., Evanston, IL 60201–4370. Randy Mink, Man. Ed. Robert Meyers, Ed. Features, 800 to 1,200 words, on U.S. vacation destinations; also essays, nostalgia, humor, travel tips, and service articles, 800 to 1,000 words. Pays up to $300, on acceptance. Top-quality color slides a must. Query.

TRAVEL & LEISURE—1120 Ave. of the Americas, New York, NY 10036. Nancy Novogrod, Ed.-in-Chief. Articles, 800 to 3,000 words, on destinations and travel-related activities. Regional pieces for regional editions. Short pieces for "Athletic Traveler" and "T&L Reports." Pays on acceptance: $2,500 to $5,000 for features; $750 to $1,500 for regionals; $50 to $300 for short pieces. Query; articles on assignment.

TRAVEL SMART—Dobbs Ferry, NY 10522. Attn: Ed. Short pieces, 250 to 1,000 words, about interesting, unusual and/or economical places. Give specific details on hotels, restaurants, transportation, and costs. Pays on publication. Query.

WESTWAYS—2601 S. Figueroa St., Los Angeles, CA 90007. Eric Seyfarth, Ed. Travel articles, 1,300 to 3,000 words, on where to go, what to see, and how to get there, with an emphasis on southern California and the West. Domestic and foreign travel articles are also of interest. Pays 75¢ a word, on acceptance.

YANKEE MAGAZINE'S TRAVEL GUIDE TO NEW ENGLAND—33 Union St., Boston, MA 02108. Janice Brand, Ed. Articles, 500 to 2,000 words, on destinations in New England. Photos. Pays on acceptance. Query with outline and writing samples.

INFLIGHT MAGAZINES

ABOARD—100 Almeria Ave., Suite 220, Coral Gables, FL 33134. Roberto Casin, Ed. Inflight magazine of 11 Latin American international airlines in Chile, Dominican Republic, Ecuador, Guatemala, El Salvador, Bolivia, Nicaragua, Honduras, Peru, Uruguay, and Paraguay. Articles, 1,200 to 1,500 words, with photos, on these countries and on science, sports, home, fashion, business, ecology, and gastronomy. No political stories. Pays $150, on acceptance and on publication. Query required.

ALASKA AIRLINES MAGAZINE—2701 First Ave., Suite 250, Seattle, WA 98121. Paul Frichtl, Ed. Articles, 250 to 2,500 words, on lifestyle topics, business, travel, and profiles of regional personalities for West Coast business travelers. Query. Payment varies, on publication.

AMERICA WEST AIRLINES MAGAZINE—Skyword Marketing, Inc., 7500 N. Dreamy Draw Dr., Suite 240, Phoenix, AZ 85020. Michael Derr, Ed. Mostly business articles; some arts, travel, 500 to 2,000 words. Pays from $250, on publication. Clips and SASE required. Guidelines. Limited market.

AMERICAN WAY—P.O. Box 619640, DFW Airport, TX 75261–9640. John Ostdick, Ed. American Airlines' inflight magazine. Features of interest to the business traveler, emphasizing travel, adventure, business, and the arts/culture. Pays from $900, on acceptance. Query.

CANADIAN—199 Avenue Rd., Third Fl., Toronto, Ontario, Canada M5R 2J3. Grant N. R. Geall, Pres./Pub. Articles, 1,000 words, on travel for Canadian Airlines International travelers. Payment varies, on acceptance. Query.

SKY—600 Corporate Dr., Ft. Lauderdale, FL 33334. Lidia de Leon, Ed. Delta Air Lines' inflight magazine. Articles on business, lifestyle, high tech, sports, the arts, etc. Color slides. Pays varying rates, on acceptance. Query with SASE. Guidelines.

USAIR MAGAZINE—New York Times Custom Publishing, 590 Madison Ave., 32nd Fl., New York, NY 10022. Catherine Sabino, Ed. Kathy Passero, Man. Ed. Articles on travel, trends in health and fitness, sports, personality profiles, food and wine, family and children, fashion and shopping, the arts and culture. "Our goal is to provide readers with lively and colorful, yet practical articles that will make their lives and their leisure time more rewarding." Query with clips; no unsolicited manuscripts. Pays $1 a word, within 60 days of acceptance.

WOMEN'S PUBLICATIONS

BBW: BIG BEAUTIFUL WOMAN—9171 Wilshire Blvd., Suite 300, Beverly Hills, CA 90210. Linda Arroz, Ed.-in-Chief. Janey Milstead, Exec. Ed. Articles, 1,500 words, of interest to women ages 25 to 50, especially large-size women, including interviews with successful large-size women and personal accounts of how to cope with difficult situations. Tips on restaurants, airlines, stores, etc., that treat large women with respect. Query. Payment varies, on publication.

BLACK ELEGANCE—475 Park Ave. S., New York, NY 10016. Sonia Alleyne, Ed. Articles, 1,000 to 2,000 words, on fashion, beauty, relationships, home design, careers, personal finance, and personalities, for black women ages 25 to 45. Short interviews. Include photos if available. Query. Pays $150 to $225, on publication. Guidelines.

BRIDAL GUIDE—Globe Communications Corp., 441 Lexington Ave., New York, NY 10017. Stephanie Wood, Ed.-in-Chief. Lisa Leffler Gabor, Travel Ed. Bimonthly. Articles, 1,500 to 3,000 words, on relationships, sexuality, health and nutrition, psychology, travel, and finance. No wedding planning, beauty, fashion articles; no fiction, essays, poetry. Query with SASE. Pays on acceptance.

BRIDE'S & YOUR NEW HOME—140 E. 45th St., New York, NY 10017. Andrea Feld, Man. Ed. Articles, 800 to 3,000 words, for engaged couples or newly-weds, on wedding planning, relationships, communication, sex, housing, redecorating, finances, careers, remarriage, step-parenting, health, birth control, pregnancy, religion, in-laws. Three major editorial subjects: home, wedding, and honeymoon. Pays $200 to $1,000, on acceptance.

CHATELAINE—Maclean Hunter Bldg., 777 Bay St., Toronto, Ont., Canada M5W 1A7. Elizabeth Parr, Sr. Ed. Articles, 1,500 to 2,500 words, on current issues and personalities of interest to Canadian women. Send query, outline, or complete manuscript; include international reply coupon. Pays from $1,200 for articles; from $350 for 500-word "Up-front" columns (relationships, health, parents/kids), on acceptance.

COMPLETE WOMAN—1165 N. Clark, Chicago, IL 60610. Jean Iversen, Asst. Ed. Articles, 1,000 to 2,000 words, with how-to sidebars, giving practical advice to women on love, sex, careers, health, personal relationships, etc. Also interested in reprints. Pays varying rates, on publication.

COSMOPOLITAN—224 W. 57th St., New York, NY 10019. Helen Gurley Brown, Ed. Betty Nichols Kelly, Fiction and Books Ed. Articles, to 3,000 words, and features, 500 to 2,000 words, on issues affecting young career women, with emphasis on jobs and personal life. Fiction on male-female relationships: short shorts, 1,500 to 3,000 words; short stories, 3,000 to 4,000 words; condensed published novels, 25,000 words. SASE required. Payment varies.

COUNTRY WOMAN—P.O. Box 989, Greendale, WI 53129. Kathy Pohl, Man. Ed. Profiles of country women (photo-feature packages), inspirational, reflective pieces. Personal-experience, nostalgia, humor, service-oriented articles, original crafts, and how-to features, to 1,000 words, of interest to country women. Pays $40 to $150, on acceptance.

THE CREATIVE WOMAN—TAPP Group, 126 E. Wing, Suite 288, Arlington Hts., IL 60004. Margaret Choudhury, Ed. Quarterly. Essays, fiction, poetry, criticism, graphic arts, and photography, from a feminist perspective. SASE for upcoming themes. Payment varies, on publication.

ELLE—1633 Broadway, New York, NY 10019. Ruth La Ferla, Exec. Ed. Articles, varying lengths, for fashion-conscious women, ages 20 to 50. Subjects include beauty, health, fitness, travel, entertainment, and lifestyles. Pays top rates, on publication. Query required.

ESSENCE—1500 Broadway, New York, NY 10036. Susan L. Taylor, Ed.-in-Chief. Linda Villarosa, Ed. Provocative articles, 800 to 2,500 words, about black women in America today: self-help, how-to pieces, business and finance, health, celebrity profiles, art, travel, and political issues. Short items, 500 to 750 words, on work, parenting, and health. Fiction, 800 to 2,500 words. Pays varying rates, on acceptance. Query for articles.

EXECUTIVE FEMALE—30 Irving Pl., New York, NY 10003. Basia Hellwig, Ed.-in-Chief. Articles, 750 to 2,500 words, on managing people, time, money, and careers, for women in business. Pays varying rates, on acceptance. Query.

FAMILY—169 Lexington Ave., New York, NY 10016. Liz DeFranco, Ed. Articles, 1,000 to 2,000 words, of interest to military women with children. Pays to $200, on publication. Guidelines.

FAMILY CIRCLE—110 Fifth Ave., New York, NY 10011. Susan Kelliher Ungaro, Ed.-in-Chief. Articles, to 2,000 words, on "women who have made a difference," marriage, family, and child-care and elder-care issues; consumer affairs, psychology, humor, health, nutrition, and fitness. Query required. Pays top rates, on acceptance.

FIRST FOR WOMEN—270 Sylvan Ave., Englewood Cliffs, NJ 07632. Jane Traulsen, Ed. Articles and mainstream stories, 1,500 to 2,500 words, reflecting the concerns of contemporary women; no formula or experimental fiction. "A humorous twist is welcome in fiction." Query for articles. Send manuscript for fiction. Pay varies, on acceptance. Allow 8 to 12 weeks for response.

GLAMOUR—350 Madison Ave., New York, NY 10017. Pamela Evens, Articles Ed. Ruth Whitney, Ed.-in-Chief. Priscilla Flood, Man. Ed. How-to articles, from 1,500 words, on careers, health, psychology, interpersonal relationships, etc., for women ages 18 to 35. Fashion, entertainment, and beauty pieces staff-written. Query Articles Ed. Pays from $500, on acceptance.

GOOD HOUSEKEEPING—959 Eighth Ave., New York, NY 10019. Joan Thursh, Articles Ed. Lee Quarfoot, Fiction Ed. In-depth articles and features, about 2,500 words, on controversial problems, topical social issues; dramatic personal narratives of unusual experiences of average families; new or unusual medical information, personal medical stories. No submissions on food, beauty, needlework, or crafts. Short stories, 2,000 to 5,000 words, with strong identification for women. Unsolicited fiction not returned; if no response in 6 weeks, assume work was unsuitable. Query with SASE for nonfiction. Pays top rates, on acceptance. Guidelines.

HARPER'S BAZAAR—1700 Broadway, New York, NY 10019. Elizabeth Tilberis, Ed.-in-Chief. Articles, 1,500 to 2,500 words, for active, sophisticated women: the arts, world affairs, food, wine, travel, families, education, careers, health, and sexuality. No unsolicited manuscripts; query with SASE. Payment varies, on acceptance.

IOWA WOMAN—P.O. Box 680, Iowa City, IA 52244. Marianne Abel, Ed. Fiction, poetry, book reviews, and personal essays; articles, to 6,500 words, on midwestern history; interviews with prominent women; current social, economic, artistic, and environmental issues. Poems, any length (submit up to 5); photos and drawings. Queries preferred for articles. Pays $5 a page, $15 for illustrations, on publication. Guidelines.

THE JOYFUL WOMAN—P.O. Box 90028, Chattanooga, TN 37412. Joy Rice Martin, Ed. Holly Martin, Ed. Asst. Articles and fiction, 500 to 1,500 words, for "women with a Christian commitment." First-person inspirational true stories, profiles of Christian women, practical and biblically oriented how-to articles. Queries preferred. Pays 3¢ to 4¢ a word, on publication.

LADIES' HOME JOURNAL—100 Park Ave., New York, NY 10017. Myrna Blyth, Pub. Dir./Ed.-in-Chief. Articles of interest to women. Send queries to: Jane Farrell, Articles Ed. (news/general interest); Mary Hickey, Sr. Ed. (health/medical); Melanie Berger, Assoc. Ed. (celebrity/entertainment); Pamela Guthrie O'Brien, Features Ed. (sex/psychology); Lois Johnson, Beauty Dir. (beauty/fashion/fitness); Jan Hazard, Food Ed. (food); Shana Aborn, Features Ed. (personal experience); Mary Mohler, Man. Ed. (children and families). Fiction accepted through literary agents only. Brief, true anecdotes about amusing things children say for "Kidspeak." True, first-person accounts, 1,000 words, "about the most intimate aspects of our lives" for anonymous "Woman to Woman": Submit typed, double-spaced manuscript with SASE to Box WW, c/o address above; pays $750. Guidelines.

LADY'S CIRCLE—152 Madison Ave., Suite 906, New York, NY 10016. Mary F. Bemis, Ed. How-to, food, and crafts articles for homemakers. Short fiction. "Upbeat" pieces for over-50 audience. Pays $125 for articles, $10 for pet peeves, $5 for recipes or helpful hints, on publication.

MCCALL'S—110 Fifth Ave., New York, NY 10011. Attn: Articles Ed. Articles, 1,000 to 3,000 words, on current issues, human interest, family relationships. Payment varies, on acceptance.

MADEMOISELLE—350 Madison Ave., New York, NY 10017. Dana Cowin, Man. Ed. Articles, 1,500 to 2,500 words, on work, relationships, health, and trends of interest to single, working women in their mid-twenties. Reporting pieces, essays, first-person accounts, and humor. No how-to or fiction. Submit query with clips and SASE. Pays excellent rates, on acceptance.

MODERN BRIDE—249 W. 17th St., New York, NY 10011. Mary Ann Cavlin, Man. Ed. Articles, 1,500 to 2,000 words, for bride and groom, on wedding planning, financial planning, juggling career and home, etc. Pays $600 to $1,200, on acceptance.

MS.: THE WORLD OF WOMEN—230 Park Ave., 7th Fl., New York, NY 10169. Attn: Manuscript Ed. Articles relating to feminism, women's roles, and social change; national and international news reporting, profiles, essays, theory, and analysis. Query with resumé, published clips, and SASE required. No fiction or poetry accepted, acknowledged, or returned.

NA'AMAT WOMAN—200 Madison Ave., Suite 2120, New York, NY 10016. Judith A. Sokoloff, Ed. Articles on Jewish culture, women's issues, social and political topics, and Israel, 1,500 to 3,000 words. Short stories with a Jewish theme. Pays 10¢ a word, on publication.

NEW WOMAN—215 Lexington Ave., New York, NY 10016. Karen Walden, Ed.-in-Chief. Articles for women ages 25 to 49, on self-discovery, self-development, and self-esteem. Features: relationships, careers, health and fitness, money, fashion, beauty, food and nutrition, travel features with self-growth angle, and essays by and about women pacesetters. Query. Pays about $1 a word, on acceptance.

ON THE ISSUES—Choices Women's Medical Center, Inc., 97–77 Queens Blvd., Forest Hills, NY 11374–3317. Ronni Sandroff, Ed. "The Progressive

Woman's Quarterly." Articles, to 2,500 words, on political or social issues. Movie, music, and book reviews, 500 to 750 words. Query. Payment varies, on publication.

PLAYGIRL—801 Second Ave., New York, NY 10017. Charmian Carl, Ed.-in-Chief. In-depth articles for contemporary women. Humor, celebrity interviews, fiction. Pays varying rates. Query with clips. Guidelines.

RADIANCE: THE MAGAZINE FOR LARGE WOMEN—P.O. Box 30246, Oakland, CA 94604. Alice Ansfield, Ed./Pub. Quarterly. Articles, 1,500 to 2,500 words, that provide information, inspiration, and resources for women all sizes of large. Features include information on health, media, fashion, and politics that relate to issues of body size. Fiction and poetry also welcome. Pays to $100, on publication.

REDBOOK—224 W. 57th St., New York, NY 10019. Diane Salvatore, Sally Lee, Sr. Eds. Dawn Raffel, Fiction Ed. Toni Hope, Health Ed. For mothers, ages 25 to 45. Short stories, to 25 typed pages; dramatic narratives, 1,000 to 2,000 words, for "A Mother's Story" and "Happy Endings." Query with writing samples for articles. SASE required. Pays excellent rates.

SELF—350 Madison Ave., New York, NY 10017. Alexandra Penney, Ed.-in-Chief. "We no longer accept unsolicited manuscripts or queries."

TODAY'S CHRISTIAN WOMAN—465 Gundersen Dr., Carol Stream, IL 60188. Ramona Cramer Tucker, Ed. Articles, 1,500 words, that are "warm and personal in tone, full of real-life anecdotes that deal with the following relationships: marriage, parenting, friendship, spiritual life, and self." Humorous anecdotes, 150 words, that have a Christian slant. Queries required. Payment varies, on acceptance. Guidelines.

VIRTUE: THE CHRISTIAN MAGAZINE FOR WOMEN—P.O. Box 36630, Colorado Springs, CO 80936–3663. Nancie Carmichael, Man. Ed. Articles and stories, 1,200 to 1,400 words, that explore women's lives, their spiritual journeys, and their relationships with family, friends, and God. Pays 15¢ to 22¢ a word, on publication.

VOGUE—350 Madison Ave., New York, NY 10017. Attn: Features Ed. Articles, to 1,500 words, on women, entertainment and the arts, travel, medicine, and health. General features. Query; no unsolicited manuscripts. Pays good rates, on acceptance.

WOMAN OF POWER—P.O. Box 2785, Orleans, MA 02653. Charlene McKee, Ed. A magazine of feminism, spirituality, and politics. Articles, to 3,500 words. Each issue explores a special theme. Send SASE for themes and guidelines. Pays in copies and subscription.

WOMAN'S DAY—1633 Broadway, New York, NY 10019. Rebecca Greer, Sr. Articles Ed. Human-interest or helpful articles, to 2,000 words, on marriage, child-rearing, health, careers, relationships, money management. Dramatic first-person narratives of medical miracles, rescues, women's experiences, etc. "We respond to queries promptly; unsolicited manuscripts are returned unread." Pays top rates, on acceptance.

WOMAN'S OWN—1115 Broadway, New York, NY 10010. Carla Merolla, Man. Ed. Articles, 1,500 to 2,000 words, offering inspirational and practical advice on relationships and career and lifestyle choices for women 25 to 35. Common subjects: staying together, second marriages, working women, asserting yourself, meeting new men, "love-styles," sex, etc. Columns, 800 words, for "Suddenly Single," "Moving Up," "Round-Up," "Mindpower," "Dieter's Notes," "Fashion

Advisor," and "Financial Advisor." Profiles, 250 to 500 words, of women who have overcome great odds for "Woman in the News." Fun, in-depth quizzes. Short pieces on trends and breakthroughs for "Let's Put Our Heads Together." Query. Pays $75 to $300, on acceptance.

WOMAN'S TOUCH—1445 Boonville, Springfield, MO 65802–1894. Peggy Musgrove, Ed. Aleda Swartzendruber, Assoc. Ed. Inspirational articles, 500 to 1,200 words, for Christian women. Uses some poetry, 50 to 150 words. Submit complete manuscript. Pays on acceptance. Allow 3 months for response. Guidelines and editorial calendar.

WOMAN'S WORLD—270 Sylvan Ave., Englewood Cliffs, NJ 07632. Andrea Bien, Feature Ed. Fast-moving short stories, about 1,900 words, with light romantic theme. (Specify "short story" on outside of envelope.) Mini-mysteries, 950 words, with "whodunit" or "howdunit" theme. No science fiction, fantasy, horror, ghost stories, or gratuitous violence. Pays $1,000 for short stories, $500 for mini-mysteries, on acceptance. SASE.

WOMEN & RECOVERY—Need to Know Press, P.O. Box 151947–2, Cupertino, CA 95015–1947. Sara V. Cole, Ed. Quarterly. Essays, exposés, humor, self-help articles, product or treatment profiles and reviews, opinion pieces, and personal-experience pieces, 1,000 to 2,000 words, related to women's recovery issues (physical, emotional, and spiritual). Poems, cartoons, B&W photos and drawings. Pays $35 to $100 for articles; $15 to $50 for poetry and art, on publication.

WOMEN IN BUSINESS—American Business Women's Assn., 9100 Ward Pkwy., Box 8728, Kansas City, MO 64114–0728. Wendy S. Myers, Ed. Features, 1,000 to 1,500 words, for working women ages 35 to 55. No profiles. Query required. Pays on acceptance.

WOMEN'S CIRCLE—P.O. Box 299, Lynnfield, MA 01940. Marjorie Pearl, Ed. Success stories on home-based female entrepreneurs. How-to articles on contemporary craft and needlework projects. Unique money-saving ideas and recipes. Pays varying rates, on acceptance.

WOMEN'S SPORTS & FITNESS—2025 Pearl St., Boulder, CO 80302. Mary Duffy, Ed. Outdoor sports how-tos, profiles, adventure travel, and controversial issues in women's sports, 500 to 2,000 words. Fitness, nutrition, and health. Pays on publication.

WORKING MOTHER—Lang Communications, 230 Park Ave., New York, NY 10169. Attn: Ed. Dept. Articles, to 2,000 words, that help women in their task of juggling job, home, and family. "We like pieces that solve or illuminate a problem unique to our readers." Payment varies, on acceptance.

WORKING WOMAN—230 Park Ave., New York, NY 10169. Lynn Povich, Ed.-in-Chief. Articles, 1,000 to 2,500 words, on business and personal aspects of the lives of executive and managerial women and entrepreneurs. Pays from $400, on acceptance.

MEN'S PUBLICATIONS

ESQUIRE—250 W. 55th St., New York, NY 10019. Edward Kosner, Ed.-in-Chief. David Hirshey, Deputy Ed. Articles, 2,500 to 4,000 words, for intelligent audience. Pays varying rates, on acceptance. Query with clips and SASE.

GALLERY—401 Park Ave. S., New York, NY 10016–8802. Barry Janoff, Ed.-in-Chief. Rich Friedman, Man. Ed. Articles, investigative pieces, interviews,

595

profiles, to 2,500 words, for sophisticated men. Short humor, satire, service pieces, and fiction. Photos. Pays varying rates, on publication. Query. Guidelines.

GQ—350 Madison Ave., New York, NY 10017. No free-lance queries or manuscripts.

INSIDE EDGE—50 Church St., Cambridge, MA 02138. Josie Roth, Ed. Fiction, nonfiction, and humor, 1,000 words, for young men ages 18 to 24. Queries preferred. Pays $250, on publication of second article; first published article receives no payment.

IRIS MAGAZINE—Iris Publications, Inc., P.O. Box 7263, Atlanta, GA 30357. Glenn Crawford, Assoc. Ed. Quarterly. Gay men's literary review of fiction, to 5,000 words, poetry to 60 lines, and B&W photography and art.

MEN'S FITNESS—21100 Erwin St., Woodland Hills, CA 91367. Peter Sikowitz, Ed.-in-Chief. Authoritative and practical articles, 1,500 to 1,800 words, and department pieces, 1,200 to 1,500 words, on fitness, health, and men's issues. Pays $500 to $1,000, on acceptance.

MEN'S HEALTH—Rodale Press, 33 E. Minor St., Emmaus, PA 18098. Jeff Csatari, Sr. Ed. Articles, 1,000 to 2,500 words, on fitness, diet, health, relationships, sports, and travel for men ages 25 to 55. Pays from 50¢ a word, on acceptance. Query.

PENTHOUSE—1965 Broadway, New York, NY 10023–5965. Peter Bloch, Ed. Lavada Blanton, Features and Fashion Ed. General-interest profiles, interviews, and investigative articles, to 5,000 words. No unsolicited fiction. Pays on acceptance.

PLAYBOY—680 N. Lakeshore Dr., Chicago, IL 60611. Peter Moore, Stephen Randall, Eds. Articles, 3,500 to 6,000 words, and sophisticated fiction, 1,000 to 10,000 words (5,000 preferred), for urban men. Humor; satire. Science fiction. Pays to $5,000 for articles and fiction, $2,000 for short-shorts, on acceptance. SASE required.

PLAYERS—8060 Melrose Ave., Los Angeles, CA 90046. Cecil Wills, Ed. Articles, 1,000 to 3,000 words, for black men: politics, economics, travel, fashion, grooming, entertainment, sports, interviews, fiction, humor, satire, health, and sex. Photos a plus. Pays on publication.

ROBB REPORT—1 Acton Pl., Acton, MA 01720. Robert R. Feeman, Ed. Lifestyle magazine for men. Feature articles and regular columns on investment opportunities, exotic cars, classic and collectible autos, investibles and collectibles, technology, lifestyles (fashion, home, trends, food, books, personalities, pets, etc.), boats, travel, business profiles, etc. Pays on publication. Query with SASE and clips.

SENIORS MAGAZINES

KEY HORIZONS—Gateway Plaza, 950 N. Meridian, Suite 1200, Indianapolis, IN 46204. Joan Todd, Man. Ed. General-interest articles and department pieces, 300 to 1,500 words, for readers ages 50 and over in the Midwest, East, and Southwest. Departments include money, health, finance, domestic travel (no first-person pieces), and better living (gardening, cooking, etc.). No nostalgia or first-person retrospectives. Pays $50 to $500, on publication.

MATURE LIVING—127 Ninth Ave. N., Nashville, TN 37234. Al Shackleford, Ed. Fiction and human-interest articles, to 1,200 words, for senior adults. Must be consistent with Christian principles. Payment varies, on acceptance.

MATURE YEARS—201 Eighth Ave. S., P.O. Box 801, Nashville, TN 37202. Marvin W. Cropsey, Ed. Articles of interest to older adults: health and fitness, personal finance, hobbies and inspiration. Anecdotes, to 300 words, poems, cartoons, jokes, and puzzles for older adults. Allow 2 months for response. "A Christian magazine that seeks to build faith. We always show older adults in a favorable light." Include name, address, and social security number with all submissions.

MODERN MATURITY—3200 E. Carson St., Lakewood, CA 90712. J. Henry Fenwick, Ed. Articles, to 2,000 words, on careers, workplace, human interest, living, finance, relationships, and consumerism for readers over 50. Query with SASE. Pays $500 to $2,500, on acceptance.

NEW CHOICES FOR RETIREMENT LIVING—28 W. 23rd St., New York, NY 10010. David A. Sendler, Ed.-in-Chief. News and service magazine for people ages 50 to 65. Articles on planning for retirement, health and fitness, financial strategies, housing options, travel, profiles/interviews (celebrities and newsmakers), relationships, leisure pursuits, etc. Query or send complete manuscript. SASE required. Payment varies, on acceptance.

THE RETIRED OFFICER MAGAZINE—201 N. Washington St., Alexandria, VA 22314. Attn: Manuscripts Ed. Articles, 800 to 2,000 words, of interest to military retirees and their families. Current military/political affairs, recent military history (especially Vietnam and Korea), military family lifestyles, health, money, second careers. Photos a plus. Pays from $750, on acceptance. Queries required. Guidelines.

RX REMEDY—120 Post Rd. W., Westport, CT 06880. Val Weaver, Ed. Bimonthly. Articles, 600 to 2,500 words, on health and medication issues for readers 55 and older. Regular columns include "The Fitness Prescription" and "The Nutrition Prescription." Query. Pays $1 to $1.25 a word, on acceptance.

SENIOR HIGHLIGHTS—26081 Merit Cir., Suite 101, Laguna Hills, CA 92653. Lee McCamon, Ed. Articles, 500 to 800 words, on health, money, retirement lifestyles, travel, and nostalgia. Queries preferred. No payment.

SENIOR MAGAZINE—3565 S. Higuera St., San Luis Obispo, CA 93401. Attn: Ed. Articles, 600 to 900 words, of interest to senior citizens in California: profiles, travel pieces, articles about new things, places, business, sports, movies, television, and health; reviews of new or outstanding older books. Pays $1.50 per inch; $10 to $25 for B&W photos, on publication.

YESTERDAY'S MAGAZETTE—P.O. Box 15126, Sarasota, FL 34277. Ned Burke, Ed. Articles and stories, 500 to 1,000 words, set in the 1920s to '70s. Photos a plus. Traditional poetry, to 24 lines. Pays $5 to $25, for articles, on publication. Pays in copies for short pieces and poetry.

HOME & GARDEN/FOOD & WINE

AMERICAN HOMESTYLE—(formerly *Decorating Remodeling*) 110 Fifth Ave., New York, NY 10011. Kathryn George, Karen Saks, Eds.-in-Chief. Articles on interior design, remodeling, architecture, and the decorative arts. Query. Payment varies, on acceptance.

AMERICAN ROSE—P.O. Box 30,000, Shreveport, LA 71130. Ed Gage, Man. Ed. Articles on home rose gardens: varieties, products, helpful advice, rose care, etc.

BETTER HOMES AND GARDENS—1716 Locust St., Des Moines, IA 50309–3023. Jean Lemmon, Ed. Articles, to 2,000 words, on money management, health, travel, pets, and cars. Pays top rates, on acceptance. Query.

BRIDE'S & YOUR NEW HOME—140 E. 45th St., New York, NY 10017. Andrea Feld, Man. Ed. Articles, 800 to 3,000 words, for engaged couples or newly-weds on home (housing, redecorating, etc.), wedding, and honeymoon. Pays $200 to $1,000, on acceptance.

CANADIAN WORKSHOP MAGAZINE—130 Spy Ct., Markham, Ont., Canada L3R 5H6. Jo Currie, Ed. Articles, 1,500 to 2,800 words, on do-it-yourself home renovations, energy saving projects, etc., with photos. Pays varying rates, on acceptance.

CHILE PEPPER—P.O. Box 4278, Albuquerque, NM 87196. Melissa Jackson, Assoc. Ed. Food and travel articles, 1,000 to 1,500 words. "No general and obvious articles, such as 'My Favorite Chile Con Carne.' We want first-person articles about spicy world cuisine." Queries required. No fillers. Payment varies, on publication.

CHOCOLATIER—Haymarket, Ltd., 45 W. 34th St., New York, NY 10001. Michael Schneider, Ed. Articles related to chocolate and desserts, cooking and baking techniques, lifestyle and travel. Pays varying rates, on acceptance. Query required.

DECORATING REMODELING—See *American HomeStyle*.

EATING WELL—Ferry Rd., P.O. Box 1001, Charlotte, VT 05445. Scott Mowbray, Ed. Bimonthly. Feature articles, 2,000 to 5,000 words. Department pieces, 100 to 200 words, for "Nutrition News" and "Marketplace." "We look for strong journalistic voice; authoritative, timely coverage of nutrition issues; healthful recipes that emphasize good ingredients, simple preparation, and full flavor; and a sense of humor." Query. Payment varies, 45 days after acceptance.

ELLE DECOR—1633 Broadway, New York, NY 10019. Charles Bricker, Exec. Ed. Articles, 300 to 1,000 words, on designers and craftspeople (query with photos of the designers and their work) and on houses and apartments "notable for their quirkiness or their beauty, preferably an eclectic combination of the two." Query. Pays $1.25 a word, on publication.

FLOWER & GARDEN MAGAZINE—700 W. 47th St., Suite 310, Kansas City, MO 64112. Attn: Ed. Practical how-to articles, 1,000 words, on lawn and garden advice. Query. Photos a plus. Pays varying rates, on acceptance (on publication for photos).

FOOD & WINE—1120 Ave. of the Americas, New York, NY 10036. Mary Simons, Ed.-in-Chief. Mary Ellen Ward, Man. Ed. Current culinary or beverage ideas for dining and entertaining at home and out. Food-related travel pieces. Submit detailed proposal.

GOURMET: THE MAGAZINE OF GOOD LIVING—Conde Nast, 360 Madison Ave., New York, NY 10017. Attn: Ed. Query; no unsolicited manuscripts.

HARROWSMITH COUNTRY LIFE—Ferry Rd., Charlotte, VT 05445. Attn: Ed. Dept. Features, 3,000 to 4,000 words, on community/small town issues, the environment, rural life, gardening, energy-efficient housing, and healthful food. Short pieces for "Screed" (opinions) and "Gazette" (news briefs). Pays $500 to $1,500 for features, $50 to $600 for department pieces, on acceptance. Query required. Guidelines.

THE HERB COMPANION—Interweave Press, 201 E. Fourth St., Loveland, CO 80537. David Merrill, Man. Ed. Bimonthly. Articles, 1,500 to 3,000 words; fillers, 75 to 150 words. Practical horticultural information, original recipes illustrating the use of herbs, thoroughly researched historical insights, step-by-step instructions for herbal craft projects, profiles of notable individuals in the field, book reviews. Pays $100 per published page, on publication.

THE HERB QUARTERLY—P. O. Box 689, San Anselmo, CA 94960. Linda Sparrowe, Ed. Articles, 2,000 to 4,000 words, on herbs: practical uses, cultivation, gourmet cooking, landscaping, herb tradition, medicinal herbs, crafts ideas, unique garden designs; profiles of herb garden experts; practical how-tos for the herb businessperson. Include garden design when possible. Pays on publication. Guidelines; send SASE.

HOME MAGAZINE—1633 Broadway, 44th Fl., New York, NY 10019. Gale Steves, Ed-in-Chief. Linda Lentz, Articles Ed. Articles of interest to homeowners: architecture, remodeling, decorating, products, project ideas, landscaping and gardening, financial aspects of home ownership, home offices, home-related environmental and ecological topics. Query, with 50- to 200-word summary. Pays varying rates, on acceptance.

HOME MECHANIX—2 Park Ave., New York, NY 10016. Michael Chotiner, Ed. Home improvement articles. Time- or money-saving tips for the home, garage, or yard; seasonal reminders for homeowners. Pays $50, on acceptance.

HORTICULTURE—98 N. Washington St., Boston, MA 02114. Deborah Starr, Exec. Ed. Published 10 times a year. Authoritative, well-written articles, 500 to 2,500 words, on all aspects of gardening. Pays competitive rates, on publication. Query.

HOUSE BEAUTIFUL—1700 Broadway, New York, NY 10019. Elaine Greene, Features Ed. Service articles related to the home. Pieces on design, travel, and gardening. Query with detailed outline. SASE required. Guidelines.

HOUSEPLANT MAGAZINE—P.O. Box 1638, Elkins, WV 26241. Larry Hodgson, Ed.-in-Chief. Articles, 700 to 1,500 words, on indoor gardening, travel, humor, hydroponics, plant portraits. Query. Payment varies, on publication.

LOG HOME LIVING—P.O. Box 220039, Chantilly, VA 22022. Roland Sweet, Ed. Articles, 1,000 to 1,500 words, on modern manufactured and hand-crafted kit log homes: homeowner profiles, design and decor features. Pays $200 to $500, on acceptance.

METROPOLITAN HOME—1633 Broadway, New York, NY 10019. Barbara Graustark, Articles Ed. Service and informational articles for residents of houses, co-ops, lofts, and condominiums, on real estate, equity, wine and spirits, collecting, trends, travel, etc. Interior design and home furnishing articles with emphasis on lifestyle. Query. Payment varies.

THE MOTHER EARTH NEWS—24 E. 23rd St., 5th Fl., New York, NY 10010. Michelle Silver, Assoc. Ed. Articles on country living: home improvement and construction, how-tos, indoor and outdoor gardening, crafts and projects, etc. Also health, ecology, energy, and consumerism pieces; profiles. Payment varies.

NATIONAL GARDENING MAGAZINE—180 Flynn Ave., Burlington, VT 05401. Michael MacCaskey, Ed. Articles, 1,000 to 2,500 words, and departments, 800 to 1,000 words, for advanced and beginning gardeners: the latest on fruits, vegetables, and flowers; seed-to-table profiles of major crops; first-hand reports from experienced gardeners; profiles; easy-to-follow gardening techniques and building projects; recipes. Personal opinion for "View from the Garden." Reflective or humorous essays for "The Last Leaf." Query preferred. Pays $150 to $500, on acceptance. Guidelines.

SELECT HOMES & FOODS—(formerly *Select Homes*) 50 Holly St., Toronto, Ontario, Canada M4S 3B3. Lynette Jennings, Ed. How-to articles, profiles of Canadian homes, renovation, decor, and gardening features, 800 to 1,500 words. Canadian content and locations only. Query with international reply coupons. Pays from $400 to $900 (Canadian), on acceptance. Send SAE with international reply coupons for guidelines.

VEGGIE LIFE—1041 Shary Cir., Concord, CA 94518. Margo Lemas, Ed. Bimonthly. Features and profiles, 2,500 words, for "people interested in American and ethnic meatless cuisine, organic gardening, environmental issues, and healthy living." Food features (include 8 to 10 recipes); department pieces, 250 to 1,000 words. Queries preferred. Payment varies, on acceptance.

WINE SPECTATOR—387 Park Ave. S., New York, NY 10016. Jim Gordon, Man. Ed. Features, 600 to 2,000 words, preferably with photos, on news and people in the wine world, travel, food, and other lifestyle topics. Query required. Pays from $400, extra for photos, on publication.

WINES & VINES—1800 Lincoln Ave., San Rafael, CA 94901. Philip E. Hiaring, Ed. Articles, 2,000 words, on grape and wine industry, emphasizing marketing, management, and production. Pays 5¢ a word, on acceptance.

WORKBENCH—700 W. 47th St., Suite 310, Kansas City, MO 64112. Robert N. Hoffman, Exec. Ed. Illustrated how-to articles on home improvement and woodworking, with detailed instructions. Pays from $150 per printed page, on acceptance. Guidelines.

YOUR HOME/INDOORS & OUT—P.O. Box 10010, Ogden, UT 84409. Attn: Ed. Dept. Articles, 1,000 words, with good color transparencies and fresh ideas in all areas of home decor: the latest in home construction (exteriors, interiors, building materials, design); the outdoors at home (landscaping, pools, patios, gardening); home management, buying, and selling. "We are especially interested in articles on choosing a realtor or home builder." No do-it-yourself pieces. Query required. Payment varies.

FAMILY & PARENTING MAGAZINES

AMERICAN BABY—Cahners Childcare Group, 475 Park Ave. S., New York, NY 10016. Judith Nolte, Ed. Articles, 1,000 to 2,000 words, for new or expectant parents on prenatal and infant care. Pays varying rates, on acceptance.

BABY TALK—636 Ave. of the Americas, New York, NY 10011. Susan Strecker, Ed. Articles, 1,000 to 1,500 words, by parents or professionals, on babies, baby care, etc. No poetry. Pays varying rates, on acceptance. SASE required.

BAY AREA PARENT—401 Alberto Way, Suite A, Los Gatos, CA 95032–5404. Mary Brence Martin, Ed. Articles, 1,200 to 1,400 words, on local parenting issues for readers in California's Santa Clara County and the South Bay area. Query. Mention availability of B&W photos. Pays 6¢ a word, $10 to $15 for photos, on publication. Also publishes *Valley Parent* for central Contra Costa County and the tri-valley area of Alameda County.

THE BIG APPLE PARENTS' PAPER—36 E. 12th St., New York, NY 10003. Susan Hodara, Ed. Articles, 600 to 750 words, for NYC parents. Pays $35 to $50, on publication. Buys first NY-area rights.

CAPPER'S—1503 S.W. 42nd St., Topeka, KS 66609–1265. Nancy Peavler, Ed. Human-interest, personal-experience, historical articles, 300 to 700 words. Poetry, to 15 lines, on nature, home, family. Novel-length fiction for serialization. Letters on women's interests, recipes, and hints for "Heart of the Home." Jokes. Children's writing and art section. Pays varying rates, on publication.

CATHOLIC PARENT—Our Sunday Visitor, Inc., 200 Noll Plaza, Huntington, IN 46750. Woodeene Koenig-Bricker, Ed. Features, how-tos, and general-interest articles, 800 to 1,000 words, dealing with the issues of raising children "with solid values in today's changing world. Keep it anecdotal and practical with an emphasis on values and family life." Payment varies, on acceptance. Guidelines.

CENTRAL CALIFORNIA PARENT—2059 W. Bullard, #131, Fresno, CA 93711. Sally Cook, Pub. Articles, 500 to 1,500 words, of interest to parents of children of all ages. Payment varies, on publication.

CHRISTIAN HOME & SCHOOL—3350 E. Paris Ave. S.E., Grand Rapids, MI 49512. Gordon L. Bordewyk, Ed. Articles for parents in Canada and the U.S. who send their children to Christian schools and are concerned about the challenges facing Christian families today. Pays $75 to $150, on publication. Guidelines.

CHRISTIAN PARENTING TODAY—P.O. Box 850, Sisters, OR 97759. Brad Lewis, Ed. Articles, 900 to 1,500 words, dealing with raising children with Christian principles. Departments: "Parent Exchange," 25 to 100 words, on problem-solving ideas that have worked for parents; "My Story," 800 to 1,500 words, first-person accounts of how one family or parent faced a parenting challenge; "Life in our House," insightful anecdotes, 25 to 100 words, about humorous things said at home. Queries preferred for articles. Pays 15¢ to 25¢ a word, on publication. Pays $40 for "Parent Exchange," $25 for "Life in our House." Guidelines; enclose SASE.

EASTSIDE PARENT—Northwest Parent Publishing, 2107 Elliott Ave., #303, Seattle, WA 98121. Ann Bergman, Ed. Articles, 300 to 2,500 words, for parents of children under 12. Readers tend to be professional, two-career families. Queries are preferred. Pays $25 to $200, on publication. Also publishes *Seattle's Child, Portland Parent*, and *Pierce County Parent*.

EXCEPTIONAL PARENT—209 Harvard St., Suite 303, Brookline, MA 02146–5005. Stanley D. Klein, Ed. Articles, 1,000 to 1,500 words, for parents raising children with disabilities. Practical ideas and techniques on parenting, as well as the latest in technology, research, and rehabilitation. Pays $25, on publication. Query.

FAMILY—169 Lexington Ave., New York, NY 10016. Liz DeFranco, Ed. Articles, 1,000 to 2,000 words, of interest to women with children. Topics include: military lifestyle, home decorating, travel, moving, food, personal finances, career, relationships, family, parenting, health and fitness. Pays to $200, on publication.

THE FAMILY: A CATHOLIC PERSPECTIVE—50 St. Pauls Ave., Boston, MA 02130. Sr. Theresa Frances Myers, Ed. Articles, 800 to 2,000 words, on a broad range of family topics, including marital relationships, parenting, profiles of role-models for Catholic families. Upbeat, thought-provoking, family-oriented fiction, 1,000 to 1,200 words. Views, columns, personal reflections, 800 words; fillers, 50 to 500 words. "Our readers are primarily Roman Catholic parents with children at home." Submit complete manuscripts; no queries and no simultaneous submissions. Pays 6¢ to 8¢ a word, on publication. (Pays for fillers on acceptance.) Does not read submissions in July or August.

FAMILY FUN—Walt Disney Publishing Group, Box 929, Northampton, MA 01061. Alexandra Kennedy, Ed. Read-aloud stories, to 750 words, and articles, to 1,500 words, on family activities and "creative parenting." Payment varies, on acceptance. Queries preferred.

FAMILY LIFE—Wenner Media, 1290 Ave. of the Americas, New York, NY 10104–0298. Attn: Ed. Dept. Articles, 1,000 to 4,000 words, on education, travel, money, health, community service, and other subjects of interest to active parents of children ages 3 to 12. Service pieces, 700 to 1,500 words, on sports, lessons, field trips, toys, parties, and pets. Short pieces, 250 to 800 words, on news and activities. Query with clips.

GROWING CHILD/GROWING PARENT—22 N. Second St., P.O. Box 620, Lafayette, IN 47902–0620. Nancy Kleckner, Ed. Articles, to 1,500 words, on subjects of interest to parents of children under 6. No personal experience pieces or poetry. Guidelines.

HOME LIFE—127 Ninth Ave. N., Nashville, TN 37234. Charlie Warren, Ed.-in-Chief. Southern Baptist. Articles, to 1,500 words, on Christian marriage, parenting, and family relationships. Pays from $75 for articles, on acceptance.

JOYFUL CHILD JOURNAL—34 Russell Ave., Buffalo, NY 14214. Karen Spring Stevens, Exec. Ed. Quarterly. Fiction and nonfiction, 500 to 1,000 words, that "explore how society and education can more effectively nurture children (and adults) to express their fullest potential, thus releasing their inner joy. Articles on educating and parenting the whole child (body, mind, and spirit)." Some short poetry. Guidelines. Pays in copies. Queries preferred.

L.A. BABY—See *Wingate Enterprises, Ltd.*

L.A. PARENT—See *Wingate Enterprises, Ltd.*

LIVING WITH PRESCHOOLERS—See *ParentLife*.

LIVING WITH TEENAGERS—127 Ninth Ave. N., Nashville, TN 37234. Attn: Ed. Articles from a Christian perspective for parents of teenagers. Send resumé only.

OURS: THE MAGAZINE OF ADOPTIVE FAMILIES—Adoptive Families of America, 3333 Hwy. 100 N., Minneapolis, MN 55422. Jolene L. Roehlkepartain, Ed. Bimonthly. Articles, 800 to 1,700 words, on living in an adoptive family and other adoption issues. B&W photos of families, adults, or children. No payment. Query.

PARENTGUIDE NEWS—475 Park Ave. S., New York, NY 10016. Leslie Elgort, Ed. Articles, 1,000 to 1,500 words, related to families and parenting issues: trends, profiles, special programs, products, etc. Humor and photos also considered.

PARENTING—See *Wingate Enterprises, Ltd.*

PARENTING—301 Howard St., 17th Fl., San Francisco, CA 94105. Attn: Articles Ed. Articles, 500 to 3,500 words, on education, health, fitness, nutrition, child development, psychology, and social issues for parents of young children. Query.

PARENTLIFE—(formerly *Living with Preschoolers*) MSN 140, 127 Ninth Ave. N., Nashville, TN 37234. Attn: Ed. Articles on Christian family issues. Resumés only.

PARENTS—685 Third Ave., New York, NY 10017. Ann Pleshette Murphy, Ed. Articles, 1,500 to 2,500 words, on parenting, family, women's and community issues, etc. Informal style with quotes from experts. Pays from $1,000, on acceptance. Query.

PARENT'S DIGEST—100 Park Ave., New York, NY 10017. Mary E. Mohler, Ed.-in-Chief. Published 3 times a year by *Ladies' Home Journal.* Articles, 250 to 2,500 words, for parents; frequently uses reprints. Payment varies, on acceptance. Query.

PIERCE COUNTY PARENT—See *Eastside Parent.*

PORTLAND PARENT—See *Eastside Parent.*

QUICK 'N EASY COUNTRY COOKIN'—Parkside Publications, Inc., P.O. Box 66, Davis, SD 57021–0066. Judith Friese, Copy/Production Ed. Family-oriented articles, 400 to 500 words, on cooking, and articles with a human-interest/Christian perspective. "We also accept short verse, puzzles, and humorous fillers, up to 50 words." Pays $10 for articles, on publication.

RETIRED MILITARY FAMILY—169 Lexington Ave., New York, NY 10016. Liz DeFranco, Ed. Articles, 1,000 to 1,500 words, of interest to military retirees and their families: travel, finance, food, hobbies, second careers, grandparenting, etc. Pays to $200, on publication.

SAN DIEGO PARENT—See *Wingate Enterprises, Ltd.*

SEATTLE'S CHILD—Northwest Parent Publishing, 2107 Elliott Ave., #303, Seattle, WA 98121. Ann Bergman, Ed. Articles, 400 to 2,500 words, of interest to parents, educators, and childcare providers of children under 12, plus investigative reports and consumer tips on issues affecting families in the Puget Sound region. Pays $75 to $400, on publication. Query required.

SESAME STREET PARENTS' GUIDE—One Lincoln Plaza, New York, NY 10023. Valerie Monroe, Exec. Ed. Articles, 800 to 2,500 words, on medical, psychological, and educational issues for families with young children (up to 8 years old). First-person pieces on parenting for "Family Portrait." "A Conversation With . . . " columns, to 1,500 words, of questions and answers with professionals (educators, psychologists, authors) who affect the lives of children. Pays 50¢ to $1 per word, up to 6 weeks after acceptance.

THE SINGLE PARENT—Parents Without Partners, Inc., 401 N. Michigan Ave., Chicago, IL 60611. Mercedes M. Vance, Ed. Quarterly. Articles, 500 to 1,000 words, addressing the concerns of single parents, including physical and emotional wellness, careers (for adults and youths), and intergenerational issues. Fillers, 300 to 500 words. Prefers pieces that "enlighten and entertain busy people"; no "cutesy or sob stories." No payment.

STEPFAMILIES—Stepfamily Assn. of America, 215 Centennial Mall S., Suite 212, Lincoln, NE 68508–1834. Attn: Exec. Dir. Quarterly. Articles, 2 to 4 pages, relevant to stepfamily living. Fillers and poetry. No payment.

TODAY'S FAMILY—3585 W. Lexington Ave., Suite 328, Arden Hills, MN 55126. Valerie Hockert, Pub./Man. Ed. Quarterly. Articles, 750 to 2,000 words, on "hot topics and fun for every family." Pays $10 to $50, on publication. Query preferred.

TWINS—6740 Antioch, Suite 155, Merriam, KS 66204. Jean Cerne, Man. Ed. Bimonthly. Features, 6 to 8 double-spaced pages; columns, 4 to 6 pages. "Twin-specific parenting information, from both the professional (research-based) and personal (hands-on experience) perspectives." Pays varying rates, on publication. Query.

VALLEY PARENT—See *Bay Area Parent.*

VIRTUE: THE CHRISTIAN MAGAZINE FOR WOMEN—P. O. Box 36630, Colorado Springs, CO 80936–3663. Nancie Carmichael, Man. Ed. Articles, 1,200 to 1,500 words, on family, marriage, self-esteem, working mothers, opinions, crafts. Fiction and poetry. Pays 15¢ to 22¢ a word, $25 to $50 for poetry, on publication. Query with SASE required.

WINGATE ENTERPRISES, LTD.—P.O. Box 3204, 443 E. Irving Dr., Burbank, CA 91504. Attn: Eds. Publishes city-based parenting magazines with strong "service-to-parent" slant. Articles, 1,200 words, on child development, health, nutrition, and education. *San Diego Parent* covers San Diego area. *Parenting* covers the Orange County, CA, area. *L.A. Parent* is geared toward parents of children to age 10; *L.A. Baby* to expectant parents and parents of newborns. Pays $100 to $300, on acceptance. Query.

WORKING MOTHER—Lang Communications, 230 Park Ave., New York, NY 10169. Attn: Ed. Dept. Articles, to 2,000 words, that help women juggle job, home, and family. Payment varies, on acceptance.

LIFESTYLE MAGAZINES

AMERICAN HEALTH—28 W. 23rd St., New York, NY 10010. Attn: Ed. Dept. Lively, authoritative articles, 1,000 to 3,000 words, on scientific and lifestyle aspects of health and fitness; 100- to 500-word news reports. Query with clips. Pays $150 to $250 for news stories; payment varies for features, on acceptance.

CHANGES—U.S. Journal, Inc., 3201 S.W. 15th St., Deerfield Beach, FL 33442–8190. Jeffrey Laign, Ed. "The Recovery Lifestyle Magazine." Bimonthly. Recovery-oriented fiction, 1,500 words, and poetry. Query for nonfiction, 2,000 words. Pays 15¢ a word, on publication.

THE CHRISTIAN SCIENCE MONITOR—One Norway St., Boston, MA 02115. Lawrence Goodrich, Features Ed. Newspaper. Articles on lifestyle trends, women's rights, family, and parenting. Pays varying rates, on acceptance.

COUNTRY—5400 S. 60th St., Greendale, WI 53129. Dan Matel, Man. Ed. Pieces, 500 to 1,500 words, on interesting rural and country people who have unusual hobbies; liberal use of direct quotes. Good, candid color photos required. Pays on acceptance.

COUNTRY AMERICA—1716 Locust St., Des Moines, IA 50309–3023. Dick Sowienski, General Interest Ed. Mike Hood, Outdoors Ed. Neil Pond and Peg Brinkhoff, Entertainment Eds. Diane Yanney, Food Ed. Curt Goettsch, Travel/ Crafts Ed. Features on travel, cooking, recreation, crafts, homes, gardening, and personalities. "Articles should be light on copy with potential for several color photos." Queries preferred.

FELLOWSHIP—Box 271, Nyack, NY 10960–0271. Richard Deats, Ed. Bimonthly published by the Fellowship of Reconciliation, an interfaith, pacifist organization. Features, 1,500 to 2,000 words, and articles, 750 words, "dealing with nonviolence, opposition to war, and a just and peaceful world community." Photo essays (B&W photos, include caption information). Pays in copies and subscription. Queries preferred. SASE required.

GERMAN LIFE—Zeitgeist Publishing, 1 Corporate Dr., Grantsville, MD 21536. Michael Koch, Ed. Bimonthly. Articles, 200 to 2,000 words, on German culture, its past and present, and how America has been influenced by its German immigrants: history, travel, people, the arts, and social and political issues. Fillers,

50 to 200 words. Pays $300 to $400, to $80 for fillers, on publication. Queries preferred.

HEART & SOUL—Rodale Press, Inc., 33 E. Minor St., Emmaus, PA 18098. Catherine Cassidy, Man. Ed. Articles, 800 to 2,000 words, on health, beauty, fitness, nutrition, and relationships for African-American readers. "We aim to be the African-American's ultimate guide to a healthy lifestyle." Payment varies, on acceptance. Queries preferred.

INDEPENDENT LIVING—150 Motor Parkway, Suite 420, Hauppauge, NY 11788–5145. Anne Kelly, Ed. Articles, 1,000 to 2,000 words, addressing lifestyles of persons who have disabilities. Possible topics: home health care, careers, travel, sports, family life, and sexuality. Pays 10¢ a word, $15 per photo, on publication. Query.

INSIDE MAGAZINE—226 S. 16th St., Philadelphia, PA 19102–3392. Jane Biberman, Ed. Jewish lifestyle magazine. Articles, 1,500 to 3,000 words, on Jewish issues, health, finance, and the arts. Queries required; send clips if available. Pays $75 to $600, after publication.

JEWISH CURRENTS—22 E. 17th St., #601, New York, NY 10003. Morris U. Schappes, Ed. Articles, 2,400 to 3,000 words, on Jewish culture or history: Holocaust, resistance commemoration, Black-Jewish relations, Jewish labor struggles. "We are a secular Jewish magazine." No fiction. No payment.

LEFTHANDER MAGAZINE—P.O. Box 8249, Topeka, KS 66608–0249. Kim Kipers, Ed. Bimonthly. Articles, 1,500 to 1,800 words, related to left-handedness: profiles of left-handed personalities; research on performing specific tasks or sports as a lefty; teaching left-handed children. Personal experience pieces for "Perspective." SASE for guidelines. Pays $80 to $100, on publication. Buys all rights. Query.

LIFEPRINTS—P.O. Box 5181, Salem, OR 97304. Carol McCarl, Ed. Quarterly. Articles, 1,200 to 1,800 words, and poetry, 20 lines, for visually impaired youth and adults. Career opportunities, educational skills, and recreational activities. "We want to give readers an opportunity to learn about interesting and successful people who happen to be blind." Pays $15 for articles; $10 for poetry, on publication. Queries are preferred.

LINK, THE COLLEGE MAGAZINE—The Soho Bldg., 110 Greene St., Suite 407, New York, NY 10012. Ty Wenger, Man. Ed. Lifestyle magazine for college students. Short features and essays, 500 to 800 words, on dating, college road trips, trends, and lifestyles. First-person pieces, 600 to 700 words, written by recent graduates with interesting employment stories for "So You Want My Job." Guidelines. Pays $100 to $500, on publication. Queries preferred.

MAGICAL BLEND—Box 421130, San Francisco, CA 94142. Jerry Snider, Lit. Ed. Positive, uplifting articles, to 3,000 words, on spiritual exploration, lifestyles, occult, white magic, New Age thought.

MILITARY LIFESTYLE MAGAZINE—4800 Montgomery Ln., Suite 710, Bethesda, MD 20814. Hope Daniels, Ed. Articles, 800 to 1,500 words, for active-duty and retired military families; pieces on child raising, marriage, health, fitness, food, and issues concerning military families; home decor and "portable" or "instant" gardening articles; fiction. Pays $300 to $700, on publication. Query.

NATIVE PEOPLES MAGAZINE—5333 N. 7th St., Suite C-224, Phoenix, AZ 85014–2804. Gary Avey, Ed. Quarterly. Articles, 1,800 to 2,800 words, on the "arts and lifeways" of the native peoples of the Americas; authenticity and positive portrayals of present traditional and cultural practices necessary. Pays 25¢ a word, on publication. Query, including availability of photos.

NATURAL HEALTH: THE GUIDE TO WELL-BEING—17 Station St., Box 1200, Brookline, MA 02147. Attn: Ed. Bimonthly. Features, 1,500 to 3,000 words: practical information, new discoveries, and current trends on natural health and living. Topics include natural goods and medicine, alternative health care, nutrition, wellness, personal fitness, and modern holistic teachings. Departments and columns, 250 to 1,000 words. Payment varies, on acceptance.

NEW AGE JOURNAL—342 Western Ave., Brighton, MA 02135. Peggy Taylor, Ed. Articles for readers who take an active interest in social change, personal growth, health, and contemporary issues. Features, 2,000 to 4,000 words; columns, 750 to 1,500 words; short news items, 50 words; and first-person narratives, 750 to 1,500 words. Pays varying rates.

NEW CHOICES FOR RETIREMENT LIVING—28 W. 23rd St., New York, NY 10010. Allen J. Sheinman, Articles Ed. David A. Sendler, Ed.-in-Chief. News and service magazine for people ages 50 to 65. Articles on planning for retirement, health and fitness, financial strategies, housing options, travel, profiles/interviews (celebrities and newsmakers), relationships, leisure pursuits, etc. SASE required. Payment varies, on acceptance. Query or send complete manuscript.

OUT—The Soho Bldg., 110 Greene St., Suite 800, New York, NY 10012. Michael Goff, Ed.-in-Chief. Bimonthly. Articles, 50 to 8,000 words, on various subjects (current affairs, culture, fitness, finance, etc.) of interest to gay and lesbian readers. "The best guide to what we publish is to read previous issues." Guidelines. Payment varies, on publication. Query.

OUT YOUR BACKDOOR—4686 Meridian Rd., Williamston, MI 48895. Jeff Potter, Ed. Articles and fiction, 2,500 words, for thrifty, down-to-earth culture enthusiasts. "Budget travel, second-hand goods, and homespun but high-quality culture all combine to yield an energetic, practical, folksy post-modern magazine." Study sample issue before submitting. Pays in copies.

PALM SPRINGS LIFE—Desert Publications, 303 North Indian Canyon Dr., P.O. Box 2724, Palm Springs, CA 92263. Jamie Pricer, Ed. Articles, 1,000 to 3,000 words, of interest to "wealthy, upscale people who live and/or play in the desert." Pays $150 to $400 for features, $50 to $75 for short profiles, on publication. Query required.

ROBB REPORT—1 Acton Pl., Acton, MA 01720. Robert R. Feeman, Ed. Feature articles on lifestyles, home interiors, boats, travel, investment opportunities, exotic automobiles, business, technology, etc. Payment varies, on publication. Query with SASE and published clips.

USAIR MAGAZINE—NYT Custom Publishing, 590 Madison Ave., 32nd Fl., New York, NY 10022. Catherine Sabino, Ed. Kathy Passero, Man. Ed. USAir inflight magazine. Articles on travel, trends in health and fitness, sports, personality profiles, food and wine, family and children, fashion and shopping, the arts and culture. "Our goal is to provide readers with lively and colorful, yet practical articles that will make their lives and their leisure time more rewarding." Pays $1 a word, within 60 days of acceptance. Query with clips; no unsolicited manuscripts.

WEIGHT WATCHERS MAGAZINE—360 Lexington Ave., New York, NY 10017. Deborah Kotz, Health Ed. Articles on health, nutrition, fitness, and weight-loss motivation and success. Pays from $500. Query with clips required. Guidelines.

WILDFIRE—Bear Tribe Publishing, P.O. Box 199, Devon, PA 19333. Judith Trustone, Man. Ed. Articles, 1,000 to 2,500 words, with a strong nature-based focus on spirituality, personal development, alternative lifestyles, natural healings, and ecology. Poetry, 20 lines. Pay varies, on publication.

WIRED—544 Second St., San Francisco, CA 94107–1427. Jessie Scanlon, Ed. Assoc. Lifestyle magazine for the "digital generation." Articles, essays, profiles, fiction, and other material that discusses the "meaning and context" of digital technology in today's world. Guidelines. Payment varies, on publication.

YOGA JOURNAL—2054 University Ave., Berkeley, CA 94704. Rick Fields, Ed. Articles, 1,200 to 4,000 words, on holistic health, spirituality, yoga, and transpersonal psychology; New Age profiles; interviews. Pays $75 to $800, on publication.

SPORTS AND RECREATION

ADVENTURE CYCLIST—(formerly *Bikereport*) Adventure Cycling Assn., P.O. Box 8308, Missoula, MT 59807. Daniel D'Ambrosio, Ed. Articles, 1,200 to 2,500 words: accounts of bicycle tours in the U.S. and overseas, interviews, personal-experience pieces, humor, and news shorts. Pays $25 to $65 per published page.

THE AMERICAN FIELD—542 S. Dearborn, Chicago, IL 60605. B.J. Matthys, Man. Ed. Yarns about hunting trips, bird-shooting; articles to 1,500 words, on dogs and field trials, emphasizing conservation of game resources. Pays varying rates, on acceptance.

AMERICAN MOTORCYCLIST—American Motorcyclist Assn., Box 6114, Westerville, OH 43081–6114. Greg Harrison, Ed. Articles and fiction, to 3,000 words, on motorcycling: news coverage, personalities, tours. Photos. Pays varying rates, on publication. Query with SASE.

AMERICAN SQUAREDANCE MAGAZINE—661 Middlefield Rd., Salinas, CA 93906–1004. Jon Sanborn, Ed. Articles and fiction, 1,000 to 1,500 words, related to square dancing. Poetry. Fillers, to 100 words. Pays $1.50 per column inch.

ATLANTIC SALMON JOURNAL—P.O. Box 429, St. Andrews, N.B., Canada E0G 2X0. Harry Bruce, Ed. Articles, 1,500 to 3,000 words, related to Atlantic salmon: fishing, conservation, ecology, travel, politics, biology, how-tos, anecdotes. Pays $100 to $400, on publication.

BACKPACKER MAGAZINE—Rodale Press, 33 E. Minor St., Emmaus, PA 18098. John Viehman, Exec. Ed. Articles, 250 to 3,000 words, on self-propelled backcountry travel: backpacking, kayaking/canoeing, mountaineering, Nordic skiing; technique, health, natural science. Photos. Pays varying rates. Query.

THE BACKSTRETCH—19899 W. 9 Mile Rd., Southfield, MI 48075–3960. Harriet Dalley, Ed. United Thoroughbred Trainers of America. Feature articles, with photos, on subjects related to thoroughbred horse racing. Pays after publication. Sample issue and guidelines on request.

BASEBALL FORECAST, BASEBALL ILLUSTRATED—See *Hockey Illustrated.*

BASKETBALL FORECAST—See *Hockey Illustrated.*

BASSIN'—NatCom, Inc., 5300 CityPlex Tower, 2448 E. 81st St., Tulsa, OK 74137–4207. Mark Chesnut, Man. Ed. Articles, 1,200 to 1,400 words, on how and where to bass fish, for the amateur fisherman. Pays $300 to $500, on acceptance.

BASSMASTER MAGAZINE—B.A.S.S. Publications, P.O. Box 17900, Montgomery, AL 36141. Dave Precht, Ed. Articles, 1,500 to 2,000 words, with photos, on freshwater black bass and striped bass. "Short Casts" pieces, 400 to 800 words, on news, views, and items of interest. Pays $200 to $400, on acceptance. Query.

BAY & DELTA YACHTSMAN—2019 Clement Ave., Alameda, CA 94501. Connie Skoog, Ed. Cruising stories and features, how-tos. Must have northern California tie-in. Photos and illustrations. Pays varying rates.

BC OUTDOORS—1132 Hamilton St., #202, Vancouver, B.C., Canada V6B 2S2. Karl Bruhn, Ed. Articles, to 2,000 words, on fishing, hunting, conservation, and all forms of non-competitive outdoor recreation in British Columbia and Yukon. Photos. Pays from 20¢ to 27¢ a word, on acceptance.

BICYCLING—33 E. Minor St., Emmaus, PA 18098. Bill Strickland, Man. Ed. Articles, 500 to 2,500 words, for serious cyclists, on recreational riding, fitness training, nutrition, bike maintenance, equipment, racing and touring, covering all aspects of the sport: road, mountain biking, track racing, etc. Photos, illustrations. Pays $25 to $1,000, on acceptance. Guidelines.

BIKEREPORT—See *Adventure Cyclist.*

BIRD WATCHER'S DIGEST—P.O. Box 110, Marietta, OH 45750. William H. Thompson, III, Ed. Articles, 600 to 2,500 words, for bird watchers: first-person accounts; how-tos; pieces on endangered species; profiles. Cartoons. Pays from $50, on publication.

BLACK BELT—P.O. Box 918, Santa Clarita, CA 91380–9018. Attn: Ed. Articles related to self-defense: how-tos on fitness and technique; historical, travel, philosophical subjects. Pays $100 to $300, on publication. Guidelines.

BOAT PENNSYLVANIA—Pennsylvania Fish and Boat Commission, P.O. Box 67000, Harrisburg, PA 17106–7000. Art Michaels, Ed. Articles, 200 to 2,500 words, with photos, on boating in Pennsylvania: motorboating, sailing, waterskiing, canoeing, kayaking, and personal watercraft. No pieces on fishing. Pays $50 to $250, on acceptance. Query. Guidelines.

BOUNDARY WATERS JOURNAL—9396 Rocky Ledge Rd., Ely, MN 55731. Stuart Osthoff, Ed. Articles, 2,000 to 3,000 words, on wilderness, recreation, nature, and conservation in Minnesota's Boundary Waters Canoe Area Wilderness and Ontario's Quetico Provincial Park. Regular features include canoe-route journals, fishing, camping, hiking, cross-country skiing, wildlife and nature, regional lifestyles, history, and events. Pays $200 to $400, on publication; $50 to $150 for photos.

BOW & ARROW HUNTING—Box 2429, 34249 Camino Capistrano, Capistrano Beach, CA 92624–0429. Roger Combs, Ed. Dir. Articles, 1,200 to 2,500 words, with B&W photos, on bowhunting; profiles and technical pieces. Pays $100 to $300, on acceptance. Same address and mechanical requirements for *Gun World.*

BOWHUNTER MAGAZINE—Box 8200, Harrisburg, PA 17105–8200. M.R. James, Ed. Informative, entertaining features, 500 to 2,000 words, on bow-and-arrow hunting. Fillers. Photos. "Study magazine first." Pays $50 to $300, on acceptance.

BOWHUNTING WORLD—Dept. OU, 601 Lakeshore Pkwy., Suite 600, Minnetonka, MN 55305. Mike Strandlund, Ed. Articles, 1,800 to 3,000 words, on all aspects of bowhunting and competitive archery equipment, with photos. "We're interested in how-to articles on bowhunting techniques and feature articles that cover the romance or mechanics of all types of archery gear, from traditional to high tech." Also mini-features, 1,000 to 1,600 words. Pays from $325, on acceptance. Query. Guidelines.

BOWLERS JOURNAL—200 S. Michigan Ave., Chicago, IL 60604. Jim Dressel, Ed. Trade and consumer articles, 1,200 to 2,200 words, with photos, on bowling. Pays $75 to $200, on acceptance.

BOWLING—5301 S. 76th St., Greendale, WI 53129. Bill Vint, Ed. Articles, to 1,500 words, on all aspects of bowling, especially human interest. Profiles. "We're looking for unique, unusual stories about bowling people and places and occasionally publish business articles." Pays varying rates, on publication. Query required.

BUCKMASTERS WHITETAIL MAGAZINE—1114 Princeton Pl., Euless, TX 76040. Russell Thornberry, Exec. Ed. Semiannual. Articles and fiction, 2,500 words, for serious sportsmen. "Big Buck Adventures" articles capture the details and the adventure of the hunt of a newly discovered trophy. Fresh, new whitetail hunting how-tos; new biological information about whitetail deer that might help hunters; entertaining deer stories; and other department pieces. Photos a plus. Guidelines. Pay $250 to $400 for articles, on acceptance.

CALIFORNIA HORSE REVIEW—P.O. Box 1238, Rancho Cordova, CA 95741-1238. Attn: Ed. Articles, 750 to 2,500 words, on horse training, for professional horsemen; profiles of prominent West Coast horses and riders. Pays $35 to $125, on publication.

CANADIAN DIVER & WATERSPORT—See *Diver Magazine.*

CANOE AND KAYAK MAGAZINE—(formerly *Canoe*) P.O. Box 3146, Kirkland, WA 98083. Jim Thompson, Man. Ed. Features, 1,100 to 2,000 words; department pieces, 500 to 1,000 words. Topics include canoeing or kayaking adventures, destinations, boat and equipment reviews, techniques and how-tos, short essays, camping, environment, humor, health, history, etc. Pays $5 per column inch, on publication. Query preferred. Guidelines.

CAR AND DRIVER—2002 Hogback Rd., Ann Arbor, MI 48105. Csaba Csere, Ed.-in-Chief. Articles, to 2,500 words, for enthusiasts, on new cars, classic cars, industry topics. "Ninety percent staff-written. Query with clips. No unsolicited manuscripts." Pays to $2,500, on acceptance.

CAR CRAFT—6420 Wilshire Blvd., Los Angeles, CA 90048. Chuck Schifsky, Ed. Articles and photo-features on high performance street machines, drag cars, racing events; technical pieces; action photos. Pays from $150 per page, on publication.

CASCADES EAST—716 N.E. Fourth St., P.O. Box 5784, Bend, OR 97708. Geoff Hill, Ed./Pub. Articles, 1,000 to 2,000 words, on outdoor activities (fishing, hunting, golfing, backpacking, rafting, skiing, snowmobiling, etc.), history, special events, and scenic tours in central Oregon Cascades. Photos. Pays 5¢ to 10¢ a word, extra for photos, on publication.

CASINO PLAYER—Bayport One, Suite 470, 8025 Black Horse Pike, W. Atlantic City, NJ 08232. Adam Fine, Ed. Articles, 500 to 1,000 words, accompanied by photos, for beginning to intermediate gamblers, on slots, video poker, and table games. No first-person or real-life gambling stories. Pays $100, on publication.

CHESAPEAKE BAY MAGAZINE—1819 Bay Ridge Ave., Annapolis, MD 21403. Jean Waller, Ed. Articles, to 1,500 words, on boating and fishing on Chesapeake Bay. Photos. Pays $100 to $150, on publication. Query.

CITY SPORTS MAGAZINE—2201 Third St., San Francisco, CA 94107. Craig Bystrynski, Ed. Articles, 300 to 3,000 words, on participant sports, family recreation, travel, and the active lifestyle. Pays $50 to $500, on publication. Query. Limited market.

CROSSTRAINER—505-H Saddle River Rd., Saddle Brook, NJ 07662. Alan Paul, Ed. Articles, 5 to 10 double-spaced pages, geared to fitness and sports training, nutrition, running, weight training, etc. Photos. Pays $50 to $400, on publication. Query.

CURRENTS—212 W. Cheyenne Mountain Blvd., Colorado Springs, CO 80906. Greg Moore, Ed. Quarterly. "Voice of the National Organization for River Sports." Articles, 500 to 2,000 words, for kayakers, rafters, and river canoeists, pertaining to whitewater rivers and/or river running. Fillers. B&W action photos. Pays $40 and up for articles, $30 to $50 for photos, on publication. Queries preferred.

CYCLE WORLD—1499 Monrovia Ave., Newport Beach, CA 92663. David Edwards, Ed. Technical and feature articles, 1,500 to 2,500 words, for motorcycle enthusiasts. Photos. Pays on publication. Query.

CYCLING U.S.A.—U.S. Cycling Federation, One Olympic Plaza, Colorado Springs, CO 80909. Jason Anderson, Ed. Articles, 500 to 1,000 words, on bicycle racing. Pays 10¢ to 15¢ a word, on publication. Query.

THE DIVER—P.O. Box 313, Portland, CT 06480. Bob Taylor, Ed. Articles on divers, coaches, officials, springboard and platform techniques, training tips, etc. Pays $15 to $35, extra for photos ($5 to $10 for cartoons), on publication.

DIVER MAGAZINE—295–10991 Shellbridge Way, Richmond, B.C., Canada V6X 3C6. Peter Vassilopoulos, Pub./Ed. Illustrated articles, 500 to 1,000 words, on dive destinations. Shorter pieces are also welcome. "Travel features should be brief and accompanied by excellent slides and/or prints and a map. Unsolicited articles will be reviewed only from August to October and will be considered for *Diver Magazine* and *Canadian Diver & Watersport*." Pays $2.50 per column inch, on publication. Guidelines. Limited market.

EQUUS—Fleet Street Corp., 656 Quince Orchard Rd., Gaithersburg, MD 20878. Laurie Prinz, Man. Ed. Articles, 1,000 to 3,000 words, on all breeds of horses, covering their health, care, the latest advances in equine medicine and research. "Attempt to speak as one horseperson to another." Pays $100 to $400, on publication.

FAMILY MOTOR COACHING—8291 Clough Pike, Cincinnati, OH 45244–2796. Pamela Wisby Kay, Ed. Articles, 1,500 to 2,000 words, on technical topics and travel routes and destinations accessible by motorhome. Query preferred. Payment varies, on acceptance.

FIELD & STREAM—2 Park Ave., New York, NY 10016. Duncan Barnes, Ed. Articles, 1,500 to 2,000 words, with photos, on hunting, fishing. Short articles, to 1,000 words. Fillers, 75 to 500 words. Cartoons. Pays from $800 for feature articles with photos, $75 to $500 for fillers, $100 for cartoons, on acceptance. Query for articles.

FLY FISHERMAN—6405 Flank Dr., Box 8200, Harrisburg, PA 17105. Philip Hanyok, Man. Ed. Query.

FLY ROD & REEL—P.O. Box 370, Camden, ME 04843. James E. Butler, Ed. Fly-fishing pieces, 2,000 to 2,500 words, and occasional fiction; articles on the culture and history of the areas being fished. Pays on acceptance. Query.

610

FOOTBALL DIGEST—Century Publishing Co., 990 Grove St., Evanston, IL 60201. Kenneth Leiker, Sr. Ed. John Hareas, Sr. Assoc. Ed. William Wagner, Assoc. Ed. Profiles of pro and college stars, nostalgia, trends in the sport, 1,500 to 2,500 words, aimed at the hard-core football fan. Pays on publication.

FOOTBALL FORECAST—See *Hockey Illustrated.*

FUR-FISH-GAME—2878 E. Main St., Columbus, OH 43209. Mitch Cox, Ed. Illustrated articles, 800 to 2,500 words, preferably with how-to angle, on hunting, fishing, trapping, dogs, camping, or other outdoor topics. Some humorous or where-to articles. Pays $40 to $150, on acceptance.

GAME AND FISH PUBLICATIONS—P.O. Box 741, Marietta, GA 30061. Attn: Ed. Dept. Publishes 30 monthly outdoor magazines for 48 states. Articles, 1,500 to 2,500 words, on hunting and fishing. How-tos, where-tos, and adventure pieces. Profiles of successful hunters and fishermen. No hiking, canoeing, camping, or backpacking pieces. Pays $125 to $175 for state-specific articles, $200 to $250 for multi-state articles, before publication. Pays $25 to $75 for photos.

GOLF FOR WOMEN—P.O. Box 951989, Lake Mary, FL 32795–1989. Pat Baldwin, Ed.-in-Chief. Golf-related articles of interest to women; fillers and humor. Instructional pieces are staff-written. Pays from 40¢ a word, on publication. Query.

GOLF JOURNAL—Golf House, P.O. Box 708, Far Hills, NJ 07931–0708. David Earl, Ed. Articles on golf personalities, history, travel. Humor. Photos. Pays varying rates, on publication.

GOLF MAGAZINE—2 Park Ave., New York, NY 10016. Jim Frank, Ed. Articles, 1,000 words with photos, on golf history and travel (places to play around the world); profiles of professional tour players. Shorts, to 500 words. Pays 75¢ a word, on acceptance. Queries preferred.

GOLF TIPS—Werner Publishing Corp., 12121 Wilshire Blvd., #1220, Los Angeles, CA 90025–1175. Nick Mastroni, Ed. Articles, 500 to 1,500 words, for serious golfers: unique golf instruction, golf products, interviews with pro players. Fillers: short "shotmaking" instruction tips. Queries preferred. Pays $200 to $600, on publication.

THE GREYHOUND REVIEW—National Greyhound Assn., Box 543, Abilene, KS 67410. Tim Horan, Man. Ed. Articles, 1,000 to 10,000 words, pertaining to the greyhound racing industry: how-to, historical nostalgia, interviews. Pays $85 to $150, on publication.

GULF COAST GOLFER—See *North Texas Golfer.*

GUN DIGEST—4092 Commercial Ave., Northbrook, IL 60062. Ken Warner, Ed. Well-researched articles, to 5,000 words, on guns and shooting, equipment, etc. Photos. Pays from 10¢ a word, on acceptance. Query.

GUN WORLD—See *Bow & Arrow Hunting.*

HANG GLIDING—U.S. Hang Gliding Assn., P.O. Box 8300, Colorado Springs, CO 80933–8300. Gilbert Dodgen, Ed. Articles, 2 to 3 pages, on hang gliding. Pays to $50, on publication. Query.

HOCKEY ILLUSTRATED—Lexington Library, Inc., 233 Park Ave. S., New York, NY 10003. Stephen Ciacciarelli, Ed. Articles, 2,500 words, on hockey players and teams. Pays $125, on publication. Query. Same address and requirements for *Baseball Illustrated, Wrestling World, Pro Basketball Illustrated, Pro Football Illustrated, Baseball Forecast, Pro Football Preview, Football Forecast,* and *Basketball Forecast.*

HORSE & RIDER—1060 Calle Cordillera, Suite 103, San Clemente, CA 92673. Juli S. Thorson, Ed. Articles, 500 to 3,000 words, with photos, on western riding and general horse care geared to the performance horse: training, feeding, grooming, health, etc. Pays varying rates, on publication. Buys one-time rights. Guidelines.

HORSEMEN'S YANKEE PEDLAR—785 Southbridge St., Auburn, MA 01501. Nancy L. Khoury, Pub. News and feature-length articles, about horses and horsemen in the Northeast. Photos. Pays $2 per published inch, on publication. Query.

HORSEPLAY—P.O. Box 130, Gaithersburg, MD 20884. Lisa Kiser, Man. Ed. Articles, 700 to 3,000 words, on eventing, show jumping, horse shows, and dressage for riders, horse owners, and sport horse enthusiasts. Profiles, instructional articles, occasional humor, and competition reports. Pays 10¢ a word for all rights, 9¢ a word for first North American rights, after publication. Query. SASE required. Guidelines.

HOT ROD—6420 Wilshire Blvd., Los Angeles, CA 90048-5515. Drew Hardin, Ed. How-to pieces and articles, 500 to 5,000 words, on auto mechanics, hot rods, track and drag racing. Photo-features on custom or performance-modified cars. Pays to $200 per page, on publication.

HUNTING—6420 Wilshire Blvd., Los Angeles, CA 90048-5515. Todd Smith, Ed. How-to articles on practical aspects of hunting. At least 15 photos required with articles. Query required. Guidelines. Pays $250 to $500 for articles with B&W photos, extra for color photos, on publication.

INSIDE SPORTS—990 Grove St., Evanston, IL 60201. Kenneth Leiker, Sr. Ed. In-depth, insightful sports articles, player profiles, fillers, and humor. Payment varies, on acceptance. Query.

INSIDE TEXAS RUNNING—9514 Bristlebrook Dr., Houston, TX 77083-6193. Joanne Schmidt, Ed. Articles and fillers on running in Texas. Pays $35 to $100, $10 for photos, on acceptance.

KITPLANES—P.O. Box 6050, Mission Viejo, CA 92690. Dave Martin, Ed. Articles, 1,000 to 4,000 words, on all aspects of design, construction, and performance of aircraft built from kits and plans by home craftsmen. Pays $60 per page, on publication.

LAKELAND BOATING—1560 Sherman Ave., Suite 1220, Evanston, IL 60201-5047. John Wooldridge, Ed. Articles for powerboat owners on the Great Lakes and other area waterways, on long-distance cruising, short trips, maintenance, equipment, history, regional personalities and events, and environment. Photos. Pays on publication. Query. Guidelines.

MEN'S FITNESS—21100 Erwin St., Woodland Hills, CA 91367. Peter Sikowitz, Ed.-in-Chief. Features, 1,500 to 1,800 words, and department pieces, 1,200 to 1,500 words: authoritative and practical articles dealing with fitness, health, and men's issues. Pays $500 to $1,000, on acceptance.

MEN'S HEALTH—Rodale Press, 33 E. Minor St., Emmaus, PA 18098. Jeff Csatari, Sr. Ed. Articles, 1,000 to 2,500 words, on sports, fitness, diet, health, nutrition, relationships, and travel, for men ages 25 to 55. Pays from 50¢ a word, on acceptance. Query.

MICHIGAN OUT-OF-DOORS—P.O. Box 30235, Lansing, MI 48909. Kenneth S. Lowe, Ed. Features, 1,500 to 2,500 words, on hunting, fishing, camping, and conservation in Michigan. Pays $75 to $150, on acceptance.

MID-WEST OUTDOORS—111 Shore Dr., Hinsdale, IL 60521–5885. Gene Laulunen, Ed. Articles, 1,000 to 1,500 words, with photos, on where, when, and how to fish and hunt in the Midwest. No Canadian material. Pays $15 to $35, on publication.

MOTOR TREND—6420 Wilshire Blvd., Los Angeles, CA 90048–5515. Leonard Emanuelson, Ed. Articles, 250 to 2,000 words, on autos, racing, events, and profiles. Photos. Pay varies, on acceptance. Query.

MOTORCYCLIST—6420 Wilshire Blvd., Los Angeles, CA 90048–5515. Mitch Boehm, Ed. Articles, 1,000 to 3,000 words. Photos. Pays $150 to $300 per published page, on publication.

MOTORHOME MAGAZINE—3601 Calle Tecate, Camarillo, CA 93012. Barbara Leonard, Ed. Dir. Articles, to 1,500 words, with color slides, on motorhomes. Also travel and how-to pieces. Pays to $600, on acceptance.

MUSCULAR DEVELOPMENT—505-H Saddle River Rd., Saddle Brook, NJ 07662. Alan Paul, Ed. Articles, 1,000 to 2,500 words, on competitive bodybuilding, power lifting, sports, and nutrition for serious weight training athletes; personality profiles, training features, and diet and nutrition pieces. Photos. Pays $100 to $400, on publication. Query.

MUSHING—P.O. Box 149, Ester, AK 99725–0149. Todd Hoener, Ed. Dogdriving how-tos, profiles, and features, 1,500 to 2,000 words; and department pieces, 500 to 1,000 words, for competitive and recreational dogsled drivers, weight pullers, and skijorers. International audience. Photos. Pays $20 to $250, on publication. Queries preferred. Guidelines and sample issue on request.

NATIONAL PARKS MAGAZINE—1776 Massachusetts Ave., Washington, DC 20036. Sue E. Dodge, Ed. Articles, 1,500 to 2,500 words, on natural history, wildlife, and conservation as they relate to national parks; illustrated features on the natural, historic, and cultural resources of the National Park System. Pieces about legislation and other issues and events related to the parks. Pays $100 to $800, on acceptance. Query. Guidelines.

THE NEW ENGLAND SKIERS GUIDE—Box 1125, Waitsfield, VT 05673. Tim Etchells, Ed. Annual (June deadline for submissions). Articles on alpine and Nordic skiing, equipment, and winter vacations at New England resorts. Rates vary.

NEW YORK OUTDOORS—51 Atlantic Ave., Floral Park, NY 11001. Scott Shane, Pub. Jon Tsaovsis, Ed. Articles, 600 to 1,500 words, with B&W photos on all outdoor activities (include technique and equipment) in and around New York State. Pays to $350.

NORTH TEXAS GOLFER—9182 Old Katy Rd., Suite 212, Houston, TX 77055. Steve Hunter, Ed./Pub. Articles, 800 to 1,500 words, of interest to golfers in north Texas. Pays $50 to $250, on publication. Queries required. Same requirements for *Gulf Coast Golfer* (for golfers in south Texas).

NORTHEAST OUTDOORS—P.O. Box 2180, Waterbury, CT 06722–2180. John Florian, Ed. Dir. Articles, 500 to 1,000 words, preferably with B&W photos, on camping and recreational vehicle (RV) touring in northeast U.S.: recommended private campgrounds, camp cookery, recreational vehicle hints. Stress how-to, where-to. Cartoons. Pays $20 to $80, on publication. Guidelines.

OFFSHORE—220 Reservoir St., Needham Heights, MA 02194. Herbert Gliick, Ed. Articles, 1,200 to 2,500 words, on boats, people, places, maritime history, and events along the New England, New York, and New Jersey coasts. Writers should be knowledgeable boaters. Photos a plus. Pays $250 to $500.

613

ON TRACK—17165 Newhope St., "M", Fountain Valley, CA 92708. Jon Gunn and Tim Tuttle, Eds. Features and race reports, 500 to 2,500 words. Pays $5.25 per column inch, 2 weeks after publication. Query.

OPEN WHEEL—47 S. Main St., Ipswich, MA 01938. Dick Berggren, Ed. Articles, to 6,000 words, on open wheel drivers, races, and vehicles. Photos. Pays to $400 on publication.

OUTDOOR CANADA—703 Evans Ave., Suite 202, Toronto, Ont., Canada M9C 5E9. Ms. Teddi Brown, Ed. Published 8 times yearly. Articles, 1,500 to 2,000 words, on fishing, camping, hiking, canoeing, hunting, and wildlife. Pays $200 to $600, on publication.

OUTDOOR LIFE—2 Park Ave., New York, NY 10016. Vin T. Sparano, Ed.-in-Chief. Articles, 1,400 to 1,700 words, and short, instructive items, 900 to 1,100 words, on hunting, fishing, boats, outdoor equipment, and related subjects. Pays $300 to $550, on acceptance. Query.

OUTSIDE—1165 N. Clark, Chicago, IL 60610. No unsolicited material.

PENNSYLVANIA ANGLER—Pennsylvania Fish and Boat Commission, P.O. Box 67000, Harrisburg, PA 17106–7000. Attn: Art Michaels, Ed. Articles, 500 to 3,000 words, with photos, on freshwater fishing in Pennsylvania. Pays $50 to $250, on acceptance. Must send SASE with all material. Query. Guidelines.

PENNSYLVANIA GAME NEWS—Game Commission, 2001 Elmerton Ave., Harrisburg, PA 17110–9797. Bob Mitchell, Ed. Articles, to 2,500 words, on outdoor subjects, except fishing and boating. Photos. Pays from 6¢ a word, extra for photos, on acceptance.

PETERSEN'S BOWHUNTING—6420 Wilshire Blvd., Los Angeles, CA 90048–5515. Greg Tinsley, Ed. How-to articles, 2,000 to 2,500 words, on bowhunting. Also pieces on where to bowhunt, unusual techniques and equipment, and profiles of successful bowhunters will also be considered. Photos must accompany all manuscripts. Pays $300 to $400, on acceptance. Query.

PLANE & PILOT—12121 Wilshire Blvd., #1220, Los Angeles, CA 90025–1175. Steve Higginson, Features Ed. Aviation related articles, 1,500 to 3,000 words, targeted to the single engine, piston powered recreational pilot. Training, maintenance, travel, equipment, pilot reports. Occasional features on antique, classic, and kit- or home-built aircraft. Payment varies, on publication. Query preferred.

POWER AND MOTORYACHT—245 W. 17th St., New York, NY 10011. Diane M. Byrne, Assoc. Ed. Articles, 1,000 to 2,000 words, for owners of powerboats, 24 feet and larger. Seamanship, ship's systems, maintenance, sportfishing news, travel destinations, profiles of individuals working to improve the marine environment. "For our readers, powerboating is truly a lifestyle, not just a hobby." Pays $500 to $1,000, on acceptance. Query required.

POWERBOAT—1691 Spinnaker Dr., Suite 206, Ventura, CA 93001. Eric Colby, Ed. Articles, to 1,500 words, with photos, for high performance powerboat owners, on outstanding achievements, water-skiing, competitions; technical articles on hull and engine developments; how-to pieces. Pays $300 to $1,000, on acceptance. Query.

PRACTICAL HORSEMAN—Box 589, Unionville, PA 19375. Mandy Lorraine, Ed. How-to articles conveying experts' advice on English riding, training, and horse care. Pays on acceptance. Query with clips.

PRIVATE PILOT—P.O. Box 6050, Mission Viejo, CA 92690–6050. Joseph P. O'Leary, Ed. Technically based aviation articles, 1,000 to 4,000 words, for general aviation pilots, aircraft owners, and aviation enthusiasts. Photos. Pays $75 to $250, on publication. Query.

PRO BASKETBALL ILLUSTRATED—See *Hockey Illustrated.*

PRO FOOTBALL ILLUSTRATED, PRO FOOTBALL PREVIEW—See *Hockey Illustrated.*

PURE-BRED DOGS/AMERICAN KENNEL GAZETTE—51 Madison Ave., New York, NY 10010. Beth Adelman, Exec. Ed. Articles, 1,000 to 2,500 words, relating to pure-bred dogs, for serious fanciers. Pays $100 to $300, on acceptance. Queries preferred.

RESTORATION—P.O. Box 50046, Tucson, AZ 85703–1046. W.R. Haessner, Ed. Articles, 1,200 to 1,800 words, on restoration of autos, trucks, planes, trains, etc., and related building (bridges and structures). Photos. Pays from $25 per page, on publication. Queries required.

RIDER—3601 Calle Tecate, Camarillo, CA 93012. Mark Tuttle Jr., Ed. Articles, to 3,000 words, with slides, on travel, touring, commuting, and camping motorcyclists. Pays $100 to $750, on publication. Query.

ROCK + ICE MAGAZINE—603A S. Broadway, Boulder, CO 80303. Marjorie McCloy, Ed. Bimonthly. Articles, 500 to 6,000 words, and fiction, 1,500 to 4,000 words, for technical rock and ice climbers: sport climbers, mountaineers, alpinists, and other adventurists. Slides and B&W photos considered. Query. Pays $200 per published page.

RUNNER TRIATHLETE NEWS—P.O. Box 19909, Houston, TX 77224. Lance Phegley, Ed. Articles on running for road racing and multi-sport enthusiasts in TX, OK, NM, LA, and AR. Payment varies, on publication.

RUNNER'S WORLD—Rodale Press, 33 E. Minor St., Emmaus, PA 18098. Bob Wischnia, Sr. Ed. Articles for "Human Race" (submit to Eileen Shovlin), "Finish Line" (to Cristina Negron), and "Health Watch" (to Adam Bean) columns. Send feature articles or queries to Bob Wischnia. Payment varies, on acceptance. Query.

SAFARI—4800 W. Gates Pass Rd., Tucson, AZ 85745. William Quimby, Publications Dir. Articles, 2,000 words, on worldwide big game hunting. Pays $200, extra for photos, on publication.

SAIL—275 Washington St., Newton, MA 02158–1630. Patience Wales, Ed. Articles, 1,500 to 3,500 words, features, 1,000 to 2,500 words, with photos, on sailboats, equipment, racing, and cruising. How-tos on navigation, sail trim, etc. Pays $75 to $1,000 on publication. Guidelines.

SAILING—125 E. Main St., Port Washington, WI 53074. M. L. Hutchins, Ed. Features, 700 to 1,500 words, with photos, on cruising and racing; first-person accounts; profiles of boats and regattas. Query for technical or how-to pieces. Pays varying rates, 30 days after publication. Guidelines.

SALT WATER SPORTSMAN—77 Franklin St, Boston, MA 02110. Barry Gibson, Ed. Articles, 1,200 to 1,500 words, on how anglers can improve their skills, and on new places to fish off the coast of the U.S. and Canada, Central America, the Caribbean, and Bermuda. Photos a plus. Pays $350 to $700, on acceptance. Query.

SEA, BEST OF BOATING IN THE WEST—17782 Cowan, Suite C, Irvine, CA 92714. Attn: Ed. Features, 800 to 1,500 words, and news articles, 200 to 250 words, of interest to West Coast powerboaters: profiles of boating personalities, cruise destinations, analyses of marine environmental issues, technical pieces on navigation and seamanship, news from western harbors. No fiction, poetry, or cartoons. Pays varying rates, on acceptance.

SEA KAYAKER—P.O. Box 17170, Seattle, WA 98107–0860. Christopher Cunningham, Ed. Articles, 400 to 4,500 words, on ocean kayaking. Related fiction. Pays about 10¢ a word, on publication. Query with clips and international reply coupons.

SHOTGUN SPORTS—P.O. Box 6810, Auburn, CA 95604. Frank Kodl, Ed. Articles with photos, on trap and skeet shooting, sporting clays, hunting with shotguns, reloading, gun tests, and instructional shooting. Pays $25 to $200, on publication.

SILENT SPORTS—717 10th St., P.O. Box 152, Waupaca, WI 54981–9990. Attn: Ed. Articles, 1,000 to 2,000 words, on bicycling, cross country skiing, running, canoeing, hiking, backpacking, and other "silent" sports. Must have regional (upper Midwest) focus. Pays $50 to $100 for features; $20 to $50 for fillers, on publication. Query.

SKI RACING INTERNATIONAL—Box 1125, Rt. 100, Waitsfield, VT 05673. Attn: Ed. Articles by experts on race techniques and conditioning secrets. Coverage of World Cup, Pro, Collegiate, and Junior competition. Comprehensive race information. Photos. Rates vary.

SKYDIVING MAGAZINE—1725 N. Lexington Ave., DeLand, FL 32724. Michael Truffer, Ed. Timely news articles, 300 to 800 words, relating to sport and military parachuting. Fillers. Photos. Pays $25 to $200, extra for photos, on publication.

SNOWEST—520 Park Ave., Idaho Falls, ID 83402. Steve Janes, Ed. Articles, 1,200 words, on snowmobiling in the western states. Pays to $100, on publication.

SOCCER JR.—27 Unquowa Rd., Fairfield, CT 06430. Joe Provey, Ed. Articles, fiction, and fillers related to soccer for readers in 5th and 6th grade. Query. Pays $450 for features; $250 for department pieces, on acceptance.

SOUTH CAROLINA WILDLIFE—P. O. Box 167, Columbia, SC 29202–0167. John E. Davis, Ed. Articles, 1,000 to 2,000 words, with state and regional outdoor focus: conservation, natural history, wildlife, and recreation. Profiles, how-tos. Pays on acceptance.

SOUTHERN OUTDOORS—5845 Carmichael Rd., Montgomery, AL 36117. Larry Teague, Ed. Essays, 1,200 to 1,500 words, related to the outdoors. Pays 15¢ to 20¢ a word, on acceptance.

SPORT MAGAZINE—6420 Wilshire Blvd., Los Angeles, CA 90048. Cam Benty, Ed. Dir. Query with clips. No fiction, poetry, or first person.

SPORTS ILLUSTRATED—1271 Ave. of the Americas, New York, NY 10020. Chris Hunt, Articles Ed. Query. Rarely uses free-lance material.

SPUR MAGAZINE—P. O. Box 2123, Augusta, GA 30903–2123. Attn: Ed. Dept. Articles, 300 to 5,000 words, on thoroughbred racing, breeding, polo, show jumping, eventing, and steeplechasing. Profiles of people and farms. Historical and nostalgia pieces. Pays $50 to $400, on publication. Query.

STARTING LINE—P.O. Box 19909, Houston, TX 77224. Lance Phegley, Ed. Quarterly. Articles, 800 to 1,200 words, for coaches, parents, and children, 8 to 18, on training for track and field, cross country, and racewalking, including techniques, health and fitness, nutrition, sports medicine, and related issues. Payment varies, on publication.

STOCK CAR RACING—47 S. Main St., Ipswich, MA 01938. Dick Berggren, Feature Ed. Articles, to 6,000 words, on stock car drivers, races, and vehicles. Photos. Pays to $400, on publication.

SURFER MAGAZINE—P. O. Box 1028, Dana Point, CA 92629. Court Overin, Pub. Steve Hawk, Ed. Articles, 500 to 5,000 words, on surfing, surfers, etc. Photos. Pays 20¢ to 30¢ a word, $10 to $600 for photos, on publication.

SURFING—P. O. Box 3010, San Clemente, CA 92674. Nick Carroll, Ed. Skip Snead, Asst. Ed. Short newsy and humorous articles, 200 to 500 words. No first-person travel articles. "Knowledge of the sport is essential." Pays varying rates, on publication.

TENNIS—5520 Park Ave., P. O. Box 0395, Trumbull, CT 06611–0395. Donna Doherty, Ed. Instructional articles, features, profiles of tennis stars, grass-roots articles, humor, 800 to 2,000 words. Photos. Pays from $300, on publication. Query.

TENNIS WEEK—124 E. 40th St., Suite 1101, New York, NY 10016. Eugene L. Scott, Pub. Kim Kodl, Cherry V. Masih, Merrill Chapman, Man. Eds. In-depth, researched articles, from 1,000 words, on current issues and personalities in the game. Pays $125, on publication.

TRAILER BOATS—20700 Belshaw Ave., Carson, CA 90746–3510. Randy Scott, Ed. Technical and how-to articles, 500 to 2,000 words, on boat, trailer, or tow vehicle maintenance and operation; skiing, fishing, and cruising. Fillers, humor. Pays $100 to $700, on acceptance.

TRAILER LIFE—3601 Calle Tecate, Camarillo, CA 93012. Barbara Leonard, Ed. Articles, to 2,000 words, with photos, on trailering, truck campers, motorhomes, hobbies, and RV lifestyles. How-to pieces. Pays to $600, on acceptance. Guidelines.

TRAILS-A-WAY—Woodall Publishing Co., P.O. Box 5000, Lake Forest, IL 60045–5000. Ann Emerson, Ed. RV-related travel articles, 1,000 to 1,200 words, for midwest camping families. Pay varies, on publication.

THE WATER SKIER—799 Overlook Dr., Winter Haven, FL 33884. Greg Nixon, Ed. Feature articles on waterskiing. Pays varying rates, on acceptance.

THE WESTERN HORSEMAN—P.O. Box 7980, Colorado Springs, CO 80933–7980. Pat Close, Ed. Articles, about 1,500 words, with photos, on care and training of horses; farm, ranch, and stable management; health care and veterinary medicine. Pays to $400, on acceptance.

WESTERN SPORTSMAN—P.O. Box 737, Regina, Sask., Canada S4P 3A8. Brian Bowman, Ed. Articles, to 2,500 words, on hunting and fishing in Alberta, Saskatchewan, and Manitoba; how-to pieces. Photos. Pays $75 to $300, on publication.

WINDSURFING—P.O. Box 2456, Winter Park, FL 32790. Debbie Snow, Ed. Features, instructional pieces, and tips, by experienced boardsailors. Fast action photos. Pays $50 to $75 for tips, $250 to $300 for features, extra for photos. SASE for guidelines.

WINDY CITY SPORTS—1450 W. Randolph, Chicago, IL 60607. Shelley Berryhill, Ed. Articles, 1,000 words, on amateur sports in Chicago. Pays $100, on publication. Query required.

WOMAN BOWLER—1912 Grand Ave., Des Moines, IA 50309. Paul Marshall, Ed. Profiles, interviews, and news articles, to 1,000 words, for women bowlers. Pays varying rates, on acceptance. Query with outline.

WOMEN'S SPORTS & FITNESS—2025 Pearl St., Boulder, CO 80302. Mary Duffy, Ed. Outdoor sports how-tos, profiles, adventure travel, and controversial issues in women's sports, 500 to 2,000 words. Fitness, nutrition, and health pieces also considered. Pays on publication.

WRESTLING WORLD—See *Hockey Illustrated.*

YACHTING—2 Park Ave., New York, NY 10016. Charles Barthold, Ed. Articles, 1,500 words, on upscale recreational power and sail boating. How-to and personal-experience pieces. Photos. Pays $350 to $1,000, on acceptance. Queries preferred.

AUTOMOTIVE MAGAZINES

AAA WORLD—AAA Headquarters, 1000 AAA Dr., Heathrow, FL 32746–5063. Douglas Damerst, Ed. Automobile and travel concerns, including automotive travel, purchasing, and upkeep, 750 to 1,500 words. Pays $300 to $600, on acceptance. Query with clips; articles are by assignment only.

AMERICAN MOTORCYCLIST—American Motorcyclist Assn., Box 6114, Westerville, OH 43081–6114. Greg Harrison, Ed. Articles and fiction, to 3,000 words, on motorcycling: news coverage, personalities, tours. Photos. Pays varying rates, on publication. Query with SASE.

CAR AND DRIVER—2002 Hogback Rd., Ann Arbor, MI 48105. Csaba Csere, Ed. Articles, to 2,500 words, for enthusiasts, on new cars, classic cars, industry topics. "Ninety percent staff-written. Query with clips. No unsolicited manuscripts." Pays to $2,500, on acceptance.

CAR AUDIO AND ELECTRONICS—21700 Oxnard St., Woodland Hills, CA 91367. Bill Neill, Ed. Features, 1,000 to 2,000 words, on electronic products for the car: audio systems, cellular telephones, security systems, CBs, radar detectors, etc.; how to buy them; how they work; how to use them. "To write for us, you must know this subject thoroughly." Pays $200 to $1,000, on acceptance.

CAR CRAFT—6420 Wilshire Blvd., Los Angeles, CA 90048. Chuck Schifsky, Ed. Articles and photo-features on high performance street machines, drag cars, racing events; technical pieces; action photos. Pays from $150 per page, on publication.

CYCLE WORLD—1499 Monrovia Ave., Newport Beach, CA 92663. David Edwards, Ed. Technical and feature articles, 1,500 to 2,500 words, for motorcycle enthusiasts. Photos. Pays $100 to $200 per page, on publication. Query.

EASYRIDERS MAGAZINE—Box 3000, Agoura Hills, CA 91376–3000. Keith R. Ball, Ed. Articles, 500 to 1,500 words, that stress the good times of owning a motorcycle. Technical articles, slice-of-life pieces, and humor; motorcycle news, history, and accomplishments. Hard-hitting, rugged, bike-oriented fiction, 1,200 to 2,000 words. Query. Pays 10¢ to 25¢ a word, on publication. Guidelines.

HOT ROD—6420 Wilshire Blvd., Los Angeles, CA 90048–5515. Drew Hardin, Ed. How-to pieces and articles, 500 to 5,000 words, on auto mechanics, hot rods, track and drag racing. Photo-features on custom or performance-modified cars. Pays $200 per page, on publication.

MOTOR TREND—6420 Wilshire Blvd., Los Angeles, CA 90048–5515. Leonard Emanuelson, Ed. Articles, 250 to 2,000 words, on autos, racing, events, and profiles. Photos. Pay varies, on acceptance. Query.

MOTORCYCLIST—6420 Wilshire Blvd., Los Angeles, CA 90048–5515. Mitch Boehm, Ed. Articles, 1,000 to 3,000 words. Photos. Pays $150 to $300 per published page, on publication.

OPEN WHEEL—See *Stock Car Racing.*

RESTORATION—P.O. Box 50046, Tucson, AZ 85703–1046. W.R. Haessner, Ed. Articles, 1,200 to 1,800 words, on restoration of autos, trucks, planes, trains, etc., and related building (bridges, structures, etc.). Photos. Pays from $25 per page, on publication. Queries required.

RIDER—3601 Calle Tecate, Camarillo, CA 93012. Mark Tuttle Jr., Ed. Articles, to 3,000 words, with color slides, on travel, touring, commuting, and camping motorcyclists. Pays $100 to $750, on publication. Query.

ROAD & TRACK—1499 Monrovia Ave., Newport Beach, CA 92663. Ellida Maki, Man. Ed. Short automotive articles, to 450 words, of a "timeless nature" for knowledgeable car enthusiasts. Pays on publication. Query.

ROAD KING—Hammock Publishing, 3322 W. End Ave., Suite 700, Nashville, TN 37203. George Friend, Ed. Bimonthly. Articles, 300 to 1,500 articles, on business of trucking from a driver's point of view; profiles of drivers and their rigs; technical aspects of trucking equipment; trucking history; travel destinations near major interstates; humor; fillers. No fiction. Include clips with submission. Pays negotiable rates, on publication.

STOCK CAR RACING—47 S. Main St., Ipswich, MA 01938. Dick Berggren, Ed. Features, technical automotive pieces, and profiles of interesting racing personalities, to 6,000 words, for oval track racing enthusiasts. Fillers. Pays $75 to $350, on publication. Same requirements for *Open Wheel.*

FITNESS MAGAZINES

AMERICAN FITNESS—15250 Ventura Blvd., Suite 200, Sherman Oaks, CA 91403. Peg Jordan, Ed. Rhonda Wilson, Man. Ed. Articles, 500 to 1,500 words, on exercise, health, sports, nutrition, etc. Illustrations, photos.

CROSSTRAINER—505-H Saddle River Rd., Saddle Brook, NJ 07662. Alan Paul, Ed. Articles, 5 to 10 double-spaced pages, geared to fitness and sports training, nutrition, running, weight training, etc. Photos. Pays $50 to $400, on publication. Query.

FITNESS—The New York Times Company Women's Magazines, 110 Fifth Ave., New York, NY 10011. Rona Cherry, Ed. Articles, 500 to 2,000 words, on health, exercise, sports, nutrition, diet, psychological well-being, sex, and beauty for readers around 30 years old. Queries required. Pays $1 per word, on acceptance.

IDEA PERSONAL TRAINER—6190 Cornerstone Ct. E., Suite 204, San Diego, CA 92121–3773. Terese Hannon, Asst. Ed. Association publication for personal fitness trainers. Articles on exercise science; program design; profiles of successful trainers; business, legal, and marketing topics; tips for networking with other trainers and with allied medical professionals; client counseling; and training tips. "What's New" column includes industry news, products, and research. Query. Payment varies, on acceptance.

619

IDEA TODAY—6190 Cornerstone Ct. E., Suite 204, San Diego, CA 92121–3773. Terese Hannon, Asst. Ed. Practical articles, 1,000 to 3,000 words, on new exercise programs, business management, nutrition, sports medicine, dance-exercise, and one-to-one training techniques. Articles must be geared toward the aerobics instructor, exercise studio owner or manager, or personal trainer. Don't query for consumer or general health articles. Payment is negotiable, on acceptance. Query preferred.

INSIDE TEXAS RUNNING—9514 Bristlebrook Dr., Houston, TX 77083–6193. Joanne Schmidt, Ed. Articles and fillers on running in Texas. Pays $35 to $100, $10 to $25 for photos, on acceptance.

MEN'S FITNESS—21100 Erwin St., Woodland Hills, CA 91367. Peter Sikowitz, Ed.-in-Chief. Features, 1,500 to 1,800 words, and department pieces, 1,200 to 1,500 words: "authoritative and practical articles dealing with fitness, health, and men's issues." Pays $500 to $1,000, on acceptance.

MEN'S HEALTH— Rodale Press, 33 E. Minor St., Emmaus, PA 18098. Jeff Csatari, Sr. Ed. Articles, 1,000 to 2,500 words, on fitness, diet, health, relationships, sports, and travel, for men ages 25 to 55. Pays from 50¢ a word, on acceptance. Query.

MUSCULAR DEVELOPMENT—505-H Saddle River Rd., Saddle Brook, NJ 07662. Alan Paul, Ed. Articles, 1,000 to 2,500 words, on competitive bodybuilding, power lifting, sports, and nutrition for serious weight training athletes: personality profiles, training features, and diet and nutrition pieces. Photos. Pays $100 to $400, on publication. Query.

NATURAL HEALTH: THE GUIDE TO WELL-BEING—17 Station St., Box 1200, Brookline, MA 02147. Bimonthly. Features, 1,500 to 3,000 words: practical information, new discoveries, and current trends about natural health and living. Topics include: natural goods and medicines, alternative health care, nutrition, wellness, personal fitness, and modern holistic teachings. Departments and columns, 250 to 1,000 words. Pays varying rates, on acceptance.

NEW BODY—1700 Broadway, New York, NY 10019. Nicole Dorsey, Ed. Lively, readable service-oriented articles, 800 to 1,200 words, on exercise, nutrition, lifestyle, diet, and health for women ages 18 to 35. Writers should have some background in or knowledge of the health field. Also considers 500- to 600-word essays for "How I Lost It" column by writers who have lost weight and kept it off. Pays $100 to $300, on publication. Query.

THE PHYSICIAN AND SPORTSMEDICINE—4530 W. 77th St., Minneapolis, MN 55435. Terry Monahan, Man. Ed. News and feature articles. Clinical articles must be co-authored by physicians. Sports medicine angle necessary. Pays $150 to $1,000, on acceptance. Query. Guidelines.

VEGETARIAN TIMES—P.O. Box 570, Oak Park, IL 60303. Toni Apgar, Pub. Articles, 1,200 to 2,500 words, on vegetarian cooking, nutrition, health and fitness, and profiles of prominent vegetarians. "News Items" and "In Print" (book reviews), to 500 words. "Herbalist" pieces, to 1,800 words, on medicinal uses of herbs. Queries required. Pays $75 to $1,000, on acceptance. Guidelines.

VIM & VIGOR—8805 N. 23rd Ave., Suite 11, Phoenix, AZ 85021. Fred Petrovsky, Ed. Positive articles, with accurate medical facts, on health and fitness, 1,200 to 2,000 words, by assignment only. Writers may submit qualifications for assignment. Pays $450, on acceptance. Guidelines.

WEIGHT WATCHERS MAGAZINE—360 Lexington Ave., New York, NY 10017. Deborah Kotz, Health Ed. Articles on health, nutrition, fitness, and weight-loss motivation and success. Pays from $500. Query with clips required. Guidelines.

WOMEN'S SPORTS & FITNESS—2025 Pearl St., Boulder, CO 80302. Mary Duffy, Ed. Outdoor sports how-tos, profiles, adventure travel, and controversial issues in women's sports, 500 to 2,000 words. Fitness, nutrition, and health pieces. Pays on publication.

YOGA JOURNAL—2054 University Ave., Berkeley, CA 94704. Rick Fields, Ed. Articles, 1,200 to 4,000 words, on holistic health, meditation, consciousness, spirituality, and yoga. Pays $50 to $800, on publication.

CONSUMER/PERSONAL FINANCE

BETTER HOMES AND GARDENS—750 Third Ave., New York, NY 10017. Margaret V. Daly, Exec. Features Ed. Articles, 750 to 1,000 words, on "any and all topics that would be of interest to family-oriented, middle-income people."

BLACK ENTERPRISE—130 Fifth Ave., New York, NY 10011. Earl G. Graves, Ed. Articles on money management, careers, political issues, entrepreneurship, high technology, and lifestyles for black professionals. Profiles. Pays on acceptance. Query.

CONSUMERS DIGEST—5705 N. Lincoln Ave., Chicago, IL 60659. John Manos, Ed. Articles, 500 to 3,000 words, on subjects of interest to consumers: products and services, automobiles, travel, health, fitness, consumer legal affairs, and personal money management. Photos. Pays from 35¢ to 50¢ a word, extra for photos, on acceptance. Query with resumé and clips.

FAMILY CIRCLE—110 Fifth Ave., New York, NY 10011. Susan Ungaro, Ed.-in-Chief. Susan Sherry, Sr. Ed. Enterprising, creative, and practical articles, 1,000 to 1,500 words, on investing, smart ways to save money, secrets of successful entrepreneurs, and consumer news on smart shopping. Pays $1 a word, on acceptance. Query with clips.

HOME MECHANIX—2 Park Ave., New York, NY 10016. Michael Chotiner, Ed. Home improvement, remodeling, maintenance, home finances. Pays $250 per page, on acceptance.

KEY HORIZONS—Gateway Plaza, 950 N. Meridian, Suite 1200, Indianapolis, IN 46204. Joan Todd, Man. Ed. Quarterly. General-interest articles and department pieces, 300 to 2,500 words, for readers 50 and older. Topics include personal finance, cooking, health, and domestic travel. Pays $25 to $500, $25 to $50 for photos, on publication.

KIPLINGER'S PERSONAL FINANCE MAGAZINE—1729 H St. N.W., Washington, DC 20006. Attn: Ed. Dept. Articles on personal finance (i.e., buying insurance, mutual funds). Pays varying rates, on acceptance. Query required.

KIWANIS—3636 Woodview Trace, Indianapolis, IN 46468. Chuck Jonak, Man. Ed. Articles, 2,500 to 3,000 words, on financial planning for younger families and retirement planning for older people. Pays $400 to $1,000, on acceptance. Query required.

MODERN MATURITY—3200 E. Carson St., Lakewood, CA 90712. Annette Winter, Sr. Ed. Articles, 300 to 2,000 words, on a wide range of financial topics of interest to people over 50. Pays to $1 a word, on acceptance. Query required.

THE MONEYPAPER—1010 Mamaroneck Ave., Mamaroneck, NY 10543. Vita Nelson, Ed. Financial news and money-saving ideas; particularly interested in information about companies with dividend reinvestment plans. Brief, well-researched articles on personal finance, money management: saving, earning, invest-

621

ing, taxes, insurance, and related subjects. Pays $75 for articles, on publication. Query with resumé and writing sample.

SELF—350 Madison Ave., New York, NY 10017. Beth Howard, Money/ Careers Ed. "We no longer accept unsolicited manuscripts or queries."

WOMAN'S DAY—1633 Broadway, New York, NY 10019. Rebecca Greer, Articles Ed. Articles, to 2,500 words, on financial matters of interest to a broad range of women. Pays top rates, on acceptance. Query. No unsolicited manuscripts.

WORTH—575 Lexington Ave., New York, NY 10022. John Koten, Ed. Dir. Clear, timely, well-argued articles on personal finance. Payment varies, on acceptance. Query with clips and SASE.

YOUR MONEY—5705 N. Lincoln Ave., Chicago, IL 60659. Dennis Fertig, Ed. Informative, jargon-free personal finance articles, to 2,500 words, for the general reader, on investment opportunities and personal finance. Pays 30¢ a word, on acceptance. Query with clips for assignment. (Do not send manuscripts on disks.)

BUSINESS AND TRADE PUBLICATIONS

ABA JOURNAL—American Bar Assn., 750 N. Lake Shore Dr., Chicago, IL 60611. Gary A. Hengstler, Ed./Pub. Articles, to 3,000 words, on law-related topics: current events in the law and ideas that will help lawyers practice better and more efficiently. Writing should be in an informal, journalistic style. Pays from $1,000, on acceptance; buys all rights.

ACCESSORIES MAGAZINE—50 Day St., Norwalk, CT 06854. Reenie Brown, Ed. Dir. Articles, with photos, for women's fashion accessories buyers and manufacturers. Profiles of retailers, designers, manufacturers; articles on merchandising and marketing. Pays $75 to $100 for short articles, from $100 to $300 for features, on publication. Query.

ACROSS THE BOARD—845 Third Ave., New York, NY 10022. John Ramos, Asst. Ed. Articles, 1,000 to 4,000 words, on a variety of topics of interest to business executives; straight business angle not required. Payment varies, on publication.

ALTERNATIVE ENERGY RETAILER—P.O. Box 2180, Waterbury, CT 06722. John Florian, Ed. Dir. Feature articles, 1,000 words, for retailers of hearth products, including appliances that burn wood, coal, pellets, and gas, and hearth accessories and services. Interviews with successful retailers, stressing the how-to. B&W photos. Pays $200, extra for photos, on publication. Query.

AMERICAN BANKER—One State Street Plaza, New York, NY 10004. Tom Ferris, Man. Ed. Articles, 1,000 to 3,000 words, on banking and financial services, technology in banking, consumer financial services, investment products. Pays varying rates, on publication. Query preferred.

AMERICAN COIN-OP—500 N. Dearborn St., Chicago, IL 60610–9988. Laurance Cohen, Ed. Articles, to 2,500 words, with photos, on successful coin-operated laundries: management, promotion, decor, maintenance, etc. Pays from 8¢ a word, $8 per B&W photo, 2 weeks prior to publication. Query. Guidelines.

AMERICAN DEMOGRAPHICS—P.O. Box 68, Ithaca, NY 14851–9989. Brad Edmondson, Ed.-in-Chief. Articles, 500 to 2,000 words, on the 4 key elements of a consumer market (its size, its needs and wants, its ability to pay, and how it can be reached), with specific examples of how companies market to consumers.

Readers include marketers, advertisers, and strategic planners. Pays $100 to $500, on acceptance. Query.

AMERICAN FARRIERS JOURNAL—P.O. Box 624, Brookfield, WI 53008–0624. Frank Lessiter, Ed. Articles, 800 to 2,000 words, on general farriery issues, hoof care, tool selection, equine lameness, and horse handling. Pays 50¢ per published line, $13 per published illustration or photo, on publication. Query.

AMERICAN MEDICAL NEWS—515 N. State St., Chicago, IL 60610. Ronni Scheier, Topic Ed. Public health articles, 1,000 to 3,000 words, on socioeconomic developments of interest to physicians across the country. No pieces on health, clinical treatments, or research. Query required. Pays $500 to $1,500, on acceptance. Guidelines.

THE AMERICAN SALESMAN—P.O. Box 1, Burlington, IA 52601–0001. Barbara Boeding, Ed. Articles, 900 to 1,200 words, on techniques for increasing sales. Author photos requested on article acceptance. Buys all rights. Pays 3¢ a word, on publication. Guidelines.

AMERICAN SALON—270 Madison Ave., New York, NY 10016. Kathy McFarland, Ed. Official publication of the National Cosmetology Assoc. No longer considering unsolicited manuscripts.

AMERICAN SCHOOL & UNIVERSITY—401 N. Broad St., Philadelphia, PA 19108. Joe Agron, Ed. Articles and case studies, 1,200 to 1,500 words, on design, construction, operation, and management of school and university facilities. Queries preferred.

AREA DEVELOPMENT MAGAZINE—400 Post Ave., Westbury, NY 11590. Tom Bergeron, Ed. Articles for top executives of industrial companies on sites and facility planning. Pays $60 per manuscript page. Query.

ART BUSINESS NEWS—19 Old King's Hwy. S., Darien, CT 06820. Sarah Seamark, Ed. Articles, 1,000 words, for art dealers and framers, on trends and events of national importance to the art industry, and relevant business subjects. Pays from $100, on publication. Query preferred.

ARTS & CRAFTS RETAILER—6151 Powers Ferry Rd. N.W., Atlanta, GA 30339–2941. Ben Johnson, Ed. Articles, from 800 words, for dealers, wholesalers, and manufacturers of arts and crafts materials; must be specific to trade. Pays to 15¢ a word, on publication. Query.

AUTOMATED BUILDER—P.O. Box 120, Carpinteria, CA 93014. Don Carlson, Ed. Articles, 500 to 750 words, on various types of home manufacturers and dealers. Query required. Pays $300, on acceptance, for articles with slides.

BARRON'S—200 Liberty St., New York, NY 10281. James P. Meagher, Ed. Investment-interest articles. Query.

BICYCLE RETAILER AND INDUSTRY NEWS—1547 South St. Francis Dr., Santa Fe, NM 87505. Marc Sani, Ed. Articles, 50 to 1,200 words, on employee management, employment strategies, and general business subjects for bicycle manufacturers, distributors, and retailers. Pays 17¢ a word (higher rates for more complex articles), plus expenses, on publication. Query.

BOATING INDUSTRY—Argus Business, 5 Penn Plaza, 13th Fl., New York, NY 10001–1810. Richard W. Porter, Ed. Articles, 1,000 to 2,500 words, on recreational marine products, management, merchandising and selling, for boat dealers. Photos. Pays varying rates, on publication. Query.

623

BOOKPAGE—ProMotion, Inc., 2501 21st Ave. S., Suite 5, Nashville, TN 37212. Ann Meador Shayne, Ed. Book reviews, 500 words, for a tabloid used by booksellers to promote new titles, authors, and bookstores. Query with writing samples and areas of interest; Editor will make assignments for reviews. Guidelines. Pays in copies.

BUILDER—Hanley-Wood, Inc., One Thomas Cir. N.W., Suite 600, Washington, DC 20005. Noreen S. Welle, Ed. Articles, to 1,500 words, on trends and news in home building: design, marketing, new products, etc. Pays negotiable rates, on acceptance. Query.

BUSINESS—(formerly *Business Today*) P.O. Box 10010, 1720 Washington Blvd., Ogden, UT 84409. Address Editorial Staff. Informative articles, 1,000 words, on business concerns of the businessperson/entrepreneur in U.S. and Canada. Color photos. Pays 15¢ a word, $35 for photos, $50 for cover photos, on acceptance. Query. Guidelines.

BUSINESS ATLANTA—6151 Powers Ferry Rd., Atlanta, GA 30339–2941. John Sequerth, Ed. Articles, 1,000 to 3,000 words, with Atlanta business angle, strong marketing slant that will be useful to top Atlanta executives and business people. Pays $300 to $1,000, on publication. Query with clips.

BUSINESS MARKETING—740 N. Rush St., Chicago, IL 60611. Steve Yahn, Ed. Articles on selling, advertising, and promoting products and services to business buyers. Pays competitive rates, on acceptance. Queries required.

BUSINESS TIMES—P.O. Box 580, 315 Peck St., New Haven, CT 06513. Joel MacClaren, Ed. Articles on Connecticut-based businesses and corporations. Query.

BUSINESS TODAY—See *Business.*

CAMPGROUND MANAGEMENT—P.O. Box 5000, Lake Forest, IL 60045–5000. Mike Byrnes, Ed. Detailed articles, 500 to 2,000 words, on managing recreational vehicle campgrounds. Photos. Pays $50 to $200, after publication.

CHEESE MARKET NEWS—See *Dairy Foods Magazine.*

CHIEF EXECUTIVE—733 Third Ave., 21st Fl., New York, NY 10017. J.P. Donlon, Ed. CEO bylines. Articles, 2,500 to 3,000 words, on management, financial, or business strategies. Departments, 1,200 to 1,500 words, on investments, amenities, and travel. Features on CEOs at leisure, Q&A's with CEOs, other topics. Pays varying rates, on acceptance. Query required.

CHINA, GLASS & TABLEWARE—368 Essex Ave., Bloomfield, NJ 07003. Amy Stavis, Ed. Case histories and interviews, 1,500 to 2,500 words, with photos, on merchandising of china and glassware. Pays $65 per page, on publication. Query.

CHRISTIAN RETAILING—600 Rinehart Rd., Lake Mary, FL 32746. Brian Peterson, Ed. Articles, 1,000 to 2,000 words, on new products, industry news, or topics related to running a profitable Christian retail store. Pays $50 to $300, on publication.

CLEANING MANAGEMENT MAGAZINE—13 Century Hill Dr., Latham, NY 12110–2197. Tom Williams, Ed. Articles, 500 to 1,200 words, on managing efficient cleaning and custodial/maintenance operations, profiles, photo-features, or general-interest articles directly related to the industry; also technical/mechanical how-tos. Photos encouraged. Query. Pays to $200 for features, on publication. Guidelines.

CLUB MANAGEMENT—(formerly *CMAA*) 8730 Big Bend Blvd., St. Louis, MO 63114. Tom Finan, Pub. The official magazine of the Club Managers Assoc. of America. Features, to 2,000 words, and news items, from 100 words, on management, budget, cuisine, personnel, government regulations, etc., for executives who run private clubs. "Writing should be tight and conversational, with liberal use of quotes." Color photos usually required with manuscript. Query preferred. Guidelines.

CMAA—See *Club Management.*

COMMERCIAL CARRIER JOURNAL—Chilton Way, Radnor, PA 19089. Jerry Standley, Ed. Thoroughly researched articles on private fleets and for-hire trucking operations. Pays from $50, on acceptance. Queries required.

COMPUTER GRAPHICS WORLD—10 Tara Blvd., Suite 500, Nashua, NH 03062–2801. Stephen Porter, Ed. Articles, 1,000 to 3,000 words, on computer graphics technology and its use in science, engineering, architecture, film and broadcast, and graphic arts areas. Photos. Pays $600 to $1,000 per article, on acceptance. Query.

CONCORD NORTH—See *Network Publications.*

CONCRETE INTERNATIONAL—Box 19150, 22400 W. Seven Mile Rd., Detroit, MI 48219–1849. William J. Semioli, Assoc. Pub./Ed. Articles, 6 to 12 double-spaced pages, on concrete construction, design, and technology with drawings and/or photos. Pays $100 per printed page, on publication. Query.

THE CONSTRUCTION SPECIFIER—Construction Specifications Institute, 601 Madison St., Alexandria, VA 22314. Kristina A. Kessler, Ed. Technical articles, 1,000 to 3,000 words, on the "nuts and bolts" of commercial construction, for architects, engineers, specifiers, contractors, and manufacturers. Pays 15¢ per word, on publication.

CONVENIENCE STORE NEWS—7 Penn Plaza, New York, NY 10001. Maureen Azzato, Ed. Features and news items, 500 to 750 words, for convenience store owners, and operators. Photos, with captions. Pays $3 per column inch or negotiated price for features; extra for photos, on publication. Query.

COOKING FOR PROFIT—P.O. Box 267, Fond du Lac, WI 54936–0267. Colleen Phalen, Pub./Ed.-in-Chief. Practical how-to articles, 1,500 words, on natural gas energy management related to food service, case studies, etc. Pays $75 to $250, on publication.

CRAIN'S CHICAGO BUSINESS—740 Rush St., Chicago, IL 60611. Jay McCormick, Man. Ed. Business articles about the Chicago metropolitan area exclusively. Pays $12 per column inch, on acceptance.

CREDIT AND COLLECTION MANAGER'S LETTER—Bureau of Business Practice, 24 Rope Ferry Rd., Waterford, CT 06386. Russell Case, Ed. Interviews, 500 to 1,250 words, for commercial and consumer credit managers, on innovations, successes, and problem solving. Query.

DAIRY FOODS MAGAZINE —Delta Communications, 455 N. Cityfront Pl., Chicago, IL 60611. Ellen Dexheimer, Ed. Articles, to 2,500 words, on innovative dairies, dairy processing operations, marketing successes, new products for milk handlers and makers of dairy products. Fillers, 25 to 150 words. Payment varies. Same requirements for *Cheese Market News.*

DEALERSCOPE MERCHANDISING—North American Publishing Co., 401 N. Broad St., Philadelphia, PA 19108. Richard Sherwin, Ed. Articles, 750 to

3,000 words, on sales, marketing, and finance for dealers and distributors of audio and video equipment, personal computers for the home and office, satellite TV systems for the home, major appliances. How-tos for retailers. Spot news on electronics retailing. Pays varying rates, on publication. Query with clips. Same requirements for *Dealerscope Merchandising First of the Month.*

DENTAL ECONOMICS—P.O. Box 3408, Tulsa, OK 74101. Dick Hale, Ed. Articles, 1,200 to 3,500 words, on business side of dental practice, patient and staff communication, personal investments, etc. Pays $100 to $400, on acceptance.

DRAPERIES & WINDOW COVERINGS—450 Skokie Blvd., Suite 507, Northbrook, IL 60062. Katie Sosnowchik, Ed. Articles, 1,000 to 2,000 words, for retailers, wholesalers, designers, and manufacturers of draperies and window, wall, and floor coverings. Profiles, with photos, of successful businesses in the industry; management and marketing related articles. Pays $150 to $250, after acceptance. Query.

DRUG TOPICS—5 Paragon Dr., Montvale, NJ 07645–1742. Valentine A. Cardinale, Ed. News items, 500 words, with photos, on drug retailers and associations. Merchandising features, 1,000 to 1,500 words. Pays $100 to $150 for news, $200 to $400 for features, on acceptance. Query for features.

EMERGENCY—6300 Yarrow Dr., Carlsbad, CA 92009–1597. Doug Fiske, Ed. Features, to 3,000 words, and department pieces, to 2,000 words, of interest to paramedics, emergency medical technicians, flight nurses, and other pre-hospital personnel: disaster management, advanced and basic life support, assessment, treatment. Pays $100 to $400 for features, $50 to $250 for departments. Photos are a plus. Guidelines and editorial calendar available.

EMPLOYEE SERVICES MANAGEMENT—NESRA, 2211 York Rd., Suite 207, Oak Brook, IL 60521–2371. Cynthia M. Helson, Ed. Articles, 1,200 to 2,500 words, for human resource, and employee service professionals.

THE ENGRAVERS JOURNAL—26 Summit St., P.O. Box 318, Brighton, MI 48116. Rosemary Farrell, Man. Ed. Articles, of varying lengths, on topics related to the engraving industry or small business. Pays $60 to $175, on acceptance. Query.

ENTREPRENEUR—P.O. Box 19787, Irvine, CA 92713–9438. Rieva Lesonsky, Ed.-in-Chief. Articles for established and aspiring independent business owners, on all aspects of running a business. Pay varies, on acceptance. Query required.

EXECUTIVE FEMALE—30 Irving Pl., New York, NY 10003. Basia Hellwig, Ed.-in-Chief. Articles, 750 to 2,500 words, on managing people, time, money, and careers, for women in business. Pays varying rates, on acceptance. Query.

FARM JOURNAL—230 W. Washington Sq., Philadelphia, PA 19106. Earl Ainsworth, Ed. Practical business articles, 500 to 1,500 words, with photos, on growing crops and raising livestock. Pays 20¢ to 50¢ a word, on acceptance. Query required.

FINANCIAL WORLD—1328 Broadway, New York, NY 10001. Douglas A. McIntyre, Pub. Features and profiles of large companies and financial institutions and the people who run them. Pays varying rates, on publication. Query required.

FISHING TACKLE RETAILER MAGAZINE—P.O. Box 17151, Montgomery, AL 36141–0151. Dave Ellison, Ed. Articles, 300 to 1,250 words, for merchants who carry angling equipment. Business focus is required, and writers should provide practical information for improving management and merchandising. Pays varying rates, on acceptance.

FITNESS MANAGEMENT—P.O. Box 1198, Solana Beach, CA 92075. Edward H. Pitts, Ed. Authoritative features, 750 to 2,500 words, and news shorts, 100 to 750 words, for owners, managers, and program directors of fitness centers. Content must be in keeping with current medical practice; no fads. Pays 8¢ a word, on publication. Query.

FLORIST—29200 Northwestern Hwy., P.O. Box 2227, Southfield, MI 48037-2227. Barbara Koch, Man. Ed. Articles, to 2,000 words, with photos, on retail florist shop management.

FLOWERS &—Teleflora Plaza, Suite 118, 12233 W. Olympic Blvd., Los Angeles, CA 90064. Marie Moneysmith, Ed.-in-Chief. Articles, 1,000 to 3,500 words, with how-to information for retail florists. Pays from $500, on acceptance. Query with clips.

FOOD MANAGEMENT—122 E. 42nd St., Suite 900, New York, NY 10168. Donna Boss, Ed. Articles on food service in hospitals, nursing homes, schools, colleges, prisons, businesses, and industrial sites. Trends, legislative issues, and how-to pieces, with management tie-in. Query.

THE FUTURE, NOW: INNOVATIVE VIDEO—Blue Feather Co., N8494 Poplar Grove Rd., P.O. Box 669, New Glarus, WI 53574–0669. Jennifer M. Jarik, Ed. Bimonthly. Articles, to 2 pages, on new ideas in the video industry. Pays from $75 to $100, on publication.

GENERAL AVIATION NEWS & FLYER—P.O. Box 39099, Tacoma, WA 98439–0099. Dave Sclair, Pub. Articles, 500 to 2,500 words, of interest to "general aviation" pilots. Pays to $3 per column inch (approximately 40 words); $10 for B&W photos; to $50 for color photos; within the first month of publication.

GENETIC ENGINEERING NEWS– 1651 Third Ave., New York, NY 10128. John Sterling, Man. Ed. Features and news articles on all aspects of biotechnology. Pays varying rates, on acceptance. Query.

GOLF COURSE NEWS—38 Lafayette St., Yarmouth, ME 04096. Hal Phillips, Ed. Features, 500 to 1,000 words, on all aspects of golf course maintenance, design, building, and management. Pays $200, on acceptance.

GOVERNMENT EXECUTIVE—1501 M St. N.W., Washington, DC 20005. Timothy Clark, Ed. Articles, 1,500 to 3,000 words, for civilian and military government workers at the management level.

GREENHOUSE MANAGEMENT & PRODUCTION—P.O. Box 1868, Fort Worth, TX 76101–1868. David Kuack, Ed. How-to articles, innovative production and/or marketing techniques, 500 to 1,800 words, accompanied by color slides, of interest to professional greenhouse growers. Pays $50 to $300, on acceptance. Query required.

HAMPSHIRE EAST—See *Network Publications.*

HARDWARE TRADE—10510 France Ave. S., #225, Bloomington, MN 55431. Patt Patterson, Ed. Dir. Articles, 800 to 1,000 words, on unusual hardware and home center stores and promotions in the Northwest and Midwest. Photos. Query.

627

HEALTH FOODS BUSINESS—2 University Plaza, Suite 111, Hackensack, NJ 07601. Gina Geslewitz, Ed. Articles, 1,200 words, with photos, profiling health food stores. Pays on publication. Query. Guidelines.

HEALTH PROGRESS—4455 Woodson Rd., St. Louis, MO 63134–3797. Judy Cassidy, Ed. Journal of the Catholic Health Association. Features, 2,000 to 4,000 words, on hospital and nursing home management and administration, medical-moral questions, health care, public policy, technological developments in health care and their effects, nursing, financial and human resource management for health-care administrators, and innovative programs in hospitals and long-term care facilities. Payment negotiable. Query.

HEATING/PIPING/AIR CONDITIONING—2 Prudential Plaza, 180 N. Stetson Ave., Suite 2555, Chicago, IL 60601. Robert T. Korte, Ed. Articles, to 5,000 words, on heating, piping, and air conditioning systems in industrial plants and large buildings; engineering information. Pays $60 per printed page, on publication. Query.

HOME OFFICE COMPUTING—Scholastic, Inc., 411 Lafayette St., New York, NY 10003. Cathy G. Brower, Man. Ed. Articles, 3,000 words, that provide readers with practical information on how to run their businesses and use technology more effectively. Profiles of home-based entrepreneurs. Education and entertainment pieces, 800 to 1,500 words, for "Family Computing" section. Writers must be familiar with microcomputers and software, home office products, and issues affecting small and home businesses. Payment varies, on acceptance.

HOSPITALS & HEALTH NETWORKS—(formerly *Hospitals*) 737 N. Michigan Ave., Chicago, IL 60611. Mary Grayson, Ed. Articles, 800 to 900 words, for hospital administrators. Query.

HUMAN RESOURCE EXECUTIVE—Axon Group, 747 Dresher Rd., Horsham, PA 19044–0980. David Shadovitz, Ed. Profiles and case stories, 1,800 to 2,200 words, of interest to people in the personnel profession. Pays varying rates, on acceptance. Queries required.

INC.—38 Commercial Wharf, Boston, MA 02110. George Gendron, Ed. No free-lance material.

INCOME OPPORTUNITIES—1500 Broadway, New York, NY 10036–4015. Stephen Wagner, Ed. Helpful articles, 1,000 to 2,500 words, on how to make money full- or part-time; how to start a successful small business, improve sales, work at home, mail order, franchising, etc. Pays varying rates, on acceptance.

INCOME PLUS—73 Spring St., Suite 303, New York, NY 10012. Donna Ruffini, Ed. How-to articles on starting a small business, franchise, or mail-order operation. Payment varies, on publication. Query.

INDEPENDENT BUSINESS—125 Auburn Ct., Suite 100, Thousand Oaks, CA 91362. Daniel Kehrer, Ed. Articles, 500 to 2,000 words, of practical interest and value to small business owners. Pays $200 to $1,500, on acceptance. Query.

INSTANT & SMALL COMMERCIAL PRINTER—P.O. Box 1387, Northbrook, IL 60065. Jeanette Clinkunbroomer, Ed. Articles, 3 to 6 typed pages, for operators and employees of printing businesses specializing in retail printing and/or small commercial printing: case histories, how-tos, technical pieces, small-business management. Pays $150 to $250, extra for photos, on publication. Query.

INTERNATIONAL BUSINESS—500 Mamaroneck Ave., Suite 314, Harrison, NY 10528. David E. Moore, Chairman/Ed. Dir. Articles, 1,000 to 1,500 words, on global marketing strategies. Short pieces, 500 words, with tips on operating abroad. Profiles, 750 to 3,000 words, on individuals or companies. Pays 80¢ to $1 a word, on acceptance and on publication. Query with clips.

JEMS, JOURNAL OF EMERGENCY MEDICAL SERVICES—P.O. Box 2789, Carlsbad, CA 92018. Tara Regan, Man. Ed. Articles, 1,500 to 3,000 words, of interest to emergency medical providers (from EMTs to paramedics to nurses and physicians) who work in the EMS industry worldwide.

LAUNDRY NEWS—Mill Hollow Corp., 19 W. 21st St., New York, NY 10010. Richard Merli, Ed. Articles, 500 to 1,500 words, on the institutional laundering trade as practiced in hotels, hospitals, correctional facilities, and nursing homes. Infection control, government regulation, new technology, major projects, industrial accidents, litigation, and mergers and acquisitions. Query. Pays $100 to $300, on publication.

LLAMAS—P.O. Box 100, Herald, CA 95638. Cheryl Dal Porto, Ed. "The International Camelid Journal," published 7 times yearly. Articles, 300 to 3,000 words, of interest to llama and alpaca owners. Pays $25 to $300, extra for photos, on acceptance. Query.

LOTUS—See *PC World Lotus Edition*.

LP-GAS MAGAZINE—131 W. First St., Duluth, MN 55802. Zane Chastain, Ed. Articles, 1,500 to 2,500 words, with photos, on LP-gas dealer operations: marketing, management, etc. Photos. Pays to 15¢ a word, extra for photos, on acceptance. Query.

MACHINE DESIGN—Penton Publications, 1100 Superior Ave., Cleveland, OH 44114. Ronald Khol, Ed. Articles, to 10 typed pages, on design-related topics for engineers. Pays varying rates, on publication. Submit outline or brief description.

MAINTENANCE TECHNOLOGY—1300 S. Grove Ave., Barrington, IL 60010. Robert C. Baldwin, Ed. Technical articles with how-to information on increasing the reliability and maintainability of electrical and electronic systems, mechanical systems and equipment, and plant facilities. Readers are managers, supervisors, and engineers in all industries and facilities. Payment varies, on acceptance. Query.

MANAGE—2210 Arbor Blvd., Dayton, OH 45439. Doug Shaw, Ed. Articles, 800 to 1,000 words, on management and supervision for first-line and middle managers. "Please indicate word count on manuscript and enclose SASE." Pays 5¢ a word.

MANAGING OFFICE TECHNOLOGY—(formerly *Modern Office Technology*) 1100 Superior Ave., Cleveland, OH 44114. Lura Romei, Ed. Articles, 3 to 4 double-spaced, typed pages, on new concepts, management techniques, technologies, and applications for management executives. Payment varies, on acceptance. Query preferred.

MANCHESTER—See *Network Publications*.

MANUFACTURING SYSTEMS—191 S. Gary, Carol Stream, IL 60188. Barbara Dutton, Man. Ed. Articles, 500 to 2,000 words, on computer and information systems for industry executives seeking to increase productivity in manufacturing firms. Pays 10¢ to 20¢ a word, on acceptance. Query required.

MEMPHIS BUSINESS JOURNAL—88 Union, Suite 102, Memphis, TN 38103. Barney DuBois, Ed. Articles, to 2,000 words, on business, industry trade, agri-business and finance in the mid-South trade area. Pays $80 to $200, on acceptance.

MIX MAGAZINE—6400 Hollis St., Suite 12, Emeryville, CA 94608. Blair Jackson, Ed. Articles, varying lengths, for professionals, on audio, video, and music entertainment technology. Pay varies, on publication. Query.

MODERN HEALTHCARE—740 N. Rush St., Chicago, IL 60611. Clark Bell, Ed. Features on management, finance, building design and construction, and new technology for hospitals, health maintenance organizations, nursing homes, and other health care institutions. Query. Pays $200 to $400, on publication. Very limited free-lance market.

MODERN OFFICE TECHNOLOGY—See *Managing Office Technology*.

MODERN TIRE DEALER—P.O. Box 8391, 341 White Pond Dr., Akron, OH 44320. Lloyd Stoyor, Ed. Tire retailing and automotive service articles, 1,000 to 1,500 words, with photos, on independent tire dealers and retreaders. Query; articles by assignment only. Pays $300 to $350, on publication.

NASHUA—See *Network Publications*.

NATIONAL FISHERMAN—120 Tillson Ave., Rockland, ME 04841. James W. Fullilove, Ed. Articles, 200 to 2,000 words, aimed at commercial fishermen and boat builders. Pays $4 to $6 per inch, extra for photos, on publication. Query preferred.

NATION'S BUSINESS—1615 H St. N.W., Washington, DC 20062. Articles on small-business topics, including management advice and success stories. Pays negotiable rates, on acceptance. Guidelines available.

NEEDLEWORK RETAILER—P.O. Box 2438, Ames, IA 50010. Heidi A. Bomgarden, Ed. Bimonthly. Articles, 500 to 1,000 words, on how to run a small needlework business. Pays varying rates, on acceptance.

NEPHROLOGY NEWS & ISSUES/NORTH AMERICA—15150 N. Hayden Rd., Suite 101, Scottsdale, AZ 85260. Mark E. Neumann, Ed. News articles, human-interest features, and opinion essays on dialysis, kidney transplants, and kidney disease. Pays $50 to $100. Also publishes *Nephrology News & Issues/Europe* for the European renal care community.

NETWORK PUBLICATIONS—100 Main St., Nashua, NH 03060. Rick Broussard, Ed. Nancy Williamson, Man. Ed. Lifestyle and business articles with a New Hampshire angle, with sources from all regions of the state, for the company's 4 regional monthlies: *Nashua, Manchester, Concord North,* and *Hampshire East.* Payment varies, on acceptance.

NEW CAREER WAYS NEWSLETTER—67 Melrose Ave., Haverhill, MA 01830. William J. Bond, Ed. How-to articles, 1,500 to 2,000 words, on new ways to succeed at work in the 1990s. Pays varying rates, on publication. Query with outline and SASE. Same address and requirements for *Workskills Newsletter*.

THE NORTHERN LOGGER AND TIMBER PROCESSOR--Northeastern Logger's Assn., Inc., P.O. Box 69, Old Forge, NY 13420. Eric A. Johnson, Ed. Features, 1,000 to 2,000 words, of interest to the forest product industry. Photos. Pays varying rates, on monthly publication. Query preferred.

NSGA RETAIL FOCUS—National Sporting Goods Assoc., 1699 Wall St., Suite 700, Mt. Prospect, IL 60056. Bob Nieman, Ed. Members magazine. Articles,

1,000 to 1,500 words, on sporting goods industry news and trends, the latest in new product information, and management and store operations. Payment varies, on publication. Query.

NURSINGWORLD JOURNAL—470 Boston Post Rd., Weston, MA 02193. R. Patrick Gates, Ed. Articles, 800 to 1,500 words, for nurses, nurse educators, and students of nursing, etc., on all aspects of nursing. B&W photos. Pays $35, on publication.

OPPORTUNITY MAGAZINE—73 Spring St., Suite 303, New York, NY 10012. Donna Ruffini, Ed. Articles, 900 to 1,500 words, on sales psychology, sales techniques, successful small business careers, self-improvement. Pays $25 to $50, on publication.

OPTOMETRIC ECONOMICS—American Optometric Assn., 243 N. Lindbergh Blvd., St. Louis, MO 63141–7881. Dr. Jack Runninger, Ed. Articles, 1,000 to 2,000 words, on private practice management for optometrists; direct, conversational style with how-to advice on how optometrists can build, improve, better manage, and enjoy their practices. Short humor and photos. Query. Payment varies, on acceptance.

PARTY & PAPER RETAILER—70 New Canaan Ave., Norwalk, CT 06850. Trisha McMahon Drain, Ed. Articles, 800 to 1,000 words, that offer employee, management, and retail marketing advice to the party or stationery store owner: display ideas, success stories, financial advice, legal advice. "Articles grounded in facts and anecdotes are appreciated." Pay varies, on publication. Query with published clips.

PC WORLD LOTUS EDITION—(formerly *Lotus*) 77 Franklin St., Boston, MA 02110. Eric Bender, Exec. Ed. Articles, 1,500 to 2,000 words, on business and professional applications of Lotus software. Query with outline required. Pay varies, on final approval.

PET BUSINESS—5400 N.W. 84th Ave., Miami, FL 33166. Elizabeth McKey, Ed. Brief, documented articles on animals and products found in pet stores; research findings; legislative/regulatory actions; business and marketing tips and trends. Pays $4 per column inch, on publication; pays $20 for photos.

PET PRODUCT NEWS & PSM—(formerly *Pets/Supplies/Marketing*) P.O. Box 6050, Mission Viejo, CA 92690. Scott McElhaney, Ed. Articles, 1,000 to 1,200 words, with photos, on pet shops, and pet and product merchandising. Pays $175 to $350, extra for photos. No fiction or news clippings. Query.

PETS/SUPPLIES/MARKETING—See *Pet Product News & PSM*.

PHOTO MARKETING—3000 Picture Pl., Jackson, MI 49201. Margaret Hooks, Man. Ed. Business articles, 1,000 to 3,500 words, for owners and managers of camera/video stores or photo processing labs. Pays $150 to $500, extra for photos, on publication.

PHYSICIAN'S MANAGEMENT—7500 Old Oak Blvd., Cleveland, OH 44130. Bob Feigenbaum, Ed. Articles, 1,500 words, on finance, investments, malpractice, and office management for primary care physicians. No clinical pieces. Pays $125 per printed page, on acceptance. Query with SASE.

PIZZA TODAY—P.O. Box 1347, New Albany, IN 47151. James E. Reed, Ed. Articles, to 2,500 words, on pizza business management for pizza entrepreneurs. Pizza business profiles. Pays $75 to $150 per published page, on publication. Query.

P.O.B.—5820 Lilley Rd., Suite 5, Canton, MI 48187–3623. Victoria L. Dickinson, Ed. Technical and business articles, 1,000 to 4,000 words, for professionals and technicians in the surveying and mapping fields. Technical tips on field and office procedures and equipment maintenance. Pays $150 to $400, on acceptance.

POLICE MAGAZINE—6300 Yarrow Dr., Carlsbad, CA 92009–1597. Dan Burger, Ed. Articles and profiles, 1,000 to 3,000 words, on specialized groups, equipment, issues, and trends of interest to people in the law enforcement profession. Pays $100 to $300, on acceptance.

POOL & SPA NEWS—3923 W. Sixth St., Los Angeles, CA 90020. News articles for the swimming pool, spa, and hot tub industry. Pays from 10¢ to 15¢ a word, extra for photos, on publication. Query.

PROGRESSIVE GROCER—4 Stamford Forum, Stamford, CT 06901. Priscilla Donegan, Man. Ed. Articles related to retail food operations; ideas for successful merchandising, promotions, and displays. Short pieces preferred. Payment varies, on acceptance.

QUICK PRINTING—1680 S. W. Bayshore Blvd., Port St. Lucie, FL 34984. Tara Marini, Man. Ed. Articles, 1,500 to 3,000 words, of interest to owners and operators of quick print shops, copy shops, and small commercial printers, on how to make their businesses more profitable; include figures. Pays from $75, on acceptance.

REAL ESTATE TODAY—National Assoc. of Realtors, 430 N. Michigan Ave., Chicago, IL 60611–4087. Educational, how-to articles, to 1,500 words, on all aspects of residential real estate, real estate finance, commercial-investment real estate, and real estate brokerage-management. Query required.

REGARDIE'S—1010 Wisconsin Ave. N.W., Suite 600, Washington, DC 20007. Richard Blow, Ed. Profiles and investigations of the "high and mighty" in the DC area. "We require aggressive reporting and imaginative, entertaining writing." Pays 75¢ a word, on publication. Queries required.

REMODELING—Hanley-Wood, Inc., One Thomas Cir. N.W., Suite 600, Washington, DC 20005. Wendy A. Jordan, Ed. Articles, 250 to 1,700 words, on remodeling and industry news for residential and light commercial remodelers. Pays on acceptance. Query.

RESEARCH MAGAZINE—2201 Third St., P.O. Box 77905, San Francisco, CA 94107. Anne Evers, Ed. Articles of interest to stockbrokers, 1,000 to 3,000 words, on financial products, selling, how-tos, and financial trends. Pays from $300 to $900, on publication. Query.

RESTAURANTS USA—1200 17th St. N.W., Washington, DC 20036–3097. Paul Moomaw, Ed. Publication of the National Restaurant Assn. Articles, 1,000 to 1,500 words, on the food service and restaurant business. Restaurant experience preferred. Pays $350 to $800, on acceptance. Query.

ROOFER MAGAZINE—6719 Winkler Rd., Suite 214, Ft. Myers, FL 33919. Jack Klein, Ed. Technical and non-technical articles, human-interest pieces, 1,000 to 1,500 words, on roofing-related topics: new roofing concepts, energy savings, pertinent issues, roofing contractor profiles, industry concern. Humorous items welcome. No general business or computer articles. Include photos. Pays negotiable rates, on publication. Guidelines.

THE ROTARIAN—1560 Sherman Ave., Evanston, IL 60201–3698. Willmon L. White, Ed. Articles, 1,200 to 2,000 words, on international social and economic issues, business and management, environment, science and technology. "No political or religious subjects." Pays good rates, on acceptance. Query.

RV BUSINESS—3601 Calle Tecate, Camarillo, CA 93012. Katherine Sharma, Ed. Articles, to 1,500 words, on RV industry news and product-related features. Articles on legislative matters affecting the industry. General business features rarely used. Pays varying rates.

THE SAFETY COMPLIANCE LETTER—24 Rope Ferry Rd., Waterford, CT 06386. Shelley Wolf, Ed. Interview-based articles, 800 to 1,250 words, for corporate safety managers, on successful safety and health programs in the workplace. Pays to 15¢ a word, on acceptance. Query.

SAFETY MANAGEMENT—24 Rope Ferry Rd., Waterford, CT 06386. Heather Vaughn, Ed. Interview-based articles, 1,100 to 1,500 words, for safety professionals, on improving workplace safety and health. Pays to 15¢ a word, on acceptance. Query.

SALES & MARKETING MANAGEMENT—Bill Communications, Inc., 355 Park Ave. S., New York, NY 10010. Charles Butler, Ed. Features and short articles of interest to sales and marketing executives. Looking for practical "news you can use." Pays varying rates, on acceptance. Queries preferred.

SIGN BUSINESS—P.O. Box 1416, Broomfield, CO 80038. Glen Richardson, Ed. Articles targeted to the sign business. Pays $50 to $200, on publication.

SMALL MAGAZINE REVIEW—Dustbooks, P.O. Box 100, Paradise, CA 95967. Len Fulton, Ed./Pub. Reviews, to 200 words, of small and literary magazines; tracks the publishing of small-circulation periodicals. Pays 10¢ a word, on acceptance.

SMALL PRESS REVIEW— Dustbooks, P.O. Box 100, Paradise, CA 95967. Len Fulton, Ed./Pub. News pieces and reviews, to 200 words, of books by small presses. Pays in copies.

SOFTWARE MAGAZINE —One Research Dr., Suite 400B, Westborough, MA 01581. Mike Bucken, Ed. Technical features, to 3,500 words, for computer-literate MIS audience, on how various software products are used. Pays about $750 to $1,000, on publication. Query required. Calendar of scheduled editorial features available.

SOUTHERN LUMBERMAN—P.O. Box 681629, Franklin, TN 37068–1629. Nanci P. Gregg, Man. Ed. Articles on sawmill operations, interviews with industry leaders, how-to technical pieces with an emphasis on increasing sawmill production and efficiency and new installation. "Always looking for 'sweetheart' mill stories; we publish one per month." Pays $100 to $250 for articles with B&W photos. Queries preferred.

STONE WORLD—1 Kalisa Way, Suite 205, Paramus, NJ 07652. John Sailer, Ed. Articles, 750 to 1,500 words, on new trends in installing and designing with stone. For architects, interior designers, and design professionals. Pays $115 per printed page, on publication. Query.

TEA & COFFEE TRADE JOURNAL—130 W. 42nd St., New York, NY 10036. Jane P. McCabe, Ed. Articles, 3 to 5 pages, on trade issues of importance to the tea and coffee industry. Query. Pays $5 per published inch, on publication.

TEXTILE WORLD—4170 Ashford-Dunwoody Rd. N.E., Suite 420, Atlanta, GA 30319. Mac Isaacs, Ed. Articles, 500 to 2,000 words, with photos, on manufacturing and finishing textiles. Pays varying rates, on acceptance.

TODAY'S OR NURSE—Slack, Inc., 6900 Grove Rd., Thorofare, NJ 08086. Mary Jo Krey, Man. Ed. Clinical or general articles, from 2,000 words, of direct interest to operating room nurses.

TRAILER/BODY BUILDERS—P.O. Box 66010, Houston, TX 77266. Paul Schenck, Ed. Articles on engineering, sales, and management ideas for truck body and truck trailer manufacturers. Pays from $100 per printed page, on acceptance.

TRAINING MAGAZINE—50 S. Ninth St., Minneapolis, MN 55402. Jack Gordon, Ed. Articles, 1,000 to 2,500 words, for managers of training and development activities in corporations, government, etc. Pays to 25¢ a word, on acceptance. Query.

TRAVEL COUNSELOR—CMP Publications, 600 Community Dr., Manhassett, NY 11030. Linda Ball, Ed. Business and management how-to articles, 1,000 to 1,500 words, of successful travel industry workers. Pay varies, on acceptance.

TREASURY & RISK MANAGEMENT—(formerly *Treasury*) 253 Summer St., Boston, MA 02210. Ms. Maile Hulihan, Ed. Ann Gramm, Art Dir. Bimonthly. Articles, 200 to 3,000 words, on treasury management for corporate treasurers, CFOs, and vice presidents of finance. Pays 50¢ to $1 a word, on acceptance. Query.

TRUCKERS/USA—P.O. Box 323, Windber, PA 15963. David Adams, Ed. Articles, 500 to 1,000 words, on the trucking business and marketing. Trucking-related poetry and fiction. Payment varies, on publication.

VENDING TIMES—1375 Broadway, New York, NY 10018. Arthur E. Yohalem, Ed. Features and news articles, with photos, on vending machines. Pays varying rates, on acceptance. Query.

WINES & VINES—1800 Lincoln Ave., San Rafael, CA 94901. Philip E. Hiaring, Ed. Articles, 2,000 words, on grape and wine industry, emphasizing marketing, management, and production. Pays 5¢ a word, on acceptance.

WOMEN IN BUSINESS—9100 Ward Parkway, Box 8728, Kansas City, MO 64114–0728. Wendy Myers, Ed. Publication of the American Business Women's Assn. Features, 1,000 to 2,000 words, for career women from 25 to 55 years old; no profiles. Pays 15¢ a published word, on acceptance. Query.

WOODSHOP NEWS—Pratt St., Essex, CT 06426–1185. Ian C. Bowen, Ed. Features, one to 3 typed pages, for and about people who work with wood: business stories, profiles, news. Pays from $3 per column inch, on publication. Queries preferred.

WORKBOAT—P.O. Box 1348, Mandeville, LA 70470. Don Nelson, Ed. Features, to 2,000 words, and shorts, 500 to 1,000 words, providing current, lively information for workboat owners, operators, crew, suppliers, and regulators. Topics include construction and conversion; diesel engines and electronics; politics and industry; unusual vessels; new products; and profiles. Payment varies, on acceptance and on publication. Queries preferred.

WORKSKILLS NEWSLETTER—See *New Career Ways Newsletter.*

WORLD OIL—Gulf Publishing Co., P.O. Box 2608, Houston, TX 77252–2608. Robert E. Snyder, Ed. Engineering and operations articles, 3,000 to 4,000 words, on petroleum industry exploration, drilling, or production. Photos. Pays from $50 per printed page, on acceptance. Query.

WORLD WASTES—6151 Powers Ferry Rd. N.W., Atlanta, GA 30339. Bill Wolpin, Ed./Pub. Case studies, market analysis, and how-to articles, 1,000 to 2,000 words, with photos of refuse haulers, recyclers, landfill operators, resource recovery operations, and transfer stations, with solutions to problems in the field. Pays from $125 per printed page, on publication. Query preferred.

IN-HOUSE/ASSOCIATION MAGAZINES

Publications circulated to company employees (sometimes called house magazines or house organs) and to members of associations and organizations are excellent, well-paying markets for writers at all levels of experience. Large corporations publish these magazines to promote good will, familiarize readers with the company's services and products, and interest customers in these products. And, many organizations publish house magazines designed to keep their members abreast of the issues and events concerning a particular cause or industry. Always read an in-house magazine before submitting an article; write to the editor for a sample copy (offering to pay for it) and the editorial guidelines. Stamped, self-addressed envelopes should be enclosed with any query or manuscript. The following list includes a sampling of publications in this large market.

AMERICAN DANE—The Danish Brotherhood of America, National Headquarters, 3717 Harney St., Omaha, NE 68131–3844. Jennifer Denning-Kock, Ed. Articles and fiction, to 1,500 words, with a Danish "flavor." Queries are preferred. Submit from May through August. Payment varies, to $50, on publication.

AMERICAN HOW-TO—12301 Whitewater Dr., Suite 260, Minnetonka, MN 55343. Tom Sweeney. Bimonthly magazine for members of The Handyman Club of America. Articles, 1,000 to 1,500 words, for homeowners interested in do-it-yourself projects. Carpentry, plumbing, electrical work, landscaping, masonry, tools, woodworking, and new products. Payment is 50¢ a word, on acceptance. Queries preferred. Send SASE for editorial calendar with upcoming themes.

AMOCO TRAVELER—K.L. Publications, Inc., 2001 Killebrew Dr., Suite 105, Bloomington, MN 55425. Mary Lou Brooks, Ed. Quarterly. Membership magazine for Amoco Traveler Club. Articles, 1,500 to 1,800 words, on North American travel and destinations. "Writing should be tight, reportorial, and colorful." Pays $350 to $450 for first rights; $125 to $150 for reprints, on publication.

CALIFORNIA HIGHWAY PATROLMAN—2030 V St., Sacramento, CA 95818–1730. Carol Perri, Ed. Articles on transportation safety, California history, travel, consumerism, past and present vehicles, humor, general items, etc. Photos a plus. Pays 2 ½ ¢ a word, $5 for B&W photos, on publication. Guidelines and/or sample copy with 9x11 SASE.

COLUMBIA—1 Columbus Plaza, New Haven, CT 06510–0901. Richard McMunn, Ed. Journal of the Knights of Columbus. Articles, 1,500 words, for Catholic families. Must be accompanied by color photos or transparencies. No fiction. Pays to $500 for articles and photos, on acceptance.

THE COMPASS—365 Washington Ave., Brooklyn, NY 11238. J.A. Randall, Ed. Articles, to 2,500 words, on the sea and deep sea trade; also articles on aviation. Pays to $600, on acceptance. Query with SASE.

THE ELKS MAGAZINE—425 W. Diversey Pkwy., Chicago, IL 60614. Judith L. Keogh, Man. Ed. Articles, to 1,200 to 3,000 words, on business, sports, and topics of current interest; for non-urban audience with above-average income. Informative or humorous pieces, to 2,500 words. Pays $150 to $400 for articles, on acceptance. Query.

FIREHOUSE—PTN Publishing Company, 445 Broad Hollow Rd., Melville, NY 11747. Barbara Dunleavy, Ed.-in-Chief. Articles, 500 to 2,000 words: on-the-scene accounts of fires, trends in firefighting equipment, controversial fire-service issues, and lifestyles of firefighters. Pays $100 per typeset page; extra for photos. Query.

FOCUS—Turnkey Publishing, P.O. Box 200549, Austin, TX 78720. Doug Johnson, Ed. Magazine of the North American Data General Users Group. Articles, 700 to 4,000 words, on Data General computers. Photos a plus. Pays to $50, on publication. Query required.

THE FURROW—Deere & Co., John Deere Rd., Moline, IL 61265. George R. Sollenberger, Exec. Ed. Specialized, illustrated articles on farming. Pays to $1,000, on acceptance.

IDEA PERSONAL TRAINER—6190 Cornerstone Ct. E., Suite 204, San Diego, CA 92121–3773. Therese Hannon, Asst. Ed. Association publication for personal fitness trainers. Articles on exercise science; program design; profiles of successful trainers; business, legal, and marketing topics; tips for networking with other trainers and with allied medical professionals; client counseling; and training tips. "What's New" column includes industry news, products, and research. Payment varies, on acceptance. Query.

KIWANIS—3636 Woodview Trace, Indianapolis, IN 46268. Chuck Jonak, Man. Ed. Articles, 2,500 words (sidebars, 250 to 350 words), on lifestyle, relationships, world view, education, trends, small business, religion, health, etc. No travel pieces, interviews, profiles. Pays $400 to $1,000, on acceptance. Query.

THE LION—300 22nd St., Oak Brook, IL 60521. Robert Kleinfelder, Sr. Ed. Official publication of Lions Clubs International. Articles, 800 to 2,000 words, and photo essays, on club activities. Pays from $100 to $700, including photos, on acceptance. Query.

NATURE CONSERVANCY—1815 N. Lynn St., Arlington, VA 22209. Mark Cheater, Ed. Membership publication. Articles on wildlife, people, trends in conservation or ecology. Pieces must have connection to The Nature Conservancy's activities or mission. No poetry or fiction. Query with clips required; article lengths, deadlines, and payment determined at time of assignment. Pays on acceptance. Guidelines.

NETWORK NEWS—9710 S. 700 E., Bldg. A, Suite 206, Sandy, UT 84070. Kristin King, Ed. Official magazine of the Network Professional Assn. Humorous editorial articles, 600 to 800 words, on computing, especially networking. Submit with SASE for reply only; manuscripts will not be returned. Pays 30¢ a word, after acceptance.

PUBLIC CITIZEN MAGAZINE—2000 P St. N.W., Suite 610, Washington, DC 20036. Peter Nye, Ed. Investigative reports and articles of timely political interest, for members of Public Citizen: consumer rights, health and safety, environmental protection, safe energy, tax reform, trade, and government and corporate accountability. Photos, illustrations. Payment negotiable.

RESTAURANTS USA—1200 17th St. N.W., Washington, DC 20036–3097. Paul Moomaw, Ed. Publication of the National Restaurant Assn. Articles, 1,000 to 1,500 words, on the food service and restaurant business. Restaurant experience preferred. Pays $350 to $800, on acceptance. Query.

THE RETIRED OFFICER MAGAZINE—201 N. Washington St., Alexandria, VA 22314. Address the Manuscripts Ed. Articles, 800 to 2,000 words, of interest to military retirees and their families. Current military/national affairs: recent military history, health/medicine, and second-career opportunities. No fillers. Photos a plus. Pays to $500, on acceptance. Query. Guidelines.

THE ROTARIAN—1560 Sherman Ave., Evanston, IL 60201–3698. Willmon L. White, Ed. Publication of Rotary International, world service organization of business and professional men and women. Articles, 1,200 to 2,000 words, on international social and economic issues, business and management, human relationships, travel, sports, environment, science and technology; humor. Pays good rates, on acceptance. Query.

SILVER CIRCLE—4900 Rivergrade Rd., Irwindale, CA 91706. Jay Binkly, Ed. National consumer-interest quarterly. Consumer service articles, 800 to 2,500 words, on careers, money, health, home, gardening, food, travel, hobbies, etc. Pays $250 to $1,500, on acceptance. Query.

VFW MAGAZINE—406 W. 34th St., Kansas City, MO 64111. Richard K. Kolb, Ed. Magazine for Veterans of Foreign Wars and their families. Articles, to 1,500 words, on current issues and military history, with veteran angle. Photos. Pays to $500 for unsolicited articles, extra for photos, on acceptance. Guidelines.

WOODMEN MAGAZINE—1700 Farnam St., Omaha, NE 68102. Scott J. Darling, Asst. V.P./Comm. Mgr. "We rarely purchase free-lance material."

RELIGIOUS MAGAZINES

ADVANCE—1445 Boonville Ave., Springfield, MO 65802. Harris Jansen, Ed. Articles, 1,200 words, slanted to ministers, on preaching, doctrine, practice; how-to features. Pays to 10¢ a word, on acceptance.

AMERICA—106 W. 56th St., New York, NY 10019–3893. George W. Hunt, S.J., Ed. Articles, 1,000 to 2,500 words, on current affairs, family life, literary trends. Pays $75 to $150, on acceptance.

AMERICAN BIBLE SOCIETY RECORD—1865 Broadway, New York, NY 10023. Clifford P. Macdonald, Man. Ed. Material related to work of American Bible Society: translating, publishing, distributing. Pays on acceptance. Query.

AMERICAN JEWISH HISTORY—American Jewish Historical Society, 2 Thornton Rd., Waltham, MA 02154. Dr. Marc Lee Raphael, Ed. Academic articles, 15 to 30 typed pages, on the settlement, history, and life of Jews in North and South America. Queries preferred. No payment.

AMIT WOMAN—817 Broadway, New York, NY 10003–4761. Micheline Ratzersdorfer, Ed. Articles, 1,000 to 2,000 words, of interest to Jewish women: Middle East, Israel, history, holidays, travel. Pays to $75, on publication.

ANGLICAN JOURNAL—600 Jarvis St., Toronto, Ont., Canada M4Y 2J6. Carolyn Purden, Ed. National newspaper of the Anglican Church of Canada. Articles, to 1,200 words, on current events and human-interest subjects in a religious context. Pays $200 to $500, on acceptance. Query.

ANNALS OF ST. ANNE DE BEAUPRÉ—P.O. Box 1000, St. Anne de Beaupré, Quebec, Canada G0A 3C0. Roch Achard, C.Ss.R., Ed. Articles, 1,200 to 1,500 words, that promote devotion to St. Anne and Christian family values. "Write something inspirational, educational, objective, and uplifting." No poetry. Pays 3¢ to 4¢ a word, on acceptance.

BAPTIST LEADER—American Baptist Churches-USA, P.O. Box 851, Valley Forge, PA 19482–0851. L. Isham, Ed. Practical how-to or thought-provoking

637

articles, 1,200 to 2,000 words, for local church lay leaders, pastors, and Christian education staff.

BIBLE ADVOCATE—P.O. Box 33677, Denver, CO 80233. Roy Marrs, Ed. Articles, 1,000 to 2,500 words, and fillers, 100 to 500 words, on Bible passages and Christian living. Poetry, 5 to 25 lines, on religious themes. Opinion pieces, to 700 words. "Be familiar with the doctrinal beliefs of the Church of God (Seventh Day). For example, they don't celebrate a traditional Easter or Christmas." Pays $10 per page (to $25) for articles, $5 for poetry, on publication. Guidelines.

BRIGADE LEADER—Box 150, Wheaton, IL 60189. Deborah Christensen, Man. Ed. Inspirational articles, 1,000 words, for Christian men who lead boys, with an emphasis on issues pertaining to men. "Most articles are written on assignment by experts." Pays $60 to $150. Query required.

CATECHIST—2451 E. River Rd., Dayton, OH 45439. Patricia Fischer, Ed. Informational and how-to articles, 1,200 to 1,500 words, for Catholic teachers, coordinators, and administrators in religious education programs. Pays $25 to $75, on publication.

CATHOLIC DIGEST—P.O. Box 64090, St. Paul, MN 55164–0090. Attn: Articles Ed. Articles, 1,000 to 3,500 words, on Catholic and general subjects. Fillers, to 300 words, on instances of kindness rewarded, for "Hearts Are Trumps"; accounts of good deeds, for "People Are Like That." Pays from $200 for original articles, $100 for reprints, on acceptance; $4 to $50 for fillers, on publication. Guidelines.

CATHOLIC NEAR EAST MAGAZINE—1011 First Ave., New York, NY 10022–4195. Michael La Civita, Ed. A bimonthly publication of Catholic Near East Welfare Assoc., a papal agency for humanitarian and pastoral support. Articles, 1,500 to 2,000 words, on people of the Middle East, northeast Africa, India, and eastern Europe: their faith, religious heritage, culture, and present state of affairs. Special interest in Eastern Christian churches. Color photos for all articles. Query. Pays 20¢ a word.

CATHOLIC PARENT—Our Sunday Visitor, Inc., 200 Noll Plaza, Huntington, IN 46750. Woodeene Koenig-Bricker, Ed. Features, how-tos, and general-interest articles, 800 to 1,000 words, for Catholic parents. "Keep it anecdotal and practical with an emphasis on values and family life. Don't preach." Payment varies, on acceptance.

CATHOLIC TWIN CIRCLE—15760 Ventura Blvd., Suite 1201, Encino, CA 91436. Loretta G. Seyer, Ed. Articles and interviews of interest to Catholic families, 1,000 to 2,000 words, with photos. Opinion or inspirational columns, 800 words. Strict attention to Catholic doctrine required. Enclose SASE. Pays from 10¢ a word for articles, $50 for columns, on publication.

CHARISMA & CHRISTIAN LIFE—600 Rinehart Rd., Lake Mary, FL 32746. Lee Grady, Ed. Dir. Charismatic/evangelical Christian articles, 1,500 to 2,500 words, for developing the spiritual life. News stories, 300 to 1,500 words. Photos. Pays varying rates, on publication.

THE CHRISTIAN CENTURY—407 S. Dearborn St., Chicago, IL 60605. James M. Wall, Ed. Ecumenical. Articles, 1,500 to 2,500 words, with a religious angle, on political and social issues, international affairs, culture, the arts. Poetry, to 20 lines. Photos. Pays about $25 per printed page, extra for photos, on publication.

CHRISTIAN EDUCATION COUNSELOR—(formerly *Sunday School Counselor*) 1445 Boonville Ave., Springfield, MO 65802–1894. Sylvia Lee, Ed.

Articles, 1,000 to 1,500 words, on teaching and administrating Christian education in the local church, for local Sunday school and Christian school personnel. Pays 5¢ to 10¢ a word, on acceptance.

CHRISTIAN EDUCATION JOURNAL—Scripture Press Ministries, P.O. Box 650, Glen Ellyn, IL 60138. Leslie H. Stobbe, Exec. Ed. Articles, 5 to 15 typed pages, on Christian education topics. Pays $100, on publication. Guidelines.

CHRISTIAN HOME & SCHOOL—3350 E. Paris Ave. S.E., Grand Rapids, MI 49512. Gordon L. Bordewyk, Ed. Articles for parents in Canada and the U.S. who send their children to Christian schools and are concerned about the challenges facing Christian families today. Pays $75 to $150, on publication. Guidelines.

CHRISTIAN MEDICAL & DENTAL SOCIETY JOURNAL—P.O. Box 830689, Richardson, TX 75083–0689. David B. Biebel, D. Min., Ed. Articles, 8 to 10 double-spaced pages, for Christian medical and dental professionals. Queries preferred. Pays to $50, on publication. Guidelines.

CHRISTIAN PARENTING TODAY—P.O. Box 36630, Colorado Springs, CO 80936–3663. Brad Lewis, Ed. Articles, 900 to 1,500 words, dealing with raising children with Christian principles. Departments: "Parent Exchange," 25 to 100 words on problem-solving ideas that have worked for parents; "My Story," 800 to 1,500 words, first-person accounts of how one family or parent faced a parenting challenge; "Life in Our House," insightful anecdotes, 25 to 100 words, about humorous things said at home. Pays 15¢ to 25¢ a word, on publication. Pays $40 for "Parent Exchange," $25 for "Life in our House." Guidelines; send SASE.

CHRISTIAN SINGLE—MSN 140, 127 Ninth Ave. N., Nashville, TN 37234. Stephen Felts, Ed. Articles, 600 or 1,200 words, for single adults about leisure activities, issues related to single parents, inspiring personal experiences, humor, life from a Christian perspective. Payment varies, on acceptance. Query. Guidelines.

CHRISTIAN SOCIAL ACTION—100 Maryland Ave. N.E., Washington, DC 20002. Lee Ranck, Ed. Articles, 1,500 to 2,000 words, on social issues for concerned persons of faith. Pays $75 to $125, on publication.

CHRISTIANITY TODAY—465 Gundersen Dr., Carol Stream, IL 60188. David Neff, Exec. Ed. Doctrinal social issues and interpretive essays, 1,500 to 3,000 words, from evangelical Protestant perspective. No fiction or poetry. Pays $200 to $500, on acceptance. Query.

CHURCH ADMINISTRATION—127 Ninth Ave. N., Nashville, TN 37234. Southern Baptist. How-to articles, 1,500 to 1,800 words, on administrative planning, staffing, pastoral ministry, organization, and financing. Pays 5 ½¢ a word, on acceptance. Query.

CHURCH & STATE—8120 Fenton St., Silver Spring, MD 20910. Joseph L. Conn, Man. Ed. Articles, 600 to 2,600 words, on religious liberty and church-state relations. Pays varying rates, on acceptance. Query.

CHURCH EDUCATOR—Educational Ministries, Inc., 165 Plaza Dr., Prescott, AZ 86303. Robert G. Davidson, Ed. How-to articles, to 1,750 words, on Christian education: activity projects, crafts, learning centers, games, bulletin boards, etc., for all church school, junior and high school programs, and adult study groups. Allow 3 months for response. Pays 3¢ a word, on publication.

THE CHURCH HERALD—4500 60th St. S.E., Grand Rapids, MI 49512–9642. Jeffrey Japinga, Ed. Reformed Church in America. Articles, 500 to 1,500 words, on Christianity and culture, politics, marriage, and home. Pays $50 to $125, on acceptance. Query.

THE CHURCH MUSICIAN—127 Ninth Ave. N., Nashville, TN 37234. Jere Adams, Ed. Articles for spiritual enrichment, testimonials, human-interest pieces, and other subjects of interest to music directors, pastors, organists, pianists, choir coordinators, and members of the music council in local churches. Pays to 5 ½¢ a word, on acceptance. Same address and requirements for *Glory Songs* (for adults), and *The Senior Musician* (for senior adults).

CIRCUIT RIDER—P.O. Box 801, Nashville, TN 37202–0801. J. Richard Peck, Ed. Articles for United Methodist pastors, 800 to 1,600 words. Pays $50 to $200, on acceptance. Query preferred; SASE required.

COLUMBIA—1 Columbus Plaza, New Haven, CT 06510–0901. Richard McMunn, Ed. Knights of Columbus. Articles, 1,500 words, for Catholic families. Must be accompanied by color photos or transparencies. No fiction. Pays to $500 for articles with photos, on acceptance.

COMMENTARY—165 E. 56th St., New York, NY 10022. Norman Podhoretz, Ed. Articles, 5,000 to 7,000 words, on contemporary issues, Jewish affairs, social sciences, religious thought, culture. Serious fiction; book reviews. Pays on publication.

COMMONWEAL—15 Dutch St., New York, NY 10038. Margaret O'Brien Steinfels, Ed. Catholic. Articles, to 3,000 words, on political, religious, social, and literary subjects. Pays 3¢ a word, on acceptance.

COMPASS: A JESUIT JOURNAL—10 St. Mary St., #300, Toronto, Ont., Canada M4Y 1P9. Robert Chodos, Ed. Essays, 1,500 to 2,500 words, on current religious, political, and cultural topics. "We are ecumenical in spirit and like to provide a forum for lively debate and an ethical perspective on social and religious questions." Query preferred. Pays $100 to $500, on publication.

THE COVENANT COMPANION—5101 N. Francisco Ave., Chicago, IL 60625. John E. Phelan, Ed. Articles, 1,000 words, with Christian implications published for members and attenders of Evangelical Covenant Church, "aimed at gathering, enlightening, and stimulating devotion to Jesus Christ and the living of the Christian life." Poetry. Pays $15 to $35, on publication.

CRUSADER—P.O. Box 7259, Grand Rapids, MI 49510. G. Richard Broene, Ed. Fiction, 900 to 1,500 words, and articles, 400 to 1,000 words, for boys ages 9 to 14 that show how God is at work in their lives and in the world around them. Also, short fillers. Pays 4¢ to 5¢ a word, on acceptance.

DAILY MEDITATION—Box 2710, San Antonio, TX 78299. Ruth S. Paterson, Ed. Inspirational nonsectarian articles, 650 to 2,000 words. Fillers, to 350 words; verse, to 20 lines. Pays 1 ½¢ to 2¢ a word for prose; 14¢ a line for verse, on acceptance. SASE required.

DAILY WORD—Unity Village, MO 64065. Colleen Zuck, Ed. Daily lessons, 25 lines (double-spaced), that may be based on an affirmation, a Bible text, or an idea that has been helpful in meeting some situation in your life. Pays $30, on acceptance, plus copies. Guidelines.

DAUGHTERS OF SARAH—2121 Sheridan Rd., Evanston, IL 60201. Cathi Falsani, Asst. Ed. Fiction, 750 to 2,000 words, and poetry, to 500 words, from a Christian feminist perspective. Articles, 750 to 2,000 words, on theology and social issues of Christian feminism. Guidelines. No simultaneous submissions. Query required.

DECISION—Billy Graham Evangelistic Assn., 1300 Harmon Pl., P.O. Box 779, Minneapolis, MN 55440–0779. Roger C. Palms, Ed. Christian testimonies and teaching articles on evangelism and Christian nurturing, 1,500 to 1,800 words. Vignettes, 400 to 1,000 words. Pays varying rates, on publication.

DISCOVERIES—WordAction Publishing Co., 6401 The Paseo, Kansas City, MO 64131. Attn: Ed. Asst. Weekly take-home paper designed to correlate with evangelical Sunday school curriculum. Fiction, 500 to 700 words, for 8- to 10-year-olds. Stories should feature contemporary, true-to-life characters and should illustrate character building and scriptural application. No poetry. Pays 5¢ a word, on publication. Guidelines.

DREAMS & VISIONS—Skysong Press, R. R. 1, Washago, Ontario, Canada L0K 2B0. Steve Stanton, Ed. New frontiers in Christian fiction. Eclectic fiction, 2,000 to 6,000 words, that "has literary value and is unique and relevant to Christian readers today." Pays in copies and $100 honorarium to best of the year.

EVANGEL—Light and Life Press, Box 535002, Indianapolis, IN 46253–5002. Carolyn Smith, Ed. Free Methodist. Personal experience articles, 1,000 words; short devotional items, 300 to 500 words; fiction, 1,200 words, showing personal faith in Christ to be instrumental in solving problems. Pays 4¢ a word for articles, $10 for poetry, on publication.

EVANGELIZING TODAY'S CHILD—Warrenton, MO 63383. Attn: Eds. Articles, 1,200 to 1,500 words, for Sunday school teachers, Christian education leaders, and children's workers. Feature articles should include teaching principles, instruction for the reader, and classroom illustrations. "Impact" articles, 700 to 900 words, show the power of the Gospel in or through the life of a child; "Resource Center," 200- to 300-word teaching tips. Also short stories, 800 to 1,000 words, of contemporary children dealing with problems; must have a scriptural solution. Pays 10¢ to 12¢ a word for articles; $15 to $25 for "Resource Center" pieces; 8¢ a word for short stories, on publication. Guidelines.

FAITH TODAY—Box 8800, Sta. B, Willowdale, Ontario, Canada M2K 2R6. Brian C. Stiller, Ed. Audrey Dorsch, Man. Ed. Articles, 1,500 words, on current issues relating to the church in Canada. Pays negotiable rates, on publication. Queries required.

THE FAMILY: A CATHOLIC PERSPECTIVE—50 St. Pauls Ave., Boston, MA 02130. Sister Theresa Frances Myers, Ed. Articles, 800 to 2,000 words, on a broad range of family topics, including marital relationships, parenting, profiles of role-models for Catholic families. Upbeat, thought-provoking, family-oriented fiction, 1,000 to 1,200 words. Views, columns, personal reflections, 800 words; fillers, 50 to 500 words. "Our readers are primarily Roman Catholic parents with children at home." Submit complete manuscripts; no queries and no simultaneous submissions. Pays 6¢ to 8¢ a word, on publication. (Pays for fillers on acceptance.) Does not read submissions in July or August.

THE FAMILY DIGEST—(formerly *Parish Family Digest*) P.O. Box 40137, Fort Wayne, IN 46804. Corine B. Erlandson, Ed. Articles, 750 to 1,000 words, on family life, Catholic subjects, seasonal, parish life, prayer, inspiration, etc., for the Catholic reader. Also publishes short humorous anecdotes and light-hearted cartoons. Pays 5¢ a word, on acceptance.

FELLOWSHIP—Box 271, Nyack, NY 10960–0271. Richard Deats, Ed. Bimonthly published by the Fellowship of Reconciliation, an interfaith, pacifist organization. Articles, 750 words, and features, 1,500 to 2,000 words; B&W photoessays, on active nonviolence, opposition to war. "Articles for a just and peaceful world community." Queries preferred. SASE required. Pays in copies and subscription.

FELLOWSHIP IN PRAYER—291 Witherspoon St., Princeton, NJ 08542. Articles, to 1,500 words, and poems, to 35 lines, relating to prayer, meditation, and the spiritual life as practiced by men and women of all faith traditions. Pays in copies. Guidelines.

FOURSQUARE WORLD ADVANCE—1910 W. Sunset Blvd., Suite 200, Los Angeles, CA 90026. Ronald D. Williams, Ed. Official publication of the International Church of the Foursquare Gospel. Religious fiction and nonfiction, 1,000 to 1,200 words, and religious poetry. Pays $75, on publication. Guidelines.

FRIENDS JOURNAL—1501 Cherry St., Philadelphia, PA 19102–1497. Vinton Deming, Ed. Articles and fiction, to 2,000 words, reflecting Quaker life today: commentary on social issues, experiential articles, Quaker history, world affairs. Poetry, to 25 lines, and Quaker-related humor and crossword puzzles also considered. Pays in copies. Guidelines.

THE GEM—Box 926, Findlay, OH 45839–0926. Evelyn Sloat, Ed. Articles, 300 to 1,600 words, and fiction, 1,000 to 1,600 words: true-to-life experiences of God's help, of healed relationships, and of growing maturity in faith. For adolescents through senior citizens. Pays $15 for articles and fiction, $5 to $10 for fillers, after publication.

GLORY SONGS—See *The Church Musician.*

GROUP, THE YOUTH MINISTRY MAGAZINE—Box 481, Loveland, CO 80539. Rick Lawrence, Ed. Interdenominational magazine for leaders of junior and senior high school Christian youth groups. Articles, 500 to 1,700 words, about practical youth ministry principles, techniques, or activities. Short how-to pieces, to 300 words. Pays to $150 for articles, $15 to $25 for department pieces, on acceptance. Guidelines.

GUIDE—Review and Herald Publishing Assn., 55 W. Oak Ridge Dr., Hagerstown, MD 21740. Stories, to 1,200 words, for Christian youth, ages 10 to 14. Pays 3¢ to 4¢ a word, on acceptance.

GUIDEPOSTS—16 E. 34th St., New York, NY 10016. Colleen Hughes, Features Ed. True first-person stories, 250 to 1,500 words, stressing how faith in God helps people cope with life. Anecdotal fillers, to 250 words. Pays $100 to $400, $50 for fillers, on acceptance.

HERALD OF HOLINESS—6401 The Paseo, Kansas City, MO 64131. Attn: Man. Ed. Church of the Nazarene. Articles, 800 to 2,000 words, about distinctive Nazarenes, Christian family life and marriage, a Christian approach to social issues, seasonal material, and short devotional articles. Submit complete manuscript. Pays 4¢ to 5¢ a word, within 30 days of acceptance. Guidelines.

HOME LIFE—127 Ninth Ave. N., Nashville, TN 37234. Charlie Warren, Ed.-in-Chief. Mary Paschall Darby, Man. Ed. Southern Baptist. Fiction, personal experience, and articles on Christian marriage, parenthood, and family relationships. Human-interest pieces, 200 to 500 words; cartoons and short verse related to family. Query with SASE required. Pays on acceptance.

INDIAN LIFE—Box 3765, Sta. B, Winnipeg, MB, Canada R2W 3R6. Ed Hughes, Ed. Christian teaching articles and testimonials of Native Americans, 1,000 to 1,200 words. "Our magazine is designed to help the North American Indian Church speak to the social, cultural, and spiritual needs of Native people." Writing should be at a seventh-grade reading level. "We prefer Native writers who write from within their culture." Queries preferred.

INSIDE MAGAZINE—226 S. 16th St., Philadelphia, PA 19102–3392. Jane Biberman, Ed. Articles, 1,500 to 3,000 words, and fiction, 2,000 to 3,000 words, of interest to Jewish adults. Pays $100 to $500, after publication. Query.

JEWISH CURRENTS—22 E. 17th St., #601, New York, NY 10003. Morris U. Schappes, Ed. Articles, 2,400 to 3,000 words, on Jewish history, Jewish secularism, progressivism, labor struggle, Holocaust resistance, Black-Jewish relations, Israel, Yiddish culture. "We are pro-Israel though non-Zionist and a secular magazine; no religious articles." Overstocked with fiction and poetry. No payment.

THE JEWISH HOMEMAKER—705 Foster Ave., Brooklyn, NY 11230. Mayer Bendet, Ed. Bimonthly. Articles, 1,000 words, for a traditional/Orthodox Jewish audience. Humor and fillers. Query. Payment varies, on publication.

THE JEWISH MONTHLY—B'nai B'rith International, 1640 Rhode Island Ave. N.W., Washington, DC 20036. Jeff Rubin, Ed. Articles, 500 to 3,000 words, on politics, religion, history, culture, and social issues of Jewish concern with an emphasis on people. Pays 10¢ to 25¢ a word, on publication. Query with clips.

JOURNAL OF CHRISTIAN NURSING—P.O. Box 1650, Downers Grove, IL 60515. Judy Shelly, Sr. Ed. Articles, 8 to 12 double-spaced pages, that help Christian nurses view nursing practice through the eyes of faith: spiritual care, ethics, values, healing and wholeness, psychology and religion, personal and professional ethics, etc. Priority given to nurse authors, though work by non-nurses will be considered. Opinion pieces, to 4 pages, for "The Last Word" section. Pays $25 to $80. Guidelines and editorial calendar.

THE JOYFUL WOMAN—P.O. Box 90028, Chattanooga, TN 37412. Joy Rice Martin, Ed. Articles and fiction, 500 to 1,500 words, for Christian women: first-person inspirational true stories, profiles of Christian women, practical and biblically oriented how-to articles. Pays 3¢ to 4¢ a word, on publication.

KEY TO CHRISTIAN EDUCATION—8121 Hamilton Ave., Cincinnati, OH 45231–2396. Barbara Bolton and Lowellette Lauderdale, Eds. Articles, to 1,200 words, on teaching methods, and success stories for workers in Christian education. Pays varying rates, on acceptance.

LEADERSHIP—465 Gundersen Dr., Carol Stream, IL 60188. Kevin A. Miller, Ed. Articles, 500 to 3,000 words, on administration, finance, and/or programming of interest to ministers and church leaders. Personal stories of crisis in ministry. "We deal mainly with the how-to of running a church. We're not a theological journal but a practical one." Pays $50 to $350, on acceptance.

LIBERTY MAGAZINE—12501 Old Columbia Pike, Silver Spring, MD 20904–1608. Roland R. Hegstad, Ed. Timely articles, to 2,500 words, and photoessays, on religious freedom and church-state relations. Pays 6¢ to 8¢ a word, on acceptance. Query.

LIGHT AND LIFE—P.O. Box 535002, Indianapolis, IN 46253–5002. Robert Haslam, Ed. Fresh, lively articles about practical Christian living, and sound treatments of vital issues facing the Evangelical in contemporary society. Pays 4¢ a word, on publication.

LIGUORIAN—Liguori, MO 63057–9999. Rev. Allan Weinert, Ed. Catholic. Articles and short stories, 1,500 to 2,000 words, on Christian values in modern life. Pays 10¢ to 12¢ a word, on acceptance.

THE LIVING LIGHT—U.S. Catholic Conference, Dept. of Education, 3211 4th St. N.W., Washington, DC 20017–1194. Berard L. Marthaler, Exec. Ed. Theo-

643

retical and practical articles, 1,500 to 4,000 words, on religious education, catechesis, and pastoral ministry.

LIVING WITH PRESCHOOLERS—See *ParentLife*.

LIVING WITH TEENAGERS—127 Ninth Ave. N., Nashville, TN 37234. Articles, 600 to 1,200 words, told from a Christian perspective for parents of teenagers; first-person approach preferred. Queries welcome; SASE required. Pay is negotiable and made on acceptance.

THE LOOKOUT—8121 Hamilton Ave., Cincinnati, OH 45231. Simon J. Dahlman, Ed. Articles, 500 to 2,000 words, on spiritual growth, family issues, applying Christian faith to current issues, and people overcoming problems with Christian principles. Inspirational or humorous shorts, 500 to 800 words; fiction, to 2,000 words. Pays 6¢ to 12¢ a word, on acceptance.

THE LUTHERAN—8765 W. Higgins Rd., Chicago, IL 60631. Edgar R. Trexler, Ed. Articles, to 2,000 words, on Christian ideology, personal religious experiences, social and ethical issues, family life, church, and community. Pays $100 to $600, on acceptance. Query required.

MARRIAGE PARTNERSHIP—Christianity Today, Inc., 465 Gundersen Dr., Carol Stream, IL 60188. Ron Lee, Man. Ed. Articles, 500 to 2,000 words, related to marriage, for men and women who wish to fortify their relationship. Cartoons, humor, fillers. Pays $50 to $300, on acceptance. Query required.

MARYKNOLL—Maryknoll, NY 10545. Joseph Veneroso, M. M., Ed. Frank Maurovich, Man. Ed. Magazine of the Catholic Foreign Mission Society of America. Articles, 800 to 1,000 words, and photos relating to missions or missioners overseas. Pays $150, on acceptance. Payment for photos made on publication.

MATURE LIVING—127 Ninth Ave. N., Nashville, TN 37234. Leisure magazine for senior adults. "Unique, creative manuscripts, to 900 words, characterized by human interest, Christian warmth, and humor." Pays 5 ½¢ a word (or per line for poetry).

MATURE YEARS—201 Eighth Ave. S., P.O. Box 801, Nashville, TN 37202. Marvin W. Cropsey, Ed. Nondenominational quarterly. Articles, 1,500 to 2,000 words, on retirement or related subjects, inspiration. Humorous and serious fiction, 1,500 to 1,800 words. Travel pieces with religious slant. Poetry, to 14 lines. Include social security number with manuscript. Guidelines.

THE MENNONITE—P.O. Box 347, Newton, KS 67114. Gordon Houser, Ed. Larry Penner, Asst. Ed. Articles, 1,000 words, that emphasize Christian themes. Pays 5¢ a word, on publication. Guidelines.

MESSENGER OF THE SACRED HEART—661 Greenwood Ave., Toronto, Ont., Canada M4J 4B3. Articles and short stories, about 1,500 words, for American and Canadian Catholics. Pays from 4¢ a word, on acceptance.

MIDSTREAM—110 E. 59th St., New York, NY 10022. Joel Carmichael, Ed. Jewish-interest articles and book reviews. Fiction, to 3,000 words, and poetry. Pays 5¢ a word, after publication. Allow 3 months for response.

THE MIRACULOUS MEDAL—475 E. Chelten Ave., Philadelphia, PA 19144–5785. John W. Gouldrick, C.M., Ed. Dir. Catholic. Fiction, to 2,400 words. Religious verse, to 20 lines. Pays from 2¢ a word for fiction, from 50¢ a line for poetry, on acceptance.

MODERN LITURGY—160 E. Virginia St., #290, San Jose, CA 95112. Kathi Drolet, Man. Ed. "Articles making the connection between imagination and celebration (faith expression) or worship and 'real' life." Material must be related to Roman Catholic liturgy. Query required. Pays in copies and subscription.

MOMENT—3000 Connecticut Ave. N.W., Suite 300, Washington, DC 20008. Suzanne Singer, Man. Ed. Sophisticated, issue-oriented articles, 2,000 to 4,000 words, on Jewish topics. Nonfiction only. Pays $150 to $400, on publication.

MOMENTUM—National Catholic Educational Assn., 1077 30th St. N.W., Suite 100, Washington, DC 20007–3852. Patricia Feistritzer, Ed. Articles, 500 to 1,500 words, on outstanding programs, issues, and research in education. Book reviews. Pays 4¢ a word, on publication. Query.

MOODY MAGAZINE—820 N. La Salle Blvd., Chicago, IL 60610. Andrew Scheer, Man. Ed. Anecdotal articles, 1,200 to 2,000 words, on the evangelical Christian experience in the home, the community, and the workplace. Pays 15¢ to 20¢ a word, on acceptance. Query.

THE NATIONAL CHRISTIAN REPORTER—See *The United Methodist Reporter.*

NEW COVENANT—200 Noll Plaza, Huntington, IN 46750. Jim Manney, Ed. Articles and testimonials, 1,000 to 4,000 words, that foster renewal in the Catholic Church, especially the charismatic, ecumenical, and evangelical dimensions of that renewal. Queries preferred. Pays from 15¢ a word, on acceptance.

NEW ERA—50 E. North Temple, Salt Lake City, UT 84150. Richard M. Romney, Man. Ed. Articles, 150 to 1,500 words, and fiction, to 2,000 words, for young Mormons. Poetry; photos. Pays 5¢ to 10¢ a word, 25¢ a line for poetry, on acceptance. Query.

NEW WORLD OUTLOOK—475 Riverside Dr., Rm. 1351, New York, NY 10115–0122. Alma Graham, Ed. Articles, 500 to 2,000 words, illustrated with color photos, on United Methodist missions and Methodist-related programs and ministries. Focus on national, global, and women's and children's issues, and on men and youth in missions. Query. Pays on publication.

OBLATES—15 S. 59th St., Belleville, IL 62223–4694. Mary Mohrman, Manuscripts Ed. Christine Portell, Man. Ed. Articles, 500 to 600 words, that inspire, uplift, and motivate through positive Christian values in everyday life. Inspirational poetry, to 16 lines. Send complete manuscript only. Pays $80 for articles, $30 for poems, on acceptance. Send 52¢ SASE for guidelines and sample copy.

THE OTHER SIDE—300 W. Apsley, Philadelphia, PA 19144. Doug Davidson, Nonfiction Ed. Jennifer Wilkins, Fiction Ed. Rod Jellema, Poetry Ed. Independent, ecumenical Christian magazine devoted to issues of peace, justice, and faith. Fiction, 500 to 5,000 words, that deepens readers' encounter with the mystery of God and the mystery of ourselves. Nonfiction, 500 to 4,000 words (most under 2,000 words), on contemporary social, political, economic, or racial issues in the U.S. or abroad. Poems, to 50 lines; submit up to 3 poems. Payment is 2 copies plus $20 to $350 for articles; $75 to $250 for fiction; $15 for poems, on acceptance. Guidelines.

OUR FAMILY—Box 249, Battleford, Sask., Canada S0M 0E0. Nestor Gregoire, Ed. Articles, 1,000 to 3,000 words, for Catholic families, on modern society, family, marriage, current affairs, and spiritual topics. Humor; verse. Pays 7¢ to 10¢ a word for articles, 75¢ to $1 a line for poetry, on acceptance. SAE with international reply coupons required with all submissions. Guidelines.

OUR SUNDAY VISITOR—200 Noll Plaza, Huntington, IN 46750. David Scott, Ed. In-depth features, 1,000 to 1,200 words, on the Catholic church in America today. No poetry or fiction. Pays $150 to $250, on acceptance.

PARENTLIFE—(formerly *Living with Preschoolers*) MSN 140, 127 Ninth Ave. N., Nashville, TN 37234. Attn: Ed. Informative articles and personal experience pieces, 800 to 1,200 words, relating to family and the preschool child, written with a Christian perspective. Payment varies, on acceptance.

PARISH FAMILY DIGEST—See *The Family Digest.*

PASTORAL LIFE—Box 595, Canfield, OH 44406–0595. Anthony L. Chenevey, Ed. Articles, 2,000 to 2,500 words, addressing the problems of pastoral ministry. Pays 4¢ a word, on publication. Guidelines.

PATHWAYS—Christian Board of Publication, Box 179, St. Louis, MO 63166. Christine Hershberger Miner, Ed. Fiction, 100 to 800 words; articles, 600 to 1,000 words; and poetry, to 20 lines. Accepts material for 12- to 16-year-olds. Pays 3¢ a word for prose, from $3 for poetry, on acceptance. Guidelines.

PENTECOSTAL EVANGEL—1445 Boonville Ave., Springfield, MO 65802. John Maempa, Interim Ed. Assemblies of God. Religious, personal experience, and devotional articles, 400 to 1,000 words. Pays 7¢ a word, on acceptance.

THE PENTECOSTAL MESSENGER—P.O. Box 850, Joplin, MO 64802. Peggy Allen, Man. Ed. Articles, 500 to 2,000 words, that deal with Christian commitment: human interest, inspiration, social and religious issues, Bible topics, and seasonal material. Pays 1 ½¢ per word, on publication. Guidelines.

PERSPECTIVE—Pioneer Clubs, Box 788, Wheaton, IL 60189. Rebecca Powell Parat, Ed. Articles, 750 to 1,500 words, that provide growth for adult club leaders in leadership and relationship skills and offer encouragement and practical support. Readers are lay leaders of Pioneer Clubs for boys and girls (age 2 to 12th grade). "Most articles written on assignment; writers familiar with Pioneer Clubs who would be interested in working on assignment should contact us." Queries preferred. Pays $40 to $90, on acceptance. Guidelines.

PIME WORLD—17330 Quincy St., Detroit, MI 48221. Paul W. Witte, Man. Ed. Articles, 600 to 1,200 words, on Catholic missionary work in the Orient, West Africa, and Latin America. Color photos. No fiction or poetry. Pays 6¢ a word, extra for photos, on publication.

POWER AND LIGHT—6401 The Paseo, Kansas City, MO 64131. Beula J. Postlewait, Preteen Ed. Fiction, 400 to 800 words, for grades 5 and 6, defining Christian experiences and demonstrating Christian values and beliefs. Pays 3 ½¢ a word for first rights; 5¢ a word for multi-use rights, on publication.

THE PREACHER'S MAGAZINE—10814 E. Broadway, Spokane, WA 99206. Randal E. Denny, Ed. Scholarly and practical articles, 700 to 2,500 words, on areas of interest to Christian ministers: church administration, pastoral care, professional and personal growth, church music, finance, evangelism. Pays 3 ½¢ a word, on publication. Guidelines.

PRESBYTERIAN RECORD—50 Wynford Dr., North York, Ont., Canada M3C 1J7. John Congram, Ed. Fiction and nonfiction, 1,500 words, and poetry, any length. Short items, to 800 words, of a contemporary and often controversial nature for "Full Count." The purpose of the magazine is "to provide news, not only from our church but the church-at-large, and to fulfill both a pastoral and prophetic role among our people." Queries preferred. SAE with international reply coupons required. Pays $50 (Canadian), on publication. Guidelines.

PRESBYTERIAN SURVEY—100 Witherspoon, Louisville, KY 40202–1396. Catherine Cottingham, Man. Ed. Articles, 1,200 words, of special interest to members of the Presbyterian Church. Pays to $100, before publication.

THE PRIEST—200 Noll Plaza, Huntington, IN 46750–4304. Father Owen F. Campion, Ed. Viewpoints, to 1,500 words, and articles, to 5,000 words, on life and ministry of priests, current theological developments, etc., for priests, permanent deacons, and seminarians. Pays $50 to $300, on acceptance.

PURPOSE—616 Walnut Ave., Scottdale, PA 15683–1999. James E. Horsch, Ed. Fiction and fillers, to 750 words, on Christian discipleship and church-year related themes, with good photos; pieces of history, biography, science, hobbies, from a Christian perspective; Christian problem solving. Poetry, to 12 lines. "Send complete manuscript; no queries." Pays to 5¢ a word, to $1 a line for poetry, on acceptance.

QUAKER LIFE—Friends United Meeting, 101 Quaker Hill Dr., Richmond, IN 47374–1980. Johan Maurer, Ed. Carol Beals, Man. Ed. Articles and news for members of the Society of Friends. Brief poetry considered. "Almost all material is solicited to match theme format." Pays in copies.

QUEEN OF ALL HEARTS—26 S. Saxon Ave., Bay Shore, NY 11706–8993. J. Patrick Gaffney, S.M.M., Ed. Publication of Montfort Missionaries. Articles and fiction, 1,000 to 2,000 words, related to the Virgin Mary. Poetry. Pay varies, on acceptance.

THE QUIET HOUR—850 N. Grove Ave., Elgin, IL 60120. Gary Wilde, Ed. Short devotionals. Pays $15, on acceptance. By assignment only; query.

RECONSTRUCTIONISM TODAY—30 Old Whitfield Rd., Accord, NY 12404. Lawrence Bush, Ed. Articles on contemporary Judaism and Jewish culture. Pays in copies and subscription.

RESPONSE: A CONTEMPORARY JEWISH REVIEW—27 W. 20th St., 9th Fl., New York, NY 10011–3707. Yigal Schleifer, David R. Adler, Eds. Michael Steinberg, Asst. Ed. Fiction, to 25 double-spaced pages, in which Jewish experience serves as controlling influence. Articles, to 25 pages, with a focus on Jewish issues. Poetry, to 80 lines, and book reviews. Pays in copies. Guidelines.

REVIEW FOR RELIGIOUS—3601 Lindell Blvd., St. Louis, MO 63108. David L. Fleming, S.J., Ed. Informative, practical, or inspirational articles, 1,500 to 5,000 words, from a Catholic theological or spiritual point of view. Pays $6 per page, on publication. Guidelines.

ST. ANTHONY MESSENGER—1615 Republic St., Cincinnati, OH 45210–1298. Norman Perry, O.F.M., Ed. Articles, 2,000 to 3,000 words, on personalities, major movements, education, family, religious and church issues, spiritual life, and social issues. Human-interest pieces. Humor; fiction, 2,000 to 3,000 words. Articles and stories should have religious implications. Query for nonfiction. Pays 14¢ a word, on acceptance.

ST. JOSEPH'S MESSENGER—P.O. Box 288, Jersey City, NJ 07303–0288. Sister Ursula Maphet, Ed. Inspirational articles, 500 to 1,000 words, and fiction, 1,000 to 1,500 words. Verse, 4 to 40 lines. Payment varies, on publication.

SEEK—8121 Hamilton Ave., Cincinnati, OH 45231. Eileen H. Wilmoth, Ed. Articles and fiction, to 1,200 words, on inspirational and controversial topics and timely religious issues. Christian testimonials. Pays 5¢ to 7¢ a word, on acceptance. SASE for guidelines.

THE SENIOR MUSICIAN—See *The Church Musician.*

SHARING THE VICTORY—Fellowship of Christian Athletes, 8701 Leeds Rd., Kansas City, MO 64129. John Dodderidge, Ed. Articles, interviews, and profiles, to 1,000 words, for co-ed Christian athletes and coaches in high school, college, and pros. Pays from $50, on publication. Query required.

SIGNS OF THE TIMES—P. O. Box 7000, Boise, ID 83707. Marvin Moore, Ed. Seventh-Day Adventists. Articles, 500 to 2,500 words: features on Christians who have performed community services; current issues from a biblical perspective; health, home, marriage, human-interest pieces; inspirational articles. Pays to 25¢ a word, on acceptance. Send 9x12 SASE for sample and guidelines.

SISTERS TODAY—The Liturgical Press, St. John's Abbey, Collegeville, MN 56321–7500. Articles, 500 to 3,500 words, on theology, social justice issues, and religious issues for women and the Church. Poetry, to 34 lines. Pays $5 per printed page, $10 per poem, on publication; $50 for color cover photos and $25 for B&W inside photos. Send articles to: Sister Mary Anthony Wagner, O.S.B., Ed., St. Benedict's Convent, St. Joseph, MN 56374–2099. Send poetry to: Sister Virginia Micka, C.S.J.,1884 Randolph Ave., St. Paul, MN 55105.

SOCIAL JUSTICE REVIEW—3835 Westminster Pl., St. Louis, MO 63108–3409. Rev. John H. Miller, C.S.C., Ed. Articles, 2,000 to 3,000 words, on social problems in light of Catholic teaching and current scientific studies. Pays 2¢ a word, on publication.

SPIRITUAL LIFE—2131 Lincoln Rd. N.E., Washington, DC 20002–1199. Edward O'Donnell, O.C.D., Ed. Professional religious journal. Religious essays, 3,000 to 5,000 words, on spirituality in contemporary life. Pays from $50, on acceptance. Guidelines.

STANDARD—6401 The Paseo, Kansas City, MO 64131. Attn: Ed. Articles and fiction, 300 to 1,700 words; true experiences; poetry, to 20 lines; fiction with Christian emphasis but not overtly preachy; cartoons in good taste. Pays 3 ½¢ a word, on acceptance.

SUNDAY DIGEST—850 N. Grove Ave., Elgin, IL 60120. Sharon Stultz, Ed. Articles, 1,000 to 1,800 words, on Christian faith in contemporary life; inspirational and how-to articles; free-verse poetry. Anecdotes, 500 words. Pays on acceptance.

SUNDAY SCHOOL COUNSELOR—See *Christian Education Counselor.*

TEACHERS INTERACTION—3558 S. Jefferson Ave., St. Louis, MO 63118. Jane Haas, Ed. Articles, 800 to 1,200 words; how-to pieces, to 100 words, for Lutheran volunteer church school teachers. Pays $20 to $100, on publication. Limited free-lance market.

THEOLOGY TODAY—Box 29, Princeton, NJ 08542. Thomas G. Long, Ed. Patrick D. Miller, Ed. Articles, 1,500 to 3,500 words, on theology, religion, and related social and philosophical issues. Literary criticism. Pays $75 to $200, on publication.

TODAY'S CHRISTIAN WOMAN—465 Gundersen Dr., Carol Stream, IL 60188. Ramona Cramer Tucker, Ed. Articles, 1,500 words, that are "warm and personal in tone, full of real-life anecdotes that deal with the following relationships: marriage, parenting, friendship, spiritual life, and self." Humorous anecdotes, 150 words, that have a Christian slant. Queries required. Payment varies, on acceptance. Guidelines.

THE UNITED CHURCH OBSERVER—84 Pleasant Blvd., Toronto, Ont., Canada M4T 2Z8. Attn: Ed. Factual articles, 1,500 to 2,500 words, on religious trends, human problems, social issues. No poetry. Pays after publication. Query.

THE UNITED METHODIST REPORTER—P.O. Box 660275, Dallas, TX 75266–0275. John Lovelace, Ed. United Methodist newspaper. Religious features, to 500 words. Religious verse, 4 to 12 lines. Photos. "Tight-deadline, time-sensitive, nationally circulated weekly newspaper." Pays 4¢ a word, on publication. Send for guidelines. Same address and requirements for *The National Christian Reporter* (interdenominational).

UNITED SYNAGOGUE REVIEW—155 Fifth Ave., New York, NY 10010. Lois Goldrich, Ed. Articles, 1,000 to 1,200 words, on issues of interest to Conservative Jewish community. Query.

UNITY MAGAZINE—Unity School of Christianity, Unity Village, MO 64065. Philip White, Ed. Articles, 1,000 to 1,800 words: health and healing, religious, metaphysical, Bible interpretation, and inspiration. Poems. Pays 20¢ a word, on acceptance.

VIRTUE: THE CHRISTIAN MAGAZINE FOR WOMEN—P. O. Box 36630, Colorado Springs, CO 80936–3663. Nancie Carmichael, Ed. Articles and fiction, 1,200 to 1,400 words, for Christian women. Query for articles; SASE required. Guidelines. Send 9x12 SASE with 5 stamps for sample copy.

VISTA MAGAZINE—P. O. Box 50434, Indianapolis, IN 46250–0434. Attn: Ed. Articles and adult fiction, on current Christian concerns and issues as well as fundamental issues of holiness and Christian living. First-person pieces, 500 to 1,200 words. Opinion pieces from an evangelical perspective, 500 to 650 words. Pays 4¢ a word for first rights, 2¢ a word for reprints. Send SASE for guidelines before submitting material.

THE WAR CRY—The Salvation Army, P.O. Box 269, Alexandria, VA 22313. Attn: Ed.-in-Chief. Inspirational articles, to 800 words, addressing modern life and issues. Color photos. Pays 15¢ a word for articles, $75 to $150 for photos, on acceptance.

WITH—722 Main St., Box 347, Newton, KS 67114. Eddy Hall and Carol Duerksen, Eds. Fiction, 500 to 2,000 words; nonfiction, 500 to 1,500 words; and poetry, to 50 lines for Anabaptist-Mennonite teenagers. "Wholesome humor always gets a close read." B&W 8x10 photos accepted. Payment is 4¢ a word, on acceptance (2¢ a word for reprints).

WOMAN'S TOUCH—1445 Boonville, Springfield, MO 65802–1894. Peggy Musgrove, Ed. Aleda Swartzendruber, Assoc. Ed. Articles, 500 to 1,200 words, that provide help and inspiration to Christian women, strengthening family life, and reaching out in witness to others. Uses some poetry and fillers, 50 to 150 words. Submit complete manuscript. Allow 3 months for response. Payment varies, on acceptance. Guidelines and editorial calendar.

WORLD VISION MAGAZINE—919 W. Huntington Dr., Monrovia, CA 91016. Bruce Brander, Man. Ed. Thoroughly researched articles, 1,200 to 2,000 words, on worldwide poverty, evangelism, the environment, and justice. Include reputable sources and strong anecdotes. "Turning Points," first-person articles, 450 to 700 words, about a life-changing, spiritual experience related to serving the poor. "We like articles to offer positive ways Christians can make a difference." Query required. Payment negotiable, made on acceptance.

YOUNG SALVATIONIST—The Salvation Army, 615 Slaters Ln., P.O. Box 269, Alexandria, VA 22313. Attn: Ed. Articles, 600 to 1,200 words, that teach the Christian view of everyday living, for teenagers. Short shorts, first-person testimonies, 600 to 800 words. Pays 10¢ a word, on acceptance. SASE required. Send 8 ½x11 SASE (3 stamps) for theme list, guidelines, and sample copy.

YOUR CHURCH—465 Gundersen Dr., Carol Stream, IL 60188. Richard Doebler, Man. Ed. Articles, to 1,000 words, about church business administration. Query required. Pays about 10¢ a word, on acceptance. Guidelines.

HEALTH

ACCENT ON LIVING—P. O. Box 700, Bloomington, IL 61702. Raymond C. Cheever, Pub. Betty Garee, Ed. Articles, 250 to 1,000 words, about physically disabled people, including their careers, recreation, sports, self-help devices, and ideas that can make daily routines easier. Good photos a plus. Pays 10¢ a word, on publication. Query.

AMERICAN BABY—Cahners Childcare Group, 475 Park Ave. S., New York, NY 10016. Judith Nolte, Ed. Articles, 1,000 to 2,000 words, for new or expectant parents on prenatal or infant care. Pays varying rates, on acceptance.

AMERICAN FITNESS—15250 Ventura Blvd., Suite 200, Sherman Oaks, CA 91403. Peg Jordan, Ed. Rhonda Wilson, Man. Ed. Articles, 500 to 1,500 words, on exercise, health, sports, nutrition, etc. Illustrations, photos.

AMERICAN HEALTH—28 W. 23rd St., New York, NY 10010. Attn: Ed. Dept. Lively, authoritative articles, 1,000 to 3,000 words, on scientific and lifestyle aspects of health and fitness; 100- to 500-word news reports. Query with clips. Pays $250 ($50 kill fee) for news stories; 75¢ to $1 per word for features (kill fee is 25% of assigned fee), on acceptance.

AMERICAN JOURNAL OF NURSING—555 W. 57th St., New York, NY 10019. Santa J. Crisall, Clinical Ed. Articles, 1,500 to 2,000 words, with photos, on nursing. Query.

ARTHRITIS TODAY—The Arthritis Foundation, 1314 Spring St. N.W., Atlanta, GA 30309. Cindy McDaniel, Ed. Research, self-help, how-to, general interest, general health, and lifestyle topics, and inspirational articles, 750 to 3,000 words, and short fillers, 100 to 250 words. "The magazine is written to help people with arthritis live more productive, independent, and pain-free lives." Pays $500 to $1,000 for articles, $100 to $250 for short fillers, on acceptance.

BABY TALK—636 Ave. of the Americas, New York, NY 10011. Susan Strecker, Ed. Articles, 1,000 to 1,500 words, by parents or professionals, on babies and baby care, etc. No poetry. Pay varies, on acceptance. SASE required.

BETTER HEALTH—1384 Chapel St., New Haven, CT 06511. James F. Malerba, Pub. Dir. Wellness and prevention magazine affiliated with The Hospital of Saint Raphael in New Haven. Upbeat articles, 2,000 to 2,500 words, that encourage a healthier lifestyle. Articles must contain quotes and narrative from healthcare professionals at Saint Raphael's and other local services. No first-person or personal experience articles. Pays $300 to $500, on acceptance. Query with SASE.

COMMON JOURNEYS—P.O. Box 17003, Minneapolis, MN 55417. Claire Griffler, Man. Ed. A journal by and for those living with chronic pain or illness. Personal essays, journal notes, letters between friends, to 1,200 words. Poems, to 25 lines, drawings related to the journal's theme also considered. Queries preferred. Pays in copies.

CROSSTRAINER—505-H Saddle River Rd., Saddle Brook, NJ 07662. Alan Paul, Ed. Articles, 5 to 10 double-spaced pages, geared to fitness and sports training, nutrition, running, weight training, etc. Photos. Pays $50 to $400, on publication. Query.

DIABETES SELF-MANAGEMENT—150 W. 22nd St., New York, NY 10011. James Hazlett, Ed. Articles, 2,000 to 4,000 words, for people with diabetes who want to know more about controlling and managing it. Up-to-date and authoritative information on nutrition, pharmacology, exercise physiology, technological advances, self-help, and other how-to subjects. "Articles must be useful, instructive, and must have immediate application to the day-to-day life of our readers. We do not publish personal experience, profiles, exposés, or research breakthroughs." Query with one-page rationale, outline, writing samples, and SASE. Pays from $500, on acceptance. Buys all rights.

EATING WELL—Ferry Rd., P.O. Box 1001, Charlotte, VT 05445. Scott Mowbray, Ed. Bimonthly. "A food book with a health perspective." Feature articles, 2,000 to 5,000 words, for readers who "know that what they eat directly affects their well-being, and believe that with the right approach, one can enjoy both good food and good health." Department pieces, 100 to 200 words, for "Nutrition News" and "Marketplace." "We look for strong journalistic voice; authoritative, timely coverage of nutrition issues; healthful recipes that emphasize good ingredients, simple preparation, and full flavor; and a sense of humor." Query. Pays varying rates, 45 days after acceptance.

FITNESS—The New York Times Company Women's Magazines, 110 Fifth Ave., New York, NY 10011. Rona Cherry, Ed. Articles, 500 to 2,000 words, on health, exercise, sports, nutrition, diet, psychological well-being, sex, and beauty. Average reader is 30 years old. Query required. Pays $1 a word, on acceptance.

HEALTH—(formerly *In Health*) 301 Howard St., 18th Fl., San Francisco, CA 94105. Kate Lee, Ed. Asst. Articles, 1,200 words, for "Food," "Fitness," "Vanities," "Money," "Mind," and "Family" departments. Pays $1,800, on acceptance. Query with clips and SASE required.

IDEA PERSONAL TRAINER—6190 Cornerstone Ct. E., Suite 204, San Diego, CA 92121-3773. Terese Hannon, Asst. Ed. Association publication for personal fitness trainers. Articles on exercise science; program design; profiles of successful trainers; business, legal, and marketing topics; tips for networking with other trainers and with allied medical professionals; client counseling; and training tips. "What's New" column includes industry news, products, and research. Query. Payment varies, on acceptance.

IDEA TODAY—6190 Cornerstone Ct. E., Suite 204, San Diego, CA 92121-3773. Terese Hannon, Asst. Ed. Practical articles, 1,000 to 3,000 words, on new exercise programs, business management, nutrition, sports medicine, dance-exercise, and one-to-one training techniques. Articles must be geared toward the aerobics instructor, exercise studio owner or manager, or personal trainer. No queries on topics for the consumer; no general health ideas. Payment negotiable, on acceptance. Query preferred.

IN HEALTH—See *Health*.

LET'S LIVE—P.O. Box 74908, Los Angeles, CA 90004. Patty Padilla-Gallagher, Ed.-in-Chief. Articles, 1,000 to 1,500 words, on preventive medicine and nutrition, alternative medicine, diet, vitamins, herbs, exercise, recipes, and natural beauty. Pays $150, on publication. Query.

MEDIPHORS—P.O. Box 327, Bloomsburg, PA 17815. Dr. Eugene D. Radice, Ed. "A Literary Journal of the Health Professions." Short stories, essays, and commentary, 3,000 words, related to medicine and health. Poetry, to 30 lines. "We are not a technical journal of science. We do not publish research or review articles, except of a historical nature." Pays in copies. Guidelines.

MUSCULAR DEVELOPMENT—505-H Saddle River Rd., Saddle Brook, NJ 07662. Alan Paul, Ed. Articles, 5 to 10 double-spaced typed pages, geared to serious weight training athletes, on any aspect of competitive body building, powerlifting, sports, and nutrition. Photos. Pays $50 to $400, on publication. Query.

NATURAL FOOD & FARMING—Natural Food Assoc., P.O. Box 210, Atlanta, TX 75551. Lisa Arnold, Janice Elliott, Assoc. Eds. Articles, 2,000 words, on health and nutrition with a focus on naturally grown, chemical-free foods and preventive medicine. Pays $25 on acceptance, plus 5¢ a word, immediately after publication.

NATURAL HEALTH: THE GUIDE TO WELL-BEING—17 Station St., Box 1200, Brookline, MA 02147. Attn: Ed. Bimonthly. Features, 1,500 to 3,000 words, on holistic health, natural foods, herbal remedies, etc., and interviews. Departments and columns, 250 to 1,000 words. Photos. Pays varying rates, on acceptance.

NEW BODY—1700 Broadway, New York, NY 10019. Nicole Dorsey, Ed. Well-researched, service-oriented articles, 800 to 1,200 words, on exercise, nutrition, lifestyle, diet, and health for women ages 18 to 35. Also considers submissions, 500 to 600 words, for "How I Lost It" column, in which writers tell how they lost weight and have kept it off. Writers should have some background in or knowledge of the health field. Pays $100 to $300, on publication. Send detailed query.

NURSING 95—1111 Bethlehem Pike, P.O. Box 908, Springhouse, PA 19477. Patricia Nornhold, Clinical Dir. Most articles are clinically oriented, and are written by nurses for nurses. Also covers legal, ethical, management, and career aspects of nursing; narratives about personal nursing experiences. No poetry. Pays $25 to $300, on publication. Query.

NURSINGWORLD JOURNAL—470 Boston Post Rd., Weston, MA 02193. R. Patrick Gates, Man. Ed. Articles, 500 to 1,500 words, for and by nurses and nurse-educators, on aspects of current nursing issues. Pays $35, on publication.

PATIENT CARE—5 Paragon Dr., Montvale, NJ 07645. Jeffrey H. Forster, Ed. Articles on medical care, for primary-care physicians; mostly staff-written. Pays varying rates, on publication. Query; all articles assigned.

THE PHYSICIAN AND SPORTSMEDICINE—4530 W. 77th St., Minneapolis, MN 55435. Terry Monahan, Man. Ed. News and feature articles; clinical articles coauthored with physician. Sports medicine angle necessary. Pays $150 to $1,000, on acceptance. Guidelines. Query.

A POSITIVE APPROACH—P.O. Box 910, Millville, NJ 08332. Patricia Johnson, Ed. Articles, 500 words, on all aspects of the positive-thinking disabled/ handicapped person's private and business life. Well-researched articles of interest to the visually and hearing impaired, veterans, the arthritic, and all categories of the disabled and handicapped, on interior design, barrier-free architecture, gardening, wardrobe, computers, and careers. No fiction or poetry. Pays in copies.

PREVENTION—33 E. Minor St., Emmaus, PA 18098. Lewis Vaughn, Man. Ed. Query required. No guidelines available. Limited market.

PSYCHOLOGY TODAY—49 E. First St., 11th Fl., New York, NY 10010. Hara E. Marano, Ed. Bimonthly. Articles, 4,000 words, on timely subjects and news. Pays varying rates, on publication.

RX REMEDY—120 Post Rd. W., Westport, CT 06880. Val Weaver, Ed. Bimonthly. Articles, 600 to 2,500 words, on health and medication issues for readers 55 and older. Regular columns include "The Fitness Prescription" and "The Nutrition Prescription." Query. Pays $1 to $1.25 a word, on acceptance.

TODAY'S OR NURSE—Slack Inc., 6900 Grove Rd., Thorofare, NJ 08086. Mary Jo Krey, Man. Ed. Clinical or general articles, from 2,000 words, of direct interest to operating room nurses.

VEGETARIAN TIMES—P.O. Box 570, Oak Park, IL 60303. Toni Apgar, Pub. Articles, 1,200 to 2,500 words, on vegetarian cooking, nutrition, health and fitness, and profiles of prominent vegetarians. "News Items" and "In Print" (book reviews), to 500 words. "Herbalist" pieces, to 1,800 words, on medicinal uses of herbs. Queries required. Pays $75 to $1,000, on acceptance. Guidelines.

VIBRANT LIFE—55 W. Oak Ridge Dr., Hagerstown, MD 21740. Attn: Ed. Features, 750 to 1,500 words, on total health: physical, mental, and spiritual. Upbeat articles on the family and how to live happier and healthier lives; Christian slant. Pays $80 to $250, on acceptance.

VIM & VIGOR—8805 N. 23rd Ave., Suite 11, Phoenix, AZ 85021. Fred Petrovsky, Ed. Positive health and fitness articles, 1,200 to 2,000 words, with accurate medical facts. By assignment only; writers with feature- or news-writing ability may submit qualifications for assignment. Pays $450, on acceptance. Guidelines.

WOMEN & RECOVERY—Need to Know Press, P.O. Box 151947-2, Cupertino, CA 95015-1947. Sara V. Cole, Ed. Quarterly. Essays, exposés, humor, self-help articles, product or treatment profiles and reviews, opinion pieces, 1,000 to 2,000 words, related to women's recovery issues (physical, emotional, and spiritual). Poems, cartoons, B&W photos and drawings. Pays $35 to $100 for articles; $15 to $50 for poetry and art, on publication.

YOGA JOURNAL—2054 University Ave., Berkeley, CA 94704. Rick Fields, Ed. Articles, 1,200 to 4,000 words, on holistic health, meditation, consciousness, spirituality, and yoga. Pays $75 to $800, on publication.

YOUR HEALTH—5401 N.W. Broken Sound Blvd., Boca Raton, FL 33487. Susan Gregg, Ed.-in-Chief. Health and medical articles, 1,000 to 2,000 words, for a lay audience. Queries preferred. Pays $75 to $200, on publication.

YOUR HEALTH—1720 Washington Blvd., Box 10010, Ogden, UT 84409. Attn: Ed. Staff Articles, 1,000 words, on individual health care needs: prevention, treatment, low-impact aerobics, fitness, nutrition, etc. Color photos required. Pays 15¢ a word, on acceptance. Guidelines.

EDUCATION

AMERICAN SCHOOL & UNIVERSITY—401 N. Broad St., Philadelphia, PA 19108. Joe Agron, Ed. Articles and case studies, 1,200 to 1,500 words, on design, construction, operation, and management of school and university facilities. Queries preferred.

THE BOOK REPORT—Linworth Publishing, 480 E. Wilson Bridge Rd., Suite L, Worthington, OH 43085-2372. Carolyn Hamilton, Ed./Pub. "The Journal for Secondary School Librarians." Articles by school librarians or other educators about practical aspects of running a school library. Write for themes and guidelines. Also publishes *Library Talk*, "The Magazine for Elementary School Librarians."

CAREER WOMAN—See *Minority Engineer.*

CAREERS & THE DISABLED—See *Minority Engineer.*

CHANGE—1319 18th St. N.W., Washington, DC 20036. Attn: Ed. Columns, 700 to 2,000 words, and in-depth features, 2,500 to 3,500 words, on programs, people, and institutions of higher education. "We can't usually pay for unsolicited articles."

CHRISTIAN EDUCATION JOURNAL—Scripture Press Ministries, P.O. Box 650, Glen Ellyn, IL 60138. Leslie H. Stobbe, Exec. Ed. Articles, 5 to 15 typed pages, on Christian education topics. Pays $100, on publication. Guidelines.

THE CLEARING HOUSE—Heldref Publications, 1319 18th St. N.W., Washington, DC 20036. Judy Cusick, Man. Ed. Bimonthly for middle level and high school teachers and administrators. Articles, 2,500 words, related to education: useful teaching practices, research findings, and experiments. Some opinion pieces and satirical articles related to education. Pays in copies.

EQUAL OPPORTUNITY—See *Minority Engineer.*

FOUNDATION NEWS—1828 L St. N.W., Washington, DC 20036. Arlie W. Schardt, Ed. Articles, to 2,000 words, on national or regional activities supported by, or of interest to, grant makers and the nonprofit sector. Pays to $1,500, on acceptance. Query.

GIFTED EDUCATION PRESS QUARTERLY—P.O. Box 1586, 10201 Yuma Ct., Manassas, VA 22110. Maurice Fisher, Pub. Articles, to 4,000 words, written by educators, laypersons, and parents of gifted children, on the problems of identifying and teaching gifted children and adolescents. "Interested in incisive analyses of current programs for the gifted and recommendations for improving the education of gifted students. Particularly interested in advocacy for gifted children, biographical sketches of highly gifted individuals, and the problems of teaching humanities, science, ethics, literature, and history to the gifted. Looking for highly imaginative and knowledgeable writers." Query required. Pays in subscription.

THE HISPANIC OUTLOOK IN HIGHER EDUCATION—17 Arcadian Ave., Paramus, NJ 07652. Attn: Man. Ed. Articles, 1,500 to 2,000 words, on the issues, concerns, and potential models for furthering the academic results of Hispanics in higher education. Queries are preferred. Payment varies, on publication.

HOME EDUCATION MAGAZINE—P.O. Box 1083, Tonasket, WA 98855–1083. Helen E. Hegener, Man. Ed. Informative articles, 750 to 2,000 words, on all aspects of the growing homeschool movement. Send complete manuscript or detailed query with SASE. Pays 45¢ per column inch, on publication.

THE HORN BOOK MAGAZINE—11 Beacon St., Suite 1000, Boston, MA 02108. Anita Silvey, Ed. Articles, 600 to 2,800 words, on books for young readers and related subjects for librarians, teachers, parents, etc. Payment varies, on publication. Query.

INDEPENDENT LIVING—See *Minority Engineer.*

INSTRUCTOR MAGAZINE—Scholastic, Inc., 555 Broadway, New York, NY 10012. Mickey Revenaugh, Ed. Articles, 300 to 1,500 words, for teachers in grades K through 8. Payment varies, on acceptance.

ITC COMMUNICATOR—International Training in Communication, P.O. Box 1809, Sutter Creek, CA 95685. JoAnn Levy, Ed. Educational articles, 200 to 800 words, on leadership, language, speech presentation, procedures for meetings, personal and professional development, written and spoken communication techniques. SASE required. Pays in copies.

JOYFUL CHILD JOURNAL—34 Russell Ave., Buffalo, NY 14214. Karen Spring Stevens, Exec. Ed. Quarterly. Fiction and nonfiction, 500 to 1,000 words, that "explore how society and education can more effectively nurture children (and adults) to express their fullest potential, thus releasing their inner joy. Articles on educating and parenting the whole child (body, mind, and spirit)." Some short poetry. Queries preferred. Guidelines. Pays in copies.

654

KEY TO CHRISTIAN EDUCATION—8121 Hamilton Ave., Cincinnati, OH 45231–2396. Barbara Bolton and Lowellette Lauderdale, Eds. Articles, to 1,200 words, on Christian education; tips for teachers in the local church. Pays varying rates, on acceptance.

LEADERSHIP PUBLISHERS, INC.—P.O. Box 8358, Des Moines, IA 50301–8358. Attn: Dr. Lois F. Roets. Educational materials for talented and gifted students, grades K to 12. Send SASE for catalogue and guidelines before submitting. Pays in royalty for books, and flat fee for booklets.

LEARNING 95/96—P.O. Box 9753, Greensboro, NC 27429. Charlene Gaynor, Ed. How-to, why-to, and personal-experience articles, to 3,000 words, for teachers of grades K through 8. Tested classroom ideas for curriculum roundups, to 600 words. Pays to $300 for features, on acceptance.

LIBRARY TALK—See *The Book Report.*

MEDIA & METHODS—1429 Walnut St., Philadelphia, PA 19102. Diane Falten, Man. Ed. Articles, 800 to 1,000 words, on media, technologies, and methods used to enhance instruction and learning in K through 12th-grade classrooms. Pays $50 to $200, on publication. Query required.

MINORITY ENGINEER—150 Motor Parkway, Suite 420, Hauppauge, NY 11788–5145. James Schneider, Exec. Ed. Articles, 1,000 to 1,500 words, for college students, on career opportunities in engineering, techniques of job hunting, and role-model profiles of professional minority engineers. Interviews. Pays 10¢ a word, on publication. Query. Same address and requirements for *Equal Opportunity, Career Woman* (query Eileen Nester), and *Careers & the DisABLED.* For *Woman Engineer* and *Independent Living*, query Editor Anne Kelly.

MOMENTUM—National Catholic Educational Assn., 1077 30th St. N.W., Suite 100, Washington, DC 20007–3852. Patricia Feistritzer, Ed. Articles, 500 to 1,500 words, on outstanding programs, issues, and research in education. Book reviews. Query or send complete manuscript. No simultaneous submissions. Pays 4¢ a word, on publication.

PIII DELTA KAPPAN—8th and Union St., Box 789, Bloomington, IN 47402–0789. Pauline Gough, Ed. Articles, 1,000 to 4,000 words, on educational research, service, and leadership; issues, trends, and policy. Pays from $250, on publication.

SCHOOL ARTS MAGAZINE—50 Portland St., Worcester, MA 01608. Eldon Katter, Ed. Articles, 800 to 1,000 words, on art education with special application to the classroom: successful and meaningful approaches to teaching art, innovative art projects, uncommon applications of art techniques or equipment, etc. Photos. Pays varying rates, on publication. Guidelines.

SCHOOL SAFETY—National School Safety Ctr., 4165 Thousand Oaks Blvd., Suite 290, Westlake Village, CA 91362. Ronald D. Stephens, Exec. Ed. Published 8 times during the school year. Articles, 2,000 to 3,000 words, of use to educators, law enforcers, judges, and legislators on the prevention of drugs, gangs, weapons, bullying, discipline problems, and vandalism; also on-site security and character development as they relate to students and schools. No payment made.

TEACHING K-8—40 Richards Ave., Norwalk, CT 06854. Patricia Broderick, Ed. Dir. Articles, 1,200 words, on the profession of teaching children. Queries are not necessary. Pays to $35, on publication.

TECH DIRECTIONS—Box 8623, Ann Arbor, MI 48107. Paul J. Bamford, Man. Ed. Articles, one to 10 double-spaced typed pages, for teachers and administrators in industrial, technology, and vocational educational fields, with particular interest in classroom projects, computer uses, and legislative issues. Pays $10 to $150, on publication. Guidelines.

TECHNOLOGY & LEARNING—Peter Li, Inc., 2169 E. Francisco Blvd. E., Suite A-4, San Rafael, CA 94901. Judy Salpeter, Ed. Articles, to 3,000 words, for teachers of grades K through 12, about uses of computers and related technology in the classroom: human-interest and philosophical articles, how-to pieces, software reviews, and hands-on ideas. Pay varies, on acceptance.

TODAY'S CATHOLIC TEACHER—330 Progress Rd., Dayton, OH 45449. Stephen Brittan, Ed. Articles, 600 to 800 words, 1,000 to 1,200 words, and 1,200 to 1,500 words, on education, parent-teacher relationships, innovative teaching, teaching techniques, etc., of use to educators. Pays $65 to $250, on publication. SASE required. Query. Guidelines.

WILSON LIBRARY BULLETIN—950 University Ave., Bronx, NY 10452. GraceAnne A. DeCandido, Ed. Articles, 1,800 to 3,600 words, on libraries, communications, and information systems. News, reports, features. Pays $100 to $300, extra for photos, on publication.

WOMAN ENGINEER—See *Minority Engineer.*

FARMING AND AGRICULTURE

ACRES USA—P.O. Box 8800, Metairie, CA 70011. Fred C. Walters, Ed. Articles on biological agriculture: technology, case reports, "hands-on" advice. "Our emphasis is on production of quality food without the use of toxic chemicals." Pays 6¢ a word, on acceptance.

AMERICAN BEE JOURNAL—51 N. Second St., Hamilton, IL 62341. Joe M. Graham, Ed. Articles on beekeeping, for professionals. Photos. Pays 75¢ a column inch, extra for photos, on publication.

BUCKEYE FARM NEWS—Ohio Farm Bureau Federation, Two Nationwide Plaza, Box 479, Columbus, OH 43216–0479. Lynn Echelberger, Copy Ed. Articles, to 600 words, related to agriculture. Pays on publication. Query. Limited market.

DAIRY GOAT JOURNAL—W. 2997 Markert Rd., Helenville, WI 53137. Dave Thompson, Ed. Articles, to 1,500 words, on successful dairy goat owners, youths and interesting people associated with dairy goats. "Especially interested in practical husbandry ideas." Photos. Pays $50 to $150, on publication. Query.

FARM INDUSTRY NEWS—7900 International Dr., Minneapolis, MN 55425. Joe Degnan, Ed. Articles for farmers, on new products, machinery, equipment, chemicals, and seeds. Pays $350 to $500, on acceptance. Query required.

FARM JOURNAL—230 W. Washington Sq., Philadelphia, PA 19106. Earl Ainsworth, Ed. Articles, 500 to 1,500 words, with photos, on the business of farming. Pays 20¢ to 50¢ a word, on acceptance. Query.

FLORIDA GROWER & RANCHER—1331 N. Mills Ave., Orlando, FL 32803. Frank Garner, Ed. Articles and case histories on Florida farmers, growers, and ranchers. Pays on publication. Query; buys little freelance material.

THE FURROW—Deere & Co., John Deere Rd., Moline, IL 61265. George Sollenberger, Exec. Ed. Specialized, illustrated articles on farming. Pays to $1,000, on acceptance.

HARROWSMITH—Telemedia Communications, Inc., Camden East, Ont., Canada K0K 1J0. Arlene Stacey, Ed. Articles, 700 to 3,000 words, on country life, organic gardening, and alternative energy. Pays $150 to $1,500, on acceptance. Query with SAE/international reply coupon.

HARROWSMITH COUNTRY LIFE—Ferry Rd., Charlotte, VT 05445. Attn: Ed. Dept. Articles, 3,000 to 4,000 words, on country living, community issues, health, gardening, do-it-yourself projects, and the food chain. News briefs for "Gazette." Pays $500 to $1,500 for features, $50 to $600 for department pieces, on acceptance. Query required. Send SASE for guidelines.

NATURAL FOOD & FARMING—Natural Foods Associates, P.O. Box 210, Atlanta, TX 75551. Lisa Arnold, Janice Elliott, Assoc. Eds. Articles, 2,000 words, on health and nutrition with a focus on naturally grown, chemical-free foods and preventive medicine. "We want articles that help develop the interrelationship between the living soil and human health." Pays $25 on acceptance, plus 5¢ a word, immediately after publication.

OHIO FARMER—1350 W. Fifth Ave., Columbus, OH 43212. Tim White, Ed. Articles on farming, rural living, etc., in Ohio. Pays $50 per column, on publication.

PEANUT FARMER—3000 Highwoods Blvd., Suite 300, Raleigh, NC 27604–1029. Mary Evans, Man. Ed. Articles, 500 to 2,000 words, on production and management practices in peanut farming. Pays $50 to $350, on publication.

PENNSYLVANIA FARMER—704 Lisburn Rd., Camp Hill, PA 17011. John R. Vogel, Ed. Articles on farmers in PA, NJ, DE, MD, and WV; timely business-of-farming concepts and successful farm management operations. Short pieces on humorous experiences in farming. Payment varies, on publication.

RURAL HERITAGE—281 Dean Ridge Ln., Gainesboro, TN 38562. Gail Damerow, Ed. How-to and feature articles, 1,200 to 1,600 words, related to rural living and draft horses, mules, and oxen. Short pieces, to 800 words, and special features, to 2,000 words, also considered. Pays 5¢ a word, $10 for photos, on publication. SASE for guidelines.

SHEEP! MAGAZINE—W. 2997 Markert Rd., Helenville, WI 53137. Dave Thompson, Ed. Articles, to 1,500 words, on successful shepherds, woolcrafts, sheep raising, and sheep dogs. "Especially interested in people who raise sheep successfully as a sideline enterprise." Photos. Pays $80 to $150, extra for photos, on publication. Query.

SMALL FARM TODAY—3903 W. Ridge Trail Rd., Clark, MO 65243–9525. Paul Berg, Man. Ed. Agriculture articles, 800 to 1,800 words, on preserving and promoting small farming, rural living, and "agripreneurship." How-to articles on alternative crops, livestock, and direct marketing. Pays 3 ½ ¢ a word, on publication. Query.

SUCCESSFUL FARMING—1716 Locust St., Des Moines, IA 50309–3023. Gene Johnston, Man. Ed. Articles on farm production, business, and families; also farm personalities, health, leisure, and outdoor topics. Pays varying rates, on acceptance.

TOPICS IN VETERINARY MEDICINE—812 Springdale Dr., Exton, PA 19341–2803. Kathleen Etchison, Ed. Technical articles, 1,200 to 1,500 words, and clinical features, 500 words, on veterinary medicine. Photos. Pays $300, $150 for shorter pieces, extra for photos, on publication.

WALLACES FARMER—6200 Aurora Ave., Suite 609E, Urbandale, IA 50322–2838. Monte Sesker, Ed. Features, 600 to 700 words, on farming in Iowa; methods and equipment; interviews with farmers. Query. Payment varies, on acceptance.

ENVIRONMENT AND CONSERVATION

THE AMERICAN FIELD—542 S. Dearborn, Chicago, IL 60605. B.J. Matthys, Man. Ed. Yarns about hunting trips, bird-shooting; articles, to 1,500 words, on dogs and field trials, emphasizing conservation of game resources. Pays varying rates, on acceptance.

AMERICAN FORESTS—1516 P St. N.W., Washington, DC 20005. Bill Rooney, Ed. Well-documented articles, to 2,000 words, with photos, on the use, enjoyment, and management of forests. Photos. Pays on acceptance.

THE AMICUS JOURNAL—Natural Resources Defense Council, 40 W. 20th St., New York, NY 10011. Kathrin Day Lassila, Ed. Quarterly. Articles and book reviews on national and international environmental topics. (No fiction, essays, speeches, or product reports accepted.) Query with SASE required. Pays varying rates, 30 days after publication.

ANIMALS—350 S. Huntington Ave., Boston, MA 02130. Joni Praded, Dir./ Ed. Informative, well-researched articles, to 2,500 words, on animal protection, national and international wildlife, pet care, conservation, and environmental issues that affect animals. No personal accounts or favorite pet stories. Pays from $350, on acceptance. Query.

ATLANTIC SALMON JOURNAL—P.O. Box 429, St. Andrews, N.B., Canada E0G 2X0. Harry Bruce, Ed. Articles, 1,500 to 3,000 words, related to Atlantic salmon: fishing, conservation, ecology, travel, politics, biology, how-tos, anecdotes. Pays $100 to $400, on publication.

AUDUBON—700 Broadway, New York, NY 10003. Michael W. Robbins, Ed. Bimonthly. Articles, 1,000 to 4,000 words, on conservation and environmental issues, natural history, ecology, and related subjects. Payment varies, on acceptance. Query.

BIRD WATCHER'S DIGEST—P.O. Box 110, Marietta, OH 45750. William H. Thompson, III, Ed. Articles, 600 to 2,500 words, for bird watchers: first-person accounts; how-tos; pieces on endangered species; profiles. Cartoons. Pays from $50, on publication.

EQUINOX—25 Sheppard Ave. W., Suite 100, North York, Ont., Canada M2N 6S7. Jim Cormier, Ed. Alan Morantz, "Nexus" Ed. Articles, 3,000 to 6,000 words, on popular geography, wildlife, astronomy, science, the arts, travel, and adventure. Department pieces, 300 to 800 words, for "Nexus" (science and medicine). Pays $1,500 to $3,500 for features, $100 to $500 for short pieces, on acceptance.

FLORIDA WILDLIFE—620 S. Meridian St., Tallahassee, FL 32399–1600. Attn: Ed. Bimonthly of the Florida Game and Fresh Water Fish Commission. Articles, 800 to 1,200 words, that promote native flora and fauna, hunting, fishing in Florida's fresh waters, outdoor ethics, and conservation of Florida's natural resources. Pays $50 to $400, on publication.

658

HARROWSMITH COUNTRY LIFE—Ferry Rd., Charlotte, VT 05445. Attn: Editorial Dept. Feature articles, 1,000 to 4,000 words, on practical country living, gardening, rural and community issues, natural history, house profiles (design, construction, and restoration). How-to and do-it-yourself building, country skills, gardening projects. Profiles of country careers, news briefs, and product and book reviews. Pays $500 to $1,500 for features; $50 to $600 for department pieces. Query with SASE required. Guidelines.

INTERNATIONAL WILDLIFE—8925 Leesburg Pike, Vienna, VA 22184. Donna Johnson, Assoc. Ed. Short features, 700 words, and 1,500- to 2,500-word articles that make nature, and human use and stewardship of it, understandable and interesting. Pays $500 for one-page features, $1,800 for full-length articles, on acceptance. Writers must query with writing samples. Very limited free-lance needs. Guidelines.

NATIONAL GEOGRAPHIC—17th and M Sts. N.W., Washington, DC 20036. William P.E. Graves, Ed. First-person, general-interest, heavily illustrated articles on science, natural history, exploration, and geographical regions. Written query required.

NATIONAL PARKS MAGAZINE—1776 Massachusetts Ave., Washington, DC 20036. Sue E. Dodge, Ed. Articles, 1,500 to 2,500 words, on areas in the National Park System, proposed new areas, threats to parks or park wildlife, new trends in park use, legislative issues, and endangered species of plants or animals relevant to national parks. Pays $100 to $800, on acceptance. Query. Guidelines.

NATIONAL WILDLIFE—8925 Leesburg Pike, Vienna, VA 22184. Mark Wexler, Ed. Articles, 1,000 to 2,500 words, on wildlife, conservation, environment; outdoor how-to pieces. Photos. Pays on acceptance. Query.

OUTDOOR TRAVELER, MID-ATLANTIC—WMS Publications, Inc., P.O. Box 2748, Charlottesville, VA 22902. Marianne Marks, Ed. Scott Clark, Assoc. Ed. Articles, 2,500 to 3,000 words, about outdoor recreation, travel, adventure, and nature in the mid-Atlantic region (NY, PA, NJ, MD, DE, DC, WV, VA, and NC). Departments include "Destinations," 450 to 600 words, on practical and descriptive guides to sports destinations; "Getaways," B&Bs and inns, including seasonal and outdoor activities; book reviews, 200 words. Pays $500 to $650 for features; payment varies for departments, on publication. Guidelines.

SEA FRONTIERS—400 S.E. Second Ave., 4th Fl., Miami, FL 33131. Bonnie Bilyeu Gordon, Ed. Illustrated articles, 500 to 3,000 words, on scientific advances related to the sea, biological, physical, chemical, or geological phenomena, ecology, conservation, etc., written in a popular style for lay readers. Send SASE for guidelines. Pays 25¢ a word, on acceptance. Query.

SMITHSONIAN MAGAZINE—900 Jefferson Dr., Washington, DC 20560. Marlane A. Liddell, Articles Ed. Articles on history, art, natural history, physical science, profiles, etc. Query with clips and SASE.

SPORTS AFIELD—250 W. 55th St., New York, NY 10019. Terry McDonell, Ed. Articles, 500 to 2,000 words, with quality photos, on hunting, fishing, natural history, survival, conservation, ecology, personal experiences. How-to pieces; humor, fiction. Payment varies, on acceptance.

TEXAS PARKS & WILDLIFE—Fountain Park Plaza, 3000 S. Interstate Hwy. 35, Suite 120, Austin, TX 78704. Jim Cox, Sr. Ed. Articles, 800 to 1,500 words, promoting the conservation and enjoyment of Texas wildlife, parks, waters, and all outdoors. Features on hunting, fishing, birding, camping, and the environment. Department pieces, to 1,000 words, for "Parks & Places to Go," "State of

Nature," and "Woods and Waters." Profiles of personalities who have made important contributions to the conservation in Texas. Photos a plus. Pays to $600, on acceptance; extra for photos.

VIRGINIA WILDLIFE—P.O. Box 11104, Richmond, VA 23230–1104. Attn: Ed. Articles, 1,500 to 2,000 words, on conservation and related topics, including fishing, hunting, wildlife management, outdoor safety, ethics, etc. All material must have Virginia tie-in and be accompanied by color photos. Query with SASE. Pays from 10¢ a word, extra for photos, on acceptance.

WILDLIFE CONSERVATION—The Wildlife Conservation Society, Bronx, NY 10460. Nancy Simmons, Sr. Ed. First-person articles, 1,500 to 2,000 words, on "popular" natural history, "based on author's research and experience as opposed to textbook approach." Payment varies, on acceptance. Guidelines.

MEDIA AND THE ARTS

AHA! HISPANIC ARTS NEWS—Assoc. of Hispanic Arts, 173 E. 116th St., New York, NY 10029–1302. Dolores Prida, Ed. Feature articles, editorials, reviews, and monthly calendars. Query.

AIRBRUSH ACTION—P.O. Box 2052, 1985 Swarthmore Ave., Lakewood, NJ 08701. Attn: Eds. Articles, 500 to 3,000 words, on airbrushing, graphics, and art-related topics. Pays $75 to $300, on publication. Query.

THE AMERICAN ART JOURNAL—730 Fifth Ave., Suite 205, New York, NY 10019–4105. Jayne A. Kuchna, Ed. Scholarly articles, 2,000 to 10,000 words, on American art of the 17th through the early 20th centuries. Photos. Pays $200 to $500, on acceptance.

AMERICAN INDIAN ART MAGAZINE—7314 E. Osborn Dr., Scottsdale, AZ 85251. Roanne P. Goldfein, Ed. Detailed articles, 10 double-spaced pages, on American Indian arts: painting, carving, beadwork, basketry, textiles, ceramics, jewelry, etc. Pays varying rates, on publication. Query.

AMERICAN JOURNALISM REVIEW—8701 Adelphi Rd., Adelphi, MD 20783. Rem Rieder, Ed. Articles, 500 to 5,000 words, on print or electronic journalism, ethics, and related issues. Pays 20¢ a word, on publication. Query.

AMERICAN THEATRE—355 Lexington Ave., New York, NY 10017. Jim O'Quinn, Ed. Features, 500 to 4,000 words, on the theater and theater-related subjects. Payment negotiable, on publication. Query.

AMERICAN VISIONS, THE MAGAZINE OF AFRO-AMERICAN CULTURE—2101 S St. N.W., Washington, DC 20008–4011. Joanne Harris, Ed. Articles, 1,500 words, and columns, 750 to 2,000 words, on African-American culture with a focus on the arts. Pays from $100 to $1,000, on publication. Query.

ART & ANTIQUES—919 Third Ave., 15th Fl., New York, NY 10022. Mark Mayfield, Ed. Investigative pieces or personal narratives, 1,500 words, and news items, 300 to 500 words, on art or antiques. Pays $1 a word, on publication. Query.

THE ARTIST'S MAGAZINE—1507 Dana Ave., Cincinnati, OH 45207. Mary Magnus, Ed. Features, 1,200 to 2,500 words, and department pieces for the working artist. Poems, to 20 lines, on art and creativity. Single-panel cartoons. Pays $150 to $350 for articles; $65 for cartoons, on acceptance. Guidelines. Query.

ARTS ATLANTIC—145 Richmond St., Charlottetown, P.E.I., Canada C1A 1J1. Joseph Sherman, Ed. Articles and reviews, 600 to 3,000 words, on visual,

660

performing, and literary arts in Atlantic Canada. Also, "idea and concept" articles of universal appeal. Query.

BLUEGRASS UNLIMITED—Box 111, Broad Run, VA 22014–0111. Peter V. Kuykendall, Ed. Articles, to 3,500 words, on bluegrass and traditional country music. Photos. Pays 8¢ to 10¢ a word, extra for photos.

BRIGHT LIGHTS FILM JOURNAL—P.O. Box 420987, San Francisco, CA 94142–0987. Gary Morris, Ed.-in-Chief. Quarterly. Publishes film analysis, commentary, and history, 1,000 to 10,000 words, with an emphasis on social and cultural forces that shape films, past and present. "We deal with all forms of cinema, from 'high art' films to mainstream Hollywood to independent and world cinema." Payment is in copies.

CAMERA & DARKROOM—9171 Wilshire Blvd., Suite 300, Beverly Hills, CA 90210. Ana Jones, Ed. Articles on photographic techniques and photographic portfolios, 1,000 to 2,500 words, with photos, for all levels of photographers. Pays $100 to $750. Query.

CLAVIER MAGAZINE—200 Northfield Rd., Northfield, IL 60093. James T. Rohner, Pub. Practical articles, interviews, master classes, and humor pieces, 2,000 words, for keyboard performers and teachers. Pays $40 to $80 per published page, on publication.

DANCE MAGAZINE—33 W. 60th St., New York, NY 10023. Richard Philp, Ed.-in-Chief. Features on dance, personalities, techniques, health issues, and trends. Photos. Query; limited free-lance market.

DANCE TEACHER NOW—3101 Poplarwood Ct., Suite 310, Raleigh, NC 27604. K.C. Patrick, Ed. Articles, 1,000 to 3,000 words, for professional dance educators, senior students, and other dance professionals on practical information for the teacher and/or business owner; economic and historical issues related to the profession. Profiles of schools, methods, and people who are leaving their mark on dance. Must be thoroughly researched. Photos a plus. Pays $200 to $350, on acceptance. Query preferred.

DRAMATICS—Educational Theatre Assoc., 3368 Central Pkwy., Cincinnati, OH 45225–2392. Don Corathers, Ed. Articles, interviews, how-tos, 750 to 4,000 words, for high school students on the performing arts with an emphasis on theater practice: acting, directing, playwriting, technical subjects. Prefer articles that "could be used by a better-than-average high school teacher to teach students something about the performing arts." Pays $25 to $300 honorarium. Complete manuscripts preferred; graphics and photos accepted.

THE ENGRAVERS JOURNAL—26 Summit St., P. O. Box 318, Brighton, MI 48116. Rosemary Farrell, Man. Ed. Articles, varying lengths, on topics related to the engraving industry and small business operations. Pays $60 to $175, on acceptance. Query.

FILM QUARTERLY—Univ. of California Press Journals, 2120 Berkeley Way, Berkeley, CA 94720. Ann Martin, Ed. Historical, analytical, and critical articles, to 6,000 words; film reviews, book reviews. Guidelines.

FLUTE TALK—Instrumentalist Publishing Co., 200 Northfield Rd., Northfield, IL 60093. Kathleen Goll-Wilson, Ed. Articles, 6 to 12 typed pages, on flute performance, music, and pedagogy; fillers; photos and line drawings. Thorough knowledge of music or the instrument a must. Pays honorarium, on publication. Queries preferred.

THE FUTURE, NOW: INNOVATIVE VIDEO—Blue Feather Co., N8494 Poplar Grove Rd., P.O. Box 669, New Glarus, WI 53574–0669. Jennifer M. Jarik, Ed. Bimonthly. Articles, to 2 pages, on new ideas in the video business. Pays from $75 to $100, on publication.

GUITAR PLAYER MAGAZINE—411 Borel Ave., Suite 100, San Mateo, CA 94402. Attn: Ed. Articles, 1,500 to 5,000 words, on guitarists, guitars, and related subjects. Pays $100 to $400, on acceptance. Buys one-time and reprint rights.

INDIA CURRENTS—P.O. Box 21285, San Jose, CA 95151. Arvind Kumar, Submissions Ed. Fiction, to 1,500 words, and articles, to 800 words, on Indian culture in the United States and Canada. Articles on Indian arts, entertainment, and dining. Also music and book reviews, 300 words, and commentary on national or international events affecting the lives of Indians, 800 words. Pays in subscriptions. Guidelines.

INDUSTRIAL PHOTOGRAPHY—445 Broadhollow Rd., Melville, NY 11747. Steve Shaw, Ed. Articles on techniques and trends in current professional photography, audiovisuals, etc., for industrial photographers and executives. Query.

INTERNATIONAL MUSICIAN—Paramount Bldg., 1501 Broadway, Suite 600, New York, NY 10036. Attn: Ed. Articles, 1,500 to 2,000 words, for professional musicians. Pays varying rates, on acceptance. Query.

JAZZIZ—3620 N.W. 43rd St. #D, Gainesville, FL 32606. Roy Parkhurst, Sr. Ed. Feature articles on all aspects of adult contemporary music: interviews, profiles, concept pieces. Departments include reviews of a variety of music genres, radio, and video. Emphasis on new releases. Send resumé with manuscript. Pays varying rates, on acceptance. Query.

LIVING BLUES—Hill Hall, Room 301, Univ. of Mississippi, University, MS 38677. David Nelson, Ed. Articles, 1,500 to 10,000 words, about living African-American blues artists. Interviews. Occasional retrospective/historical articles or investigative pieces. Query. Pays $75 to $200, on publication; $25 per B&W photo.

MEDIA HISTORY DIGEST—c/o *Editor & Publisher*, 11 W. 19th St., New York, NY 10011. Hiley H. Ward, Ed. Articles, 1,500 to 2,000 words, on the history of media, for wide consumer audience. Puzzles and humor related to media history. Pays varying rates, on publication. Query.

MODERN DRUMMER—870 Pompton Ave., Cedar Grove, NJ 07009. Ronald L. Spagnardi, Ed. Articles, 500 to 2,000 words, on drumming: how-tos, interviews. Pays $50 to $500, on publication.

NEW ENGLAND ENTERTAINMENT DIGEST—P.O. Box 313, Portland, CT 06480. Bob Taylor, Ed. News and features on the arts and entertainment industry in New England. Pays $10 to $25, on publication.

OPERA NEWS—The Metropolitan Opera Guild, 70 Lincoln Ctr. Plaza, New York, NY 10023–6593. Patrick J. Smith, Ed. Articles, 600 to 2,500 words, on all aspects of opera. Payment varies, on publication. Query.

PERFORMANCE—1101 University Dr., Suite 108, Fort Worth, TX 76107. Don Waitt, Pub./Ed.-in-Chief. Reports on the touring industry: concert promoters, booking agents, concert venues and clubs, as well as support services, such as lighting, sound, and staging companies.

PETERSEN'S PHOTOGRAPHIC—6420 Wilshire Blvd., Los Angeles, CA 90048–5515. Jenni Bidner, Ed. Articles and how-to pieces, with photos, on travel, video, and darkroom photography, for beginners, advanced amateurs, and professionals. Pays $100 per printed page, on publication.

PHOTO: ELECTRONIC IMAGING MAGAZINE—57 Forsyth St. N.W., Suite 1600, Atlanta, GA 30303. Kimberly Brady, Ed.-in-Chief. Articles, 1,000 to 3,000 words, on silver-halide still and cine photography, video, electronic imaging, and multimedia. Material must be directly related to professional imaging techniques for business, military, government, education, scientific, and industrial photographers. Query required; all articles on assignment only. Payment varies, on publication.

PLAY—3620 N.W. 43rd St. #D, Gainesville, FL 32606. Roy Parkhurst, Sr. Ed. Features, articles, and departments covering educational entertainment products for children: music, spoken word, video, electronics, books, computers, games, and other interactive toys. Targeted to parents; also includes clinical discussions of child development. Pays varying rates, on acceptance. Query.

PLAYBILL—52 Vanderbilt Ave., New York, NY 10017. Joan Alleman, Ed.-in-Chief. Sophisticated articles, 700 to 1,800 words, with photos, on theater and subjects of interest to theatergoers. Pays $100 to $500, on acceptance.

POPULAR PHOTOGRAPHY—1633 Broadway, New York, NY 10019. Jason Schneider, Ed.-in-Chief. How-to articles, 500 to 2,000 words, for amateur photographers. Query with outline and photos.

PREVUE—P.O. Box 974, Reading, PA 19603. J. Steranko, Ed. Lively articles, interviews, and illustrated features, 4 to 25 pages, on women and the arts (film and TV actresses, singers, comics, dancers, strippers, artists, celebrities, models, etc.). Pays varying rates, on acceptance. Query with clips.

RIFF—7011 Realm Dr., Suite A3, San Jose, CA 95119. Michael J. Vaughn, Ed. Profiles, 1,000 and 1,500 words, of jazz artists, and articles on other jazz-related subjects. Prefer articles with a San Francisco Bay area connection. Query preferred. Pays $50 to $100, on publication.

ROLLING STONE—1290 Ave. of the Americas, 2nd Fl., New York, NY 10104. Attn: Ed. Magazine of American music, culture, and politics. No fiction. Query; no unsolicited manuscripts. Rarely accepts free-lance material.

SHEET MUSIC MAGAZINE—223 Katonah Ave., Katonah, NY 10536. Josephine Sblendorio, Man. Ed. Pieces, 1,000 to 2,000 words, for pianists and organists, on musicians and composers, how-tos, and book reviews, to 500 words; no hard rock or heavy metal subjects. Pays $75 to $200, on publication.

SOUTHWEST ART—5444 Westheimer, Suite 1440, Houston, TX 77056. Susan McGarry, Ed. Articles, 1,200 to 1,800 words, on the artists, art collectors, museum exhibitions, gallery events and dealers, art history, and art trends west of the Mississippi River. Particularly interested in representational or figurative arts. Pays from $400, on acceptance. Query with slides of artwork to be featured.

STAGE DIRECTIONS—SMW Communications, Inc., 3101 Poplarwood Ct., Suite 310, Raleigh, NC 27604. Stephen Peithman, Ed. How-to articles, to 2,000 words, on costuming, makeup, lighting, set design and decoration, props, special effects, fundraising, and audience development for readers who are active in all aspects of community, regional, academic, or youth theater. Short pieces, 400 to 500 words, "are a good way to approach us first." Pays to $100, on publication. Guidelines.

STORYTELLING MAGAZINE—P.O. Box 309, Jonesborough, TN 37659. Attn: Eds. How-to articles, 800 to 1,500 words, and personal experience, 800 words, related to storytelling. One story (1,000 words) per issue. Pays in copies. "Limited market; most articles are written by members of the National Storytelling Assn. or experts in the fields related to the oral tradition."

TCI—(formerly *Theatre Crafts Magazine*) 32 W. 18th St., New York, NY 10011. Patricia MacKay, Pub. David Barbour, Ed. Articles, 500 to 2,500 words, on design, technical, and management aspects of theater, opera, dance, television, and film for those in performing arts and the entertainment trade. Pays on acceptance. Query.

TDR (THE DRAMA REVIEW): A JOURNAL OF PERFORMANCE STUDIES—721 Broadway, 6th Fl., New York, NY 10003. Richard Schechner, Ed. Eclectic articles on experimental performance and performance theory; cross-cultural, examining the social, political, historical, and theatrical contexts in which performance happens. Submit query or manuscript with SASE and disk. Pays $100 to $250, on publication.

THEATRE CRAFTS MAGAZINE—See *TCI Magazine.*

U.S. ART—220 S. Sixth St., Suite 500, Minneapolis, MN 55402. Frank J. Sisser, Ed./Pub. Features and artist profiles, 2,000 words, for collectors of limited-edition art prints. Query. Pays $400 to $450, within 30 days of acceptance.

VIDEO MAGAZINE—460 W. 34th St., New York, NY 10001. Stan Pinkwas, Man. Ed. How-to and service articles, 300 to 2,000 words, on home video equipment, technology, and programming; related human-interest features. Pays varying rates, on acceptance. Query.

VIDEOMAKER—P.O. Box 4591, Chico, CA 95927. Stephen Muratore, Ed. Authoritative, how-to articles geared to hobbyist and professional video camera/camcorder users: instructionals, editing, desktop video, audio and video production, innovative applications, tools and tips, industry developments, new products, etc. Pays varying rates, on publication. Queries preferred.

HOBBIES, CRAFTS, COLLECTING

AMERICAN HOW-TO—12301 Whitewater Dr., Suite 260, Minnetonka, MN 55343. Tom Sweeney, Ed. Bimonthly. Articles, 1,000 to 1,500 words, for homeowners interested in do-it-yourself projects. Carpentry, plumbing, electrical work, landscaping, masonry, tools, woodworking, and new products. Pays 50¢ a word, on acceptance. Queries preferred. Send SASE for editorial calendar with upcoming themes.

AMERICAN WOODWORKER—Rodale Press, 33 E. Minor St., Emmaus, PA 18098. David Sloan, Ed. "A how-to bimonthly for the woodworking enthusiast." Technical or anecdotal articles, to 2,000 words, relating to woodworking or furniture design. Fillers, drawings, slides and photos considered. Pays from $150 per published page, on publication; regular contributors paid on acceptance. Queries preferred. Guidelines.

ANCESTRY—P.O. Box 476, Salt Lake City, UT 84110. Loretto Szucs, Acquisitions Ed. Bimonthly for genealogists and hobbyists who are interested in getting the most out of their research. Articles, 1,500 to 4,000 words, that instruct (how-tos, research techniques, etc.) and inform (new research sources, new collections, etc.). No family histories, genealogies, or pedigree charts. Pays $25 to $75, on publication. Guidelines.

THE ANTIQUE TRADER WEEKLY—Box 1050, Dubuque, IA 52004. Kyle D. Husfloen, Ed. Articles, 1,000 to 2,000 words, on all types of antiques and collectors' items. Photos. Pays from $25 to $200, on publication. Query preferred. Buys all rights.

ANTIQUES & AUCTION NEWS—P.O. Box 500, Mount Joy, PA 17552. Attn: Ed. Weekly newspaper. Factual articles, 600 to 1,500 words, on antiques, collectors, collections, and places of historic interest. Photos. Query required. Pays $5 to $20, after publication.

ANTIQUEWEEK—P.O. Box 90, Knightstown, IN 46148. Tom Hoepf, Ed., Central Edition; Connie Swaim, Ed., Eastern Edition. Weekly antique, auction, and collectors' newspaper. Articles, 500 to 1,500 words, on antiques, collectibles, restorations, genealogy, auction and antique show reports. Photos. Pays from $40 to $150 for in-depth articles, on publication. Query. Guidelines.

AQUARIUM FISH—P.O. Box 6050, Mission Viejo, CA 92690. Edward Bauman, Ed. Articles, 2,000 to 4,000 words, on freshwater, saltwater, and pond fish, with or without color transparencies. (No "pet fish" stories, please.) Payment varies, on publication.

AUTOGRAPH COLLECTOR MAGAZINE—510-A S. Corona Mall, Corona, CA 91720. Kevin Sherman, Ed. Articles, 1,000 to 3,500 words, on all areas of autograph collecting: preservation, framing, and storage, specialty collections, documents and letters, collectors and dealers. Queries preferred. Payment varies.

BECKETT BASEBALL CARD MONTHLY—15850 Dallas Pkwy., Dallas, TX 75248. Mike Payne, Ed. Articles, 500 to 2,000 words, geared to baseball-card collecting, with an emphasis on the pleasures of the hobby. "We accept no stories with investment tips." Query. Pays $100 to $250, on acceptance. Guidelines.

BECKETT BASKETBALL MONTHLY—15850 Dallas Pkwy., Dallas, TX 75248. Randy Cummings, Assoc. Ed. Articles, 400 to 1,000 words, on the sports-card hobby, especially basketball card collecting for readers 10 to 25. Query. Pays $100 to $250, on acceptance. Also publishes *Beckett Football Card Monthly, Beckett Focus on Future Stars, Beckett Hockey Monthly,* and *Beckett Racing Monthly.* SASE for guidelines.

BIRD TALK—Box 6050, Mission Viejo, CA 92690. Julie Rach, Ed. Articles for pet bird owners: care and feeding, training, safety, outstanding personal adventures, exotic birds in their native countries, profiles of celebrities' pet birds, travel to bird parks or shows. Pays 10¢ a word, after publication. Query or send manuscript; good transparencies a plus.

BIRD WATCHER'S DIGEST—P.O. Box 110, Marietta, OH 45750. Mary B. Bowers, Ed. Articles, 600 to 3,000 words, on bird-watching experiences and expeditions: information about rare sightings; updates on endangered species. Pays from $50, on publication. Allow 8 weeks for response.

CANADIAN STAMP NEWS—103 Lakeshore Rd., Suite 202, St. Catharines, Ont., Canada L2N 2T6. Ellen Rodger, Ed. Biweekly. Articles, 1,000 to 2,000 words, on stamp collecting news, rare and unusual stamps, and auction and club reports. Special issues throughout the year; send for guidelines. Photos. Pays from $70, on publication.

CANADIAN WORKSHOP MAGAZINE—130 Spy Ct., Markham, Ont., Canada L3R 5H6. Jo Currie, Ed. Articles, 1,500 to 2,800 words, on do-it-yourself home renovations, energy saving projects, etc., with photos. Pays varying rates, on acceptance.

CARD COLLECTOR'S PRICE GUIDE—155 E. Ames Ct., Plainview, NY 11803. Attn: Ed. Office. Articles, from 800 words, related to non-sports cards (comic cards, TV/movie cards, science fiction cards, etc.); collecting and investing; fillers. Queries preferred. Pays 10¢ a word, on publication.

CARD PLAYER—3140 S. Polaris #8, Las Vegas, NV 89102. Linda Johnson, Pub. "The Magazine for Those Who Play to Win." Articles on poker events, personalities, legal issues, new casinos, tournaments, and prizes. Also articles on strategies, theory and game psychology to improve poker play. Occasionally uses humor, cartoons, puzzles, or anecdotal material. Pays $50 to $200, on publication; $25 to $35 for fillers. Guidelines.

THE CAROUSEL NEWS & TRADER—87 Park Ave. W., Suite 206, Mansfield, OH 44902. Attn: Ed. Features on carousel history and profiles of amusement park operators and carousel carvers of interest to band organ enthusiasts, carousel art collectors, preservationists, amusement park owners, artists, and restorationists. Pays $50 per published page, after publication. Guidelines.

CHESS LIFE—186 Rte. 9W, New Windsor, NY 12553–7698. Glenn Petersen, Ed. Articles, 500 to 3,000 words, for members of the U.S. Chess Federation, on news, profiles, technical aspects of chess. Features on all aspects of chess: history, humor, puzzles, etc. Fiction, 500 to 2,000 words, related to chess. Photos. Pays varying rates, on acceptance. Query; limited free-lance market.

CLASSIC TOY TRAINS—21027 Crossroads Cir., Waukesha, WI 53187. Attn: Ed. Articles, with photos, on toy train layouts and collections. Also train manufacturing history and repair/maintenance. Pays $75 per printed page, on acceptance. Query.

COLLECTING TOYS—21027 Crossroads Cir., Waukesha, WI 53187. Jim Bunte, Ed. Bimonthly. Articles of varying lengths for a "nostalgia/collecting magazine that recalls the great toys of the 1940s and '70s." Profiles of toy collectors, designers, and manufacturers; articles for toy collectors. Color photos. Pays $75 to $100 per page.

COLLECTOR EDITIONS—170 Fifth Ave., New York, NY 10010. Joan Muyskens Pursley, Ed. Articles, 750 to 1,500 words, on collectibles, mainly contemporary limited-edition figurines, plates, and prints. Pays $150 to $350, within 30 days of acceptance. Query with photos.

COLLECTORS JOURNAL—P.O. Box 601, Vinton, IA 52349. Cristina McCormick Hurley, Ed. Weekly tabloid. Features, to 2,000 words, on antiques and collectibles. Pays $10 for articles, $15 for articles with photos, on publication.

COLLECTORS NEWS—P.O. Box 156, Grundy Ctr., IA 50638. Linda Kruger, Ed. Articles, to 1,000 words, on private collections, antiques, and collectibles, especially 20th-century nostalgia, Americana, glass and china, music, furniture, transportation, timepieces, jewelry, farm-related collectibles, and lamps; include quality color or B&W photos. Pays $1 per column inch; $25 for front-page color photos, on publication.

COMIC BOOK COLLECTOR—155 E. Aines Ct., Plainview, NY 11803. Attn: Ed. Dept. Articles, from 800 words, related to comic books, comic characters, cartoons, etc.; collecting and investing; fillers. Queries preferred. Pays 10¢ a word, on publication.

COUNTRY FOLK ART MAGAZINE—8393 E. Holly Rd., Holly, MI 48442–8819. Tanya Lane, Man. Ed. Articles on travel, decorating, gardening, collectibles; how-to pieces, 750 to 2,000 words, with a creative slant on American folk art; profiles of artisans. Pays $150 to $300, on acceptance. Submit pieces on seasonal topics one year in advance.

COUNTRY HANDCRAFTS—5400 S. 60th St., Greendale, WI 53129. Kathleen Zimmer, Ed. All types of craft designs (needlepoint, quilting, woodworking, etc.) with complete instructions and full-size patterns. Pays from $50 to $300, on acceptance, for all rights.

CRAFTS 'N THINGS—Dept. W, 701 Lee St., Suite 1000, Des Plaines, IL 60016–4570. Julie Stephani, Ed. How-to articles on all kinds of crafts projects, with instructions. Send manuscript with instructions and photograph of the finished item. Pays $50 to $250, on acceptance.

CROSS-STITCH PLUS—306 E. Parr Rd., Berne, IN 46711. Lana Schurb, Ed. How-to and instructional counted cross-stitch. Pays varying rates.

CROSS-STITCH SAMPLER—P.O. Box 413, Chester Heights, PA 19017. Deborah N. DeSimone, Ed. Articles, 500 to 1,500 words, about counted cross-stitch, drawn thread, or themes revolving around stitching (samplers, needlework tools, etc.). Queries required. Pays varying rates, on acceptance.

DOG FANCY—P.O. Box 6050, Mission Viejo, CA 92690. Kim Thornton, Ed. Articles, 1,500 to 3,000 words, on dog care, health, grooming, breeds, activities, events, etc. Photos. Payment varies, on publication.

DOLL WORLD—306 E. Parr Rd., Berne, IN 46711. Cary Raesner, Ed. Informational articles about doll collecting.

DOLLS, THE COLLECTOR'S MAGAZINE—170 Fifth Ave., New York, NY 10010. Karen Bischoff, Man. Ed. Articles, 500 to 2,500 words, for knowledgeable doll collectors; sharply focused with a strong collecting angle, and concrete information (value, identification, restoration, etc.). Include high quality slides or transparencies. Pays $100 to $350, within 30 days of acceptance. Query.

FIBERARTS—50 College St., Asheville, NC 28801. Ann Batchelder, Ed. Published 5 times yearly. Articles, 400 to 2,000 words, on contemporary trends in fiber sculpture, weaving, surface design, quilting, stitchery, papermaking, felting, basketry, and wearable art. Query with photos of subject, outline, and synopsis. Pays varying rates, on publication.

FINESCALE MODELER—P.O. Box 1612, Waukesha, WI 53187. Bob Hayden, Ed. How-to articles for people who make nonoperating scale models of aircraft, automobiles, boats, figures. Photos and drawings should accompany articles. One-page model-building hints and tips. Pays from $40 per published page, on acceptance. Query preferred.

GAMES—19 W. 21st St., Suite 1002-W, New York, NY 10010. R. Wayne Schmittberger, Ed.-in-Chief. "The magazine for creative minds at play." Features and short articles on games and playful, offbeat subjects. Visual and verbal puzzles, pop culture quizzes, brainteasers, contests, game reviews. Pays top rates, on publication. Send SASE for guidelines; specify writer's, crosswords, variety puzzles, or brainteasers.

HERITAGE QUEST—Historic Resources, P.O. Box 329, Bountiful, UT 84011. Leland Meitzler, Ed. Bimonthly. Genealogy how-to articles, 2 to 4 pages, national, international, or regional in scope. Payment varies, on publication.

THE HOME SHOP MACHINIST—2779 Aero Park Dr., Box 1810, Traverse City, MI 49685. Joe D. Rice, Ed. How-to articles on precision metalworking and foundry work. Accuracy and attention to detail a must. Pays $40 per published page, extra for photos and illustrations, on publication. Send SASE for guidelines.

KITPLANES—P.O. Box 6050, Mission Viejo, CA 92690. Dave Martin, Ed. Articles geared to the growing market of aircraft built from kits and plans by home craftsmen, on all aspects of design, construction, and performance, 1,000 to 4,000 words. Pays $60 per page, on publication.

LOST TREASURE—P.O. Box 1589, Grove, OK 74344. Grace Michael, Man. Ed. How-to articles, legends, folklore, and stories of lost treasures. Also publishes *Treasure Facts* (bimonthly): how-to information for treasure hunters, club news, who's who in treasure hunting, tips, etc. *Treasure Cache* (annual): articles on documented treasure caches with sidebar telling how to search for cache highlighted in article. Pays 4¢ a word, $5 for photos, $100 for cover photos.

LOTTOWORLD MAGAZINE—2150 Goodlette Rd., Suite 200, Naples, FL 33940. Barry Miller, Man. Ed. Articles of interest to readers, over 18 years old, who play the lottery. Human-interest pieces on lottery winners and losers, winning systems, advice on predicting numbers and increasing your odds of winning, competition between state lotteries, etc. Payment varies, 30 days after publication.

THE MIDATLANTIC ANTIQUES MAGAZINE—P.O. Box 908, Henderson, NC 27536. Lydia Stainback, Ed. Articles, 500 to 2,000 words, on antiques, collectibles, and related subjects. "We need show and auction reporters." Queries are preferred. Payment varies, on publication.

MILITARY HISTORY—602 S. King St., Suite 300, Leesburg, VA 22075. C. Brian Kelly, Ed. Bimonthly. Features, 4,000 words, with 500-word sidebars, on the strategy, tactics, and personalities of military history. Department pieces, 2,000 words, on espionage, weaponry, perspectives, and travel. No fiction. Pays $200 to $400, on publication. Query. Guidelines.

MODEL RAILROADER—21027 Crossroads Cir., P.O. Box 1612, Waukesha, WI 53187. Andy Sperandeo, Ed. Articles on model railroads, with photos of layout and equipment. Pays $90 per printed page, on acceptance. Query.

MOTOR BOATING & SAILING—250 W. 55th St., 4th Fl., New York, NY 10019–5905. Peter A. Janssen Ed./Pub. Articles, 1,500 words, on buying, maintaining, and enjoying boats "Appeal to the dreams, adventures, and the lifestyles of committed boat owners." Hard-core, authoritative how-to. Query. Payment varies, on acceptance.

NEEDLEWORK RETAILER—117 Alexander Ave., P.O. Box 2438, Ames, IA 50010. Heidi A. Bomgarden, Ed. Articles, 500 to 1,000 words, on how to run a small needlework business or anything related to the needlework trade. "Articles must specifically address the needlework business; general articles about small businesses will not be accepted." Pays varying rates, on acceptance.

NEW ENGLAND ANTIQUES JOURNAL—4 Church St., Ware, MA 01082. Jody Young, Gen. Mgr. Julie Murkette, Man. Ed. Well-researched articles, to 2,500 words, on antiques of interest to collectors and/or dealers, auction and antiques show reviews, to 1,000 words, antiques market news, to 500 words; photos desired. Pays to $150, on publication. Query or send manuscript. Reports in 2 to 4 weeks.

PETERSEN'S PHOTOGRAPHIC—8490 Sunset Blvd., Los Angeles, CA 90069. Bill Hurter, Ed. How-to articles on all phases of still photography of interest to the amateur and advanced photographer. Pays about $100 per printed page for article accompanied by photos, on publication.

POPULAR MECHANICS—224 W. 57th St., New York, NY 10019. Deborah Frank, Man. Ed. Articles, 300 to 1,500 words, on latest developments in mechanics, industry, science, telecommunications; features on hobbies with a mechanical slant; how-tos on home and shop projects; features on outdoor adventures, boating, and electronics. Photos and sketches a plus. Pays to $1,500; to $500 for short pieces, on acceptance. Buys all rights.

POPULAR WOODWORKING—1041 Shary Cir., Concord, CA 94518. Robert C. Cook, Ed. Project articles, to 5,000 words; techniques pieces, to 1,500 words; anecdotes and essays, to 1,000 words, for the "modest production woodworker, small shop owner, wood craftsperson, advanced hobbyist and woodcarver." Pays $500 to $1,000 for large, complicated projects; $100 to $500 for small projects and other features; half on acceptance, half on publication. Query with brief outline and photo of finished project.

QUICK & EASY CRAFTS—306 E. Parr Rd., Berne, IN 46711. Beth Schwartz, Ed. How-to and instructional needlecrafts and other arts and crafts, book reviews, and tips. Photos. Pays varying rates, before publication.

RAILROAD MODEL CRAFTSMAN—P.O. Box 700, Newton, NJ 07860–0700. William C. Schaumburg, Ed. How-to articles on scale model railroading; cars, operation, scenery, etc. Pays on publication.

RESTORATION—P.O. Box 50046, Tucson, AZ 85703–1046. W.R. Haessner, Ed. Articles, 1,200 to 1,800 words, on restoring and building chairs, machines, boats, autos, trucks, planes, trains, toys, tools, etc. Photos and art required. Pays $50 per page, on publication. Query.

RUG HOOKING MAGAZINE—Stackpole Magazines, 500 Vaughn St., Harrisburg, PA 17110. MacDonald Kennedy, Ed. How-to and feature articles on rug hooking for beginners and advanced artists. No payment.

SCHOOL MATES—U.S. Chess Federation, 186 Rte. 9W, New Windsor, NY 12553–7698. Carl Simmons, Ed. Articles and fiction, to 1,000 words, and short fillers, related to chess for beginning chess players (not necessarily children). "Instructive, but there's room for fun puzzles, anecdotes, etc. All chess related. Articles on chessplaying celebrities are always of interest to us." Pays about $40 per 1,000 words, on publication. Query; limited free-lance market.

73 AMATEUR RADIO—WGI, 70 Rte. 202N, Peterborough, NH 03458. David Cassidy, Assoc. Pub./Ed. Articles, 1,500 to 3,000 words, for electronics hobbyists and amateur radio operators. Pays $50 to $250.

SEW NEWS—P.O. Box 1790, News Plaza, Peoria, IL 61656. Linda Turner Griepentrog, Ed. Articles, to 3,000 words, "that teach a specific technique, inspire a reader to try new sewing projects, or inform a reader about an interesting person, company, or project related to sewing, textiles, or fashion." Emphasis is on fashion (not craft) sewing. Pays $25 to $400, on acceptance. Queries required; no unsolicited manuscripts accepted.

SPORTS CARD TRADER—155 E. Ames Ct., Plainview, NY 11803. Attn: Ed. Office. Articles, from 1,000 words, related to baseball, football, basketball, and hockey cards; collecting and investing. Fillers. Queries preferred. Pays 10¢ a word, on publication.

SPORTS COLLECTORS DIGEST—Krause Publications, 700 E. State St., Iola, WI 54990. Tom Mortenson, Ed. Articles, 750 to 2,000 words, on old baseball card sets and other sports memorabilia and collectibles. Pays $50 to $100, on publication.

TEDDY BEAR REVIEW—Collector Communications Corp., 170 Fifth Ave., New York, NY 10010. Stephen L. Cronk, Ed. Articles on antique and contemporary teddy bears for makers, collectors, and enthusiasts. Pays $50 to $200, within 30 days of acceptance. Query with photos.

THREADS MAGAZINE—Taunton Press, 63 S. Main St., Box 5506, Newtown, CT 06470. Attn: Ed. Bimonthly. Articles and department pieces about materials, tools, techniques, people, and design in sewing and textile arts, especially in garment making, knitting, quilting, and stitchery, by writers experienced in these crafts. Pays $150 per published page, on publication.

TREASURE CACHE, TREASURE FACTS—See *Lost Treasure.*

TROPICAL FISH HOBBYIST—1 T.F.H. Plaza, Neptune City, NJ 07753. Ray Hunziker, Ed. Articles, 500 to 3,000 words, for beginning and experienced tropical and marine fish enthusiasts. Photos. Pays $35 to $250, on acceptance. Query.

WEST ART—Box 6868, Auburn, CA 95604–6868. Martha Garcia, Ed. Features, 350 to 700 words, on fine arts and crafts. No hobbies. Photos. Pays 50¢ per column inch, on publication. SASE required.

WESTERN & EASTERN TREASURES—P.O. Box 1095, Arcata, CA 95521. Rosemary Anderson, Man. Ed. Illustrated articles, to 1,500 words, on treasure hunting and how-to metal-detecting tips. Pays 2¢ a word, extra for photos, on publication.

WILDFOWL CARVING AND COLLECTING—Stackpole Magazines, 500 Vaughn St., Harrisburg, PA 17110. Cathy Hart, Ed.-in-Chief. How-to and reference articles, of varying lengths, on bird carving; collecting antique and contemporary carvings. Query. Pays varying rates, on acceptance.

WIN MAGAZINE—120 S. San Fernando Blvd., Suite 439, Burbank, CA 91502. Cecil Suzuki, Ed. Gambling-related articles, 1,600 to 2,500 words, and fiction. Pays on publication.

WOODENBOAT MAGAZINE—P.O. Box 78, Brooklin, ME 04616. Jonathan Wilson, Ed. How-to and technical articles, 4,000 words, on construction, repair, and maintenance of wooden boats; design, history, and use of wooden boats; and profiles of outstanding wooden boat builders and designers. Pays $150 to $200 per 1,000 words. Query preferred.

WOODWORK—42 Digital Dr., Suite 5, Novato, CA 94949. John McDonald, Ed. Bimonthly. Articles for woodworkers on all aspects of woodworking (simple, complex, technical, or aesthetic) with illustrations and cut lists. Topics include personalities, joinery, shows, carving, how-to, finishing, etc. Pays $150 per published page; $35 for "Techniques" department pieces, on publication. Queries or outlines preferred.

WORKBASKET MAGAZINE—700 W. 47th St., Suite 310, Kansas City, MO 64112. Kay M. Olson, Ed. Instructions and models for original knit, crochet, and tat items. (Designs must fit theme of issue.) How-tos on crafts and gardening, 400 to 1,200 words, with photos. Pays on acceptance; negotiable rates for instructional items.

WORKBENCH—700 W. 47th St., Suite 310, Kansas City, MO 64112. Robert N. Hoffman, Exec. Ed. Articles on do-it-yourself home improvement and maintenance projects and general woodworking articles for beginning and expert craftsmen. Complete working drawings with accurate dimensions, step-by-step instructions, lists of materials, in-progress photos, and photos of the finished product must accompany submission. Query. Pays from $150 per published page, on acceptance.

YELLOWBACK LIBRARY—P.O. Box 36172, Des Moines, IA 50315. Gil O'Gara, Ed. Articles, 300 to 2,000 words, on boys'/girls' series literature (Hardy Boys, Nancy Drew, Tom Swift, etc.) for collectors, researchers, and dealers. "Especially welcome are interviews with, or articles by past and present writers of juvenile series fiction." Pays in copies.

YESTERYEAR—P.O. Box 2, Princeton, WI 54968. Michael Jacobi, Ed. Articles on antiques and collectibles for readers in WI, IL, IA, MN, and surrounding states. Photos. Will consider regular columns on collecting or antiques. Pays from $10, on publication. Limited market.

ZYMURGY—Box 1679, Boulder, CO 80306–1679. Elizabeth V. Gold, Ed. Articles appealing to beer lovers and homebrewers. Pays in merchandise and books. Query.

POPULAR & TECHNICAL SCIENCE, COMPUTERS

AD ASTRA—National Space Society, 922 Pennsylvania Ave. S.E., Washington, DC 20003–2140. Richard Wagner, Ed.-in-Chief. Lively, non-technical features, to 3,000 words, on all aspects of international space program. Particularly interested in "Living in Space" articles; space settlements; lunar and Mars bases. Pays $150 to $200, on publication. Query. Guidelines.

AMERICAN HERITAGE OF INVENTION & TECHNOLOGY—60 Fifth Ave., New York, NY 10011. Frederick Allen, Ed. Quarterly. Articles, 2,000 to 5,000 words, on history of technology in America, for the sophisticated general reader. Query. Pays on acceptance.

THE ANNALS OF IMPROBABLE RESEARCH—(formerly *The Journal of Irreproducible Results*) The MIT Museum, 265 Massachusetts Ave., Cambridge, MA 02139. Marc Abrahams, Ed. Science humor, science reports and analysis, one to 4 pages. Brief science-related poetry. B&W photos. "This journal is the place to find the mischievous, funny, iconoclastic side of science." Guidelines. No payment.

ARCHAEOLOGY—135 William St., New York, NY 10038. Peter A. Young, Ed.-in-Chief. Articles on archaeology by professionals or lay people with a solid knowledge of the field. Pays $250 to $500, on publication. Query required.

ASTRONOMY—P.O. Box 1612, Waukesha, WI 53187. Robert Burnham, Ed. Articles on astronomy, astrophysics, space programs, research. Hobby pieces on equipment; short news items. Pays varying rates, on acceptance.

BIOSCIENCE—American Institute of Biological Science, 730 11th St. N.W., Washington, DC 20001. Anna Maria Gillis, Features Ed. Articles, 2 to 4 journal pages, on new developments in biology or on science policy, for professional biologists. Style should be journalistic. Pays $300 per journal page, on publication. Query required.

BYTE MAGAZINE—One Phoenix Mill Ln., Peterborough, NH 03458. Dennis Allen, Ed. Features on new technology and reviews of computers and software, varying lengths, for technically advanced users of personal computers. Payment is competitive. Query. Guidelines.

C/C++ USERS JOURNAL—1601 W. 23rd St., Suite 200, Lawrence, KS 66046–4153. Marc Briand, Man. Ed. Practical, how-to articles, 3,000 words (including 300 lines of code) on C/C++ programming. "Political or highly theoretical articles are discouraged, as are pieces about programming 'religion.'" Query required. Pays $100 per published page of text, $80 per published page of code, on publication. Guidelines.

COMPUTE GAZETTE—324 W. Wendover Ave., Suite 200, Greensboro, NC 27408. David Hensley, Man. Ed. Tom Netsel, Ed. Articles, to 2,000 words, on

Commodore 64/128, including home, education, and business applications, games, and programming. Original programs and artwork also accepted.

COMPUTERCRAFT—See *Microcomputer Journal*.

DATA COMMUNICATIONS, DATA COMMUNICATIONS INTERNATIONAL—1221 Ave. of the Americas, New York, NY 10020. Joseph Braue, Ed.-in-Chief. Technical articles, 2,000 to 5,000 words, on communications networks. Readers are managers of multinational computer networks. Payment varies; made on acceptance and on publication.

DIEHARD MAGAZINE—LynnCarthy Industry, Inc., P.O. Box 392, Boise, ID 83701. Attn: Ed. "The Flyer for Commodore 8 Bitters." Programs, reviews, tutorials, 500 to 3,000 words. Articles on all technical aspects of Commodore usage, especially on C/PM and machine language; humor. Submit disk or hard copy. Pays $20 to $200, on acceptance.

ELECTRONICS NOW—500-B Bi-County Blvd., Farmingdale, NY 11735. Brian C. Fenton, Ed. Technical articles, 1,500 to 3,000 words, on all areas related to electronics. Pays $50 to $500 or more, on acceptance.

ENVIRONMENT—1319 18th St. N.W., Washington, DC 20036–1802. Barbara T. Richman, Man. Ed. Factual articles, 2,500 to 5,000 words, on scientific, technological, and environmental policy and decision-making issues. Pays $100 to $300. Query.

FINAL FRONTIER—249 Main St., Dunedin, FL 34698. Leonard David, Ed. Articles, 1,500 to 3,000 words; columns, 800 words; and shorts, 250 words, about people, events, and "exciting possibilities" of the world's space programs. Pays about 25¢ a word, on acceptance. Query.

FOCUS—Turnkey Publishing, Inc., P.O. Box 200549, Austin, TX 78720. Doug Johnson, Ed. Articles, 700 to 4,000 words, on Data General computers. Photos a plus. Pays to $50, on publication. Query required.

THE FUTURIST—World Future Society, 7910 Woodmont Ave., Suite 450, Bethesda, MD 20814. Cynthia G. Wagner, Man. Ed. Features, 1,000 to 5,000 words, on subjects pertaining to the future: environment, education, business, science, technology, etc. Submit complete manuscript with brief bio (or CV) and SASE. Pays in copies.

GENETIC ENGINEERING NEWS—1651 Third Ave., New York, NY 10128. John Sterling, Man. Ed. Articles on all aspects of biotechnology; feature articles and news articles. Pays varying rates, on acceptance. Query.

HOBSON'S CHOICE: SCIENCE FICTION AND TECHNOLOGY—The Starwind Press, P.O. Box 98, Ripley, OH 45167. Attn: Submissions Ed. Articles and literary criticism, 1,000 to 5,000 words, for readers interested in science and technology. Also science fiction and fantasy, 2,000 to 10,000 words. Query for nonfiction. Pays 1¢ to 4¢ a word, on acceptance.

HOME OFFICE COMPUTING—Scholastic, Inc., 411 Lafayette St., New York, NY 10003. Bernadette Grey, Ed.-in-Chief. Articles, 3,000 words, that provide readers with practical information on how to run their businesses and use technology more effectively. Profiles of home-based entrepreneurs. Education and entertainment pieces, 800 to 1,500 words, for "Family Computing" section. Writers must be familiar with microcomputers and software, home office products, and issues affecting small and home buisinesses. Payment varies, on acceptance.

HOMEPC—CPM Publications, 600 Community Dr., Manhasset, NY 11030–5772. Andrea Linne, Features Ed. Articles that help home computer users get the most out of their PCs. Query with clips and resumé required. Payment varies, on acceptance.

INFOMART MAGAZINE—Infomart Corporate Communications, 1950 Stemmons Fwy., Suite 6038, Dallas, TX 75207. Aaron Woods, Ed. Articles, 800 to 1,200 words, on business applications of information systems and data processing managers. Query. Payment is negotiable.

THE JOURNAL OF IRREPRODUCIBLE RESULTS—See *The Annals of Improbable Research.*

LINK-UP—2222 River Rd., King George, VA 22485. Loraine Page, Ed. Dir. Articles about online services, bulletin board systems, and CD-ROM for the computer owner who uses this technology for business, home, and educational use. Book reviews, 500 to 800 words. Pays $90 to $220 for articles, $55 for reviews, on publication. Photos a plus.

LOTUS—See *PC World Lotus Edition.*

MACHOME JOURNAL—544 Second St., San Francisco, CA 94107. Sandra Anderson, Ed.-in-Chief. Jargon-free solutions to the information needs of Macintosh computer users. "Present technology in concise, factual, complete, non-condescending manner." Submissions on disk or over online services preferred; guidelines strongly recommended. Payment varies.

MACUSER—950 Tower Ln., Foster City, CA 94404–2121. James Bradbury, Ed. Product-oriented articles, 1,000 to 3,000 words. No case studies or personal anecdotes. Queries required. Payment varies, on acceptance.

MACWORLD—Editorial Proposals, 501 Second St., Suite 500, San Francisco, CA 94107. Reviews, news, consumer, and how-to articles, of varying lengths, related to Macintosh personal computers. Query only; no unsolicited manuscripts. Pays from $150 to $3,500, on acceptance. Guidelines.

MICROCOMPUTER JOURNAL—(formerly *Computercraft*) 76 N. Broadway, Hicksville, NY 11801. Art Salsberg, Ed.-in-Chief. How-to features, technical tutorials, servicing and construction projects related to personal computer and microcontroller equipment and software. Emphasizes enhancements, modifications, and applications. Lengths vary. Query with outline required. Pays $90 to $150 per published page, after acceptance.

MOBILE OFFICE—470 Park Ave. S., 14th Fl., New York, NY 10016. Rich Malloy, Ed.-in-Chief. Articles, 1,500 to 2,000 words, on applications for mobile electronics. Query. Payment varies, on publication.

NATURAL HISTORY—American Museum of Natural History, Central Park W. at 79th St., New York, NY 10024. Ellen Goldensohn, Man. Ed. Informative articles, to 3,000 words, by experts, on anthropology and natural sciences. "Strongly recommend that writers send SASE for guidelines and read our magazine, before querying." Pays $1,000 for features, on acceptance. Query.

NETWORK NEWS—9710 S. 700 E., Bldg. A, Suite 206, Sandy, UT 84070. Kristin King, Ed. Humorous editorial articles, 600 to 800 words, on computing, especially networking. "Readers are computer professionals who are concerned with the multivendor network computing world." Submit with SASE for reply only; manuscripts will not be returned. Pays 30¢ a word, after acceptance.

NETWORK WORLD—161 Worcester Rd., Framingham, MA 01701-9171. John Gallant, Ed. Articles, to 2,500 words, about applications of communications technology for management level users of data, voice, and video communications systems. Pays varying rates, on acceptance.

OMNI—324 W. Wendover Ave., Suite 205, Greensboro, NC 27408. Keith Ferrell, Ed. Articles, 750 to 3,500 words, on scientific aspects of the future: space colonies, cloning, machine intelligence, ESP, origin of life, future arts, lifestyles, etc. Fiction, 2,000 to 10,000 words, should be sent to Ellen Datlow, Fiction Ed., *Omni,* 1965 Broadway, New York, NY 10023. Pays $800 to $3,500, $175 for short items, on acceptance. Query.

PC GRAPHICS & VIDEO—201 E. Sandpointe Ave., Suite 600, Santa Ana, CA 92725. Gene Smarte, Ed. Applications of graphics and video on pc-compatible computers for professionals and enthusiasts. Pays flat fee. Query.

PC WORLD LOTUS EDITION—(formerly *Lotus*) 77 Franklin St., Boston, MA 02110. Eric Bender, Exec. Ed. Articles, 1,500 to 2,000 words, on business and professional applications of Lotus software. Query with outline required. Pay varies, on final approval.

PCM MAGAZINE—Falsoft, Inc., 9509 US Highway 42, P.O. Box 385, Prospect, KY 40059. Attn: Submissions Ed. Articles and computer programs for Tandy and IBM-compatible computers. Pays varying rates, on publication.

POPULAR ELECTRONICS—500-B Bi-County Blvd., Farmingdale, NY 11735. Carl Laron, Ed. Features, 1,500 to 2,500 words, for electronics hobbyists and experimenters. "Our readers are science and electronics oriented, understand computer theory and operation, and like to build electronics projects." Fillers and cartoons. Pays $25 to $500, on acceptance.

POPULAR SCIENCE—2 Park Ave., New York, NY 10016. Fred Abatemarco, Ed. Articles, with photos, on developments in applied science and technology. Short illustrated articles on new inventions and products; photo essays, book excerpts. Pays from $150 per printed page, on acceptance.

PUBLISH—Integrated Media, Inc., 501 Second St., San Francisco, CA 94107. Jake Widman, Ed.-in-Chief. Features, 1,200 to 2,000 words, and reviews, 300 to 800 words, on all aspects of computerized publishing. Pays $400 for short articles and reviews, from $900 for full-length features and reviews, on acceptance.

THE SCIENCES—2 E. 63rd St., New York, NY 10021. Peter G. Brown, Ed. Essays and features, 2,000 to 4,000 words, and book reviews, on all scientific disciplines. Pays honorarium, on publication. Query.

SEA FRONTIERS—400 S.E. Second Ave., 4th Fl., Miami, FL 33131. Bonnie Bilyeu Gordon, Ed. Illustrated articles, 500 to 3,000 words, on scientific advances related to the sea, biological, physical, chemical, or geological phenomena, ecology, conservation, etc., written in a popular style for lay readers. Send SASE for guidelines. Pays 25¢ a word, on acceptance. Query.

SKY & TELESCOPE—Sky Publishing Corp., P.O. Box 9111, Belmont, MA 02178–9111. Timothy Lyster, Man. Ed. Articles for amateur and professional astronomers worldwide. Department pieces for "Amateur Astronomers," "Astronomical Computing," "Telescope Making," "Observer's Page," and "Gallery." Also, 1,000-word opinion pieces, for "Focal Point." Mention availability of diagrams and other illustrations. Query required. Pays 10¢ to 25¢ a word, on publication.

TECHNOLOGY & LEARNING—Peter Li, Inc., 2169 E. Francisco Blvd., Suite A-4, San Rafael, CA 94901. Judy Salpeter, Ed. Articles, to 3,000 words, for teachers of grades K through 12, about uses of computers and related technology in the classroom: human-interest and philosophical articles, how-to pieces, software reviews, and hands-on ideas. Pay varies, on acceptance.

TECHNOLOGY REVIEW—MIT, W59–200, Cambridge, MA 02139. Steven J. Marcus, Ed. General-interest articles on technology and its implications. Payment varies, on acceptance. Query.

VERTICAL APPLICATION RESELLER—275 Washington St., Newton, MA 02158. John Russell, Ed. Bimonthly. Articles, 500 to 1,200 words, that emphasize new technologies and products for readers who are computer systems and software "resellers." "If you know what the title of the magazine means, you probably have a good idea of what we're looking for." Query. Pays from $100, on acceptance.

WORDPERFECT MAGAZINES—MS 7300, 1555 N. Technology Way, Orem, UT 84057–2399. Joanne Schulthies, Ed. Asst. Features, 1,400 to 1,800 words, and columns, 1,200 to 1,400 words, on how-to subjects with easy-to-follow instructions that familiarize readers with WordPerfect software. Humorous essays, 750 words, for "Final Keystrokes." Pays $400 to $700, on acceptance. Query.

ANIMALS

AMERICAN FARRIERS JOURNAL—P.O. Box 624, Brookfield, WI 53008–0624. Frank Lessiter, Ed. Articles, 800 to 2,000 words, on general farrier issues, hoof care, tool selection, equine lameness, and horse handling. Pays 50¢ per published line, $15 per published illustration or photo, on publication. Query.

ANIMAL PRESS—4180 Ruffin Rd., Suite 110, San Diego, CA 92123. Renee Vititoe, Ed. Articles and fiction, 1,000 words. Well-written human interest, educational, or newsworthy articles about pets. No animal activist material. Pays $25 to $50, after publication.

ANIMALS—350 S. Huntington Ave., Boston, MA 02130. Joni Praded, Dir./ Ed. Informative, well-researched articles, to 2,500 words, on animal protection, national and international wildlife, pet care, conservation, and environmental issues that affect animals. No personal accounts or favorite pet stories. Pays from $350, on acceptance. Query.

AQUARIUM FISH—P.O. Box 6050, Mission Viejo, CA 92690. Edward Bauman, Ed. Articles, 2,000 to 4,000 words, on freshwater, saltwater, and pond fish, with or without color transparencies. (No "pet fish" stories.) Payment varies, on publication.

BIRD TALK—Box 6050, Mission Viejo, CA 92690. Julie Rach, Ed. Articles for pet bird owners: care and feeding, training, safety, outstanding personal adventures, exotic birds in their native countries, profiles of celebrities' birds, travel to bird parks or bird shows. Query or send manuscript; good transparencies a plus. Pays 7¢ to 10¢ a word, after publication.

CAT FANCY—P.O. Box 6050, Mission Viejo, CA 92690. Debbie Phillips-Donaldson, Ed. Fiction and nonfiction, to 3,000 words, on cat care, health, grooming, etc. Pays 5¢ to 10¢ a word, on publication.

DAIRY GOAT JOURNAL—W. 2997 Markert Rd., Helenville, WI 53137. Dave Thompson, Ed. Articles, to 1,500 words, on successful dairy goat owners, youths and interesting people associated with dairy goats. "Especially interested in practical husbandry ideas." Photos. Pays $50 to $150, on publication. Query.

DOG FANCY—P.O. Box 6050, Mission Viejo, CA 92690. Kim Thornton, Ed. Articles, 1,500 to 3,000 words, on dog care, health, grooming, breeds, activities, events, etc. Photos. Payment varies, on publication.

DOG WORLD—Maclean Hunter Publishing Co., 29 N. Wacker Dr., Chicago, IL 60606–3298. Donna L. Marcel, Ed. Articles, to 3,000 words, for breeders, pet owners, exhibitors, kennel operators, veterinarians, handlers, and other pet professionals on all aspects of pet care and responsible ownership: health care, training, legal rights, animals welfare, etc. Queries required. Allow 4 months for response. Pays $50 to $500, on publication. Guidelines.

EQUUS—Fleet Street Corp., 656 Quince Orchard Rd., Gaithersburg, MD 20878. Laurie Prinz, Man. Ed. Articles, 1,000 to 3,000 words, on all breeds of horses, covering their health and care as well as the latest advances in equine medicine and research. "Attempt to speak as one horseperson to another." Pays $100 to $400, on publication.

THE FLORIDA HORSE—P.O. Box 2106, Ocala, FL 34478. F.J. Audette, Ed. Articles, 1,500 words, on Florida thoroughbred breeding and racing. Also veterinary articles, financial articles, and articles of general interest. Pays $100 to $200, on publication.

HORSE & RIDER—1060 Calle Cordillera, Suite 103, San Clemente, CA 92673. Juli Thorson, Ed. Sue M. Copeland, Man. Ed. Articles, 500 to 3,000 words, with photos, on western training and general horse care: feeding, health, grooming, etc. Pays varying rates, on publication. Buys one-time rights. Guidelines.

HORSE ILLUSTRATED—P.O. Box 6050, Mission Viejo, CA 92690. Audrey Pavia, Ed. Articles, 1,500 to 2,500 words, on all aspects of owning and caring for horses. Photos. Pays $200 to $300, on publication. Query.

HORSEMEN'S YANKEE PEDLAR—785 Southbridge St., Auburn, MA 01501. Nancy L. Khoury, Pub. News and feature-length articles, about horses and horsemen in the Northeast. Photos. Pays $2 per published inch, on publication. Query.

HORSEPLAY—P.O. Box 130, Gaithersburg, MD 20884. Lisa M. Kiser, Man. Ed. Articles, 700 to 3,000 words, on eventing, show jumping, horse shows, dressage, driving, and fox hunting for horse owners and English riders. Profiles, instructional articles, occasional humor, and competition reports. Pays 10¢ a word, buys all rights, after publication. Query with SASE. Guidelines.

LLAMAS—P.O. Box 100, Herald, CA 95638. Cheryl Dal Porto, Ed. "The International Camelid Journal," published 7 times yearly. Articles, 300 to 3,000 words, of interest to llama and alpaca owners. Pays $25 to $300, extra for photos, on publication. Query.

MUSHING—P.O. Box 149, Ester, AK 99725–0149. Todd Hoener, Pub. How-tos, innovations, history, profiles, interviews, and features, 1,500 to 2,000 words, and department pieces, 500 to 1,000 words, for competitive and recreational dog drivers and skijorers. International audience. Photos. Queries preferred. Pays $20 to $250, after acceptance. Guidelines.

PRACTICAL HORSEMAN—Box 589, Unionville, PA 19375. Mandy Lorraine, Ed. How-to articles on English riding, training, and horse care. Query with clips. Payment varies, on acceptance.

PURE-BRED DOGS/AMERICAN KENNEL GAZETTE—51 Madison Ave., New York, NY 10010. Beth Adelman, Exec. Ed. Articles, 1,000 to 2,500 words, relating to serious breeders of pure-bred dogs. Pays from $250 to $350, on acceptance. Query preferred.

SHEEP! MAGAZINE—W. 2997 Markert Rd., Helenville, WI 53137. Dave Thompson, Ed. Articles, to 1,500 words, on successful shepherds, woolcrafts, sheep raising, and sheep dogs. "Especially interested in people who raise sheep successfully as a sideline enterprise." Photos. Pays $15 to $150, extra for photos, on acceptance. Query.

TROPICAL FISH HOBBYIST—1 T.F.H. Plaza, Neptune City, NJ 07753. Ray Hunziker, Ed. Articles, 500 to 3,000 words, for beginning and experienced tropical and marine fish enthusiasts. Photos. Query. Pays $35 to $250, on acceptance.

WILDLIFE CONSERVATION—The Wildlife Conservation Society, Bronx, NY 10460. Nancy Simmons, Sr. Ed. Articles, 1,500 to 2,000 words, that "probe conservation controversies to search for answers and help save threatened species." Payment varies, on acceptance. Guidelines.

TRUE CRIME

DETECTIVE CASES—See *Globe Communications Corp.*

DETECTIVE DRAGNET—See *Globe Communications Corp.*

DETECTIVE FILES—See *Globe Communications Corp.*

FRONT PAGE DETECTIVE—Reese Communications, Inc., 460 W. 34th St., New York, NY 10001. Rose Mandelsberg, Ed.-in-Chief. True detective stories, 5,000 to 6,000 words, with detective work, mystery, and some kind of twist. No fiction. Good color photos of victim, perpetrator, crime scene, or detective may accompany article. Pays $250 to $500 for articles, to $200 for photos. Query.

FUGITIVE!—848 Dodge Ave., Suite 420, Evanston, IL 60202. Lawrence Shulruff, Ed. Articles, 600 to 800 words, on unsolved crime and criminals at large. "Provide details about case. We encourage readers to contact police with tips about cases in each issue. Articles shouldn't be gory. Photos or composites of suspect are required." Query required. Pays $50 to $150, on acceptance.

GLOBE COMMUNICATIONS CORP.—1350 Sherbrooke St. W., Suite 600, Montreal, Quebec, Canada H3G 2T4. Dominick A. Merle, Ed. Factual accounts, 3,500 to 6,000 words, of "sensational crimes, preferably sex crimes, either pre-trial or after conviction." All articles will be considered for *Startling Detective, True Police Cases, Detective Files, Headquarters Detective, Detective Dragnet*, and *Detective Cases*. Query with pertinent information, including dates, site, names, etc. Pays $250 to $350, on acceptance; buys all rights.

HEADQUARTERS DETECTIVE—See *Globe Communications Corp.*

INSIDE DETECTIVE—Reese Communications, Inc., 460 W. 34th St., New York, NY 10001. Rose Mandelsberg, Ed.-in-Chief. Timely, true detective stories, 5,000 to 6,000 words, or 10,000 words. No fiction. Color photos of victim, killer, crime scene, or officer who headed investigation. Pays $250 to $500 for articles, to $200 for photos, on acceptance. Query.

MASTER DETECTIVE—Reese Communications, Inc., 460 W. 34th St., New York, NY 10001. Rose Mandelsberg, Ed.-in-Chief. Detailed articles, 5,000 to 6,000 words, with photos, on current cases, emphasizing human motivation and detective work. Also publish longer articles, 10,000 words. No fiction. Clear, color photos of victim, crime scene, perpetrator, and officer who led case. Pays $250 to $500, to $200 for photos, on acceptance. Query.

OFFICIAL DETECTIVE—Reese Communications, Inc., 460 W. 34th St., New York, NY 10001. Rose Mandelsberg, Ed.-in-Chief. True detective stories,

5,000 to 6,000 words, on current investigations, strictly from the investigator's point of view. No fiction. Clear color photos of victim, killer, crime scene, or lead officer on case. Pays $250, to $200 for photos, on acceptance. Query.

P.I. MAGAZINE: AMERICA'S PRIVATE INVESTIGATION JOURNAL —755 Bronx Ave., Toledo, OH 43609. Bob Mackowiak, Ed. Profiles of professional investigators containing true accounts of their most difficult cases. Pays $25 to $50, plus copies, on publication.

STARTLING DETECTIVE—See *Globe Communications Corp.*

TRUE DETECTIVE—Reese Communications, Inc., 460 W. 34th St., New York, NY 10001. Rose Mandelsberg, Ed.-in-Chief. Articles, from 5,000 to 10,000 words, with photos, on current police cases, emphasizing detective work and human motivation. No fiction. Photos of perpetrator, victim, crime scene, or officer who spearheaded case. Pays $250 to $500, to $200 for photos, on acceptance. Query.

TRUE POLICE CASES—See *Globe Communications Corp.*

MILITARY

AIR FORCE TIMES—See *Times News Service.*

ARMY MAGAZINE—2425 Wilson Blvd., Arlington, VA 22201–3385. Mary B. French, Ed.-in-Chief. Features, to 2,000 words, on military subjects. Essays, humor, history (especially World War II), news reports, first-person anecdotes. Pays 12¢ to 18¢ a word, $25 to $50 for anecdotes, on publication.

ARMY RESERVE MAGAZINE—1815 N. Ft. Myer Dr., #203, Arlington, VA 22209–1805. Lt. Col. Jim Nielsen, Ed. Articles, 1,000 words, on military training and the history of the Army Reserve; profiles, 250 words, of interesting people in Army Reserve: military family life, humor, and anecdotes. Submit manuscripts with high-quality photos. Query. No payment. Guidelines.

ARMY TIMES—See *Times News Service.*

LEATHERNECK—Box 1775, Quantico, VA 22134–0776. William V.H. White, Ed. Articles, to 3,000 words, with photos, on U.S. Marines. Pays $50 per printed page, on acceptance. Query.

LIFE IN THE TIMES—See *Times News Service.*

MARINE CORPS GAZETTE—Box 1775, Quantico, VA 22134. Col. John E. Greenwood, Ed. Military articles, 500 to 2,000 and 2,500 to 5,000 words. "Our magazine serves primarily as a forum for active duty officers to exchange views on professional, Marine Corps-related topics. Opportunity for 'outside' writers is limited." Queries preferred.

MILITARY—2122 28th St., Sacramento, CA 95818. Lt. Col. Michael Mark, Ed. Articles, 600 to 2,500 words, on firsthand experience in military service: World War II, Korea, Vietnam, and all current services. "Our magazine is about military history by the people who served. They are the best historians." No payment.

MILITARY HISTORY—602 S. King St., Suite 300, Leesburg, VA 22075. C. Brian Kelly, Ed. Bimonthly. Features, 4,000 words with 500-word sidebars, on the strategy, tactics, and personalities of military history. Department pieces, 2,000 words, on espionage, weaponry, perspectives, and travel. Pays $200 to $400, on publication. Query. Guidelines.

MILITARY LIFESTYLE MAGAZINE—4800 Montgomery Ln., Suite 710, Bethesda, MD 20814–5341. Hope Daniels, Ed. Articles, 1,000 to 1,800 words, for active-duty military families in the U.S. and overseas, on lifestyles, child-raising, health, food, fashion, travel, sports and leisure; short fiction. No poetry, no historical reminiscences. Pays $300 to $800, on publication. Query.

NAVY TIMES—See *Times News Service.*

RETIRED MILITARY FAMILY—169 Lexington Ave., New York, NY 10016. Liz DeFranco, Ed. Articles, 1,000 to 1,500 words, on travel, finance, food, hobbies, second careers, grandparenting, and other topics of interest to military retirees and their families. Pays to $200, on publication.

THE RETIRED OFFICER MAGAZINE—201 N. Washington St., Alexandria, VA 22314. Attn: Manuscripts Ed. Articles, 800 to 2,000 words, of interest to military retirees and their families. Current military/political affairs: recent military history (especially Vietnam and Korea), health, money, military family lifestyles, and second-career job opportunities. Photos a plus. Pays to $1,000, on acceptance. Queries required; no unsolicited manuscripts. Guidelines.

TIMES NEWS SERVICE—Army Times Publishing Co., Springfield, VA 22159. Attn: R&R Ed. Free-lance material for "R&R" newspaper section (formerly called "Life in the Times"). Articles about military life, its problems and how to handle them as well as interesting things people are doing. Travel articles, 700 words, on places of interest to military people. Profiles, 600 to 700 words, on interesting members of the military community. Personal-experience essays, 750 words. No fiction or poetry. Pays $75 to $100, on acceptance. Also articles, 1,000 words, for supplements to *Army Times*, *Navy Times*, and *Air Force Times.* Address Supplements Ed. Pays $125 to $200, on acceptance. Guidelines.

VFW MAGAZINE—406 W. 34th St., Kansas City, MO 64111. Richard K. Kolb, Ed. Magazine for Veterans of Foreign Wars and their families. Articles, 1,500 words, on current events, veteran affairs, and military history with veteran angle. Photos. Pays to $500, extra for photos, on acceptance. Guidelines. Query .

HISTORY

ALABAMA HERITAGE—The Univ. of Alabama, Box 870342, Tuscaloosa, AL 35487–0342. Suzanne Wolfe, Ed. Quarterly. Articles, to 5,000 words, on local, state, and regional history: art, literature, language, archaeology, music, religion, architecture, and natural history. Query, mentioning availability of photos and illustrations. Pays an honorarium, on publication, plus 10 copies. Guidelines.

AMERICAN HERITAGE OF INVENTION & TECHNOLOGY—60 Fifth Ave., New York, NY 10011. Frederick Allen, Ed. Quarterly. Articles, 2,000 to 5,000 words, on history of technology in America, for the sophisticated general reader. Query. Pays on acceptance.

AMERICAN HISTORY ILLUSTRATED—6405 Flank Dr., P.O. Box 8200, Harrisburg, PA 17105. Attn: Ed. Articles, 3,000 to 5,000 words, soundly researched. Style should be popular, not scholarly. No travelogues, fiction, or puzzles. Pays $300 to $650, on acceptance. Query with SASE required.

AMERICAN JEWISH HISTORY—American Jewish Historical Society, 2 Thornton Rd., Waltham, MA 02154. Dr. Marc Lee Raphael, Ed. Articles, 15 to 30 typed pages, on American Jewish history. Queries preferred. No payment.

CAROLOGUE—South Carolina Historical Society, 100 Meeting St., Charleston, SC 29401–2299. Stephen Hoffius, Ed. General-interest articles, to 10 pages, on South Carolina history. Queries preferred. Pays in copies.

CHICAGO HISTORY—Clark St. at North Ave., Chicago, IL 60614. Claudia Lamm Wood, Ed. Articles, to 4,500 words, on political, social, and cultural history of Chicago. Pays to $250, on publication. Query.

EARLY AMERICAN LIFE—Box 8200, Harrisburg, PA 17105–8200. Mimi Handler, Ed. Illustrated articles, 1,000 to 3,000 words, on early American life: arts, crafts, furnishings, architecture; travel features about historic sites and country inns. Pays $50 to $500, on acceptance. Query.

GOLDENSEAL—The Cultural Ctr., 1900 Kanawha Blvd. E., Charleston, WV 25305–0300. Ken Sullivan, Ed. Features, 3,000 words, and shorter articles, 1,000 words, on traditional West Virginia culture and history. Oral histories, old and new B&W photos, research articles. Pays to $200, on publication. Guidelines.

THE HIGHLANDER—P.O. Box 397, Barrington, IL 60011. Angus Ray, Ed. Bimonthly. Articles, 1,300 to 1,900 words, related to Scottish history. "We are not concerned with modern Scotland or current problems in Scotland." Pays $100 to $150, on acceptance.

HISTORIC PRESERVATION—1785 Massachusetts Ave. N.W., Washington, DC 20036. Anne Elizabeth Powell, Ed. Feature articles from published writers, 1,500 to 4,000 words, on residential restoration, preservation issues, and people involved in preserving America's heritage. Mostly staff-written. Query required.

HISTORY NEWS—AASLH, 530 Church St., Suite 600, Nashville, TN 37219–2325. LuAnne Sneddon, Ed. History-related articles, 2,500 to 3,500 words, about museums, historical societies and sites, libraries, etc.; "In My Opinion" pieces, 1,000 words; "Technical Leaflets," 5,000 words. B&W photos. Submit 2 copies of manuscript. No payment made. Guidelines.

JOURNAL OF THE WEST—1531 Yuma, Manhattan, KS 66502–4228. Robin Higham, Ed. Articles, to 20 pages, devoted to the history and the culture of the West, then and now. B&W photos. Pays in copies.

LABOR'S HERITAGE—10000 New Hampshire Ave., Silver Spring, MD 20903. Stuart Kaufman, Ed. Quarterly journal of The George Meany Memorial Archives. Articles, 15 to 30 pages, for labor scholars, labor union members, and the general public. Pays in copies.

MILITARY—2122 28th St., Sacramento, CA 95818. Lt. Col. Michael Mark, Ed. Military history by people who served in the military. First-hand experiences, 600 to 2,500 words, of service in World War II, Korea, Vietnam, and more recent times. No payment.

MILITARY HISTORY—602 S. King St., Suite 300, Leesburg, VA 22075. C. Brian Kelly, Ed. Bimonthly. Features, 4,000 words, with 500-word sidebars, on the strategy, tactics, and personalities of military history. Department pieces, 2,000 words, on espionage, weaponry, personalities, perspectives, and travel. Pays $200 to $400, on publication. Query. Guidelines.

MONTANA, THE MAGAZINE OF WESTERN HISTORY—225 N. Roberts St., Box 201201, Helena, MT 59620–1201. Charles E. Rankin, Ed. Authentic articles, 3,500 to 5,500 words, on the history of the American and Canadian West; new interpretive approaches to major developments in western history. Footnotes or bibliography must accompany article. "Strict historical accuracy is essential." No fiction. Queries preferred. No payment made.

NEBRASKA HISTORY—P.O. Box 82554, Lincoln, NE 68501. James E. Potter, Ed. Articles, 3,000 to 7,000 words, relating to the history of Nebraska and the Great Plains. B&W line drawings. Allow 60 days for response. Pays in copies. Cash prize awarded to one article each year.

OLD WEST—P.O. Box 2107, Stillwater, OK 74076. John Joerschke, Ed. Thoroughly researched and documented articles, 1,500 to 4,500 words, on the history of the American West. B&W 5x7 photos to illustrate articles. Queries are preferred. Pays 3¢ to 6¢ a word, on acceptance.

PERSIMMON HILL—1700 N.E. 63rd St., Oklahoma City, OK 73111. M.J. Van Deventer, Ed. Published by the National Cowboy Hall of Fame. Articles, 1,500 to 2,000 words, on Western history and art, cowboys, ranching, and nature. Top-quality illustrations a must. Pays from $100 to $250, on publication.

PROLOGUE—National Archives, NECP, Washington, DC 20408. Dr. Henry J. Gwiazda, Ed. Quarterly. Articles, varying lengths, based on the holdings and programs of the National Archives, its regional archives, and the presidential libraries. Query. Pays in copies.

SOUTH CAROLINA HISTORICAL MAGAZINE—South Carolina Historical Society, 100 Meeting St., Charleston, SC 29401–2299. Stephen Hoffius, Ed. Scholarly articles, to 25 pages including footnotes, on South Carolina history. "Authors are encouraged to look at previous issues to be aware of previous scholarship." Pays in copies.

TRUE WEST—P.O. Box 2107, Stillwater, OK 74076–2107. John Joerschke, Ed. True stories, 500 to 4,500 words, with photos, about the Old West to 1930. Some contemporary stories with historical slant. Source list required. Pays 3¢ to 6¢ a word, extra for B&W photos, on acceptance.

THE WESTERN HISTORICAL QUARTERLY—Utah State Univ., Logan, UT 84322–0740. Clyde A. Milner II, Ed. Original articles about the American West, the Westward movement from the Atlantic to the Pacific, twentieth-century regional studies, Spanish borderlands, Canada, northern Mexico, Alaska, and Hawaii. No payment made.

YESTERDAY'S MAGAZETTE—P.O. Box 15126, Sarasota, FL 34277. Ned Burke, Ed. Articles and fiction, to 1,000 words, on the 1920s through '70s, nostalgia and memories of people, places, and things. Traditional poetry, to 24 lines. Pays $5 to $25, on publication. Pays in copies for poetry and short pieces. Guidelines.

COLLEGE, CAREERS

THE BLACK COLLEGIAN—1240 S. Broad St., New Orleans, LA 70125. K.F. Kazi, Man. Ed. Articles, to 2,000 words, on experiences of African-American students, careers, and how-to subjects. Pays on publication. Query.

BYLINE—Box 130596, Edmond, OK 73013. Marcia Preston, Ed.-in-Chief. General fiction, 2,000 to 4,000 words. Nonfiction: 1,500- to 1,800-word features and 300- to 800-word special departments. Poetry, 10 to 30 lines preferred. Nonfiction and poetry must be about writing. Humor, 400 to 800 words, about writing. "We seek practical and motivational material that tells writers how they can succeed, not why they can't. Overdone topics: writers' block, the muse, rejection slips." Pays $5 to $10 for poetry; $15 to $35 for departments; $50 for features and short fiction, on acceptance.

CAREER WOMAN—See *Minority Engineer*.

CAREER WORLD—General Learning Corp., 60 Revere Dr., Northbrook, IL 60062–1563. Carole Rubenstein, Man. Ed. Published monthly, September through May. Gender-neutral articles about specific occupations and career development for junior and senior high school audience. Query with clips and resumé. Payment varies, on publication.

CAREERS & THE DISABLED—See *Minority Engineer*.

CIRCLE K—3636 Woodview Trace, Indianapolis, IN 46268–3196. Nicholas K. Drake, Exec. Ed. Serious and light articles, 1,000 to 2,000 words, on careers, college issues, trends, leadership development, self-help, community service and involvement. Pays $225 to $400, on acceptance. Queries preferred.

COLLEGE BROADCASTER—National Assn. of College Broadcasters, 71 George St., Box 1824, Providence, RI 02912–1824. Attn: Ed. Bimonthly. Articles, 500 to 2,000 words, on college radio and TV station operations and media careers. Query. Pays in copies.

EQUAL OPPORTUNITY—See *Minority Engineer*.

FLORIDA LEADER—c/o Oxendine Publishing, P.O. Box 14081, Gainesville, FL 32604–2081. Kay Quinn, Man. Ed. Published 3 times a year. Articles, 800 to 1,000 words, for Florida college students. "Focus on leadership, career success, profiles of growth careers in Florida and the Southeast." Pays $35 to $50, on publication.

LINK: THE COLLEGE MAGAZINE—The Soho Bldg., 110 Greene St., Suite 407, New York, NY 10012. Ty Wenger, Man. Ed. Articles of interest to college students. Short features and essays, 500 to 800 words, on dating, college road trips, trends, and lifestyles. First-person pieces, 600 to 700 words, written by recent graduates with interesting employment stories for "So You Want My Job." Queries preferred. Guidelines. Pays $100 to $500, on publication.

MINORITY ENGINEER—150 Motor Parkway, Suite 420, Hauppauge, NY 11788–5145. James Schneider, Exec. Ed. Articles, 1,000 to 1,500 words, for college students, on career opportunities in engineering fields; techniques of job hunting; developments in and applications of new technologies. Interviews. Profiles. Pays 10¢ a word, on publication. Query. Same address and requirements for *Woman Engineer, Equal Opportunity, Career Woman*, and *Careers & the DisABLED*.

STUDENT LEADER—c/o Oxendine Publishing, P.O. Box 14081, Gainesville, FL 32604–2081. Kay Quinn, Man. Ed. Semiannual. "The Magazine for America's Most Outstanding Students." Articles, 800 to 1,000 words, on career and college success. "Include quotes from faculty, corporate recruiters, current students, recent alumni." Pays $50 to $150, on publication.

STUDENT LEADERSHIP—P.O. Box 7895, Madison, WI 53707–7895. Jeff Yourison, Ed. Articles, to 2,000 words, and poetry for Christian college students. All material should reflect a Christian world view. Queries required.

UCLA MAGAZINE—405 Hilgard Ave., Los Angeles, CA 90024–1391. David Greenwald, Ed. Quarterly. Articles, 2,000 words, must be related to UCLA through research, alumni, students, etc. Queries required. Pays to $2,000, on acceptance.

WOMAN ENGINEER—See *Minority Engineer*.

OP-ED MARKETS

THE ARGUS LEADER—P.O. Box 5034, Sioux Falls, SD 57117–5034. Rob Swenson, Editorial Page Ed. Articles, to 850 words, on a wide variety of subjects for "Different Voices" column. Prefer local writers with an expertise in their subject. No payment. Guidelines.

ARIZONA REPUBLIC—120 E. Van Buren, Phoenix, AZ 85004. Stephanie Robertson, Ed. Articles, 800 to 1,000 words, on domestic affairs, environment, religion, politics, law, etc. Query. Exclusive rights: AZ.

THE ATLANTA CONSTITUTION—P.O. Box 4689, Atlanta, GA 30302. Raman Narayanan, Op-Ed Ed. Articles related to the Southeast, Georgia, or the Atlanta metropolitan area, 200 to 800 words, on a variety of topics: law, economics, politics, science, environment, performing and manipulative arts, humor, education; religious and seasonal topics. Pays $50 to $150, on publication.

THE BALTIMORE SUN—P.O. Box 1377, Baltimore, MD 21278–0001. Hal Piper, Opinion-Commentary Page Ed. Articles, 600 to 1,500 words, on a wide range of topics: politics, education, foreign affairs, lifestyles, etc. Humor. Payment varies, on publication. Exclusive rights: MD and DC.

BOSTON HERALD—One Herald Sq., Boston, MA 02106. Attn: Editorial Page Ed. Pieces, 600 to 800 words, on economics, foreign affairs, politics, regional interest, and seasonal topics. Prefer submissions from regional writers. Payment varies, on publication. Exclusive rights: MA, RI, and NH.

THE CHARLOTTE OBSERVER—P.O. Box 30308, Charlotte, NC 28232–0308. Jane McAlister Pope, Ed. Well-written, thought-provoking articles, to 700 words. "We are only interested in articles on local (Carolinas) issues or that use local examples to illustrate other issues." Pays $50, on publication. No simultaneous submissions in NC or SC.

THE CHICAGO TRIBUNE—435 N. Michigan Ave., Chicago, IL 60611. Marcia Lythcott, Op-Ed Page Ed. Pieces, 800 to 1,000 words, on domestic and international affairs, environment, regional interest, and personal essays. SASE required.

THE CHRISTIAN SCIENCE MONITOR—One Norway St., Boston, MA 02115. Stacy Teicher, Opinion Page Coordinator. Pieces, 750 to 900 words, on domestic and foreign affairs, economics, education, environment, law, and politics. Pays $100, on acceptance. Retains all rights for 90 days after publication.

THE CLEVELAND PLAIN DEALER—1801 Superior Ave., Cleveland, OH 44114. Brent Larkin, Ed. Dir. Pieces, 700 to 900 words, on a wide variety of subjects. Pays $50, on publication.

DALLAS MORNING NEWS—Communications Ctr., P.O. Box 655237, Dallas, TX 75265. Bob Moos, "Viewpoints" Ed. Pieces, 750 words, on politics, education, foreign and domestic affairs, cultural trends, seasonal and regional issues. Pay averages $75, on publication. SASE required. Exclusive rights: Dallas/Ft. Worth area.

DENVER POST—P.O. Box 1709, Denver, CO 80201. Bob Ewegen, Ed. Articles, 400 to 700 words, with local or regional angle. Pays $35 to $50, on publication. Query.

DES MOINES REGISTER—P.O. Box 957, Des Moines, IA 50304. Attn: "Opinion" Page Ed. Articles, 500 to 850 words, on all topics. Prefer Iowa subjects. Pays $35 to $75, on publication. Exclusive rights: IA.

DETROIT FREE PRESS—321 W. Lafayette Blvd., Detroit, MI 48226. Attn: Op-Ed Ed. Opinion pieces, to 800 words, on domestic and foreign affairs, economics, education, environment, law, politics, and regional interest. Priority given to local writers or topics of local interest. Pays $50 to $100, on publication. Query. Exclusive rights: MI and northern OH.

THE DETROIT NEWS—615 W. Lafayette Blvd., Detroit, MI 48226. Attn: Anne Abate. Pieces, 500 to 750 words, on a wide variety of subjects. Pays $75, on publication.

THE FLINT JOURNAL—200 E. First St., Flint, MI 48502–1925. David J. Fenech, Opinion Dept. Ed. Articles, 650 words, of regional interest by local writers. Non-local writers should query. No payment. Limited market.

FRESNO BEE—1626 E St., Fresno, CA 93786–0001. Karen Baker, Ed. Articles, 750 words. Writers in central California preferred. Send complete manuscript. Pays $75, on acceptance.

THE HOUSTON POST—P.O. Box 4747, Houston, TX 77210–4747. Fred King, Op-Ed Ed. Opinion pieces, 850 words, on wide variety of topics. Send complete manuscript with SASE. Very limited market. Pays $40, on publication. Exclusive rights: Houston area.

INDIANAPOLIS STAR—P.O. Box 145, Indianapolis, IN 46206–0145. John H. Lyst, Ed. Articles, 700 to 800 words. Pays $40, on publication. Exclusive rights: IN.

LONG BEACH PRESS-TELEGRAM—604 Pine Ave., Long Beach, CA 90844. Larry Allison, Ed. Articles, 750 to 900 words, on regional topics. Pays $75, on publication. Exclusive rights: Los Angeles area.

LOS ANGELES TIMES—Times Mirror Sq., Los Angeles, CA 90053. Bob Berger, Op-Ed Ed. Commentary pieces, to 750 words, on many subjects. "Not interested in nostalgia or first-person reaction to faraway events. Pieces must be exclusive." Payment varies, on publication. Limited market. SASE required.

LOUISVILLE COURIER-JOURNAL—525 W. Broadway, Louisville, KY 40202. Attn: Op-Ed Ed. Pieces, 750 words, on regional topics. Local writers preferred. Pays $25 to $50, on publication. Very limited market.

THE NEW YORK TIMES—229 W. 43rd St., New York, NY 10036. Attn: Op-Ed Ed. Opinion pieces, 650 to 800 words, on any topic, including public policy, science, lifestyles, and ideas, etc. Include your address, daytime phone number, and social security number with submission. "If you haven't heard from us within 2 weeks, you can assume we are not using your piece. Include SASE if you want work returned." Pays on publication. Buys first North American rights.

NEWSDAY—"Viewpoints," 235 Pinelawn Rd., Melville, NY 11747. Noel Rubinton, "Viewpoints" Ed. Pieces, 700 to 800 words, on a variety of topics. Pays $150, on publication.

THE ORANGE COUNTY REGISTER—P.O. Box 11626, Santa Ana, CA 92711. K.E. Grubbs, Jr., Ed. Articles on a wide range of local and national issues and topics. Pays $50 to $100, on publication.

THE OREGONIAN—1320 S.W. Broadway, Portland, OR 97201. Address Op-Ed Ed. Articles, 900 to 1,000 words, of news analysis from Pacific Northwest writers or on regional topics. Send complete manuscript. Pays $100, on publication.

PITTSBURGH POST GAZETTE—34 Blvd. of the Allies, Pittsburgh, PA 15222. John Allison, Contributions Ed. Articles, to 800 words, on a variety of subjects. No humor. Pays $60 to $150, on publication. SASE required.

PORTLAND PRESS HERALD—P.O. Box 1460, Portland, ME 04104–5009. Attn: Op-Ed Page Ed. Articles, 750 words, on any topic with regional tie-in. No payment without prior agreement. Exclusive rights: ME.

THE REGISTER GUARD—P.O. Box 10188, Eugene, OR 97440. Don Robinson, Editorial Page Ed. All subjects; regional angle preferred. Pays $10 to $25, on publication. Very limited use of non-local writers.

THE SACRAMENTO BEE—2100 Q St., Sacramento, CA 95852. William Kahrl, Opinion Ed. Op-ed pieces, to 750 words; state and regional topics preferred. Pays $150, on publication.

ST. LOUIS POST-DISPATCH—900 N. Tucker Blvd., St. Louis, MO 63101. Donna Korando, Commentary Ed. Articles, 700 words, on economics, education, science, politics, foreign and domestic affairs, and the environment. Pays $70, on publication. "Goal is to have half of the articles by local writers."

ST. PAUL PIONEER PRESS—345 Cedar St., St. Paul, MN 55101. Ronald D. Clark, Ed. Articles, to 700 words, on a variety of topics. Strongly prefer authors with a connection to the area. Pays $75, on publication.

ST. PETERSBURG TIMES—Box 1121, 490 First Ave. S., St. Petersburg, FL 33731. Jon East, "Perspective" Section Ed. Authoritative articles, to 2,000 words, on current political, economic, and social issues. Payment varies, on publication. Query.

THE SAN FRANCISCO CHRONICLE—901 Mission St., San Francisco, CA 94103. Dean Wakefield, Open Forum Ed. Articles, 400 and 650 words, "that represent lively writing, are pertinent to public policy debates, and move the debate forward." Also, well-crafted humor pieces. Pays to $150 (usually $75 to $100 for unsolicited pieces), on publication.

SAN FRANCISCO EXAMINER—110 5th St., San Francisco, CA 94103. Attn: Op-Ed Ed. Well-written articles, 500 to 650 words, on any subject. Payment varies, on publication.

SEATTLE POST-INTELLIGENCER—P.O. Box 1909, Seattle, WA 98111. Charles J. Dunsire, Editorial Page Ed. Articles, 750 to 800 words, on foreign and domestic affairs, environment, education, politics, regional interest, religion, science, and seasonal material. Prefer writers who live in the Pacific Northwest. Pays $75 to $150, on publication. SASE required. Very limited market.

TULSA WORLD—P.O. Box 1770, Tulsa, OK 74102. Articles, about 600 words, on subjects of local or regional interest. "We prefer local or regional writers." No payment. Exclusive rights: Tulsa area.

USA TODAY—1000 Wilson Blvd., Arlington, VA 22229. Sid Hurlburt, Ed./ Columns. Articles, 400 to 600 words, on public policy issues. Very limited market. Query. Pays $125, on publication.

THE WALL STREET JOURNAL—Editorial Page, 200 Liberty St., New York, NY 10281. David B. Brooks, Op-Ed Ed. Articles, to 1,500 words, on politics, economics, law, education, environment, humor (occasionally), and foreign and domestic affairs. Articles must be timely, heavily reported, and of national interest by writers with expertise in their field. Pays $150 to $300, on publication.

WASHINGTON TIMES—3600 New York Ave. N.E., Washington, DC 20002. Frank Perley, Articles and Opinion Page Ed. Articles, 800 to 1,000 words, on a variety of subjects. No pieces written in the first-person. "Syndicated columnists cover the 'big' issues; find an area that is off the beaten path." Pays $150, on publication. Exclusive rights: Washington, DC and Baltimore area.

ADULT MAGAZINES

CHIC—9171 Wilshire Blvd., Suite 300, Beverly Hills, CA 90210. Doug Oliver, Exec. Ed. Sex-related articles, interviews, erotic fiction, 2,500 words. Query for articles. Pays $750 for articles, $500 for fiction, on acceptance.

D-CUP—Swank Publications, Inc., 210 Rt. 4 E., Suite 401, Paramus, NJ 07652. Bob Rosen, Ed. Erotic fiction and articles, 2,000 to 2,500 words. Pays $100 to $250, on publication.

FORUM, THE INTERNATIONAL JOURNAL OF HUMAN RELA-TIONS—1965 Broadway, New York, NY 10023–5965. V. K. McCarty, Assoc. Pub./Ed. Dir. Erotic fiction with "stunningly memorable, highly explicit sex sculpted with the best possible language skills. Also sexually oriented articles." Pays $600, on acceptance.

GALLERY—401 Park Ave. S., New York, NY 10016–8802. Barry Janoff, Ed.-in-Chief. Rich Friedman, Man. Ed. Articles, investigative pieces, interviews, profiles, to 2,500 words, for sophisticated men. Short humor, satire, service pieces, and fiction. Photos. Pays varying rates, on publication. Query. Guidelines.

GENESIS—110 E. 59th St., Suite 3100, New York, NY 10022. Michael Banka, Pub. Articles, 2,000 words. Sexually explicit nonfiction features, 2,000 words. Photo essays. Query with clips. Pays 60 days after acceptance.

PENTHOUSE—1965 Broadway, New York, NY 10023. Peter Bloch, Ed. Lavada Blanton, Features and Fashion Ed. Articles, to 5,000 words: general-interest profiles, interviews (with introduction), and investigative pieces. Pays on acceptance.

PLAYBOY—680 N. Lakeshore Dr., Chicago, IL 60611. Peter Moore, Stephen Randall, Articles Eds. Articles, 3,500 to 6,000 words, and sophisticated fiction, 1,000 to 10,000 words (5,000 preferred), for urban men. Humor; satire. Science fiction. Pays to $5,000 for articles, to $5,000 for fiction, $2,000 for short-shorts, on acceptance.

PLAYERS—8060 Melrose Ave., Los Angeles, CA 90046. Cecil Wills, Ed. Articles, 1,000 to 3,000 words, for black men: politics, economics, travel, fashion, grooming, entertainment, sports, interviews, fiction, humor, satire, health, and sex. Photos a plus. Pays on publication.

PLAYGIRL—801 Second Ave., New York, NY 10017. Charlene Keel, Man. Ed. Articles, 1,500 words, for women 18 to 34. Celebrity interviews, 1,500 to 2,000 words. Humor. Pays varying rates, on acceptance.

VARIATIONS, FOR LIBERATED LOVERS—1965 Broadway, New York, NY 10023–5965. V. K. McCarty, Ed. Dir./Assoc. Pub. First-person true narrative descriptions of "a couple's enthusiasm, secrets, and sex scenes squarely focused within one of the magazine's pleasure categories." Pays $400, on acceptance.

FICTION MARKETS

This list gives the fiction requirements of general- and special-interest magazines, including those that publish detective and mystery, science fiction and fantasy, romance and confession stories. Other good markets for short fiction are the *College, Literary and Little Magazines* where, though payment is modest (usually in copies only), publication can help a beginning writer achieve recognition by editors at the larger magazines. Juvenile fiction markets are listed under *Juvenile* and *Young Adult Magazines*. Publishers of book-length fiction manuscripts are listed under *Book Publishers*.

All manuscripts must be typed double-space and submitted with self-addressed envelopes bearing postage sufficient for the return of the material. If a manuscript need not be returned, note this with the submission, and enclose an SASE for editorial reply. Use good white paper; onion skin and erasable bond are not acceptable. *Always* keep a copy of the manuscript, since occasionally a manuscript is lost in the mail. Magazines may take several weeks—often longer—to read and report on submissions. If an editor has not reported on a manuscript after a reasonable amount of time, write a brief, courteous letter of inquiry.

GENERAL FICTION

ABORIGINAL SF—P.O. Box 2449, Woburn, MA 01888–0849. Charles C. Ryan, Ed. Stories, 2,500 to 7,500 words, with a unique scientific idea, human or alien character, plot, and theme of lasting value; "must be science fiction; no fantasy, horror, or sword and sorcery." Pays $250. Send SASE for guidelines.

AFRICAN VOICES—305 7th Ave., 11th Fl., New York, NY 10001–6008. Carolyn A. Butts, Exec. Ed. Bimonthly. Humorous, erotic, and dramatic fiction, 500 to 2,500 words, by ethnic writers. Nonfiction, 500 to 1,500 words, is also welcome. Investigative articles, artist profiles, essays, and first-person narratives. Poetry, to 50 lines. Pays $25 to $100, on publication.

AIM MAGAZINE—P.O. Box 20554, Chicago, IL 60620. Ruth Apilado, Ed. Short stories, 800 to 3,000 words, geared to proving that people from different backgrounds are more alike than they are different. Story should not moralize. Pays from $15 to $25, on publication. Annual contest.

ALFRED HITCHCOCK MYSTERY MAGAZINE—1540 Broadway, New York, NY 10036. Cathleen Jordan, Ed. Well-plotted, plausible mystery, suspense, detection and crime stories, to 14,000 words; "ghost stories, humor, futuristic or atmospheric tales are all possible, as long as they include a crime or the suggestion of one." Pays 7¢ a word, on acceptance. Guidelines with SASE.

ALOHA, THE MAGAZINE OF HAWAII AND THE PACIFIC—720 Kapiolani Blvd., 4th Fl., Honolulu, HI 96813. Cheryl Tsutsumi, Ed. Fiction to 4,000 words, with a Hawaii focus. Pays $150 to $300, on publication. Query.

AMAZING STORIES—Box 111, Lake Geneva, WI 53147. Mr. Kim Mohan, Ed. Original, previously unpublished science fiction, fantasy, and horror, 1,000 to 20,000 words. Pays 6¢ to 10¢ a word, on acceptance.

THE AMERICAN VOICE—332 W. Broadway, Suite 1215, Louisville, KY 40202. Frederick Smock, Ed. Avant-garde, literary fiction, nonfiction, and well-crafted poetry, any length (shorter works are preferred). "Please read our journal before attempting to submit." Payment varies, on publication.

ANALOG SCIENCE FICTION AND FACT—1540 Broadway, New York, NY 10036. Stanley Schmidt, Ed. Science fiction, with strong characters in believable future or alien setting: short stories, 2,000 to 7,500 words; novelettes, 10,000 to

20,000 words; serials, to 70,000 words. Pays 5¢ to 8¢ a word, on acceptance. Query for novels.

ASIMOV'S SCIENCE FICTION MAGAZINE—1540 Broadway, 15th Fl., New York, NY 10036. Gardner Dozois, Ed. Short science fiction and fantasies, to 15,000 words. Pays 6¢ to 8¢ a word, on acceptance. Guidelines.

THE ATLANTIC MONTHLY—745 Boylston St., Boston, MA 02116. William Whitworth, Ed. Short stories, 2,000 to 6,000 words, of highest literary quality, with "fully developed narratives, distinctive characterization, freshness in language, and a resolution of some kind." SASE required. Pays $2,500, on acceptance.

THE BELLETRIST REVIEW—Marmarc Publications, 17 Farmington Ave., Suite 290, Plainville, CT 06062. Marlene Dube, Ed. Semiannual. Fiction, 1,500 to 5,000 words: adventure, contemporary, erotica, psychological horror, humor, literary, mainstream, suspense, and mystery. No fantasy, juvenile, westerns, overblown horror, or confessional pieces. Pays in copies.

THE BOSTON GLOBE MAGAZINE—*The Boston Globe*, Boston, MA 02107. Evelynne Kramer, Ed. Short stories, to 3,000 words. Include SASE. Pays on acceptance.

BOYS' LIFE—1325 W. Walnut Hill Ln., P.O. Box 152079, Irving, TX 75015–2079. Kathleen Vilim DaGroomes, Fiction Ed. Publication of the Boy Scouts of America. Humor, mystery, science fiction, adventure, 1,200 words, for 8- to 18-year-old boys; study back issues. Pays from $750, on acceptance. Send SASE for guidelines.

BUFFALO SPREE MAGAZINE—Box 38, Buffalo, NY 14226. Johanna Van De Mark, Ed./Pub. Fiction and humor, to 2,000 words, for readers in the western New York region. Pays $100 to $125, on publication.

BYLINE—Box 130596, Edmond, OK 73013. Marcia Preston, Ed.-in-Chief. Kathryn Fanning, Man. Ed. General fiction, 2,000 to 4,000 words. Nonfiction: 1,500- to 1,800-word features and 300- to 800-word special departments. Poetry, 10 to 30 lines preferred. Nonfiction and poetry must be about writing. Humor, 400 to 800 words, about writing. "We seek practical and motivational material that tells writers how they can succeed, not why they can't. Overdone topics: writers' block, the muse, rejection slips." Pays $5 to $10 for poetry; $15 to $35 for departments; $50 for features and short fiction, on acceptance. SASE for guidelines.

CAMPUS LIFE—465 Gundersen Dr., Carol Stream, IL 60188. Harold Smith, Exec. Ed. Fiction and humor, reflecting Christian values, 1,000 to 3,000 words, for high school and college students. Pays from $150 to $400, on acceptance. Limited free-lance market. Published writers only. Queries required; SASE.

CAPPER'S—1503 S.W. 42nd St., Topeka, KS 66609–1265. Nancy Peavler, Ed. Short novel-length fiction for serialization. Pays on publication.

CAT FANCY—P.O. Box 6050, Mission Viejo, CA 92690. Debbie Phillips-Donaldson, Ed. Fiction and nonfiction, to 3,000 words, about cats. Pays 5¢ to 10¢ a word, on publication.

CATHOLIC FORESTER—355 Shuman Blvd., P.O. Box 3012, Naperville, IL 60566–7012. Dorothy Deer, Ed. Official publication of the Catholic Order of Foresters. Fiction, to 2,000 words (prefer shorter); "looking for more contemporary, meaningful stories dealing with life today." No sex or violence or "preachy" stories; religious angle not required. Pays 10¢ a word, on acceptance.

CHESS LIFE—186 Rte. 9W, New Windsor, NY 12553–7698. Glenn Petersen, Ed. Fiction, 500 to 2,000 words, related to chess for members of the U.S. Chess

Federation. Also, articles, 500 to 3,000 words, on chess news, profiles, technical aspects of chess. Pays varying rates, on acceptance. Query; limited market.

COBBLESTONE—7 School St., Peterborough, NH 03458–1454. Meg Chorlian, Ed. Fiction must relate to theme, 500 to 1,200 words, for children aged 8 to 14 years. Pays 10¢ to 17¢ a word, on publication. Send SASE for editorial guidelines.

COMMENTARY—165 E. 56th St., New York, NY 10022. Brenda Brown, Man. Ed. Fiction, of high literary quality, on contemporary social or Jewish issues. Pays on publication.

COMMON GROUND MAGAZINE—P.O. Box 99, McVeytown, PA 17051–0099. Ruth Dunmire and Pam Brumbaugh, Eds. Quarterly. Fiction, 1,000 to 2,000 words, related to Central Pennsylvania's Juniata River Valley. Pays $25 to $200, on publication. Guidelines.

COSMOPOLITAN—224 W. 57th St., New York, NY 10019. Betty Kelly, Fiction and Books Ed. No longer publishing short stories; fiction manuscripts will not be considered.

COUNTRY WOMAN—P.O. Box 989, Greendale, WI 53129. Kathy Pohl, Man. Ed. Fiction, 750 to 1,000 words, of interest to rural women; protagonist must be a country woman. "Stories should focus on life in the country, its problems and joys, as experienced by country women; must be upbeat and positive." Pays $90 to $125, on acceptance.

CRICKET—Box 300, Peru, IL 61354–0300. Marianne Carus, Ed.-in-Chief. Fiction, 200 to 1,800 words, for 9- to 14-year-olds. Pays to 25¢ a word, on publication. SASE required.

DISCOVERIES—WordAction Publishing Co., 6401 The Paseo, Kansas City, MO 64131. Attn: Ed. Asst. Weekly take-home paper designed to correlate with Evangelical Sunday school curriculum. Fiction, 500 to 700 words, for 8- to 10-year-olds. Stories should feature contemporary, true-to-life characters and should illustrate character building and scriptural application. No poetry. Pays 5¢ a word, on publication. Guidelines.

DOGWOOD TALES MAGAZINE—P.O. Box 172068, Memphis, TN 38187. Attn: Ed. Bimonthly "for the fiction lover in all of us." Short stories, 250 to 6,000 words, in any genre except religion or pornography. "Stories should be fresh, well-paced, and have strong endings." Contests. Guidelines.

EASYRIDERS MAGAZINE—P. O. Box 3000, Agoura Hills, CA 91376–3000. Keith R. Ball, Ed. Hard-hitting, rugged fiction, 1,200 to 2,000 words, that depicts bikers in a favorable light; humorous bent preferred. Pays 10¢ to 25¢ a word, on acceptance.

ELLERY QUEEN MYSTERY MAGAZINE—1540 Broadway, New York, NY 10036. Janet Hutchings, Ed. High-quality detective, crime, and mystery stories, 3,000 to 7,000 words. Also "Minute Mysteries," 250 words, short verses, limericks, and novellas, to 17,000 words. "We like a mix of classic detection and suspenseful crime." "First Stories" by unpublished writers. Pays 3¢ to 8¢ a word, on acceptance.

ESQUIRE—250 W. 55th St., New York, NY 10019. Edward Kosner, Ed.-in-Chief. Send finished manuscript of short story; submit one at a time. No full-length novels. No pornography, science fiction, or "true romance" stories.

EVANGEL—Light and Life Press, Box 535002, Indianapolis, IN 46253–5002. Carolyn Smith, Ed. Free Methodist. Fiction, to 1,200 words, with personal faith in Christ shown as instrumental in solving problems. Pays 4¢ a word, on publication.

FAITH 'N STUFF—See *Guideposts for Kids.*

FAMILY CIRCLE—110 Fifth Ave., New York, NY 10011. Kathy Sagan, Sr. Ed. Fiction is no longer being considered.

FICTION INTERNATIONAL—English Dept., San Diego State Univ., San Diego, CA 92182–0295. Harold Jaffe, Ed. Post-modernist and politically committed fiction and theory. Submit between September 1st and December 15th.

FLY ROD & REEL—P.O. Box 370, Camden, ME 04843. James E. Butler, Ed. Occasional fiction, 2,000 to 2,500 words, related to fly fishing. Special annual fiction issue published in summer. Payment varies, on acceptance.

GALLERY—401 Park Ave. S., New York, NY 10016–8802. Barry Janoff, Ed. Dir. Rich Friedman, Man. Ed. Fiction, to 3,000 words, for sophisticated men. "We are not looking for science fiction, mystery, 40s-style detective, or stories involving aliens from other planets. We do look for interesting stories that enable readers to view life in an off-beat, unusual, or insightful manner: fiction with believable characters and actions." Pays varying rates, on publication.

GENRE SAMPLER MAGAZINE—P.O. Box 6978, Denver, CO 80206. S. Wright, Ed. Quarterly. Short stories, 2,500 to 4,000 words, in the following genres: mystery, suspense, thriller; romance; horror; literary; adventure; science fiction; fantasy; western; mainstream; and young adult. Special category for high school students. Pays $10 to $20, on publication.

GLIMMER TRAIN PRESS—812 S.W. Washington St., Suite 1205, Portland, OR 97205. Susan Burmeister-Brown, Ed. Fiction, 1,200 to 7,500 words. "Eight stories in each quarterly magazine." Pays $300, on acceptance. Submit material in January, April, July, and October; allow 3 months for response. "Send SASE for guidelines before submitting."

GOLF DIGEST—5520 Park Ave., Trumbull, CT 06611. Jerry Tarde, Ed. Unusual or humorous stories, to 2,000 words, about golf; golf "fables," to 1,000 words.

GOOD HOUSEKEEPING—959 Eighth Ave., New York, NY 10019. Lee Quarfoot, Fiction Ed. Short stories, 1,000 to 3,000 words, with strong identification figures for women, by published writers and "beginners with demonstrable talent." Novel condensations or excerpts from about-to-be-published books only. "Writers whose work interests us will hear from us within 4 to 6 weeks of receipt of manuscript. Please send inexpensive copies of your work; and do not enclose SASEs or postage. We can no longer return or critique manuscripts. We do accept multiple submissions." Pays top rates, on acceptance.

GRIT—1503 S.W. 42nd St., Topeka, KS 66609. Roberta J. Peterson, Ed.-in-Chief. Short stories, 2,200 to 2,500 words; occasionally shorter stories, 800 to 2,000 words. Articles, 500 to 1,200 words, on interesting people and topics. Should be upbeat, inspirational, wholesome; of interest to all ages. No reference to drinking, smoking, drugs, sex, or violence. Also publishes some short poetry and true-story nostalgia. Pays 12¢ to 25¢ a word, extra for photos, on publication. All fiction submissions should be marked "Fiction Dept." Guidelines.

GUIDEPOSTS FOR KIDS—(formerly *Faith 'n Stuff*) P.O. Box 538A, Chesterton, IN 46304. Mary Lou Carney, Ed. Bible-based bimonthly for 7- to 12-year-olds. Problem fiction, mysteries, historicals, 1,500 words, with "realistic dialogue and sharp imagery. No preachy stories about Bible-toting children." Pays $125 to $300 for all rights, on acceptance. No reprints.

HARDBOILED—Gryphon Publications, P.O. Box 209, Brooklyn, NY 11228–0209. Gary Lovisi, Ed. Hard, cutting-edge crime fiction, to 3,000 words, "with impact." Query for articles, book and film reviews. "It's a good idea to read an issue before submitting a story." Payment varies, on publication.

HARPER'S MAGAZINE—666 Broadway, New York, NY 10012. Attn: Eds. Will consider unsolicited fiction manuscripts. Query for nonfiction (very limited market). No poetry. SASE required.

HICALL—See *Teen Life*.

HIGHLIGHTS FOR CHILDREN—803 Church St., Honesdale, PA 18431–1824. Kent L. Brown Jr., Ed. Fiction on sports, humor, adventure, mystery, etc., 900 words, for 8- to 12-year-olds. Easy rebus form, 100 to 120 words, and easy-to-read stories, to 500 words, for beginning readers. "We are partial to stories in which the protagonist solves a dilemma through his or her own resources." Pays from 14¢ a word, on acceptance. Buys all rights.

HOMETOWN PRESS—2007 Gallatin St., Huntsville, AL 35801. Jeffrey C. Hindman, M.D., Ed.-in-Chief. Fiction, 800 to 2,500 words, well-crafted and tightly written, suitable for family reading. New and unpublished writers welcome. SASE for guidelines.

LADIES' HOME JOURNAL—100 Park Ave., New York, NY 10017. Fiction generally accepted through agents only. "When submitting material or requesting guidelines, include SASE."

LOLLIPOPS—Good Apple, Inc., P. O. Box 299, Carthage, IL 62321–0299. Donna Borst, Ed. Teaching ideas and activities covering all areas of the curriculum for preschool to first-grade children. Rates vary.

THE LOOKOUT—8121 Hamilton Ave., Cincinnati, OH 45231. Simon J. Dahlman, Ed. Short-shorts, with moral or Christian themes, 500 to 2,000 words. Pays to 9¢ a word, on acceptance. No historical fiction, science fiction, or fantasy.

LOUIS L'AMOUR WESTERN MAGAZINE—1540 Broadway, New York, NY 10036. Elana Lore, Ed. Well-written western short stories, to 12,000 words. "Our focus is on traditional western short stories, but we will also consider Native American, modern, and mystery-oriented westerns." Pays 8¢ a word, on acceptance.

MADEMOISELLE—350 Madison Ave., New York, NY 10017. No longer accepts fiction.

THE MAGAZINE OF FANTASY AND SCIENCE FICTION—Box 11526, Eugene, OR 97440. Kristine Kathryn Rusch, Ed. Fantasy and science fiction stories, to 15,000 words. Pays 5¢ to 7¢ a word, on acceptance.

MATURE LIVING—127 Ninth Ave. N., Nashville, TN 37234. Al Shackleford, Ed. Fiction, 900 to 1,200 words, for senior adults. Must be consistent with Christian principles. Pays $75, on acceptance.

MIDSTREAM—110 E. 59th St., New York, NY 10022. M. S. Solow, Assoc. Ed. Fiction on Jewish themes, to 3,000 words. Pays 5¢ a word, after publication. Allow 3 months for response.

MILITARY LIFESTYLE MAGAZINE—4800 Montgomery Ln., Suite 710, Bethesda, MD 20814–5341. Hope Daniels, Ed. Fiction, to 1,500 words, for military families in the U.S. and overseas. Pays on publication. Annual fiction contest.

NA'AMAT WOMAN—200 Madison Ave., 21st Fl., New York, NY 10016. Judith A. Sokoloff, Ed. Short stories, approximately 2,500 words, with Jewish theme. Pays 8¢ a word, on publication.

NEW MYSTERY MAGAZINE—The Flatiron Bldg., 175 Fifth Ave., Suite 2001, New York, NY 10010–7703. Charles Raisch, Ed. Quarterly. Short mysteries, crime and suspense stories, 2,000 to 6,000 words, with "sympathetic characters and visual scenes." Book reviews, 250 to 2,000 words, of recently published novels. Pays 3¢ to 10¢ a word, on publication. No guidelines; study back issues.

THE NEW YORKER—20 W. 43rd St., New York, NY 10036. Attn: Fiction Dept. Short stories, humor, and satire. Payment varies, on acceptance. Include SASE.

OMNI—1965 Broadway, New York, NY 10023. Ellen Datlow, Fiction Ed. Strong, realistic science fiction. "We want to intrigue our readers with mindbroadening, thought-provoking stories that will excite their sense of wonder." Some contemporary hard-edged fantasy. No sword-and-sorcery, space opera, or supernatural stories. (Note: Nonfiction should be sent to Keith Ferrell, Ed., *Omni*, 324 W. Wendover Ave., Suite 205, Greensboro, NC 27408.) Pays from $1,300 to $2,250, on acceptance. SASE.

PENTHOUSE—1965 Broadway, New York, NY 10023. Peter Bloch, Ed. Lavada Blanton, Features and Fashion Ed. Women's erotic fiction. SASE required.

PLAYBOY—680 N. Lakeshore Dr., Chicago, IL 60611. Alice K. Turner, Fiction Ed. Limited market.

PLAYGIRL—801 Second Ave., New York, NY 10017. Judy Cole, Man. Ed. Contemporary, erotic fiction, from a female perspective, 2,000 to 3,000 words. Pays from $500, after acceptance.

POWER AND LIGHT—6401 The Paseo, Kansas City, MO 64131. Beula J. Postlewait, Preteen Ed. Fiction, 500 to 700 words, for grades 5 to 6, defining Christian experiences and values. Pays 5¢ a word for multiple-use rights, on publication.

PURPOSE—616 Walnut Ave., Scottdale, PA 15683–1999. James E. Horsch, Ed. Fiction, 750 words, on problem solving from a Christian point of view. Poetry, 3 to 12 lines. Pays to 5¢ a word for fiction; to $1 per line for poetry, on acceptance.

QUEEN'S QUARTERLY—Queens Univ., Kingston, Ont., Canada K7L 3N6. Attn: Fiction Ed. Fiction, to 4,000 words, in English and French. Pays to $300, on publication.

RANGER RICK—8925 Leesburg Pike, Vienna, VA 22184–0001. Deborah Churchman, Fiction Ed. Action-packed nature- and conservation-related fiction, for 6- to 12-year-olds. Maximum: 900 words. No anthropomorphism. "Multi-cultural stories welcome." Pays to $550, on acceptance. Usually buys all rights. Send SASE for guidelines.

REDBOOK—224 W. 57th St., New York, NY 10019. Dawn Raffel, Fiction Ed. Fresh, distinctive short stories, of interest to women. Pays from $1,500 for short stories (to 25 pages). Allow 12 weeks for reply. Manuscripts without SASE will not be returned. No unsolicited poetry, novellas, or novels accepted.

ST. ANTHONY MESSENGER—1615 Republic St., Cincinnati, OH 45210–1298. Norman Perry, O.F.M., Ed. Barbara Beckwith, Man. Ed. Fiction that makes readers think about issues, lifestyles, and values. Pays 14¢ a word, on acceptance. Queries or manuscripts accepted.

SASSY—6420 Wilshire Blvd., Los Angeles, CA 90048–5515. Attn: Kathy Colbert. Short stories written in the magazine's style, for girls age 14 to 19. Payment varies, on acceptance.

SCHOOL MATES—U.S. Chess Federation, 186 Rte. 9W, New Windsor, NY 12553–7698. Carl Simmons, Ed. Fiction and articles, to 1,000 words, and short fillers, related to chess for beginning chess players (not necessarily children). "Instructive, but there's room for fun puzzles, anecdotes, etc. All chess related." Pays about $40 per 1,000 words, on publication. Query; limited free-lance market.

SEA KAYAKER—P.O. Box 17170, Seattle, WA 98107–0860. Christopher Cunningham, Ed. Short stories exclusively related to ocean kayaking, 1,000 to 3,000 words. Pays on publication.

SEVENTEEN—850 Third Ave., New York, NY 10022. Joe Bargmann, Fiction Ed. High-quality, literary short fiction, to 4,000 words. Pays on acceptance.

SNOWBOARDER—P.O. Box 1028, Dana Point, CA 92629. Doug Palladini, Assoc. Pub. Published 5 times a year. Uses fiction, 1,000 to 1,500 words, related to snowboarding. Limited fiction market. Pays $150 to $800, on acceptance and on publication.

SPORTS AFIELD—250 W. 55th St., New York, NY 10019. Terry McDonell, Ed. Occasional fiction, 1,500 words, on hunting, fishing, and related topics. Humor. Pays top rates, on acceptance.

STRAIGHT—8121 Hamilton Ave., Cincinnati, OH 45231. Carla Crane, Ed. Well-constructed fiction, 1,000 to 1,500 words, showing Christian teens using Bible principles in everyday life. Contemporary, realistic teen characters a must. Most interested in school, church, dating, and family life stories. Pays 3¢ to 7¢ a word, on acceptance. Send SASE for guidelines.

SUNDAY DIGEST—850 N. Grove Ave., Elgin, IL 60120. Attn: Ed. Short stories, 400 to 1,800 words, with evangelical religious slant. Payment varies, on acceptance.

'TEEN—6420 Wilshire Blvd., Los Angeles, CA 90048–5515. Attn: Fiction Dept. Short stories, 2,500 to 4,000 words: mystery, teen situations, adventure, romance, humor for teens. Pays from $200, on acceptance.

TEEN LIFE—(formerly *Hicall*) 1445 Boonville Ave., Springfield, MO 65802–1894. Tammy Bicket, Ed. Fiction, to 1,000 words, for 13- to 17-year-olds. Strong evangelical emphasis a must: believable characters working out their problems according to biblical principles. Buys first rights; pays on acceptance. Reprints considered.

TQ/TEEN QUEST—2845 W. Airport Freeway, Suite 137, Irving, TX 75062. Christopher Lyon, Ed. Fiction, 1,000 to 2,000 words, for Christian teens. Pays 10¢ to 15¢ a word, on publication.

TRUCKERS/USA—P.O. Box 323, Windber, PA 15963. David Adams, Ed. Trucking related articles, poetry, and fiction, to 1,000 words. Payment varies, on acceptance.

TRUE CONFESSIONS—233 Park Ave. S., New York, NY 10003. Pat Vitucci, Ed. Romantic stories, 5,000 to 8,000 words: true-to-life drama, passion, intrigue, etc. Also short stories, 1,000 to 2,000 words. Pays after publication. Buys all rights.

VIRGINIA—The Country Publishers, Inc., P.O. Box 798, Berryville, VA 22611. Lisa Cain Curran, Asst. Ed. Quarterly. Fiction, 1,000 to 1,500 words, with Virginia setting or reference. Pays $200 to $300, 30 days after publication.

VIRTUE: THE CHRISTIAN MAGAZINE FOR WOMEN—P.O. Box 36630, Colorado Springs, CO 80936–3663. Nancie Carmichael, Man. Ed. Inspirational fiction, 1,200 to 1,400 words, with a Christian slant. Pays 15¢ to 25¢ a word, on publication. Query required for articles. SASE required.

WESTERN PEOPLE—Box 2500, Saskatoon, Sask., Canada S7K 2C4. Attn: Ed. Short stories, 1,000 to 2,500 words, on subjects or themes of interest to rural readers in western Canada. Pays $100 to $175, on acceptance. Enclose international reply coupons and SAE.

WILDFOWL—1901 Bell Ave., Suite #4, Des Moines, IA 50315. R. Sparks, Man. Ed. Occasional fiction, humor, related to duck hunters and wildfowl. Pays $400, on acceptance.

WIN MAGAZINE—120 S. San Fernando Blvd., Suite 439, Burbank, CA 91502. Cecil Suzuki, Ed. Gambling-related fiction, 1,600 to 2,500 words. Pays on publication.

WOMAN'S WORLD—270 Sylvan Ave., Englewood Cliffs, NJ 07632. Jeanne Muchnick, Fiction Ed. Fast-moving short stories, about 2,400 words, with light romantic theme. (Specify "short story" on outside of envelope.) Mini-mysteries, 1,100 words, with "whodunit" or "howdunit" theme. No science fiction, fantasy, or historical romance and no horror, ghost stories, or gratuitous violence. Pays $1,000 for short stories, $500 for mini-mysteries, on acceptance. Submit manuscript with SASE.

YANKEE—Yankee Publishing Co., Dublin, NH 03444. Judson Hale, Ed. Edie Clark, Fiction Ed. High-quality, literary short fiction, to 1,500 words, with setting in or compatible with New England; no sap buckets or lobster pot stereotypes. Pays $1,000, on acceptance.

DETECTIVE AND MYSTERY

ALFRED HITCHCOCK MYSTERY MAGAZINE—1540 Broadway, New York, NY 10036. Cathleen Jordan, Ed. Well-plotted mystery, detective, suspense, and crime fiction, to 14,000 words. Submissions by new writers strongly encouraged. Pays 7¢ a word, on acceptance. Guidelines with SASE.

ARMCHAIR DETECTIVE—129 W. 56th St., New York, NY 10019. Kate Stine, Ed.-in-Chief. Jeffrey Lorber, Man. Ed. Articles on mystery and detective fiction; biographical sketches, reviews, etc. No fiction; no short stories. Pays $10 a printed page; reviews are unpaid.

ELLERY QUEEN MYSTERY MAGAZINE—1540 Broadway, New York, NY 10036. Janet Hutchings, Ed. Detective, crime, and mystery fiction, approximately 1,500 to 12,000 words. No sex, sadism, or sensationalism. Particularly interested in new writers and "first stories." Pays 3¢ to 8¢ a word, on acceptance.

HARDBOILED—Gryphon Publications, P.O. Box 209, Brooklyn, NY 11228–0209. Gary Lovisi, Ed. Hard, cutting-edge crime fiction, to 3,000 words. Query for articles, book and film reviews. B&W drawings (send photocopies only). Payment varies, on publication.

NEW MYSTERY MAGAZINE—The Flatiron Bldg., 175 Fifth Ave., Suite 2001, New York, NY 10010–7703. Charles Raisch, Ed. Quarterly. Short mysteries, crime and suspense stories, 2,000 to 6,000 words. No true crime. Book reviews, 250 to 2,000 words, of upcoming or recently published novels. Pays $15 to $300, on publication. Guidelines.

OVER MY DEAD BODY!—P.O. Box 1778, Auburn, WA 98071–1778. Cherie Jung, Features Ed. Mystery, suspense, and crime fiction, to 4,000 words. Author profiles, interviews, and mystery-related travel, 750 to 1,500 words. Fillers, to 100 words. Include B&W photos. "We are entertainment for mystery fans, from cozy to hardboiled and everything in between." Pays 1¢ a word for fiction; $10 to $25 for nonfiction; $5 for fillers; $10 to $25 for illustrations, on publication.

SCIENCE FICTION AND FANTASY

ABERRATIONS—(formerly *Aberations*) P.O. Box 460430, San Francisco, CA 94146. Richard Blair, Man. Ed. Michael Andre-Driussi, Sr. Fiction Ed. Science fiction, horror, and fantasy, to 8,000 words. "Experimental, graphic, multi-genre is O.K. with science fiction/fantasy/horror tie-in." Guidelines. Pays ¼¢ a word, on publication.

ABORIGINAL SF—P.O. Box 2449, Woburn, MA 01888–0849. Charles C. Ryan, Ed. Short stories, 2,500 to 7,500 words, and poetry, one to 2 typed pages, with strong science content, lively, unique characters, and well-designed plots. No sword and sorcery or fantasy. Pays $250 for fiction, $20 for poetry, $4 for science fiction jokes, and $20 for cartoons, on publication.

AMAZING STORIES—Box 111, Lake Geneva, WI 53147. Mr. Kim Mohan, Ed. Original, previously unpublished science fiction, fantasy, and horror, 1,000 to 25,000 words. Pays 6¢ to 10¢ a word, on acceptance.

ANALOG SCIENCE FICTION AND FACT—1540 Broadway, New York, NY 10036. Stanley Schmidt, Ed. Science fiction with strong characters in believable future or alien setting: short stories, 2,000 to 7,500 words; novelettes, 10,000 to 20,000 words; serials, to 80,000 words. Also uses future-related articles. Pays to 7¢ a word, on acceptance. Query for serials and articles.

AREA OF OPERATIONS—Stygian Vortex Publications, 6634 Atlanta St., Hollywood, FL 33024–2965. Glenda Woodrum, Ed. in-Chief. Annual. Adult science fiction with a military slant. No length limits; query for stories over 10,000 words. Role-playing games; book, movie, and game reviews; game and science fiction convention information. "As violence is part of this genre, death and destruction are expected. Strong language and adult themes are part of this type of science fiction, too. Make certain the world you create is entirely your own." Payment is one copy. Guidelines.

ARGONAUT—P.O. Box 4201, Austin, TX 78765. Michael E. Ambrose, Ed. "Hard" science fiction, to 7,500 words, and science fiction dealing with the sciences, intergalactic or interplanetary adventure. Poetry, to 30 lines, with a science fiction focus. No fantasy, horror, interviews, reviews, or seasonal material. Reports in 6 weeks. Pays in 3 copies.

ASIMOV'S SCIENCE FICTION MAGAZINE—1540 Broadway, 15th Fl., New York, NY 10036. Gardner Dozois, Ed. Short, character-oriented science fiction and fantasy, to 15,000 words. Pays 5¢ to 8¢ a word, on acceptance. Send SASE for guidelines.

DRAGON MAGAZINE—P.O. Box 111, Lake Geneva, WI 53147. Mr. Kim Mohan, Ed. Barbara G. Young, Fiction Ed. Articles, 1,500 to 7,500 words, on fantasy and science fiction role-playing games. Fantasy, 1,500 to 8,000 words. Pays 6¢ to 8¢ a word for fiction, on acceptance. Pays 4¢ a word for articles, on publication. Send SASE for guidelines.

FANGORIA—475 Park Ave. S., 8th Fl., New York, NY 10016. Anthony Timpone, Ed. Published 10 times yearly. Movie, TV, and book previews, reviews, and interviews, 1,800 to 2,500 words, in connection with upcoming horror films. "A strong love of the genre and an appreciation and understanding of the magazine are essential." Pays $175 to $225, on publication.

FANTASY AND SCIENCE FICTION—Mercury Press, Inc., P.O. Box 11526, Eugene, OR 97440. Kristine Kathryn Rusch, Ed. Short stories, to 20,000 words. "We have no formula, but you should be familiar with the magazine before submitting." For sample copies, write to 143 W. Creamhill Rd., W. Cornwall, CT 06796. Pays 5¢ to 7¢ a word, on acceptance.

FANTASY & TERROR—See *Fantasy Macabre.*

FANTASY MACABRE—P.O. Box 20610, Seattle, WA 98102. Jessica Salmonson, Ed. Fiction, to 3,000 words, including translations. "We look for a tale that is strong in atmosphere, with menace that is suggested and threatening rather than the result of dripping blood and gore." Pays 1¢ a word, to $30 per story, on publication. Also publishes *Fantasy & Terror* for poetry-in-prose pieces.

FOOTSTEPS PRESS—P.O. Box 75, Round Top, NY 12473. Bill Munster, Ed. Horror, mystery, and ghost story chapbooks, 3,000 to 5,000 words. Royalty (usually from $350 to $500). Query.

HAUNTS—Nightshade Publications, Box 3342, Providence, RI 02906. Joseph K. Cherkes, Ed. Horror, science/fantasy, and supernatural short stories with strong characters, 1,500 to 8,000 words. No explicit sexual scenes or gratuitous violence. Pays 1/3¢ to 1¢ a word, on publication. Manuscripts read January through June.

HOBSON'S CHOICE: SCIENCE FICTION AND TECHNOLOGY—The Starwind Press, P.O. Box 98, Ripley, OH 45167. Attn: Submissions Ed. Science fiction and fantasy, 2,000 to 10,000 words. Articles and literary criticism, 1,000 to 5,000 words, for readers interested in science and technology. Query for nonfiction. Pays 1¢ to 4¢ a word, on acceptance.

THE LEADING EDGE—3163 JKHB, Provo, UT 84602. Michael Carr, Ed. Published 3 times a year. Short stories, 3,000 to 12,000 words, and some experimental fiction; poems, to 200 lines; and articles, to 8,000 words, on science, scientific speculation, and literary criticism. "Do not send originals; manuscripts are marked and critiqued by staff." Pays $10 to $100 for fiction; $10 per published page of poetry, on publication. Guidelines.

LORDS OF THE ABYSS: TALES OF SUPERNATURAL HORROR—Stygian Vortex Publications, 6634 Atlanta St., Hollywood, FL 33024–2965. Glenda Woodrum, Ed.-in-Chief. John R. Osborne, Asst. Ed. Annual. Stories by and for supernatural horror enthusiasts. No length limits on fiction; query for stories over 10,000 words. Some book, movie, and role-playing game reviews, to 500 words. "No serial killers, rapists, insane people, child molesters, or demonically possessed psycho killers." Payment is one copy. Guidelines.

THE MAGAZINE OF FANTASY AND SCIENCE FICTION—P.O. Box 11526, Eugene, OR 97440. Kristine Kathryn Rusch, Ed. Fantasy and science fiction stories, to 10,000 words. Pays 5¢ to 7¢ a word, on acceptance.

MAGIC REALISM—P.O. Box 620, Orem, UT 84059–0620. C. Darren Butler, Ed. Julie Thomas, Ed. Published 2 to 3 times a year. Stories, to 7,500 words (4,000 words preferred), of magic realism, exaggerated realism, some genre fantasy/dark fantasy. Occasionally publish glib fantasy like that found in folktales, fairy tales, and myths. No occult, sleight-of-hand magicians, or wizards/witches. Pays $2 per published page for prose; $3 per page for poetry.

MARION ZIMMER BRADLEY'S FANTASY MAGAZINE—P.O. Box 249, Berkeley, CA 94701. Marion Zimmer Bradley, Ed. Quarterly. Well-plotted stories, 3,500 to 4,000 words. Action and adventure fantasy "with no particular objection to modern settings." Send SASE for guidelines before submitting. Pays 3¢ to 10¢ a word, on acceptance.

MIDNIGHT ZOO—Box 8040, 544 Ygnacio Valley Rd., #13, Walnut Creek, CA 94596. Elizabeth Martin-Burk, Man. Ed. Science fiction, horror, and fantasy, 8,000 words. Nonfiction, 1,000 to 2,000 words, including interviews, humor, and general interest. Guidelines.

NEURONET: STORIES FROM THE CYBERLAND—Stygian Vortex Publications, 6634 Atlanta St., Hollywood, FL 33024–2965. Glenda Woodrum, Ed.-in-Chief. John R. Osborne, Asst. Ed. Annual. Cyberpunk fiction. "All stories should be hard-hitting, gritty, and filled with the grim nature of the cyberpunk future." No length limits; query for over 10,000 words. Payment is one copy. Guidelines.

NEXT PHASE—Phantom Press Publications, 33 Court St., New Haven, CT 06511. Kim Means, Ed. Science fiction, fantasy, experimental fiction, and commentary, to 3,000 words. Poetry, any length. "We prefer environmentally or socially conscious fiction." SASE required. Pays in copies.

OMNI—1965 Broadway, New York, NY 10023. Ellen Datlow, Fiction Ed. Strong, realistic science fiction, 2,000 to 10,000 words, with good characterizations. "We want to intrigue our readers with mindbroadening, thought-provoking stories that will excite their sense of wonder." Some fantasy. No horror, ghost, or sword and sorcery tales. (Nonfiction, 750 to 3,000 words, should be sent to Keith Ferrell, Ed., *Omni,* 324 W. Wendover Ave., Suite 205, Greensboro, NC 27408.) Pays $1,300 to $2,250, on acceptance. SASE.

ONYX MAGAZINE—713 E. 8th St., Hobart, IN 46342. Tim Snodgrass, Ed. Quarterly. Humorous science fiction and fantasy, to 8 pages, single-spaced. Personal-experience essays, to 8 pages, on science fiction/fantasy conventions. Poems, limericks, fillers, drawings. Pays in copies.

PIRATE WRITINGS—53 Whitman Ave., Islip, NY 11751. Edward J. McFadden, Pub./Ed. Mystery, science fiction, fantasy, humor, and light horror; shorts, 250 to 1,000 words, and stories, 1,000 to 2,500 words. Poetry, to 20 lines. Pays to 4¢ a word, on publication.

PULPHOUSE: A FICTION MAGAZINE—P.O. Box 1227, Eugene, OR 97440. Dean Wesley Smith, Pub. Jonathan Bond, Ed. Fantasy, science fiction, horror, and mysteries, 5,000 words. Pays 4¢ to 7¢, on publication.

SCIENCE FICTION CHRONICLE—P.O. Box 022730, Brooklyn, NY 11202–0056. Andrew Porter, Ed. News items, 200 to 500 words, for science fiction and fantasy readers, professionals, and booksellers. Interviews with authors, 2,500 to 4,000 words. No fiction. Pays 3 ½¢ to 5¢ a word, on publication. Query.

THE SCREAM FACTORY—Deadline Press, 16473 Redwood Lodge Rd., Los Gatos, CA 95030. Bob Morrish, Ed. Quarterly. Articles, 1,000 to 7,000 words, on all facets of horror fiction and film. Interviews, 750 to 4,000 words, with authors and directors; brief, analytical reviews, 100 to 400 words, of old and new books. Query. Pays ½¢ a word, on publication.

SHADOW SWORD—Stygian Vortex Publications, 6634 Atlanta St., Hollywood, FL 33024–2965. Glenda J. Woodrum, Ed. Quarterly. Stories, articles, and artwork by and for fantasy enthusiasts: heroic fantasy, sword and sorcery, high fantasy, and dark fantasy. Query for stories over 10,000 words. "No 'cute' stories!" Payment is one copy. Guidelines.

SHAPESHIFTER!—Stygian Vortex Publications, 6634 Atlanta St., Hollywood, FL 33024–2965. John R. Osborne, Ed. Annual. Stories, articles, and artwork on lycanthropes, shape-changers, and partly human creatures. Some role-playing game-related material. Query for stories over 10,000 words. "We prefer stories in which the shapeshifters are the heroes/protagonists, not stories in which they ravage a small town, etc." Payment is one copy. Guidelines.

TWISTED—P.O. Box 1249, Palmetto, GA 30268–1249. Christine Hoard, Ed. Fiction and articles, to 5,000 words; poetry, to one page. "No sword and sorcery or hard science fiction. We prefer adult-oriented horror and dark fantasy. Query. Send SASE for guidelines." Pays in copies.

2AM MAGAZINE—P.O. Box 6754, Rockford, IL 61125–1754. Gretta M. Anderson, Ed. Fiction, of varying lengths. "We prefer dark fantasy/horror; great science fiction and sword and sorcery stories are welcome." Profiles and intelligent commentaries. Poetry, to 50 lines. Pays from ½¢ a word, on acceptance. Guidelines.

WEIRD TALES—123 Crooked Ln., King of Prussia, PA 19406–2570. George Scithers, Pub. Darrell Schweitzer, Ed. Fantasy and horror (no science fiction), to 20,000 words. Pays 3¢ to 8¢ a word, on acceptance. Guidelines.

CONFESSION AND ROMANCE

BLACK CONFESSIONS—See *Black Romance.*

BLACK ROMANCE—233 Park Ave. S., New York, NY 10003. Tonia L. Shakespeare, Ed. Romance fiction, 5,800 to 6,700 words, and service articles on beauty, health, and relationship tips, 800 to 1,000 words, for black female readers. Queries preferred. Pays $75 to $125, on publication. Also publishes *Black Secrets, Bronze Thrills, Black Confessions,* and *Jive.* Guidelines.

BLACK SECRETS—See *Black Romance.*

BRONZE THRILLS—See *Black Romance.*

INTIMACY—233 Park Ave. S., 5th Fl., New York, NY 10003. Tonia L. Shakespeare, Ed. Fiction, 5,000 to 5,800 words, for black women ages 18 to 45; must have contemporary plot and contain two romantic and intimate love scenes. Pays $75 to $100, on publication. Guidelines.

JIVE—See *Black Romance.*

MODERN ROMANCES—233 Park Ave. S., New York, NY 10003. Cherie Clark King, Ed. Romantic and topical confession stories, 2,000 to 10,000 words, with reader-identification and strong emotional tone. Pays 5¢ a word, after publication. Buys all rights.

ROMANTIC INTERLUDES—P.O. Box 760, Germantown, MD 20875. Attn: Ed. Bimonthly. Romantic fiction, 1,200 to 6,000 words. No graphic sex or violence. Romantic poetry, 100 words. Pays half on acceptance, half on publication. Guidelines.

TRUE CONFESSIONS—233 Park Ave. S., New York, NY 10003. Pat Vitucci, Ed. Timely, emotional, first-person stories, 2,000 to 10,000 words, on romance, family life, and problems of today's young blue-collar women. Pays 5¢ a word, after publication.

TRUE EXPERIENCE—233 Park Ave. S., New York, NY 10003. Claire Cloutler LeBlanc, Ed. Jennifer Hampton, Assoc. Ed. Realistic first-person stories, 4,000 to 10,000 words (short shorts, to 2,000 words), on family life, single life, love, romance, overcoming hardships, mysteries. Pays 3¢ a word, after publication.

TRUE LOVE—233 Park Ave. S., New York, NY 10003. Cynthia Di Martino, Ed. Fresh, young, true-to-life romance stories, on love and topics of current interest. Must be written in the past tense and first person. Pays 3¢ a word, after publication. Guidelines.

TRUE ROMANCE—233 Park Ave. S., New York, NY 10003. Pat Byrdsong, Ed. True or true-to-life, dramatic and/or romantic first-person stories, 2,000 to 9,000 words. Love poems. "We enjoy working with new writers." Reports in 3 to 5 months. Pays 3¢ a word, a month after publication.

POETRY MARKETS

The following list includes markets for both serious and light verse. Although major magazines pay good rates for poetry, the competition to break into print is very stiff, since editors use only a limited number of poems in each issue. On the other hand, college, little, and literary magazines use a great deal of poetry, and though payment is modest—usually in copies—publication in these journals can establish a beginning poet's reputation, and can lead to publication in the major magazines. Poets will also find a number of competitions offering cash awards for unpublished poems in the *Literary Prize Offers* list, as well as opportunities to have their book-length poetry manuscripts published.

ALOHA, THE MAGAZINE OF HAWAII—720 Kapiolani Blvd., Fourth Fl., Honolulu, HI 96813. Cheryl Chee Tsutsumi, Ed. Poetry relating to Hawaii. Pays $30 per poem, on publication.

AMERICA—106 W. 56th St., New York, NY 10019. Patrick Samway, S.J., Literary Ed. Serious poetry, preferably in contemporary prose idiom, 10 to 25 lines. Occasional light verse. Submit 2 or 3 poems at a time. Pays $1.40 per line, on publication. Guidelines. SASE required.

THE AMERICAN SCHOLAR—1811 Q St. N.W., Washington, DC 20009–9974. Joseph Epstein, Ed. Highly original poetry for college-educated, intellectual readers. Pays $50, on acceptance.

THE ATLANTIC MONTHLY—745 Boylston St., Boston, MA 02116. Peter Davison, Poetry Ed. Previously unpublished poetry of highest quality. Limited market; only 2 to 3 poems an issue. Interested in new poets. Occasionally uses light verse. "No simultaneous submissions; we make prompt decisions." Pays excellent rates, on acceptance.

CAPPER'S—1503 S.W. 42nd St., Topeka, KS 66609–1265. Nancy Peavler, Ed. Traditional poetry and free verse, 4 to 16 lines, with simple everyday themes. Submit up to 6 poems at a time, with SASE. Payment, on acceptance.

CHILDREN'S PLAYMATE—P.O. Box 567, Indianapolis, IN 46206. Lise Hoffman, Ed. Poetry for children, 6 to 8 years old, on good health, nutrition, exercise, safety, seasonal and humorous subjects. Pays to $15, on publication. Buys all rights.

THE CHRISTIAN SCIENCE MONITOR—One Norway St., Boston, MA 02115. Alice Hummer, The Home Forum. Finely crafted poems that celebrate the extraordinary in the ordinary. Seasonal material always needed. No violence, sensuality, or racism. Short poems preferred; submit no more than 5 poems at a time. SASE required. Pays varying rates, on publication.

COMMONWEAL—15 Dutch St., New York, NY 10038. Rosemary Deen, Poetry Ed. Catholic. Serious, witty poetry. Pays 50¢ a line, on publication. SASE required. No submissions accepted June to September.

COMPLETE WOMAN—Dept. P, 1165 N. Clark St., Chicago, IL 60610. Attn: Assoc. Ed. Send poetry with SASE. Pays $10, on publication.

COSMOPOLITAN—224 W. 57th St., New York, NY 10019. Rachel Zalis, Poetry Ed. Poetry about relationships and other topics of interest to young, active women. Pays $25, on acceptance. SASE required.

COUNTRY WOMAN—P.O. Box 989, Greendale, WI 53129. Kathy Pohl, Man. Ed. Traditional rural poetry and light verse, 4 to 30 lines, on rural experiences and country living; also seasonal poetry. Poems must rhyme. Pays $10 to $25, on acceptance.

EVANGEL—Box 535002, Indianapolis, IN 46253–5002. Carolyn Smith, Ed. Free Methodist. Devotional or nature poetry, 8 to 16 lines. Pays $10, on publication.

FAMILY CIRCLE—110 Fifth Ave., New York, NY 10011. No unsolicited poetry.

GOOD HOUSEKEEPING—Light Housekeeping Page, 959 8th Ave., New York, NY 10019. Rosemary Leonard, Ed. No longer accepting material for Light Housekeeping page.

HARP-STRINGS—P.O. Box 640387, Beverly Hills, FL 34464. Madelyn Eastlund, Ed. Poems, 14 to 80 lines, on a variety of topics and in many forms. No light verse, "prose masquerading as poetry," confessions, or raw guts poems. Pays in copies.

THE ILLINOIS ARCHITECTURAL AND HISTORICAL REVIEW—202 S. Plum, Havana, IL 62644. David Alan Badger, Ed. Quarterly. Poems, to 40 lines, related to Illinois, especially its history, architecture, or historical figures. Submit to Gene Fehler, Poetry Ed., 106 Laurel Ln., Seneca, SC 29678. No other free-lance material used. Pays in copies.

LADIES' HOME JOURNAL—100 Park Ave., New York, NY 10017. No longer accepts poetry. "Last Laughs" page has been discontinued.

MATURE YEARS—201 Eighth Ave. S., P.O. Box 801, Nashville, TN 37202. Marvin W. Cropsey, Ed. United Methodist. Poetry, to 14 lines, on preretirement, retirement, Christianity, inspiration, seasonal subjects, aging. No "saccharine" poetry. Submit up to 6 poems at a time. Pays 50¢ to $1 per line.

MIDSTREAM—110 E. 59th St., New York, NY 10022. Joel Carmichael, Ed. M.S. Solow, Poetry Ed. Poetry of Jewish interest. "Brevity highly recommended." Pays $25, on publication. Allow 3 months for response.

700

THE MIRACULOUS MEDAL—475 E. Chelten Ave., Philadelphia, PA 19144–5785. John W. Gouldrick, C.M., Ed. Catholic. Religious verse, to 20 lines. Pays 50¢ a line, on acceptance.

MODERN BRIDE—249 W. 17th St., New York, NY 10011. Mary Ann Cavlin, Man. Ed. Short verse of interest to bride and groom. Pays $25 to $35, on acceptance.

THE NATION—72 Fifth Ave., New York, NY 10011. Grace Schulman, Poetry Ed. Poetry of high quality. Pays after publication. SASE requried.

NATIONAL ENQUIRER—Lantana, FL 33464. Michele Cooke, Asst. Ed. Short poems, with traditional rhyming verse, of an amusing, philosophical, or inspirational nature. No experimental poetry. Original epigrams, humorous anecdotes, and "daffynitions." Submit seasonal/holiday material at least 2 months in advance. Pays $25, after publication. SASE required.

THE NEW REPUBLIC—1220 19th St. N.W., Washington, DC 20036. Mary Jo Salter, Poetry Ed. Pays $75, after publication.

THE NEW YORKER—20 W. 43rd St., New York, NY 10036. Attn: Poetry Ed. First-rate poetry. Pays top rates, on acceptance. Include SASE.

PATHWAYS—Christian Board of Publication, Box 179, St. Louis, MO 63166. Christine Hershberger Miner, Ed. Short poems for 12- to 15-year-olds. Pays 30¢ a line, on publication.

PURPOSE—616 Walnut Ave., Scottdale, PA 15683–1999. James E. Horsch, Poetry Ed. Poetry, to 8 lines, with challenging Christian discipleship angle. Pays 50¢ to $1 a line, on acceptance.

ST. JOSEPH'S MESSENGER—P.O. Box 288, Jersey City, NJ 07303–0288. Sister Ursula Maphet, Ed. Light verse and traditional poetry, 4 to 40 lines. Pays $5 to $15, on publication.

THE SATURDAY EVENING POST—P.O. Box 567, Indianapolis, IN 46206. Steven Pettinga, Post Scripts Ed. Light verse and humor. No conventional poetry. SASE required. Pays $15, on publication.

THE UNITED METHODIST REPORTER—P.O. Box 660275, Dallas, TX 75266–0275. John Lovelace, Ed. Religious verse, 4 to 16 lines. Pays $2, on acceptance.

WESTERN PEOPLE—P.O. Box 2500, Saskatoon, Sask., Canada S7K 2C4. Michael Gillgannon, Man. Ed. Short poetry, with Western Canadian themes. Pays on acceptance. Send international reply coupons.

YANKEE—Yankee Publishing Co., Dublin, NH 03444. Jean Burden, Poetry Ed. Serious poetry of high quality, to 30 lines. Pays $50 per poem for all rights, $35 for first rights, on publication.

GREETING CARDS & NOVELTY ITEMS

Companies selling greeting cards and novelty items (T-shirts, coffee mugs, buttons, etc.) often have their own specific requirements for submitting ideas, verse, and artwork. In general, however, each verse or message should be typed, double-spaced, on a 3x5 or 4x6 card. Use only one side of the card, and be sure to put your name and address in the upper left-hand corner. Keep a copy of every verse or idea you send. (It's also advisable to keep a record of what you've submitted to each publisher.) Always enclose an SASE, and do not send out more than ten verses or ideas in a group to any one publisher. Never send original artwork.

AMBERLEY GREETING CARD COMPANY—11510 Goldcoast Dr., Cincinnati, OH 45249–1695. Ned Stern, Ed. Humorous ideas for cards: birthday, illness, friendship, anniversary, congratulations, "miss you," etc. Send SASE for market letter before submitting ideas. Pays $150. Buys all rights.

AMERICAN GREETINGS—One American Rd., Cleveland, OH 44144. Kathleen McKay, Editorial Recruitment. Study current offerings and query before submitting.

BLUE MOUNTAIN ARTS, INC.—P.O. Box 1007, Boulder, CO 80306. Attn: Ed. Staff, Dept. TW. Poetry and prose about love, friendship, family, philosophies, etc. Also material for special occasions and holidays: birthdays, get well, Christmas, Valentine's Day, Easter, etc. Submit seasonal material 4 months in advance of holiday. No artwork or rhymed verse. Include SASE. Pays $200 per poem.

BRILLIANT ENTERPRISES—117 W. Valerio St., Santa Barbara, CA 93101–2927. Ashleigh Brilliant, Ed. Illustrated epigrams. Send SASE for the price of a catalogue and samples. Pays $40, on acceptance.

CONTEMPORARY DESIGNS—P.O. Box 60, Gilbert, IA 50105–0060. Sallie Abelson, Ed. Short, positive, humorous sayings for coffee mugs, T-shirts, memo pads, etc. "We are in need of sayings that fit into the following categories: college students, Jewish, camp, teacher, working world. We are not interested in puns, gross ideas, poetry, or prose. No need to enclose artwork; however, if you have a picture idea, you may draw it out or describe it." Submit each idea separately on 3x5 cards. Include writer's name and address on each card. Responds in 6 weeks. Pays from $35, on acceptance. Guidelines.

CONTENOVA GIFTS—1239 Adanac St., Vancouver, BC, Canada V6A 2C8. Russ Morris, Ed. Catchy, humorous, and sentimental one-liners for ceramic gift mugs. Submit on 3x5 cards; up to 15 ideas at a time. Payment varies, on acceptance. Guidelines.

DAYSPRING GREETING CARDS—Outreach Publications, Inc., P.O. Box 1010, Siloam Springs, AR 72761. Attn: Ed. Inspirational messages that minister love, encouragement, and comfort to the receiver. Holidays, everyday occasions, and special-occasion cards. SASE for guidelines. Allow 4 to 6 weeks for response. Pays $30, on acceptance.

DESIGN DESIGN, INC.—P.O. Box 2266, Grand Rapids, MI 49501–2266. Don Kallil, Ed. Tom Vituj, Creative Dir. Humorous and sentimental ideas for greeting cards, mugs, T-shirts, and note pads. Everyday (birthday, get well, just for fun, etc.) and seasonal (Christmas, Valentine's Day, Easter, Mother's Day, Father's Day, Graduation, Halloween, Thanksgiving) material. Payment varies, on publication.

EPHEMERA, INC.—P.O. Box 490, Phoenix, OR 97535. Attn: Ed. Provocative, irreverent, and outrageously funny slogans for novelty buttons and magnets. Submit typed list of slogans with an SASE. Pays $25 per slogan, on publication. Guidelines.

FREEDOM GREETING CARD COMPANY—P.O. Box 715, Bristol, PA 19007. Jay Levitt, Ed. Dept. Traditional and humorous verse and love messages. Inspirational poetry for all occasions. Pays negotiable rates, on acceptance. Query with SASE.

HALLMARK CARDS, INC.—Box 419580, Mail Drop 216, Kansas City, MO 64141-6580. Write Carol King for submission agreement and guidelines; include SASE, no samples. Not currently soliciting new writers or sentiments. Work is on assignment basis only. Free lancers must show exceptional originality and style not available from in-house employees and must have previous writing experience.

OATMEAL STUDIOS—Box 138 TW, Rochester, VT 05767. Attn: Ed. Humorous, clever, and new ideas needed for all occasions. Send SASE for guidelines.

PARAMOUNT CARDS—P.O. Box 6546, Providence, RI 02940-6546. Attn: Editorial Freelance. Humorous card ideas for birthday, relative's birthday, friendship, romance, get well, Christmas, Valentine's Day, Easter, Mother's Day, Father's Day, and Graduation. Submit each idea (5 to 10 per submission) on 3x5 card with name and address on each. Enclose SASE. Payment varies, on acceptance.

RED FARM STUDIO—1135 Roosevelt Ave., P.O. Box 347, Pawtucket, RI 02862. Attn: Production Coord. Traditional cards for graduation, wedding, birthday, get well, anniversary, friendship, new baby, sympathy, and Christmas. Pays $3 a line. SASE required.

ROCKSHOTS, INC.—632 Broadway, New York, NY 10012. Bob Vesce, Ed. Adult, provocative, humorous gag lines for greeting cards. Submit on 4x5 cards. Pays $50 per line, on acceptance. Guidelines.

SANGAMON COMPANY—Route 48 W., P.O. Box 410, Taylorville, IL 62568. Attn: Ed. Dept. "We will send writer's guidelines to experienced free lancers before reviewing any submissions. We work on assignment." Pays competitive rates, on acceptance.

SUNRISE PUBLICATIONS, INC.—P.O. Box 4699, Bloomington, IN 47402. Attn: Ed. Coord. Original copy for holiday and everyday cards. "Submit up to 20 verses, one to 4 lines; simple, to-the-point ideas that could be serious, humorous, or light-hearted, but sincere, without being overly sentimental. Rhymed verse not generally used." SASE required. Allow 4 to 6 weeks for response. Send SASE for guidelines. Pays standard rates.

VAGABOND CREATIONS, INC.—2560 Lance Dr., Dayton, OH 45409. George F. Stanley, Jr., Ed. Greeting cards with graphics only on cover (no copy) and short punch line inside: birthday, everyday, Valentine's Day, Christmas, and graduation. Mildly risqué humor with double entendre acceptable. Ideas for illustrated theme stationery. Pays $15, on acceptance.

WARNER PRESS PUBLISHERS—1200 E. Fifth St., Anderson, IN 46012. Robin Fogle, Product Ed. "New free-lance system has been developed; you must send SASE for guidelines before submitting." Religious themes, sensitive prose, and inspirational verse for boxed cards, posters, and calendars. Pays $20 to $35, on acceptance. Also accepts ideas for coloring and activity books.

WEST GRAPHICS PUBLISHING—385 Oyster Point Blvd., #7, S. San Francisco, CA 94080. Attn: Production Dept. Outrageous humor concepts, all occasions (especially birthday) and holidays, for photo and illustrated card lines. Submit on 3x5 cards: concept on one side; name, address, and phone number on other. Pays $100, 30 days after publication.

703

WILLIAMHOUSE-REGENCY, INC.—28 W. 23rd St., New York, NY 10010. Nancy Boecker, Ed. Captions for wedding invitations only. Query for writing specifications sheet. Pays $25 per caption, on acceptance. SASE required.

CAROL WILSON FINE ARTS, INC.—P.O. Box 17394, Portland, OR 97217. Gary Spector, Carol Wilson, Eds. Humorous copy for greeting cards. Queries preferred. Pays $75 or negotiated royalties, on publication. Guidelines.

COLLEGE, LITERARY, AND LITTLE MAGAZINES

The thousands of literary journals, little magazines, and college quarterlies published today welcome work from novices and pros alike; editors are always interested in seeing traditional and experimental fiction, poetry, essays, reviews, short articles, criticism, and satire, and as long as the material is well-written, the fact that a writer is a beginner doesn't adversely affect his or her chances for acceptance.

Most of these smaller publications have small budgets and staffs, so they may be slow in their reporting time—several months is not unusual. In addition, they usually pay only in copies of the issue in which published work appears and some—particularly college magazines—do not read manuscripts during the summer.

Publication in the literary journals can, however, lead to recognition by editors of large-circulation magazines, who read the little magazines in their search for new talent. There is also the possibility of having one's work chosen for reprinting in one of the prestigious annual collections of work from the little magazines.

Because the requirements of these journals differ widely, it is always important to study recent issues before submitting work to one of them. Copies of magazines may be in large libraries, or a writer may send a postcard to the editor and ask the price of a sample copy. When submitting a manuscript, always enclose a self-addressed envelope, with sufficient postage for its return.

For a complete list of literary and college publications and little magazines, writers may consult such reference works as *The International Directory of Little Magazines and Small Presses*, published annually by Dustbooks (P.O. Box 100, Paradise, CA 95967).

AFRICAN AMERICAN REVIEW—(formerly *Black American Literature Forum*) Dept. of English, Indiana State Univ., Terre Haute, IN 47809. Joe Weixlmann, Ed. Essays on African American literature, theater, film, art, and culture; bibliographies; interviews; poems; fiction; and book reviews. Submit up to 6 poems. Query for book review assignments; send 3 copies of all other submissions. Pays an honorarium and copies. Responds in 3 months.

AFRICAN VOICES—305 7th Ave., 11th Fl., New York, NY 10001–6008. Carolyn A. Butts, Exec. Ed. Bimonthly. Humorous, erotic, and dramatic fiction,

500 to 2,500 words, by ethnic writers. Nonfiction, 500 to 1,500 words, including investigative articles, artist profiles, essays, and first-person narratives. Payment is $25 to $100, on publication.

AGNI—(formerly *The Agni Review*) Dept. TW, Boston Univ., Creative Writing Program, 236 Bay State Rd., Boston, MA 02215. Askold Melnyczuk, Ed. Erin Belieu, Man. Ed. Short stories, poetry, essays, and artwork. Reading period October 1 to April 30 only.

❢ **ALABAMA LITERARY REVIEW**—Troy State Univ., Smith 253, Troy, AL 36082. Theron Montgomery, Chief Ed. Semiannual. Contemporary, literary fiction and nonfiction, 3,500 words, and poetry, to 2 pages. Thought-provoking B&W photos. Pays in copies (honorarium when available). Responds within 3 months.

ALASKA QUARTERLY REVIEW—College of Arts & Sciences, Univ. of Alaska, 3211 Providence Dr., Anchorage, AK 99508. Attn: Eds. Short stories, novel excerpts, poetry (traditional and unconventional forms). Submit manuscripts between August 15 and May 15. Pays in copies.

ALBATROSS—P.O. Box 7787, North Port, FL 34287–0787. Richard Smyth, Richard Brobst, Eds. High-quality poetry; especially interested in ecological and nature poetry written in narrative form. Interviews with well-known poets. Submit 3 to 5 poems at a time with brief bio. Pays in copies.

❢**AMELIA**—329 E St., Bakersfield, CA 93304. Frederick A. Raborg, Jr., Ed. Poetry, to 100 lines; critical essays, to 2,000 words; reviews, to 500 words; belles lettres, to 1,000 words; fiction, to 4,500 words; fine pen-and-ink sketches; photos. Pays $35 for fiction and criticism, $10 to $25 for other nonfiction and artwork, $2 to $25 for poetry. Annual contest.

THE AMERICAN BOOK REVIEW—Publications Center, Univ. of Colorado, English Dept., Box 494, Boulder, CO 80309. Don Laing, Man. Ed. Literary book reviews, 700 to 1,200 words. Pays $50 honorarium and copies. Query with clips of published reviews.

❋ **AMERICAN LITERARY REVIEW**—Univ. of North Texas, P.O. Box 13615, Denton, TX 76203–3615. Scott Cairns and Barbara Rodman, Eds. Short fiction, to 30 double-spaced pages, and poetry (submit 3 to 5 poems). Pays in copies.

❥ **THE AMERICAN POETRY REVIEW**—1721 Walnut St., Philadelphia, PA 19103. Attn: Eds. Highest quality contemporary poetry. SASE required. Responds in 10 weeks.

AMERICAN QUARTERLY—National Museum of American History, Smithsonian Institution, Washington, DC 20560. Gary Kulik, Ed. Scholarly essays, 5,000 to 10,000 words, on any aspect of U.S. culture. Pays in copies.

THE AMERICAN SCHOLAR—1811 Q St. N.W., Washington, DC 20009–9974. Joseph Epstein, Ed. Articles, 3,500 to 4,000 words, on science, politics, literature, the arts, etc. Book reviews. Pays to $500 for articles, $100 for reviews, on publication.

THE AMERICAN VOICE—332 W. Broadway, Suite 1215, Louisville, KY 40202. Frederick Smock, Ed. Published 3 times per year. Avant-garde, literary fiction, nonfiction, and well-crafted poetry, any length (shorter works are preferred). "Please read our journal before attempting to submit." Payment varies, on publication.

❢**AMERICAN WRITING**—4343 Manayunk Ave., Philadelphia, PA 19128. Alexandra Grilikhes, Ed. Semiannual. "We encourage experimentation, new writing that takes risks with form, point of view, language, perceptions. We're interested in the voice of the loner, states of being, and initiation." Fiction and nonfiction, to 3,500 words, and poetry. Pays in copies.

AMHERST REVIEW—P.O. Box 1811, Amherst College, Amherst, MA 01002. Molly Lyons, Ed. Fiction, to 6,000 words. Pays in copies. Manuscripts read September to February.

ANOTHER CHICAGO MAGAZINE—3709 N. Kenmore, Chicago, IL 60613. Attn: Ed. Semiannual. Fiction, essays on literature, and poetry. "We want writing that's urgent, new, and lives in the world." Pays $5 to $50, on acceptance.

ANTIETAM REVIEW—7 W. Franklin St., Hagerstown, MD 21740. Susanne Kass and Ann Knox, Eds.-in-Chief. Fiction, to 5,000 words; poetry and photography. Submissions from regional artists only (MD, PA, WV, VA, DE, DC). Pays from $20 to $100. Guidelines. Manuscripts read September through January. SASE required.

THE ANTIGONISH REVIEW—St. Francis Xavier Univ., Antigonish, N.S., Canada B2G 1C0. George Sanderson, Ed. Poetry; short stories, essays, book reviews, 1,800 to 2,500 words. Pays in copies.

ANTIOCH REVIEW—P.O. Box 148, Yellow Springs, OH 45387–0148. Robert S. Fogarty, Ed. Timely articles, 2,000 to 8,000 words, on social sciences, literature, and humanities. Quality fiction. Poetry. No inspirational poetry. Pays $15 per printed page, on publication. Poetry considered from September to May; other material considered year-round.

❋ APALACHEE QUARTERLY—Apalachee Press, P.O. Box 20106, Tallahassee, FL 32316. Barbara Hamby, Mary Jane Ryals, Bruce Boehrer, Paul McCall, Monifa Love, Eds. Experimental fiction, to 30 manuscript pages; poems (submit 3 to 5). Pays in copies. Manuscripts read year-round.

ARACHNE—162 Sturges St., Jamestown, NY 14701–3233. Susan L. Leach, Ed. Quarterly. Fiction, to 1,500 words. Poems (submit up to 7). "We are looking for rural material and would like first publication rights." No simultaneous submissions. Pays in copies. Manuscripts read January, March, July, and October.

ARIZONA COWBOY POETS MAGAZINE—P.O. Box 498, Prescott, AZ 86302. Sally Harper Bates, Geri Davis, Eds. Cowboy and western poetry, any length. Nonfiction, 250 to 500 words, on cowboy views, themes, lifestyles, and attitudes. Pays in copies.

ARIZONA QUARTERLY—Univ. of Arizona, Main Library B-541, Tucson, AZ 85721. Edgar A. Dryden, Ed. Criticism of American literature and culture from a theoretical perspective. No poetry or fiction. Pays in copies.

❋ ARTFUL DODGE—College of Wooster, Wooster, OH 44691. Daniel Bourne, Ed. Annual. Fiction, to 20 pages. Literary essays, especially those involving nonfiction personal narrative, to 15 pages. Poetry, including translations of contemporary poets; submit 3 to 6 poems at a time; long poems encouraged. Pays $5 per page, on publication, plus 2 copies. Manuscripts read year-round.

THE ATLANTEAN PRESS REVIEW—354 Tramway Dr., P.O. Box 361116, Milpitas, CA 95036. Patricia LeChevalier, Ed. Romantic-realism: adventure, suspense, detective and romance stories, and serious fiction. Essays on various aspects of romantic art and art history. Structured rhyming poems. No horror, supernatural, erotica, or religious material. Pays $15 to $125, half on acceptance, half on publication.

706

♪ AURA LITERARY/ARTS REVIEW—P.O. Box 76, Univ. Center, UAB, Birmingham, AL 35294. Mark Valenta, Ed. Amy Robinson, Poetry Ed. Leigh Steele, Fiction Ed. Fiction and essays on literature, to 5,000 words; book reviews, to 4,000 words; poetry; photos. Pays in copies. Guidelines.

BAD HAIRCUT—P.O. Box 2827, Olympia, WA 98507. Ray and Kim Goforth, Eds. Articles and fiction, to 4,000 words (2,000 words preferred). Focus on politics, human rights, and environmental themes. Unrhymed poetry, to one page, and drawings also accepted. "We hope that by creating art with these themes we can influence society and help create a better world." Pays in copies.

BAMBOO RIDGE, THE HAWAII WRITERS' QUARTERLY—Bamboo Ridge Press, P.O. Box 61781, Honolulu, HI 96839–1781. Eric Chock, Ed. Poetry, to 10 pages, and short stories, 25 pages, by writers in U.S. and abroad. Submit with SASE. Reports in 3 to 6 months. Pays in small honorarium and 2 copies. Manuscripts read year-round.

BELLES LETTRES—11151 Captain's Walk Ct., N. Potomac, MD 20878–0441. Janet Mullaney, Ed. Quarterly devoted to literature by or about women. Articles, 250 to 2,000 words: reviews, interviews, rediscoveries, and retrospectives; columns on publishing news, reprints, and nonfiction titles. Query required. Pays in copies (plus honorarium if funds available).

♪ THE BELLINGHAM REVIEW—The Signpost Press Inc., 1007 Queen St., Bellingham, WA 98226. Knute Skinner, Ed. Semiannual. Fiction, to 5,000 words, and poetry, any length. Pays in copies and subscription. Manuscripts read from September 1 to March 1.

♪ BELLOWING ARK—P.O. Box 45637, Seattle, WA 98145. Robert R. Ward, Ed. Bimonthly. Short fiction, poetry, and essays of varying lengths, that portray life as a positive, meaningful process. B&W photos; line drawings. Pays in copies. Manuscripts read year-round.

THE BELOIT FICTION JOURNAL—Box 11, Beloit College, Beloit, WI 53511. Clint McCown, Ed. Short fiction, one to 35 pages, on all themes. No pornography, political propaganda, religious dogma. Pays in copies. Manuscripts read September to May.

♪ BELOIT POETRY JOURNAL—RFD 2, Box 154, Ellsworth, ME 04605. Attn: Ed. Strong contemporary poetry, of any length or in any mode. Pays in copies. Guidelines.

BLACK AMERICAN LITERATURE FORUM—See *African American Review*.

♪ BLACK BEAR REVIEW—Black Bear Publications, 1916 Lincoln St., Croydon, PA 19021–8026. Ave Jeanne, Ed. Semiannual. Book reviews and contemporary poetry. "We publish poems with social awareness, but any well-written piece is considered." Pays in one copy.

♪ BLACK BOUGH—P.O. Box 465, Somerville, NJ 08876. Kevin Walker, Charles Easter, Eds. Semiannual. Haiku and related forms: tanka, senryu, and haibun. Send up to 20 haiku per submission, with several haiku per page. SASE required. Pays $1 per verse; up to $4 for long poem or sequence, on acceptance. No free contributor's copies.

BLACK RIVER REVIEW—855 Mildred Ave., Lorain, OH 44052–1213. Deborah Glaefke Gilbert, Ed. Contemporary poetry, fiction (to 4,000 words), essays, short book reviews, B&W artwork. No greeting card verse or slick magazine

707

prose. Submit between January 1 and May 1. Pays in copies. Guidelines. SASE required.

THE BLACK WARRIOR REVIEW—The Univ. of Alabama, P.O. Box 2936, Tuscaloosa, AL 35486–2936. Mark S. Drew, Ed. Fiction; poetry; translations; reviews and essays. Annual awards. SASE required. Manuscripts read year-round.

⁕ THE BLOOMSBURY REVIEW—1028 Bannock St., Denver, CO 80204–4037. Tom Auer, Ed. Marilyn Auer, Assoc. Ed. Book reviews, publishing features, interviews, essays, poetry. Pays $5 to $25, on publication.

⁑ BLUE UNICORN—22 Avon Rd., Kensington, CA 94707. Attn: Ed. Published in October, February, and June. "We are looking for originality of image, thought, and music; we rarely use poems over a page long." Submit up to 5 poems with SASE. Artwork used occasionally. Pays in one copy.

BLUELINE—English Dept., SUNY, Potsdam, NY 13676. Anthony Tyler, Ed. Essays, fiction, to 3,500 words, on Adirondack region or similar areas. Poems, to 75 lines; submit no more than 5. Pays in copies. Manuscripts read September to November 30.

BORDERLANDS: TEXAS POETRY REVIEW—P.O. Box 49818, Austin, TX 78765. Attn: Ed. Semiannual. "Outward-looking" poetry of a political, spiritual, or social nature. Writers from Texas, the Southwest, and bilingual writers given special attention. Send up to 5 pages of poetry. Essays, to 3,000 words, on contemporary poets, especially those from the Southwest. Query for essays. Pays one copy.

⁂ BOSTON REVIEW—33 Harrison Ave., Boston, MA 02111–2008. Kim Cooper, Man. Ed. Reviews and essays, 800 to 3,000 words, on literature, art, music, film, photography. Original fiction, to 5,000 words. Poetry. Pays $40 to $100. Manuscripts read year-round.

🏹 BOTTOMFISH—21250 Stevens Creek Blvd., Cupertino, CA 95014. Robert Scott, Ed. Annual. Stories, vignettes, and experimental fiction, to 5,000 words. Free verse or traditional poetry, any subject, any length. "Our purpose is to give national exposure to new writers and new styles of creative writing. We publish at the end of March each year." Pays in copies. Manuscripts read July 1 to February 1.

⁋ BOULEVARD—P.O. Box 30386, Philadelphia, PA 19103. Richard Burgin, Ed. Published 3 times a year. High-quality fiction and articles, to 30 pages; poetry. Pays to $250, on publication.

⁑ THE BRIDGE—14050 Vernon St., Oak Park, MI 48237. Jack Zucker, Ed. Helen Zucker, Fiction Ed. Mitzi Alvin, Poetry Ed. Manon Meilgaard, Assoc. Fiction Ed. Semiannual. Fiction, 7,500 words, and poetry, to 200 lines. Pays in copies.

BUCKNELL REVIEW—Bucknell Univ., Lewisburg, PA 17837. Attn: Ed. Interdisciplinary journal in book form. Scholarly articles on arts, science, and letters. Pays in copies.

CALIFORNIA STATE POETRY QUARTERLY—California State Poetry Society, Box 7126, Orange, CA 92613. Attn: Ed. Board. Poetry, to 60 lines. Pays in one copy.

CALLALOO—Dept. of English, Univ. of Virginia, Charlottesville, VA 22903. Charles H. Rowell, Ed. Fiction, poetry, drama, and popular essays by, and critical studies and bibliographies on Afro-American, Caribbean, and African artists and writers. Payment varies, on publication.

*CALLIOPE—Creative Writing Program, Roger Williams Univ., Bristol, RI 02809–2921. Martha Christina, Ed. Short stories, to 2,500 words; poetry. Pays in copies and subscription. No submissions April through July.

CALYX, A JOURNAL OF ART & LITERATURE BY WOMEN—P.O. Box B, Corvallis, OR 97339. M. Donnelly, Man. Ed. Fiction, 5,000 words; book reviews, 1,000 words (please query with SASE about reviews); poetry, to 6 poems. Include short bio and SASE. Guidelines. Pays in copies. Submissions accepted October 1 to November 15.

CANADIAN FICTION MAGAZINE—Box 1061, Toronto, Ontario, Canada K7L 3R1. Attn: Ed. High-quality short stories, novel excerpts, and experimental fiction, to 5,000 words, by Canadians. Interviews with Canadian authors; translations. Pays $10 per page, on publication. Annual prize, $500. Manuscripts read year-round.

*THE CAPE ROCK—Dept. of English, Southeast Missouri State Univ., Cape Girardeau, MO 63701. Harvey E. Hecht, Ed. Semiannual. Poetry, to 70 lines, and B&W photography. (One photographer per issue; pays $100.) Pays in copies and $200 for best poem in each issue. Manuscripts read August to April.

THE CARIBBEAN WRITER—Univ. of the Virgin Islands, RR 02, Box 10,000, Kingshill, St. Croix, Virgin Islands, U.S. 00850. Erika J. Waters, Ed. Annual. Fiction (to 15 pages, submit up to 2 stories) and poems (no more than 5); the Caribbean should be central to the work. Blind submissions policy: place title only on manuscript; name, address, and title of manuscripts on separate sheet. Pays in copies. Manuscripts read September through December.

*THE CAROLINA QUARTERLY—Greenlaw Hall CB#3520, Univ. of North Carolina, Chapel Hill, NC 27599–3520. Amber Vogel, Ed. Fiction, to 7,000 words, by new or established writers. Poetry, to 300 lines. Manuscripts read year-round.

*CATALYST—Atlanta Fulton Public Library, 1 Margaret Mitchell Sq., Atlanta, GA 30303. Pearl Cleage, Ed. Semiannual. Fiction, to 3,000 words, and poetry. Pays to $200, on publication. Send SASE for guidelines and themes.

THE CENTENNIAL REVIEW—312 Linton Hall, Michigan State Univ., East Lansing, MI 48824–1044. R.K. Meiners, Ed. Articles, 3,000 to 5,000 words, on sciences, humanities, and interdisciplinary topics. Pays in copies.

*THE CHARITON REVIEW—Northeast Missouri State Univ., Kirksville, MO 63501. Jim Barnes, Ed. Highest quality poetry and fiction, to 6,000 words. Modern and contemporary translations. "The only guideline is excellence in all matters."

*CHICAGO REVIEW—5801 S. Kenwood Ave., Chicago, IL 60637. David Nicholls, Ed. Andy Winston, Fiction Ed. Angela Sorby, Poetry Ed. Mark Morrison, Nonfiction Ed. Essays, interviews, reviews, fiction, translations, poetry. Pays in copies plus one year's subscription. Manuscripts read year-round; replies in 2 to 3 months.

*CHIRON REVIEW—Route 2, Box 111, St. John, KS 67576–2212. Michael Hathaway, Ed. Contemporary fiction, to 4,000 words; articles, 500 to 1,000 words; and poetry, to 30 lines. Photos. Pays in copies.

*CICADA—329 E St., Bakersfield, CA 93304. Frederick A. Raborg, Jr., Ed. Quarterly. Single haiku, sequences, or garlands; essays about the forms; haibun and fiction (one story per issue) related to haiku or Japan. Pays in copies.

᠈ **CIMARRON REVIEW**—205 Morrill Hall, Oklahoma State Univ., Stillwater, OK 74078–0135. Gordon Weaver, Ed. Poetry, fiction, essays. Seeks an individual, innovative style that focuses on contemporary themes. Pays $50 for stories and essays; $15 for poems, plus one-year subscription. Manuscripts read year-round.

● **CLOCKWATCH REVIEW**—Dept. of English, Illinois Wesleyan Univ., Bloomington, IL 61702–2900. James Plath, Ed. Semiannual. Fiction, to 4,000 words, and poetry, to 36 lines. "Our preference is for fresh language, a believable voice, a mature style, and a sense of the unusual in the subject matter." Pays $25 for fiction, $5 for poetry, on acceptance, plus copies. Manuscripts read year-round.

᠈ **COLLAGES & BRICOLAGES**—P.O. Box 86, Clarion, PA 16214. Marie-José Fortis, Ed. Annual. Fiction and nonfiction, plays, interviews, book reviews, and poetry. Surrealistic and expressionistic drawings in ink. "I seek writers who are politically and socially aware and whose writing is not egocentric." Pays in copies. Manuscripts read August through October.

COLORADO REVIEW—English Dept., Colorado State Univ., Fort Collins, CO 80523. David Milofsky, Ed. Short fiction on contemporary themes. Pays $5 per printed page for fiction; $10 for poetry. Manuscripts read September to April 15.

COLUMBIA: A MAGAZINE OF POETRY & PROSE—404 Dodge, Columbia Univ., New York, NY 10027. Attn: Ed. Semiannual. Fiction and nonfiction; poetry; essays; interviews; visual art. Pays in copies. SASE required. Guidelines. Manuscripts read September to May.

THE COMICS JOURNAL—Fantagraphics, Inc., 7563 Lake City Way, Seattle, WA 98115. Attn: Man. Ed. "Looking for free-lancers with working knowledge of the diversity and history of the comics medium." Reviews, 2,500 to 5,000 words; domestic and international news, 500 to 7,000 words; "Opening Shots" editorials, 500 to 1,500 words; interviews; and features, 2,500 to 5,000 words. Query for news and interviews. Pays 1 ½¢ a word, on publication. Guidelines.

᠈ **CONFRONTATION**—Dept. of English, C.W. Post of L. I. U., Brookville, NY 11548. Martin Tucker, Ed. Serious fiction, 750 to 6,000 words. Crafted poetry, 10 to 200 lines. Pays $10 to $100, on publication.

THE CONNECTICUT POETRY REVIEW—P.O. Box 818, Stonington, CT 06378. J. Claire White and Harley More, Eds. Poetry, 5 to 20 lines, and reviews, 700 words. Pays $5 per poem, $10 per review, on acceptance. Manuscripts read September to January and April to June.

CONNECTICUT RIVER REVIEW—327 Seabury Dr., Bloomfield, CT 06002. Ben Brodinsky, Ed. Semiannual. Poetry. Submit 3 to 5 poems, to 40 lines. Pays in one copy. Guidelines.

THE COOL TRAVELER—P.O. Box 273, Selinsgrove, PA 17870. Bob Moore, Pub./Ed. Bimonthly. Articles, 800 words, including excerpts from diaries and letters written while traveling. "We are a literary newsletter about place and experience; we emphasize 'what happened' rather than 'what to see.'" Travel-related poetry. Pays to $20, on publication.

· **CQ/CALIFORNIA STATE POETRY QUARTERLY**—California State Poetry Society, Box 7126, Orange, CA 92613. Attn: Ed. Board. Submit poetry of no more than 60 lines. Payment is one copy. SASE for contest information.

᠈ **CRAZY QUILT**—P.O. Box 632729, San Diego, CA 92163–2729. Attn: Eds. Fiction, to 4,000 words, poetry, one-act plays, and literary criticism. Also B&W art, photographs. Pays in copies. Manuscripts read year-round.

710

THE CREAM CITY REVIEW—Box 413, Univ. of Wisconsin, Milwaukee, WI 53201. Mark Drechsler and Brian Jung, Eds.-in-Chief. Semiannual. "We serve a national audience interested in a diversity of writing (in terms of style, subject, genre) and writers (gender, race, class, publishing history, etc.). Both well-known and newly published writers of fiction, poetry, and essays are featured, along with B&W artwork." Payment varies, usually $5 a page plus 2 copies. SASE required. Manuscripts read year-round; responds in 8 weeks (not as quickly during the summer).

THE CREATIVE WOMAN—TAPP Group, 126 East Wing, Suite 288, Arlington Hgts., IL 60004. Margaret Choudhury, Ed. Quarterly. Essays, fiction, poetry, criticism, graphic arts, and photography, from a feminist perspective. SASE for upcoming themes. Payment varies, on publication.

THE CRESCENT REVIEW—1445 Old Town Rd., Winston-Salem, NC 27106–3143. Guy Nancekeville, Ed. Semiannual. Short stories only. Pays in copies. No submissions May to June or November to December.

CRITICAL INQUIRY—Univ. of Chicago Press, Wieboldt Hall, 1050 E. 59th St., Chicago, IL 60637. W. J. T. Mitchell, Ed. Critical essays that offer a theoretical perspective on literature, music, visual arts, and popular culture. No fiction, poetry, or autobiography. Pays in copies. Manuscripts read year-round.

⁕ CUMBERLAND POETRY REVIEW—P.O. Box 120128, Acklen Sta., Nashville, TN 37212. Attn: Eds. High-quality poetry and criticism; translations. Send up to 6 poems with brief bio. No restrictions on form, style, or subject matter. Pays in copies.

DENVER QUARTERLY—Univ. of Denver, Denver, CO 80208. Bin Ramke, Ed. Literary, cultural essays and articles; poetry; book reviews; fiction. Pays $5 per printed page, after publication.

DESCANT—Texas Christian Univ., T.C.U. Sta., Fort Worth, TX 76129. Betsy Colquitt, Stanley Trachtenberg, Harry Opperman, and Steve Sherwood, Eds. Fiction, to 6,000 words. Poetry, to 40 lines. No restriction on form or subject. Pays in copies. Frank O'Connor Award ($500) is given each year for best short story published in the volume. Submit material September through May only.

THE DEVIL'S MILLHOPPER—The Devil's Millhopper Press, USC/Aiken, 171 University Pkwy., Aiken, SC 29801–6399. Stephen Gardner, Ed. Poetry. Send SASE for guidelines and contest information. Pays in copies.

DEXTER REVIEW—P.O. Box 8418, Ann Arbor, MI 48107. Ronald Farrington Sharp, Ed. Annual. Non-genre fiction, to 3,000 words; poetry, to 3 pages; art-related essays and short interviews, to 3,000 words. No formula romances, detectives, space aliens. Pays in copies. Guidelines.

◊ THE DISTILLERY—Motlow State Community College, P.O. Box 88100, Tullahoma, TN 37388. Tony Hays, Ed. Semiannual. Essays on history, literary criticism, and fiction, 4,000 words; also poetry, 100 lines. Photos and drawings. Southern authors preferred. Pays in copies.

▸ DOG RIVER REVIEW—5976 Billings Rd., Parkdale, OR 97041–9610. Laurence F. Hawkins, Ed. Poetry, fiction, plays, book reviews, and related articles, to 2,500 words. B&W art. No religious or greeting card verse. Pays in copies.

▴ DREAMS & VISIONS—Skysong Press, R. R. 1, Washago, Ontario, Canada L0K 2B0. Steve Stanton, Ed. Eclectic fiction, 2,000 to 6,000 words, that is "in some way unique and relevant to Christian readers today." Pays in copies, with $100 honorarium to best of the year.

711

EARTH'S DAUGHTERS—P.O. Box 41, Central Park Sta., Buffalo, NY 14215. Attn: Ed. Published 3 times a year. Fiction, to 1,000 words, poetry, to 40 lines, and B&W photos or drawings. "Finely crafted work with a feminist theme." Pays in copies. SASE for guidelines and themes.

⁕ **ELF: ECLECTIC LITERARY FORUM**—ELF Associates, Inc., P.O. Box 392, Tonawanda, NY 14150. C. K. Erbes, Ed. Fiction, 3,500 words. Essays on literary themes, 3,500 words. Poetry, to 30 lines. Allow 4 to 6 weeks for response. Pays in 2 copies.

⁕ **EMBERS**—Box 404, Guilford, CT 06437. Katrina Van Tassel, Mark Johnston, Charlotte Garrett, Eds. Semiannual. Poetry. Interested in original new voices as well as published poets. Chapbook contest in December. Manuscripts read year-round.

⁕ **EUREKA LITERARY MAGAZINE**—Eureka College, P.O. Box 280, Eureka, CA 61530. Loren Logsdon, Ed. Semiannual. Fiction, 25 to 30 pages, and poetry, submit up to 4 poems at a time. "We seek to promote no specific political agenda or literary theory. We strive to publish the best of the fiction and poetry submitted to us." Pays in copies.

EVENT—Douglas College, Box 2503, New Westminster, BC, Canada V3L 5B2. David Zieroth, Ed. Short fiction, reviews, poetry. Pays $22 per printed page, on publication.

⁕ **FALL CREEK PRESS**—P.O. Box 1127, Fall Creek, OR 97438. Helen Wirth, Ed.-in-Chief. Short stories through which the reader is sensitized to an opportunity for spiritual growth. Stories used in anthologies. Guidelines very specific; send SASE for author's guide before submitting. Nominal advance plus royalty.

⁕ **FARMER'S MARKET**—P.O. Box 1272, Galesburg, IL 61402. Attn: Ed. Short stories, to 40 pages, and poetry. Pays in copies and subscription.

⁕ **FATHOMS**—2020 W. Pensacola, Unit 46, #549, Tallahassee, FL 32304. Rex West, Poetry Ed. Todd Pierce, Fiction Ed. Semiannual. Short stories and "flash" fiction, to 2,000 words. Creative nonfiction, to 2,000 words. Poetry, to 100 lines. Pays in one copy.

⁕ **FEELINGS**—Anderie Poetry Press, P.O. Box 85, Easton, PA 18044–0085. Carl and Carole Heffley, Eds. "America's Beautiful Poetry Magazine." Quarterly. Submit up to 3 poems, 25 lines each, in rhymed or blank verse, "that convey an immediate sense of recognition, intensity of thought, and heart-to-heart communication." Three editor's choice awards of $10, plus readers' choice award of $10 each issue.

FICTION INTERNATIONAL—English Dept., San Diego State Univ., San Diego, CA 92182–0295. Harold Jaffe, Ed. Post-modernist and politically committed fiction and theory. Pays in copies. Manuscripts read from September 1 to December 15.

THE FIDDLEHEAD—Campus House, Univ. of New Brunswick, Fredericton, N.B., Canada E3B 5A3. Attn: Ed. Serious fiction, 2,500 words, preferably by Canadians. Pays about $10 per printed page, on publication. SAE with international reply coupons required. Manuscripts read year-round.

⁕ **FIELD**—Rice Hall, Oberlin College, Oberlin, OH 44074. Stuart Friebert, David Young, Eds. Serious poetry, any length, by established and unknown poets; essays on poetics by poets. Translations by qualified translators. Payment varies, on publication. Manuscripts read year-round.

FINE MADNESS—P.O. Box 31138, Seattle, WA 98103–1138. Attn: Ed. Poetry, any length; short fiction. Pays in copies. No simultaneous submissions. Guidelines.

FOLIO—Dept. of Literature, American Univ., Washington, DC 20016. Julie Langsdorf, Wayne Scott, Eds. Semiannual. Fiction, poetry, translations, and essays. Photos and drawings. Pays in 2 copies. Submissions read September through March. Contest.

FOOTWORK, THE PATERSON LITERARY REVIEW—Cultural Affairs Dept., Passaic County Comm. College, College Blvd., Paterson, NJ 07505–1179. Maria Mazziotti Gillan, Ed. High-quality fiction and poetry, to 10 pages. Pays in copies. Manuscripts read January through May.

THE FORMALIST—320 Hunter Dr., Evansville, IN 47711. William Baer, Ed. Metrical poetry, to 2 pages, including blank verse, couplets, and traditional forms such as sonnets, ballads, villanelles, etc. "Sound and rhythm make poetry what it is." SASE required.

FREE INQUIRY—P.O. Box 664, Buffalo, NY 14226. Paul Kurtz, Ed. Tim Madigan, Exec. Ed. Articles, 500 to 5,000 words, for "literate and lively readership. Focus is on criticisms of religious belief systems, and how to lead an ethical life without a supernatural basis." Pays in copies.

THE GEORGIA REVIEW—Univ. of Georgia, Athens, GA 30602–9009. Stanley W. Lindberg, Ed. Stephen Corey, Assoc. Ed. Short fiction; personal and interdisciplinary essays; book reviews; poetry. Novel excerpts discouraged. Manuscripts read October through May.

THE GETTYSBURG REVIEW—Gettysburg College, Gettysburg, PA 17325. Peter Stitt, Ed. Quarterly. Poetry, fiction, essays, and essay-reviews, 1,000 to 20,000 words. "Review sample copy before submitting." Pays $2 a line for poetry; $25 per printed page for fiction and nonfiction. Allow 3 to 6 months for response. SASE required.

GLIMMER TRAIN PRESS—812 S.W. Washington St., Suite 1205, Portland, OR 97205. Susan Burmeister-Brown, Ed. Quarterly. Fiction, 1,200 to 7,500 words. Eight stories in each issue. Pays $300, on acceptance. Submit material in January, April, July, and October. Allow 3 months for response.

GOTHIC JOURNAL—19210 Forest Rd. N., Forest Lake, MN 55025–9766. Kristi Lyn Glass, Pub. Bimonthly. News and reviews for readers, writers, and publishers of all types of gothic novels. Articles, 1,000 to 2,000 words, on gothic and romantic suspense topics, author profiles, and book reviews (250 to 500 words). Pays in copies.

GRAHAM HOUSE REVIEW—Box 5000, Colgate Univ., Hamilton, NY 13346. Peter Balakian, Ed. Bruce Smith, Ed. Poetry, translations, and essays on modern poets. Payment depends on grants. Manuscripts read year-round; responds in 2 to 4 weeks.

GRAIN—Box 1154, Regina, Sask., Canada S4P 3B4. Geoffrey Ursell, Ed. Short stories, to 30 typed pages; poems, send up to 8; visual art. Pays $30 to $100 for stories, $100 for cover art, $30 for other art. SAE with international reply coupons required. Manuscripts read year-round.

GRAND STREET—131 Varick St., #906, New York, NY 10013. Jean Stein, Ed. Quarterly. Poetry, any length. Pays $3 a line, on publication. Will not read unsolicited fiction or essays.

713

GREEN'S MAGAZINE—P.O. Box 3236, Regina, Sask., Canada S4P 3H1. David Green, Ed. Fiction for family reading, 1,500 to 4,000 words. Poetry, to 40 lines. Pays in copies. International reply coupons must accompany U.S. manuscripts. Manuscripts read year-round.

THE GREENSBORO REVIEW—Dept. of English, Univ. of North Carolina, Greensboro, NC 27412–5001. Jim Clark, Ed. Semiannual. Poetry and fiction. Submission deadlines: September 15 and February 15. Pays in copies. Writer's guidelines and guidelines for literary awards issue available on request.

HALF TONES TO JUBILEE—Pensacola Junior College, English Dept., 1000 College Blvd., Pensacola, FL 32504. Walter F. Spara, Ed. Fiction, to 1,500 words, and poetry, to 60 lines. Pays in copies. Manuscripts read August 15 to May 15. Contest.

HAUNTS—Nightshade Publications, Box 3342, Providence, RI 02906–0742. Joseph K. Cherkes, Ed. Short stories, 1,500 to 8,000 words: horror, science-fantasy, and supernatural tales with strong characters. Pays 1/3¢ to 1¢ a word, on publication. Manuscripts read January 1 to June 1.

HAWAII REVIEW—Dept. of English, Univ. of Hawaii, 1733 Donagho Rd., Honolulu, HI 96822. Carrie Hoshino, Ed.-in-Chief. Quality fiction, poetry, interviews, essays, and literary criticism reflecting both regional and global concerns. Manuscripts read year-round.

HAYDEN'S FERRY REVIEW—Box 871502, Arizona State Univ., Tempe, AZ 85287–1502. Attn: Ed. Semiannual. Fiction, essays, and poetry (submit up to 6 poems). Include brief bio and SASE. Deadline for Spring/Summer issue is September 30; Fall/Winter issue, February 28. Pays in copies.

THE HEARTLANDS TODAY—Firelands Writing Center of Firelands College, Huron, OH 44839. Larry Smith and Nancy Dunham, Eds. Fiction, 1,000 to 4,500 words, and nonfiction, 1,000 to 3,000 words, about the contemporary Midwest. Poetry (submit 3 to 5 poems). "Writing must be set in the Midwest, but can include a variety of themes." B&W photos. Query for current themes. Pays $10 to $20 honorarium, plus copies.

HERESIES: A FEMINIST PUBLICATION ON ART AND POLITICS— Box 1306, Canal Street Sta., New York, NY 10013. Attn: Ed. Thematic issues. Accepts work by women only. Fiction, to 15 double-spaced typed pages; nonfiction; poetry; visual arts; photography. "Do not send original artwork." SASE required. Guidelines.

THE HIGHLANDER—P.O. Box 397, Barrington, IL 60011. Angus Ray, Ed. Bimonthly. Articles, 1,300 to 1,900 words, related to Scottish history. "We are not concerned with modern Scotland or current problems in Scotland." Pays $100 to $150, on acceptance.

THE HOLLINS CRITIC—P.O. Box 9538, Hollins College, VA 24020. John Rees Moore, Ed. Published 5 times a year. Features an essay on a contemporary fiction writer or poet, cover sketch, brief biography, and book list. Also, book reviews and poetry. Pays $25 for poetry, on publication.

HOME LIFE—127 Ninth Ave. N., Nashville, TN 37234. Charlie Warren, Ed.-in-Chief. Mary Paschall Darby, Man. Ed. Southern Baptist. Short lyrical verse: humorous, marriage and family, seasonal, and inspirational. Pays to $24 for poetry, from $75 for articles, on acceptance.

HOME PLANET NEWS—P.O. Box 415, Stuyvesant Sta., New York, NY 10009. Enid Dame and Donald Lev, Eds. Quarterly art tabloid. Fiction, to 8 typed pages; reviews, 3 to 5 pages; and poetry, any length. "We are looking for quality poetry, fiction, and discerning literary and art reviews." Query for nonfiction. Pays in copies and gift subscription. Manuscripts read year-round.

HURRICANE ALICE: A FEMINIST QUARTERLY—207 Lind Hall, 207 Church St. S.E., Minneapolis, MN 55455. Attn: Ed. Articles, fiction, essays, interviews, and reviews, 500 to 3,000 words, with feminist perspective. Pays in copies.

HYPHEN MAGAZINE—P.O. Box 516, Somonauk, IL 60552. Attn: Ed. Original fiction, poetry, interviews, articles, reviews, and columns, as well as artwork. Pays in copies.

THE ILLINOIS REVIEW—42401 English Dept., Illinois State Univ., Normal, IL 61790-4240. Jim Elledge, Ed. Semiannual. Poems, prose poems, stories, novel excerpts, one-act plays, translations, essays, and book reviews. "Open to mainstream and alternative material by established or unknown writers." B&W cover art and photos. Pays in copies. Manuscripts read August 1 to May 1; responds in one to 2 months.

IN THE COMPANY OF POETS—P.O. Box 10786, Oakland, CA 94610. Jacalyn Robinson, Ed./Pub. Quarterly. Fiction and creative essays, to 2,500 words, for a wide multicultural range of readers. Poems of any length. Drawings and photos. Pays in 3 copies. Guidelines. Manuscripts read year-round.

INDIANA REVIEW—316 N. Jordan Ave., Indiana Univ., Bloomington, IN 47405. Gretchen Knapp, Ed.-in-Chief. Cara Diaconoff, Ed. Fiction with an emphasis on storytelling and sophistication of language. Poems that are well-executed and ambitious. Pays $5 per page. SASE required. Manuscripts read year-round.

INTERGALACTIC POETRY MESSENGER—Flutter By Press, 252 Nassau St., Princeton, NJ 08540. Bruce Wilson, Ed. Fiction and nonfiction, to 10 pages; poetry, submit up to 10. Essays, cartoons, photos, illustrations, short humor. "Readership includes poets, writers, the young at heart. Our aim is to expand the readership of poetry journals with our graphics parade. We desire to publish serious work in a mirthful, accessible format." Queries preferred. Payment varies, on publication.

INTERIM—Dept. of English, Univ. of Nevada, Las Vegas, NV 89154-5034. A. Wilber Stevens, Ed. Semiannual. Fiction, to 5,000 words, and poetry. Pays in copies and 2-year subscription. Responds in 2 months.

THE IOWA REVIEW—EPB 308, Univ. of Iowa, Iowa City, IA 52242. David Hamilton, Ed. Essays, poems, stories, reviews. Pays $10 a page for fiction and nonfiction, $1 a line for poetry, on publication. Manuscripts read August 15 through April 15.

IOWA WOMAN—P.O. Box 680, Iowa City, IA 52244. Marianne Abel, Ed. Fiction, poetry, book reviews, and personal essays; articles, to 6,500 words, on midwestern history; interviews with prominent women; current social, economic, artistic, and environmental issues. Poems, any length (submit up to 5); photos and drawings. Queries preferred for articles. Pays $5 a page, $15 for illustrations, on publication. Guidelines; send SASE.

IRIS MAGAZINE—Iris Publications, Inc., P.O. Box 7263, Atlanta, GA 30357. Glenn Crawford, Assoc. Ed. Quarterly. A gay men's literary review of fiction, to 5,000 words, poetry to 60 lines, and B&W photography and art. Pays in copies.

JACARANDA REVIEW—Dept. of English, Univ. of California, Los Angeles, CA 90024. Bruce Kijewski, Ed. Laurence Roth, Poetry Ed. Semiannual. Fiction, to 50 pages, and poetry (submit up to 3 poems). No payment.

THE JAMES WHITE REVIEW—P.O. Box 3356, Traffic Sta., Minneapolis, MN 55403. Phil Willkie, Pub. "A Gay Men's Literary Quarterly." Short stories, to 9,000 words, and poetry, to 250 lines. Book reviews. Responds in 3 months.

JAPANOPHILE—Box 223, Okemos, MI 48864. Earl R. Snodgrass, Ed. Fiction, to 4,000 words, with a Japanese setting. Each story should have at least one Japanese character and at least one non-Japanese. Articles, 2,000 words, that celebrate Japanese culture. "We seek to promote Japanese-American understanding. We are not about Japan-bashing or fatuous praise." Pays to $20, on publication. Annual short story contest; deadline December 31.

JOYFUL NOISE—31 St. Anthony Ln., Glenville, NY 12302. Fred Dandino, Pub. Carole Dandino, Ed. Quarterly. Fiction, 500 words; nonfiction, 250 to 500 words; poetry, anecdotes, recipes, limericks, puzzles, and letters, any length. "We accept only material from people who are physically challenged. When submitting, please tell us what your disability is. We're always on the lookout for humorous stories." Send complete manuscript; no queries. Responds in 2 months. Pays in copies. Guidelines.

A JOYFUL NOISE—Spiritual Quest Publishing, 249 Tamiami Trail S., Venice, FL 34285. Michael Jones, Ed. Inspirational and religious poetry, to 30 lines. Submit up to four poems at a time. "We like upbeat, nontraditional free-verse. Poems should be moving, dramatic, humorous, and thought-provoking. We use all forms of poetry." Guidelines. No payment.

KALEIDOSCOPE—United Disability Services, 326 Locust St., Akron, OH 44302–1876. Darshan Perusek, Ph.D., Ed.-in-Chief. Semiannual. Fiction, essays, interviews, articles, and poetry relating to disability and the arts, to 5,000 words. Photos a plus. "We present balanced, realistic images of people with disabilities and publish pieces that challenge stereotypes." Submissions accepted from writers with or without disabilities. Pays $10 to $125. Guidelines recommended. Manuscripts read year-round; response may take up to 6 months.

KALLIOPE: A JOURNAL OF WOMEN'S ART—Florida Community College at Jacksonville, 3939 Roosevelt Blvd., Jacksonville, FL 32205. Attn: Ed. Fiction, to 2,500 words; poetry; interviews of women writers, to 2,000 words; and B&W photos of fine art. Query for interviews only. Pays in copies.

KANSAS QUARTERLY—English Dept., Kansas State Univ., Manhattan, KS 66506. Attn: Ed. Literary criticism, art, and history. Fiction and poetry. Pays in copies. Two series of annual awards.

KARAMU—Dept. of English, Eastern Illinois Univ., Charleston, IL 61920. Peggy Brayfield, Ed. Contemporary or experimental fiction. Creative nonfiction prose, personal essays, and memoir pieces. Poetry. Pays in copies. Manuscripts read year-round; best time to submit is January to May.

THE KENYON REVIEW—Kenyon College, Gambier, OH 43022. David H. Lynn, Ed. Quarterly. Fiction, poetry, essays, literary criticism, and reviews. "We appreciate manuscripts from writers who read the magazine." Pays $10 a printed page for prose, $15 a printed page for poetry and reviews, on publication. Manuscripts read September to March.

KINESIS—P.O. Box 4007, Whitefish, MT 59937. Leif Peterson, Ed./Pub. Fiction and articles, 2,000 to 6,000 words, and poetry, to 60 lines. "Make sure it moves!" Pays in copies.

KIOSK—c/o English Dept., 306 Clemens Hall, SUNY Buffalo, Buffalo, NY 14226. Mary Obropta, Ed. Robert Rebein, Fiction Ed. A.M. Allcott, Poetry Ed.

Fiction, to 20 pages, with a "strong sense of voice, narrative direction, and craftsmanship." Poetry "that builds possibilities for dramatic dialogue." Address appropriate editor. Pays in copies. Manuscripts read September 1 to April 15.

LAMBDA BOOK REPORT—1625 Connecticut Ave. N.W., Washington, DC 20009. Jim Marks, Ed. Reviews and features, 500 to 1,100 words, of gay and lesbian books. Queries preferred. Pays $15 to $60, 30 days after publication.

LATINO STUFF REVIEW—P.O. Box 440195, Miami, FL 33144. Nilda Cepero-Llevada, Ed./Pub. Short stories, 3,000 words; poetry, to one page; criticism and essays on literature, the arts, social issues. Bilingual publication focusing on Latino topics. Pays in copies.

THE LEADING EDGE—3163 JKHB, Provo, UT 84602. Michael Carr, Ed. Science fiction and fantasy magazine published 3 times a year. Short stories, 3,000 to 12,000 words; poetry, to 200 lines; and articles, to 8,000 words, on science, scientific speculation, and literary criticism. "Do not send originals; manuscripts are marked and critiqued by staff." Pays $10 to $100 for fiction; $10 per published page of poetry; $2 to $4 for fillers; on publication. SASE for guidelines.

LIGHT—Box 7500, Chicago, IL 60680. John Mella, Ed. Quarterly. Light verse. Also fiction, reviews, and essays, to 2,000 words. Fillers, humor, jokes, quips. "If it has wit, point, edge, or barb, it will find a home here." Cartoons and line drawings. Query for nonfiction. Pays in copies.

LILITH, THE INDEPENDENT JEWISH WOMEN'S MAGAZINE—250 W. 57th St., New York, NY 10107. Susan Weidman Schneider, Ed. Fiction, 1,500 to 2,000 words, on issues of interest to Jewish women.

LITERARY MAGAZINE REVIEW—English Dept., Kansas State Univ., Manhattan, KS 66506. Attn: Ed. Reviews and articles concerning literary magazines, 1,000 to 1,500 words, for writers and readers of contemporary literature. Pays modest fees and in copies. Query.

THE LITERARY REVIEW—Fairleigh Dickinson Univ., 285 Madison Ave., Madison, NJ 07940. Walter Cummins, Martin Green, Harry Keyishian, William Zander, Eds. Jill Kushner, Man. Ed. Serious fiction; poetry; translations; essays and reviews on contemporary literature. Pays in copies.

LONG NEWS: IN THE SHORT CENTURY—P.O. Box 150–455, Brooklyn, NY 11215. Barbara Henning, Ed. Annual. Visual art, poetry, and prose with an emphasis on language, theory, and experimentation. Pays in copies.

LONG SHOT—P.O. Box 6238, Hoboken, NJ 07030. Danny Shot, Jack Wiler, Nancy Mercado, Tom Pulhamus, Eds. Fiction, poetry, and nonfiction, to 10 pages. B&W photos and drawings. Pays in copies.

THE LONG STORY—18 Eaton St., Lawrence, MA 01843. Attn: Ed. Stories, 8,000 to 20,000 words; prefer stories about poor and working class people. Pays in copies. Manuscripts read year-round.

THE LONGNECK—208 S. Crawford Rd., Vermillion, SD 57069. J.D. Erickson, Ed. Essays and fiction, 2,000 words. Vignettes, nostalgia. Poetry; submit no more than 5 poems. No religious material. Deadline: March 1 annually. Payment is in copies.

MAGIC REALISM—P.O. Box 620, Orem, UT 84059–0620. C. Darren Butler and Julie Thomas, Eds. Published 3 times a year. Stories, to 7,500 words (4,000 words preferred), and poetry, any length, of magic realism, exaggerated realism, some genre fantasy/dark fantasy. Occasionally publish glib fantasy like that found in folktales, fairy tales, and myths. No occult, sleight-of-hand magicians, or wizards/witches. Pays $2 per published page, plus copy.

THE MALAHAT REVIEW—Univ. of Victoria, P.O. Box 1700, MS 8524, Victoria, BC, Canada V8W 2Y2. Derk Wynand, Ed. Fiction and poetry, including translations. Pays from $25 per page, on acceptance.

THE MANHATTAN REVIEW—440 Riverside Dr., #45, New York, NY 10027. Attn: Ed. Highest quality poetry. Pays in copies.

MASSACHUSETTS REVIEW—Memorial Hall, Univ. of Massachusetts, Amherst, MA 01003. Attn: Ed. Literary criticism; articles on public affairs, scholarly disciplines. Short fiction, 15 to 25 pages. Poetry. Pays $50, on publication. SASE required. No submissions between June and October.

MEDIPHORS—P.O. Box 327, Bloomsburg, PA 17815. Eugene D. Radice, MD, Ed. "A literary journal of the health professions." Short stories, essays, and commentary, 3,000 words. "Topics should have some relation to medicine and health, but may be quite broad." Poems, to 30 lines. Humor. Pays in copies. Guidelines.

MICHIGAN HISTORICAL REVIEW—Clarke Historical Library, Central Michigan Univ., Mt. Pleasant, MI 48859. Attn: Ed. Semiannual. Scholarly articles related to Michigan's political, social, economic, and cultural history; articles on American, Canadian, and Midwestern history that directly or indirectly explore themes related to Michigan's past. Manuscripts read year-round.

MID-AMERICAN REVIEW—Dept. of English, Bowling Green State Univ., Bowling Green, OH 43403. George Looney, Ed. Wayne Barham, Assoc. Ed. High-quality fiction, poetry, articles, translations, and reviews of contemporary writing. Fiction to 5,000 words, (query for longer work). Reviews, articles, 500 to 2,500 words. Pays to $50, on publication (pending funding). Manuscripts read September through May.

MIDWEST QUARTERLY—Pittsburg State Univ., Pittsburg, KS 66762. James B. M. Schick, Ed. Scholarly articles, 2,500 to 5,000 words, on contemporary academic and public issues; poetry. Pays in copies. Manuscripts read year-round.

THE MINNESOTA REVIEW—Dept. of English, East Carolina Univ., Greenville, NC 27858. Attn: Ed. "Politically committed fiction, 1,000 to 6,000 words, nonfiction, 5,000 to 7,500 words, and poetry, 3 pages maximum, for readers committed to social issues, including feminism, neomarxism, etc." Pays in copies. Responds in 2 to 4 months.

MISSISSIPPI REVIEW—Ctr. for Writers, Univ. of Southern Mississippi, Southern Sta., Box 5144, Hattiesburg, MS 39406–5144. Frederick Barthelme, Ed. Serious fiction, poetry, criticism, interviews. Pays in copies.

THE MISSISSIPPI VALLEY REVIEW—Dept. of English, Western Illinois Univ., Macomb, IL 61455. John Mann and Tama Baldwin, Eds. Short fiction, nonfiction, and poetry (send 3 to 5 poems). Pays in copies. Manuscripts read September to May.

THE MISSOURI REVIEW—1507 Hillcrest Hall, Univ. of Missouri-Columbia, Columbia, MO 65211. Greg Michalson, Man. Ed. Speer Morgan, Ed. Poems, of any length. Fiction and essays. Pays $20 per printed page, on contract. Manuscripts read year-round.

MODERN HAIKU—P.O. Box 1752, Madison, WI 53701–1752. Robert Spiess, Ed. Haiku and articles about haiku. Pays $1 per haiku, $5 a page for articles. Manuscripts read year-round.

718

MONTHLY REVIEW—122 W. 27th St., New York, NY 10001. Paul M. Sweezy, Harry Magdoff, Eds. Analytical articles, 5,000 words, on politics and economics, from independent socialist viewpoint. Pays $25 for reviews, $50 for articles, on publication.

NEBO: A LITERARY JOURNAL—Dept. of English and Foreign Languages, Arkansas Tech. Univ., Russellville, AR 72801–2222. Attn: Ed. Poems (submit up to 5); mainstream fiction, to 3,000 words; critical essays, to 10 pages. Pays in one copy. SASE required. Guidelines. Offices closed May through August. "Best time to submit is November through February."

NEGATIVE CAPABILITY—62 Ridgelawn Dr. E., Mobile, AL 36608. Sue Walker, Ed. Poetry, any length; fiction, essays, art. Pays $20 per story. Contests.

NEW AUTHOR'S JOURNAL—1542 Tibbits Ave., Troy, NY 12180. Mario V. Farina, Ed. Fiction, to 3,000 words, and poetry. Topical nonfiction, to 1,000 words. Pays in copies and subscription. Manuscripts read year-round.

NEW DELTA REVIEW—c/o Dept. of English, Louisiana State Univ., Baton Rouge, LA 70803–5001. Nicola Mason, Catherine Williamson, Eds. Semiannual. Fiction and nonfiction, to 5,000 words. Submit up to 4 poems, any length. Also essays, interviews, reviews, and B&W photos or drawings. "We want to see your best work, even if it's been rejected elsewhere." Pays in copies. Manuscripts read year-round.

NEW ENGLAND REVIEW—Middlebury College, Middlebury, VT 05753. David Huddle, Ed. William Lychack and Devon Jersild, Assoc. Eds. Fiction, nonfiction, and poetry of varying lengths. "National, international, literary, political, effectively radical writing." Pays $10 per page, on acceptance, and in copies and subscription. Manuscripts read September to May.

NEW ENGLAND WRITERS' NETWORK—P.O. Box 483, Hudson, MA 01749–0483. Glenda Baker, Nonfiction Ed. Fiction, to 2,000 words. Creative technique articles, to 1,800 words, on the art or craft of writing. Personal essays, to 1,000 words; humorous essays, to 1,000 words; how-tos, to 500 words; nonfiction fillers, to 200 words; personal experience, to 500 words; creative poetry, to 32 lines. "No religious, political, sexual, or racially offensive material." Include cover letter. Query for interviews. Submit nonfiction to Ms. Baker at address above; fiction to: Donna Clark, Fiction Ed., 93 Medford St., Malden, MA 02148. Pays $10 for stories; pays in copies for other material.

NEW LAUREL REVIEW—828 Lesseps St., New Orleans, LA 70117. Lee Meitzen Grue, Ed. Annual. Fiction, 10 to 20 pages; nonfiction, to 10 pages; poetry, any length. Library market. No inspirational verse. International readership. Pays in one copy.

NEW LETTERS—Univ. of Missouri-Kansas City, Univ. House, Kansas City, MO 64110–2499. James McKinley, Ed.-in-Chief. Fiction, 3,500 to 5,000 words. Poetry, submit 3 to 6 poems at a time. Send SASE for literary awards guidelines. Manuscripts read October 15 to May 15.

NEW ORLEANS REVIEW—Loyola Univ., New Orleans, LA 70118. Attn: Ed. Literary or film criticism, to 6,000 words. Serious fiction and poetry.

THE NEW PRESS LITERARY QUARTERLY—53–35 Hollis Court Blvd., Flushing, NY 11365. Bob Abramson, Pub. Quarterly. Fiction and nonfiction, to 2,500 words. Poetry to 200 lines. Pays $15 for prose. Contests.

THE NEW RENAISSANCE—9 Heath Rd., Arlington, MA 02174. Louise T. Reynolds, Ed. An international magazine of ideas and opinions, emphasizing literature and the arts. Query with SASE, outline, and writing sample for articles; send complete manuscript for fiction and essays. Payment varies, after publication. Manuscripts read from January 2 to March 1.

THE NEW YORK QUARTERLY—P.O. Box 693, Old Chelsea Sta., New York, NY 10113. William Packard, Ed. Published 3 times a year by The National Poetry Foundation. Poems of any style and persuasion, well written and well intentioned. Pays in copies. Manuscripts read year-round.

NIGHTSUN—School of Arts & Humanities, Frostburg State Univ., Frostburg, MD 21532–1099. Douglas DeMars, Ed. Annual. Short stories, about 3 pages; poems, to 40 lines. Payment is 2 copies. Manuscripts read September 1 to May 1.

NIMROD—2210 S. Main St., Tulsa, OK 74114–1190. Attn: Ed. Publishes 2 issues annually, one awards and one thematic. Quality poetry and fiction, experimental and traditional. Pays $5 a page (to $25) and copies. Annual awards for poetry and fiction. Send SASE for guidelines.

96 INC—P.O. Box 15559, Boston, MA 02215. Attn: Ed. Semiannual. Fiction, 1,000 to 7,500 words, interviews, and poetry of varying length. Pays $10 to $25, on publication.

THE NORTH AMERICAN REVIEW—Univ. of Northern Iowa, Cedar Falls, IA 50614–0516. Peter Cooley, Poetry Ed. Poetry of high quality. Pays from $20 per poem, on publication. Manuscripts read year-round.

NORTH ATLANTIC REVIEW—15 Arbutus Ln., Stony Brook, NY 11790–1408. John Gill, Ed. Annual. Fiction and nonfiction, to 5,000 words; poetry, any length; fillers, humor, photographs and illustrations. A special section on social or literary issues is a part of each issue. Pays in copies. Responds in 5 or 6 months.

THE NORTH DAKOTA QUARTERLY—Univ. of North Dakota, Grand Forks, ND 58202–7209. Attn: Ed. Essays in the humanities; fiction, reviews, and poetry. Limited market. Pays in copies and subscription.

NORTHEASTARTS—Boston Arts Organization, Inc., JFK Sta., P.O. Box 6061, Boston, MA 02114. Mr. Leigh Donaldson, Ed. Fiction and nonfiction, to 750 words; poetry, to 30 lines; and brief humor. "Both professional and beginning writers are considered. No obscene or offensive material." Payment is one copy.

THE NORTHERN READER—Savage Press, Box 115, Superior, WI 54880. Mike Savage, Ed. Bimonthly. Reminiscence pieces, to 1,500 words. Fiction, to 2,000 words. Free verse and metrical poetry, essays, and fillers. Pays in copies. Guidelines.

NORTHWEST REVIEW—369 PLC, Univ. of Oregon, Eugene, OR 97403. Hannah Wilson, Fiction Ed. Fiction, commentary, essays, and poetry. Reviews. Pays in copies. Send SASE for guidelines.

OASIS—P.O. Box 626, Largo, FL 34649–0626. Neal Storrs, Ed. Short fiction and literary essays, to 7,000 words, poetry, and translations from French, German, Italian, or Spanish. Nonfiction on any subject. No children's stories. Complete manuscripts preferred. Pays $15 to $50 for prose, $5 per poem, on publication. Guidelines.

OBJECT LESSON—Bluestone Press, P.O. Box 1186, Hampshire College, Amherst, MA 01002. Joshua Saul Beckman, Man. Ed. Semiannual. Fiction and poetry, to 100 pages, one-act plays, essays, interviews, B&W artwork. Annual poetry and fiction contests. Pays in copies.

THE OHIO REVIEW—Ellis Hall, Ohio Univ., Athens, OH 45701–2979. Wayne Dodd, Ed. Short stories, poetry, essays, reviews. Pays $5 per page for prose,

$1 a line for poetry, plus copies, on publication. SASE required. Submissions read September through May.

ONIONHEAD—Arts on the Park, Inc., 115 N. Kentucky Ave., Lakeland, FL 33801–5044. Attn: Ed. Council. Short stories, to 4,000 words; essays, to 2,500 words; and poetry, to 60 lines; on provocative social, political, and cultural observations and hypotheses. Pays in copies. Send SASE for Wordart poetry contest information. Manuscripts read year-round; responds in 8 weeks.

OREGON EAST—Hoke College Ctr., EOSC, La Grande, OR 97850. Attn: Ed. Short fiction, nonfiction, to 3,000 words, one-act plays, poetry, and high-contrast graphics. Pays in copies. Manuscripts read September through March.

ORPHIC LUTE—Dreamcatcher Multiple Arts, Inc., 1713 14th Ave., Seattle, WA 98112. David Sparenberg, Ed. Lyric poetry, to 40 lines. Special interests include ethnic, ecological, mythic, and dream-related themes. Pays in copies. Submissions read year-round.

OTHER VOICES—Univ. of Illinois at Chicago, Dept. of English (M/C 162), 601 S. Morgan St., Chicago, IL 60607–7120. Lois Hauselman, Sharon Fiffer, Eds. Semiannual. Fresh, accessible short stories, one-act plays, and novel excerpts, to 5,000 words. Pays in copies and modest honorarium. Reading period is October 1 to April 1.

OUTERBRIDGE—College of Staten Island, English Dept. 25–218, 2800 Victory Blvd., Staten Island, NY 10314. Charlotte Alexander, Ed. Annual. Well-crafted stories, about 20 pages, and poetry, to 4 pages, "directed to a wide audience of literate adult readers." Pays in 2 copies. Manuscripts read September to June.

PAINTED BRIDE QUARTERLY—230 Vine St., Philadelphia, PA 19106. Marion Wren, Kathleen Volk-Miller, Brian Brown, Eds. Fiction and poetry of varying lengths. Pays in subscription.

PAINTED HILLS REVIEW— 2950 Portage Bay W. #411, Davis, CA 95616. Michael Ishii and Kara Kosmatka, Eds. Well-crafted fiction and creative nonfiction, to 4,000 words. Poetry, to 100 lines. Pays in one or 2 copies. Manuscripts read year-round. Contests.

PANHANDLER—English Dept., Univ. of West Florida, Pensacola, FL 32514–5751. Michael Yots, Stanton Millet, and Laurie O'Brien, Eds. Semiannual. Fiction, 1,500 to 3,000 words; poetry, any length. Pays in copies. Responds in one to 3 months.

THE PARIS REVIEW—541 E. 72nd St., New York, NY 10021. Attn: Fiction and Poetry Eds. Fiction and poetry of high literary quality. Pays on publication.

PARNASSUS—41 Union Sq. W., Rm. 804, New York, NY 10003. Herbert Leibowitz, Ed. Critical essays and reviews on contemporary poetry. International in scope. Pays in cash and copies. Manuscripts read year-round.

PARTISAN REVIEW—Boston Univ., 236 Bay State Rd., Boston, MA 02215. William Phillips, Ed. Serious fiction, poetry, and essays. Payment varies. No simultaneous submissions. Manuscripts read year-round.

PASSAGER: A JOURNAL OF REMEMBRANCE AND DISCOVERY— c/o Univ. of Baltimore, 1420 N. Charles St., Baltimore, MD 21201–5779. Kendra Kopelke, Ed. Fiction and essays, 4,000 words, and poetry, to 60 lines. "We publish writers of all ages, but with an emphasis on new older writers." Pays in copies.

PASSAGES NORTH—Kalamazoo College, 1200 Academy St., Kalamazoo, MI 49006. Michael Barrett, Ed. Semiannual; published in December and June.

Poetry, fiction, essays, interviews, visual art. Pays in copies. Manuscripts read September to June.

THE PENNSYLVANIA REVIEW—Univ. of Pittsburgh, Dept. of English, 526 Cathedral of Learning, Pittsburgh, PA 15260. Attn: Ed. Fiction, to 5,000 words, book reviews, interviews with authors, and poems (send up to 6). Pays in copies. Manuscripts read September through March only.

PIEDMONT LITERARY REVIEW—Bluebird Ln., Rt. #1, Box 1014, Forest, VA 24551. Evelyn Miles, Man. Ed. Quarterly. Poems, any length and style; submit up to 5 poems to Evelyn Miles at above address. Submit Asian verse to Dorothy McLaughlin, 10 Atlantic Rd., Somerset, NJ 08873. Submit prose, to 2,500 words, to Dr. Olga Kronmeyer, 25 W. Dale Dr., Lynchburg, VA 24501. No pornography. Pays one copy.

PIG IRON PRESS—P.O. Box 237, Youngstown, OH 44501–0237. Jim Villani, Ed. Fiction and nonfiction, to 8,000 words. Poetry, to 100 lines. Write for upcoming themes. Pays $5 per published page or poem, on publication. Manuscripts read year-round. Responds in 3 months.

THE PINEHURST JOURNAL—Pinehurst Press, P.O. Box 360747, Milpitas, CA 95036–0747. Michael K. McNamara, Ed. Quarterly. Contemporary and experimental fiction, 750 to 4,000 words. Articles, 1,500 to 3,500 words, on art, music, literature, and theater; profiles and essays. Poetry, to 24 lines. Line art (no photos). Pays $5, on publication, plus one copy, for fiction and nonfiction; pays one copy for poetry and art. Send #10 SASE for guidelines. Manuscripts read year-round.

PIRATE WRITINGS—53 Whitman Ave., Islip, NY 11751. Edward J. McFadden, Pub./Ed. Shorts, 250 to 1,000 words, and stories, 1,000 to 2,500 words: mystery, science fiction, fantasy, literary, humor, light horror. Poetry, to 20 lines. Pays to 4¢ a word, on publication.

PIVOT—250 Riverside Dr., #23, New York, NY 10025. Martin Mitchell, Ed. Annual. Poetry, to 75 lines. Payment is 2 copies. Manuscripts read January 1 to June 1.

PLAINS POETRY JOURNAL—Box 2337, Bismarck, ND 58502–2337. Jane Greer, Ed. Poetry using traditional conventions in vigorous, compelling ways; no greeting card-type verse or prosaic "free" verse. No subject is taboo. Pays in copies.

PLOUGHSHARES—Emerson College, 100 Beacon St., Boston, MA 02116–1596. Attn: Ed. Serious fiction, to 6,000 words. Pays $10 per page ($40 to $200), on publication, plus 2 copies and subscription. Manuscripts read August through March. Guidelines.

POEM—c/o English Dept., U.A.H., Huntsville, AL 35899. Nancy Frey Dillard, Ed. Serious lyric poetry. Pays in copies. Manuscripts read year-round (best times to submit are December to March and June to September).

POET AND CRITIC—203 Ross Hall, Iowa State Univ., Ames, IA 50011–1201. Neal Bowers, Ed. Poetry, reviews, essays on contemporary poetry. Pays in copies. No manuscripts read June through August.

POET LORE—The Writer's Ctr., 4508 Walsh St., Bethesda, MD 20815. Philip K. Jason, Exec. Ed. Sunil Freeman, Man. Ed. Original poetry, all kinds. Translations, reviews, and critical essays. Pays in copies. Annual narrative poetry contest.

POET MAGAZINE—P.O. Box 54947, Oklahoma City, OK 73154. Attn: Ed. Quarterly. "Dedicated to publishing poets at all levels. New and experienced poets encouraged to submit." Submit copies (not originals) of up to 5 poems, any form, and articles of any length on subjects related to poetry. Include one loose stamp (not SASE) for editorial reply; manuscripts will not be returned. Payment is one copy. Guidelines.

POETRY—60 W. Walton St., Chicago, IL 60610. Joseph Parisi, Ed. Poetry of highest quality. Submit 3 to 4 poems. Allow 10 to 12 weeks for response. Pays $2 a line, on publication.

POETRY EAST—DePaul Univ., 802 W. Belden Ave., Chicago, IL 60614–3214. Marilyn Woitel, Man. Ed. Semiannual. Poetry, essays, and translations. "Please send a sampling of your best work. Do not send book-length manuscripts without querying first." Pays in copies.

THE POET'S PAGE—821 S. First St., Princeton, NJ 61356. Ione Kolm Pence, Ed./Pub. Quarterly. Poetry, any length, any style, any topic. Articles and essays on poetry and poetic forms, poets, styles, etc. Pays in copies.

PORTLAND REVIEW—c/o Portland State Univ., P.O. Box 751, Portland, OR 97207. Attn: Ed. Semiannual. Short fiction, essays, poetry, one-act plays (to 5 pages), photography, and artwork. "Please include a bio." Payment is one copy.

POTOMAC REVIEW—P.O. Box 134, McLean, VA 22101–0134. Jack Harrison, Ed. Quarterly. Fiction and literary essays, to 2,500 words. Poetry, to 2 pages. B&W photos. Pays in copies.

PRAIRIE SCHOONER—201 Andrews Hall, Univ. of Nebraska, Lincoln, NE 68588–0334. Hilda Raz, Ed. Short stories, poetry, essays, book reviews, and translations. Pays in copies. SASE required. Manuscripts read year-round; responds in 3 months. Annual contests.

PRIMAVERA—Box 37–7547, Chicago, IL 60637. Attn: Editorial Board. Annual. Fiction and poetry that focuses on the experiences of women; "author need not be female." B&W photos and drawings. No simultaneous submissions. Pays in 2 copies. Responds within 3 months.

PRISM INTERNATIONAL—E459–1866 Main Mall, Dept. of Creative Writing, Univ. of British Columbia, Vancouver, B.C., Canada V6T 1Z1. Attn: Ed. High-quality fiction, poetry, drama, creative nonfiction, and literature in translation, varying lengths. Include international reply coupons. Pays $20 per published page. Annual short fiction contest.

PROOF ROCK—P.O. Box 607, Halifax, VA 24558. Don Conner, Fiction Ed. Serena Fusek, Poetry Ed. Fiction, to 2,500 words. Poetry, to 32 lines. Reviews. Pays in copies.

PUCKERBRUSH REVIEW—76 Main St., Orono, ME 04473–1430. Constance Hunting, Ed. Semiannual. Literary fiction, criticism, and poetry of various lengths, "to bring literary Maine news to readers." Pays in 2 copies. Manuscripts read year-round.

PUDDING MAGAZINE: THE INTERNATIONAL JOURNAL OF APPLIED POETRY—c/o Pudding House Bed & Breakfast for Writers and Writers Resource Ctr., 60 N. Main St., Johnstown, OH 43031. Jennifer Bosveld, Ed. Poems on popular culture, social concerns, personal struggle; poetry therapy that has been revised for art's sake; articles/essays on poetry in the human services. Manuscripts read year-round.

PUERTO DEL SOL—New Mexico State Univ., Box 3E, Las Cruces, NM 88003–0001. Kevin McIlvoy, Ed. Short stories and personal essays, to 30 pages; novel excerpts, to 65 pages; articles, to 45 pages, and reviews, to 15 pages. Poetry, photos. Pays in copies. Manuscripts read September 1 to April 1.

PULPHOUSE: A FICTION MAGAZINE—P.O. Box 1227, Eugene, OR 97440. Dean Wesley Smith, Pub. Jonathan Bond, Ed. Fiction, 5,000 words: science fiction, fantasy, horror, mystery, romance, western, and mainstream. Occasionally uses poetry. Pays 4¢ to 7¢ a word, on publication.

QUARTERLY WEST—317 Olpin Union, Univ. of Utah, Salt Lake City, UT 84112. M.L. Williams, Ed. Fiction, short-shorts, poetry, translations, and reviews. Pays $25 to $50 for stories, $15 to $50 for poems. Manuscripts read year-round. Biennial novella competition in even-numbered years.

RAG MAG—P.O. Box 12, Goodhue, MN 55027–0158. Beverly Voldseth, Ed. Semiannual. Eclectic fiction and nonfiction, art, photos. Poetry, any length. No religious writing. Pays in copies. Manuscripts read year-round.

RAMBUNCTIOUS REVIEW—1221 W. Pratt Blvd., Chicago, IL 60626. Mary Dellutri, Richard Goldman, Nancy Lennon, Beth Hausler, Eds. Fiction, to 12 pages; poems, submit up to 5 at a time. Pays in copies. Manuscripts read September through May. Contests.

RED CEDAR REVIEW—Dept. of English, 17-C Morrill Hall, Michigan State Univ., East Lansing, MI 48824–1036. Laura Klynstra, Ed. Fiction, to 5,000 words, and poetry (submit up to 5 poems). Pays in copies. Manuscripts read year-round.

THE REDNECK REVIEW OF LITERATURE—1326 W. Sheridan Ct., Milwaukee, WI 53209. Penelope Reedy, Ed. Semiannual. Fiction, to 2,500 words, of the contemporary American West; essays and book reviews, 300 to 1,500 words; poetry and drama. Pays in copies. Manuscripts read year-round.

RESONANCE—P.O. Box 215, Beacon, NY 12508. Evan Pritchard, Ed. Published sporadically. Fiction, to 1,200 words; thematic nonfiction, to 1,200 words. Pays one copy.

REVIEW: LATIN AMERICAN LITERATURE AND ARTS—Americas Society, 680 Park Ave., New York, NY 10021. Alfred J. MacAdam, Ed. Semiannual. Work in English translation by and about young and established Latin American writers; essays and book reviews considered. Send queries for 1,000- to 1,500-word manuscripts, and short poem translations. Payment varies, on acceptance.

RHINO—1808 N. Larrabee St., Chicago, IL 60614. Kay Meier and Don Hoffman, Eds. "Authentic emotion in well-crafted poetry." Pays in copies. Manuscripts read year-round.

RIVER CITY—Dept. of English, Memphis State Univ., Memphis, TN 38152. J.P. Craig, Joey Flamm, and Greg Heartman, Ed. Staff. Poems, short stories, essays, and interviews. No novel excerpts. Pay varies according to grants. Manuscripts read September through April. Contests.

RIVER STYX—3207 Washington Ave., St. Louis, MO 63103. Attn: Ed. Published 3 times a year. Fiction, personal essays, literary interviews, poetry, and B&W photos. Payment is $8 per printed page and 2 copies. Manuscripts read September 1 to October 31; reports in 12 weeks.

RIVERSIDE QUARTERLY—Box 958, Big Sandy, TX 75755. Leland Sapiro, Ed. Science fiction and fantasy, to 3,500 words; reviews, criticism, any

724

length; poetry and letters. "Read magazine before submitting." Send poetry to Sheryl Smith, 515 Saratoga #2, Santa Clara, CA 95050. Pays in copies.

ROANOKE REVIEW—Roanoke College, Salem, VA 24153. Robert R. Walter, Ed. Quality short fiction, to 7,500 words, and poetry, to 100 lines. Pays in copies.

ROCKFORD REVIEW—P.O. Box 858, Rockford, IL 61105. David Ross, Ed.-in-Chief. Quarterly. Fiction, essays, and satire, 250 to 1,300 words. Experimental and traditional poetry, to 50 lines (shorter works preferred). One-act plays and other dramatic forms, to 10 pages. "We prefer genuine or satirical human dilemmas with coping or non-coping outcomes that ring the reader's bell." Submit up to 3 works at a time. Pays in copies; $25 Editor's Choice Prizes awarded each issue.

ROSEBUD—P.O. Box 459, Cambridge, WI 53523. Rod Clark, Ed. Quarterly. Fiction, articles, profiles, 1,200 to 1,800 words, and poems of love, alienation, travel, humor, nostalgia, and unexpected revelation. Guidelines. Pays $45 plus copies, on publication.

SAN FERNANDO POETRY JOURNAL—18301 Halstead St., Northridge, CA 91325. Richard Cloke, Ed. Quality poetry, 20 to 100 lines, with social content; scientific, philosophical, and historical themes. Pays in copies.

SAN JOSE STUDIES—c/o English Dept., San Jose State Univ., San Jose, CA 95192. John Engell and David Mesher, Eds. Poetry, fiction, and essays on interdisciplinary topics, focusing on Bay Area and California cultures. Occasionally publishes photos and art. Pays in copies. Annual awards. Responds in 2 to 3 months.

SANSKRIT LITERARY/ART PUBLICATION—Univ. of North Carolina/Charlotte, Charlotte, NC 28223–0001. Attn: Ed. Annual. Poetry, short fiction, photos, and fine art.

SANTA BARBARA REVIEW—P.O. Box 536, Summerland, CA 93067. Shelly Lowenkopf, Ed. Short stories, novellas, and occasionally plays. Biographies and essays, to 6,500 words. Poems (no epics). Query for novellas and nonfiction. Pays in copies.

SATYAGRAHA MAGAZINE—P.O. Box 11275, Berkeley, CA 94701. Darren Richardson, Ed. Quarterly. Articles, to 1,200 words, on progressive issues and poetry, to 50 lines. Fillers; B&W photos and art. "We are especially interested in writings by females and minorities." Pays in copies.

SCANDINAVIAN REVIEW—725 Park Ave., New York, NY 10021. Attn: Ed. Published 3 times a year. Essays on contemporary Scandinavia: arts, sciences, business, politics, and culture of Scandinavia. Fiction and poetry, translated from Nordic languages. Pays from $100, on publication.

SCRIVENER—McGill Univ., 853 Sherbrooke St. W., Montreal, Quebec, Canada H3A 2T6. Susan Brekelmans, Ed. Poems, submit 5 to 15; prose, to 20 pages; reviews, to 5 pages; essays, to 10 pages. Photography and graphics. Pays in copies.

THE SEATTLE REVIEW—Padelford Hall, GN-30, Univ. of Washington, Seattle, WA 98195. Donna Gerstenberger, Ed. Short stories, to 20 pages, poetry, essays on the craft of writing, and interviews with northwest writers. Payment varies. Manuscripts read September 1 through May 31.

SENECA REVIEW—Hobart & William Smith Colleges, Geneva, NY 14456. Deborah Tall, Ed. Poetry, translations, and essays on contemporary poetry. Pays in copies. Manuscripts read September 1 to May 1.

SHOOTING STAR REVIEW—7123 Race St., Pittsburgh, PA 15208. Sandra Gould Ford, Pub. Fiction and folktales, to 3,000 words, essays, to 2,000 words, and poetry, to 50 lines, on the African-American experience. Query for book reviews only. Pays $5 for poems; $10 for essays; $10 to $20 for fiction. Send SASE for topic deadlines. Responds to queries in 3 weeks; manuscripts in 4 months.

SHORT FICTION BY WOMEN—Box 1276, Stuyvesant Sta., New York, NY 10009. Rachel Whalen, Ed. Semiannual. Short stories, novellas, and novel excerpts, to 20,000 words, by women writers. No horror, romance, or mystery fiction. Payment varies, on publication. Manuscripts read year-round. Guidelines.

SING HEAVENLY MUSE! WOMEN'S POETRY & PROSE—P.O. Box 13320, Minneapolis, MN 55414. Attn: Ed. Short stories and essays, to 5,000 words. Poetry. Query for themes and reading periods. Pays in copies.

SKYLARK—2200 169th St., Hammond, IN 46323-2094. Pamela Hunter, Ed. "The Fine Arts Annual of Purdue Calumet." Fiction and articles, to 4,000 words. Poetry, to 21 lines. B&W prints and drawings. Pays in one copy. Manuscripts read November 1 through May 31 for fall publication.

SLIPSTREAM—Box 2071, Niagara Falls, NY 14301. Attn: Ed. Contemporary poetry, any length. Pays in copies. Query for themes. (Also accepting cassette tape submissions for audio poetics tape series: spoken word, collaborations, songs, audio experimentation.) Guidelines. Annual poetry chapbook contest has a December 1 deadline; send SASE for details. Query for fiction.

SMALL MAGAZINE REVIEW—Dustbooks, P.O. Box 100, Paradise, CA 95967. Len Fulton, Ed./Pub. Reviews, 200 words, of small and literary magazines. Query. Pays 10¢ a word, on acceptance.

THE SMALL POND MAGAZINE—P.O. Box 664, Stratford, CT 06497-0664. Napoleon St. Cyr, Ed. Published 3 times a year. Fiction, to 2,500 words; poetry, to 100 lines. Query for nonfiction. SASE required. Include short bio. Pays in copies. Manuscripts read year-round.

SMALL PRESS REVIEW—Box 100, Paradise, CA 95967. Len Fulton, Ed. News pieces and reviews of books, to 200 words, by small presses. Pays in copies.

SNAKE NATION REVIEW—Snake Nation Press, 110 #2 W. Force, Valdosta, GA 31601. Roberta George, Ed. Quarterly. Short stories, novel chapters, and informal essays, 5,000 words, and poetry, to 60 lines. Pays in copies and prizes.

SNOWY EGRET—P.O. Box 9, Bowling Green, IN 47833. Karl Barnebey and Philip Repp, Eds. Poetry, fiction, and nonfiction, to 10,000 words. Natural history from artistic, literary, philosophical, and historical perspectives. Pays $2 per page for prose; $2 to $4 for poetry, on publication. Manuscripts read year-round.

SONORA REVIEW—Dept. of English, Univ. of Arizona, Tucson, AZ 85721. Attn: Fiction, Poetry, or Nonfiction Ed. Fiction, poetry, translations, interviews, literary nonfiction. Personal essays, memoirs, creative nonfiction. Pays in copies. Annual prizes for fiction, poetry, and nonfiction. Manuscripts read year-round.

THE SOUTH CAROLINA REVIEW—Dept. of English, Clemson Univ., Clemson, SC 29634-1503. Richard J. Calhoun, Exec. Ed. Semiannual. Fiction, essays, reviews, and interviews of up to 4,000 words. Short poems. Send complete manuscript; query Mark Royden Winchell for book reviews. Pays in copies. Response time is 6 to 9 months. Manuscripts read September through May (but not in December).

SOUTH COAST POETRY JOURNAL—English Dept., CSUF, Fullerton, CA 92634. John J. Brugaletta, Ed. Semiannual. Poetry, to 40 lines. Only unpublished and uncommitted poetry, please. "Our editorial tastes are eclectic, ranging from the strictly metered and rhymed to free verse and including virtually every mixture in between." Payment is in one copy. Manuscripts read September through May.

SOUTH DAKOTA REVIEW—Box 111, Univ. Exchange, Vermillion, SD 57069–2390. John R. Milton, Ed. Exceptional fiction, 3,000 to 5,000 words, and poetry, 10 to 25 lines. Critical articles, especially on American literature, Western American literature, theory and esthetics, 3,000 to 5,000 words. Pays in copies. Manuscripts read year-round; slower response time in the summer.

THE SOUTHERN CALIFORNIA ANTHOLOGY—c/o Master of Professional Writing Program, WPH 404, Univ. of Southern California, Los Angeles, CA 90089–4034. James Ragan, Ed.-in-Chief. Fiction, to 20 pages, and poetry, to 5 pages. Pays in copies. Manuscripts read September to May.

SOUTHERN EXPOSURE—P.O. Box 531, Durham, NC 27702. Eric Bates, Ed. Quarterly forum on "Southern movements for social change." Short stories, to 4,500 words, essays, investigative journalism, and oral histories, 500 to 4,500 words. Pays $25 to $200, on publication. Query.

SOUTHERN HUMANITIES REVIEW—9088 Haley Ctr., Auburn Univ., Auburn, AL 36849. Dan R. Latimer, R. T. Smith, Eds. Short stories, essays, and criticism, 3,500 to 15,000 words; poetry, to 2 pages. Responds within 3 months. SASE required.

SOUTHERN POETRY REVIEW—Dept. of English, Univ. of North Carolina, Charlotte, NC 28223. Ken McLaurin, Ed. Poems. No restrictions on style, length, or content. Manuscripts read September through May.

THE SOUTHERN REVIEW—43 Allen Hall, Louisiana State Univ., Baton Rouge, LA 70803. James Olney and Dave Smith, Eds. Emphasis on contemporary literature in United States and abroad with special interest in southern culture and history. Fiction and essays, 4,000 to 8,000 words. Serious poetry of highest quality. Pays $12 a page for prose, $20 a page for poetry, on publication. No manuscripts read in the summer.

SOUTHWEST REVIEW—307 Fondren Library W., Box 374, Southern Methodist Univ., Dallas, TX 75275. Elizabeth Mills, Sr. Fiction Ed. "A quarterly that serves the interests of the region but is not bound by them." Fiction, essays, poetry, and interviews with well-known writers, 3,000 to 7,500 words. Pays varying rates. Manuscripts read September 1 through May 31.

SOU'WESTER—Southern Illinois Univ. at Edwardsville, Edwardsville, IL 62026–1438. Fred W. Robbins, Ed. Fiction, to 8,000 words. Poetry, any length. Pays in copies. Manuscripts read year-round; slower response time in the summer.

THE SOW'S EAR POETRY REVIEW—19535 Pleasant View Dr., Abingdon, VA 24210–6827. Attn: Ed. Quarterly. Eclectic poetry and art. Submit 1 to 5 poems, any length, plus a brief biographical note. Interviews, essays, and articles, any length, about poets and poetry are also considered. B&W photos and drawings. Payment is one copy. Poetry and chapbook contests; write for guidelines.

SPARROW MAGAZINE—Sparrow Press, 103 Waldron St., W. Lafayette, IN 47906. Felix Stefanile, Ed./Pub. Contemporary (14-line) sonnets, and occasionally formal poems in other structures. Submit up to 5 poems. Pays $3 per poem, on publication. A $25 sonnet prize is awarded to a contributor in each issue.

SPECTRUM—Univ. of California/ Santa Barbara, Box 14800, Santa Barbara, CA 93107. Attn: Ed. Short stories, to 12 pages, essays on literature, memoirs, poetry. Pays in copies. Annual contest. Manuscripts read September 20 to January 31.

SPECTRUM—Anna Maria College, Box 72-A, Paxton, MA 01612–1198. Robert H. Goepfert, Ed. Scholarly articles, 3,000 to 15,000 words; short stories, to 10 pages; and poetry, to 2 pages; book reviews, photos, and artwork. Pays $20 plus 2 copies. SASE required. Manuscripts read September 1 to May 10.

THE SPOON RIVER POETRY REVIEW—Dept. of English, Stevenson Hall, Illinois State Univ., Normal, IL 61790–4240. Lucia Cordell Getsi, Ed. Poetry, any length. Pays in copies.

SPSM&H—329 E St., Bakersfield, CA 93304. Frederick A. Raborg, Jr., Ed. Single sonnets, sequences, essays about the sonnet form, short fiction in which the sonnet plays a part, books, and anthologies. Pays $10, plus copies, for fiction and essays.

STAND MAGAZINE—122 Morris Rd., Lacey's Spring, AL 35754. Daniel Schenker and Amanda Kay, Eds. Fiction, 2,000 to 4,000 words, and poetry to 100 lines (submit up to 6 poems). No formulaic verse.

STATE STREET REVIEW—FCCJ North Campus, 4501 Capper Rd., Jacksonville, FL 32218–4499. John Hunt, Exec. Ed. Vickie Swindling, Man. Ed. Semiannual. Fiction, to 6,000 words. Nonfiction, 2,000 words, on writers, poets, or on writing itself. Poetry. Pays in copies.

STORY QUARTERLY—P.O. Box 1416, Northbrook, IL 60065. Anne Brashler, Diane Williams, Eds. Short stories and interviews. Pays in copies. Manuscripts read year-round.

THE STYLUS—9412 Huron Ave., Richmond, VA 23294. Roger Reus, Ed. Annual. "An open forum for intelligent, well-researched articles on a variety of authors and literary topics." Query preferred. Limited fiction market. Pays in copies.

THE SUN—The Sun Publishing Co., 107 N. Roberson St., Chapel Hill, NC 27516. Sy Safransky, Ed. Articles, essays, interviews, and fiction, to 10,000 words; poetry; photos, illustrations, and cartoons. "We're interested in all writing that makes sense and enriches our common space." Pays $100 for fiction and essays, $25 for poetry, on publication.

SYCAMORE REVIEW—Purdue Univ., Dept. of English, West Lafayette, IN 47907. Michael S. Manley, Ed.-in-Chief. Semiannual. Poetry, short fiction (no genre fiction), personal essays, and translations, to 10,000 words. Pays in copies. Manuscripts read September to April.

TAR RIVER POETRY—Dept. of English, East Carolina Univ., Greenville, NC 27834. Peter Makuck, Ed. Poetry and reviews. "Interested in skillful use of language, vivid imagery. Less academic, more powerful poetry preferred." Pays in copies. Submit from September to November or January to April.

THE TEXAS REVIEW—English Dept., Sam Houston State Univ., Huntsville, TX 77341. Paul Ruffin, Ed. Fiction, poetry, articles, to 20 typed pages. Reviews. Pays in copies and subscription.

THEMA—Box 74109, Metairie, LA 70033–4109. Virginia Howard, Ed. Fiction, to 20 pages, and poetry, to two pages, related to theme. Pays $25 per story; $10 per short-short; $10 per poem; $10 for B&W art/photo, on acceptance. Send SASE for themes and guidelines.

THIRTEEN—Box 392, Portlandville, NY 13834–0392. Ken Stone, Ed. Quarterly. Thirteen-line poetry. Pays in one copy. Manuscripts read year-round.

360 DEGREES—Art & Literary Review, Union Bank Bldg., 17800 Castleton St., Suite 190, City of Industry, CA 91748. Karen Kinnison, Ed. Quarterly art and literary review, featuring fiction and poetry (any length), artwork, graphic imagery, and "art-text', words mixed with images. Send photocopies and photographs only. Pays in copies.

THE THREEPENNY REVIEW—P.O. Box 9131, Berkeley, CA 94709. Wendy Lesser, Ed. Fiction, to 5,000 words. Poetry, to 100 lines. Essays, 1,500 to 3,000 words, on books, theater, film, dance, music, art, television, and politics. Pays to $200, on acceptance. Limited market. Send SASE for guidelines.

TIGHTROPE—323 Pelham Rd., Amherst, MA 01002. Ed Rayher, Ed. Limited-edition, letterpress semiannual. Fiction and nonfiction, to 10 pages; poetry, any length. Pays in copies. Manuscripts read year-round.

TOMORROW MAGAZINE—P.O. Box 148486, Chicago, IL 60614–8486. Tim W. Brown, Ed. Fiction and novel excerpts, 2,000 words. Poetry. Pays in copies.

TOUCHSTONE—P.O. Box 8308, Spring, TX 77387. Bill Laufer, Pub. Annual. Fiction, 750 to 2,000 words: mainstream, experimental. Interviews, essays, reviews. Poetry, to 40 lines. Pays in copies. Manuscripts read year-round.

TREASURE HOUSE—Treasure House Publishing, 1106 Oak Hill Ave., #3A, Hagerstown, MD 21742. Attn: Ed.-in-Chief. Fiction, 1,500 to 3,000 words, and poetry. Submit poems (up to 10) to: Ed., *Treasure House,* c/o 1420 N St. N.W., #912-E, Washington, DC 20005. (Submit fiction to Hagerstown address.) Pays in copies. Guidelines.

TRIQUARTERLY—Northwestern Univ., 2020 Ridge Ave., Evanston, IL 60208–4302. Attn: Ed. Serious, aesthetically informed and inventive poetry and prose, for an international and literate audience. Pays $20 per page for prose, $1.50 per line for poetry. Reading period October 1 to March 31. Allow 10 to 12 weeks for reply.

TRIVIA—P.O. Box 9606, N. Amherst, MA 01059–9606. Erin Rice, Kay Parkhurst, Eds. Semiannual journal of radical feminist writing. Literary essays, experimental prose, translations, interviews, and reviews. "After-readings": personal accounts of the writer's reaction to books or other writings by women. Pays in copies. Guidelines. Manuscripts read year-round.

2AM MAGAZINE—P.O. Box 6754, Rockford, IL 61125–1754. Gretta Anderson, Ed. Poetry, articles, reviews, and personality profiles, 500 to 2,000 words, as well as fantasy, horror, and some science fiction/sword-and-sorcery short stories, 500 to 5,000 words. Pays ½¢ a word, on acceptance. Manuscripts read year-round.

THE UNIVERSITY OF WINDSOR REVIEW—See *Windsor Review.*

UNSOMA—349 Davis Rd., Pelzer, SC 29669. Penegashega Nick, Ed. Articles, poetry, essays, prose, B&W art, exposé, erotica. "Radical, political, A to Z, anything and everything that twists the mind, soothes the soul, enlightens the lost." Pays in copies.

URBANUS/RAIZIRR—P.O. Box 192561, San Francisco, CA 94119. Peter Drizhal, Ed. Semiannual. Fiction and nonfiction, 1,000 to 5,000 words, and poetry, to 40 lines, that reflect post-modernist influences for a "readership generally impatient with the mainstream approach." B&W photos and drawings. Pays $10 to $25 for fiction and nonfiction, on acceptance; pays in copies for poetry.

729

VERVE—P.O. Box 3205, Simi Valley, CA 93093. Ron Reichick, Ed. Contemporary fiction and nonfiction, to 1,000 words, that fits the theme of the issue. Poetry, to two pages; submit up to 5 poems. Pays in one copy. Query for themes.

THE VILLAGER—135 Midland Ave., Bronxville, NY 10708. Amy Murphy, Ed. Mary Hazzah, Fiction/Articles Ed. Mrs. Joseph Aiello, Poetry Ed. Fiction, 900 to 1,500 words: mystery, adventure, humor, romance. Short, preferably seasonal poetry. Pays in copies.

VINCENT BROTHERS REVIEW—4566 Northern Cir., Mad River Township, Dayton, OH 45424–5733. Kimberly Willardson, Ed. Published three times a year. Fiction, nonfiction, poetry, fillers, and B&W art. "Read back issues before submitting." Pays from $10 for fiction and nonfiction, plus two copies; payment for all other work is two copies. Guidelines.

VIRGINIA QUARTERLY REVIEW—One W. Range, Charlottesville, VA 22903. Attn: Ed. Quality fiction and poetry. Serious essays and articles, 3,000 to 6,000 words, on literature, science, politics, economics, etc. Pays $10 per page for prose, $1 per line for poetry, on publication.

VISIONS INTERNATIONAL—1110 Seaton Ln., Falls Church, VA 22046. Bradley R. Strahan, Ed. Published 3 times a year. Poetry, to 30 lines, and B&W drawings. (Query first for art.) "Nothing amateur or previously published. Read magazine before submitting." Pays in copies. Manuscripts read year-round.

WASCANA REVIEW—c/o Dept. of English, Univ. of Regina, Regina, Sask., Canada S4S 0A2. Kathleen Wall, Ed. Short stories, 2,000 to 6,000 words; critical articles on short fiction and poetry; poetry. Pays $3 per page for prose, $10 for poetry, after publication.

WASHINGTON REVIEW—P.O. Box 50132, Washington, DC 20091–0132. Clarissa Wittenberg, Ed. Poetry; articles on literary, performing and fine arts in the Washington, D.C., area. Fiction, 1,000 to 2,500 words. Area writers preferred. Pays in copies. Responds in 3 months.

WEBSTER REVIEW—English Dept., SLCC—Meramec, 11333 Big Bend Rd., St. Louis, MO 63122. Nancy Schapiro, Robert Boyd, Greg Marshall, Eds. Fiction; poetry; interviews; essays; translations. Pays in copies. Manuscripts read year-round.

WEST BRANCH—Bucknell Hall, Bucknell Univ., Lewisburg, PA 17837. Karl Patten, Robert Taylor, Eds. Poetry and fiction. Pays in copies and subscriptions.

WESTERN HUMANITIES REVIEW—Univ. of Utah, Salt Lake City, UT 84112. Dawn Corrigan, Man. Ed. Quarterly. Fiction and essays, to 30 pages, and poetry. Pays $50 for poetry, $150 for short stories and essays, on acceptance. Manuscripts read year-round; responds in 3 to 6 months.

THE WILLIAM AND MARY REVIEW—P.O. Box 8795, College of William and Mary, Williamsburg, VA 23187–8795. Andrew Zawacki, Ed. Annual. Fiction, critical essays, and interviews, 2,500 to 7,500 words; poetry, all genres (submit 5 to 8 poems). Pays in copies. Manuscripts read September through April. Responds in 3 months.

WILLOW SPRINGS—MS-1, Eastern Washington Univ., Cheney, WA 99004–2496. Attn: Ed. Fiction, poetry, translation, and art. Length and subject matter are open. Pays $10 for poetry; $35 for prose, on publication. Manuscripts read September 15 to May 15.

WIND MAGAZINE—RFD #1-Box 809K, Pikeville, KY 41501. Steven R. Cope and Charlie G. Hughes, Eds. Semiannual. Short stories and poems. Reviews of books from small presses, to 250 words, and news of interest to the literary community. Pays in copies. Manuscripts read year-round.

THE WINDLESS ORCHARD—Dept. of English, Indiana-Purdue Univ., Ft. Wayne, IN 46805. Robert Novak, Ed. Contemporary poetry. Pays in copies. SASE required. Manuscripts read year-round.

WINDSOR REVIEW—(formerly *The University of Windsor Review*) Dept. of English, Univ. of Windsor, Windsor, Ont., Canada N9B 3P4. Wanda Campbell, General Ed. Short stories, poetry, and original art. Pays $15 to $50, on publication. Responds in one to 3 months.

WITHOUT HALOS—Ocean County Poets Collective, P.O. Box 1342, Point Pleasant Beach, NJ 08742. Frank Finale, Ed. Submit 3 to 5 poems (to 2 pages) between January 1 and June 30. Pays in copies.

WITNESS—Oakland Community College, 27055 Orchard Lake Rd., Farmington Hills, MI 48334. Peter Stine, Ed. Thematic journal. Fiction and essays, 5 to 20 pages, and poems (submit up to 3). Pays $6 per page for prose, $10 per page for poetry, on publication.

WOMAN OF POWER—P.O. Box 2785, Orleans, MA 02653. Charlene McKee, Ed. A magazine of feminism, spirituality, and politics. Nonfiction, to 5,000 words. Send SASE for issue themes and guidelines. Pays in copies and subscription. Manuscripts read year-round.

THE WORCESTER REVIEW—6 Chatham St., Worcester, MA 01609. Rodger Martin, Ed. Poetry (submit up to 5 poems at a time), fiction, critical articles about poetry, and articles and reviews with a New England connection. Pays in copies. Responds within 6 months.

THE WORMWOOD REVIEW—P.O. Box 4698, Stockton, CA 95204-0698. Marvin Malone, Ed. Quarterly. Poetry and prose-poetry, 4 to 400 lines. "We encourage wit and conciseness." Pays 3 to 20 copies or cash equivalent.

WRITERS FORUM—Univ. of Colorado, 1420 Austin Bluffs Pkwy., Colorado Springs, CO 80933-7150. Alex Blackburn, Ed. Annual. Mainstream and experimental fiction, 1,000 to 8,000 words. Poetry (one to 5 poems per submission). Emphasis on western themes and writers. Pays in copies. Manuscripts read September through February.

WRITERS ON THE RIVER—P.O. Box 40828, Memphis, TN 38174. Miss Demaris C. Smith, Ed. Catherine Hudgens, Prose Ed. Ouida Simmons, Poetry Ed. Fiction (adventure, fantasy, historical, humor, mainstream, mystery/suspense), and nonfiction (profiles, scholarly essays, regional history), to 2,500 words. All types of poetry considered; submit up to 6. "We try to promote good writing and act as a sounding board for Southern writers." Submit 2 copies of manuscripts. Submissions accepted from: AR, AL, MS, LA, TN, KY, and MO only. Pays in copies. Manuscripts read year-round.

XANADU: A LITERARY JOURNAL—Box 773, Huntington, NY 11743-0773. Barry Fruchter, Articles Ed. Mildred Jeffrey, Barbara Lucas, Weslea Sidon, Mitzie Grossman, Lois V. Walker, Sue Kain, Eds. Poetry on a variety of topics; no length restrictions. Scholarly articles on fiction and poetry. Pays in copies. Manuscripts read September through June.

YALE REVIEW—Yale Univ., P.O. Box 208243, New Haven, CT 06520-8243. J.D. McClatchy, Ed. Serious poetry, to 200 lines, and fiction, 3,000 to 5,000 words. Pays average of $300.

YARROW—English Dept., Lytle Hall, Kutztown State Univ., Kutztown, PA 19530. Harry Humes, Ed. Semiannual. Poetry. "Just good, solid, clear writing. We don't have room for long poems." Pays in copies. Manuscripts read year-round.

ZYZZYVA—41 Sutter, Suite 1400, San Francisco, CA 94104. Howard Junker, Ed. Publishes work of West Coast writers only: fiction, essays, and poetry. Pays $50 to $250, on acceptance. Manuscripts read year-round.

HUMOR, FILLERS, AND SHORT ITEMS

Magazines noted for their excellent filler departments, plus a cross-section of publications using humor, short items, jokes, quizzes, and cartoons, follow. However, almost all magazines use some type of filler material, and writers can find dozens of markets by studying copies of magazines at a library or newsstand.

THE ANNALS OF IMPROBABLE RESEARCH—(formerly *The Journal of Irreproducible Results*) The MIT Museum, 265 Massachusetts Ave., Cambridge, MA 02139. Marc Abrahams, Ed. Science humor, science reports and analysis, one to 4 pages. B&W photos. "This journal is the place to find the mischievous, funny, iconoclastic side of science. An insider's journal that lets anyone sneak into the company of wonderfully mad scientists." Guidelines. No payment.

ARMY MAGAZINE—2425 Wilson Blvd., Arlington, VA 22201–3385. Mary B. French, Ed.-in-Chief. True anecdotes on military subjects. Pays $25 to $50, on publication.

THE ATLANTIC MONTHLY—745 Boylston St., Boston, MA 02116. Attn: Ed. Sophisticated humorous or satirical pieces, 1,000 to 3,000 words. Some light poetry. Pays from $500 for prose, on acceptance.

ATLANTIC SALMON JOURNAL—P.O. Box 429, St. Andrews, N.B., Canada E0G 2X0. Harry Bruce, Ed. Fillers, 50 to 100 words, on salmon politics, conservation, and nature. Pays $25 for fillers, on publication.

BICYCLING—33 E. Minor St., Emmaus, PA 18098. Attn: Eds. Anecdotes, helpful cycling tips, and other items for "Paceline" and "Tip Talk" sections, 150 to 250 words. Pays $25 to $50, on acceptance.

BYLINE—Box 130596, Edmond, OK 73013. Marcia Preston, Ed.-in-Chief. Humor, 300 to 800 words, about writing. Pays $15 to $35 for humor, on acceptance.

CAPPER'S—1503 S.W. 42nd St., Topeka, KS 66609–1265. Nancy Peavler, Ed. Household hints, recipes, jokes. Pays varying rates, on publication.

CASCADES EAST—716 N. E. 4th St., P. O. Box 5784, Bend, OR 97708. Geoff Hill, Ed. Fillers related to travel, history, and recreation in central Oregon. Pays 5¢ to 10¢ a word, extra for photos, on publication.

CATHOLIC DIGEST—P.O. Box 64090, St. Paul, MN 55164–0090. Attn: Ed. Articles, 200 to 500 words, on instances of kindness rewarded for "Hearts Are Trumps." Stories about conversions, for "Open Door." Reports of tactful remarks or actions, for "The Perfect Assist." Accounts of good deeds, for "People Are Like

That." Humorous pieces, 50 to 300 words, on parish life, for "In Our Parish." Amusing signs, for "Signs of the Times." Jokes; fillers. No fiction. Pays $4 to $50, on publication. Manuscripts cannot be acknowledged or returned.

CHICKADEE—179 John St., Suite 500, Toronto, Ont., Canada M5T 3G5. Lizann Flatt, Ed. Juvenile poetry, 10 to 15 lines. Fiction, 800 words. Pays on acceptance. Enclose international reply coupons.

CHILDREN'S PLAYMATE—1100 Waterway Blvd., P. O. Box 567, Indianapolis, IN 46206. Lise Hoffman, Ed. Articles and fiction, puzzles, games, mazes for children, ages 6 to 8, emphasizing health, fitness, sports, safety, and nutrition. Pays to 17¢ a word (varies on puzzles), on publication.

COLUMBIA JOURNALISM REVIEW—Columbia Univ., 700 Journalism Bldg., New York, NY 10027. Gloria Cooper, Man. Ed. Amusing mistakes in news stories, headlines, photos, etc. (original clippings required), for "Lower Case." Pays $25, on publication.

COUNTRY WOMAN—P. O. Box 989, Greendale, WI 53129. Kathy Pohl, Man. Ed. Short rhymed verse, 4 to 20 lines, seasonal and country-related. All material must be positive and upbeat. Pays $10 to $15, on acceptance.

CRACKED—Globe Communications, Inc., 441 Lexington Ave., 2nd Fl., New York, NY 10017. Lou Silverstone, Andy Simmons, Eds. Humor, one to 5 pages, for 12- to 15-year-old readers. "Queries are not necessary, but read the magazine before submitting material!" Pays from $100 per page, on acceptance.

CURRENT COMEDY—See *Speaker's Idea File.*

CYCLE WORLD—1499 Monrovia Ave., Newport Beach, CA 92663. David Edwards, Ed. News items on motorcycle industry, legislation, trends. Pays on publication.

THE ELKS MAGAZINE—425 W. Diversey Pkwy., Chicago, IL 60614. Fred D. Oakes, Ed. Informative or humorous pieces, to 2,500 words. No fillers. Pays from $150, on acceptance. Query required.

FACES—Cobblestone Publishing, 7 School St., Peterborough, NH 03458–1454. Carolyn P. Yoder, Ed. Puzzles, mazes, crosswords, and picture puzzles for children. Send SASE for list of themes before submitting.

THE FAMILY DIGEST—P.O. Box 40137, Fort Wayne, IN 46804. Corine B. Erlandson, Ed. Family- or Catholic parish-oriented humor. Anecdotes, to 250 words, of funny or unusual real-life parish and family experiences. Pays $5 to $10, on acceptance.

FARM AND RANCH LIVING—5400 S. 60th St., Greendale, WI 53129. Nick Pobst, Ed. Fillers on rural people and living, 200 words. Pays from $15, on acceptance and publication.

FATE—P.O. Box 64383, St. Paul, MN 55164–0383. Attn: Ed. Factual fillers, to 300 words, on strange or psychic happenings. True stories, to 500 words, on proof of survival or mystic personal experiences. Pays 10¢ a word. Send SASE for guidelines.

FIELD & STREAM—2 Park Ave., New York, NY 10016. Duncan Barnes, Ed. Fillers on hunting, fishing, camping, etc., to 500 words. Cartoons. Pays $75 to $250 for fillers, $100 for cartoons, on acceptance.

GALLERY—401 Park Ave. S., New York, NY 10016–8802. Barry Janoff, Ed. Dir. Rich Friedman, Man. Ed. Short humor, satire, and short service features for men. Pays varying rates, on publication. Query. Guidelines.

733

GAMES—19 W. 21st St., Suite 1002, New York, NY 10010. R. Wayne Schmittberger, Ed.-in-Chief. Pencil puzzles, visual brainteasers, and pop culture tests. Humor and playfulness a plus; quality a must. Pays top rates, on publication.

GLAMOUR—350 Madison Ave., New York, NY 10017. Attn: Viewpoint Ed. Articles, 1,000 words, for "Viewpoint" section: opinion pieces for women. Pays $500, on acceptance. SASE required.

GOOD HOUSEKEEPING—959 Eighth Ave., New York, NY 10019. Rosemary Leonard, Ed. No longer accepting verse, poems, or quips for the Light Housekeeping page.

INDEPENDENT LIVING—150 Motor Pkwy., Suite 420, Hauppauge, NY 11788–5145. Anne Kelly, Ed. Short humor, to 500 words, and cartoons for magazine addressing lifestyles and home health care of persons who have disabilities. Pays 10¢ a word, on publication. Query.

THE JOURNAL OF IRREPRODUCIBLE RESULTS—See *The Annals of Improbable Research.*

LADIES' HOME JOURNAL—"Kidspeak," 100 Park Ave., 3rd Fl., New York, NY 10017. Attn: Eds. Brief, true anecdotes about the amusing things children say. All material must be original. Pays $50 for children's anecdotes. Due to the volume of mail received, submissions cannot be acknowledged or returned.

MAD MAGAZINE—485 Madison Ave., New York, NY 10022. Attn: Eds. Humorous pieces on a wide variety of topics. Two- to 8-panel cartoons (not necessary to include sketches with submission). SASE for guidelines strongly recommended. Pays top rates, on acceptance.

MATURE LIVING—127 Ninth Ave. N., MSN 140, Nashville, TN 37234. Attn: Ed. Brief, humorous, original items; 25-line profiles with action color photos; "Grandparents Brag Board" items; Christian inspirational pieces for senior adults, 125 words. Pays $10 to $20.

MATURE YEARS—201 Eighth Ave. S., P.O. Box 801, Nashville, TN 37202. Marvin W. Cropsey, Ed. Poems, cartoons, puzzles, jokes, anecdotes, to 300 words, for older adults. Allow 2 months for manuscript evaluation. "A Christian magazine that seeks to build faith. We always show older adults in a favorable light." Include name, address, social security number with all submissions.

MID-WEST OUTDOORS—111 Shore Dr., Hinsdale, IL 60521–5885. Gene Laulunen, Man. Ed. Where to and how to fish and hunt in the Midwest, 700 to 1,500 words, with 2 photos (no slides). Pays $15 to $35, on publication.

MODERN BRIDE—249 W. 17th St., New York, NY 10011. Mary Ann Cavlin, Man. Ed. Humorous pieces, 500 to 1,000 words, for brides. Pays on acceptance.

THE NEW HUMOR MAGAZINE—Box 216, Lafayette Hill, PA 19444. Edward Savaria, Jr., Ed. Quarterly. Fiction, interviews, and profiles, up to 1,000 words; short poetry, jokes, and fillers. "We would edit out all truly gross humor and anything that elicits loud groans. Please, no X-rated jokes or stories." Pays $50 to $300 for stories and articles, $5 to $25 for jokes and fillers, on acceptance.

NEW YORK—755 Second Ave., New York, NY 10017. Kurt Andersen, Ed. Sarah Jewler, Man. Ed. Short, lively pieces, to 400 words, highlighting events and trends in New York City for "Fast Track." Profiles, to 300 words, for "Brief Lives." Pays $25 to $300, on publication. Include SASE.

THE NEW YORKER—20 W. 43rd St., New York, NY 10036. Attn: Newsbreaks Dept. Amusing mistakes in newspapers, books, magazines, etc. Pays from $10, extra for headings and tags, on acceptance. Material returned only with SASE.

THE NOSE—Acme Publishing Co., Inc., 60 Federal St., Suite 502, San Francisco, CA 94107. Jack Boulware, Ed. Humorous/investigative pieces with "a shoot-from-the-hip attitude." Features, 1,500 to 4,000 words. Interviews, 1,000 to 3,000 words. "The Beat," first-person experiences, 350 words. "Wild West," 300 words, random satirical pieces, rewrites of actual news items. Also short, witty reviews of recent videos, books, magazines, CDs, and software, 150 words. Payment negotiable. Guidelines.

OPTOMETRIC ECONOMICS—American Optometric Assn., 243 N. Lindbergh Blvd., St. Louis, MO 63141. Dr. Jack Runninger, Ed. Short humor for optometrists. Payment varies, on acceptance.

OUTDOOR LIFE—2 Park Ave., New York, NY 10016. Vin T. Sparano, Ed. Short instructive items, 900 to 1,100 words, on hunting, fishing, boating, and outdoor equipment; regional pieces on lakes, rivers, specific geographic areas of special interest to hunters and fishermen. Photos. No fiction or poetry. Pays $300 to $350, on acceptance.

PARENTS—685 Third Ave., New York, NY 10017. Ann Pleshette Murphy, Ed. Short items on solutions of child care problems for "Parents Exchange." Pays $50, on publication.

PLAYBOY—680 N. Lakeshore Dr., Chicago, IL 60611. Attn: Party Jokes Ed. or After Hours Ed. Jokes; short original material on new trends, lifestyles, personalities; humorous news items. Pays $100 for jokes, on publication; $50 to $350 for "After Hours" items, on publication.

PLAYGIRL—801 Second Ave., New York, NY 10017. Attn: Man. Ed. Humorous looks at daily life, sex, romance, and relationships from male or female perspective, 800 to 1,000 words, for "The Men's Room" and "The Women's Room." Pays varying rates.

PUNCH DIGEST FOR CANADIAN DOCTORS—See *Stitches, The Journal of Medical Humour.*

READER'S DIGEST—Pleasantville, NY 10570. Consult "Contributor's Corner" page for guidelines. No submissions acknowledged or returned.

REAL PEOPLE—950 Third Ave., 16th Fl., New York, NY 10022. Brad Hamilton, Ed. True stories, to 500 words, about interesting people for "Real Shorts" column; strange occurrences, everyday weirdness, etc., may be funny, sad, or hairraising. Also humorous items, to 75 words, taken from small-circulation magazines, newspapers, etc. Pays $25 to $50, on publication.

RHODE ISLAND MONTHLY—18 Imperial Pl., Providence, RI 02903. Vicki Sanders, Man. Ed. Short pieces, to 250 words, on Rhode Island and southeastern Massachusetts: places, customs, people and events. Pieces, to 150 words, on products and services; to 200 words on food, chefs, and restaurants. Pays $25 to $50, on publication. Query.

ROAD & TRACK—1499 Monrovia Ave., Newport Beach, CA 92663. Ellida Maki, Man. Ed. Short automotive articles, to 450 words, of "timeless nature" for knowledgeable car enthusiasts. Pays on publication. Query.

ROAD KING—Hammock Publishing, 3322 W. End Ave., Suite 700, Nashville, TN 37203. Attn: Fillers Ed. Trucking-related cartoons and fillers. Payment is negotiable, on publication. SASE required.

735

THE ROTARIAN—1560 Sherman Ave., Evanston, IL 60201–3698. Willmon L. White, Ed. Occasional humor articles. Payment varies, on acceptance. No payment for fillers, anecdotes, or jokes.

SACRAMENTO MAGAZINE—4471 D St., Sacramento, CA 95819. Karen Coe, Ed. "City Lights," interesting and unusual people, places, and behind-the-scenes news items, to 400 words. All material must have Sacramento tie-in. Payment varies, on publication.

SOAP OPERA UPDATE—270 Sylvan Ave., Englewood Cliffs, NJ 07632. Dawn Mazzurco, Exec. Ed. Soap opera oriented fillers, to 500 words. Payment varies, on publication.

SPEAKER'S IDEA FILE—(formerly *Current Comedy*) 165 W. 47th St., New York, NY 10036. Gary Apple, Humor Ed. Original, funny, performable jokes on news, fads, topical subjects, business, etc. Jokes for roasts, retirement dinners, and for speaking engagements. Humorous material specifically geared for public speaking situations such as microphone feedback, introductions, long events, etc. Also interested in longer original jokes and anecdotes that can be used by public speakers. Pays $12, after publication.

SPORTS AFIELD—250 W. 55th St., New York, NY 10019. Attn: Ed. Unusual, useful tips, anecdotes, 100 to 300 words, for "Almanac" section: hunting, fishing, camping, boating, etc. Photos. Pays on publication.

SPORTS CARD TRADER—155 E. Ames Ct., Plainview, NY 11803. Douglas Kale, Ed. Fillers related to collecting and investing in baseball, football, basketball, and hockey cards. (Also articles on investing in sports cards or memorabilia.) Pays 10¢ a word, on publication.

STAR—660 White Plains Rd., Tarrytown, NY 10591. Attn: Ed. Topical articles, 50 to 800 words, on human-interest subjects, show business, lifestyles, the sciences, etc., for family audience. Pays varying rates.

STITCHES, THE JOURNAL OF MEDICAL HUMOUR—(formerly *Punch Digest for Canadian Doctors*) 14845 Yonge St., Suite 300, Aurora, Ontario, Canada L4G 6H8. Simon Hally, Ed. Humorous pieces, 250 to 2,000 words, for physicians. "Most articles have something to do with medicine." Short humorous verse and original jokes. Pays 30¢ to 40¢ (Canadian) a word; $50 (Canadian) for cartoons, on publication.

TECH DIRECTIONS—Box 8623, Ann Arbor, MI 48107. Paul J. Bamford, Man. Ed. Cartoons, puzzles, brainteasers, and humorous anecdotes of interest to technology and industrial education teachers and administrators. Pays $20 for cartoons; $25 for puzzles, brainteasers, and other short classroom activities; $5 for humorous anecdotes, on publication.

THOUGHTS FOR ALL SEASONS: THE MAGAZINE OF EPIGRAMS—478 N.E. 56th St., Miami, FL 33137. Michel P. Richard, Ed. Epigrams and puns, one to 4 lines, and poetry, to one page. "Writers are advised not to submit material until they have examined a copy of the magazine." Payment is one copy.

TOUCH—Box 7259, Grand Rapids, MI 49510. Carol Smith, Man. Ed. Puzzles based on the NIV Bible, for Christian girls ages 8 to 14. Pays $10 to $15 per puzzle, on acceptance. Send SASE for theme update.

TRAVEL SMART—Dobbs Ferry, NY 10522. Attn: Ed. Interesting, unusual travel-related tips. Practical information for vacation or business travel. Pays $5 to $150. Query for over 250 words.

TRUE CONFESSIONS—233 Park Ave. S., New York, NY 10003. Pat Vitucci, Ed. Warm, inspirational first-person fillers, 300 to 700 words, about love, marriage, family life, for "The Feminine Side of Things," "My Man," and "Incredible But True." Short stories, 1,000 to 2,000 words. Pays after publication. Buys all rights.

THE UTNE READER—Lens Publishing Co., 1624 Harmon Pl., Fawkes Bldg., Minneapolis, MN 55403–1906. Josh Glenn, Ed. Asst. Short summary pieces and reviews, 300 to 1,000 words. Primarily a reprint publication. Limited market; query preferred. Pays $100 to $500, on publication.

WISCONSIN TRAILS—P.O. Box 5650, Madison, WI 53705. Attn: Ed. Short fillers, 300 words, about Wisconsin: places to go, things to see, etc. Pays $75, on publication.

WOMEN'S GLIB—P.O. Box 259, Bala Cynwyd, PA 19004. Rosalind Warren, Ed. Annual. Feminist humor, 2 to 10 pages, funny one-liners, and brief, rhymed poems. Submissions accepted from women only. No pieces on diet, weight loss, body image, or romance. Cartoons. Pays from $5 per page, on publication, plus copies.

JUVENILE AND YOUNG ADULT MAGAZINES

JUVENILE MAGAZINES

AMERICAN GIRL—8400 Fairway Pl., P.O. Box 998, Middleton, WI 53562–0998. Attn: Ed. Dept. Asst. Bimonthly. Articles, to 800 words, and contemporary or historical fiction, to 3,000 words, for girls ages 7 to 12. "We do not want 'teenage' material, i.e. articles on romance, make-up, dating, etc." Payment varies, on acceptance. Query for articles.

CALLIOPE: WORLD HISTORY FOR YOUNG PEOPLE—Cobblestone Publishing, Inc., 7 School St., Peterborough, NH 03458. Carolyn P. Yoder, Ed.-in-Chief. Theme-based magazine, published five times yearly. Articles, 750 words, with lively, original approach to world history (East/West) through the Renaissance. Shorts, 200 to 750 words, on little-known information related to issue's theme. Fiction, to 1,200 words: historical, biographical, adventure, or retold legends. Activities for children, to 800 words. Poetry, to 100 lines. Puzzles and games. Send SASE for guidelines and themes. Pays 10¢ to 17¢ a word, on publication.

CHICKADEE—The Young Naturalist Foundation, 179 John St., Suite 500, Toronto, Ont., Canada M5T 3G5. Lizann Flatt, Ed. Animal and adventure stories for 3- to 9-year-olds. Also puzzles, activities, and observation games. Pays varying rates, on acceptance. Submit complete manuscript with $1.50 check or money order for return postage.

CHILD LIFE—1100 Waterway Blvd., P.O. Box 567, Indianapolis, IN 46206. Stan Zukowski, Ed. Articles, 500 to 1,000 words, for 9- to 11-year-olds. Fiction and humor, to 1,200 words, with emphasis on health, fitness, and sports. General interest. Poetry. Puzzles. Photos. Pays 10¢ a word, extra for photos, on publication. Buys all rights.

CHILDREN'S DIGEST—1100 Waterway Blvd., P.O. Box 567, Indianapolis, IN 46206. Elizabeth Rinck, Ed. Health and general-interest publication for preteens. Informative articles, 500 to 1,200 words, and fiction (especially realistic, adventure, mystery, and humorous), 500 to 1,500 words. Historical and biographical articles. Poetry and activities. Pays from 10¢ a word, from $15 for poems, on publication.

CHILDREN'S PLAYMATE—1100 Waterway Blvd., P.O. Box 567, Indianapolis, IN 46206. Lise Hoffman, Ed. General-interest and health-related short stories, 500 to 700 words, for 6- to 8-year-olds. Simple science articles and how-to crafts pieces with brief instructions. "All About" features, about 500 words, on health, fitness, nutrition, safety, and exercise. Poems, puzzles, dot-to-dots, mazes, hidden pictures. Pays to 17¢ a word, from $15 for poetry, on publication.

CLUBHOUSE—Box 15, Berrien Springs, MI 49103. Elaine Trumbo, Ed. Action-oriented Christian stories, 800 to 1,200 words. Children in stories should be wise, brave, funny, kind, etc. Pays $30 to $35 for stories.

COBBLESTONE—7 School St., Peterborough, NH 03458–1454. Samuel Mead, Ed. Theme-related articles, biographies, fiction, and short accounts of historical events, to 1,000 words, for 8- to 15-year-olds. Pays 10¢ to 17¢ a word, on publication. Send SASE for guidelines and themes.

CRAYOLA KIDS—Meredith Publishing, 1912 Grand Ave., Des Moines, IA 50309–3379. Deborah Gore Ohrn, Ed. Bimonthly for readers 3 to 8 years old. Stories, 150 to 250 words; hands-on crafts and activities, one to 4 pages. Interviews. Pays $100 to $250, on publication. Query with resumé and work samples.

CRICKET—Box 300, Peru, IL 61354–0300. Marianne Carus, Pub./Ed.-in-Chief. Articles and fiction, 200 to 1,500 words, for 9- to 14-year-olds. Poetry, to 30 lines. Pays to 25¢ a word, to $3 a line for poetry, on publication. SASE required. Guidelines.

DISCOVERIES—WordAction Publishing Co., 6401 The Paseo, Kansas City, MO 64131. Attn: Ed. Asst. Weekly designed to correlate with Evangelical Sunday school curriculum. Fiction, 500 to 700 words, for 8- to 10-year-olds should feature contemporary, true-to-life character and illustrate character building and scriptural application. No poetry. Pays 5¢ a word, on publication. Guidelines.

FACES—Cobblestone Publishing, 7 School St., Peterborough, NH 03458–1454. Carolyn P. Yoder, Ed.-in-Chief. In-depth feature articles, 800 to 1,200 words, with an anthropology theme. Shorts, 200 to 800 words, related to themes. Fiction, to 1,500 words, on legends, folktales, stories from around the world, etc., related to theme. Activities, to 1,000 words, including recipes, crafts, games, etc., for children. Pays 13¢ to 17¢ a word for features; 10¢ to 12¢ a word for shorts; 10¢ to 15¢ a word for fiction. Send for guidelines and themes.

FAITH 'N STUFF—See *Guideposts for Kids.*

FIELD & STREAM—2 Park Ave., New York, NY 10016. Duncan Barnes, Ed. Articles, to 600 words, on hunting and fishing, real-life adventure, how-to projects, natural phenomena and history, conservation, and sporting ethics for *Field and Stream Jr.*, a special section aimed at 8- to 12-year-olds. Puzzles and fillers, 25 to 100 words. Pays from $75 to $650, on acceptance. Queries preferred.

THE FRIEND—50 E. North Temple, 23rd Fl., Salt Lake City, UT 84150. Vivian Paulsen, Man. Ed. Stories and articles, 1,000 to 1,200 words. Stories, to 250 words, for younger readers and preschool children. Pays from 9¢ a word, from $25 per poem, on acceptance. Prefers completed manuscripts.

GUIDEPOSTS FOR KIDS—(formerly *Faith 'n Stuff*) P.O. Box 538A, Chesterton, IN 46304. Mary Lou Carney, Ed. True, action-packed, value-driven stories that either feature kids or would be of interest to kids. Stories must be suitable for scripting as brief comic books. Fiction: historicals and mysteries, approximately 1,500 words. Contemporary stories, 1,000 words. Kids interacting with kids;not preachy. Payment varies. Query with SASE.

HIGHLIGHTS FOR CHILDREN—803 Church St., Honesdale, PA 18431–1824. Beth Troop, Manuscript Coord. Christine Clark, Assoc. Ed. Stories and articles, to 900 words, for 2- to 12-year-olds. Fiction should have strong plot, believable characters, story line that holds reader's interest from beginning to end. No crime or violence. For articles, cite references used and qualifications. Easy rebus-form stories. Easy-to-read stories, 300 to 600 words, with strong plots. Pays from 14¢ a word, on acceptance.

HIGHWAYS—Presbyterian Publishing House, 100 Witherspoon St., Louisville, KY 40202. James S. Clinefelter, Ed. Quarterly church education resource. Articles, 100 to 600 words, and poetry, to 20 lines, for 15- to 18-year-olds. Payment varies. Limited market.

HOPSCOTCH, THE MAGAZINE FOR GIRLS—P.O. Box 164, Bluffton, OH 45817–0164. Marilyn Edwards, Ed. Bimonthly. Articles and fiction, 600 to 1,200 words, and short poetry for girls ages 6 to 12. Special interest in articles, with photos, about girls involved in worthwhile activities. "We believe young girls deserve the right to enjoy a season of childhood before they become young adults; we are not interested in such topics as sex, romance, cosmetics, hairstyles, etc." Pays 5¢ to 7¢ a word, on publication.

HUMPTY DUMPTY'S MAGAZINE—1100 Waterway Blvd., P.O. Box 567, Indianapolis, IN 46206. Christine French Clark, Ed. General-interest publication with an emphasis on health and fitness for 4- to 6-year-olds. Easy-to-read fiction, to 600 words, some with health and nutrition, safety, exercise, or hygiene as theme; humor and light approach preferred. Creative nonfiction, including photo stories. Crafts with clear, brief instructions. No-cook recipes using healthful ingredients. Short verse, narrative poems. Pays to 20¢ a word, from $15 for poems, on publication. Buys all rights.

JACK AND JILL—1100 Waterway Blvd., P.O. Box 567, Indianapolis, IN 46206. Steve Charles, Ed. Articles, 500 to 800 words, for 7- to 10-year-olds, on sports, fitness, health, nutrition, safety, exercise. Features, 500 to 700 words, on history, biography, life in other countries, etc. Fiction, to 700 words. Short poems, games, puzzles, projects, recipes. Photos. Pays 10¢ to 20¢ a word, extra for photos, on publication.

JUNIOR TRAILS—1445 Boonville Ave., Springfield, MO 65802–1894. Sinda Zinn, Ed. Fiction, 1,000 to 1,500 words, with a Christian focus, believable characters, and moral emphasis. Articles, 300 to 500 words, on science, nature, biography. Pays 2¢ or 3¢ a word, on acceptance.

KID CITY—Children's Television Workshop, 1 Lincoln Plaza, New York, NY 10023. Attn: Ed. Short stories, to 500 words; factual articles; interviews/features on kids in sports, TV, or movies; animal stories; crafts, activities, games and comics that teach. Send complete manuscript for fiction; query for nonfiction. Pays $250 to $350, on acceptance. Guidelines.

LADYBUG—P.O. Box 300, Peru, IL 61354–0300. Marianne Carus, Pub./ Ed.-in-Chief. Paula Morrow, Assoc. Ed. Picture stories, read-aloud stories, fantasy, folk and fairy tales, 300 to 750 words, for 2- to 6-year-olds; poetry, to 20 lines; songs and rhymes; crafts, activities, and games, to 4 pages. Pays to 25¢ a word for stories and articles; to $3 a line for poetry, on publication. SASE required. Guidelines.

MY FRIEND—Daughters of St. Paul, 50 St. Pauls Ave., Boston, MA 02130. Sister Anne Joan, Ed. "The Catholic Magazine for Kids." Readers are 6 to 12 years old. Fiction, to 400 words, for primary readers; 400 to 600 words for intermediate readers. Nonfiction: general-information articles, media literacy, lives of saints, etc., 150 to 600 words. Some humorous poetry, 6 to 8 lines. Buys first rights. Pays $20 to $150 for stories and articles, $5 to $20 for fillers. Query for artwork. Guidelines available.

NATIONAL GEOGRAPHIC WORLD—1145 17th St. N.W., Washington, DC 20036–4688. Susan Tejada, Ed. Picture magazine for young readers, ages 8 and older. Natural history, adventure, archaeology, geography, science, the environment, and human interest. Proposals for picture stories only. No unsolicited manuscripts.

NEW MOON, THE MAGAZINE FOR GIRLS AND THEIR DREAMS— P.O. Box 3587, Duluth, MN 55803–3587. Joe Kelly, Man. Ed. "Our goal is to celebrate girls and support their efforts to hang onto their voices, strengths, and dreams as they move from being girls to becoming women." Profiles of girls and women, 300 to 1,000 words. Science and math experiments, 300 to 600 words. Submissions from both girls and adults. Queries preferred. Pays 5¢ to 8¢ a word, on publication. Also publishes companion letter, *New Moon Parenting*.

ODYSSEY: SCIENCE THAT'S OUT OF THIS WORLD—Cobblestone Publishing, 7 School St., Peterborough, NH 03458–1454. Carolyn P. Yoder, Ed.-in-Chief. Beth Lindstrom, Ed. Features, 250 to 750 words, on astronomy and space science for 8- to 14-year-olds. Short experiments, projects, and games. Send SASE for guidelines and themes. Pays 10¢ to 17¢ a word, on publication.

ON THE LINE—616 Walnut, Scottdale, PA 15683–1999. Mary Clemens Meyer, Ed. Weekly paper for 10- to 14-year-olds. Nature, general nonfiction, and how-to articles, 350 to 500 words; fiction, 900 to 1,200 words; poetry, puzzles, cartoons. Pays to 4¢ a word, on acceptance.

PLAYS, THE DRAMA MAGAZINE FOR YOUNG PEOPLE—120 Boylston St., Boston, MA 02116–4615. Elizabeth Preston, Man. Ed. Wholesome one-act comedies, dramas, skits, satires, farces, and creative dramatic material suitable for school productions at junior high, middle, and lower grade levels. Plays with modern settings preferred. Also uses dramatized classics, folktales and fairy tales, puppet plays. No religious plays or musicals. Pays good rates, on acceptance. Buys all rights. Query first for classics, folk and fairy tales. Guidelines; send SASE.

POCKETS—1908 Grand Ave., Box 189, Nashville, TN 37202–0189. Janet McNish, Ed. Ecumenical magazine for 6- to 12-year-olds. Fiction and scripture stories, 600 to 1,500 words; short poems; and articles about the Bible, 400 to 600 words. Pays from 12¢ a word, $25 to $50 for poetry, on acceptance. Guidelines and themes. Annual fiction contest; send SASE for details.

POWER AND LIGHT—6401 The Paseo, Kansas City, MO 64131. Beula J. Postlewait, Preteen Ed. Fiction, 500 to 800 words, for grades 5 and 6, with Christian emphasis. Cartoons and puzzles. Pays 5¢ a word for multi-use rights, 1 3/4¢ a word for reprints. Pays $15 for cartoons and puzzles. Send SASE with manuscript.

RADAR—Standard Publishing, 8121 Hamilton Ave., Cincinnati, OH 45231. Margaret Williams, Ed. Weekly Sunday school take-home paper. Articles, 400 to

650 words, on nature, hobbies, crafts. Short stories, 900 to 1,000 words: mystery, sports, school, family, with 12-year-old as main character; serials, 2,000 words. Christian emphasis. Poems to 12 lines. Pays to 7¢ a word, to 50¢ a line for poetry, on acceptance.

RANGER RICK—National Wildlife Federation, 8925 Leesburg Pike, Vienna, VA 22184–0001. Gerald Bishop, Ed. Articles, to 900 words, on wildlife, conservation, natural sciences, and kids in the outdoors, for 6- to 9-year-olds. Nature-related fiction, mysteries, fantasies, and science fiction welcome. Games (no crosswords or word-finds), crafts, humorous poems, outdoor activities, and puzzles. For nonfiction, query with sample lead, list of references, and names of experts you plan to contact. Guidelines. Pays to $550, on acceptance.

SHOFAR—43 Northcote Dr., Melville, NY 11747. Gerald H. Grayson, Ed. Short stories, 500 to 750 words; articles, 250 to 750 words; poetry, to 50 lines; short fillers, games, puzzles, and cartoons for Jewish children, 8 to 13. All material must have a Jewish theme. Pays 10¢ a word, on publication. Submit holiday pieces at least 6 months in advance.

SKIPPING STONES—P.O. Box 3939, Eugene, OR 97403. Arun N. Toké, Exec. Ed. "A Multi-Cultural Children's Quarterly." Articles, approximately 500 words, relating to community and family, religions, culture, nature, traditions, and cultural celebrations in other countries, for 7- to 15-year-olds. "Especially invited to submit are children from cultural backgrounds other than European-American and/or those with physical challenges. We print art, poetry, songs, games, stories, and photographs from around the world and include many different languages (with English translation)." Payment is one copy, on publication. Send SASE for guidelines.

SOCCER JR.—27 Unquowa Rd., Fairfield, CT 06430. Joe Provey, Ed. Fiction and fillers about soccer for readers ages 8 and up. Pays $450 for a feature or story; $250 for department pieces, on acceptance. Query.

SPIDER—P.O. Box 300, Peru, IL 61354. Attn: Submissions Ed. Fiction, 300 to 1,000 words, for 6- to 9-year-olds: realistic, easy-to-read stories, fantasy, folk and fairy tales, science fiction, fables, myths. Articles, 300 to 800 words, on nature, animals, science, technology, environment, foreign culture, history (include short bibliography with articles). Serious, humorous, or nonsense poetry, to 20 lines. Puzzles, activities, and games, to 4 pages, also considered. Pays 25¢ a word, $3 per line for poetry, on publication.

SPORTS ILLUSTRATED FOR KIDS—Time & Life Bldg., Rockefeller Ctr., New York, NY 10020. Stephen Malley, Sr. Ed. Articles, 1,000 to 1,500 words, and short features, 500 to 600 words, for 8- to 13-year-olds. "Most articles are staff-written. Department pieces are the best bet for free lancers." Departments: "My Worst Day," 600 words, an athlete's account as told to a writer; "Curveballs," 150 words, wacky sports trivia; "Tips from the Pros" and "Legends," 400 words, about sports figures of the past. Pays $500 for departments, $1,000 to $1,250 for articles, on acceptance. Query required.

STONE SOUP, THE MAGAZINE BY CHILDREN—Box 83, Santa Cruz, CA 95063–0083. Gerry Mandel, Ed. Stories, free-verse poems, plays, book reviews by children under 14. "Preference given to writing based on real-life experiences." Pays $10.

STORY FRIENDS—Mennonite Publishing House, Scottdale, PA 15683. Marjorie Waybill, Ed. Stories, 350 to 800 words, for 4- to 9-year-olds, on Christian faith and values in everyday experiences. Poetry. Pays to 5¢ a word, to $10 per poem, on acceptance.

SUPERSCIENCE BLUE—Scholastic, Inc., 555 Broadway, New York, NY 10012. Attn: Ed. Science news and hands-on experiments for grades 4 through 6. Article topics are staff-generated and assigned to writers. For consideration, send children's and science writing clips to Editor. Include SASE for editorial calendar. Pays $50 to $500, on acceptance.

3–2–1 CONTACT—Children's Television Workshop, 1 Lincoln Plaza, New York, NY 10023. Curtis Slepian, Ed. Entertaining and informative articles, 600 to 1,000 words, for 8- to 14-year-olds, on all aspects of science, computers, scientists, and children who are learning about or practicing science. Pays $75 to $500, on acceptance. No fiction. Query.

TOUCH—Box 7259, Grand Rapids, MI 49510. Carol Smith, Man. Ed. Upbeat fiction and features, 500 to 1,000 words, for Christian girls ages 8 to 14; personal life, nature, crafts. Poetry, puzzles. Pays 2 ½¢ a word, extra for photos, on acceptance. Query with SASE for theme update.

TURTLE MAGAZINE FOR PRESCHOOL KIDS—1100 Waterway Blvd., Box 567, Indianapolis, IN 46206. Christine French Clark, Ed. Heavily illustrated articles with an emphasis on health and nutrition for 2- to 5-year-olds. Humorous, entertaining fiction. Also crafts and activities pieces and simple science experiments. Simple poems. Stories-in-rhyme and read-aloud stories, to 500 words. Pays to 20¢ a word for stories; from $15 for poems; payment varies for activities, on publication. Buys all rights. Send SASE for guidelines.

U.S. KIDS—1100 Waterway Blvd., P.O. Box 567, Indianapolis, IN 46206. Steve Charles, Health/Fitness Ed. Articles, to 1,000 words, on issues related to kids ages 5 to 10, fiction, true-life adventures, science and nature topics. Special emphasis on health and fitness. Fiction with real-world focus; no fantasy.

VENTURE—Christian Service Brigade, P.O. Box 150, Wheaton, IL 60189. Deborah Christensen, Ed. Fiction and nonfiction, 1,000 words, for 10- to 15-year-old boys involved in Stockade and Battalion. "Think like a boy this age. They want action, adventure, and humor. They also need to see how faith in God affects every area of life and is more than just a prayer to get out of trouble." Humor and fillers; B&W 8x10 photos also accepted. Pays 5¢ to 10¢ a word, on publication.

WONDER TIME—6401 The Paseo, Kansas City, MO 64131. Lois Perrigo, Ed. Stories, 250 to 350 words, for 6-to 8-year-olds, with Christian emphasis to correlate with Sunday school curriculum. Pays $25 stories, on production.

YOUTH UPDATE—St. Anthony Messenger Press, 1615 Republic St., Cincinnati, OH 45210. Attn: Ed. "Articles for Catholic teens that address timely topics. Avoid cuteness; glib phrases and cliches; academic or erudite approaches; preachiness. Pays on acceptance, 14 ¢ a word." Query with outline and SASE.

YOUNG ADULT MAGAZINES

ALIVE NOW!—P.O. Box 189, Nashville, TN 37202. Attn: Ed. Short essays, 250 to 400 words, with Christian emphasis for adults and young adults. Poetry, one page. B&W photos. Query with SASE for themes. Pays $20 to $30, on publication.

BOYS' LIFE—1325 W. Walnut Hill Ln., P.O. Box 152079, Irving, TX 75015–2079. Attn: Ed. Publication of Boy Scouts of America. Articles and fiction, 500 to 1,500 words, for 8- to 18-year-old boys. Pays from $350 for major articles, $750 for fiction, on acceptance. Query for articles; send complete manuscript for fiction.

BREAKAWAY—8605 Explorer Dr., Colorado Springs, CO 80920. Michael Ross, Ed. Fiction, to 1,800 words, and real-life adventure articles, to 1,500 words. Humor and interesting facts, 500 to 800 words. Readers are 12- to 16-year-old Christian boys. "Must have a male slant." Pays 12¢ to 15¢ a word, on acceptance. Guidelines.

BRIO—Focus on Family, 8605 Explorer Dr., Colorado Springs, CO 80920. Susie Shellenberger, Ed. Articles of interest to Christian teen girls: profiles, how-to pieces, adventures that show the fun Christian teens can have together. Fiction, to 2,000 words, with realistic character development, good dialogue, and a plot that teen girls will be drawn to. Stories may contain a spiritual slant but should not be preachy. Short humorous pieces. Pays 8¢ to 12¢ a word, on acceptance.

CAMPUS LIFE—465 Gundersen Dr., Carol Stream, IL 60188. Harold Smith, V.P./Ed. Articles reflecting Christian values and world view, for high school and college students. Humor, general fiction, and true, first-person experiences. "If we have a choice of fiction, how-to, and a strong first-person story, we'll go with the true story every time." Photo essays, cartoons. Pays 10¢ to 20¢ a word, on acceptance. Query.

CHALLENGE—1548 Poplar Ave., Memphis, TN 38104–2493. Jeno Smith, Ed. Southern Baptist. Articles, to 800 words, for 12- and 18-year-old boys, on teen issues, current events. Photo essays on Christian sports personalities. Pays 4 ½¢ a word, extra for photos, on acceptance.

CRACKED—Globe Communications, Inc., 441 Lexington Ave., 2nd Fl., New York, NY 10017. Lou Silverstone, Andy Simmons, Eds. Humor, one to 5 pages, for 12- to 15-year-old readers. "Read magazine before submitting." Pays $100 per page, on acceptance.

EXPLORING—P.O. Box 152079, 1325 W. Walnut Hill Ln., Irving, TX 75015–2079. Scott Daniels, Exec. Ed. Publication of Boy Scouts of America. Articles, 500 to 1,500 words, for 14- to 21-year-old boys and girls, on teenage trends, college, computer games, music, education, careers, "Explorer" activities (hiking, canoeing, camping), and program ideas for meetings. No controversial subjects. Pays $150 to $500, on acceptance. Query. Send SASE for guidelines.

FREEWAY—Box 632, Glen Ellyn, IL 60138. Amy J. Cox, Ed. First-person true stories, personal experience, how-tos, fillers, humor, fiction, to 1,200 words, for 15- to 22-year-olds. Send photos, if available. Occasionally publishes poetry. Must have Christian emphasis. Pays 7¢ to 10¢ a word.

HICALL—See *Teen Life.*

KEYNOTER—3636 Woodview Trace, Indianapolis, IN 46268. Julie A. Carson, Exec. Ed. Articles, 1,500 to 1,800 words, for high school leaders: general-interest features; self-help; contemporary teenage problems. No fillers, poetry, first-person accounts, or fiction. Pays $150 to $300, on acceptance. Query preferred.

LISTEN MAGAZINE—55 W. Oak Ridge Dr., Hagerstown, MD 21740. Lincoln Steed, Ed. Articles, 1,200 to 1,500 words, providing teens with "a vigorous, positive, educational approach to the problems arising from the use of tobacco, alcohol, and other drugs." Pays 5¢ to 7¢ a word, on acceptance.

MERLYN'S PEN: THE NATIONAL MAGAZINES OF STUDENT WRITING—P.O. Box 1058, Dept. WR, East Greenwich, RI 02818. R. James Stahl, Ed. *Intermediate Edition*: writing by students in grades 6 through 9. Short stories, to 3,500 words; reviews; travel pieces; and poetry, to 100 lines. *Senior Edition*: for writers in grades 9 through 12. Fiction, 3,500 words. Poetry, to 200 lines. Responds with a brief critique in 10 weeks. Pays in copies. Guidelines available.

NEW ERA—50 E. North Temple, Salt Lake City, UT 84150. Richard M. Romney, Ed. Articles, 150 to 1,500 words, and fiction, to 2,000 words, for young Mormons. Poetry. Photos. Pays 5¢ to 20¢ a word, 25¢ a line for poetry, on acceptance. Query.

SASSY—6420 Wilshire Blvd., Los Angeles, CA 90048–5515. Attn: Kathy Colbert. Short stories written in the magazine's style, for girls ages 14 to 19. Payment varies, on acceptance.

SEVENTEEN—850 Third Ave., New York, NY 10022. Catherine Cavender, Exec. Ed. Articles, to 2,500 words, on subjects of interest to teenagers. Sophisticated, well-written fiction, 1,500 to 4,000 words, for young adults. Articles, to 1,200 words, by writers 21 and younger for "Voice." Pays varying rates, on acceptance.

STRAIGHT—8121 Hamilton Ave., Cincinnati, OH 45231. Carla J. Crane, Ed. Articles on current situations and issues for Christian teens. Humor. Well-constructed fiction, 1,000 to 1,200 words, showing teens using Christian principles. Poetry by teenagers. Photos. Pays about 3¢ to 7¢ a word, on acceptance. Send SASE for guidelines.

'TEEN—6420 Wilshire Blvd., Los Angeles, CA 90048–5515. Attn: Ed. Short stories, 2,500 to 4,000 words: mystery, teen situations, adventure, romance, humor for teens. Pays $200, on acceptance. Buys all rights.

TEEN LIFE—(formerly *Hicall*) 1445 Boonville Ave., Springfield, MO 65802–1894. Tammy Bicket, Ed. Articles, 500 to 1,000 words, and fiction, to 1,200 words, for 13- to 17-year-olds; strong evangelical emphasis. Interviews with Christian athletes and other well-known Christians; true stories; up-to-date factual articles. "Send SASE for list of topics we're interested in using." Pays on acceptance.

TEEN POWER—Box 632, Glen Ellyn, IL 60138. Amy J. Cox, Ed. Take-home Sunday school paper. True-to-life fiction or first-person (as told to), true teen experience stories with Christian insights and conclusion, 700 to 1,000 words. Include photos. Pays 7¢ to 10¢ a word, extra for photos, on acceptance.

TIGER BEAT—Sterling/MacFadden Partnership, 233 Park Ave. S., New York, NY 10003. Louise Barile, Ed. Articles, to 4 pages, on young people in show business and music industry. Pays varying rates, on acceptance. Query. SASE required.

TQ/TEEN QUEST—2845 W. Airport Freeway, Suite 137, Irving, TX 75062. Christopher Lyon, Ed. Articles and well-crafted fiction, 2,000 words, for Christian teens. Cartoons and color slides. Pays 10¢ to 15¢ a word, on publication.

YM—685 Third Ave., New York, NY 10017. Catherine Romano, Man. Ed. Articles, to 2,500 words, on entertainment, lifestyle, fashion, beauty, relationships, health, for women ages 14 to 19. Payment varies, on acceptance. Query with clips, SASE.

YOUNG AND ALIVE—4444 S. 52nd St., Lincoln, NE 68506. Richard J. Kaiser, Man. Ed. M. Marilyn Brown, Ed. Quarterly. Feature articles, 800 to 1,400 words, for blind and visually impaired young adults on adventure, biography, camping, careers, health, history, hobbies, holidays, marriage, nature, practical Christianity, sports, and travel. Photos. Pays 3¢ to 5¢ a word, $5 to $20 for photos, on acceptance. Guidelines.

YOUNG SALVATIONIST—The Salvation Army, 615 Slaters Ln., P.O. Box 269, Alexandria, VA 22313. Deborah Sedlar, Ed. Articles for teens, 800 to 1,200 words, with Christian perspective; fiction, 800 to 1,200 words; short fillers. Pays 10¢ a word, on acceptance.

YOUNG SCHOLAR—Suite 1, 4905 Pine Cone Dr., Durham, NC 27707. Greg Sanders, Man. Ed. Articles, 1,200 to 1,500 words, for bright high school students. Departments include "New to Use," 325 to 350 words; "Performance," 750 words; "Mindstuff," 350 word-reviews of books or CD-ROM; "What's Hot Now," 150 to 275 words, on interesting, worthwhile products. "The magazine is not about school; it's about learning and living the learning lifestyle. Our readers are very sophisticated. Don't write anything elementary, preachy, or thoughtless." Pays $300 to $500 for articles, $25 to $100 for department pieces, on acceptance. Queries preferred. Guidelines.

THE DRAMA MARKET

Community, regional, and civic theaters and college dramatic groups offer the best opportunities today for playwrights to see their plays produced, whether for staged production or for dramatic readings. Indeed, aspiring playwrights who can get their work produced by any of these have taken an important step toward breaking into the competitive dramatic field —many well-known playwrights received their first recognition in the regional theaters. Payment is generally nominal, but regional and university theaters usually buy only the right to produce a play, and all further rights revert to the author. Since most directors like to work closely with the authors on any revisions necessary, theaters will often pay the playwright's expenses while in residence during rehearsals. The thrill of seeing your play come to life on the stage is one of the pleasures of being on hand for rehearsals and performances.

Aspiring playwrights should query college and community theaters in their region to find out which ones are interested in seeing original scripts. Dramatic associations of interest to playwrights include the Dramatists Guild (234 W. 44th St., New York, NY 10036), and Theatre Communications Group, Inc. (355 Lexington Ave., New York, NY 10017), which publishes the annual *Dramatists Sourcebook*. *The Playwright's Companion*, published by Feedback Theatrebooks (305 Madison Ave., Suite 1146, New York, NY 10165), is an annual directory of theaters and prize contests seeking scripts. See the *Organizations for Writers* list for details on dramatists' associations.

Some of the theaters on the following list require that playwrights submit all or some of the following with scripts—cast list, synopsis, resumé, recommendations, return postcard—and with scripts and queries, SASEs must always be enclosed. Playwrights may also wish to register their material with the U.S. Copyright Office. For additional information about this, write Register of Copyrights, Library of Congress, Washington, DC 20559.

REGIONAL AND UNIVERSITY THEATERS

A. D. PLAYERS—2710 W. Alabama, Houston, TX 77098. Martha Doolittle, Lit. Mgr. Jeannette Clift George, Artistic Dir. Full-length or one-act comedies, dramas, musicals, children's plays, and adaptations with Christian world view. Submit resumé, cast list, and synopsis with SASE. Readings. Pays negotiable rates.

ACTORS THEATRE OF LOUISVILLE—316 W. Main St., Louisville, KY 40202. Michael Bigelow Dixon, Lit. Mgr. Ten-minute comedies and dramas, to 10 pages; include SASE. Annual contest. Guidelines.

ALABAMA SHAKESPEARE FESTIVAL—The State Theatre, #1 Festival Dr., Montgomery, AL 36117–4605. Bob Vardaman, Lit. Assoc. Full-length adaptations and plays dealing with southern or black issues. Send resumé and synopsis in June.

ALLEY THEATRE—615 Texas Ave., Houston, TX 77002. Christopher Baker, Lit. Dir. Full-length plays and musicals, including translations and adaptations. No unsolicited scripts; agent submissions or professional recommendations only.

ALLIANCE THEATRE COMPANY—1280 Peachtree St. N.E., Atlanta, GA 30309. Walter Bilderback, Dramaturg. Full-length comedies and dramas especially those that "deal with moral/spiritual questions of life in multicultural America." Query with synopsis and cast list. Pay varies.

AMERICAN LITERATURE THEATRE LAB—Fountain Theatre, 5060 Fountain Ave., Los Angeles, CA 90029. Simon Levy, Assoc. Prod. Dir. One-act and full-length stage adaptations of classic and contemporary American literature. Sets and cast size are unrestricted. Send synopsis and SAS postcard. Rate of payment is standard, as set by the Dramatists Guild.

AMERICAN LIVING HISTORY THEATER—P.O. Box 2677, Hollywood, CA 90078. Dorene Ludwig, Artistic Dir. One-act, historically accurate (primary source materials only) dramas dealing with marketable or known American historical and literary characters and events. Submit treatment and letter with SASE. Responds within 6 months. Pays varying rates.

AMERICAN PLACE THEATRE—111 W. 46th St., New York, NY 10036. Elise Thoron, Artistic Assoc. "No unsolicited manuscripts accepted. Writers may send a synopsis and the first 20 pages with SASE. We seek challenging, innovative works and do not favor obviously commercial material."

AMERICAN REPERTORY THEATRE—64 Brattle St., Cambridge, MA 02138. Robert Scanlan, Lit. Dir. No unsolicited manuscripts. Submit one-page description of play with 10-page sample. SASE required. Allow 2 to 4 weeks for response.

AMERICAN STAGE COMPANY—FDU, Box 336, Teaneck, NJ 07666. James Vagias, Exec. Prod. Full-length comedies, dramas, and musicals for cast of 5 or 6 and single set. No unsolicited scripts.

AMERICAN STANISLAVSKI THEATRE—485 Park Ave., #6A, New York, NY 10022. Sonia Moore, Artistic Dir. Full-length or one-act dramas with important message, for cast ages 16 to 45. No offensive language. Submit script with SAS postcard in April and May; reports in September. No payment.

AMERICAN THEATRE OF ACTORS—314 W. 54th St., New York, NY 10019. James Jennings, Artistic Dir. Full-length dramas for a cast of 2 to 6. Submit complete play and SASE. Reports in one to 2 months.

MAXWELL ANDERSON PLAYWRIGHTS SERIES, INC.—11 Esquire Rd., Norwalk, CT 06851. Muriel Nussbaum, Ken Parker, Artistic Dirs. Produces 6 professional staged readings of new plays each year in Greenwich, CT. Send complete script with SASE.

ARENA STAGE—Sixth and Maine Ave. S.W., Washington, DC 20024. Laurence Maslen, Assoc. Artistic Dir. No unsolicited manuscripts; send synopsis and first 10 pages of dialogue. Allow 3 to 6 months for reply.

ARKANSAS ARTS CENTER CHILDREN'S THEATRE—Box 2137, Little Rock, AR 72203. Bradley Anderson, Artistic Dir. Seeks solid, professional full-length or one-act scripts, especially work adapted from contemporary and classic literature. Some original work.

ARKANSAS REPERTORY THEATRE COMPANY—601 S. Main, P.O. Box 110, Little Rock, AR 72203–0110. Brad Mooy, Lit. Mgr. Full-length comedies, dramas, and musicals; prefer up to 8 characters. Send synopsis, cast list, resumé, and return postage; do not send complete manuscript. Reports in 3 months.

ARTREACH TOURING THEATRE—3074 Madison Rd., Cincinnati, OH 45209. Kathryn Schultz Miller, Artistic Dir. One-act dramas and adaptations for touring children's theater; up to 3 cast members, simple sets. Submit script with synopsis, cast list, resumé, recommendations, and SASE. Payment varies.

BARTER THEATER—P.O. Box 867, Abingdon, VA 24210. Richard Rose, Producing Dir. Full-length dramas, comedies, adaptations, musicals, and children's plays. Submit synopsis, dialogue sample, and SASE. Allow 6 to 8 months for report. Payment rates negotiable.

BERKELEY REPERTORY THEATRE—2025 Addison St., Berkeley, CA 94704. Sharon Ott, Artistic Dir. No unsolicited manuscripts; agent submissions or professional recommendations only. Responds in 3 to 4 months.

BERKSHIRE THEATRE FESTIVAL—Box 797, Stockbridge, MA 01262. Julianne Boyd, Artistic Dir. Full-length comedies, musicals, and dramas; cast to 8. Submit through agent only.

BOARSHEAD THEATER—425 Cesar Chavez Ave., Lansing, MI 48933. John Peakes, Artistic Dir. Full-length comedies and dramas with simple sets and cast of up to 10. Send precis, 5 to 10 pages of dialogue, cast list with descriptions. SAS postcard for reply.

BRISTOL RIVERSIDE THEATRE—Box 1250, Bristol, PA 19007. Susan D. Atkinson, Producing/Artistic Dir. Full-length plays with up to 10 actors and a simple set. Not accepting new scripts until June, 1995.

CALIFORNIA UNIVERSITY THEATRE—California, PA 15419. Dr. Richard J. Helldobler, Chairman. Unusual, avant-garde, and experimental one-act and full-length comedies and dramas, children's plays, and adaptations. Cast size varies. Submit synopsis with short, sample scene(s). Payment available.

CENTER STAGE—700 N. Calvert St., Baltimore, MD 21202. James Magruder, Resident Dramaturg. Full-length comedies, dramas, translations, adaptations. No unsolicited manuscripts. Send synopsis, a few sample pages, resumé, cast list, and production history. Pays varying rates. Allow 8 to 10 weeks for reply.

CHILDSPLAY, INC.—Box 517, Tempe, AZ 85280. David Saar, Artistic Dir. Multigenerational plays running 45 to 120 minutes: dramas, musicals, and adaptations for young audiences. Productions may need to travel. Cast of 4 to 8. Submissions accepted July through December. Reports in 2 to 6 months. Payment varies.

CIRCLE IN THE SQUARE/UPTOWN—1633 Broadway, New York, NY 10019–6795. Nancy Bosco, Lit. Advisor. Full-length comedies, dramas, and adaptations. Send synopsis with resumé, cast list, and 10-page dialogue sample; no unsolicited scripts. SASE required.

CIRCLE REPERTORY COMPANY—632 Broadway, 6th Fl., New York, NY 10012. Lynn Thomson, Dramaturg/Lit. Mgr. "We accept scripts submitted by agents." Offers criticism "as often as possible." Reports in 6 months. Readings.

CITY THEATRE COMPANY—57 S. 13th St., Pittsburgh, PA 15203. Gwen Orel, Lit. Dir. Full-length cutting-edge comedies and dramas; especially interested in women and minorities. Cast to 10; simple sets. Query September to May. Royalty.

CLASSIC STAGE COMPANY—136 E. 13th St., New York, NY 10003. Patricia Taylor, Man. Dir. David Esbjornson, Artistic Dir. Full-length adaptations and translations of existing classic literature. Submit synopsis with cast list and SASE, September to May. Offers readings. Pays on royalty basis.

THE CONSERVATORY THEATRE ENSEMBLE—(formerly *Ensemble Theatre Company of Marin*) c/o Tamalpais High School, 700 Miller Ave., Mill Valley, CA 94941. Daniel Caldwell, Artistic Dir. Comedies, dramas, children's plays, adaptations, and scripts addressing high school issues for largely female cast (approx. 3 women per man). "One-act plays of approximately 30 minutes are especially needed, as we produce 40 short plays each season using teenage actors." Send synopsis and resumé.

CREATIVE THEATRE—102 Witherspoon St., Princeton, NJ 08540. Eloise Bruce, Artistic Dir. Participatory plays for children, grades K through 6; cast of 4 to 6; arena or thrust stage. Submit manuscript with synopsis and cast list. Pay varies.

CROSSROADS THEATRE CO.—7 Livingston Ave., New Brunswick, NJ 08901. Ricardo Khan, Artistic Dir. Sydné Mahone, Dir. of Play Development. Full-length and one-act dramas, comedies, musicals, and adaptations; issue-oriented experimental plays that offer honest, imaginative, and insightful examinations of the African-American experience. Also interested in African and Caribbean plays. Queries only, with synopsis, cast list, resumé, and SASE.

DELAWARE THEATRE COMPANY—200 Water St., Wilmington, DE 19801–5030. Cleveland Morris, Artistic Dir. Full-length comedies, dramas, and musicals dealing with interracial dynamics in America. Contemporary or historical settings. Prefer cast of no more than 10. Send synopsis or complete script; SASE required. Reports in 6 months. Write for details of Connections competition.

DENVER CENTER THEATRE COMPANY—1050 13th St., Denver, CO 80204. Attn: Lit. Dir. Readings and productions of new works presented throughout the year. Send letter of inquiry, synopsis, 10 pages of dialogue, and resumé of writing experience. Stipend and housing provided for workshops.

DETROIT REPERTORY THEATRE—13103 Woodrow Wilson Ave., Detroit, MI 48238. Barbara Busby, Lit. Mgr. Full-length comedies and dramas. Enclose SASE. Pays royalty.

STEVE DOBBINS PRODUCTIONS—650 Geary Blvd., San Francisco, CA 94102. Chuck Hilbert, Lit. Dir. Full-length comedies, dramas, and musicals. Cast of up to 12. Query with synopsis and resumé. No unsolicited manuscripts. Reports in 6 months. Offers workshops and readings. Pays 6% of gross.

DORSET THEATRE FESTIVAL—Box 519, Dorset, VT 05251. Jill Charles, Artistic Dir. Full-length comedies, musicals, dramas, and adaptations for up to 8 cast members; simple set preferred. Agent submissions and professional recommendations only. Pays varying rates. Residencies at Dorset Colony House for Writers available October to June; inquire.

DRIFTWOOD SHOWBOAT—Box 1032, Kingston, NY 12401. Fred Hall, Resident Company Artistic Dir. Full-length family comedies for 2- to 6-person cast, single setting. No profanity. Submit cast list, synopsis, and return postcard September to June.

EAST WEST PLAYERS—4424 Santa Monica Blvd., Los Angeles, CA 90029. Tim Dang, Artistic Dir. Brian Nelson, Dramaturg. Produces 4 to 5 new plays annually. Original plays, translations, adaptations, musicals, and youth theater, "all of which must illuminate the Asian or Asian-American experience, or resonate in a significant fashion if cast with Asian-American actors." Readings. Prefer to see query letter with synopsis and 10 pages of dialogue; complete scripts also considered. Reports in 5 to 6 weeks for query; 6 months for complete script.

ECCENTRIC CIRCLES THEATRE—400 W. 43rd St., #4N, New York, NY 10036. Rosemary Hopkins, Artistic Dir. Full-length and one-act comedies and dramas with simple sets and a cast of no more than 10. Submit manuscript or synopsis with resumé and SASE. Reports in 6 weeks.

ENSEMBLE STUDIO THEATRE—549 W. 52nd St., New York, NY 10019. Attn: Lit. Mgr. Send full-length or one-act comedies and dramas with resumé and SASE, September to April. Rarely pays for scripts. Fifteen readings of new plays per year.

ENSEMBLE THEATRE COMPANY OF MARIN—See *The Conservatory Theatre Ensemble.*

FLORIDA STUDIO THEATRE—1241 N. Palm Ave., Sarasota, FL 33577. Chris Angermann, New Play Development. Innovative plays that are pertinent and contemporary. Query first with synopsis and SASE. Also accepting musicals.

EMMY GIFFORD CHILDREN'S THEATER—3504 Center St., Omaha, NE 68105. James Larson, Artistic Dir. Theatre for young audiences. Referrals only.

THE GOODMAN THEATRE—200 S. Columbus Dr., Chicago, IL 60603. Susan V. Booth, Lit. Mgr. Queries from recognized literary agents or producing organizations required for full-length comedies or dramas. No unsolicited scripts or synopses accepted.

THE GROUP, SEATTLE'S MULTICULTURAL THEATRE—305 Harrison St., Seattle, WA 98109. Attn: Lit. Dir. Full-length satires, dramas, musicals, and translations, with no more than 10-person cast and simple set. Special interest in plays suitable for multi-ethnic cast; serious plays on social/cultural issues; satires and comedies with bite. Query with synopsis, sample dialogue, resumé, and SASE required. Reporting time: 6 weeks.

THE GUTHRIE THEATER—725 Vineland Pl., Minneapolis, MN 55403. Attn: Lit. Dir. Full-length comedies, dramas, and adaptations. Manuscripts accepted only from recognized theatrical agents. Query with detailed synopsis and cast size. Reports in 2 to 4 months.

HIPPODROME STATE THEATRE—25 S.E. Second Pl., Gainesville, FL 32601. David Boyce, Dramaturg. Full-length plays with unit sets and casts of up to 10. Submit synopsis and resumé August through November. Enclose return postcard.

HOLLYWOOD THESPIAN COMPANY—(formerly *Hollywood Theater Company*) 12838 Kling St., Studio City, CA 91604–1127. Rai Tasco, Artistic Dir.

Full-length comedies and dramas for integrated cast. Include cast list and SAS postcard with submission.

HONOLULU THEATRE FOR YOUTH—2846 Ualena St., Honolulu, HI 96819. Pam Sterling, Artistic Dir. Plays, 60 to 90 minutes, for young people and family audiences. Adult casts. Contemporary issues, Pacific themes, etc. Unit sets, small cast. Query or send cover letter with synopsis, cast list, and SASE. Royalties negotiable.

HORIZON THEATRE COMPANY—P. O. Box 5376, Station E, Atlanta, GA 31107. Jeffrey and Lisa Adler, Artistic Dirs. Full-length comedies, dramas, and satires. Encourages submissions by women writers. Cast of no more than 10. Submit synopsis with cast list, resumé, and recommendations. Pays percentage. Readings. Reports in 6 months.

HUNTINGTON THEATRE COMPANY—252 Huntington Ave., Boston, MA 02115. Jayme Koszyn, Dramaturg. Full-length comedies and dramas. Query with synopsis, cast list, resumé, recommendations, and SAS postcard.

ILLINOIS THEATRE CENTER—400 Lakewood Blvd., Park Forest, IL 60466. Steve S. Billig, Artistic Dir. Full-length comedies, dramas, musicals, and adaptations, for unit/fragmentary sets, and up to 8 cast members. Send summary and SAS postcard. No unsolicited manuscripts. Pays negotiable rates. Workshops and readings offered.

INVISIBLE THEATRE—1400 N. First Ave, Tucson, AZ 85719. Deborah Dickey, Lit. Mgr. Letter of introduction from theatre professional must accompany submissions for full-length comedies, dramas, musicals, and adaptations. Submit January to May. Cast of up to 10; simple set. Also one-act plays. Pays royalty.

JEWISH REPERTORY THEATRE—1395 Lexington Ave., New York, NY 10128. Ran Avni, Artistic Dir. Full-length comedies, dramas, musicals, and adaptations, with up to 10 cast members, relating to the Jewish experience. Pays varying rates. Enclose SASE.

KUMU KAHUA—Kennedy Theatre, Univ. of Hawaii at Manoa, 1770 East-West Rd., Honolulu, HI 96822. Dennis Carroll, Man. Dir. Full-length plays especially relevant to life in Hawaii. Prefer simple sets for arena and in-the-round productions. Submit resumé and synopsis January through April. Pays $35 per performance. Readings. Contests.

LIVE OAK THEATRE—200 Colorado, Austin, TX 78701. Ms. Amparo Garcia, Tom Byrne, Lit. Mgrs. Full-length plays, translations, and adaptations. "Special interest in producing works of Texan and southern topics and new American plays." No unsolicited scripts; send letter of inquiry. Contest. Guidelines.

LOS ANGELES DESIGNERS' THEATRE—P. O. Box 1883, Studio City, CA 91614–0883. Richard Niederberg, Artistic Dir. Full-length comedies, dramas, musicals, fantasies, or adaptations. Religious, political, social, and controversial themes encouraged. Nudity, "adult" language, etc., O.K. "Please detail in the cover letter what the writer's proposed involvement with the production would be beyond the usual. Do not submit material that needs to be returned." Payment varies.

THE MAGIC THEATRE—Fort Mason Ctr., Bldg. D, San Francisco, CA 94123. Cathy Clark, Lit. Mgr. Comedies and dramas. "Special interest in poetic, non-linear, and multicultural work for mainstage productions, workshops, and readings." Query with synopsis, resumé, first 10 to 20 pages of script, and SASE. No unsolicited manuscripts. Pays varying rates.

750

MANHATTAN THEATRE CLUB—453 W. 16th, New York, NY 10011. Attn: Kate Loewald. Full-length and one-act comedies, dramas, and musicals. No unsolicited manuscripts. Send synopsis with 10 to 15 pages of dialogue, cast list, resumé, and SASE. Allow 6 months for reply.

METROPOLITAN THEATRICAL SOCIETY, INC.—(formerly *Takoma Players, Inc.*) Box 56512, Washington, DC 20012. Gaynelle Reed Lewis, Lit. Dir. Realistic, full-length dramas, comedies, and musicals. Special interest in plays suitable multi-ethnic casts. Submit manuscript with SASE. Payment negotiable.

MILL MOUNTAIN THEATRE—One Market Sq., Second Fl., Roanoke, VA 24011–1437. Jo Weinstein, Lit. Mgr. One-act comedies and dramas, 25 to 40 minutes. For full-length plays, send letter, resumé, and synopsis. Payment varies.

MISSOURI REPERTORY THEATRE—4949 Cherry St., Kansas City, MO 64110. Felicia Londré, Dramaturg. Full-length comedies and dramas. Query with synopsis, cast list, resumé, and SAS postcard. Royalty. Allow 6 months for response.

MUSIC-THEATRE GROUP—29 Bethune St., New York, NY 10014. Attn: Lit. Dir. Innovative works of music-theatre, to 90 minutes. Query only, with synopsis and SAS postcard. Best submission time: September to December.

MUSICAL THEATRE WORKS—440 Lafayette St., New York, NY 10003. Andrew Barrett, Lit. Mgr. Full-length musicals, for a cast of up to 15. Submit manuscript and cassette score with SASE. Responds in 4 to 6 months.

NATIONAL BLACK THEATRE—2033 Fifth Ave., Harlem, NY 10035. Attn: Tunde Samuel. Drama, musicals, and children's plays. "Scripts should reflect African and African-American lifestyle. Historical, inspirational, and ritualistic forms appreciated." Workshops and readings.

NATIONAL PLAYWRIGHTS CONFERENCE, EUGENE O'NEILL THEATRE CENTER—234 W. 44th St., Suite 901, New York, NY 10036. Attn: Lit. Dir. Annual competition to select new stage plays and teleplays/screenplays for development during the summer at organization's Waterford, CT location. Submission deadline: December 1. Send #10-size SASE in the fall for guidelines. Pays stipend, plus travel/living expenses during conference.

NEW THEATRE, INC.—169 Massachusetts Ave., Boston, MA 02115. Attn: Lit. Dir. New full-length scripts for readings, workshop, and main stage productions. Include SASE. Address to NEWorks Submissions Program.

NEW TUNERS/PERFORMANCE COMMUNITY—1225 W. Belmont Ave., Chicago, IL 60657. Allan Chambers, Artistic Dir. of Development. Full-length musicals only, for cast to 15; no wing/fly space. Send query with brief synopsis, cassette tape of score, cast list, resumé, SASE, and SAS postcard. Pays on royalty basis.

NEW YORK SHAKESPEARE FESTIVAL/JOSEPH PAPP PUBLIC THEATER—425 Lafayette St., New York, NY 10003. Shelby Jiggetts, Lit. Mgr. Plays and musical works for the theater, translations, and adaptations. Submit sample dialogue with synopsis, cassette (for musicals), and SASE. Allow 4 to 6 months for response.

NEW YORK STATE THEATRE INSTITUTE—P.O. Box 28, Troy, NY 12181–0028. Attn: Lit. Dir. Query for new musicals and plays for family audiences, with synopsis, cast list. Submit between April and August. Payment varies.

ODYSSEY THEATRE ENSEMBLE—2055 S. Sepulveda Blvd., Los Angeles, CA 90025. Ron Sossi, Artistic Dir. Full-length comedies, dramas, musicals,

751

and adaptations: provocative subject matter, or plays that stretch and explore the possibilities of theater. Query Jan Lewis, Lit. Mgr., with synopsis, 8 to 10 pages of sample dialogue, and resumé. Pays variable rates. Allow 2 to 6 months for reply to script; 2 to 4 weeks for queries. Workshops and readings.

OLDCASTLE THEATRE COMPANY—Bennington Center for the Arts, P.O. Box 1555, Bennington, VT 05201. Eric Peterson, Dir. Full-length comedies, dramas, and musicals for a small cast (up to 10) and a single stage set. Submit synopsis and cast list in the winter. Reports in 6 months. Offers workshops and readings. Pays expenses for playwright to attend rehearsals. Royalty.

PENGUIN REPERTORY COMPANY—Box 91, Stony Point, Rockland County, NY 10980. Joe Brancato, Artistic Dir. Full-length comedies and dramas with cast size to 5. Submit script, resumé, and SASE. Payment varies.

PENNSYLVANIA STAGE—837 Linden St., Allentown, PA 18101. Attn: Lit. Dir. Full-length plays with cast of 4 to 10; no more than 2 sets. Send synopsis, cast list, and SASE to Outreach/Literary Dept. Pays negotiable rates. Allow 6 months for reply. Staged readings possible.

PEOPLE'S LIGHT AND THEATRE COMPANY—39 Conestoga Rd., Malvern, PA 19355. Alda Cortese, Lit. Mgr. One-act or full-length comedies, dramas, adaptations. No unsolicited manuscripts; query with synopsis, 10 pages of script required. Reports in 6 months. Payment negotiable.

PIER ONE THEATRE—Box 894, Homer, AK 99603. Lance Petersen, Lit. Dir. Full-length and one-act comedies, dramas, musicals, children's plays, and adaptations. Submit complete script; include piano score with musicals. New works given staged readings. "We think new works in the theater are extremely important!" Pays 8% of ticket sales for mainstage musicals; other payment varies.

PLAYHOUSE ON THE SQUARE—51 S. Cooper in Overton Sq., Memphis, TN 38104. Jackie Nichols, Artistic Dir. Full-length comedies, dramas; cast of up to 15. Contest deadline is April for fall production. Pays $500.

PLAYWRIGHTS' PLATFORM—164 Brayton Rd., Boston, MA 02135. Attn: Lit. Dir. Script development workshops and public readings for New England playwrights only. Full-length and one-act plays of all kinds. No sexist or racist material accepted. Residents of New England send scripts with short synopsis, resumé, SAS postcard, and SASE. Readings conducted at Massachusetts College of Art.

POPE THEATRE COMPANY—262 S. Ocean Blvd., Manalapan, FL 33462. J. Barry Lewis, Lit. Mgr. Full-length comedies, dramas, musicals, and children's plays. Query with synopsis, cast list (up to 10 actors), resumé, and SASE from October through May. Royalty. Allow 6 months for response.

POPLAR PIKE PLAYHOUSE—7653 Old Poplar Pike, Germantown, TN 38138. Frank Bluestein, Artistic Dir. Full-length and one-act comedies, dramas, musicals, and children's plays. Submit synopsis with SAS postcard and resumé. Pays $300.

PORTLAND STAGE COMPANY—Box 1458, Portland, ME 04104. Attn: Lit. Dir. Not accepting unsolicited material at this time.

PRINCETON REPERTORY COMPANY—17 Hulfish St., Suite 260, Palmer Sq. N., Princeton, NJ 08542. Victoria Liberatori, Artistic Dir. Full-length comedies and dramas for a cast of up to 5. One set. Submit synopsis with resumé, cast list, and 3-page dialogue sample. Do not submit complete script. "Scripts with socially relevant themes that move beyond domestic drama preferred. The treatment of these themes might be lyrical, surreal, realistic, or high concept." Readings offered. Responds within one year.

THE PUERTO RICAN TRAVELING THEATRE—141 W. 94th St., New York, NY 10025. Miriam Colon Valle, Artistic Dir. Full-length and one-act comedies, dramas, and musicals; cast of up to 8; simple sets. "We prefer plays based on the contemporary Hispanic experience, material with social, cultural, or psychological content." Payment negotiable.

THE REPERTORY THEATRE OF ST. LOUIS—Box 191730, St. Louis, MO 63119. Attn: Lit. Dir. Query with brief synopsis, technical requirements, and cast size. Unsolicited manuscripts will be returned unread.

THE ROAD COMPANY—Box 5278 EKS, Johnson City, TN 37603. Robert H. Leonard, Artistic Dir. Christine Murdock, Lit. Mgr. Full-length and one-act comedies, dramas with social/political relevance to small-town audiences. Send synopsis, cast list, and production history, if any. Pays negotiable rates. Reports in 6 to 12 months.

ROUND HOUSE THEATRE—12210 Bushey Dr., Silver Spring, MD 20902. Attn: Production Office Mgr. Full-length comedies, dramas, adaptations, and musicals; cast of up to 10; prefer simple set. Send one-page synopsis. No unsolicited manuscripts.

SALT AND PEPPER MIME COMPANY/NEW ENSEMBLE ACTORS THEATRE—320 E. 90th St., #1B, New York, NY 10128. Ms. Scottie Davis, Man. Prod. One-acts, all types, especially those conducive to "nontraditional" casting. "Very interested in pieces suitable to surrealistic or mimetic concept in philosophy or visual style." One- or 2-person cast. Send resumé, SAS postcard, cast list, and synopsis to 250 W. 65th St., New York, NY 10023. Scripts reviewed from May to September. Works also considered for readings, storyplayers, experimental development, and readers' theater. Royalty.

SEATTLE REPERTORY THEATRE—155 Mercer St., Seattle, WA 98109. Daniel Sullivan, Artistic Dir. Full-length comedies, dramas, and adaptations. Submit synopsis, 10-page sample, SAS postcard, and resumé to Kurt Beattie, Artistic Assoc. New plays series with workshops each spring.

SOCIETY HILL PLAYHOUSE—507 S. 8th St., Philadelphia, PA 19147. Walter Vail, Dramaturg. Full-length dramas, comedies, and musicals with up to 6 cast members and simple set. Submit synopsis and SASE. Reports in 6 months. Nominal payment.

SOUTH COAST REPERTORY—P. O. Box 2197, Costa Mesa, CA 92628. John Glore, Lit. Mgr. Full-length comedies, dramas, musicals, juveniles. Query with synopsis and resumé. Payment varies.

SOUTHERN APPALACHIAN REPERTORY THEATRE—P.O. Box 620, Mars Hill, NC 28754. James W. Thomas, Artistic Dir. Full-length comedies, dramas, musicals, and plays with Appalachian theme. Submit resumé, recommendations, full script, and SASE. Send SASE for information on Southern Appalachian Playwright's Conference (held in January each year). Pays $500 royalty if play is selected for production during the summer season. Deadline for submissions is October 1 each year.

THE SPUYTEN DUYVIL THEATRE CO.—P.O. Box 1024, New York, NY 10024. Attn: Lit. Dir. Full-length comedies and dramas with single set and cast size to 10. "Good women's roles needed." SASE required.

STAGE LEFT THEATRE—1633 N. Halsted, Suite 304, Chicago, IL 60614. Laura Knight, Lit. Mgr. Full-length comedies, dramas, and adaptations for cast of one to 12. "We are committed to producing material that provokes debate about political or social issues." Offers workshops and readings. No unsolicited scripts. Payment varies.

STAGE ONE: THE LOUISVILLE CHILDREN'S THEATRE—425 W. Market St., Louisville, KY 40202. Attn: Lit. Dir. Adaptations of classics and original plays for children ages 4 to 18. Submit script with resumé and SASE. Reports in 4 months.

STAGES REPERTORY THEATRE—3201 Allen Pkwy., #101, Houston, TX 77019. Beth Sanford, Assoc. Dir. Unproduced new works: full-length dramas, comedies, translations, and adaptations, with small casts and simple sets. Submit synopsis; no unsolicited scripts. Send for guidelines for Texas playwrights' festival held in the spring.

TAKOMA PLAYERS, INC.—See *Metropolitan Theatrical Society, Inc.*

MARK TAPER FORUM—135 N. Grand Ave., Los Angeles, CA 90012. Oliver Mayer, Lit. Assoc. Full-length comedies, dramas, musicals, juveniles, adaptations. Query.

THE TEN MINUTE MUSICALS PROJECT—Box 461194, W. Hollywood, CA 90046. Michael Koppy, Prod. One-act musicals. Include audio cassette, libretto, and lead sheets with submission. "We are looking for complete short musicals." Pays $250.

THEATER ARTISTS OF MARIN—Box 150473, San Rafael, CA 94915. Charles Brousse, Artistic Dir. Full-length comedies, dramas, and musicals for a cast of 2 to 8. Submit complete script with SASE. Reports in 4 to 6 months. Three showcase productions each year.

THEATRE AMERICANA—Box 245, Altadena, CA 91001. Attn: Lit. Dir. Full-length comedies and dramas, preferably with American theme. No children's plays. Language and subject matter should be suitable for a community audience. Send bound manuscript with cast list, resumé, and SASE, by January 31. No payment. Allow 3 to 6 months for reply. Submit no more than 2 entries per season.

THEATRE/TEATRO—Bilingual Foundation of the Arts, 421 N. Ave., #19, Los Angeles, CA 90031. Guillermo Reyes, Lit. Mgr. Margarita Galban, Artistic Dir. Full-length plays about Hispanic experience; small casts. Submit manuscript with SASE. Pays negotiable rates.

THEATREWORKS—470 San Antonio Rd., Palo Alto, CA 94306. Attn: Lit. Dept. Full-length comedies, dramas, and musicals. Submit complete script or synopsis with SAS postcard and SASE, cast list, theatre resumé, and production history. For musicals, include cassette of up to 6 songs and lyrics for all songs. Responds in 2 months for submissions made March to August; 4 months for submissions September to February. Payment is negotiable.

THEATREWORKS/USA—890 Broadway, 7th Fl., New York, NY 10003. Barbara Pasternack, Lit. Mgr. One-hour children's musicals and plays with music for 5-person cast. Playwrights must be within commutable distance to New York City. Submit outline or treatment, sample scenes, and music in spring, summer. Pays royalty and commission.

WALNUT STREET THEATRE COMPANY—9th and Walnut Sts., Philadelphia, PA 19107. Beverly Elliott, Lit. Mgr. Full-length comedies, dramas, musicals, and adaptations; also, one- to 4-character plays for studio stage. Submit 20 sample pages with SAS postcard, cast list, and synopsis. Musical submissions must include an audio tape. Reports in 5 months. Payment varies.

THE WESTERN STAGE—156 Homestead Ave., Salinas, CA 93901. Tom Humphrey, Artistic Dir. Joyce Lower, Dramaturg. The Salinas River Playwriting Festival, September through October. Presentations in theater, dance, music, the visual arts, film, poetry. Also workshops, classes, displays, etc. Write for guidelines and required application.

WOOLLY MAMMOTH THEATRE COMPANY—1401 Church St. N.W., Washington, DC 20005. James C. Byrnes, Lit. Mgr. Looking for offbeat material, unusual writing. Unsolicited scripts accepted. Payment varies.

GARY YOUNG MIME THEATRE—23724 Park Madrid, Calabasas, CA 91302. Gary Young, Artistic Dir. Comedy monologues and vignettes, for children and adults, one to 90 minutes; casts of one man or one man and one woman, and portable set. Pays varying rates. Enclose SAS postcard, resumé, recommendations, cast list, and synopsis.

PLAY PUBLISHERS

ALABAMA LITERARY REVIEW—Troy State Univ., 253 Smith Hall, Troy, AL 36082. Theron Montgomery, Ed. Full-length and one-act comedies and dramas, to 50 pages. Query preferred. Responds to queries in 2 weeks; 2 to 3 months for complete manuscripts. Do not submit material in August. Payment is in copies.

AMELIA—329 E St., Bakersfield, CA 93304. Frederick A. Raborg, Jr., Ed. One-act comedies and dramas; no longer than 45 minutes running time. Responds in 2 to 3 months. Payment is $35, on acceptance.

ANCHORAGE PRESS—Box 8067, New Orleans, LA 70182. Attn: Ed. Plays and musicals that have been proven in multiple production, for children ages 8 to 14. "We publish 8 to 10 new playbooks and one to 3 new hardcover books each year." Royalty.

ART CRAFT PUBLISHING COMPANY—(formerly *Art Craft Play Company*) P.O. Box 1058, Cedar Rapids, IA 52406. Attn: Ed. Two- and three-act comedies, mysteries, farces, and musicals and one-act comedies or dramas, with one interior setting and a large cast for production by middle, junior, and senior high school students. Pays royalty or flat fee.

BAKER'S PLAYS—100 Chauncy St., Boston, MA 02111. Attn: Ed. Scripts for amateur production: one-act plays, children's plays, musicals, religious drama, full-length plays for high school production. Allow 4 months for response.

BLIZZARD PUBLISHING—301-89 Princess St., Winnipeg, Manitoba, Canada R3B 1K6. Anna Synenko, Acquisitions Ed. One-act and full-length dramas, children's plays, and adaptations. Queries preferred. Responds in 3 to 4 months. Royalty.

CALLALOO—Dept. of English, Univ. of Virginia, Charlottesville, VA 22903. Charles H. Rowell, Ed. One-act dramas by and about African-American, Caribbean, and African writers. Scripts read September through May. Responds in 3 to 6 months. Payment varies, on publication.

CHICAGO PLAYS, INC.—2632 N. Lincoln Ave., Chicago, IL 60614. Jill Murray, Pres. Full-length and one-act comedies, dramas, musicals, children's plays, and adaptations. "Submissions must have received a professional production in the Chicago area." Responds in 4 to 6 months. Royalty.

E. I. CLARK, PUBLISHERS—St. John's Rd., P.O. Box 246, Schulenburg, TX 78956. Carol Drabek, Ed. One-act and full-length plays and musicals, for children, young adults, and adults. Serious drama, comedies, classics, fairytales, melodramas, and holiday plays. "We seldom publish a play that has not been produced." Responds in 2 to 6 months. Royalty.

COLLAGES AND BRICOLAGES—P.O. Box 86, Clarion, PA 16214. Marie-José Fortis, Ed. One-act comedies and dramas. Manuscripts read August through November; responds in one to 3 months. Payment is in copies. Include SASE.

CONFRONTATION—Dept. of English, C.W. Post of L.I.U., Greenvale, NY 11548. Martin Tucker, Ed. One-act comedies, dramas, and adaptations. Manuscripts read September through May. Include SASE. Responds in 6 to 8 weeks. Pays, $25 to $100, on publication.

CONTEMPORARY DRAMA SERVICE—Meriwether Publishing Co., Box 7710, 885 Elkton Dr., Colorado Springs, CO 80903. Arthur Zapel, Ed. Easy-to-stage comedies, skits, one-acts, musicals, puppet scripts, and full-length plays for schools and churches. (Junior high through college level; no elementary level material.) Adaptations of classics and improvised material for classroom use. Comedy monologues and duets. Chancel drama for Christmas and Easter church use. Enclose synopsis. Books on theater arts subjects and anthologies. Textbooks for speech and drama. Pays by fee arrangement or royalty.

DRAMATIC PUBLISHING —311 Washington St., Woodstock, IL 60098. Sarah Clark, Ed. Full-length and one-act plays and musicals for the stock, amateur, and children's theater market. Royalty. Responds within 16 weeks.

DRAMATICS—Educational Theatre Assoc., 3368 Central Pkwy., Cincinnati, OH 45225–2392. Don Corathers, Ed. One-act and full-length plays for high school production. Pays $100 to $400, on acceptance.

ELDRIDGE PUBLISHING COMPANY—P. O. Box 1595, Venice, FL 34284. Nancy Vorhis, Ed. Dept. One-act and full-length plays and musicals suitable for performance by schools, churches, and community theatre groups. Comedies, tragedies, dramas, skits, spoofs, and religious plays (Christmas and Easter); easy costuming and scenery. Submit complete manuscript with cover letter, biography, and SASE. Responds in 2 months. Flat fee for one-act and religious plays, on publication; royalties for full-length plays.

SAMUEL FRENCH, INC.—45 W. 25th St., New York, NY 10010. Lawrence R. Harbison, Ed. Full-length plays for dinner, community, stock, college, and high school theaters. One-act plays (30 to 45 minutes). Children's plays, 45 to 60 minutes. Royalty.

HEUER PUBLISHING COMPANY—Drawer 248, Cedar Rapids, IA 52406. C. Emmett McMullen, Ed. One-act comedies and dramas for contest work; three-act comedies, mysteries, or farces, and musicals, with one interior setting, for high school production. Pays royalty or flat fee.

INSTITUTE FOR CONTEMPORARY EASTERN EUROPEAN DRAMA AND THEATRE—Graduate Ctr., 33 W. 42nd St., Rm. 801, New York, NY 10036. Daniel C. Gerould, Co-Dir. Full-length and one-act translations of contemporary Eastern European plays. Query. Payment varies.

MODERN INTERNATIONAL DRAMA—Theatre Dept., SUNY, P.O. Box 6000, Binghamton, NY 13902–6000. George E. Wellwarth, Man. Ed. Semiannual.

Full-length and one-act translations of previously untranslated modern (20th century) plays. No adaptations. Queries preferred. Responds in one month. Pays in copies, on publication.

NATIONAL DRAMA SERVICE—MSN 158, 127 Ninth Ave. N., Nashville, TN 37234. Attn: Ed. Scripts, 2 to 7 minutes long: drama, puppet shows, clown shows, Christian comedy, responsive readings, and monologues. "We publish dramatic material that communicates the message of Christ. We want scripts that will give even the smallest church the opportunity to enhance their ministry with drama." Payment varies, on acceptance. Guidelines.

PIONEER DRAMA SERVICE—P. O. Box 4267, Englewood, CO 80155. Attn: Ed. Full-length and one-act plays; plays for young audiences; musicals, melodramas, and Christmas plays. No unproduced plays or plays with largely male casts or multiple sets. Query. Outright purchase or royalty.

PLAYERS PRESS, INC.—P.O. Box 1132, Studio City, CA 91614–0132. Robert W. Gordon, Ed. One-act and full-length comedies, dramas, and musicals. "No manuscript will be considered unless it has been produced." Query with manuscript-size SASE and two #10 SASEs for correspondence. Include resumé and/or biography. Responds in 3 to 12 months. Royalty.

PLAYS, THE DRAMA MAGAZINE FOR YOUNG PEOPLE—120 Boylston St., Boston, MA 02116–4615. Elizabeth Preston, Man. Ed. One-act plays, with simple sets, for production by young people, 7 to 17: comedies, dramas, farces, skits, holiday plays, adaptations of classics, biography plays, puppet plays, and creative dramatics. No musicals or plays with religious themes. Maximum lengths: lower grades, 10 double-spaced pages; middle grades, 15 pages; junior and senior high, 20 pages. Send SASE for guidelines. Query for adaptations. Pays good rates, on acceptance. Buys all rights.

PRISM INTERNATIONAL—Dept. of Creative Writing, Univ. of British Columbia Buch E462–1866 Main Mall, Vancouver, BC, Canada V6T 1Z1. Attn: Ed. One-act plays. Responds in 2 to 3 months. Pays $20 per page, on publication.

THE RADIO PLAY—Suite 230, 100 Boylston St., Boston, MA 02116. Stanley Richardson, Lit. Mgr. Original radio plays and radio adaptations of American classics in the public domain, 30 to 32 pages, to fit a 30-minute program format. Query for adaptations only. Responds within 4 months for complete manuscripts. Payment varies, on acceptance. Send SASE for style sheet.

RAG MAG—P.O. Box 12, Goodhue, MN 55027. Beverly Voldseth, Ed. Semiannual. Full-length and one-act comedies and dramas. Query with 3 to 7 pages of play. Pays in copies.

ROCKFORD REVIEW—P.O. Box 858, Rockford, IL 61105. David Ross, Ed. One-act comedies, dramas, and satires, to 1,300 words. "We prefer genuine or satirical human dilemmas with coping or non-coping outcomes that ring true." Pays in copies (plus invitation to attend reading-reception in the fall).

SINISTER WISDOM—P.O. Box 3252, Berkeley, CA 94703. Elana Dykewomon, Ed. Quarterly. One-act (no longer than 15 pages) lesbian drama. "We are particularly interested in work that reflects the diversity of our experiences: as lesbians of color, ethnic lesbians, Jewish, old, young, working class, poor, disabled, fat. Only material by born-woman lesbians is considered." Responds in 3 to 9 months; write for upcoming themes. Payment is in 2 copies, on publication. SASE.

TURTLE MAGAZINE—1100 Waterway Blvd., P.O. Box 567, Indianapolis, IN 46206. Elizabeth Rinck, Ed. One-act children's plays. Responds in 10 weeks. Payment is 12¢ to 22¢ per word, on publication. Send SASE for guidelines.

THE TV AND FILM SCRIPT MARKET

The almost round-the-clock television offerings on commercial, educational, and cable TV stations, in addition to the hundreds of films released yearly, may lead free-lance writers to believe that opportunities to sell scripts or program ideas are infinite. Unfortunately, this is not true. With few exceptions, producers and programmers do not consider scripts submitted directly to them, no matter how good they are. In general, free lancers can achieve success in this nearly closed field by concentrating on getting their fiction (short stories and novels) and nonfiction published in magazines or books, combed diligently by producers for possible adaptations. A large percentage of the material offered over all types of networks (in addition to the motion pictures made in Hollywood) is in the form of adaptations of published material.

Writers who want to try their hand at writing directly for this very limited market should be prepared to learn the special techniques and acceptable format of scriptwriting, and several books have been written on this subject. Also, experience in playwriting and a knowledge of dramatic structure gained through working in amateur, community, or professional theaters can be helpful.

A knowledge of the TV and film industry is necessary to the script writer, and trade magazines will keep the writer abreast of current events. *The Hollywood Reporter* (5055 Wilshire Blvd., Los Angeles, CA 90036–4396) publishes daily industry news, including information on rewrites underway, book adaptations, deal-making, etc. Writers may also want to check the *Daily Variety* (5700 Wilshire Blvd., Suite 120, Los Angeles, CA 90036) for trade news.

Writers may wish to register their story, treatment, series format, or script with the Writers Guild of America; to protect themselves from legal battles, many producers will not look at a script unless it has been registered with the guild. This registration does not confer statutory rights, but it does supply evidence and date of authorship. Registration is effective for ten years, and is renewable after that. The WGA's registration service is available for a fee of $10 to $23 for members and $17 to $57 for non-members. For more information, write to: Registration Service, Writers Guild of America East, Inc., 555 W. 57th St., New York, NY 10019. Dramatic material can also be registered with the U.S. Copyright Office (Register of Copyrights, Library of Congress, Washington, DC 20559).

Since virtually all TV and film producers will read scripts and queries submitted only through recognized agents, we've included a list of agents who have indicated to us that they are willing to read queries for TV scripts or screenplays. The agents on this list have indicated that they do not charge a reading fee, and charge the standard 10% commission for dramatic material; however, writers are advised to write directly for details on each agent's policy. Most of the major film studios will deal only with those agents who are Writers Guild of America signatories; such agents are required, under contract with the guild, to charge their clients no more than a 10% commission. Writers seeking representation for their screenplays

758

should note, therefore, that an agent charging over 10% commission on a screenplay will be unable to show that script to the major studios.

The Association of Authors' Representatives (10 Astor Pl., 3rd Floor, New York, NY 10003) will send a list of member agents upon receipt of a self-addressed, legal-sized envelope with enough postage for two ounces, and a $5 check or money order. *Literary Market Place* (Bowker), available in most libraries, includes a list of agents; and *Literary Agents of North America, Fifth Edition* [Author Aid/Research Associates International, 340 E. 52nd St., New York, NY 10022; (212) 758–4213)] provides detailed information on agents and their needs and is available through the publisher. Most of the agents listed below prefer queries and/or synopses, and will not reply unless the standard SASE has been enclosed; never send a complete manuscript unless it has been requested. Agents indicating they will consider multiple queries (i.e., queries the author has sent simultaneously to other agents) do so with the understanding that the author has made note of it in the query. A list of network (ABC, NBC, CBS, FOX) shows, agents, and production companies may be found in *Ross Reports Television*, published monthly by Television Index, Inc., [40–29 27th St., Long Island City, NY 11101; (718) 937–3990].

TV AND FILM SCRIPT AGENTS

AARDVARK LITERARY AGENTS—5330 Main St., Suite 270, Williamsville, NY 14221. Attn: Kate Berman or Jim Fair. Screenplays. Query with bio/resumé; no multiple queries. Commission: 10%. Fees: photocopying, shipping.

LEE ALLAN AGENCY—P.O. Box 18617, Milwaukee, WI 53218. Attn: Mr. Lee A. Matthias. Screenplays. Send query only; multiple queries O.K. Commission: 10%. Fees: photocopying, shipping.

MICHAEL AMATO AGENCY—1650 Broadway, Rm. 307, New York, NY 10019. Attn: Michael Amato. Screenplays. Send query or complete manuscript. Commission: 10%. Fees: none.

MARCIA AMSTERDAM AGENCY—41 W. 82nd St., #9A, New York, NY 10024. Attn: Marcia Amsterdam. Screenplays and teleplays: comedy, romance, psychological suspense. Query with resumé; multiple queries O.K.; three-week exclusive for requested submissions. Commission: 10%, screenplays. Fees: photocopying, shipping.

LOIS BERMAN & JUDY BOALS—Writers House, Inc., 21 W. 26th St., New York, NY 10010. Screenplays, teleplays, and stage plays. Unpublished, unproduced writers considered. Query with bio and resumé. Commission: 10%. Fees: photocopying.

DOUGLAS, GORMAN, ROTHACKER & WILHELM, INC.—1501 Broadway, Suite 703, New York, NY 10036. Screenplays and full-length teleplays. Query with synopsis, bio/resumé; multiple queries O.K. Commission: 10%. Fees: none.

ROBERT A. FREEDMAN DRAMATIC AGENCY, INC.—1501 Broadway, Suite 2310, New York, NY 10036. Attn: Robert A. Freedman or Selma Luttinger. Screenplays and teleplays. Send query only; multiple queries O.K. Commission: standard. Fees: photocopying.

THE CHARLOTTE GUSAY LITERARY AGENCY—10532 Blythe, Los Angeles, CA 90064. Screenplays. Query with outline, sample pages, and bio/resumé; no multiple queries. Commission: 10%. Fees: photocopying, shipping.

OTTO R. KOZAK LITERARY AGENCY—P.O. Box 152, Long Beach, NY 11561. Screenplays and teleplays. Unpublished and unproduced writers considered. Query with outline or treatment; no multiple queries. Commission: 10%. Fees: none.

LUCY KROLL AGENCY—390 West End Ave., New York, NY 10024. Attn: Lucy Kroll. Screenplays, teleplays, and stage plays. Query with bio and resumé; multiple queries O.K. Commission: 10%. Fees: none.

MONTGOMERY LITERARY AGENCY—P.O. Box 8822, Silver Spring, MD 20907–8822. Attn: M.E. Olsen, Pres. Screenplays and teleplays, all commercial types. Query with synopsis, sample pages, bio/resumé. Commission: 10%. Fees: none.

H.N. SWANSON, INC.—8523 Sunset Blvd., Los Angeles, CA 90069. Attn: Thomas J. Shanks, Pres. Screenplays and teleplays. Unpublished, unproduced writers sometimes considered. Query first; no multiple queries. Commission: 10%.

THE TANTLEFF OFFICE—375 Greenwich St., Suite 700, New York, NY 10013. Attn: Jill Bock. Screenplays and teleplays. Query with synopsis, up to 10 sample pages, bio/resumé; multiple queries O.K. Commission: 10%. Fees: none.

ANN WRIGHT REPRESENTATIVES—136 E. 56th St., Suite 9J, New York, NY 10022–3619. Attn: Dan Wright. Screenplays and teleplays. Query with bio/resumé; no multiple queries. Commission: 10%. Fees: photocopying, shipping.

BOOK PUBLISHERS

The following list includes the major book publishers for adult and juvenile fiction and nonfiction and a representative number of small publishers from across the country.

Before sending a complete manuscript to an editor, it is advisable to send a brief query letter describing the proposed book. The letter should also include information about the author's special qualifications for dealing with a particular topic and any previous publication credits. An outline of the book (or a synopsis for fiction) and a sample chapter may also be included.

It is common practice to submit a book manuscript to only one publisher at a time, although it is becoming more and more acceptable for writers, even those without agents, to submit the same query or proposal to more than one editor at the same time. When sending multiple queries, *always* make note of it in each submission.

Book manuscripts may be sent in typing paper boxes (available from a stationery store) and sent by first-class mail, or, more common and less expensive, by "Special Fourth Class Rate—Manuscript." For rates, details of insurance, and so forth, inquire at your local post office. With any submission to a publisher, be sure to enclose sufficient postage for the manuscript's return.

Royalty rates for hardcover books usually start at 10% of the retail price of the book and increase after a certain number of copies have been sold. Paperbacks generally have a somewhat lower rate, about 5% to 8%. It is customary for the publishing company to pay the author a cash advance against royalties when the book contract is signed or when the finished manuscript is received. Some publishers pay on a flat-fee basis.

While most of the publishers on this list consider either unsolicited manuscripts or queries, more and more publishers now read only agented submissions. Since finding an agent is often not an easy task, especially for newcomers, writers are advised to try to sell their manuscripts directly to the publisher first. Should this fail, the *Literary Agents* list notes, among many other details, whether unpublished writers are considered.

ABBEY PRESS—St. Meinrad, IN 47577. Karen Katafiasz, Books Ed. Not considering any new material at this time.

ABINGDON PRESS—Imprint of The United Methodist Publishing House, P.O. Box 801, Nashville, TN 37202. Mary Catherine Dean, Sr. Ed. General-interest books: mainline, social issues, marriage/family, self-help, exceptional people. Query with outline and one or 2 sample chapters. Guidelines.

ACADEMIC PRESS—Div. of Harcourt Brace, 525 B St., Suite 1900, San Diego, CA 92101. Attn: Ed. Dept. Scientific and technical books and journals for research-level scientists, students, and professionals; upper-level undergraduate and graduate science texts. Query.

ACCENT PUBLICATIONS—Box 15337, 12100 W. 6th Ave., Denver, CO 80215. Mary Nelson, Exec. Ed. Nonfiction church resources from evangelical Christian perspective; no trade books. "Request guidelines before querying." Query with sample chapters and SASE. Royalty. Paperback only.

ACE BOOKS —Imprint of Berkley Publishing Group, 200 Madison Ave., New York, NY 10016. Laura Anne Gilman, Asst. Ed. Science fiction and fantasy. Query with first 3 chapters and outline. Royalty.

ADAMA BOOKS—See *Modan Publishing.*

ADDISON-WESLEY PUBLISHING CO.—One Jacob Way, Reading, MA 01867-3999. Attn: Ed. Dept. Adult nonfiction on current topics including science, health, psychology, business, biography, child care, etc. Specializing in literary nonfiction. Royalty.

ALADDIN BOOKS—See *Simon & Schuster Children's Publishing Division.*

ALASKA NORTHWEST BOOKS—An imprint of Graphic Arts Center Publishing Co., 2208 N.W. Market St., Suite 300, Seattle, WA 98107. Marlene Blessing, Ed.-in-Chief. Nonfiction, 50,000 to 100,000 words, with an emphasis on natural world and history of Alaska, Western Canada, Pacific Northwest, and Pacific Rim: travel books; cookbooks; field guides; children's books; outdoor recreation; natural history; native culture; lifestyle. Send query or sample chapters with outline. Guidelines.

ALGONQUIN BOOKS OF CHAPEL HILL—Div. of Workman Publishing Co., Inc., Box 2225, Chapel Hill, NC 27515. Shannon Ravenel, Ed. Dir. Trade books, fiction and nonfiction, for adults.

761

ALYSON PUBLICATIONS—40 Plympton, Boston, MA 02118. Anthony Grima, Ed. Gay and lesbian adult fiction and nonfiction books, from 65,000 words. *Alyson Wonderland* imprint: Children's picture books with gay and lesbian themes; young adult titles, from 65,000 words. Query with outline and sample chapters. Royalty.

ALYSON WONDERLAND—See *Alyson Publications.*

AMERICAN PARADISE PUBLISHING—P.O. Box 37, St. John, USVI 00831. Gary M. Goodlander, Ed. "We are interested in 'hopelessly local' books, between 80 and 300 pages. We need useful, practical books that help our Virgin Island readers lead better and more enjoyable lives." Guidebooks, cookbooks, how-to books, books on sailing, yacht cruising, hiking, snorkeling, sportfishing, local history, and West Indian culture, specifically aimed at Caribbean readers/tourists. Query with outline and sample chapters. Royalty.

THE AMERICAN PSYCHIATRIC PRESS—1400 K St. N.W., Washington, DC 20005. Carol C. Nadelson, M.D., Ed.-in-Chief. Books that interpret scientific and medical aspects of psychiatry for a lay audience and that address specific psychiatric problems. Authors must have appropriate credentials to write on medical topics. Query required. Royalty.

ANCHOR BOOKS—Imprint of Doubleday and Co., 1540 Broadway, New York, NY 10036. Martha K. Levin, Pub. Adult trade paperbacks and hardcovers. Nonfiction, multicultural, sociology, psychology, philosophy, women's interest, etc. No unsolicited manuscripts.

ANCHORAGE PRESS—Box 8067, New Orleans, LA 70182. Attn: Acquisitions Ed. Dramatic publishers. Plays for children ages 4 to 18. "We publish 8 to 10 new playbooks and one to 3 new hardcover books each year." Royalty.

AND BOOKS—702 S. Michigan, South Bend, IN 46601. Janos Szebedinsky, Ed. Adult nonfiction. Topics include computers, fine arts, health, philosophy, regional subjects, and social justice.

ANHINGA PRESS—P.O. Box 10595, Tallahassee, FL 32302–0595. Rick Campbell, Ed. Poetry books. (Publishes 2 books a year.) Query or send complete manuscripts. Flat fee. Annual poetry prize; send SASE for details.

APPALACHIAN MOUNTAIN CLUB BOOKS—5 Joy St., Boston, MA 02108. Attn: Ed. Dept. Regional (New England) and national nonfiction titles, 250 to 400 pages, for adult audience; juvenile and young adult nonfiction. Topics include guidebooks on non-motorized backcountry recreation, nature, mountain history/ biography, search and rescue, conservation, and environmental management. Query with outline and sample chapters. Multiple queries considered. Royalty.

APPLE SOUP BOOKS—Imprint of Alfred A. Knopf Books for Young Readers, 201 E. 50th St., New York, NY 10022. Anne Schwartz, Ed. Dept. Mostly picture books; some middle grade and young adult novels. Unsolicited manuscripts welcome. Royalty.

ARCADE PUBLISHING—141 Fifth Ave., New York, NY 10010. Richard Seaver, Pub./Ed. Fiction and nonfiction. No longer accepting children's books. No unsolicited manuscripts. Query.

ARCHWAY PAPERBACKS—Pocket Books, 1230 Ave. of the Americas, New York, NY 10020. Attn: Manuscript Proposals. Young adult contemporary fiction (suspense thrillers, romances) and nonfiction (popular current topics), for ages 12 to 16. Send query, outline, and sample chapters.

762

ARCO PUBLISHING—Prentice Hall General Reference Group, Paramount Communications Bldg., 15 Columbus Cir., New York, NY 10023. Charles Wall, Ed.-in-Chief. Nonfiction, originals and reprints, from 50,000 words. Career guides, test preparation. Query; unsolicited manuscripts not accepted. Royalty.

ARCSOFT PUBLISHERS—P.O. Box 179, Hebron, MD 21830. Anthony Curtis, Pres. Nonfiction hobby books for beginners: personal computing, space science, desktop publishing, journalism. Hobby electronics for laymen and consumers, beginners and novices. Query. Outright purchase and royalty basis. Paperback only.

ARMSTRONG PUBLISHING CORP.—55 Old Post Rd., #2, P.O. Box 1678, Greenwich, CT 06836. Herbert M. Johnson, Ed. George F. Johnson, Ed. Children's books. Fiction and picture books, to 48 pages, for readers ages 3 to 11. Royalty.

ASTARTE SHELL PRESS—P.O. Box 10453, Portland, ME 04104. Sapphire, Ed. Books on theology, politics, and social issues from a feminist/woman's perspective. No poetry. Send sample chapters or complete manuscripts. Royalty.

AVALON BOOKS—Imprint of Thomas Bouregy & Co., Inc., 401 Lafayette St., New York, NY 10003. Hank Kennedy, Pres. Marcia Markland VP/Pub. Suzanne Rose, Ed. Hardcover books, 40,000 to 50,000 words: romances, mysteries, and westerns. No explicit sex. Query with first 3 chapters and outline; nonreturnable. SASE for guidelines.

AVERY PUBLISHING GROUP—120 Old Broadway, Garden City Park, NY 11040. Attn: Man. Ed. Nonfiction, from 40,000 words, on health, childbirth, child care, healthful cooking. Query with SASE. Royalty.

AVON BOOKS—1350 Ave. of the Americas, New York, NY 10019. Robert Mecoy, Ed.-in-Chief. Genre fiction, general nonfiction, historical romance, 60,000 to 200,000 words. *AvoNova*: science fiction, 75,000 to 100,000 words. Query with synopsis and sample chapters. Ellen Edwards, Historical Romance; John Douglas, Science Fiction; Chris Miller, Fantasy. *Camelot Books*: Ellen Krieger, Ed. Fiction and nonfiction for 7- to 10-year-olds. Query. *Flare Books*: Ellen Krieger, Ed. Fiction and nonfiction for 12-year-olds and up. Query. Royalty. Paperback only.

BACKCOUNTRY PUBLICATIONS—Div. of The Countryman Press, Inc., P. O. Box 175, Woodstock, VT 05091–0175. Helen Whybrow, Man. Ed. Regional guidebooks on hiking, walking, canoeing, bicycling, mountain biking, cross-country skiing, and fishing covering New England, the mid-Atlantic states, and the Midwest; gardening, rural living, environmental ethics, and Shaker life. Send outline and sample chapter with SASE. Royalty.

BAEN BOOKS—Baen Enterprises, P.O. Box 1403, Riverdale, NY 10471–1403. Jim Baen, Pres./Ed.-in-Chief. Strongly plotted science fiction; innovative fantasy. Query with synopsis and manuscript. Advance and royalty. Guidelines available for letter-sized SASE.

BAKER BOOK HOUSE—P. O. Box 6287, Grand Rapids, MI 49516–6287. Allan Fisher, Dir. of Publications. Religious nonfiction: books for trade, clergy, seminarians, collegians. Religious fiction. Royalty.

BALBOA—See *Tiare Publications.*

BALLANTINE BOOKS—201 E. 50th St., New York, NY 10022. Clare Ferraro, Ed.-in-Chief. General fiction and nonfiction. Query.

BALSAM PRESS—One Madison Ave., 25th Fl., New York, NY 10010. Barbara Krohn, Exec. Ed. General and illustrated adult nonfiction. Query. Royalty.

BANTAM BOOKS—Div. of Bantam, Doubleday, Dell, 1540 Broadway, New York, NY 10036. Irwyn Applebaum, Pres./Pub. Adult fiction and nonfiction. Mass-market titles, submit queries to the following imprints: *Crime Line*, crime and mystery fiction; *Domain*, frontier fiction, historical sagas, traditional westerns; *Spectra*, science fiction and fantasy; *Fanfare*, romance; *Bantam Nonfiction*, wide variety of commercial nonfiction, including true crime, health and nutrition, sports, reference. Agented queries and manuscripts only.

BARRICADE BOOKS—61 4th Ave., New York, NY 10003. Lyle Stuart, Pub. General nonfiction, celebrity biographies, controversial subjects. No fiction. Send synopsis with SASE. Modest advances against royalties.

BARRON'S—250 Wireless Blvd., Hauppauge, NY 11788. Grace Freedson, Acquisitions Ed. Nonfiction for juveniles (science, nature, history, hobbies, and how-to) and picture books for ages 3 to 6. Nonfiction for adults (business, childcare, sports). Query with SASE. Guidelines.

BAUHAN, PUBLISHER, WILLIAM L.—Box 443, Dublin, NH 03444. William L. Bauhan, Ed. Biographies, fine arts, gardening, architecture, and history books with an emphasis on New England. Submit query with outline and sample chapter.

BEACON PRESS—25 Beacon St., Boston, MA 02108. Wendy Strothman, Dir. Deb Chasman, Sr. Ed. General nonfiction: world affairs, women's studies, anthropology, history, philosophy, religion, gay and lesbian studies, environment, nature writing, African-American studies, Asian-American studies, Native-American studies. Series: Concord Library (nature writing); Barnard New Women Poets; Black Women Writers (fiction); Men and Masculinity (nonfiction). Query. SASE required.

BEAR & COMPANY, INC.—P.O. Drawer 2860, Santa Fe, NM 87504. Barbara Clow, Ed. Nonfiction "that will help transform our culture philosophically, environmentally, and spiritually." Query with outline and sample chapters. SASE required. Royalty.

BEECH TREE BOOKS—See *William Morrow and Co., Inc.*

BEHRMAN HOUSE—235 Watchung Ave., W. Orange, NJ 07052. Adam Siegel, Projects Ed. Adult and juvenile nonfiction, varying lengths, in English and in Hebrew, on Jewish subject matter. Query with outline and sample chapters. Flat fee.

BERKLEY PUBLISHING GROUP —Div. of The Putnam Berkley Group, Inc., 200 Madison Ave., New York, NY 10016. Lou Aronica, Pub. General-interest fiction and nonfiction; science fiction, suspense, and mystery novels; romance. Submit through agent only. Publishes both reprints and originals. Paperback books, except for some hardcover mysteries.

BETHANY HOUSE PUBLISHERS—11300 Hampshire Ave. S., Minneapolis, MN 55438. Attn: Ed. Dept. Religious fiction and nonfiction. Query with sample chapters. Royalty.

BINFORD & MORT PUBLISHING—1202 N.W. 17th Ave., Portland, OR 97209. J.F. Roberts, Ed. Books on subjects related to the Pacific Coast and the Northwest. Lengths vary. Query. Royalty.

BIRCH LANE PRESS—See *Carol Publishing Group.*

BLACK BUTTERFLY CHILDREN'S BOOKS—Writers and Readers Publishing, 625 Broadway, New York, NY 10012. Attn: Deborah Dyson or Beth Smith.

Titles featuring black children and other children of color. Picture books for children up to 11; board books for toddlers; juvenile fiction for all ages. Query. Royalty.

BLACK BUZZARD PRESS—1110 Seaton Ln., Falls Church, VA 22046. Bradley R. Strahan, Ed. Poetry manuscripts, to 60 pages. Query. Royalty.

BLAIR, PUBLISHER, JOHN F.—1406 Plaza Dr., Winston-Salem, NC 27103. Carolyn Sakowski, Pres. Books from 50,000 words: biography, history, folklore, and guidebooks, with southeastern tie-in. Query. Royalty.

BLUE DOLPHIN PUBLISHING, INC.—P.O. Box 1920, Nevada City, NV 95959. Paul M. Clemens, Ed. Books, 200 to 300 pages, on comparative spiritual traditions, lay and transpersonal psychology, self-help, health, and healing. Send complete manuscript or query with outline and sample chapters. Royalty.

BLUE MOON BOOKS, INC.—61 Fourth Ave., New York, NY 10003. Barney Rosset, Pub. Erotic fiction and nonfiction on a variety of topics. Send synopsis and sample chapters and SASE.

BONUS BOOKS—160 E. Illinois St., Chicago, IL 60611. Anne Barthel, Assoc. Ed. Nonfiction; topics vary widely. Query with sample chapters and SASE. Royalty.

BOYDS MILLS PRESS—815 Church St., Honesdale, PA 18431. Beth Troop, Manuscript Coord. Hardcover trade books for children. Fiction: picture books; middle-grade fiction with fresh ideas and involving story; young adult novels of literary merit. Nonfiction should be "fun, entertaining, and informative." Send outline and sample chapters for young adult novels and nonfiction, complete manuscripts for all other categories. Royalty.

BRADBURY PRESS—See *Simon & Schuster Children's Publishing Division.*

BRANDEN PUBLISHING COMPANY—17 Station St., Box 843, Brookline Village, MA 02147. Attn: Ed. Dept. Novels, biographies, and autobiographies. Especially books by or about women, 250 to 350 pages. Also considers queries on history, computers, business, performance arts, and translations. Query only with SASE. Royalty.

BRAZILLER PUBLISHERS, GEORGE—60 Madison Ave., New York, NY 10010. Attn: Ed. Dept. Fiction and nonfiction. Mostly art, art history; some profiles of writers, collection of essays and short stories, anthologies. Send art history manuscripts to Adrienne Baxter, Ed.; others to Fiction Editor. Send outline with sample chapters. Payment varies, usually flat fee for art books, advance and royalty for fiction.

BRETT BOOKS, INC.—P.O. Box 290–637, Brooklyn, NY 11229–0011. Barbara J. Brett, Pres./Pub. Nonfiction for adult trade market. "Submit a query letter of no more than two pages, stating your professional background and summarizing your book proposal in 2 to 4 paragraphs." SASE. Royalty.

BRIDGEWATER BOOKS—Imprint of Troll Associates, 100 Corporate Dr., Mahwah, NJ 07430. Attn: Ed. Dept. Hardcover picture books, novels, and anthologies.

BRISTOL PUBLISHING ENTERPRISES—P.O. Box 1737, San Leandro, CA 94577. Patricia J. Hall, Ed. Nitty Gritty Cookbooks: 120-recipe manuscripts. Query with outline, sample chapters, SASE. Royalty.

BROADMAN AND HOLMAN PUBLISHERS—127 Ninth Ave. N., Nashville, TN 37234. Richard P. Rosenbaum Jr., Ed. Dir. Religious and inspirational nonfiction. Query with SASE. Royalty.

BROWNDEER PRESS—Imprint of Harcourt Brace & Co. Children's Books, P.O. Box 80160, Portland, OR 97280–1160. Linda Zuckerman, Ed. Dir. Picture books, humorous middle-grade fiction, and young adult material written from an unusual perspective or about an unusual subject. Only considers submissions from agents, published authors, or members of SCBWI. Query for nonfiction with cover letter, resumé, and sample chapter; send complete manuscript for picture books (avoid rhyming text). For longer fiction, send first 3 chapters, synopsis, and short cover letter with biographical information. SASE required for all correspondence.

BUCKNELL UNIVERSITY PRESS—Bucknell Univ., Lewisburg, PA 17837. Mills F. Edgerton, Jr., Dir. Scholarly nonfiction. Query. Royalty.

BULFINCH PRESS—Div. of Little, Brown & Co., 34 Beacon St., Boston, MA 02108. Attn: Ed. Dept. Books on fine arts and photography. Query with outline or proposal and vita.

BYRON PREISS VISUAL PUBLICATIONS—24 W. 25th St., New York, NY 10010. Attn: Ed. Dept. Book packager. "We are primarily interested in seeing samples from established authors willing to work to specifications on firm deadlines." Genres: science fiction, fantasy, horror, juvenile, young adult, nonfiction. Pays competitive advance against royalties for commissioned work.

C&T PUBLISHING—5021 Blum Rd., #1, Martinez, CA 94553. Todd Hensley, Pres. Quilting books, 64 to 200 finished pages. "Our focus is how-to, although we will consider picture, inspirational, or history books on quilting." Send query, outline, or sample chapters. Multiple queries considered. Royalty.

CALYX BOOKS—P.O. Box B, Corvallis, OR 97339. Margarita Donnelly, Ed. Beverly McFarland, Ed. Feminist publisher. Novels, short stories, poetry, nonfiction, translations, and anthologies by women. "We are committed to publishing the work of all women, including women of color, lesbians, older women, etc." Query with outline and sample chapters. Guidelines. Royalty.

CAMELOT BOOKS—See *Avon Books.*

CANDLEWICK PRESS—2067 Massachusetts Ave., Cambridge, MA 02140. Attn: Ed. Dept. "Unfortunately, we are no longer able to consider unsolicited material; unsolicited manuscripts will be returned unread."

CAPSTONE PRESS, INC.—P.O. Box 669, N. Mankato, MN 56001–0669. Attn: Ed. Dept. Juvenile theme-books for children in preschool to grade 6. Send SASE for catalogue of series themes. Query required. Flat fee.

CAROL PUBLISHING—600 Madison Ave., New York, NY 10022. Allan J. Wilson, Ed. General nonfiction. *Citadel Press*: biography, film, history, no fiction. *Birch Lane Press*: Nonfiction, 75,000 words. *Lyle Stuart*: Nonfiction, 75,000 words, of "a controversial nature; gaming." Query with outline required. Royalty.

CAROLRHODA BOOKS—241 First Ave. N., Minneapolis, MN 55401. Rebecca Poole, Ed. Complete manuscripts for ages 4 to 12: biography, science, nature, history, photo essays; historical fiction, 10 to 15 pages, for ages 6 to 10. Guidelines. Hardcover.

CASSANDRA PRESS—P.O. Box 150868, San Rafael, CA 94915. Attn: Ed. Dept. New Age, holistic health, metaphysical, and psychological books. Query with outline and sample chapters, or complete manuscript. Include SASE. Royalty (no advance).

THE CATHOLIC UNIVERSITY OF AMERICA PRESS—620 Michigan Ave. N.E., Washington, DC 20064. David J. McGonagle, Dir. Scholarly nonfiction:

American and European history (both ecclesiastical and secular); Irish studies; American and European literature; philosophy; political theory; theology. Query with prospectus, annotated table of contents, or introduction and resumé. Royalty.

CHATHAM PRESS—P. O. Box A, Old Greenwich, CT 06870. Roger H. Lourie, Man. Dir. Books on the Northeast coast, New England maritime subjects, and the ocean. Large photography volumes. Query with outline, sample chapters, illustrations, and SASE large enough for the return of material. Royalty.

CHELSEA GREEN PUBLISHING CO.—Route 113, P.O. Box 130, Post Mills, VT 05058–0130. Jim Schley, Ed. Primarily nonfiction: natural history, environmental issues, outdoor recreation, and lifestyle books with strong backlist potential. Query with outline and SASE. Not considering any unsolicited manuscripts at this time. Royalty.

CHICAGO REVIEW PRESS—814 N. Franklin St., Chicago, IL 60610. Amy Teschner, Ed. Nonfiction: activity books for young children, project books for ages 10 to 18, general nonfiction, architecture, adoption, how-to, popular science, and regional topics. Query with outline and sample chapters.

CHILDREN'S LIBRARY PRESS—P.O. Box 1919, Joshua Tree, CA 92252. Attn: Acquisition Ed. Texts for picture books. Submit complete manuscript. Royalty.

CHILTON BOOK CO.—One Chilton Way, Radnor, PA 19089. Christopher J. Kuppig, Gen. Mgr. Antiques and collectibles, sewing and crafts, professional/technical, and automotive topics. Query with outline, sample chapter, and return postage. *Wallace-Homestead Books.*

CHINA BOOKS—2929 24th St., San Francisco, CA 94110. Wendy K. Lee, Sr. Ed. Books relating to China or Chinese culture. Adult nonfiction, varying lengths. Juvenile picture books, fiction, nonfiction, and young adult books. Query. Royalty.

CHRONICLE BOOKS—275 Fifth St., San Francisco, CA 94103. Attn: Ed. Dept. Topical nonfiction, history, biography, fiction, art, photography, architecture, design, nature, food, regional, and children's books. Send proposal with SASE.

CITADEL PRESS—See *Carol Publishing Group.*

CLARION BOOKS—215 Park Ave. S., New York, NY 10003. Dorothy Briley, Ed.-in-Chief/Pub. Fiction, nonfiction, and picture books: short novels and lively stories for ages 6 to 10 and 8 to 12, historical fiction, humor; picture books for infants and children to age 7; biography, natural history, social studies, American and world history for readers 5 to 8, and 9 and up. Royalty. Hardcover.

CLARK CITY PRESS—P.O. Box 1358, Livingston, MT 59047. Attn: Ed. Dept. Collections of poems, short stories, and essays; novels, biographies, and some children's books. No unsolicited manuscripts. Royalty.

CLEIS PRESS—P.O. Box 14684, San Francisco, CA 94114. Frédérique Delacoste, Ed. Fiction and nonfiction, 200 pages, by women. No poetry. Send SASE with two first-class stamps for catalogue before querying. Royalty.

CLOVERDALE PRESS—48 Eighth Ave., Suite 401, New York, NY 10014. Book packager. "Since our requirements vary considerably and frequently according to our publishers' needs, please send query letter before submitting material." Address young adult and juvenile to Marion Vaarn; adult to Lisa Howell.

COBBLEHILL BOOKS—375 Hudson St., New York, NY 10014. Joe Ann Daly, Ed. Dir. Rosanne Lauer, Exec. Ed. Fiction and nonfiction for preschoolers through junior high school. Query for manuscripts longer than picture books; send complete manuscript for picture books. Royalty.

COFFEE HOUSE PRESS—27 N. 4th St., Suite 400, Minneapolis, MN 55401. Attn: D. Caligiuri. Literary fiction (no genres). Query with SASE.

COLLIER BOOKS FOR YOUNG ADULTS—See *Simon & Schuster Children's Publishing Division.*

COMPCARE PUBLISHERS—3850 Annapolis Ln., Suite 100, Minneapolis, MN 55447. Margaret Marsh, Ed. Dir. Adult nonfiction: books on positive living; emotional health; growth in personal, couple, and family relationships. Young adult nonfiction. Submit proposal and 2 sample chapters or complete manuscript. Royalty.

COMPUTE BOOKS—324 West Wendover Ave., Greensboro, NC 27408. Attn: Ed. Dept. PC game books, video game books. Also specializes in PC application books.

CONCORDIA PUBLISHING HOUSE—3558 S. Jefferson Ave., St. Louis, MO 63118. Attn: Ed. Dept. Practical nonfiction with explicit religious content, conservative Lutheran doctrine. Children's fiction with explicit Christian content. No poetry. Query. Royalty.

CONFLUENCE PRESS—Spalding Hall, Lewis Clark State College, 500 8th Ave., Lewiston, ID 83502–2698. James Hepworth, Dir. Fiction, nonfiction, and poetry, of varying lengths, "to promote and nourish young writers in particular, to achieve literary and artistic excellence." Send query, outline, and sample chapters. Flat fee or royalty.

CONSUMER REPORTS BOOKS—101 Truman Ave., Yonkers, NY 10703. Mark Hoffman, Exec. Ed. Medicine/health, finances, automotive, homeowners. Submit complete manuscript, or send contents, outline, 3 chapters, and resumé.

CONTEMPORARY BOOKS, INC.—2 Prudential Plaza, Suite 1200, Chicago, IL 60601–6790. Nancy Crossman, Ed. Dir. Trade nonfiction, 100 to 400 pages, on health, fitness, sports, cooking, humor, business, popular culture, biography, real estate, finance, women's issues. Query with outline, sample chapters, and SASE. Royalty.

COUNCIL FOR INDIAN EDUCATION—2032 Woody Dr., Billings, MT 59102. Hap Gilliland, Ed. Books dealing with Native-American life and culture, for children ages 5 to 18. Picture books, 30 to 60 pages; fiction, nonfiction, and young adult books, 30 to 300 pages. Query or send complete manuscript. Flat fee for short stories included in anthologies; royalty for books. Guidelines. Manuscripts read October through May.

COUNTRYMAN PRESS—Div. of The Countryman Press, Inc., P.O. Box 175, Woodstock, VT 05091–0175. Helen Whybrow, Ed. Adult books of varying lengths on travel, outdoor recreation, fishing, gardening, nature, environment, rural how-to, and New Englandiana. Query with outline and sample chapters. Multiple queries considered. Royalty.

CRAFTSMAN BOOK COMPANY—6058 Corte del Cedro, P.O. Box 6500, Carlsbad, CA 92018. Laurence D. Jacobs, Ed. How-to construction and estimating manuals and software for professional builders, 450 pages. Query. Royalty. Paperback.

CREATIVE ARTS BOOK CO.—833 Bancroft Way, Berkeley, CA 94710. Donald S. Ellis, Pub. Adult nonfiction: women's issues, music; African-American, Asian, and California topics. Query with outline, sample chapters, SASE. Royalty.

CRESTWOOD HOUSE—See *Simon & Schuster Children's Publishing Division.*

CRIME LINE—See *Bantam Books.*

THE CROSSING PRESS—P.O. Box 1048, Freedom, CA 95019. Elaine Goldman Gill, John Gill, Pubs. Health, holistic health, men's studies, feminist studies, spiritual works, gay topics, cookbooks. Royalty.

CROWN BOOKS FOR YOUNG READERS—201 E. 50th St., New York, NY 10022. Simon Boughton, Ed.-in-Chief. Children's nonfiction (science, sports, nature, music, and history), and picture books for ages 3 and up. Send manuscript for picture books. Guidelines.

CRYSTAL RIVER PRESS—P.O. Box 1382, Healdsburg, CA 95448. Tom Watson, Ed.-in-Chief. Juvenile books. Picture books for preschoolers to age 6. Fiction and nonfiction for K through 12. Young adult books, 60,000 words, for readers 13 to 18. *Starling Line,* to 60,000 words, for easy and beginning readers. Royalty.

DANIEL AND COMPANY, JOHN—P.O. Box 21922, Santa Barbara, CA 93121. John Daniel, Pub. Books, to 200 pages, in the field of belles lettres and literary memoirs; stylish and elegant writing; essays and short fiction dealing with social issues; one poetry title per year. Send synopsis or outline with no more than 50 sample pages and SASE. Allow 6 to 8 weeks for response. Royalty.

DAVIS PUBLICATIONS, INC.—50 Portland St., Worcester, MA 01608. Wyatt Wade, Ed. Books for the art education market; mainly for teachers of art, grades K through 12, 100 to 300 manuscript pages. Must have an educational component. Grades K through 8, address Claire M. Golding; grades 9 through 12, address Helen Ronan. Query with outline and sample chapters. Royalty.

DAW BOOKS, INC.—375 Hudson St., 3rd Fl., New York, NY 10014-3658. Elizabeth R. Wollheim, Ed.-in-Chief. Sheila E. Gilbert, Sr. Ed. Peter Stampfel, Submissions Ed. Science fiction and fantasy, 60,000 to 120,000 words. Royalty.

DAWN PUBLICATIONS—14618 Tyler Foote Rd., Nevada City, CA 95959. Glenn J. Hovemann, Ed. Dept. Nature awareness books highlighting nature's power to enliven the human soul. Health and healing books that aim to help people rise to their highest potential, physically, mentally, and spiritually. Children's books with a positive, uplifting message that will inspire the child's soul; no lectures. "We are open to other themes that are helpful and inspiring, including manuscripts with more explicitly spiritual content." Submit table of contents, synopsis, sample chapters. For children's works, submit complete manuscript and specify intended age. Guidelines. Royalty.

DEARBORN FINANCIAL PUBLISHING, INC.—Div. of Dearborn Publishing Group Inc., 520 N. Dearborn St., Chicago, IL 60610. Anita A. Constant, Sr. V.P. Books on financial services, real estate, banking, small business, etc. Query with outline and sample chapters. Royalty and flat fee.

DEL REY BOOKS—201 E. 50th St., New York, NY 10022. Shelly Shapiro, Exec. Ed. Veronica Chapman, Sr. Ed. Science fiction and fantasy, 60,000 to 120,000 words; first novelists welcome. Material must be well paced with logical resolutions. Fantasy with magic basic to plotline. Send manuscript or outline with 3 sample chapters. Include manuscript-size SASE. Royalty.

DELACORTE PRESS—1540 Broadway, New York, NY 10036. Leslie Schnur, Jackie Farber, Trish Todd, Jackie Cantor, Eds. Adult fiction and nonfiction.

Juvenile and young adult fiction (Craig Virden, Ed.). Accepts fiction (mystery, young adult, romance, fantasy, etc.) from agents only.

DELANCEY PRESS—P.O. Box 40285, Philadelphia, PA 19106. Wesley Morrison, Ed. Dir. All types of nonfiction, 60,000 words. Query. Royalty.

DELL BOOKS—1540 Broadway, New York, NY 10036. Attn: Ed. Dept., Book Proposal. Commercial fiction and nonfiction, family sagas, historical romances, war action, general fiction, occult/horror/psychological suspense, true crime, men's adventure. Send four-page narrative synopsis for fiction, or an outline for nonfiction. Enclose SASE. Address submissions to Dell Books, Ed. Dept., Book Proposal. Allow 2 to 3 months for response.

DELTA BOOKS—1540 Broadway, New York, NY 10036. Attn: Ed. Dept., Book Proposal. General-interest nonfiction: psychology, feminism, health, nutrition, child care, science, self-help, and how-to. Send an outline with SASE.

DEVIN-ADAIR PUBLISHERS, INC.—6 N. Water St., Greenwich, CT 06830. C. de la Belle Issue, Pub. J. Andrassi, Ed. Books on conservative affairs, Irish topics, photography, Americana, self-help, health, gardening, cooking, and ecology. Send outline, sample chapters, and SASE. Royalty.

DI CAPUA BOOKS—See *HarperCollins Children's Books.*

DIAL PRESS—Imprint of Dell Publishing, 1540 Broadway, New York, NY 10036. Susan Kamil, Ed. Dir. Quality fiction and nonfiction. No unsolicited material.

DIAMOND BOOKS—Imprint of Berkley Publishing Co., 200 Madison Ave., New York, NY 10012. Attn: Ed. Dept. Suspense fiction, historical romances, regencies, women's contemporary fiction. Westerns. No unagented manuscripts. Paperback.

DILLON PRESS—See *Simon & Schuster Children's Publishing Division.*

DOMAIN—See *Bantam Books.*

DORLING KINDERSLEY PUBLISHING, INC.—95 Madison Ave., New York, NY 10016. Attn: B. Alison Weir. Preschool and children's picture books. Submit through agent only.

DOUBLEDAY AND CO.—1540 Broadway, New York, NY 10036. Stephen Rubin, Pub./Pres. David Gernert, Ed.-in-Chief. No unsolicited manuscripts.

DOWN HOME PRESS—P.O. Box 4126, Asheboro, NC 27204. Jerry Bledsoe, Ed. Nonfiction books related to the Carolinas and the South. Query or send complete manuscript. Royalty.

DREW BOOKS, LISA—See *Scribner.*

DUNNE BOOKS, THOMAS—Imprint of St. Martin's Press, 175 Fifth Ave., New York, NY 10010. Thomas L. Dunne, Ed. Adult fiction (mysteries, trade, etc.) and nonfiction (history, biographies, science, politics, etc.). Query with outline, sample chapters, and SASE. Royalty.

DUQUESNE UNIVERSITY PRESS—600 Forbes Ave., Pittsburgh, PA 15282–0101. Attn: Ed. Dept. Scholarly publications in the humanities and social sciences.

DUTTON ADULT—Div. of Penguin USA, 375 Hudson St., New York, NY 10014. Arnold Dolin, Ed. Dir. Fiction and nonfiction books. Manuscripts accepted only from agents or on personal recommendation.

DUTTON CHILDREN'S BOOKS—Div. of Penguin USA, 375 Hudson St., New York, NY 10014. Lucia Monfried, Ed.-in-Chief. Picture books, easy-to-read books; fiction and nonfiction for preschoolers to young adults. Submit outline and first 3 chapters with query for fiction and nonfiction, complete manuscripts for picture books and easy-to-read books. Manuscripts should be well written with fresh ideas and child appeal. Include SASE.

EAKIN PRESS—P.O. Drawer 90159, Austin, TX 78709–0159. Melissa Roberts, Sr. Ed. Adult nonfiction, 60,000 to 80,000 words: Texana, regional cookbooks, Mexico and the Southwest. Children's books: history, culture, geography, etc. of Texas and the Southwest. Juvenile picture books, 5,000 to 10,000 words; fiction, 20,000 to 30,000 words; young adult fiction, 25,000 to 40,000 words. Currently overstocked; query. Royalty.

THE ECCO PRESS—100 W. Broad St., Hopewell, NJ 08525. Daniel Halpern, Ed. Fiction, poetry, literary criticism, and translations. Send query and sample chapter.

EERDMANS PUBLISHING COMPANY, INC., WM. B.—255 Jefferson Ave. S.E., Grand Rapids, MI 49503. Jon Pott, Ed.-in-Chief. Protestant, Roman Catholic, and Orthodox theological nonfiction; American religious history; some fiction. For children's religious books, query Amy Eerdmans, Children's Book Ed. Royalty.

ELDER BOOKS—P.O. Box 490, Forest Knolls, CA 94933. Attn: Ed. Books related to aging, health, and Alzheimer's and other conditions related to aging. How-to and inspirational books. Send complete manuscript; no multiple submissions. Royalty.

ELEMENT BOOKS—42 Broadway, Rockport, MA 01966. Paul Cash, Acquisitions Ed. Books on world religions, ancient wisdom, astrology, meditation, and women's studies. Study recent catalogue. Query with outline and sample chapters. Royalty.

ENSLOW PUBLISHERS, INC.—Bloy St. & Ramsey Ave., Box 777, Hillside, NJ 07205. Brian D. Enslow, Ed./Pub. Nonfiction books for young people. Areas of emphasis are children's and young adult books for ages 10 to 18 in the fields of social studies, science, and biography. Also reference books for all ages and easy reading books for teenagers.

EPICENTER PRESS—P.O. Box 60529, Fairbanks, AK 99706. Lael Morgan, Ed. Quality nonfiction trade books, contemporary western art and photography titles, and destination travel guides emphasizing the Pacific Northwest. "We are a regional press whose interests include but are not limited to the arts, history, environment, and diverse cultures and lifestyles of the North Pacific and high latitudes." Flat fee.

ERIKSSON, PUBLISHER, PAUL S.—P.O. Box 62, Forest Dale, VT 05745. Attn: Ed. Dept. General nonfiction (send outline and cover letter); some fiction (send three chapters with query). Royalty.

ESTRIN PUBLISHING—1900 Ave. of the Stars, Suite 670, Los Angeles, CA 90067. Dana Graves, Ed. Books, 300 to 400 pages, for paralegals and attorneys. Query with outline and sample chapters; multiple queries considered. Royalty.

EVANS & CO., INC., M.—216 E. 49th St., New York, NY 10017. Attn: Ed. Dept. Books on humor, health, self-help, popular psychology, and cookbooks. Western fiction for adults; fiction and nonfiction for young adults. Query with outline, sample chapter, and SASE. Royalty.

EVENT HORIZON PRESS—P.O. Box 867, Desert Hot Springs, CA 92240. Joseph Cowles, Pub. Adult fiction and nonfiction. Poetry books, from 50 pages. Not accepting any new material at this time.

EXCALIBUR PUBLICATIONS—Box 36, Latham, NY 12110–0036. Alan M. Petrillo, Ed. Books on military history, firearms history, tactics and strategy, history of battles. Query with outline and sample chapters. SASE. Royalty or flat fee.

FABER AND FABER—50 Cross St., Winchester, MA 01890. Attn: Ed. Dept. Novels, anthologies, and nonfiction books on topics of popular culture and general interest. Query with SASE. Royalty.

FACTS ON FILE PUBLICATIONS—460 Park Ave. S., New York, NY 10016. Susan Schwartz, Ed. Dir. Reference and trade books on science, health, literature, language, history, the performing arts, ethnic studies, popular culture, sports, etc. (No fiction, poetry, computer books, technical books or cookbooks.) Query with outline, sample chapter, and SASE. Royalty. Hardcover.

FALL CREEK PRESS—P.O. Box 1127, Fall Creek, OR 97438. Sharon Rock, Pub. "We publish book anthologies of short stories (no single-author collections) demonstrating the role of personal choice in opening the door to spiritual growth." Request Author Guide before submitting. Royalty.

FANFARE—Imprint of Bantam Books, 1540 Broadway, New York, NY 10036. Beth DeGuzman, Wendy McCurdy, Sr. Eds. Historical and contemporary adult women's fiction, 90,000 to 150,000 words. Study field before submitting. Query. Paperback and hardcover.

FARRAR, STRAUS & GIROUX—19 Union Sq. W., New York, NY 10003. Attn: Ed. Dept. Adult and juvenile literary fiction and nonfiction. No guidelines or catalogues sent to writers.

FAWCETT/IVY BOOKS—Imprint of Ballantine Books, 201 E. 50th St., New York, NY 10022. Barbara Dicks, Exec. Ed. Adult mysteries, regencies, and historical romances, 75,000 to 120,000 words. Mysteries and problem novels, 60,000 to 70,000 words, for young adults. Query with outline and sample chapters. Average response time is 3 to 6 months. Royalty.

THE FEMINIST PRESS AT THE CITY UNIVERSITY OF NEW YORK —311 E. 94th St., New York, NY 10128. Florence Howe, Pub. Reprints of significant "lost" fiction, original memoirs, autobiographies, biographies; multicultural anthologies; handbooks; bibliographies. "We are especially interested in international literature, women and peace, women and music, and women of color." Royalty.

FINE, INC., DONALD I.—19 W. 21st St., New York, NY 10010. Attn: Ed. Dept. Literary and commercial fiction. General nonfiction. No queries or unsolicited manuscripts. Submit through agent only.

FIREBRAND BOOKS—141 The Commons, Ithaca, NY 14850. Nancy K. Bereano, Ed. Feminist and lesbian fiction and nonfiction. Royalty. Paperback and library edition cloth.

FLARE BOOKS—See *Avon Books*.

FLORES PUBLICATIONS, J.—P.O. Box 830131, Miami, FL 33283–0131. Eli Flores, Ed. Books, 30,000 to 80,000 words, on business, personal finance. Query with outline and sample chapters. Royalty.

772

FONT & CENTER PRESS—P.O. Box 95, Weston, MA 02193. Ilene Horowitz, Ed./Pub. Children's picture books, with a special emphasis on multicultural themes; general nonfiction topics for young readers. Cookbooks. How-to books. Alternative history for adults and young adults. Send complete manuscript for picture books; proposal, outline, and sample chapter for other books. Response in 3 months. SASE. Royalty.

FORTRESS PRESS—426 S. Fifth St., Box 1209, Minneapolis, MN 55440. Dr. Marshall D. Johnson, Dir. Books in the areas of biblical studies, theology, ethics, and church history for academic and professional markets, including libraries. Query.

FOUL PLAY PRESS—The Countryman Press, Inc., Lincoln Corners, Rt. 4 W., P.O. Box 175, Woodstock, VT 05091. Lou Kannenstine, Ed. Adult mystery fiction, 180 to 240 pages, "of high literary quality," including cozy, suspense, and hard boiled. No true crime. Query with synopsis and one sample chapter.

FOUR WALLS EIGHT WINDOWS—39 W. 14th, #503, New York, NY 10011. No unsolicited material.

FOUR WINDS PRESS—See *Simon & Schuster Children's Publishing Division.*

THE FREE PRESS—See *Macmillan Publishing Co., Inc.*

FULCRUM PUBLISHING—350 Indiana St., Suite 350, Golden, CO 80401. Attn: Submissions Dept. Adult trade nonfiction: travel, nature, American history, biography, self-help, and gardening. No fiction. Send cover letter, sample chapters, outline, table of contents, and author credentials. Royalty.

GARRETT PARK PRESS—P.O. Box 190, Garrett Park, MD 20896. Robert Calvert, Jr., Pub. Reference books on career education, occupational guidance, and financial aid only. Query required. Multiple queries considered but not encouraged. Royalty.

GEORGIA STATE UNIVERSITY BUSINESS PRESS—University Plaza, Atlanta, GA 30303–3093. Attn: Ed. Dept. Books, software, research monographs, and directories in the business sciences and related disciplines.

GERINGER BOOKS, LAURA—See *HarperCollins Publishing.*

GIBBS SMITH PUBLISHER/PEREGRINE SMITH BOOKS—P.O. Box 667, Layton, UT 84041. Madge Baird, Ed. Dir. Adult nonfiction. Query. Royalty.

GINIGER CO. INC., THE K.S.—250 W. 57th St., Suite 519, New York, NY 10107. Attn: Ed. Dept. General nonfiction. Query with SASE; no unsolicited manuscripts. Royalty.

GLENBRIDGE PUBLISHING LTD.—6010 W. Jewell Ave., Lakewood, CO 80232. James A. Keene, Ed. Nonfiction books on a variety of topics, including business, history, and psychology. Query with sample chapter. Royalty.

GLOBE PEQUOT PRESS, THE—6 Business Park Rd., Box 833, Old Saybrook, CT 06475. Laura Strom, Acquisitions Ed. Nonfiction with national and regional focus; travel; outdoor recreation; personal finance; business; cooking; home how-to; gardening; gift books. Query with sample chapter, contents, and one-page synopsis. SASE required. Royalty.

GOLD EAGLE—See *Worldwide Library.*

GOLDEN PRESS—See *Western Publishing Co., Inc.*

GOLDEN WEST PUBLISHERS—4113 N. Longview, Phoenix, AZ 85014. Hal Mitchell, Ed. Cookbooks and Western history and travel books. Query. Royalty or flat fee.

GRAYWOLF PRESS—2402 University Ave., Suite 203, St. Paul, MN 55114. Attn: Ed. Dept. Literary fiction (short story collections and novels), poetry, and essays. Not considering manuscripts at this time.

GREAT QUOTATIONS—1967 Quincy Ct., Glendale Hgts., IL 60139. Ringo Suek, Ed. General adult titles, 100 to 300 pages; children's books of up to 300 pages for ages 5 and older. Query with outline and sample chapters, or send complete manuscript. Royalty.

GREEN TIGER PRESS—See *Simon & Schuster Children's Publishing Division.*

GREENWILLOW BOOKS—Imprint of William Morrow and Co., Inc., 1350 Ave. of the Americas, New York, NY 10019. Susan Hirschman, Ed.-in-Chief. Children's books for all ages. Picture books.

GROSSET AND DUNLAP, INC.—Div. of Putnam & Grosset Books, 200 Madison Ave., New York, NY 10016. Craig Walker, Pub. Mass-market children's books. Query required. Royalty.

GROVE/ATLANTIC MONTHLY PRESS—841 Broadway, New York, NY 10003–4793. Morgan Entrekin, Pub. Distinguished fiction and nonfiction. Query.

GULLIVER BOOKS—See *Harcourt Brace.*

HAMMOND, INC.—515 Valley St., Maplewood, NJ 07040. Charles Lees, Ed. Nonfiction: cartographic reference, travel. Query with outline and sample chapters. SASE required. Payment varies.

HANCOCK HOUSE PUBLISHERS, LTD.—1431 Harrison Ave., Box 959, Blaine, WA 98231–0959. Attn: Ed. Dept. Adult nonfiction: guide books, cookbooks, biographies, natural history, and sports. Some juvenile nonfiction. Query with outline and sample chapters. Multiple queries considered. Royalty.

HARCOURT BRACE—525 B St., Suite 1900, San Diego, CA 92101. Attn: Ed. Dept. Adult trade nonfiction and fiction. Books for Professionals: test preparation guides and other student self-help materials. Juvenile fiction and nonfiction for beginning readers through young adults under the following imprints: *HB Children's Books, Gulliver Books, Browndeer Press, Jane Yolen Books, Odyssey Paperbacks,* and *Voyager Paperbacks.* Adult books: no unsolicited manuscripts or queries. Children's books: queries and manuscripts from agents only. No simultaneous submissions. Send query to Manuscript Submissions, Children's Book Division, 525 B St., Suite 1900, San Diego, CA 92101–4495. SASE required.

HARCOURT BRACE PROFESSIONAL PUBLISHING—Imprint of Harcourt Brace, 525 B St., Suite 1900, San Diego, CA 92101. Attn: Ed. Dept. Professional books for practitioners in accounting, auditing, tax. Query required. Royalty.

HARLEQUIN BOOKS/CANADA—225 Duncan Mill Rd., Don Mills, Ont., Canada M3B 3K9. *Harlequin Glitz*: Dianne Moggy, Sr. Ed. Intense, sensuous dramas set against a backdrop of "glitz and glamour," 100,000 words plus. Query. *Harlequin Superromance*: Paula Eykelhof, Sr. Ed. Contemporary romance, 85,000 words, with a mainstream edge. Query. *Harlequin Temptation*: Birgit Davis-Todd, Sr. Ed. Sensuous, humorous contemporary romances, 60,000 words. Query.

HARLEQUIN BOOKS/U.S.—300 E. 42nd St., 6th Fl., New York, NY 10017. Debra Matteucci, Sr. Ed. Contemporary romances, 70,000 to 75,000 words. Send for tip sheets. *Harlequin American Romances*: bold, exciting romantic adventures, "where anything is possible and dreams come true." *Harlequin Intrigue*: set against a backdrop of mystery and suspense, worldwide locals. Query. Paperback.

HARPER PAPERBACKS—HarperCollins, 10 E. 53rd St., New York, NY 10022. Geoff Hannell, Pub. Karen Solem, Ed.-in-Chief. Carolyn Marino, Exec. Ed. Jessica Lichtenstein, Sr. Ed., Katie Tso, Ed., John Silbersack, Sci. Fic./Fantasy/ Horror Ed., Abigail Kamen, Ed.

HARPERCOLLINS CHILDREN'S BOOKS—10 E. 53rd St., New York, NY 10022–5299. Katrin Magnusson, Admin. Coord. Picture books, chapter books, and fiction and nonfiction for middle-grade and young adult readers. "Our imprints (*HarperTrophy* paperbacks, *Michael di Capua Books*, and *Laura Geringer Books*) are committed to producing imaginative and responsible children's books. All publish from preschool to young adult titles." Guidelines. Query, send sample chapters, or complete manuscript. Royalty.

HARPERCOLLINS PUBLISHERS—10 E. 53rd St., New York, NY 10022–5299. Adult Trade Department: Address Man. Ed. Fiction, nonfiction (biography, history, etc.), reference. Submissions from agents only. College texts: Address College Dept. Children's books: Address *Harper Junior Books*; Religion, theology, etc.: Address *Harper San Francisco*, Ice House One-401, 151 Union St., San Francisco, CA 94111–1299. No unsolicited manuscripts; query only.

HARPERPRISM—Imprint of HarperCollins, 10 East 53rd St., New York, NY 10022–5299. John Silbersack, Ed.-in-Chief. Christopher Schelling, Exec. Ed. Science fiction/fantasy. 50 titles per year in hardcover, trade paper, and mass market. No unsolicited manuscripts; query.

HARPERTROPHY—See *HarperCollins Children's Books.*

HARVARD COMMON PRESS—535 Albany St., Boston, MA 02118. Bruce Shaw, Ed. Adult nonfiction: cookbooks, travel guides, books on family matters, health, small business, etc. Send outline and sample chapters or complete manuscript. SASE. Royalty.

HARVARD UNIVERSITY PRESS—79 Garden St., Cambridge, MA 02138–1499. No free-lance submissions or queries.

HARVEST HOUSE PUBLISHERS—1075 Arrowsmith, Eugene, OR 97402. Eileen L. Mason, V.P. Editorial. Nonfiction with evangelical theme: how-tos, marriage, women, contemporary issues. Fiction. Children's fiction (ages 9 to 13). No biographies, autobiographies, history, music books, or poetry. Query with SASE.

HAWORTH PRESS, INC—10 Alice St., Binghamton, NY 13904–1580. Bill Palmer, Ed. Scholarly press interested in research-based adult nonfiction: psychology, social work, women's studies, family and marriage; some recreation and entertainment. Send outline with sample chapters or complete manuscript. Royalty.

HAY HOUSE—P.O. Box 6204, Carson, CA 90749–6204. Dan Olmos, Ed. Dir. Metaphysical books on health, self-awareness, spiritual growth, and the environment. Query with outline and sample chapters. Royalty.

HAZELDEN EDUCATIONAL MATERIALS—Box 176, Center City, MN 55012. Attn: Ed. Dept. Self-help books, 100 to 400 pages, relating to addiction, recovery, and wholeness. Query with outline and sample chapters. Multiple queries considered. Royalty.

HB CHILDREN'S BOOKS—See *Harcourt Brace.*

HEALTH COMMUNICATIONS, INC.—3201 S.W. 15th St., Deerfield Beach, FL 33442. Christine Belleris, Ed. Dir. Books on self-help recovery and personal growth for adults (250 pages). Query with outline and sample chapter, or send manuscript with SASE. Royalty.

HEALTH PLUS PUBLISHERS—P.O. Box 1027, Sherwood, OR 97140. Paula E. Clure, Ed. No longer considering unsolicited material.

HEALTH PRESS—P.O. Box 1388, Santa Fe, NM 87501. Kathleen Schwartz, Ed. Health-related adult books, 100 to 300 finished pages. "We're seeking cutting-edge, original manuscripts that will excite and help readers. Author must have credentials, or preface/intro must be written by M.D., Ph.D., etc. Controversial topics are desired; must be well researched and documented." Prefer completed manuscript, but will consider queries with outline and sample chapters. Multiple queries considered. Royalty.

HEARST BOOKS—See *William Morrow and Co.*

HEINEMANN—361 Hanover St., Portsmouth, NH 03801. Attn: Ed. Dept. Practical theatre, world literature, and literacy education. Query.

HEMINGWAY WESTERN STUDIES SERIES—Boise State Univ., 1910 University Dr., Boise, ID 83725. Tom Trusky, Ed. Artists' and eccentric books (multiple editions) relating to Rocky Mountain environmental, racial, religious, gender and other public issues. Guidelines.

HERALD PRESS—616 Walnut Ave., Scottdale, PA 15683. Attn: Ed. Dept. Christian books for adults and children: inspiration, Bible study, self-help, devotionals, current issues, peace studies, church history, missions, evangelism, family life, fiction, and personal experience. Send one-page summary and 2 sample chapters. Royalty.

HIGGINSON BOOK COMPANY—148 Washington St., Salem, MA 01970. E. Wheeldon, Ed. Dept. Nonfiction genealogy and local history, 20 to 1,000 pages. Specializes in reprints. Query. Royalty.

HIGHSMITH PRESS—P.O. Box 800, Fort Atkinson, WI 53538–0800. Donald Sager, Pub. Adult books, 80 to 360 text pages, on professional library science, education, and reference. Books on multicultural themes or subjects for preschoolers (32 pages) through young adults (120 to 240 pages). Query with outline and sample chapters. Royalty.

HIPPOCRENE BOOKS—171 Madison Ave., New York, NY 10016. George Blagowidow, Ed. Dir. Language instruction books and foreign language dictionaries, travel guides, and military history. Send outline and sample chapters with SASE for reply. Multiple queries considered. Royalty.

HOLIDAY HOUSE, INC.—425 Madison Ave., New York, NY 10017. Margery S. Cuyler, V. P. Ashley Mason, Assoc. Ed. General juvenile fiction and nonfiction. Submit complete manuscript or 3 sample chapters and summary. Royalty. Hardcover only.

HOLT AND CO., HENRY—115 W. 18th St., New York, NY 10011. Bruno Quinson, Pub. Distinguished works of biography, history, fiction, and natural history; humor; child activity books; parenting books; books for the entrepreneurial business person; and health books. "Virtually all submissions come from literary agents or from writers whom we publish. We do not accept unsolicited submissions."

HOME BUILDER PRESS—National Assoc. of Home Builders, 1201 15th St. N.W., Washington, DC 20005–2800. Doris M. Tennyson, Sr. Ed. How-to and business management books, 150 to 200 manuscript pages, for builders, remodelers, and developers. Writers should be experts in homebuilding, remodeling, land development and related aspects of the building industry. Query with outline and sample chapter. Royalty. For guidelines send SASE with $2 postage to Carolyn Poindester, Ed. Asst.

HOUGHTON MIFFLIN COMPANY—222 Berkeley St., Boston, MA 02116–3764. Attn: Ed. Dept. Fiction: literary, historical. Nonfiction: history, biography, psychology. No unsolicited submissions. Children's book division, address Children's Trade Books: picture books, fiction, and nonfiction for all ages. Query. Royalty.

HP BOOKS—Div. of The Berkley Publishing Group, 200 Madison Ave., New York, NY 10016. Attn: Ed. Dept. Illustrated how-tos on cooking, gardening, automotive topics. Query with SASE. Royalty.

HUNTER PUBLISHING, INC.—300 Raritan Center Pkwy., Edison, NJ 08818. Michael Hunter, Ed. Travel guides. Query with outline.

HYPERION—114 Fifth Ave., New York, NY 10011. Material accepted from agents only. No unsolicited manuscripts or queries considered.

IMPACT PUBLISHERS, INC.—P.O. Box 1094, San Luis Obispo, CA 93406. Attn: Acquisitions Ed. Popular psychology books, from 200 pages, on personal growth, relationships, families, communities, and health for adults. Children's books for "Little Imp" series on issues of self-esteem. "Writers must have advanced degrees and professional experience in human-service fields." Query with outline and sample chapters. Royalty.

INDIANA UNIVERSITY PRESS—601 N. Morton St., Bloomington, IN 47404–3797. Attn: Ed. Dept. Scholarly nonfiction, especially cultural studies, literary criticism, music, history, women's studies, African-American studies, science, philosophy, African studies, Middle East studies, Russian studies, anthropology, regional, etc. Query with outline and sample chapters. Royalty.

INSTRUCTOR BOOKS—See *Scholastic Professional Books.*

INTERNATIONAL MARINE—Box 220, Camden, ME 04843. Jonathan Eaton, Ed. Dir., James Babb, Acquisitions Ed. Books on boating (sailing and power).

INTIMATE MOMENTS—See *Silhouette Books.*

IRON CROWN ENTERPRISES—P.O. Box 1605, Charlottesville, VA 22902. Jessica Ney-Grimm, Ed. Supplemental texts, 80,000 to 230,000 words, to accompany fantasy role-playing games. Extremely specific market. "Study one of our existing products before querying." Royalty or flat fee.

ISLAND PRESS—1718 Connecticut Ave. N.W., Suite 300, Washington, DC 20009. Charles C. Savitt, Pub. Nonfiction focusing on natural history, literary science, the environment, and natural resource management. "We want solution-oriented material to solve environmental problems. For *Shearwater Books*, we want books that express new insights about nature and the environment." Query or send manuscript. SASE required.

JAI PRESS, INC.—55 Old Post Rd., #2, P.O. Box 1678, Greenwich, CT 06836. Herbert Johnson, Ed. Research and technical reference books on such subjects as business, economics, management, sociology, political science, and computer science. Query or send complete manuscript. Royalty.

777

JALMAR PRESS—2625 Skypark Dr., Suite 204, Torrance, CA 90505. Catherine Montgomery, Dir. Acquisitions & Development. Nonfiction books for parents and teachers. "Our emphasis is self-esteem, under which we publish books to enhance a student's self-awareness." Multiple queries considered. Submit outline. Royalty.

JAMES BOOKS, ALICE—98 Main St., Farmington, ME 04938. Sean Amaral, Program Dir. "Shared-work cooperative" publishes books of poetry (72 to 80 pages) by writers living in New England. Manuscripts read in September and January. "We emphasize the publication of poetry by women, but also welcome and publish manuscripts by men." Authors paid with 100 copies of their books. Write for guidelines. Holds national competition for Beatrice Hawley Award.

THE JOHNS HOPKINS UNIVERSITY PRESS—2715 N. Charles St., Baltimore, MD 21218. No unsolicited poetry or fiction considered.

JOHNSON BOOKS, INC.—1880 S. 57th Ct., Boulder, CO 80301. Walt Borneman, Man. Ed. Nonfiction: environmental subjects, archaeology, geology, natural history, astronomy, travel guides, outdoor guidebooks, fly fishing, regional. Query. Royalty.

JONATHAN DAVID PUBLISHERS, INC.—68–22 Eliot Ave., Middle Village, NY 11379. Alfred J. Kolatch, Ed.-in-Chief. General nonfiction (how-to, sports, cooking and food, self-help, etc.) and books specializing in Judaica. Query with outline, sample chapter, and resumé required. SASE. Royalty or outright purchase.

JUST US BOOKS—301 Main St., Orange, NJ 07050. Cheryl Hudson, Ed. Children's books celebrating African-American heritage. Picture books, 24 to 32 pages. Chapter books and biographies, from 2,500 words. Queries with SASE required. Royalty or flat fee.

KALMBACH PUBLISHING COMPANY—21027 Crossroads Cir., Waukesha, WI 53187. Terry Spohn, Sr. Acquisitions Ed. Adult nonfiction, 18,000 to 50,000 words, on scale modeling, model railroading, miniatures, and astronomy. Send outline with sample chapters. Accepts multiple queries. Royalty.

KAR-BEN COPIES—6800 Tildenwood Ln., Rockville, MD 20852. Judye Groner, Ed. Books on Jewish themes for preschool and elementary children (to age 9): picture books, fiction, and nonfiction. Complete manuscript preferred. SASE. Flat fee and royalty.

KEATS PUBLISHING, INC.—27 Pine St., Box 876, New Canaan, CT 06840. Nathan Keats, Pub. Nonfiction: health, how-to. Query. Royalty.

KENSINGTON BOOKS—(formerly *Zebra Hardcovers*) Imprint of Kensington Publishing Corp., 850 Third Ave., New York, NY 10022. Sarah Gallick, Exec. Ed. Mainstream fiction and nonfiction. Mysteries. Send synopsis and sample chapters. Royalty.

KENT STATE UNIVERSITY PRESS—Kent State Univ., Kent, OH 44242. John T. Hubbell, Dir. Julia Morton, Sr. Ed. Publishes hardcover and paperback originals and some reprints. Especially interested in scholarly works in history and literary studies of high quality, any titles of regional interest for Ohio, scholarly biographies, archaeological research, the arts, and general nonfiction.

KIVAKI PRESS—585 E. 31st St., Durango, CA 81301. Greg Cumberford, Pub. Nonfiction books for the academic, holistic health, and environmental markets. Complete manuscript may be submitted on disk with hard copy of synopsis. If not submitting on disk, send synopsis only for manuscripts over 200 pages. Royalty.

778

KNOPF BOOKS FOR YOUNG READERS, ALFRED A.—201 E. 50th St., New York, NY 10022. Janet Schulman, Pub. Stephanie Spinner, Assoc. Pub. Frances Foster, Ed.-at-Large. Anne Schwartz, Exec. Ed. Reg Kahney, Sr. Ed. Distinguished juvenile fiction and nonfiction. Query. Royalty. Guidelines.

KNOPF, INC., ALFRED A.—201 E. 50th St., New York, NY 10022. Attn: Sr. Ed. Distinguished adult fiction and general nonfiction. Query. Royalty.

KODANSHA AMERICA, INC.—114 Fifth Ave., New York, NY 10011. Attn: Ed. Dept. Books, 50,000 to 200,000 words, on cross-cultural, Asian and other international subjects. Query with outline, sample chapters, and SASE. Royalty.

LADYBIRD BOOKS, INC.—840 Washington St., P.O. Box 1690, Auburn, ME 04210. Attn: Ed. Dept. Books for babies, toddlers, and preschoolers. Picture books, storybooks, nursery rhymes, fairy tales, activity and coloring books. Rarely accepts unsolicited manuscripts. Query required.

LAREDO PUBLISHING—22930 Lockness Ave., Torrance, CA 90501. Clara Kohen, Ed. Bilingual and ESL (English as a second language) titles in Spanish and English. Children's fiction and young adult titles. Query with outline. Royalty.

LARK BOOKS—50 College St., Asheville, NC 28801. Rob Pulleyn, Pub. Distinctive books for creative people in crafts, how-to, leisure activities, and "coffee table" categories. Query with outline. Royalty.

LAUREL BOOKS—Imprint of Bantam, Doubleday, Dell Publishing Co., 1540 Broadway, New York, NY 10036. Attn: Ed. Dept. Contemporary fiction, reprints from *Delacorte Press.*

LAUREL-LEAF—Imprint of Bantam, Doubleday, Dell Publishing Co., 1540 Broadway, New York, NY 10036. Attn: Ed. Dept. Unsolicited young adult manuscripts are accepted only for the Delacorte Press Prize for a first young adult novel. This must be a work of fiction written for ages 12 to 18, by a previously unpublished author. Send SASE for rules and guidelines.

LEADERSHIP PUBLISHERS, INC.—P.O. Box 8358, Des Moines, IA 50301–8358. Attn: Dr. Lois F. Roets. Educational materials for talented and gifted students, grades K to 12, and teacher reference books. No fiction or poetry. Send SASE for catalogue and writer's guidelines before submitting. Query or send complete manuscript. Royalty for books; flat fee for booklets.

LEE & LOW BOOKS—228 E. 45th St., 14th Fl., New York, NY 10017. Philip Lee, Pub. Elizabeth Szabla, Ed.-in-Chief. Focus is on fiction and nonfiction picture books for children ages 4 to 10. "Our goal is to meet the growing need for books that address children of color and to provide books on subjects and stories they can identify with. Of special interest are stories set in contemporary America. Folklore and animal stories discouraged." Query with resumé, writing samples, and SASE. Royalty or flat fee.

LEISURE BOOKS—Div. of Dorchester Publishing Co., Inc., 276 Fifth Ave., New York, NY 10001. Kim Mattson, Ed. Historical romances, from 110,000 words; *Love Spell,* futuristic, time-travel, and historical romances from 100,000 words. Query with synopsis, sample chapters, and SASE. Royalty.

LIFETIME BOOKS, INC.—2131 Hollywood Blvd., Hollywood, FL 33020. H. Allen Etling, Ed. Nonfiction (100 to 300 pages): general interest, how-tos, business, health, and inspiration. Query with letter or outline and sample chapter, SASE. Royalty.

LIMELIGHT—See *Tiare Publications.*

779

LINCOLN-HERNDON PRESS, INC.—818 S. Dirksen Pkwy., Springfield, IL 62703. Shirley A. Buscher, Asst. Pub. American humor that reveals American history. Humor collections. Query.

LITTLE, BROWN & CO.—1271 Ave. of the Americas, New York, NY 10020. Laura Barnes, Ed. Dept. Fiction, general nonfiction, sports books; divisions for law and medical texts. Query only.

LITTLE, BROWN & CO. CHILDREN'S BOOKS DEPT.—34 Beacon St., Boston, MA 02108. Attn: Ed. Dept. Juvenile fiction and nonfiction and picture books. No unsolicited manuscripts. Agented material only.

LLEWELLYN PUBLICATIONS—P.O. Box 64383, St. Paul, MN 55164–0383. Nancy J. Mostad, Acquisitions Mgr. Books, from 75,000 words, on subjects of self-help, how-to, alternative health, astrology, metaphysics, new age, and the occult. Metaphysical/occult fiction. "We're interested in any kind of story (romance, mystery, historical, gothic, science, adventure), just as long as the theme is some aspect of authentic occultism." Query with sample chapters. Multiple queries considered. Royalty.

LODESTAR—An affiliate of Dutton Children's Books, a Div. of Penguin Books USA, Inc., 375 Hudson St., New York, NY 10014. Virginia Buckley, Ed. Dir. Fiction (picture books to young adult, mystery, fantasy, science fiction, western) and nonfiction (science, contemporary issues, nature, history) considered for ages 9 to 11, 10 to 14, and 12 and up. Also fiction and nonfiction picture books for ages 4 to 8. "We are not accepting submissions at this time, but writers may query."

LONGMEADOW PRESS—P.O. Box 10218, 201 High Ridge Rd., Stamford, CT 06904. Attn: Juvenile Ed. Board books, picture books, young fiction, and nonfiction for children. Send complete manuscript. Royalty or flat fee.

LOTHROP, LEE & SHEPARD BOOKS—Imprint of William Morrow & Co., Inc., 1350 Ave. of the Americas, New York, NY 10019. Susan Pearson, Ed.-in-Chief. Juvenile fiction and nonfiction, picture books. Does not review unsolicited material. Royalty.

LOUISIANA STATE UNIVERSITY PRESS—P.O. Box 25053, Baton Rouge, LA 70894–5053. Margaret Dalrymple, Ed. Scholarly adult nonfiction, dealing with the U.S. South, its history, and its culture. Query with outline and sample chapters. Royalty.

LOVE SPELL—See *Leisure Books.*

LOVEGRAM ROMANCES—See *Zebra Books.*

LOVESWEPT—Imprint of Bantam Books, 1540 Broadway, New York, NY 10036. Beth DeGuzman, Sr. Ed. Adult contemporary romances, approximately 55,000 words. Study field before submitting. Query required. Paperback only.

LOYOLA UNIVERSITY PRESS—3441 N. Ashland Ave., Chicago, IL 60657–1397. Joseph Downey, S.J., Ed. Religious and ethics-related material for college-educated Christian readers. "Campion Book Series": art, literature, and religion; contemporary Christian concerns; Jesuit studies; Chicago books. "Values and Ethics Series": scholarly books centered on the theme of values and ethics, but stressing readability and topical relevance. Nonfiction, 200 to 400 pages. Query with outline. Royalty.

LUCENT BOOKS—P.O. Box 289011, San Diego, CA 92198–0011. Bonnie Szumski, Man. Ed. Lori Shein, Ed. Books, 18,000 to 25,000 words, at 7th- to 12th-grade reading level. "Overview" series: political, social, cultural, economic, moral, historical, and environmental topics. "The Importance Of" biography series presents the lives of the world's most influential men and women in all areas of endeavor. "The Importance Of" world history series presents historical events and their importance to society. Query required; work by assignment only. Flat fee. Guidelines and catalogue available.

LYLE STUART—See *Carol Publishing Group.*

LYONS & BURFORD, PUBLISHERS—31 W. 21st St., New York, NY 10010. Peter Burford, Ed. Books, 100 to 300 pages, related to the outdoors (camping, gardening, natural history, etc.) or sports. Query with outline. Royalty.

MCFARLAND & COMPANY, INC., PUBLISHERS—Box 611, Jefferson, NC 28640. Robert Franklin, Ed.-in-Chief. Scholarly and reference books in many fields, except mathematical sciences. Please do not send new age, inspirational, children's, poetry, fiction, or exposés. Submit double-spaced manuscripts, 225 pages and up, or query with outline and sample chapters. Royalty.

MCGUINN & MCGUIRE PUBLISHING, INC.—P.O. Box 20603, Bradenton, FL 34203. Christopher Carroll, Man. Ed. Books, 45,000 to 100,000 words: business, history, and biography titles. "We especially like to see authors who have researched the market as completely as they researched their topic." Send complete manuscript or query with outline and sample chapters. Royalty.

MCKAY COMPANY, DAVID—201 E. 50th St., New York, NY 10022. No unsolicited manuscripts.

MACMILLAN CHILDREN'S BOOK GROUP—See *Simon & Schuster Children's Publishing Division.*

MACMILLAN PUBLISHING CO., INC.—866 Third Avenue, New York, NY 10022. Attn: Ed. Dept. General Book Division: Religious, sports, science, and reference books. No fiction. Paperbacks: *Collier Books.* History, psychology, contemporary issues, sports, popular information, childcare, health. *The Free Press.* College texts and professional books in social sciences, humanities. Query. Royalty.

MACMURRAY & BECK, INC.—P.O. Box 150717, Lakewood, CO 80215. Frederick Ramey, Exec. Dir. Quality fiction and nonfiction. Royalty.

MADISON BOOKS—4720 Boston Way, Lanham, MD 20706. James E. Lyons, Pub. Full-length nonfiction: history, biography, contemporary affairs, trade reference. Query required. Royalty.

MARKOWSKI INTERNATIONAL PUBLISHERS—One Oakglade Cir., Hummelstown, PA 17036. Michael A. Markowski, Ed. Nonfiction, from 30,000 words: popular health and fitness, marriage and human relations, human development, self-help, personal growth, sales and marketing, leadership training, network marketing, motivation and success. Also various aviation and model aviation topics. "We are interested in how-to, motivational, and instructional books of short to medium length that will serve recognized and emerging needs of society." Query with outline and three sample chapters. Royalty.

MCELDERRY BOOKS, MARGARET K.—Simon & Schuster Children's Publishing Division 15 Columbus Circle, New York, NY 10023. Margaret K. McElderry, Ed. Picture books; quality fiction, including fantasy, science fiction, beginning chapter books, humor, realism; and nonfiction.

MEADOWBROOK PRESS—18318 Minnetonka Blvd., Deephaven, MN 55391. Attn: Ed. Dept. Upbeat, useful books, 60,000 words, on pregnancy, childbirth, and parenting; shorter works of humor, party planning, children's activities. Query with outline, sample chapters, and qualifications. Royalty or flat fee.

MEGA-BOOKS OF NEW YORK—116 E. 19th St., New York, NY 10003. Carol Gilbert, Man. Ed. Book packager. Young adult books, 150 pages, children's books. Query for guidelines. SASE with resumé. Flat fee.

MENTOR BOOKS—Imprint of Penguin USA, 375 Hudson St., New York, NY 10014. Attn: Eds. Nonfiction originals for the college and high school market. Query required. Royalty.

MERCURY HOUSE—201 Filbert St., Suite 400, San Francisco, CA 94133. Thomas Christensen, Exec. Ed. Quality fiction and nonfiction (international politics, literary travel, environment, philosophy/personal growth, and performing arts). Query with outline, sample chapters, and SASE. Limited fiction market.

MEREDITH CORP. BOOK GROUP—(*Better Homes and Gardens Books*) 1716 Locust St., Des Moines, IA 50309–3023. Nancy Green, Exec. Ed. Books on gardening, crafts, health, decorating, etc., mostly staff-written. "Interested in freelance writers with expertise in these areas." Limited market. Query with SASE.

MESSNER, JULIAN—Paramount Communications, 250 James St., Morristown, NJ 07046. John Doolings, Assoc. Pub. Curriculum-oriented nonfiction. General nonfiction, ages 8 to 14: science, nature, biography, history, and hobbies. Lengths vary. Royalty.

THE MICHIGAN STATE UNIVERSITY PRESS—1405 S. Harrison Rd., Suite 25, E. Lansing, MI 48823–5202. Attn: Ed. Dept. Scholarly nonfiction, with concentrations in history, regional history, African sources, business, and Civil War. Submit prospectus, table of contents, and sample chapters to Editor-in-Chief. Authors should refer to *The Chicago Manual of Style, 14th Edition*, for formats and styles.

MILKWEED EDITIONS—430 First Ave. N., Suite 400, Minneapolis, MN 55401–1743. Emilie Buchwald, Ed. "We publish excellent award-winning fiction, poetry, essays, and nonfiction, the kind of writing that makes for good reading." Publishes about 12 books a year. Query with sample chapters. Royalty. Also publishes *Milkweeds for Young Readers*: novels and biographies for middle grades.

THE MILLBROOK PRESS—2 Old New Milford Rd., Brookfield, CT 06804. Tricia Bauer, Manuscript Coord. Nonfiction for early elementary grades through grades 7 and up, appropriate for the school and public library market, encompassing curriculum-related topics and extracurricular interests. Query with outline and sample chapter. Royalty.

MILLS & SANDERSON, PUBLISHERS—41 North Rd., #201, Bedford, MA 01730–1021. Jan H. Anthony, Pub. Books, 250 pages, on family problem-solving. Query. Royalty.

MINSTREL BOOKS—Imprint of Pocket Books, 1230 Ave. of the Americas, New York, NY 10020. Patricia MacDonald, Ed. Dir. Middle-grade fiction and nonfiction for ages 7 to 11. Scary stories, fantasies, school stories, adventures, animal stories; no picture books. Send query, outline, sample chapters to Attn: Manuscript Proposals.

THE MIT PRESS—55 Hayward St., Cambridge, MA 02142. Attn: Acquisitions Dept. Books on computer science/artificial intelligence; cognitive sciences; economics; architecture; aesthetic and social theory; linguistics; technology studies; environmental studies; and neuroscience.

MODAN PUBLISHING—P.O. Box 1202, Bellmore, NY 11710. Bennett Shelkowitz, Man. Dir. Adult nonfiction. Young adult fiction and nonfiction. Children's picture books. Books with international focus or related to political or social issues. Judaica and Hebrew books from Israel, *Adama Books*.

MOON HANDBOOKS—Moon Publications, Inc., 330 Wall St., #1, Chico, CA 95928. Taran March, Exec. Ed. Travel guides, 400 to 600 pages. Will consider multiple submissions. Query. Royalty.

MOREHOUSE PUBLISHING—871 Ethan Allen Hwy., Suite 204, Ridgefield, CT 06877. Deborah Grahame-Smith, Ed. E. Allen Kelley, Pub. Theology, pastoral care, church administration, spirituality, Anglican studies, history of religion, books for children, youth, elders, etc. Query with outline, contents, and sample chapter. SASE required. Royalty.

MORRIS, JOSHUA—See *Reader's Digest Young Families, Inc.*

MORROW AND CO., INC., WILLIAM—1350 Ave. of the Americas, New York, NY 10019. Attn: Eds. Adult fiction and nonfiction: no unsolicited manuscripts. *Beech Tree Books* and *Mulberry Books* (children's paperbacks), Amy Cohn, Ed. Dir.; *Hearst Books* (general nonfiction) and *Hearst Marine Books*, Ann Bramsom, Ed. Dir.; *Morrow Junior Books* (children's books for all ages), David Reuther, Ed.-in-Chief.

MOUNTAIN PRESS PUBLISHING—1301 S. 3rd W., P.O. Box 2399, Missoula, MT 59806. Attn: John Rimel. Nonfiction, 300 pages: natural history, field guides, geology, horses, Western history, Americana, outdoor guides, and fur trade lore. Query with outline and sample chapters; multiple queries considered. Royalty.

THE MOUNTAINEERS BOOKS—1011 S.W. Klickitat Way, Suite 107, Seattle, WA 98134. Margaret Foster, Ed./Acquisitions Mgr. Nonfiction books on noncompetitive aspects of outdoor sports such as mountaineering, backpacking, walking, trekking, canoeing, kayaking, bicycling, skiing; independent adventure travel. Field guides, how-to and where-to guidebooks, biographies of outdoor people; accounts of expeditions. Natural history and conservation. Submit sample chapters and outline. Royalty.

MUIR PUBLICATIONS, JOHN—P.O. Box 613, Santa Fe, NM 87504-0613. Ken Luboff, Ed. Travel guidebooks for adults. Nonfiction books for children, 8 to 12, primarily in the areas of science and intercultural issues. Send manuscript or query with sample chapters. No fiction. Royalty or work for hire.

MULBERRY BOOKS—See *William Morrow and Co.*

MUSTANG PUBLISHING CO., INC.—Box 3004, Memphis, TN 38173. Rollin A. Riggs, Ed. Nonfiction for 18- to 40-year-olds, specializing in travel, humor, and how-to. Send queries for 100- to 300-page books, with outlines and sample chapters. Royalty. SASE required.

THE MYSTERIOUS PRESS—Imprint of Warner Books, Time and Life Bldg., 1271 Ave. of the Americas, New York, NY 10020. William Malloy, Ed.-in-Chief. Mystery/suspense novels. Agented manuscripts only.

NAIAD PRESS, INC.—Box 10543, Tallahassee, FL 32302. Barbara Grier, Ed. Adult fiction, 52,000 to 60,000 words, with lesbian themes and characters: mysteries, romances, gothics, ghost stories, westerns, regencies, spy novels, etc. Query with letter and one-page précis only. Royalty.

NATIONAL PRESS—7200 Wisconsin Ave., Suite 212, Bethesda, MD 20814. Talia Greenberg, Ed. Nonfiction: history, criminology, reference and health; parenting; business, management, and automotive titles (*Plain English Press*). Query with outline and sample chapters. Royalty.

NATUREGRAPH PUBLISHERS—P.O. Box 1075, Happy Camp, CA 96039. Barbara Brown, Ed. Nonfiction: Native-American culture, natural history, outdoor living, land, gardening, health, Indian lore, and how-to. Query. Royalty.

THE NAVAL INSTITUTE PRESS—Annapolis, MD 21402. Attn: Ed. Dept. Nonfiction, 60,000 to 100,000 words: military histories; biographies; ship guides; how-tos on boating and navigation. Occasional fiction, 75,000 to 110,000 words. Query with outline and sample chapters. Royalty.

NELSON, INC., THOMAS—Nelson Pl. at Elm Hill Pike, P.O. Box 141000, Nashville, TN 37214–1000. Attn: Submissions Ed. Religious and secular fiction and nonfiction for adults. Fiction and nonfiction for teens. Query with outline, sample chapter, and SASE.

NEW DISCOVERY BOOKS—See *Simon & Schuster Children's Publishing Division.*

NEW LEAF PRESS, INC.—P.O. Box 311, Green Forest, AR 72638. Jim Fletcher, Acquisitions Ed. Nonfiction, 100 to 400 pages, for Christian readers: self-help, how to live the Christian life, devotionals, gift books. Query with outline and sample chapters, or submit complete manuscript. Royalty.

THE NEW PRESS—450 W. 41st St., New York, NY 10036. Andre Schiffrin, Dir. Serious nonfiction: history, economics, education, politics. Fiction in translation. Query required.

NEW READERS PRESS—1320 Jamesville Ave., Box 131, Syracuse, NY 13210. Jennifer Lashley, Office Mgr. Fiction and nonfiction, 5,000 to 9,000 words, and poetry for adults who read at low levels, for use in adult basic education programs, volunteer literacy organizations, and job training programs. Query with outline, synopsis, and sample chapters. Read guidelines first. Do not submit material for juvenile or teenage readers. Royalty or flat fee.

NEW RIVERS PRESS—420 N. 5th St., Suite 910, Minneapolis, MN 55401. C.W. Truesdale, Ed./Pub. Collections of short stories, essays, and poems from emerging writers in Upper Midwest. Query.

NEW SOCIETY PUBLISHERS—4527 Springfield Ave., Philadelphia, PA 19143. Attn: Ed. Dept. Nonfiction books on fundamental social change through nonviolent social action. Request guidelines before submitting proposal. SASE required.

NEW WORLD LIBRARY—58 Paul Dr., San Rafael, CA 94903. Attn: Submissions Ed. Nonfiction, especially leading-edge inspirational/self-help books, enlightened business, Native American, classic wisdom, environmental awareness. "Aim for intelligent, aware audience, interested in personal and planetary transformation." Query with outline and SASE. Multiple queries accepted. Royalty.

NEW YORK UNIVERSITY PRESS—70 Washington Sq. S., New York, NY 10012. Niko Pfund, Ed.-in-Chief. Scholarly nonfiction. Submit manuscript and/or proposal with sample chapters and curriculum vitae.

NEWCASTLE PUBLISHING—13419 Saticoy St., N. Hollywood, CA 91605. Al Saunders, Pub. Nonfiction manuscripts, 200 to 250 pages, for older adults on personal health, health care issues, and relationships. "We are not looking for fads or trends. We want books with a long shelf life." Multiple queries considered. Royalty.

NEWMARKET PRESS—18 E. 48th St., New York, NY 10017. Esther Margolis, Pub. Nonfiction on health, psychology, self-help, child care, parenting, music, and film. Query required. Royalty.

784

NORTH COUNTRY PRESS—P.O. Box 440, Belfast, ME 04915. William M. Johnson, Pub. Nonfiction with a Maine and/or New England tie-in with emphasis on the outdoors; also limited fiction (Maine-based mystery). "Our goal is to publish high-quality books for people who love New England." Query with SASE, outline, and sample chapters. No unsolicited manuscripts. Royalty.

NORTHLAND PUBLISHING—P.O. Box 1389, Flagstaff, AZ 86001. Erin Murphy, Ed. Nonfiction books on natural history; fine arts; Native-American culture, myth, art, and crafts; and cookbooks. Unique children's books, to 1,500 words, preferably with a Southwest/West regional theme. Query with outline, sample chapter, potential market for proposed book, and SASE for adult books. For children's books, send complete manuscript. Royalty.

NORTHWORD PRESS, INC.—Box 1360, 7520 Highway 51, Minocqua, WI 54548. Donna F. Lebrecht, Ed. Nonfiction nature and wildlife books, from 25,000 words. Send for catalogue. Royalty or flat fee.

NORTON AND CO., INC., W.W.—500 Fifth Ave., New York, NY 10110. Liz Malcolm, Ed. High-quality fiction and nonfiction. No occult, paranormal, religious, genre fiction (formula romance, science fiction, westerns), cookbooks, arts and crafts, young adult, or children's books. Query with synopsis, 2 to 3 chapters (including first chapter), and resumé. Return postage and packaging required. Royalty.

ODYSSEY PAPERBACKS—See *Harcourt Brace.*

THE OLIVER PRESS—Josiah King House, 2709 Lyndale Ave. S., Minneapolis, MN 55408. James Satter, Ed. Collective biographies for young adults. Submit proposals for books, 20,000 words, on people who have made an impact in such areas as history, politics, crime, science, and business. Flat fee (approximately $1,000).

OPEN COURT PUBLISHING CO.—Box 599, Peru, IL 61354. Attn: Ed. Dept. Scholarly books on philosophy, psychology, religion, eastern thought, history, public policy, education, science, and related topics. Send sample chapters with outline and resumé. Royalty.

OPEN HAND PUBLISHING—P.O. Box 22048, Seattle, WA 98122. P. Anna Johnson, Pub. Books that reflect the diverse cultures within the United States, with emphasis upon the African American. "Our mission is to publish books which will promote positive social change as well as better understanding between all people." Submit complete manuscript. Royalty.

ORCHARD BOOKS—95 Madison Ave., New York, NY 10016. Neal Porter, Pres./Pub. Hardcover picture books. Fiction for middle grades and young adults. Nonfiction and photo essays for young children. Submit complete manuscript. Royalty.

OREGON STATE UNIVERSITY PRESS—101 Waldo Hall, Corvallis, OR 97331. Attn: Ed. Dept. Scholarly books in a limited range of disciplines and books of particular importance to the Pacific Northwest. Query with summary.

OSBORNE/MCGRAW HILL—2600 Tenth St., Berkeley, CA 94710. Jeffrey M. Pepper, Ed.-in-Chief. Microcomputer books for general audience. Query. Royalty.

OUR SUNDAY VISITOR PUBLISHING—200 Noll Plaza, Huntington, IN 46750. Mary Machall, Ed. Asst. Catholic-oriented books of various lengths. No fiction. Query with outline and sample chapters. Royalty.

THE OVERLOOK PRESS—149 Wooster St., New York, NY 10012. Tracy Carns, Ed. Dir. Literary fiction, some fantasy/science fiction, foreign literature in translation, general nonfiction, including art, architecture, design, film, history, biography, crafts/lifestyle, martial arts, Hudson Valley regional interest, and children's books. Query with outline and sample chapters. Royalty.

OWEN PUBLISHERS, INC., RICHARD C.—P.O. Box 585, Katonah, NY 10536. Janice Boland, Ed., Dept. TW. Fiction and nonfiction. Brief storybooks, approximately 45 to 100 words, suitable for 5-, 6-, and 7-year-old beginning readers for the "Ready to Read" program. Royalties for writers. Flat fee for illustrators. Writers must send SASE for guidelines before submitting.

OXFORD UNIVERSITY PRESS—200 Madison Ave., New York, NY 10016. Attn: Ed. Dept. Authoritative books on literature, history, philosophy, etc.; college textbooks, medical, scientific, technical and reference books. Query. Royalty.

PACER BOOKS FOR YOUNG ADULTS—Imprint of Berkley Publishing Group, 200 Madison Ave., New York, NY 10016. Melinda Metz, Ed. Fiction: horror, suspense, romance, and role-playing fantasy gamebooks. No unsolicited manuscripts; queries only. Paperback only.

PANTHEON BOOKS—Div. of Random House, 201 E. 50th St., New York, NY 10022. Attn: Ed. Dept. Quality fiction and nonfiction. Query required. Royalty.

PAPIER-MACHE PRESS—135 Aviation Way, #14, Watsonville, CA 95076. Sandra Martz, Ed. Fiction, poetry, and nonfiction books; 4 to 6 books annually. "We emphasize, but are not limited to, the publication of books and related items for midlife and older women." Write for guidelines. Query. Royalty for single-author books; pays in copies for anthologies, plus royalty if book goes into second printing.

PARA PUBLISHING—P.O. Box 4232, Santa Barbara, CA 93140–4232. Dan Poynter, Ed. Adult nonfiction books on parachutes and skydiving only. Author must present evidence of having made at least 1,000 jumps. Query. Royalty.

PARAGON HOUSE—370 Lexington Ave., New York, NY 10017. Michael Giampaoli, Pub. Serious nonfiction, including history, reference, literature, philosophy, religion, and current affairs. Query. Royalty.

PARENTING PRESS—#F, P.O. Box 75267, Seattle, WA 98125. John Shoemaker, Ed. Choice-oriented parenting books, 112 pages. Skill-building and problem-solving children's books, 30 to 60 pages. "Send SASE for guidelines, then query with outline and sample chapters." Royalty.

PASSPORT BOOKS—4255 W. Touhy Ave., Lincolnwood, IL 60646–1975. Constance Rajala, Ed. Dir. Adult nonfiction, 200 to 400 pages, picture books up to 120 pages, and juvenile nonfiction. Send outline and sample chapters for books on foreign language, travel, and culture. Multiple queries considered. Royalty and flat fee.

PEACHTREE PUBLISHERS, LTD.—494 Armour Cir. N.E., Atlanta, GA 30324. Attn: Ed. Dept. Wide variety of children's books, humor, fiction and nonfiction. No religious material, science fiction/fantasy, romance, mystery/detective, historical fiction; no business, scientific, or technical books. Send outline and sample chapters. SASE required. Royalty. No unsolicited submissions at this time.

PELICAN PUBLISHING CO., INC.—1101 Monroe St., Gretna, LA 70053. Nina Kooij, Ed. General nonfiction: Americana, regional, architecture, how-to, travel, cookbooks. Royalty.

PELION PRESS—See *Rosen Publishing Group.*

PENGUIN BOOKS—Imprint of Penguin USA, 375 Hudson St., New York, NY 10014. Attn: Ed. Dept. Adult fiction and nonfiction paperbacks. Royalty.

PENZLER BOOKS, OTTO—See *Scribner.*

PEREGRINE SMITH BOOKS—Imprint of Gibbs Smith, P.O. Box 667, Layton, UT 84041. Madge Baird, Ed. Dir. Juvenile books. Fiction picture books, to 3,000 words, and nonfiction picture books, to 4,000 words, as well as chapter books, to 10,000 words, for children ages 5 to 11: western/cowboy, activity, how-to, nature and environment, and biography and ethnic. Query with sample chapters or send complete manuscript. Royalty.

THE PERMANENT PRESS—Noyac Rd., Sag Harbor, NY 11963. Judith Shepard, Ed. Seeks original and arresting novels, biographies. Query. Royalty.

PERSPECTIVES PRESS—P.O. Box 90318, Indianapolis, IN 46290–0318. Pat Johnston, Pub. Books on infertility, adoption, closely related child welfare issues (foster care, etc.), and reproductive health. Also picture books, 32 pages, for children up to 10 years old. "Writers must read our guidelines before submitting." Query. Royalty.

PHILOMEL BOOKS—Div. of The Putnam & Grosset Group, 200 Madison Ave., New York, NY 10016. Patricia Lee Gauch, Ed. Dir. Paula Wiseman, Ed.-in.-Chief. Juvenile picture books, young adult fiction, and some biographies. Fresh, original work with compelling characters and "a truly childlike spirit." Query required.

PINEAPPLE PRESS—P.O. Drawer 16008, Southside Sta., Sarasota, FL 34239. June Cussen, Ed. Serious fiction and nonfiction, Florida-oriented, 60,000 to 125,000 words. Query with outline, sample chapters, and SASE. Royalty.

PINNACLE BOOKS—Imprint of Kensington Publishing Corp., 850 Third Ave., New York, NY 10022. Paul Dinas, Ed. Nonfiction books: true crime, celebrity biographies, and humor. Romance: alternative romances; romance from a man's point of view; multicultural romances. Send synopsis and sample chapters. Royalty.

PIPPIN PRESS—229 E. 85th St., Gracie Sta., Box 1347, New York, NY 10028. Barbara Francis, Pub. High-quality picture books for preschoolers; small chapter books for ages 6 to 10, emphasizing humor and fantasy, humorous mysteries; imaginative nonfiction for children of all ages. Query with SASE. Royalty.

PLAIN ENGLISH PRESS—See *National Press.*

PLAYERS PRESS, INC.—P.O. Box 1132, Studio City, CA 91614. Robert Gordon, Ed. Plays and musicals for children and adults; juvenile and adult nonfiction related to theatre, film, television, and the performing arts. Lengths vary. Query. Royalty.

PLENUM PUBLISHING CORP.—233 Spring St., New York, NY 10013. Linda Greenspan Regan, Sr. Ed. Trade nonfiction, approximately 300 pages, on popular science, criminology, psychology, sociology, anthropology, and health. Query required. Royalty. Hardcover.

PLUME BOOKS—Imprint of Penguin USA, 375 Hudson St., New York, NY 10014. Attn: Ed. Dept. Nonfiction: hobbies, business, health, cooking, child care, psychology, history, popular culture, biography, and politics. Fiction: serious literary and gay. Query.

POCKET BOOKS—A Paramount Communications Co., 1230 Ave. of the Americas, New York, NY 10020. No unsolicited material.

787

POPULAR PRESS—Bowling Green State University, Bowling Green, OH 43403. Ms. Pat Browne, Ed. Nonfiction, 250 to 400 pages, examining some aspect of popular culture. Query with outline. Flat fee or royalty.

POTTER, CLARKSON —201 E. 50th St., New York, NY 10022. Lauren Shakely, Ed.-in-Chief. General trade books. Submissions accepted through agents only.

PRAEGER PUBLISHERS—Imprint of Greenwood Publishing Group, 88 Post Rd. W., Westport, CT 06880–4232. James Dunton, Pub. General nonfiction; scholarly and text books. Query with outline. Royalty.

PRENTICE HALL PRESS—A Paramount Communications Co., 15 Columbus Circle, New York, NY 10023. Attn: Ed. Dept. General reference and travel books. Query required. Royalty.

PRESIDIO PRESS—505B San Marin Dr., Suite 300, Novato, CA 94945–1340. Attn: Ed. Dept. Nonfiction: military history and military affairs, from 90,000 words. Fiction: selected military and action-adventure works and mysteries, from 100,000 words. Query. Royalty.

PRICE STERN SLOAN, INC.—11150 Olympic Blvd., Los Angeles, CA 90064. Attn: Ed. Dept. Children's books; adult trade nonfiction, including humor and calendars. Imprint includes *Troubador Press.* Query with SASE required. Royalty.

PRIMA PUBLISHING—P.O. Box 1260, Rocklin, CA 95677. Ben Dominitz, Pub. Jennifer Basye, Ed. Nonfiction on variety of subjects, including business, health, and cookbooks. "We want books with originality, written by highly qualified individuals." Royalty.

PROMPT PUBLICATIONS—An imprint of Howard W. Sams & Co., 2647 Waterfront Pkwy. E. Dr., Suite 300, Indianapolis, IN 46214–2041. Attn: Acquisitions Ed. Nonfiction softcover technical books on electronics, how-to, troubleshooting and repair, electrical engineering, video and sound equipment, cellular technology, etc., for all levels of technical experience. Query with outline, sample chapters, author bio, and SASE. Royalty.

PRUETT PUBLISHING COMPANY—2928 Pearl, Boulder, CO 80301. Jim Pruett, Pres. Nonfiction: outdoors and recreation, western U.S. history, travel, natural history and the environment, fly fishing. Query. Royalty.

PUFFIN BOOKS—Imprint of Penguin USA, 375 Hudson St., New York, NY 10014. Attn: Ed. Dept. Children's fiction and nonfiction paperbacks. Query with SASE. Royalty.

PUTNAM'S SONS, G.P.—200 Madison Ave., New York, NY 10016. Attn: Ed. Dept. General trade nonfiction, fiction. Query Arthur Levine, Ed.-in-Chief, for children's books. No unsolicited manuscripts. Royalty.

QUEST BOOKS—Imprint of The Theosophical Publishing House, 306 W. Geneva Rd., P. O. Box 270, Wheaton, IL 60189–0270. Brenda Rosen, Sr. Ed. Nonfiction books on Eastern and Western religion and philosophy, holism, healing, transpersonal psychology, men's and women's spirituality, Native-American spirituality, meditation, yoga, ancient wisdom. Query. Royalty.

QUILL TRADE PAPERBACKS—Imprint of William Morrow and Co., Inc., 1350 Ave. of the Americas, New York, NY 10019. Andrew Dutter, Ed. Trade paperback adult nonfiction. Submit through agent only.

RAGGED MOUNTAIN PRESS—Box 220, Camden, ME 04843. Jonathan Eaton, Ed. Dir. James Barb, Acquisitions Ed. Books on outdoor recreation.

RAINTREE STECK-VAUGHN PUBLISHERS—Div. of Steck-Vaughn Co., National Education Corp., 466 Southern Blvd., Chatham, NJ 07928. Walter Kossmann, Ed. Nonfiction books, 5,000 to 30,000 words, for school and library market: biographies for grades 3 and up; and science, social studies, and history books for primary grades through high school. Query with outline and sample chapters; SASE required. Flat fee and royalty.

RANDOM HOUSE, INC.—201 E. 50th St., New York, NY 10022. Attn: Ed. Dept. General fiction and nonfiction. Query with three chapters and outline for nonfiction; complete manuscript for fiction. SASE required. Royalty.

RANDOM HOUSE JUVENILE DIV.—201 E. 50th St., New York, NY 10022. Kate Klimo, Ed.-in-Chief. Fiction and nonfiction for beginning readers; paperback fiction line for 7- to 9-year-olds. No unsolicited manuscripts. Agented material only.

READER'S DIGEST YOUNG FAMILIES, INC.—221 Danbury Rd., Wilton, CT 06897. Willy Derraugh, Pub. Children's books for readers ages 2 to 11. Imprints include: *Reader's Digest Kids,* high-quality, fully illustrated information and reference books; *Joshua Morris,* imaginative and uniquely formatted novelty books and book kits, with an emphasis on information and learning; *Wishing Well,* novelty formats. Address submissions to an imprint's Acquisitions Ed.

THE RED SEA PRESS—11-D Princess Rd., Suites D, E, F, Lawrenceville, NJ 08648. Kassahun Checole, Pub. Adult nonfiction, 360 double-spaced manuscript pages. "We focus on nonfiction material with a specialty on the Horn of Africa." Query. Royalty.

REGNERY PUBLISHING, INC.—(formerly *Regnery Gateway*) 422 First St. S.E., Suite 300, Washington, DC 20003. Attn: Ed. Dept. Nonfiction books on public policy. Query. Royalty.

RENAISSANCE HOUSE—541 Oak St., P. O. Box 177, Frederick, CO 80530. Eleanor H. Ayer, Ed. Regional guidebooks. Currently publishing guidebooks on Colorado, Arizona, California, and the Southwest. "We use only manuscripts written to our specifications for new or ongoing series." Submit outline and short bio. Royalty.

RISING TIDE PRESS—5 Kivy St., Huntington Sta., New York, NY 11746. Lee Boojamra, Ed. Books for, by, and about lesbians. Fiction, 60,000 to 70,000 words: romance, mystery, and science fiction/fantasy. Nonfiction, 40,000 to 60,000 words. Royalty. Reports in 3 months.

RIZZOLI INTERNATIONAL PUBLICATIONS, INC.—300 Park Ave. S., New York, NY 10010. Manuela Soares, Children's Book Ed. Seeks manuscripts that introduce children to fine art, folk art, and architecture of all cultures for a small, specialized list. Publishes nonfiction and fiction for all ages. "Particularly interested in stories that can be illustrated with museum art. Fiction should use storytelling as a way of putting art and culture into a vivid, exciting context for kids." Query with SASE or response card. Royalty.

ROC—Imprint of Penguin USA, 375 Hudson St., New York, NY 10014. Amy Stout, Exec. Ed. Science fiction, fantasy; some horror. Query.

RODALE PRESS—33 E. Minor St., Emmaus, PA 18098. Pat Corpora, Pub. Books on health, gardening, homeowner projects, cookbooks, inspirational topics, pop psychology, woodworking, natural history. Query with outline and sample chapter. Royalty and outright purchase. In addition: "We're always looking for truly competent free lancers to write chapters for books conceived and developed in-house"; payment on a work-for-hire basis; address Bill Gottlieb, V.P.

ROSEN PUBLISHING GROUP—29 E. 21st St., New York, NY 10010. Roger Rosen, Pres. Gina Strazzabosco, Ed. Young adult books, 8,000 to 40,000 words, on career and personal guidance, journalism, self-help, etc. *Pelion Press*: music, art, history. Pays varying rates.

ROYAL FIREWORKS PRESS—1 First Ave., Unionville, NY 10988. Charles Morgan, Ed. Adult science fiction and mysteries. Juvenile and young adult fiction, biography, and educational nonfiction. Submit complete manuscripts. No multiple queries. Royalty.

RUNNING PRESS—125 S. 22nd St., Philadelphia, PA 19103. Attn: Exec. Ed. Trade nonfiction: art, craft, how-to, self-help, science, lifestyles. Children's books and interactive packages. Query. Royalty.

RUTLEDGE HILL PRESS—211 Seventh Ave. N., Nashville, TN 37217. Ronald E. Pitkin, V.P. Southern-interest fiction and market-specific nonfiction. Query with outline and sample chapters. Royalty.

ST. ANTHONY MESSENGER PRESS—1615 Republic St., Cincinnati, OH 45210–1298. Lisa Biedenbach, Man. Ed. Inspirational nonfiction for Catholics, supporting a Christian lifestyle in our culture; prayer aids, education, practical spirituality, parish ministry, liturgy resources. Query with 500-word summary. Royalty.

ST. MARTIN'S PRESS—175 Fifth Ave., New York, NY 10010. Attn: Ed. Dept. General adult fiction and nonfiction. Query. Royalty.

SANDLAPPER PUBLISHING, INC.—P.O. Drawer 730, Orangeburg, SC 29116–0730. Amanda Gallman, Book Ed. Nonfiction books on South Carolina history, culture, cuisine. Query with outline, sample chapters, and SASE.

SASQUATCH BOOKS—1008 Western Ave., #300, Seattle, WA 98104. Attn: Ed. Dept. Regional books by West Coast authors on a wide range of nonfiction topics: travel, natural history, gardening, cooking, history, children's and public affairs. Books must have a West Coast angle. Query with SASE. Royalty.

SCARECROW PRESS—P.O. Box 4167, Metuchen, NJ 08840. Norman Horrocks, V.P./Editorial. Reference works and bibliographies, from 150 pages, especially in the areas of cinema, TV, radio, and theater, mainly for use by libraries. Query or send complete manuscript; multiple queries considered. Royalty.

SCHOCKEN BOOKS—Div. of Pantheon Books, 201 E. 50th St., New York, NY 10022. Attn: Ed. Dept. General nonfiction: Judaica, women's studies, education, art history. Query with outline and sample chapter. Royalty.

SCHOLASTIC, INC.—555 Broadway, New York, NY 10012. No unsolicited manuscripts.

SCHOLASTIC PROFESSIONAL BOOKS—411 Lafayette St., New York, NY 10003. Attn: Shawn Richardson. Books by and for teachers of kindergarten through eighth grade. *Instructor Books*: practical, activity/resource books on teaching reading, science, math, etc. *Teaching Strategies Books*: 64 to 96 pages on new ideas, practices, and approaches to teaching. Query with outline, sample chapters or activities, contents page, and resumé. Flat fee or royalty. Multiple queries considered. SASE for guidelines.

SCOTT, FORESMAN AND CO.—1900 E. Lake Ave., Glenview, IL 60025. Kate Nyquist, Pres. Elementary and secondary textbooks. Royalty or flat fee.

SCRIBNER—(formerly *Charles Scribner's Sons*) A Div. of Paramount Publishing Consumer Group, 866 Third Ave., New York, NY 10022. Attn: Ed. Dept. Fiction, general nonfiction, science, history, mysteries, and biography; query. Books for Young Readers: fantasy, mystery, science fiction, and problem novels; picture books for ages 5 up; and nonfiction (science and how-tos). Imprints include *Lisa Drew Books* and *Otto Penzler Books*. Query with outline and sample chapter.

SHAW PUBLISHERS, HAROLD—388 Gunderson Dr., Box 567, Wheaton, IL 60189. Ramona Cramer Tucker, Dir. of Ed. Services. Nonfiction, 120 to 220 pages, with an evangelical Christian perspective. Some teen and adult fiction and literary books. Query. Flat fee or royalty.

SHEARWATER BOOKS—See *Island Press.*

SIERRA CLUB BOOKS—100 Bush St., San Francisco, CA 94104. Attn: Ed. Dept. Nonfiction: environment, natural history, the sciences, outdoors and regional guidebooks, nature photography; juvenile fiction and nonfiction. Query with SASE. Royalty.

SIGNATURE BOOKS, INC.—564 West 400 North, Salt Lake City, UT 84116. Attn: Board of Dirs. Adult fiction and nonfiction, from 100 pages. Adult poetry from 80 pages. Royalty.

SIGNET BOOKS AND SIGNET CLASSIC—Imprint of Penguin USA, 375 Hudson St., New York, NY 10014. Attn: Ed. Dept. Commercial fiction (historicals, sagas, thrillers, action/adventure novels, westerns) and nonfiction (self-help, how-to, true crime, etc.). Royalty.

SILHOUETTE BOOKS—300 E. 42nd St., New York, NY 10017. Isabel Swift, Ed. Dir. *Silhouette Romances*: Anne Canadeo, Sr. Ed. Contemporary romances, 53,000 to 58,000 words. *Special Edition*: Tara Gavin, Sr. Ed. Sophisticated contemporary romances, 75,000 to 80,000 words. *Silhouette Desire*: Lucia Macro, Sr. Ed. Sensuous contemporary romances, 53,000 to 60,000 words. *Intimate Moments*: Leslie Wainger, Sr. Ed./Ed. Coord. Sensuous, exciting contemporary romances, 80,000 to 85,000 words. *Silhouette Shadows*: Contemporary gothic style romances, 70,000 to 75,000 words. *Historical romance*: 95,000 to 105,000 words, and more; query with synopsis and 3 sample chapters to Tracy Farrell, Sr. Ed. Query with synopsis and SASE to appropriate editor. Tipsheets available.

SILVER MOON PRESS—126 Fifth Ave., Suite 803, New York, NY 10011. Theresa Desmond, Ed. Juvenile titles for a multicultural audience, ages 6 to 9 and 8 to 12. Historical fiction, 64 to 80 pages, and books on science also considered. Query with outline; multiple queries acceptable. Payment varies.

SIMON & SCHUSTER—A Div. of Paramount Publishing Consumer Group, 1230 Ave. of the Americas, New York, NY 10020. Adult books: No unsolicited material.

SIMON & SCHUSTER CHILDREN'S PUBLISHING DIVISION—A Div. of Paramount Publishing Consumer Group, 1230 Ave. of the Americas, New York, NY 10020. Stephanie Owens Lurie, V.P./Ed. Dir. Books for ages preschool through high school: picture books to young adult; nonfiction for all age levels.

Hardcover only. Imprints include: *Aladdin Books, Bradbury Press, Collier Books for Young Adults, Crestwood House, Dillon Press, Four Winds Press, Green Tiger Press* and *New Discovery Books*. Send complete manuscript for picture books; synopsis and 3 chapters for novels; query for nonfiction. SASE required for reply.

SINGER MEDIA CORP.—Seaview Business Park, 1030 Calle Cordillera, #106, San Clemente, CA 92673. Kurt Singer, Pres. Foreign reprint rights to books in fields of business, management, self-help, romance and mysteries, psychology, and documentary videos. Royalty.

SKYLARK BOOKS—See *Yearling Books.*

THE SMITH—69 Joralemon St., Brooklyn, NY 11201. Harry Smith, Ed. Fiction and nonfiction, from 64 pages, and poetry, 48 to 112 pages. "While publishing at a high level of craftsmanship, we have pursued the increasingly difficult, expensive and now relatively rare policy of keeping our titles in print over the decades." Query with outline and sample chapters. Royalty.

SMITH AND KRAUS, INC.—P.O. Box 10, Main St., Newbury, VT 05051. Marisa Smith, Pres. Books related to theater, including anthologies of monologues, works by modern playwrights, and career development for actors. Full-length or one-act dramas. Also, books for young actors. Send query and synopsis. Allow 3 months for response. Payment is made on acceptance and on publication.

SOHO PRESS—853 Broadway, New York, NY 10003. Juris Jurjevics, Ed. Novels, mysteries, and nonfiction, from 60,000 words. Send SASE and complete manuscript. Royalty.

SOUTHERN ILLINOIS UNIVERSITY PRESS—P.O. Box 3697, Carbondale, IL 62902–3697. Curtis L. Clark, Ed. Dir. Nonfiction in the humanities, 200 to 400 pages. Query with outline and sample chapters. Royalty.

SOUTHERN METHODIST UNIVERSITY PRESS—Box 415, Dallas, TX 75275. Kathryn Lang, Sr. Ed. Serious literary fiction. Nonfiction: scholarly studies in religion, medical ethics (death and dying); film, theater; scholarly works on Texas or Southwest. No juvenile material, science fiction, or poetry. Query. Royalty.

SPECTACLE LANE PRESS—Box 34, Georgetown, CT 06829. Attn: Ed. Dept. Humor books, 500 to 5000 words, on subjects of strong, current interest, illustrated with cartoons. Buys text or text/cartoon packages. Royalty.

SPECTRA BOOKS—Imprint of Bantam Books, 1540 Broadway, New York, NY 10036. Jennifer Hershey, Exec. Ed. Tom Dupree, Ed. Science fiction and fantasy, with emphasis on storytelling and characterization. Query with SASE; no unsolicited manuscripts. Royalty.

STANDARD PUBLISHING—8121 Hamilton Ave., Cincinnati, OH 45231. Attn: Acquisitions Coord. Fiction: juveniles based on Bible or with moral tone. Christian education. Conservative evangelical.

STANFORD UNIVERSITY PRESS—Stanford Univ., Stanford, CA 94305–2235. Norris Pope, Ed. "For the most part, we publish academic scholarship." No original fiction or poetry. Query with outline and sample chapters. Royalty.

STARLING LINE—See *Crystal River Press.*

STEERFORTH PRESS—105–106 Chelsea St., Box 70, S. Royalton, VT 05068. Attn: Ed. Dept. Adult fiction and nonfiction; no specific category or field. "Our test of a book's worth is whether it has been written well, is intended to engage the full attention of the reader, and has something new or important to say." Query. Royalty.

STEMMER HOUSE PUBLISHERS, INC.—2627 Caves Rd., Owings Mills, MD 21117. Barbara Holdridge, Ed. Juvenile picture books and adult nonfiction. Specializes in art, design, cookbooks, children's, and horticultural titles. Query with SASE. Royalty.

STERLING PUBLISHING CO., INC.—387 Park Ave. S., New York, NY 10016. Sheila Anne Barry, Acquisitions Mgr. How-to, hobby, woodworking, health, fiber arts, craft, wine, nature, oddities, new age, puzzles, juvenile humor and activities, juvenile science, medieval history, Celtic topics, gardening, alternative lifestyle, business, pets, recreation, sports and games books, reference, and military topics. Query with outline, sample chapter, and sample illustrations. Royalty.

STONEYDALE PRESS—205 Main St., Drawer B, Stevensville, MT 59870. Dale A. Burk, Ed. Adult nonfiction, primarily how-to, on outdoor recreation with emphasis on big game hunting. "We're a very specialized market. Query with outline and sample chapters essential." Royalty.

STOREY COMMUNICATIONS—Schoolhouse Rd., Pownal, VT 05261. Gwen Steege, Sr. Ed. How-to books for country living. Adult books, 100 to 350 pages, on gardening, crafts, building, cooking, nature, and how-to. Juvenile nonfiction, 100 to 250 pages, on gardening, crafts, and cooking. Royalty or flat fee.

STORY LINE PRESS—Three Oaks Farm, Brownsville, OR 97327-9718. Robert McDowell, Ed. Fiction, nonfiction, and poetry of varying lengths. Query. Royalty.

STRAWBERRY HILL PRESS—3848 S.E. Division St., Portland, OR 97202-1641. Carolyn Soto, Ed. Nonfiction: biography, autobiography, history, cooking, health, how-to, philosophy, performance arts, and Third World. Query with sample chapters, outline, and SASE. Royalty.

SUNDANCE PUBLISHERS & DISTRIBUTORS—P.O. Box 1326, Newtown Rd., Littleton, MA 01460. Gare Thompson, Publisher. "We publish 'literature-based' classroom learning programs." Picture books, 16 to 48 pages; children's fiction, 64 to 120 pages; and juvenile nonfiction, 16 to 48 pages. Series include "Sundance Big Books," which illustrate multicultural characters and themes, for grades K through 2, and "Info Power," fact-based nonfiction on various subjects for grades 5 through 8. Query. Royalty or flat fee.

TSR, INC.—P.O. Box 756, Lake Geneva, WI 53147. Attn: Manuscript Ed. Epic high fantasy, gritty, action-oriented fantasy, Gothic horror, some humorous young adult fantasy, some science fiction, approx. 100,000 words. Query. Royalty.

TAB BOOKS—Prof. Book Group, McGraw-Hill, Inc., Blue Ridge Summit, PA 17294. Ron Powers, Ed. Dir. Nonfiction: electronics, computers, vocational how-to, aviation, science fair projects, business start up, science and technology, juvenile science, technician-level automotive, marine and outdoor life, military history, and engineering. Royalty or flat fee.

TAMBOURINE BOOKS—Imprint of William Morrow & Co., Inc., 1350 Ave. of the Americas, New York, NY 10019. Paulette C. Kaufmann, V.P./Ed.-in-Chief. Picture books, fiction, and nonfiction for all ages in general trade market. "We hope to find new talented writers and illustrators who are working outside the New York area."

TAYLOR PUBLISHING CO.—1550 W. Mockingbird Ln., Dallas, TX 75235. Macy Jaggers, Asst. Ed. Adult nonfiction: gardening, sports and recreation, health, popular culture, parenting, home improvement, nature/outdoors. Query with outline, sample chapters, relevant author bio, and SASE. Royalty.

TEACHING STRATEGIES BOOKS—See *Scholastic Professional Books.*

TEMPLE UNIVERSITY PRESS—Broad and Oxford Sts., Philadelphia, PA 19122. Michael Ames, Ed. Adult nonfiction. Query with outline and sample chapters. Royalty.

TEN SPEED PRESS—P.O. Box 7123, Berkeley, CA 94707. Attn: Ed. Dept. Self-help and how-to on careers, recreation, etc.; natural science, history, cookbooks. Query with outline, sample chapters, and SASE. Paperback. Royalty.

THUNDER'S MOUTH PRESS—632 Broadway, 7th Fl., New York, NY 10012. Neil Ortenberg, Ed. Mainly nonfiction: current affairs, popular culture, memoirs, and biography, to 300 pages. Royalty.

TIARE PUBLICATIONS—P.O. Box 493, Lake Geneva, WI 53147. Gerry L. Dexter, Ed. Books of interest to radio hobbyists, 60,000 to 100,000 words. Practical and how-to nonfiction, *Limelight* imprint; jazz discographies and commentaries, *Balboa* imprint. Query with outline and sample chapters. Royalties.

TIMES BOOKS—Div. of Random House, Inc., 201 E. 50th St., New York, NY 10022. Steve Wasserman, Ed. Dir. General nonfiction specializing in economics, politics, science, and current affairs. No unsolicited manuscripts or queries accepted.

TO LOVE AGAIN—See *Zebra Books.*

TOPAZ—Imprint of Penguin USA, 375 Hudson St., New York, NY 10014. Attn: Eds. Historical romance. Query.

TOR BOOKS—175 Fifth Ave., 14th Fl., New York, NY 10010. Robert Gleason, Ed.-in-Chief. Patrick Nielsen Hayden, Sr. Ed., science fiction and fantasy. Melissa Ann Singer, Sr. Ed., general fiction. Books from 60,000 words. Query with outline and sample chapters. Royalty.

TRICYCLE PRESS—Imprint of *Ten Speed Press,* P.O. Box 7123, Berkeley, CA 94707. Nicole Geiger, Ed. Children's books: Picture books, submit complete manuscripts. Activity books, submit about 20 pages and complete outline. Chapter fiction, submit 3 chapters and complete outline. "Real life" books that help children cope with issues. SASE required. Responds in 10 weeks. Royalty.

TROLL ASSOCIATES—100 Corporate Dr., Mahwah, NJ 07430. M. Francis, Ed. Juvenile fiction and nonfiction. Query preferred. Royalty or flat fee.

TROUBADOR PRESS—See *Price Stern Sloan, Inc.*

TUDOR PUBLISHERS, INC.—P.O. Box 38366, Greensboro, NC 27438. Eugene E. Pfaff, Jr., Ed. Helpful nonfiction books for senior citizens, teenagers, and minorities. Young adult biographies and occasional young adult novels. Reference library titles. Occasional high-quality adult fiction. Send proposal or query with sample chapters. Royalty.

TYNDALE HOUSE—351 Executive Dr., Box 80, Wheaton, IL 60189. Ron Beers, V.P. Juvenile and adult fiction and nonfiction on subjects of concern to Christians. Picture books with religious focus for preschool and early readers. Query.

UAHC PRESS—838 Fifth Ave., New York, NY 10021. Aron Hirt-Manheimer, Ed. Religious educational titles on or related to Judaism. Adult nonfiction; juvenile picture books, fiction, nonfiction, and young adult titles. Query with outline. Royalty.

UNIVERSE PUBLISHING—300 Park Ave. S., New York, NY 10010. Susan Carpenter, Ed. Dir. Fine arts, art history, art criticism, women's studies, and children's books. Query with SASE. Royalty.

UNIVERSITY OF ALABAMA PRESS—P.O. Box 870380, Tuscaloosa, AL 35487–0380. Attn: Ed. Dept. Scholarly and general regional nonfiction. Submit to appropriate editor: Malcolm MacDonald, Ed. (history, public administration, political science); Nicole Mitchell, Ed. (English, rhetoric and communication, Judaic studies, women's studies); Judith Knight, Ed. (archaeology, anthropology). Send complete manuscript. Royalty.

UNIVERSITY OF ARIZONA PRESS—1230 N. Park Ave., Suite 102, Tucson, AZ 85719. Stephen Cox, Dir., Joanne O'Hare, Sr. Ed. Christine R. Szuter, Acquiring Ed. Amy Chapman Smith, Acquiring Ed. Scholarly and popular nonfiction: Arizona, American West, anthropology, archaeology, environmental science, Latin America, Native Americans, natural history, space sciences, women's studies. Query with outline and sample chapters or send complete manuscript. Royalty.

UNIVERSITY OF CALIFORNIA PRESS—2120 Berkeley Way, Berkeley, CA 94720. Attn: Acquisitions' Dept. Scholarly nonfiction. Query with cover letter, outline, sample chapters, curriculum vitae, and SASE.

UNIVERSITY OF GEORGIA PRESS—330 Research Dr., Athens, GA 30602–4901. Karen Orchard, Ed. Short story collections and poetry, scholarly nonfiction and literary criticism, Southern and American history, regional studies, biography and autobiography. For nonfiction, query with outline and sample chapters. Poetry collections considered in Sept. and Jan. only; short fiction in June and July only. A $10 fee is required for all poetry and fiction submissions. Royalty. SASE for competition guidelines.

UNIVERSITY OF ILLINOIS PRESS—1325 S. Oak St., Champaign, IL 61820. Richard L. Wentworth, Ed.-in-Chief. Short story collections, 140 to 180 pages; nonfiction; and poetry, 70 to 100 pages. Rarely considers multiple submissions. Query. Royalty. "Not accepting unsolicited manuscripts at this time."

UNIVERSITY OF MASSACHUSETTS PRESS—Box 429, Amherst, MA 01004–0429. Clark Dougan, Sr. Ed. Query with SASE.

UNIVERSITY OF MINNESOTA PRESS—2037 University Ave. S.E., Minneapolis, MN 55455. Biodun Iginla, Ed. Janaki Bakhle, Ed. Nonfiction: media studies, literary theory, critical aesthetics, philosophy, cultural criticism, regional titles, 50,000 to 225,000 words. Query with detailed prospectus or introduction, table of contents, sample chapter, and recent resumé. Royalty.

UNIVERSITY OF MISSOURI PRESS—2910 LeMone Blvd., Columbia, MO 65201–8227. Attn: Ed. Dept. Scholarly books on American and European history; American, British, and Latin American literary criticism; political philosophy; intellectual history; regional studies; and poetry and short fiction. Query Beverly Jarrett, Dir. and Ed.-in-Chief, for scholarly studies and creative nonfiction. Query Mr. Clair Willcox, Poetry and Fiction Editor, with 4 to 6 sample poems or one short story, table of contents for entire manuscript, and cover letter describing the work and author's professional background.

UNIVERSITY OF NEBRASKA PRESS—312 N. 14th St., Lincoln, NE 68588–0484. Attn: Eds. Specializes in the history of the American West, Native-American studies, and literary criticism. Send proposals with summary, 2 sample chapters, and resumé. Write for guidelines for annual North American Indian Prose Award.

UNIVERSITY OF NEW MEXICO PRESS—Univ. of New Mexico, Albuquerque, NM 87131. Elizabeth C. Hadas, Ed. Dir. David V. Holtby, Larry Ball, Dana Asbury, and Barbara Guth, Eds. Scholarly nonfiction on social and cultural anthropology, archaeology, Western history, art, and photography. Query. Royalty.

795

UNIVERSITY OF NORTH CAROLINA PRESS—P.O. Box 2288, Chapel Hill, NC 27515–2288. David Perry, Ed. General-interest books (75,000 to 125,000 words) on the lore, crafts, cooking, gardening, travel, and natural history of the Southeast. No fiction or poetry. Query preferred. Royalty.

UNIVERSITY OF NORTH TEXAS PRESS—P.O. Box 13856, Denton, TX 76203–6586. Frances B. Vick, Dir. Charlotte M. Wright, Ed. Books on Western Americana, Texan culture, women's studies, multicultural studies, and folklore. Series include: "War and the Southwest" (perspectives, histories, and memories of war from authors living in the Southwest); "Western Life Series"; "Philosophy and the Environment Series"; "Texas Poets" (poetry by Native Texans only); and "Texas Writers" (critical biographies of Texas writers). Send manuscript or query with sample chapters; no multiple queries. Royalty.

UNIVERSITY OF OKLAHOMA PRESS—1005 Asp Ave., Norman, OK 73019–0445. John Drayton, Asst. Dir. Books, to 300 pages, on the history of the American West, Indians of the Americas, congressional studies, classical studies, literary criticism, and natural history. Query. Royalty.

UNIVERSITY OF PITTSBURGH PRESS—127 N. Bellefield Ave., Pittsburgh, PA 15260. Attn: Eds. Scholarly nonfiction; poetry. Query.

UNIVERSITY OF TENNESSEE PRESS—293 Communications Bldg., Knoxville, TN 37996–0325. Attn: Ed. Dept. Nonfiction, regional trade, 200 to 300 manuscript pages. Query with outline and sample chapters. Royalty.

UNIVERSITY OF WISCONSIN PRESS—114 N. Murray St., Madison, WI 53715–1199. Attn: Acquisitions Ed. Scholarly nonfiction and regional books.

UNIVERSITY PRESS OF COLORADO—P.O. Box 849, Niwot, CO 80544. Attn: Ed. Dept. Scholarly books in the humanities, social sciences, and applied sciences. No fiction or poetry.

UNIVERSITY PRESS OF FLORIDA—15 N.W. 15th St., Gainesville, FL 32611–2079. Walda Metcalf, Ed.-in-Chief/Assoc. Dir. Nonfiction, 150 to 450 manuscript pages, on regional studies, Native Americans, folklore, women's studies, Latin-American studies, contemporary literary criticism, sociology, anthropology, archaeology, international affairs, labor studies, and history. Poetry. Royalty.

THE UNIVERSITY PRESS OF KENTUCKY—663 S. Limestone St., Lexington, KY 40508–4008. Nancy Grayson Holmes, Ed.-in-Chief. Scholarly books in the major fields. Serious nonfiction of general interest. Books related to Kentucky and the Ohio Valley, the Appalachians, and the South. No fiction, drama, or poetry. Query.

UNIVERSITY PRESS OF MISSISSIPPI—3825 Ridgewood Rd., Jackson, MS 39211–6492. Seetha Srinivasan, Ed.-in-Chief. Scholarly and trade titles in American literature, history, and culture; southern studies; African-American, women's and American studies; social sciences; popular culture; folklife; art and architecture; natural sciences; and other liberal arts.

UNIVERSITY PRESS OF NEW ENGLAND—23 S. Main St., Hanover, NH 03755–2048. Attn: Ed. Dept. General and scholarly nonfiction. American, British, and European history, literature, literary criticism, creative fiction and nonfiction, and cultural studies. Jewish studies, women's studies, studies of the New England region, environmental studies, and other policy issues.

VAN NOSTRAND REINHOLD—115 Fifth Ave., New York, NY 10003. Brian D. Heer, Pres./CEO, Marianne Russell, VP-Editorial. Business, professional, scientific, and technical publishers of applied reference works. Hospitality, culinary, architecture, graphic and interior design, industrial and environmental health and safety, computer science, engineering, and technical management.

VANDAMERE PRESS—P.O. Box 5243, Arlington, VA 22205. Jerry Frank, Assoc. Acquisitions Ed. General trade, fiction and nonfiction, including history, military, parenting, career guides, and travel. Also books about the nation's capital for a national audience. Prefer to see outline with sample chapter for nonfiction; for fiction send 4 or 5 sample chapters. Multiple queries considered. Royalty. SASE required.

VICTOR BOOKS—Div. of Scripture Press Publications, 1825 College Ave., Wheaton, IL 60187. Greg Clouse, Acquisitions Ed. Fiction and nonfiction, 100,000 words, for evangelical Christian readers. Also, picture books and fiction for children. Query with outline and sample chapters. Royalty.

VIKING—Imprint of Penguin USA, 375 Hudson St., New York, NY 10014. No unagented manuscripts.

VIKING CHILDREN'S BOOKS—Imprint of Penguin USA, 375 Hudson St., New York, NY 10014. Attn: Ed. Dept. Fiction and nonfiction, including biography, history, and sports, for ages 7 to 14. Humor and picture books for ages 2 to 6. Query Children's Book Dept. with outline and sample chapter. SASE required. Royalty.

VILLARD BOOKS—Div. of Random House, 201 E. 50th St., New York, NY 10022. Diane Reverand, V.P./Pub./Ed.-in-Chief. Fiction, sports, inspiration, how-to, biography, humor, etc. "We do look for authors who are promotable and books we feel we can market well." Royalty.

VINTAGE BOOKS—Div. of Random House, 201 E. 50th St., New York, NY 10022. Attn: Ed. Dept. Quality fiction and serious nonfiction. Please query with sample chapters for fiction; query for non-fiction.

VOYAGER PAPERBACKS—See *Harcourt Brace.*

WALKER AND COMPANY—435 Hudson St., New York, NY 10014. Attn: Ed. Dept. Adult fiction: mysteries, westerns. Adult nonfiction: Americana, biography, history, science, natural history, medicine, psychology, parenting, sports, outdoors, reference, popular science, self-help, business, and music. Juvenile nonfiction, including biography, science, history, music, and nature. Juvenile fiction: Middle grade and young adult novels. Query with synopsis and SASE. Royalty.

WALLACE-HOMESTEAD BOOKS—See *Chilton Book Co.*

WARNER BOOKS—1271 Ave. of the Americas, New York, NY 10020. Mel Parker, Pub., Warner Paperbacks. No unsolicited manuscripts or proposals.

WASHINGTON STATE UNIVERSITY PRESS—Cooper Publications Bldg., Pullman, WA 99164–5910. Glen Lindeman and Keith Petersen, Eds. Books on northwest history, prehistory, and culture, 100 to 250 pages. Send complete manuscript. Royalty.

WASHINGTON WRITERS PUBLISHING HOUSE—P.O. Box 15271, Washington, DC 20003. Attn: Ed. Dept. Poetry books, 50 to 60 pages, by writers in the greater Washington, DC area. Send SASE for guidelines.

WATTS, FRANKLIN—95 Madison Ave., New York, NY 10016. Emily Dolbear, Submissions. Curriculum-oriented nonfiction for grades 4 to 12, including science, history, social studies, and biography. Query with SASE required.

WEISS ASSOCIATES, DANIEL—33 W. 17th St., New York, NY 10011. Sigrid Berg, Ed. Asst. Book packager. Parenting and self-help books. Young adult books, 45,000 words; middle-grade books, 33,000 words; elementary books, 10,000 to 12,000 words. Query with outline and sample chapter. Royalty and flat fee.

WESLEYAN UNIVERSITY PRESS—110 Mt. Vernon St., Middletown, CT 06459–0433. Suzanna Tamminen, Ed. *Wesleyan Poetry*: 64 to 80 pages. Query. Royalty.

WESTERN PUBLISHING CO., INC.—850 Third Ave., New York, NY 10022. Robin Warner, V.P./Pub., Children's Books; Audrey Cusson, Assoc. Pub; Alice Bregman, Marilyn Salomon, Ed. Dirs., Children's Books. Children's books, fiction and nonfiction: picture books, storybooks, concept books, novelty books. Adult nonfiction: field guides. No unsolicited manuscripts. Same address and requirements for *Golden Press*. Royalty or flat fee.

WESTMINSTER/JOHN KNOX PRESS—100 Witherspoon St., Louisville, KY 40202. Davis Perkins, Dir. Stephanie Egnotovich, Man. Ed. Books that inform, interpret, challenge, and encourage Christian faith and living. Royalty. Send SASE for guidelines.

WHISPERING COYOTE PRESS—480 Newbury St., Suite 104, Danvers, MA 01923. Ms. Lou Alpert, Ed. Picture books, 32 pages, for readers ages 4 to 12. Submit complete manuscript with SASE. Royalty.

WHITMAN, ALBERT—6340 Oakton, Morton Grove, IL 60053. Kathleen Tucker, Ed. Picture books for preschool children; novels, biographies, mysteries, and general nonfiction for middle-grade readers. Submit complete manuscript for picture books, 3 chapters and outline for longer fiction; query for nonfiction. Royalty.

WILDERNESS PRESS—2440 Bancroft Way, Berkeley, CA 94704. Thomas Winnett, Ed. Nonfiction: outdoor sports, recreation, and travel in the western U.S. Royalty.

WILEY & SONS, JOHN—605 Third Ave., New York, NY 10158–0012. Attn: Ed. Dept. Nonfiction: science/technology; business/management; real estate; travel; cooking; biography; psychology; computers; language; history; current affairs; health; finance. Send proposals with outline, author vita, market information, and sample chapter. Royalty.

WILLIAMSON PUBLISHING CO.—Church Hill Rd., Charlotte, VT 05445. Attn: Ed. Activity books for children. Adult hands-on books for country living. Writers must send for guidelines before submitting material.

WILLOW CREEK PRESS—Number 1, Fifty One Centre, P.O. Box 881, Minocqua, WI 54548. Tom Petrie, Ed. Books, 25,000 to 50,000 words, on nature, wildlife, and outdoor sports. Also children's picture books and nonfiction for readers 9 to 12 years old. Submit queries and sample chapters. No fiction. Royalty.

WILLOWISP PRESS, INC.—801 94th Ave. N., St. Petersburg, FL 33702. Attn: Acquisitions Ed. Juvenile books for children in grades pre-K through 8. Picture books, 300 to 800 words. Fiction, 14,000 to 18,000 words for grades 3 through 5; 20,000 to 24,000 words for grades 5 through 8. Requirements for nonfiction vary. Query with outline, sample chapter, and SASE. Guidelines. Royalty or flat fee.

WILSHIRE BOOK COMPANY—12015 Sherman Rd., N. Hollywood, CA 91605. Melvin Powers, Pub. Nonfiction: self-help, motivation, inspiration, psychology, how-to, entrepreneurship, mail order, and horsemanship. Fiction: adult fables, 35,000 to 45,000 words, that teach principles of psychological growth or offer guidance in living. Send synopsis/detailed chapter outline, 3 chapters, and SASE. Royalty.

WINDSWEPT HOUSE PUBLISHERS—Mt. Desert, ME 04660. Jane Weinberger, Pub. Children's picture books; young adult novels; adult fiction and nonfiction. Query. Overstocked; not considering new material until 1996.

WINGBOW PRESS—7900 Edgewater Dr., Oakland, CA 94621. Randy Fingland, Ed. Nonfiction: women's interests, health, psychology. No fiction or poetry. Query preferred. Royalty.

WISHING WELL—See *Reader's Digest Young Families, Inc.*

WOODBINE HOUSE—5615 Fishers Ln., Rockville, MD 20852. Susan Stokes, Ed. "Emphasis is increasingly on books for or about people with disabilities, but will consider nonfiction of all types. No personal accounts, poetry, or books that can be marketed only through bookstores." Query or submit complete manuscript with SASE. Guidelines for SASE. Royalty.

WORKMAN PUBLISHING CO., INC.—708 Broadway, New York, NY 10003. Attn: Ed. Dept. General nonfiction. Normal contractual terms based on agreement.

WORLDWIDE LIBRARY—Div. of Harlequin Books, 225 Duncan Mill Rd., Don Mills, Ont., Canada M3B 3K9. Randall Toye, Ed. Dir. Feroze Mohammed, Sr. Ed. Action adventure series for *Gold Eagle* imprint; mystery fiction reprints only. No unsolicited manuscripts or queries.

YEARLING BOOKS—Imprint of Dell Publishing Co., 1540 Broadway, New York, NY 10036. Attn: Ed. Dept. Books for K through 6. Manuscripts accepted from agents only. Same address and requirements for *Skylark Books.*

YOLEN BOOKS, JANE—See *Harcourt Brace.*

ZEBRA BOOKS—Imprint of Kensington Publishing Corp., 850 Third Ave., New York, NY 10022. Ann LaFarge, Exec. Ed. Popular fiction: horror; historical romance; *Lovegram Romances* (120,000 words); regencies (80,000 to 120,000 words); sagas; westerns. Also *To Love Again* aimed at women over 45. Query with synopsis and sample chapters preferred.

ZEBRA HARDCOVERS—See *Kensington Books.*

ZFAVE—Imprint of Kensington Publishing Corp., 850 Third Ave., 16th Floor, New York, NY 10022. Elise Donner, Exec. Ed. Series and single titles for 8- to 16-year-olds . Send complete synopsis and sample chapters or complete synopsis and complete manuscript. Royalty.

ZONDERVAN PUBLISHING HOUSE—5300 Patterson S.E., Grand Rapids, MI 49530. Attn: Manuscript Review. Christian titles. General fiction and nonfiction; academic and professional books. Query with outline, sample chapter, and SASE. Royalty. Guidelines.

UNIVERSITY PRESSES

University presses generally publish books of a scholarly nature or of specialized interest by authorities in a given field. A few publish fiction and

799

poetry. Many publish only a handful of titles a year. Always query first. Do not send a manuscript until you have been invited to do so by the editor. Several of the following presses and their detailed editorial submission requirements are included in the *Book Publishers* list.

BOISE STATE UNIVERSITY—See Hemingway Western Studies Series.

BOWLING GREEN STATE UNIVERSITY—See Popular Press.

BUCKNELL UNIVERSITY PRESS—Bucknell University, Lewisburg, PA 17837.

CAMBRIDGE UNIVERSITY PRESS—40 W. 20th St., New York, NY 10011–4211.

THE CATHOLIC UNIVERSITY OF AMERICA PRESS—620 Michigan Ave. N.E., Washington, DC 20064.

DUKE UNIVERSITY PRESS—Box 90660, Durham, NC 27708–0660.

DUQUESNE UNIVERSITY PRESS—600 Forbes Ave., Pittsburgh, PA 15282–0101.

FORDHAM UNIVERSITY PRESS—University Box L, Bronx, NY 10458–5172.

GEORGIA STATE UNIVERSITY BUSINESS PRESS—University Plaza, Atlanta, GA 30303–3093.

HEMINGWAY WESTERN STUDIES SERIES—Boise State Univ., 1910 University Dr., Boise, ID 83725.

INDIANA UNIVERSITY PRESS—601 N. Morton St., Bloomington, IN 47404–3797.

THE JOHNS HOPKINS UNIVERSITY PRESS—2715 N. Charles St., Baltimore, MD 21218.

KENT STATE UNIVERSITY PRESS—Kent State Univ., Kent, OH 44242.

LOUISIANA STATE UNIVERSITY PRESS—P.O. Box 25053, Baton Rouge, LA 70894–5053.

LOYOLA UNIVERSITY PRESS—3441 N. Ashland Ave., Chicago, IL 60657–1397.

THE MICHIGAN STATE UNIVERSITY PRESS—1405 S. Harrison Rd., Suite 25, E. Lansing, MI 48823–5202.

THE MIT PRESS—Acquisitions Dept., 55 Hayward St., Cambridge, MA 02142.

NEW YORK UNIVERSITY PRESS—70 Washington Sq. S., New York, NY 10012.

OHIO STATE UNIVERSITY PRESS—180 Pressey Hall, 1070 Carmack Rd., Columbus, OH 43210.

OREGON STATE UNIVERSITY PRESS—101 Waldo Hall, Corvallis, OR 97331.

THE PENNSYLVANIA STATE UNIVERSITY PRESS—820 N. University Dr., University Park, PA 16802.

POPULAR PRESS—Bowling Green State Univ., Bowling Green, OH 43403.

PRINCETON UNIVERSITY PRESS—41 William St., Princeton, NJ 08540.

SOUTHERN ILLINOIS UNIVERSITY PRESS—Box 3697, Carbondale, IL 62902–3697.

SOUTHERN METHODIST UNIVERSITY PRESS—Box 415, Dallas, TX 75275.

STANFORD UNIVERSITY PRESS—Stanford University, Stanford, CA 94305–2235.

SYRACUSE UNIVERSITY PRESS—1600 Jamesville Ave., Syracuse, NY 13244–5160.

TEMPLE UNIVERSITY PRESS—Broad and Oxford Sts., Philadelphia, PA 19122.

UNIVERSITY OF ALABAMA PRESS—P.O. Box 870380, Tuscaloosa, AL 35487–0380.

UNIVERSITY OF ARIZONA PRESS—1230 N. Park Ave., Suite 102, Tucson, AZ 85719.

UNIVERSITY OF CALIFORNIA PRESS—2120 Berkeley Way, Berkeley, CA 94720.

UNIVERSITY OF CHICAGO PRESS—5801 Ellis Ave., Chicago, IL 60637–1496.

UNIVERSITY OF GEORGIA PRESS—330 Research Dr., Athens, GA 30602–4901.

UNIVERSITY OF ILLINOIS PRESS—1325 S. Oak St., Champaign, IL 61820.

UNIVERSITY OF MASSACHUSETTS PRESS—Box 429, Amherst, MA 01004–0429.

UNIVERSITY OF MINNESOTA PRESS—2037 University Ave. S.E., Minneapolis, MN 55455.

UNIVERSITY OF MISSOURI PRESS—2910 LeMone Blvd., Columbia, MO 65201–8227.

UNIVERSITY OF NEBRASKA PRESS—312 N. 14th St., Lincoln, NE 68588–0484.

UNIVERSITY OF NEW MEXICO PRESS—University of New Mexico, Albuquerque, NM 87131.

UNIVERSITY OF NORTH CAROLINA PRESS—P.O. Box 2288, Chapel Hill, NC 27515–2288.

UNIVERSITY OF NORTH TEXAS PRESS—P.O. Box 13856, Denton, TX 76203–6586.

UNIVERSITY OF OKLAHOMA PRESS—1005 Asp Ave., Norman, OK 73019–0445.

UNIVERSITY OF PITTSBURGH PRESS—127 N. Bellefield Ave., Pittsburgh, PA 15260.

UNIVERSITY OF SOUTH CAROLINA PRESS—University of South Carolina, 1716 College St., Columbia, SC 29208.

UNIVERSITY OF TENNESSEE PRESS—293 Communications Bldg., Knoxville, TN 37996–0325.

UNIVERSITY OF WASHINGTON PRESS—P.O. Box 50096, Seattle, WA 98145–5096.

UNIVERSITY OF WISCONSIN PRESS—114 N. Murray St., Madison, WI 53715–1199.

UNIVERSITY PRESS OF COLORADO—P.O. Box 849, Niwot, CO 80544.

UNIVERSITY PRESS OF FLORIDA—15 N.W. 15th St., Gainesville, FL 32611–2079.

THE UNIVERSITY PRESS OF KENTUCKY—663 S. Limestone St., Lexington, KY 40508–4008.

UNIVERSITY PRESS OF MISSISSIPPI—3825 Ridgewood Rd., Jackson, MS 39211–6492.

UNIVERSITY PRESS OF NEW ENGLAND—23 S. Main St., Hanover, NH 03755–2048.

THE UNIVERSITY PRESS OF VIRGINIA—Box 3608, Univ. Sta., Charlottesville, VA 22903.

WASHINGTON STATE UNIVERSITY PRESS—Cooper Publications Bldg., Pullman, WA 99164–5910.

WAYNE STATE UNIVERSITY PRESS—4809 Woodward Ave., Detroit, MI 48201.

WESLEYAN UNIVERSITY PRESS—110 Mt.Vernon St., Middletown, CT 06459–0433.

YALE UNIVERSITY PRESS—Box 209040, Yale Sta., New Haven, CT 06520–9040.

SYNDICATES

Syndicates are business organizations that buy material from writers and artists to sell to newspapers all over the country and the world. Authors are paid either a percentage of the gross proceeds or an outright fee.

Of course, features by people well known in their fields have the best chance of being syndicated. In general, syndicates want columns that have been popular in a local newspaper, perhaps, or magazine. Since most syndicated fiction has been published previously in magazines or books, beginning fiction writers should try to sell their stories to magazines before submitting them to syndicates.

Always query syndicates before sending manuscripts, since their needs change frequently, and be sure to enclose SASEs with queries and manuscripts.

ARKIN MAGAZINE SYNDICATE—500 Bayview Dr., N. Miami Beach, FL 33160. Joseph Arkin, Ed. Dir. Articles, 750 to 2,200 words, for trade and professional magazines. Must have small-business slant, be written in layman's language, and offer solutions to business problems. Articles should apply to many businesses, not just a specific industry. No columns. Pays 3¢ to 10¢ a word, on acceptance. SASE required; query not necessary.

CONTEMPORARY FEATURES SYNDICATE—P. O. Box 1258, Jackson, TN 38302–1258. Lloyd Russell, Ed. Articles, 1,000 to 10,000 words: how-to, money savers, business, etc. Self-help pieces for small business. Query. Pays from $25, on acceptance.

HARRIS & ASSOCIATES FEATURES—12084 Caminito Campana, San Diego, CA 92128. Dick Harris, Ed. Sports- and family-oriented features, to 1,200 words; fillers and short humor, 500 to 800 words. Queries preferred. Pays varying rates.

HISPANIC LINK NEWS SERVICE—1420 N St. N.W., Washington, DC 20005. Charles A. Ericksen, Ed. Trend articles, opinion and personal experience pieces, and general features with Hispanic focus, 650 to 700 words; editorial cartoons. Pays $25 for op-ed columns and cartoons, on acceptance. Send SASE for guidelines.

THE HOLLYWOOD INSIDE SYNDICATE—Box 49957, Los Angeles, CA 90049. John Austin, Dir. Feature articles, 750 to 2,500 words, on TV and film personalities with B&W photo(s). Article suggestions for three-part series. Pieces on unusual medical and scientific breakthroughs. Pays on percentage basis for features, negotiated rates for ideas, on publication.

LOS ANGELES TIMES SYNDICATE—Times Mirror Sq., Los Angeles, CA 90053. Commentary, features, columns, editorial cartoons, comics, puzzles and games; news services. Send SASE for submission guidelines.

NATIONAL NEWS BUREAU—P.O. Box 43039, Philadelphia, PA 19129. Harry Jay Katz, Ed. Articles, 500 to 1,500 words, interviews, consumer news, how-tos, travel pieces, reviews, entertainment pieces, features, etc. Pays on publication.

NEW YORK TIMES SYNDICATION SALES—122 E. 42nd St., New York, NY 10168. Gloria Brown Anderson, Exec. Ed. Previously published health, lifestyle, and entertainment articles only, to 1,500 words. Query with published article or tear sheet and SASE. Pays varying rates, on publication.

OCEANIC PRESS SERVICE—Seaview Business Park, 1030 Calle Cordillera, Unit #106, San Clemente, CA 92673. Peter Carbone, General Mgr. Buys reprint rights for foreign markets, on previously published novels, self-help, and how-to books; interviews with celebrities; illustrated features on celebrities, family, health, beauty, personal relationships, etc.; cartoons, comic strips. Pays on acceptance or half on acceptance, half on syndication. Query.

SINGER MEDIA CORP.—#106, 1030 Calle Cordillera, San Clemente, CA 92673. Helen J. Lee, Ed. U.S. and/or foreign reprint rights to published romance books, historical novels, gothics, westerns, and mysteries (published during last 25 years); business management titles, self-help, and computer. Biography, women's interest, all lengths. Home repair, real estate, psychological quizzes. Interviews with celebrities. Humor. Illustrated columns, cartoons, comic strips. Pays on percentage basis or by outright purchase.

TRIBUNE MEDIA SERVICES—435 N. Michigan Ave. #1500, Chicago, IL 60611. Michael Silver, Ed. Continuing columns, comic strips, features, electronic databases.

UNITED FEATURE SYNDICATE—200 Park Ave., New York, NY 10166. Diana Loevy, V.P./ Exec. Ed. Syndicated columns; no one-shots or series. Payment by contractual arrangement. Send samples with SASE.

UNITED PRESS INTERNATIONAL—1400 Eye St. N.W., Washington, DC 20005. Robert A. Martin, Man. Ed. No free-lance material.

UNIVERSAL PRESS SYNDICATE—4900 Main St., Kansas City, MO 64112. Attn: Paula Reichler Parker. Articles for kiosk feature service, covering lifestyles, trends, health, fashion, parenting, business, humor, the home, entertainment, and personalities. Query. Payment varies.

LITERARY PRIZE OFFERS

Each year many important literary contests are open to free-lance writers from all genres. Writers seeking publication of their book-length poetry manuscripts are encouraged to enter the several contests in this list that offer publication as the prize; many presses that once considered unsolicited poetry manuscripts by emerging or unpublished writers now limit their reading of such manuscripts to those entered in their contests for new writers. The short summaries given below are intended merely as guides; closing dates, requirements, and rules are tentative. Every effort has been made to ensure the accuracy of information provided here. Since submission requirements are more detailed than space allows, writers should send SASE for complete guidelines before entering any contest. Writers are also advised to check the monthly "Prize Offers" column of *The Writer* Magazine (120 Boylston St., Boston, MA 02116–4615) for additional contest listings and up-to-date contest requirements. Deadlines are annual unless otherwise noted.

ACADEMY OF AMERICAN POETS—Walt Whitman Award, 584 Broadway, Suite 1208, New York, NY 10012–3250. An award of $1,000 plus publication is offered for a book-length poetry manuscript by a poet who has not yet published a volume of poetry. Deadline: November 15.

ACADEMY OF MOTION PICTURE ARTS AND SCIENCES—The Nicholl Fellowships, Dept. WR, 8949 Wilshire Blvd., Beverly Hills, CA 90211–1972. Up to five fellowships of $25,000 each are awarded for original screenplays that display exceptional craft and engaging storytelling. Deadline: May 1.

ACTORS' PLAYHOUSE—National Children's Theatre Festival, 8851 Southwest 107th Ave., Miami, FL 33176. Attn: Suzanne Roberts, Chairman. Prizes of $1,200 plus production, $500, and $250 are awarded for plays 40 to 50 minutes long, for ages 12 to 17; and musicals 45 to 60 minutes long, for ages 5 to 12. Deadline: June 1.

ACTORS THEATRE OF LOUISVILLE—Ten-Minute Play Contest, 316 W. Main St., Louisville, KY 40202–4218. A prize of $1,000 is offered for a previously unproduced ten-page script. Deadline: December 1.

AMELIA MAGAZINE—329 E St., Bakersfield, CA 93304. Attn: Frederick A. Raborg, Jr., Ed. Offers writing awards year round in poetry, short fiction, and nonfiction, with prizes of up to $250. Deadline: varies.

AMERICAN ACADEMY OF ARTS AND LETTERS—Richard Rogers Awards, 633 W. 155th St., New York, NY 10032. Offers subsidized productions or staged readings in New York City by a nonprofit theater for a musical, play with music, thematic review, or any comparable work other than opera. Deadline: November 1.

AMERICAN FICTION/NEW RIVERS PRESS—Fiction Awards, P.O. Box 229, Moorhead State Univ., Moorhead, MN 56563. Attn: Alan Davis, Ed. Prizes of $1,000, $500, and $250 are awarded for short stories, to 10,000 words. The stories of up to 25 finalists are published in *American Fiction* anthology. Deadline: May 1.

AMERICAN RADIO THEATRE—Radio Script Writers' Competition, 3035 23rd St., San Francisco, CA 94110–3315. Prizes of $250, $100, and three $50 awards are offered for the top five radio plays submitted. Deadline: August 31.

THE AMERICAN-SCANDINAVIAN FOUNDATION—Translation Prize, 725 Park Ave., New York, NY 10021. A prize of $2,000 is awarded for an outstanding English translation of poetry, fiction, drama, or literary prose originally written in Danish, Finnish, Icelandic, Norwegian, or Swedish. Deadline: June 1.

ANHINGA PRESS—Anhinga Prize for Poetry, P.O. Box 10595, Tallahassee, FL 32302–0595. A $1,000 prize will be awarded for an unpublished full-length collection of poetry, 48 to 64 pages, by a poet who has published no more than one full-length collection. Deadline: March 1.

THE ASSOCIATED WRITING PROGRAMS—Awards Series, Tallwood House, Mail Stop 1E3, George Mason Univ., Fairfax, VA 22030. In the categories of poetry, short fiction, the novel, and nonfiction, the prize is book publication and a $2,000 honorarium. Deadline: February 28.

ASSOCIATION OF JEWISH LIBRARIES—Sydney Taylor Manuscript Competition, 15 Goldsmith St., Providence, RI 02906. Attn: Lillian Schwartz, Coordinator. Offers $1,000 for the best fiction manuscript, 64 to 200 pages, by an unpublished book author, writing for readers 8 to 11. Stories must have a positive Jewish focus. Deadline: January 15.

ASTRAEA NATIONAL LESBIAN ACTION FOUNDATION—Emerging Writers Awards, Lesbian Writers Fund, 666 Broadway, Suite 520, New York, NY 10012. Five awards of $11,000 each are given to lesbian writers of fiction or poetry whose work includes some lesbian content. Writers must have published at least one piece in a newspaper, periodical, or anthology, and must not have published more than one book. Deadline: March 1.

AUSTIN PEAY STATE UNIVERSITY—Rainmaker Awards in Poetry, P.O. Box 4565, Clarksville, TN 37044. A prize of $500 plus publication in *Zone 3* is awarded for the best poem. Deadline: January 1.

BAKER'S PLAYS—High School Playwriting Contest, 100 Chauncy St., Boston, MA 02111. Plays about the high school experience, written by high school students, are eligible for awards of $500, $250, and $100. Deadline: January 31.

BANTAM DOUBLEDAY DELL BOOKS FOR YOUNG READERS—Marguerite de Angeli Prize, Dept. BFYR, 1540 Broadway, New York, NY 10036. A prize of $1,500 and a $3,500 advance against royalties is awarded for a middle-grade fiction manuscript that explores the diversity of the American experience. Open to U.S. and Canadian writers who have not previously published a novel for middle-grade readers. Deadline: June 30.

BARNARD COLLEGE—New Women Poets Prize, Women Poets at Barnard, Columbia University, 3009 Broadway, New York, NY 10027–6598. Attn: Directors. A prize of $1,500 and publication by Beacon Press is offered for an unpublished poetry manuscript, 50 to 100 pages, by a female poet who has never published a book of poetry. Deadline: October 1.

BELLES LETTRES—Personal Essay Contest, 11151 Captain's Walk Ct., N. Potomac, MD 20878. A prize of publication plus $500 is awarded for the best personal essay of up to 2,000 words, on any topic. Deadline: August 31.

THE BELLINGHAM REVIEW—Contest Entry, 49th Parallel Poetry Contest, 1007 Queen St., Bellingham, WA 98226. Publication and prizes of $150, $100, and $50 are awarded for poems up to 40 lines, any style or subject. Deadline: December 1.

BEVERLY HILLS THEATRE GUILD/JULIE HARRIS PLAYWRIGHT AWARD—2815 N. Beachwood Dr., Los Angeles, CA 90068. Attn: Marcella Meharg. Offers prize of $5,000, plus possible $2,000 for productions in Los Angeles area, for previously unproduced and unpublished full-length play. A $2,000 second prize and $1,000 third prize are also offered. Deadline: November 1.

BIRMINGHAM-SOUTHERN COLLEGE—Hackney Literary Awards, BSC A-3, Birmingham, AL 35254. A prize of $2,000 is awarded for an unpublished novel, any length. Deadline: September 30. Also, a $2,000 prize is shared for the winning short story, to 5,000 words, and poem of up to 50 lines. Deadline: December 31.

BOISE STATE UNIVERSITY—Eccentric Book Competition, Hemingway Western Studies Center, Boise, ID 83725. Tom Trusky, Ed. A prize of $500 and publication is awarded for up to three books; manuscripts (text and/or visual content) and proposals are considered for the short-run printing of books on public issues, especially the Inter-Mountain West. Deadline: December 1.

BOSTON MAGAZINE—Fiction Contest, 300 Massachusetts Ave., Boston, MA 02115. Publication and $500 are awarded for the best short story on a given theme, up to 3,000 words, set in or around Boston. Deadline: September 1.

THE BOSTON REVIEW—Short Story Contest, 33 Harrison Ave., Boston, MA 02111. A prize of $300 plus publication is awarded for the best previously unpublished story of up to 4,000 words. Deadline: October 1.

BUCKNELL UNIVERSITY—The Philip Roth Residence in Creative Writing, Stadler Center for Poetry, Bucknell University, Lewisburg, PA 17837. Attn: John Wheatcroft, Dir. The fall residency may be used by a writer, over 21, not currently enrolled in a university, to work on a first or second book. The residency is awarded in odd-numbered years to a fiction writer, and in even-numbered years to a poet. Deadline: March 1.

CASE WESTERN RESERVE UNIVERSITY—Marc A. Klein Playwriting Award, Dept. of Theater Arts, 10900 Euclid Ave., Cleveland, OH 44106–7077. A prize of $1,000 plus production is offered for an original, previously unproduced full-length play by a student currently enrolled at an American college or university. Deadline: May 15.

CHELSEA AWARDS COMPETITION—P.O. Box 1040, York Beach, ME 03910. Attn: Ed. Prizes of $500 plus publication are awarded for the best unpublished short fiction and poetry. Deadlines: June 15 (fiction); December 15 (poetry).

CHICAGO TRIBUNE—Nelson Algren Awards, 435 N. Michigan Ave., Chicago, IL 60611. A first prize of $5,000 and three runner-up prizes of $1,000 are awarded for outstanding unpublished short stories, 2,500 to 10,000 words, by American writers. Deadline: February 1.

CLAUDER COMPETITION—P.O. Box 383259, Cambridge, MA 02238–3259. Awards $3,000 plus professional production for a full-length play by a New England writer. Runner-up prizes of $500 and a staged reading also awarded. Deadline: June 30 (of odd-numbered years).

CLEVELAND STATE UNIVERSITY POETRY CENTER—Poetry Center Prize, Dept. of English, Rhodes Tower, Room 1815, Cleveland, OH 44115. Attn: Prof. Nuala Archer. Publication and $1,000 are awarded for a previously unpublished volume of poetry. Deadline: March 1.

CMH LITERARY NETWORK—Contests, 360 Connecticut Ave., Suite 115, Norwalk, CT 06854. Offers a number of contests for beginning writers throughout the year. Deadline: varies.

COALITION FOR THE ADVANCEMENT OF JEWISH EDUCATION—David Dornstein Memorial Creative Writing Contest, 261 W. 35th St., Floor 12A, New York, NY 10001. A prize of publication and $1,000 is awarded for the best original, previously unpublished short story, to 5,000 words, on a Jewish theme or topic, by a writer age 18 to 35. Deadline: December 31.

COLONIAL PLAYERS, INC.—Promising Playwright Award, 99 Great Lake Dr., Annapolis, MD 21403. Attn: Frank Moorman. A prize of $750 plus possible production will be awarded for the best full-length play by a resident of MD, DC, VA, WV, DE, or PA. Deadline: December 31 (of even-numbered years).

COLORADO CHRISTIAN UNIVERSITY—New Christian Plays Award, 180 S. Garrison St., Lakewood, CO 80226. Attn: Patrick Rainville Dorn, Literary Mgr. Full-length or one-act plays, musicals, readers' theater or children's plays are considered for a prize of $200. First place and runners up are considered for production. Deadline: March 31.

COMMUNITY CHILDREN'S THEATRE OF KANSAS CITY—8021 E. 129th Terrace, Grandview, MO 64030. Attn: Mrs. Blanche Sellens, Dir. A prize of $500, plus production, is awarded for the best play, up to one hour long, to be performed by adults for elementary school audiences. Deadline: January 31.

THE CRITIC—Short Story Contest, Thomas More Assoc., 205 W. Monroe St., 6th Floor, Chicago, IL 60606–5097. Original, upublished short stories are eligible for the prize of $500 plus publication. Deadline: September 1 (of even-numbered years).

CUMBERLAND POETRY REVIEW—Robert Penn Warren Poetry Prize Competition, P.O. Box 120128, Nashville, TN 37212. Three poems of up to 100 lines each may be submitted for prizes of $500, $300, and $200. Deadline: March 15.

EUGENE V. DEBS FOUNDATION—Bryant Spann Memorial Prize, Dept. of History, Indiana State Univ., Terre Haute, IN 47809. Offers a prize of $1,000 for a published or unpublished article or essay on themes relating to social protest or human equality. Deadline: April 30.

DEEP SOUTH WRITERS CONFERENCE—Contest Clerk, Drawer 44691, Univ. of Southwestern Louisianna, Lafayette, LA 70504–4691. Prizes ranging from

$50 to $300 are offered for unpublished manuscripts in the following categories: short fiction, novel, nonfiction, poetry, drama, and French literature. Deadline: July 15. Miller Award: offers $500 for a play dealing with some aspect of the life of Edward de Vere (1550–1604), the 17th Earl of Oxford. Deadline: July 15 (of odd-numbered years).

DELACORTE PRESS—Prize for First Young Adult Novel, Bantam Doubleday Dell BFYR, 1540 Broadway, New York, NY 10036. A writer who has not previously published a young adult novel may submit a book-length manuscript with a contemporary setting suitable for readers ages 12 to 18. The prize is $1,500 plus a $6,000 advance, plus hardcover and paperback publication. Deadline: December 31.

BARBARA DEMING MEMORIAL FUND, INC.—Money for Women, P.O. Box 40–1043, Brooklyn, NY 11240–1043. Attn: Pam McAllister, Administrator. Grants of up to $1,000 are awarded semiannually to individual feminists in the arts whose work addresses women's concerns and/or speaks for peace and justice from a feminist perspective. Deadlines: June 30; December 31.

DRURY COLLEGE—Playwriting Contest, 900 N. Benton Ave., Springfield, MO 65802. Attn: Sandy Asher, Writer-in-Residence. Prizes of $300 and two $150 honorable mentions, plus possible production, are awarded for original, previously unproduced one-act plays. Deadline: December 1 (of even-numbered years).

DUBUQUE FINE ARTS PLAYERS—One-Act Playwriting Contest, 569 S. Grandview Ave., Dubuque, IA 52003. Attn: Sally T. Ryan, Coordinator. Prizes of $600, $300 and $200 plus possible production are awarded for unproduced, original one-act plays of up to 40 minutes. Deadline: January 31.

DUKE UNIVERSITY—Dorothea Lange-Paul Taylor Prize, Prize Committee, Center for Documentary Studies, Box 90802, Duke University, Durham, NC 27708–0802. A grant of up to $10,000 is awarded to a writer and photographer working together in the formative stages of a documentary project that will ultimately result in a publishable work. Deadline: January 31.

EIGHTH MOUNTAIN PRESS—Poetry Prize, 624 Southeast 29th Ave., Portland, OR 97214. A prize of a $1,000 advance plus publication is awarded for a poetry manuscript, 50 to 120 pages, by a woman writer. Deadline: February 1 (of even-numbered years).

ELF: ECLECTIC LITERARY FORUM—Ruth Cable Memorial Prize, P.O. Box 392, Tonawanda, NY 14150. Awards of $500 and three $50 prizes are given for poems up to 50 lines. Deadline: March 31.

ELMIRA COLLEGE—Playwriting Award, Dept. of Theatre, Elmira College, Elmira, NY 14901. Attn: Prof. Amnon Kabatchnik, Artistic Dir. A prize of $1,000 plus production is awarded for the best original full-length play. Deadline: June 1 (of even-numbered years).

EMPORIA STATE UNIVERSITY—Bluestem Award, English Dept., Emporia State Univ., Emporia, KS 66801–5087. A prize of $1,000 plus publication is awarded for a previously unpublished book of poems by a U.S. author. Deadline: March 1.

ENSEMBLE THEATRE—George Hawkins Play Contest, 3535 Main St., Houston, TX 77002. Offers $500 plus production for an original one-act play or musical, using adult actors, for African-American audiences, ages 6 to 16. Deadline: March 15.

FAMILY CIRCLE—Annual Mystery/Suspense Short Story Contest, 110 Fifth Ave., New York, NY 10011. A first prize of $2,000 plus publication, and a $1,000 second prize are awarded for short stories of mystery or suspense. Deadline: November 1.

THE FLORIDA REVIEW—Short Fiction Contest, Dept. of English, Univ. of Central Florida, Orlando, FL 32816–0001. Attn: Russell Kesler, Ed. A $500 first prize, plus publication, and a $200 second prize are offered for short stories of up to 7,500 words. Deadline: May 15.

FLORIDA STATE UNIVERSITY—World's Best Short Short Story Contest, English Dept., Florida State University, Tallahassee, FL 32306. Attn: Jerome Stern. A prize of $100, a box of Florida oranges, and publication are offered for the best short short story, 250 words. Deadline: February 15.

FLORIDA STUDIO THEATRE—Shorts Contest, 1241 N. Palm Ave., Sarasota, FL 34236. Attn: Christian Angermann. Short scripts, songs, and other performance pieces on a given theme are eligible for a prize of $500. Deadline: June 15.

THE FORMALIST—Howard Nemerov Sonnet Award, 320 Hunter Dr., Evansville, IN 47711. A prize of $1,000 plus publication is offered for a previously unpublished, original sonnet. Deadline: May 31.

FOUR WAY BOOKS—Poetry Contests, P.O. Box 607, Marshfield, MA 02050. Intro Series in Poetry: A prize of $1,000 plus publication is awarded for a book-length collection of poems by a poet who has not previously published a book of poetry. Award Series in Poetry: A prize of $1,500 plus publication is awarded for a book-length collection of poems by a poet who as published at least one collection of poetry. Deadline: April 30.

GALLERY PLAYERS—The Leo Yassenoff Jewish Community of Greater Columbus, 1125 College Ave., Columbus, OH 43209. A $1,000 award plus possible production is offered for the best original, previously unproduced and unpublished full-length play; musicals are not eligible. Deadline: September 1 (of odd-numbered years).

GEORGE MASON UNIVERSITY—Greg Grummer Award in Poetry, *Phoebe: A Journal of Literary Arts*, 4400 Univ. Dr., Fairfax, VA 22030. A prize of $500 plus publication is offered for an outstanding previously unpublished poem. Deadline: October 15.

GLIMMER TRAIN PRESS—Semi-Annal Short Story Award for New Writers, 812 S.W. Washington St., #1205, Portland, OR 97205. Writers whose fiction has never appeared in a nationally distributed publication are eligible to enter their stories of 1,200 to 7,500 words. Prizes are $1,200 plus publication, $500, and $300. Deadlines: March 31; September 30.

GROLIER POETRY PRIZE—6 Plympton St., Cambridge, MA 02138. Two $150 honorariums are awarded for poetry manuscripts of up to 10 pages by writers who have not yet published a book of poems. Deadline: May 1.

HEEKIN GROUP FOUNDATION—Fiction Fellowships Competition, 68860 Goodrich Rd., Sisters, OR 97759. Offers the $5,000 Tara Fellowship in Short Fiction, the $10,000 James Fellowship for the Novel in Progress, and the $4,000 Mary Molloy Fellowship for the Children's Working Novel to writers who have never published a novel, and have not published more than three short stories. Deadline: December 1.

809

HELICON NINE EDITIONS—Literary Prizes, 9000 W. 64th Terrace, Merriam, KS 66202. Attn: Gloria Vando Hickok. Marianne Moore Poetry Prize: offers $1,000 for an original unpublished poetry manuscript of at least 50 pages. Willa Cather Fiction Prize: offers $1,000 for an original novella or short story collection, from 150 to 300 pages. Deadline: January 30.

HEMINGWAY SHORT STORY COMPETITION—Hemingway Days Festival, P.O. Box 4045, Key West, FL 33041. A $1,000 first prize, and two $500 runner-up prizes are offered for short stories, 2,500 words or fewer, of any form or style. Deadline: July 1.

HIGHLIGHTS FOR CHILDREN—Fiction Contest, 803 Church St., Honesdale, PA 18431. Three $1,000 prizes plus publication are offered for stories on a given subject, up to 900 words. Deadline: February 28.

HILTON-LONG POETRY FOUNDATION—Naomi Long Madgett Poetry Award, c/o Lotus Press, Inc., P.O. Box 21607, Detroit, MI 48221. A prize of $500 plus publication will be awarded to an African-American writer for a previously unpublished collection of poems, 60 to 80 pages. Deadline: April 1.

RUTH HINDMAN FOUNDATION—H.E. Francis Award, Dept. of English, Univ. of Alabama, Huntsville, AL 35899. A prize of $1,000 plus publication is awarded for a short story of up to 5,000 words. Deadline: December 1.

HUMBOLDT STATE UNIVERSITY—Raymond Carver Short Story Contest, English Dept., Arcata, CA 95521–4957. Offers a $500 first prize, plus publication in the literary journal *Toyon*, and a $250 second prize for an unpublished short story, to 25 pages, by a writer living in the U.S. Deadline: November 1.

ICS BOOKS, INC.—"No S---! There I Was Again" Contest, 1370 E. 86th Pl., Merrillville, IN 46410. Prizes of $1,200 and $400 plus publication are offered for humorous, tall tales. Deadline: December 1.

IOWA WOMAN MAGAZINE—Writing Contest for Women, P.O. Box 2938, Waterloo, IA 50704. Women writers may enter short fiction, essays, or poems for a $300 first prize, $150 second prize, and publication. Deadline: December 31.

IUPUI CHILDREN'S THEATRE—Playwriting Competition, Indiana University-Purdue University at Indianapolis, 525 N. Blackford St., Indianapolis, IN 46202–3120. Offers four $1,000 prizes plus staged readings for plays for young people. Deadline: September 1 (of even-numbered years).

ALICE JAMES BOOKS—Beatrice Hawley Award, 98 Main St., Farmington, ME 04938. A prize of publication plus 100 free copies is offered for the best poetry manuscript, 60 to 70 pages. Deadline: January 15.

JEWISH COMMUNITY CENTER THEATRE—Dorothy Silver Playwriting Competition, 3505 Mayfield Rd., Cleveland Heights, OH 44118. Attn: Elaine Rembrandt, Dir. Offers $1,000 and a staged reading for an original, previously unproduced full-length play, on some aspect of the Jewish experience. Deadline: December 15.

THE CHESTER H. JONES FOUNDATION—National Poetry Competition, P. O. Box 498, Chardon, OH 44024. Prizes of $1,000, $750, $500, and $250, as well as several $50 and $10 prizes are awarded for original, unpublished poems of up to 32 lines. Deadline: March 31.

JAMES JONES SOCIETY—First Novel Fellowship, c/o Dept. of English, Wilkes Univ., Wilkes-Barre, PA 18766. An award of $2,000 is offered for a first novel-in-progress by an American. Deadline: April 1.

THE JOURNAL: THE LITERARY MAGAZINE OF O.S.U.—The Ohio State University Press, 180 Pressey Hall, 1070 Carmack Rd., Columbus, OH 43210–1002. Attn: David Citino, Poetry Ed. Awards $1,000 plus publication for at least 48 pages of original, unpublished poetry. Deadline: September 30.

KALLIOPE—Sue Saniel Elkind Poetry Contest, Florida Community College at Jacksonville, 3939 Roosevelt Blvd., Jacksonville, FL 32205. Publication and $1,000 are awarded for the best poem, under 40 lines, written by a woman. Deadline: November 1.

KEATS/KERLAN MEMORIAL FELLOWSHIP—The Ezra Jack Keats/Kerlan Collection Memorial Fellowship Committee, 109 Walter Library, 117 Pleasant St. S.E., Univ. of Minnesota, Minneapolis, MN 55455. A $1,500 fellowship is awarded to a talented writer and/or illustrator of children's books who wishes to use the Kerlan Collection for furtherance of his or her artistic development. Deadline: May 1.

JACK KEROUAC LITERARY PRIZE—Lowell Historic Preservation Commission, 222 Merrimack St., Suite 310, Lowell, MA 01852. A prize of $500 and festival reading are awarded for an unpublished work of fiction, nonfiction, or poetry relating to themes expressed in Kerouac's work. Deadline: August 1.

LA JOLLA FESTIVAL—International Imitation Raymond Chandler Writing Competition, c/o Friends of the La Jolla Library, 3129 Bremerton Pl., La Jolla, CA 92037. Prizes of $700, $500, and $300 will be awarded for manuscripts, 500 words, that imitate or parody Raymond Chandler's writing style and subject matter. Deadline: August 1.

LINCOLN COLLEGE—Billee Murray Denny Poetry Award, Lincoln, IL 62656. Attn: Janet Overton. Prizes of $1,000, $500, and $250 are offered for original, unpublished poems by poets who have never published a book of poetry. Deadline: May 31.

LIVE OAK THEATRE—New Play Award, 311 Nueces St., Austin, TX 78701. Offers $1,000 plus possible production for the best full-length, unproduced, unpublished play. Deadline: November 1.

LODI ARTS COMMISSION—Drama Festival, 125 S. Hutchins St., Lodi, CA 95240. A prize of $1,000 plus production is awarded for a full-length play; a prize of $500 plus production is awarded for a children's play. Deadline: April 1 (of odd-numbered years).

LOVE CREEK PRODUCTIONS—Short Play Festival & One-Act Mini Festivals, 47 El Dorado Pl., Weehawken, NJ 07087–7004. Gay and Lesbian One-Acts: Finalists receive showcase production; the winner receives a $200 prize. Deadline: May 31. One-Acts on Religion and Spirituality: Finalists receive production; the winner receives a $200 prize. Deadline: July 31. Short Plays: At least 30 scripts, up to 40 minutes long, are chosen for festival performance; the winner receives a $300 prize. Deadline: September 30.

AMY LOWELL POETRY TRAVELLING SCHOLARSHIP—Choate, Hall & Stewart, Exchange Pl., 53 State St., Boston, MA 02109–2891. Attn: F. Davis Dassori, Jr., Esq. A scholarship of approximately $29,000 is awarded for a poet to spend the year abroad to advance the art of poetry. Deadline: October 15.

THE MADISON REVIEW—Dept. of English, 600 N. Park St., Helen C. White Hall, Univ. of Wisconsin-Madison, Madison, WI 53706. Phyllis Smart Young Prize in Poetry: awards $500 plus publication for a group of three unpublished poems. Chris O'Malley Prize in Fiction: awards $500 plus publication for an unpublished short story. Deadline: September 30.

MASQUE THEATRE OF TEMPLE TERRACE—Playwriting Competition, P.O. Box 291212, Tampa, FL 33687–1212. Attn: Contest Coordinator. Prizes of $500 plus production, $100, and $50 are awarded for previously unpublished, unproduced, full-length plays; no children's plays or musicals. Deadline: February 28.

MIDWEST RADIO THEATRE WORKSHOP—MRTW Script Contests, 915 E. Broadway, Columbia, MO 65201. The Workshop Script Contest: offers $800 in prizes, to be divided among two to four winners, and free workshop participation for contemporary radio scripts, 25–30 minutes long. Deadline: November 15. Public Service Announcement Contest: offers $100 plus production for a 60-second script using radio theater to increase AIDS awareness. Deadline: November 15.

MIDWEST THEATRE NETWORK—Rochester Playwright Festival, 5031 Tongen Ave. N.W., Rochester, MN 55901. Seven scripts of various lengths and types are chosen for festival production. Deadline: January 31.

MILKWEED EDITIONS—430 First Ave. N., Suite 400, Minneapolis, MN 55401–1743. Prize for Children's Literature: A cash prize plus publication with negotiated advance and royalties are offered for a children's novel or biography that embodies humane values and insights that contribute to cultural understanding; writers who have published book-length fiction or nonfiction for children or adults, or at least three short stories are eligible to enter. Deadline: Entries accepted year round. National Fiction Prize: A prize of $3,000 plus publication is offered for a novel, novella, or collection of short fiction by a writer who has previously published a book-length collection of fiction or at least three short stories or novellas in nationally distributed journals. Deadline: July 15.

MILL MOUNTAIN THEATRE—New Play Competition, 2nd Floor, One Market Square, Roanoke, VA 24011–1437. Attn: Jo Weinstein. Sponsors New Play Competition with a $1,000 prize and staged reading, with possible full production, for an unpublished, unproduced, full-length or one-act play. Cast size to ten. Deadline: January 1.

THE MISSOURI REVIEW—Editors' Prize, 1507 Hillcrest Hall, UMC, Columbia, MO 65211. Publication plus $1,000 is awarded for short fiction and essay manuscripts, 25 pages, and $500 for the winning poetry manuscript, 10 pages. Deadline: October 15.

THE MOUNTAINEERS BOOKS—The Barbara Savage/"Miles from Nowhere" Memorial Award, 1011 S. W. Klickitat Way, Suite 107, Seattle, WA 98134. Attn: Donna DeShazo, Dir. Offers a $3,000 cash award, plus publication and a $12,000 guaranteed advance against royalties for an outstanding unpublished, book-length manuscript of a nonfiction, personal-adventure narrative. Deadline: February 1 (of even-numbered years).

MULBERRY PRESS—Poetry Prize, 105 Betty Rd., East Meadow, NY 11554–1601. Attn: Contest Chairperson. Offers $500 plus broadside publication for the best previously unpublished poem. Deadline: March 31.

NATIONAL ENDOWMENT FOR THE ARTS—Nancy Hanks Center, 1100 Pennsylvania Ave. N.W., Room 722, Washington, DC 20506. Attn: Dir., Literature Program. Offers fellowships to writers and translators of poetry, fiction, plays, and creative nonfiction. Deadline: varies.

NATIONAL POETRY SERIES—P.O. Box G, Hopewell, NJ 08525. Attn: Amanda Ford, Coordinator. Sponsors Annual Open Competition for unpublished book-length poetry manuscripts. Five manuscripts are selected for publication, and each winner receives a $1,000 award. Deadline: February 15.

NATIONAL REPERTORY THEATRE FOUNDATION—National Play Award, P.O. Box 71011, Los Angeles, CA 90071. Attn: R. Espinoza. A prize of $5,000 plus five runner-up awards of $500 each are awarded for an original, previously unproduced play. Deadline: June 30 (of odd-numbered years).

NEGATIVE CAPABILITY MAGAZINE—Fiction/Poetry Contests, 62 Ridgelawn Dr. East, Mobile, AL 36608. Attn: Sue Walker. Eve of St. Agnes Poetry Award: offers $1,000 plus publication for an original, unpublished poem. Deadline: January 15. Short Fiction Award: offers $1,000 for a previously unpublished story, 1,500 to 4,500 words. Deadline: December 1.

NEW DRAMATISTS—L. Arnold Weissberger Playwriting Competition, 424 W. 44th St., New York, NY 10036. A prize of $5,000 is offered for full-length, unpublished, unproduced script. Deadline: May 31.

NEW ENGLAND POETRY CLUB—P.O. Box 81275, Wellesley Hills, MA 02181–0002. Prizes range from $500 to $100 in various contests for members and nonmembers. Deadline: June 30.

NEW ENGLAND THEATRE CONFERENCE—John Gassner Memorial Playwriting Award, c/o Dept. of Theatre, Northeastern Univ., 360 Huntington Ave., Boston, MA 02115. A $500 first prize and a $250 second prize are offered for unpublished, unproduced full-length plays. Deadline: April 15.

NEW LETTERS—University of Missouri-Kansas City, 5100 Rockhill Rd., Kansas City, MO 64110. Offers $750 for the best short story, to 5,000 words; $750 for the best group of three to six poems; $500 for the best essay, to 5,000 words. The work of each winner and first runner-up will be published. Deadline: May 15.

NEWPORT WRITERS CONFERENCE—Spirit of Newport Writing Contest, P.O. Box 12, Newport, RI 02840. A prize of $250 plus free writers conference tuition is offered for short stories, to 2,000 words, and poetry, any length, using a Newport theme or setting. Deadline: August 1.

NIMROD/HARDMAN AWARDS—Arts and Humanities Council of Tulsa, 2210 S. Main St., Tulsa, OK 74114. Katherine Anne Porter Prize: offers prizes of $1,000 and $500 for fiction, to 7,500 words. Pablo Neruda Prize: offers prizes of $1,000 and $500 for one long poem or a selection of poems. Deadline: April 15.

NORTH CAROLINA WRITERS' NETWORK—Writing Contests, 3501 Hwy. 54 West, Studio C, Chapel Hill, NC 27516. Thomas Wolfe Fiction Prize: offers $500 for a previously unpublished short story or novel excerpt. Deadline: August 31. Randall Jarrell Poetry Prize: offers $500 for a previously unpublished poem. Deadline: November 1.

NORTHEASTERN UNIVERSITY PRESS—Samuel French Morse Poetry Prize, English Dept., 406 Holmes, Northeastern Univ., Boston, MA 02115. Attn: Prof. Guy Rotella, Chairman. Offers $500 plus publication for a full-length poetry manuscript by a U.S. poet who has published no more than one book of poems. Deadline: August 1 (for inquiries); September 15 (for entries).

NORTHERN KENTUCKY UNIVERSITY—Y.E.S. New Play Festival, Dept. of Theatre, Highland Hts., KY 41099–1007. Attn: Mike King, Project Dir. Awards three $400 prizes plus production for previously unproduced full-length plays and musicals. Deadline: October 15 (of even-numbered years).

NORTHERN MICHIGAN UNIVERSITY—Mildred & Albert Panowski Playwriting Competition, Forest Roberts Theatre, Northern Michigan Univ., 1401 Presque Isle Ave., Marquette, MI 49855–5364. Awards $2,000, plus production for an original, full-length, previously unproduced and unpublished play. Deadline: November 15.

O'NEILL THEATER CENTER—National Playwrights Conference, 234 W. 44th St., Suite 901, New York, NY 10036. Offers stipend, staged readings, and room and board at the conference, for new stage and television plays. Deadline: December 1.

THE PARIS REVIEW—Poetry and Fiction Prizes, 541 E. 72nd St., New York, NY 10021. Bernard F. Connors Prize: offers $1,000 plus publication for a previously unpublished poem. Deadline: May 1. Aga Khan Prize: offers $1,000 plus publication for a previously unpublished short story. Deadline: June 1.

PEN/JERARD FUND AWARD—PEN American Center, 568 Broadway, New York, NY 10012. Attn: John Morrone, Programs & Publications. Offers $4,000 to beginning female writers for a work-in-progress of general nonfiction. Applicants must have published at least one article in a national magazine or major literary magazine, but not more than one book of any kind. Deadline: January 15 (of odd-numbered years).

PEN WRITERS FUND—PEN American Center, 568 Broadway, New York, NY 10012. Attn: Karen Hwa, Coordinator. Grants and interest-free loans of up to $1,000 are available to published writers or produced playwrights facing unanticipated financial emergencies. If the emergency is due to HIV- and AIDS-related illness, professional writers and editors qualify through the Fund for Writers and Editors with AIDS; all decisions are confidential. Deadline: applications accepted year-round.

PEN WRITING AWARDS FOR PRISONERS—PEN American Center, 568 Broadway, New York, NY 10012. County, state, and federal prisoners are eligible to enter one published manuscript in each of four categories: poetry, to 100 lines, fiction, drama, and nonfiction, to 5,000 words. Prizes of $100, $50, and $25 are awarded in each category. Deadline: September 1.

PEREGRINE SMITH POETRY SERIES—Gibbs Smith, Publisher, P.O. Box 667, Layton, UT 84041. Offers a $500 prize plus publication for a previously unpublished 64-page poetry manuscript. Deadline: April 30.

PETERLOO POETS—Open Competition, 2 Kelly Gardens, Calstock, Cornwall PL18 9SA, U.K. Attn: Harry Chambers. Prizes totalling 4,100 British pounds, including a grand prize of £2,000 plus publication, are awarded for poems of up to 40 lines. Deadline: March 1.

PIG IRON PRESS—Kenneth Patchen Competition, P.O. Box 237, Youngstown, OH 44501. Awards paperback publication, $100, and 50 copies of the winning manuscript of fiction (in even-numbered years) and poetry (in odd-numbered years). Deadline: October 31.

PIONEER DRAMA SERVICE—Shubert Fendrich Memorial Playwriting Contest, P.O. Box 4267, Englewood, CO 80155–4267. A prize of publication plus a $1,000 advance is offered for a previously produced, though unpublished, full-length play suitable for community theater. Deadline: March 1.

PIRATE'S ALLEY FAULKNER PRIZES FOR FICTION—632 Pirate's Alley, New Orleans, LA 70116. Prizes are $5,000 for an unpublished novel of over 50,000 words; $1,500 for a novellas of under 50,000 words; and $1,250 for a short story of under 15,000 words. All awards include additional prize money to be used as an advance against royalties to encourage publisher interest. Deadline: April 1.

PLAYBOY MAGAZINE—College Fiction Contest, 680 N. Lakeshore Dr., Chicago, IL 60611. Prizes of $3,000 plus publication, and $500, are offered for a short story, up to 25 pages, by a college student. Deadline: January 1.

PLAYHOUSE-ON-THE-SQUARE—New Play Competition, 51 S. Cooper, Memphis, TN 38104. Attn: Mr. Jackie Nichols, Exec. Dir. A stipend plus production is awarded for a full-length, previously unproduced play or musical. Deadline: April 1.

THE PLAYWRIGHTS' CENTER—Jerome Fellowships, 2301 Franklin Ave. East, Minneapolis, MN 55406. Six emerging playwrights are offered a $5,000 stipend and 12-month residency; housing and travel are not provided. Deadline: November 1.

THE PLUM REVIEW—Poetry Contest, P.O. Box 1347, Philadelphia, PA 19105–1347. Publication and $500 are awarded for previously unpublished poems in any form or style. Deadline: February 28.

POCKETS MAGAZINE—Fiction Contest, c/o Lynn W. Gilliam, Assoc. Ed., P.O. Box 189, Nashville, TN 37202–0189. A $1,000 prize goes to the author of the winning 1,000- to 1,600-word story for children in grades 1 to 6. Deadline: September 1.

POET LORE—John Williams Andrews Narrative Poetry Competition, The Writer's Center, 4508 Walsh St., Bethesda, MD 20815. A prize of $350 plus publication is awarded for the best unpublished, original narrative poem of at least 100 lines. Deadline: November 30.

POETRY SOCIETY OF AMERICA—15 Gramercy Park, New York, NY 10003. Prizes ranging from $2,750 to $100 are offered in contests for unpublished poems, open to members and nonmembers: Celia B. Wagner Memorial Award; John Masefield Memorial Award; Elias Lieberman Student Poetry Award; George Bogin Memorial Award; Robert H. Winner Memorial Award; Ruth Lake Memorial Award. Deadline: December 15.

EMILY POWELL LITERARY AWARDS—8F Hudson Harbour Dr., Poughkeepsie, NY 12601. Attn: Victor L. Gregurick. Prizes of $200, $150, $100, and $50 are awarded for unpublished poems, up to 100 lines. Deadline: August 15.

PRISM INTERNATIONAL—Short Fiction Contest, Creative Writing Dept., Univ. of B.C., E466–1866 Main Mall, Vancouver, B.C., V6T 1Z1. Publication, a $2,000 first prize, and five $200 prizes are awarded for stories of up to 25 pages. Deadline: December 1.

PURDUE UNIVERSITY PRESS—Verna Emery Poetry Award, 1532 South Campus Courts-B, W. Lafayette, IN 47907–1532. Unpublished collections of original poetry, 60 to 90 pages, are considered for an award of publication plus royalties. Deadline: January 31.

QUARTERLY REVIEW OF LITERATURE—Poetry Awards, 26 Haslet Ave., Princeton, NJ 08540. Four to six prizes of $1,000, publication, and 100 books are awarded for 60- to 100-page manuscripts of poetry, poetic plays, long poems, or poetry in translation. Deadlines: May 31; November 30.

QUICK BROWN FOX PUBLISHERS—Short Story and Poetry Contest, Dept. TW, P.O. Box 7894, Athens, GA 30604–7894. Attn: Dr. Charles Connor. Prizes of $500 and $100 are awarded for stories of up to 3,000 words. A $100 prize is awarded for the best poem of up to 16 lines. Deadline: February 1.

RANDOM HOUSE JUVENILE BOOKS—Dr. Seuss Picturebook Award Contest, 201 E. 50th St., New York, NY 10022. A prize of $25,000 plus publication is awarded for a picturebook manuscript by an author/illustrator who has not published more than one book. Deadline: December 1 (of even-numbered years).

THE RETURNING THE GIFT FOUNDATION—North American Native Authors First Book Awards, The Greenfield Review Literary Center, P.O. Box 308, 2 Middle Grove Rd., Greenfield Center, NY 12833. Attn: Joseph Bruchac, Dir. Native Americans of American Indian, Aleut, Inuit, or Metis ancestry who have not yet published a book are eligible to enter poetry, 48 to 100 pages, and prose, up to 100 pages of fiction or nonfiction, for publication. Deadline: May 1.

RIVER CITY MAGAZINE—Writing Awards in Fiction, Dept. of English, Memphis State University, Memphis, TN 38152. Attn: Sharon Bryan, Ed. Awards a $2,000 first prize, plus publication, a $500 second prize, and a $300 third prize, for previously unpublished short stories, to 7,500 words. Deadline: December 1.

ROME ART & COMMUNITY CENTER—Milton Dorfman Poetry Prize, 308 W. Bloomfield St., Rome, NY 13440. Offers prizes of $500, $200, and $100 plus publication for the best original, unpublished poems. Deadline: November 1.

IAN ST JAMES AWARDS—c/o The New Writers' Club Ltd., P.O. Box 101, Tunbridge Wells, Kent TN4 8YD, England. Attn: Merric Davidson. Offers twenty prizes of 250 to 5,000 British pounds plus publication for short stories. Deadline: February 28.

ST. MARTIN'S PRESS/MALICE DOMESTIC CONTEST—Thomas Dunne Books, 175 Fifth Ave., New York, NY 10010. Offers publication plus a $10,000 advance against royalties, for Best First Traditional Mystery Novel. Deadline: October 15.

ST. MARTIN'S PRESS/PRIVATE EYE NOVEL CONTEST—Private Eye Novel Contest, 175 Fifth Ave., New York, NY 10010. Co-sponsored by Private Eye Writers of America. Winner of the Best First Private Eye Novel Contest receives publication plus $10,000 against royalties; open to previously unpublished writers of private eye novels. Deadline: August 1.

SIENA COLLEGE—International Playwrights' Competition, Siena College, 515 Loudon Rd., Loudonville, NY 12211–1462. Offers $2,000 plus campus residency expenses for the winning full-length script; no musicals. Deadline: June 30 (of even-numbered years).

SIERRA REPERTORY THEATRE—Taylor Playwriting Award, P. O. Box 3030, Sonora, CA 95370. Attn: Dennis Jones, Producing Dir. Offers $500, plus possible production, for full-length plays or musicals that have received no more than two productions or staged readings. Deadline: August 31.

SLIPSTREAM—Poetry Chapbook Contest, P.O. Box 2071, Niagara Falls, NY 14301. Attn: Dan Sicoli. A prize of $500 plus 50 chapbook copies is offered for the best poetry manuscript of up to 40 pages. Deadline: December 1.

SMOKEBRUSH CENTER FOR ARTS AND THEATER—Festival of New Plays for Children, 235 South Nevada, Colorado Springs, CO 80903. An expense-paid trip to view production is awarded for an original, unpublished, previously unproduced children's play. Deadline: February 28.

SNAKE NATION PRESS—Violet Reed Haas Poetry Prize, 110 #2 West Force, Valdosta, GA 31601. Attn: Nancy Phillips. A prize of publication plus $500 is awarded for a previously unpublished book of poetry, 50 to 75 pages. Deadline: January 1.

SOCIETY OF AMERICAN TRAVEL WRITERS FOUNDATION—Lowell Thomas Travel Journalism Award, 4101 Lake Boone Trail, Suite 201, Raleigh, NC 27607. Prizes totalling $11,000 are offered for published and broadcast work by U.S. and Canadian travel journalists. Deadline: February 28.

SONORA REVIEW—Contests, Univ. of Arizona, Dept. of English, Tucson, AZ 85721. Poetry Contest: offers $500 plus publication for the best poem. Deadline: July 1. Short Story Contest: offers $500 plus publication for the best short story. Deadline: December 1.

SONS OF THE REPUBLIC OF TEXAS—Summerfield G. Roberts Award, General Office, 5942 Abrams Rd., Suite 222, Dallas, TX 75231. A prize of $2,500 is awarded for published or unpublished creative writing on the Republic of Texas, 1836–1846. Deadline: January 15.

SOUTH COAST POETRY JOURNAL—Annual Poetry Contest, English Dept., California State University at Fullerton, Fullerton, CA 92634. Previously unpublished, original poems, to 40 lines, will be considered for prizes of $200, $100, and $50, plus publication. Deadline: March 31.

SOUTHERN APPALACHIAN REPERTORY THEATRE—Playwrights' Conference, P.O. Box 620, Mars Hill, NC 28754–0620. Attn: Ms. Gaynelle M. Caldwell, Jr. Unproduced, unpublished scripts will be considered; up to five playwrights are selected to attend the conference and hear their plays read by professional actors; full production is possible. Deadline: October 1.

SOUTHERN POETRY REVIEW—Guy Owen Poetry Prize, Dept. of English, UNCC, Charlotte, NC 28223. Attn: Ken McLaurin, Ed. A prize of publication plus $500 is awarded for the best original, previously unpublished poem. Deadline: April 30.

THE SOW'S EAR PRESS—19535 Pleasant View Dr., Abingdon, VA 24211–6827. Chapbook Competition: offers a prize of $500 plus 50 published copies for the best poetry manuscript. Deadline: April 30. Poetry Competition: offers prizes of $500, $100, and $50 for a previously unpublished poem of any length. Deadline: October 31.

STAND MAGAZINE—Short Story Competition, 179 Wingrove Rd., Newcastle upon Tyne, NE4 9DA, U.K. Prizes totalling 2,250 British pounds, including a £1,250 first prize, are awarded for previously unpublished stories under 8,000 words. Winning stories are published in *Stand Magazine*. Deadline: March 31 (of odd-numbered years).

STORY LINE PRESS—Nicholas Roerich Prize, 27006 Gap Rd., Three Oaks Farm, Brownsville, OR 97327–9718. A prize of $1,000 plus publication is awarded for an original book of poetry by a poet who has never before published a book. Deadline: October 15.

SUNY FARMINGDALE—Paumanok Poetry Award, Visiting Writers Program, Knapp Hall, SUNY Farmingdale, Farmingdale, NY 11735. Prizes of $750 and two $300 prizes are offered for entries of five to seven poems. Deadline: September 15.

SYRACUSE UNIVERSITY PRESS—John Ben Snow Prize, 1600 Jamesville Ave., Syracuse, NY 13244–5160. Attn: Dir. Awards a $1,500 advance, plus publication, for an unpublished book-length nonfiction manuscript about New York State, especially upstate or central New York. Deadline: December 31.

TAKESHI KAIKO AWARD—Takeshi Kaiko Award Secretariat, c/o TBS Britannica Co., Ltd., Shuwa Sanbancho Bldg., 28–1 Sanbancho, Chiyoda-ku, Tokyo

102, Japan. A prize of three million yen is awarded for a previously unpublished manuscript relating to the observation of human nature; fiction, nonfiction, reviews, or reports up to 60,000 words are eligible. Deadline: August 31.

TEN-MINUTE MUSICALS PROJECT—Box 461194, W. Hollywood, CA 90046. Attn: Michael Koppy, Prod. Musicals of 7 to 14 minutes are eligible for a $250 advance against royalties and musical anthology productions at theaters in the U.S. and Canada. Deadline: August 31.

THE WRITERS' WORKSHOP—Poetry, Fiction, and Nonfiction Contests, P.O. Box 696, Asheville, NC 28802. International Poetry and Fiction Contests: A $500 first prize, $250 second prize, and $100 third prize are offered for unpublished stories of up to 30 typed, double-spaced pages, and poetry of up to three typed, double-spaced pages per poem. Deadline: February 15. Isak Dinesen Creative Nonfiction Contest: offers $500, $250, and $100 for unpublished essays of up to 20 typed, double-spaced pages. Deadline: August 31.

THEATRE MEMPHIS—New Play Competition, P.O. Box 240117, Memphis, TN 38124–0117. The prize is $1,500 plus production for the best full-length play or group of related one-acts. Deadline: July 1, 1996 (held every three years).

THEATREWORKS—Playwrights' Forum Awards, Univ. of Colorado, P.O. Box 7150, Colorado Springs, CO 80933–7150. Attn: Whit Andrews, Producing Dir. Two unpublished, unproduced short plays are selected for production; playwrights are awarded $250 plus travel expenses. Deadline: December 1.

THE THURBER HOUSE—Thurber House Residencies, 77 Jefferson Ave., Columbus, OH 43215. Attn: Michael J. Rosen, Lit. Dir. Three-month residencies and stipends of $5,000 each are awarded in the categories of writing, playwriting, and journalism. Winners have limited teaching responsibilities with The Ohio State University. Deadline: December 15.

TOWNGATE THEATRE—Playwriting Contest, Oglebay Institute, Oglebay, Wheeling, WV 26003. Offers $300 plus production for an unproduced, full-length, non-musical play. Deadline: January 1.

TRIQUARTERLY—Northwestern University, 2020 Ridge Ave., Evanston, IL 60208–4302. William Goyen Prize for Fiction: offers $3,000 plus publication for an unpublished novel, novella, or short story collection, 150 to 400 pages. Deadline: June 30 (of odd-numbered years). Terrence Des Pres Prize for Poetry: offers $2,000 plus publication for unpublished poetry manuscripts of at least 48 pages. Deadline: August 31 (of even-numbered years).

TRITON COLLEGE—Salute to the Arts Poetry Contest, 2000 Fifth Ave., River Grove, IL 60171–1995. Winning original, unpublished poems, to 60 lines, on designated themes, are published by Triton College. Deadline: April 1.

UNICO NATIONAL—Ella T. Grasso Literary Award Contest, 72 Burroughs Pl., Bloomfield, NJ 07003. A prize of $1,000 is awarded for the best essay or short story, 1,500 to 2,000 words, on the Italian-American experience. Deadline: April 1.

U.S. NAVAL INSTITUTE—Arleigh Burke Essay Contest, *Proceedings Magazine*, 118 Maryland Ave., Annapolis, MD 21402–5035. Attn: Bert Hubinger. Awards prizes of $3,000, $2,000, and $1,000 plus publication, for essays on the advancement of professional, literary, or scientific knowledge in the naval or maritime services, and the advancement of the knowledge of sea power. Deadline: December 1. Also sponsors several smaller contests; deadlines vary.

UNIVERSITY OF ARKANSAS PRESS—Arkansas Poetry Award, 201 Ozark Ave., Fayetteville, AR 72701. Awards publication of a 50- to 80-page poetry manuscript to a writer who has never had a book of poetry published. Deadline: May 1.

UNIVERSITY OF CALIFORNIA IRVINE—Chicano/Latino Literary Contest, Dept. of Spanish and Portuguese, UCI Irvine, CA 92717. Attn: Juan Bruce-Novoa, Dir. A first prize of $1,000 plus publication, and prizes of $500 and $250 are awarded in alternating years for poetry, drama, novels, and short stories. Deadline: April 30.

UNIVERSITY OF COLORADO—Nilon Award for Excellence in Minority Fiction, Fiction Collective Two, English Dept. Publications Ctr., Campus Box 494, Boulder, CO 80309–0494. Awards $1,000 plus joint publication for original, unpublished, book-length fiction, in English, by a U.S. citizen of the following ethnic minorities: African American, Hispanic, Asian, Native American or Alaskan Native, and Pacific Islander. Deadline: November 30.

UNIVERSITY OF GEORGIA PRESS—Flannery O'Connor Award for Short Fiction, Athens, GA 30602. Two prizes of $1,000 plus publication are awarded for a book-length collection of short fiction. Deadline: July 31.

UNIVERSITY OF GEORGIA PRESS CONTEMPORARY POETRY SERIES—Athens, GA 30602–4901. Offers publication of manuscripts from poets who have published at least one volume of poetry. Deadline: January 31. Publication of book-length poetry manuscripts is offered to poets who have never had a book of poems published. Deadline: September 30.

UNIVERSITY OF HAWAII AT MANOA—Kumu Kahua Playwriting Contest, Dept. of Drama and Theatre, 1770 East-West Rd., Honolulu, HI 96822. Awards $500 for a full-length play, and $200 for a one-act, set in Hawaii and dealing with some aspect of the Hawaiian experience. Also conducts contest for plays written by Hawaiian residents. Deadline: January 1.

UNIVERSITY OF IOWA—Iowa Publication Awards for Short Fiction, Dept. of English, 308 English Philosophy Bldg., Iowa City, IA 52242–1492. The John Simmons Short Fiction Award and the Iowa Short Fiction Award, both for unpublished full-length collections of short stories, offer publication under a standard contract. Deadline: September 30.

UNIVERSITY OF IOWA PRESS—The Iowa Poetry Prize, 119 W. Park Rd., 100 Kuhl House, Iowa City, IA 52242–1000. Two $1,000 prizes, plus publication, are awarded for poetry manuscripts, 50 to 150 pages, by writers who have published at least one book of poetry. Deadline: March 31.

UNIVERSITY OF MASSACHUSETTS PRESS—Juniper Prize, Amherst, MA 01003. Offers a prize of $1,000 plus publication for a book-length manuscript of poetry; awarded in odd-numbered years to writers who have never published a book of poetry, and in even-numbered years to writers who have published a book or chapbook of poetry. Deadline: September 30.

UNIVERSITY OF NEBRASKA PRESS—North American Indian Prose Award, 327 Nebraska Hall, 901 N. 17th St., Lincoln, NE 68588–0520. Previously unpublished book-length manuscripts of biography, autobiography, history, literary criticism, and essays will be judged for originality, literary merit, and familiarity with North American Indian life. A $1,000 advance and publication are offered. Deadline: July 1.

UNIVERSITY OF NORTH TEXAS PRESS—Katherine Anne Porter Prize in Short Fiction, ALR Books/ Short Fiction Series, UNT Box 13827, Denton, TX 76203–6827. Attn: William Cobb, Ed. A prize of $500 plus publication is awarded for a fiction manuscript of 150 to 300 pages. Deadline: April 30. The Vassar Miller Prize in Poetry (c/o Scott Cairns, Series Ed., ALR Books/ Poetry Series, English Dept., Old Dominion Univ., Norfolk, VA 23529) offers $500 plus publication for a book-length poetry manuscript of 50 to 80 pages. Deadline: February 28.

UNIVERSITY OF PITTSBURGH PRESS—127 N. Bellefield Ave., Pittsburgh, PA 15260. Agnes Lynch Starrett Poetry Prize: offers $2,500 plus publication in the Pitt Poetry Series for a book-length collection of poems by a poet who has not yet published a volume of poetry. Deadline: April 30. Drue Heinz Literature Prize: offers $10,000 plus publication and royalty contract, for an unpublished collection of short stories or novellas, 150 to 300 pages. Deadline: August 31.

UNIVERSITY OF SOUTHERN CALIFORNIA—Ann Stanford Poetry Prize, Master of Professional Writing Program, WPH 404, University of Southern California, Los Angeles, CA 90089–4034. Publication plus prizes of $750, $250, and $100 are awarded; submit up to five poems. Deadline: April 15.

UNIVERSITY OF WISCONSIN PRESS POETRY SERIES—114 N. Murray St., Madison, WI 53715. Attn: Ronald Wallace, Ed. Previously unpublished manuscripts, 50 to 80 pages, are considered for the Brittingham Prize in Poetry and the Felix Pollak Prize in Poetry, each offering $1,000 plus publication. Deadline: October 1.

THE UNTERBERG POETRY CENTER OF THE 92ND STREET Y— "Discovery"/*The Nation*, 1395 Lexington Ave., New York, NY 10128. Four prizes of $300, publication, and a reading are awarded for original 10-page manuscripts by poets who have not yet published a book of poetry. Deadline: February 1.

VETERANS OF FOREIGN WARS—Voice of Democracy Audio Essay Competition, VFW National Headquarters, 406 W. 34th St., Kansas City, MO 64111. Several national scholarships totalling $99,000 are awarded to high school students for short, tape-recorded essays. Themes change annually. Deadline: November 15.

VILLA MONTALVO—Biennial Poetry Competition, P.O. Box 158, Saratoga, CA 95071. Residents of CA, NV, OR, and WA are eligible to enter poems in any style for prizes of: $1,000 plus an artist residency at Villa Montalvo, $500, and $300, as well as eight prizes of $25. Deadline: October 1 (of odd-numbered years).

WAGNER COLLEGE—Stanley Drama Award, Dept. of Humanities, Howard Ave. and Campus Rd., Staten Island, NY 10301. Awards $2,000 plus possible production for an original, previously unpublished and unproduced full-length play or musical. Deadline: September 1.

WASHINGTON PRIZE FOR FICTION—1301 S. Scott St., Arlington, VA 22204. Attn: Larry Kaltman, Dir. Offers $3,000, $2,000, and $1,000 for unpublished novels or short story collections, at least 65,000 words. Deadline: November 30.

WHITE PINE PRESS—Poetry Prize, 10 Village Sq., Fredonia, NY 14063. A prize of publication plus $500 is awarded for an original book-length manuscript of poetry. Deadline: December 1.

WHITE-WILLIS THEATRE—New Playwrights Contest, 5266 Gate Lake Rd., Ft. Lauderdale, FL 33319. Offered are a $500 prize plus production for the winning unpublished, unproduced full-length play. Deadline: August 1.

TENNESSEE WILLIAMS FESTIVAL—University of New Orleans, Metro College Conference Services, ED 122, New Orleans, LA 70148. A $1,000 prize plus a staged reading and full production are offered for an original, unpublished one-act play on an American subject. Deadline: December 31.

WORD WORKS—Washington Prize for Fiction, P. O. Box 42164, Washington, DC 20015. A prize of $1,000 plus publication is offered for an unpublished volume of poetry by a living American poet. Deadline: March 1.

WRITERS AT WORK—Fellowship Competition, P.O. Box 1146, Centerville, UT 84014–5146. Prizes of $1,500 plus publication, and $500, in fiction, nonfiction, and poetry categories, are awarded for excerpts of unpublished short stories, novels, essays, or poetry. Open to any writer who has not yet published a book-length volume of original work. Deadline: February 28.

YALE UNIVERSITY PRESS—Yale Series of Younger Poets Prize, Box 92A, Yale Sta., New Haven, CT 06520. Attn: Ed. Series publication is awarded for a book-length manuscript of poetry written by a poet under 40 who has not previously published a volume of poems. Deadline: February 28.

YOUNG PLAYWRIGHTS, INC.—Young Playwrights Festival, 321 W. 44th St., Suite 906, New York, NY 10036. Festival productions and readings are awarded for the best plays by writers under 19. Deadline: October 15.

WRITERS COLONIES

Writers colonies offer isolation and freedom from everyday distractions and a quiet place for writers to concentrate on their work. Though some colonies are quite small, with space for just three or four writers at a time, others can provide accommodations for as many as thirty or forty. The length of a residency may vary, too, from a couple of weeks to five or six months. These programs have strict admissions policies, and writers must submit a formal application or letter of intent, a resumé, writing samples, and letters of recommendation. As an alternative to the traditional writers colony, a few of the organizations listed offer writing rooms for writers who live nearby. Write for application information first, enclosing a stamped, self-addressed envelope. Residency fees listed are subject to change.

THE EDWARD F. ALBEE FOUNDATION, INC.
14 Harrison St.
New York, NY 10013
(212) 266–2020
David Briggs, *Foundation Secretary*
    Located on Long Island, "The Barn," or the William Flanagan Memorial Creative Persons Center, is maintained by the Albee Foundation. "The standards for admission are, simply, talent and need." Sixteen writers are accepted each season for one-month residencies, available from June 1 to October 1; applications, including writing samples, project description, and resumé, are accepted from January 1 to April 1. There is no fee, though residents are responsible for their own food and travel expenses.

ATLANTIC CENTER FOR THE ARTS
1414 Art Center Ave.
New Smyrna Beach, FL 32168
(904) 427–6975
Nicholas Conroy, *Program Director*
   The center is located on the east coast of central Florida, with 67 acres of pristine hammockland on a tidal estuary. All buildings, connected by raised wooden walkways, are handicapped accessible and air conditioned. The center provides a unique environment for sharing ideas, learning, and collaborating on interdisciplinary projects. Master artists meet with mid-career artists for readings and critiques, with time out for individual work. Residencies are three weeks. Fees are $600 for private room/bath; $200 for off-site (tuition only); financial aid is limited. Application deadlines vary.

BELLAGIO STUDY AND CONFERENCE CENTER
Program for Scholars and Artists in Residence
Bellagio Center Office
The Rockefeller Foundation
420 Fifth Ave.
New York, NY 10018–2702
(212) 852–8431
Susan E. Garfield, *Manager*
   Located on Lake Como in the Italian Alps, the Center offers about 140 residencies annually to writers, artists, scholars, and scientists who expect their stay to result in publication, exhibition, or performance. Spouses may stay at no cost. Four-week residencies, with free room and board, are available from February 1 to December 20. Residents must provide their own travel and other expenses. Brochure available; do not send SASE. Applicants chosen on the basis of project description, resumé, one sample of published work, and up to three published reviews. Apply one year in advance. Deadlines are March 1, May 25, August 25, and December 1.

BERLINER KUNSTLERPROGRAM
Artists-in-Berlin Program
950 Third Ave.
New York, NY 10022
(212) 758–3223
Dr. Heidrun Suhr, *Director*
   One-year residencies are offered to well-known and emerging writers, painters, sculptors, and composers to promote cultural exchange. Up to 20 residencies are offered for periods beginning between January 1 and June 30. Room, board, travel, and living expenses are awarded. Residents may bring spouse and children. Application, project description, and copies of publications are due by January 1 of the year preceding the residency.

BLUE MOUNTAIN CENTER
Blue Mountain Lake, NY 12812
(518) 352–7391
Harriet Barlow, *Director*
   Hosts month-long residencies for artists and writers from mid-June to late October. Established fiction and nonfiction writers whose work evinces social and ecological concern are among the 14 residents accepted per session. A brochure is available on request. There is no charge to residents for their time at Blue Mountain, although all visitors are invited to contribute to the studio construction fund. There is no application form; apply by sending

822

a brief biographical sketch, a plan for work at Blue Mountain, five slides or approximately 10 pages of work, an indication of preference for an early summer, late summer, or fall residence, and a $20 application fee; applications due February 1.

BYRDCLIFFE ARTS COLONY
Artists' Residency Program
Woodstock Guild
34 Tinker St.
Woodstock, NY 12498
(914) 679-2079
Attn: *Director*
The Villetta Inn, located on the 600-acre arts colony, offers private rooms, a communal kitchen, and a peaceful environment for fiction writers, poets, playwrights, and visual artists. Residencies from one to four months are offered from June to September. Fees are $400 to $500 per month; limited financial assistance available. Submit application, resumé, writing sample, reviews, and references; the deadline is in mid-April.

THE CAMARGO FOUNDATION
W-1050 First National Bank Bldg.
332 Minnesota St.
St. Paul, MN 55106-1314
Ricardo Bloch, *Administrative Assistant*
The Camargo Foundation maintains a center of studies in France for the benefit of nine scholars and graduate students each semester who wish to pursue projects in the humanities relative to France. In addition, one artist, one composer, and one writer are accepted each semester. The foundation offers furnished apartments and a reference library in the city of Cassis. Research should be at an advanced stage and not require resources unavailable in the Marseilles-Aix-Cassis region. Fellows must be in residence at the foundation; the award is exclusively a residential grant. Application materials include: application form, curriculum vitae, three letters of recommendation, and project description. Writers, artists, and composers are required to send work samples. Applications due March 1.

CENTRUM
P.O. Box 1158
Port Townsend, WA 98368
(206) 385-3102
Attn: *Program Coordinator*
The Centrum residency program for writers has been temporarily suspended.

CHATEAU DE LESVAULT
Writers Retreat Program
Onlay
58370 Villapourcon
France
(33) 86-84-32-91; Fax: (33) 86-84-35-78
Bibbi Lee, *Director*
This French country residence is located in western Burgundy, in the national park of Le Morvan. Five large rooms, fully equipped for living and working, are available October through April, for one month or longer. Residents in this small artists' community have access to the entire chateau, including the salon, library, and grounds. The fee is 4,500 francs (approximately

$900) per month, or 2,500 francs for two weeks, and includes room, board, and utilities. Apply by writing to the selection committee, including project description, two references, writing samples, and publications list, if available. Applications handled on a first-come basis.

COTTAGES AT HEDGEBROOK
2197 E. Millman Rd.
Langley, WA 98260
(206) 321–4786
Attn: *Director*

Cottages at Hedgebrook provides for women writers, published or not, of all ages and from all cultural backgrounds, a natural place to work. Established in 1988, the retreat is part of Hedgebrook Farm, thirty acres of farmland and woods located on Whidbey Island in Washington State. Each writer has her own cottage, equipped with electricity and woodstove. A bathhouse serves all six cottages. Writers gather for dinner in the farmhouse every evening and frequently read in the living room/library afterwards. Limited travel scholarships are available. Residencies range from one week to three months. April 1 is the application deadline for residencies from mid-June to mid-December; October 1 for mid-January to late May. Applicants are chosen by a selection committee composed of writers.

CURRY HILL/GEORGIA
c/o 404 Crestmont Ave.
Hattiesburg, MS 39401–7211
(601) 264–7034
Mrs. Elizabeth Bowne, *Director*

This retreat for eight fiction and nonfiction writers is offered for one week each spring (March 26 to April 1, 1995) by writer/teacher Elizabeth Bowne. "I care about writers and am delighted and enthusiastic when I can help develop talent." A $400 fee covers meals and lodging at Curry Hill, a family plantation home near Bainbridge, Georgia. Applications should be sent in early January; qualified applicants accepted on a first-come basis.

DJERASSI RESIDENT ARTISTS PROGRAM
2325 Bear Gulch Rd.
Woodside, CA 94062–4405
(415) 851–8395
Attn: *Executive Director*

The Djerassi Program offers living and work spaces in a rural, isolated setting to writers, visual artists, choreographers, and composers seeking undisturbed time for creative work. Residencies usually last one month; 45 artists are accepted each year. There are no fees other than the $20 application fee. Applications, with resumé and documentation of recent creative work, are due February 15.

DORLAND MOUNTAIN ARTS COLONY
Box 6
Temecula, CA 92593
(909) 676–5039
Attn: *Admissions Committee*

Dorland is a nature preserve and "primitive retreat for creative people" located in the Palomar Mountains of Southern California. "Without electricity, residents find a new, natural rhythm for their work." Novelists, playwrights, poets, nonfiction writers, composers, and visual artists are encouraged to apply for residencies of two weeks to two months. Fee of $150 a month includes cottage, fuel, and firewood. Application deadlines are March 1 and September 1.

DORSET COLONY HOUSE
Box 519
Dorset, VT 05251
(802) 867–2223
John Nassivera, *Director*
Writers and playwrights are offered low-cost room with kitchen facilities at the historic Colony House in Dorset, Vermont. Residencies are one week to two months, and are available between September 15 and June 1. Applications are accepted year round, and up to eight writers stay at a time. The fee is $95 per week; financial aid is limited. For more information, send SASE.

FINE ARTS WORK CENTER IN PROVINCETOWN
24 Pearl St.
Provincetown, MA 02657
Fred Leebron, *Acting Director*
Fellowships, including living and studio space and monthly stipends, are available at the Fine Arts Work Center on Cape Cod, for writers to work independently. Residencies are for seven months, October through May; apply before February 1 deadline. Eight first-year fellows and two second-year fellows are accepted. Send SASE for details.

THE GELL WRITERS CENTER
Writers & Books
740 University Ave.
Rochester, NY 14607
(716) 473–2590
Joe Flaherty, *Director*
The Center, on Canandaigua Lake, is found in the Finger Lakes region of New York, and includes 24 acres of woodlands. Two separate living quarters, with private bath and work area, are available for $35 per night. All serious writers are welcome; reservations made on a first-come basis.

GLENESSENCE WRITERS COLONY
1447 W. Ward Ave.
Ridgecrest, CA 93555
(619) 446–5894
Allison Swift, *Director*
Glenessence is a luxury villa located in the Upper Mojave Desert, offering private rooms with bath, pool, spa, courtyard, shared kitchen, fitness center, and library. Children, pets, and smoking are prohibited. Residencies are offered at $565 per month; meals are not provided. Reservations made on a first-come basis.

THE TYRONE GUTHRIE CENTRE
Annaghmakerrig, Newbliss
County Monaghan
Ireland
(353) 47–54003; Fax: (353) 47–54380
Bernard Loughlin, *Director*
Set on a 400-acre country estate, the center offers peace and seclusion to writers and other artists to enable them to get on with their work. All art forms are represented. One- to three-month residencies are offered throughout the year, at the rate of 1,200 to 1,600 Irish pounds (about $1, 920 to $2,560) per

month, depending on the season; financial assistance available to Irish citizens only. A number of longer term self-catering houses in the old farmyard are also available at £300 pounds per week. Writers may apply for acceptance year round.

THE HAMBIDGE CENTER
P.O. Box 339
Rabun Gap, GA 30568
(706) 746–5718
Judy Barber, *Director*

The Hambidge Center for Creative Arts and Sciences is located on 650 acres of quiet woods in the north Georgia mountains. Seven private cottages are available for fellows, who are asked to contribute $125 per week. Two-week to two-month residencies, from May to October, and limited winter residencies are offered to serious artists from all disciplines. Send SASE for application form. Application deadline: January 31.

HAWTHORNDEN CASTLE INTERNATIONAL RETREAT FOR WRITERS
Hawthornden Castle
Lasswade, Midlothian EH18 1EG
Scotland
(031) 440–2180
Attn: *Administrator*

Hawthornden Castle stands on a secluded crag overlooking the valley of the River North Esk. The retreat provides a peaceful setting where creative writers can work without disturbance. The castle houses five writers at a time, and is open ten months out of the year. Writers from any part of the world may apply for full fellowships. Application forms due September 15 for residencies in the following year.

HOMESTEAD GUEST HOUSE
P.O. Box 343
Town Hall Rd.
Beloit, WI 53511
(608) 362–8055
Rolf Lund, *Proprietor*

The Homestead is located on farmland in southern Wisconsin and is run by three working artists. A two-bedroom cottage and private guest rooms are available for rent at $35 a night; meals are not provided. Reserve at least one week in advance.

KALANI HONUA RETREAT & CULTURAL CENTER
Artist-in-Residence Program
RR2, Box 4500
Pahoa, HI 96778
(808) 965–7828
Richard Koob, *Program Coordinator*

Located in a rural coastal setting of 20 botanical acres, Kalani Honua hosts and sponsors educational programs "with the aloha experience that is its namesake: harmony of heaven and earth." Residencies range from two weeks to two months and are available throughout the year. Fees range from $26 to $43 per day, excluding meals. Applications accepted year round.

LEIGHTON STUDIOS
Office of the Registrar
The Banff Centre for the Arts

Box 1020, Station 28
107 Tunnel Mountain Dr.
Banff, Alberta T0L 0C0
Canada
(403) 762–6180; (800) 565–9989; Fax: (403) 762–6345
Teresa Boychuck, *Registrar*
The Leighton Studios are open year round, providing time and space for artists to produce new work. Established writers, composers, musicians, and visual artists of all nationalities are encouraged to apply. Artists working in other mediums at the conceptual state of a project will also be considered. Weekly fees (Canadian dollars): $273 studio; $182 single room; $92 meals. Applications are accepted at any time. Space is limited; apply at least six months prior to preferred starting date. Write for application form.

THE MACDOWELL COLONY
100 High St.
Peterborough, NH 03458
(603) 924–3886
Pat Dodge, *Admissions Coordinator*
Studios, room, and board are available for writers to work without interruption in a woodland setting. Selection is competitive. Apply by January 15 for stays May through August; April 15 for September through December; and September 15 for January through April. Residencies last up to eight weeks, and 80 to 90 writers are accepted each year. Send SASE for application form.

THE MILLAY COLONY FOR THE ARTS
P.O. Box 3
Austerlitz, NY 12017–0003
(518) 392–3103
Gail Giles, *Assistant Director*
At Steepletop, the former home of Edna St. Vincent Millay, writers are provided studios, living quarters, and meals at no cost. Residencies last one month. Application deadlines are February 1, May 1, and September 1. Send SASE for more information and an application form.

MOLASSES POND WRITERS' RETREAT AND WORKSHOP
RR 1, Box 85C
Milbridge, ME 04658
(207) 546–2506
Martha Barron Barrett and Sue Wheeler, *Coordinators*
Led by published authors who teach writing at the University of New Hampshire. The one-week workshop is held in June and includes time set aside for writing, as well as manuscript critique and writing classes. Up to 10 writers participate, staying in five lakeside cottages with private work space and kitchen. Classes and communal dinner held in the main lodge. The $350 fee covers lodging, dinners, and tuition. Applicants must be serious about their work; no children's literature or poetry. Submit statement of purpose and 15 to 20 pages of fiction or nonfiction between March 1 and May 1.

THE N.A.L.L. ASSOCIATION
232, Boulevard de Lattre
06140 Vence
France
(33) 93–58-13–26; Fax: (33) 93–58-09–00
Attn: *Director*
This international center for writers and artists is located on eight acres of the Mediterranean village of Vence. Residents stay in cottages equipped with

827

kitchen, bath, and private garden. One afternoon a week is set aside for residents to discuss their work with local artists over tea. Six-month residencies are encouraged. Cottages are rented at various rates, to members of the N.A.L.L. (Nature, Art, and Life League); membership is 500 francs (about $100) per year. Meals are not included. Submit resumé, writing sample, and project description. Applications accepted year round.

THE NORTHWOOD UNIVERSITY
Alden B. Dow Creativity Center
3225 Cook Rd.
Midland, MI 48640–2398
(517) 837–4478
Carol B. Coppage, *Director*

The Fellowship Program allows individuals time away from their ongoing daily routines to pursue their project ideas without interruption. A project idea should be innovative, creative, and have potential for impact in its field. Four eight-week residencies, lasting from early-June to early-August, are awarded yearly. There is a $10 application fee. A $750 stipend plus room and board are provided. No spouses or families. Applications are due December 31.

PALENVILLE INTERARTS COLONY
2 Bond St.
New York, NY 10012
(518) 678–3332
Joanna Sherman, *Artistic Director*

Support is provided for artists of the highest calibre in all disciplines, either working alone or in groups. The admissions panel is interested in interartistic collaboration and intercultural projects. Residencies last from one to eight weeks, and fees range from $125 to $200 per week; scholarships are available. About 50 applicants are accepted for the May through October season. Applications due in April; send SASE for details.

RAGDALE FOUNDATION
1260 N. Green Bay Rd.
Lake Forest, IL 60045
(708) 234–1063
Michael Wilkerson, *Director*

Uninterrupted time and peaceful space allow writers a chance to finish works in progress, to begin new works, to solve thorny creative problems, and to experiment in new genres. The foundation is located 30 miles north of Chicago, on 40 acres of prairie. Residencies of two weeks to two months are available for writers, artists, and composers. The fee is $12 per day; some full and partial fee waivers available, based solely on financial need. Send SASE for deadline information. Late applications considered when space is available. Application fee: $20.

SASKATCHEWAN WRITERS' GUILD
Artists Colonies and Retreats
P.O. Box 3986
Regina, Saskatchewan S4P 3R9
Canada
(306) 757–6310
Attn: *Director*

Colonies are at two locations: St. Peter's Abbey, near Muenster, provides month-long retreats year round, as well as a summer colony, with two- to eight-week residencies available; and Emma Lake, near Prince Albert, is the site of a two-week residency in August. A fee of $100 per week includes room and board. Submit application form, resumé, project description, references, and writing samples. Saskatchewan residents are given preference. The deadline is April 1 for the St. Peter's summer colony; otherwise, apply up to three weeks in advance of starting date.

THE JOHN STEINBECK ROOM
Long Island University
Southampton Campus Library
Southampton, NY 11968
(516) 287–8379
Robert Gerbereux, *Library Director*
The John Steinbeck Room at Long Island University provides a basic research facility to writers who have either a current contract with a book publisher or a confirmed assignment from a magazine editor. The room is available for a period of six months with one six-month renewal permissible. Send SASE for application.

SYVENNA FOUNDATION
Rte. 1, Box 193
Linden, TX 75563
(903) 835–8252
The Syvenna Foundation's residency program for writers has been discontinued.

THE THURBER HOUSE RESIDENCIES
c/o Thurber House
77 Jefferson Ave.
Columbus, OH 43215
(614) 464–1032
Michael J. Rosen, *Literary Director*
Residencies in the restored home of James Thurber are awarded to journalists, writers, and playwrights. Residents work on their own writing projects, and in addition to other duties, teach one class at the Ohio State University. A stipend of $5,000 per quarter is provided. A letter of interest and curriculum vitae must be received by December 15, at which time applications are reviewed for the upcoming academic year.

UCROSS FOUNDATION
Residency Program
2836 U.S. Hwy. 14–16 East
Clearmont, WY 82835
(307) 737–2291
Elizabeth Guheen, *Executive Director*
Residencies, two to eight weeks, in the foothills of the Big Horn Mountains in Wyoming, allow writers, artists, and scholars to concentrate on their work without interruption. Two residency sessions are scheduled annually: February to June and August to December. There is no charge for room, board, or studio space. Application deadlines are March 1 for the fall session and October 1 for the spring session. Send SASE for more information.

VERMONT STUDIO CENTER
P.O. Box 613NW
Johnson, VT 05656
(802) 635–2727
Attn: *Registrar*

The Vermont Studio Center offers two-week writing studio sessions from February through April, led by prominent writers and teachers focusing on the craft of writing. Independent writers' retreats are also available year round for those seeking more solitude. Room, working studio, and meals are included in all programs. Work-exchange fellowships are available. Applications are accepted year-round. Send SASE for fee schedule and brochure.

VILLA MONTALVO ARTIST RESIDENCY PROGRAM
P.O. Box 158
Saratoga, CA 95071
(408) 741–3421
Lori A. Wood, *Program Manager*

Villa Montalvo, in the foothills of the Santa Cruz Mountains, offers one-to three-month, free residencies to writers and artists. Several merit-based fellowships are available. September 1 and March 1 are the application deadlines. Send SASE for application forms.

VIRGINIA CENTER FOR THE CREATIVE ARTS
Sweet Briar, VA 24595
(804) 946–7236
William Smart, *Director*

A working retreat for writers, composers, and visual artists in Virginia's Blue Ridge Mountains. Residencies from one week to three months are available year round. Application deadlines are the 15th of January, May, and September; about 300 residents are accepted each year. A limited amount of financial assistance is available. Send SASE for more information.

THE WRITERS ROOM
153 Waverly Pl., 5th Floor
New York, NY 10014
(212) 807–9519
Renata Miller, *Executive Director*

Located in Greenwich Village, the Writers Room provides "highly subsidized work space to all types of writers at all stages of their careers. We offer urban writers a quiet, benevolent oasis, a place to escape from noisy neighbors, children, roommates, and other distractions of city life." The room holds 24 desks separated by partitions, a smokers' room with four desks, a kitchen, library, and lounge. Open 24 hours a day, 365 days a year. Fee is $165 quarter; several scholarships are available.

THE WRITERS STUDIO
The Mercantile Library Association
17 E. 47th St.
New York, NY 10017
(212) 755–6710
Harold Augenbraum, *Director*

The Writers Studio is a quiet place in which writers can rent space conducive to the production of good work. A carrel, locker, small reference collection, electrical outlets, and membership in the Mercantile Library of New York are available at the cost of $200 per three-month residency. Submit application, resumé, and writing samples; applications considered year round.

HELENE WURLITZER FOUNDATION OF NEW MEXICO
Box 545
Taos, NM 87571
(505) 758–2413
Henry A. Sauerwein, Jr., *Executive Director*

Rent-free and utility-free studios in Taos are offered to creative writers and artists in all media. "All artists are given the opportunity to be free of the shackles of a 9-to-5 routine." Length of residency varies from three to six months. The foundation is open from April 1 through September 30.

YADDO
Box 395
Saratoga Springs, NY 12866–0395
(518) 584–0746
Attn: *Admissions Committee*
Visual artists, writers, choreographers, dancers, composers, and collaborators are invited for stays from two weeks to two months. Room, board, and studio space are provided. Voluntary payment of $20 a day is suggested. No artist deemed worthy of admission by the judging panels will be denied admission on the basis of an inability to contribute. Deadlines are January 15 and August 1. Send SASE for application. An application fee of $20 is required.

WRITERS CONFERENCES

Each year, hundreds of writers conferences are held across the country. The following list, arranged geographically, represents a sampling of conferences; each listing includes the location of the conference, the month during which it is usually held, and the name of the person from whom specific information may be received. Additional conferences are listed annually in the May issue of *The Writer* Magazine (120 Boylston St., Boston, MA 02116–4615).

ALABAMA

AL/GA SCBWI 3RD ANNUAL SPRING CONFERENCE—Tallassee, AL. March. Send SASE to Joan Broerman, Reg. Advisor, SCBWI, 1616 Kestwick Dr., Birmingham, AL 35226–2350.

WRITING TODAY—Birmingham, AL. March. Write Martha Andrews, Dir., Birmingham Southern College, BSC-A3, Birmingham, AL 35254.

THE ALABAMA WRITERS' CONCLAVE—Montevallo, AL. August. Write Harriette Moon Dawkins, 117 Hanover Rd., Homewood, AL 35209.

ALASKA

SITKA SYMPOSIUM ON HUMAN VALUES AND THE WRITTEN WORD—Sitka, AK. June. Write Carolyn Servid, Dir., Island Institute, Box 2420, Sitka, AK 99835.

1995 NWA CRUISE CONFERENCE—Cruise on Alaskan Inland, AK. June. Write Sandy Whelchel, Dir., 1450 S. Havana, Ste. 424, Aurora, CO 80012.

ARIZONA

AMERICAN CHRISTIAN WRITERS CONFERENCE—Various locations and dates throughout the year. Write Reg Forder, Dir., American Christian Writers, Box 5168, Phoenix, AZ 85010.

ARKANSAS

NATIONAL FEDERATION OF STATE POETRY SOCIETIES—Little Rock, AR. June. Write Verna Lee Hinegardner, Dir., 605 Higdon Ferry Rd., Apt. 109, Hot Springs, AR 71913.

ARKANSAS WRITERS CONFERENCE—Little Rock, AR. June. Write Clovita Rice, Dir., 1115 Gillette Dr., Little Rock, AR 72207.

OZARK CREATIVE WRITERS CONFERENCE—Eureka Springs, AR. October. Write Peggy Vining, Dir., 6817 Gingerbread La., Little Rock, AR 72204.

CALIFORNIA

2ND WEST COAST WRITERS' CONFERENCE—Los Angeles, CA. February. Write Alexandra Cantor, Exec. Dir., ASJA, 1501 Broadway, Ste. 302, New York, NY 10036.

HOW TO GET AND STAY PUBLISHED—Fresno, CA. March. Write Linda Kay Weber, Dir., Win-Win, P.O. Box 5331, Fresno, CA 93755–5331.

WRITERS' FORUM—Pasadena, CA. March. Write Meredith Brucker, Dir., Pasadena City College, Community Education, 1570 E. Colorado Blvd., Pasadena, CA 91106.

EARLY SPRING IN CALIFORNIA WORKSHOP—Sonoma, CA. March. Write Hannelore Hahn, Dir., International Women's Writing Guild, Box 810, Gracie Station, New York, NY 10028.

MOUNT HERMON CHRISTIAN WRITERS CONFERENCE—Mount Hermon, CA. April. Write David Talbott, Dir., Mount Hermon Assn., P.O. Box 413, Mount Hermon, CA 95041.

SANTA BARBARA WRITERS CONFERENCE—Santa Barbara, CA. June. Write Barnaby Conrad, Dir., Box 304, Carpinteria, CA 93014.

CALIFORNIA WRITERS' CONFERENCE—Pacific Grove, CA. June. Write Carol O'Hara, California Writers' Club, 2214 Derby St., Berkeley, CA 94705.

"WRITE TO BE READ" WORKSHOP—Hume Lake, CA. July. Write Norman B. Rohrer, Dir., 260 Fern La., Hume Lake, CA 93628.

THE CHRISTIAN COMMUNICATORS CONFERENCE—Fullerton, CA. July. Write Susan Titus Osborn, Dir., 3133 Puente St., Fullerton, CA 92635.

SQUAW VALLEY COMMUNITY OF WRITERS—Squaw Valley, CA. July, August. Write Oakley Hall, Dir., Squaw Valley Community of Writers, P.O. Box 2352, Olympic Valley, CA 96146.

GENE PERRET'S ROUND TABLE COMEDY WRITERS CONVENTION—Palm Springs, CA. July. Write Linda Perret, Dir., 30941 W. Agoura Rd., Ste. 228, Westlake Village, CA 91361.

NAPA VALLEY WRITERS' CONFERENCE—St. Helena, CA. August. Write Sherri Hallgren, Man. Dir., Napa Valley College, Upper Valley Campus, 1088 College Ave., St. Helena, CA 94574.

WRITERS AND ILLUSTRATORS CONFERENCE IN CHILDREN'S LITERATURE—Marina Del Rey, CA. August. Write Lin Oliver, Dir., SCBWI, 22736 Vanowen, Ste. 106, West Hills, CA 91307.

WRITERS IN THE REDWOODS RETREAT—Occidental, CA. November. Write Elaine Wright Colvin, Dir., Alliance Redwoods, 6250 Bohemian Hwy., Occidental, CA 95465.

COLORADO

COLORADO CHRISTIAN WRITERS CONFERENCE—Boulder, CO. March. Write Debbie Barker, Dir., 67 Seminole Ct., Lyons, CO 80540.

STEAMBOAT SPRINGS WRITERS CONFERENCE—Steamboat Springs, CO. July. Write Harriet Freiberger, Dir., P.O. Box 774284, Steamboat Springs, CO 80477.

COLORADO GOLD CONFERENCE—Denver, CO. September. Write Leslie O'Kane, Dir., Rocky Mountain Fiction Writers, P.O. Box 260244, Denver, CO 80226–0244.

CONNECTICUT

WESLEYAN WRITERS CONFERENCE—Middletown, CT. June. Write Anne Greene, Dir., Wesleyan Writers Conference, Wesleyan Univ., Middletown, CT 06459.

FLORIDA

13TH ANNUAL KEY WEST LITERARY SEMINAR—Key West, FL. January. Write Monica Haskell, Dir., Key West Literary Seminar, 419 Petronia St., Key West, FL 33040.

CHRISTIAN WRITERS' INSTITUTE FLORIDA CONFERENCE—Orlando, FL. February. Write Dottie McBroom, Dir., Christian Writers' Institute, 177 E. Crystal Lake Ave., Lake Mary, FL 32746.

15TH ANNUAL SOUTHWEST FLORIDA WRITERS' CONFERENCE—Fort Myers, FL. February. Write Joanne Hartke, Dir., Edison Community College, P.O. Box 60210, Fort Myers, FL 33906–6210.

SCBWI CONFERENCE—Palm Springs, FL. September. Write Barbara Casey, Dir., 2158 Portland Ave., Wellington, FL 33414.

SPACE COAST WRITERS GUILD 15TH ANNUAL CONFERENCE—Cocoa Beach, FL. November. Write Dr. Edwin J. Kirschner, Pres., Space Coast Writers Guild, Box 804, Melbourne, FL 32902.

GEORGIA

CURRY HILL PLANTATION WRITER'S RETREAT—Bainbridge, GA. March. Write Elizabeth Bowne, Dir., 404 Crestmont Ave., Hattiesburg, MS 39401–7211.

SANDHILLS WRITERS' CONFERENCE—Augusta, GA. May. Write Anthony Kellman, Dir., Augusta College, Cont. Education, 2500 Walton Way, Augusta, GA 30904–2200.

SOUTHEASTERN WRITER'S CONFERENCE—St. Simons Island, GA. June. Write Pat Laye, Rt. 1, Box 102, Cuthbert, GA 31740.

1995 HARRIETTE AUSTIN WRITERS CONFERENCE—Athens, GA. July. Write Dr. Charles Connor, Dir., Quick Brown Fox Publishers, P.O. Box 7894, Athens, GA 30604–7894.

MOONLIGHT AND MAGNOLIAS CONFERENCE—Atlanta, GA. September. Send SASE to Carol Springston, Dir., 4378 Karls Gate Dr., Marietta, GA 30068.

HAWAII

WEEKEND SEMINARS—Maui, HI. January. Write Weekend Seminars, 315 E. Water St., Cambridge, WI 53523.

A WRITER'S PARADISE—Honolulu, HI. July. Write Janis Reams Hudson, Dir., RWA, 13700 Veterans Memorial Dr., Ste. 315, Houston, TX 77014.

ILLINOIS

INTERNATIONAL WOMEN'S WRITING GUILD MIDWEST CONFERENCE—Chicago, IL. May. Write Hannelore Hahn, Dir., I.W.W.G., Box 810, Gracie Station, New York, NY 10028.

CHRISTIAN WRITERS' INSTITUTE 47TH ANNUAL CONFERENCE—Wheaton, IL. June. Write Dottie McBroom, Dir., Christian Writers' Institute, 177 E. Crystal Lake Ave., Lake Mary, FL 32746.

MISSISSIPPI VALLEY WRITERS CONFERENCE—Rock Island, IL. June. Write Bess Pierce, 734 18th Ave. A, Moline, IL 61265.

BLOOMING GROVE 19TH ANNUAL WRITERS' CONFERENCE—Bloomington, IL. July, August. Write Bettie Wilson Story, Dir., P.O. Box 515, Bloomington, IL 61702.

AUTUMN AUTHORS' AFFAIR XIII—Lisle, IL. October. Write Nancy McCann, Dir., Autumn Authors' Affair, 1507 Burnham Ave., Calumet City, IL 60409.

INDIANA

MIDWEST WRITERS WORKSHOP—Muncie, IN. July. Write Earl L. Conn, Dir., Midwest Writers Workshop, Dept. of Journalism, Ball State Univ., Muncie, IN 47306.

IOWA

IOWA SUMMER WRITING FESTIVAL—Iowa City, IA. June, July. Write Peggy Houston, Dir., 116 International Center, Univ. of Iowa, Iowa City, IA 52245.

KANSAS

WRITERS WORKSHOP IN SCIENCE FICTION—Lawrence, KS. July. Write James Gunn, Dir., English Dept., Univ. of Kansas, Lawrence, KS 66045.

KENTUCKY

18TH ANNUAL APPALACHIAN WRITERS WORKSHOP—Hindman, KY. August. Write Mike Mullins, Dir., Box 844, Hindman Settlement School, Hindman, KY 41822.

LOUISIANA

WRITE NOW!—Lafayette, LA. March. Write Leigh Simmons, Dir., Writers' Guild of Acadiana, P.O. Box 51532, Lafayette, LA 70505–1532.

WRITERS' GUILD OF ACADIANA SUMMER WORKSHOP—Lafayette, LA. August. Write Leigh Simmons, Dir., Writers' Guild of Acadiana, P.O. Box 51532, Lafayette, LA 70505–1532.

MAINE

WELLS WRITERS' WORKSHOP—Wells, ME. May, September. Write Victor A. Levine, Dir., 69 Broadway, Concord, NH 03301.

ANNUAL STONECOAST WRITERS' CONFERENCE—Freeport, ME. July. Write Barbara Hope, Dir., Univ. of Southern Maine, Stonecoast Writers' Conference, 96 Falmouth St., Portland, ME 04103.

55TH STATE OF MAINE WRITERS' CONFERENCE—Ocean Park, ME. August. Write Richard F. Burns, Dir., P.O. Box 296, Ocean Park, ME 04063.

MARYLAND

AMERICAN MEDICAL WRITERS ASSN. ANNUAL CONFERENCE—Baltimore, MD. October. Write Lillian Sablack, Dir., AMWA, 9650 Rockville Pike, Bethesda, MD 20814–3995.

SANDY COVE CHRISTIAN WRITERS CONFERENCE—North East, MD. October. Write Gayle Roper, Dir., R.D. #6, Box 112, Coatesville, PA 19320.

MASSACHUSETTS

MOUNT HOLYOKE WRITERS' CONFERENCE—South Hadley, MA. June. Write Michael Pettit, Dir., Box 3213-W, Mount Holyoke College, S. Hadley, MA 01075.

CAPE LITERARY WORKSHOPS—Barnstable, MA. August. Write Marion Vuilleumier, Dir., Cape Cod Writers' Center, c/o Conservatory, Rte. 132, W. Barnstable, MA 02668.

CAPE COD WRITERS' CONFERENCE—Craigville, MA. August. Write Marion Vuilleumier, Dir., Cape Cod Writers' Center, c/o Conservatory, Rte. 132, W. Barnstable, MA 02668.

AMHERST BOOK AND PLOW FESTIVAL—Amherst, MA. September. Write Diane Mandle, Dir., 11 Spring St., Amherst, MA 01002.

MICHIGAN

MIDLAND WRITERS CONFERENCE—Midland, MI. June. Write Barbara Brennan, Dir., Grace A. Dow Memorial Library, 1710 W. St. Andrews, Midland, MI 48640.

MINNESOTA

SPLIT ROCK ARTS PROGRAM—Duluth, MN. July, August. Write Andrea Gilats, Dir., 306 Wesbrook Hall, Univ. of Minnesota, 77 Pleasant St. S.E., Minneapolis, MN 55455.

MINNEAPOLIS WRITERS' WORKSHOP—Minneapolis, MN. August. Write Director, P.O. Box 24356, Minneapolis, MN 55424.

MISSOURI

ANNUAL MARK TWAIN WRITERS CONFERENCE—Hannibal, MO. June. Write Dr. James C. Hefley, Dir., Hannibal-LaGrange College, 921 Center St., Hannibal, MO 63401.

SCBWI WRITING FOR CHILDREN WORKSHOP—Springfield, MO. October. Write Sandy Asher, Dir., Drury College, 900 N. Benton, Springfield, MO 65802.

MONTANA

ENVIRONMENTAL WRITING INSTITUTE—Corvallis, MT. May. Write Henry Harrington, Dir., Center for Cont. Education, Univ. of Montana, Missoula, MT 59812.

YELLOW BAY WRITER'S WORKSHOP—Flathead Lake, MT. August. Write Annick Smith and Judy Jones, Dirs., Center for Cont. Education, Univ. of Montana, Missoula, MT 59812.

NEVADA

READING AND WRITING THE WEST—Reno, NV. July. Write Stephen Tchudi, Dir., Dept. of English, Univ. of Nevada, Reno, NV 89557.

NEW HAMPSHIRE

17TH ANNUAL FESTIVAL OF POETRY—Franconia, NH. July, August. Write Donald Sheehan, Dir., The Frost Place, Franconia, NH 03580.

ANNUAL SEACOAST WRITERS CONFERENCE—Chester, NH. October. Write Lynn Makowicz, Dir., Seacoast Writers Assn., P.O. Box 6553, Portsmouth, NH 03802–6553.

NEW JERSEY

TRENTON STATE COLLEGE WRITERS CONFERENCE—Trenton, NJ. April. Write Jean Hollander, Dir., Dept. of English, Trenton State College, Hillwood Lakes 4700, Trenton, NJ 08650–4700.

WRITING BY THE SEA—Stone Harbor, NJ. November. Write Natalic Newton, Dir., 7 Chestnut Oak Dr., Cape May Court House, NJ 08210.

NEW MEXICO

WRITERS' CONFERENCE AT SANTA FE—Santa Fe, NM. February. Write Ruth Crowley, Dir., Santa Fe Community College, P.O. Box 4187, Santa Fe, NM 87502–4187.

SOUTHWEST WRITERS CONFERENCE—Albuquerque, NM. August. Write JoAnn Hamlin, Dir., 1338 Wyoming Blvd. N.E., Ste. B., Albuquerque, NM 87112.

NEW YORK

"MEET THE AGENTS/BIG APPLE" WORKSHOPS—New York, NY. April, October. Write Hannelore Hahn, Dir., International Women's Writing Guild, Box 810, Gracie Station, New York, NY 10028.

CHILDREN'S LITERATURE CONFERENCE—Hempstead, NY. April, July. Write Lewis Shena, Dir., Cont. Education, 110 Hofstra Univ., Hempstead, NY 11550.

24TH ANNUAL WRITERS' CONFERENCE—New York, NY. May. Write Kate Kelly, Dir., ASJA, 1501 Broadway, Ste. 302, New York, NY 10036.

MANHATTANVILLE WRITERS' WEEK—Purchase, NY. June. Write Dean Ruth Dowd, Dir., Manhattanville College, 2900 Purchase St., Purchase, NY 10577.

HIGHLIGHTS FOUNDATION WRITERS WORKSHOP—Chautauqua, NY. July. Write Jan Keen, Dir., Highlights Foundation, 814 Court St., Honesdale, PA 18431.

ROBERT QUACKENBUSH'S CHILDREN'S BOOK WRITING AND IL-LUSTRATING WORKSHOPS—New York, NY. July. Write Robert Quackenbush, Dir., 460 E. 79th St., New York, NY 10021.

18TH ANNUAL "REMEMBER THE MAGIC" SUMMER CONFER-ENCE—Saratoga Springs, NY. August. Write Hannelore Hahn, Dir., International Women's Writing Guild, Box 810, Gracie Station, New York, NY 10028.

NORTH CAROLINA

DUKE UNIVERSITY WRITERS' WORKSHOP—Durham, NC. June. Write Georgann Eubanks, Dir., Box 90703, Durham, NC 27708–0703.

APPALACHIAN WRITERS ASSOCIATION—Cullowhee, NC. July. Write Steve Eberly and Darnell Arnaut, Chairs., P.O. Box 2019, Cullowhee, NC 28723.

THE WRITER'S ROUNDTABLE—Wilmington, NC. Summer. Write Jack Fryar, Dir., Writer's Roundtable, 2801 Lyndon Ave., Wilmington, NC 28405.

OHIO

WESTERN RESERVE WRITERS CONFERENCE—Mentor, OH. March, September. Write Lea Leever Oldham, Dir., 34200 Ridge Rd., #110, Willoughby, OH 44095.

THE HEIGHTS WRITERS CONFERENCE—Cleveland, OH. May. Write Lavern Hall, Dir., Writer's World Press, P.O. Box 24684-WH, Cleveland, OH 44124–0684.

ANTIOCH WRITERS' WORKSHOP—Yellow Springs, OH. July. Write Judy DaPolito, Dir., Antioch Writers' Workshop, P.O. Box 494, Yellow Springs, OH 45387.

27TH ANNUAL MIDWEST WRITERS' CONFERENCE—Canton, OH. October. Write Gregg L. Andrews, Dir., Midwest Writers' Conference, 6000 Frank Ave. N.W., Canton, OH 44721.

THE COLUMBUS WRITERS CONFERENCE—Columbus, OH. October. Write Angela Palazzolo and JoAnn Judy, Dirs., The Writer's Connection, P.O. Box 20548, Columbus, OH 43220.

OKLAHOMA

OPPORTUNUTY '95—Norman, OK. March. Write Betty Culpepper, Dir., National League of Pen Women, 828 Cruce St., Norman, OK 73069.

4TH ANNUAL NORTHWEST OKLAHOMA WRITER'S WORKSHOP —Enid, OK. Spring. Write Dr. Earl Mabry, Dir., P.O. Box 1308, Enid, OK 73702.

OKLAHOMA FALL ARTS INSTITUTES WRITING WORKSHOP— Lone Wolf, OK. October. Write Mary Gordon Taft, Dir., Oklahoma Arts Institute, P.O. Box 18154, Oklahoma City, OK 73154.

OREGON

WINTER AND SUMMER FISHTRAP—Wallowa Lake, OR. February, July. Write Rich Wandschneider, Dir., Fishtrap, P.O. Box 38, Enterprise, OR 97828.

HAYSTACK PROGRAM IN THE ARTS AND SCIENCES—Cannon Beach, OR. June, August. Write Portland State Univ., Extended Studies, P.O. Box 1491, Portland, OR 97207.

PENNSYLVANIA

PENNWRITERS ANNUAL CONFERENCE—Pittsburgh, PA. May. Write Joy Hopkins, Dir., 108 Jaspen Way, Canonsburg, PA 15317.

PHILADELPHIA WRITERS' CONFERENCE—Philadelphia, PA. June. Write Michael Sharp, Dir., 1995 PWC Registrar, P.O. Box 7171, Elkins Park, PA 19027.

CUMBERLAND VALLEY FICTION WRITERS WORKSHOP—Carlisle, PA. June. Write Judy Gill, Dir., Dept. of English, Dickinson College, Carlisle, PA 17013–2896.

MONTROSE CHRISTIAN WRITER'S CONFERENCE—Montrose, PA. July. Write Jill Meyers, Dir., P.O. Box 159, Montrose, PA 18801–0159.

LIGONIER VALLEY WRITERS CONFERENCE—Ligonier, PA. July. Write Dr. Tina Thoburn, Dir., R.R. 4, Box 8, Ligonier, PA 15658.

SOUTH CAROLINA

WRITE TO SELL V—Rock Hill, SC. February. Write Ron Chepesiuk, Dir., 782 Wofford St., Rock Hill, SC 29730.

TENNESSEE

YOUNG SCHOLARS AND WRITERS CAMP—Memphis, TN. June. Write Dr. Beth Kamhi, Dir., Dept. of English, Rhodes College, 2000 North Pkwy., Memphis, TN 38112.

838

OUTDOOR WRITERS ASSN. ANNUAL CONFERENCE—Chattanooga, TN. June. Write James W. Rainey, Dir., 2017 Cato Ave., Ste. 101, State College, PA 16801.

TEXAS

AUSTIN WRITERS' LEAGUE WORKSHOPS—Austin, TX. March through November. Write Angela Smith, Dir., Austin Writers' League, 1501 W. 5th St., Ste. E-2, Austin, TX 78703.

TCU/CHISHOLM TRAIL WESTERN SEMINAR—Fort Worth, TX. June. Write Judy Alter, Dir., Office of Extended Education, Texas Christian Univ., Box 32927, Fort Worth, TX 76129.

CRAFT OF WRITING CONFERENCE—Richardson, TX. September. Write Janet Harris, Dir., Univ. of Texas, P.O. Box 830688, CN1.1, Richardson, TX 75083–0688.

VERMONT

7TH ANNUAL NEW ENGLAND WRITERS CONFERENCE—Windsor, VT. July. Write Dr. Frank Anthony, Dir., P.O. Box 483, Windsor, VT 05089.

ANNUAL BREAD LOAF WRITERS' CONFERENCE —Ripton, VT. August. Write Michael Collier, Dir., Bread Loaf Writers' Conference, Middlebury College, Adirondack House, Middlebury, VT 05753.

VIRGINIA

CHRISTOPHER NEWPORT UNIV. WRITERS CONFERENCE—Newport News, VA. April. Write Terry Cox, Dir., Office of Cont. Education, Christopher Newport Univ., 50 Shoe La., Newport News, VA 23606.

SHENANDOAH VALLEY WRITERS' GUILD—Middletown, VA. May. Write Prof. F.H. Cogan, Dir., P.O. Box 47, Middletown, VA 22645.

HIGHLAND SUMMER CONFERENCE—Radford, VA. June. Write Dr. Grace Toney Edwards, Dir., Box 6935, Radford Univ., Radford, VA 24142.

SHENANDOAH PLAYWRIGHTS RETREAT—Staunton, VA. July, August. Write Robert Graham Small, Dir., Pennyroyal Farm, Rt. 5, Box 167F, Staunton, VA 24401.

WASHINGTON

WRITER'S WEEKEND AT THE BEACH—Ocean Park, WA. February. Write Birdie Etchison, P.O. Box 877, Ocean Park, WA 98640.

CLARION WEST FANTASY AND SCIENCE FICTION WRITERS WORKSHOP—Seattle, WA. June, July. Write Leslie Howle, Dir., 340 15th Ave. E., Ste. 350, Seattle, WA 98112.

PACIFIC NORTHWEST WRITERS CONFERENCE—Seattle, WA. July. Write Director, PNWC, 2033 6th Ave., #804, Seattle, WA 98121.

PORT TOWNSEND WRITERS' CONFERENCE—Port Townsend, WA. July. Write Carol Jane Bangs, Dir., Centrum, Box 1158, Port Townsend, WA 98368.

1995 FALL CHRISTIAN WRITERS CONFERENCE—Seattle, WA. September. Write Elaine Wright Colvin, Dir., Writers Information Network, P.O. Box 11337, Bainbridge Island, WA 98110.

WISCONSIN

THE WRITE TOUCH VIII—Oconomowoc, WI. April. Write Kathleen Smith, Dir., 5464 N. Port Washington Rd., Ste. 109, Glendale, WI 53217.

GREEN LAKE CHRISTIAN WRITERS CONFERENCE—Green Lake, WI. July. Write Jan DeWitt, Dir., W2511 State Hwy. 23, Green Lake, WI 54941–9300.

SCBWI WISCONSIN FALL RETREAT—Racine, WI. October. Send SASE to Sheri Cooper Sinykin, Dir., 26 Lancaster Ct., Madison, WI 53719–1433.

STATE ARTS COUNCILS

State arts councils sponsor grants, fellowships, and other programs for writers. To be eligible for funding, a writer *must* be a resident of the state in which he is applying. For more information, write to the addresses below. Telephone numbers are listed; 1–800 numbers are toll free for in-state calls only; numbers preceded by TDD indicate Telecommunications Device for the Deaf; TTY indicates Teletypewriter.

ALABAMA STATE COUNCIL ON THE ARTS
One Dexter Ave.
Montgomery, AL 36130
(205) 242–4076
Albert B. Head, *Executive Director*

ALASKA STATE COUNCIL ON THE ARTS
411 W. 4th Ave., Suite 1E
Anchorage, AK 99501–2343
(907) 269–6610
Jean Palmer, *Grants Officer*

ARIZONA COMMISSION ON THE ARTS
417 W. Roosevelt
Phoenix, AZ 85003
(602) 255–5882
Tonda Gorton, *Literature Director*

ARKANSAS ARTS COUNCIL
1500 Tower Bldg.
323 Center St.
Little Rock, AR 72201
(501) 324–9766
Mona Hughes, *Assistant Director*

CALIFORNIA ARTS COUNCIL
Public Information Office
2411 Alhambra Blvd.
Sacramento, CA 95817
(916) 227–2550

COLORADO COUNCIL ON THE ARTS
750 Pennsylvania St.
Denver, CO 80203–3699
(303) 894–2617
Barbara Neal, *Executive Director*

CONNECTICUT COMMISSION ON THE ARTS
227 Lawrence St.
Hartford, CT 06106
(203) 566–4770
John Ostrout, *Executive Director*

DELAWARE DIVISION OF THE ARTS
Carvel State Building
820 N. French St.
Wilmington, DE 19801
(302) 577–3540
Barbara King, *Artist Fellowship Coordinator*

FLORIDA ARTS COUNCIL
Dept. of State
Div. of Cultural Affairs
The Capitol
Tallahassee, FL 32399–0250
(904) 487–2980
Attn: Ms. Peyton Fearington

GEORGIA COUNCIL FOR THE ARTS
530 Means St. N.W., Suite 115
Atlanta, GA 30318
(404) 651–7920
Caroline Ballard Leake, *Executive Director*

HAWAII STATE FOUNDATION ON CULTURE AND THE ARTS
44 Merchant St.
Honolulu, HI 96813
(808) 586–0300
Wendell P.K. Silva, *Executive Director*

IDAHO COMMISSION ON THE ARTS
Box 83720
Boise, ID 83720–0008
(208) 334–2119
Attn: Diane Josephy Peavey

ILLINOIS ARTS COUNCIL
James R. Thompson Center
100 W. Randolph, Suite 10–500
Chicago, IL 60601
(312) 814–4990; (800) 237–6994
Richard Gage, *Director of Communication Arts*

INDIANA ARTS COMMISSION
402 W. Washington St., Rm. 072
Indianapolis, IN 46204–2741
(317) 232–1268; TDD: (317) 233–3001
Julie Murphy, *Director of Programs*

IOWA ARTS COUNCIL
Capitol Complex
Des Moines, IA 50319–0290
(515) 281–4451

KANSAS ARTS COMMISSION
Jayhawk Tower
700 S.W. Jackson, Suite 1004
Topeka, KS 66603–3758
(913) 296–3335
Robert T. Burtch, *Editor*

KENTUCKY ARTS COUNCIL
31 Fountain Pl.
Frankfort, KY 40601
(502) 564–3757; TDD: (502) 564–3757
Louis S. DeLuca, *Executive Director*

LOUISIANA STATE ARTS COUNCIL
Box 44247
Baton Rouge, LA 70804
(504) 342–8200; Fax: (504) 342–8173
Gerri Hobdy, *Interim Director*

MAINE ARTS COMMISSION
State House, Station 25
Augusta, ME 04333–0025
(207) 287–2724
Alden C. Wilson, *Director*

MARYLAND STATE ARTS COUNCIL
Artists-in-Education
601 N. Howard St.
Baltimore, MD 21201
(410) 333–8232
Linda Vlasak, *Program Director*
Pamela Dunne, *AIE Program Assistant*

MASSACHUSETTS CULTURAL COUNCIL
80 Boylston St., 10th Floor
Boston, MA 02116–4802
(617) 727–3668; (800) 232–0960; TTY: (617) 338–9153
Robert Ayres, *Literature Coordinator*

MICHIGAN COUNCIL FOR ARTS AND CULTURAL AFFAIRS
1200 Sixth St., Suite 1180
Detroit, MI 48226–2461
(313) 256–3731
Betty Boone, *Executive Director*

842

MINNESOTA STATE ARTS BOARD
432 Summit Ave.
St. Paul, MN 55102
(612) 297–2603; (800) 866–2787
Karen Mueller, *Artist Assistance Program Associate*

COMPAS: WRITERS & ARTISTS IN THE SCHOOLS
305 Landmark Center
75 W. Fifth St.
St. Paul, MN 55102
(612) 292–3254
Daniel Gabriel, *Director*

MISSISSIPPI ARTS COMMISSION
239 N. Lamar St., Suite 207
Jackson, MS 39201
(601) 359–6030
Jane Crater Hiatt, *Executive Director*

MISSOURI ARTS COUNCIL
Wainwright Office Complex
111 N. 7th St., Suite 105
St. Louis, MO 63101–2188
(314) 340–6845
Michael Hunt, *Program Administrator for Literature*

MONTANA ARTS COUNCIL
316 N. Park Ave., Suite 252
Helena, MT 59620
(406) 444–6430
Fran Morrow, *Director of Artists Services*

NEBRASKA ARTS COUNCIL
3838 Davenport St.
Omaha, NE 68131–2329
(402) 595–2122
Jennifer Severin, *Executive Director*

NEVADA STATE COUNCIL ON THE ARTS
Capitol Complex
100 Stewart St.
Carson City, NV 89710
(702) 687–6680; Fax: (702) 687–6688
Susan Boskoff, *Executive Director*

NEW HAMPSHIRE STATE COUNCIL ON THE ARTS
Phenix Hall
40 N. Main St.
Concord, NH 03301–4974
(603) 271–2789; TDD (800) 735–2964; Fax: (603) 271–3584
Audrey Sylvester, *Artist Services Coordinator*

NEW JERSEY STATE COUNCIL ON THE ARTS
Grants Office, Fellowships
CN 306
Trenton, NJ 08625
(609) 292–6130

843

NEW MEXICO ARTS DIVISION
228 E. Palace Ave.
Santa Fe, NM 87501
(505) 827–6490
Randy Forrester, *Operations Director*

NEW YORK STATE COUNCIL ON THE ARTS
915 Broadway
New York, NY 10010
(212) 387–7023
Michael G. Albano, *Director, Literature Program*

NORTH CAROLINA ARTS COUNCIL
Dept. of Cultural Resources
Raleigh, NC 27601–2807
(919) 733–7897
Deborah McGill, *Literature Director*

NORTH DAKOTA COUNCIL ON THE ARTS
418 E. Broadway, Suite 70
Bismark, ND 58501
(701) 244–3954
Patsy Thompson, *Executive Director*

OHIO ARTS COUNCIL
727 E. Main St.
Columbus, OH 43205–1796
(614) 466–2613
Bob Fox, *Literature Program Coordinator*

STATE ARTS COUNCIL OF OKLAHOMA
Jim Thorpe Bldg., Room 640
Oklahoma City, OK 73105
(405) 521–2931
Betty Price, *Executive Director*

OREGON ARTS COMMISSION
775 Summer St. N.E.
Salem, OR 97310
(503) 986–0082
Attn: Peter Sears

PENNSYLVANIA COUNCIL ON THE ARTS
Room 216, Finance Bldg.
Harrisburg, PA 17120
(717) 787–6883
Marcia Salvatore, *Literature and Theatre Programs*
Diane Young, *Artists-in-Education Program*

RHODE ISLAND STATE COUNCIL ON THE ARTS
95 Cedar St., Suite 103
Providence, RI 02903
(401) 277–3880
Karolye White, *Acting Executive Director*

SOUTH CAROLINA ARTS COMMISSION
1800 Gervais St.
Columbia, SC 29201
(803) 734–8696
Steven Lewis, *Director, Literary Arts Program*

844

SOUTH DAKOTA ARTS COUNCIL
230 S. Phillips Ave., Suite 204
Sioux Falls, SD 57102–0788
(605) 339–6646
Attn: Dennis Holub

TENNESSEE ARTS COMMISSION
320 Sixth Ave. N., Suite 100
Nashville, TN 37243–0780
(615) 741–1701; Fax: (615) 741–8559
Attn: Alice Swanson

TEXAS COMMISSION ON THE ARTS
Visual and Communication Arts
P.O. Box 13406
Austin, TX 78711–3406
(512) 463–5535
Rita Starpattern, *Program Administrator*

UTAH ARTS COUNCIL
617 E. South Temple
Salt Lake City, UT 84102–1177
(801) 533–5895; Fax: (801) 533–6196
G. Barnes, *Literary Coordinator*

VERMONT COUNCIL ON THE ARTS
136 State St.
Montpelier, VT 05602
(802) 828–3291
Cornelia Carey, *Grants Officer*

VIRGINIA COMMISSION FOR THE ARTS
223 Governor St.
Richmond, VA 23219
(804) 225–3132
Peggy J. Baggett, *Executive Director*

WASHINGTON STATE ARTS COMMISSION
234 E. 8th Ave.
Olympia, WA 98504–2675
(206) 753–3860
Bitsy Bidwell, *Community Arts Development Manager*

WEST VIRGINIA DEPT. OF EDUCATION AND THE ARTS
1900 Kanawha Blvd. E.
Charleston, WV 25305
(304) 558–0220
Lakin Ray Cook, *Executive Director*

WISCONSIN ARTS BOARD
101 E. Wilson St., 1st Floor
Madison, WI 53703
(608) 266–0190
Dean Amhaus, *Executive Director*

WYOMING ARTS COUNCIL
2320 Capitol Ave.
Cheyenne, WY 82002
(307) 777–7742
Guy Lebeda, *Literature Program Manager*

ORGANIZATIONS FOR WRITERS

ACADEMY OF AMERICAN POETS
584 Broadway, Suite 1208
New York, NY 10012
(212) 274–0343
Mrs. Edward T. Chase, *President*

Founded in 1934 to promote American poetry through fellowships, awards programs, public programs, and publications. The academy offers an annual fellowship for distinguished poetic achievement, the Peter I. B. Lavan Younger Poet Awards, four major book awards, and sponsors prizes for poetry at 150 universities and colleges nationwide. Readings, lectures, and regional symposia take place at various New York City locations and other locations in the United States. Membership is open to all: $45 annual fee includes subscription to the quarterly, *Poetry Pilot*, and complimentary copies of award-winning books.

AMERICAN CRIME WRITERS LEAGUE
219 Tuxedo
San Antonio, TX 78209
Barbara Mertz, *President*
Jay Brandon, *Membership Chair*

A national organization of working professional mystery authors. To be eligible for membership in ACWL you must have published at least one of the following: one full-length work of crime fiction or nonfiction; three short stories; or three nonfiction crime articles. The bimonthly *ACWL BULLETin* features articles by reliable experts and an exchange of information and advice among professional writers. Annual dues: $35.

AMERICAN MEDICAL WRITERS ASSOCIATION
9650 Rockville Pike
Bethesda, MD 20814
(301) 493–0003; Fax: (301) 493–6384
Lillian Sablack, *Executive Director*

Members of the association are engaged in biomedical communications. Any person actively interested in or professionally associated with any medium of medical communication is eligible for membership. Annual dues: $75.

AMERICAN SOCIETY OF JOURNALISTS AND AUTHORS, INC.
1501 Broadway, Suite 302
New York, NY 10036
(212) 997–0947
Alexandra Cantor, *Executive Director*

A nationwide organization of independent writers of nonfiction dedicated to promoting high standards of nonfiction writing through monthly meetings, annual writers' conferences, etc. The ASJA offers extensive benefits and services including referral services, numerous discount services, and the opportunity to explore professional issues and concerns with other writers. Members also receive a monthly newsletter with confidential market information. Membership is open to professional free-lance writers of nonfiction; qualifications are judged by the membership committee. Call or write for application details.

ASSOCIATION OF HISPANIC ARTS, INC.
173 E. 116th St.
New York, NY 10029
(212) 860–5445
Jane Arce Bello, *Executive Director*

Founded in 1975, the AHA serves both Hispanic arts organizations and individual artists at various stages of development, to ensure that the rich array of Hispanic arts and cultural expressions will be preserved. Publishes *Hispanic Arts News*, providing information on events, job opportunities, and other issues. Individual subscription: $20.

THE AUTHORS GUILD, INC.
330 W. 42nd St.
New York, NY 10036–6902
(212) 563–5904; Fax: (212) 564–5363; E-mail: Authors@pipeline.com
Attn: *Membership Committee*

Membership offers writers of all genres legal advice, reviews of publishing and agency contracts, and access to seminars and symposiums around the country on subjects of concern to authors. The Authors Guild also lobbies on behalf of all authors on issues such as copyright, taxation, and freedom of expression. A writer who has published a book in the last seven years with an established publisher, or has published three articles in periodicals of general circulation within the last eighteen months is eligible for active voting membership. An unpublished writer who has just received a contract offer may be eligible for associate membership. Membership is also to those who wish to have access to Authors Guild events and its quarterly *Bulletin*. All members of the Authors Guild automatically become members of its parent organization, the Authors League of America. Annual dues: $90.

THE AUTHORS LEAGUE OF AMERICA, INC.
330 W. 42nd St.
New York, NY 10036–6902
(212) 564–8350; Fax: (212) 564–5363; E-mail: Authors@pipeline.com
Attn: *Membership Committee*

A national organization representing over 14,000 authors and dramatists on matters of joint concern, such as copyright, taxes, and freedom of expression. Membership is restricted to authors and dramatists who are members of the Authors Guild and the Dramatists Guild. Matters such as contract terms and subsidiary rights are in the province of the two guilds.

BLACK THEATRE NETWORK
Box 11502
Fisher Bldg. Station
Detroit, MI 48211
(313) 577–7906
Lundeana Thomas, *President*

The Black Theatre Network is a national non-profit organization devoted to exposing all people to the beauty and complexity of black theater, and to preserving the art form for future generations. The BTN sponsors an annual national conference, and the Randolph Edmonds Young Scholars Competition. Publications include the quarterly *BTNews*, *The Black Theatre Directory*, and *Black Voices*, a guide to plays by black authors. Annual dues: $25, *student & retiree*; $40, *individual*; $75, *organization*.

847

BRITISH AMERICAN ARTS ASSOCIATION
116 Commercial St.
London E1 6NF
England
(071) 247–5385
Jennifer Williams, *Executive Director*
An information service and clearing house for exchange between British and American cultural activities in all arts fields, the BAAA provides advocacy and technical assistance to professional artists. The BAAA does not give funds and is not a membership organization.

THE DRAMATISTS GUILD
234 W. 44th St.
New York, NY 10036–3909
(212) 398–9366
Peter Stone, *President*; Todd Neal, *Director of Membership*
A professional association of playwrights, composers, and lyricists, the guild was established to protect dramatists' rights and to improve working conditions. Services include use of the guild's contracts; a toll-free number for members in need of business counseling; a discount ticket service; access to two health insurance programs and a group term life insurance plan; a reference library; and a Committee for Women. Publications include *The Dramatists Guild Quarterly*, *The Dramatists Guild Resource Directory*, and *The Dramatists Guild Newsletter*. All playwrights, produced or not, are eligible for membership. All active or associate members of the Dramatists Guild automatically become members of its parent organization, the Authors League. Annual dues: $125, *active*; $75, *associate*; $50, *subscribing*; $35, *student*.

INTERNATIONAL ASSOCIATION OF THEATRE FOR CHILDREN AND YOUNG PEOPLE
2707 E. Union
Seattle, WA 98122
(206) 860–9212
Jolly Sue Baker, *Executive Director*
The development of professional theater for young audiences and international exchange are the organization's primary mandates. Provides a link between professional theaters, artists, directors, training institutions, and arts agencies; sponsors festivals and forums for interchange among theaters and theater artists. Annual dues: $50, *individual*; $25, *student and retiree*.

THE INTERNATIONAL WOMEN'S WRITING GUILD
Box 810, Gracie Station
New York, NY 10028–0082
(212) 737–7536; Fax: (212) 737–9469
Hannelore Hahn, *Executive Director & Founder*
Founded in 1976, serving as a network for the personal and professional empowerment of women through writing. Services include six issues of a 28-page newsletter, a list of literary agents and publishing services, access to health insurance plans at group rates, access to writing conferences and related events throughout the U.S., including the annual summer conference at Skidmore College in Saratoga Springs, NY, regional writing clusters, and year-round supportive networking. Any woman may join regardless of portfolio. Annual dues: $35; $45 *international*.

MIDWEST RADIO THEATRE WORKSHOP
KOPN
915 E. Broadway
Columbia, MO 65201
(314) 874–5676; Fax: (314) 499–1662
Steve Donofrio, *Director*
  Founded in 1979, the MRTW is the only national resource for American radio dramatists, providing referrals, technical assistance, educational materials, and workshops. MRTW coordinates an annual national radio script contest, publishes an annual radio scriptbook, and distributes a script anthology with primer. Send SASE for more information.

MYSTERY WRITERS OF AMERICA, INC.
17 E. 47th St., 6th Floor
New York, NY 10017
(212) 888–8171
Priscilla Ridgway, *Executive Director*
  The MWA exists for the purpose of raising the prestige of mystery and detective writing, and of defending the rights and increasing the income of all writers in the field of mystery, detection, and fact crime writing. Each year, the MWA presents the Edgar Allan Poe Awards for the best mystery writing in a variety of fields. The four classifications of membership are: *active*, open to any writer who has made a sale in the field of mystery, suspense, or crime writing; *associate*, for professionals in allied fields/writers in other fields; *corresponding*, for writers living outside the U.S.; *affiliate*, for unpublished writers. Annual dues: $65; $32.50 *corresponding members*.

NATIONAL ASSOCIATION OF SCIENCE WRITERS, INC.
P.O. Box 294
Greenlawn, NY 11740
(516) 757–5664
Diane McGurgan, *Administrative Secretary*
  The NASW promotes the dissemination of accurate information regarding science through all media, and conducts a varied program to increase the flow of news from scientists, to improve the quality of its presentation, and to communicate its meaning to the reading public. Anyone who has been actively engaged in the dissemination of science information is eligible to apply for membership. Active members must be principally involved in reporting on science through newspapers, magazines, TV, or other media that reach the public directly. Associate members report on science through limited-circulation publications and other media. Annual dues: $60.

NATIONAL LEAGUE OF AMERICAN PEN WOMEN
1300 17th St. N.W.
Washington, DC 20036–1973
(202) 785–1997
Dr. Frances T. Carter, *National President*
  Promotes development of the creative talents of professional women in the arts. Membership is through local chapters, available by invitation from current members.

THE NATIONAL WRITERS ASSOCIATION
1450 S. Havana, Suite 424
Aurora, CO 80012
(303) 751–7844
Sandy Whelchel, *Executive Director*

849

New and established writers, poets, and playwrights throughout the U.S. and Canada may become members of the NWA, a full-time, customer-service-oriented association founded in 1937. Members receive a bimonthly newsletter, *Authorship*, and may attend the annual June conference. Annual dues: $60, *professional*; $50, *regular*; add $20 outside the U.S., Canada, and Mexico.

NATIONAL WRITERS UNION
873 Broadway, #203
New York, NY 10003
(212) 254–0279
Maria Pallante, *Executive Director*

Dedicated to bringing about equitable payment and fair treatment of free-lance writers through collective action. Membership is over 4,000 and includes book authors, poets, cartoonists, journalists, and technical writers in 13 chapters nationwide. The union offers its members contract and agent information, group health insurance, press credentials, grievance handling, a quarterly magazine, and sample contracts and resource materials. It sponsors workshops and seminars across the country. Membership is open to writers who have published a book, play, three articles, five poems, one short story or an equivalent amount of newsletter, publicity, technical, commercial, government, or institutional copy, or have written an equivalent amount of unpublished material and are actively seeking publication. Annual dues: $75 to $175.

NEW DRAMATISTS
424 W. 44th St.
New York, NY 10036
(212) 757–6960
Elana Greenfield, *Director of Artistic Programs*

New Dramatists is dedicated to finding gifted playwrights and giving them the time, space, and tools to develop their craft. Services include readings and workshops; a director-in-residence program; national script distribution for members; artist work spaces; international playwright exchange programs; script copying facilities; and a free ticket program. Membership is open to residents of New York City and the surrounding tri-state area. National memberships are offered to those outside the area who can spend time in NYC in order to take advantage of programs. Apply between July 15 and September 15. No annual dues.

NORTHWEST PLAYWRIGHTS GUILD
Box 9218
Portland, OR 97207–9218
(503) 222–7010
Bill Johnson, *Office Manager*

The guild supports and promotes playwrights living in the Northwest through play development, staged readings, and networking for play competitions and production opportunities. Members receive monthly and quarterly newsletters. Annual dues: $20.

OUTDOOR WRITERS ASSOCIATION OF AMERICA, INC.
2017 Cato Ave., Suite 101
State College, PA 16801–2768
(814) 234–1011
James W. Rainey, *Executive Director*

A non-profit, international organization representing professional communicators who report and reflect upon America's diverse interests in the outdoors. Membership, by nomination only, includes a monthly publication,

Outdoors Unlimited; annual conference; annual membership directory; contests. The association also provides scholarships to qualified students.

PEN AMERICAN CENTER
568 Broadway
New York, NY 10012
(212) 334–1660
Karen Kennerly, *Executive Director*
   PEN American Center is one of more than 120 centers worldwide that compose International PEN. The 2,700 members of the American Center are poets, playwrights, essayists, editors, and novelists, as well as literary translators and those agents who have made a substantial contribution to the literary community. PEN American headquarters is in New York City, and branches are located in Boston, Chicago, New Orleans, Portland, Oregon, and San Francisco. Among the activities, programs, and services sponsored are literary events and awards, outreach projects to encourage reading, assistance to writers in financial need, and international and domestic human rights campaigns on behalf of many writers, editors, and journalists censored or imprisoned because of their writing. Membership is open to writers who have published two books of literary merit, as well as editors, agents, playwrights, and translators who meet specific standards; apply to membership committee.

THE PLAYWRIGHTS' CENTER
2301 Franklin Ave. E.
Minneapolis, MN 55406
(612) 332–7481
David Moore, Jr., *Executive Director*
   The Playwrights' Center fuels the contemporary theater by providing services that support the development and public appreciation of playwrights and playwriting. Members receive applications for all programs, a calendar of events, eligibility to participate in special activities, including classes, outreach programs, and PlayLabs. Annual dues: $35.

POETRY SOCIETY OF AMERICA
15 Gramercy Park
New York, NY 10003
(212) 254–9628
Elise Paschen, *Executive Director*
   Founded in 1910, the PSA seeks through a variety of programs to gain a wider audience for American poetry. The PSA conducts several annual contests for poetry, many open to non-members, and offers workshops, poetry readings, and publications. Maintains the Van Voorhis Library of American Poetry. Annual dues: $40.

POETS AND WRITERS, INC.
72 Spring St.
New York, NY 10012
(212) 226–3586
Elliot Figman, *Executive Director*
   Poets & Writers, Inc., was founded in 1970 to foster the development of poets and fiction writers and to promote communication throughout the literary community. A non-membership organization, it offers a nationwide information center for writers; *Poets & Writers Magazine* and other publications; as well support for readings and workshops at a wide range of venues.

PRIVATE EYE WRITERS OF AMERICA
407 W. Third St.
Moorestown, NJ 08057
(609) 235–8261
Robert J. Randisi, *Executive Director*
Martha L. Derickson, *Membership Chairman*
A national organization that seeks to promote a wider recognition and appreciation of private eye literature. Sponsors the annual Shamus Award for the best in P.I. fiction. Writers who have published a work of fiction (short story, novel, TV script, or movie screenplay) with a private eye as the central character are eligible to join as active members. Serious devotees of the P.I. story may become associate members. Annual dues: $50, *active*; $40, *associate*; $50, *international*.

ROMANCE WRITERS OF AMERICA
13700 Veterans Memorial Dr., Suite 315
Houston, TX 77014
(713) 440–6885
Linda Fisher, *Office Supervisor*
An international organization with over 140 local chapters across the U.S. and Canada; membership is open to any writer, published or unpublished, interested in the field of romantic fiction. Annual dues of $60, plus $10 application fee for new members; benefits include annual conference, contest, market information, and bimonthly newsmagazine, *Romance Writers' Report*.

SCIENCE-FICTION AND FANTASY WRITERS OF AMERICA, INC.
5 Winding Brook Dr., #1B
Guilderland, NY 12084
Peter Dennis Pautz, *Executive Secretary*
An organization whose purpose it is to foster and further the professional interests of science fiction and fantasy writers. Presents the annual Nebula Award for excellence in the field and publishes the *Bulletin* for its members (also available to nonmembers).
Any writer who has sold a work of science fiction or fantasy is eligible for membership. Annual dues: $50, *active* ; $35, *affiliate*; plus $10 installation fee; send for application and information.

SMALL PRESS GENRE ASSOCIATION
P.O. Box 6301
Concord, CA 94524
(510) 254–7442
Joe Morey, *President*
The SPGA is a new international service organization for writers of any genre, illustrators, editors, and publishers of material related to the genres of science fiction, fantasy, horror, western, mystery and its subgenres. Members receive six issues of the *Genre Press Digest*, critique services, grievance arbitration, research assistance, and membership in COSMEP: The International Association of Independent Publishers. Annual dues: $25, U.S. and Canada; $30, international.

SOCIETY FOR TECHNICAL COMMUNICATION
901 N. Stuart St., #904
Arlington, VA 22203–1854
(703) 522–4114
William C. Stolgitis, *Executive Director*
A professional organization dedicated to the advancement of the theory

and practice of technical communication in all media. The 19,000 members in the U.S. and other countries include technical writers and editors, publishers, artists and draftsmen, researchers, educators, and audiovisual specialists. Annual dues: $95.

SOCIETY OF AMERICAN TRAVEL WRITERS
4101 Lake Boone Trail, Suite 201
Raleigh, NC 27607
(919) 787–5181
Susan Rexer, *Administrative Coordinator*

The Society of American Travel Writers represents writers and other professionals who strive to provide travelers with accurate reports on destinations, facilities, and services. Membership is by invitation. Active membership is limited to salaried travel writers and free lancers who have a steady volume of published or distributed work about travel. Initiation fees: $200, *active*; $400, *associate*. Annual dues: $120, *active*; $240, *associate*.

SOCIETY OF CHILDREN'S BOOK WRITERS & ILLUSTRATORS
22736 Vanowen St., Suite 106
West Hills, CA 91307
(818) 888–8760
Lin Oliver, *Executive Director*

A national organization of authors, editors, publishers, illustrators, filmmakers, librarians, and educators, the SCBWI offers a variety of services to people who write, illustrate, or share an interest in children's literature. Full memberships are open to those who have had at least one children's book or story published. Associate memberships are open to all those with an interest in children's literature. Annual dues: $40.

SOCIETY OF ENVIRONMENTAL JOURNALISTS
9425 Stenton Ave., Suite 209
Philadelphia, PA 19118
(215) 247–9710; Fax: (215) 247–9712; E-mail: SEJOffice@AOL.com
Beth Parke, *Executive Director*

Dedicated to enhancing the quality and accuracy of environmental reporting, the society serves 900 members with a quarterly journal, national and regional conferences, computer bulletin board service, a mentoring program, and an annual directory. Annual dues: $30.

SOCIETY OF PROFESSIONAL JOURNALISTS
16 S. Jackson St.
Greencastle, IN 46135–0077
(317) 653–3333
Greg Christopher, *Executive Director*

With 13,500 members and 300 chapters, the society serves the interests of print, broadcast, and wire journalists. Services include legal counsel on journalism issues, jobs-for-journalists career search program, professional development seminars, and awards that encourage journalism. Members receive *Quill*, a monthly magazine that explores current issues in the field. SPJ promotes ethics and freedom of information programs. Annual dues: $64, *professional*; $32, *student*.

THE SONGWRITERS GUILD FOUNDATION
1560 Broadway, Suite 1306
New York, NY 10036
(212) 768–7902; Fax: (212) 768–9048
George Wurzbach, *National Projects Director*

Open to published and unpublished songwriters, the Guild provides members with contracts, reviews contracts, collects royalties from publishers, offers group health and life insurance plans, conducts workshops and critique sessions, and provides a songwriting collaboration service. Annual dues: $55, *associate*; $70 and up, *full member*.

THEATRE COMMUNICATIONS GROUP
355 Lexington Ave.
New York, NY 10017
(212) 697–5230
Peter Zeisler, *Executive Director*
TCG, a national organization for the American theater, provides services to facilitate the work of playwrights, literary managers, and other theater professionals and journalists. Publications include the quarterly bulletin *Play-Source*, which circulates information on new plays, translations, and adaptations to more than 300 TCG constituent theaters and to potential producers. Also publishes the annual *Dramatists Sourcebook*. Individual members receive *American Theatre* Magazine. Annual dues: $35, *individual*.

WESTERN WRITERS OF AMERICA, INC.
1012 Fair St.
Franklin, TN 37064
(615) 791–1444
James A. Crutchfield, *Secretary/Treasurer*
Membership is open to qualified professional writers of fiction and nonfiction related to the history and literature of the American West. Its chief purpose is to promote a more widespread distribution, readership, and appreciation of the West and its literature. Holds annual convention in the last week of June. Sponsors annual Spur Awards, Owen Wister Award, and Medicine Pipe Bearer's Award for published work and produced screenplays. Annual dues: $60.

WRITERS GUILD OF AMERICA, EAST, INC.
555 W. 57th St.
New York, NY 10019
(212) 767–7800
Mona Mangan, *Executive Director*

WRITERS GUILD OF AMERICA, WEST, INC.
8955 Beverly Blvd.
West Hollywood, CA 90048
(310) 550–1000
Brian Walton, *Executive Director*
The Writers Guild of America (East and West) represents writers in motion pictures, broadcast, cable and new media industries, including news and entertainment. In order to qualify for membership, a writer must fulfill current requirements for employment or sale of material in one of these fields.
The basic dues are $25 per quarter for WGA West and $12.50 per quarter for WGAE. In addition, there are quarterly dues based on percentage of the member's earnings in any one of the fields over which the guild has jurisdiction. The initiation fee is $1,000 for WGAE, for writers living east of the Mississippi, and $2,500 for WGA West, for those living west of the Mississippi.

WRITERS INFORMATION NETWORK
P.O. Box 11337
Bainbridge Island, WA 98110
(206) 842–9103
Elaine Wright Colvin, *Director*
W.I.N. was founded in 1983 to provide a link between Christian writers and the religious publishing industry. Offered are a bimonthly newsletter, market news, editorial services, advocacy and grievance procedures, referral services, and conferences. Annual dues: $20; $25, *foreign*.

LITERARY AGENTS

As more and more book publishers will consider only agented submissions, more writers are turning to agents to sell their manuscripts. The following is an expanded list of agents that handle literary material and in some cases, stage plays. Included in each listing are such important details as type of material represented, submission procedure, and commission. Since the agent's income is a percentage of the amount received from the sales of a client's work, agents must represent writers who are selling fairly regularly to good markets. Nonetheless, many of the agents listed here note they will consider unpublished writers. Always query an agent first, and enclose a self-addressed, stamped envelope; most agents will not respond without an SASE. Do not send any manuscripts until the agent has asked you to do so; and be wary of agents who charge fees for reading manuscripts. All of the following agents have indicated they do *not* charge reading fees, and those who pass on postage, phone, or photocopying fees to their clients have indicated such.

To learn more about agents and their role in publishing, the Association of Authors' Representatives, Inc., publishes a code of ethics as well as an up-to-date list of AAR members, available for $5 (check or money order) and a 52¢ legal-size SASE. Write to: Association of Authors' Representatives, Inc., 10 Astor Pl., 3rd Floor, New York, NY 10003.

Other lists of agents and their policies can be found in *Literary Market Place*, a directory found in most libraries, and in *Literary Agents of North America, Fifth Edition* (Author Aid/Research Associates International, 340 E. 52nd St., New York, NY 10022).

AARDVARK LITERARY AGENTS—5330 Main St., Suite 270, Williamsville, NY 14221. Attn: Kate Berman, Jim Fair. Adult fiction, nonfiction, and plays. Young adult novels considered; no children's stories. Unpublished writers considered. Query with outline, three chapters, and bio/resumé. Multiple queries O.K. Commission: 10%. Fees: photocopying, shipping.

LEE ALLAN AGENCY—P.O. Box 18617, Milwaukee, WI 53218. Attn: Mr. Lee A. Matthias. Adult fiction, nonfiction, and juvenile for all ages. Unpublished writers considered. Query; multiple queries O.K. Commission: 15%. Fees: photocopying, overnight shipping, telephone. "Go to a bookstore and locate the exact place in the store where your book would be displayed. If it realistically fits a popular market niche, is not derivative or imitative, meets the size constraints, and you can't make it any better yourself, you are ready to find an agent."

JAMES ALLEN LITERARY AGENT—538 East Hartford St., P.O. Box 278, Milford, PA 18337. Attn: James Allen. Adult fiction. Unpublished writers considered. Query; no multiple queries. Commission: 10% domestic, 20% foreign. Fees: photocopying, shipping. "My list is quite full; though I'm always willing to consider material, I'm mainly interested in taking on only people with previous booklength fiction publishing credits."

MARCIA AMSTERDAM AGENCY—41 W. 82nd St. #9A, New York, NY 10024. Attn: Marcia Amsterdam. Adult and young adult fiction. Query; will read multiple queries, "but if we request a submission, we request a 2- or 3- week exclusive." Commission: 15% domestic. Fees: standard costs.

ARCADIA—20A Old Neversink Rd., Danbury, CT 06811. Attn: Victoria Gould Pryor. Adult fiction and nonfiction. Unpublished writers considered. Query; multiple queries O.K. Commission: 15%. Fees: photocopying.

THE AXELROD AGENCY—54 Church St., Lenox, MA 01240. Adult fiction and nonfiction. Unpublished writers considered. Query; multiple queries O.K. Commission: 10% U.S., 20% foreign. Fees: photocopying.

MALAGA BALDI LITERARY AGENCY, INC.—Box 591, Radio City Station, New York, NY 10101. Attn: Malaga Baldi. Adult fiction and nonfiction. Unpublished writers considered. Query first; "if I am interested, I ask for proposal, outline, and sample pages for nonfiction, complete manuscript for fiction." Multiple queries O.K. Commission: 15%. Fees: none.

THE BALKIN AGENCY—P.O. Box 222, Amherst, MA 01004. Attn: Rick Balkin. Adult nonfiction. Unpublished writers considered. Query with outline; no multiple queries. Commission: 15% domestic, 20% foreign. Fees: none. "Most interested in serious nonfiction."

VIRGINIA BARBER AGENCY—101 Fifth Ave., New York, NY 10003. Adult fiction and nonfiction. Query with outline, sample pages, and bio/resumé. No multiple queries. Commission: 15% domestic, 20% foreign. Fees: photocopying.

LORETTA BARRETT BOOKS—101 Fifth Ave., New York, NY 10003. Attn: Loretta Barrett. Adult fiction and nonfiction. Unpublished writers considered. Query with outline and bio/resumé; no multiple queries. Commission: 15%. Fees: telephone. "Response time is approximately 4 to 8 weeks. Please do not call before then."

REID BOATES LITERARY AGENCY—Box 328, 69 Cooks Crossroad, Pittstown, NJ 08867–0328. Attn: Reid Boates. Adult fiction and nonfiction. Unpublished writers considered. Query; no multiple queries. Commission: 15%. Fees: none.

GEORGES BORCHARDT, INC.—136 E. 57th St., New York, NY 10022. Adult fiction and nonfiction. Unpublished writers considered by recommendation only. No unsolicited queries or submissions. Commission: 10%. Fees: photocopying, shipping.

BRANDT & BRANDT LITERARY AGENTS—1501 Broadway, New York, NY 10036. Adult fiction and nonfiction. Unpublished writers considered occasion-

856

ally. Unsolicited query by letter only; no multiple queries. Commission: 10%. Fees: photocopying.

THE HELEN BRANN AGENCY, INC.—94 Curtis Rd., Bridgewater, CT 06752. Attn: Carolyn Feusferer. Adult fiction and nonfiction. Unpublished writers considered. Query; no multiple queries. Commission: 15%. Fees: none.

PATTI BREITMAN PUBLISHING PROJECTS—12 Rally Ct., Fairfax, CA 94930. Attn: Patti Breitman. Nonfiction: self-help only. Unpublished writers considered. Query; multiple queries O.K. Commission: 15% domestic, 30% foreign. Fees: photocopying, shipping. " Keep it brief and lively."

CURTIS BROWN LTD.—10 Astor Place, New York, NY 10003. General trade fiction and nonfiction; also juvenile. Unpublished writers considered. Query; no multiple queries. Commission: 15% domestic, 10% foreign. Fees: photocopying; express mail.

JANE JORDAN BROWNE—Multimedia Product Development, 410 S. Michigan Ave., Rm. 724, Chicago, IL 60605. Attn: Jane Jordan Browne. Adult fiction and nonfiction; juvenile, all ages. Query; multiple queries O.K. Commission: 15% domestic, 20% foreign. Fees: photocopying; foreign fax, telephone, and postage.

KNOX BURGER ASSOCIATES, LTD.—39 ½ Washington Square S., New York, NY 10012. Adult fiction and nonfiction; no science fiction, fantasy, or romance. Unpublished writers considered. Query; no multiple queries. Commission: 15%. Fees: photocopying.

SHEREE BYKOFSKY ASSOCIATES, INC.—211 East 51st St., Suite 11D, New York, NY 10022. Adult nonfiction. Unpublished writers considered. Query with outline, up to 3 sample pages or proposal. Multiple queries O.K.. Commission: 15%. Fees: none.

MARTHA CASSELMAN—P.O. Box 342, Calistoga, CA 94515–0342. Nonfiction, especially interested in cookbooks. Also young adult. Unpublished writers considered. Query with outline, sample pages, and bio/resumé. Multiple queries O.K. Commission: 15%. Fees: photocopying.

JULIE CASTIGLIA AGENCY—1155 Camino del Mar, Suite 510, Del Mar, CA 92014. Attn: Julie Castiglia. Fiction: mainstream, commercial mysteries/thrillers. Nonfiction: psychology, women's issues, science, biography, business, parenting. Query with outline, sample pages, and bio/resumé. No multiple queries. Commission: 15%. Fees: photocopying, shipping. "Please do not query on the phone. Attend workshops and writers' conferences before approaching an agent."

DIANE CLEAVER, INC.—55 Fifth Ave., New York, NY 10003. Adult fiction and nonfiction. Unpublished writers considered. Query; multiple queries O.K. Commission: 15%. Fees: photocopying.

HY COHEN LITERARY AGENCY, LTD.—111 West 57th St., New York, NY 10019. Attn: Hy Cohen. Adult fiction, nonfiction, and juvenile. Unpublished writers considered. Unsolicited queries and manuscripts O.K. Multiple submissions considered. Commission: 10% domestic, 20% foreign. Fees: phone, photocopying, postage. "I rarely respond well to first-person narrative. Good luck!"

JOANNA LEWIS COLE—404 Riverside Dr., New York, NY 10025. Attn: Joanna Cole. Juvenile fiction and nonfiction, all ages. Unpublished writers considered. Query; multiple queries O.K. Commission 10 to15%. Fees: photocopying, shipping.

COLUMBIA LITERARY ASSOCIATES—7902 Nottingham Way, Ellicott City, MD 21043. "Due to a very active client list, CLA is currently reviewing new projects only through professional referrals."

DON CONGDON ASSOCIATES, INC.—156 Fifth Ave., Suite 625, New York, NY 10010. Adult fiction and nonfiction. Unpublished writers considered occasionally. Query with outline; no multiple queries. Commission: 10% domestic. Fees: photocopying.

THE DOE COOVER AGENCY—58 Sagamore Ave., Medford, MA 02155. Attn: Doe Coover, Colleen Mohyde. Adult fiction and general nonfiction. Unpublished writers considered. Query with outline, sample pages, and bio/resumé; multiple queries O.K. Commission: 15%. Fees: photocopying.

RICHARD CURTIS ASSOCIATES, INC.—171 E. 74th St., New York, NY 10021. Adult nonfiction. Unpublished writers considered. Query with bio/resumé; no multiple queries. Commission: 15% domestic, 20% foreign. Fees: photocopying, shipping.

DARHANSOFF & VERRILL LITERARY AGENCY—1220 Park Ave., New York, NY 10128. Adult fiction and nonfiction. Unpublished writers considered. Unsolicited queries "only with recommendations." Commission: 10% domestic, 20% foreign. Fees: none.

ELAINE DAVIE LITERARY AGENCY—Village Gate Square, 274 N. Goodman St., Rochester, NY 14607. Attn: Elaine Davie. Adult fiction and nonfiction; "we specialize in books by and for women, especially romance." Unpublished writers considered. Query with outline and sample pages. Multiple submissions O.K. Commission: 15%. Fees: none.

ANITA DIAMANT AGENCY, INC.—310 Madison Ave # 1508, New York, NY 10017. Attn: Anita Diamant. Adult fiction: literary, mystery, romance. Also nonfiction "anything not technical," and young adult. Query with outline, sample pages, and bio/resumé. No multiple queries. Commission: 15%. Fees: none.

SANDRA DIJKSTRA LITERARY AGENCY—1155 Camino del Mar, Suite 515C, Del Mar, CA 92014. Attn: Beverly Fisher. Adult fiction and nonfiction. Query outline and bio/resumé. For fiction, submit first 50 pages and synopsis; for nonfiction, submit proposal. Commission: 15% domestic, 20% foreign. Fees: none.

THE JONATHAN DOLGER AGENCY—49 E. 96th St., #9B, New York, NY 10128. Attn: Tom Wilson. Adult trade fiction and nonfiction. Considers unpublished writers. Query with outline. Commission: 15%. Fees: photocopying, shipping. "No category mysteries, romance, or science fiction."

DWYER & O'GRADY, INC.—P.O. Box 239, East Lempster, NH 03605. Attn: Elizabeth O'Grady. Branch office: P.O. Box 790, Cedar Key, FL 32625. Children's picture books for ages 6 to 12; require strong story line, dialogue, and character development. Unpublished writers considered. Query with bio/resumé; no multiple queries. Commission: 15%. Fees: photocopying, shipping. "Our primary focus is the representation of illustrators who also write their own stories; however, we represent several adult authors who write for the children's market."

JANE DYSTEL LITERARY MANAGEMENT—One Union Square West, New York, NY 10003. Attn: Jane Dystel. Adult fiction and nonfiction. Unpublished writers considered. Query with bio/resumé; no multiple queries. Commission: 15%. Fees: shipping.

EDUCATIONAL DESIGN SERVICES—P.O. Box 253, Wantaugh, NY 11793. Attn: Bertam L. Linder. Educational texts only. Unpublished writers considered. Query with outline, sample pages or complete manuscript, and bio/resumé. No multiple queries. Commission: 15%. Fees: none.

ETHAN ELLENBERG LITERARY AGENCY—548 Broadway, Suite 5E, New York, NY 10012. Attn: Steve Seitz. Adult fiction and nonfiction; juvenile. Unpublished writers considered. Query with outline and sample pages; multiple queries O.K. Commission: 15%. Fees: photocopying, shipping.

ANN ELMO AGENCY—60 E. 42nd St., New York, NY 10165. Attn: Lettie Lee. Branch office: 756 Neilson St., Berkeley, CA 94707. Adult fiction, nonfiction, and plays. Juvenile books for middle grades and up; no picture books. Unpublished writers considered. Query with outline, sample pages, and bio/resumé. No multiple queries. Commission: 15%. Fees: none.

FELICIA ETH—555 Bryant St., Suite 350, Palo Alto, CA 94301. Attn: Felicia Eth. Adult fiction, "highly selective, mostly contemporary." Also nonfiction. Unpublished writers considered. Query with outline, sample pages, and bio/resumé. Multiple queries O.K. if noted. Commission: 15% domestic, 20% foreign. Fees: photocopying. "I am a small, highly personal agent, not right for everyone but very committed to those I work with. I tend to work with writers based either on the West Coast or at least west of the Mississippi."

FARBER LITERARY AGENCY—14 E. 75th Ave. S.E., New York, NY 10021. Attn: Ann Farber. Adult fiction, nonfiction, and stage plays; juvenile books. Considers unpublished writers. Query with outline and sample pages. Commission: 15% "with services of attorney." Fees: photocopying.

FLANNERY LITERARY—34–36 28th St. #5, Long Island City, NY 11106–3516. Attn: Jennifer Flannery. Adult fiction and nonfiction; juvenile books for all ages. Unpublished writers considered. Query; multiple queries O.K. Commission: 15%. Fees: none.

ROBERT A. FREEDMAN DRAMATIC AGENCY, INC.—1501 Broadway, Suite 2310, New York, NY 10036. Attn: Robert A. Freedman or Selma Luttinger. Stage plays. Send query only; multiple queries O.K. Commission: standard. Fees: photocopying.

SAMUEL FRENCH, INC.—45 W. 25th St., New York, NY 10010. Attn: Lawrence Harbison, Ed.. Stage plays. Unpublished writers considered. Query with complete manuscript; unsolicited and multiple queries O.K. Commission: 10%. Fees: none.

JAY GARON-BROOKE ASSOCIATES—101 W. 55th St. #5K, New York, NY 10019. Attn: Jay Garon. Adult fiction and nonfiction. Unpublished writers considered. Query with outline and bio/resumé; no multiple queries. Commission: 15% domestic, 30% foreign. Fees: photocopying.

GOLDFARB & GRAYBILL—918 16th St. N.W., Suite 400, Washington, DC 20006. Attn: Nina Goldfarb. Adult fiction and nonfiction. No poetry, romance, science fiction, or children's books. Query with bio/resumé; for fiction, include a synopsis, sample chapter. Multiple queries O.K. Commission: 15%. Fees: photocopying, shipping. "We appreciate clear, succinct, well-written, grammatical query letters and samples."

GOODMAN ASSOCIATES—500 West End Ave., New York, NY 10024. Attn: Daniele Boucher. Adult fiction and nonfiction. Unpublished writers considered. Query with outline, sample pages, and bio/resumé. Multiple queries O.K. Commission: 15% domestic, 20% foreign. Fees: photocopying, long-distance telephone, postage.

MAIA GREGORY ASSOCIATES—311 East 72nd St., New York, NY 10021. Adult nonfiction only. Unpublished writers considered. Query with sample pages and bio/resumé. No multiple queries. Commission: 15%. Fees: none.

HEACOCK LITERARY AGENCY, INC.—1523 Sixth St., Suite 14, Santa Monica, CA 90401. Attn: Jim Heacock, Pres. Adult nonfiction. Unpublished writers considered. Query with outline, sample pages, and bio/resumé. Multiple queries O.K. Commission: 10% to 15%. Fees: out-of-pocket expenses. "Make your query letter original, interesting, and clear as to the 'hook' that makes it different from others, conventional wisdom, or common sense."

FREDERICK HILL ASSOCIATES—1842 Union St., San Francisco, CA 94123. Attn: Bonnie Nadell. Branch office: 8446 ½ Melrose Pl., Los Angeles, CA 90069. Adult fiction and nonfiction. Unpublished writers considered. Query with outline and bio/resumé; mulitple queries O.K. Commission: 15%. Fees: photocopying, postage.

JOHN L. HOCHMANN BOOKS—320 E. 58th St., New York, NY 10022. Attn: John L. Hochmann. Nonfiction: biography, social history, college textbook. Unpublished writers considered, "provided they present evidence of expertise in the field they are writing about." Query with outline, sample pages, and bio/resumé. No multiple queries. Commission: 15% for U.S./Canadian, 15% foreign language and U.K. Fees: none. "Do not submit jacket copy. Submit outlines and proposals that include evaluations of competing books."

HULL HOUSE LITERARY AGENCY—240 East 82nd St., New York, NY 10028. Attn: David Stewart Hull, Pres. New writers contact Lydia Mortimer, Associate. Nonfiction: true crime, biography, military, general history. Fiction, especially crime fiction. Query with outline and bio/resumé; include sample pages with nonfiction queries only. Multiple queries O.K. Commission: 15% domestic, 20% foreign. Fees: photocopying, overseas fax and postage.

IMG/JULIAN BACH LITERARY AGENCY—22 E. 71st St., New York, NY 10021. Attn: Julian Bach, Trish Lande, Carolyn Krupp, or Mark Reiter. Adult fiction and nonfiction; juvenile books for young readers through young adult. Unpublished writers considered. Query with outline, sample pages, and bio/resumé. No multiple queries. Commission: 15%. Fees: photocopying.

INTERNATIONAL PUBLISHER ASSOCIATES, INC.—289 Mt. Hope Ave., Suite V-13, Dover, NJ 07801. Attn: J. DeRogatis, Exec. V. P. Adult nonfiction. Unpublished writers considered. Query with outline and sample pages; multiple queries O.K. Commission: 15% domestic, 20% foreign. Fees: photocopying, shipping.

SHARON JARVIS & CO.—Toad Hall, Inc., Laceyville, PA 18623. Adult fiction and nonfiction. Unpublished writers considered. Query with bio and resumé; no multiple queries. Commission: 15%. Fees: photocopying. "Pay attention to what's selling and what's commercial."

JCA LITERARY AGENCY, INC.—27 W. 20th St., Suite 1103, New York, NY 10011. Adult fiction and nonfiction. Unpublished writers considered. Query with sample pages; multiple queries O.K. Commission: 10% domestic, 20% foreign. Fees: photocopying, shipping. "Be as straightforward and to-the-point as possible. Don't try to hype us or bury us in detail."

LOUISE B. KETZ AGENCY—1485 First Ave., Suite 4B, New York, NY 10021. Attn: Louise B. Ketz. Adult nonfiction on science, business, sports, history, and reference. Considers unpublished writers "with proper credentials." Query with outline and bio/resumé; multiple queries occasionally considered. Commission: 10% to 15%. Fees: photocopying, shipping.

KIDDE, HOYT & PICARD—335 E. 51st St., New York, NY 10022. Attn: Katharine Kidde, Wendy Wylegala. General interest/trade nonfiction on current affairs, social sciences, and the arts. Adult mainstream fiction; some literary, mysteries, romances, thrillers. No science fiction, horror, or poetry. Unpublished writers not considered, "but we'll consider writers who have published short fiction or nonfiction—a published book is not necessary." Query with 2 or 3 chapters and synopsis; also include writing experience. Multiple queries O.K. Commission: 10%. Fees: photocopying, postage.

KIRCHOFF/WOHLBERG, INC.—866 United Nations Plaza, Suite 525, New York, NY 10017. Attn: Liza Voges. Juvenile fiction and nonfiction only. Unpublished writers considered. Query; multiple submissions O.K. Commission: 15%. Fees: none.

HARVEY KLINGER, INC.—301 W. 53rd St., New York, NY 10019. Attn: Harvey Klinger. Adult fiction and nonfiction. Unpublished writers considered. Query with outline, sample pages, and bio/resumé. No multiple queries. Commission: 15% domestic, 25% foreign. Fees: photocopying, shipping.

BARBARA S. KOUTS—P.O. Box 558, Bellport, NY 11713. Attn: Barbara S. Kouts. Adult fiction, nonfiction, and juvenile books for all ages. Unpublished writers considered. Query with bio/resumé. Multiple queries O.K. Commission: 10%. Fees: photocopying. "Send your best work always!"

LUCY KROLL AGENCY—390 West End Ave., New York, NY 10024. Attn: Barbara Hogenson. Adult fiction, nonfiction, and plays. Unpublished writers considered. Query; multiple queries O.K. Commission: 15% books, 10% dramatic. Fees: none.

PETER LAMPACK AGENCY, INC.—551 Fifth Ave., Suite 1613, New York, NY 10176. Attn: Sandra Blanton, Agent. Deborah T. Brown, Assoc. Agent. Literary and commercial fiction; "We like both contemporary relationship works and historical fiction in addition to suspense, mystery, action-adventure." No romance, science fiction, or horror. Nonfiction: biography/autobiography, politics, finance, and law, written by experts in the fields. Unpublished writers considered. Query with synopsis; outline and bio/resumé for nonfiction. Sample pages will be solicited after queries. Multiple queries O.K. Commission: 15%. Fees: photocopying.

THE ROBERT LANTZ-JOY HARRIS AGENCY—156 Fifth Ave., Suite 617, New York, NY 10010. Adult fiction and nonfiction. Unpublished writers considered. Query with outline, sample pages, and bio/resumé. No multiple queries. Commission: 15%. Fees: photocopying, shipping.

MICHAEL LARSEN/ELIZABETH POMADA—1029 Jones St., San Francisco, CA 94109. Attn: M. Larsen, nonfiction; E. Pomada, fiction. Fiction: literary, commercial, and genre. Nonfiction: pop psychology and science, biography, business, nature, health, history, arts, travel. Unpublished writers considered. Query for fiction with first 30 pages, synopsis, SASE, and phone number. For nonfiction, query by phone: (415) 673–0939. Multiple queries O.K., "as long as we're told." Commission: 15%. Fees: none.

THE MAUREEN LASHER AGENCY—P.O. Box 888, Pacific Palisades, CA 90272. Attn: Ann Cashman. Adult fiction and nonfiction. Unpublished writers considered. Query with outline, sample pages, and bio/resumé. No multiple queries. Commission: 15%. Fees: none.

LEVANT & WALES, INC.—108 Hayes St., Seattle, WA 98108. Attn: Elizabeth Wales, Valerie Griffith. Adult fiction and nonfiction. Unpublished writers considered. Query with outline, sample pages, and bio/resumé. Mulitple queries O.K. Commission: 15%. Fees: photocopying.

LICHTMAN, TRISTER, SINGER & ROSS—1666 Connecticut Ave. N.W., Suite 501, Washington, DC 20009. Attn: Gail Ross, Howard Yoon. Adult nonfiction. Unpublished writers considered. Query with outline, sample pages, bio, and resumé. Multiple queries O.K. Commission: 15%. Fees: none.

NANCY LOVE LITERARY AGENCY—250 E. 65th St, New York, NY 10021. Mostly nonfiction; some fiction, but no genre except mysteries and thrillers. Unpublished writers considered. Query; no multiple queries on novels. Commission: 15%. Fees: photocopying.

DONALD MAASS LITERARY AGENCY—157 W. 57th St., Suite 1003, New York, NY 10019. Attn: Donald Maass, Pres. Jennifer Jackson, Asst. Adult fiction, specializing in genres: science fiction, fantasy, mystery, suspense, historical. Unpublished writers considered. Query; multiple queries O.K. Commission: 15% domestic, 20% foreign. Fees: none.

GERARD MCCAULEY AGENCY, INC.—P.O. Box 844, Katonah, NY 10536. Attn: Gerard F. McCauley, Henry Houghton. Adult fiction and nonfiction. Unpublished writers considered. Query; no multiple queries. Commission: 15%. Fees: postage.

GINA MACCOBY LITERARY AGENCY—1123 Broadway, Suite 1010, New York, NY 10010. Adult fiction and nonfiction; juvenile for all ages. Unpublished writers considered. Query; multiple queries O.K. Commission: 10%. Fees: photocopying, airmail postage, bank charges for converting foreign currencies.

CAROL MANN LITERARY AGENCY—55 Fifth Ave., New York, NY 10003. Attn: Carol Mann. Deborah Clifford, subsidiary rights. Fiction, 10%; nonfiction, 90%. Query; multiple queries O.K. commission: 15%. Fees: photocopying, shipping.

MANUS ASSOCIATES INC.—417 East 57th St., Suite 5D, New York, NY 10022. Attn: Janet Manus. Branch office: 430 Cowper St., Palo Alto, CA 94301. Adult fiction and nonfiction. No science fiction, category romance, or military books. Unpublished writers considered. Query with outline, sample pages, and bio/resumé. Multiple queries O.K., "on occasion." Commission: 15%. Fees: photocopying, shipping.

MILDRED MARMUR ASSOCIATES LTD.—Suite 127, 2005 Palmer Ave., Larchmont, NY 10538. Attn: M. Marmur. Adult fiction, nonfiction, and juvenile books. No poetry, science fiction, or illustrated juvenile books. Unpublished writers considered. Query with outline, sample pages, and bio/resumé. No multiple queries. Commission: 15%. Fees: photocopying, shipping.

ELISABETH MARTON AGENCY—One Union Square W., Rm. 612, New York, NY 10003–3303. Attn: Tonda Marton. Plays only. Unproduced playwrights considered. Query; multiple queries O.K. Commission: 10%. Fees: none.

JED MATTES, INC.—200 West 72nd St., Suite 50, New York, NY 10023. Adult fiction and nonfiction. Unpublished writers considered. Query; multiple queries O.K. Commission: 15% domestic, 20% foreign. Fees: none.

HELMUT MEYER LITERARY AGENCY—330 East 79th St, New York, NY 10021. Attn: Helmut Meyer. Adult fiction and nonfiction. Unpublished writers considered. Telephone queries preferred: (212) 288-2421. For mailed queries, include outline, sample pages, and bio/resumé. No multiple queries. Commission: 15%. Fees: none.

MONTGOMERY LITERARY AGENCY—P.O. Box 8822, Silver Spring, MD 20907–8822. Attn: M.E. Olsen, Pres. Novels, general-interest nonfiction, how-to, new age, humor, and some plays. Juvenile books for all ages. Unpublished writers considered. Query; complete manuscript preferred with synopsis. Multiple queries O.K. Commission: 15%. Fees: none. "We're interested in material from new or established writers."

HOWARD MORHAIM LITERARY AGENCY—175 Fifth Ave., Suite 709, New York, NY 10010. Attn: Howard Morhaim, Allison Mulen. Quality adult fiction, especially mysteries, thrillers, and suspense novels, and nonfiction. No children's books. Unpublished writers considered. Query with outline and first 3 chapters for fiction, detailed proposal for nonfiction. Multiple queries O.K. Commission: 15%. Fees: photocopying.

HENRY MORRISON, INC.—Box 235, Bedford Hills, NY 10507. Adult fiction and nonfiction books. Unpublished writers considered. Query with outline; multiple queries O.K. Commission: 15% U.S., 20% foreign. Fees: photocopying, shipping. "We are concentrating on a relatively small list of clients, and work toward building them in the U.S. and international marketplaces. We tend to avoid autobiographical novels and extremely literary novels, but always seek good nonfiction on major political and historical subjects."

RUTH NATHAN AGENCY—80 Fifth Ave., Suite 706, New York, NY 10011. Adult nonfiction: art books, decorative arts, show business, biography. Commission: 15%. Fees: photocopying, shipping. "To writers seeking an agent: Please note what my specialties are. Do not send science fiction, fantasy, children's books, or business books."

NEW ENGLAND PUBLISHING ASSOCIATES, INC.—P.O. Box 5, Chester, CT 06412. Attn: Elizabeth Knappman. Adult nonfiction. Unpublished writers considered. Query; "send a carefully thought-out, market-driven proposal with concept statement, market analysis, competitive survey, author bio, annotated chapter outline, and 50–70 pages of sample chapters." No multiple queries. Commission: 15%. Fees: none.

EDWARD A. NOVAK III—711 North Second St., #1, Harrisburg, PA 17102. Attn: Ed Novak. Adult fiction and nonfiction. Unpublished writers considered. Query; multiple submissions O.K. Commission: 15% domestic; 19% foreign. Fees: photocopying.

THE RICHARD PARKS AGENCY—138 E. 16th St., #5B, New York, NY 10003. Adult nonfiction; fiction by referral only. Unpublished writers considered. Query; multiple queries O.K. Commission: 15% domestic, 20% foreign. Fees: photocopying. "No phone calls or faxed queries, please."

JAMES PETER ASSOCIATES, INC.—P.O. Box 772, Tenafly, NJ 07670. Attn: Bert Holtje. Adult nonfiction. Unpublished writers considered. Query with outline, sample pages, and bio/resumé. No multiple queries. Commission: 15%. Fees: none.

ALISON PICARD, LITERARY AGENT—P.O. Box 2000, Cotuit, MA 02635. Attn: Alison Picard. Adult fiction, nonfiction, and juvenile books. Unpublished writers considered. Query; multiple queries O.K. Commission: 15%. Fees: none.

SUSAN ANN PROTTER—110 W. 40th St., Suite 1408, New York, NY 10018. Adult fiction and nonfiction. Unpublished writers considered. Query with project description, resumé, and publishing history; multiple queries O.K. Commission: 15%. Fees: none.

ROBERTA PRYOR, INC.—24 W. 55th St., New York, NY 10019. Attn: Roberta Pryor. Adult fiction, nonfiction; juvenile general interest for all age levels. Unpublished writers considered. Query with outline, sample pages, and bio/resumé. Multiple queries O.K. Commission: 15% domestic, 10% foreign. Fees: photocopying, overnight shipping. "When submitting book proposals, taboo is the coy refusal to give away any plot resolution. How do we know the author can resolve his plot, take care of loose ends? Some applicants feel a copywriter's approach, i.e., jacket copy come-on, will tickle our fancy. Not so."

RAINES & RAINES—71 Park Ave., Suite 44A, New York, NY 10016. Attn: Keith Korman, Joan Raines, Theron Raines. Adult fiction, nonfiction, and juvenile for all ages. No unpublished writers considered. Send one-page query; no multiple queries. Commission: 15% domestic, 20% foreign. Fees: photocopying.

HELEN REES LITERARY AGENCY—308 Commonwealth Ave., Boston, MA 02115. Adult fiction and nonfiction. Unpublished writers considered. Query with outline, bio/resumé, and up to 50 sample pages; no multiple queries. Commission: 15%. Fees: none.

JANE ROTROSEN AGENCY—318 E. 51st St., New York, NY 10022. Attn: Ruth Kagle. Branch office: P.O. Box 1331, Taos, NM 87571. Attn: Stephanie Laidman. Adult fiction and nonfiction. Unpublished writers considered. Query; multiple queries O.K. Commission: 15% U.S. and Canada, 20% overseas. Fees: none.

PESHA RUBENSTEIN—37 Overlook Terr., #1D, New York, NY 10033. Attn: Pesha Rubenstein. Women's fiction; juvenile books; no young adult fiction. Unpublished writers considered. Query with first 10 pages; multiple queries O.K. Commission: 15% domestic, 20% foreign. Fees: photocopying. "Don't tell me you'll make me rich. Do tell me the ending of the story in the synopsis."

RUSSELL & VOLKENING, INC.—50 W. 29th St., New York, NY 10001. Adult and juvenile fiction and nonfiction. Unpublished writers considered. Query with outline and sample pages. No multiple queries. Commission: 10%. Fees: none.

RUSSELL-SIMENAUER LITERARY AGENCY, INC.—P.O. Box 43267, Upper Monclair, NJ 07043. Attn: Jacqueline Simenauer, Margaret Russell. Adult fiction: literary, commercial, mystery, humorous, historical novels, first novels. Adult nonfiction: pop psychology, self-help, medical, nutrition, sexuality, new-age spirituality, women's and men's issues, investigative journalism, true crime, military, adventure, business, celebrities. Some children's books. Query with outline, sample pages, bio/resumé; muliple queries O.K. Commission: 15% domestic, 25% foreign. Fees: shipping, phone, photocopying.

SANDUM & ASSOCIATES—144 E. 84th St., New York, NY 10028. Attn: Howard E. Sandum. Adult fiction and nonfiction. Unpublished writers considered. Query with sample pages and bio/resumé; multiple queries O.K. Commission: 15% domestic, 10% foreign. "We do not consider manuscripts in genres such as science fiction, romance, or horror unless surpassing literary qualities are present."

THE SHUKAT AGENCY—340 W. 55th St., Suite 1A, New York, NY 10019. Attn: Scott Shukat, Pat McLaughlin. Stage plays. Unpublished writers considered occasionally. Query with outline and sample pages; no multiple queries. Commission: 15%. Fees: none.

BOBBE SIEGEL, RIGHTS LITERARY AGENT—41 W. 83rd St., New York, NY 10024. Attn: Bobbe Siegel. Adult fiction and nonfiction. Unpublished writers considered. Query; multiple queries O.K. Commission: 15%. Fees: photocopying. "Keep query short, to the point, and literate. Don't sing your own praises; manuscript should speak for itself."

F. JOSEPH SPIELER LITERARY AGENCY—154 W. 57th St., Rm.135, New York, NY 10019. Adult fiction and nonfiction; juvenile books for all ages. Unpublished writers considered. Query with outline; no multiple queries. Commission: 15%. Fees: none.

GLORIA STERN AGENCY—2929 Buffalo Speedway, #2111, Houston, TX 77098. Attn: Gloria Stern. Adult nonfiction. Query with short outline, bio/resumé, and one double-spaced chapter; multiple queries O.K. Commission: 15%. Fees: photocopying.

GUNTHER STUHLMANN, AUTHOR'S REPRESENTATIVE—P.O. Box 276, Becket, MA 01223. Attn: Barbara Ward. Fiction and nonfiction, especially biography, letters, and history. No mysteries, romance, adventure. Unpublished writers sometimes considered. Query; no multiple queries. Commission: 10% North America; 15% Britain and Commonwealth; 20% foreign. "We take on few new clients at this time."

H.N. SWANSON, INC.—8523 Sunset Blvd., Los Angeles, CA 90069. Attn: Thomas J. Shanks, Pres. Jim Anderson, Steve Fisher, Larry Kennar, Anna Courtney. Adult fiction and nonfiction. Unpublished writers sometimes considered. Query; no multiple queries. Commission: 15% domestic; 20% foreign. Fees: none.

THE TANTLEFF OFFICE—375 Greenwich St., Suite 700, New York, NY 10013. Attn: John Santoianni, stage plays; Anthony Gardner, books. Adult fiction and nonfiction; stage plays. Unpublished writers considered. Query with synopsis, up to 10 sample pages, bio/resumé; multiple queries O.K. Commission: 10% plays, 15% books. Fees: none.

TARC LITERARY AGENCY—4725 E. Sunrise Dr. #215, Tucson, AZ 85718. Attn: Martha Gore. Adult fiction and nonfiction, multicultural juvenile books. Unpublished writers considered. Query with bio/resumé; multiple queries O.K. Commission: 15% U.S.; 20% foreign. Fees: photocopying, shipping.

SUSAN P. URSTADT, INC.—103 Brushy Ridge Rd., New Canaan, CT 06840. Attn: Susan Urstadt, Jeanne Fredericks. Adult nonfiction; juvenile books. Unpublished writers considered. Query with outline, sample pages, and bio/resumé. No multiple queries. Commission:15%. Fees: none. "We look for dedicated, cheerful, long-term authors who want to build writing careers with care."

JOHN A. WARE LITERARY AGENCY—392 Central Park West, New York, NY 10025. Attn: John Ware. Literate, accessible noncategory adult fiction, as well as thrillers and mysteries. Adult nonfiction: biography, history, current affairs, investigative journalism, social criticism, Americana and folklore, science, medicine, sports, and memoirs. Unpublished writers considered. Query; multiple queries O.K. Commission: 15% domestic, 20% foreign. Fees: photocopying. "No telephone queries, please, without referral."

WATKINS/LOOMIS AGENCY—133 E. 35th St., Suite 1, New York, NY 10016. Attn: Nicole Aragi. Adult fiction and nonfiction. Unpublished writers considered. Query; no multiple queries. Commission: 15%. Fees: none.

SANDRA WATT & ASSOCIATES—8033 Sunset Blvd., Suite 4053, Los Angeles, CA 90046. Attn: Sandra Watt. Adult fiction and nonfiction. Unpublished writers considered. Query with bio/resumé; multiple submissions O.K. Commission: 15%. Fees: marketing fees for shipping, telephone, faxes, for new writers only. "We're old fashioned. We love good writing."

WIESER & WIESER, INC.—118 E. 25th St., 2nd Floor, New York, NY 10010. Attn: Olga Wieser. Adult fiction and nonfiction. Unpublished writers considered. Query with outline and bio/resumé; no multiple queries. Commission: 15%. Fees: photocopying, shipping.

TODD WIGGINS—436 Anderson Ave., Suite 9, Cliffside Park, NJ 07010. Attn: Todd Wiggins. Adult fiction and nonfiction. Unpublished writers considered. Query with bio/resumé; multiple queries O.K. Commission: 15% domestic, 20% foreign. "No cookbooks, business management strategies, or how-to books. Prefer serious fiction and nonfiction by writers who are willing to work hard."

WITHERSPOON ASSOCIATES—157 W. 57th St., Suite 700, New York, NY 10019. Adult fiction and nonfiction. Unpublished writers considered. Query with sample pages; no multiple queries. Commission: 15%. Fees: none.

RUTH WRESCHNER, AUTHORS' REPRESENTATIVE—10 W. 74th St., New York, NY 10023. Attn: Ruth Wreschner. Adult fiction: mainstream novels, genre books, mysteries, romance. Adult nonfiction by experts in a particular field. Young adult books, ages 12 and up. No pornography, incest, or sexual abuse. Unpublished writers considered. Query with outline, sample pages, and bio/resumé. Multiple queries O.K. Commission: 15% domestic, 20% foreign. Fees: photocopying, postage.

ANN WRIGHT REPRESENTATIVES—136 E. 56th St., #9J, New York, NY 10022–3619. Attn: Dan Wright, Literary Dept. Adult fiction with strong film potential. Unpublished writers considered. Query with bio/resumé; no multiple queries. Commission: 10% to 20%. Fees: photocopying, shipping.

WRITERS HOUSE—21 W. 26th St., New York, NY 10010. Attn: John Abraham, fiction. John Hodgeman, nonfiction; Beth Feinberg, juvenile and young adult. Adult fiction, nonfiction, and stage plays; also juvenile for all ages, and young adult. Unpublished writers considered. Query with bio/resumé; no multiple queries. Commission: 15% domestic; 20% foreign; 10% stage plays. Fees: out-of-pocket expenses only.

WRITERS' PRODUCTIONS—P.O. Box 630, Westport, CT 06881. Attn: David L. Meth. Adult fiction and nonfiction, both of literary quality. Unpublished writers considered. Query with outline, 30 to 50 sample pages, and bio/resumé. Multiple queries considered, but not preferred. Commission: 15% domestic, 25% foreign and multimedia. Fees: photocopying, shipping. "Send your best, most professional written work. Research your market, know your field."

SUSAN ZECKENDORF ASSOCIATES, INC.—171 W. 57th St., New York, NY 10019. Attn: Susan Zeckendorf. Fiction: literary fiction; mysteries; thrillers; women's commercial fiction. Nonfiction: science; music; biography; social history. Unpublished writers considered. Query with outline, sample pages, bio/resumé; multiple queries O.K. Commission: 15% domestic; 20% foreign. Fees: photocopying. "Keep your description of the work brief."

GEORGE ZIEGLER—160 E. 97th St., Suite 4A, New York, NY 10029. Nonfiction and stage plays. Unpublished writers considered. Query; multiple queries O.K. Commission: 15%. Fees: none. "The query should tell me what the project is about, not how good the author thinks it is. If the query package costs more than 29¢ to mail, you are sending too much."

INDEX TO MARKETS

870

872

875

881